ALEXANDER POPE

A pastel of Alexander Pope made for Martha Blount in about 1739. Private Collection.

ALEXANDER POPE

A LIFE

MAYNARD MACK

W. W. NORTON & COMPANY
NEW YORK · LONDON

in association with

YALE UNIVERSITY PRESS
NEW HAVEN · LONDON
1985

© 1986 by Maynard Mack

First Edition

All rights reserved. No part of this publication may be reproduced, stored in a
retrieval system or transmitted in any form or by any means, electronic, mechanical,
photocopying, recording or otherwise, without prior permission in writing of the
publisher.

The text of this book is composed in Linotron Bembo.
Composition by The Bath Press, Avon. Book design by John Nicoll.

Published in the United States of America in 1985 by W. W. Norton & Company, Inc.,
500 Fifth Avenue, New York, NY 10110.

ISBN 0-393-02208-0

Library of Congress Cataloging in Publication Data

Mack, Maynard, 1909–
Alexander Pope: a life.
1. Pope, Alexander, 1688–1744—Biography.
2. Poets, English—18th century—Biography. I. Title.
PR3633.M27 1985   821'.5 [B]   85–2941

Published simultaneously in Canada by Penguin Books Canada Ltd,
2801 John Street, Markham, Ontario L3R 1B4.

1 2 3 4 5 6 7 8 9 0

For F B M

"Whose love indulg'd my labours past,
Matures my present, and shall bound my last!"

He was a poet and hated the approximate.

Rilke

Never say you know the last word about any human heart.

Henry James

I! fuge! sed poteras tutior esse domi.

Martial

PREFACE

Though close to a hundred volumes, large and small, have been devoted to Pope's poetry since World War II, I believe this to be the first completed attempt (a word I wish to emphasize) since 1900 to give a comprehensive account of the man in his times, from his birth in 1688 to his death in 1744. There exists, of course, George Sherburn's *The Early Career of Alexander Pope*, now fifty years old, but even that book, wonderful as it is, belongs, as he intended, rather more to the genre of literary career than to that of biography, and moreover, leaves off at 1727, when Pope was only thirty-nine. Otherwise, so far as I know, only one writer has been sufficiently venturesome to undertake a full-scale life, and even that undertaking seems to have been abandoned following the appearance of its first volume in 1968. In the meantime, Swift has attracted the three brilliant volumes of Irvin Ehrenpreis, not to mention the work of earlier chroniclers from Carl Van Doren and Ricardo Quintana to Middleton Murry. As for Johnson, the other towering literary figure of eighteenth-century England, he not only is the subject of the greatest biography ever written, but continues to receive the warm and sensitive attention of biographers of the highest distinction as well as the immense circumstantial homage represented by such works as Alleyn Reade's eleven volumes of *Johnsonian Gleanings*. Gleanings! and in eleven volumes! No wonder true-blue Johnsonians can play at Twenty Questions with each other—as, for instance, what was the name of the cat that succeeded Hodge?—whereas even the most admiring readers of Pope rarely know the family name of his mother, let alone the name of the dog whose puppy when given to the Prince of Wales bore the famous inscription on its collar:

> I am his Highness' Dog at Kew,
> Pray tell me Sir, whose Dog are you?

I like to imagine, therefore, that this book may be found useful and perhaps even entertaining by readers fond of biography as well as by those with a specific interest in the eighteenth century. It is blest, at any rate, in having for subject a fascinating figure who exercised through his powerful friends and his own drive and imagination an important influence on English poetry, publishing, bookmaking, and gardening. If his life was a "long disease," as he remarks in his verse-letter to his friend Dr. Arbuthnot, owing to the tuberculosis of the bone that he presumably contracted from his foster nurse soon after birth, it remains also one of the great literary success stories of all time. Disadvantaged politically as a Roman Catholic and socially as a hunchback and cripple, he managed nevertheless to win the friendship of an astonishing variety of gifted men and women along with a position of authority in his own age that later practitioners of the poetic art can only envy. In the words of Lord Byron, hyperbole perhaps but worth meditating, "Neither time, nor distance, nor grief, nor age can ever diminish my veneration for him who is the great moral poet of all times, of all climes, of all feelings, and of all stages of existence. ... His poetry is the Book of Life." At the very least, it is a book worth looking into, as is the life of the poet who produced it.

In the exploration of these matters which follows, I have sought to give equal treatment to both, and I have here and there borrowed from my own earlier work. Pope's writings I have made an effort to place, so far as may be done at this late date, in the context of feelings, personalities, and events which precipitated even if it can never altogether account for them; the stratum of mystery in works of art is real and like the sacred underground river of Coleridge's *Kubla Khan* does not lend itself readily to measurement. Pope's life has its mysteries too, which I have tried to view fairly. Without concealing his warts, I have consciously avoided magnifying them or dwelling on them to the exclusion of all else; and where there are extenuating circumstances to be considered, as for most discreditable actions there are, few of us being dyed-in-the-wool villains, I have thought it proper to consider them. Pope's worst faults were grievous, but so are the faults of most of us; and I believe he has suffered long enough from a species of self-righteousness in his commentators that one must make every effort to avoid. If the results of the effort in my case are dismissed as special pleading, so be it. There are few poets who cannot use an advocate.

As others have learned before me, certain thoughts sit troublingly in the mind as a work long in preparation draws to its close. For me, one is of the large amounts of fascinating material that have had to be jettisoned along the way in order to keep some degree of proportion in the whole: enough material to supply almost any number of other biographical studies, which I warmly hope will be forthcoming and will set me right where I have strayed. My other thought, which cuts far deeper, is of the friends who cheered this undertaking when it began, would have rejoiced to see it finished, but have not survived to do so. I think particularly of James L. Clifford, James M. Osborn, and William K. Wimsatt. *Ubi amici, sunt ibidem opes.*

To acknowledge the living whose acts of generosity have helped improve these pages is like numbering the stars. I shall certainly not escape overlooking someone, perhaps many more than one, and for that discourtesy I ask pardon in advance. Nevertheless, dear Daughters of Memory, Muse of History, Muse of Biography (if any), speak loud as many of their names as you can. For reading the entire final text, or most of it, with patient resignation but scrupulously helpful advice, sing rapturously these: Laurine and Andrew Bongiorno, Nina Bouis, Frank Brady, Morris Brownell, Andrew Davis, Howard Erskine-Hill, Ellen Graham, Donald Lamm, John Nicoll, Martin Price, Claude Rawson, Pat Rogers, Patricia Meyer Spacks, Barry Wade. For experienced judgment on small portions or assistance with individual problems, let these names too be gratefully recalled: Margot Butt, George Clarke, Rosemary Cowler, Donald Greene, Robert Halsband, William Kellaway, William Kinsley, James Means, Ruthe Battestin, Beth Riely, John Riely, Valerie Rumbold, John Ryden, Arthur Sherbo, Victoria Thys, Joseph Trapp, Eugene Waith, Aubrey Williams, James Winn. And for those little unremembered acts of kindness and of love that make so large a portion of a good librarian's life, acclaim in golden tones the staffs of the Beinecke, Bodleian, British, Clark, Houghton, Huntington, Princeton, and Sterling libraries.

Praise and thanks be also given to those who over the years have helped me with research. They are many: Kathryn Cook, Stephen Cushman, Ruth Grdseloff, Ann Joyce, Leslie Moore, Julie Peters, Barbara Will, Mark Wollaeger. But my debt is greatest to three: A. D. K. Hawkyard, Catherine Sharrock, and Ann Waters. And greatest of all to one: Annetta Boyett. To her labors, and, most especially, her keen researches in documentary sources, almost every page of this book is in debt.

Nor is it, Muses, ever just to forget the generosity of the Olympians: of my own university, of the National Endowment for the Humanities, of the John Simon Guggenheim Memorial Foundation, of the Andrew W. Mellon Foundation, of the Henry E. Huntington Library and Art Gallery, of the William Andrews Clark Memorial Library. Singly and collectively they have bestowed on me the greatest of blessings: time. For their kindness to me and to countless others, I salute them.

Always, however, when the captains and the kings depart, and all
other debts have been acknowledged, a creditor remains for whose
bounty one can only thank God. To her this book is dedicated.

M.M.

I am grateful for permission from the following publishers to quote
from copyright materials: to Faber and Faber, London, and Harcourt
Brace Jovanovich, New York, for lines from T. S. Eliot's *The Waste
Land* from *Collected Poems 1909–62* © 1936, 1963, 1964; to J. M. Dent,
London, and New Directions Publishing Corporation, New York,
for lines from Dylan Thomas's "Fern Hill" from *Collected Poems*
© 1945; and to the Wesleyan University Press, Middletown,
Connecticut, for the poem by James Wright, "Written in a Copy of
Swift's Poems for Wayne Burns" from *Collected Poems* © 1969.

CONTENTS

Part Four: "My Countrys Poet," 1733–1744

PART ONE

BEGINNINGS

1688–1708

CHAPTER 1

A LONDON CHILDHOOD

"Heretick Dogs"

It was the best of times and it was the worst of times.

In the London household of Alexander and Edith Pope, Edith was expecting her first child. Just short of ten years earlier, on 12 August 1679, Alexander had buried his first wife, Magdalen, in the parish of St. Benet Fink in London, where he plied his business as an importer and exporter of linens—"Hollands," as they were then often called, from their being manufactured in Flanders. For her funeral he paid a sizable extra fee to have the Great Bell of St. Benet Fink tolled, an available special tribute, rarely offered by those bereaved. His two children by Magdalen, a daughter of the same name and a son Alexander, he entrusted on her death to the care of his sister Mary, wife of the Rev. Ambrose Staveley, rector of Pangbourne in Berkshire.

So, at least, we may infer. For the Rev. Mr. Staveley noted in his parish register three years later: "Alexander Pope a childe of my Brother in law Alexander Pope a Merchant of London was buried September ye first 1682." If, as so often happened in the seventeenth century, Magdalen's death came about in childbirth, it is all the more understandable that a busy City widower should have turned to a close relative in the country, well out of London's notoriously insalubrious air, which was also at the moment an air of panic, for the keeping of his newborn infant and its sibling while he looked about for a second wife to mother them.

We do not know when the search concluded in his marriage with Edith Turner; but it appears from the foregoing that by the time he was able to resume domestic life, his only son was dead. This circumstance undoubtedly lent an extra tingle of anticipation to the feelings with which he now awaited the new arrival—feelings that cannot have been free of some sharp anxieties as well. The spring of 1688 had been exceptionally wet and cold, filled with dangerous distempers, and who could tell what this might presage in the months ahead for a helpless infant fresh from the womb, or, as parents of that day were likelier to say, from the hand of God? Edith, moreover, now only a month away from her forty-fifth birthday, was substantially older than was usually thought safe for delivery of a first child. There could be serious danger in this event for her, and perhaps yet more for the newcomer, who was all too plainly their last hope of having a child of their own.

A quiet and reflective man from all accounts, Mr. Pope was almost certainly beset by other worries too. These extended well beyond his own doorstep to the state of the nation into which his child was to be born and in which it would grow up. He and his wife were Roman Catholics. Edith belonged to a large Yorkshire family whose religious sympathies, at least among the children who reached adulthood, had divided down the middle, five of ten surviving daughters becoming Catholic and five Protestant. Five wise virgins and five foolish ones, their brother had once said. In seventeenth-century families, such divisions were not rare. Though Edith appears to have chosen the Roman side, even if she had not it would have been customary for her in those patriarchal days to assume the faith of her husband when she married, along with his name and protection. Alexander, for his part, had been born (posthumously) into the family of an Anglican clergyman in Hampshire, also named Alexander Pope. But at some point during his merchandising career, he had converted to Rome, possibly during his apprenticeship in the textile trade, which, according to one tradition had been passed in Lisbon, according to another, in Flanders.

As a Catholic merchant living in the part of London called the City, then a stronghold of English Protestantism, Mr. Pope must already have met with much to make him apprehensive. His residency in the parish of St. Benet Fink during the period of mass hysteria triggered by the alleged "Popish Plot" (at which time—1678–81—it was claimed that Jesuits and other Catholics planned to assassinate Charles II and butcher all the Protestants in England) had exposed him to sounds, sights, and deeds horrible for any member of a persecuted minority to contemplate. The more so because there was never any certainty that the same ugly passions, open always to arousal by unforeseen events or unscrupulous politicians, would not recur. Some twenty-four of his co-religionists, mostly secular priests and Jesuits but including also an elderly and ailing Irish archbishop and a peer of the realm, had been tried for treason during those lunatic months, testified against by witnesses whose word, as John Evelyn later confided to his *Diary*, "should not be taken against the life of a Dog," bullied by judges who all but insisted on verdicts of guilty, and (with the exception of the peer, for whom the penalties of treason were commuted to beheading) condemned, carted, hanged, castrated, disemboweled, and exposed in quarters to the gaze of the passersby. Many others had been thrown into prison and left to rot there without trial. So great became the panic, even among the educated as the plot scare rose toward its climax, that if Magdalen Pope had died some months earlier than she did, her coffin would have been forced open by any soldiers who met with it, a parliamentary order having gone out (on 4 November 1678) to stop all funeral processions and ransack the coffins for contraband arms.*

Even more frightening for a Catholic (because closer home) were the Pope-burning processions. These, serving the crowds who attended them as a sort of popular street-theater, had been reintroduced about 1673 by various Protestant groups to express an antipapal solidarity against the "Romanizing" drift of Charles II's court, and they became particularly popular after the conversion of his brother James (widely guessed at from 1673) had been confirmed by James's marriage in the same year to a Catholic princess, Mary Beatrice of Modena. During the political maneuvers undertaken in the next half-dozen years to exclude James from the throne, Pope-burnings

---

* It is difficult to exaggerate either the degree of panic or the fury of the rhetoric which fanned it. For an extreme example, see *An Appeal from the country to the city, for the preservation of his Majesty's person, liberty, property, and the Protestant religion* (1679), pp. 2–4: "First, Imagine you see the whole Town in a flame, occasioned this second time by the same Popish malice which set it on fire before. At the same instant fancy, that amongst the distracted Crowd you behold Troops of Papists, ravishing your Wives and your Daughters, dashing your little Childrens brains out against the walls, plundering your Houses and cutting your own Throats, by the name of *Heretick Dogs*. . . . Also, casting your eye towards *Smithfield*, imagine you see your Father, or your Mother, or some of your nearest and dearest Relations, tyed to a Stake in the midst of flames, when with hand and eyes lifted up to Heaven, they scream and cry out to that God for whose Cause they die; which was a frequent spectacle the last time Popery reign'd amongst us. Fancy the Ministers of God's holy Word torn in pieces before your very eyes. . . . Then the only Commodity will be Fire and Sword; the only object, Women running with their hair about their ears, Men cover'd with blood, Children sprawling under Horses feet. . . . In fine, what the Devil himself would do, were he here upon Earth, will in his absence infallibly be acted by his Agents the Papists. . . . There is no such thing as an *English* Papist who is not in the Plot, at least in his good wishes." The pamphlet has been attributed to Charles Blount.

1. Anti-Catholic propaganda in 1680 during the "Popish Plot" scare.
   By permission of the British Library.

became an almost standard feature of the street celebrations held on November 5, the day set apart to commemorate the nation's escape earlier from a genuine Roman Catholic conspiracy in 1605. This is the conspiracy associated with the name of Guy Fawkes, whose intention had been to usher in a general restoration of the old religion by first blowing up the king and Parliament. Similar burnings had become attached to November 17, accession day of Elizabeth I; for this was now being increasingly observed, in tacit and sometimes not so tacit censure of the Stuart court, to honor her role as architect of the *true* religion.

One of the biggest of these outings, on 17 November 1679, involved two hundred porters carrying torches, a statue of Elizabeth decked out with "Magna Carta" and "Protestant Religion," effigies of cardinals, friars, and Jesuits along with a massive effigy of the Pope, who was made to bow to Elizabeth and then set ablaze after being hooted by a throng, it was claimed, of two hundred thousand.★ On November 17 two years earlier, while the debates about Exclusion were heatedly going on but long before there was any question of a "Plot," the Pope's effigy was presented with "2 divells

---

★ *Londons Defiance to Rome* (*A Perfect Narrative of the Magnificent Processions, and Solemn Burnings of the Pope at Temple Barr, Nov. 17th 1679*), (1679), p. 3. At the end of a parade of persons garbed in the attire of Catholic religious orders and others sumptuously costumed as bishops and cardinals, the papal effigy appeared "in a lofty glorious *Pageant*, representing a Chair of State covered with *Scarlet*, the Chair richly Embroidered and Fringed, and bedeck'd with Golden Balls and *Crosses*; At his Feet a *Cushion of State*, and two *Boys* in Surplices with White Silk Banners, and *Bloody Crucifixes* and *Daggers*, with an Incense-Pot before them, *Censing* his Holiness, who was arrayed in a splendid Scarlet Gown, lined through with *Ermin*, and richly daubed with Gold and Silver Lace; on his Head a Tripple *Crown* of Gold, and a glorious Collar of *Gold and precious Stones*, *St. Peters Keys*, a number of *Beads*, *Agnus Dei's*, and other Catholic *Trumpery*. At his back, his Holinesses privy Councellor (The *degraded Seraphim*) *Anglice* the *Devil*, frequently Caressing, *Hugging*, and Whispering him, and oft-times instructing him aloud to destroy His Majesty; to forge a *Protestant Plot*, and to *Fire the City* again, to which purpose he held an *Infernal Torch* in his hand."

The description sufficiently indicates how carefully and expensively these occasions were manufactured to perpetuate hostility towards papists. To a degree, however, they may also have functioned as a festal substitute for the processions and ceremonials of the old faith, the solemnities of one age becoming the entertainments of the next. Though perhaps not consciously intended to do so, they could also defuse any latent attractions that papal authority and pomp might exercise on the popular imagination by first ridiculing and then "vanquishing" them.

whispering in his eares, his belly filled full of live catts who squawled most hideously as soone as they felt the fire; the common [people] saying all ye while it was ye language of ye Pope and ye Divel in a dialogue betwixt them." Though modern historians of these events have insisted with reason that they did not often result in mob violence and had no appreciable influence on the government, their effect as well as their intent was obviously to intimidate Roman Catholics, and the intensity of the aggressions released may be plainly read in the screams of those burning cats.

A Pope-burning on Guy Fawkes Day, 1673, took place in the Poultry, no great distance from where Alexander and Magdalen Pope were apparently living at that time. Another Pope-burning, in 1677, again on Guy Fawkes Day, took place at the Monument. This was the great pillar (still standing today) erected on Fish Street Hill by Christopher Wren to memorialize the undaunted spirit of the city after the great fire of 1666, only a moderate walk from Broad Street, where we know the Popes were situated. Today one can only guess at the feelings such displays of fear and hatred aroused in Roman Catholics living within eyeshot or earshot. A year later, on Elizabeth I's accession day, even Mary Beatrice's Catholic ladies-in-waiting sat trembling behind bolted doors at Somerset House, expecting an assault that fortunately never came.

Hardest of all to bear for an adherent of the old faith was the perpetual consciousness of being held up, on the one hand, as a sport and mockery, a devotee of practices and beliefs that the rest of the nation held in derision, and, on the other, as the Pandora's box from which all moral, political, and social evils sprang. Protestants, almost to a man, blamed Catholics for the Great Fire of 1666. Extremer minds, either deluded or believing the best defense to be a good offense, unburdened themselves of responsibility for the Civil Wars and the execution of Charles I by laying it at the door of Jesuits and "Romish" intrigues. Such intrigues, they subsequently insisted at the time of the alleged "Plot," had all but brought about the assassination of Charles II as well, and a general massacre of Protestants, save that its dark intent had been blessedly exposed by that great deliverer of the people, Titus Oates.

Though after 1685, during the three years of James's reign, Pope-burnings along with other traditional stimulants of anti-Catholic sentiment were outlawed, this did not prevent their occasional recurrence and only increased the political and psychological tensions. Typical of the city's mood as well as the plight of its Roman Catholic minority, the following news item, published in March

1688, scarcely two months before Edith Pope was to be delivered, speaks volumes:

> Of a corpse whose fragments were found in divers quarters of the city, the homicide and murderess has been discovered in the person of its wife, and thus all suspicion and discourse imputing the crime to the Jesuit Fathers and the Catholics, ceases.

Yet by a trick of the mind well known to psychologists, the same minority that evoked such dread and hate in times of stress was in other moods patronized and ridiculed for observances that all reasonable men agreed to scorn. Possibly it would be truer to say, affected to scorn. Where the taboo is formidable, it may be that the attraction is more so. In any case, men like William, Lord Russell, a staunch Whig, did not scruple to declare in Commons (with blissful indifference to Anglicanism's own straddling position on the Real Presence in the Mass):

> I despise such a ridiculous and nonsensical religion. A piece of wafer, broken betwixt a priest's fingers, to be our Saviour! And what becomes of it when eaten, and taken down, you know.

Andrew Marvell was yet more extreme:

> *Popery* is such a thing as cannot, but for want of a word to express it, be called a *Religion*, nor is it to be mentioned with what civility is otherwise decent to be used, in speaking of the differences of *humane Opinion* about Divine Matters.

So much for the charity of poets! Even John Tillotson, eventually archbishop of Canterbury, though able at one moment to tell the Commons that he doubted not that "*Papists* are made like other men," found himself uncertain at another whether the Pope was or was not Antichrist. Lately, the biggest jest among Protestants had been that the Pope was sending to Queen Mary Beatrice, who like Edith was pregnant, "the Virgin Mary's smo[c]k and hallowed bairn cloaths," this following (it was claimed) the Virgin's appearing to the Queen in her own person to announce that "that holy thing that shall be born of her shall be a son."

Not a friendly jest! But "God's English-men," as Milton had proudly dubbed them, were not in a frame of mind just now to expend much friendship on fellow countrymen loyal to the Pope. Now that their throne held the first confessedly Catholic monarch the country had known since Mary I's time, who could guess what his devious designs might be? Or yet more worrisome, who could not? Those who asserted with the anonymous author of a *Letter to a Dissenter* (1687) and *The Anatomy of an Equivalent* (1688) that under no circumstances could a Catholic king be trusted to allow liberty of worship except as a mask for absolutist and eventually exclusivist intentions had seemed during the past year to gain credence for their view from James's own actions in supplanting numbers of justices of the peace, heads of colleges, and officers in the armed forces with representatives of his own faith. Now, if the Queen should be delivered safely of her child, this unpredictable monarch might have a male heir, and that heir would at once take precedence over his Protestant half-sisters, Princess Mary, wife to William of Orange, and Princess Anne (later Queen Anne), wife to George of Denmark. Hence if the father failed to bring in popery and slavery, the son could be counted on to make the omission good. On the whole, it was much more attractive to imagine, as many did, that the Queen had never actually been pregnant at all; or if she had, that she had lost the child by miscarriage, to which she had always been liable and about which anxieties had been expressed as early as the past November and as late as this present May. The virtue of such reasoning was that it allowed the whole accouchement to be written off as a Romish trick, and whatever should eventually be produced from it to be branded an imposture.★

★ This did of course occur. The infant was immediately alleged by the Protestant interest to have been smuggled into the Queen's bedroom in a warming pan. As F. R. Turner points out (*James II*, London: Eyre and Spottiswoode, 1948, p. 405), "It is difficult to believe that the doubts which were immediately cast on the genuineness of the birth arose spontaneously; the phenomenon of a fanatically held belief in what we now know to be utterly untrue, in fact, is almost exactly a repetition of what happened ten years earlier in connection with the so-called Popish Plot."

By October the fanatically held belief became so powerful that James felt obliged to hold a special council at which some forty-odd witnesses testified to the genuineness of the birth. Many people, however, continued to prefer the lie. One of them was James's own daughter, the future Queen Anne, who, while acknowledging "tis possible it may be her [Mary Beatrice's] child," told her elder sister Mary, consort to William III: "I shall never now be satisfied whether the child be true or false"; adding comfortably in a later letter (after citing numerous witnesses to the genuineness of the birth including the queen's bedchamber-woman and members of the king's privy council): "methinks it is wonderful if it is no cheat, that they never took no pains to convince me of it." (18 June and 24 July 1688; in B. C. Brown, *The Letters and Diplomatic Instructions of Queen Anne*, London: Cassell, 1935, pp.

In these ways, for English Protestants too, the spring of 1688 was a season of apprehension. And there was no comfort to be had, for those so inclined, from the planetary signs. In March the celestial positions had appeared to imply (or at any rate to invite interpretation in terms of) antagonisms in the state:

> Still the *Superiors* move in *Card'nal* Signs;
> Bright *Sol*, and *Hermes* th' Aequinoctial mount,
> Opposing *Saturn*'s Whiggish deep-Designs:
> And for 's *Rebellion* bring him to Account.
> *Mars* is turn'd *Politician*, and discovers
> The Frauds of *Trimming Subjects* and false *Lovers*.

But now, in May, it was obvious to initiates that personal and private ease were also under threat:

> If *Mars* the *Gall* doth rule, and *Jove* the *Blood*,
> And *Chronus* the wise *Spleen*, and all at Strife,
> Astrologers have ever understood
> Such dire Positions *Fatal* unto Life;
> At least to the *Comforts* of it. *Card'nal* Stars
> Ne'er fail of raising *Micro-Cosmal* Wars.

Seven months later, the author of these riddling rhymes could have proclaimed them prophecy. By then, Princess Mary's husband, the future William III, had landed with his Dutch army at Torbay, and following a solemn largely triumphal progress through the south counties, had arrived at St. James's to assume the throne from which James II had lately fled. By then, too, it was apparent to some (most notably Roman Catholics, and those who for their loyalty either to the house of Stuart or to the idea of a legally inheriting king would become nonjurors, [i.e., would refuse the oaths of allegiance] in the next reign) that "Positions"—whether astrological or merely political and religious—had in fact become fatal to life or at least to the comforts of it. The stream of exiles flowing into England during

---

37, 42.) Mary too continued to believe in her father's perfidy as a way of justifying what she knew to be her husband's treacherous intention "to dethrone him by force." See Mechtild Comtesse Bentinck, ed., *Marie, Reine d'Angleterre, Lettres et Mémoires* (The Hague, 1880), pp. 74–5; Marjorie Bowen, *The Third Mary Stuart . . . with Memoirs and Letters of Queen Mary II of England*, 1662–1694 (London: John Lane, 1929), p. 126; and Henri and Barbara van der Zee, *William and Mary* (London: Macmillan, 1973) pp. 235–7.

the past three years from the French king's persecutions of the Huguenots would be replaced, at various times during the next half century or so, by exiles fleeing (for similar reasons) the other way.

A life in danger

Into this unpromising conjuncture of events, Alexander Pope the future poet was born. The time was 6:45 P.M. on the twenty-first of May 1688. The place, though somewhat less certain, seems pretty clearly to have been no. 2 Plough Court, just off Lombard Street in what is now usually thought of by Londoners as the City.

Some weeks earlier, close to but probably not actually on All Fools Day (much though it would have pleased Pope at a later time to think so), Lewis Theobald was born, in Sittingbourne, Kent. He would be the hero of the first *Dunciad*, assigned a shadowy throne in Dull-town by the doughty little king-maker who had just arrived in Plough Court. There is something touching as well as funny in the thought of these two, each (according to the theories of their time) a blank sheet of paper awaiting the inscriptions of experience, yet each blindly strengthening day by day toward a confrontation that would initiate the last great English poem in the Renaissance tradition.

Twenty days after Pope's birth, Mary Beatrice presented her delighted husband with James Francis Edward Stuart, later to be known in England as the Old Pretender but officially recognized in France as James III. Though he would never meet or (perhaps) even hear of Edith Pope's offspring, he too would have some influence on the poet's life and fortunes and on the lives and fortunes of other Englishmen. His very presence just across the Channel, and especially Louis XIV's support of his dynastic claims on his father's death in 1701, fueled continuously and sometimes justified the fears of English Protestants that they could lose the benefits of their visitation by Dutch William in a further visitation by French Louis and James III. Two of Pope's closest friends-to-be, Henry St. John and Francis Atterbury, eventually spent time in the service of the Old Pretender, and, as the succession of sometimes serious Jacobite plots and uprisings from 1708 to 1745 makes clear, were not altogether alone in preferring a native to a foreign prince and in adhering (for whatever worldly personal reasons) to a mystique of kingship that was in fact the last failing bulwark against secularization of the political process. These tensions nourished antipathies that might otherwise have withered, kept "popery" a dirty word throughout Pope's lifetime, and on occasion caused him acute embarrassment if not anguish.

Had he come into the world a century later, more about Pope's childhood would undoubtedly be known—if for no other reason than that it might then have seemed to him a stage of his life worth memorializing. Nineteenth-century writers are at some pains to recall this aspect of their experience, often to the extent of several hundred pages. By a few it is remembered as a time of deep Wordsworthian stirrings and communion with mysterious powers; by many more, as a glorious interlude of leisure, innocence, and freedom from responsibility before the onset of adult cares. Some, notably those who suffered an unhappy childhood, lament that life's supremest blessing was cruelly denied them, while others, De Quincey especially, address this period of their lives in such extravagant terms that one is obliged to wonder what reality they refer to. My narrative, De Quincey warns in his preface to *Autobiographic Sketches* (1853), will sometimes rise into "a far higher key," and never more so than when I deal with that portion of my existence in which there is "nothing on the stage but a solitary infant, and its solitary combat with grief—a mighty darkness, and a sorrow without a voice." Today, such language seems better suited to the anguish of a King Lear than to the oral and anal preoccupations of one who, as Shakespeare with his never-failing sanity reminds us, spends much of this phase "mewling and puking in the nurse's arms."

For better or worse, attitudes toward childhood in Pope's day differed markedly from these. The goal, especially for boys, was to attain as fast as possible the grown-up condition, the full socialized state that was required before one could make one's contribution to society, and the years prior to this effort were granted little intrinsic value of their own. When Pope sits down at the age of fifty-one to reminisce about his past with his good friend Jonathan Richardson, the portrait painter, taking notes, it is characteristic both of the age and the man that his first sentence gets him born, his second educated, and his third launched on his career as a poet. With the same indifference, his young friend Joseph Spence, who at one time intended to do a biography of him, passes over his early childhood with a single entry, and that not from the poet himself but from his older half-sister Magdalen.

Still, there is much in Pope's infancy and early years of which we may be reasonably sure. Immediately after birth, unless his father strongly opposed it, he would have been swaddled—encased, that is to say, in linen wrappings that held his arms and legs immobile for the first ten to fourteen weeks. This treatment, a tradition of child care over many centuries, was thought to prevent an infant's weak bones from being bent and thus to be of some assistance against rickets, which along with smallpox was the disease most dreaded during infancy and whose actual dietary causes were of course unknown. Swaddling was also a device of some convenience to nurse or parent. Not only did it guard against injury to eyes and ears from scratching, but it made for less crying since, as we now know, it slows the heartbeat and prolongs sleep; further, it enabled the infant to be easily moved from place to place, or even to be hung up on a hook. Some have proposed on this evidence (with a glance at eighteenth-century Russia) that swaddling produces political docility. But this notion accords so poorly with the facts of life in other European countries where it was practiced that it seems wisest to conclude with the most recent historian of these matters that the psychological results of swaddling (if any) remain unknown. If the treatment had effects on Pope, docility seems not to have been among them. Ironically, however, during his last years, he had once again to put up with indignities of this kind in the form of stiff canvas bodices—"being scarce able to hold himself erect till they were laced . . ."—owing to the ravages of the tubercle bacillus in his bones.

Almost equally a fixture in the regimen of seventeenth-century infants, if at all well born, was nursing by a woman other than the mother: a wet nurse. In Pope's case her name was Mary Beach. Though we know little else about her, she was probably recommended by some of Edith's female kin, as the custom then was, and if she possessed the characteristics usually most sought after in a foster nurse, she was of a wholesome brown complexion; had good teeth, a sweet breath, and a broad but not fat bosom; had at some time in her past recovered from the smallpox; and was delivered of her own child (often already now dead either of some doctor or disease) three or four months earlier. Foster nurses were mostly engaged by upper-class women who could afford it, and for a multitude of reasons. These could include one's own and one's husband's vanity about one's breasts; or the traditional notion, derived from Galen, that a nursing woman's milk is adversely affected by sexual activity; or the fashionable conviction that nursing is a labor unfit for gentlewomen; or a lingering belief in the greater efficacy of a vigorous lower-class woman's milk; or the inability of the mother to provide sufficient nourishment from her own supply; or any combination of these. At

Edith Pope's age of forty-five, this last consideration may have been decisive.

Only five years younger than her mistress when she moved into the Pope household to look after the new arrival, Mary Beach remained in the family till she died at the age of seventy-seven. "Nutrix mea fidelissima, M. Beach," Pope writes in the *Memorial List of Departed Relations and Friends* that he kept in his Elzevir Vergil, "obiit 5 Nov. 1725, aet. 77." ["My most faithful nurse, M. Beach died 5 November 1725, aged 77."] Later—we do not know exactly when—Elizabeth Turner, Edith's spinster sister, joined the household. Since we know that she taught Pope how to read, she must have made part of the family from an early stage in the poet's life. She too remained with them until her death and was remembered with affection in the Elzevir list: "Anno 1710, Jan. 24, Avita mea piissimae mem., Eliz. Turner, migravit in coelum, annum agens 74." ["On January 24, 1710, my aunt of most blessed memory, Eliz. Turner, passed into heaven in her 74th year."]

Looking back on this era from the latter decades of the twentieth century, we may well consider it remarkable that the young Pope (or any other child) survived. These were times when a man of learning like Elias Ashmole, founder of Oxford's Ashmolean Museum (perhaps the earliest public museum of natural history in the world), could say that he had held a piece of bryony root (a notable cathartic) in his hand and it had freed him of the bellyache, and when prescriptions for relieving infant colic were likely as not to call for some such talisman as a cold marble stone on which the sun has never shone. Writing to his son Edward, like himself a physician, only seven years before Pope was born, Sir Thomas Browne notes with satisfaction that Edward has prescribed an "issue"—in other words, a wound surgically procured—for his little niece aged two months. This is to be kept open and running by the insertion of foreign matter (such as fragments of root known to seventeenth-century physicians as issue-pease) as long as necessary. Though the child is clearly too young, he agrees, to take any but very dilute decoctions of "china, sarsa, eryingium, rad. osmundae, agrimonie, hartstong, betonica" to combat what appear to be her rachitical symptoms, chalybeates (salts of iron) will surely do her more good than harm, as will bleeding her at the ear.

But even such prescriptions pale beside many of those receiving sanction from the distinguished chemist Robert Boyle in his *Medicinal Experiments* of 1692, one of the most popular family handbooks of the period. Among other recipes more palatable, one for sore throat, as common an ailment among children then as now, proposes "a drachm of white dog's turd" worked up with honey of roses into "a linctus, to be very slowly let down the throat." Another—"For Convulsions, especially in Children"—requires ground dried earthworms fortified with "a pretty number of grains of ambergrease" to moderate the stench. A third—"For the Cholic and diverse other Distempers"—features an infusion made of "four or five balls of fresh stone-horse dung" steeped in a pint of white wine, to be drunk "from a quarter to half a pint" at a dose. Easily the Mount Everest and Mona Lisa among these unappealing remedies is the following, used "To clear the Eyes, even of films": Take human fecal matter "of good Colour and consistence," dry it slowly "till it be pulverable," then reduce it "into an impalpable powder, which is to be blown once, twice, or thrice a day . . . into the patient's Eyes." Since a copy of this handbook survives, carrying what I take to be the signature of Pope's father, one can only hope that its being of the third edition of 1696 means that the poet, at least during infancy, escaped acquaintance with its cures.

All this, and no doubt a good deal else, the young Pope survived. The only serious peril he seems to have met with in these earliest years came from quite a different source. This is the account given to Joseph Spence in Pope's presence by his half-sister Magdalen in 1728:

> Mr. Pope's life . . . was in danger several times, and the first so early as when he was a child in coats. A wild cow that was driven by the place where he was at play struck at him with her horns, tore off his hat which was tied under his chin, wounded him in the throat, beat him down, and trampled over him.

Magdalen was "by," she says, when it happened, probably assigned, as older sisters so often have been, to baby-sit her small brother while he played. When she retells the story to Spence fourteen years later, she adds that her brother was then "about three years old," was "filling a little cart with stones," and wore a hat with a feather in it. The cow, we may reasonably suppose, was being driven to Smithfield or, more likely, Leadenhall Market. Both markets are approachable by routes that would have brought the cow and her drover to the vicinity of Plough Court, situated less than a mile from Smithfield and only a few steps from Leadenhall. Along any of these routes Pope may have been gathering stones under his sister's supervision. An alternative possibility is that the cow was one of those sometimes driven about the streets by milkwomen who sold milk fresh from the udder.

From the "coats" mentioned by Magdalen—a womanish attire worn by all young children at this period, male or female—a boy could count on graduating at some time between his third and seventh year to the specifically male breeches. These were immensely coveted, John Locke notes, "not for their Cut, or Ease, but because the having them is a Mark of a Step towards Manhood." In affluent households like the Popes' a good deal was usually made of this occasion. Lady North, for example, writes in 1679 to her son Sir Francis about the "breeching" of his son and her grandson, "little Frank":

> You cannot believe the great concern that was in the whole family here last Wednesday, it being the day that the tailor was to help dress little Frank in his breeches. . . . Never had any bride that was to be dressed upon her wedding night more hands about her, some the legs and some the arms, the tailor buttoning and others putting on the sword, and so many looking on that had I not had a finger amongst them I could not have seen him.
>
> They are very fit, everything, and he looks taller and prettier than in his coats.

Proud parents, at least one aunt, a sister, and probably other relatives, servants, and neighbors may easily be imagined in a similar scene surrounding the son and heir of the Pope family, who would now gravitate increasingly from the society and care of the household women to that of his father and other men. It seems quite conceivable, in fact, that the earliest portrait we have of Pope, painted when he was seven, was commissioned to register this particular *rite de passage*, though its showing him only to the waist may argue against this. The sitter has, at any rate, a fashionable chevalier-like coiffure and pose, and this, together with the sumptuous silks of the costume, the self-conscious somewhat swaggering air of command on the handsome face (appropriate to a small boy's day of triumph), and the fact that children, even noble children, were rarely painted in England at this time, suggests that in some respect this is an adoring family's tribute to its only man-child, even if not explicitly a commemoration of his actual breeching. At the same time, the high quality of the painting, attributed guessingly at present to the French émigré artist Simon Dubois, reminds us that the poet's uncle on his mother's side was Samuel Cooper the miniaturist, known variously to his contemporaries as "the prince of limners" and "the van Dyke in little," and that, accordingly, we need not be surprised to find the Pope family so soon in touch with painters.

2. Alexander Pope, aged seven. By an unknown artist, possibly Simon
Dubois, *c.* 1695. The sprig of laurel was painted in by Jervas later. Wimsatt,
1.

Osborn Collection, Beinecke Library, Yale University. By kind
permission.

Cooper, described by Prince Cosimo de Medici, who sat to him in 1669, as "a tiny man, all wit and courtesy," acquired early in his career an international reputation for the delicacy and precision of his art. Though they were not blood relatives and never knew each other, his gifted nephew was soon to follow him in each of these respects.

"The Language of the Heart"

If Edith Pope when young resembled her sister Christiana Cooper, the miniaturist's wife, she was a vivacious and pretty woman. A charming miniature of Christiana, executed by her husband, shows an elegantly dressed young lady, possibly in her early thirties, with delicately cut features, set off by a string of pearls about her slim neck and curls as devastating as Belinda's in *The Rape of the Lock*. On her death in 1693, she bequeathed this necklace to Edith along with a miniature of their mother (probably also her husband's work) and a "grinding stone"—the latter perhaps indicative that Edith had talent, or perhaps only aspirations, as an amateur painter in her own right. To her nephew and godson, then going on six, Christiana left "my china dish with the silver foote and a dish to sette it in"—something the boy must have expressed a special fancy for—and, on the death of her sister Elizabeth, who is allowed life use, "all my books pictures and Medalls sett in gold or otherwise." A story goes, unverifiable now, that Edith also received from her sister at some point Samuel Cooper's sketchbooks, color boxes, and other artist's paraphernalia including his cups (for grinding and compounding) "of precious agate." If the story is true, the gift was presumably destined in the long run, like the books, pictures, and medals, for her godson and nephew, who may have been showing at five or six some early signs of the interest in drawing and sketching that we know he had developed by the time he was nine or ten. What seems clear, at any rate, is that Christiana Cooper's relationship with the Pope family was close, possibly close enough to lend credence to the further tradition that the handsome monument commemorating her and her husband which is still viewable in London, in St. Pancras Old Church, was erected at the poet's father's expense.

Of Edith herself, the most revealing of the three images now known (all dating from her old age) is a drawing made of her at age eighty-seven or eighty-eight by Pope's friend Jonathan Richardson. The face has squared, the cheeks have dropped, the chin sags; but under these ruins is clearly visible the substructure of what was certainly a serene and possibly a beautiful face, with the alert untroubled gaze of one who has accepted what life offers without wincing, and who, we happen to know, was both mischievous enough to call Spencer Compton, Speaker of the House of Commons, "the Prater" and compassionate enough to be named by her son "a parent to the poor and me." Pope himself thought her beautiful at any age. One of the recurrent images in his letters to friends as she grows into her eighties is of his mother as a lighted taper—reflecting, one presumes, the verse in Ecclesiasticus: "As the clear light upon the holy candlestick, so is the beauty of the face in ripe age." When she died on 7 June 1733, probably just eight days short of ninety, he urged Richardson to come at once to draw her—"before this winter flower is faded."

We may guess that after her father's death in 1665, Edith stayed on with her mother and her sister Elizabeth in the comfortable family house in York until her mother also died in 1681. At that point, social decorum would have decreed that she and her sister remove elsewhere to the protection of relatives. Since at least three households of Turner kin were by this time established in London, the presumption is strong that Edith, probably still in Elizabeth's company, settled in one of them, there in due course, through Catholic relatives or friends, to make the acquaintance of Alexander Pope and become his wife.

Alexander's own origins lay farther south. Though the blood in his veins was by herald's count less "ancient" than hers, he too sprang from a sturdy stock. His grandfather, Richard Pope, was a substantial citizen of Andover (in Hampshire), at that period an important market town and cloth-making center astride the highroad from London to the west in the midst of green hills gleaming with the white fells of sheep. There he kept the Angel Inn, a valuable hostelry near the top of the High Street, which southward became the Winchester Road and northward rambled on to Newbury. By his wife, Mary West Pope, he had five children, managing his domestic economy so well that he was able to portion his two daughters with £300 each when they married and send at least one of his three sons to university: achievements of no mean order for a provincial innkeeper in the early decades of the seventeenth century. He was also elected four times the town's bailiff or chief magistrate and died holding that office in 1633. Something of his standing in the community may be gathered from the fact that in old deeds and documents he is often styled "gentleman."

The innkeeper's university-educated son—so far as we know, the first of the family to be named Alexander—enjoyed an equally prosperous career in the church. B.A. of Oriel College, Oxford, and M.A. of Gloucester Hall (now Worcester College), he was preferred in 1631 at the age of thirty-two to a good living at Thruxton, a few miles southwest of Andover. By the time he died fifteen years later, at the height of the Civil War, he had accumulated two additional livings and was able to leave his wife Dorothy Pyne Pope a very handsome annual income of £250. (Though his wife says he was "of gentle disposition," he was certainly litigious, as was she, and perhaps testy when put upon—conceivably an omen of things to come.) He also left her four young children to rear: Dorothy, eleven, named after her mother, Mary, ten, William, three, and a fourth yet unborn who arrived in April 1646, two months after his father's death, and was christened Alexander in his memory. This was the poet's father.

Dorothy Pope died in 1670. Of her two daughters, her namesake died unmarried in 1695 and Mary became the wife of the Reverend Ambrose Staveley of Pangbourne in Berkshire, to whose household, it will be recalled, her brother Alexander, the poet's father, entrusted his children by his first wife when bereft in 1679. By that period in his life, Alexander had obtained whatever formal education was to be his lot, probably at the village school in Micheldever (just north of Winchester), where Dorothy Pope had moved soon after she lost her husband to be near her father, who was vicar of St. Mary's there. By this date also, Alexander had been for about a decade in partnership with his elder brother, William, trading in linens as far afield as Virginia. In 1684, we know, William was in chancery undertaking to collect payment from their Virginia agent for a shipment of linens and other goods, for which the agreed-upon *quid pro quo* was to have been some thousands of pounds of tobacco. The upshot of this suit we do not know, nor do we hear thereafter of either William or the partnership. There is, however, in the poet's later capsule history of himself, composed and sent to Lord Hervey at the time of their quarrel in 1733, a sentence hinting some sort of rift between the two brothers on grounds that Pope obviously thought discreditable to William. My father (he tells Hervey)—and in this sentence he is not being ironic, for he had much admired Hervey's elder brother—was like you in having an elder brother, "though he had one who wanted some of those good qualities which yours possessed." If the rift had come about by 1688, it may have offered an additional reason for Alexander Pope's retirement from commerce in that year. Equally cogent motives must have been the immediate crackdown by William and Mary's government on London papists, together with the bleak trading outlook for a Roman Catholic merchant under the new circumstances and what were sure to seem to any foresighted business man the certain prospects of war with France, impeding

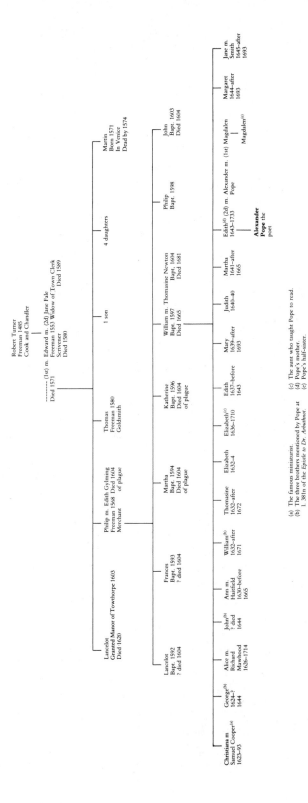

3. Genealogy of the Turner family to which Pope's mother belonged.

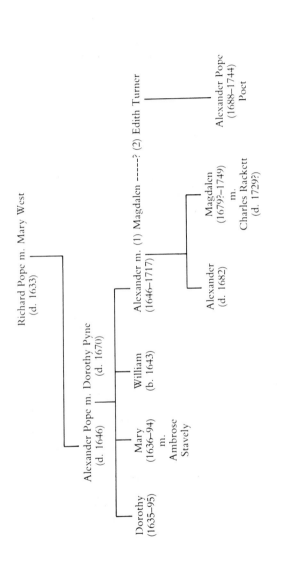

4. Genealogy of the Pope family.

cross-channel trade. Conceivably, the birth of his son and heir had something to do with the decision as well. He had prospered. He was worth some £10,000—a fortune in those days. He could afford the ease that would enable him to take a larger role in the life of his household.

At any rate, whatever his reasons, retire he did, and from that time on, as one of his death notices is said to have observed in 1717, "passed twenty-nine years in privacy."

We have no likeness of Pope's father apart from a bare outline drawing of his face in death, which tells us little or nothing. Such other slight evidence as survives suggests that, though apparently as wise in the ways of the world as we would expect a merchant to be (he is credited with advising his son to refuse to correct other men's verses for them: "You'll do nothing but get enemies by it"—and was of course proved right), he was himself a man of precisest rectitude. The portrait his son gives of him toward the close of *An Epistle to Dr. Arbuthnot*, however much we may discount it for the role it plays in the architecture of the poem, shows us a distinctly open and guileless personality, self-effacing, unbelligerent, one who evidently took his Christian commitment with sufficient seriousness to try to live by it, and in whom the exclusions and penalties attached to an outlawed religion had perhaps induced a species of social and political quietism, or at least the habit of marching unobtrusively to his own inner drum:

> Born to no Pride, inheriting no Strife,
> Nor marrying Discord in a Noble Wife,
> Stranger to Civil and Religious Rage,
> The good Man walk'd innoxious thro' his Age.
> No Courts he saw, no Suits would ever try,
> Nor dar'd an Oath, nor hazarded a Lye:
> Un-learn'd, he knew no Schoolman's subtle Art,
> No Language, but the Language of the Heart.
> By Nature honest, by Experience wise,
> Healthy by Temp'rance and by Exercise:
> His Life, tho' long, to sickness past unknown,
> His Death was instant, and without a groan.

(ll. 392–403)

A document only recently come to light gives us much the same picture of the man, though in prose. Rather bald disjointed prose, for the speaker is Magdalen, the poet's half-sister, reminiscing in her old age for the ear of Jonathan Richardson, who has apparently been putting questions to her. Of her father, Magdalen had this to say, tucking in at the close an anecdote (of a sort very likely to have stuck in a child's mind) which probably tells us a good deal about Mr. Pope's character and perhaps something about what it may have been like to live with him:

> Mr. Pope's father died of a *Polypus* [i.e., blood clot] on ye Heart; was very Well the Day before, & had never known Pain. In the Night told Mrs *Pope*, He had a touch of her Disorder, shortness of Breath; took a little Mint-Water, Syrrop, & Brandy, & settled to Sleep; in an hour wak'd, & said He was Worse; she rose & rang for Pope's Nurse, who allways Liv'd wth them, & as she rais'd him in the Bed, He fell back, & Dyed.
>
> Never in Drink, nor told a Lye in all his Life, & most Honest in all things; made his Wife soon after they were Married, send 2.^sh after a Mantua maker, Mrs Shepherd who had come to decay, because if She said She gave but 10 where others gave 12, She would injure the Woman's character with those that might not know it was on account of her having employ'd her of the first, before She raised her Price; if She said 12, She would tell a Lye.★

Clearly the senior Mr. Pope had a somewhat demanding personality, with austere standards of performance for others as well as himself—witness further his wife's statement to Spence many years after his death about his setting their young son to make verses: "He was pretty difficult in being pleased and used often to send him back to new turn them. 'These are not good rhymes' [he would say]."

Our one other intimate glimpse of the poet's father shows what seems to be a related side of him. This comes in a letter of the playwright William Wycherley to Pope in 1707. The veteran playwright, aged now in his early sixties (himself twice a convert to Catholicism but one on whom such commitments sat lightly) had taken up young Pope as his protégé and was corresponding with him regularly. To judge from this letter, he had just recently visited him and his parents

---

★ Bodleian Library, MS. English Letters d. 59, f. 89. Printed in "New Anecdotes," pp. 348–9. I take the anecdote to mean that Mrs. Pope paid the woman at the rate of 10 shillings, as had been her habit in the past. She was then, however, required by her husband to make this up to the new rate of 12 shillings on the ground that if word got about that the woman had taken 10 shillings from Mrs. Pope, her now asking 12 would be seen as price-gouging. If, to counter this, either the woman or Mrs. Pope (it is not altogether clear which one is meant, but it does not matter) *claimed* that the amount accepted had been 12 shillings, this would be a lie, unless and until Mrs. Pope made up the difference.

at the house in Berkshire where by this time they resided—not, it may be, without causing a certain consternation among the poet's elders by the exposition of views deriving from a long libertine career in the Restoration theater. Religious discussion, apparently, had not been avoided, and whatever was actually said, it seems clear that Mr. Pope had staunchly stood his ground. For the playwright now writes to the poet in a tone only partly facetious, "As for the Good Book you sent me, I took it as kindly as the Reprimand from the Good Man, (which I think you heard,) and was that I should not stand in my own light, which was spoken with the Zeal, and Simplicity of a Prophet."

Without pressing the remark too far, one may perhaps see reflected in it that degree of reluctant respect which guileless people sometimes win by their very simplicity and sincerity from those who feel themselves to be of a more sophisticated breed. To stand in one's own light is a quasi-proverbial way of saying "to prejudice one's chances"—can it have been salvation that was under discussion? But the phrase can also mean "to be obtuse while (or especially because) one imagines oneself to be clever," as when the narrator says in Lyly's *Euphues*, "Here ye may behold, gentlemen, how lewdly"—i.e., ignorantly—"wit standeth in its own light." The felicity of the image, so appropriate to Wycherley's religious situation from Mr. Pope's point of view, so pointed yet so gentle, so complimentary and critical at once, may serve to remind us, as it seems to have reminded Wycherley, that to speak with the zeal and sincerity of a prophet is not necessarily to speak without finesse.

How such episodes—and others like it, if there were others—affected the young Pope, it is more difficult to say. Perhaps not at all. Evidence abounds that he adored both his parents, always spoke of his father as "the best of men," and was profoundly moved when he lost him. Still—to consider only the present incident—there must have been embarrassment for a young man of nineteen, eager no doubt, as most young men are, to appear liberated and modish, in seeing an admired celebrity put down (however gracefully) by an upstanding old-fashioned father (however much cherished) for views that were possibly more congenial to the son than he would have cared to say. For though he was consistently respectful of his parents' faith, so much so that to spare them pain seems to be always in the forefront of his reasons for not acting on the many invitations he received to make himself eligible for pensions and other emoluments by converting to the established church, it is not clear that he deeply shared their convictions except in the loose sense that he was to remain all his life a theist and probably, in some way not very sharply defined even to himself, a Christian.

Especially now in these days, as he was growing out of his teens and making more and more regularly under the wing of friends like Wycherley those forays into the London world of taste and fashion on which literary success depended, the realization must often have come home to him that between the House of Holiness and Vanity Fair there is a great gulf fixed; and that if the vicissitudes of his parents' experience and particularly the century into which they were born had committed them for the most part to one side in this ancient polarity, his own interests, the demands of his career, and the charac-ter of the century he was growing up into must increasingly commit him to the other. It is some such consciousness as this, one is inclined to think, that gives the tribute to his father above quoted its special nostalgia (even its hyperbole). It seems to lament not simply a loved parent but an entire world gone, a world as appealing in its bright simplicities and certainties, yet also as unattainable, as the luminous world of Hamlet's father is to Hamlet. In both instances a shrewd, skeptical, highly self-reflexive personality with a mind as supple as a fine blade manages to create itself in some sort of succession—or is it in some sort of antithesis, like the parson's son who becomes the village delinquent?—to a father cut on simpler, and perhaps even in Pope's father's case, more "heroic" if more limited lines.

But all this lies well ahead in the future. We may turn back now to Plough Court and the young boy growing there.

CHAPTER 2

LESSONS

"The finest City in the World"

If it is true, as many twentieth-century developmental psychologists now think, that the optimum condition for fostering a child's creativity is the company of intelligent and loving adults fortified by limited contact with peer groups during the earliest years, Pope's childhood was fortunate. The cherished offspring of elderly parents—darling likewise (we may guess) of an old nurse and an older maiden aunt—sole boy in a household comfortably well off and in need of a male heir to continue the family name: under such circumstances, he can hardly have escaped a great deal of cosseting even in those pediatrically harsh times. So much adult attention can hardly have been good for him socially, but he undoubtedly received along with it all those stimuli to linguistic precocity and intensified fantasy life that such environments normally provide.

For despite its involvement in the feasts, fasts, vigils, and prayers at which the poet will later glance smilingly in one of his poems to Teresa Blount, the Pope household seems on the evidence to have been remarkably affectionate, tightly knit, and, in comparison with the severities obtaining in a large number of seventeenth-century families, easygoing. The tone of Pope's few remaining letters to his father is altogether relaxed, and such limited communications to Edith Pope as are now extant show her being addressed simply and intimately, as well by her step-daughter as by her son, as "Dear Mother." This stands in marked contrast with the usages of many households of Pope's day and after—that of Elizabeth Montagu, for instance, the future Bluestocking, who still in the 1730s called her parents "Sir" and "Madam"; or of Samuel Johnson, who as late as 1759, when almost fifty, begins a letter to his mother "Honour'd Madam."

To the softer style of milieu in which Pope grew up, the family's Catholicism may have contributed. In Catholic homes, patriarchal absolutism and the repressive disciplines often accompanying it, so marked a feature of life in families of Puritan background during the seventeenth century and of Evangelical families in the nineteenth, were often countered by the women. Women enjoyed special status in Catholic households owing to their central role as guardians and transmitters of the devotional practices honoring Mary and, more particularly, of the dietary observances, centered in the kitchen, by which from Reformation times Roman Catholics had maintained an identity for themselves and a supportive community for each other. What plainly needs to be added to this picture in Pope's case is that the only potential autocrat was a father who was gentle and unassuming and who, even if he had not been, might have found himself over-matched by the collective maternal solicitude of the three women who surrounded him. The poet's own profound and delicate appreci-ation of women (which cannot be entirely dissociated from a certain fear or mistrust of them), and also that quality of his sensibility that some critics have called feminine for lack of an exacter term, may owe something to his early and prolonged experience of a household strongly colored by womanly influence.

As for the house in which he spent his earliest years, that can have been only a delight. Suitably spacious, it was arranged on three floors with a garret above and a large storage cellar underneath that must once have been crammed with the bales and bundles of Mr. Pope's import-export trade and perhaps, on rainy days, still kept a faint redolence of Virginia tobacco, if indeed that missing shipment, or others of the kind, had ever been received. It was, at any rate, the kind of place that small boys love to prowl in and people in imagination with grotesque and scary forms concocted out of humdrum realities like old teapots; while above it, in the "Yard," lay an inviting mish-mash of conduits, pipes, basins, and chutes for storage of water and draining the roof. These, we are told, included "two large leaden cisterns," a "leaden sink under the Cistern," "a large bottle rack," "one ball cock, two brass cocks," "a leaden pipe from the Cistern to the copper [i.e., a large copper vessel]," "[a] leaden pipe from Mrs. Matthin's Yard to the Cisterns and to the Cistern up one pair of stairs," and a downspout—or in the language of the time, a "trunk" (i.e., wooden chute) from the "flat" (i.e., eavestrough) into the yard—surely for any boy a paradise of dainty devices.

Some parts of this maze of plumbing penetrated the cellar, which actually enclosed several smaller rooms, and conveyed rain-water through them from the roof by means of "a large Vault arched with brick," in which "a trough, leaded," ran "from the back Yard to the front to bring the water away." Although it cannot have crossed his mind at the time and we have no reason to suppose that it ever did,

5. Pope's birthplace, 2 Plough Court. Watercolor by J. L. Stewart, *c.* 1870. Courtesy of the Guildhall Library, London.

this was in actual fact Pope's first grotto, hardly the progenitor but at any rate the forerunner of all those other caverns and subterranean territories that were to strike his fancy, from the "Cave of Spleen" in *The Rape of the Lock*, the "Cave of Poverty and Poetry" in the *Dunciad*, and the grottoes encountered in classical epic, to that unique underground creation at Twickenham (also crammed with plumbing) which Robert Dodsley was to call "The Cave of Pope."

Upstairs, though we know nothing whatever about its furnishings apart from Mr. Pope's collection of religious controversy ("all that had been written on both sides in the reign of King James the second"), the house was elegantly fitted with several part-marble hearths (the chimney-pieces set with Dutch tiles and having painted landscape scenes above), and wainscoting all round. At the very top of the house, an attic lit by a skylight also beckoned. Over its parapet, if one were tall enough, or through its fenestrations, if one were not, it was possible to stare at passersby some twenty-five or thirty feet below and shiver happily at the thought of plummeting down among them, *not* to crack like an egg on the paving stones but to arise unharmed to applause without even splintering one's wand; or, still more intoxicating, to soar away over the house tops like a bird. Like Icarus, one would be forced to admit later, as one's acquaintance with both myth and natural law improved. Or like Phaeton. Then as now, growing up included the unwelcome news that most myths are caramelized fragments of common sense. In one's house, as also (one would learn later) in the microcosm of one's self, neither cellar nor attic, however delicious as locations to visit, however essential in what they contribute to life, can count on adult approval as places to go for long stays. The lot of the grown-up, they tell us, is not creeping or soaring but hanging in there—between. And they, alas, are right.

The house lay almost at the bottom of Plough Court, itself a cul-de-sac (the name derived at some earlier time from a street sign featuring a plough) that elbowed south off Lombard Street at a point a few steps west of Gracechurch Street. Gracechurch was an important artery flowing north across Cornhill to become Bishopsgate Street thereafter, and south, in a gradually steepening incline, to become New Fish Street, the main thoroughfare to London Bridge, at that time the only bridge joining the City to the Surrey side. Lombard Street was also important, but for other reasons. It had been for centuries the center of the City's banking trade, in the beginning that of the Lombard goldsmiths themselves, later that of their English successors. Here, Sir Thomas Gresham, founder of the Royal Exchange under Elizabeth I, had lived, his ancestral house sign the grasshopper (though an odd emblem for a family of bankers!) still to be seen at Barclays Bank on the north side of the street and on the weather vane of the Exchange. Here too, according to street-ballad lore, came the lecherous King Edward IV to seduce the vivacious and stunningly beautiful Jane Shore from her goldsmith husband; though in this matter, history has so far betrayed legend as to declare that William Shore was actually a mercer, his wife's real name Elizabeth, and their residence in Lombard Street probably supposititious.

Where Lombard ends to the east at Gracechurch Street, Fenchurch Street begins, the street where Samuel Pepys first became conscious of the inroads of the Great Plague during the ill-starred summer of 1665. Where it ends in the west, it merges with Cornhill; and the two streets, after appropriating Threadneedle Street, which slants into their intersection from the northeast, empty into the broad Poultry, which in turn unburdens further west in Cheapside. Thus Lombard Street, running somewhat northwest, and Threadneedle Street, running somewhat southwest, make two sides of a triangle, of which Gracechurch Street (if pieced out with a fragment of Bishopsgate Street on the north) forms the base, and Cornhill a sort of hypotenuse separating the large triangle into two smaller ones. In Pope's day this whole area swarmed with shops, well-stocked markets, taverns, coffee houses (Lloyd's, ancestor of the great insurance market, had already relocated from Tower Street to no. 16 Lombard Street), and residences of substantial merchants, many of whom had been or one day would be Lord Mayor. Small internal courts abounded, resonant sounding boards for hawkers. Lanes and alleys with inviting names laced the area in all directions: Abchurch, Bearbinder, Birchin, Pope's Head, to choose only a few. The last, in particular, named for some long-ago merchants of the Pope who had set up trade near Lombard Street (and bearing no doubt at that earlier stage, or perhaps still, a sign showing a head crowned with the papal tiara) must have sometimes occasioned sobering thoughts in Alexander Pope senior, remembering the Popish plot scare, and might have done so in his small son's mind as well, could he have guessed that one day a hostile publisher named Edmund Curll would set up *his* portrait for a house sign, calling it "Popes Head."

But everywhere now, when the child glanced up at such emblems, his eye would be caught only by the glittering spires (so he would call them later on in *Windsor-Forest*) of the new Wren churches, some of them—St. Paul's cathedral, most evidently—still building. Less than thirty years before, everything he now beheld—in fact, almost the whole City, from Pudding Lane just east of Gracechurch Street to

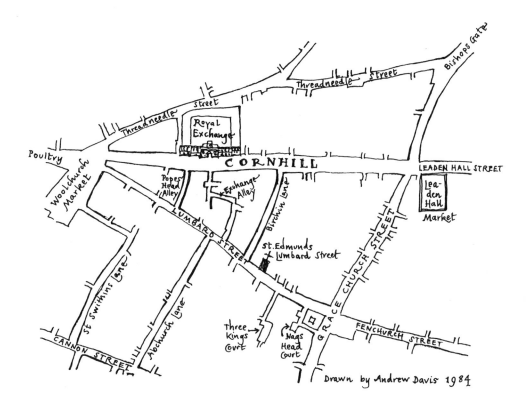

6. Map of the Lombard Street area. Adapted from the London map by John Ogilby and William Morgan, 1677.

Plough Court apparently lay between Three Kings Court and Nags Head Court. It is not shown on William Morgan's map.

By kind permission of Andrew Davis.

Temple Church off Fleet Street and Pie Corner west of Smithfield—had been leveled by the Great Fire, only a crowd of blacksooted house-chimneys left standing like mourners in a sea of rubble. (London, said the dean of Rochester in his next Sunday's sermon, which Pepys thought in bad taste, had been shrunk "from a large Folio to a Decimo tertio.") But now, all had been made new again or was in the process of becoming so. The phoenix, as the poets of the time never tired of reiterating, had consumed itself only to rise more glorious than ever from its ashes. Lombard Street, now for the first time declared one of the City's "High Streets," was again "throughout graced with good and lofty Buildings"; and in Plough Court, with "a good Free Stone Pavement," the new houses were "well builded and inhabited." Euphoria was universal. If the fire had been a judgment, it had also been a blessing. "However disastrous it might be to the then inhabitants," wrote one of Pope's contemporaries in 1707, it had proved 'infinitely beneficial to their Posterity":

> By means of the Inlargements of the Streets, of the Great Plenty of good Water, convey'd to all Parts; of the common Sewers, and other like Contrivances, such Provision is made for a free Access and Passage of the Air, for Sweetness, Cleanness, and for Salubrity, that it is not only the finest, but the most healthy City in the World.

Bliss was it, therefore, in that dawn to be alive, and to be a child (oblivious yet of religious history) was very heaven. London offered in those times what must have seemed an almost continuous theater. On Guy Fawkes Day, cannon boomed at the nearby Tower mixed with the roars of the affrighted lions confined there in the king's menagerie; bonfires sprang up all over the City at selected street corners; and the bells from a dozen steeples near, and twice as many far, pealed for hours, sometimes all day—the great bells of St. Mary le Bow ("loud Bow's stupendous Bells," says Pope in the *Dunciad*, possibly recalling a moment of childhoood amazement) echoing among them to declare all inhabitants within range true Cits and cockneys. Twelve days later, on Elizabeth I's accession day, the celebrations might be even greater. On both occasions, there were usually fireworks, and when there was a military victory, or a peace, as there sometimes was during the long wars with France in the 1690s, the City would respond for a day or two as if the circus had come to town. At William III's homecoming from the Peace of Ryswick, for example, his cavalcade "marcht thro' the citty" in a manner to rejoice any small boy's heart:

> a troop of horse grenadiers, the two citty marshalls with their men, 3 trumpets, the sherifs officers with javelins, the lord mayors officers on foot in their gowns, 2 trumpets, citty banner, citty officers in their proper habits on horseback, 2 trumpets, kings

drummer, common hunt, citty sword bearer, then the aldermen, recorder, and sherifs all on horseback in their scarlet gowns, knight marshalls men, messengers of the chamber, deputy knight marshall, kettle drums and trumpets, serjeant trumpet with his mace, serjeant at arms, heralds and purs[u]ivants at arms uncovered, gentleman usher of the black rodd, lord mayor bearing the citty sword, garter king at arms, king in his coach, attended by the gentlemen pentioners, footmen and [e]querries, nobility and gentry, &c. in coaches with 6 horses each to the number of 80.

In a period when governments everywhere ruled as much by sumptuous and intimidating display as by actual exercise of police power, exhibitions of this kind were not exceptional. Most memorable among such displays for Pope himself, if we may judge from the impression it left upon his best-known poem, was that of the Lord Mayor. During his term of office, this magistrate might be sighted unexpectedly anywhere within the City, for his public appearances were ordinarily on horseback, "himself always in long Robes, sometimes of fine Scarlet Cloath richly furr'd, sometimes Purple, sometimes Puke [i.e., puce], and over his Robes a Hood of Black Velvet, which is said to be a Badge of a Baron of the Realm, with a great Chain of Gold about his Neck, or Collar of SS's with a great rich Jewel Pendant thereon, with many Officers walking before, and on all sides of him."

"Knottier Points we knew not half so well"

Such extreme pomp at a time when attitudes were secularizing—such effulgences of surface encasing a face and body (indeed, many faces and bodies in that showy age) which were not usually to the manner born—invited parody, and, as every reader of the *Dunciad* knows, parody they received, from a master hand:

'Twas on the day, when Thorold,★ rich and grave,
Like Cimon triumph'd both on land and wave:
(Pomps without guilt, of bloodless swords and maces,
Glad chains, warm furs, broad banners, and broad faces).

(1: 83–6)

★ Sir George Thorold was Lord Mayor in 1720. The Lord Mayor's Procession made its way to Whitehall by land and water. Hence Thorold is ironically compared to the Athenian general, Cimon, who defeated the "barbarian" Persians by land and sea on the same day.

7. "A view of the Mansion House, appointed for the Residence of the Lord Mayor of London, during the Year of his Mayoralty." (Under construction, 1733–49.) Engraving by Thomas Bowles, 1751.

Lombard Street is immediately to viewer's left.

Courtesy of the Guildhall Library, London.

This is mockery, obviously; and the mockery expands until the route by which Dulness and her minions move westward from the City to be welcomed by the Hanoverian court at Whitehall becomes a surreal rendering of the route by which the Lord Mayor and *his* minions journey on Lord Mayor's Day to pay their respects to the reigning monarch, and then return to the City.

On the other hand, a manuscript version of these lines may point to residues of a more primitive response, reaching far back into a child's mixed sensations of delight and terror as he stares up from some lowly perch at what seem to be towering figures gliding by:

> 'Twas on the day when thro' the broad Cheapside
> Gigantic Forms in Cars triumphal ride. . . .

"Gigantic Forms" adds to the mockery, to be sure, evoking both the kind of personage we expect to find in epic poetry and the comfortable embonpoint of City Mayors. Yet readers who recall the lingering effect of certain of their own childhood experiences may reasonably wonder if the quality of the poem to which recent criticism has rightly called attention—"[Pope's] Dul-town is inhabited not by starving poets but by vividly felt, if faceless, presences who are sometimes infantile and sometimes maniac"— does not owe something to deeply buried memories. Memories of shadowy personages moving in crowds with a fierce concentration on the business in hand, and particularly impressive when seen by torchlight, as on the Lord Mayor's Day they often were. It would hardly be surprising if their vague menace as sensed at the time by a child were to surface later on, giving physical body to what the rational (now grown-up) mind of the poet interpreted as solely an intellectual and cultural threat.

However this may be, it is useful to recall that if the Catholic youth growing up in his country's greatest city viewed much that he saw with a child's delight, he was likely before many more years had passed to modify these impressions. One is driven to speculation here, for we have no secure knowledge even of Pope's whereabouts between the ages of four and eight, much less of any part of his personal experience. The house in Plough Court passed into other hands during the late spring or early summer of 1692, though "Mr Popes serv[an]t [Mary Beach?] & Jo[h]n Taverner [the family's priest]" stayed on with its new occupant into early 1693, perhaps while a new accommodation was being found and readied. Presumably, the Popes elected to move at this time because of the repeated proclamations during the early years of the new reign requiring Romanists to keep at a distance of ten miles from Hyde Park Corner. Presumably, too, the poet's father being the conscientious man he was, the family did not attempt to go underground but removed immediately, as a first step, to nearby Hammersmith, which had a certain reputation in those days as a Roman Catholic refuge. There, it appears, Pope's half-sister Magdalen met and married Charles Rackett of an affluent Hammersmith family and in the fall of 1695 bore him a daughter Mary (born 16 September, buried the following April). In the same year, Rackett purchased a property at Binfield in Berkshire, whose prior three-year lease to a tenant expired only in September 1697. At that date, the Racketts must have removed briefly to Binfield, for when in July of 1698 he sold the Binfield property to his father-in-law, he is named in the deed as "late of Hammersmith, . . . now of Binfield," and his father-in-law as "of Hammersmith aforesaid Merchant."

But though all signs thus point to the probability that Pope spent some part of his childhood at Hammersmith, that village was close enough to London to allow frequent comings and goings, sometimes no doubt to visit Edith Pope's several London relations, the future poet's uncles, aunts, and cousins; sometimes perhaps to see friends in the old haunts about Lombard Street; or even possibly, now and then, to join the crush of spectators at one or other of the great street spectacles, which, as we have seen, accompanied every holiday, every military success, and even the first entry of every new foreign ambassador with his vast gleaming company of welcomers, guardsmen, and retainers. That Pope nowhere at any time mentions a sojourn in Hammersmith, but in his one statement to Spence gives the clear impression that he went directly from London to Binfield at about age twelve may signify only his chronic forgetfulness by the time, years later, when these conversations occurred. Or it may equally suggest that his vivid early memories of London, to which he must have added substantially during his return there for two or three years of schooling at about age nine, blottted out all else.

It would be at this latter period, in any case, that he would begin to view some of the sights about him with new eyes. If at one time or other he walked with his father by the new Royal Exchange, with its fascinating shops and busy hum of wheeling and dealing, it would sooner or later be made clear that there were reasons for his father's life having changed from what it had once been, some of them not reassuring. Or if they ventured afield in the direction of the Thames along Suffolk Lane, they would pass the Merchant Taylors' School, generally considered the best City school of its time, and it would need to be explained that there were reasons why certain boys could not attend there even if their parents were to desire it. Then, too, on every side in the rebuilding metropolis those glittering new Wren spires arose, all the way from St. Benet Fink, off Threadneedle, to where, just above the entry to London Bridge (as a poet of our own century has it),

> the walls of Magnus Martyr hold
> Inexplicable splendor of Ionian white and gold.

Under all those spires, there were spaces that some children had gradually to discover it was weaseling or apostasy to enter.

These, possibly, were among the early impressions salted down in a young boy's assessment of the world around him; and to these, during the late 1690s especially, others yet more disquieting would join. Though we have no reason to suppose that the Pope family's loyalties were other than staunchly British, it cannot have been easy to respond without reserve to the foreign successes of a king whose levies of money, widely resented at times even by the Protestant side, fell most heavily on Roman Catholics, and whose parliaments almost year by year multiplied their difficulties with new legislation. If, as was very possibly the case, there lingered in the Pope family an attachment to James II, who was still felt by many Protestants as well as Roman Catholics to be their proper king *de jure*, it must have been less easy to cheer at the defeats of Louis XIV, the only monarch powerful enough to have restored a Stuart king to his throne. One did not, however, need to go as far as this in one's sympathies to resent the elaborate penal system by which the Establishment majority sought to keep all religious minorities—and with special invidiousness the Roman Catholic one—from competing in the open market for positions in the professional and public service: a system in which, as Pope would put it some forty years later, when his own position was secure enough to allow him to say *almost* anything he pleased,

> certain Laws, by Suff'rers thought unjust,
> Deny'd all Posts of Profit or of Trust.
>
> (*Imit. of Hor., Ep.* II, ii, 60–61)

Nor did one need to be stubbornly opposed to the new Williamite regime to feel that for all its promises of freedom of conscience (unrealized through the intransigence of Parliament), it had actually worsened the position of Roman Catholics by reducing to zero the moderating influence on their treatment sometimes exercised earlier by Louis XIV and his ministers:

> Hopes after hopes of pious Papists fail'd,
> While mighty William's thundring Arm prevail'd.
>
> (*Ibid.,* 62–3)

After 1688, as noticed above, legislation was enacted, and periodically reactivated, requiring papists to remove themselves from the cities of London and Westminster by a distance of not less than ten miles. No Roman Catholic could remain oblivious of the mistrust implicit in such action and of the potential dangers it posed. The new government also remitted the oaths of supremacy and allegiance (long a stumbling block to Protestant as well as Catholic recusants) so far as to allow Protestant dissenters to serve in either house of Parliament, while substituting other oaths specifically to exclude papists. To all justices of the peace, power was given to authorize daytime forcible entry of papists' houses in search of firearms, with confiscation and three months' imprisonment if any were found, a fine equal to the value of the arms to be paid to the informer (a notable encouragement to tattling on the one side and stealth on the other) and a further fine equal to three times their value to be paid to the crown. For ownership of a horse above the value of £5, penalties were the same.

Later on during William's reign, the economic straitjacket tightened. Legislation excluded Roman Catholic barristers from access to the courts. Lords lieutenant in the shires were empowered to draft horse and foot soldiers from papist estates and charge the cost upon the estate owner. Toward the close of the reign, a particularly notorious act disqualified Roman Catholics from inheriting landed property or buildings, a provision that made it advisable for Pope's father in acquiring the Binfield property to convey it to two of his wife's Protestant nephews to be held in trust for his son. Worse, any Catholic child was allowed, and therefore in substance invited, to repudiate his family's faith and by this means constitute himself its sole heir, requiring from his father such annual maintenance as the lord chancellor might think fit until his coming of age. Another stipulation of the act allotted a reward of £100 for any substantiated report of a Catholic child being sent abroad to be educated. This had been a usual recourse for affluent papist families, since a Catholic education was difficult to come by in the surreptitious and sometimes fly-by-night schools that managed to evade the ordinances against them in England. To make doubly sure that a Catholic education would be difficult to obtain, a further provision prohibited Catholic priests from saying mass, and Catholic schoolmasters from teaching school, on pain of perpetual imprisonment, with again £100 to any person informing on them.

To grow up in England in these circumstances was to be torn, and probably on occasion bitterly torn, between one's natural loyalty to one's native land and one's resentment of what must always have seemed to the individual peace-loving Catholic such as Pope's father an unwarranted exclusion and distrust, branding one an alien. Just how much an alien, if the young Pope retained any naive curiosity about it, he could easily reassure himself by walking hardly more than an ordinary city block from his former residence in Plough Court to the vicinity of Wren's great pillar commemorating the rebirth of the city after the great fire. There, at no. 25 Pudding Lane, site of the house where the fire was believed to have started in the kitchen of Thomas Farynor the king's baker, a plaque in the wall informed all comers:

> Here, by the Permission of Heaven, Hell broke loose upon this Protestant City, from the malicious Hearts of barbarous Papists, by the Hand of their Agent Hubert, who confessed, and on the Ruins of this Place declared the Fact, for which he was hanged, viz. That here begun that dreadful Fire, which is described and perpetuated on and by the Neighbouring Pillar.

This plaque was placed during the Plot scare in 1681, removed during the reign of James II, replaced when William came in, and taken down about the middle of the next century—not from any refinements of feeling, but because "the stoppage of passengers to read it" interfered with traffic. Nearby, on the pillar itself, also incised in 1681, razed under James, re-incised more deeply under William, and not removed till 21 January 1831, following the Catholic Emancipation Act, an inscription ran:

> This Pillar was set up in Perpetual Remembrance of that most dreadful burning of this Protestant City, begun and carried on by the Treachery and Malice of the Popish Faction, in the beginning of September, in the Year of our Lord 1666, in order to the carrying on of their horrid Plot for extirpating the Protestant Religion and Old English Liberty, and the introducing Popery and Slavery.

In 1733, when in his forty-fifth year Pope at last took notice of this inscription, the image he chose is revealing. It is the image of a small boy confronting a persecutor—

> Where London's column, pointing at the skies,
> Like a tall bully, lifts the head, and lyes—
> (*Epistle to Bathurst*, 339–40)

which is perhaps put yet more tellingly in one of its manuscript forms:

> Where London's Monum^t is reared so high
> Like some tall Bully, to look big & lye.

The comparison tells us something, I suspect, about the feelings and thoughts that churned in the young Pope's brain as he began to grasp, with increasing years and experience, both the intensity and the falsity

8. The Monument.

> Where London's column, pointing at the skies,
> Like a tall bully, lifts the head, and lyes.
>
> *Epistle to Bathurst*, 339–40.

Courtesy of the Guildhall Library, London.

of the Catholic myth, of which his and thousands of other families had been and would be scapegoats. Conceivably, too, it registers some early stirrings of that feistiness which would one day help make him the satirist he became.

This is not to say that at this or any other time Pope was filled with religious zeal. On this point, during his earlier years, we have no clues whatever, though it is usually the case that, at least up to puberty, children reflect what their parents feel (with more passion because they less know why) and that injustice always seems particularly outrageous to those whom life has not yet hardened to it. It is also fair to point out that provocative events helped fuel the hysteria that led to anti-Catholic strictures and fears. During the nineties, Jacobite plots and rumors of plots (including one genuinely serious conspiracy against the king's life) came and went like foam on an angry sea. In such circumstances, papists were always the first to be thought treasonable, whether they were or not and despite the fact that certain influential Protestant magnates were in closer touch than most Catholics with James II's court-in-exile, buttering their bread on both sides. Enforcement of the anti-Catholic laws, moreover, was always spasmodic and usually inefficient, sometimes enabling families in the counties—less often in London because of the concentration there of militant Protestants both Establishment and Dissenting—to survive for long periods without being seriously touched by them. How the Popes actually fared, we do not know. Apart from the right not to be persecuted for their beliefs and the right to worship when, where, and as they pleased—rights not acknowledged anywhere at that time save in one or two German principalities and the Low Countries—they may have fared well.

On the other hand, compulsory exclusion from most of the institutions of one's own country is deeply humiliating, and the humiliation is not likely to have been lost on an observant child, whenever he began to entertain thoughts about what he would do when grown up. To cite the shrewd observation of the first Marquis of Halifax, the only Church of England man of the time who seems to have recognized the psychological burden that the penal system imposed on Roman Catholics (which he thought ought to convert them!) the prospects of any talented and ambitious adherent of the old faith were dim:

> To have no share in business, no opportunity of showing his own value to the world; to live at best an useless, and by others to be thought a dangerous member of the nation where he was born, is a

burden to a generous mind that cannot be taken off by all the pleasure of a lazy unmanly life, or by the nauseous enjoyment of a dull plenty that produceth no food for the mind, which will ever be considered in the first place by a man that hath a soul.

Thus all things considered, it is not surprising that in the late years of William's reign Pope's father began to consider removal of his family to an area more sequestered than Hammersmith from the angry passions of the day. Nor is it surprising that the boy himself, at an age when most boys have other dreams, embraced with alacrity—an alacrity supported by precocious talent, but probably also by predictable constraints on other outlets—a career in poetry. There, at any rate, the Tests he would face would be of an acceptable kind.

"A sort of rapture"

It is reported of John Keats that when he was learning to talk he answered everything that was said to him with a rhyme or a chime on the last word spoken. Though the story may be apocryphal, it is not implausible. Children generally, when beginning to acquire language, have a fondness for repeating certain sounds, and since they rarely manage to get them exactly right, the result can easily be misunderstood by a hopeful bystander as a conscious rhyme. A good many family nicknames come into being by this route, and it seems possible that the senior Mr. Pope's early interest in setting his son to make verses may have come about, or at any rate have been encouraged, through some such experience, interpreted—at the time groundlessly, though, as it turned out, correctly in the long run—for a sign of poetic genius. As most children also love strong rhythms and seek to imitate them, Pope's notion that he "lisp'd in numbers, for the numbers came" perhaps had a similar foundation in the ordinary responses of young children to language, though no doubt in his case intensified to a degree.

The event that by his own account made him "catch the itch of poetry" was Homer—"when I read him in my childhood." He was then about eight, it appears, and the Homer he met with was John Ogilby's translation of the *Iliad*, "in that great edition with pictures." Great is the right word. The pages of an average copy of Ogilby's *Iliad* measure some seventeen by eleven inches, allowing the type in which the verse is set to run about the same size as that in a modern first-grade primer and supplying to the full-page engravings all the space necessary for a commanding clarity of design—again as in a good modern children's book except that the color is limited to black and white. Not that Ogilby intended his book for children. Far from it. His elegant column of verse (eight to twenty lines on a page) is surrounded like a tiny peninusula by a vast weedy sea of commentary rising against it from three sides: an offense to the eye that Pope was careful not to repeat in his Homer translations, where the commentary is placed at the back.

Nevertheless, one may easily see why he still spoke of this book in the next to last year of his life with "a sort of rapture only in reflecting on it." Homer's *Iliad*—as Pope had himself noted for his readers in his famous Preface (using a comparison that may owe something both to that early rapture and to Ogilby's crowded page)—was "a wild Paradise, where if one cannot see all the Beauties so distinctly as in an order'd Garden, it is only because the Number of them is infinitely greater." If the poem had an "action" in Aristotle's sense, it also had "actions" in a boy's sense—several hundred of them, all involving collective or individual mayhem, and an equal number of ways of dying in battle, each different from the one before. Its heroes, outsize in stature, gigantic in strength, were either favorites or offspring of the pagan gods and hence, for a seventeenth-century imagination, available counterparts of the modern child's Batman, Superman, and all the electronic heroes who have succeeded them. Yet at the same time, these great personages were "wonderfully diversify'd" (as the Preface had put it); they possessed developed personalities that enacted and were acted upon by a variety of easily graspable everyday passions: pride, rage, terror, greed, pity, lust; and they were required, as in our real world, though not in the magical world of their present-day descendants, to purchase their brief bright moments of ascendancy at tragic cost.

Add to this the poignancy of certain great scenes in the poem, such as Hector's parting from his wife Andromache, their infant son Astyanax recoiling in fright at the great crested helmet on his father's brow; or the reconciliation of Trojan Priam with Greek Achilles over Hector's dead body in the common human bond of suffering. Add also the vividness and variety of dozens of epic similes, some bringing what human beings do to each other in battle into ironic proximity with what natural forces at their cruelest and most savage do to human beings; others holding up as foil to the iron self-discipline of the heroic code all those peacetime sweetnesses (enjoyed earlier or elsewhere or by others) that measure both what is lost by that code and what gained. Collect these enticements together, infuse throughout a breathtaking lucidity of style matched by an altogether unselfconscious nobility of vision, and it becomes possible to understand why Homer was regarded in the ancient world as comprising in himself a whole curriculum of humane studies, and why Keats, in our world, discovering him for the first time in translation, could only compare him to a new planet or a boundless sea.

In Ogilby's great edition of the *Iliad* with pictures, all these attractions came reinforced. First of all, for a child's taste, by the forty-eight engravings. There mighty warriors struggled hotly for their lives among plunging half-frantic horses and the twisted bodies of those already fallen, vultures gathering visibly in the sky to their feast. There the naked corpse of Hector lay fixed by thongs to the rear of Achilles' chariot, while his parents looked on from the Trojan wall in unbelieving dismay and grief. There too one saw the cloud-borne deathless gods serenely quaffing nectar far above the tears and sweat of the dying men who carried out their great opposeless wills below. These were images not easily forgotten—images of a harsh world to which Pope later became so attuned when translating the poem that it is sometimes impossible to distinguish his interpolations in this vein from Homer's own expressions of it.

But the great joy, of course, for a lively mind like Pope's must have been discovery—the discovery of learning. Ogilby's commentary, when one got really down to it, was not so forbidding after all, and while it contained much that a child's eye might glide past, swarmed with alluring glimpses into odd corners of history and myth. There, on a single page, an inquiring child could learn that even women of high estate in that lost ancient world were skilled in spinning and weaving. He could learn that to speak of Apollo as God of the Silver Bow, as Homer did, or God of the Golden Bow, as Pindar did, was to mean only that he was the Shining God, "a bow of either [gold or silver], pure & unmixt, being wholly useless." Still on the subject of Apollo, he could also learn that the god is sometimes called Smintheus, the Mouse-God, after a temple built for him by the people of Teucros. Why did they build that Temple? Because the Teucrians were told during one of their migrations that they would know their destined home whenever a great force rose out of the earth to assault them. One night while they slept, it did: it ate through all the leather fastenings of their shields and greaves. Taking this for their sign, they settled in that place and built a temple to Apollo, whom they thereafter (having realized what their great "earth force" had been) called the Mouse-God and to whom they erected a statue showing him with a mouse beneath his foot.

On the same page, a curious reader could discover that the island of Tenedos took its name from a young prince named Tennes, who had refused to go to bed with his step-mother though invited by her to do so. In retaliation, she persuaded his father that he had attempted to rape her and was not satisfied till he was set adrift on the sea in an open chest. But Neptune looked after him and brought him safely to shore on an island called Leucophrys ["White Beach"]. There, soon after, the people received him for their king and lawgiver (he later won renown for the rigor of his laws) and renamed their island Tenedos in his honor.

As if this were not sufficient for any reader, however eager, one could even on that same page learn something about psychological warfare. At the opening of the *Iliad*, only Agamemnon has offended the Trojan priest Chryses by withholding the priest's daughter to be his concubine. Why then should Chryses call down Apollo's punishment on the entire Greek army? Answer: this was the one sure way of getting his daughter back. If Agamemnon alone were struck down by the god, the Greeks, lacking their leader, would probably decamp and go home, taking the priest's daughter with them. By contrast, if the Greek army suffered generally, the weight of public opinion would compel Agamemnon to yield. We are not to forget, however, warns Ogilby (who like all of Homer's translators views the author through the spectacles of his own time) that Homer is ordinarily a staunch asserter and supporter of the sovereignty of kings.

In 1707, when Pope was just short of twenty and first toying with the thought of translating the *Iliad*, he spoke glowingly to a friend of Homer's "Rapture and Fire, which carries you away with him, with that wonderfull Force, that no man who has a true Poetical spirit is Master of himself, while he reads him." If, with Ogilby's assistance, his absorption was equally intense at age eight, as we may guess it was from his pleasure in recalling it in middle age, it is easy to see why, on his being sent to school, he found more formal studies dull and unrewarding.

He had earlier (as we saw) learned to read from the aunt who made her home with the family and had taught himself to write "by copying printed books". He had also spent a year—perhaps more, though such studies did not usually begin till around age seven—under the regular tutelage of a family priest. The priest's name was Edward Taverner, alias Banister and John Davies (all Roman priests used aliases because their presence in England had been a criminal offense since Elizabethan days), and there is reason to believe he had lived with the Popes since 1692, when Pope was four. From him, at any rate, by the time he was seven or eight, Pope had acquired the rudiments of Latin rhetoric and Latin grammar together with some smatterings of Greek—on the Jesuit plan of education, which was to introduce both ancient languages at once. Once this had been accomplished, he was packed off to school.

Schools

Despite the severe penalties, Catholic schools survived. Some surreptitiously, some because the authorities winked at them. Pope's first school was at Twyford, then a country village in Hampshire about three miles from Winchester. The area around Winchester had enjoyed a certain reputation as a refuge for Catholics, and at the time of Pope's arrival there in 1696 or 1697, three Roman Catholic schools were in fact operating. The largest, at nearby Silkstead, had something like eighty boys. Twyford had about thirty and was being conducted at the time by a "Mr. Wait" with the assistance of a "Mr. John Grove." Very shortly before Pope came, there had been bad blood between the two schools, apparently because Twyford had formerly been content to be a feeder-school for Silkstead, taking younger boys, but had now begun seriously to compete with it. Not far from Twyford, a third school was also establishing itself under the direction of one Mr. Barlow in a residence called Longwood House.

Of Pope's stay at Twyford, we know little. It lasted, he told Spence, "only one year." Possibly it lasted even less, for we know that he wrote "a satire on some faults of his master," and was "whipped and ill-used ... and taken from thence on that account." It is tempting to exaggerate this incident because it seems symbolically so suitable a beginning for one who would eventually make a reputation in satire. Many years later, a letter not wholly to be trusted (because designed to mislead his enemy, the rascally bookseller and publisher Edmund Curll) tells us that this satire was in verse and over a hundred lines long. But this can as well have been a leg-pull. We do not know, in fact, whether the satire was in verse or in prose; whether it was directed at Mr. Wait or Mr. Grove (both names offer interesting possibilities) or some third person. Nor do we know whether it was the culmination and "last straw" in a sequence of incidents or a nonce effort in which Pope, either as the most gifted writer in his form or wanting to show in this field of endeavor a prowess denied him in others, singled himself out to play the role of tyrannicide for the common gratification of all. The questionable letter already mentioned tells us that the satire was found in the culprit's pocket through the tattling of a schoolmate. If this is true, the episode may have added its farthing's worth of caution to what eventually became in Pope a distinctive taste for secrecy, dissimulation, and surreptitious action.

Following the Twyford fiasco, the young rebel was sent to study under Thomas Deane, who from at least 1696 had kept a struggling school at Marylebone. Deane, formerly Fellow of University College, Oxford, had, like John Dryden, converted to Catholicism with the coming of James II, and had remained a convert, again like Dryden, on the coming of William III. He had therefore lost his Oxford post in 1688, was more than once thereafter, according to report, "in prison upon Account of his Religion, and the Notion of his being in Popish Orders," and in 1691 had been sentenced to the pillory under the name of Thomas Franks "for concealing a libel"—apparently some sort of censure of the Williamite government—"printed by one who lodg'd in the same House with him." Further hostile attentions, this time from "a busy Justice in that neighbourhood," compelled him to move his school during Pope's attendance there from Marylebone to Hyde Park Corner, "on the very Spot where Down-street was afterwards built."

Mr. Deane's school seems to have been a more relaxed institution than Twyford. Certainly it was if there is any truth in Johnson's story that Pope used to stroll from there to the playhouse. All that seems entirely clear is that during the two or three years of his attendance, Pope made a number of permanent friends, whose families we find him soliciting some thirty years later for financial aid for their former master, once again in prison for a "seditious" pamphlet; and that in the course of his stay he wielded enough influence with some of his associates to persuade them to participate in an epic play he had compounded out of "a number of speeches from the *Iliad*, tacked together with verses of my own." Since the master's gardener is said to have been called upon to play Ajax in this vehicle, one may guess that the episode chosen was one in which exceptional size and brawn were of some moment, possibly the celebration of Ajax in Book 7, where he duels with Hector, almost vanquishing him, but more probably the dramatic scene in Book 17, where Ajax and his diminutive brother (a role taken by Pope himself?) hold the entire Trojan army at bay while Patroclus's body is removed. Since, in addition, the young impressario "contrived to have all the actors dressed after the pictures in his favourite Ogilby"—this requiring an extraordinary complement of household materials to represent helmets, greaves, tunics, spears, and shields—one may further guess that such elaborate preparation was not carried on without approval of the master himself. All of which may suggest that Pope was right—though he was certainly not thinking of his own project at the time—in saying of Deane in his letter soliciting support for him that he had been "all his life a dupe to some project or other."

Along with the classical authors abovementioned, both schools must have offered religious training, of which no record today survives. We do know, however, something of the religious regimen at Standon School, opened in 1753 as a successor to Twyford after the latter had been closed down by the renewed hostility toward Catholics raised by the invasion of the Young Pretender in 1745; and the routines at Twyford and Hyde Park Corner probably did not vary greatly from these. Here at 6:30 A.M. prayers and mass were said, after which, at eight, all students took part in "some Catechism suitable to their Age & Capacity, as 1st the Doway [Douai] Abstract, with Mr. Gother's Instructions for Children, 2ndly, Fleury's Historical Catechism, 3rdly, Turberville's &c." The content of all these books is substantially the Christian doctrine of the Roman church arranged catechistically and spiced from time to time with exegesis and moral precept. Thus Turberville, for instance, instructs his readers that the Savior was born at midnight "to take away the darkness of our sins," and in a poor stable "to teach us the love of poverty, and contempt of the world." But he proceeds then to sixty pages of "Exposition of the Creed," twelve pages expounding the Lord's Prayer, some forty-eight expounding the Ten Commandments, fifty-eight expounding the Seven Catholic Sacraments, fifteen expounding the Seven Deadly Sins, twenty-five expounding the Ceremonies of the Mass, and twenty expounding the meaning of the Festival Days of the Year.

After this period of instruction, secular studies of ancient authors and a period of recreation occupied the remainder of the day; but at 6 P.M. the Master "is to ring the Bell for Evening Prayers, consisting of the Litany of the Saints, the Rosary or Mona Mors with the night Exercises & Reflection or Meditation for the following Day, all of which are to be read leisurely and distinctly by the best Readers amongst the Scholars in their Turns." Supper followed, with again a period of recreation. Then at 8 P.M. (8:30 from June to September 1):

> "At the Sound of the Bell all go quietly to their Chambers, & after a short Prayer said on their knees, by their own Bed Side, undress themselves modestly, without romping, noise, or going into each other's Chambers."

And so to bed.

Looking back on his schooldays from a distance of more than thirty years, Pope told Spence he had not gained much from either Twyford or Mr. Deane's. This assessment may in part, of course, be the product of other considerations than intellectual ones. Poets, and bookish types generally, have never been altogether comfortable with the quasi-tribal life-style (often accented by bullying, hazing, and other rituals of male hardihood) which flourished in a majority of boys' schools in times past. Pope was clearly a slight youth even before his illness set in, and having been brought up largely by women, like Shelley a century later, may have been as ignorant as he of the games his contemporaries knew and may equally have earned their scorn. A brief biography published in the year of his death (1744), said to contain contributions "from one who was [his] School-Fellow," remarks plausibly that "at the Hours of Recreation, whilst the Rest of his School-fellows were diverting themselves at such Games and Sports as was usual with Boys of their Age," the future poet "used to amuse himself with Drawing." Such withdrawals can hardly have been the whole story, as the Homeric play testifies; but if they took place, and took place often, as the 1744 *Life* implies, they cannot have increased his popularity with his peers. Similar unrecorded experiences of being a misfit, or of being lonely, or of being persecuted may have influenced his dour appraisal of what he gained from formal school life, and so of course may the natural inclination of one who was largely self-educated to appear entirely so.

Still, the curriculum of studies in a late seventeenth-century school was not well calculated for the meridian of a lively imagination, an imagination that had been browsing freely through an English Homer and probably through other books as well, better suited to his interests and capacity than Cicero's *De Officiis* in Latin, a favorite school text of the day on "Duties." Not that the works chosen for attention in such schools were necessarily unsuited to young minds. There was always the *Metamorphoses* of Ovid, even more inviting than Homer as an introduction to classical myth as well as certain other matters on which boys usually begin to show an interest at about ten; there was Vergil's *Aeneid* in whole or part; and sometimes, if the school offered Greek, a bit of work on Xenophon's *Anabasis* and Aesop.

Essentially, it was not the books that were at fault, but the method of instruction. This called for constant parsing of Latin sentences, construing of inflections, memorizing of rhetorical figures, and composing of Latin verses. Rote-minded, heavily insistent on the forms of language for their own sake, everywhere emphasizing fragments over wholes and means instead of ends, the system could not prevent a bright student from getting an education, for no system can; but it could make the process intellectually wasteful and physically a torture. It was made to work, and perhaps could only have been made to work, by several generations of schoolmasters who managed to thrive, in Ben Jonson's picturesque phrase, by "sweeping [their] living from the posteriors of little children." Flogging was the order of the day; if Pope got by with being whipped only once during his schooling (we do not know that he did), he was fortunate. At the big Establishment schools where masters like Busby reigned—"Dripping with Infant's blood, and Mother's Tears," as Pope would later describe him in the *Dunciad*—flogging was so much a way of life that Snarl, the vicious old roué in Shadwell's *Virtuoso*, can announce to the audience, with every expectation of being understood, that he comes to the brothel to be flogged because "I was so us'd to 't at *Westminster* School, I cou'd never leave it off since."

Even with all the violence, the educational effects were rarely comforting. In the eighteenth century, Lord Ashley, future third Earl of Shaftesbury, complains that after seven years at Winchester his brother can neither construe nor write a Latin sentence. Montaigne complains, in the sixteenth, that after making a very good beginning with Latin at home, he was shipped off to school, and when he finally emerged at age thirteen, "I had run thorough my whole Course (as they call it) . . . without any manner of Improvement." Jotted beside these sentences in his own copy of Montaigne, Pope's manuscript memorandum acknowledges that essentially this is his story too: "mutato nomine de me Fabula narratur ["Change the name and it's my story too"].

By around 1700, in short, when Pope left Mr. Deane's school and moved with his family to Binfield, he knew that much remained to be done. He would have to find a new and more demanding master, and that master would have to be himself.

CHAPTER 3

TRADITIONS

"Thy forests, Windsor"

The village of Binfield in Berkshire, when the Pope family moved there, was a thriving agricultural community of some three hundred fifty to four hundred souls, situated about seven or eight miles southwest as the crow flies from Windsor Castle and about thirty from Hyde Park Corner. Their house, still standing today but so much altered as to be unrecognizable, seems to have been originally a rather modest red-brick affair of a sort that might have descended in a family of prosperous yeomen and probably had. "Very small" is the considered opinion of an observer who eighty-odd years ago was able to view the two rooms remaining at that time of the original structure; and this tallies with the poet's own reference in a letter of 1711 inviting his friend Henry Cromwell to stay: "A little Room and a little Heart are both at your Service, and you may be secure of being easy in 'em at least . . . For you shall go just your own Way, and keep your own Hours, which is more than can be done often in Places of greater Entertainment." Even so early Pope sounds his characteristic note of (in this case unavoidable!) freedom from the punctilios and servilities of courts and great houses. It is a note that will often recur.

The house, known in those days as "Whitehill House," stands toward the southern tip of the village roughly two miles from its parish church and just north of the (then) main road from London through Bracknell and Wokingham to Reading. Around it in Pope's time were spread some fourteen acres of arable land and meadow, which two small parcels divided from the rest brought to a total of nineteen. Immediately to the north lay the village common lands— lands sometimes referred to in premodern England as the heath or the waste—and, to the northeast, a few hundred yards further into the countryside, a grove of mature beeches straddled a pretty rise with a view. Here, we are told, the young Pope often retreated to read or write under a favorite tree, and it may indeed be to this grove that he refers in 1717, when, on revisiting Binfield, he evokes for the Blount sisters, with perhaps a certain (mock?) wistfulness looking through the jest, "those Woods where I have so often enjoyd—An Author & a Book; and begot such Sons upon the Muses, as I hope will live to see their father what he never was yet, an old and a good man." Renamed "Pope's Wood," this grove became in due course a frequent destination of literary pilgrimages; and the favored tree (or one taken for it), with an assist from one of its younger neighbors, seems to have conveyed well into the nineteenth century the announcement, deeply incised and often renewed: "Here Pope sung."

Away from Binfield in all directions, but particularly to the south and east, the royal forest of Windsor stretched for miles. Encompassing at least a hundred thousand acres, it was not a forest as most of us today think of forests; it was a mixture of individual woods and woodland rides with pasturage and meadow, scatterings of grove and coppice, and immense dark reaches of heathery moor, punctuated sometimes by green belts of farms with neat hedgerows and pollarded willows along the banks of drainage ditch or stream, and sometimes by outcroppings of bush and bracken so tall and dense that even deer, not to mention smaller game, could hide in them and shake off pursuers. Granted the idealization of the English countryside that Pope's youthful poem *Windsor-Forest* asks us to accept in honor of Queen Anne, last of the Stuart monarchs and regarded by some as England's first rightful ruler since 1688, when Dutch William ousted her father James II, the scenery it describes corresponds with remarkable accuracy to features actually present in the landscape about Binfield:

> Here waving Groves a checquer'd Scene display,
> And part admit and part exclude the Day;
> As some coy Nymph her Lover's warm Address
> Nor quite indulges, nor can quite repress.
> There, interspers'd in Lawns and opening Glades,
> Thin Trees arise that shun each others Shades.
> Here in full Light the russet Plains extend;
> There wrapt in Clouds the blueish Hills ascend:
> Ev'n the wild Heath displays her purple Dies,
> And 'midst the Desart fruitful Fields arise,
> That crown'd with tufted Trees and springing Corn,
> Like verdant Isles the sable Waste adorn.
>
> (ll. 17–28)

This is, of course, a "poetic" landscape carefully composed, as has often been observed. In its subtle concern with color, "its quiet range of tint and tone" (says a late commentator with a professional competence in these matters), it marks a new moment in the history of landscape description:

9. Pope's House: Binfield.

A little House, with Trees a-row,
And like its Master, very low.

Imit. Hor., Ep.I, vii: 77–8

From Dugdale's *England and Wales Delineated* (1852). No earlier view is known. By permission of the British Library.

"See (Pope seems to cry) how the wide sunburnt fields here in the foreground stretch away yonder; and yonder how the rugged moorland glows with the bloom of the heather; while there, look! on the far-off horizon are the hills, barely seen—not blue, with all those clouds about, nor yet insubstantial enough for pale blue; more grey than blue, really, but a colder grey than the surrounding clouds—blueish, to be precise." Only a painter, actual or potential, would have patience enough to analyse—or would bother enough to render—such niceties.

We may perhaps catch also, in the second couplet of the passage, a gleam of that long-lived pastoral eroticism—Ovidian nymph with god or mortal, country or court nymph (or milkmaid) with shepherd or courtier, fragment of *fête champêtre* or *fête galante* snatched here in a simile—which evidently answers to something deeply ingrained in the human imagination and in various modifications has played a considerable role in landscape art from Giorgione to Manet, but perhaps most particularly in the tradition of Watteau, Lancret, Boucher, and Fragonard. Yet for all their painterly and literary artifice, the lines refer unmistakably to scenes about Binfield in Pope's time.

For a boy city bred, life in the country was a brave new world. True, he was working hard at his books in these years, so hard that (recalling this period forty years later) his sister Magdalen told Spence that he "did nothing but write and read." But unbookish folk are prone to such exaggerations about bookish ones, and we may safely guess that even so studious a youth enjoyed occasional distractions. One of these he doubtless found close home; for his father had settled into gardening at Whitehill as if born to it and soon acquired, it appears, as much local fame for the size of his "Hartichokes" (still in the early 1700s a recherché item in the English diet, though introduced as far back as Henry VIII's time) as his son was to do later at Twickenham for his efforts with melons, broccoli, and pineapples. Since it seems unlikely that so consuming an avocation in the man had no roots in the experience of the boy, we are perhaps justified in picturing the young Pope, before ill health overtook him, as sometimes at work in the kitchen garden alongside his admired father, or at any rate marveling at his father's horticultural skills, as Odysseus on his homecoming marvels at those of Laertes:

> Great is thy skill, oh father! great thy toil,
> Thy careful hand is stamp'd on all the soil,
> Thy squadron'd vineyards well thy art declare,

The olive green, blue fig, and pendent pear;
And not one empty spot escapes thy care.

(24: 287–91)

The produce would be different enough at Whitehill, but not (as anyone who has ever kept a garden knows) the toil or care.

On similar grounds, though nothing can be certainly stated in either case, we may suspect that the Binfield neighborhood as a whole, with its numerous glades and groves, open prospects, "beautiful hills and vales intermixed with fine lawns and herbage for cattle," together with its great variety of tree forms and shades of verdure (beech, oak, poplar, willow, fir, and more) threw images of pleasure on a boy's retina, and eventually on his mind, that later, however obliquely, took effect in the grown man's leanings toward an open and "natural" style of landscaping at Twickenham.

Binfield may have brought other formative experiences as well. Windsor and Windsor Castle, as mentioned earlier, lay close at hand, and Pope's visits there would help foster in him that rapturous pride of country which blazes up so strikingly in *Windsor-Forest*, never altogether to fade. At Windsor Castle, especially in the Chapel of St. George, he would encounter exciting moments of his country's past, incorporated in forms not likely to leave a youthful imagination untouched, from the time of William the Conqueror, who first established a royal residence at Windsor, to that of "My Queen *Anne*" (as he calls her in a poem written late in life), who now made the castle her chief abode and hunted regularly in the forest. Here Edward III was born—warrior king and, with his son the Black Prince, first vanquisher of France, the enemy with whom England was again at war during most of Pope's Binfield years. Here Edward had founded his world-renowned Order of the Garter, the crests, swords, and banners of whose current members, overhanging the richly carved oak stalls in St. George's choir, furnished as dazzling a spectacle for a young poet in the first years of the eighteenth century as they remain for visitors today. The time was coming when a British statesman would remark that he liked the Garter because there was no damned humbug about merit in it. But that time was not yet. A certain aura of distinction still, in Pope's youth, attended the wearers of the "Silver Star" (line 290), and many of the names of past holders, recorded on brasses at the rear of each stall, evoked events and personalities that in the climate of the early 1700s, when Marlborough was winning his great victories at Blenheim and Ramillies, could hardly fail to quicken an English pulse: all those bustling internal factions and foreign wars over which in the history plays Shakespeare had already cast his golden spell.

Sad stories of the death of kings could also be read in that chapel. There, under one roof, Henry VI and Edward IV, victim and victor, Lancastrian and Yorkist, bitter rivals for the throne throughout the Wars of the Roses, lay at peace with each other at last—as Pope would duly note in his poem with all the sententiousness that the seventeenth and eighteenth centuries savored on such occasions:

> Here o'er the Martyr-King the Marble weeps,
> And fast beside him, once-fear'd *Edward* sleeps:
> Whom not th' extended *Albion* could contain,
> From old *Belerium*★ to the *Northern* Main,
> The Grave unites; where ev'n the Great find Rest,
> And blended lie th' Oppressor and th' Opprest!
>
> (ll. 313–18)

Another king whom a majority of Englishmen in the 1700s held to have been martyred, Charles I, was likewise buried in the Chapel. Buried, in fact, in the same vault with Henry VIII, his opposite in almost every imaginable respect. In Pope's lifetime the exact location of his body remained unknown—"(Obscure the Place, and uninscrib'd the Stone)," says the poem at line 320—and it was not until 1813 that Charles's skeleton and severed head were found together in the plain leaden coffin where they had been hastily tucked away in hugger-mugger, hard by the skeleton of his Tudor predecessor: "heartless Henry" (as Byron put it in some scathing verses of that period on the English royal house in general) beside "headless Charles."

Pope's own view of Charles was of course very different. In *Windsor-Forest*, the "Fact"—i.e., crime—"accurst" of his execution is clearly implied to have been the sin from which followed the rest of England's seventeenth-century trials and disorders (plague, fire, internal divisiveness), till at last Anne brought the country's warring factions together:

> Oh Fact accurst! What Tears has *Albion* shed,
> Heav'ns! what new Wounds, and how her old have bled?
> She saw her Sons with purple Deaths expire,
> Her sacred Domes involv'd in rolling Fire,
> A dreadful Series of Intestine Wars,

★Land's End in Cornwall.

Inglorious Triumphs, and dishonest Scars.
At length great ANNA said—Let Discord cease!
She said, the World obey'd, and all was *Peace*!

(ll. 321–8)

A ridiculous hope, obviously, in any political sense! Yet as an expression of the mood that for a time attended Anne's accession and the great military successes abroad (and perhaps too of that search for "something evermore about to be" with which poetry as opposed to history deals), not entirely without foundation. Walking up Thames Street and then Church Street from the Castle, a visitor to Windsor in Pope's day was unlikely to overlook its new classical Town Hall, recently completed by Sir Christopher Wren; and there in a niche on the north facade (on any visit made after 1706) a statue of Anne might catch his eye, bearing a Latin inscription altogether in the vein of Pope's attitudes as expressed in the poem:

Arte tua, sculptor, non est imitabilis Anna;
Annae vis similem sculpere, sculpe deam.★

"An Occasional Conformist"

Oddly enough, Pope's catalogue of monarchs associated with Windsor contains the name of no Tudor. The omission seems striking in view of the fact that Henry VIII is buried in a monument impossible to overlook in the same chapel with the kings already mentioned, and that both he and his daughter Elizabeth I had left their mark on the castle fabric. Elizabeth, it is true, receives a glancing reference (without name) as formerly an arbiter among nations in Father Thames's vision of the dawning Pax Britannica, when (that arbitership having been assumed by Anne)

Kings shall sue, and suppliant States be seen
Once more to bend before a *British* QUEEN.

(ll. 383–4)

But no other attention is given her, despite her standing then as now, and nothing at all is said of her brilliant father, unless, as the poem's editors in the Twickenham edition suggest, the un-Saxon grandeur attributed to the buildings laid waste by William I in expanding his hunting grounds—

★ ["Not by your art, sculptor, can Anne be portrayed;
You would carve a likeness of Anne? Then carve a goddess."]

> The levell'd Towns with Weeds lie cover'd o'er,
> The hollow Winds thro' naked Temples roar;
> Round broken Columns clasping Ivy twin'd;
> O'er Heaps of Ruin stalk'd the stately Hind;
> The Fox obscene to gaping Tombs retires,
> And savage Howlings fill the sacred Quires—
>
> (ll. 67–72)

is intended to carry our minds four centuries onward to Henry's dissolution of the monasteries. The intention cannot be taken for granted:
Pope may simply be elevating his diction to keep decorum with the
deeds of kings. On the other hand, the reference is by no means implausible. Pope may have known through early friends, one of whom,
as we shall see, was a Forest verderer, that the depredations attributed
by the *Chronicles* to William were modest beside those actually carried
out by Henry, who swallowed up manors, villages, and churches with
a ruthlessness quite comparable to that deplored in the poem.

Living in Berkshire, moreover, Pope was probably witness at first
hand to the sad consequences of Henry's greed in the looting of the
great abbeys. No traveler to Reading, then a small market and manu-
facturing town about as far west of Binfield as Windsor lay to the
east, could fail to notice the relics of the great Benedictine abbey
there, once a jewel among English religious houses, center of public
charities and sound liberal education (the place, it is said, where the
enchanting "Somer is y-comen in" was composed) now in the 1700s a
thirty-acre precinct of broken columns, bits of tracery, decaying
vaults and spandrels, rubble. To secure the wealth of this place in its
heyday, Henry's agent Thomas Cromwell wove his usual net of
intrigue about the presiding abbot Hugh Faringdon (as he had earlier
done about Thomas More) and then (acting as even Froude had to
concede, as "prosecutor, judge, and jury") had him executed illegally
on his own personal order. Faringdon was hanged, quartered, the
pieces thrown into burning pitch, then swung in chains from the
abbey gates. The abbey itself, which Faringdon, unlike many of his
confrères, could not be cajoled into surrendering voluntarily, was
promptly pillaged, yielding tapestries, manuscripts, books, and
2,645 ounces of silver and gold in church vessels, besides an income
from the lands of just under £2,000 a year, in a period when the annual
wage of a house servant was likely to be a suit of clothes plus twenty-
five shillings.

Pope may or may not have been acquainted with the fate of Hugh
Faringdon, which was also shared by the abbots of Colchester and

Glastonbury. But the ruins of the great Reading abbey remained for all to see, as did those of a number of other religious foundations in Berkshire, which had been well furnished with them—one reason, it may be, for the original establishment in that area of a cluster of prominent Roman Catholic families: Blounts, Dancastles, Englefields south of the Thames in Berkshire, Fermors, Stonors, Talbots, and Webbs just north of it in Oxfordshire. In such circles, a consciousness of past injustices, kept alive by present privations, was not likely to nourish the warmest of regards for those who, like Henry and Elizabeth, had contributed largely to the alienated status of the group. It may well be therefore that Pope's omission of the Tudor monarchs from his blazon of British glories in *Windsor-Forest*, and perhaps even the veiled allusion to the destruction of the monasteries (if that is what it is), tacitly express a point of view.

The consciousness of having been relegated to something like second-class citizenship was not, however, the only or even the most powerful tie uniting the English Roman Catholic community—in Berkshire or elsewhere. Among the determinedly zealous, a subtler and stricter bond was the not altogether healthy conviction (to which beleaguered ethnic and religious minorities have always been susceptible) that they formed part of a "saving remnant," bore witness to a reality that others had betrayed, guarded a pure flame that must be passed on at all costs undimmed. Such an outlook, whether in our day or Pope's, invites intolerance of whatever it chooses to identify as deviationism or innovation, and Pope found himself in trouble with it (Catholics of this persuasion censured him severely for his verses on monkish ignorance in the *Essay on Criticism*) almost from the moment he began to publish. Fortunately, it was not widely shared. For most Catholics by 1700, a century and a half of enforced withdrawal from the satisfactions of consensus behavior with their countrymen—taking food together, for instance (which had become a particularly sensitive area in view of Protestant disapproval of most mealtime religious observances)—had gradually given rise to a characteristic attitude, a received form of worship, and a more or less uniform style of living.

The characteristic attitude, except among pockets of the very zealous, was largely one of unmilitant acceptance of the status quo, something like that which Pope ascribes to his father in the lines earlier quoted from his *Epistle to Dr. Arbuthnot*. The attitude could accommodate vague longings and even sometimes preciser hopes for a change of dynasty to bring Catholics their freedom, but in general it held very little solid expectation of this event and even less ambition to risk serious trouble on behalf of it. So at any rate most historians now believe. At the time, matters were far less clear. The maneuverings of Jacobite zealots at home and the ambitions of the Stuart claimant abroad eventuated just often enough in invasion or threat of invasion during the next half century to lend credence to old fears. Fears, as we saw earlier, that could be and sometimes were played upon by those in authority for political ends. Walpole as first minister proved to be a master at this game, and even Gilbert Burnet, Whig Bishop of Sarum, sought to frighten Queen Anne from the peace that eventually became the Peace of Utrecht by assuring her it would bring back the fires of Smithfield. It was to be a very long time before English Protestants could compel themselves to recognize that loyalty to a displaced dynasty in preference to a foreign one, or to a faith that had earlier been that of their own forefathers, did not carry with it automatically any intention to disestablish the English church, massacre the Protestant population, or reclaim the abbey lands. Stereotypes, especially those that can be counted on to curtail competition from gifted minorities, die hard.

The received form of Roman Catholic worship by 1700 had become the private mass. It was performed in the household by a resident priest, who might also serve in some other capacity such as tutor—this would help conceal his true function from the law—or as pastor to whatever small company of Catholic faithful his immediate neighborhood afforded. The private mass as an institution obviously had its shortcomings, for Catholic writers of the time complain equally of those who, as if "stepping out of Bed to the Altar," attend in such "disrespectful undress that it would be an affront to the meanest Friend" and of those who, at some later time of day, "approach the Holy Table powdered, patch'd, perfumed, barenecked, or any other ways so set forth as seems more suitable for a Ball." Among Catholics of Pope's time, as among later Catholics till recently, few worshippers felt impelled to follow what the priest did at the altar. The Catholic writer just quoted, though urging in his *Instructions* that those present "accompany" the priest, acknowledges that in fact most persons regard mass-time as a time for their own personal acts of worship, "some saying their Beads all the time of the Mass, others their Morning Prayers, others the Offices of the Day or some private Devotion."

Related to devotion but partly also the outcome of long custom, the way of life of a rural English Roman Catholic household in 1700 made substantial demands on the individual member. It was based on the liturgical calendar; and while by 1700 the fast days and days of abstinence from meat, which had once comprised over a third of the year, together with the feast days or holy days, which numbered about forty, were settling into a pattern economically more practicable because less disruptive of farm labor, the great fasts of Lent and the great feasts centered on Whitsun, Saints Peter and Paul (June 29), Assumption of the Virgin (August 15), Michaelmas (September 29), and All Saints, but particularly Christmas and Easter, could be complex and sometimes all-consuming. As late as 1799, by which time Catholic devotional practices had generally relaxed, Frances, Lady Jerningham, could joke with her daughter that her brother Arthur, long a colonel in the French army but lately home for an Easter-week visit, had interrupted his stay by Maundy Thursday because "the fasting and praying this week was too much for him." Pope, also jokingly, confides a similar embarrassment in 1710 to his fashionable London friend Henry Cromwell, who was not a Roman Catholic:

> I had written to you sooner but that I made some Scruple of sending Profane [non-devotional] Things to You in Holy Week. Besides Our Family wou'd have been Scandalizd to see me write, who take it for granted I write nothing but ungodly Verses; and They say here so many Pray'rs, that I can make but few Poems; For in this point of Praying, I am an Occasional Conformist [the cant phrase applied to Catholic or Protestant recusants who took the Anglican sacrament just often enough to be excepted from the usual penalties and exclusions]. So just as I am drunk or Scandalous in Town, according to my Company I am for the same reason Grave & Godly here.

This is clearly Pope the chameleon putting on a face to meet the faces that he meets, possibly under the impression (voiced to Cromwell six months earlier) that it is "the chief point of Friendship to comply with [a] Friend's Motions & Inclinations." In any case, the frank acknowledgment that he inclines to behave according to the company he is in represents (in my view) a basic truth about himself of which it is interesting to see him conscious so early.

With his Roman Catholic friend John Caryll, the joking could be more intimate. Pope thanks him for a gift of oysters, without which, he claims, his family Lent in Binfield would have been austere:

> But you have taken care I should not have this at least to complain of, by the kind present you sent me; without which, had I kept Lent here, I must have submitted to the common fate of my brethren, and have starved: yet I should (I think) have been the first poet that ever

starved for the sake of religion. Now as your lady is pleased to say of my present, that St. Luke himself never drew such a Madonna [Pope has evidently just sent Mrs. Caryll a specimen of his drawing skills]; so I may say of yours, that the prince of the apostles himself, tho' he was a fisherman all his life, never eat so good oysters. And as she tells me that I did a thing I never thought of, and excelled a saint, I may tell you that you have done a thing you was not aware of, and reclaimed a sinner; for you'll be the cause that I shall obey a precept of the Church, and fast this Lent, which I have not done many years before. Which (with my hearty thanks) is all I can say on this subject, for I find upon scratching my head three times, that 'tis not so hard to get pearls out of oysters, as wit.

It is not easy to read between the lines of such a letter to discover what Pope really felt about the religious practices among which he grew up. To turn a witty compliment (by now everywhere expected of him) was obviously a first concern; and the reference to his not having fasted in Lent "for many years before," at first glance revealing, is actually an in-joke for the benefit of his co-religionist, fasting not being required of a Roman Catholic till age twenty-one and Pope being now just a few months past twenty-two. The playful tone of the passage is the tone he takes toward these matters usually and may be seen again in instances as diverse as the image he summons up for John Caryll's son, a young man of about his own age, of escaping the family prayer bell by professing urgent business in the "necessary-house," and the regimen he imagines for a young Catholic coquette of his acquaintance condemned to forgo the delights of social London for a sojourn in the country:

> She went, to plain-work, and to purling brooks,
> Old-fashion'd halls, dull aunts, and croaking rooks,
> She went from Op'ra, park, assembly, play,
> To morning walks, and pray'rs three hours a day;
> To pass her time 'twixt reading and Bohea,★
> To muse, and spill her solitary Tea,
> Or o'er cold coffee trifle with the spoon,
> Count the slow clock, and dine exact at noon;
> Divert her eyes with pictures in the fire,
> Hum half a tune, tell stories to the squire;
> Up to her godly garret after sev'n,
> There starve and pray, for that's the way to heav'n.

★In the early eighteenth century, a tea of the highest quality.

Plainly not the words of an impassioned votary! Yet it would be a gross mistake to take any of these statements at face value. The jocularity that Pope assumes for such occasions, like the smile of Lady Jerningham instanced earlier, has much the quality of an elder brother's condescension to a younger brother or sister, whom he feels free to censure at will but about whom he is fiercely loyal if another ventures the same liberty. It is with a similar jocularity, one notices, that Pope confronts his ugly body after the tubercular disease takes hold of him, and the need in both cases may have been the same. To manage a humorous attitude toward any inconvenient datum of existence, particularly one that may occasion mockery, hostility, or embarrassment in others, is to declare a certain detachment from it for oneself, and to make the claim (usually, no more than a courageous social pose) that it is *not* a sensitive area to be avoided by one's friends or fastened on as vulnerable by one's enemies.

But these are matters for later consideration. Suffice it to say here that Pope's response to the devotional life of his parent's pious household, so far as it is ever expressed publicly, contains as much affection as amusement. If he found their regimen excessive, or even inhibiting at times, as the remark to Cromwell may imply (or may not: for the chameleon tendency to which Pope refers in the earlier letter may be at work in this case too), there is no evidence that it interfered appreciably with his studies or his writing, or, for that matter, with what must have been on his first arriving in Binfield a boy's delighted explorations of country life.

CHAPTER 4

PREPARATIONS

"The happiest part of my life"

Of Pope's impressions of his new home, his *Windsor-Forest* affords a fascinating glimpse. Much in the poem obviously reflects his reading at the time. Much also, however, attests to such feelings, thoughts, and fancies as any observant and imaginative youth may be counted on to entertain in a rural setting, particularly in the unspoiled agricultural countryside of those days. "I followed everywhere as my fancy led me," he confided to Spence toward the end of his life, recalling this early period in Binfield, "and was like a boy gathering flowers in the woods and fields just as they fall in his way. I still look upon these five or six years as the happiest part of my life." The primary reference is to the unstructured character of his reading; but we may guess that the accompanying image of a child's delicious freedom in exploring woods and fields is equally a remembrance from that time.

There was much for a child to rejoice in. At first, no doubt, the simplest pleasures of the out-of-doors. "Thick new-born Violets [in] a soft Carpet spread" along the margins of coppices and groves where the sun strikes; wild "Pinks and Daisies" in the meadows; "Hawthorns" blossoming in the hedgerows; in the orchard, the "exalted scents" of ripe pears yet dangling from the tree; bronzed grain "nodding" in the wind in the nearest open field, as if consenting to the sickle; in the deep woods, those puzzling reversed reflections on the surfaces of pools and quiet streams: all these experiences appear at one time or other in Pope's poetry, and the last-named experience, almost always one of childhood's earliest and most memorable encounters with the riddles of appearance and reality, seems to have impressed him sufficiently to be noticed in one of the first poems he ever wrote (at about age fifteen) as well as (in a maturer formulation) in *Windsor-Forest*. There, stopping on the banks of the Loddon, a small river running north to the Thames only a stroll away from Binfield, "the musing Shepherd"

spies
The headlong Mountains and the downward Skies,
The watry Landskip of the pendant Woods,
And absent Trees that tremble in the Floods;
In the clear azure Gleam the Flocks are seen,
And floating Forests paint the Waves with Green.

(ll. 211–116)

The passage draws on some lines from the Latin poet Ausonius describing the Moselle. Yet, like the painterly description of the Binfield landscape, provided we remember that what we call hills Pope's contemporaries regularly (in verse) called mountains, it manages to cull out landscape features actually to be found locally without compromising their capacity to call up a succession of similar landscape moments stretching back to Vergil. In Pope's work generally, scene as 'idea,' as landscape transformed to inscape in the manner of Poussin or Lorrain, takes precedence over topography. So, too, does scene as a dance of verbal energies. Notable in this passage, in particular, is the swirl of paradoxical and even self-contradictory activities set going in the midst of ostensible quiet by the musing consciousness of the shepherd, which creates while it "spies."

Experiences more inward must also have come thronging in these early Binfield years. Intoxicating escapes, we may imagine, such as a country life invites, into a child's private kingdoms of forest and field. A rapturous sense of seclusions, enclaves, inaccessible retreats—"Thy Forests, *Windsor*! and thy green Retreats" (line 1)—at a time of life when the symbolic "green" is as much within as without; when (to quote a predecessor of Pope's)

the raw blossome of my youth was yet
In my first childhood's green enclosure bound;

and when all raptures are made more rapturous by golden intimations of secret powers ripening. Premonitions, moreover, there must have been (for these come to all of us in our youth) of presences in earth, air, stream, and in the mind itself. Not Wordsworthian presences in Pope's case, obviously, but not the inert rubble of a classical education either: invented perhaps but also discovered; mysteries of the imagination that haunt us still, though we no longer objectify some of them as nymphs and dryads ("Be present, Sylvan Maids!" the poem urges in line 3), others as Muses ("Your Aid, O Muses bring!" line 5), still others as tutelary deities and Geniuses of the Place.

When in *Windsor-Forest* the huntress-nymph Lodona is transformed into the Berkshire river Loddon to escape the lustful pursuit of Pan (a quiet stream, the Loddon curls up from Hampshire to join the Thames about six miles from Binfield), we would be rash to suppose that we are dealing *merely* (as Pope's nineteenth-century editors liked to think) with a piece of "mythological trash" inspired by too much reading in Ovid's *Metamorphoses*. "As a child," observes a respected critic and poet of our own day, "I became a confirmed believer in the ancient gods simply because as between the reality of fact and the reality of myth I chose myth." It is a choice that has always been congenial to poets, and it was one much easier to sustain in Pope's time, when "Nature" was still usually held to be a spiritualized and animistic order, than it has become since. We may therefore reasonably conjecture that a poet whose major works would regularly consist in investing realities of fact—a forest, a lock of hair, bad writers, the England of Robert Walpole, Twickenham, and himself—with some of the characteristics of myth responded as receptively as his predecessors and successors to intuitions of mysterious powers in nature. And though it would be quite beside the point to identify Pope's intentions in the Lodona episode with the revelations made in our own ecologically embarrassed century by such lay-prophets as Faulkner's Ike McCaslin (who discovers that absolute possession of anything in nature, whether wilderness or bear, imperils both the object possessed and something in oneself), it is very much to the point, I think, to notice the anticipation in the Lodona incident, and in all its Ovidian counterparts, of the central situation in *The Rape of the Lock*: a rape or threat of rape precipitates a metamorphosis in which loss is balanced against gain.

Speculations of a very different sort about the Lodona passage will occur to readers who remember Byron's amusing stanzas on the education provided by Donna Inez for her son Don Juan—a situation not altogether remote from Pope's as sole son of godly parents in a household where three elderly females kept up the pieties and proprieties:

> But that which Donna Inez most desired,
> And saw into herself each day before all
> The learned tutors whom for him she hired,
> Was, that his breeding should be strictly moral:
> Much into all his studies she inquired,
> And so they were submitted first to her, all
> Arts, sciences—no branch was made a mystery
> To Juan's eyes, excepting natural history.

His classic studies made a little puzzle,
Because of filthy loves of gods and goddesses,
Who in the earlier ages raised a bustle,
But never put on pantaloons or bodices;
His reverend tutors had at times a tussle;
And for their *Aeneids*, *Iliads*, and *Odysseys*
Were forced to make an odd sort of apology,
For Donna Inez dreaded the Mythology.
                    (*Don Juan*, Canto 1, stanzas 39, 41)

Ovid's rendering of "the Mythology" has had so colorful a history
as the educator of precocious schoolboys (not merely in the niceties of
Latin syntax) that a careful reader of the Lodona passage—

Now fainting, sinking, pale, the Nymph appears;
Now close behind his sounding Steps she hears;
And now his Shadow reach'd her as she run,
(His Shadow lengthen'd by the setting Sun)
And now his shorter Breath with sultry Air
Pants on her Neck—

                                             (ll. 191–6)

might well be forgiven for wondering if it does not in some degree
(besides reflecting the central hunter-becomes-hunted metaphor of
the poem) show the effects of certain early stirrings that at about the
same time were finding a more explicit outlet in a translation of
Ovid's story of Arethusa. In this story, another huntress-nymph,
Arethusa, pauses to bathe in an inviting stream—

I came, and in the Brink my Foot I dipp'd;
Then to the Knee in dimpling Curls I slipp'd;
Nor cool'd, upon a Bough my Veil I hung:
And, on the Bank my airy Garments flung;
Into the bounding Tyde I naked leap—

                                             (ll. 23–7)

only to find herself, as she "frisk'd and wanton'd," the object of
amorous advances from the river-god Alpheus:

Just as I was, without my Cloaths I fled;
(Upon the other Bank my Cloaths were laid)
The more did he with raging Passion burn,
Naked he thought me fitter for his Turn.

                                             (ll. 35–8)

Here again, though it is always impossible to be sure, a careful reader may be tempted to conclude that the scene is handled not simply *con amore* but with a particularity (as in those paintings of naked nymphs or busty tragic heroines found acceptable even in pious households for their literary associations) that seems to have as much to do with personal reverie or fantasy as with an ancient text. Some details in fact are striking. In Ovid's narrative, there is nothing quite so exactly observed as "dimpling Curls" to describe the flow of water about an object plunged into it; there is no suggestion of a "Veil," though this can easily have come from other accounts of Roman costume; and though Ovid's Arethusa plays about in the stream, "gliding in a thousand turns," the overtones of "frisk'd and wanton'd" conceivably extend further.

At about these years too, for most of us, begin those first awesome transactions with time. Time, the arch-enemy and depredator—"Years foll'wing Years, steal something ev'ry day," Pope will say later, adopting an image of Milton's that was earlier Shakespeare's and, of course, Horace's. Time the old gypsy man and pied-piper, as some poets of our own day have perceived him, who allows

> In all his tuneful turning so few and such morning songs
> Before the children green and golden
> Follow him out of grace.

But time also the revealer and healer, the creator and improver, as Pope rarely forgets; who gives as he takes; replaces old dreams with new; and helps make poems as well as landscapes:

> Spontaneous beauties all around advance,
> Start ev'n from Difficulty, strike from Chance;
> Nature shall join you, Time shall make it grow
> A Work to wonder at—perhaps a Stow;
>
> (ll. 67–70)

or perhaps such a poem as that from which these verses come: *An Epistle to the Right Honourable Earl of Burlington.*

In a touching passage from an unrevised draft of his 1717 *Preface*, Pope looks back on these younger days with a certain ruefulness:

> I was very innocently in love with myself wn [when] I began to write & my first productions were the children of Self-Love upon Innocence. . . . I had made an Epic poem, & panegyrics on all the Princes of Europe, & thought myself the greatest Genius tht [that]

ever was. I cant but regret those visions of my childhood, which, like the fine Colours I then saw when my Eyes shut, are vanishd for ever.

But this is far from being the whole story. Vanished forever? On the contrary! Ever reappearing in new shapes, like those other painted clouds that beautify our days. Hence when he assures himself at the close of *Windsor-Forest* that his humble Muse, content to have made this pastoral hymn to the peace and plenty of a Stuart reign, has now no further or higher ambitions, we know better. And so did he—however great his gratifications on first completing the poem may have been.

"Short is his Joy!"

Equally conducive to reflection (we gather from *Windsor-Forest*) as he grew into his middle teens, was the seasonal procession of rural sports. Spring, the poem tells us, brings out the patient fisherman, "his Angle trembling in his Hand" (138). Observation of the man leads to observation of his catch, or at least of such creatures as were available for catching in the local Berkshire streams. Pope describes them with a loving attention to pictorial effect, rising from purple through silver to gold and then falling away to crimson, without, however, ignoring the actual characteristics of the species concerned. "Bright-ey'd Perch," touched at the spread of the fins with "Tyrian Dye," usher in the silver eels, wet and glistening, "in shining Volumes roll'd"; and these in turn set off the yellow carp, scales agleam in the sun as if "bedrop'd with Gold," which are flanked by "Swift Trouts, diversify'd with Crimson Stains," and, almost pre- dictably, by "Pykes," long established piscatorially as "Tyrants" because of their appetite for other fish, including their own kind (ll. 137–46). The allusion to tyranny is not, however, simply pic- turesque. It appropriates the pictorial to the moral, which is the method of the poem as a whole, and it defines in miniature the prin- ciple of despotic rule ("Th' enormous faith of many made for one," as he will put it later in the *Essay on Man*) that is throughout being contrasted with the harmonies and felicities of the reign of Anne.

Summer's sport has a more sociable cast: the deer hunt. In the royal forests, this was the queen's prerogative, and Swift gives an unfor- gettable picture of her in her later years, careening along (because too corpulent to hunt otherwise) "in a chaise with one horse, which she drives herself, and drives furiously, like Jehu, and is a mighty hunter, like Nimrod." Accompanying her, at least in Pope's version of the chase, is an escort of young hunters, who "rowze" the game, cheer the hounds as they catch the scent and "open" [i.e., give cry], then take off at a gallop on impatient mounts that have already in anticipation run the course: "Hills, Vales, and Floods appear already crost."

> See! the bold Youth strain up the threatning Steep,
> Rush thro' the Thickets, down the Vallies sweep,
> Hang o'er their Coursers Heads with eager Speed,
> And Earth rolls back beneath the flying Steed.
>
> (ll. 155–58)

Living where he did, Pope must often have witnessed such scenes, very possibly including glimpses of the queen in her chariot. From about sixteen or seventeen, moreover, he had taken to riding regularly for his health with his elderly friend Sir William Trumbull, official verderer of the Forest's Easthamstead Walk, and so very likely had learned at first hand how the earth rolls back when glimpsed from a fast gallop and what a different sensation there is under the saddle when the horse is straining up a hillside as against sweeping down a valley. Certainly, at any rate by the time he composed *Windsor-Forest*, he had learned what a poet most needs to know about such differences, which is how to represent them by means of rhythm and sound, as in the enormous contrast of lines 1 and 2 above.

Autumn sports, as Pope records them, contribute a note of melancholy. After the harvest, feeding in the stubble of the "new-shorn Field" for the grain yet lodged there, partridges offer an easy mark, first for the "ready Spaniel" that sets the birds, then for the hunter who unfurls over their heads "the swelling Net," into which they rise and by which they become entangled (ll. 98–104). At the same season the hare circles to elude the "well-breath'd Beagles" in hot pursuit. The pheasant, flushed from his thicket but confident at first in his imagined power to escape, "mounts exulting on triumphant Wings," only to be struck down by an invention still comparatively recent in the early 1700s—the fowling piece firing a volley of small pellets—which was rapidly proving to be the nemesis of game birds in general:

> Oft, as in Airy Rings they skim the Heath,
> The clam'rous Lapwings feel the Leaden Death:
> Oft as the mounting Larks their Notes prepare,
> They fall, and leave their little Lives in Air.
>
> (ll. 131–34)

With what sensations Pope himself came to view these activities, we may perhaps gauge from a paper he contributed to Richard Steele's short-lived periodical *The Guardian* in 1713. In that essay, more than a century in advance of the movements that eventually sprang up to encourage humane treatment of animals, he protested eloquently against both the cruelties that uninstructed children often inflict on birds and beasts and the more sophisticated cruelties of adults, perpetuated equally (he points out) in the eighteenth-century manorial kitchen, "filled with the Cries of Creatures expiring in Tortures," and in the hunting field, particularly in connection with the stag hunt: "a Diversion," he says, "which has such Authority and Custom to support it" that he dares not attack it frontally, but only "that Savage Compliment our Huntsmen pass upon Ladies of Quality, who are present at the Death . . ., when they put the Knife in their Hands to cut the Throat of a helpless, trembling and weeping Creature." His own personal attitude on these matters, he puts forward in a passage translated from Plutarch's *Moralia*:

> Yet if . . . we are ashamed to be so out of Fashion as not to Offend [i.e., refrain from killing altogether], let us at least Offend with some Discretion and Measure. If we kill an Animal for our Provision, let us do it with the Meltings of Compassion and without tormenting it. Let us consider, that 'tis in its own Nature Cruelty to put a living Creature to Death; we at least destroy a Soul that has Sense and Perception.

Very similar views of human responsibility govern *Windsor-Forest*. None of the usual eighteenth-century field-sports is actually disapproved. All are said to be "pleasing Toils" (line 120), and may, indeed, have pleased the poet himself, either personally or vicariously, when in the intervals of his reading he wandered about Binfield with his spaniel at his heels ("a little one, a lean one, and none of the finest Shap'd," he tells Cromwell, evidently remarking a certain affinity between master and dog) or accompanied a hunting friend. "I often," he writes reminiscingly to Thomas Dancastle in early 1717, following the family's removal from Binfield,

> give a Range to my Imagination, & goe a strolling with . . . you, up and down Binfield Wood, or over Bagshot Heath. I wish you all health, not you only, but your Horse, your Dog Lilly, &c. May your gun never fail, and your aim never miss. May your Pouch come swagging home, laden with woodcocks, and may those woodcocks be so fatt & good as to please Mr. Philips [the

Dancastles' family priest, evidently the object of some teasing about his appetite].

These seem hardly the words of a young man who condemns hunting altogether (though here too a lifelong inclination to take on the coloring of his correspondents should perhaps be allowed for); and we know, further, from his having carried pistols for a time after the first appearance of the *Dunciad*, that he was not without experience of firearms, presumably acquired during the Binfield years. Yet if hunting is accepted in the poem as something that human beings enjoy doing, and even as something that it is better for them to do than to kill each other in war, the stress nevertheless falls heavily on the creaturely attractions of the victims, or, alternatively, as in the verses on the larks and lapwings, on the pathos of their unexpected deaths. The most often admired passage in the poem, that on the shooting of the pheasant already alluded to, combines both these elements:

> See! from the Brake the whirring Pheasant springs,
> And mounts exulting on triumphant Wings;
> Short is his Joy! he feels the fiery Wound,
> Flutters in Blood, and panting beats the Ground.
> Ah! what avail his glossie, varying Dyes,
> His Purple Crest, and Scarlet-circled Eyes,
> The vivid Green his shining Plumes unfold;
> His painted Wings, and Breast that flames with Gold?
>
> (ll. 111–18)

Here, as earlier, color is assigned a moral function, and the beauty of the created image, as one critic has sensitively though perhaps too rhetorically observed, "cries out for ever against the pitiful destruction it depicts." At the same time, however, Pope accentuates the pathos of the unexpected death by appropriating it to a formula of feeling to which (as Samuel Johnson would say somewhat later in a similar connection) "every bosom returns an echo." Originating in Homeric epic, where time and again gifts that might have been expected to save a warrior's life—extreme youth, courage, goodness, high birth, great wealth, or all together—fail him, this formula became a commonplace of Roman and later poetry, appearing essentially unchanged (though with slightly shifting accents) in poems as different from each other as Gray's *Elegy in a Country Churchyard*:

> The boast of heraldry, the pomp of pow'r,
> And all that beauty, all that wealth e'er gave,
> Awaits alike th' inevitable hour—

and Landor's lament for the woman he calls Rose Aylmer:

> Ah, what avails the sceptered Race!
> Ah, what the form divine!
> What every virtue, every grace!
> Rose Aylmer, all were thine.

But nowhere except in *Windsor-Forest*, so far as I am aware, is this particular complex of feelings applied to a bird.

The oddity of that circumstance, together with the fact that the pheasant's death is unmistakably described at first hand, even to the details of panting and drumming, inclines one to wonder if by any chance the episode had personal significance. Not that we should expect to see in Pope's pheasant a forerunner of Coleridge's albatross! Far from it—though it is true that the fellowship of creatures that Coleridge's mariner violates was by no means a new conception with the nineteenth century, having been a feature of classical and Renaissance accounts of the Golden Age which reappears also in the *Essay on Man*. The emphasis of the *Windsor-Forest* passage is clearly different. Pope concentrates on the slain, not the slayer: first on the abrupt reversal of the bird's attributed feelings as it rises on triumphant wings, and then on the loss and waste of its death, realized and communicated not, through any commentary but simply by pointing to its vitality and beauty when alive. Guilt, if guilt there is, attaches in Pope's lines not to a particular individual in a particular set of circumstances, as in the mariner's case, or in the case of the boy in Robert Penn Warren's moving poem who shoots, for reasons he does not himself understand, a beautiful red-tailed hawk only to find that he is ever after in some sense haunted by its "Gold eyes, unforgiving." The agent of violence in the pheasant passage never, as a moral sensibility, appears. His act is neither mysterious nor particularly wanton, but commonplace in a sport that is regularly followed and has been through centuries. Whatever judgment, therefore, one may care to infer from the poet's obvious sympathy with the victim must be assumed to speak (like the deaths of the warriors in Homer) less of a single mind's moral experience than of some ultimate irony or contrariety in the nature of things that renders us helpless to save what is precious from that in ourselves which does not prize it, or from that which prizes it, as Pan in the poem prizes Lodona, only as prize.

"A maddish way with him"

For some, says Francis Bacon (recording all the wrong motives for learning before identifying the right one), knowledge is a couch—"whereupon to rest a searching and restless spirit." For others, variable and wandering intelligences, it is a terrace—on which "to walk up and down with a fair prospect." For yet others, it is a tower of state ("for a proud mind to raise itself upon"), a fort ("for strife and contention"), a shop ("for profit or sale"). The *true* aim of learning for a Renaissance mind like Bacon's is of course to foster both the private and the public life—"a conjunction like that of the two highest planets, Saturn the planet of rest and contemplation, and Jupiter the planet of civil society and action."

Though Pope shared Bacon's views on combining contemplation and action (for "in the former," he writes in a *Spectator* paper, "Men generally grow useless by too much Rest, and in the latter are des-troy'd by too much Precipitation"), it would be reckless to assert of him, or perhaps of any human being, that none of Bacon's disap-proved objectives ever contaminated his educational ambitions. Sheer pleasure seems to have been at first his guide:

> In a few years I had dipped into a great number of the English, French, Italian, Latin, and Greek poets. This I did without any design but that of pleasing myself, and got the languages by hunting after the stories . . . rather than read the books to get the languages.

Looking back later on this inversion of a contemporary school-education, he concluded that, "in some respects," he had gained, because he had been left free to read for the sense, whereas at school he would have been taught for so many years to read only for words. His convictions on this matter are reflected in one of the best-known passages in the final *Dunciad*:

> Plac'd at the doors of Learning, youth to guide,
> We never suffer it to stand too wide.
> To ask, to guess, to know, as they commence,
> As Fancy opens the quick springs of Sense,
> We ply the Memory, we load the brain,
> Bind rebel Wit, and double chain on chain,
> Confine the thought, to exercise the breath;
> And keep them in the pale of Words till death.
>
> (Book 4, ll. 153–60)

In the poet's conversations with Spence, to which we owe much of our information about his early reading, he speaks chiefly of his readings in the poets—again not a diet of which Bacon could approve. Between the ages of seven or eight and twenty or twenty-one, poetry seems to have been in fact the principal object of his concentration. From eight until about twelve, Homer in the Ogilby translation, Ovid's *Metamorphoses* in the standard seventeenth-century translation of George Sandys, and the *Thebaid* of Statius in an abbreviated version "by some very bad hand" were his favorites among the classical poets, as Waller, Spenser, and Dryden (the *Fables*, no doubt, which took him into the story worlds of Chaucer, Bocaccio, and Ovid) are said to have been among the English. During these same years he was engaged with his priests and at school in learning the rudiments of the classical languages—an occupation sufficiently glanced at in chapter 2. Then at twelve or thirteen he began the self-conducted tour of the poets that we have just heard him describe, carrying it on uninterruptedly until roughly his majority; though it is fair to point out that from the very beginning he diversified his stints of reading with efforts to render passages in the Latin poets that especially pleased him into English verse and to imitate the styles, or sometimes even particular poems, of the English poets he admired. All this was eventually topped off, he told both Spence and Warburton, by seven more years spent "in unlearning all he had been acquiring for twice seven." What he meant by this, one gathers, is that it cost him several years of further systematic study to correct, extend, and "methodize" the lopsided and haphazard education he had got at first.

Interruptions of this strict regimen were in the early years rare. At about fifteen or sixteen he went up to London to learn French and Italian, but this was rather a change of scene than of work habits. Where he stayed or how long he remained in the city, we do not know. The visit apparently ran counter to the advice of members of his family, who took the practical view that his poor health, already to be reckoned with, would never permit him to travel to countries where those languages were spoken. But the same stubbornness that enabled him during a lifetime of illness to produce a body of verse now collected in ten volumes, a correspondence collected in five, and a series of prose pieces that, when collected, will amount to three, came to his aid: "He stuck to it, went thither, and mastered both these languages with a surprising dispatch."

This is a family priest and friend speaking, and we may wonder how much beyond skin-deep Pope's Italian actually was, though he did absorb enough of the language to quote Tasso appositely (in the original) in his *Iliad* notes, and, nearly twenty years later, to make the visiting poet and playwright Scipio Maffei the compliment of at least appearing to translate his play *La Merope*. French he seems to have battened down more securely. His oral French was perhaps not up to sustaining a rapid conversation "with a Voltaire in his own tongue," says the French scholar who has studied this matter closely, but without doubt he knew the language sufficiently "to read our authors in the original." In one way or other, at any rate, with the help of English and neo-Latin translations, he managed on the Italian side a degree of acquaintance with such major figures as Ariosto, Petrarch, and Tasso, and with at least some poems by Bembo, Bonarelli, Castiglione, Fracastoro, Guarini, Marino, Molza, Poliziano, Sadoleto, Sannazaro, Strada, and Vida. In fact, his enthusiasm for the minor Italians who wrote in Latin was so durable as to cause him to collect and publish an anthology of their work toward the end of his life.

As for the French, they had produced during the sixteenth and seventeenth centuries a literature far more accessible to English readers of Pope's day than the Renaissance Italians, and Pope became tolerably (though I think never more than tolerably) well read in it, prose as well as verse, but notably verse. To this one must add that his grasp of his own native literature has rarely been excelled, as the notes in almost any edition of his works abundantly show. His love of the ancients never dampened his admiration (as sometimes happened with his contemporaries) for the achievements of his great English predecessors; nor did his own consciousness that he would one day be among the English poets obscure what he owed to them. "I know too well," he wrote in a letter of 1711, "the vast difference betwixt those who truly deserve the name of poets and men of wit, and one who is nothing but what he owes to them; and I keep the pictures of Dryden, Milton, Shakespeare, &c., in my chamber, round about me, that the constant remembrance of 'em may keep me always humble."

Throughout this long orgy of poetical assimilation, a wild "rapture" (in the literal sense), perhaps almost a frenzy, seems to have made itself visible in the young Pope and to have caused comment. "To speak plain to you," Pope's sister confided to Spence in 1728, referring to this early period, "my brother has a maddish way with him;" Spence then added, in what was apparently intended to be an interpretation of the remark: "Little people mistook the excess of his genius for madness." A pronouncement strikingly similar comes to us from a different source. At some point between his fourteenth and nineteenth year, Pope made the acquaintance of Edmund Smith, a poet of considerable reputation in his own day, who for his carelessness about dress was variously known as "the handsome sloven" and "Captain Rag." "Igad," the Captain is reported to have exclaimed after an unspecified period in Pope's company, "that young fellow will either be a madman or make a very great poet."

These comments allude to something not easy to define. Perhaps they point only to the raptness already mentioned, to an extreme fixedness on the matter in hand, such as the poet himself describes when, later, his imagination became totally absorbed in the *Iliad* translation:

> Like a Witch, whose Carcase lies motionless on the floor, while she keeps her airy Sabbaths, . . . in this world, & in others, I seem to sleep in the midst of the Hurry, even as you would say a Top stands still, when tis in the Whirle of its giddy motion. 'Tis . . . a serious truth I tell you when I say that my Days & Nights are . . . so equally insensible of any Moving Power but Fancy, that I have sometimes spoke of things in our family as Truths & real accidents [i.e., events], which I only Dreamt of; & again when some things that actually happen'd came into my head, have thought (till I enquire) that I had only dream'd of them.

Or perhaps what Captain Rag and Magdalen were struck by was no more than the fanatical application of a young man making his way; who now understood more fully and vividly than when a child how many doors were closed to him. A nagging consciousness of exclusion, experience tells us, can produce in different personalities very different effects. One effect can be anger, sometimes so deeply internalized as to vent itself only much later in adult life in such varying forms as fits of depression, unexplained bouts of irritability, sweeping irresistible impulses to throw a few bricks at the stained-glass attitudes of the excluding Establishment. As everybody knows, there are hints of this effect in Pope's career, though I do not in any way wish to mitigate his responsibility for his actions by conjecturing that some of them, like Belinda's, may have had their origin in a Cave of Spleen. A related effect of exclusion can of course be acquiescence in defeat. This effect is possibly to be recognized in the extreme languor and fragility of certain Victorian women and many heroines of nineteenth-century popular fiction, barred by their society from all but token participation in the hurly-burly of their times. It is certainly the effect singled out by Halifax, we may recall, when he implied that every *manly* soul would of course choose to escape the indolence that the Penal Laws imposed on Roman Catholics by going over to the Established Church. Though Pope never capitulated to this pressure, he may have felt its challenge and have been compelled to deal with it in another way.

For surely the most predictable result of an exclusionary policy is to generate in at least some of those victimized by it a massive determination to overcome it, to *force* an entry into the excluding group or at least into some of the freedoms and privileges associated with it. "*Envy* must own, I live among the Great," Pope observed in 1733, at the age of forty-five; and though the sentiment translates a verse in the Horatian satire he was at the moment imitating, it clearly recognizes with satisfaction the eminence conferred on him by his Twickenham villa and garden, from which in these poems of the 1730s he had already begun to speak to his peers. That eminence he had won in the face of the most dismaying odds, including not only successive bouts of serious illness and chronic headache together with a steady drumbeat of attacks on his religion, character, competence, family origins, and twisted frame, but also the monumental difficulty of bringing off the vast Homeric task he had set himself in the translating of the *Iliad*. If, therefore, among the impulses that drove Pope in his student years elements of sheer testiness and pugnacity were mixed in, we need not be surprised. Cripple and Roman Catholic he might be, but he *would* beat a path into his society's high places and bask in its applause.

To "carry the culture with you"

Meanwhile, the intense self-preparation went on.

In his teens, Pope tells us, he ran through all the books in his father's library. Books of religious controversy, these, often breathing hellfire, while stating and restating with much deployment of learned texts the main points at issue between the Roman and English churches. Pope "warm'd" his head with them, he confided to a friend later on (packing into that verb the low opinion of theological hair-splitting that he retained all his life),

and the consequence was, that I found my self a Papist and a Protestant by turns, according to the last book I read. I am afraid most Seekers are in the same case, and when they stop, they are not so properly converted, as out-witted.

One such volume that he purchased for himself (we happen to know because the book survives) was compiled by the French Roman Catholic apologist George Touchet in 1674 and bears the sufficiently explanatory title: *Historical collections, Out of several grave Protestant historians, concerning the changes of religion, and the strange confusions following from thence; in the reigns of King Henry the Eighth, Edward the Sixth, Queen Mary, and Elizabeth.* The absence of the royal title before Edward and Elizabeth is, of course, part of the argument.

Erasmus he seems to have read too at about this time, and—in what had now become for some of his more zealous coreligionists (perhaps understandably in view of the pressures put on them by the Protestant majority) superannuated Erasmian virtues of tolerance, moderation, civility, and wit, together with a learning lightly worn—found his own preferred model of Catholic behavior. And not only this, but a literary model as well. One of the great ironists of all time, Erasmus had perfected in his best-known work, *The Praise of Folly* (1509), a satirical formula of almost infinite adaptability: a foolish speaker (in Erasmus, the figure of Folly herself) engages in a chatter of self-congratulation, which like the progress of dawn gradually discovers that folly is wisdom, wisdom is folly, and the whole world a great stage of fools. "For what that passes among mortals everywhere is not full of folly, done by fools in the presence of fools?" It would be difficult to prove that this work was not sometimes at the back of Shakespeare's mind, particularly in writing *Twelfth Night* and *King Lear.* It was certainly at the back of Swift's when replaying the Erasmian theme, more bitterly and reductively, through his arrogant "Modern" in *A Tale of a Tub.* And, unmistakably, both the figure of Dulness in Pope's *Dunciad* and the Martinus Scriblerus who composes a majority of its notes (along with that other Martinus, product of the Scriblerians as a group, who gave the world his *Memoirs*) owe something to Erasmus's invention.

On all these counts, Erasmus became a lifelong hero for Pope. He singles him out for religious rehabilitation in his *Essay on Criticism:* "The Glory of the Priesthood, and the Shame!"—"the Shame" because Erasmus's denunciation of papal and ecclesiastical abuses, which preceded Luther's by several years, brought him only obloquy from fellow Catholics. He hopes to emulate Erasmus's moderation—"Like good Erasmus in an honest Mean"—in charting what he still liked to suppose in his first Horatian satire (1733) could be a *via media* through the factional disputes of his time, though he was already in that very poem taking sides. And he finds in him, as a member of his own church, a rock behind which he can on occasion shelter. "I will set before me," he assures a Roman Catholic friend in 1711, defending the severe position he had taken on sectarianism in the *Essay on Criticism*, "that excellent example of that great man and great saint, Erasmus, who in the midst of calumny proceeded with all the calmness of innocence, the unrevenging spirit of primitive Christianity." Though Erasmus was by no means as guileless as his admirer here presents him, and though Pope like the rest of us fell short of his professions of innocence and forgiveness fully as often as he met them, his early attachment to one of the greatest of the six-teenth-century Christian humanists clearly left its impress and helped strengthen the emphasis on charity in religious matters that runs like a golden thread through his life:

> In Faith and Hope the world will disagree,
> But all Mankind's concern is Charity.
> All must be false that thwart this One great End,
> And all of God, that bless Mankind or mend.
>
> (*Essay on Man*, 3: 307–10.)

On the whole, not a bad rule of thumb.

Montaigne, another lifelong admiration, also swam into Pope's ken at about this period. In 1706, when he was eighteen, he bought a copy of the three-volume English translation of the *Essays* (1685–93) by Charles Cotton. Though doubtless he browsed in its pages many times, he worked his way through it thoroughly at least once, scat-tering down the margins of most pages the inverted commas and double commas that in his books always evince special interest, and appending inside the back cover a suitably "considered" estimate:

> This is (in my Opinion) the very best Book for Information of Manners, that has been writ. This Author says nothing but what every one feels att the Heart. Whoever deny it, are not more Wise than Montaigne, but less honest.

Pope was no exception to the general rule that readers of the *Essays*, always at some point and usually at many, encounter themselves. The young Frenchman's unprofitable formal schooling after a much better grounding informally at home struck him, we may recall, as the very image of his own disappointing experiences at Twyford and Mr. Dean's. Similarly applicable to himself, or so he seems to have thought, was the trait of Montaigne's youthful personality which prompted his associates to set him down as lazy. "There was no fear that I would do ill," Montaigne writes, looking back on these early years in his famous essay on education (1: 26), "but that I would do nothing; nobody suspected that I would be wicked, but useless"—words beside which his enthusiastic reader in Binfield, presumably with a certain excitement, jotted *Alter Ego* ["Just like me!"]. For the beginning of wisdom in education, the essay continues, in a sentence that its Binfield reader sprinkles with commas and double commas, is to understand that nothing succeeds

> like alluring the Appetite and Affection, otherwise you make nothing but so many Asses loaded with Books, and by virtue of the Lash, give them their Pocket full of Learning to keep; Whereas, to do well, you should not only lodge it with them, but make them to espouse it.

One suspects that Pope may have had this passage among others in mind when commissioning for his *Dunciad Variorum* in 1729 a title-page plate showing an ass precisely thus "loaden," with an Horatian motto translatable freely (and punningly) to mean both "Our destination is Rag Fair, where the pages of our worthless publications are used to wrap merchandise" and "We are the authors who supply flatteries for a price."

But such affinities were superficial. What must have struck Pope far more forcibly at this stage of his development, when he was not yet far removed from his saturation in Catholic–Protestant controversy, was that Montaigne offered, like Erasmus, the example of a loyal Catholic who despised bigotry. He had kept up an admiring friendship with France's Protestant king, Henry of Navarre. He had managed with sympathy the religious divisions in his own family: both a brother and a sister had converted (as, of course, had several of Pope's kin). And he too had tried hard to walk a peaceable middle course between warring political factions, in consequence of which (as later for Pope) he became suspect to both sides: "To the Gibelin [Ghibelline] I was a Guelph, and to the Guelph a Gibelin"—a way of putting it that Pope possibly recalls in describing, much later, his own efforts at neutrality:

> In Moderation placing all my Glory,
> While Tories call me Whig, and Whigs a Tory.

Most creditable of all, perhaps, Montaigne had not hesitated to speak out against those evils to which, in a favorite phrase of his Binfield reader's, borrowed from Lucretius, religion can "persuade":

> There is no hostility so admirable, as the Christian. Our Zeal performs Wonders, when it seconds our Inclinations to Hatred, Cruelty, Ambition, Avarice, Detraction and Rebellion: But when

it moves against the Hair towards Bounty, Benignity and Tem-
perance, . . . we stir neither hand nor foot. Our religion is intended
to extirpate Vices: Whereas it skreens, nourishes and incites them.

One can readily see why a young Roman Catholic, looking about
him in the first decade or so of the eighteenth century and pardonably
uneasy about both the problematic future awaiting any writer who
hopes to live by his pen and the legalized closure against him of most
alternative careers, might find in these words matter for reflection.
Certain it is, at any rate, that many aspects of Montaigne's religious
thought—his humbling of human reason, his impatience with doctrinal niceties even while submitting to the teachings of his church in
some large general sense well removed from life's ordinary arenas, his
founding of a personal ethic on the nature of the visible world and of
men and women as they are rather than on ecclesiastical or scriptural
fiats, his strong stress on just and compassionate behavior as the
primary obligation of a religious life, and his conviction that such
behavior is not only God's will but man's happiness—accord
extremely well with the "system of ethics" that Pope was eventually
to work out in his *Essay on Man*, and beyond question helped stimu-
late the kind of thinking from which that poem grew.
    One further characteristic of Montaigne's thought that we may
safely guess woke an echo in his Binfield admirer was its thorough
permeation by the learning of the Ancients. Not alone in the
aphorisms, anecdotes, and verses with which the author of the *Essays*
continuously refracts his image of himself in a wilderness of Greek
and Roman mirrors; but in the profound sense of human frailty and
limitation, fortified by his own skepticism, which he had ingested
from a body of literature that was always intensely conscious of the
finiteness of human capacities, and despite occasional upward gazings
at Jove's aether in its more exalted moments never actually flew away
into the circumambient gas. Montaigne's chief contribution, indeed,
for many in the first two centuries after his death (rather like Freud
later on, who was himself a careful student of the *Essays*) was to
render vivid and irrefutable, as most of the classical poets had done,
the sub- and nonrational dimensions of human personality: not only
the fragility of its hold on order but the importance of recognizing
this deficiency lest in the intoxication of its rational pride it destroy
itself—a message that has lost none of its urgency with the passing of
time.
    Part of what we know about Pope's reading at this period comes (as
with this copy of Montaigne) through books surviving from his

library. Roughly a hundred and seventy of these are now known, perhaps about a quarter to a third of his collection. Montaigne, according to his own account, had a thousand volumes ranged about him on the five rows of shelves lining his tower-study, amounting, even if we allow for works of more than one volume, to some eight or nine hundred separate titles. But this was exceptional, especially in his century. The catalogue of Swift's library runs to six hundred and fifty-seven items, that of Congreve's to six hundred and fifty-nine. It seems likely that Pope's belongs roughly in this range.

Though he was anything but a prolific annotator while reading, Pope occasionally volunteers, as we have seen, a brief verbal comment, a pointing hand, a cross, or scatterings of single and double inverted commas—especially in books that there is reason to believe he read in youth. Among the earliest books owned by him personally must have been the 1598 black-letter Chaucer given him by a Roman Catholic neighbor in 1701, when he was thirteen. He had, however, the year before, purchased for himself a 1641 sixth edition of the poems of George Herbert (the age of contemporary reprints had not yet arrived), and he had also bought the first two volumes of *Don Quixote* in the translation by Peter Motteux, which had just appeared. (Volumes three and four were not published till 1703.) For a young man susceptible to "raptures" and other seductions by the power of imagination, here was an admonitory example indeed, and one notes with interest that Pope peppers with inverted commas the passage in which the Don's niece, his barber, and the local curate weed his library of romances of knight-errantry after they have learned from his initial adventures what madness his reading has brought. But surely this lot, says the curate, approaching a new portion of the books, can be spared:

> these cannot be books of Knight Errantry; they are too small: You'll find they are only Poets. . . . Oh! good Sir, cry'd the Niece, burn 'em with the rest, I beseech you; for shou'd my Unkle get cur'd of his Knight-Errant Frenzy, and betake himself to the reading of these Books, we shou'd have him turn Shepherd, and so wander thro' the Woods and Fields, nay, and what wou'd be worse yet, turn Poet, which they say is a catching and an incurable Disease.

The niece's sentiment that poetry is a madness yet more desperate than knight-errantry, Pope embraces with double commas.

Few of his books contain, like these, a date of purchase or gift. But if it is true, as it appears to be, that an entry of price paid or a signature written down in some form other than the "A. Pope" he finally settled for indicate acquisitions made during his boyhood and adolescence, then it is clear that by the time he reached his majority in 1709, he had been pretty thoroughly through Latin literature including the neo-Latin writers mentioned earlier. He also knew in translation, on the Greek side, Herodotus, Homer, Lucian, and Theocritus. He was working seriously at Homer in the original. And just possibly he had attempted the Greek text of Pindar and other early lyricists, which he owned. He had further digested a fair number of European authors down to Boileau and had applied the minute attention of an apprentice-poet to his major English predecessors: Chaucer, Spenser, Sidney, probably Shakespeare, though his copy is not now known, Jonson, Milton, and Dryden.

Still, the utility of so feverish an application to books remains debatable unless one has a tenacious memory and sufficient judgment to call up from it only what is germane to the subject in hand. Pope had both. While yet in his teens, he could identify an obscure neo-Latin verse about which two much older friends were puzzling, both men of substantial learning. "I forgot, I think, to tell you," one of the friends writes to the other in 1707, "that our said little Poet [Pope] (to whom in all the mighty extent of Poetical Territories, there is no Terra Incognita) found out our *Ridet anhelantem, &c.* He says it is in one of the Silvas of Angelicus Policianus, and in that called Ambra, and that you have the Book."

This was far from being the mechanical total recall of the stereotypical whiz kid. Politian's "Ambra" was a great favorite of Pope's and contributed much later a Latin inscription to his plan for a renovation of his Twickenham waterfront that he did not live to carry out. Down in that "deep well of unconscious cerebration," as Henry James once described it, the nursery of all imaginative inventions, Pope's reading had a way of remaining sensitively alive and of surfacing in ways either smiling or grave but seldom impertinent. Thirty years after his encounter with *Don Quixote* (it is, of course, likely that he returned to the book at some time in the interval), he is able to draw on one of its lesser-known episodes to convey the essentially antihuman ostentation of certain contemporary ways of life. And even longer after he had first met with Montaigne's moving juxtaposition of what the passing of the years is doing to his mental and physical powers with Horace's similar lament, he is able to recall that conjunction, adjusted to his own experience of time's thieveries, with both a beauty of phrase and a psychological profundity that neither of his predecessors had quite achieved.

It is to this aspect of Pope's genius that his best poetry owes its deep resonances, as voices from many places and times arise from the deep well in a thrilling unison, fortifying, qualifying, complicating each other. One need not distinguish the voices precisely, though frequently it is Pope's intent that one should. Poetry for him, as for his great predecessors, is emphatically more a social than a personal institution; its proper audience a cross section of educated readers; its proper subject the shared common life. To write in a public idiom, and always within a program of reference calculated to draw poet and reader into a community of experience, first with each other and then with other poets and readers of a valued past (or, as it was put the other day in a dialogue between two American poets, to "carry the culture with you"): this was the poet's task, as Pope understood it, and for this in the Forest he was readying his powers.

CHAPTER 5

FIRST HEROES

John Caryll and Thomas Betterton

A farther feature of Pope's life in Binfield—one that belongs with any account of his education as well as one that tells us something about his personal attractiveness as a youth and young man—is the wide circle of friends he managed to accumulate in that retired spot.

Earliest among these, we may be reasonably sure, were fellow Roman Catholics living in the neighborhood, to whom from the outset his family would be drawn by common practices and beliefs. The manor of Binfield, for instance, had been held by the Roman Catholic Dancastle family since late in the sixteenth century. Its present owner was John Dancastle, whose younger brother Thomas we have already met as the hunter to whose dog and gun Pope in 1717 wishes success. Evidently a friend of uncommon generosity, Thomas Dancastle often allowed himself to be used as Pope's amanuensis during the progress of the *Iliad* translation, making fair copies of the poet's draft texts in the full knowledge that they would be speedily reduced again to rubble by additional revisions. Later, after the Popes had left Binfield for Chiswick (probably to be closer to London, but also, probably, in view of anti-Catholic sentiment following the Jacobite invasion of 1715, to put themselves under the powerful Whig protection of the Earl of Burlington), gifts of grapes from the manor, along with fair copies of books of the *Iliad* for the younger Pope and "white strabery plants" for the elder, followed them for some years; while in those same years Pope recalled in his letters to the brothers the happy days when he had used to see them "tossing wheatsheaves and raising Reeks [ricks]," or, as on frosty days in the Christmas season, when "we drank metheglin [mead] and chatted together."

Further but not far away, about two miles south of Reading, lay Whiteknights, seat of the Englefield family. This too had been a Roman Catholic property for a century. Anthony Englefield, its current owner, was "a good natur'd, merry conceited, Learned & Politique Gentleman," with mathematical and astronomical interests extending at least to the fabrication of sundials. He was further skilled, Pope tells us, "in composing of quaint Madrigalls, & Anagramms," and, according to his granddaughter, a great lover of poetry and poets, who heartily admired Pope. From the echo in "merry conceited" of Elizabethan jest books and in "Learned & Politique" of sober seventeenth-century discourses on affairs of state, we may picture a lively old gentleman (he died at 75 in 1712) with a child's zest for jokes, riddles, comic songs, and possibly burlesque imitations of solemn coxcombs. (In the Memorial List of dead friends kept in his Elzevir Vergil, Pope speaks of him as the joy of his youth, a great wit and wag: *vir facetissimus, juventutis meae deliciae*.) At his house, in due course, Pope would meet the granddaughter above quoted, Martha Blount of Mapledurham House across the Thames, a young woman two years younger than he who became his lifelong friend—some like to think, his wife or mistress. Somewhat earlier, he would also meet there Martha's sister Teresa, a girl of his own age, very beautiful, vivacious, a great flirt, with whom at least for a number of years he thought himself to be, and perhaps was, seriously in love.

Probably at Whiteknights too, by the time he was fifteen, Pope had met Englefield's kinsman, John Caryll, twenty-one years his senior. With Caryll he was to conduct a correspondence lasting over two decades, which provides us with many of the best clues we have to his interior world—though as usual allowances must be made for his instinctive adaptation of himself to his correspondent's "Motions & Inclinations." Caryll had keen literary interests and a literary acquaintance that included at various times Dryden, Wycherley, and the actor Thomas Betterton. Pope never became acquainted with Dryden, though he told Spence that he had once *seen* him, when taken as a boy to Will's coffee house, where Dryden held court. Wycherley he perhaps met through Caryll, whose family seats at Ladyholt and West Grinstead were only a comfortable journey to the south in Sussex. And he may have met Betterton, who had a farm near Reading, at Whiteknights.

Reputed the greatest actor of his time, and standing (it would be said later) in the direct line of genius from Shakespeare's Richard Burbage through Charles Hart (Shakespeare's grandnephew) to David Garrick, Betterton was in his late sixties by the time Pope knew him, and lived, between engagements, which were becoming fewer, in semiretirement on his Reading farm. His physical frame, always stocky, had thickened, his face had broadened, his shoulders were stooped, he was partly crippled with gout, and his voice had lost

10. Thomas Betterton (1635?–1710). Studio of Sir Godfrey Kneller, *c.* 1695.

Roscius sui temporis, exit omnium cum plausu bonorum, aet. 74 ["The Roscius of his age, he left the stage to the applause of all good men, aged 74."] Pope's entry on the obituary page of his Elzevir Vergil.

Courtesy of the National Portrait Gallery, London.

11. Thomas Betterton (1635?–1710). By Alexander Pope, after Kneller, 1713.

"I find my hand most successful in drawing of friends and those I most esteem; in so much that my masterpiece has been one of Dr. Swift and one [of?] Mr. Betterton." Pope to Caryll, 31 August 1713.

By kind permission of the Earl of Mansfield.

something of its variety and harmony, though he could still tune it when he wished to "an artful *Climax*" that electrified everyone in the theater from fops to orange girls. In his heyday, he is said to have acted with equal facility and effect roles as unlike as those of Hamlet and Sir Toby Belch. In the scene in Gertrude's closet, says a contemporary, where Hamlet sees his father's ghost for the second time, Betterton's usually ruddy complexion would turn

> as pale as his Neckcloth, when every Article of his Body seem'd to be affected with a Tremor inexpressible; so that, had his Father's Ghost actually risen before him, he could not have been seized with more real Agonies; and this was felt so strongly by the Audience, that the Blood seem'd to shudder in their Veins likewise, and they in some Measure partook of the Astonishment and Horror, with which they saw this excellent Actor affected.

But the last word on Betterton belongs rightly to Colley Cibber, who worked for and with him during the first third of his own career and, whatever his own failings onstage, brought a professional's appreciation to the art of others. "*Betterton*," Cibber says, "was an Actor, as *Shakespear* was an Author: both without Competitors!"

For a young country poet, eager for news of the great world, such a man radiated glamour even in decay, and his stories of the past age must have held Pope spellbound. Betterton had known and worked with Dryden, Pope's man of men. He had been leading actor of the Duke's Company under Sir William Davenant, last of the Jacobeans, Shakespeare's reputed godson—some would say (among them, apparently, Davenant himself) his natural son. He had been friendly with Charles II, who had given him his coronation suit in which to play the part of Prince Alvaro in Davenant's *Love and Honour*. From Davenant by way of Betterton Pope received much of the lore that he passed on to Spence about "the Giant Race before the Flood" (Dryden's phrase for the playwrights of the pre–Civil War period), and it is possible that by way of Betterton he acquired the interest in Jacobean and Caroline drama generally that is signaled by the presence in his library of individual plays by Brome, Chapman, Davenport, Habington, May, Massinger, Randolph, Rowley, and Shirley, and of complete collections by Jonson, Beaumont and Fletcher, and Dryden. After Betterton's death in 1710, Pope served his widow in the office of literary executor, bringing out for her financial interest some Chaucerian adaptations by her husband (probably with extensive revisions by himself) in a miscellany of 1712 along with his own first version of the *Rape of the Lock*. Johnson reports that Pope's friend

Elijah Fenton was so convinced the adaptations were actually by Pope that he offered him £5 if he could show them "in the hand of Betterton." This may be gossip, but it suggests the loyalty Pope felt to Betterton, and one notes with added interest his statement of the following year, while studying painting under Charles Jervas, that his best successes came when picturing those he most esteemed—"insomuch that my masterpieces have been one [portrait] of Dr. Swift and one [of] Mr. Betterton." (The latter, based on a portrait of Betterton by Kneller, is reproduced above, p. 91).

Betterton's advice to Pope was to write for the stage, and in these earliest days it appears that Pope felt some attraction from that quarter. He had written when very young "something toward a tragedy" (conceivably the *Iliad* potpourri acted at Mr. Deane's school) and afterward an entire tragedy "on a very moving story in the legend of Saint Genevieve." At eighteen, he was urged by a friend who had read his *Pastorals* to try his hand at a pastoral comedy, something on the order of Tasso's *Aminta* or Guarini's *Faithful Shepherd* (*Il Pastor Fido*); at nineteen he seems to have toyed with the idea of a play on Gaius Gracchus, the revolutionary agrarian reformer of late second-century Rome; and at twenty-three he was admonished by another friend to have a fling in the tragic vein—

> Leave Elegy and Translation to the inferior Class, on whom the Muses only glance now and then like our Winter-Sun, and then leave 'em in the dark. Think on the Dignity of Tragedy. . . . Every one wonders that a Genius like yours will not support the sinking *Drama*—

flatteries calculated to turn any young writer's head.

That Pope, after his salad days, was proof against such solicitations was doubtless not owing to any want of vanity. Nor was it, one suspects, entirely for the reasons he gave Betterton:

> I had taken such strong resolutions against any thing of that kind, from seeing how much everybody that did write for the stage was obliged to subject themselves to the players and the town.

Even if so fierce an independence played some part in the decision, there must have been other considerations. Fear of public failure, for one thing: a prospect not easily borne by one whom even his friends—affectionately no doubt but also patronizingly—now called "little Pope." For another thing (we may guess), certain legitimate apprehensions of the short shrift that any theater audience of those days might be inclined by the variable winds of politics to give to the work of a confessed Roman Catholic. And for a third—possibly the greatest dissuasive of all—a firm sense of his own limits. This was deeply ingrained in Pope from boyhood (perhaps a by-product of his physical situation) and enabled him not merely to resist writing for the stage, but to burn—though late and not without regret—the darling composition of his youth, an unfinished epic on Alcander Prince of Rhodes;★ and to leave unexecuted the most formidable scheme of his latter years, which was to write a blank verse epic on Brutus, great grandson of Aeneas, legendary founder of the British race. Visions of his English homeland as a land of destiny, so clearly set forth in *Windsor-Forest*, never altogether deserted Pope's imagination, even in the darker moods of his maturity and old age.

William Wycherly

Additional dissuasives against writing for the stage may have come from Wycherley. Wycherley had known in the 1670s all the glitter that a quick succession of four plays, three of them rousing popular successes, can bring a man. In 1671, *Love in a Wood* had fixed a new playwright of genius on London's admiring attention, including the attention of Barbara Villiers, the king's mistress, who (it is said) speedily became Wycherley's mistress as well. This was followed in 1672 by his one comparative failure, *The Gentleman Dancing Master*, a wide-ranging satire centered (with characteristic British enthusiasm) on the affectations of the French. Then came in 1675 *The Country Wife*, wherein a triumphant conjugation of lubricity with wit impaled the whole of fashionable society on its own favorite horn; and, the following year (his most impressive work though not his best play) *The Plain Dealer*, to which the comment of a perceptive contemporary on his writing as a whole admirably applies: "His Muse is not led forth as to a Review, but as to battle. ... Like Your Heroes of Antiquity, he charges in iron." Having shown the beau

---

★ Spence, nos. 37n., 38–40. "My epic poem was about two years in hand. ... I endeavoured (says he, smiling) in this poem to collect all the beauties of the great epic writers into one piece. There was Milton's style in one part and Cowley's in another, here the style of Spenser imitated and there Statius, here Homer and Virgil, and there Ovid and Claudian." Ruffhead (*Life of Pope*, 1769, p. 27), confirming the poet's later attitude of amusement toward the poem's extravagances, cites in particular "a description of a Scythian hero, who contemned a pillow, though of snow, as luxury and effeminacy." One may imagine the trumpet tones.

12. William Wycherley (1640?–1716). Attributed to Lawrence Crosse.

Whose Sense instructs us, and whose Manner charms.

Pastorals: Autumn, 9.

Courtesy of the National Portrait Gallery, London.

monde in *The Country Wife* that its system of huckstering marriages and its ruthless sensuality were obverse and reverse of the same coin, he now carved out in *The Plain Dealer* a world of court sycophants and bourgeois *arrivistes*, whose interacting greed, lust, malice, and faithlessness were making their London a waste land.

Like most playwrights before modern times, Wycherley received little remuneration from his work, and, being an accomplished spendthrift, occupied a great deal of his time following his decade of glory in search of an affluence that continued to elude him. By the time he and Pope came to be acquainted, possibly in late 1704, when Pope was going on seventeen, he had run through an unsuccessful marriage, served time in debtors' prison, suffered a severe illness (whose effects along with those of age rendered him increasingly forgetful), and, finally, after a delay of years, had brought out shortly before he met Pope a collection of verse called *Miscellany Poems*, from which he hoped to recoup his fortunes. The book failed badly, for cause. Its versification was lumpish—Wycherley's forte had always been prose. Its wit—much of it stumbling heavily among para-doxes—must have struck even a well-disposed audience as embarrassingly self-conscious: for example, "*Upon the* Discretion *of* Folly, *by which Men are Fortunate and Innocent, which is better than to be Wise. To a Lady, who, in Contradiction to the* Author, *said*, It was not better to be Happy, than Wise." And its themes—"*To a Fine Young* Woman, *who being ask'd by her Lover*, Why she kept so filthy a Thing as a Snake in her Bosom; *answer'd* 'Twas to keep a filthier thing out of it, his Hand"; or again: "*Upon a* Lady's Fall *over a* Stile, *gotten by running from her* Lover; *by which she show'd* her Fair Back-side, *which was her best Side, and made him more her Pursuer than he was before*"—were (many of them) comically ill-suited to a new national sensibility that had brought forth during the 1690s under William and Mary a Society for the Reformation of Manners, a Society for the Propaga-tion of the Gospel, and Jeremy Collier's *Short View of the Profaneness and Immorality of the English Stage*, where characters from *The Country Wife* and *The Plain Dealer* were featured on the opening page.

For Pope, Wycherley, like Betterton, represented the great world of affairs and, perhaps more especially, the gratifications of literary fame. Though a has-been in the sense that he was now reduced to grinding out verses in an obsolete vein, he had earned his niche among the English dramatists, and his plays, up to the time when Pope met him, held the stage almost without interruption. Through him as through Betterton Pope could make imaginative contact with the literary lions of the past age, hear anecdotes of the conversations at Will's and similar places of resort, and become schooled in, perhaps even absorb some colorings from, Wycherley's views of courtiers and literary critics, while responding (with a warmth born of understandable insecurities about his own appeal to women) to the old playwright's stress on the preeminence of masculine friendship. Wycherley could also serve Pope as a seasoned judge of the work he was now engaged in, that quartet of *Pastorals* representing the four seasons in a tradition deriving from Virgil's *Eclogues* and Spenser's *Shepheardes Calendar.*

There was thus every reason why Pope, after meeting Wycherley, should pursue his acquaintance by addressing an admiring letter to him. And there was equal reason, in turn, why Wycherley should be at the trouble of a reply. It cannot have been other than soothing to an elderly ego, battered by the ill success of many enterprises including the volume of *Miscellany Poems*, to be viewed through the admiring eyes of a youth who hung upon his every word. A youth, moreover, of obvious talent, who gave every indication of making a place for himself among the new generation of writers coming on, and was very good company to boot. Though slight in stature, and by this time (so far as we can tell) beginning to be stooped, the young Pope had a fine expressive eye, a sweetness in his look and temper that the tooth of pain had not yet scarred, and a voice so musical that the playwright Thomas Southerne, who must have met Pope through Wycherley or Betterton, used to call him "*The little Nightingale*". Persons intimate with him at this period found him, Spence tells us, "excessively gay and lively"—"excessively" perhaps meaning only "exceedingly," but possibly that he was nervous about how people would respond to his disability, and hence put forth a visible effort to please. Though the self-portrait he sketched in the 1730s refers to a period around 1712, the young man conjured up there (however much touched in the poem by the idealizing brush of recollection) cannot be much unlike the youth whom Wycherley met in 1704. "I hope it is your Resolution," the poet says to the friend whom he addresses in this poem,

> To give me back my Constitution!
> The sprightly Wit, the lively Eye,
> Th' engaging Smile, the Gaiety,
> That laugh'd down many a Summer's Sun,
> And kept you up so oft till one;
> And all that voluntary Vein,
> As when Belinda rais'd my Strain.
>
> *Imit. Hor., Ep.* I, vii, 43–50

It is an ancient cry: *Eheu, fugaces, Postume, Postume* ["Alas, the fleeting years, Postumus, Postumus"].

A very probable additional reason for Wycherley's cordial reception of Pope's overture was his failed book of *Miscellany Poems*. He still had by him a swarm of similar materials: poems, pieces of poems, ideas for poems in the shape of prose maxims, epigrams, and aphorisms. These could easily be assembled in a second offering, but it would be necessary this time to improve the verse and avoid the longueurs and repetitions of the earlier poems. Who so well qualified to give him a hand with this as the young country poet whose manuscript *Pastorals* Wycherley's close friend, the critic William Walsh, was even now pronouncing to be superior to anything Vergil had done at the same age? A safe claim on Walsh's part, since it is not recorded that at seventeen Virgil had written anything at all; but nevertheless the highest possible compliment in intent. Obviously, the young man had what Wycherley could use.

The resulting friendship was inevitably a curiosity. Apart from the extreme difference in age, the contrast of size bordered on the risible. Wycherley was of powerful build ("brawny," says the contemporary epithet) and tall, though in the years when Pope knew him inclining to corpulence. Pope, on the other hand, skinny as an eel, was of extremely delicate build and short—after his stoop had taken effect, no more than four and a half feet high. The sight of the two of them together must have awakened in the minds of at least some of their friends—Betterton's, for instance, who knew his Shakespeare well—Falstaff's description of himself walking in front of his page like a sow that hath o'erwhelmed all her farrow but one. Pope's own amused consciousness of the figure they made comes through obliquely in a letter written from Binfield to a London friend in 1709, where he observes that his small dog follows him about as constantly in the country "as I was us'd to do Mr. W[ycherley] in the Town."

The letters that this ill-matched pair exchanged, spasmodically, over a period of a dozen years underscore the oddity of the relationship. Pope labors to be witty in a style that he must have known either from Wycherley's conversation or published letters to be suitable to the man, while endeavoring at the same time to express appreciation of Wycherley's interest in him, becoming diffidence about his present abilities as an author, and a wish (entirely characteristic of him throughout his life, but probably at this age not unmixed with satisfaction at so much ritual applause) to get quickly past the barriers of compliment to plain talk. "Praise to a young Wit," he solemnly admonishes his correspondent in the second of his surviving letters, drawing on an imagery of garden and orchard highly expressive of his rural situation at this time,

> is like Rain to a tender Flower; if it be moderately bestow'd, it chears and revives, but if too lavishly, overcharges and depresses him. Most Men in years, as they are generally discouragers of Youth, are like old Trees, that being past Bearing themselves will suffer no young Plants to flourish beneath them. But as if it were not enough to have out-done all your Coævals in Wit, you will excel them in good Nature too. As for my green Essays, if you find any pleasure in 'em, it must be such as a Man naturally takes in observing the first Shoots and Buddings of a Tree which he has rais'd himself; and tis impossible they should be esteem'd any otherwise, than as we value Fruits for being early; which nevertheless are the most insipid, and the worst of the Year. In a word, I must blame you for treating me with so much Compliment, which is at best but the Smoak of Friendship.

To an apparently similar caveat of ten days later that has not survived, Wycherley replies:

> I have receiv'd yours . . ., wherein your Modesty refuses the just Praise I give you, by which you lay claim to more, as a Bishop gains his Bishoprick by saying he will not Episcopate: But I must confess, whilst I displease you by commending you, I please my self; just as Incense is sweeter to the Offerer than the Deity to whom 'tis offered, by his being so much above it: For indeed, every Man partakes of the Praise he gives, when it is so justly given.

Much posturing here on both sides; much false modesty; perhaps some consulting of commonplace books. On Pope's part, additionally, there is either a moment of oversight or a gleam of the complacence of youth in the allusion to old trees "past Bearing"; while from Wycherley's court comes a cunning stroke in the matter of the cleric who gains his end by saying he will not episcopate, as well as a sharp drive to the baseline in the incense that is sweeter to the offerer than to the deity, the latter being "so much above it." A stunning put-down—if that is what it is. Wycherley had not spent five years of his youth among the French *précieuses* for nothing.

Yet despite all such sparring the acquaintance prospered and a genuine affection sprang up. Wycherley visited Binfield at least once, as we have seen, and we know that during one of Pope's long winter stays in London he visited the old man almost twice a day. True, there were strains. Correcting another man's verses, as his father had warned him, brought exasperation and resentment. Wycherley grew angry because his "Dear Little Great Friend" kept making, as he thought, too many and too radical changes in the poems he was revising. Pope chafed in turn under almost two years of time-consuming labor—it was nearly half a dozen years before the project was let drop altogether—for which the reward was sometimes mere petulance; and he found particularly trying his mentor's faulty memory, which allowed him to versify in the morning passages he had been reading the night before in Montaigne, La Rochefoucauld, Gracian, or Seneca (his favorite authors) without realizing they were not his own: "all their thoughts, only expressed in a different turn." Though these circumstances led occasionally to tart remarks by both correspondents and there may have been a certain coolness for a year or more following the spring of 1710, Pope sprang warmly to Wycherley's defense when his poems were disparaged publicly in 1708 by the translator John Ozell and the playwright Nicholas Rowe, lent him money during his last poverty-stricken days, kept throughout his life Wycherley's portrait in his house, and in 1730 gave Spence a retrospective account of their relationship that seems plausible as well as fair:

> We were pretty well together to the last, only his memory was so totally bad that he did not remember a kindness done to him from minute to minute. He was peevish too, latterly, so that sometimes we were out a little and sometimes in. He never did any unjust thing to me in his whole life, and I went to see him on his death-bed.

In fact, Pope was twice with Wycherley during his last days and set down afterwards in the Elzevir list: "Anno 1715 [16], mens Martio, decessit Gul. Wycherley, poeta morum scientia clarus, ille meos primus qui habebat amores, aet. 75." ["In March 1716 Will. Wycherley departed this life, a poet renowned for his understanding of character, the first to have my affections, his age 75."] Whatever his reservations about Wycherley's verse-making may have been, he confers on him here the title of poet in the radical sense, praises him rightly for his understanding of human behavior, and recognizes him as the first of his (literary) friends.

Dr. Samuel Garth

Other men of letters and affairs who took a friendly interest in Pope during these early years were the physician Dr. Samuel Garth, the former envoy and secretary of state Sir William Trumbull, and

13. Samuel Garth (1661–1719). By Sir Godfrey Kneller, *c.* 1710.

... the best good Christian he
Altho' he knows it not.

A Farewell to London, 15–16.

Courtesy of the National Portrait Gallery, London.

William Walsh, declared by Dryden in a possibly too expansive moment "the best Critick of our Nation."

Garth, later knighted by George I and appointed physician-in-ordinary to the royal household, was at the time best known for a literary work: *The Dispensary*. This was a six-canto mock-heroic poem describing with a fine gusto (and many entertaining applications of traditional epic episodes and conventions to the modern urban scene) the efforts of the London apothecaries and certain of their physician sympathizers to block the establishment by the Royal College of Physicians of a free dispensary for the poor, the apothecaries believing their livelihood thus threatened. Published in 1699, the poem met with instant public success, reaching a third edition the same year and continuing in demand for half a century.

The Dispensary's mock-heroic impulse was not of course new. The practice of ridiculing human pettiness and pretension by treating them in a highfalutin style had enjoyed a long history by 1699, including among its more considerable recent examples Boileau's *Le Lutrin* of 1674, which had held up to laughter the fierce antagonisms of some priests about the positioning of a lectern in their chapel. Several of Garth's inventions in the poem were, however, new, as were a number of delicate and colorful details that Pope subsequently borrowed and improved on in the *Rape of the Lock*. More important, the poem's success in investing London settings with moral and aesthetic values furnished cues, when the time came, for similar procedures in the *Dunciad*.

Under what circumstances Pope met Garth we do not know. Evidently they were acquainted early, perhaps as early as 1703, when Pope was fifteen: an edition of *The Dispensary* of that year survives from his library, inscribed "*Donum Autoris.*" In any event, the relation prospered. Garth (according to Lady Mary Wortley Montagu, "known by his red cloak and superior frown") was a witty man, with a reputation for *bons mots*. When, for example, his excessively rich and overbearing colleague Dr. John Radcliffe ("that puppy," Swift called him on one occasion) died leaving money to Oxford for a library, he noted that it was like a eunuch's founding a seraglio. Yet he was at the same time kindly and warm-hearted, much admired for "Humanity, Generosity, and Charitable Temper" in the practice of his profession, and a man who cherished literary talent wherever found, even if (as was soon clear in the case of Pope) it much excelled his own. He had been a close friend of Dryden's, one of the group at Will's, and had helped procure for him the honor of a public funeral by arranging that his body lie in state for some days at the College of

Physicians, at the end of which time he had pronounced over it an elegant Latin oration to "great Approbation and Applause." Before long, he was showing himself equally appreciative of Pope. He was among those through whose approving hands the manuscript of the *Pastorals* passed, and the preface of his own later topographical poem *Claremont* pays glowing tribute to the author of *Windsor-Forest*.

Pope returned Garth's warm regard. We may guess that he was drawn to him as much by Garth's appetite for good works as by his wit—traits they both shared. Yet the quality that is always uppermost in his commendations of the doctor is good nature, by which he clearly means not simply a sanguine temperament and kindly disposition but a frankness and openness of address such as he himself aspired to, liked to fancy himself possessed of, but only fitfully achieved. We meet here one of the most perplexing aspects of Pope's career and personality. Though he assures the world constantly that he loves to pour himself out

as plain

As downright *Shippen*, or as old *Montagne*,
Imit. Hor., Sat. II, i, 51–2

there remains a reserve in him that in some circumstances can edge over into evasiveness, deceit, or chicanery. Even in his letters, as we have seen, he often shows himself intensely conscious of the other person, intensely concerned about the impression he himself will make, and thus to an extent on guard, even while he may be urging with complete sincerity the mutual opening of hearts. In the poems, the case is similar. Certainly few writers approach us in their work with a voice and presence so ingratiatingly ingenuous yet so artful.

For such a cast of mind, what explanation? Without presuming that the heart of this or any other psychic mystery may be confidently plucked out, one may venture a few guesses. Surely something should be allowed to a habit of self-protection developed by an only child with a normal taste for privacy in a household of solicitous adults, the more solicitous for having a genius on their hands. Something may be owing also to the caution and circumspection bred by circumstance into the practices and—one might add without exaggeration—into the very bones of Roman Catholic families at this period, especially those who had known the suspicions attending them (sometimes understandably in a country at war) under William III. Pope's early acquaintance with so many men of distinguished reputation is possibly a further factor to be reckoned with. What more likely than that a youth caressed and praised by a variety of individuals of note should almost unawares fall to practicing a coloration agreeable to each, and so, over a period of impressionable years, build a habit of "performance," ever seeking to oblige and please, ever wary of missteps and of presuming too far, yet perhaps always genuinely hankering for a degree of intimacy and informal interchange made impossible by the disparity of age and the austerity of the social code.

Most important of all, I am inclined to think, are the insecurities that we now know become exceptionally acute in all persons who are set apart physically or culturally (in Pope's case, it was both) from the norms of those around them. Men and women who by some mark or other—deafness, blindness, mutilation, a deformity like Pope's or merely a black skin—register with the rest of us as "different" are almost inevitably, modern studies tell us, more self-conscious than we "normals" about being on parade, tend therefore to become acute observers of our responses to them and thus more situation-conscious, more detached, more studied in their own responses than the normal person needs to be. Something within them is kept from surfacing for fear of rebuffs, yet all the more on that account they long to break through to a phase of candor and spontaneity where they can be sure what others really think of them and how far their apparent acceptance is trustworthy. All these impulses seem very clear in Pope and give to the epitaph reserved for Garth in the Memorial List of departed friends a special poignancy: *Homo candidus* ["A guileless man"]. This is, I believe, the highest compliment Pope knew how to pay and the one he most cherished whenever (rightly or wrongly) it was paid to him.

Sir William Trumbull

Pope's friendship with Trumbull, perhaps the most intimate and affectionate of his early career, came about through their being neighbors in the Forest. Easthamstead Park, the Trumbull family estate, lay only a mile or two away from Binfield at Easthamstead, where Sir William, after a considerable career in diplomacy under Charles II, James II, and William III (topped off under William by service on the privy council and as a secretary of state) now amused himself with gardening and literature. His admiration of the size of Pope's father's "Hartichokes" we have already encountered. That was in June 1706, by which date it appears that he and the younger Pope were already on easy terms, exchanging books and conversation, perhaps occasionally competing at translations, and riding out together in the Forest "three or four days in the week, and at last almost every day." Trumbull, as mentioned earlier, was a verderer, charged with the judicial disposition of trespasses upon the Forest, "either of vert or venison." In the Forest of Windsor there were twelve such officers, each having jurisdiction over a district or "Walk," Sir William's being Easthamstead Walk. Since for villagers and farmers, the vert (i.e., the trees and other vegetation giving cover to the deer) was almost as tempting a source of fuel as the deer were of food, and since the gentry too were not above nibbling in this area of the Crown's prerogatives, the verderer's task was a demanding one, requiring a nice balance between the claims of the law and the realities of both human need in the poor and political clout in the squires. Later, as we shall see, offenses against the royal forests assumed for a time a more specific political complexion, becoming a form of protest, tinged perhaps with Jacobitism, that seriously affected the family of Pope's sister.

According to such evidence as survives, Trumbull was a model verderer, never taking deer except upon warrant of the Chief Huntsman. He seems also to have been a model patron, a term applied to him by at least one French writer, and by Wycherley, who refers to him additionally as "that most Ingenious, humane, most honourable, and most learned Gentleman." Dryden too had possibly known his benefactions, or if not, at any rate his enthusiasm for literature, acknowledging in the Postscript to his Vergil:

> If the last *Aeneid* shine among its Fellows, 'tis owing to the Commands of Sir *William Trumbull*, one of the Principal Secretaries of State, who recommended it, as his Favourite, to my Care: and for his sake particularly I have made it mine.

For Pope, Trumbull played the role of a second father, or perhaps more accurately, of a solicitous grandfather and great uncle. His education and interests—in his early years he had taken a degree at St. John's, Oxford, been chosen Fellow of All Souls, and traveled widely through France and Italy accompanied by Edward Browne, son of the author of *Religio Medici*—qualified him admirably for this role, as did his general benignity of temperament and his age—he was just short of a half century older than Pope. One hears frequently in his correspondence with his nephew Ralph Bridges (chaplain at Fulham to the Bishop of London) of his growing affection for his precocious little neighbor ("The little Creature is my darling more and more," September 18, 1707) and of his concern for Pope's frail physique ("He

Sr WILLIAM TRUMBULL K.^t
Principal Secretary of State to King William III.

14. Sir William Trumbull (1639–1716). Engraving by George Vertue (1724) after Sir Godfrey Kneller (1694–95?).

> *You*, that too wise for Pride, too good for Pow'r,
> Enjoy the Glory to be Great no more.
>
> *Pastorals: Spring*, 7–8.

Courtesy of the National Portrait Gallery, London.

look'd & really was no more than a shaddow," August 5, 1707; "Poor little Pope has been ill; He was abroad last week with me to take the Aire & a Puff of Wind had almost blown him away," June 8, 1708). Later, when Pope has begun to make extended stays in London, there are avuncular warnings against dissipation:

> I . . . beg of you earnestly to get out of all Tavern-company, and fly away *tanquam ex incendio* ["as you would from a conflagration"]. What a misery it is for you to be destroy'd by the foolish kindness ('tis all one whether real or pretended) of those who are able to bear the Poison of bad Wine; and to engage you in so unequal a combat.

To which (the record shows) his "darling" paid such heed as young men customarily do.

Trumbull's contribution to Pope's education and to the direction of his career may have been considerable. His guidance and his interest may have helped in some measure to replace the formal university training denied Pope by his religion, though it is also plain that the instruction went both ways. We find Trumbull expressing astonishment to his nephew at the range of Pope's reading, asking him to look about in London for copies of books that Pope has recommended to him, and being introduced to such delights as the 1645 collection of Milton's minor poems, which Pope was among the first in his time to value. On the other side of the interchange, it was Trumbull who put Pope on to writing the topographical and scenic parts of *Windsor-Forest*, many of which possibly derive from their rides together, and it was Trumbull again who urged on him the translation of Homer. The first fragment of that translation, Sarpedon's speech to Glaucus from Iliad XII, published in 1709 along with the *Pastorals*, probably owes something, perhaps much, to Trumbull as well as to his learned clerical nephew, who vetted it for fidelity to the Greek.

There are other ways in which the long association with Trumbull may have affected Pope's thinking. His admired friend Garth, for instance, was a self-proclaimed atheist, or possibly what we would nowadays call agnostic—the two positions were by no means adequately distinguished in those religiously militant days. His admired friend Trumbull, on the other hand, was a believer and staunch supporter of the Anglican establishment. Sheltered through boyhood and adolescence in a pious Roman Catholic household associating mainly with other such households, a youth so observant as Pope can hardly have failed to be impressed, as his acquaintance broadened, by the uniformity of decent and even virtuous behavior that seemed to emerge from systems of belief and unbelief popularly held to be radically opposed and to be productive of totally different sorts of moral conduct. Reflections of this nature must have played some part, one thinks, in settling his views (implied in the *Essay on Criticism* and repeated in the *Essay on Man*) so early in the track blazed by the Cambridge Platonists and other "Latitude men," not to mention his readings in Erasmus and Montaigne. As Benjamin Whichcote, in some sense the founder of the Cambridge Platonists, had put it: "*Nothing is desperate in the condition of good men*; they will not live and die in any dangerous error."

Trumbull, moreover, had served James II as a special envoy to the French court after the revocation of the Edict of Nantes, when suddenly French Protestants were subjected to brutalities such as had been the lot of Roman Catholics in England only in the wake of the Gunpowder and Popish Plots. It cannot be said that Britain's special envoy, only perfunctorily backed by his royal master, accomplished a great deal politically—certainly nothing at all to soften Louis XIV's harsh measures—but he returned with a clear sense of what religious persecution meant for its victims, and the experience may have mellowed him for the kindness he showed later to Catholics like Dryden and Pope. If, during their woodland rides, such subjects surfaced in Trumbull's conversation, they may have further enforced his protégé's hostility to what in the *Essay on Criticism* is called sectarianism:

> (Thus Wit, like Faith, by each man is apply'd
> To *one small Sect*, and All are *damn'd beside*)
>
> (ll.396–7)

and in the *Essay on Man*, religious zeal:

> Zeal then, not charity, became the guide,
> And hell was built on spite, and heav'n on pride. . . .
> With Heav'n's own thunders shook the world below,
> And play'd the God an engine on his foe.
>
> (ll. 261–2; 267–8)

A more precise image of bigotry would be hard to find.

Perhaps the clearest evidence we have of the range of issues on which the association with Trumbull set Pope thinking is the following from a letter of 1714:

> For Fame [Pope is apparently replying to some compliments on the success of the *Rape of the Lock*] tho' it be as *Milton* finely calls it, *The last Infirmity of noble Minds*, is scarce so strong a temptation as to

warrant our loss of time here: It can never make us lie down contentedly on a death-bed (as some of the ancients are said to have done with that thought). You Sir have your self taught me, that an easy situation at that hour, can proceed from no ambition less noble than that of an eternal felicity, which is unattainable by the strongest endeavours of the Wit, but may be gain'd by the sincere intentions of the Heart only. As in the next world, so in this, the only solid blessings are owing to the goodness of the mind, not the extent of the capacity: Friendship here is an emanation from the same source as Beatitude there: the same benevolence and grateful disposition that qualifies us for the one, if extended farther, makes us partakers of the other.

To be sure, there may be an element of pose and coloration here, a young man striking before a respected elder attitudes he knows will draw approval—as who among us has not on occasion done? Still, this is a young man who at least once already has shaken hands with death and who is sensing, however insecurely, the first pressures of a question that will haunt him throughout his career, as it has other creative personalities before and since. Which matters more: to be a great artist? or to be a good man? to be valued for one's writings or for oneself? to achieve (in Yeats's phrase) perfection of the work or of the life? Though Pope's assiduous attention to his texts shows him unwilling to give up some semblance of the former, his expressed convictions invariably support the latter; and however much our current romantic idolatry of art may incline us to dismiss all this as lip-service, we are quite wrong to deny to him, or to anyone, the genuineness of an aspiration on the ground that it sometimes failed of being realized. As a matter of fact, the statement he makes to Trumbull seems in part to be a rendering in his own terms of the passage in *Lycidas* that his quotation of its most famous line shows him to be reflecting on:

> *Fame* is no plant that grows on mortal soil,
> Nor in the glistering foil
> Set off to th' world, nor in broad rumour lies,
> But lives and spreads aloft by those pure eyes,
> And perfet witnes of all-judging *Jove*;
> As he pronounces lastly on each deed,
> Of so much fame in Heav'n expect thy meed.
>
> (ll. 78–84)

This is not the last time that Pope will take his cue from the great predecessor whose portrait he hung in his chamber to keep him humble.

William Walsh

Walsh's influence on Pope's early years, like Trumbull's, was probably
general as well as literary. In his youth he had been something of a beau.
Tall and well made, with light hair set off by dark eyes and a ruddy
complexion (if we may believe the hints dropped in his *Letters Gallant
and Amorous* of 1692), gifted also, as these letters show, with all the
blandishments of witty small talk, he had committed in his youth, he
tells us, every amorous indiscretion except marriage. By the time Pope
knew him, however, he had "left *Cupid* in the lurch" for politics and
literature. He was now in his forties, had served in two parliaments as a
Whig M.P. for Worcestershire (1698–1702), been appointed to a post
in the royal household (as Gentleman of the Horse) on the accession of
Queen Anne, and was about to stand in the parliamentary elections of
1705 for Richmond in Yorkshire.

Thus like most of Pope's early acquaintances he was preeminently a
man of affairs and in this capacity may have helped fortify in his young
friend some of those aristocratic attitudes toward the writer's profession (which he would have found also in his Montaigne) that crop out
so incongruously from time to time in his statements about his
work—that he wrote only because it pleased him, gave up no serious
calling for "this idle trade," lisped (as a child) in numbers "for the
numbers came," and began to publish merely because he was told he
"might please such as it was a credit to please." All this seems laughable
coming from one of the most painstaking of craftsmen, one who was
also a canny publisher as well as a shrewd judge of timing and public
taste, and who, having masterminded the most successful subscription
undertaking of his time, knocked himself out summer after summer to
make good on his commitment.

Laughable, it may be, yet deeply felt. And while there is probably (it
is difficult to be entirely sure) some element of snobbery in this claim to
lofty self-sufficiency, there is plainly some clinging also to an ideal of
serene detachment cherished by almost everyone in this age and
memorably voiced by Congreve when visited by Voltaire:

> Mr. *Congreve* [Voltaire wrote afterwards] had one Defect, which
> was his entertaining too mean an Idea of his first Profession, . . . tho'
> 'twas to this he ow'd his Fame and Fortune. He spoke of his Works as
> of Trifles that were beneath him; and hinted to me in our first Con-
> versation, that I should visit him on no other Foot than that of a
> Gentleman, who led a Life of Plainness and Simplicity. I answer'd,
> that had he been so unfortunate as to be a mere Gentleman, I should

never have come to see him; and I was very much disgusted at so unseasonable a Piece of Vanity.

We may sympathize, I think, with both men. From today's perspectives, Voltaire has by far the better of the argument, and Congreve's remonstrance, if not the "despicable foppery" that Johnson thought it, seems at any rate a disagreeable form of cant. On the other hand, from the point of view that we have seen Milton taking up in *Lycidas*—whether the highest good be conceived in seventeenth-century religious terms as the approbation of "all-judging Jove" or in Renaissance and classical terms as cultivation of the virtues and peaceful possession of one's soul—

> One self-approving hour whole years out-weighs
> Of stupid starers, and of loud huzzas—

Congreve's position has its claims, and "the impertinent Frenchman," as Charles Lamb tartly put it, "was properly answer'd."

What we have here, plainly, is a clash of worlds, one vanishing, the other emerging—"No man but a blockhead ever wrote except for money," declared Samuel Johnson on 5 April 1776, though he too was capable of other opinions on other occasions. Both worlds had a strong attraction for Pope. Few poets, if any, have more self-consciously pursued an immortality in art than he, to say nothing of a settled livelihood. Yet when a trying acquaintance taxes him in his mature years as Voltaire taxed Congreve—

> I am sorry to hear you say, You never thought any great Matters of your *Poetry*.—It is, in my Opinion, the Characteristic you are to hope your *Distinction* from: To be *Honest* is the Duty of every *plain Man*! . . . But your *Honesty* you possess in common with a *Million*, who will never be *remember'd*; whereas your *Poetry* is a Peculiar, that will make it impossible, you should be forgotten—

he unhesitatingly responds:

> I am very sensible that my *Poetical* Talent is all that may make me *remembered*: But it is my *Morality* only [my being a good man] that must make me *Beloved*, or *Happy*.

Discount it as we may, there is a residue of authenticity in this longing that remains with him all his life and possibly accounts for this extraordinary success in making and keeping friends.

The character of Walsh's more strictly literary influence on Pope is less easy to guess at. "He encouraged me much," Pope told Spence late in his life, "and used to tell me that there was one way left of excelling, for though we had several great poets, we never had any one great poet that was correct—and he desired me to make that my study and aim." The statement unfortunately leaves us quite in the dark as to what Walsh meant by correctness. Perhaps he had in mind technicalities like the hiatus, placing of the caesura, the exclusion of triplet rhymes or lines of six feet from couplet paragraphs, the niceties of sound echoing sense, and such like. Or perhaps, alternatively, he was concerned for the keeping of various decorums in the choice of diction, the separation of genres, the harmonizing of style with subject (as, for instance, not using language too "heroic" in an elegiac poem), or even the avoidance of low, indelicate, or specialized locutions. Or perhaps both.

The one point that seems certain in Walsh's indoctrination is that it stressed the taking of infinite pains. In the letter to Wycherley already quoted in which he finds Pope's *Pastorals* superior to anything Vergil had written at the same age, he urges the poet to call that he may "read the Verses over with him, and give him my opinion of the particulars." That he repeatedly offered this kind of meticulous attention is borne out by Pope's statement that his translation of the first book of Statius's *Thebaid*, when published, carried the corrections of Walsh, and also by some leaves surviving with the manuscript of the *Pastorals* in which Pope submits to Walsh's judgment minute points of versification and decorum, and receives, though often without explanation, a considered answer.

Typical are the following exchanges. They are worth pausing on for a moment because they probably offer as clear examples as may be had of what Walsh—and Pope at this point in his career—considered correctness to be; and also because they help revive for us certain aspects of the now all-but-forgotten poetics of the rhymed closed couplet, in which, as in eighteenth-century music, much is made of minute variations. In each instance Pope presents his current manuscript text, names an objection that a friend or his own cooler judgment has raised, and submits an alternative. The focus of his question he signalizes by underscoring the relevant word or words. Walsh's reply is given here in italics.

The first exchange concerns the opening lines of *Spring*, which also introduce the four poems as a group:

> First in these Fields I *sing* the Sylvan Strains,
> Nor blush to sport on Windsor's *peaceful* Plains;
> Fair Thames flow gently from thy sacred Spring,
> While on thy Banks Sicilian Muses *sing*.

Objection. That the Letter [alliteration] is hunted too much—Sing the Sylvan—Peaceful Plains—and that the word *Sing* is us'd two lines after, Sicilian Muses sing.

Alteration. First in these Fields I *try* the Sylvan Strains,
   Nor blush to sport on Windsor's *happy* Plains. &c.

Quere. If *Try* be not properer in relation to *First*; as, we first attempt a thing; and more modest? and if *Happy* be not more than *Peaceful*?

[Walsh's comment]: *Try is better than sing—Happy does not sound right, yᵉ first Syllable being short, perhaps you may finde a better word than Peaceful as Flowry.*

Walsh evidently favors modesty, but his ear is troubled, I think rightly, by the snip-snap effect of "happy"; wrongly, however, he seems willing to settle for the commonplace "Flowry" in order to lengthen the vowel and catch up toward the close of line 2 the *f* sound in "First" at the beginning of line 1. In the text finally sent to the printer, Pope solved the problem to his own satisfaction by replacing "happy" with "blissful" and so catching up both the *f* sound at the beginning of the couplet and the *bl* sound at the beginning of the line.

The second example, which I take from *Summer*, shows Walsh's taste more favorably. The passage includes four of the best-known lines in the *Pastorals* (73–6), which were later excerpted and set to music in Handel's oratorio *Semele*. In *Summer*, the shepherd hero implores his absent loved one to return:

   Oh deign to grace our happy rural Seats,
   Our mossy Fountains, and our green Retreats:
   While you yʳ Presence to the Groves deny,
   Our flow'rs are faded, and our Brooks are dry;
   Tho' withring Herbs lay dying on the Plain,
   At yʳ Return they shall be green again.
   Or, Oh deign to grace our happy Rural Seats,   ⋆Or,
   Our mossy Fountains, & our green Retreats: Where'er you
   ⋆Winds, where you walk, shall gently fann the Glade,   walk, fresh
   Trees, where you sit, shall crowd into a Shade,   Gales shall
   ⋆Flow'rs, where you tread, in painted Pride shall rise,   fann ye Glade,
   And all things flourish where you turn your Eyes:

                                                                                              ⋆Or,
                                                                                     Where'er you
   Quere. Which of these you like better?   tread, the purple
   [Walsh's comment]: *The second, with the alterations*   flow'rs shall
   on yᵉ side.   rise,

Unquestionably, Walsh casts his vote for the best choice of the three, a version that was altered in the published text only by the substitution of "cool Gales" for "fresh Gales" (abandoning the insistent f-G/f-G alliteration for a subtler echo that at the same time lengthens the caesura by catching up the k sound of "cool" in "walk") and "blushing Flow'rs" for "purple flow'rs," which assigns to the flowers a responsiveness—a shy, deferential reticent responsiveness—contrasting delicately with the more aggressive and muscular response of the trees.

As a final instance, I choose an exchange about the closing lines of *Autumn*, which ends in the evening as the previous two *Pastorals* had ended in the morning and at noon.

> Thus sung the Swains, while Day yet strove with Night,   *Quere
> And Heav'n yet *languish'd* with departing light;   if lan-
> When falling Dews with Spangles deck'd the Glade,   guish be a
> And the *low Sun* had lengthen'd ev'ry Shade.   proper word?

Objection. That to mention the *Sunsett* after Twilight (Day yet strove wth Night) is improper, Is the following Alteration any thing better?

> Thus sung the Swains while Day yet strove wth Night,
> The Sky still blushing wth departing light;
> When falling Dews with Spangles deck'd the Glade,
> And the *brown Evening* lengthen'd ev'ry Shade.

[Walsh's comment]: *Tis not ye Evening but ye Sun being low y^t* [that] *lengthens ye Shades. Otherwise ye second please mee best.*

Walsh's laconic reply to the marginal query about "languish" is: *Not very proper.* We may reasonably guess, I think, that his objection here has to do with what he sees as a fault against genre and hence springs from the same theoretical base as his objection in another of these exchanges to Pope's saying (of the death of the shepherdess Daphne) that "the Clouds have put their Mourning on." This, he says, is "too conceited" for pastoral, meaning, presumably, too ingenious, sophisticated, witty, "polite"—not the sort of metaphorizing that in his view accords with "the Truth, Sincerity and Innocence" of a shepherd's life, or with the "simple," "easie," and "humble" thoughts becoming to it. The "languishing" of "Heav'n" evidently struck him in the same way. His comment on the main question, on the other hand, which is slightly more forthcoming, rests fairly on the classical and neoclassical axiom that the task of poetry is to imitate things as they actually are. If it is a low sun that

15. William Walsh (1663–1708). By Sir Godfrey Kneller and his studio, *c.* 1708.

> . . . the Muse's Judge and Friend.
>
> *Essay on Criticism,* 729.

Courtesy of the National Portrait Gallery.

stretches out the shadows, no brown evening will do. In the upshot, his advice led to the reappearance of "the low Sun" in the published version of the fourth line, but, less happily, to a revamping of the first line that divested it of interest: "Thus sung the Shepherds till th' Approach of Night."

On the whole, in this matter of practical criticism, it is probably fair to say that Walsh did little for Pope but the one thing needful: he took him seriously, read him carefully, and offered the support of a formed (if narrow) taste to a tyro whose practice of the couplet and the established genres was still diffident and experimental. Beyond this, it is probable that he furthered Pope's acquaintance with the ancient and modern European critics. For unless we suppose that Dryden's tribute to him as the best critic of our nation sprang merely from gratitude (perhaps for the same kind of attention to the verse of the *Aeneid* translation that he later gave to Pope?), the preeminence that Dryden accords him presumably lay in this area. He had, moreover, a degree of familiarity with Italian writers and Renaissance neo-Latinists, from whose example he may, in fact, have derived his admiration for correctness—Pietro Bembo, to name only one example, having been in the habit of keeping some forty portfolios through which every page of his Latin verse was successively sieved, picking up polish at each stage.

It may have been particularly the critics, then—Aristotle, Longinus, Horace, Quintilian, Vida, Boileau, and some others in that formidable line—that the two friends discussed and explored when in August of 1707, after "a dreadful long Journey" from Binfield, presumably via Oxford, the Vale of Evesham ("famous for Fertility and bad Roads"), and the cathedral city of Worcester, Pope arrived for a visit at Abberley Lodge, the Walsh family seat in Worcestershire, hard by the hill on which Owen Glendower once planted his Welsh banner in defiance of the English. That he should have undertaken such a trip at all (looking, Trumbull told his nephew, so frail at his setting out that he wondered if he should ever lay eyes on him again) is probably a tribute to the determination with which at this period of his life he seized every opportunity to extend his education. Once at Abberley, he stayed close to six weeks. This likewise must be a tribute of sorts: possibly to Pope for the attractiveness of his zeal, wit, and talent, certainly to Walsh for his patience and generosity. A few months later Walsh was dead.

Small wonder that in the *Essay on Criticism*, some early drafts of which Pope tells us he showed to Walsh on this occasion, the place of honor at the end of a long line of critics whose works Walsh may have helped him digest is reserved for "the Muse's Judge and Friend":

Such late was *Walsh*,—the Muse's Judge and Friend,
Who justly knew to blame or to commend;
To Failings *mild*, but *zealous* for Desert;
The *clearest Head*, and the *sincerest Heart*.
This humble Praise, lamented *Shade*! receive,
This Praise at least a grateful Muse may give!

Though Pope would soon write maturer verse than this, it is quite possible that Walsh's best legacy to him is the fastidious skill with which he has made the *d* and *t* sounds in these lines play off against the *s* and *z* sounds, while the larger verse rhythms coil and uncoil in a manner already distinctively his own.

Returning from Abberley in September of 1707, Pope was far along toward a final text of the *Pastorals*, had begun the planning for and probably some snatches of the *Essay on Criticism*, was in process of revising his translation of Statius, to which Walsh had evidently contributed, and at the urging of Trumbull had begun (or would very soon begin) the masterly rendering of some fragments of Homer that was to lead in a few years to his undertaking the *Iliad*. The first phases of his preparation for a career in poetry were now over, and he was ready to try those wings in public that Walsh and his other early friends had helped him "prune."

PART TWO

THE ROAD TO FAME

1709–1720

CHAPTER 6

FIRST PUBLICATIONS

"So Pimps grow rich, while Gallants are undone"

On the second of May 1709, a little less than three weeks before his twenty-first birthday, *Poetical Miscellanies, The Sixth Part,* launched Pope on his public career as a poet. It was an elegant little volume, neatly printed with much grateful white space on paper thin enough to accommodate its 752 pages in a compass roughly that of a middling-sized modern paperback. As issued, it was in fact a paperback, as most eighteenth century books were, the glowing calf binding in which it is usually found today supplied at purchaser's expense.

During the three years since Tonson had first solicited the *Pastorals* for this volume, publication had been more than once delayed. In a letter to a friend following the last postponement in late 1708, Pope amuses himself by comparing his situation to that of a condemned man receiving a succession of royal pardons:

> Beyond all my Expectations, & far above my Demerits, I have been most mercifully repriev'd by the Sovereign Power of Jacob Tonson, from being brought forth to publick Punishment and respited from Time to Time from the hands of those barbarous Executioners of the Muses [i.e., the coffee-house critics].

He is similarly amused by the bold claim on the collection's title page that all its contributions are by "Eminent Hands." Writing to Wycherley soon after its appearance—Wycherley has assured him that "all the best Judges . . . like your part of the Book so well, that the rest is lik'd the worse"—he assumes first of all the posture of aristocratic detachment we have met with before:

> I shall be satisfy'd if I can lose my Time agreeably this way, without losing my reputation: As for gaining any, I am as indifferent in the Matter as *Falstaffe* was, and may say of *Fame* as he did of *Honour*, *If it comes, it comes unlook'd for; and there's an End on 't.*

Then he adds, a propos of Tonson's boast:

> I can be content with a bare saving [i.e., neither winning nor losing] game, without being thought an Eminent hand, (with which Title *Jacob* has graciously dignify'd his adventurers and voluntiers in Poetry). *Jacob* creates Poets, as Kings sometimes do Knights, not for their honour, but for money. Certainly he ought to be esteem'd a worker of Miracles, who is grown rich by Poetry.
>
> > What Authors lose, their Booksellers have won,
> > So Pimps grow rich, while Gallants are undone.

Notable in these passages, apart from a young man's nervous concern for the reception of his work (here disguised as unconcern) is an emphatic questioning of the power lodged in those days in publisher and bookseller—in his case, the elder Jacob Tonson. Tonson, described by one of his contemporaries as "Chief Merchant to the Muses" (a title not intended to be honorific), had indeed managed the miracle that Pope attributes to him: he had grown rich by poetry—or, more exactly, by poets. Dryden's publisher for twenty years, he had profited from the series of poetical miscellanies that Dryden had overseen for him, from the immense topical appeal of Dryden's political satires, from the continuing market for his plays, and especially from his sinewy translations of Juvenal and Vergil (surely among the glories of seventeenth-century versification), in executing the latter of which, it is fair to say, the translator quite literally wore himself out. At an early date, Tonson had also bought a piece of the copyright of *Paradise Lost*, eventually acquiring it entire and reissuing the poem in its first illustrated edition in 1688, its first annotated edition in 1695 (along with the other poems), and thereafter for half a century in various formats as part of Milton's *Poetical Works*, to which he had similarly acquired the rights. Later, having added the copyright of Shakespeare to his holdings, he commissioned from the playwright Nicholas Rowe the first fully "edited" edition of the plays (1709), complete with an introduction based on information from Betterton that became the standard life of Shakespeare before the nineteenth century.

Tonson prospered partly because the composing and perusing of neatly turned verses were at this time still numbered among the accomplishments of an English gentleman, though the tradition was fading fast. Partly too because he was aggressive, shrewd, and a boon companion. He seems to have founded, for example, what is probably the first expense-account publisher's dinner on record: a weekly feast at a local mutton-pie house, which, with bumptious heartiness and "always a sharp Eye towards his own Interest," he nursed gradually into the distinguished gathering of Whig writers and politicians known as the Kit-Kats, many of whom he could count on to supply hints or copy toward his printing ventures. Some writers, like Sir Richard Blackmore, himself a Whig, took a comparatively benign view of the Tonson empire:

> Now crowds to Founder *Bocaj* [Jacob] did resort,
> And for his Favour humbly made their Court.
> The little Wits attended at his Gate,
> And Men of Title did his Levee wait;
> For he, as Sovereign by Prerogative,
> Old Members did exclude, and new receive.
> He judg'd who most were for the Order fit,
> And Chapters held to make new Knights of Wit.

But many disagreed. A Tory poet, depicting him scornfully under the name *Bibliopolo* (i.e., "Bookseller"), assailed his domineering ways, interpolating three unsavory lines written about him earlier by Dryden:

> Now the Assembly [the Kit-Kats] to adjourn prepar'd,
> When *Bibliopolo* from behind appear'd
> As well describ'd by th' old Satyrick Bard,
> *With leering Looks, Bull-fac'd, and Freckled fair,*
> *With two left Legs; and Judas-colour'd* [red] *Hair,*
> *With Frowzy Pores, that taint the ambient Air.*
> Sweating and Puffing for a-while he stood.
> And then broke forth in this insulting Mood:
> I am the Touchstone of all Modern Wit,
> Without my Stamp in vain your Poets write.
> Those only purchase everliving Fame,
> That in my Miscellany plant their Name.

Pope seems to recall this passage and its planting metaphor in the letter first quoted above.

> That Poet were a happy Man who cou'd but obtain a Grant to preserve His [fame] for Ninety nine Years: for those Names very rarely last so many Days, which are planted either in Jacob Tonson's, or the Ordinary of Newgate's, Miscellanies.★

★The Newgate chaplain's occasional publications of condemned persons' confessions and last words.

The criticism was not, however, personal. Despite the enormous discrepancy in age (Tonson was born in 1655), the two men became fast friends. Towards the end of the publisher's life, in fact, when the poet was inviting two other friends to dine at Twickenham, he promises them as his third guest "a Phaenomenon worth seeing & hearing, Old Jacob Tonson, who is the perfect Image & Likeness of Bayle's Dictionary [the first English translation of which Tonson had published]; so full of Matter, Secret History, & Wit & Spirit; att almost fourscore." It is notable, nonetheless, that save for one or two small pieces in other Tonson anthologies and his edition of Shakespeare (to whose works Tonson continued to claim copyright), Pope never published with old Jacob, very probably, as the latter's most recent biographer has said, because they were "too well matched in the art of driving shrewd bargains." Tonson, Pope well knew, had not made his fortune merely through sagacity or merely through the market for poetry. He had made it in considerable part through the inequitable scheme of things that then governed publishing, whereby publisher or bookseller, who were often the same man, normally purchased each work outright or for a certain period, and the author, no matter how well it then sold and continued to sell in successive editions, perhaps through generations, received little or no further remuneration. Under this scheme, Milton contracted with Samuel Simmons for a total emolument of £20 if *Paradise Lost* sold out three editions. Of this money, he was actually paid only £5, his widow only £8 more, making the rate of compensation for the greatest long poem in the language slightly more than a farthing per line. Rates had improved (though partly through inflation) by Pope's time, and Pope received for his contribution to *Poetical Miscellanies, The Sixth Part* thirteen guineas, or something over twopence a line; while for the two versions of the *Rape of the Lock*, as dazzling among mock-epics as Milton's poem among epics, he managed to squeeze out of Bernard Lintot all of fivepence a line. Though these figures appear less outrageous when adjusted for the depreciation of money over the past two centuries, they remain heavily weighted in favor of the processor and against the producer, and the seeds of rebellion had already begun to take root in Pope by the time he published his first poems, as the letters quoted make clear. Over his lifetime, as we shall see, he managed to turn this traditional system of rewards almost on its head, becoming to all intents and purposes his own publisher and probably, by his example, doing more than any other eighteenth-century writer to improve the prospects of the writing class.

"There lived in Lombardy, as Authors write"

Like most anthologies of current poetry, *Poetical Miscellanies, The Sixth Part* featured mainly the work of writers born to be forgotten. It contained, however, two poems by Swift, one of them his delightfully astringent retelling of Ovid's *Baucis and Philemon*, and three by Pope. On pp. 172–224 appeared *January and May; Or, The Merchant's Tale. From Chaucer*, originally undertaken, we may presume, as part of his program for learning to write by practicing the styles of other poets. Pages 301–323 carried one of the Homer translations that his elderly friend Trumbull had long been urging him to undertake: *The Episode of Sarpedon, Translated from the Twelfth and Sixteenth Books of Homer's Iliads*. The four *Pastorals*, occupying pp. 721–751, closed the book and were evidently intended by Tonson to balance another set of pastorals (of which we shall hear more) that he placed at the beginning.

From early boyhood Chaucer had been a favorite with Pope. At thirteen, as mentioned earlier, he was given by a Binfield neighbor a copy of Thomas Speght's 1598 edition, the only text (along with its several reprints) in which Chaucer was at the time available. Though it was a forbidding book, crudely printed in double column and Gothic letter, and bristling with what we now know are misprints and misreadings and containing works not by Chaucer, Pope's markings in his copy show that he read it attentively and more than once. "I read Chaucer still," he told Spence as late as 1730, "with as much pleasure as almost any of our poets. He is a master of manners and of description, and the first tale-teller in the true enlivened natural way."

Since every age, however, views the past through its own interests (usually choosing to believe there are no others), it is idle to look in Pope for the Chaucer we think we know today. Our Chaucer is the sly ironist, the dapper and droll observer standing so thoroughly above and apart from his tales that if any flaws of redundancy or shapelessness appear they must be assigned not to the artist but the tale-teller. The Chaucer of eighteenth-century readers was vastly different. For them he was a true primitive, an admired but somewhat unfastidious ancestor, a great comic moralist who was, however, at the same time a rough diamond, requiring, as Dryden had put it, to be "polish'd, ere he shines." His verse, in the only texts the early eighteenth century knew, appeared not to scan—indeed, in many instances, owing to scribal carelessness or contemporary ignorance of the sounded final e, could not be made to. The Chaucerian open couplet, moreover, lacked the enclosed antiphonies of sound to which the contemporary ear, after Waller, Denham, and Dryden, was attuned. Neither was Chaucer's manner—loquacious, even self-indulgent, as it seemed to some—free of occasional longueurs; while his tales, often as broad in language as in situation, were such as a "polite" audience containing increasing numbers of women (still held officially even if not always privately to be vessels of a finer clay) could hardly digest without embarrassment.

Unquestionably, here was an ancestor who in some sense deserved every title of Dryden's famous tribute:

> In the first place, As he is the Father of *English* Poetry, so I hold him in the same Degree of Veneration as the *Grecians* held *Homer*, or the *Romans Virgil*: He is a perpetual Fountain of good Sense; learn'd in all Sciences [branches of knowledge]; and therefore speaks properly on all Subjects: . . . [Moreover] he must have been a Man of a most wonderful comprehensive Nature, because . . . he has taken into the Compass of his *Canterbury Tales* the various Manners and Humours (as we now call them) of the whole *English* Nation, in his Age . . . Even the Ribaldry of the Low Characters is different: The *Reeve*, the *Miller*, and the *Cook*, are several Men, and distinguish'd from each other, as much as the mincing Lady Prioress, and the broad-speaking gap-tooth'd Wife of *Bathe*. . . . 'Tis sufficient to say according to the Proverb, that here is God's Plenty.

But unquestionably, too, this was an ancestor to whose work and world certain mutings and mutations would have to be applied to make him acceptable to contemporary readers.

It is with these ends in view that Pope sets out to translate the *Merchant's Tale*. In its bare bones, it is simply the story of an old man (January) who takes a young wife (May) and is cuckolded for his pains when she climbs into a pear tree to gather its fruit and surrenders herself there by prearrangement to Damian, her husband's young squire—high romance indeed. But as Chaucer tells it, the crude jest at the center is so delectably pranked out with vivid details of medieval life and droll quirks of human nature, so well supplied with what Pope's readers would have called "celestial machinery" in the form of a battle of wills between Pluto the Fairy King and Proserpina the Fairy Queen, so mischievously interwoven with tongue-in-cheek discussions of the relative merits of the wedded and single states —above all, so brilliantly climaxed by the same sort of womanly resourcefulness as that with which Shakespeare's Rosalind teases his Orlando:

You shall never take her without her answer, unless you take her without her tongue. O that woman who cannot make her fault her husband's occasion [i.e., a stick to beat him with], let her never nurse her child herself, for she will breed it like a fool—

that it is not surprising to find Landor, four and a half centuries after Chaucer's death, convinced that only one other Englishman had walked the English roads

<blockquote>
with step
So active, so inquiring eye, or tongue
So varied in discourse.
</blockquote>

The story of an old man's cuckolding by a young wife was calculated to appeal to readers in Pope's time. It acted out in the form of caricature (and perhaps thereby helped exorcise) an anxiety pervasive in most male-dominated societies, where arranged marriages are the cultural norm, particularly arranged marriages of desirable young women with rich dotards. The sympathy of those who deplored such unions could be slanted toward the bride, as with Chaucer and in Pope's imitation, or toward the betrayed husband, as in Swift's *The Progress of Marriage*, but in either case the implicit moral of the tale came down hard against forced marriage and on the side of more sensitive procedures. Since the genre gradually disappeared as the practice of forced marriage declined and a conception of the family as a form of individual fulfilment took precedence over conceptions of the family as a social and economic institution, one is moved to wonder whether such tales were not among the means by which popular literature, then as now, held the mirror up to nature and showed virtue her own feature, scorn her own image. How far Pope himself might have subscribed to such a view of the *Merchant's Tale* is anyone's guess. He may have been drawn to the story (as to *The Wife of Bath Her Prologue*, not published till three years later but doubtless undertaken when he undertook *The Merchant's Tale*) simply by the fascination blended of sympathy and mistrust—the latter perhaps predictable in a dwarf and cripple—that invariably characterizes his evocations of women. Or he may have chosen it on the merest whim. As Horatio reminds Hamlet, it can be dangerous in biography to consider too curiously.

Though much of Chaucer's poem reappears in Pope's, the differences are significant. Where Chaucer leans steadily away from fable toward story—which is to say toward a fully realized fiction about an old gaffer's experience in desiring and marrying a beautiful young woman—Pope leans away from story toward satirical exemplum, in a manner that his first lines announce:

> There liv'd in *Lombardy*, as Authors write,
> In Days of old, a wise and worthy Knight;
> Of gentle Manners, as of gen'rous Race,
> Blest with much Sense, more Riches, and some Grace.
>
> (ll. 1–4)

Where Chaucer, moreover, sidles into his material, letting it gradually appear how far his January is to be considered "wise," gentle in his manner, or generous in his bloodlines, Pope marshals all these attributes up front to focus ironies of a coarser kind: "much Sense, more Riches, and some Grace." In line with his other sly obliquities, Chaucer leaves much to be read between the lines. His young May (and young indeed she may have been by the marrying habits of those times) lies waiting for old January's embraces on her wedding night "as stille as stone." And when the story ends, Chaucer gives us simply a deluded happy husband, leading his (as he thinks) vindicated spouse back to his house from the pear-tree; whereas Pope, concluding what he takes to be a didactic comic yarn, finds it indispensable to spell out its topsy-turvy moral:

> Thus ends our Tale, whose Moral next to make,
> Let all wise Husbands hence Example take;
> And pray, to crown the Pleasure of their Lives,
> To be so well deluded by their Wives.
>
> (ll. 817–20)

Despite such losses—and there are others—*January and May* remains a stunning accomplishment for a poet who was probably no more than seventeen or eighteen when he began it and twenty when he revised it for publication. Though his language is more predictable than Chaucer's—"He cry'd, he roar'd, he storm'd, he tore his Hair": this is Pope's version of Chaucer's "he yaf a roryng and a cry" (spoken of January as he sees his wife whored in the tree)—he is often finely responsive to Chaucer's lead. And in one passage—Pope's version of the rendezvous of the Fairy King and Queen—it might indeed be argued that in his own mode he has outclassed his original. Chaucer has:

> And so bifel, that brighte morwe-tyde,
> That in that gardyn, in the ferther syde,
> Pluto, that is kyng of Fayerye,
> And many a lady in his compaignye,
> Folwynge his wyf, the queene Proserpyna,
> Which that he ravysshed out of Ethna

> Whil that she gadered floures in the mede—
> In Claudyan ye may the stories rede,
> How in his grisely carte he hire fette—
> This kyng of Fairye thanne adoun hym sette
> Upon a bench of turves, fressh and grene,
> And right anon thus seyde he to his queene.
>
> (IV, E: 2225–2236)

Inimitable, of course. But Pope's lines have a special deliciousness of their own:

> It so befel, in that fair Morning-tide,
> The Fairies sported on the Garden's Side,
> And, in the midst, their Monarch and his Bride.
> So featly tripp'd the light-foot Ladies round,
> The Knights so nimbly o'er the Greensword bound,
> That scarce they bent the Flow'rs, or touch'd the Ground.
> The Dances ended, all the Fairy Train
> For Pinks and Daisies search'd the flow'ry Plain;
> While on a Bank reclin'd of rising Green,
> Thus, with a Frown, the King bespoke his Queen.
>
> (ll. 617–26)

For melody and rhythm few verses in English are more bewitching than Pope's fourth and fifth.

One is left wondering, nevertheless, what were the thoughts of the devout family in Binfield on their son's making his literary debut in the bawdy company of *January and May*, soon to be companioned by *The Wife of Bath Her Prologue*. Were they (like many a later parent) conditioned to accepting in their offspring what might have troubled them in others? Or did they comfort themselves by turning at once to the magnificent lines from Homer that followed in mid-volume?

"But since, alas, ignoble age must come"

On the plains of Troy, fighting to save from ruin that golden city by the sea, Homer's Sarpedon addresses his comrade Glaucus: Why, he asks, are we kings honored by our countrymen almost as gods, and why do we stand possessed of great tracts of orchard and ploughland, if it be not that by our conduct in battle we persuade all who serve under us that our privileges are earned? Then he adds, in phrases that have haunted the Western imagination for centuries, phrases that have become synonymous not only with the principle of *noblesse oblige* but with what is sometimes called "the heroic view of tragic life":

> Ah, friend, if once escaped from this battle we were for ever to be ageless and immortal, neither should I fight myself amid the foremost, nor should I send thee into battle where men win glory; but now—for in any case fates of death beset us, fates past counting, which no mortal may escape or avoid—now let us go forward, whether we shall give glory to another, or another to us.

This, a principal turning point of the *Iliad*, Pope has fastened on with the insight that all his work with Homer shows. Hector and his fellow warriors have driven the Greeks behind the wall erected to protect their beached ships. The question now is whether to try to breach the wall and fire the Greek navy or withdraw. An omen appears in the sky: the bird of Zeus, an eagle, struggles with a great snake that it holds in its talons, but then, stung, lets it drop. Hector's companion Polydamas interprets the omen as a signal to withdraw. But Hector refuses to take instruction from a bird. "One omen is best," he replies: "to fight for one's country." He is trusting in Zeus' promise of victory made only some hours before. But he forgets, or chooses to forget, that Zeus has promised victory only until the Trojans reach the ships.

It is at this moment that Homer puts into Sarpedon's mouth the words already quoted—reflecting in them the heroic mood that equally inflames Hector. Hector has known from the outset that Troy and he and all its people are doomed. But he knows also that he is its chief defender, a king's son, and for all these reasons together he elects, in the spirit of Sarpedon's charge to Glaucus, not to withdraw but to press on, though the way of prudence lies back to the city. In the eloquent words of one of the best of Homer's commentators:

> [Homer] has been careful to keep reminding us that [Hector] is choosing the way of death; he presents the plain foolishness of the thing, confronts it with prudent words, with the wisdom that looks before and after, and then drowns out these voices in the applause of Hector's world. ... It is as if above the voice of prudence and common sense, the trumpets of heroism sounding the charge rang out triumphantly around Hector as he leapt within the gates.

Pope's rendering of this trumpet music—music with a sigh in its throat—is muted but unforgettable:

> Cou'd all our Care elude the greedy Grave,
> Which claims no less the Fearful than the Brave,
> For Lust of Fame I shou'd not vainly dare
> In fighting Fields, nor urge thy Soul to War.
> But since, alas, ignoble Age must come,
> Disease, and Death's inexorable Doom;
> The Life which others pay, let Us bestow,
> And give to Fame what we to Nature owe;
> Brave, tho' we fall; and honour'd, if we live;
> Or let us Glory gain, or Glory give!
>
> (ll. 43–52)

The shape that Pope gives to the *Episode* as a whole indicates that he knows precisely what the function of Sarpedon in the poem is and how his destiny typifies the larger action; for he adds now to the passage from Book 12 celebrating Sarpedon's moment of glory the passage in Book 16 that narrates his death. Here again, as in a glass, Sarpedon's fate shows us Hector's and prepares us for it. As Sarpedon is slain by Patroclus, who is drawn into battle by the breaching of the wall that Sarpedon helps Hector achieve, so Hector will be slain by Achilles, roused by Patroclus' death at Hector's hands. Though deeply lamented by his father Zeus, Sarpedon cannot be saved because he is a mortal doomed to the fate of mortals. So much also proves true of Hector. All that Zeus *can* do is to see that the body of his son undergoes no further indignities and is returned for burial to his native land, where funeral rites will be observed and a monument erected to his bravery. Again—and owing likewise to a father's grief—this will be the course of events for Hector.

Through Sarpedon, then, Homer sketches out well in advance of the denouement the curve of action begun in glory and closed by death (repeated again and again in the poem) that defines the heroic code. Also through Sarpedon, he is able to compress into two moving episodes, which Pope combines in one, that code's answer to the overwhelming question to which every individual and society must work out its own responses: what values are worth defending? and, if it comes to that, worth dying for? Hence when a few years later, in the *Rape of the Lock*, Pope brings Sarpedon's challenge into the fashionable drawing-rooms of Hampton Court and makes its phrases echo and re-echo beyond the chitchat we hear there, the tantrums we witness there, and the decidedly shrunken moral application it receives there, it is a moment of revelation and judgment, as electric in its own way as when Hamlet says to the skull of Yorick: "Now get you to my lady's chamber and tell her, let her paint an inch thick, to this favour she must come. Make her laugh at that!"

> Oh! if to dance all Night, and dress all Day,
> Charm'd the Small-pox, or chas'd old Age away;
> Who would not scorn what Huswife's Cares produce,
> Or who would learn one earthly Thing of Use?
> To patch, nay ogle, might become a Saint,
> Nor could it sure be such a Sin to paint.
> But since, alas! frail Beauty must decay,
> Curl'd or uncurl'd, since Locks will turn to grey,
> Since painted, or not painted, all shall fade,
> And she who scorns a Man, must die a Maid;
> What then remains, but well our Pow'r to use,
> And keep good Humour still whate'er we lose?
> And trust me, Dear! good Humour can prevail,
> When Airs, and Flights, and Screams, and Scolding fail.
> Beauties in vain their pretty eyes may roll;
> Charms strike the Sight, but Merit wins the Soul.
>
> (ll. 19–34)

In 1709, the *Rape of the Lock* and this passage in particular lie well ahead. But Pope's choice of the Sarpedon episode for his first published essay at Homer shows how well he already understands the poem without which the *Rape of the Lock* would be unimaginable, and how deeply he is laying the groundwork, though as yet unconsciously, for those brilliant reinterpretations of contemporary by past experience that so distinguish his later work. He was also at the time, perhaps somewhat less unconsciously, preparing himself for the two great Homeric undertakings that would eventually occupy some ten years of his life and bring him more fame and fortune in his own day than any other of his accomplishments. It might be argued further that in tackling the Sarpedon speech he was himself following its counsel. The best-known translation of that speech before Pope wrote was by John Denham, a much-admired poet of Dryden's generation; and for a mere boy to vie openly with a writer of such standing was to open himself to charges of immodesty. Pope is conscious of this, and in the synopsis prefixed to his translation refers to Denham—"after whom," he says, he would not have "the Vanity to attempt it for any other reason, than that the Episode must have been very imperfect without so Noble a part of it." Disarming, yes. And probably expressive of genuine trepidations. Still, the apology does leave open (not to say advertise!) an invitation to carry out the necessary comparisons, and Pope must have known, being the accomplished poet he already was, how any contest would have to come out between his own verses and these:

> Could the declining of this Fate (oh friend)
> Our Date to Immortality extend?
> Or if Death sought not them, who seek not Death,
> Would I advance? Or should my vainer breath
> With such a Glorious Folly thee inspire?
> But since with Fortune Nature doth conspire,
> Since Age, Disease, or some less noble End,
> Though not less certain, doth our days attend;
> Since 'tis decreed, and to this period lead
> A thousand ways, the noblest path we'll tread;
> And bravely on, till they, or we, or all,
> A common Sacrifice to Honour fall.

Even the coffee-house critics must have sensed, when they recalled those lines and then read Pope's, that a new star of some magnitude was rising in their sky.

An "Agreeable Place"

But it was of course on the four *Pastorals* that Pope had chiefly pinned his hopes. They had the advantage of being original work rather than translation and of representing a kind of poem that the example of Vergil and his Renaissance followers, including Spenser in *The Shepheardes Calendar*, had marked out as the appropriate first test for aspiring poets—"the Bow," said a contemporary critic, alluding to the great bow of Odysseus that none of Penelope's wooers could string, "at which most of our young Dabblers in Rhime have try'd their Strength"—and, he added, failed. Pope's own struggle with this reluctant instrument was not to be crowned by any such masterpiece as Milton's *Lycidas*, written roughly seventy years earlier by a greater poet on the threshold of full maturity. Pope's excursions into formal pastoral are the intricate compositions of a precocious boy who has temporarily submitted his imagination to a largely moribund tradition: possibly to see what could still be made of it, possibly out of enthusiasm for his predecessors' great achievements in that tradition and a wish to learn by emulating them, possibly even (as the remark of the critic just quoted may suggest) because neither the young poet nor his first readers quite realized how thoroughly exhausted as a genre the formal pastoral was. As T. S. Eliot once observed, speaking of the early poems of Blake, they "are not, as usually supposed, crude attempts to do something beyond a boy's capacity; they are . . . quite mature and successful attempts to do something small."

Nowadays, pastoral, like satire, survives mainly as an outlook—a cluster of attitudes and feelings. At its center beats a sophisticated longing for something that is experienced as "missing": a way of life, a power of seeing, a desired condition of things now viewed as lost (though possibly recoverable), even though it may never actually have existed or been in fact enjoyed. Explanations of this state of affairs abound. Some see in it the normal cantankerous human addiction to whatever it is we do not presently have: the grass in the last pasture, the good old days, the Golden Age, the Earthly Paradise, the security of the womb (Boethius's sixth-century lament, "O that our times would go back to the old ways!"—*Utinam modo nostra redirent In mores tempora priscos*—seems to be a cultural constant since earliest times); or, alternatively, if the orientation of the moment is toward the future, the grass in the next pasture, the millennium, the City of God, Utopia, matriarchy, the triumph of the proletariat. Other analysts, remembering Freud, locate in this habit of mind "the discontent of the civilized with civilization," an ineradicable malaise contracted from the repressions and inhibitions necessary to the socializing of the individual and the development of a stable personality. Still others associate it with a primal urge to be reborn, made new—to recover, or discover, some such wholeness of being as Matthew Arnold, in a "pastoral" of his own, ascribes to a seventeenth-century wandering scholar, whom he imagines living on through the centuries in the byways of Oxfordshire untouched by Victorian *angst*:

> O born in days when wits were fresh and clear,
> And life ran gaily as the sparkling Thames;
> Before this strange disease of modern life,
> With its sick hurry, its divided aims,
> Its heads o'ertax'd, its palsied hearts, was rife—
> Fly hence, our contact fear!

On this view, such events as the flight to the woods of the 1960s, the multiplication of communes, the assiduous application to handicrafts, even the regression of several generations of youth to a costume derived largely from the American "Western" (itself an expression of nostalgia for the vanished simplicities and hardihoods of the frontier) may be claimed to be as solid symptoms of the pastoralizing impulse as the games that Marie Antoinette used to play with her court shepherdesses in La Bergerie at Versailles.

But whatever the truth may be about pastoralism as an outlook, the form in which we meet with it in Pope's *Pastorals* is that of the conventional classical eclogue, derived from Theocritus and Vergil, and peopled with the usual *dramatis personae* of gods, goddesses, nymphs, satyrs, sheep, shepherds (mostly lovelorn), and country maidens (mostly coy), tucked away in a succession of inviting variations of what used to be called the *locus amoenus*: the Agreeable Place. The shepherds exist there to sing, for the eclogue is especially a poet's world as well as a world of poets. The maidens exist there —they are seldom present in person—to be longed for and pursued, because the eclogue features love-longing rather than love. Its eroticism, uncomplicated by the rituals and legalisms of organized societies, yearns toward such freedoms as the presence of nymphs and satyrs hints at even if it never actually depicts. In the eclogue as in heaven, there is no marrying or giving in marriage: wives, husbands, squalling—even laughing—infants are quite unknown within its tidy precincts. The sheep, apart from their value as stage properties and their appropriateness to a time when, as Pope puts it, "the best of men follow'd the employment" of sheep herding, exist to provide a dumb sympathy for the suffering shepherds, or sometimes to let their own eloquent impassiveness contrast with the twittering rhetorical flights of their masters, or sometimes even (to compare great things with small, as Vergil recommends) to complete a metaphor in which sheep and shepherd together image forth people and king, or, in the case of *Lycidas*, people and responsible presbyter.

It is the landscapes, however, that best express the nostalgia of the form. There the gods visit—sure proof along with the nymphs and satyrs that this is enchanted ground. There the poet-shepherd receives Orphic power, so that everything animate or inanimate responds to his singing: winds hush, waterfalls suspend their motion, rivers stop in their channels; and if he burns with love, all nature burns with him, not excepting his sheep: "They parch'd with Heat, and I inflam'd by thee," (*Summer*, line 20). Beauty shares this power. As we saw earlier when Pope was practicing his woodnotes for the criticism of Walsh, if the cold-hearted beloved will only consent to enter the poet's world, nature will respond to her too:

> Where-e'er you walk, cool Gales shall fan the Glade,
> Trees, where you sit, shall crowd into a Shade,
> Where-e'er you tread, the blushing Flow'rs shall rise,
> And all things flourish where you turn your Eyes.
>
> (*Summer*, 73–6)

In these Agreeable Places, remote from war, remote too from what the Romans called *negotium* or business, a man may lie under his favorite beech tree (as Pope is said to have done under the great beech near Binfield) and finger his flute, or try his skill against that of another shepherd, or wander at will and at ease among meadow flowers, shady groves with cooling breezes, crystalline fountains, fields where oxen plough, and small cottages with smoke rising from their roofs, registering on his consciousness (apart from praise of his mistress or distress at her loss) only the slow passage of the day from dawn through noon and afternoon to evening, the movement of the "rowling Year" from spring through summer and autumn into winter, and the cycle of human life from fresh youth to death. Love and death, as has often been pointed out, are the two chief stops on the shepherd-poet's pipe.

Pope's own delicate adaptations of the eclogue landscape have drawn considerable interest of late years. "Rococo vignettes in a gilt scrollwork," one critic calls them, by no means disapprovingly. "As gorgeous as those court masques which had carried on the pastoral tradition a century earlier," writes another. "We are reminded," says a third, "of the dance gestures and poses of nymphs and shepherds and deities in the twilight landscapes of Poussin and Zuccarelli." These are sound perceptions, particularly in their suggestion that Pope's eclogue landscapes are as carefully "pictorialized" and adjusted to convey "mood" as the arranged scenes of the Caroline masque or the manipulation of distance in baroque painting:

> Resound ye Hills, resound my mournful Strain!
> Of perjur'd *Doris*, dying I complain:
> Here where the *Mountains* less'ning as they rise,
> Lose the low Vales, and steal into the Skies;
> While lab'ring Oxen, spent with Toil and Heat,
> In their loose Traces from the Field retreat;
> While curling Smokes from Village-Tops are seen,
> And the fleet Shades glide o'er the dusky Green.
>
> (*Autumn*, 57–64)

Most of these particulars come to Pope from a common stock of rural imagery, originated by Vergil and Theocritus and expanded by the neo-Latin pastoralists, that had been accumulating in English poetry since Spenser's time. The misty effect of a range of hills at dusk, a yoke of oxen with their weary master bound for home, wisps of smoke curling from cottage chimneys as supper is got ready, the eerie lengthening of shadows at sunset: such images will appear and reappear among Pope's successors, painters as well as poets. That remarkable change we call Romanticism, which will impel Wordsworth to complain of the scarcity of new images from nature in eighteenth-century poetry, lay at this time well ahead. For Pope, and for his contemporaries in the other arts (architecture, sculpture, painting, but also those arts which produced the furniture, silver, and porcelain that are the envy of the modern world), the aim is still to work within a known vocabulary of motifs and patterns, extending their reach by the individuality and diversity with which one disposes and applies them but not forgetting (to borrow an image that would have fascinated Pope had he known of it) that like the genetic double helix they contain much encapsulated wisdom, and therefore not neglecting to appropriate their strength. In this sense, Pope's poetry is as profoundly "conservative" as that of the Romantics is revolutionary.

In planning the *Pastorals* as a group, Pope may also have had in mind, being as visually sensitive as he was, those representations of the four seasons as an allegory of human life that circulated so widely in his time in paintings and engravings as well as garden sculptures, and of which a particularly influential series was in fact painted by Poussin. He may even have known, though here we enter the Acrasian bower of pure speculation, one or both of the Poussin paintings (unconnected with the four seasons series) in which a group of shepherds is seen, in the one discovering, in the other raptly contemplating, a tomb bearing the inscription (now, alas, become almost a cliché): *Et in Arcadia ego*—"Even in Arcadia, I Death am with you." A passage in *Winter*, where Lycidas urges Thyrsis to sing a threnody for Daphne, seems suggestive in this respect:

> Begin: this Charge the dying *Daphne* gave,
> And said: "Ye Shepherds, sing around my Grave!"
> Sing, while beside the shaded Tomb I mourn,
> And with fresh Bays her Rural Shrine adorn.
>
> (*Winter*, 17–20)

But though it may be instructive to remember Poussin when considering the progress of the four *Pastorals* as a group from spring to winter, dawn to evening, joy to mourning, Pope had grounds more relative than this for that "constant braving ... of death," which pervades his work from its beginnings in the *Pastorals* and in the *Episode of Sarpedon* to the final *Dunciad*, where "Universal Darkness" buries all. He had, so far as the *Pastorals* are concerned, the traditional melancholy of the genre, where Joy's hand is ever at his lips bidding adieu and grief for the dead shepherd is a recurrent theme; and he had too, by the time he wrote any of the four *Dunciads*, the experience of years of illness punctuated by moments that brought him very close to that ague of the skeleton of which the pastoralists merely sing.

We may reasonably guess, in any case, that a contemporary reader of the *Pastorals* was less impressed by the pictorializing of their scenery, to which he was quite used from the example of Vergil, than by their fledgling author's success in acclimatizing Arcadia to England. It is not simply that the poems situate Vergilian pastoral names, activities, and landscape features in English settings, among English trees, flowers, birds, rivers, and poets. The effort is considerably more complex than this and quite evidently has for one of its aims the investment of the native countryside with some of the symbolic associations of classic ground:

> First in these Fields I try the Sylvan Strains,
> Nor blush to sport on *Windsor*'s blissful Plains:
> Fair *Thames* flow gently from thy sacred Spring,
> While on thy Banks *Sicilian* Muses sing;
> Let Vernal Airs thro' trembling Osiers play,
> And *Albion's* Cliffs resound the Rural Lay.
>
> (*Spring*, ll. 1–6)

This is Pope's "general Exordium" to the four poems. Greek Helicon (it says, or at least implies), grandsire of all sacred springs and symbolic fountainhead of the poetic art, has now an heir, even a rival, in the Thames. Around its sacred spring, the Sicilian Muses of Theocritus are presently thronging, summoned there by this poet's art as the art of Vergil had summoned them formerly to Rome and the art of Spenser to Britain. Pope evokes the example of Spenser by the reminiscence of his "Prothalamion" in line 3 ("Sweete Themmes runne softly till I end my song"), and the example of Vergil by the first couplet, alluding to the opening of his sixth eclogue, believed generally at this time to have been the earliest composed. "My Muse thought fit to toy first with Sicilian strains and blushed not to dwell in the woods," Vergil had written—which Dryden had interpreted in translating:

I first transferr'd to *Rome Sicilian* Strains,
Nor blushed the *Dorick* Muse to dwell on *Mantuan* Plains.

Pope's interpretation builds on these. The beauty of Windsor's "blissful Plains"—successors now to Mantua's, his lines suggest—is such that no poet need blush to have adopted them for his pastoral settings; and the famed hospitality of the Thames (symbol and haunt of native poetry) to importations from every clime guarantees its untroubled "gentle" acceptance of the foreign "Airs" now playing and echoing among its responsive willows, and reflected with a right-English resonance from the white cliffs of Dover to the nations of the world.

To participate in this way, significantly, in the process of accommodating the great ancients and the classical past to one's own clime, time, and tongue had been the ambition of most European poets of the Renaissance. Sharing that ambition, many English poets cherished a second, that of endowing a small island-nation, still dwarfed by the long-standing cultural dominance of the Sun King's France and dazzled by the imaginative radiance of Greece and Rome, with a poetic character, a national myth, a stratum of "dream" that had appropriated some of these glories and then surpassed them. As two of Pope's shepherds insist in *Spring*, and as he insists in his own person in *Windsor-Forest*, the great rivers of ancient lore may foam with gold like the Pactolus or be lined with Arabian trees dropping their med'cinable gum like the Eridanus: they are still no match for England, either in the beauty of their women:

> Celestial *Venus* haunts *Idalia*'s Groves,
> *Diana Cynthus, Ceres Hybla* loves;
> If *Windsor*-Shades delight the matchless Maid,
> *Cynthus* and *Hybla* yield to *Windsor*-Shade.
>
> (ll. 65–8)

or the wealth of their commerce:

> Let *India* boast her Plants, nor envy we
> The weeping Amber or the balmy Tree,
> While by our Oaks the precious Loads are born[e],
> And realms commanded which those Trees adorn.
> (*Windsor-Forest*, 29–32)

The formula is traditional of course. Vergil had used it to establish the amenities of his own native land:

> But neither Media's groves, land of wondrous wealth,
> nor beauteous Ganges, nor Hermus, thick with gold,
> may vie with Italy's glories—not Bactra, nor India,
> nor all Panchaia, rich in incense-bearing land.

With Vergil's Renaissance followers, the formula becomes a commonplace, and this is precisely what gives it life for Pope: it comes to him trailing a long history; it has known the play of many minds, it records the struggle of more than one imagination to give the world a human face. The humanist poets of the Renaissance, it has been well said, were notably sensitive to the interplay of times and cultures—of the self and what was alien to the self. For them, the beginnings of creativity lay not in some solipsistic Cartesian *cogito* or other version of the Narcissus myth, but in a "double groping"—both toward the "otherness" of the ancient text and toward "a modern sensibility," a personal voice, to mediate it. In this respect, Pope's affinities with the humanist poets go deep, and his works—not simply these first undertakings but also his finest achievements, from the expanded *Rape of the Lock* to the Horatian poems and the *Dunciad*—are best read, like theirs, in the light of that double perspective.

In the *Pastorals*, the mediating modern voice is largely that of a representative early eighteenth-century poet struggling to show his mastery of a genre by distilling into his own adaptation of it as much as possible of its honored past. To this end he packs his lines with reminiscences and evocations, not simply of his three great pastoral models but of a host of other poets, including admired contemporaries and near-contemporaries from Dryden and Milton to Congreve and Garth. He could hardly, in fact, have made the four poems more allusive if he had consciously intended them to serve as a modern "Musaeum" of the pastoral form—as conceivably he did. Yet the modern voice is also, as we saw, the voice of one determined to capture for his own day and place the appeal to the imagination that even as late as Wordsworth's time the old poetical names and presences could sometimes exercise. Even in Wordsworth they could inspire nostalgia for a pagan creed, alternative to that of the frantic "real" world where getting and spending laid waste the mind's mythopoeic powers:

> So might I, standing on this pleasant lea,
> Have visions that would make me less forlorn:
> Have sight of Proteus rising from the sea,
> Or hear old Triton blow his wreathed horn.

For the young man in Binfield, the twilight of the old gods had not yet gone so far. He could still claim, as he does in the Preface to his *Iliad* of 1715, that the Homeric gods, "after all the various Changes of Times and Religion, continue to this Day the Gods of Poetry," even though he may well have sensed by that date—what his subsequent practice seems to confess—how much he was whistling in the dark. And he could also still try, by superimposing a poetical Arcadia on Windsor plains and a poetical Golden Age on the reign of Queen Anne (as well as by the other equations and transpositions effected in the *Pastorals*), to carve out for himself a defensible position between contemporary actuality and ancient dream.

On the whole, this part of the experiment must be pronounced a failure. The dream is too much with him and quite stifles whatever individual new voice a neophyte poet was equipped to muster. Hints of a deeper personal engagement with the traditional materials occasionally surface, as perhaps in the symbolic loneliness and long-ingness of the shepherd-poet in *Summer*, whose name, significantly, is "Alexis." Just possibly something personal surfaces again in the closing verses of *Winter*, where it would be pleasant to think that the new poet is not simply following Vergil and Milton in bidding farewell to the pastoral mode in favor of greater undertakings to come, but is recognizing a sobering change in the prospects for this kind of poetry:

> Sharp *Boreas* blows, and Nature feels decay,
> Time conquers All, and We must Time obey.
> Adieu, ye *Vales*, ye *Mountains*, *Streams* and *Groves*,
> Adieu, ye Shepherd's rural *Lays* and *Loves*,
> Adieu, my Flocks, farewell ye *Sylvan* Crew,
> *Daphne* farewell, and all the World adieu!
>
> (ll. 87–92)

But such hints are scattered and at best inconclusive. We fare better with these poems if we do not ask of them what they have not to offer, but look instead, as Eliot advised with Blake, for a reasonably mature and successful attempt to do something small. For the "small" thing that an adolescent poet needs to do most and can do best is to master the management of words, and particularly the interplay of their sounds and sensations and meanings as they form on the tongue, in the ear, in the brain. It is customary for many of us today to disvalue this species of virtuosity, being born into a country and indeed into a century that on the whole underplays the formalities of verse-making as it underplays the formalities of behavior and dress. Still, it requires only a leisurely and friendly inspection of the *Pastorals* to be struck by the enormous skill with which euphonious combinations have been interwoven to create the illusion of polyphony controlled by harmony as in a chorale or cello suite. "Linkèd sweetness, long drawn out"—Keats's phrase for the music of the *Faerie Queene*—is not inappropriate to large sections of the *Pastorals*, and it is in this respect, primarily, that Pope can be credited with having left a distinctively personal signature on the pastoral mode.

CHAPTER 7

DELUDING FANCIES, REAL DISCOMFORTS

Henry Cromwell

In July, two months after the *Pastorals* appeared, Pope enclosed the following stanzas in a letter to a friend. (In the letter they lack a title, but eventually, when published, they were to be called an *Ode on Solitude*.)

> Happy the Man, who free from Care,
> The Business and the Noise of Towns,
> Contented breaths his Native Air,
>   In his own Grounds:
>
> Whose Herds with Milk, whose Fields with Bread,
> Whose Flocks supply him with Attire,
> Whose Trees in Summer yield him Shade,
>   In Winter, Fire.
>
> Blest, who can unconcern'dly find
> His Years slide silently away,
> In Health of Body, Peace of Mind,
>   Quiet by Day,
>
> Repose at Night; Study & Ease,
> Together mixt; sweet Recreation;
> And Innocence, which most does please,
>   With Meditation.
>
> Thus, let me live, unseen, unknown,
> Thus, unlamented, let me die,
> Steal from the World, & not a Stone
>   Tell where I lye.

As with the *Pastorals*, the themes touched on in these stanzas had enjoyed a long past. They reach back through Abraham Cowley and other seventeenth-century poets to various sources in antiquity, particularly the odes of Horace. But unlike most of the traditions prominent in the *Pastorals*, these had a future. After Pope's time, and indeed well before, the figure of the poet as shepherd increasingly gives way, as here, to the figure of the poet as countryman, gentleman farmer, *promeneur solitaire*. Nymphs, satyrs, gods and goddesses, all the relics of the old animism and polytheism, evaporate (many of them to reappear, however, in other forms under other names). And the Agreeable Place, even if still essentially a country of the mind to which the imagination retreats for refreshment from the hurly-burly of Court or City, comes to resemble more and more some actual locality—Pope's own Twickenham villa along the Thames, say; or Gray's playing fields of Eton; or Burns's Ayrshire and Wordsworth's Lake Country; or Frost's New Hampshire. At about the same time, the Arcadian impulse turns visibly more inward. It incorporates itself with that intensifying strain of self-consciousness and individualism that we associate with Montaigne, or with Milton's "paradise within thee happier far," which is to compensate for the lost garden. The Arcadian dream shifts now to a life of quiet study, self-examination and self-cultivation, together with increasingly worshipful observation of the natural world—as in Gilbert White of Selborne and ultimately the Romantics. Above all, it becomes a dream of social and economic independence. Ben Jonson had put the point in an Horatian adaptation of his own, drawing on the same epode that undergirds Pope's, and many a later poet would repeat it after him:

> Happie is he, that from all Businesse cleare,
> As the old race of Mankind were,
> With his own Oxen tills his Sires left lands,
> And is not in Usurer's bands:
> Nor Souldier-like started with rough alarmes,
> Nor dreads the Seas enraged harmes:
> But flies the Barre and Courts, with the proud bords,
> And waiting Chambers of great Lords.

The object of a poet's fantasies from now on, in short, is not an incumbency under the inevitable spreading beech, but enough un-earned increment from "left lands" to free him from debt, soldiering, merchant-venturing, lawyering, and sycophancy, or, as Samuel Johnson would sum it all up some five years after Pope's death, from "toil, envy, want, the garret, and the jail." The Arcadian dream flows into and for a time becomes part of the history of the writer's trade and the sociology of literature.

The recipient of the ode was a friend of some years' standing whose life must have represented for Pope the antithesis of most of the values the poem was intended to honor, and to whom, in communicating it, he felt called upon to add that he had written it before age twelve—"that you may perceive how long I have continued in my Passion for a rural life, & in the same Employments of it." The friend in question was Henry Cromwell, whom we have met before, a first cousin once removed of the redoubtable Oliver. Pope may have met him through George Granville, one of the early readers and praisers of the *Pastorals* when they were still circulating in manuscript, a distant kinsman of the Sir Richard Grenville whose proud conduct of the *Revenge* against an entire squadron of the Spanish armada is celebrated by Tennyson in what used to be a famous school piece. More probably, Pope encountered Cromwell through Wycherley, in whose company as early as 1705 he had visited Will's, the coffee house just off Covent Garden that Dryden's presence some years earlier had made the center of literary London and the haunt of such poetically inclined idlers as Cromwell was. Having a sufficiency of "left lands" in Lincolnshire, Cromwell, like many gentlemen of his stamp, lived almost exclusively in London, where he lounged in the coffee houses (Pope mentions the "Speculative Angle" reserved for him in one of them, meaning his chair with a commanding view), read the newspapers, attended the theaters, played a fashionable hand at picquet or ombre, now and then contributed to the Miscellanies a translation from Ovid's how-to-do-it repertory of amorous addresses, and womanized.

Johnson assures us he could learn no more of Cromwell than that he rode to the hunt in a tye-wig; but Johnson was too easily discouraged. Gay, picturing him among those waiting to greet Pope on his "return" from his long labors on the *Iliad*, supplies some colorful and possibly significant details in the line: "And honest, hatless *Cromwell*, with red Breeches"; and one of Pope's verse-letters to the man himself, which the unscrupulous bookseller Curll got hold of and twice printed in the poet's lifetime, yields many more: that he was somewhat deaf, took snuff, and favored a crow quill over a goose quill; that he frequented the ladies of easy virtue who patrolled the precincts of Drury Lane and the theater named after it, and had once (according to his own account) contested for a bird of this feather with the great Dryden; and that he kept company with a covey of obscure figures, mainly poetasters, of whom we know little except that they must have been crashing bores. One, named Fowler, was nicknamed Howler from his habit of appearing uninvited at any lodging to which he could obtain admittance—his "Pockets stuffed out with Poetry like an Attorney's Term-bag"—ready to bestow it all generously on whatever audience he could find. Of another, named Brocas, Pope writes in the verse letter aforesaid:

> Since your Acquaintance with one *Brocas*,
> Who needs will back the Muses Cock-horse,
> I know you dread all those who write,
> And both with Mouth and Hand recite;
> Who slow, and leisurely rehearse,
> As loath t'enrich you with their Verse;
> Just as a Still, with Simples in it,
> Betwixt each Drop stays half a Minute.
> (That Simile is not my own,
> But lawfully belongs to *Donne*)
> (You see how well I can contrive a
> *Interpolatio furtiva*). . . .
> In vain he strains to reach your Ear,
> With what it wisely, will not hear:
> You bless the Powers who made that Organ
> Deaf to the Voice of such a *Gorgon*,
> (For so one sure may call that Head,
> Which does not Look, but Read Men dead.)

Out of such minute occasions, repeated *ad nauseam* for Pope himself as his fame grew and his good word became the next best thing to a writ of *imprimatur*, would spring at long last those droll lines of comical counsel in the *Epistle to Dr. Arbuthnot*:

> A dire Dilemma! either way I'm sped,
> If Foes, they write, if Friends, they read me dead.
> Seiz'd and ty'd down to judge, how wretched I!
> Who can't be silent, and who will not lye;
> To laugh, were want of Goodness and of Grace,
> And to be grave, exceeds all Pow'r of Face.
> I sit with sad Civility, I read
> With honest anguish, and an aking head;
> And drop at last, but in unwilling ears,
> This saving counsel, "Keep your Piece nine years."
>   Nine years! cries he, who high in *Drury-lane*
> Lull'd by soft Zephyrs thro' the broken Pane,

Rymes ere he wakes, and prints before *Term* ends,
Oblig'd by hunger and Request of friends:
"The Piece you think is incorrect? why take it,
"I'm all submission, what you'd have it, make it."

(ll. 31–46)

These are sentiments that prominent writers of any period (not to mention teachers) are likely to peruse with a sympathetic smile.

From other sources it is clear that Cromwell was considerably the dandy. He often wore or carried, as the fashion then was, a nosegay from the flower-booths in Covent Garden; favored a full-bottomed wig built so high at the parting that it resembled, says a feminine observer, the twin peaks of Parnassus; and walked, according to the same observer, mincingly, or even with a sort of dancing gait as if he were "leading up a *Spanish-Pavan* in the *Minuet-Step*." In addressing the ladies, he apparently behaved with a high old-fashioned and no doubt by the early 1700s quite risible excess of courtesy, just possibly combined with a certain disposition toward the laying on of hands—"creeping advances, clinging embraces," comments his friend Wycherley, not entirely, it would appear, in jest. He was evidently of a dark or sallow complexion with a thin longish face—a satyr's face, to quote Wycherley again, who also jokingly compares him in appearance to the Devil. As in dress and bearing, so in speech. Extending his services to Pope in Binfield, Wycherley adds those of Cromwell and another mutual friend (Major-General John Tidcomb) in a parody of each: "My hearty service to your good Father, and Mother, whilst your Allys, and Friends of the Coffee house, Titcomb the rough, and Cromwell the Gentle, send you theirs; The one swearing (by God) you are a pretty Fellow, and t' other (y gad) that you are a polite Person."

Add to this that a correspondent of the female observer just cited sees him as a species of Don Quixote ("His weasle Carcase was so thin") and calls him Don Diego; add further that the lady herself dubs him "the Knight" while comparing him at the same time to Taffety Trippit the Fortune-Hunter, Squire Easy the Amorous Bard, and Sir Timothy Tittle the Critick (three satiric personalities created by Addison and Steele in the *Tatler*); and a more or less recognizable Restoration man-about-town (Cromwell was born in 1659) begins to appear. One third amorous fop "intended for a Jest to the rest of the World, whilst he poor Soul is wholly insensible of it." One third stiff pedant and arch-critic, mortgaged to the principle that even laughter at a comedy must be authorized by some rule. And one third amiable companion, carrying perhaps under all his layers of affectation a kind of benign innocence, rather like that of Don Armado in Shakespeare's *Love's Labours Lost*. Pope, at any rate, became fond of him—"the soft, beneficent, and Curteous Mr Cromwell," he addresses him in one letter; "the gentlest too, the best-naturd of Mortalls."

"That little Alexander the women laugh at"

If we may judge from their correspondence, which seems to have begun in Pope's eighteenth or nineteenth year and to have ended in his twenty-fourth, the two men were useful to each other and enjoyed each other's company despite the discrepancy of age. Cromwell, however quaint or fantastic in himself, was undoubtedly a storehouse of information about London life, women, fashions, gossip, and genteel behavior, and may even have played a significant role in helping reurbanize the young "country putt," as Pope sometimes liked to call himself, whom a hostile source describes at this period (when he was still making short forays about London in the company of Wycherley) as "a little *Aesopic* sort of animal in his own cropt Hair, and Dress agreeable to the Forest he came from."

> I thought indeed he might be some Tenant's Son of his [Wycherley's], who might make his Court for continuance in his Lease on the Decease of his Rustick Parent, but was sufficiently surpriz'd when Mr. *Wycherley* afterwards told me he was Poetically inclin'd, and writ tolerably smooth Verses.

Though an enemy's report, there seems no reason to reject its glimpse of an awkward hunchbacked boy, possibly somewhat abashed by his own lack of suitable sartorial and tonsorial splendors.

With Cromwell, a solid Latinist, Pope would try out during the next few years much of his work in progress, most especially a translation of the first book of Statius's *Thebaid* and (to this he had again been invited by Tonson) of one of Ovid's imaginary love-letters, *Sapho to Phaon*. The manuscript of the latter, which survives, bears on its margin in Cromwell's hand a small hailstorm of compliments—"Pulchrè," "Benè," "Rectè"—with only an occasional less euphoric notation: "Tautologicè," "Jejunè," "Remittite." From these criticisms Pope obviously benefited. In May, for example, only a few days after the appearance of the *Miscellany*, he encloses in a packet from Binfield a new segment of the *Thebaid*, assuring his correspondent that the portions he has been good enough to work over earlier are already "corrected to your Sense." Not that the two friends easily agreed. Cromwell was a stickler for literal exactitudes, and Pope confesses in the same letter that he has been a little refractory to some of his suggestions in the past, promising hereafter more "Obedience." It seems doubtful that he made good on this promise. Only a month later, a further letter shows him defending his free rendering of one of Statius's temporal references on the ground that it accords better with that author's generally relaxed attitude toward the unity of time. Pope was not one to give ground when he believed himself in the right, either then or later. On the other hand, he was tireless—particularly as a young man—in seeking advice. One of the most interesting features of his working papers is the frequency with which a marginal *Quaere* appears: *quaere* if this passage should be omitted or postponed? *quaere* if these lines are obscure? *quaere* (even when the query remains implicit, expressed only by layer on layer of revision) in what way can this poem or this verse be improved by soliciting the views of other readers? It is the right question for a poet to ask who aspires, as Pope did, to speak not for a school of visionaries or a club of initiates but for the commonalty of literate men and women.

In Cromwell, too, Pope found a friend whose presence did not require him to be graver than is congenial to adolescence. With Cromwell he could let out sail, indulge what has been called the "habitual outrageousness" of his fancy; trifle, joke, talk bawdy, even so far break down the usual reserves and deferences of one eighteenth-century gentleman to another, especially an elder, that later he felt called on to apologize:

> To be serious, you have extreamly obliged me by your Frankness and Kindness to me in Town: And if I have abus'd it by too much Freedome on my part I hope you will attribute it to the natural Openness of my Temper, which hardly knows how to show Respect, where I feel Affection.

It is in letters to Cromwell, accordingly, that Pope feels free to talk of his dogs, whose fidelity, he is beginning to learn (if he did not know already), surpasses that of many presumed acquaintances and friends. One such "acquaintance," seemingly the same Charles Gildon who commented above on his rusticity, has (so he hears) been insinuating "malicious untruths" of him to Wycherley, who has not written in some time. Likewise, it is to Cromwell he confesses—or pretends—that he hopes for a life not over-regular, not constricted like a play written to the rules—"let it be a good merry Farce, a G-ds name, and a figg for the Critical Unities"—though on the other hand, not actually disorderly:

> I wou'd as soon write like Durfey [Thomas Durfey, playwright and songwriter], as live like Tidcombe; whose beastly, laughable Life is (if you will excuse such a Similitude) not unlike a Fart, at once nasty & diverting.

It is with Cromwell, too, no doubt with some encouragement, that Pope often unbuttons into what one of his Victorian admirers has amusingly called his "sad-dog" pose. The passage just quoted above on friendly "freedoms" goes on to conclude, for example: "I would love my Friend, as my Mistress, without Ceremony; and hope a little Rough Usage sometimes may not be more displeasing to one than it is to the other." For Cromwell likewise, following one of his stays in London, he makes up, or at the very least pruriently dresses up, an alleged adventure with a handsome young gentlewoman on his way home by stagecoach. The woman, who has been in London consulting her doctors, feels nauseated (probably from the coach's lurching), and Pope offers her some fruit:

> In short, I tempted, and she Eat; nor was I more like the Devil, than she like Eve. Having the good Success of the foresaid Gentleman before my eyes, I put on the Gallantry of the old Serpent, & in spite of my Evil Forme, accosted her with all the Gayety I was master of; which had so good Effect, that in less than an hour she grew pleasant, her Colour return'd, & she was pleas'd to say, my Pre-scription had wrought an Immediate Cure. In a Word, I had the pleasantest Journey imaginable, so that now, as once of yore, by means of the *forbidden Fruit*, the *Devil* got into *Paradise*—I shou'd not have us'd this last Phrase but that I know your civill Appre-hension will not put any ill Construction upon it, & you will firmly believe that we were as modest—even as Sapho & Mr. Cromwell.

On another occasion, to a jocular paragraph on the pains and penalties of being "Pygmaean" of stature, he appends an anecdote that is possibly yet more suspect, accompanied by a rondeau adapted from Voiture, who like himself was small:

> I was the other day in company with a Lady, who rally'd my Person so much, as to cause a total Subversion of my Countenance: some days after, to be reveng'd on her, I presented her amongst

other Company the following Rondeau on that occasion, which I desire you to show Sappho.

> You know where you did despise
> (Tother day) my little Eyes,
> Little Legs, and little Thighs,
> And some things, of little Size,
>   You know where.
> You, tis true, have fine black eyes,
> Taper Legs, and tempting Thighs,
> Yet what more than all we prize
> Is a Thing of little Size,
>   You know where.

For a final specimen, here is Pope at twenty-three penning a letter to Cromwell from Mapledurham House, sitting now in the company of the Blount sisters, the two young women he loved best in the world, who were apparently at the moment similarly engaged in correspondence or perhaps in handiwork:

> . . . every moment my Eyes are employed upon this paper, they are taken off from Two of the finest faces in the Universe: For I am at this instant placd betwixt Two such Ladies that in good faith 'tis all I'm able to do, to keep my self in my Skin [i.e., foreskin]. *He! Monsieur Cromvell! Entendez-vous bien?* ["Do you get me?"]

Sad-dog stuff indeed! But then he continues in a much more forthcoming manner, the mock-heroic banter covering but not concealing some genuine urgencies beneath:

> You that are so nice an Admirer of Beauty, or (as a Critic wou'd say) so *Elegant a Spectator of Forms*? You must have a sober Dish of Coffee, and a Solitary Candle at your side, to write an Epistle Lucubratory to your Friend; whereas I can do it as well with two Pair of radiant Lights, that outshine the Golden God of Day. . . . You fancy now that *Sapho*'s Eyes are a Couple of these my Tapers, but 'tis no such matter Sir; these are Eyes that have more Persuasion in one Glance than all *Sapho*'s Oratory and Gesture together, let her put her Body into what *moving Postures* she pleases. . . . How gladly wou'd I give all I am worth, that is to say, my *Pastorals* for *one* of their *Maidenheads*, & my *Essay* [his *Essay on Criticism*, published a few months earlier] for the other? I wou'd lay out all my *Poetry* in *Love*; an *Original* for a *Lady*, & a *Translation* for a *Waiting Maid*!

The amusing discrimination of hierarchies in the last sentence should not blind us to the fact that Pope raises here, at a discreet distance, a question that often troubled him and perhaps at one time or other troubles most writers—as indeed it had troubled Milton:

> Alas! What boots it with uncessant care
> To tend the homely slighted Shepherd's trade,
> And strictly meditate the thankless Muse?
> Were it not better done as others use,
> To sport with *Amaryllis* in the shade,
> Or with the tangles of *Neæra's* hair?

But then, as so often with Pope, a wild grotesquerie of fancy, rising probably from what seems to have been Cromwell's repeated urging that he write for the stage, dissipates all serious undercurrents in a burst of self-deprecating laughter:

And now (since you find what a blessed disposition I am in)

> Tell me, by all the melting joys of Love,
> By the warm Transports & entrancing Languors,
> By the soft Fannings of the wafting sheets,
> By the dear Tremblings of the Bed of Bliss;
> By all these tender Adjurations tell me,
> —Am I not fit to write a Tragedy?

And wou'd not these Lines sound admirably in the Mouth of *Wilks*, especially if he humourd each period with his Leg, & stamp'd with just alacrity at the Cadences. But alas! what have I to do with *Jane Gray*? as long as Miss *Molly*, Miss *Betty*, or Miss *Patty*, are in this World? Shall I write of *Beauties murderd long ago*, when there are those at this instant that *murder me*? I'll e'en compose my own Tragedy, & the Poet shall appear in his own Person to move Compassion.

Though the sad-dog pose appears only sporadically in Pope and, as might be expected, mainly between the ages of nineteen and twenty-five, it reminds us that there is a certain pathos lurking under the silliness of his attempts to appear before friends as a seasoned man of the world. Perhaps it emerges most touchingly of all in a passing confidence of this same period to John Caryll: "'Tis certain the greatest magnifying glasses in the world are a mans own eyes, when they look upon his own person; yet even in those, I appear not the great Alexander Mr. Caryll is so civil to, but that little Alexander the women laugh at." By "the women," Pope did not mean the ladies—who doubtless laughed too, but inwardly, or behind their fans.

"This long Disease, my Life"

Pope's references to himself in the preceding section make it clear that by the time he began to be known as a successful poet he was already established in his own mind and in the minds of others as a dwarf and cripple. The disease that crippled him and fixed his stature permanently at about that of a twelve-year-old boy was almost certainly (as mentioned earlier) tuberculosis of the bone, or what is now called Pott's disease. The chances are good that it was contracted during infancy from the milk of Mary Beach his nurse; less probably, from cow's milk.

The disease itself, mentioned by Hippocrates and Galen, and found in Egyptian mummies, is among the oldest known to medical history, though its source in the tubercle bacillus could not of course be demonstrated till after the isolation of that bacillus by Robert Koch in 1882. Percival Pott (1714–88), the eighteenth-century English surgeon whose name the disease now bears, inevitably knew nothing of its bacterial origins, but was an acute observer of its effects. These could include at various stages of its progress debilitating bouts of high fever, severe inflammation of the eyes, a harsh cough, abdominal pain, and a persistent chill and numbness in the legs that frequently brought on in later years a considerable or total loss of use. In addition, the disease usually produced respiratory problems, owing to the cramping of the contents of the thorax as the weakening spine and vertebrae collapsed—in Pope's case, evidently, both sidewise and backwards into what is clinically called a kyphoscoliosis. Respiratory problems, in turn, rarely failed to cause cardiac weakness.

Chronically or fitfully, Pope suffered from all these complications, many of them worsened by commoner ills (such as colds, indigestion, and hemorrhoids) and made more incapacitating by a shortness of sight that was already giving him serious trouble by the time he was nineteen. Joshua Reynolds, who viewed him with a promising young painter's attention at age fifty-two or so, describes him thus:

> He was ... about four feet six high; very humpbacked and deformed; he wore a black coat; and, according to the fashion of the time, had on a little sword. . . . He had a large and very fine eye,

16. Alexander Pope, at full length. Drawn surreptitiously by William Hoare at Bath, *c.* 1741. Wimsatt, 64.1a.

Courtesy of the National Portrait Gallery, London.

and a long handsome nose; his mouth had those peculiar marks which are always found in the mouths of crooked persons; and the muscles that run across the cheek were so strongly marked as to appear like small cords. Roubiliac, who made a bust of him from life, observed that his countenance was that of a person who had been much afflicted with headache, and he should have known the fact from the contracted appearance of the skin between his eyebrows.

The affliction made what appears to have been the first memorable announcement of its presence at about the time he reached puberty. He himself attributed the illnesses that then struck him to the intensity of his application to his studies, telling Spence in 1728 that these had "reduced him in four or five years' time to so sad a state of health that after trying physicians for a good while in vain, he resolved to give way to his distemper, and sat down calmly, in a full expectation of death in a short time." Fortunately, he also decided to write farewell letters to his "more particular friends," among them a Benedictine named Thomas Southcote, who at once sought medical advice in London and carried it himself to Binfield. "The chief thing the doctor ordered him was to apply less and to ride every day, and the following his advice soon restored him to his health." Such was Pope's subsequent report to Spence. Spence adds that the cure took place when the poet was about seventeen—an age that seems to accord with the dramatic first appearance of the malady at age twelve or thirteen and the four- to five-year duration of the first series of attacks. The seeming "cure" was of course temporary, and while perhaps assisted by exercise, must have come about mainly through one of the remissions that are characteristic of this disease. The doctor's prescription did, however, as we saw, have the excellent side-effect of fostering Pope's acquaintance and regular ridings-out with Sir William Trumbull, and so, in a sense, furthered the inception of such works as *Windsor-Forest* and the translation of Homer.

Recurrent flare-ups of the tubercular infection and the gradual worsening of symptoms as the years rolled past make Pope's allusion to "this long Disease, my Life" in his *Epistle to Dr. Arbuthnot* (line 132) something more than a casual jest. Apart from the standard horrors of eighteenth-century medical practice—purgings, vomitings, bleedings—"evacuations and plasters and phlebotomy and blisters"—always to be endured and (what was harder) survived whenever an attack was judged to be serious, Pope was afflicted with constant headaches, sometimes so severe that he could barely see the

paper he wrote upon, frequent violent pain at bone and muscle joints
—thought then to be rheumatic but known now to be linked to
skeletal deterioration—shortness of breath, increasing inability to
ride horseback or even walk for exercise ("I can walk 8 or ten Miles a
day," Swift writes to Pope as early as 1731, "& ride 30 Irish ones. You
cannot ride a mile nor walk two"), recalcitrant wasting fevers, and
such an exquisite sensitivity to cold as to require in winter almost a
cocoon of waistcoats, in which "I live like an Insect, in hope of
reviving with the Spring." Though doubtless only a usage picked up
in boyhood, his habitual expletive "by way of oath" was, appropriately, " God mend me!"

Pope's usual response to illnesses was to try to pass them off as
good-humoredly as possible. To John Caryll, during one of them, he
pictures his spirits rising and falling within his thin frame, according
to the degree of warmth around it, like the column of wine or spirit in
an eighteenth-century thermometer. For Caryll's son, whom he
imagines in the midst of a rousing fox-hunt, blood boiling, heart
pounding, he declares himself to be "just in the reverse of all this
Spirit & Life, confin'd to a narrow Closet, lolling on an Arm Chair,
nodding away my Days over a Fire, like the picture of January in an
old Salisbury Primer." Informing Martha Blount that he is "in a very
odd course for the pain in my side," he adds:

> I mean a course of brickbats and tiles, which they apply to me
> piping hot, morning and night; and sure it is very satisfactory to
> one who loves architecture at his heart, to be built round in his very
> bed.

And he writes to Burlington, in the severe winter of 1743–44, contemplating a journey from Twickenham to Chiswick to visit him:

> If my Lord Burlington goes to Chiswick on Saturday or Sunday, &
> cares to be troubled with me, I will, upon his sending a warm
> Chariot (for I dare not go in a Chaise) put my self into his power,
> like a small Bird half starved, in this miserable weather.

But the smile was sometimes wan. To Bathurst, in the year he
turned forty, he confides:

> I do not think I ever shall enjoy any health four days together, for
> the remaining Sand I have to run. The Bath was tryed after all other
> remedies, as a last remedy, and that has proved totally ineffectuall.
> I never had more long or more violent Headakes, &c. than three
> fits since my return.

17. Alexander Pope, at cards in his old age. Attributed to the Countess of Burlington, *c.* 1738–42?

The object over Pope's head, possibly a private joke, is more probably an earlier doodle. Wimsatt, 65.

By kind permission of the Trustees of the Chatsworth Settlement. Photograph: Courtauld Institute of Art.

And to Fortescue in the same year:

> I am in the condition of an old fellow of Threescore, with a Complication of Diseases upon me; A constant Headake; ruind Tone of the Stomach; the Piles; a Vomiting & Looseness; & an Excess of Wind. Some of these succeed, the moment I get quit of the others: & upon the whole, indeed I am in a very uncomfortable way.

In the upshot, the disease brought him close to total invalidism. A report evidently gleaned from maidservants of the earl of Oxford, with whom he often stayed during his forties and early fifties (Oxford died three years earlier than Pope), portrays the aging poet as

> unable to dress or undress himself, or get into bed without help; nor could he stand upright till a kind of stays, made of stiff linen, were laced on him, one of his sides being contracted almost to the backbone. He wanted much waiting on, but was very liberal to the Maid-servants about him [according to Johnson, "Lord Oxford's servant declared that in a house where her business was to answer his call she would not ask for wages"], so that he had never reason to complain of being neglected. These females attended him at night, and, in the morning, brought him his writing desk to bed, lighted his fire, drew on his stockings ["His legs were so slender," Johnson's account adds, "that he enlarged their bulk with three pair"], etc. which offices he often summoned them to perform at very early hours; so that, when any part of their business was left undone, their common excuse was, that they had been employed with Mr. Pope, and then no farther reprehension was to be dreaded.

When we pause to reflect how much of Pope's finest poetry stems from this period and from these conditions, we begin to get some measure of the quality of the sword (to borrow an image applied by Wycherley to his little friend) that gleamed so brightly inside its decaying scabbard.

CHAPTER 8

NEW WINE IN OLD BOTTLES AND THE DISCOVERY OF ENVY

"O Thebes! for thee what Fates remain?"

Somewhat surprisingly, Pope did not go up to London for the publication of his first poems in Tonson's *Miscellany*. If he was apprehensive about their reception, it was probably with cause. Many minds likely to show an interest in poetry were taken up that spring with antagonisms between Whig and Tory (to concern us more fully later) and with the arguments of the two parties about the necessity or folly (Tories thought it folly) of continuing the war against Louis XIV, in progress with only brief recesses for twenty years. Or perhaps it was only that Pope was unwell. He had visited the city the preceding January, lodging, it seems likely, at a certain Mrs. Bamber's in the chamber next to Wycherley, and had gone home from there ill, as was more often than not his fate following a winter visit. London's sooty air, compared by John Evelyn to the atmosphere of Italy's Lake Avernus, which was said to asphyxiate birds in flight, was no help to a respiratory system as troublesome as Pope's. Nor did late hours, smoky rooms, and the accompanying indulgences of food and drink agree with him. He would always need London for its stimulus—its news, gossip, glitter, friendships, publishers, and literary conversations. But he would always need plain living and the country more. All which suggests forcibly that the lines on solitude quoted earlier and sent to Cromwell immediately following a second trip to London in late June speak with a personal as well as Horatian accent. "Health of Body," "Peace of Mind," "Quiet by Day," "Repose at Night," "Study & Ease, Together mixt," "sweet Recreation," and

"Innocence"—these were precisely what London had not to offer at any time of year, at least not to one of Pope's unreliable constitution.

He was at work just now on three new projects. One was the translation, mentioned earlier, of Statius's *Thebaid*. The *Thebaid*, as its title announces, deals with what used to be called "the matter of Thebes," in this case that part of it comprising the bloody struggle of Eteocles and Polynices, sons of Oedipus, for the Theban throne. A favorite poem of Chaucer, as apparently also of Dante, who quite unhistorically presents its author in the *Purgatorio* as having been converted to Christianity, it attracted Pope's attention in his boyhood at about the same time as Ogilby's Homer and probably for the same reasons: its exciting episodes, its vocabulary of pathos and horror, its larger-than-life personalities driven by passion (Statius's psychology is strongly Stoic) to their doom. Later—for he continued to honor the poem above all Latin epics save the *Aeneid*—Pope was probably attracted by the virtuosity of the Statian style. This, though purporting to imitate Vergil, is far more figural, hyberbolic, and "conceited"; abounds in electrifying phrases (such as *saeva dies animi*, "the cruel daylight of the mind," for the pitiless clarity with which a mind tortured by passion replays its guilt as well as its losses); and exhibits a skill in pictorial description that much resembles Pope's own and from which undoubtedly he learned.

For Statius, court poet to Domitian, last of the Flavian emperors, this story of an accursed royal house seems to have had the interest of topical allusion. It considerably paralleled the story of intrafamilial rivalry, tyranny, and murder that had haunted the Julio–Claudian line (Tiberius, Caligula, Claudius, Nero) and had then—this was the official Flavian propaganda—been brought to a propitious close by the orderly succession of Vespasian, Titus, and Domitian. If Pope was unconscious of the political coloring, as he may well have been, ignorance did not prevent his rendering a few passages of the original with what is possibly a political undercurrent of his own. The Theban story of two kinsmen rivaling for a throne, one of them actually invading to oust the other, carried just enough potential analogy with the events of 1688 in England to invite "interpretation." The following lines, for instance, describing Polynices's consuming ambition to occupy the throne even before his turn comes up, might easily be read by a reader so inclined as a reference to William III, who was popularly and on the whole rightly suspected of having maneuvered for the English throne from the time of the Exclusion crisis, even though, until the birth of his father-in-law's male heir in 1688, he had only to bide his time to succeed:

> Forbidden *Thebes* appears before his Eye,
> From whence he sees his absent Brother fly,
> With Transport views the airy Rule his own,
> And swells on an imaginary Throne.
> Fain wou'd he cast a tedious Age away,
> And live out all in one triumphant Day.

(ll. 447–52)

"Fly" in this passage could seem particularly significant to Jacobite readers, for in their view this was all that James had done—he had not abdicated, he had only saved his life by eluding a usurper—and about either flying or fleeing the Latin original said nothing. Even the word "Brother" could be appropriated to the cause if one took it, in the common phrase of the time, to mean simply Brother Monarch—which of course made the act of treachery worse.

Yet more applicable to 1688, particularly for readers who remembered Dryden on the headstrong moody London populace that supported the would-be usurper Monmouth against his father Charles II (James II was of course Dutch William's "father"-in-law), were the lines on Theban complainants against the present ruler Eteocles:

> But the vile Vulgar, ever discontent,
> Their growing Fears in secret Murmurs vent,
> Still prone to change, tho' still the Slaves of State,
> And sure the Monarch whom they have, to hate;
> New Lords they madly make, then tamely bear,
> And softly curse the Tyrants whom they fear.
> And one of those who groan beneath the Sway
> Of Kings impos'd, and grudgingly obey,
> (Whom Envy to the Great, and vulgar Spight
> With Scandal arm'd, th' Ignoble Mind's Delight,)
> Exclaim'd—O *Thebes!* for thee what Fates remain,
> What Woes attend this inauspicious Reign?
> Must we, alas! our doubtful Necks prepare,
> Each haughty Master's Yoke by turns to bear,
> And still to change whom chang'd we still must fear?

(ll. 224–38)

Such verses might even be imagined to include a warning against the new Hanoverian "haughty Master" or "King impos'd," who by the Act of Succession of 1701 had been invited to assume the throne on Anne's death.

There is no way, I think, of establishing Pope's intentions in such passages beyond doubt. If they are consciously political, then his efforts in the mode of innuendo begin earlier than has been supposed. What is more reliably to be observed in the Statius translation is the poet's increasing mastery of his medium. There is a new energy in his verbs. The scenes he is capable of realizing are more various. He can control now many kinds of mood, shifting with some ease from passages like this, which enacts the finality of Jove's will in the unusual placing of the caesura in line 3 and the part rhyme of *fix'd* with *Styx*:

> For by the black infernal *Styx* I swear,
> (That dreadful Oath which binds the Thunderer)
> 'Tis fix'd; th' irrevocable Doom of *Jove*;
> No Force can bend me, no Persuasion move—
>
> (ll. 411–14)

to passages like this, catching at the twilit stillness of moonrise:

> Wide o'er the World in solemn Pomp she drew
> Her airy Chariot, hung with Pearly Dew;
> All Birds and Beasts lye hush'd; Sleep steals away
> The wild Desires of Men, and Toils of Day,
> And brings, descending thro' the silent Air,
> A sweet Forgetfulness of Human Care—
>
> (ll. 476–81)

to this, which describes the abduction of Ganymede, sculptured in gold on a drinking cup:

> There from the Chace *Jove*'s tow'ring Eagle bears
> On golden Wings, the *Phrygian* to the Stars;
> Still as he rises in th' Aethereal Height,
> His native Mountains lessen to his Sight;
> While all his sad Companions upward gaze,
> Fix'd on the Glorious Scene in wild Amaze,
> And the swift Hounds, affrighted as he flies,
> Run to the Shade, and bark against the Skies.
>
> (ll. 640–47)

Meanwhile, the gift Pope had always had of charging his lines with sounds and rhythms felt as much upon the tongue and teeth as heard by the ear grew more assured. This passage, for example, evoking the irony of the brothers' struggle by stressing the poverty of the contested prize, exhibits part of its brilliance in a veritable fugue of *s* and *z* formations, interlaced with formations of the several vowels plus *r* (and vice versa) and tolling throughout with internal rhyme and repetition:

> Yet then *no proud aspiring* Piles *were rais'd*,
> *No fretted Roofs* with polish'd Metals blaz'd,
> *No* labour'd Columns in long *Order* plac'd,
> *No Grecian Stone* the pompous *Arches grac'd;*
> *No* nightly Bands in glitt'ring *Armour* wait
> Before the sleepless Tyrant's guarded Gate;
> *No* Chargers then were *wrought* in burnish'd Gold,
> Nor silver Vases took the forming Mold,
> Nor Gems on Bowls emboss'd were seen to shine,
> Blaze on the *Brims*, and *Sparkle* in the Wine—
> Say, *wretched Rivals!* What *provokes your Rage?*
> Say, to what End *your* impious *Arms* engage?
> Not All *bright Phoebus* views in *early Morn*,
> *Or* when his Evening Beams the West adorn,
> When the South glows with his *Meridian Ray*,
> And the cold North receives a fainter Day;
> For *Crimes* like these, not all those *Realms* suffice,
> W *ere* all those *Realms* the guilty Victor's Prize!
>
> (ll. 200–217)

Here the translator of Homer, of whom Johnson would say that he had "tuned the English tongue," begins umistakably to emerge.

"For who so fond as youthful Bards of Fame?"

A more seasoned virtuosity appears in *The Temple of Fame*, a poem of some five hundred lines on which the young Pope was also working at this time, and of which an early draft was probably extant by the autumn of 1710. Here, in contrast to his earlier "translations," Pope uses a Chaucerian dream-poem, *The Hous of Fame*, partly as a point of reference against which to measure his successes in compression (to some of these he cannot forbear calling attention in his notes), but mainly to assert an ambivalence about poetic fame that will remain a distinctive attribute of his literary personality throughout his life.

Chaucer's *Hous* is a poem about famous lovers, or such at least it sets out to be, but then breaks off, unfinished, "Love's folke" having been met with only in murals. The ambling, somewhat garrulous (though in detail often charming) narrative with which Chaucer fills the intervening space apparently appealed to Pope as little as it does to most twentieth-century readers apart from specialists. It is therefore only on the last book, where Chaucer's dream finally encompasses the visionary structures housing Fame and Rumor, that Pope draws, and even there with such rearrangements and shifts of emphasis as throw into relief what is beginning to be recognizable as a characteristic Popian theme. Particulars—ephemera—the flotsam and jetsam of experience: all are fascinating but have value for an artist only in so far as they can be organized in a patterned whole. Thus in the dream itself "A Train of Phantoms in wild Order rose," but could yield no meaning till rearranged and interpreted by mind: "And, join'd, this Intellectual Scene compose."

The notion of "composition," put forward here at the poem's opening, becomes its central motif. Chaucer's poem, unfinished, bristling with delightful but extraneous particulars, "clog'd," from an eighteenth-century point of view, "with trivial Circumstances," is pruned and reshaped to make a rounded moral parable. Much is lost in the exchange, but much is gained. In the same way, Chaucer's Hous, with its "Babewinnes and pinacles, Ymageries and tabernacles," is reformed into a structure vaguely on the order of the Pantheon or Rome's St. Peter's, though far excelling any building "rear'd by mortal Hands." Each of its four massive entrances honors with sculptures the founders of civilization in that quarter of the world on which it opens: West, East, South, North. For these, too, were masters of the art of composition, disciplining the anarchic passions of mankind as the dreamer's "Intellectual Scene" disciplines the unruly phantoms. The collective memory of mankind views them accordingly as composing a "venerable Order":

> Here fabled Chiefs in darker Ages born,
> Or Worthys old, whom Arms or Arts adorn,
> Who Cities rais'd, or tam'd a monstrous Race;
> The Walls in venerable Order grace:
> Heroes in animated Marble frown,
> And Legislators seem to think in Stone.
>
> (ll. 69–74)

Within the gates, in concentric circles of increasing worthiness, the great figures of Greek and Roman history appear. (If it was a severe limitation in Western culture up to our own century that it knew only its own tradition—an obliviousness expressed unconsciously in Pope's poem by the fact that no one given honor on his Eastern, Southern, or Northern gates obtains a place inside—it is perhaps our own equivalent limitation to be aware of many, familiar in depth with none.) Pope's selection of individuals again points up the pre-eminence of "composition" in the sense of anarchy controlled. Alexander the Great is present, of course ("The Youth that all things but himself subdu'd"), but outshone by Caesar ("Caesar, the World's great Master, and his own"). They are outshone in turn by leaders who made the safety of their peoples their highest law: *salus populi suprema lex*: Epaminondas, Timoleon, Scipio, Aurelius. These too, are outshone by those in the next circle, figures of "less . . . noisy Fame)" such as Socrates and Aristides, Cato and Brutus (ll. 151–78). Finally, as might be expected in a poet's pantheon, the inmost circle discovers a tableau of six great ancient writers, each throned in majesty on a mighty column wreathed round with symbols of his work or life. For Pope, it goes without saying, the highest rank belongs to Homer, the next to Vergil—two epic poets. Then follow Pindar and Horace—two lyric poets—and after them Aristotle and Cicero (ll. 179–243). Aristotle is here, one gathers, as the master of those who know, a man who could "look all Nature thro'" and by the power of contemplation compose from the formless data of everyday experience "intellectual scenes": his *Poetics*, *Ethics*, *Politics*, and the like. Cicero, on the other hand, presumably demonstrates the power of civic action, having quelled the thrust to power of Catiline and his conspirators and restored composure to the Roman state. Throughout these characterizations, as in the later Preface to his translation of the *Iliad*, the poet balances the "fire" of Greece against the poise of Rome.

Up to this point, the dreamer's vision reflects his first and superficial supposition that fame is a desirable even if probably unattainable objective. This changes when at last he descries Fame herself on a throne higher than all the rest, blazing with jewels whose colors refract upon the dome to produce a rainbow. The impression of instability and transience thus conveyed (a reprise of the dreamer's earlier discovery that the hill on which the Temple sits is made of ice) is speedily confirmed as both Fame and her Temple surrealistically dilate ("Upward the Columns shoot, the Roofs ascend"), while suitors for her favor assemble from all the globe, only to become victims of her caprice:

> Their Pleas were diff'rent, their Request the same;
> For Good and Bad alike are fond of Fame.
> Some she disgrac'd, and some with Honours crown'd;
> Unlike Successes equal Merits found.

> Thus her blind Sister, fickle *Fortune* reigns,
> And undiscerning, scatters Crowns and Chains.
>
> (ll. 292–97)

Fame, in short, begins to act like rumor, and as if to underscore the change the dreamer is abruptly snatched away to Rumor's abode, a whirling mansion notable primarily for its countless doors and its walls ceaselessly ringing with "various News":

> The flying Rumours gather'd as they roll'd,
> Scarce any Tale was sooner heard than told;
> And all who told it, added something new,
> And all who heard it, made Enlargements too,
> In ev'ry Ear it spread, on ev'ry Tongue it grew.
> Thus flying East and West, and North and South,
> News travel'd with Increase from Mouth to Mouth;
> So from a Spark that kindled first by Chance,
> With gath'ring Force the quick'ning Flames advance;
> Till to the Clouds their curling Heads aspire,
> And Tow'rs and Temples sink in Floods of Fire.
>
> (ll. 468–78)

Pope may have had in mind the misinformation about the Trojan Horse that brought down Troy in flames. Modern readers will be reminded rather of the more difficult kinds of misinformation that press in heavily on the nuclear button:

> There, at one Passage, oft you might survey
> A Lye and Truth contending for the way;
> And long 'twas doubtful, both so closely pent,
> Which first should issue thro the narrow Vent:
> At last agreed, together out they fly,
> Inseparable now, the Truth and Lye.
>
> (ll. 489–94)

At this juncture, an unidentified "One" accosts the dreamer to ask why he has come: "Art thou, fond Youth, a Candidate for Praise?" The dreamer's answer is implicit already in his poem's progress from the mighty columns, impervious to time, which proclaim the glory of the greatest ancients, to the whirling seat of Rumor, where

> Above, below, without, within, around,
> Confus'd, unnumber'd Multitudes are found,
> Who pass, repass, advance, and glide away;
> Hosts rais'd by Fear, and Phantoms of a Day.
>
> (ll. 458–61)

Nevertheless, he makes the reply that becomes him as a beginner:

> 'Tis true, said I, not void of Hopes I came,
> For who so fond as youthful Bards of Fame?

He is a beginner, however, whose dream has already pictured for him the long-run risks:

> How vain that second Life in others' Breath,
> Th' Estate which Wits inherit after Death!
> Ease, Health, and Life, for this they must resign,
> (Unsure the Tenure, but how vast the Fine!) . . .
> All luckless Wits their Enemies profest,
> And all successful, jealous Friends at best.

It is possible that Pope added the last two lines after a betrayal we shall come to presently. Even so, the next to last shows an uncanny anticipation of what lay ahead in the long succession of attacks that began with his first successes and lasted till after his death; and the two verses preceding phrase an attitude toward the writer's life that will never leave him, though it will never deter him either. The poem ends, appropriately, with what I believe we must consider a heartfelt prayer; yet it is a prayer by which the suppliant would surely have been as much discomfited as cheered had it been fulfilled:

> Unblemish'd let me live, or die unknown,
> Oh, grant an honest Fame, or grant me none!

Here too time would insist on a composition of costs and gains.

"Nature Methodiz'd"

The largest project occupying Pope's attention at this time was a poem to which Johnson would later ascribe "such extent of comprehension, such nicety of distinction, such acquaintance with mankind, and such knowledge both of ancient and modern learning as are not often attained by the maturest age and longest experience"—let alone by a youth just turning twenty-three. He was speaking of *An Essay on Criticism.*

The poem had been long in gestation. The interests it reflects were doubtless first kindled by the poet's early reading in "all the best critics," especially, it would seem, Quintilian, Rapin, and Bossu. Later, we know, there had been extended conversations with Walsh, to whom Pope subsequently recalled he had shown a version of the

Essay (can it have been more than early drafts of some passages on "correctness" in versification?) during his summer visit to Abberley in 1707. Following this, the guidance he had sought to give Wycherley in versifying, or reversifying, his collection of bons mots and apothegms inevitably directed his attention to some of the problems of practical criticism and perhaps to some of the attitudes toward criticism and poetry that the *Essay* treats. His friendship with Cromwell may well have had a similar effect. As a strict constructionist in criticism, a favorer in particular of the methodizing French, Cromwell seems to have represented the kind of rule-bound conservatism in literary matters that any practicing poet, even one so respectful of the past as Pope, had to find ways to break free of; and when Pope urges that

> Some Beauties yet, no Precepts can declare, (141)

or that a good writer must

> Neglect the Rules each *Verbal Critick* lays, (261)

it is tempting to imagine that he has Cromwell in mind.

He had, at any rate, the contemporary critical situation in mind: confused, contentious, anarchic, bedeviled by dogma and narrow views. There is not, Addison was soon to declare in a paper for Steele's *Tatler*, "a more importunate, empty, and conceited animal than that which is generally known by the name of a critic":

> This, in the common Acceptation of the Word, is one that, without entering into the Sense and Soul of an Author, has a few general Rules, which, like mechanical Instruments, he applies to the Works of every Writer, and as they quadrate with them, pronounces the Author perfect or defective. . . . The Marks you may know him by are, an elevated Eye, and dogmatical Brow, a positive Voice, and a Contempt for everything that comes out, whether he has read it or not.

Although Addison's "critic" was not peculiar to the eighteenth century, he flourished in it. The high repute in which literary skills were held and the smattering (occasionally the reality) of a literary education that every well-born gentleman picked up at school as a dog's tail picks up burrs insured a considerable vogue for protractor-and-T-square approaches to poetry. One of the special delights of Pope's *Essay*, in fact, is the sharply drawn picture it gives of the bustling, contentious, opinionated London scene, conveyed in an idiom that retains something of the informal sparkle as well as the high spit and polish of the best comic speech of the stage—whole worlds away from the flaccid banalities of the actual Sir Timothy Tittles of contemporary coffee house and drawing room.

As often, critical confusions were further confounded at the time by ideological change. There had been springing up, for instance, a troublesome estrangement in critical conceptions of the creative process. Though the old term "wit" still weakly flourished its quiverful of disparate senses, ranging from smart repartee to artistic invention, genius, and insight, its chief sense as applied to literature was tilting increasingly to the side of decorum—"a propriety of thoughts and words," as Dryden had finally summed it up. This in preference to the more free-wheeling acts of imagination that the sensibility of an earlier era had packed into puns, paradoxes, subversive ambiguities, outrageous metaphors, explosive yokings of opposites, and all those other linguistic romps for which Johnson was to chide even Shakespeare: "A quibble . . . was to him the fatal Cleopatra for which he lost the world and was content to lose it."

By the time Pope's career began, wit in this older more maverick sense was rapidly losing ground. By representatives of middle-class gravity like Sir Richard Blackmore, author of interminable Whiggish epics and of *A Satyr Against Wit* published in 1699, wit seems to have been reckoned the exclusionary badge of a leisure caste. It implied a kind of intellectual playfulness not quite suited to an oncoming, soberer, more deeply Protestant world of serious men of business; and from an evangelical point of view it gave every evidence of being one of the cultural blandishments by which effete gentlemen, Tory high churchmen, and overweening aristocrats (along with the "lewd" stage of Wycherley, Dryden, and Congreve that they and their hangers-on supported and even sometimes wrote for) were managing to seduce British virtue to its ruin. Still more injurious to wit's higher claims—because widely read and respected in even the most sophisticated groups—was John Locke's verdict in his *Essay Concerning Human Understanding* (published in 1690, three editions by 1695) that wit's contribution to the life of the mind lay merely in the assembling of resembling "Ideas"—"thereby to make up pleasant Pictures and agreeable Visions." On similar grounds, its expressive effects in language, declared in the same essay to be misleaders of the passions and therefore "perfect cheats," were being more and more often ascribed to "false wit" (a somewhat id-like literary bad boy of early eighteenth-century literary theory), while the operations of the more decorous (superego-like) wit were defined in ways that made it less and less distinguishable from "judgment." Judgment, the mind's power not to associate but to discriminate and analyze, inevitably the idol of the new sciences in their then stage of taxonomy, had become the chief beneficiary of wit's losses. In the words of Thomas Hobbes, enunciated prophetically a half century before, "Judgement. . . without Fancy is Wit, but Fancy without Judgement not." Taken seriously, this meant the demotion of almost all that wit in its largest sweep had previously embraced, including especially those aspects of creativity that we associate with genius, inspiration, fire, rapture, ecstasy, serendipity, and the Muse, to second-class citizenship in one's mental economy. Eventually, by further encroachments that were already taking place before Pope died and have continued into our own day, the term would be shrunk down to signify little more than a "joke" or a "joker."

The effort to work out conciliatory positions in the poem by no means ends with this attempt to rehabilitate some of the older latitudes of wit. That was a losing cause, despite the fact that Pope's use of the term in such a dazzle of different senses wonderfully illustrates, whether consciously or not, the absurdity of conducting criticism as if it were a branch of logic or mathematics and thus, in a way, "acts out" the poem's main theme. With the maturity of insight so much admired by Johnson, he seems also to have sensed the general crisis of authority in his time that the scientific, political, social, cultural, and psychological developments of the preceding century were beginning to effect in all departments of life. The new cosmology, associated with Newton; the new "scientific" learning fostered by the Royal Society; the "Glorious Revolution" of 1688 on behalf of liberty and property (a phrase in which liberty usually meant the free consolidation of property in the hands of a few); the execution of one *de jure* monarch and the exiling of another, with all the disturbance to ancient loyalties that this entailed; the growing economic power of the dissenting groups, who were now beginning to constitute the larger part of a new moneyed as opposed to landed class; the steady expansion of forms of individualism both ethical and esthetic, affecting taste as well as conscience and gradually redefining roles and values within the family: all these changes were fracturing traditional consensuses, leaving most lines of authority apart from personal self-assertion tentative and insecure.

Partly, at least, in response to all this, the *Essay* shows a pervasive concern for corporateness: for the responsibility of the individual member, whether a person, idea, work of art, or critical term, to some sort of community or whole. This concern is expressed in some highly visible ways, of which one is the poem's studied depersonalization of the views put forward, another its carefully assimilative treatment of diverse and divergent doctrines. It also appears, perhaps less obviously, in the eclectic nature of the imagery, which reaches around and beyond the specialist concerns of poetry and criticism to incorporate the ordinary man or woman's every-day experience. All these are ways of emphasizing the importance of deference to a larger communal One.

To depersonalize (or impersonalize) the author's own views seems to be the chief function of the classical reminiscences with which the poem swarms. From Aristotle, Horace, Quintilian, and Longinus, to name the principal ancient sources. From at least one Italian Renaissance poet and critic, Vida. From several French writers of the age of Louis XIV, especially Boileau. And in the English past, besides a multitude of minor authors (including the authors of such earlier verse-treatises as *An Essay upon Poetry*, *An Essay on Translated Verse*, *An Essay on Unnatural Flights in Poetry*, and an English *Art of Poetry* based on Boileau's *Art poétique*), from Ben Jonson and Dryden. This plenitude of authorities should not mislead us. Pope was no more interested in plagiarizing here than in his *Pastorals* or his *Ode on Solitude*. On the contrary. He relies on his readers to recognize the traditional sources of his doctrines—he could do so because they were already "soaked" in them thanks to their education and their reading—and to make sure there was no mistake about this he named a reasonable number of them in notes.

Still less was he interested in airing what De Quincey would later call mouldy commonplaces. Commonplaces, as Johnson's enthusiasm for the *Essay* makes clear, are not mouldy so long as they remain the vehicle of live values, and for Pope and his century the classical values were exuberantly alive. It is precisely to underscore his acceptance of them that he lays stress on his precedents. To keep the great voices sounding behind his own was to identify his poem with the collective classical tradition, and thus with the sensibility of the society formed by that tradition, whose spokesman in this work he was offering to become. It was also to practice the critical philosophy that the poem preaches—to acknowledge that the idiosyncrasies of individual intelligence and taste must be tried, and normalized, against the collective principles of the community of educated men.

This is a point that the *Essay* reiterates in its assimilation of critical terms and doctrines. In Part I, the theoretical portion of the poem, two questions are asked and answered that go to the root of the critical problem in Pope's time and perhaps any time. First: how can literature and criticism meet? How can anything as subjective as

18. Alexander Pope, wearing "the Critick's Ivy." Charcoal and chalk, by Sir Godfrey Kneller, *c.* 1721. Wimsatt, 6.1.

"wit" (meaning by wit in this context the creative imagination of the artist, or its result, the work of art) ever mesh except fortuitously with anything as subjective as the judgment, or the taste, of the individual critic and reader? What common denominator enables literature to communicate, criticism to be practiced? The satisfying answer in Pope's day was always "Nature." This was a peculiarly honorific term and concept, carrying a multitude of meanings but always tending to imply the creative operations of a quasi-divine agency that made for order, universality, and permanence, alike in man, in art, and in the cosmos. Literature and criticism have therefore a common ground (the poem says)—not only because each of these activities is underlain by the same two powers or manifestations of one power, wit and judgment, but because the characteristic power or manifestation expressed in each activity—wit in art, judgment in criticism—derives from a common source, "Unerring Nature," by which it may be normalized as one normalizes one's watch (ll. 9–10) by the true time of the sun (ll. 13, 68 ff).

Second: how may we reconcile modern "Reason" (our own sense of what makes sense) with ancient Authority, current artistic insights with past ones; or, to give the issue a twentieth-century coloring, the individual talent with the tradition? Again, the poem points to a resolution through the mercurial term Nature. "Reason," for Pope's contemporaries, being the name of the universal and permanent when considered in its intellectual aspect, was by definition one of Nature's manifestations. So was Authority. For since the ancients participate with the modern in this universal and permanent Reason and have left behind them works whose permanent and universal character many centuries have proved, ancient literature must like-wise be considered one of Nature's manifestations: "*Nature* and *Homer* were, he found, the *same*" (line 135). This in turn meant that the Rules—the principles of effective writing that a long line of critics had derived from Homer and other poets—were by no means impositions of a dead hand upon the present: they were "*Nature* still, but *Nature Methodiz'd*." (line 89). And it meant also that the surest route to a sound art and criticism was the study of these authors and these principles: "To copy *Nature* is to copy *Them*" (line 140).

Pope does not intend by this a theory of servile imitation. He means rather that every new generation must strive to assimilate the art of those whose success in rendering our common humanity ("Nature") time has demonstrated; the individual talent must steep itself in the tradition; and in Pope's day, when the only internation-ally accepted literature was that of Greece and Rome (and when serious poets were as agreed on the primacy of the epic poem as they appear to be now on the primacy of the poem of personal reflection), Homer and Vergil naturally comprised the heart of this tradition. Pope knows, of course, that criticism cannot afford to let a live tradition degenerate into formulae, dictating "dull *Receits* how Poems may be made" (line 115); or lose the contemporary élan (the "wit" in judging) that alone enables it to discern and applaud the "Beauties . . . no Precepts can declare" (line 141). But he knows with equal firmness that the individual writer's imagination must be guided by his judgment, reflecting the collective experience hived up in the principles of good writing—the Rules (ll. 84 ff); and that true wit, to quote the best remembered and most misunderstood line in the poem, is always "*Nature* to Advantage drest" (line 297)—i.e., experience so rendered that its universality comes home.

In the *Essay* as a whole, this ideal of corporateness, of subjective (watch) time continuously regulating itself against universal (sun) time, becomes the major imaginative theme. One aspect of it presides in the evolution of the poem's argument, as it marches from what a critic is supposed to know—Part I, concluding significantly with a celebration of the ancients ("Still green with Bays each *ancient* Altar stands," line 181)—to what a critic is supposed to be and do: Part III, in which the ideal critic is described and the great practitioners of criticism are reviewed. This is a development extending theory to practice and esthetics to ethics, which by its climactic emphasis on good manners in criticism underscores again the social and corporate ideal. A complementary aspect of the theme is not far to seek in Part II. As the opening simile of the Alps suggests, followed by the anecdote about Don Quixote, the positives behind the satire in this section are humility in the presence of what is greater than ourselves and intelligence to rectify our personal vision by collective wisdom. All the ways of straying in criticism (and poetry) that constitute this portion of the *Essay* arise from indifference to the commonalty; self-conceit, a love to parts, eccentricity, sectarianism—in short, a self-confidence about windmills of which Don Quixote (ll. 267 ff) is an appropriate symbol.

The poem's final extensions of this theme are carried by the imagery. One pattern, involving especially images that are physiological or institutional, widens the relation of part to whole that the poem declares to be necessary for a healthy criticism to encompass the more generic relations of part to whole that in an individual are called health and in a society a healthy social order. Literary norms, these images suggest—announcing a pasionate conviction that will mark

Pope's whole career—are not ultimately dissociable from greater norms. A perverse criticism and a corrupt art are equivalent in their own way to other symptoms of deterioration: tyranny in the state, bigotry and schism in the church, impotence, nausea, flatulence, jaundice in the individual organism.

Meantime, another line of images invites our appropriation of these separate instances of whole-and-part to the larger concept of the One-and-Many. The crucial image here is that of light emanating from the sun, which in turn is identified with light emanating into the human mind from "Nature," and these in turn are associated by implication with something resembling Grace. This last analogy must not be pushed very far. The poem's language never leaves a naturalistic base. Yet in the recurrent references to the great light by which men's little lights are fed; or in the presentation of the ancients as altars burning with celestial fire (ll. 181, 195)—men who have talked with heaven and brought back commandments (ll. 98–99)—beings in whom "Nature" was fully incarnate and may still be known (ll. 135, 140); or in the stress on pride as cause of the falling off from critical "grace" recorded in Part II; or in the amusing likeness to a catalogue of the saved that it is perhaps permissible to see in Part III; or, finally, in the progress of the poem's argument from self-will ("each believes his own," line 10) to submission before a corporate Truth—in all these respects Pope extends his literary-critical ideal to its widest implications.

Not that the *Essay* is altogether so tidy an argument as may appear from the above summary. It is after all a poem and has the familiar strengths and weaknesses of its species. Just how far "true wit" is to preserve its old insouciance, how far be penetrated by the propriety and decorum associated with sense and judgement, is never clearly established, as many a critic has pointed out. The relationship—and especially the division of authority—between the principles derived by critics from the great ancient poets and those derivable from the same sources with the same light of "nature" by the studious later artist also remains ultimately clouded, as does the critical status of the "*nameless Graces* which no Methods teach." For if these last, as claimed, lie "beyond the Reach of Art" and are inaccessible to "Methods," they can hardly (despite the poem's insistence on this) be either dispensations or invasions of the methodizing rules (ll. 161–2); still less can a "Grace" be honestly accounted either a "licence" or a new "Rule" (ll. 146–9).

Other grounds for cavil easily suggest themselves. However great our respect for ancient authors generally, why must we genuflect before "each," as ll. 119 and 181 appear to propose? Here a young author's enthusiasm for Homer, Vergil, Horace, and some others has propelled him into a veneration altogether too undiscriminating, not to say servile. Likewise, though sometimes useful as a rule of thumb, can it be laid down as an unexceptionable truth that only creative artists are good critics? Surely not, especially in a poem that reserves much of its highest praise for Aristotle, Quintilian, Longinus, Petronius, and the commentaries of Dionysius of Halicarnassus on Homer.

Yet these and other lapses seem finally beside the point. What gives the *Essay on Criticism* continuing vitality—apart from a catholicity of outlook that insists on honoring creator with critic, original genius with the rules, and wit with judgment, apart too from its often scintillating burlesques of critical and artistic failings that are as unacceptable today as they were in 1711—is the felt presence in almost every line of a spirited performer who has at last found himself, exulting like a dancer or skilled gymnast in the fascination of what's difficult.

Sometimes he will strike off (as if at a blow) a portrait as doctrinal to our times nearly three centuries later as to his own—that, for instance, of the ideal critic:

> But where's the Man, who Counsel *can* bestow,
> Still *pleas'd* to *teach*, and yet not *proud* to *know*?
> Unbiass'd, or by *Favour* or by *Spite*;
> Not *dully prepossesst*, nor *blindly right*;
> Tho' Learn'd, well-bred; and tho' well-bred, sincere;
> Modestly bold, and Humanly severe?
> Who to a *Friend* his Faults can freely show,
> And gladly praise the Merit of a *Foe*?
> Blest with a *Taste* exact, yet unconfin'd;
> A *Knowledge* both of *Books* and *Humankind*;
> *Gen'rous Converse*; a *Soul* exempt from *Pride*;
> And *Love* to *Praise*, with *Reason* on his Side?
>
> (ll. 631–42)

The desire of the moth for the star, obviously, since Pope shared with most of us a total inability to attain this ideal; yet it is touching to see it so vividly sketched.

Or sometimes he will glide with seeming effortlessness into a similitude that, even though it is surely not, as Johnson held, "perhaps the best that English poetry can shew," nevertheless expresses so magisterially the experience of all who have ever entered upon any area of learning—

> Fir'd at first Sight with what the *Muse* imparts,
> In *fearless Youth* we tempt the Heights of Arts,
> While from the bounded *Level* of our Mind,
> *Short Views* we take, nor see the *Lengths behind*,
> But *more advanc'd*, behold with strange Surprize
> New, distant Scenes of *endless* Science rise!
> So pleas'd at first, the tow'ring *Alps* we try,
> Mount o'er the Vales, and seem to tread the Sky;
> Th' Eternal Snows appear already past,
> And the first *Clouds* and *Mountains* seem the last:
> But *those attain'd*, we tremble to survey
> The growing Labours of the lengthen'd Way,
> Th' *increasing* Prospect *tires* our wandring Eyes,
> Hills peep o'er Hills, and *Alps* on *Alps* arise!—
>
> (ll. 219–232)

that it seems to exemplify and incorporate, like so much else in this poem, the precise excellence that it elsewhere calls "true wit":

> *Something*, whose Truth convinc'd at Sight we find,
> That gives us back the Image of our Mind.
>
> (ll. 299–300)

The simile of the Alps must have recurred often to Pope's mind once he had begun his task with Homer.

And then again, with a happiness as well as care, he will sometimes manage a verbal maneuver so simple in appearance, so breathtaking on reflection, that the common sense of mankind has plucked it out of the poem and made it a part of speech: "A *little Learning* is a dang'rous Thing" (215); "To Err is *Humane*; to Forgive, *Divine* (525); "For *Fools* rush in where *Angels* fear to tread" (625). And several more. Next to Shakespeare, we may recall, Pope has contributed more to our common language than any other poet. It is a gift not lightly to be dismissed.

A "hunchback'd Toad"

The poem was published on May 15, 1711, following a year made somewhat melancholy for Pope by the loss of his friend Betterton and of his aunt Elizabeth Turner as well as by two protracted and dangerous illnesses. "I may say one good thing of Sickness," he confided feelingly to Cromwell after the second bout, "that it is the best Cure in the world for Ambition." But such moods lasted in him as in most of us only as long as the illness that caused them, and accordingly we may guess with what high hopes he looked forward to the *Essay*'s reception as the day of publication drew near. Hopes qualified, we may justifiably imagine, by certain anxieties. This would be, after all, his first appearance in print since the Tonson *Miscellany Poems* and a much riskier venture than that. The content of this poem would be quite new to its readers so far as treatment in verse was concerned, there being extant several reputable versified "Arts" of poetry, including Horace's, but nothing quite like a critical "Art." The poem's style, moreover, while not precisely new (since it is formed on the racy vernacular of Dryden's prologues and epilogues), was his own first effort at a fully contemporary "conversational" idiom, pithy, pointed, witty, and smart, yet, for all its air of unruffled detachment, passionate. Would the pundits of the Town who made and unmade literary reputations warm to such fervor? Would they grasp the poet's deep concern for the good health of both criticism and poetry? would they recognize the generosity of his conception of criticism, a conception that reinstated above the carping censor and the tavern witling the broad sympathies and generosity of outlook that had distinguished the great Dryden? And would they appreciate the work's basic originality despite its surface dependence on predecessors—"less," it has been well said, "a response to tradition than an original engagement with his own time, in the light of traditional knowledge"? What, moreover, would they say of the sheer audacity of this undertaking by a youth who even at the moment of publication was still a few days short of twenty-three?

One answer to these questions was provided on June 20, not by Town pundits but by John Dennis, in a pamphlet entitled *Reflections Critical and Satyrical, upon a late Rhapsody, call'd, an Essay upon Criticism*. Dennis at this juncture was fifty-three. In Dryden's day, he had made one of the crowd at Will's, had won the esteem of several of the best writers of the age, and had published poems, plays, familiar letters, and criticism in rapid succession, the last with deserved success. In criticism, Dennis had a talent. Many a passage of his *Impartial Critick* (1693) is as shrewdly perceived as it is sharply put, and his major critical contribution—*The Advancement and Reformation of Poetry* (1701), enlarged and somewhat modified in his *Grounds of Criticism in Poetry* (1704)—though far from systematic and sometimes clinging, as an intelligent critic often must, to both halves of an arrant contradiction, has assured him of an honorable if modest place among Milton critics, students of the psychology of poetic creation, theorists of the sublime, and proponents of poetical "Passion" and "Enthusiasm"—which it is not, however, clear that he invariably distinguished from rant. In general, like Pope, Dennis believed in the known principles of good writing—"For if Poetry is not an Art, tis a meer whimsey. . . . If tis an Art it must have a System of rules, as evry art has"—yet recognized that native genius, Milton's in particular, might depart from or transcend them. Like Pope, too, he assumed that literature could be divided into "kinds"—for Dennis, tragedy, comedy, epic, satire, and the great ode were the only kinds that counted—each aiming at a specific effect on its audience and therefore having its own time-tried means for attaining that effect. He also venerated the ancients this side of idolatry—once more like Pope, despite the poetic overstatement cited earlier from the *Essay*. Above all, Dennis shared with Pope a genuine lifelong love of literature. In many ways it is ironic that he should have become Pope's enemy.

All that Dennis lacked was self-knowledge, good manners, and a sense of humor. Vain to the point of paranoia, he could not easily tolerate the opinions of others when they differed from his own, or their success if it were greater than what he had himself met with. He was "irritable, suspicious and envious," says the most sympathetic of his editors, ever imagining slights where they did not exist and attaching an importance to himself and his critical ideas that gradually, over the years, made him something of a laughingstock to the new literary generation forming in the London of Addison and Steele. "There," says a contemporary poet, describing a scene at Will's:

> There *Dennis*, censuring with dogmatick Tone,
> Was deaf to every Merit but his own.

And even one of his closest friends, asserting in an obituary tribute that his criticism would endure to all ages, felt obliged to mention his personal conduct:

> Th' impotent envy, the disdainful air,
> The front malignant, and the captious stare!
> The furious petulance, the jealous start.

For reasons that will soon be clear, "furious" became a term regularly applied to Dennis, along with his own favorite qualifier "tremendous" and his favorite oath "'Sdeath [God's Death]!"

By 1711, Dennis had fallen on somber days. His best work was behind him, several of his friendships had cooled, and he was living in an attic near Charing Cross, in disgrace with fortune and men's eyes.

His total imprudence in financial matters—occasion of a complaint of nonsupport brought against his own mother in the Court of Chancery when he was already twenty-eight—had plunged him by 1710 into practices hardly distinguishable from embezzlement, despite an annual emolument of £52 from a small place in the Customs (£29 more than the salary on which Fielding's Parson Adams supported a wife and six children) and occasional gifts from noble well-wishers, whom he was not above flattering obsequiously. His delusions of grandeur had so grown by this time that he was reported to believe his extradition to Paris for trial (as a stout Whig and Williamite, he had lampooned the French nation throughout most of his career) would be a central stipulation of the French government in agreeing to the Peace of Utrecht. It was further reported that, being on the coast and seeing a French ship approach, he had fled the place in the notion it was come for him. Such stories, though of dubious authenticity, indicate the degree of self-delusion of which he was thought by contemporaries to be capable.

By this time, his persecution mania had also ballooned, as old fashions changed with the new century and his ideas for the salvation of Britain through literature met with knowing smiles. Ridiculed very slightly by Steele in an early *Tatler* of 1709 for his phobia against opera, he began to think himself ridiculed whenever criticism and critics were mentioned. In the spring of 1711, he took Addison's *Spectator* of April 16 repudiating poetic justice as a principle of tragedy (a principle that in some degree Dennis approved) to be a personal affront. On April 24, making a point about raillery but with no sign whatever of an *arrière pensée*, Addison quoted a humorous couplet written by Dennis in his youth. This too he took as an affront. Three weeks later, the *Essay on Criticism* appeared, bearing its brief but memorable sketch of an overbearing critic named Appius, an obvious reminder of one of Dennis's failed tragedies, *Appius and Virginia*:

> 'Twere well, might Criticks still this Freedom take;
> But *Appius* reddens at each word you speak,
> And *stares, Tremendous*! with a *threatning Eye*,
> Like some *fierce Tyrant* in *Old Tapestry*!

In view of his peculiar mental set, Dennis may understandably have wondered whether he was not being made the victim of a conspiracy or cabal.

What evoked Pope's lines, we are not likely at this late date to learn. The two men knew each other. Dennis, in a play for sympathy,

19 John Dennis (1657–1734). Engraving after William Hogarth(?).

Like some *fierce Tyrant* in *Old Tapestry*!

Essay on Criticism, 587.

Photograph: Courtauld Institute of Art.

claims in the pamphlet that the insult came from one "wholly a Stranger to me," but confessed later that through an introduction by their mutual friend Cromwell he had been "about thrice" in Pope's company before the *Essay* was published. Did Dennis on one of these occasions verbally browbeat one whom he took to be only a little hunchbacked puppy whose first excursions with the Muse were receiving far too much attention? Quite possibly so. There is a circumstantiality in the passage that may suggest an incident drawn from life; and since Pope was never a young man to cringe, tart words may have followed. Or are the lines simply the thoughtless jeer of unbruised youth at an established—and painfully overweening—figure of fun? That also seems possible, for the imperious critic that Dennis was (few who knew him ever fully understood that his doctrines were considerably more palatable than the arrogance with which they were delivered) made him almost inevitably the antitype of everything the *Essay* proposed, and when he is cited earlier in the poem by name (line 270), it is predictably as the inflexible strict constructionist of the Rules that his authoritarian manners made him seem.

Whatever the explanation of the lines, it is the tyrannical spirit of Dennis, or what was taken, not without cause, to be his tyrannical spirit, that the entire third part of the *Essay on Criticism* implicitly seeks to exorcise. And considering Dennis's penchant for discovering slights, it is difficult to believe he would have left the new poem unscathed had it made no mention of him at all. It was too obviously, he was bound to think, an encroachment on territories over which he had long claimed to rule. It contained a few sentiments with which he could not agree, some whose meaning he took to be ambiguous, others that made no sense to him or were greatly exaggerated, and still others that, intentionally or not, he elaborately misconstrued. Most important for Dennis—and this must not be forgotten in judging him—it contained a thinly veiled public insult, all the more insulting for being true. By any standard, Pope had violated precisely those precepts about critical generosity that the poem advocated.

In replying, Dennis followed the scorched-earth policy that had brought him his uncomfortable notoriety. Not one stone of his opponent's raising should be left upon another. Thanks to his usual keen eye for logical nonsequiturs and poetic sleights of hand—like many in his time, Dennis read poetry as if it were a legal brief—he managed to turn up a handful of genuine oddities and obscurities, which, true to his advice in the poem about consulting foe as well as friend, Pope corrected in subsequent editions. Dennis also noted, rightly, that the poem's deference to the ancients was insufficiently selective, that it contradicted its own tenets in praising critics like Quintilian who could not by any stretch of imagination be called poets, and that it was absurd to pretend that an individual can excel in only one activity or branch of learning ("One *Science* only will one *Genius* fit," line 60). In this last instance, he touched on one of Pope's most deeply held convictions, reiterated in his Preface of 1717 and in some sense made the implicit burden of all his later work: we excel by giving up. It is a sentiment with which few artists will disagree.

Beyond this, Dennis's critique of the *Essay* is pedantic nit-picking and his conclusion determinedly perverse:

> Thus are his Assertions, and his Precepts frequently false and trivial, or both, his Thoughts very often crude and abortive, his Expressions absurd, his Numbers often harsh and unmusical, without Cadence and without Variety, his Rhimes trivial and common. . . . Instead of Simplicity we have little Conceit and Epigram, and Affectation. Instead of Majesty we have something that is very mean, and instead of Gravity we have something that is very boyish. And instead of Perspicuity and lucid Order, we have but too often Obscurity and Confusion.

Had Dennis stopped there, it would be easier to sympathize with him. A work once published is public property of a sort and must endure the suffrages of its readers. But the habits of years were evidently too much for him. Having demolished the work, he would now crush the author. "As there is no Creature so venomous, there is nothing so stupid and impotent as a hunch-back'd Toad," he begins, and from this beginning runs through such a repertory as was later to become for Pope a familiar litany, taunting him for being a Roman Catholic, accusing him of Jacobitism, and slandering him with "politickly setting up for Poet-Laureat against the coming over the the Pretender, which by his insolence he seems to believe approaching." Walsh, Dennis suddenly remembers, used to take this little poetaster into his company "as a double Foil to his Person, and his Capacity." Wycherley, too, in his later years, was haunted by "a certain Spectre exactly in the shape of that little Gentleman," reckoned by those around him to be his "evil Genius." The hors d'oeuvres out of the way, Dennis brings on the roast:

> And now if you have a mind to enquire between *Sunning-Hill* and *Ockingham*, for a young, squab, short Gentleman, with the forementioned Qualifications, an eternal Writer of Amorous Pastoral

Madrigals, and the very Bow of the God of Love, you will be soon directed to him. And pray as soon as you have taken a Survey of him, tell me whether he is a proper Author to make personal Reflections on others; and tell him if he does not like my Person, 'tis because he is an ungrateful Creature, since his Conscience tells him, that I have been always infinitely delighted with his: So delighted, that I have lately drawn a very graphical Picture of it; but I believe I shall keep the *Dutch* Piece from ever seeing the Light, as a certain old Gentleman in *Windsor-Forest* would have done by the Original, if he durst have been half as impartial to his own Draught as I have been to mine. This little Author may extol the Ancients as much and as long as he pleases, but he has reason to thank the good Gods that he was born a Modern. For had he been born of *Graecian* Parents, and his Father by consequence had by Law had the absolute Disposal of him, his Life had been no longer than that of one of his Poems, the Life of half a Day.

There is more, but more is not needed. Many poets have met with foolish reviewers, all the more if their work was original—Lockhart and Croker on *Endymion*, Sir John Squire on *The Waste Land*, to name only two—yet it is probably fair to say with the best informed biographer of Pope in this century that no more cruel review ever greeted a young beginner than Dennis's *Reflections*. The savage censure of the poem Pope might laugh off—it was in fact self-destroying. But the sneers at his religion, his father, his old friendships, his political loyalty, and his crippled body were another matter. If there is any truth in the findings of present-day psychology about men and women who suffer from highly visible handicaps or who differ from the majority in their deepest convictions, the assault on these inner bastions of confidence must have been deeply embittering. The hiss of the branding iron enters the soul.

CHAPTER 9

"A FEW LASTING DEPENDABLE FRIENDSHIPS" AND A DREAM FOR ENGLAND

"No sunshine but in the face of a friend"

The next three years were undoubtedly among the most exhilarating of Pope's life. He was in his early twenties and beginning to be famous. Within a few months of Dennis's attack, his *Essay on Criticism* had won the accolade of the influential *Spectator*, which named it "a Master-piece in its kind"; and within a few more months, after the publication of *Windsor-Forest* in early 1713, Sir William Trumbull's clerical nephew Ralph Bridges was able to inform his uncle that knowledge-able Londoners already spoke of "our Mr. Pope" as "one of the greatest genius's that this nation has bred." At about the same period, William Fortescue, up from Devon since 1710 to pursue the legal career that eventually brought him to be Master of the Rolls, pictures Pope (in a dream-vision written for his friend and former schoolfellow John Gay) as having succeeded to the chair of Apollo. In the course of the supposed dream, Fortescue sees a happy garden atop a forbidding mountain to which only a narrow gate admits. Gay, after several fruit-less approaches, is allowed to enter on the strength of his *Rural Sports*, published in January 1713. Pope is already inside:

> Among those few that were entred I observed A young Person of a small Stature, but a wonderful sweetness and Vivacity in his look, sitting with Nine beautiful maids dancing round him: Criticym

stood at his right hand and Pastoral on his left, he was crowned with Lawrel and seemed ye Genius of ye Place.

Silly though it is, the passage affords an arresting glimpse of the admiration with which Pope was now regarded and of the personal attraction that despite his twisted body drew others to him.

For these years were, of course, the springtime of his most devoted friendships as well as of his fame. He had an unusual talent for friendship. One wonders where among the poets (that *genus irritabile!*) another may be found who succeeded so happily over periods of many years in binding to himself and in binding himself to, such a diversity of men and women, young and old, literary and otherwise: Atterbury, Arbuthnot, Congreve, Jervas, Gay, Parnell, and Swift; Peterborow, Bathurst, Bolingbroke, Oxford, Orrery, the Burlingtons; Martha Blount, Ann Craggs, Anastasia Robinson, Henrietta Howard, even finally the old duchess of Marlborough; Mallet, Harte, Savage, Spence; Cornbury, Lyttelton, Wyndham, Marchmont, Murray; Garth, Wycherley, Trumbull, Betterton, Walsh; Blount, Bethel, Caryll, Fortescue, Richardson, Allen, and Warburton. The record has its blemishes, even its failures (though these were not always Pope's failures), as another list shows: Addison, Fenton, Broome, Hill, Lady Mary Wortley Montagu. But none of these had been an intimate friend save possibly Lady Mary, and only with her was some sort of rapprochement never achieved.

Blemishes or not, one has only to read a few pages in Pope's correspondence to understand that the ground for his success in this relationship (as probably also for most of his failures) lay in the warmth of an expressive and volatile personality. He writes to his friends, not only when he has something exigent to say but also when he does not, because he would be talking with them. "Business" is subsidiary to the important sense of being in affectionate communication with someone very dear. Friendship itself becomes often the undisguised theme. "I see no sunshine but in the face of a friend," he writes to Swift, following Swift's first visit to Twickenham in 1726, and after the second visit, "Your kind letter left for me at Mr. Gay's affected me so much, that it made me like a girl. . . . We are to believe, we shall have something better than even a friend, there"—that is, in a future life, a favorite topic between these two, who were condemned to lack each other's company on earth—"but certainly here we have nothing so good." To Gay he confides in 1730: "Nature, temper, and habit, from my youth made me have but one strong desire; all other ambitions my person, education, constitution, religion, etc. conspir'd to remove far from me. That desire was to fix and preserve a few lasting, dependable friendships." Though he leaves unmentioned here his consuming passion to be numbered among the English poets, he speaks from the heart. And on the morrow of Gay's death, to Martha Blount: "Let us comfort one another, and if possible, study to add as much more friendship to each other, as death has depriv'd us of in him." Sentences, paragraphs, and indeed whole letters of this temper recur again and again. Reading them, we grasp what is meant by that odd-sounding phrase in the first of the Horatian imitations, "the flow of soul"; and why Gay said of him, after speaking of a friend lately deceased, "But there is none like you, living or dead."

John Gay and William Fortescue

It was in the spring of 1711, perhaps on a visit to London for the publication of his *Essay*, that Pope met Gay, and, to judge from the sequel, it was a happy conjuncture of personalities at first sight. Only three years his senior, Gay resembled Pope in wit and vivacity, and in a boy's zest for puns, spoofs, jokes, double entendres, and highjinks generally —"With Laughing Eyes that twinkled in his head," runs Pope's description of him. In other respects, the two young men differed as the grasshopper from the ant. Gay was happy-go-lucky, infinitely good-natured, distinctly a *bon vivant*—*Edit, ergo est* ["He eats, therefore he is"], Congreve is reputed to have said of him—and already at twenty-six inclining to fat. He was also improvident, as careless in money matters, Swift grumbled, as if "Providence never design'd him to be above two and twenty," and during much of his life the means to his support, for he had expensive tastes, were the anxious concern and sometimes the free gift (through the patronage they helped him to) of his more provident friends, Swift and Pope in particular. His last years, after the great success of his *Beggar's Opera* in 1728, were spent under the wing of the Queensberrys, who kept him in their ducal house and, by doling out from his small accumulations only what he actually required, enabled him to die "worth upward of £3000."

Through all the vicissitudes of a preferment-seeker's life, high hopes of a place or pension ending time after time in disappointment, Gay passed relatively unsoured, always affectionate, always, by those who knew him, beloved. If he lacked, as Johnson claims, something of "the dignity of genius"—by which is meant perhaps no more than the stubborn independence Johnson himself had in such abundance—this may be simply the debit side of the remarkable disengagement from

20. John Gay (1685–1732). Engraving by William Smith after a miniature by C. F. Zincke, published 1775.

> With Laughing Eyes that twinkled in his head.
> *Dunciad*, 2: 39 (MS version).

By kind permission of the Henry E. Huntington Library and Art Galleries.

self-interest (either native to his temperament or acquired through disappointment) which makes him such a superb observer of the passing show and which found its characteristically jocose expression in the epitaph he once asked his friend Pope—"whom I love as my own Soul"—to place on his tomb:

> Life is a Jest, and all Things show it;
> I thought so once, but now I know it.

Pope evidently guessed how easily that sentiment could be misread as the mark of a cynical personality and, accordingly, when the tomb was subsequently erected in the poets' corner of Westminster Abbey, added below Gay's couplet an epitaph of his own, drawing for its first lines on the conceit of the *puer senex* or Aged Boy—

> Of Manners gentle, of Affections mild,
> In Wit a Man; Simplicity a Child—

and for its close on the traditional notion that the true resting place of the dead is not in tombs but in the hearts of their friends:

> These are Thy Honours! Not that here thy Bust
> Is mix'd with Heroes, or with Kings thy dust;
> But that the Worthy and the Good shall say,
> Striking their pensive bosoms—*Here* lies Gay.

Through Gay, Pope met Fortescue, Gay's fellow Devonian and Barnstaple schoolmate, who became not only a lifelong friend but a confidant to whom in later years he unburdened himself perhaps more freely than to any other friend save Martha Blount and Richardson. On subjects not political, we are probably to understand. For Fortescue, soon a declared supporter of the Whig establishment and of Robert Walpole, whose private secretary for some time he was, found it inexpedient in later years to appear at Pope's house in Twickenham when the Tory Bolingbroke was there, and possibly on similar grounds seems at long last to have withdrawn from an offer to serve as Pope's executor. It speaks well for both men that they could maintain a friendship in such potentially explosive circumstances. The poet of the Horatian satires of the thirties, all in one way or other attacking the Hanoverian court and ministry, can only have been an acute embarrassment for Fortescue, and one notices that Pope, as if conscious of this danger, never publicly associated Fortescue's name with the first and perhaps most daring of these, despite having warned him at the time of publication that he was the poem's counterpart of Trebatius in Horace's original:

Have you seen my imitation of Horace? I fancy it will make you smile, but though, when I first began it, I thought of you; before I came to end it, I considered it might be too ludicrous, to a man of your situation and grave acquaintance [i.e., in the Ministry?], to make you Trebatius, who was yet one of the most considerable lawyers of his time, and a particular friend of a poet. In both which circumstances I rejoice that you resemble him, but am chiefly pleased that you do it in the latter.

Considering Pope's usual practice of showing poems to his friends while yet in manuscript, especially those in which they were themselves concerned, we may wonder whether the question "Have you seen . . . ?" is not disingenuous (a way of distancing Fortescue from foreknowledge and responsibility in case the letter should be opened by one of Walpole's Treasury men), and whether the reminder that Trebatius stood friend to a poet in the reign of an earlier Augustus has not an undermeaning as well.

However this may be, Fortescue was welcome company in these happy years. A contemporary's description—*Ridens Fortescuvius* ["laughing Fortescue"]—probably says much about his personality, as do also his playful if strained efforts to compose the *Spectator*-like "vision" already cited and his early participation with Pope in a prose romp on legal quibbling called *Stradling versus Stiles*. In this remarkable document, "Matthew Stradling, Gent." has received as legacy all of a certain testator's black and white horses—of which the said testator possessed six black, six white, and six pied. Question: does the bequest rightfully include the pied horses?

Of course! says counsel for the plaintiff:

Whatever is black and white is pyed, and whatever is pyed, is black and white; *ergo*, black and white is pyed, and *vice versa*, pyed is black and white.
If therefore black and white horses are devised, pyed horses shall pass by such devise; but black and white horses are devised; *ergo*, the Pl. shall have the pyed horses.

Not at all! says counsel for the defense.

. . . For if by the devise of black and white horses, not only black and white horses, but horses of any colour, between these two extremes, may pass, then not only pyed and grey horses, but also red or bay horses [here counsel plies the gambit known to lawyer-watchers as *piscis ruber* or *hareng rouge* ("red herring")] would pass likewise, which would be absurd and against reason. And this is another strong argument in law, *nihil, quod est contra rationem, est licitum* ["Nothing that is contrary to reason is allowable"]; for reason is the life of the law, nay the Common Law is nothing but reason. . . .

In the upshot, judgment is rendered for the plaintiff, only to be stayed by a defense proposal that the pied horses are really mares. Upon which, the spoof ends. But the case (the Court having adjourned to "take advice") continues by implication into a long future of further flim-flams and delays, to meld at last, in some jurisprudential Platonic heaven, with the case of Jarndyce vs. Jarndyce in Dickens' *Bleak House*. To a rapidly developing young satirist, one can see why Fortescue appealed.

John Arbuthnot and Jonathan Swift

Others of Pope's closest friendships reaching back to this period are those with Arbuthnot and Swift. "Arbuthnot so tall"—as he is called ironically in a rhyme of 1714—came from an ancient Jacobite family of Kincardineshire. His father, a minister, had lost his living at the Revolution, and his next younger brother Robert, after a last stand for James II at Killiecrankie (17 July 1689), had fled to France, where he became over the ensuing years a successful merchant-banker and, in fact, the Old Pretender's Paris agent. John, eldest of the eight Arbuthnot sons, marched to a different drum. By the time Pope knew him in or about 1712, he had taken a medical degree at St. Andrews and been appointed Physician Extraordinary to the Queen, with lodgings set aside for him in St. James's. He had also established a distinguished reputation as mathematician and student of the natural sciences (he was elected Fellow of the Royal Society in 1704) and was now publishing, in support of the Tory effort to bring the long wars with France to a negotiated close, an allegory in five instalments entitled *The History of John Bull*—judged by Macaulay to be "the most ingenious and humorous political satire extant in our language." Under the form of a lawsuit conducted by Bull and his Dutch colleague Nicholas Frog against the Baboon [i.e., Bourbon] family, the satire touched shrewdly on the sacrifices exacted of the English country gentry by the land tax (first levied for prosecution of the French wars in 1692 and still in place), voicing at the same time a long-standing English hostility to the Dutch that had only been exacerbated by the recent "Plague of Frogs," as it was sometimes called, brought in by William III. In the person of its protagonist Bull, moreover—long-suffering, gullible, moody, but formidable when roused—the satire managed to confer a local habitation and a name on that more or less edifying composite of British characteristics which is Arbuthnot's permanent contribution to the folklore of nations:

> ... *Bull*, in the main, was an honest plain-dealing Fellow, Cholerick, Bold, and of a very unconstant Temper, he dreaded not old *Lewis* [Baboon, i.e., Louis XIV] either at Back-Sword, single Faulcion, or Cudgel-play; but then he was very apt to quarrel with his best Friends, especially if they pretended to govern him: If you flatter'd him, you might lead him like a Child. John's Temper depended very much upon the Air; his Spirits rose and fell with the Weather-glass. *John* was quick, and understood his business very well, but no Man alive was more careless, in looking into his Accounts, or more cheated by Partners, Apprentices, and Servants: This was occasion'd by his being a Boon-Companion, loving his Bottle and his Diversion. . . .
>
> *Nic. Frog* was a cunning sly Whoreson, quite the reverse of *John* in many Particulars.

By this time, in his personal world, Arbuthnot had buried six of his children (of the four who survived two, George and Anne, were also among Pope's close friends in adult life) and, at forty-five, was beginning to be subject to exquisitely painful attacks of kidney stone as well as mysterious fevers, both possibly the long-run effects of much good food and wine. His overindulgence in these pleasures, with the ensuing renal consequences, may account for what his friend Swift refers to variously as the "slouch" or "shuffle" of his gait. But from all this, like Gay, he had somehow distilled an inner tranquility and outer cheerfulness that warmed all who came near him. Gay describes him in *Mr. Popes Welcome from Greece* as one "Whose company drives Sorrow from the Heart." He was skilled in music, played cards devotedly, and laughed much—"as jovially," wrote a younger friend, "as an attendant on Bacchus." He was also spectacularly absent-minded. Swift calls him "the King of inattention," and in one of the most delightful glimpses of eighteenth-century domestic life that has come down to us he is seen sitting happily at his writing desk, apparently in the brownest of brown studies, while his children make kites of his scattered manuscripts on the floor.

Like Gay, too, in the spirit of the jesting Abbey epitaph, Arbuthnot had formulated what he called his "theory of human Virtue." On the Queen's death in August 1714, it was strongly confirmed, he tells us, by the pell-mell rush of those who hoped preferment from the

21. John Arbuthnot (1667–1735). Attributed (wrongly?) to Charles Jervas. Undated.

> Farewell Arbuthnot's Raillery
> On every learned Sot.
> *A Farewell to London, in the Year 1715.*

Under Arbuthnot's hand lies the manuscript of a satire, *An Essay on an Apothecary*, that he is not otherwise known past doubt to have written.

Courtesy of the Wellcome Institute Medical Museum, London.

22. John Arbuthnot (1667–1735). By Sir Godfrey Kneller. This portrait hung in Pope's house and was later given by him to George Arbuthnot.

> Friend to my Life, (which did not you prolong,
> The World had wanted many an idle Song) . . ..
> > *Epistle to Dr. Arbuthnot*, 77–78.

By kind permission of the Hunterian Art Gallery, Glasgow.

new Whig government of George I to place an exculpating distance between themselves and their former Tory friends:

> I have an opportunity calmly & philosophically to consider That treasure of vileness & baseness that I allways believed to be in the heart of man; & to behold them exert their insolence & baseness, every new instance, instead of surprising & grieving me, as it does some of my friends, really diverts me, & in a manner improves my Theory.

But the revealing sentence follows: "God knows I write this with tears in my eyes." One is inevitably reminded of Swift's *Vive la bagatelle* and Pope's "ninth beatitude": "Blessed is the man who expects nothing, for he shall never be disappointed." Like the beetle encased in his shards, each of these gifted men found it expedient to protect something inward and precious, some final cherished residue of idealism, optimism, or hope, with what he could pretend was a shock-proof unconcern.

Perhaps the least securely armed of any of them against fortune's blows, as it finally turned out, was Swift. Swift of the piercing blue eyes—"very particular eyes," said Pope, who in these early years studied his friend's face carefully for the portraits he was then learning how to paint, "quite azure as the heavens." Eyes that in a surviving picture of about 1718, when the sitter was fifty-one, look out on the world with an unswerving gaze into which it is tempting to read both the fascination and the disdain that seem always to have characterized his estimate of life's offerings. He had come to London from his Irish living at Laracor, an emissary of the primate to see what could be done about gaining for the church in Ireland what Anne recently had granted to the church in England. This was a remission of the "first fruits" and the accompanying annual tax that the crown had levied on its clergy since the Reformation, amounting (in Ireland) to one twentieth of each year's income plus the entire income of the first year of each new appointment.

While waiting for the government to respond, Swift immersed himself in the intellectual life of the city—at that time, for a commoner, still the surest entrance to its centers of power—and by a succession of brilliant performances, political, ecclesiastical, and poetic, quickly established himself as the most versatile writer of the age. In the beginning, he cast his lot with the Whigs—Garth, Congreve, Steele, Addison, Rowe (plus several more now known chiefly to antiquarians but then still glistering), who on his arrival in 1707 and for some time thereafter easily dominated the literary scene.

Gradually, however, his allegiance cooled. The Whig ministry pro-crastinated about remission of the Irish church taxes, seemed in fact more concerned with placating dissenters than with shoring up the established church and, where Swift's own future was concerned, promised much but offered nothing. Accordingly, in 1710, when the Whigs fell from power, Swift addressed his efforts to the new Tory ministry of Robert Harley, and from him began to receive not only encouragement in his efforts to obtain remission of the "first fruits and twentieths," but the headier satisfactions that came from being taken (even if not so completely as he himself imagined) into the counsels of the powerful and great.

By the time he met Pope in early 1713, Swift had established himself as the chief Tory spokesman of "the four last years of the queen." (So he would call this period in a violently partisan remin-iscence dating from this time but not published till long after his death.) During three of those years, first in *The Examiner* (October 1710 through May 1711) and then in a succession of pamphlets begin-ning with *The Conduct of the Allies* (27 November 1711), not to mention several verse lampoons, he had put the case cogently for the Harley ministry and the Tory peace. Put it with all the eloquence of an accomplished rhetorician and all the fervor of a man who hated war, all war, quite as heartily as did his later mouthpiece, the King of Brobdingnag. But he put it also, it has to be admitted, with a lavish infusion of that ingredient for which another of his mouthpieces, Gulliver's Houyhnhnm Master, was proud that the Houyhnhnm lan-guage had no word: the lie. Sometimes with downright falsehoods, which it is difficult to believe he did not know were falsehoods, sometimes with calculated distortions or magnifications of a truth, sometimes with stunning innuendoes, Swift sought to make it appear that the motives of the Whig leaders in wishing to prolong the war came down to simple greed. For this he had in his favor only the indisputable fact that Marlborough, and not he alone, did indeed vastly profit from the war, though mainly by the received practices of those days in farming out the contracts for military and naval supply. To the circumstance that England was committed to continuing the war by solemn covenants with her allies, Swift paid scant attention, and allowed no hint to escape of the negotiations with France for a separate peace by which she was already in the act of betraying those allies.

He further aimed to make it appear that the emergence at home of a comparatively new, largely urban, élite moneyed group, with votes in Parliament and lucrative investments in the public funds, was

23. Jonathan Swift (1667–1745). By Charles Jervas, *c*. 1718.

O thou! whatever Title please thine ear,
Dean, Drapier, Bickerstaff, or Gulliver.

Dunciad, 1: 17–18.

evidence of a war-assisted Whig conspiracy to restructure the social and political foundations of the state. Here he had going for him the relative strangeness of the machinery of public credit, much of it invented during the 1690s to support the earlier war effort, and most of it in Whig control. Though not strictly new by Anne's reign, such institutions as the Bank of England and the New East India Company, and such fiscal and fiduciary instruments as paper credit, trading capital, joint-stock, exchequer bills, money sub-scriptions, bonus funds, sinking funds, circulation allowances, and lottery loans were still sufficiently confusing and esoteric to give point to Swift's description of them as "a Mystery of Iniquity," masked in "such an unintelligible *Jargon* of Terms ... as were never known in any other Age or Country of the World." The contemporary perception that landowners were realizing at this period only about 3 percent on their investment in land, whereas the small moneyed group with investments in the national debt or in government-sponsored trading companies could realize as much as 8 percent or even 10 percent, seemed only to confirm the argu-ment. Indeed, from the landowners' point of view, the tax they paid on land (in wartime, 20 percent of income) both secured the loans made to the government by the moneyed group and supplied the interest that the moneyed group received.

There was, to be sure, a great deal else in the parson of Laracor's sophistical masterpieces. Much justified emphasis on the perfidy of the allies in not meeting their promised contributions of money and men. Much emphasis on the spectacular war-incurred national debt:

> It will, no doubt, be a mighty Comfort to our Grand-children, when they see a few Rags [i.e., such enemy flags as Marl-borough had taken at Blenheim and Ramillies] hang up in *Westminster-Hall*, which cost an hundred Millions, whereof they are paying the Arrears, and boasting, as Beggars do, that their Grandfathers were Rich and Great.

And much emphasis on the folly of the Whig insistence that Louis XIV must buy his peace by removing Philip V (his own grandson) from the Spanish throne to replace him with a Hapsburg: "As if Princes and Great Ministers could find no way of settling the Public Tranquillity, without ... forcing Sovereigns upon a People against their Inclinations." Yet the point to which Swift's thoughts seem regularly drawn is the charge of a grand domestic conspiracy:

If we must now Surrender *Spain*, what have we been Fighting for all this while? The Answer is ready: We have been Fighting for the Ruin of the Public Interest and the Advancement of a Private. We have been fighting to raise the Wealth and Grandeur of a particular Family [the Marlboroughs]; to enrich Usurers and Stock-jobbers; and to cultivate the pernicious Designs of a Faction [the Whigs], by destroying the Landed-Interest.

So strong indeed throughout these pamphlets is the appeal to prejudice and passion that one cannot but wonder whether Swift's later praise of the passionless Houyhnhnms, who always speak truth, did not serve some deeply buried psychological need, even if only the need of expiation.

"Peace descending"

Swift's earliest mention of Pope occurs in a letter to Stella on 9 March 1713, two days after the appearance of *Windsor-Forest*. "Mr. Pope has published a fine poem called Windsor Forest," he informs her; "read it." Though by this time Pope had already published not only his *Pastorals* and *Essay on Criticism*, but also his translation *Sapho to Phaon*, his Biblical-Vergilian pastoral *The Messiah*, and the first version of the *Rape of the Locke*, it is fitting that his first recorded link with Swift should come through a work that he had transformed, possibly under the influence of Swift's *Conduct of the Allies*, from a quasi-georgic on the Binfield countryside to a brilliant celebration of the Tory Peace.

Of the original poem, composed probably between 1704 and 1707, when Pope was still riding out with Sir William Trumbull, we have seen snatches in an earlier chapter. That poem, he himself tells us, comprised roughly the first two thirds of the poem we have now (ll. 1–290), plus the twelve-line personal coda with which the present poem ends. In revising this work to celebrate the peace, Pope had mainly to elaborate ideas that were implicit in it. It was already a poem that praised rural England, described the seasonal pleasures of country squires, intimated that hunting, however deplorable, might be a cut above war, and delighted in the "tow'ring Oaks" contributed to British shipping. It was also a poem deeply touched with royalist emotion. All these attributes had come to be associated in the acrimonious politics of 1710–14 with Tory thinking. At the same time, it had much to say about the savagery of (some) kings and the evils of despotic rule generally—always an important Whig concern. And it praised glowingly the world trade—dearest of all Whig interests—that preeminence on the seas was bringing home:

> Not *Neptune*'s self from all his Streams receives
> A Wealthier Tribute, than to thine [the Thames] he gives.
>
> (ll. 223–4)

In the prophecy of "Father Thames" (ll. 329 ff: the poet's chief addition to the early poem, designed to register the various blessings expected from the Peace), Pope was careful to expand this vein into a romantic picture of English merchant venturing:

> Thy Trees, fair *Windsor*! now shall leave their Woods,
> And half thy Forests rush into my Floods,
> Bear *Britain's* Thunder, and her Cross display,
> To the bright Regions of the rising Day;
> Tempt Icy Seas, where scarce the Waters roll,
> Where clearer Flames glow round the frozen Pole;
> Or under Southern Skies exalt their Sails,
> Led by new Stars, and born [e] by spicy Gales!
>
> (ll. 385–92)

This thrilling picture climaxed in a fantasy that London—as "A Free Port" without customs duties (very much a Whig hope at the time)—would become emporium to the world:

> The Time shall come, when free as Seas or Wind
> Unbounded *Thames* shall flow for all Mankind,
> Whole Nations enter with each swelling Tyde,
> And Seas but join the Regions they divide;
> Earth's distant Ends our Glory shall behold,
> And the new World launch forth to seek the Old.
> Then Ships of uncouth Form shall stem the Tyde,
> And Feather'd People crowd my wealthy Side,
> And naked Youths and painted Chiefs admire
> Our Speech, our Colour, and our strange Attire!
>
> (ll. 397–406)

In this way, the poem manages to pay homage to both the agricultural interest of the Tories and the mercantile interest of the Whigs: the second is presented as simply the natural outreach of the first, as in the political tracts of Swift. There is, however, a serious difference. Whatever Pope's personal leanings at this date, and it would be rash to pretend we know them, the poem as it stands in print is ecumenical and conciliatory, like the *Essay on Criticism*. It avoids mention of either party. Its sympathies flow throughout to victims as well as to victors. Apart from one line, it indulges no triumphing (as was usual in other poems on the Peace written at this time) over the fall of Louis XIV and France, and even the triumph of that line is distanced to be remembered among the exploits of the Black Prince and Edward III. Thus in celebrating the Peace, the poem is also peace making. Its handsome register of Windsor-related rivers (ll. 337–48), a further addition to the early version, shows them uniting their individual currents in the Thames, creating again a conspicuous image of a united commonwealth in which the waters of the Tory countryside contribute significantly, like its oaks, to the Whiggish City's global trade, on which the countryside in turn depends.

But if the poem looks at contemporary politics—or, perhaps more accurately, looks through contemporary politics to the human ends that politics addresses itself to—it also looks beyond and at a different *polis*. As an essay in the georgic vein, glimmering from its first lines with quiet allusions to the great Roman original that educated contemporaries sometimes knew by heart, *Windsor-Forest* carried in its very makeup the apocalyptic dream. Vergil, like Pope after him, had set the seasonal order, fertility, and quiet of Italian country life over against the upheaval and pain of the great wars that were now ending with the triumph of Octavian, to usher in (the poet hints) a Golden Age. In a passage already quoted in these pages, and applied by Pope to England, Vergil had exulted in the inimitable glories of his homeland, far greater than any opulences of the East. In a passage close following that was also reapplied by Pope, he had hailed Octavian ("now already victor at Asia's farthest frontier") and the Italian motherland that produced him, evoking, with his reference to Saturn, the presiding deity of the *first* Golden Age: "Hail, land of Saturn, great mother of earth's fruits, great mother of men!" Shortly after, in some of the most influential lines ever written in Latin, he had praised the Italian farmers for the simplicity and innocence of their lives, placing them anachronistically in a revived Golden Age all their own, and describing their blessings in phrases that Pope's contemporaries can hardly have avoided sensing just beneath or beyond his own idealized opening depiction of the Forest under Anne:

O happy husbandmen! too happy, should they come to know their blessings! for whom, far from the clash of arms, most righteous Earth, unbidden, pours forth from her soil an easy sustenance.... They have woodland glades and the haunts of game; a youth hardened to toil and inured to scanty fare; worship of gods and reverence for age. Among them, as she quitted the earth, Justice planted her latest steps.

These implications Pope also gathers up at the poem's conclusion. To the Peace as a peace of this world, a British triumph, an achievement within history reminiscent of the Pax Romana of Augustus, he had already paid his respects in the first part of the speech of the Thames, predicting—quite wrongly, as it turned out—the rebuilding of Whitehall Palace, of which after the fire of 1698 only Inigo Jones's Banqueting House remained, to be the restored center of British power:

> There mighty Nations shall inquire their Doom,
> The World's great Oracle in Times to come;
> There Kings shall sue, and suppliant States be seen
> Once more to bend before a *British* QUEEN.
>
> (ll. 381–4)

But in the final portion of Thames's speech he turns to the other *polis*, of which men and women have dreamed since Old Testament times:

> O stretch thy Reign, fair *Peace*! from Shore to Shore,
> Till Conquest cease, and Slav'ry be no more:
> Till the freed *Indians* in their native Groves
> Reap their own Fruits, and woo their Sable Loves,
> *Peru* once more a Race of Kings behold,
> And other *Mexico*'s be roof'd with Gold.
>
> (ll. 407–12)

At the same time he turns to a series of allegorical figures traditionally tied to the triumphs of good monarchy, some of them, indeed, suggestive of figures found in the allegorical ceiling commissioned of Rubens for that same Banqueting House by Charles I in honor of his father James:

> Exil'd by Thee from Earth to deepest Hell,
> In Brazen Bonds shall barb'rous *Discord* dwell:
> Gigantick *Pride*, pale *Terror*, gloomy *Care*,
> And mad *Ambition*, shall attend her there.
> There purple *Vengeance* bath'd in Gore retires,
> Her Weapons blunted, and extinct her Fires:

There hateful *Envy* her own Snakes shall feel,
And *Persecution* mourn her broken Wheel:
There Faction roar, *Rebellion* bite her Chain,
And gasping Furies thirst for Blood in vain.

(ll. 413–22)

Memories of Vergil's imagined temple to Augustus in the second *Georgic*, its sculptures showing Envy cowering before the Furies in hell, jostle in these lines with memories of Jove's decree in the first *Aeneid* that under Augustus the gates of war shall be closed, and Wrath sit bound with a hundred brazen knots. These interweave in turn, particularly in the first passage and those immediately leading up to it, with imagery from the most apocalyptic of all Vergil's writings, the fourth eclogue, a poem once thought to prophesy the birth of Christ:

Now comes the farthest period foretold in the Sibyl's song. The great cycle of the ages begins again. Now Justice the Virgin returns, the reign of Saturn renews. Now a new generation is sent down from the skies. Smile now, Lucina [patroness of women in labor and sister of Apollo], on the birth of the child under whom the Iron Race shall vanish and the Golden Race spring up throughout the world! Thy own Apollo reigns!

The Messianic visions of Isaiah (on which at approximately the same time Pope drew for his *Messiah*) are also summoned. Many passages from Isaiah throw light on the close of *Windsor-Forest*, but particularly relevant to the matters Pope has in hand are the verses in which it is said that "out of Zion shall go forth the law, and the word of the Lord from Jerusalem"; that swords shall be beaten into plowshares and the nations shall not learn war any more; that after the foundation of the New Jerusalem men shall build houses and live in them, plant vineyards and eat the fruit of them ("They shall not build and another inhabit, they shall not plant and another eat"); and that the princes of the Gentiles will acknowledge Zion's glory, coming from afar by ship and camel, bearing the treasures of the earth:

The Gentiles shall come to thy light, and kings to the brightness of thy rising. . . . Then shalt thou see, and flow together, and thine heart shall fear and be enlarged; because the abundance of the sea shall be converted unto thee, the forces of the Gentiles shall come unto thee. . . . Therefore thy gates shall be open continually; they shall not be shut day or night; that men may bring unto thee the forces of the Gentiles, and that their kings may be brought.

Or under Southern Skies exalt their Sails,
Led by new Stars, and born by balmy Gales.
X For me shall. Gums congeal and Spices blow,
The Coral redden, and the Ruby glow,
The Pearly Shell its lucid Globe infold,
And Phœbus warm the ripening Oar to Gold.
The Time shall come, when free as Seas or Wind
Unbounded Thames shall flow for all Mankind,
Whole Nations enter with each swelling Tyde,
(397) And Seas but joyn whom they did first divide:
Earth's distant Ends our Glory shall behold,
And the new World launch forth to seek the Old.
Then Ships of uncouth Form shall stem the Tyde,
And Feather'd People crowd my wealthy Side,
While naked Youth and painted Chiefs admire
Our Speech, our Colour, and our strange Attire!

Oh stretch thy Reign, fair Peace! from Shore to Shore,
Till Conquest cease, and Slav'ry be no more:
Till the freed Indians in their Native Groves,
Reap their own Fruits, and wooe their sable Loves,
Peru once more a Race of Kings behold;
And other Mexico's be roof'd with Gold!
Exil'd by Thee from Earth to deepest Hell,
In Brazen Bonds shall barb'rous Discord dwell:
Gigantick Pride, pale Terror, gloomy Care,
And mad Ambition, shall attend her there.

There

24. (a) and (b) *Windsor-Forest*. Recto and verso of the final leaf of the manuscript (till now supposed lost) showing Pope's beautiful fair-copy hand, with printer's calculations in the margin.

By kind permission of the Houghton Library, Harvard University.

18

There purple Vengeance, bath'd in Gore, retires;
Her Weapons blunted, and extinct her Fires.
There hateful Envy her own Snakes shall feel,
And Persecution mourn her broken Wheel:
There Faction roars, Rebellion bites her Chain,
And gasping Furies thirst for Blood in vain.

Here cease thy Flight! nor wth unhallow'd Lays
Touch the fair Fame of Albion's Golden Days:
The Thoughts of Gods let Granville's Verse recite,
And bring the Scenes of opening Fate to Light.
My humble Muse, in unambitious Strains,
Paints the green Forests and the flow'ry Plains,
Where Peace descending bids her Olives spring,
And scatters Blessings from her Dove-like Wing.
Ev'n I more sweetly pass my careless Days,
Pleas'd in the silent Shade with empty Praise;
Enough for me, that to the listning Swains
First in these Fields I sung the Sylvan Strains.

FINIS.

by Mr Pope Mr
His Hand

Pope, of course, develops the apocalytic dream with a difference. Isaiah, in part, has in mind the future humiliation of kings and people who have humiliated Israel; Pope, in part, the restoration of kings and peoples who have been plundered by Europeans. Likewise, Vergil in the fourth eclogue foresees for a time the old spoliations renewing—another Argo, another Troy—whereas Pope turns his reminiscence of these lines into a program of reconstruction: the restoration of the Incas, the rebuilding of Mexico. Worth stressing, too, is his projection of a world without slavery, though the Asiento clause of the actual Treaty of Utrecht assured England's share in the profitable slave trade. But the similarities are as important as the differences. The dream of the good community—of the shining city set upon a hill—is not dead, these lines insist; it lives, and for that very reason changes. "Although the poet speaks with prophetic confidence," runs an eloquent comment on the fourth eclogue, "his intention is to create a model for the future in terms of the deficiencies and strengths of the past and the needs of the present." As much may be said of Pope.

For the poet's role as Pope defines it here is to remember the past (Memory being Mother to the Muses) in such a way as to make it live again to contemplation, and so, in a sense, redeem it. Milton—says the poem's second paragraph (saying it, of course, in the pastoral-georgic idiom of verdure)—by "remembering" an ancient story, made it "green" once more:

> The Groves of *Eden*, vanish'd now so long,
> Live in Description, and look green in Song.
>
> (ll. 7–8)

Eden represents here, to be sure, the pastoralist's Agreeable Place. But as subsequent developments in the poem make clear, it represents also a moral center, where the lessons history teaches about our capacity for failure and its causes are gathered into an enduring myth. To the same end, the minor poet George Granville, to whom *Windsor-Forest* is dedicated, lately elevated to the peerage by Queen Anne to ensure a winning vote in the Lords for the Tory Peace, is urged to remember in his "singing" certain events of the English past which also exemplify that capacity for failure, from the civil wars of the houses of Lancaster and York down through the civil wars of the seventeenth century, the execution of the king, London's plague and fire, and whatever else may be thought to be included under the phrase "Inglorious Triumphs, and dishonest Scars" (line 326).

So also in Pope's personal coda. Though now wearing like a shepherd's garland the traditional modesty of the pastoral-georgic singer, he manages to remind us that what Milton's poetry did for Eden (and all that it represents) and what Granville's ought to do for the British monarchy (and what it represents), his own poetry has attempted to do for the Forest and the England *it* represents. By remembering it with a poet's memory, he seeks to make it available to contemplation:

> The Thoughts of Gods let *Granville*'s Verse recite,
> And bring the Scenes of opening Fate to Light.
> My humble Muse, in unambitious Strains,
> Paints the green Forests and the flow'ry Plains,
> Where Peace descending bids her Olives spring,
> And scatters Blessings from her Dove-like Wing.
>
> (ll. 425–30)

He will rejoice in the coming Pax Britannica, but he will put it in perspective by setting beside it the "Peace descending" from the city upon a hill.

CHAPTER 10

SOLEMNITIES AND FRIVOLITIES

"Rise, crown'd with Light"

At about the time he met Gay, in the late spring of 1711, Pope also met Steele. Steele was fresh from his triumph with the *Tatler*, a thrice-weekly paper that (in Gay's words) had "ventur'd to tell the Town, that they were a parcel of Fops, Fools, and vain Cocquets; but in such a manner as even pleased them, and made them more than half enclin'd to believe that he spoke Truth." He was now busy—for Steele was always busy: a tireless entrepreneur and preferment-seeker, he was ever in the midst of new schemes, from alchemical experiments to a project for bringing ocean fish to London in floating fish ponds that would have done credit to Swift's Grand Academy of Lagado—with the *Tatler's* more famous six-times-weekly successor *The Spectator*. This had commenced publication in March, with Addison again as chief collaborator, and other friends, including eventually Pope, contributing from time to time. When the puff for the *Essay on Criticism* appeared in its issue of December 20, Pope, assuming it to be from the pen of Steele, wrote thanking him. To which Steele replied (apparently concerned to preserve Addison's anonymity) that the compliment had been bestowed by "one with whome I will make you acquainted."

Thereafter, Pope's friendship with both men seems to have matured rapidly. There is nothing to show, however, that it approached, particularly with Addison, the degree of easy-going bonhomie that he favored in such associations. Addison, besides being his elder by sixteen years, as was Steele, carried himself with a self-conscious dignity not surprising in one brought up in the clerical household of Lancelot Addison, dean of Lichfield from the time Joseph Addison was eleven. It was certainly not surprising in a man of forty for whom his own talents and the favor of the great Whig

25. Sir Richard Steele 1672–1729. By Sir Godfrey Kneller, *c*. 1710.

Unable Heads that Sleep & Wake by fits
Win *Steel*[e] well sifted from all Alien Wits.

Rejected *Dunciad* couplet referring to Steele's failure to recognize the irony of *Guardian*, No. 40: see *The Last and Greatest Art*, p. 146.

Courtesy of the National Portrait Gallery, London.

magnates had won undisputed leadership of the literary coterie in London together with the financial "competence," as it was then called, of which all authors in all ages fondly dream. Not that Addison's aloofness was impenetrable. "With any mixture of strangers," Pope tell us, reminiscing with Spence some twenty years later, "and sometimes with only one, or with any man he was too jealous of [Pope here reflects the later strain in their relations], he seemed to preserve his dignity much, with a stiff sort of silence"; with intimates, on the other hand, he "had something more charming in his conversation than I ever knew in any other man." In view of Pope's acquaintance with such other men of exceptional charm as Swift, Gay, Bathurst, and Arbuthnot, this is high praise.

A primary source of Addison's conversational charm was a well-stocked mind. While still at Oxford, he had gained a deserved reputation for his classical scholarship and shortly after had been helped to foreign study and the Grand Tour by a pension obtained for him from the ministry—ancestor of the modern "travel grant." He had also the gift of fluency. The poet Edward Young, who knew him well and who confirms Pope's story of his silence and stiffness in the presence of strangers, speaks of "his noble stream of thoughts and language" once he was at ease, and Steele tells us further that as soon as he had fixed the design of anything he was composing, he "would walk about the Room and dictate it into Language with as much freedom and ease as any one could write it down." If we may judge from his work as an essayist, a delicate sense of the world's absurdities accompanied these other attributes, though it was unfortunately a sense that converted easily to condescension, not to say hostility, where women were concerned, and was all too rarely (since we know from other sources than Pope that he was easily jealous and throve on the flattery of satellites) applied to himself.

Steele was the easier companion. He was pudgy, warm-hearted, impulsive, indestructibly cheerful. A schoolmate of Addison's at the Charterhouse and subsequently at Oxford, he had left the university (without a degree) for the military, had left the military for the theater, and the theater for journalism. By the time he began the *Spectator*, he had fought a duel, written three plays, married twice (once, apparently, for *both* love and fortune), edited the official government newspaper *The Gazette*, and—always indigent despite considerable employments, emoluments, and the properties of wives—had been arrested at least once for debt. Though in no sense a devout man and caring little for the Anglican establishment, as a staunch Irish Protestant he had the usual Protestant respect for the

Scriptures, and it may have been he (just as possibly it was Caryll) who encouraged Pope to write the *Messiah*, which the *Spectator* published in its issue of 14 May 1712 (no. 378).

In some not easily traceable way, the *Messiah* springs from the same impulses that moved Pope, probably early in his boyhood, to buy a copy of the *De Imitatione Christi* attributed to Thomas à Kempis and to compose at various times during his youth and young manhood such poems and translations as *A Paraphrase on Thomas à Kempis, L. 3. C. 2*; *The Dying Christian to his Soul* (later set to music); *Hymn of St. Francis Xavier*; *Psalm xci*; *From Boetius, de consol. philos. Lib. 3. Met. 9*; and the *Universal Prayer*—to say nothing of *Eloisa to Abelard*, which in several respects belongs in this list. Pope says that the first of these was written when he was twelve, and though he was prone, like the young Milton before him and indeed many other geniuses, to underscore his precocity, the style in this instance, and some typically seventeenth-century rhymes, confirm an early date. As one of Pope's least-known juvenilia, in a devotional mode he is not known otherwise to have pursued, it warrants partial quotation—if for no other reason than to show what a considerable hymn writer Pope might have made had he tried. It voices the familiar meditative theme that Truth speaks inwardly without the noise of words (*Quod veritas intus loquitur sine strepitu verborum*):

> Speak, Gracious Lord, oh speak; thy Servant hears:
> For I'm thy Servant, and I'l[l] still be so:
> Speak Words of Comfort in my willing Ears;
> And since my Tongue is in thy praises slow,
> And since that thine all Rhetorick exceeds;
> Speak thou in words, but let me speak in deeds!
>
> Moses indeed may say the words but Thou
> Must give the Spirit, and the Life inspire;
> Our Love to thee his fervent Breath may blow,
> But 'tis thy self alone can give the fire:
> Thou without them may'st speak and profit too;
> But without thee, what could the Prophets do?
>
> Let them be silent then; and thou alone
> (My God) speak comfort to my ravish'd Ears;
> Light of my eyes, my Consolation,
> Speak when thou wilt, for still thy Servant hears.
> What-ere thou speak'st, let this be understood;
> Thy greater Glory, and my greater Good!
>
> (ll. 1–6, 19–24, 31–36)

The *Messiah*, it goes without saying, belongs to a more public tradition. The subtitle Pope gave it in the *Spectator*—"*A sacred Eclogue, compos'd of several Passages of Isaiah the Prophet. Written in Imitation of Vergil's Pollio* [i.e., *Eclogue IV*]—states clearly its dependence on the apocalyptic texts drawn on in revising *Windsor-Forest*. But the poem also participates in a long tradition of Biblical paraphrase reaching upward from Sir Philip Sidney's adaptations of the Psalms along the uneventful valleys of Joshua Sylvester and George Sandys to the royal peaks of Milton, whence it debouches on the hither side into the hollows and abysses of Tate and Brady, Sir Richard Blackmore, and Aaron Hill. Fulfilling the promise in its title, Pope's paraphrase begins with an invocation to the nymphs of Biblical Jerusalem that at the same time parallels Vergil's invocation in *Eclogue IV*:

> Sicilian Muses, let us sing a somewhat loftier strain. Not everyone is pleased with orchards and lowly tamarisks.
>
> (Eclogue IV, ll. 1–2)

> Ye Nymphs of *Solyma*! begin the Song:
> To heav'nly Themes sublimer Strains belong.
> The Mossie Fountains and the Sylvan Shades,
> The Dreams of *Pindus* and th' *Aonian* Maids,
> Delight no more—O Thou my Voice inspire
> Who touch'd *Isaiah*'s hallow'd Lips with Fire!
>
> (Messiah, ll. 1–6)

Before he finishes, the poet has intricately intertwined variations on twenty-seven passages from sixteen different chapters of Isaiah with translations and allusions derived from some thirty lines (out of 63) of *Eclogue IV*. And though the main themes touched on at the close of *Windsor-Forest* inevitably reappear—an end to war, an end to exploitation—the versification shows Pope summoning new kinds of verbal energy and managing a climax at the close that for all its rhetorical display movingly records the assumption of lesser in greater which is prayed for in the paraphrase on à Kempis, pervades the argument of the *Essay on Criticism*, reappears in the *Essay on Man* and *Dunciad*, and has always played a central role in the history of religious feeling:

> Rise, crown'd with Light, Imperial *Salem* rise!
> Exalt thy Tow'ry Head, and lift thy Eyes!
> See, a long Race thy spatious Courts adorn;
> See future Sons, and Daughters yet unborn

In crowding Ranks on ev'ry Side arise,
Demanding Life, impatient for the Skies!
See barb'rous Nations at thy Gates attend,
Walk in thy Light, and in thy Temple bend.
See thy bright Altars throng'd with prostrate Kings,
And heap'd with Products of *Sabaean* Springs! . . .
No more the rising *Sun* shall gild the Morn,
Nor Evening *Cynthia* fill her silver Horn,
But lost, dissolv'd in thy superior Rays;
One Tyde of Glory, one unclouded Blaze,
O'er flow thy Courts: The LIGHT HIMSELF shall shine
Reveal'd; and God's eternal Day be thine!
The Seas shall waste; the Skies in Smoke decay;
Rocks fall to Dust, and Mountains melt away;
But fix'd *His* Word, *His* saving Pow'r remains:
Thy *Realm* for ever lasts! thy own *Messiah* reigns!

(ll. 85–94, 99–108)

"That beautiful Rusticity"

Four months after the *Spectator* ceased publication in December 1712, Steele founded the *Guardian*. As in the earlier undertakings, Addison was chief collaborator, with occasional papers counted on from other friends, of which Pope contributed seven, possibly more. Two of his best (apart from the essay against cruelty to animals looked at earlier) are a piece on poetry-to-formula called "A Receipt to make an Epick Poem," which he later collected in his *Art of Sinking in Poetry*, and an essay on gardens that praises the "naturalness" of Alcinous' gardens in the *Odyssey* while satirically contrasting them with the current taste for topiary—for instance, the sort of item alleged to be available at a local nurseryman's:

> *Adam* and *Eve* in Yew; *Adam* a little shatter'd by the fall of the Tree of Knowledge in the great Storm; *Eve* and the Serpent very flourishing.

Two successive papers give an account of one of the newer London Clubs, the Club of Little Men. Its members, who keep their annual Founders' Day feast on the shortest day of the year over a dish of shrimps, are sworn to uphold "the Dignity of Littleness under the Noses of those Enormous Engrossers of Manhood, those Hyperbolical Monsters of the Species, the tall Fellows that overlook us." A paragraph of particular interest, since it initiates the ironical public image of Pope's physical affliction on which he will ring changes all his life, describes the Club's poet—one

> *Dick Distick* by Name, [whom] we have elected President, not only as he is the shortest of us all, but because he has entertain'd so just a Sense of the Stature, as to go generally in Black that he may appear yet Less. Nay, to that Perfection is he arriv'd, that he *stoops* as he walks. The Figure of the Man is odd enough; he is a lively little Creature, with long Arms and Legs: A Spider is no ill Emblem of him. He has been taken at a Distance for a *small Windmill*. But indeed what principally moved us in his Favour was his Talent in Poetry, for he hath promised to undertake a long Work in *short Verse* to celebrate the Heroes of our Size. He has entertained so great a Respect for *Statius*, on the Score of that Line, *Major in exiguo regnabat corpore virtus* ["Great courage was sovereign in that tiny frame"], that he once designed to translate the whole *Thebaid* for the sake of little *Tydeus*.

The one other *Guardian* that can be assigned to Pope with assurance is no. 40, published on 27 April 1713. This piece of mischief, in fact, got him into trouble. The Tonson *Miscellany* of 1709, which closed with Pope's pastorals, opened, it will be remembered, with another set of pastorals by another hand. Their author was Ambrose Philips, educated at Shrewsbury School and Cambridge, of whom we happen to know that he favored red stockings, was "of a lean make, pale complexion, extremely neat in his dress, and five feet seven inches high"—two inches taller than Swift. After a short career with the British Expeditionary Force in Spain (1706–7), where he was captured and escaped, he was now back in London, seeing much of Addison, contributing to the *Guardian*, and seeking, like every other young Briton of good family and education in straitened circumstances, a government employment. Pope had thought well of Philips's pastorals soon after they appeared. "In the whole," he told Cromwell in 1710, "we have no better Eclogs in our Language." The opinion was given, we must charitably assume, in a blind rush of generosity to the brain and a total forgetfulness of Spenser, not to mention Drayton, with whose work in this genre Pope may, however, at the time have been unfamiliar.

The two and a half years intervening between this favorable pronouncement and his paper on Philips in the *Guardian* would very probably have tempered Pope's enthusiasm in any case. His own powers both critical and creative were sharpening fast, and work that might have held absorbing interest for a young poet when he had published no original poetry except his own pastorals was likely to seem less impressive to one who had now been acclaimed for his *Essay on Criticism* and *Windsor-Forest* as well as the first version of the *Rape of the Locke*. There were other stimulants to reappraisal, too. In the *Tatler*, five days after the appearance of the Tonson volume, Steele had complimented Philips on his contribution to it without mentioning that the book also contained pastorals by Pope, and three years later had given it a second puff. In *Spectators* of November 1711 and October 1712, Addison seconded Steele's praises, in the issue of October 30 denouncing all use of "pagan mythology" as "unpardonable in a Poet that is past Sixteen" and paying tribute to Philips for avoiding it. Pope—whose pastorals and as yet unpublished *Windsor-Forest* held to the Renaissance ideal of creating for and in England a fostering myth—must have winced.

Worse was to come. Five anonymous papers devoted to pastoral poetry in the early issues of the *Guardian*—which Pope, understandably, thought were Steele's—pedestaled Philips's pastorals alongside those of Theocritus and Vergil and declared his poems, together with Spenser's, to be the touchstones of the genre in English: "To their Works I refer my Reader to make Observations upon the Pastoral Stile; where he will sooner find that Secret than from a Folio of Criticisms." Amyntas, the supposed originator of pastoral, the writer went on to add, had for his heir Theocritus, "who left his Dominions to *Virgil*, *Virgil* left his to his Son *Spencer*, and *Spencer* was succeeded by his eldest-born *Philips*." Once more, no mention of Pope. That there was malice in all this seems doubtful, though perhaps not impossible, since the writer to whom the five papers are today ascribed, Thomas Tickell, later connived with Addison in his attempt to depreciate Pope's Homer. Certainly, at any rate, there was astonishing obtuseness to another writer's feelings, for the one passage cited from Pope among the many cited from Philips is (pointedly?) taken not from his pastorals but from his *January and May*. Almost as disturbing to Pope as the author's neglect, we may guess, was his tone. For him, pastoral was not, as for Pope, an evocation of the magical world of Vergil's Arcadians, which has haunted many imaginations besides Pope's during the past two millennia; nor, as for both Spenser and Pope, a young artist's first manifesto of his dedication to the high calling of a poet. It was instead a ticket to "a kind of *Fairy Land*," a "Dream" that gratifies our taste for ease, innocence, and the country, its shepherds "Pretty Triflers" and its language best when when expressing a "pretty Rusticity."

Implied, of course, was a harsh truth, of which the author appears to have been as little aware as was Pope himself. What Tickell communicates in these papers (like Addison in his prohibition of mythology, Johnson in his discomfort before *Lycidas*, and the best writers of the century generally in their efforts to redefine the genre) is a sense, however oddly or perversely expressed, that the classical pastoral as a vehicle of serious thought and feeling is dead. That sense was encouraged, no doubt, by other much broader realignments of the European sensibility (among them the so-called Battle of the Books, or Quarrel of Ancients versus Moderns), which over the past three centuries have brought about all those rationalizing and secularizing changes that have gained us and cost us so much. To Pope the cost might well have seemed *too* high. He was always a conservative where the ancients were concerned; he held idealizing views of poetry's social and even of its political functions; and he would not have been pleased with a world in which myth has been exiled to its last stronghold in the unconscious.

Whatever his motives, which were undoubtedly mixed, Pope wrote a sixth and culminating essay as if by the same critic and sent it, evidently anonymously and in a copyist's hand, to Steele. Steele—rather like the bishop who is reputed to have said of *Gulliver's Travels* that he scarcely believed a word of it—printed the piece without catching its satirical tone. His emotions, when he tumbled to the trick, we can only surmise. Warm-hearted and forgiving as he was, he may well have joined in any sport that was made of him in the coffee houses, for the number of those who spotted the game Pope played is bound to have been small, and the number who would have been bothered by it in that age of disguises, shams, counterfeits, roles and put-ons still smaller. Yet the deception must have rankled a little, once Steele had decided that the anonymous contributor had to be Pope; Addison, with his firm ideal of gentlemanly conduct, could hardly have been pleased; and Tickell, unquestionably, along with Philips, was either considerably peeved or furious. All four must have recognized from then on that Pope could be a formidable opponent.

What the essayist was represented as saying in this sixth contribution was that he had omitted consideration of Pope's pastorals on the ground that, like most of those by Vergil or Theocritus, they did not follow the guidelines he had laid down for this genre and were, besides, "fallen into the same Error" with Vergil in not imitating true country speech. This error, to his credit, Philips had avoided, calling his shepherds by real down-on-the-farm English names like

"*Hobbinol, Lobbin, Cuddy*, and *Colin Clout*," and couching their complaints in the unspoiled vernacular of:

> O woeful Day! O Day of Woe! quoth he;
> And Woeful I, who live the Day to see—

wherein the "Simplicity of Diction, the Melancholy Flowing of the Numbers, the Sublimity of the Sound, and the easie Turn of the Words" combine to create "That beautiful Rusticity" all along desiderated in the earlier essays for this species of poem. Perhaps even superior to Philips in its command of the vernacular, the writer went on to say, was a fine Pastoral Ballad written in the Somerset dialect and recently unearthed from a pile of old manuscripts, where Cicily the milkmaid instructs Roger the farmboy:

> Rager, go vetch tha Kee, or else tha Zun
> Will quite be go, be vore c' have half a don—

and "Rager" responds:

> Thou shouldst not ax ma tweece, but I've a be
> To dreave our Bull to Bull tha Parson's Kee.

All things considered, then,

> I hope none can think it any Injustice to Mr. *Pope*, that I forbore to mention him as a Pastoral Writer; since upon the whole, he is of the same Class with *Moschus* and *Bion*, whom we have excluded that Rank; and of whose Eclogues, as well as some of Virgil's, it may be said, that according to the Description we have given of this sort of Poetry, they are by no means *Pastorals*, but *something Better*.

Under the badinage—which is directed fully as much at the author of the *Guardian* papers as at Philips—Pope raises a critical question of some moment, which he would probably himself have expressed in terms of nature and art. How far can unmitigated reality, or nature, be made compatible with the significant forms sought by art? Rephrased in our terms it might read: how far can any writer reflect the unpruned inanities of actual life and conversation, whether of barnyard or billiard room, without lapsing into what criticism recognizes as the fallacy of imitative form, and readers recognize by falling asleep? Like Steele in printing the essay, Tickell seems curiously obtuse to the fact that the "rustic" English names he so fancies are as much a literary convention as Daphnis, Alexis, and Thyrsis; and that no poem's excellence was ever constituted by pretty little touches of native life and scene (or even by any galaxy of fresh images) apart from a unifying decorum—which may consist, indeed, in the artful defiance of decorum.

This was the handle by which Gay took hold of the matter when, some months after Pope's *Guardian*, no. 40, was published, he set about producing six pastorals of his own (significantly the same number as Philips) to be published in 1714 as *The Shepherd's Week*. Quick to realize that Philips's error lay in having flung together a grotesque mélange of vocabularies, styles, and conventions—cute poeticisms like "Kidlins," "Younglins," and "Steerlings" rubbing elbows incongruously with Spenserianisms like "dampy," "steepy," "cooly," "banky" [having banks], while being jostled in turn, often within the same speech, by epithetical clichés like "Silver" floods and "Crystal" waters, plumped down to flow beside an actual herdsman's sod-roofed "Hut"—Gay glimpsed the rich vein of burlesque humor that was latent in Philips's patchwork practice and claimed it for his own. "That principally, courteous Reader," he observes in his "Proeme," with what seems to be a glance throughout at both Philips and Tickell,

> whereof I would have thee to be advised ... is touching the Language of my Shepherds; which is, soothly to say, such as is neither spoken by the country Maiden nor the courtly Dame; nay, not only such as in the present Times is not uttered, but was never uttered in Times past; and if I judge aright, will never be uttered in Times future. It having too much of the Country to be fit for the Court, too much of the Court to be fit for the Country; too much of the Language of old Times to be fit for the Present, too much of the Present to have been fit for the Old, and too much of both to be fit for any time to come. Granted also it is, that in this my Language, I seem unto myself, as a *London* Mason, who calculateth his Work for a Term of Years, when he buildeth with old Materials upon a Ground-rent that is not his own, which soon turneth to Rubbish and Ruins. For this point no Reason can I alledge, only deep learned Ensamples having led me thereunto.

As everyone who has read *The Shepherd's Week* will recall, however, Gay bought out the freehold by the drollery of his inventions and erected the only lasting edifice based on country life and peasant folkways between *The Shepheardes Calendar* and *Michael*.

"A brave man struggling in the storms of fate"

On 14 April 1713, roughly a fortnight before *Guardian*, no. 40, appeared, Addison's *Cato* was acted at Drury Lane. Its hero was the

poker-spined stoic defender of Roman republicanism, Marcus Por-
cius Cato Uticensis—called so partly from his service as governor of
Utica, Carthage's Roman rival on the North African coast, partly to
distinguish him from his great grandfather, the yet sterner Cato,
famed in school Latin texts as much for his warcry against Carthage
(*Carthago delenda est*) as for his saner aphorism on prose style (*Rem
tene, verba sequentur*: "Have something to say and the words will take
care of themselves"). From the beginning, the younger Cato opposed
what he took to be the imperial ambitions of Julius Caesar, casting his
lot finally with Pompey, and after Pompey's defeat and death, with
Pompey's followers. In the end, as Caesar's victorious armies were
approaching Utica, he read over Plato's *Phaedo* on the immortality of
the soul and then stabbed himself.

With its strong stress on freedom from "tyranny," the story had a
clear appositeness to the aims of the Glorious Revolution as the Whig
interest saw them, and possibly this connection is what suggested it
to Addison as a suitable vehicle for a tragedy while he was yet at
Oxford in the 1690s. Four acts of the play are reported to have been in
draft by 1703, following his Grand Tour, but he had no resolute
intention of bringing it to the stage (so says his editor, the Thomas
Tickell of the *Guardian* papers on pastoral) " 'till his friends of the first
quality and distinction prevailed with him to put the last finishing to
it at a time when they thought the doctrine of Liberty very seasonable."

Along with "Liberty," the source story offered the appealing
image of a martyr to principle, a theme capable of being handled with
tragic imagination as a study of the overreacher or self-doubter in us
all, or, more crassly, as a gallery of heroic attitudes to be struck with
appropriate declamation. Addison chose the second plan, or perhaps
the plan chose him. At any rate, to twentieth-century sensibilities the
play now seems a vast echoing museum filled with plaster casts. Not
so to the sensibilities of 1713, or for a long time after. That spring
political passions ran high. The Peace was regarded by many Whigs as
a sell-out of the national interest; the Queen's addition of twelve
Tory votes to the peerage the year before to guarantee a favorable
reception for the Peace in the Lords was seen as a machination of
Harley's to keep himself in power, perhaps even to bring back the
Stuarts; and the removal of Marlborough from his posts on the same
day (1 January 1712) lent itself to every sort of frightening speculation, including, again, fears of a Stuart restoration. On the birthday
of the electress Sophia (3 October 1712), through whom the Protestant line ran from James I to George Louis, Elector of Hanover (the

next king of England if the Act of Settlement held, as some feared and others hoped it would not do), London crowds shrilled through half the night their battle song: "Over, over, Hanover, over!" and when, the following May, the Harley ministry advanced Swift to be Dean of St. Patrick's and the Tory high-flyer Henry Sacheverell to the pulpit of St. Andrew's, Holborn, even a comparatively reputable Whig journalist like Abel Boyer, editor of *The Political State of Great Britain*, could comment:

> Thus in this Month of *May* Two famous Divines, *Sacheverl* and *Swift*, were advanc'd, the one for Beginning the other for Compleating (as they were said to have boasted) the Ruin of the WHIG Party.

With London in this frame of mind, *Cato* was assured a sensational success. It played for nineteen performances consecutively (almost a month in elapsed time), a record for those days, and even as late as April 25, after the initial excitement had worn off, we find the wife of a peer complaining in a letter to her husband that she can send him no London news because "I don't know a mortal that is not gone to the Play that coud get places, either in boxes, pit, or gallery." For despite its obvious availability to Whiggish interpretations—so obvious that Addison felt called on to assure the Tory ministry in advance that he "never in the least designed it as a party-play"—both parties claimed its patriotic sentiments for their own, and in a "home stroak" at the Whigs (as one correspondent put it), Bolingbroke invited Booth, who played Cato, into his box during one of the early performances, and presented him with fifty guineas—"in acknowledgment (as he expressed it) for his defending the cause of liberty so well against a *perpetuall dictator.*" The move was a shrewd hit at Marlborough, whose application to be appointed Captain General for life the Queen had refused, and made the play's encroaching Caesar appear to be a Whig.

There is every probability that Pope was present at the play's opening night, since he contributed its rousing prologue. A good account of that occasion comes from the pen of George Berkeley, the philosopher and future bishop of Cloyne, who had arrived in London from Dublin only shortly before:

> On Tuesday last Mr Addison's play entitled Cato was acted for the first time. I am informed the front boxes were all bespoke for nine days, a fortnight before the play was acted. I was present with Mr Addison, and two or three more friends in a side box, where we

had a table and two or three flasks of burgundy and champagne, with which the author (who is a very sober man) thought it necessary to support his spirits in the concern he was then under; and indeed it was a pleasant refreshment to us all between the acts. He has performed a very difficult task with great success, having introduced the noblest ideas of virtue and religion upon the stage with the greatest applause, and in the fullest audience that ever was known. The actors were at the expence of new habits, which were very magnificent, and Mr Addison takes no part of the profit, which will be very great, to himself. Some parts of the prologue, which were written by Mr Pope, a Tory and even a Papist, were hissed, being thought to savour of whiggism, but the clap got much [i.e., outdid] the hiss. My Lord Harley, who sat in the next box to us, was observed to clap as loud as any in the house all the time of the play.

Pope founded his prologue on the traditional theme that self-conquest is the conquest that matters—a theme he was to return to at length in the *Essay on Man* and, by implication, throughout the Horatian poems. Hence:

> A brave man struggling in the storms of fate,
> And greatly falling with a falling state!
>
> (ll. 21–2)

becomes a figure far more admirable than any triumphant Caesar. At the sight of Cato's effigy, in fact, drawn in state in Julius Caesar's triumph:

> The triumph ceas'd—Tears gush'd from ev'ry eye;
> The World's great Victor pass'd unheeded by;
> Her last good man dejected *Rome* ador'd,
> And honor'd *Caesar*'s less than *Cato*'s sword.
>
> (ll. 33–6)

If these, and particularly the two lines first quoted, were thought by some Tories to allude to the duke of Marlborough, lately fallen from his honors, we can understand the Tory hisses.

"Taken ill of a violent Frenzy last April"

Indirectly, the fanfare surrounding *Cato* became the occasion of Pope's getting into further mischief. On its publication, some days after the premiere at Drury Lane, there was such a rush to obtain copies of the text that (as Pope told Caryll) "the orange wenches and fruit women in the Park offer the books at the side of the coaches, and the Prologue and Epilogue [the latter by Dr. Garth] are cried about the streets by the common hawkers"—eight printings, as a matter of fact, were demanded that first year. Irritated by so much approbation of what he saw to be a defective work, John Dennis characteristically published a pamphlet of *Remarks upon Cato* in early July to counteract its evil effects on the "Tragick Stage"—for "the great Success of one very faulty Play prognosticates its Ruin more than the Miscarriage of twenty good ones." Many of his censures are well taken, even if somewhat pedantically neoclassical in character, and some of what he says makes sense by any standard. But the tone is heavily sarcastic. The critical objective is not to assess the play's defects and virtues but to bury it in the rubble of its exploded faults. And the argument is so opportunistic that Addison is damned both when he violates the tragic "rules" and when he observes them. All in all, though the *Remarks* is sounder and less petulant, this is the Dennis of the *Reflections* on the *Essay on Criticism*: "a Man" (as he put it himself in what he meant to be a demurrer) "conceitedly resolv'd to like nothing which others like" and unshakably convinced that he is never at fault: "having made a great many Enemies by former Disputes of this Nature, is a certain Proof that I have been right in those Disputes, and that they who hate me for asserting Truth are resolv'd to remain in the wrong."

Little wonder that Pope saw in Dennis's pamphlet an opportunity to even scores. Borrowing a hint from Swift's trick on Partridge the astrologer, which proved the man dead even if he were in fact alive, he would publish a pamphlet proving Dennis insane even if—as the *Remarks upon Cato*, and notably the sentences just quoted from it, might incline readers to doubt—he were in fact sane. It was a jest that would settle personal scores, be a friendly gesture on behalf of Addison, with whom, as the *Cato* prologue indicates, he was still on excellent terms, and make tasty gossip in the coffee houses. One must never entirely dismiss with Pope the claims—or what he took to be the claims—of friendship. He was quick to rise to the defense of his friends and eager to do them good—*over*quick and *over*eager, I think we must conclude, partly from a naturally combative temper, but partly too, perhaps, from a need to show that for all his dwarfish size he could meet the obligations that friendship entailed. He might not be able to stand second in a duel, but he had clout of another sort.

The consequence of all this was the anonymous *Narrative of Dr. Robert Norris, Concerning the Strange and Deplorable Frenzy of Mr. John*

Denn[*is*], written probably by Pope alone though possibly with Arbuthnot's assistance, and published only seventeen days after the *Remarks upon Cato*. Robert Norris of Snow-hill and later of Hatton-Garden was a genuine quack, who for some years had advertised in the London papers his "Experience and good Success in the Cure of Lunaticks." According to the *Narrative*, he was visited on July 20 by an old woman much concerned about her master. He had been "taken ill of a violent Frenzy last *April*"—date of *Cato*'s first performances and publication—and ever since he had done nothing but mutter "*Cator*, or *Cato*, or some such thing" (which she took to be the name of a witch: "for I have heard him say *Cator* has bewitch'd the whole Nation") and run to the window whenever anyone knocked, "crying out *S'death! a Messenger from the French King! I shall die in the* Bastile."

When Norris accompanies the old woman to her master's lodging, he finds him heavily bearded because he will not allow himself to be shaved, "believing the modern Dramatick Poets had corrupted all the Barbers in the Town to take the first Opportunity of cutting his Throat"—whether from fear of his prowess as a rival playwright or from outrage at his criticisms is not specified. His room is hung with old tapestry with great holes in it, "caus'd ... by his having cut out of it the Heads of divers *Tyrants*, the Fierceness of whose Visages had much provoked him"—an allusion to the lines that had angered Dennis in Pope's *Essay*. Pinned to the walls likewise are many leaves of Cato, annotated "*Absurd, Monstrous, Execrable*," and behind the door lie bundles of *Spectators* that the old woman keeps out of sight—"for her Master never read in them, but he was either quite mop'd [depressed], or in raving Fits." The only books in the room, "very well bound and gilded," had "Names I had never before heard of"—they are of course Dennis's own works—but the floor was littered with manuscripts, and on the table sat (a detail of pointed particularity, hinting at a dual inspiration for Dennis's criticism) "a Pot of half-dead Ale cover'd with a *Longinus*."

There ensues a remarkable bit of comic dialogue at cross purposes as Norris tries to find out how Dennis got into this condition, Dennis (who at first takes him for an agent from the Bastille) roars at his prescriptions, the old woman continues to mistake Cato for an evil spirit, and the bookseller, Bernard Lintot, publisher of the *Remarks*, who is also present, begins to fear his author is mad in earnest—"If he should be really mad," he asks, "who the Devil will buy the *Remarks*?" In the end, there is a literal battle-of-the-books with huge folios, everyone is injured, and Norris retreats, taking

Lintot home with him to dress his wounds. At which time, "he gave me the following remarkable Relation":

> That on the 17th of *May*, 1712, between the Hours of 10 and 11 in the Morning, Mr. *John Denn[is]* enter'd into his Shop, and opening one of the Volumes of the *Spectator*, . . . did suddenly, without the least Provocation, tear out that of No. [40] where the Author treats of Poetical Justice and cast it into the Street. That the said Mr. *John Denn[is]* on the 27th of *March*, 1712, finding on the said Mr. *Lintott*'s Counter a Book called an *Essay on Criticism*, just then publish'd, he read a Page or two with much Frowning and Gesticulation, till coming to these two Lines:
>
> > Some have at first for Wits, then Poets past,
> > Turn'd Criticks next, and prov'd plain Fools at last—
>
> He flung down the Book in a terrible Fury, and cried out *By G— he means Me.*
>
> That being in his Company on a certain Time, when *Shakespear* was mention'd as of a contrary Opinion to Mr. *Denn[is]* he swore the said Shakespear was a *Rascal*, with other defamatory Expressions, which gave Mr. *Lintott* a very ill Opinion of the said *Shakespear.* . . .
>
> Upon recollecting all these Circumstances, Mr. *Lintott* was entirely of Opinion, that he had been Mad for some Time, and I doubt not but this whole Narrative must sufficiently convince the World of the Excess of his Frenzy.

This résumé does scant justice to the piece, which is high-spirited, funny, and, though it makes Dennis ridiculous, free of bitterness. Pope was evidently proud of it, for he is said to have offered Addison a view of the manuscript, which, understandably, Addison is said to have refused: young men of twenty-five are inclined to (and can afford) behavior that men of forty-one, especially if committed as Addison was to playing the part of bellwether among a heterogeneous flock of Whig authors, feel compelled to reject. Our only solid evidence on either point is a somewhat puzzling letter from Steele to Lintot, dated 4 August 1713, which Dennis published in 1729 as part of a more than usually self-serving effort to persuade himself and the world that it was Pope, not he, who should bear responsibility for his having attacked *Cato*. Pope, he alleged, had persuaded Lintot to persuade *him* to write against the play because its success had aroused Pope's envy! And Pope's "Gratitude" to Dennis for "complying with his Request" (!) was the scurrilous *Narrative of Dr. Robert Norris,* which, when he had offered to show it to Addison, Addison had so far disapproved as to engage Steele to express his disapproval in the aforesaid letter:

> Mr. *Addison* desir'd me to tell you, that he wholly disapproves the Manner of Treating Mr. *Dennis* in a little Pamphlet, by way of Dr. *Norris*'s Account. When he thinks fit to take Notice of Mr. *Dennis*'s Objections to his Writings, he will do it in a Way Mr. *Dennis* shall have no just Reason to complain of. But when the Papers above-mentioned, were offer'd to be communicated to him, he said he could not, either in Honour or Conscience, be privy to such a Treatment, and was sorry to hear of it.

One must sympathize with Addison's wish to detach himself from Pope's prank. Still, the letter is an oddity and raises questions. On the one hand, why did not Dennis publish it while the episode was still fresh and his wrath at its fiercest? Or if he did not then possess it, how did he happen to come by it so much later? On the other hand, why did Addison not write the letter himself? Why, also, did he not address Dennis directly, which would have been the more natural and considerate thing to do? And why did he not, when Pope offered to communicate the manuscript, express his disapproval so forcibly as to decide Pope against publishing? Pope was exceptionally responsive to the judgments of friends; and even if he had not been it is difficult to believe he would have thought it in his interest at this time in his career, with Homer looming, to refuse an outright request from Addison. Does this add up, on Addison's part, to "something very like the behaviour of those who 'without sneering teach [or at least *permit*] the rest to sneer'?" as Pope's most distinguished biographer concluded a half century ago. Very possibly. Yet—where we know so little and where intentions count for so much—just possibly not. The significance of Steele's letter seems destined to remain a nagging mystery.

All that can be said certainly is that Addison and Pope continued, for a while, on easy terms and that from this time on Dennis fastened himself like a giant tick to Pope's poetry and reputation, feeding his revenge with a succession of scathing "Remarks" till well into old age.

CHAPTER 11

IN THE STUDIO AND ON THE TOWN

"I have thrown away three Dr. Swifts"

By the time the *Narrative of Dr. Robert Norris* appeared, Pope had been living for some months (whenever he was in London, which now was much of the time) in the house of the fashionable portrait painter Charles Jervas, in Cleveland Court, St. James's. Probably they had become acquainted through Steele or Addison, inasmuch as Jervas, a firm Whig from Dublin, was friendly with both, and later, when Addison and Pope became estranged, did what he could to reconcile them.

Pope, as we know, had shown since schooldays an interest in drawing, and in his *Pastorals* and *Windsor-Forest* had managed pictorial arrangements of landscape that have some claim to be considered forerunners of the picturesque vein in later eighteenth-century poetry. Jervas, in his youth a student of Kneller's, had studied subsequently in Paris and Rome, and now, at about thirty-eight, was in the first bloom of his fame. As early as 1709, possibly by way of reaching a friendly hand to a fellow Whig, Steele had acclaimed him in the *Tatler* "the last great painter Italy has sent us," going on to describe two of his current representations of reigning London beauties (one as a shepherdess, one as a country girl) in glowing terms. In 1711—pinnacle of socialite approbation—the duke of Marlborough had chosen him to paint his four daughters, Henrietta, Anne, Elizabeth, and Mary. After Kneller's death in 1722, Jervas would succeed as King's Painter to both George I and George II, though his uncertain touch in fetching off likenesses eventually displeased them. Kneller is reported to have said of him, having heard that he had set himself up with a coach-and-four, "Ah, mein Gott, if his horses draw no better than he does, he will never get to his journey's end"; and, further, with reference to Jervas's undisguised scorn of the decalogue: that he could not possibly break the *second* commandment, "because he cd. not make a Figure that was like anything in Heaven or in Earth."

Nevertheless, Jervas flourished. Not being a great painter—his best work, however, is far better than Kneller allowed, and tolerable portraits by him of Addison, Newton, Pope, and Swift have come down to us, along with one or two brilliant images of fashionable women—he was probably less impatient than he might otherwise have been with Pope's very minor talent, even if this was made somewhat more acceptable, as one imagines it was, by the awe with which the neophyte in painting usually views his master—even a second- or third-rate master. At any rate, a friendship grew, and Bridgewater House, Cleveland Court, St. James's, became Pope's usual residence when in London from 1713 till Jervas married in 1727.

On the learning side, Pope's exercises seem to have been largely confined to copying the work of others—the beginner's standard curriculum—with special attention apparently to the work of Jervas himself. But they did teach him to observe more sharply, or at least he believed they did. By August of 1713, he is excitedly writing Gay that he begins "to discover Beauties that were till now imperceptible to me":

Every Corner of an Eye, or Turn of a Nose or Ear, the smallest degree of Light or Shade on a Cheek, or in a dimple, have charms to distract me. I no longer look on Lord *Plausible* as ridiculous, for admiring a Lady's fine Tip of an Ear and pretty Elbow (as the *Plain-dealer* has it) but am in some danger even from the Ugly and Disagreeable, since they may have their retired beauties, in one Trait or other about 'em.

All the more reason for the novice's predictable discouragement—

You may guess in how uneasy a state I am, when every day the performances of others appear more beautiful and excellent, and my own more despicable. I have thrown away three Dr. *Swift's*, each of which was once my Vanity, two lady *Bridgwaters* [Elizabeth Churchill, third eldest of Marlborough's daughters], a Dutchess of *Montagu* [Mary Churchill, his youngest], besides half a dozen Earls, and one Knight of the Garter. I have crucify'd *Christ* over-again in effigie, and made a *Madona* as old as her mother St. *Anne*. Nay, what is yet more miraculous, I have rival'd St. *Luke* himself in Painting, and as 'tis said an Angel came and finish'd his Piece, so you would swear a Devil put the last hand to mine, 'tis so begrim'd and smutted.

26. Charles Jervas (1675–1739). Engraving by G. van der Gucht (1740) for an advertisement of the sale of Jervas's collections of "Pictures, Prints, Drawings, Bustos, Relievos," after his death. No other likeness is known. Wimsatt, ex. 1.

> What flatt'ring Scenes our wand'ring Fancy wrought,
> *Rome's* pompous Glories rising to our thought!
> *Epistle to Mr. Jervas*, 23–24.

Courtesy of the National Portrait Gallery, London.

Then he applies to himself the jest about Jervas just quoted, which one suspects has been a commonplace in every painter's atelier from Leonardo down:

> However[,] I comfort my self with a christian Reflection, that, I have not broken the Commandment, for my Pictures are not the likeness of any thing in heaven above, or in earth below, or in the waters under the earth.

In a letter to Caryll of the same week, he makes the observation noted in an earlier chapter: his hand is most successful in the drawing of friends and those he most esteems—"insomuch that my masterpieces have been one of Dr. Swift, and one of Mr. Betterton." If the Betterton portrait is the one today ascribed to Pope (p. 91)—itself a copy of Kneller's Betterton (p. 90)—it establishes beyond doubt that he was no Leonardo. The significant effects of his visual training show where one would expect to find them, in the later poems and notably in the Homer translations.

All the same, the months in London with Jervas seem to have been for Pope a most rewarding time. Mornings they spent in the studio. Jervas would perhaps be entertaining one of his aristocratic sitters or working alone toward the finished portrait, Pope watching and listening—possibly storing up in his memory some of those little quirks of spoiled femininity of which he would make such compelling use in his *Epistle to a Lady*; or even already formulating in verse what appear to be some early tentatives toward that gallery of lost souls—as, for instance, Artimesia:

> She wears no Colours (sign of Grace)
> On any Part except her Face;
> All white and black beside:
> Dauntless her Look, her Gesture proud,
> Her Voice theatrically loud,
> And masculine her Stride.
>
> (ll. 13–18)

Or Phryne, the professional call girl who has finally netted a rich husband—sufficient reminder of how little the ways of the world change:

> Phryne had Talents for Mankind,
> Open she was, and unconfin'd,
> Like some free Port of Trade:
> Merchants unloaded here their Freight,
> And Agents from each foreign State,
> Here first their Entry made.
>
> (ll. 1–8)

It is easy to imagine the women of whom these are caricatures on view in Jervas's studio, either as clients or (as the fashion then was) as visitors sampling his work finished and in progress.

Quieter and happier moments there were, of course. Looking back on these months from the austere Alps-on-Alps of the Homer undertaking, Pope remembers chiefly the delights of the interchange between painter and poet, each working in his own medium—Pope may at this time have been revising his *Temple of Fame*; he was certainly thinking seriously of and perhaps already working on the *Iliad*:

> Smit with the love of Sister-arts we came,
> And met congenial, mingling flame with flame;
> Like friendly colours found them both unite,
> And each from each contract new strength and light.
> How oft' in pleasing tasks we wear the day,
> While summer suns roll unperceiv'd away?
> How oft' our slowly-growing works impart,
> While images reflect from art to art?
> How oft' review; each finding like a friend
> Something to blame, and something to commend?
>
> (ll. 13–22)

These exchanges Pope remembers, and also the shared dream of travel. Till the end of his life, Pope longed to see Italy, to walk on "classic Ground." And with Jervas's Roman memories to kindle his imagination, and the collection of drawings Jervas had made there and the objects that like most artists on the European tour he had brought back with him, little wonder that Pope spends the most touching lines of his tribute to his mentor—one of a long line of passages and poems written explicitly to celebrate friends—in a fantasy of an Italian tour:

> Together o'er the *Alps* methinks we fly,
> Fir'd with ideas of fair *Italy*.
> With thee, on *Raphael*'s Monument I mourn,
> Or wait inspiring dreams at *Maro*'s Urn:
> With thee repose, where *Tully* once was laid,
> Or seek some ruin's formidable shade;
> While fancy brings the vanish'd piles to view,
> And builds imaginary *Rome* a-new.
> Here thy well-study'd Marbles fix our eye;
> A fading Fresco here demands a sigh:
> Each heav'nly piece unweary'd we compare,

> Match *Raphael*'s gràce, with thy lov'd *Guido*'s air,
> *Caracci*'s strength, *Correggio*'s softer line,
> *Paulo*'s free stroke, and *Titian*'s warmth divine.
>
> (ll. 25–38)

The months with Jervas at least gave Pope the current appreciative clichés.

"What an April weather in the mind!"

In the evenings, to relax from his pictorial and poetic labors, he sought out "conversation." During at least the first months of his stay in Cleveland Court, this was likely to include a visit to Button's, the coffee house that Addison had helped a former serving man establish in Russell Street, Covent Garden, just opposite the old Will's, which had by now lost much of its prestige as a literary center. Button's expressed admirably Addison's need for a congenial space, free of rowdy argument and warmed by the presence of a friendly and politically like-minded coterie. Regulars there—the little senate, as they were called after the success of *Cato* brought the analogy to mind—were Addison himself; Steele, who sometimes came on crutches because of his recurrent gout; an ill-starred cousin of Addison's named Eustace Budgell, who later on suffered from fits of insanity and eventually drowned himself; Ambrose Philips and Thomas Tickell, whom we have met; the minor poet and playwright John Hughes, Charles Johnson, another and lesser playwright, and three or four more. Droppers-in and occasional visitors included, besides Pope, Nicholas Rowe, in whose company Pope found exceptional pleasure ("He [grave]? Why, he would laugh all day long! He would do nothing else but laugh") and with whom he exchanged house visits during the late summer of this year. There was also Edward Young, a cultural amphibian from Oxford, who several years in the future would show himself not only a competent minor master of the satiric couplet but also an adept at the exclamatory, heavily segmented medium that passed with poets of the mid-century for blank verse. Pope's thumbnail sketch of a Buttonian he calls Umbra—which obviously antedates the ill feeling engendered later by the little senate—gives an ominous glimpse of a certain kind of toadyism endemic to associations of this stamp:

> Close to the best known Author, *Umbra* sits,
> The constant Index to all *Button*'s Wits.
> *Who's here?* cries *Umbra*: "Only *Johnson*"—*Oh!*

> *Your Slave*, and *exit*; but returns with *Rowe*,
> *Dear* Rowe, *let's sit and talk of Tragedies*:
> Not long, *Pope* enters, and to *Pope* he flies.
> Then up comes *Steele*; he turns upon his *Heel*,
> And in a Moment fastens upon *Steele*.
> But cries as soon, *Dear* Dick, *I must be gone*,
> *For, if I know his Tread, here's Addison.*
> Says *Addison* to *Steele*, 'Tis Time to go.
> *Pope* to the Closet steps aside with *Rowe*.
> Poor *Umbra*, left in this abandon'd Pickle,
> E'en sits him down, and writes to honest *T*[ickell].
>
> (ll. 1–14)

Sometimes Button's was the scene of more gratifying entertainments. In July, Pope heard lectures there by William Whiston, the astronomer-divine who had not long since been deprived of his Lucasian professorship at Cambridge, in which he had succeeded Newton, for imputed heresy, and was now by the kindness of Addison and Steele being provided a London platform for a series of subscription lectures. Whiston's speculations, always inclining to the oracular and prophetic, seem to have set Pope's mind awhirl. In his next letter to Caryll, echoes of the Psalmist's "What is man?" tumble together with fragments of Shakespeare and what may be reminiscences of Pascal and Montaigne in an extraordinary preview of the main themes of the *Essay on Man* nearly twenty years before the composition of that poem—all as newly charged with vitality by the increasing revelations of telescope and microscope (which Whiston had apparently described) as were the first chapters of Genesis in 1945 by the bomb dropped on Hiroshima. "Every hour of my life," he writes Caryll, "my mind is strangely divided."

> This minute, perhaps, I am above the stars, with a thousand systems round about me, looking forward into the vast abyss of eternity, and losing my whole comprehension in the boundless spaces of the extended Creation, in dialogues with Whiston and the astronomers; the next moment I am below all trifles, even grovelling with Tidcombe in the very center of nonsense. . . .
> Good God! what an Incongruous Animal is Man? how unsettled in his best part, his soul; and how changing and variable in his frame of body? The constancy of the one, shook by every notion, the temperature of the other, affected by every blast of wind. What an April weather in the mind! . . .
> What a bustle we make about passing our time, when all our

space is but a point? What aims and ambitions are crowded into this little instant of our life, which (as Shakespear finely words it) is *rounded with a sleep?* . . . Those animals whose circle of living and date of perception is limited to three or four hours, as the naturalists assure us, are yet as long-lived and possess as wide a scene of action as man, if we consider him with an eye to eternity. Who knows what plots, what achievements a mite may perform, in his kingdom of a grain of dust, within his life of some minutes? And of how much less consideration than even this, is the life of man in the sight of that God, who is from ever, and for ever!

Who that thinks in this train, but must see the world and its contemptible grandeurs lessen before him at every thought? 'Tis enough to make one remain stupified in a poise of inaction, void of all desires, of all designs, of all friendships. But we must return (thro' our very condition of being) to our narrow selves, and those things that affect ourselves. Our passions, our interests, flow in upon us, and unphilosophize us into mere mortals.

It is possibly in the interstices of such confessions that we should seek for some of the deeper impulses underlying Pope's career as satirist and perhaps much satire of the period. Emotions of transcendence, and the visions of human significance, even grandeur, that they traditionally have fostered, remain powerful enough in these sentences, as in the age itself, to invest all forms of pettiness with a compelling fascination, both the kinds that had come lately to recognition, like the mite, and the kinds that the human mind has always found distressing in its more exalted moods, like Pope and Tidcombe grovelling (the judgment is significant) in nonsense. Mixed, as here, with something like the scepticism of Erasmus and Montaigne, and indeed of Renaissance thought generally, in whose perception of reality the fool's cap is usually visible peering from beneath the crown or mitre (or, as in the case of Midas, to whose story Pope alludes pointedly in the *Epistle to Dr. Arbuthnot*, the ass's ears), wonder and exaltation make satire possible. So long as the passing show remains a passing show, apprehensible and appraisable from some accredited still point of vantage, it is difficult for certain types of mind *not* to write satire. On the other hand, when, as today, the passing show is perceived to be the only show in town, satire lacks a place to stand, and sulks and withers. This is essentially, perhaps, what Dryden had in mind in associating satire with the world of epic.

However this may be, there clearly runs through the age and through Pope's work in particular a need to qualify, or test, the elegance, dignity, propriety, formality, and "good sense" that constitute the norms of eighteenth-century decorum in conduct as well as literature against the sharpened edge of mockery, parody, derision. Students of social psychology in our own day assert that societies where the structures of social interchange are numerous and firm, where the propositions by which the society affects to guide itself are spacious, resonant, and perhaps a little pompous, and where the expectation of conformity is severe, develop a high degree of underlife, which, like the Roman saturnalia or Carnival at Shrovetide, serves the function of release. Hence, we may suppose, the importance of mock-heroic for a society still oriented "heroically" (even in its gilt carriages, costumes, and parades) toward responses of admiration, awe, and wonder. And hence too, on a lesser plane, the innumerable lampoons, libels, burlesques, blasphemies, and other *jeux d'esprit* flung off by men in elegant cloaks—pillars of the establishment—in coffee houses. A useful instance is the epigram probably written by Pope and Rowe, or possibly by Pope alone, *On a Lady who P—st at the Tragedy of Cato.* The genuine admiration with which Pope viewed Addison's play in its moral aspect is not in doubt. It is evidenced both in his prologue and in a private letter. The play allows us, he wrote Caryll, "that which Plato thought the greatest pleasure an exalted soul could be capable of, a view of virtue itself, great in person, colour, and action. The emotion which the mind will feel from this character and the sentiments of humanity which the distress of such a person as Cato will stir up in us, must necessarily fill an audience with so glorious a disposition, and so warm a love of virtue, that I question if any play has ever conduced so immediately to morals as this." Yet the very intensity of his official response provoked, or at any rate was able to accommodate, the reaction in the lines below, where we find an underlife indeed:

> While maudlin Whigs deplor'd their *Cato's* Fate,
> Still with dry Eyes the Tory *Celia* sate,
> But while her Pride forbids her Tears to flow,
> The gushing Waters find a Vent below:
> Tho' secret, yet with copious Grief she mourns,
> Like twenty River-Gods with all their Urns.
> Let others screw their Hypocritick Face,
> She shews her Grief in a sincerer Place;
> There Nature reigns, and Passion void of Art,
> For that Road leads directly to the Heart.

This duality of attitude, continuously demanded by a world in which titled coxcombs exacted deference and debauched kings and queens the most fulsome flatteries, shows itself with etched clarity in a theatrical incongruity that drew from Pope some further scurrilous verses inspired by the success of *Cato*. In the play, Cato has a daughter of spotless virtue named Marcia. On stage, the part was acted brilliantly by Anne Oldfield. Off stage, as everyone knew, Anne Oldfield was a beautiful and charming strumpet. (As a matter of fact, she was so far along in a pregnancy at the time that a midwife had to be stationed behind the scenes.) A young student of Oxford, as it happened, had fallen in love with the figure played by Oldfield and so attended all performances. Pope's epigram takes the problem of duality from there:

> You ask why Damon does the College seek?
> 'Tis because *Cato*'s not rehearsed this week;
> How long at Oxford then will Damon stay?
> Damon returns not till they *Cato* play:
> Oldfield wants Damon—when will he be at her?
> Oh, not till Oldfield shall be Cato's daughter:
> Why then, if I can guess what may ensue,
> When Cato's clapped, Damon will be so too.

Though the vehicle is tawdry enough, the tension between perceived reality and official image, present in all societies but magnified a hundredfold by the hierarchical character of Pope's, has rarely been summed up more vividly than in the mocking pun of line 8.

"Injudiciously in each"

More and more often, as autumn wore into winter, Pope found himself drawn away from the Whig group at Button's to the magnetic Toryism of Swift. From these encounters a new short-lived association came into being: the Scriblerus Club. Its members were Swift, Arbuthnot, Gay, Parnell, and Pope. Its original "founding" purpose, first broached by Pope in a humorous letter to the *Spectator* in 1712, was to issue a satirical monthly periodical entitled *The Works of the Unlearned* in imitation of an existing journal called *The Works of the Learned*. By January 1714, when the group of five seem to have begun meeting fairly regularly on successive Saturdays and were occasionally joined by Harley, still head of the Tory ministry, the club's project had altered to one more practical. They would draw up a mock biography of a certain Martinus Scriblerus, learned fool or

The Reverend *Thomas Parnell*. **D.D.** *Archdeacon of Clogher.*
From an Original Painting in the Possession of S.ʳ John Parnell.
To whom this Plate is Dedicated by his very humble Servant Thomas Davies.

27. Thomas Parnell (1672–1729).

> With softest Manners, gentlest Arts adorn'd.
> *Epistle to Robert Earl of Oxford and Mortimer*, 4.

"From an Original Painting in the possession of Sir John Parnell." Engraving dated 1771, but engraver unknown and artist unknown.

Courtesy of the Trustees of the British Museum.

lunatic philomath, who had "dipped in every art and science, but injudiciously in each." Through this fictive character, and through the adventures that could be attributed to him as well as the works he could be claimed to have written (including, of course, genuine current publications by dunces and learned pedants), they would have at their disposal an instrument flexible enough to be turned on almost any learned folly: astrology, alchemy (Steele, as we have seen, invested in alchemical experiments, as did Newton), scholastic physics and metaphysics (still taught at Oxford), millennialism, Cartesian vortices, medical quackeries, and, of course, the abuses of language in bad writing.

Some sense of the range of the plan and of the multiple contemporary absurdities it was intended to engage may be had from a letter of Arbuthnot's to Swift in the early summer of 1714, after Swift, despairing of the political situation, had gone back to Dublin. Martin, says Arbuthnot, speaking only of the medical aspects of the satire (on which as a physician he had been meditating but which he now hoped Swift would absorb into the narrative), might consider ascertaining the weight of ancient men by the size of the doses of physic they had downed; or he might publish a pathological map, on which "the Great diseases are like capital Citys, with their symptoms all like streets & suburbs, with the Roads that lead to other diseases." Or he might find

> an excellent subject of ridicule from some of the German physicians, who set up a sensitive soul as a sort of a first Minister to the rational. Helmont [1618–99] calls him Archaeus. Dolaeus [1651–1707] calls him Microcosmetor. He has under him several Genii, that reside in particular parts of the body, particularly Prince Cardimelech in the heart; Gasteronax in the stomach; & the plastic [i.e., procreative] Prince in the organs of Generation. I believe I could make you laugh at the explication of distempers from the wars & Allyances of those Princes, & how the first Minister gets the better of his Mistress anima rationalis.

Not that the group's meetings were self-consciously solemn. Much time went to wining and dining, much to batting about ideas for Martinus's works, much to jests and jollity. There were entertaining doggerel invitations to Harley to come join in the fun:

> Then come and take part in
> The Memoirs of Martin,
> Lay by your White staff & gray Habit,

> For trust us, friend Mortimer,
> Should you live years forty more
> Haec olim meminisse juvabit. ★

And there was lively conversation, of which sadly we have no record:

> Swift, Dr. Arbuthnot, and Pope were conversationalists of the
> first order, while Parnell and Gay were so witty, amiable, fun
> loving, and appreciative as to be highly prized for their company.
> . . . All, including the Earl of Oxford, loved the jesting spirit and
> were fertile in stratagems and jeux d'esprit.

One such *jeu*, if we may believe an anecdote preserved by Goldsmith, took place when Pope read aloud his revised *Rape of the Lock*, to be issued in early March 1714. Parnell, always keen for a jape, managed to keep the passage on Belinda's *toilette* sufficiently in mind to translate it into corrupt Latin. Not long after, when Pope was again reading the poem aloud, Parnell interrupted to assert that the whole *toilette* episode was stolen from an old monkish manuscript—producing in evidence the Latin he had just composed.

How much of the Club's project was actually carried through under these circumstances, no one today knows. Probably there was a skeleton outline of Scriblerus's adventures (perhaps there were even several different outlines), with here and there a chapter finished or partly finished in rough draft, and a huge sheaf of undeveloped hints for it and other chapters. In the end, as often, Pope became its literary executor by default or death of the other participants, and the *Memoirs of Scriblerus* that appeared in Volume 2 of his *Prose Works* in 1741, along with his and Bolingbroke's correspondence with Swift, bears unmistakably the marks of his oversight.

Readers sufficiently familiar with the intellectual ferment of the period will find in the *Memoirs* fascinating glimpses into the prehistory of many now established disciplines. But it is not for the *Memoirs* that the Scriblerus Club remains memorable. From the meetings of inventive minds that it facilitated and from its proposed biography of a fool, after incubations lasting many years in the varied personalities of the group, works as unlike each other as Swift's *Gulliver*, Pope's *Art of Sinking in Poetry* and his *Dunciads*, eventually were hatched.

★ "One day it will be useful to remember all this" (*Aeneid*, 1: 203).

CHAPTER 12

"HUMOUR, WIT, A NATIVE EASE AND GRACE"

"Still in Constraint your suff'ring Sex remains"

Not all of Pope's friendships in these years were formed with men. Whether or not there is significance in the circumstance that one of his earliest juvenile pieces deals with an episode in which a loyal wife is turned away by a credulous and tyrannical husband who accepts a friend's word that she is unfaithful, Pope had always a special sympathy for the lot of women. Over a number of years, beginning in this period, we find him interesting himself, perhaps with his usual excess of warmth, in the fortunes of Elizabeth Gage, sacrificed on the altar (as he saw it) by a negligent guardian who married her to a boorish husband, John Weston. Though the rights of the story are not entirely clear and both the Englefields and the Racketts, his half-sister's family, sided with the husband, Pope was able to enlist Caryll's assistance in befriending her and stuck resolutely to his own view, even to interrupting his stay with the Racketts several years afterward when he learned John Weston was coming to dinner. Though no doubt it was imprudent of him to ascribe all the wrong to one side in any affair of this kind, his position on assisting the unfortunate can hardly be faulted. "The business and study of the happy and easy," he writes Caryll, deploring his sister's unwillingness to lend Mrs. Weston support, "should be to divert and humour, as well as pity and comfort, the distressed."

From about this same period until her death by cancer in 1728, Pope took an equal interest in one of John Caryll's cousins, Anne Cope (again the victim of an unfortunate marriage to a "Rascall" —Caryll's term), to whom he sent £20 a year to enable her to subsist in France. Both interventions, it should be noted—since they were on behalf of married women—were in that age acts of courage as well as of compassion. Before the law, a husband's rights were all but absolute, and anyone interfering on a wife's behalf could find himself in trouble—which perhaps partly accounts for the stand taken by the Englefields and Racketts.

Like other men of his time, but possibly the more persistently because his shape and size left him in some doubt as to how women might respond to him, Pope developed early in life (apparently as a way of facilitating both approach and unscathed withdrawal if need be) an exaggerated teasing style of gallantry. Thus to a Mrs. Marriot of Sturston, Suffolk, about whom we know little except that she had a handsome young daughter named Betty, evidently in her mid-teens, he explains that he has been delayed in answering her letter by his rambling about a good deal, but chiefly by the arduousness of the task:

> ... I assure you I have every day Thought of writing to you. But, Madam, you ought to consider, that to reply to a very witty Epistle, such as yours, requires of necessity a good deal of Time. If I were so wise as to proceed cautiously, I should summon a Council of all the Witts at Button's Coffee house before I attempted it. In plain terms, Madam, I am but a lone man, and no match for you.

This having been satisfactorily established, he goes on to admit he has not in fact seen her letter at all:

> It came to Binfield when I was in Town, & my Politick Father detained it there to be a motive of drawing me into the Country. I have manfully resisted the Temptation these three weeks.

He has, however, dreamed repeatedly of the "many fine things" she must have said to him in the letter, so much so that when he dreamed the other night that "Mrs. Betty Marryot (like a Wagg as she is) snatched it out of my hand & offered me a Kiss to part with it," he refused—"though, in my conscience, she looked more amiable in that Dream than I had ever thought her awake; she was then handsomer than Herself, and before she was only handsomer than all others."

There is further adroit compliment to the Marriots of both generations, but this sufficiently gives the tone. Writing later to the younger Mrs. Marriot, he points out that he has chosen to write to her rather than to her mother partly because she can be counted on to spell better, having been at school more recently, but mainly because occupying herself with his letter will keep her from employing herself worse. For the conversation of men is dangerous; books either bore or kindle romantic feelings, trees set a bad example by clasping in embraces, birds and beasts make love, the sun warms the blood, and the moon melts it to yielding and melancholy.

> Therefore, I say once more, cast your Eyes upon Paper, and read only such Letters as I write, which convey no darts, no flames, but proceed from Innocence of soul, and simplicity of heart.

As for making a visit to Sturston, unthinkable! Only when his informant in that place lets him know that she has had the smallpox, or is heavily freckled or very pale, will he adventure himself in her company, dare to take her by the hand without gloves, or follow her into an arbor "without calling the company."

> This, Madam, is the top of my wishes, but how differently are our desires inclined! You sigh out in the ardour of your heart, Oh Playhouses, Parks, Opera's, Assemblies, *London*! I cry with rapture, Oh Woods, Gardens, Rookeries, Fishponds, Arbours, Mrs *Betty M[arriot]*!

Yet under the raillery of most of Pope's letters to women, of which these are characteristic examples, resides a deep concern. How sympathetically he understood the choices facing a marriageable young woman of good family may be seen in his *To a Young Lady, with the Works of Voiture*, which he seems to have been formulating in his mind by 1709 or 1710, when he was twenty-one or twenty-two, and which he published at twenty-four. Here, leading up to the portrait of "Paméla" (which also chronicles the fate of a young woman offered up to Baal in the name of Eros), a long verse paragraph summarizes the situation of women. Before marriage they are bound by the tyrannical "forms" of their society—"Custom, grown blind with Age"—designed to bring them virgins to the altar. After marriage, though it dissipates these particular restrictions, they become subject (by eighteenth-century legal statutes) to a yet greater tyrant, the husband:

> Still in Constraint your suff'ring Sex remains,
> Or bound in formal, or in real Chains.

(ll. 41–2)

No twentieth-century feminist could have said it better. In view of this, he urges the young lady not to quit

> the free Innocence of Life!
> For the dull Glory of a virtuous Wife!

(ll. 45–6)

and to withstand the lures of wealth and title that caused Paméla to mate herself with a fool. Yet if the fates rule against her and she is compelled or persuaded to marry, then only patience, cheerfulness, a sense of the ridiculous, an ability to laugh at herself, and all those other attributes that Pope crams into the words "good humor," will serve:

> Love, rais'd on Beauty, will like That decay,
> Our Hearts may bear its slender Chain a Day,
> As flow'ry Bands in Wantonness are worn;
> A Morning's Pleasure, and at Evening torn:
> *This* [good humor] binds in Ties more easie, yet more strong. . . .
>
> (ll. 63–67)

"The brightest Eyes of Britain"

The recipient of these prudent sentiments was, it seems probable, Teresa Blount, the dark-haired vivacious elder of the two sisters Pope sat between while writing his letter to Cromwell about giving his poems for maidenheads. By 1713–14, Pope had been acquainted with the sisters for some years. A riddling calculation in one of his letters to Teresa may mean that he had known them since 1707, Teresa some three months longer than Martha. Their mother, Martha Englefield, was a daughter of the Popes' Roman Catholic neighbor, the facetious Anthony Englefield of Whiteknights near Reading, under whose hospitable roof he may first have met them, or if not there, at Caryll's, whose goddaughter Martha was. Their father was Lyster Blount, of an ancient Roman Catholic family whose seat since 1490 had been Mapledurham Manor, sprawled comfortably along an elbow of the Thames about two miles northwest of Reading. He had died, in 1710, when Teresa was twenty-two, Martha only twenty. The estate, it turned out, was greatly impoverished. It had suffered sequestration by Parliament during the Commonwealth years, and the house—a stately somewhat rambling Tudor-brick affair built in the 1590s—had been besieged and sacked by Roundheads in 1643. Possibly Lyster Blount, to whom the house and manor descended from a cousin in 1671, was not the best of managers. He seems at any rate to have died unaware that the provisions made for his daughters in his will could not possibly be met—a circumstance that necessarily affected their prospects for making suitable marriages.

In a portrait of 1716 by Jervas, the two young women appear side by side, "caught in a pose of lively reaching arms" (to borrow a description from the distinguished historian of Pope's portraits), "in the hands of one a wreath and a ribbon, bearing the appropriate Jervas-like words: Martha Teresa Blount. Sic positae quoniam suaves." Appropriate Pope-like words, we should probably say instead. For the Latin is from the eclogues of his favorite Vergil—

> et vos, o lauri, carpam et te, proxima myrte,
> sic positae quoniam suaves miscetis odores

(2: 55–6)

> ["You also, O laurels, I shall seize on, and you,
> neighboring myrtle, for together you mix sweet odors"]—

and the iconographic implications are better suited to Pope's feelings than to those of Jervas, who knew the sisters only casually. The wreath in Teresa's hand is of myrtle, a plant sacred to Venus; while clasped in Martha's is the other plant of the eclogue lines, Apollo's plant, a sprig of laurel seemingly plucked from a laurel tree and shrub visible behind her. The emblems correspond admirably to distinctions of personality that Pope and others record. Martha was in mien and outlook strikingly virginal, as the name Parthenissa applied to her in another of Pope's poems to Teresa testifies, and thus may be thought to have a claim to the plant into which Daphne was metamorphosed when defending her chastity from Apollo. Martha seems to have been, in fact, something of a prude, either genuinely uncomfortable in the presence of the jokes and innuendoes she was often teased with, or convinced she should be, and hence much given to blushes that became her (Pope assured her) "the best of any Lady in England." She was blonde, blue-eyed, shy, modest, docile, tender-hearted, even-tempered, fearful of thunder, and a voracious reader, especially of French romances with their *sentiments délicats* and *tendresses soupirantes*.

Not so her sultrier dark-haired sister. Teresa, if Pope is to be believed, read nothing. Unlike Martha, she had been educated by nuns at the English Convent in Paris and, possibly in reaction, had grown a rebellious temper, a salty tongue, a love of the good things of this world (it is interesting and appropriate that the inventory taken of the furnishings of their bedrooms at the time of their father's death shows that Teresa's were valued at more than twice Martha's—containing many coverings of watered silk and, instead of Martha's dressing glass framed in sound English walnut, a dressing glass in a frame fashionably japanned) together with an insatiable

28. Teresa Blount as a child. Artist unknown.

By kind permission of J. J. Eyston, Mapledurham House. Photograph: Courtauld Institute of Art.

29. Martha Blount as a child. Artist unknown.

By kind permission of J. J. Eyston, Mapledurham House. Photograph:
Courtauld Institute of Art.

30. Martha and Teresa Blount. By Charles Jervas, *c.* 1716.

> Just when his fancy points your sprightly eyes,
>   Or sees the blush of soft *Parthenia* rise.
> *To a Young Lady, On her leaving the Town, after the Coronation,* 45–46.

By kind permission of J. J. Eyston, Mapledurham House. Photograph: Courtauld Institute of Art.

appetite for London gossip and some touches of that sexual pride which desirable young women take in the manpower of their attractions. From the age of sixteen, if not earlier, she had been the object of successive male raptures and had shown herself an accomplished coquette. It is by no means beyond possibility, in fact, that *To a Young Lady, with the Works of Voiture* was occasioned by some tender, or possibility, of marriage in the air between 1709 and 1712 which the families concerned chose finally not to embrace.

If the poem has personal overtones, we should expect them to be sidelong and disguised because well-bred young women of the period were trained not to countenance direct amorous addresses and therefore knew how to relish all the more the sly caressing compliment, the oblique confession. Some such confession is possibly implicit in the analogy between Pope's own poem, accompanied by a copy of Voiture, and Letter 7 in the Voiture collection, which was accompanied, when sent, by a copy of *Orlando Furioso*, the letter writer pointing out that the feelings of Ariosto's mad lover are intended to convey his own: "Il est, ce me semble, bien juste, puisque je lui donne moyen de vous entretenir de ses passions, qu'il vous raconte quelque chose de[s] miennes" ["It is altogether just, it seems to me, since I am enabling you to be entertained by *his* passions, that he should tell you something of mine"]. Thus what Voiture says about himself in his love letters is perhaps to be attributed by the young lady to Pope. Similar analogies lurk elsewhere. As Voiture "play'd the Trifle, Life, away" (line 12), sharing his heart with his mistress and his friend, his time with "the Muse, the Witty, and the Fair" (line 10), so it is Pope's wish (in an adaptation of a thought we have met with already in a letter to Cromwell) to imitate his spontaneity:

> Let the strict Life of graver Mortals be
> A long, exact, and serious Comedy,
> In ev'ry Scene some Moral let it teach,
> And, if it can, at once both Please and Preach:
> Let mine, an innocent gay Farce appear,
> And more Diverting still than Regular,
> Have Humour, Wit, a native Ease and Grace....
>
> (ll. 21–30)

That Pope, arch-moralist and indefatigable planner, could imagine himself settling for such a frolic (however much, like the rest of us, he might entertain it as a momentary dream) may be the finest compliment Teresa Blount ever received, though we may wonder if she appreciated it. The compliment at the close of the poem, on the other hand, she could hardly miss, which again appropriates the life and letters of Voiture to the present feelings of Mr. Pope:

> Now crown'd with Myrtle, on th' *Elysian* Coast,
> Amid those Lovers [the women he had addressed in his letters],
> joys his gentle Ghost,
> Pleas'd while with Smiles his happy Lines you view,
> And finds a fairer *Rambouillet* in you.
> The brightest Eyes of *France* inspir'd his Muse,
> The brightest Eyes of *Britain* now peruse, .
> And dead as living, 'tis our Author's Pride,
> Still to charm those who charm the World beside.
>
> (ll. 73–80)

It cannot have required more than a reasonable self-esteem on Teresa's part to understand that the "happy Lines" she had been given to view were as much those of Pope's poem as of Voiture's works; that the "Muse" inspired by the brightest eyes of France had also been inspired by some bright eyes in England (as had an English "Author's Pride"); and that Voiture's "Ghost" was not alone in finding her more enchanting than even "la princesse Julie," darling of the salonniers, whom Wycherley and Voiture had known at Angoulême.

"Favours to none, to all she Smiles extends"

All these experiences together, I am inclined to think—the exhilaration of making new friends, of living long periods in London, of growing in fame and prestige, of frequenting as a marked man the entertainments, studios, and drawing rooms where men and women of fashion gathered—above all, perhaps, the sensation of being in love, or believing himself to be in love, with one or both of the Blount sisters, though more probably with Teresa—all these experiences, I think, blossom indirectly in the masterpiece of Pope's youth, *The Rape of the Lock.* It is a happy poem from a happy interlude, the last such poem he will write.

The story of its composition is well known. John Caryll, something of a mediating figure among the Catholic gentry of the time, was sufficiently disturbed by an estrangement caused between the Petre and Fermor families when Robert Lord Petre cut a love-lock from the pretty head of Arabella Fermor that he asked Pope to write something to make a jest of the incident, "and laugh them together." Pope complied with the request by producing first the two-canto version of the poem entitled *The Rape of the Locke* (with an *e*), which he

Mᴿˢ ARABELLA FERMER
Heroine of Pope's
Rape of the Lock.

31. Arabella Fermor (1690?–1738). Undated painting. Artist unknown.

And soft Belinda's blush for ever glow.

Epistle to Jervas, 62.

Private Collection.

published along with his translation of Statius, *To a Young Lady, with the Works of Voiture*, and a few lesser pieces in a miscellany of Bernard Lintot's on 20 May 1712. Two years later, on March 4, he republished the poem separately, enlarged chiefly by the game of Ombre and the celestial machinery of sylphs and gnomes.

For contemporaries, the poem had attractions both general and particular. On the one hand, the broad satisfaction of seeing the style and folkways of one's own society brilliantly and affectionately recorded, however teasingly or mockingly; on the other, the specifically esthetic pleasure of recognizing the varied lights cast upon that record when set against familiar episodes from the world of heroic derring-do. Pope's parodies of epic convention in the poem are too numerous to mention, but the following may be singled out as especially effective in conflating battlefield with boudoir and parlor: the dream message from the gods and the arming of the champion (1: 23 ff., 121 ff.); the sacrifice to the gods and the "charge" to the troops (2: 35 ff., 73 ff.); the single combat at Ombre and the epic feast (3: 25 ff., 105 ff.); the journey to the underworld (4: 11 ff.); the general combat or mêlée, the intervention of the gods, and the apotheosis of the lock (5: 35 ff., 71 ff., 113 ff.) Those among Pope's first readers who were familiar with *Paradise Lost*, as many were after Addison's series of eighteen *Spectators* on the subject during 1711–12, would notice a particularly large number of mock parallels with that poem—for example, between the situation of the fallen angels at the opening of Milton's first book (not to mention the victims of the classical underworld and Shakespeare's Sycorax) and the punishments promised by Pope's Ariel to careless sylphs:

> Whatever Spirit, careless of his Charge,
> His Post neglects, or leaves the Fair at large,
> Shall feel sharp Vengeance soon o'ertake his Sins,
> Be stopt in *Vials*, or transfixt with *Pins*;
> Or plung'd in Lakes of bitter *Washes* lie,
> Or wedg'd whole ages in a *Bodkin's* Eye:
> *Gums* and *Pomatums* shall his Flight restrain,
> While clog'd he beats his silken Wings in vain;
> Or Alom-*Stypticks* with contracting Power
> Shrink his thin Essence like a rivell'd Flower.
> Or as *Ixion* fix'd, the Wretch shall feel
> The giddy Motion of the whirling Mill,
> In Fumes of burning Chocolate shall glow,
> And tremble at the Sea that froaths below!
>
> (2: 123–36)

As for the sylphs themselves, though borrowed from a little manual of contemporary Rosicrucian lore, they recreate in high-society terms the divine powers who watch over the fortunes of epic heroes. They are also, of course, a brilliant way of rendering, in their luminosity, fragility, and grace, the womanliness of an eighteenth-century belle:

> Transparent Forms, too fine for mortal Sight,
> Their fluid Bodies half dissolv'd in Light.
> Loose to the Wind their airy Garments flew,
> Thin glitt'ring Textures of the filmy Dew;
> Dipt in the richest Tincture of the Skies. . . .
>
> (2: 61–65)

The "action" of the poem has many layers. The surface layer is a narrative of Belinda's day: she awakes, dresses for conquest, and is conveyed down the Thames to Hampton Court palace:

> Fair Nymphs, and well-drest Youths around her shone,
> But ev'ry Eye was fix'd on her alone.
> On her white Breast a sparkling *Cross* she wore,
> Which *Jews* might kiss, and Infidels adore.
> Her lively Looks a sprightly Mind disclose,
> Quick as her Eyes, and as unfix'd as those;
> Favours to none, to all she Smiles extends,
> Oft she rejects but never once offends.
> Bright as the Sun, her Eyes the Gazers strike,
> And, like the Sun, they shine on all alike.
>
> (2: 5–14)

Once arrived, she bests the Baron at Ombre, exults with epic hubris and suffers an Aristotelian reversal in the loss of her lock, screams, collapses in a tantrum. Thereupon (after 1717, when this episode was first added) she receives good if somewhat patronizing advice from Clarissa but fails to take it, and finally participates in the general huffing and puffing of polite indignation (Pope's satire on the behavior of the families) which finds its only plausible termination in the poet's apotheosis (and Ovidian metamorphosis) of the lock, which suffers a second rape in being rapt away to become a constellation in the heavens:

> But trust the Muse—she saw it upward rise,
> Tho' mark'd by none but quick Poetic Eyes. . . .
> Not all the Tresses that fair Head can boast
> Shall draw such Envy as the Lock you lost.

> For after all the Murders of your Eye,
> When, after Millions slain, your self shall die;
> When those fair Suns shall sett, as sett they must,
> And all those Tresses shall be laid in Dust;
> *This Lock*, the Muse shall consecrate to Fame,
> And mid'st the Stars inscribe *Belinda*'s Name!
>
> (5: 123–4, 143–50)

The progress of Belinda's day is denoted, as here, by references to the sun, the last of these (5: 147) binding the pattern of her day to the pattern of human life. The epic analogue in the background is that of the hero's "day" in Homer: his aristeia or show of heroic virtue, his moment on the glory-wheel, before death, defeat, or failure overtake him, as they overtook Sarpedon. There are, of course, many other layers beneath the narrative of Belinda's day. In one of its dimensions, the poem is concerned with the elaborate rituals that once surrounded courtship: "She who scorns a man, must die a maid"—a fate that was not excitingly attractive in a world with no employments and very little respect for spinsters, even if, as in Roman Catholic families, they frequently became nuns. The game of Ombre (Spanish for "man"), with its aftermath, brings into delicate focus the pathos of this situation—Belinda's and, by extension, that of all the young belles in Pope's society, the Blount sisters included. For the choice she faces, perhaps not altogether consciously, like the one which Sarpedon in full consciousness sets forth to Glaucus, is a choice by which she loses in the long run, whichever way it goes. To be an eighteenth-century wife and the mere chattel of one's husband could be, as Pope had pointed out to Teresa in the poem addressed to her, a destiny even bleaker than to be a spinster lacking both social function and social status.

Hence the element of serious risk for those participating in the courtship rituals, a risk clearly reflected in the epic language used as Belinda

> *Burns* to encounter two adventrous Knights,
> At *Ombre* singly to decide their *Doom*. [Emphasis mine]
>
> (3: 26–27)

And hence, too, the erotic shimmer that hangs over the entire poem like a heat haze over a meadow on an April afternoon. For this dimension, Pope appropriates the teasing innuendo that plays throughout the contemporary *Tatler*, *Spectator*, and *Guardian* papers on women and women's dress. Nothing so flat-footed, to be sure, as the *Guardian*'s loving protest against hoop-petticoats: that they hurt men's shins, upset the wares in street-barrows, and, when a young lady falls down in one, make her look like "an overturned bell without a clapper." Nothing so broad as that. Instead, Ariel's instructions to his elite corps of Green Berets:

> To fifty chosen *Sylphs*, of special Note,
> We trust th' important Charge, the *Petticoat*:
> Oft have we known that sev'nfold Fence to fail,
> Tho' stiff with Hoops, and arm'd with Ribs of Whale.
> Form a strong Line about the Silver Bound,
> And guard the wide Circumference around.
>
> (2: 117–22)

The verses obviously glance at the inordinate value placed by this society on a nubile young woman's virginity beyond all other values, as the author of *Pamela* and *Clarissa Harlowe* will in due course rather vulgarly confirm. Yet Ariel's instructions invite our attention at the same time to a version of this entity less abstract (the enclosed garden, or paradise, to borrow terms that a long tradition stemming from the *Song of Songs* had established)—do they not? Or do they?

   Throughout the *Rape*, as here, Pope leaves much unstated, therefore the more vulnerable to interpretation. Betty, for instance, Belinda's maid, who helps her dress. How far should this scene summon up before us (along with the arming of the epic hero and the traditional emblem of *Vanitas*) the painter's favorite *topos*: "Venus, or Beauty, at her Toilet"—the Beauty in question being, or about to be, attired by her attendant(s) and thus making us ever more aware of the nakedness she covers? "Now awful Beauty puts on all its Arms." Or consider Shock, Belinda's dog. Is he to be considered merely the quintessential lady's lapdog? or is he the privileged voyeur? surrogate of the absent suitor? and his effect in the poem more like that of the cat in Manet's *Olympia* or the little canine in Carpaccio's *Courtesans on a Balcony*? But the point needs no laboring. Eroticism suffuses the poem like a sea, quite appropriately considering its subject, but the insistent delicacy of its strategy calls for a similar delicacy in the reader. As the foregoing samples all too sadly show, the moment one tries to capture the iridescent bubbles of its innuendo "in russet yeas and honest kersey noes," they explode to soapy water.

"Honour forbid!"

In a more inward way of viewing it, the poem's movement is psychological. We first see Belinda fancy-free—which is to say, surrounded by the protection of the sylphs (her maidenly coquetries?), whose continued power depends on her remaining fancy-free.

> Haste then ye Spirits! to your Charge repair;
> The flutt'ring Fan be *Zephyretta*'s Care;
> The Drops to thee, *Brillante*, we consign;
> And, *Momentilla*, let the Watch be thine;
> Do thou, *Crispissa*, tend her fav'rite Lock.
>
> (2: 111–15)

At the critical moment, however, the sylphs are helpless to save the lock because Belinda's affections have been preempted: an earthly lover lurks at her heart, and the lock of maidenliness is forfeit. As this is the purpose for which courtship rituals exist, it is prudish in Belinda to affect horror. Accordingly, Ariel the sylph is replaced by Umbriel the gnome—the gnomes being reincarnations of women who when alive were prudes. It is Umbriel who enters that dusky cavern of neuroses, the Cave of Spleen, one of Pope's most remarkable inventions:

> No cheerful Breeze this sullen Region knows,
> The dreadful *East* is all the Wind that blows.
> Here, in a Grotto, sheltred close from Air,
> And screen'd in Shades from Day's detested Glare,
> She [Spleen] sighs for ever on her pensive Bed,
> *Pain* at her Side, and *Megrim* at her Head. . . .
> Unnumber'd Throngs on ev'ry side are seen
> Of Bodies chang'd to various Forms by *Spleen*.
> Here living *Teapots* stand, one Arm held out,
> One bent; the Handle this, and that the Spout:
> A Pipkin there like *Homer*'s *Tripod* walks;
> Here sighs a Jar, and there a Goose-pye talks;
> Men prove with Child, as pow'rful Fancy works,
> And Maids turn'd Bottels, call aloud for Corks.
>
> (4: 19–24, 47–54)

Thence Umbriel returns with "furies" that are largely affectation to preside "on a sconce's height" over the fracas of the last canto, which affectation has precipitated. The nature of the affectation is made clear in Thalestris's speech, where we see on what a confusion of ideals rests the pose of outraged innocence she urges Belinda to adopt. "Honour," in her vocabulary, does not mean the reality of chastity, but the reputation, in the interest of which she is prepared to sacrifice the reality itself:

> *Honour* forbid! at whose unrival'd Shrine
> Ease, Pleasure, Virtue, All, our Sex resign.
>
> (4: 105–6)

Belinda's final couplet in this canto shows that she has learned Thalestris's lesson well:

> Oh hadst thou, Cruel! been content to seize
> . Hairs less in sight, or any Hairs but these!
>
> (4: 125–6)

A final web of implication takes us to the social criticism that glitters in the poem's background, where confusion of values is paramount on a broader scale. Pope represents the absurdities of the fashionable world with affection, and with an eye to the delicate beauties that its best graces unfold. We recognize too the shrewdness of his perception that the contemporary counterpart of the epic hero in his own society—in prestige, influence, authority, and tribute exacted—is the beautiful, marriageable, well-dowered young woman: the profitable "match." As Addison had once written with his usual condescension in the *Tatler*, in a preview of the spoils spread out upon Belinda's dressing table, woman is a beautiful romantic animal to be adorned by men "with Furs and Feathers, Pearls and Diamonds, Ores and Silks":

> The Lynx shall cast its Skin at her Feet to make her a Tippet; the Peacock, Parrot, and Swan, shall pay Contributions to her Muff; the Seas shall be searched for Shells, and the Rocks for Gems; and every Part of Nature furnish out its Share towards the Embellishment of a Creature that is the most consummate Work of it.

All this Pope contemplates with sympathy. But he never allows us to forget that in such a world ethical judgments have reached a sad disarray. Hearts and necklaces, lapdogs and lovers, statesmanship and tea, queens and Indian screens, the hunger of jurymen and justice, Bibles and billets-doux: his verse entangles the trifling and the serious to reflect a similar entanglement in this society's mind. And it is just here, in the presentation of moral muddle, that the mock-heroic structure proves itself invaluable. By juxtaposing the contemporary with the heroic, the poet can emphasize both the epic proportions to which this society has magnified its trifles (such as the estrangement of families over a lock of hair) and also their real triviality. Furthermore, by the contrast between the social ephemera that his verse licks up as it flows along—watches, sedan chairs, cosmetics, curling irons, men, monkeys, parrots, snuff boxes, bodkins—and the quite

32. Teresa Blount (1688–1759). By Sir Godfrey Kneller, *c.* 1712.

Trust not too much your now resistless Charms.
To a Young Lady, with the Works of Voiture, 59.

By kind permission of Lucy Bredin.

different world of heroic activity evoked through the epic parodies and the high style, he can remind us of the inexorable conditions of life, death, and self-giving that not even the most glittering civilization can afford to ignore.

Pope never knew Arabella Fermor. It is not even clear that he had ever seen her. What *is* clear, in the picture of the two Blounts mentioned earlier, is that down the fine curve of Teresa's throat, on the side turned toward us, and lying like a "hairy Sprindge" on her white shoulder, is a most beautifully displayed dark curl. What is equally clear, in my view, is that the poem's deep currents of affection and sexual attraction, not to mention its finely observed particulars both teasing and admiring, owe as much to its author's personal experience of the sparkling young women at Mapledurham as to his imagination.

CHAPTER 13

INSURRECTIONS LARGE AND SMALL

"God bless the King!"

On Sunday, 1 August 1714, the *Rape of the Lock* having just gone into its third edition, Queen Anne died. Though the event was not unexpected (she had been failing in health for some years and dangerously ill as recently as the preceding December), it sent shock waves through Britain that continued to be felt, sometimes sharply, for the next thirty years. Only in 1746, when a few companies of brave but indecisive Scotsmen, as poorly armed as led, gathered on Culloden Moor under the banner of Prince Charles Edward, the Young Pretender, and were cut down by the crossfire of the Duke of Cumberland's disciplined Hanoverians, did the last hope of a second Stuart Restoration wither. Until then, that hope, or terror, depending on the point of view, had life in it.

The Jacobite movement has sometimes been dismissed as the treasonable work of a few ambitious reactionaries, romantic loyalists, and implacable soreheads. There is truth in this conception, but it is essentially naive. Treasonable the movement certainly was, yet hardly more so than the actions of many a government-in-exile with home support from an active underground. The world has seen numbers of these since, to which honorable men have not hesitated to apply honorable names, often with reason. In their own view, supporters of the two Pretenders decidedly had honor on their side. Many felt that they were helping to rectify a great wrong done in the disinheritance of the Stuart kings in 1688—a wrong some held to be a sin. And though self-interest weighed as heavily in Jacobite deliberations as in human affairs generally (and in certain individuals, perhaps almost exclusively), other claims made themselves felt. What if Parliament *had* enacted guarantees establishing the succession in a foreign house? Those were the laws of men. Much of the stubborn strength of the Jacobite resistance sprang precisely from the conviction that there were other laws to which men and women must be left free to respond. We can see now, though doubtless no one at the time would have expressed it in these terms, that deep down in the recesses of the Jacobite–Hanoverian struggle issues were dimly stirring that still vex us. How avoid a tyranny of the majority? Or, for that matter, the tyranny of a minority? How respect civil disobedience, conscientious objection, and religious commitment without inviting anarchy? And, of course, the issue that underlies all others: how far can human beings live together bearably at all if, as for Creon in Sophocles' *Antigone*, the sole arbiter of moral law is the power of the state.

In August 1714, naturally enough, the burning question was homelier: Who should now rule? Whigs, almost to a man, supported the Hanoverian succession passionately, though some among their leaders buttered their bread on both sides and others kept open an escape route by corresponding with the enemy. Tories, on the other hand, to their cost, divided. One wing warmly favored the Hanoverians. Another, more conservative, containing many but not all the Roman Catholics, was Jacobite in varying degrees. The vast majority fell between. Ardent for the English Church, they were resolute against James's Catholicism, which he had refused to abandon; yet many were not insensitive to the dilemma summed up in a Jacobite epigram of the day:

> God bless the King!—I mean the Faith's Defender;
> God bless—no Harm in blessing!—the Pretender.
> Who that Pretender is, and who that King,
> God bless us all! is quite another thing.

A degree of comparative uncertainty as to how some segments of the Tory population would actually respond to the arrival of a disciplined, well-armed, well-publicized invasion force led by one whose *de jure* title could be argued to be at least as compelling as his German rival's was destined to keep Whitehall and its European intelligence network on the *qui vive* through the remainder of Pope's lifetime. As Robert Walpole later warned the Commons, a successful insurrection would take no great effort:

> Five or six thousand men may be embarked in such a small number of ships, and so speedily, that it is impossible to guard against it by means of our fleet. Such a number may be landed in some part of the island, before we can hear of their embarkation: and if such a

number were landed, with the Pretender at their head, there is no question that they would meet with many, especially the meaner sort, to join them. In such a case, we could not march our whole army against those invaders and their assistants; because, if we should draw all our regular forces away from the other parts of the Kingdom, the disaffected would rise in every county so left destitute of regular troops.

At the time of this address in the late 1730s, Walpole may have been exaggerating the ease of invasion to justify larger appropriations for the secret service. Still, his terms make very clear the nature of the powder keg on which, at some periods, and particularly during the first decade after Anne's death, the legally constituted government sat. The "meaner sort," as he observes, could scarcely be counted on. Rarely political in a committed sense, though capable of fanatical enthusiasms, they constituted the large underclass whose old men had dreamed dreams and whose young men had seen visions at the time of the Civil Wars, only to be deprived at the Restoration and then shut out altogether by a so-called Glorious Revolution, which replaced the divine right of kings with the divine right of property. For a long time now, they had supplied the army with its foot soldiers and the navy with its able-bodied seamen, too often by a process of forced draft that amounted to abduction. From their ranks came the landlord's farm labor, the urban aristocrat's footmen, draymen and haulers for the city merchant, the tapsters and ostlers of the country inn, Thames bargemen and Tyne keelers, not to mention the North Country miners, who with a little luck could earn five pence a day. To their ranks belonged also a majority of the thieves on the roads, the derelicts outside the alehouse (later it would be the gin shop), and the desperate young women impelled to abandon their newborn infants in the ditches and backstreets of London: hardly surprising when one considers that the punishment for bearing an illegitimate child, who might become a charge upon the rates, was to be stripped to the waist and whipped until bloody. It was "Wretches" of this class, as Pope had put it in his *Rape*, who were likeliest to "hang that Jurymen may Dine," and it was their bodies that appeared most abundantly among the monstrous annual harvests of the Tyburn tree. As Walpole knew, they were unreliable, and for cause.

As for those he calls the "disaffected," they were noblemen and squires either Jacobite by long conviction or nudged in that direction by personal discontents. By 1714–15, the northern counties contained a fair number of such persons. The Newcastle coal trade, from which many a landowner had become accustomed to piece out his revenues, was in the doldrums; harvests had lately been mediocre to poor; the land tax still imposed its burden, had done so for years. As a consequence many of the smaller estates were now heavily mortgaged, in some instances even taken over by their creditors. Further to fan resentment, the advantageous marriage, one of the best established avenues toward rehabilitating or enhancing capital in land, was becoming more difficult to arrange, at least in the landowner's perception of it, because of competition from the sons and daughters of the urban moneymen, who had made fortunes in the recent wars. If one were Roman Catholic, escape from financial straits was blocked in yet another way: there was no hope of recouping the family fortunes through the perquisites that accompanied civic office or government sinecure. Thus grounds for restlessness existed among parts of the propertied group as well.

In the event, however, Tory fears of popery and its links with continental despotisms overcame all else. Slogging down through Cumberland and Westmorland in the fall of the following year, the largely impromptu forces of the first serious Jacobite effort to contest the new king's control met with a generally chilly reception. The government had been kept informed of the rebels' plans by its agents and had taken the necessary steps, civil as well as military. Hence despite a few initial successes, the support drawn was scattered, there was no general rising, and most of the men of substance who came in were known papists. This was fatal. Roman Catholics, as the most recent study of these events reminds us, were all very well as "stiffening" in a visibly Protestant force, but by themselves "the kiss of death." Before the end of November, the wavering thrust into England had been broken by the government's battalions at Preston in Lancashire. Its Scots counterpart, which the Pretender himself joined (as he did most other things) only after much shilly-shallying and when it was far too late, succumbed the following spring.

Where Pope himself stood on these matters can probably never be confidently known. Roman Catholics did not wear their hearts on their sleeves in such times and were circumspect in their letters, never more so than if they had Stuart sympathies. From a sentence in a letter to Gay of late September 1714, we might take it that Pope was among those who briefly expected a Stuart intervention immediately following the queen's death. "The late universal Concern in publick affairs," he writes, recapitulating for his friend what has been happening in England during his absence on embassy to Hanover with Lord Clarendon, "threw us all into a hurry of Spirits; even I who am

33. James Francis Edward Stuart, the Old Pretender (1688–1766). Studio of A. S. Belle, *c.* 1712.

"Mrs. [Nelson] expects the Pretender at her Lodgings, by Saturday sennight."
Pope (jesting) to Teresa and Martha Blount, 23 July 1715.

Courtesy of the National Portrait Gallery, London.

more a Philosopher than to expect any thing from any Reign, was born[e] away with the current, and full of the expectation of the Successor." The studied obliquity of the reference, which will fit either "Successor," is possibly revealing.

On the other hand, some ten months later, when in the guise of a London newsmonger he entertains Teresa Blount with the preparations being made in London against the Pretender, including establishment of a full military encampment in Hyde Park, his facetious tone seems calculated to explode the whole possibility of invasion as chimerical. Though your well-known "Barbarity," he tells his correspondent, referring evidently to her firmness in withstanding amorous advances, may now be gratified to see "the pretty windings of the Thames about *Mapledurham*, staind with the blood of Men," there is one aspect of warfare of which you should seriously bethink yourself, those "many Rapes committed, or to be committed, upon those unfortunate Women that delight in War." An eventuality, he adds, so irresistible to contemplation that—"God forgive me"—he would buy himself a regiment, if he could, to have part in it: "for your sake—and Mrs Patty's [i.e., Martha's]—& some others, whom I have cause to fear no fair Means will prevail upon."

As for other London tidbits, it is confidently being asserted that their Catholic mutual friend, Mrs. Nelson of Binfield, presently in town, "expects the Pretender at her Lodgings, by Saturday sennight"—and (apparently with the thought of becoming to the Pretender what the most pious of the Sun King's mistresses was to him) "has bought a Picture of Madame Maintenon to sett her features by." London gossip maintains also that the Honorable Thomas Gage's fine Flanders mares have been seized—a penalty to which Roman Catholics were subject in times of crisis. Whereupon, say the latest advices,

> he seem'd more than ordinarily disturbd for some hours, sent for his Ghostly father, & resolvd to bear his Loss like a Christian. Till about the hours of seven or eight, the Coaches & Horses of several of the Nobility passing by his Window towards Hyde park [scene of the daily early-evening promenade of fine gentlemen and ladies in their equipages], he could no longer endure the disapointment, but instantly went out, took the Oathe of Abjuration, & recover'd his dear Horses which carryd him in triumph to the Ring.

It is currently reported that, "having renouncd the Errors of the Romish Communion," he is to be made Groom Porter in the new government, "& that Alex. Pope, Gent. being ready to do the same, will be chosen City-Poet."

All this, of course, is Pope frolicking. Our best clue to his soberer thoughts on Jacobite agitation lies probably in his deep dislike of all forms of blind partisanship, whether civil or religious. Writing to Caryll soon after the queen's death, when the Catholic minority were understandably disquieted about what the future held for them in view of the incoming regime's emphatic Protestantism and the general inclination to lay all Jacobite dissidence at their door, he goes out of his way to commend conciliation:

> Common charity of man to man, and universal good will to all, are the points I have most at heart; and I am sure those are not to be broken for the sake of any governors or government ... If all Whigs and all Tories had the spirit of one Roman Catholic that I know, it would be well for all Roman Catholics; and if all Roman Catholics had ever had that spirit, it had been well for all others; and we had never been charged with so wicked a spirit as that of persecution.

A year later, with Sir William Trumbull, to whom he perhaps expresses himself more freely about the rebellion than to Caryll because of the Caryll family's Jacobite history, he is extremely explicit:

> Quiet in the state, ... like charity in religion, is too much the perfection and happiness of either, to be broken or violated on any pretence or prospect whatsoever: Fire and sword, and fire and faggot are equally my aversion. I can pray for opposite parties, and for opposite religions, with great sincerity.

Whenever he and Jervas, he adds, at whose house he is again staying, drink Sir William's health, it is "a truly Catholick health; which far excels the poor narrow-spirited, ridiculous healths now in fashion" to this church or that. "Whatever our teachers may say, they must give us leave at least to *wish* generously."

That these statements represent Pope's settled convictions is strongly confirmed by a letter in which his Devonshire friend, Edward Blount (distant kin to the Blounts of Mapledurham) reflects on the foolhardiness of the 1715 rising, at that moment just crushed:

> What a dismal scene has there been open'd in the North? what ruin have those unfortunate rash gentlemen drawn upon themselves and their miserable followers, and perchance upon many others too, who upon no account would be their followers? ... I don't remember you and I ever used to trouble our selves about politicks,

but when any matter happen'd to fall into our discourse, we us'd to condemn all undertakings that tended towards the disturbing the peace and quiet of our country, as contrary to the notions we had of morality and religion, which oblige us on no pretence whatsoever to violate the laws of charity: how many lives have there been lost in hot blood [in the rebellion], and how many more are there like to be taken off in cold [in reprisals at the gallows and scaffold]?

We may reasonably conclude, therefore, that Pope was in essentials simply a Roman Catholic nonjuror. A nonjuror capable of deep sympathy with friends more Jacobite than he; capable too, it may be, of secret hopes when an invasion loomed; and obviously affronted by the indiscriminate legalized oppression of his kind; yet—for whatever reasons, expedient or principled—stoutly opposed to the kind of agitation that might bring on social unrest and civil war. Admittedly, his imagination found nothing to kindle it in the royal house of Hanover, except to satire, and here or there in the early poems his language reflects an active distaste for the Hanoverian succession. But one did not need to be a Jacobite for that. He took little stock in kings generally, and his references to the Stuart line, apart from Anne, are either noncommittal or quite uncomplimentary. The Whig effort to make all Catholics and the entire Tory party scapegoats after the '15 naturally struck him as unjust. "If the whole religious business of mankind," he wrote to Caryll in the spring of 1716, when the extent of the Whig revenge was becoming visible (Caryll, evidently, had just incurred or was expecting to incur some form of penalty for belonging to a family with a history of Jacobite service), "be included in resignation to our Maker, and charity to our fellow creatures; there are now some people, who give us the opportunity of affording as bright an example in practising the one, as themselves have given an infamous instance of the violation of the other." Even so, the right response is not resentment, but doing what one can to contain the damage:

> The misfortunes of private families, the misunderstandings of people whom distresses make suspicious [i.e., fear of the informer], the coldness of relations whom change of religion may disunite [pressure on Roman Catholic heirs to convert to save the family lands from sequestration or confiscation at such times was of course intense], or the necessities of half-ruined estates render unkind to each other,—these at least may be softened some degree, by a general well-managed humanity among ourselves.... I would gladly relieve any distressed, conscientious French [i.e.,

Huguenot Protestant] refugee at this instant: what must my concern then be, when I perceive so many anxieties just now springing in those hearts which I have desired a place in, and such clouds of melancholy rising on those faces I have so long looked upon with affection?

These are hardly the remarks of a man who believes that insurrection pays.

Essentially his own publisher

While these events were taking place in the political world around him, Pope was hard at work on the project that his friend Trumbull had long ago proposed: a translation of the entire *Iliad*. He had publicized this undertaking in late 1713, still basking in the glow of Whig approval for his Prologue to *Cato* and of Tory approval for his poem on the Peace. With the friends he now enjoyed in high places as well—Oxford and Bolingbroke in the ministry; Swift intimately involved in their counsels, already made dean of St. Patrick's and expected to go higher; Arbuthnot, whose profession and lodgings in St. James's gave him frequent access to the queen; not to mention such eminent patrons and pundits as the Whig earl of Halifax and the Tory duke of Buckinghamshire, whom he had probably known since the days when they first read his *Pastorals* in manuscript—the moment must have seemed particularly auspicious for the kind of publishing venture he had planned.

It was to be a subscription book, issued one volume per year over six years at a guinea a volume. The initial down payment was set at two guineas to defray the translator's out-of-pocket expense in collecting "the several Editions, Cricks and Commentators, which are very numerous upon this Author"; after which one guinea was due on delivery of each successive volume except the last, which would be free. In return for this investment, subscribers were to receive their six volumes in a large quarto format, "printed . . . on the finest Paper, and on a Letter new Cast on purpose, with Ornaments and initial Letters engraven on Copper." There would be four books of the poem to each volume, "with Notes to each Book."

Subscription editions had appeared before—Dryden's translation of Vergil, for instance, in 1697—but never one like this. Instead of a single large volume in folio, six of a more manageable size. Instead of one payment, wholly in advance with no recourse, five payments spread over five years, offering the opportunity (from the purchaser's point of view) of canceling later volumes if the first displeased and (from the translator's) of fixing a larger total charge. These were not the only innovations. Quality of paper and design of type were to be such as the translator chose, and the engraved initials and headpieces and tailpieces were to be produced "in such manner and by such graver" as he should determine. By a further revolutionary step taken in the work itself, Pope transformed the engraved printer's headpieces, traditional ornaments of quality books, into illustrations of the Homeric text, thus gathering letterpress and ornament toward a tighter unity of effect. At the same time, no doubt influenced by Tonson's editions of the Latin classics, where in contrast to contemporary practice capital letters appear only at the opening of sentences and proper names, and italic letters do not appear at all, he came down firmly for typographical simplicity—a preference about which he was often to vacillate before espousing it again definitively in the 1743 editions of the *Essay on Man* and *Dunciad*. By such ceaseless experimentation and keen attention to the appearance of his work in print throughout a long career, a notable authority has recently pointed out, Pope "changed the face of printed English."

Still, the most remarkable of his new departures lay in the reward reserved to the author—in this case, the translator. By the contract signed with Lintot on 23 March 1714, he was to receive two hundred guineas per volume and, in addition, *gratis*, seven hundred and fifty copies printed in the manner above described for distribution to his subscribers. The subscribers' payments thus belonged to the translator, unencumbered. In return, Lintot held the copyright and might publish whatever editions of the translation in whatever formats he pleased (the quarto size excepted), but not on royal paper with engravings, and not sooner than a month after the quarto had appeared. For the subscribers' edition, in other words, Pope became essentially his own publisher, hiring Lintot by his other concessions to serve as agent.

That Lintot acceded to these terms is a measure either of his determination to rival Tonson or of his confidence in Pope (of whose *Rape* he had just sold three thousand copies in four days), or of both. At any rate, he grandly overestimated the market for his own folio edition, which was to follow Pope's quarto—largely, one suspects, because he failed to appreciate the extent to which subscriptions to the quarto might cream off that part of the reading public having both an interest in Homer and the price of an expensive book. Not that he lost money. An edition in annual installments significantly reduced the working capital required of him and enabled the proceeds of each volume to meet the expense of the next. After meeting his costs for Pope's subscribers' quarto, his folio edition still brought him a profit of £600 to £700, perhaps as much as £25,000 to £30,000 in today's inflated currency, and his later duodecimo editions did handsomely. His profit on the folio was small, however, compared to Pope's on the quarto, which by the most conservative estimates one can make amounted to upwards of £4000—in today's money, though such comparisons are always misleading, probably £80,000 to £100,000.

For all its magnitude, the reward was well earned. Subscribers to the Homer "did not fall out of heaven." Pope or one of his friends had to obtain them. A Homeric audience required to be "found," almost, in a sense, "created"; and this was uphill work. In mid-December 1713, some ten weeks after the first announcement, we find Pope trying to assure himself and Caryll that a disappointment in the subscription will not occasion him "any great mortification." This is surely evidence that the subscription list had been slow in growing, particularly when taken in conjunction with Swift's optimistic promise in the queen's own antechamber, six weeks before, that he would himself obtain a thousand subscription guineas for the new translator. Gradually, nevertheless, Pope's own tireless efforts combined with those of his warmest friends made headway. By early 1714, he was able to tell Caryll that he now believes he will be "warmly supported on all sides," which presumably means by both political parties. By March he can add that "mortification" will be his only if he fails in the translation, for future times will learn from his subscription list that even if he was not a good poet he was "the happiest . . . in the good opinion of such a number of persons." And by April he can joke about it.

> I find subscribing much superior to writing [he tells Caryll], and there are a sort of little epigrams I more especially delight in, after the manner of rondeaus, which begin and end all in the same words; viz. Received—and A: Pope. These epigrams end smartly, and are each of 'em tagged with two guineas.

We may notice, all the same, that his preliminary list of subscribers, intended for publication in February to attract the laggards by the number and eminence of its names, did not actually appear till May. Even then, much remained to do. All but a handful of Pope's letters during the next twelvemonth before Volume 1 was released to subscribers on 6 June 1715 bear witness to intense subscription activity; and long after 1715, as each subsequent volume appeared, he was busy retrieving copies from the rare defaulter, supplying back copies to subscribers who came into the program late, and discharging other obligations of this kind.

Yet all such labor, however arduous, was merely administrative. The staggering task lay in the translation itself. Here were some sixteen thousand lines of Greek to be confronted, roughly twenty-seven hundred for each of his volumes. Each verse, each image, each episode required careful study in the commentaries and earlier translations, not forgetting what Vergil, Tasso, and Milton, Homer's greatest successors in the epic form, who often borrowed from him, might have made of one of his effects or hints. Next would come restructuring. He would have to identify the contribution of any given feature, first to its several contexts of line, paragraph, or book, and then to that distinctive configuration of attributes we call the *Iliad*, asking himself continuously how far and by what means he might hope to capture some equivalence or shadow of the integrity of the original in his version. Finally—though all three stages would necessarily be present to the mind simultaneously—he would face the problem (always the most vexing because never more than minimally soluble in translating poetry from one language, let alone one epoch, to another) of inventing an idiom that could mediate effectively between disparate worlds—in his own case, between an elevated style held to be required by the epic genre and the deeds of heroes on the one hand, and the settled speech habits, cultural expectations, and social mores of current readers on the other.

Little wonder that the scope and complexity of the undertaking he had got himself into gave him nightmares. He dreamed repeatedly, often years after the job was finished, of being engaged on a long journey (his Alps simile in the *Essay on Criticism* must at times have seemed prophetic), "puzzled which way to take" and frightened lest it never end. The vast quantity of learned lumber besetting the path of a Homer translator oppressed him: "Eustathius," Spondanus "with all his Auxiliaries," "Dacier's three Volumes, Barnes's two, Valterie's three, Cuperus half in Greek, Leo Allatius three parts in Greek, Scaliger, Macrobius, & (worse than 'em all) Aulus Gellius." Confronted with these, and with the scores on scores of other authorities cited in his informative notes, he was pained by the poverty of his personal resources. "You are a Generous Author," he wrote to Parnell, who had lent him a hand with some of the Greek commentators while Volume 1 was in progress, "I a Hackney Scribler, You are a Grecian & bred at a University, I a poor Englishman of my own Educating." The infinitude of detail to be attended to brought moments at first when he imagined the translation would cure him of poetry for ever and hardly cared if it should, when he wished that somebody would "hang" him, and when he surmised from his perpetual headaches that he might be fated to imitate Homer in only one way—"his blindness."

Yet the stamina that genius seems always able to lend its beneficiaries somehow saw him through. Stamina, yes; but also (as he told Spence) a want of money, even to buy books. We do not know how his father's fortune fared after his retirement in 1688. Conceivably not well, since we know that some part of it was invested in the French national debt, and that at least once, what with Louis XIV's wars and other extravagances, the rate of return was substantially reduced. Equally plausible is the possibility that Pope simply found it embarrassing after he was grown up to be beholden to his parent for cash outlays. At any rate, money played its part, as it does for most of us, and so did that passionate aversion to dependence which speaks so often in Pope's work, from the prayer that closes *The Temple of Fame* (1715)—

> Oh! if the Muse must flatter lawless Sway,
> And follow still where Fortune leads the way; . . .
> Then teach me, Heaven! to scorn the guilty Bays—
> (ll. 517–18, 521)

to the amusing *Dunciad* lines (1728) that took on new meaning when applied in 1743 to the Hanoverian laureate, Colley Cibber:

> Like the vile straw that's blown about the streets
> The needy Poet sticks to all he meets,
> Coach'd, carted, trod upon, now loose, now fast,
> In the Dog's tail his progress ends at last.
> (3: 291–94)

The equivalent of "the Dog's tail" for the needy poet remains unspecified but guessable. Pope was resolved *not* to be a needy poet. And though the hierarchical society he lived in was heavily fueled by flatteries, a department in which he could hold his witty own as often as he wished, he was equally resolved it should be only when he wished:

> "Praise undeserv'd is scandal in disguise":
> Well may he blush, who gives it, or receives;
> And when I flatter, let my dirty leaves
> (Like Journals, Odes, and such forgotten things

As Eusden, Philips, Settle, writ of Kings)
Cloath spice, line trunks, or flutt'ring in a row,
Befringe the rails of Bedlam and Sohoe.

(Epistle to Augustus, 413–19)

An incident of this early period gives so clear a picture of the trials an aspiring poet faced in that society and of the rituals of obeisance Pope rebelled against that it is worth recording. When he was well started on the translation, the earl of Halifax asked him to his house to read what he had done, assembling for the occasion Addison, Congreve, Garth, and possibly others of the Whig literary establishment. As Pope read,

> in four or five places Lord Halifax stopped me very civilly, and with a speech each time much of the same kind: "I beg your pardon, Mr. Pope, but there is something in that passage that does not quite please me. Be so good as to mark the place and consider it a little at your leisure. I'm sure you can give it a better turn."

Afterward, while being conveyed to Jervas's by Garth in his chariot, the poet expressed concern that he could not for the life of him puzzle out what exactly Halifax had been objecting to. Whereupon, Garth laughed, told him not to worry, but to call on Halifax again in two or three months and read the same passages as if altered:

> I followed his advice, waited on Lord Halifax some time after, said "I hoped he would find his objections to those passages removed," read them to him exactly as they were at first, and his lordship was extremely pleased with them and cried out: "Ay, now they are perfectly right! Nothing can be better."★

It would not be surprising if we were someday to learn that the first

---

★ Spence, no. 204. (It is not altogether clear from Spence's jottings whether Pope's adviser was Garth or Congreve.) Stories of the clever artist tactfully outwitting the bumptious patron naturally abounded during the great centuries of patronage. Vasari tells a similar tale of Michelangelo and Piero Soderini, a mayor of Florence. Soderini having admired Michelangelo's David but declared the nose too long, Michelangelo climbed to his scaffold, scooped up with his chisel the handful of marble dust it lay in, and made motions of reshaping the nose while letting the marble dust trickle through his fingers. Soderini was delighted with the result. "And so Michelangelo came down, laughing to himself at having satisfied that lord, for he had compassion on those who, in order to appear full of knowledge, talk about things of which they know nothing." Lives of the Artists, tr., Gaston de Vere (10 vols., London: Macmillan, 1912–15), 9: 16–17.

lineaments of "Bufo," Pope's composite portrait in the *Epistle to Dr. Arbuthnot* of the self-satisfied aristocratic patron, began to take shape in his mind at this time:

> Proud, as *Apollo* on his forked hill,
> Sate full-blown *Bufo*, puff'd by ev'ry quill;
> Fed with soft Dedication all day long. . . .
>
> (ll. 231–33)

"Well said, Dick"

Whatever the date of Halifax's gathering, Pope's encounter there with Addison is likely to have been cool. The two men had been moving for some months toward open rupture of a friendship that can never have been altogether secure. They were too much alike in some ways: both vain, both exquisitely sensitive to criticism, both too fond of the aristocratic pose of the literary amateur for whom writing is simply an amusement, both secretive and on some occasions devious. At the same time, they were such clear opposites in temperament (Pope had a streak of pugnacity not found in Addison), in way of life, and in their responses to experience that misunderstandings could almost be counted on. Pope, at least as a young man and when he was feeling well, had a marked partiality for horseplay and tomfoolery, and what he himself once called "fine Flamms"—very probably the name he would have applied to such light-hearted deceits as that in which he connived with Dr. Arbuthnot to persuade Gay that he had got a clap. According to Jervas, he and Gay had so accustomed themselves to humorous lying that neither could entirely believe the other, "tho' upon never so serious an Occasion."

In any company in which he felt at home, moreover—company, that is, which left him free to forget protocol and follow impulse—he could be irresistibly charming, though it may be that sometimes he tried too hard: this last, at any rate, is what his enemy Lord Hervey thought and said. He is also known to have drunk too much now and then, and when drunk, if we may judge by his letter to the Duchess of Hamilton headed "London, October the —— Between day and night —— The writer drunk" (where he manages to compliment her ladyship while comparing her to an elephant), he was yet more charming than when sober. Not infrequently, if quite at his ease, he fell asleep in company, his thin frame, though as capable as a violin string of putting out immense energies when called on, evidently requiring regular refreshment. "I have often thought myself the better for your company," his friend Bathurst once observed dryly, "though you have slept all the time you have been with me."

And then, too, Pope was mischievous, or could be—the natural result, perhaps, of a childhood spent too much in the shadow of adult solemnities, or—as with Ruskin later—conceivably a way of laying claim, subconsciously, to the laughing childhood he never had. Between the covert wink or smirk by which children assert their view of and often their triumph over the alien fixated world that occupies their elders and the assumed naivety of the seasoned satirist who, refusing to be put upon, cries out like the boy in the tale of *The Emperor's New Clothes*, "But he hasn't got *anything* on," there may be connections deeper than we know. At any rate, whatever the source, Pope had an iconoclastic streak in him. Skilled though he was in the ways of his world, capable of the most polished behavior—his manners "delicate, easy, and engaging," says a contemporary—many of that world's postures and preachments, which he tended to approve with one part of his being and to which he conformed, seem to have had the same fascination for another part of him as the proverbial parson in top hat for the street urchin with a snowball.

Almost everything about such a personality was calculated to irritate Addison, not least the genius that in Pope's case accompanied it. A man of the highest ideals, Addison had evolved over the years an image of himself as a model of the great and good man, rational, moderate, upright, "correct" in all senses, and in the main had lived up to it: his friend Tickell was not alone in admiring him as "the first man of the age." And though there is much in Lord Macaulay's famous essay that seems fatuous enough today, including the pronouncement that had Addison written a novel it would have been the greatest novel in the language, his tribute to Addison's "balance" makes an important point:

> Men may easily be named, in whom some particular good disposition has been more conspicuous than in Addison. But the just harmony of qualities, the exact temper between the stern and the human virtues, the habitual observance of every law, not only of moral rectitude, but of moral grace and dignity, distinguishes him from all men who have been tried by equally strong temptations, and about whose conduct we possess equally full information.

There were, however, temptations that Addison could not resist. For he had also developed an image of himself as a man with a magical touch, a writer successful in all genres who with a few strokes of his pen could transmute dross to gold. In this way, like many before and since, he mistook a very considerable talent, reinforced by good connections and a certain amount of luck, for a genius deserving universal homage, and (in part no doubt through the influence of his ingratiating personality and high moral code) quite innocently imposed this view on others. Something of the coloring of his authority over his associates is caught amusingly by Fielding in an episode of *A Journey from This World to the Next*. There Addison is found in the Elysian Fields arm in arm with Vergil, who teases him a little for his ignorance of the part played by the Eleusinian mysteries in *Aeneid* 6. Whereupon:

> I thought the Critic looked a little out of countenance, and [he] turned aside to a very merry Spirit, one *Dick Steele*, who embraced him, and told him, He had been the greatest Man upon Earth; that he readily resigned up all the Merit of his own Works to him. Upon which, *Addison* gave him a gracious Smile, and clapping him on the Back with much Solemnity, cried out, *Well said, Dick*.

To such a man, consciously or otherwise—yet more to his loyal satellites—Pope's rise to eminence inevitably appeared a threat. During 1713, ingrained political animosities exacerbated these emotions. Pope was believed to be veering to the Tories, and because of his religion became increasingly suspect to the habitués of Button's, most of whom had invested their literary futures in the Hanoverian succession and therefore doubly feared the Pretender. Pope's own conduct made matters worse. He had embarrassed Addison that year with his *Narrative of Dr. Robert Norris* in mockery of Dennis's attack on *Cato*. He had authored two epigrams, both scurrilous, which, though they in no way impugned the merits of that play, could be held to have approached its sacred precincts with something less than awe. (Neither epigram was owned by Pope, but the one on the incontinent Tory lady was instantly attributed to him by one of Addison's friends.) And as if this were not enough, he had exposed Philips's pastorals and Tickell's *Guardian* puff for them to ridicule, while at the same time, unintentionally, making Steele look foolish for not having recognized the spoof.

Precisely when Addison turned on Pope, it is impossible to be sure. One may discern, if one chooses, a certain coolness or, perhaps more reliably, an odd frugality of response in an unpublished letter of 11 February 1713, apparently acknowledging Pope's gift of an advance copy of *Windsor-Forest*. But this may be simply Addisonian reserve

("Alike reserv'd to blame, or to commend"). He was still warmly supportive of the *Iliad* translation following its announcement in October 1713, so much so that Pope could state in the Preface of his first volume, without fear of contradiction by any Buttonian:

> Mr. *Addison* was the first whose Advice determin'd me to undertake this Task, who was pleas'd to write to me upon that Occasion in such Terms as I cannot repeat without Vanity.

What Addison had in fact written, on 26 October, was that the quality of Pope's other performances showed that the new undertaking must "enrich our Tongue and do Honour to our Country," and that if Pope did not assume the task, it would probably "never be executed by any other, at least I know none of this age that is equal to it." Having, he said, "an ambition of having it known that you are my Friend," he had further offered to do all he could to forward the subscription. This may or may not have been lip service at the time. At any rate, nothing came of it. Pope was indebted to Jervas for subscription efforts among the Whigs, probably also to Congreve, Halifax, and Garth; but Addison sat on his hands. By May 1714, Pope knew that from Addison's friendship he could expect no deeds, only words. By fall, perhaps earlier, he knew he could expect competition as well.

"There had been a coldness between Mr. Addison and me," he explained to Spence in 1735:

> We had not been in company together for a good while anywhere but at Button's Coffee House, where I used to see him almost every day. On his meeting me there one day in particular, he took me aside and said he should be glad to dine with me at such [and such] a tavern if I would stay till those people (Budgell and Philips) were gone. We went . . . accordingly and Mr. Addison abused those two gentlemen . . . very much. He said he hoped nobody could think that he esteemed them heartily. After dinner Addison said that he had wanted for some time to talk with me, that his friend Tickell had formerly, whilst at Oxford, translated the first book of the *Iliad*, that he now designed to print it, and had desired him to look it over. He must therefore beg that I would not desire him to look over my first book, because if he did it would have the air of double dealing. I assured him that "I did not take it ill of Mr. Tickell that he was going to publish his translation, that he certainly had as much right to translate any author as myself, and that publishing both was entering on a fair stage [i.e., contest]." I then added that

"I would not desire him to look over my first book of the *Iliad* because he had looked over Mr. Tickell's, but could wish to have the benefit of his observations on my second, which I had then finished, and which Mr. Tickell had not touched upon." Accordingly I sent him the second book the next morning, and Mr. Addison a few days after returned it with very high commendations.

Details here may be open to question. A circumstance about which there is no doubt, however, is that Pope at some point discovered a competing Buttonian, or "Whig," translation to be in progress, which it is kinder to Addison to suppose he was informed of by Addison himself. What Addison did not think fit to reveal to him was that on the last day of May 1714, some two months after Pope's own contract with Lintot, Tickell had contracted with Tonson to translate not just Book I but the entire *Iliad*. This can only mean that the Buttonians and their leader hoped, or believed, despite Addison's praises, that Pope would prove unequal to the challenge (university men seldom underestimate their own distinction), and that when the first volume failed to win public approbation, their successor to his translation would be in place, ready to go forward without delay.

"Who would not weep?"

Pope seems never to have learned the full extent of Addison's double-dealing. He realized soon after their conversation that Tickell's translation of Book I, whether or not it had an Oxford origin (which he came to doubt) was part of a general Buttonian effort to discredit his own work when published. And by the time of publication the following June, he realized also (for the whole town buzzed with the news) that Addison had been deeply involved in the rival translation. Many, at the time and later, claimed it was entirely Addison's. Even Steele, in a moment of resentment (for he and Addison had likewise parted company), embraced this view. But surely the most reliable evidence is that of the printer Watts, who said "the translation of the first book of the *Iliad* was in Tickell's handwriting, but much corrected and interlined by Addison."

We may guess, then, that in the days leading up to June, Pope's mood ran the gamut from disappointment to anger to panic. Panic, because his standing as a poet as well as his financial future were visibly at stake. As the winter of 1714 edged into spring, pamphlets sprang up around him like wire grass to ridicule his venture. It was to be, said one, a Roman Catholic translation, regulated from St. Omer's [chief training school for English Catholics educated abroad], its reading of the poem's first word to be "Church" instead of "Wrath." It was actually, said another (with a gibe at Pope's size) "The first Book of *Tom Thumb*, transform'd from the original Nonsense into *Greek Heroicks.*" A third attack taunted him with wanting to make money from his labors, substituting his "Brass" (in daring to undertake the *Iliad*) for subscribers' "Gold," and warned that while only a madman would have embarked on "a Work, which not all the Poets of our Island durst jointly attempt," there was no way out for him now:

> No! not only your attending Subscribers, whose Expectations have been raised in Proportion to what their Pockets have been drained of, but even the industrious, prudent *Bernard* [*Lintot*], who has advanced no small Sum of Money for the Copy, require the Performance of your Articles.

The two men who collaborated in these pleasantries were friends of Addison's, and one of them, at least, a Buttonian. Their pamphlet was originally entitled *The Hump Conference*, with reference to Pope's back, and embodied other reflections in the same key on his person. All these, we know, were at Addison's suggestion struck out before publication and the title was altered to *Homerides*. A kindness, one likes to think. But as they were removed to avoid eliciting sympathy for the victim—"For *Pope* as he is a fellow of a Contemptible figure is the object of the Town's Pity"—and as no move to quash the piece entirely is recorded, we are left to wonder about Addison's intentions—as earlier about his disapproval of Pope's mockery of Dennis. The Greek motto of the pamphlet—four lines from Homer's description of Thersites—

> He was the ugliest man who came to Troy: bow-legged, lame in one foot, his humped shoulders stooping over his chest, with a pointed head above on which a thin stubble grew—

remained in place.

All this was frightening. Plainly the intention had been to riddle his first volume, publicly announced for March 1, with a fusillade of ridicule. What for some time had been becoming equally plain was that the opposition Homer was being held back so as to come out simultaneously with his own, thus insisting on public comparison of the work done by "a Hackney Scribler, . . . a poor Englishman of my own Educating" with work done by a university graduate properly trained. In the end, this was what happened. After a delay of three months, caused by the slow drying of the printed sheets but possibly also by a hope of drawing out the opposition entry, Pope published on June 6. Two days later, Tickell published, and the contest was on. Three days after that, retired to Binfield to work on the next volume but perhaps also to avoid embarrassment if embarrassment there were to be, Pope received from Lintot a note that must have sounded to him like the music of the spheres:

> You have Mr Tickles Book to divert one Hour—It is allready condemn'd here and the malice & juggle at Buttons is the conversation of those who have spare moments from Politicks.

From Gay on July 8 came further details:

> I have just set down Sir *Samuel Garth* at the Opera. He bid me tell you, that every body is pleas'd with your Translation, but a few at *Button*'s; and that Sir *Richard Steele* told him, that Mr. *Addison* said *Tickel*'s translation was the best that ever was in any language. . . . I am inform'd that at *Button*'s your character is made very free with as to morals, &c. and Mr. *A* —— says, that your translation and *Tickel*'s are both very well done, but that the latter has more of *Homer*.

Such a protracted series of hostilities aroused, predictably enough, not only anxiety but anger. And anger, as an earlier Lord Halifax had said, "raiseth Invention" though it "overheateth the Oven." Soon Pope began to believe that Addison's former advice not to tamper with the two-canto *Rape of the Locke* had been given to forestall the triumph that the enlarged *Rape* turned out to be. Later, he credited Addison—not, it is true, without what must have seemed at the time compelling evidence since it came from Addison's future step-son—with having rewarded his old enemy Gildon for publishing an attack characterizing him as "Sawney Dapper—A young Poet of the Modern stamp, an easy Versifyer, Conceited and a Contemner secretly of all others," who had mastered the art of translating Homer without any Greek and of raising a name in poetry without any poetry, primarily (in his later *Rape of the Lock*) by addressing his work to the ladies and making them "speak Bawdy." Doubtless Pope also recalled when in anger the very first slight Addison had paid him. For the *Spectator*'s encomium of the *Essay on Criticism* in 1711 had been accompanied with a censure that rankled. In the Rome of Augustus, Addison had remarked, men of letters were each other's friends and admirers; whereas in his own day writers too often sought notice by detraction of their brothers in the art, altogether contrary to the generous spirit celebrated by Denham in praising the dramatist John Fletcher, whose fame was *not*

> on lesser Ruins built,
> Nor needs thy juster Title the foul Guilt
> Of Eastern Kings, who to secure their Reign
> Must have their Brothers, Sons, and Kindred Slain.

Then, with obvious reference to Pope's four lines on "Appius," came the barb:

> I am sorry to find that an Author, who is very justly esteemed among the best Judges, has admitted some Stroaks of this Nature into a very fine Poem, I mean *The Art of Criticism*.

From Pope's point of view, the reference was uncalled for on two counts. The *Spectator* had never itself been notably protective of John Dennis's feelings—rather the reverse; and to assign envy as motive constituted a wanton (because unverified and unverifiable) affront to character that no amount of acclamation of poetic skill could easily assuage.

There was another mood at work besides anger and fear, I am inclined to think: disappointment. The story goes that at some unspecified date, probably in the early 1730s, Pope took his young friend the poet Walter Harte into Fleet Street to visit the garret where Addison had written his most famous poem, *The Campaign* (1705). Though the anecdote may be apocryphal (Addison did, however, have garret lodgings in Fleet Street at the time of writing that poem), it suggests a certain tenderness for Addison on Pope's part, a degree of respect for his memory, conceivably a touch of something resembling filial piety that must be weighed into any complete account of their relationship. Long after the quarrel, it will be recalled (in 1730), Pope spoke to Spence of Addison as one who "had something more charming in his conversation than I ever knew in any other man." Some years later (in 1737), reminding George II of the social utility of poets, he singled out Addison for the position of highest honor along with Swift. Even before Addison's death in 1719, moreover, when wounds were still fresh, a tribute to Addison (perhaps originally intended to introduce his as yet unpublished *Dialogues upon Ancient Medals*) pairs his name with that of the Roman poet whom the eighteenth century loved best. Pope imagines an England that will be as scrupulously conscious of her great men as Rome, and will lovingly commemorate them in sculptured medals of the kind the *Dialogues* had described:

> Here, rising bold, the Patriot's honest face;
> There Warriors frowning in historic brass:
> Then future ages with delight shall see
> How Plato's, Bacon's, Newton's looks agree;
> Or in fair series laurell'd Bards be shown,
> A Virgil there, and here an Addison.
>
> (*To Mr. Addison, Occasioned by his Dialogues on Medals*, 57–62)

It is this background sense of admiration—of Addison as a young man's hero and role model, a figure of magisterial powers crippled by a single frailty, a type of the lost leader—which lends such poignancy, and even a suggestion of tragic waste, to the lines that all these differences and misunderstandings at length precipitated—

> Peace to all such! But were there One whose fires
> True Genius kindles, and fair Fame inspires,
> Blest with each Talent and each Art to please,
> And born to write, converse, and live with ease:
> Shou'd such a man, too fond to rule alone,
> Bear, like the *Turk*, no brother near the throne,
> View him with scornful, yet with jealous eyes,
> And hate for Arts that caus'd himself to rise;
> Damn with faint praise, assent with civil leer,
> And without sneering, teach the rest to sneer;
> Willing to wound, and yet afraid to strike,
> Just hint a fault, and hesitate dislike;
> Alike reserv'd to blame, or to commend,
> A tim'rous foe, and a suspicious friend,
> Dreading ev'n fools, by Flatterers besieg'd,
> And so obliging that he ne'er oblig'd;
> Like *Cato*, give his little Senate laws,
> And sit attentive to his own applause;
> While Wits and Templers ev'ry sentence raise,
> And wonder with a foolish face of praise.
> Who but must laugh, if such a man there be?
> Who would not weep, if *Atticus* were he!
>
> (*Epistle to Dr. Arbuthnot*, 193–214)

As has often been remarked, these are verses that not only describe the man, but in a sense and to a degree impersonate him. The hovering subjunctives that frame the picture, the repeated antitheses that

34. Joseph Addison (1672–1719). By Michael Dahl, *c.* 1719.

> Or in fair series laurell'd Bards be shown,
> A VIRGIL there, and here an ADDISON.
> > *To Mr. Addison, Occasion'd by his Dialogues on Medals.*

> Who but must laugh, if such a man there be?
> Who would not weep, if *Atticus* were he!
> > *Epistle to Dr. Arbuthnot*, 213–14.

Courtesy of the National Portrait Gallery, London.

take back with one hand what they offer with the other, the hesitancies of rhythm (brought about by sense and sound: "Just hint a fault, and hesitate dislike") which invite attention to equivalent hesitancies in the man; the manner in which the evolving portrait gradually yields the identity of the sitter yet is never unequivocally identified with him ("Who but must laugh, if such a man there be?"): by these means and others Pope makes his analysis reflect even in its syntax and grammar the insinuating, tentative, never fully committed friend/enemy whom he had discovered in the author of *Cato*. According to Pope's own accounts, after he had been informed (though almost certainly misinformed) of Gildon's being paid to satirize him, he wrote to Addison a letter indicating what he had been told and saying that if he were to retaliate he would do it openly and in such a way as to deal fairly with good qualities as well as faults—"something in the following manner"—appending then the sketch. Pope himself believed that this action was responsible for the suspension of hostilities that followed. He may have been right; though we must allow too, in fairness, for Addison's having probably some second thoughts about his behavior and about the damage done his standing and that of the entire coterie by their chicanery. At any rate, whatever the reasons, a reconciliation of sorts took place. Addison inserted in his new journal, *The Freeholder*, on May 7, 1716, a somewhat guarded compliment to Pope's translation and, with an instrumentalism altogether characteristic of him, prevailed on a fellow Buttonian to pay a less reserved compliment in the second edition of *Homerides*, published later that month. By June, we hear from that same Buttonian (Thomas Burnet) that he has "seen Addison caressing Pope, whom . . . he hates worse than Belzeebub," that he and "the rest of the Rhiming Gang" have now dropped their hostility, and that, in fact, Garth has compelled him [Burnet] to dine with Pope, who, he grudgingly admits, though "an ill natured little false Dog," has an entertaining wit.

For it was, after all, only a reconciliation of sorts. Pope, later on, could give high praise to Addison on a number of occasions, as we have seen; but he could never quite bring himself to suppress the portrait altogether—perhaps not surprisingly since he must have been conscious of its brilliance. And Addison, on his side, though as he was dying he called in Gay to apologize for an unspecified injury done him (evidently some interference with the Hanoverian patronage Gay had long hoped for), never, so far as can be ascertained, meditated a similar apology to Pope.

CHAPTER 14

HIGH LIFE

"For Right Hereditary tax'd and fin'd"

The queen's death, and the consequent rapid decline in the political fortunes of the Tories, with whom the new king rightly associated his opposition, brought profound changes to Pope's life and perhaps to his literary career as well. The festive Scriblerus meetings came to an abrupt end. Arbuthnot lost his royal appointment (along with a legacy the queen had promised him) and the rooms in St. James's where those meetings were often held. On 10 June 1715, the day Lintot wrote to Pope that his Homer was being well received, Harley was indicted by a new Whig ministry and Parliament bent upon revenge, and on the sixteenth he was committed to the Tower. There he would remain for nearly two years while the effort to prove him guilty of high treason and high crimes and misdemeanors fizzled out. St. John, never a Scriblerian but already one of Pope's friends, anticipating a yet harsher fate, fled to France in late March 1715 and accepted there the post of Secretary of State to the Pretender. Though he soon left that service, the move dishonored him for life and gave the Whigs an additional pretext on which to hang the charge that the entire Tory party was Jacobite.

As for Parnell and Swift, they were now back in Ireland. Parnell had helped Pope with the first volume of the Homer during the spring and summer of 1714, then shared a holiday with him in Bath, and after returning to London for George I's coronation, proceeded home. He would return to visit his old friends in England only once, in 1718. Swift had preceded him. Some months before the queen's death, weary of the ruinous infighting and cut-throat jealousy of Harley and St. John, and disenchanted too, perhaps, by an evident decline in his personal influence, he had retreated to a friend's parsonage at Letcombe Bassett to nurse his wounds and signal his disapproval of what was happening in the ministry. There, in July, Pope and Parnell visited him, getting soaked for their pains (as Pope reported humorously to Arbuthnot in a parody of bad pastoral)—

> How foolish Men on Expeditions goe!
> Unweeting Wantons of their wetting Woe!
> For drizling Damps descend adown the Plain
> And seem a thicker Dew, or thinner Rain;
> Yet Dew or Rain may wett us to the shift
> We'll not be slow to visit Dr Swift—

but much enjoying their host's wine, his cider, his "usual Chidings," and a conversation of some days wherein he "talked of Politicks over Coffee, with the Air & Stile of an old Statesman, who had known something formerly; but was shamefully ignorant of the Three last weekes." A fortnight or so later, when the queen died, the old statesman's game was up, and he knew it. By the sixteenth of August, Swift was off to Holyhead, reaching Dublin on the twenty-fourth. Twelve years were to elapse before he and Pope saw each other again.

Friends were not Pope's only loss from the events of these years. On 20 March, 1716, during a season much punctuated by state trials, beheadings, hangings, disembowellings, and other residuals of the late rebellion, he reported to Caryll:

> I write this from Windsor Forest, which I am come to take my last look and leave of. We here bid our papist-neighbours adieu, much as those who go to be hanged do their fellow-prisoners, who are condemned to follow 'em a few weeks after.

Then from two verses in Vergil's first eclogue he quotes words that during the Latin centuries of English and European education have probably comforted more displaced persons than any other poetry ever written: "Perhaps now I have learnt so far as—*Nos dulcia linquimus arva* [We are leaving behind our sweet tilled fields], the next may be—*Nos patriam fugimus* [We flee our fatherland]. Let that, and all else be as Heaven pleases!"

In a letter to his fellow-poet Parnell, the description of his mood becomes more self-consciously literary:

> I can easily image to my thoughts the Solitary hours of your Eremitical Life in the [Irish] mountains from something so parellel to it, in my own retirement at Binfield—but Binfield, alas! is no more and the Muse is driven, from those Forests of which she sung. the day may shortly come, when your Friend may too literally apply

> nos Patriae fines, & dulcia linquimus arva

when he may look back with regret, on the Paradise he has lost, and have only the consolation of poor Adam

> The world lies all before him, where to chuse
> His place of rest, & Providence his Guide.

The posture of alienation struck here—by no means all posture, since the mood in the country was vindictive and no one could tell how far the bill currently pending in Parliament for collecting punitive damages from Roman Catholics might be carried—is a useful reminder of the extent to which the society Pope grew up in imprinted on his experience the themes of renunciation and loss so pervasive in his work.

What seems to have happened (though we have no details) is that Pope or his father responded to the new effort to register Roman Catholic estates for the imposition of further tax penalties by ridding themselves of their Binfield property. Possibly, too, they wished to escape what was certain to be renewed pressure to take the oaths; oaths acceptable to many Catholics at the time including, one suspects, the Popes, had they not been carefully tailored to require repudiation of a central doctrinal principle as well. In the words of the Popes' neighbor at Whiteknights, Henry Englefield, who drew up a clarifying position paper when registering his estate, it was indeed a

> Duty to be Actively Obedient where I cann without Offense to God & passively where I cannot to whatever Government God permits to reine over me And ... therefore I would willingly take an Oath of Fidelity to King George; But in as much as the reall presense of the Body & Blood of our Saviour in the Sacrament of the Eucharist was alwayes beleived by the Holy Catholick Church, ... And that the Tenn Commandments of God fully & Absolutely forbid Perjery, ... I cannot take the Test & Abjuration Oathes Enjoyned by Acts of parliament whatever I suffer.

Pope's father's position was very likely similar to Henry Englefield's. Whatever Pope's own was (we shall never know for certain), there is no evidence that he took the oaths at this or any other time. Perhaps he refused, perhaps he evaded them. Indeed, in the margin of his Montaigne, just at the point where Montaigne records the answer of the Lacedaemonians to their conqueror Antipater—

You may impose as heavy and ruinous Taxes upon us as you please, but to
command us to do shameful and dishonest things, you will lose your time—

Pope comments: "The case of those who pay double Taxes." It seems
not impossible that for Pope the Lacedaemonians' "shameful and
dishonest things" were represented by the oaths.

At Binfield, Pope had relied on Sir William Trumbull's authority
to protect his parents from the sorts of insult to which Roman Catholics were liable in periods of stress. Their new protector, following
the sale of Whitehill House, was to be Richard Boyle, third Earl of
Burlington, a prominent Whig six years Pope's junior, under whose
"wing" at Chiswick, as he explained to Caryll about a month after his
farewell to Binfield, he had found an "asylum for their old age."
There he had bought or leased the corner dwelling (no. 110, now part
of the Fox and Hounds public house) in a recently built terrace of five
at the junction of Chiswick Lane with Mawson's Lane. Chiswick
Lane, only a stone's throw south of the Great West Road, lay at about
the same distance from the Thames, whose current at this point (says
a contemporary guide) was so interrupted by several little islets that it
"but gently Salutes this Place," and so made personal traffic up and
down river with a boatman very simple. Burlington's country house,
formerly the seat of young Monmouth, Charles II's bastard son by
Lucy Walter, the "Absalom" of Dryden's *Absalom and Achitophel*,
rose not far off on the opposite side of the highway, built "after the
antient Manner very regular and strong," with "many spatious
Rooms in it, and large Gardens behind."

It is likely that Pope's friendship with Burlington began through
Jervas, possibly in early 1714 when the latter was canvassing sub-
scriptions to the Homer; more probably in May 1715, when he
returned with Burlington from the continent. On 17 May 1714,
Burlington had set out on the Grand Tour, taking Jervas with him to
keep a graphic record of notable things seen and presumably also to
advise him on purchases. When they came back the following May,
Burlington had in his retinue the sculptor G. B. Guelfi, the violinist
Pietro Castrucci, the cellist Filippo Amadei, a goodly number of
Italian craftsmen, and 878 trunks and crates containing works of art,
besides two Paris-made harpsichords, an instrument on which Burlington himself was apparently a tyro performer. One suspects there
was a celebratory dinner at this point to welcome the wayfarers
home, doubtless at Burlington House, Piccadilly, and that through
Jervas's good offices Pope was present. In his *A Farewell to London*, at
any rate—a rollicking tavern-poem written between May 19 and June

35. Richard Boyle, 3rd Earl of Burlington (1694–1753). Attributed to Jonathan Richardson, *c.* 1717–19.

> You too proceed! make falling Arts your care . . . .
> *Epistle to Burlington*, 191.

Courtesy of the National Portrait Gallery, London.

12 to make playful adieus to friends in London before retiring with
Homer for (as it turned out) his last summer in Binfield—what he
chiefly particularizes about Burlington is the quality of his chef:

> Laborious Lobster-nights, farewell!
> For sober, studious Days;
> And *Burlington*'s delicious Meal,
> For Sallads, Tarts, and Pease!
>
> (ll. 45–8)

A year later, invited to share in a three- or four-day party of pleasure
at Burlington's house in Chiswick (this may have been the moment
when he settled upon Chiswick as a place to live), he had broadened
his view. "We are," he tells Martha Blount, obviously with some
pride, "to walk, ride, ramble, dine, drink, & lye together. His gardens are delightfull, his musick [of which at this period Handel was in
charge] ravishing."

From this point, the friendship ripened fast. That summer we hear
from Pope how Burlington's gardens flourish, his structures rise, his
paintings arrive, and, from Gay, how Pope, in one of those gardens,
"unloads the Bough within his reach [Gay's emphasis on the singular
is a delightful touch], Of purple Grape, blue Plumb, or blushing
Peach." By November Burlington and he are off together to visit
Burlington's estates in Yorkshire. That same month he entertains the
earl and his countess with a dramatic invention based on a journey to
Oxford with his publisher (having borrowed one of Burlington's
mares for the occasion) that belongs among the great humorous
letters of the world. One paragraph will give its flavor. Pope,
drawing Lintot out on the problems of his trade, asks him how he
handles critics:

> "Sir (said he) nothing more easy. I can silence the most formidable
> of them; the rich one's for a sheet apiece of the blotted manuscript,
> which costs me nothing. They'll go about with it to their
> acquaintance, and pretend they had it from the author, who
> submitted to their correction: this has given some of them such an
> air, that in time they come to be consulted with, and dedicated to,
> as the top critics of the town.—As for the poor Critics, I'll give you
> one instance of my management, by which you may guess at the
> rest. A lean man that look'd like a very good scholar came to me
> t'other day; he turn'd over *Homer* [i.e., Pope's], shook his head,
> shrug'd up his shoulders, and pish'd at every line of it: *One would
> wonder* (says he) *at the strange presumption of men*; Homer *is no such*

easy task, that every *Stripling,* every *Versifier*—he was going on
when my Wife call'd to dinner: Sir, said I, will you please to eat a
piece of beef with me? Mr. *Lintott,* said he, *I am sorry you should be at
the expence of this great Book, I am really concern'd on your
account*—Sir I am oblig'd to you: if you can dine upon a piece of
beef, together with a slice of pudding—*Mr.* Lintott, *I do not say
but Mr.* Pope, *if he would condescend to advise with men of learning*—Sir, the *pudding* is upon the table, if you please to go in—My
critic complies, he comes to a taste of your poetry, and tells me in
the same breath, that the *Book* is commendable, and the *Pudding*
excellent."

The friendship with Burlington was one of Pope's happiest. It was
genuinely affectionate despite the difference in rank and lasted
Pope's lifetime. It may have been one of Burlington's happiest too:
in 1731 Pope made him the dedicatee of a superb poem on architecture, gardening, and the wise use of wealth, complimenting him as
reviver of the true classical style:

> You too proceed! make falling Arts your care,
> Erect new wonders, and the old repair,
> Jones and Palladio to themselves restore,
> And be whate'er Vitruvius was before:
> Till Kings call forth th' Idea's of your mind. . . .
> (*Epistle to Burlington,* 191–95)

Keeping "foolish company"

Though it lacked the peace of Binfield, Chiswick had advantages for
Pope. Five miles from London instead of thirty, it gave far easier
access to printer, publisher, and bookseller. Moreover, as one of the
riverside villages rapidly attracting new seats and villas within easy
reach of royalty's summer residence at Hampton Court, it brought
him into closer touch with the upper layers of society to which his
success and fame were now admitting him. After eight months, he
was already on such familiar terms with the three reigning beauties
among Princess Caroline's maids of honor (Mary Bellenden, Anne
Griffith, and Mary Lepell), that he could address them in a charming
ballad, not without a few gallant double entendres, expressing his
inability to accept their invitation to court and his hope that Gay
and he may meet them elsewhere:

In Leister fields, in house full nigh,
With door all painted green,
Where Ribbans wave upon the tye,
(A Milliner's I ween)
There you may meet us three to three,
For Gay can well make two of me.
                    With a fa, la, la.
But shou'd you catch the Prudish itch,
And each become a coward,
Bring sometimes with you Lady R[ich]
And sometimes Mistress H[owar]d,
For Virgins, to keep chaste, must go
Abroad with such as are not so.
                    With a fa, la, la.
And thus fair Maids, my ballad ends,
God send the K[ing] safe landing,
And make all honest ladies friends,
To Armies that are Standing.
Preserve the Limits of these nations,
And take off Ladies Limitations.
                    With a fa, la, la.

                                                    (ll. 36–56)

The following September finds him on a visit to the palace at
Hampton Court, obviously not his first, and soon thereafter consoling the Blount sisters with stories of the hard lives of court ladies
and their lack of all those gaieties by which particularly Teresa set
such store:

I met the Prince with all his Ladies . . . on horseback coming from
Hunting. Mrs Bellendine and Mrs Lepell took me into protection
(contrary to the Laws against harbouring Papists), & gave me a
Dinner. . . . We all agreed that the life of a Maid of Honor was of all
things the most miserable; & wished that every Woman who
envyd it had a Specimen of it. To eat Westphalia Ham [the sort of
food popular with the new German court but not yet with the
English] in a morning, ride over Hedges & ditches on borrowed
Hacks, come home in the heat of the day with a Feavor, & what is
worse a hundred times, a red Mark in the forehead with a Beaver
hatt; all this may qualify them to make excellent Wives for Fox-
hunters, & bear abundance of ruddy-complexion'd Children. As
soon as they can wipe off the Sweat of the day, they must simper an

hour, & catch cold, in the Princesses apartment; from thence *To Dinner, with what appetite they may*—And after that, till midnight, walk, work, or think, which they please? I can easily believe, no lone House in Wales, with a Mountain & a Rookery, is more contemplative than this Court; and as a proof of it I need only tell you Mrs Lepell walk'd all alone with me three or 4 hours, by moonlight; and we mett no Creature of any quality, but the King, who gave audience all alone to the Vice-chamberlen, under the Garden-wall.

In short, I heard of no Ball, Assembly, Basset-Table, or any place where two or three were gatherd together, except Mad[am] Kilmanzech's [George I's illegitimate half-sister, Madame Kielmansegge was known from her girth as "the Elephant and Castle"], to which I had the honour to be invited, & the grace to stay away.

During the Chiswick years, for reasons that will be by now apparent, a new note of frantic hurry occasionally enters the correspondence, together with an understandable but not particularly appealing complacence as he reports to the country gentleman Caryll (with whom it must, however, be remembered he is excusing himself for not having made a visit to Ladyholt) all the fashionable city folk who challenge his attention:

I have been indispensably obliged to pass some days at almost every house along the Thames; half my acquaintance being upon the breaking up of the Parliament become my neighbours. After some attendance on my Lord Burlington, I have been at the Duke of Shrewsbury's, Duke of Argyle's, Lady Rochester's, Lord Percival's, Mr Stonor's, Lord Winchelsea's, Sir Godfrey Kneller's (who has made me a fine present of a picture) and Dutchess Hamilton's. All these have indispensable claims to me, under penalty of the imputation of direct rudeness, living within 2 hours sail of Chiswick.

One cannot but wonder what the aging little family at the corner of Chiswick and Mawson Lanes thought of all this! More attractive by far is the characteristic melancholy of a report to Caryll some five months later:

I have passed almost all my time here of late [at Chiswick] being pretty much sick of the vanities of the town which agree as little with my constitution as the madness and political fury does with my judgement. I took my last leave of impertinence at a masquerade some time ago, the true epitome of all absurdities; and of all shows to no purpose, the greatest show to the least purpose. I was led thither, as one is to all foolish things, by keeping foolish company.

Keeping foolish company on another occasion during these years may have brought Pope something more lasting than self-reproach. Through his young manhood, as we saw, he tried to maintain the gay-dog image sought after at the time by most men during their twenties (and frequently long after), particularly when in the presence of women; and if we were to accept at face value the verses he then tossed off for the entertainment of friends, we should have to conclude that he was a devil of a fellow indeed. Thus his *Farewell to London*, quoted above, opens with the swagger:

> Dear, damn'd, distracting Town, farewell!
> Thy Fools no more I'll teize:
> This Year in Peace, ye Critics, dwell,
> Ye Harlots, sleep at Ease!
>
> Soft B[*ethel*?] and rough C[*ragg?*]*s*, adieu!
> Earl *Warwick* make your Moan,
> The lively H[*inchinbro*]k[*e*] and you
> May knock up★ Whores alone.
>
> (ll. 1–8)

And his very beautiful poem, *To a Young Lady, On her leaving the Town, after the Coronation*, allegedly had a coda, or perhaps simply an alternative ending, in which Teresa's presence was credited with inspiring her admirers to sublimation while her absence drove them to fleshlier outlets, and which closed with a yet broader flourish: "And if poor *Pope* is cl[a]pt, the Fault is yours."

It is possible that these and other such allusions contain a modicum of truth. A story goes—though the episode is problematical and was first published to the world by an enemy of long standing, Colley Cibber, some twenty-five years after the event—that in the course of an apparently vinous evening at Button's Pope was cajoled by three of his companions (Cibber himself, the dissolute young earl of Warwick, already or about to be Addison's stepson, and an unidentified participant) into accompanying them to a bawdy house. The object, according to Cibber—for jokes were rough-and-tumble

★ I.e., "wake up"—not the current slang American sense.

in Augustan England—was to have a laugh at the diminutive poet's expense. This (also according to Cibber) they had, he himself drawing Pope away from his chosen nymph in order, as he put it, to save him from venereal "danger" and so ensure the completion of the Homer.

How far the story is true, it is impossible to say. Pope did not repudiate it out of hand. His own account to Spence at the time the scandal was published was that it was a lie "as to the main point":

> I do remember that I was invited by Lord Warwick to pass an evening with him. He carried me and Cibber in his coach to a bawdy-house. There was a woman there, but I had nothing to do with her of the kind that Cibber mentions, to the best of my memory—and I had so few things of that kind ever on my hands that I could scarce have forgot it, especially so circumstanced as he pretends.

In later life, Pope did suffer from some form of strangury, of which one possible cause is the stricture left by a healed gonorrheal infection, and in 1740 underwent painful surgery for it. Yet the difficulty, as with many men, could well have been the effect of acute prostatitis. The evidence of William Cheselden, the most eminent surgeon of his day, who performed the operation, points entirely, though his terms are not ours, in the latter direction:

> I could give a more particular account of his [Pope's] health than perhaps any man. Cibber's slander of a carnosity [a fleshy urethral obstruction, which can be caused by venereal disease] [is] false. [He] had been gay, but left it on his acquaintance with Mrs. Blount. [He] had been in fear of a c[lap], but even that [was] without grounds.

Since Pope is supposed by some in our own day to have been impotent, Cheselden's testimony is worth noting. The wren goes to 't with as much prosperity as the swan.

A kind of chivalry

Sometime in the first six months of 1715, Pope met Edward Wortley Montagu, an eminent Whig now scrambling for favor with the new court, and his wife, Lady Mary Wortley Montagu. The Wortley Montagus had been married three years and were, at least on Lady Mary's side, now repenting at leisure. Though she had chosen her

36. Lady Mary Wortley Montagu (1689–1762). Attributed to Charles Jervas.

Joy lives not here; to happier seats it flies,
And only dwells where WORTLEY casts her eyes.
To Mr. Gay, 5–6.

From furious *Sappho* scarce a milder Fate,
P—x'd by her Love, or libell'd by her Hate.
Imit. Hor., Sat. II, i: 83–84.

Present location unknown.

husband freely, eloping with Wortley against her father the marquess's interdiction, she had managed to acquire for herself, with a
lack of perspicacity quite astonishing in one ordinarily so astute, a
rather dull man who was also considerably a boor and who treated her
much of the time with a cool preoccupied indifference. She herself
was vivacious, ambitious, aggressive, self-educated far beyond the
attainments of most women of her time, and beautiful. Her beauty,
in fact, was beginning to catch the eye of royalty, from whom might
be hoped advancement for her husband and whatever else royal persons have it in their power to bestow. But then in December 1715 she
contracted smallpox. On recovery her face was deeply pitted and she
had permanently lost her eyelashes. Pitted, not pitied, ran a pun of the
time, because, though she had been resident in London for less than a
year, her sharp tongue in the censure of others, particularly other
women, had gained a certain renown.

Her pen was soon to do likewise. By the time she took ill, she had
composed three mock pastorals in the new style of the "town
eclogue," centering on the loves and vexations of fashionable court-
nymphs and court-swains. In one of these, a speaker named
"Roxana" (easily recognizable as Mary Ker, duchess of Roxburghe,
a Scotswoman and Tory) complains of being overlooked for the post
of Lady of the Bedchamber by the Princess of Wales, who is accused
of having awarded it to an unworthy recipient. During her tirade, she
hints at the notorious breach (not yet public) dividing the Prince and
Princess of Wales from the king, attributes sexual immorality to the
princess's entourage ("A vertuous Princesse with a Court so lewd"),
and remarks the comparative unpopularity of the new German
regime with the English aristocracy:

> Oft had your drawing room been sadly thin
> And Merchants Wives close by the Chair had been,
> Had not I amply fill'd the empty Space.
>
> (ll. 35–37)

There was also a vein of cruelty at work. The duchess of Roxburghe
was a large ungainly woman ("amply fill'd"), and the opening of the
poem allowed no one to forget it:

> Roxana from the Court returning late
> Sigh'd her soft sorrows at St. James's Gate;
> Such heavy thoughts lay brooding in her Breast[,]
> Not her own Chairmen with more weight oppress'd;

> They groan the cruel load they're doom'd to bear,
> She, in these gentler Sounds, express'd her Care.
>
> (ll. 1–6)

Dangerous stuff—most notably the allusion to the lewdness of the court! And still more dangerous when, after a few weeks of circulating in manuscript, the three poems fell into the hands of Edmund Curll and were immediately published as *Court Poems*—with them a preface intimating that they were the work of Gay, or Pope, or a "Lady of Quality." Curll issued the volume on 26 March 1716. Two days later, while visiting Lintot's shop on a matter of business, where he also found Pope, he is said to have been first roundly scolded by the poet for this knavery and then, in what purported to be a peace-making "Glass of Sack," given some sort of violent emetic. Or, as Pope put it laconically in a letter to Caryll: "I contrived to save a fellow a beating by giving him a vomit." A history of this incident, he added, had been set down for posterity by "a late Grub-street author." This was, of course, himself.

What pangs Curll actually suffered, we have no way of knowing. Doubtless many. In Pope's "history," entitled *A Full and True Account of a Horrid and Barbarous Revenge by Poison, On the Body of Mr. Edm. Curll*, they are so severe that Curll supposes himself dying and so makes a deathbed confession of all his publishing delinquencies and frauds, justifying some as charities (because he publishes authors that no one else will), the rest as means to "an honest livelihood." Despite an occasional bright sentence, it is not a particularly funny pamphlet—in some of its clinical details quite the reverse—and the revenge it celebrates, though undoubtedly less reprehensible in an age in which "vomits" were a common course of medical treatment and in which gentlemen considered it their privilege to subject obstreperous rascals to immediate physical punishment, was brutal. It was also stupid. It provoked Curll to a long series of retaliations. Scarcely more than three weeks after *A Full and True Account*, he managed to get hold of and publish a light-hearted *jeu d'esprit* of Pope's addressed to a quack named John Moore, whose advertisements of an infallible medicine for eliminating worms from the intestinal tract appeared regularly in London newspapers. Whimsically supporting Moore, the poem purports to show that "worms" are indeed universal:

> The Learn'd themselves we Book-Worms name;
> The Blockhead is a Slow-worm;
> The Nymph whose Tail is all on Flame
> Is aptly term'd a Glow-worm:

The Fops are painted Butterflies,
That flutter for a Day;
First from a Worm [silkworm] they take their Rise,
And in a worm decay.

(ll. 13–20)

But (the poem continues) even Moore's nostrum will not avail for long:

O learned Friend of *Abchurch-Lane*,
Who sett'st our Entrails free!
Vain is thy Art, thy Powder vain,
Since Worms shall eat ev'n thee.

Our Fate thou only can'st adjourn
Some few short Years, no more!
Ev'n *Button*'s Wits to Worms shall turn,
Who Maggots were before.

(ll. 33–40)

Innocent enough? Not at all. This poem, published repeatedly in Curll's collections, was to haunt Pope for life. By enemies it was stubbornly misrepresented as Pope's "satire on mankind" (a title chosen to associate it with the earl of Rochester's allegedly atheistic and libertine original), and it was through their abuse and misuse of it that Pope first encountered the dilemma of satire in his day: "Personal satire was lampoon, and the result of spite; general satire was indiscriminating and the result of venomous and impious misanthropy."

Worse was to come. One of Pope's most mischievous inspirations, possibly a tavern piece but just as possibly a tickler tossed off for Teresa Blount, whose merry spirit was not averse to bawdy puns, was a burlesque of the first psalm, in the sixteenth-century version by Thomas Sternhold, still in Pope's day much sung in Protestant churches. In the King James version, the first verses of Psalm 1 read like this:

1. Blessed is the man that walketh not in the counsel of the ungodly, nor standeth in the way of sinners, nor sitteth in the seat of the scornful.
2. But his delight is in the law of the Lord; and in his law doth he meditate day and night.
3. And he shall be like a tree planted by the rivers of water, that bringeth forth his fruit in his season; his leaf also shall not wither; and whatsoever he doeth shall prosper.

In the Sternhold version, like this:

> The man is blest that hath not bent
> to wicked rede [advice] his eare:
> Nor led his life as sinners do
> nor sat in scorners chaire.
>
> But in the law of God the Lord
> doth set his whole delight:
> And in that law doth exercise
> himselfe both day and night.
>
> He shall be like the tree that growes
> fast by the rivers side:
> Which bringeth forth most pleasant fruit
> in her due time and tide.
>
> Whose leafe shall never fade nor fall
> but flourish still and stand:
> Even so all things shall prosper well
> that this man takes in hand.

And in Pope's parody like this:

> The Maid is blest that will not hear
> Of Masquerading Tricks,
> Nor lends to Wanton Songs an Ear,
> Nor sighs for Coach and Six.
>
> To please her shall her Husband strive
> With all his Main and Might,
> And in her Love shall Exercise
> Himself both Day and Night.
>
> *She* shall bring forth most Pleasant Fruit,
> *He* Flourish still and Stand,
> Ev'n so all Things shall prosper well,
> That this Maid takes in Hand.

How far—or if—Pope meant to have fun with Scripture, we can only guess. That he intended to mock the sixth-grade singsong of Sternhold, the evidence makes clear. The entire collection of versified psalms linked with Sternhold's name had early become a laughing-stock, Milton's nephew Edward Phillips comparing them to "a crackt Sans-bell [i.e., Sanctus bell] jarring in the Steeple," and even the gentle Thomas Fuller acknowledging that the authors had drunk more of Jordan than of Helicon. That it might have given Pope a degree of satisfaction to jest (from the vantage point of the Mass) at a religious culture that gave such banalities houseroom is conceivable. What is certain is that he ought to have realized the opening this ribald prank gave Curll, the group at Button's, and all others who begrudged his success as a Roman Catholic poet in a Protestant community—an opening soon seized by a correspondent of the chief Whig newspaper of the day:

> Mr. Pope having writ a prophane Ballad by way of Burlesque, on the first Psalm in Metre, as it is sung in the Churches, it may be of Service to put a stop to a farther design, which it seems he has to burlesque the Penitential Psalms [specified because held in special reverence. The charge, pure fiction, was of course intended to confirm the blasphemous character of Pope and popery].

To this Pope's parody was appended under the title *A Version of the First Psalm, for the Use of a Popish Lady*, followed by a so-called *Eccho*:

We have a Pope, than both [the Roman Pope and the Devil] more vile,
Who dares God's Word Blaspheme,
By lewd, prophane, uncleanly Style,
In Terms, I dare not Name.

The Royal David's Harp he takes,
To play his Wanton Song,
And screws and strains its strings, so makes
His smutty Notes sound strong.

No Atheist, Deist, Devil yet,
Thus rudely touch'd that Lyre;
To prostitute thus Holy Writ,
As do's this POPISH Squire.

(ll. 13–24)

Curll published Pope's "Worms," as he called it, on 1 May 1716, and his "Psalm" on June 30. All that spring—a season when religious and political passions were fierce owing to the current trials, sentencings, and executions of Jacobite rebels—he kept up a running attack in the newspapers, insinuating that Pope was a Stuart sympathizer, and his Homer (of which Volume 2 had appeared in March) a piece of Roman Catholic propaganda. The intention was obviously to annoy Pope, but more particularly to frighten his subscribers into withdrawing their support. On May 31 Curll played his trumps. *The*

Catholic Poet; Or, Protestant Barnaby's [i.e., Bernard Lintot's] *Sorrowful Lamentation*, written and issued by Curll's minions and allegedly addressed "To all Gentlemen, Authors, Translators, or Translating Poets, who are Protestants, and well affected to the present Establishment in the Most Illustrious House of Hanover," represented itself to be Lintot's *Miserere* for the failure of the Homer undertaking. The translator, he confessed, had been found ignorant of Greek, popish in intention ('*This Papish Dog . . . has translated HOMER for the Use of the PRETENDER*"), and treacherous ("this true *Catholick*, after he had got a Number of Subscriptions, by the Recommendation of our *Protestant Authors*, who are Men of Honour; he immediately betray'd all their private Conversations to the Late Ministry, . . . for which Reasons these Gentlemen have very justly forsaken him, and all the Books lye upon my Hands"). As for his person,

> My Song is of SAWNEY, The Poet of *Windsor*,
> Whose HOMER will sell, when the *Devil is blind*, *Sir*;
> And the *Hump* is *before* him, that now is *behind*, *Sir*;
>   *Which no Body can deny*.

Curll's other trump was the product of negotiations with Dennis. Issued on the same day with *The Catholic Poet*, it was entitled *A True Character of Mr. Pope* and offered the coffee houses fifteen tightly packed pages of abuse, set down, an earlier student of Pope's history has noted, "*Dennisissime*." A few sentences will give its effect, provided one imagines oneself in Pope's skin while reading them:

> But if anyone appears to be concern'd at our upbraiding him with his Natural Deformity, which did not come by his own Fault, but Seems to be the Curse of God upon him; we desire that Person to consider that this little Monster has upbraided People with their Calamities and their Diseases, . . . which he himself gave them by administring Poison to them [a glance at Curll's emetic]; we desire that Person to consider, that there is no one Disease but what all the rest of Men are subject to; whereas the Deformity of this Libeller, is Visible, Present, Lasting, Unalterable, and Peculiar to himself. 'Tis the mark of God and Nature upon him, to give us warning that we should hold no Society with him, as a Creature not of our Original, nor of our Species.

Pope's ministration of the emetic was certainly prompted in part by the natural hostility of the professional writer to the scavenging publisher—perceived not merely as a general blot on the dignity of the writing trade but as a snapper-up of unconsidered trifles who might at any time by this activity plague a reputable author personally, as he had done with *Court Poems*. The attribution of these to Pope could be nothing but an embarrassment to him, both as translator of Homer who could ill afford to disquiet his Establishment subscribers and as Roman Catholic citizen who was persistently alleged to be a Jacobite. For Gay, too, the attribution would be troublesome, since he was at this time particularly hopeful of obtaining a place or pension from the new government. As for Lady Mary, their actual author, a sound Whig frequenter of the Court and its circle, solicitous for her husband's advancement yet already suspect in some quarters for her wit and sharp tongue, the lodging of the poems at her door could be injurious indeed.

That Pope elected to look after Curll's "punishment" himself was probably less owing to his resentment, though doubtless he had worked up a quite adequate supply of that emotion, than to the image he wished to foster of himself as a man: one who "if he pleas'd, . . . pleas'd by manly ways," as he put it later in the *Epistle to Dr. Arbuthnot* (line 337); one who, despite his crazy carcass, could acquit himself with honor of the obligations of a friend. He might be incapable of giving Curll the caning he deserved, but he could make him suffer physically all the same—which, in the eighteenth century, was normally reckoned to be all a rascal would understand. And if part of the obligation involved chivalry to a female, this could only enhance a crippled poet's pride in meeting it. We may legitimately guess, indeed, that in Lady Mary's case Pope's chivalric impulses were fortified by a deep vein of fellow-feeling; for she too, following her bout with smallpox, could be looked upon as in some way "damaged," even if far more leniently than himself. Two years earlier, when Martha Blount had suffered from the disease, it had pleased him to assure her through Teresa that his affection would remain undiminished: "Whatever Ravages a merciless Distemper may commit, I dare promise her boldly what few (if any) of her Makers of Visits & Complements, dare to do; she shall have one man as much her Admirer as ever." Since this promise shows Pope in one of his favorite mental attitudes (derived perhaps from his long childhood immersion in Homer), that of the lone warrior holding a gate or a pass or a principle against all comers and vicissitudes, it may have colored his feelings of attraction to Lady Mary as well.

Such feelings he clearly had. Lady Mary, with her charm, learning, wit, knack with a verse, and aristocratic glamour had dazzled him. In what was to have been his portion of a joint letter to their mutual friend Lady Rich, leaving the facing half of the sheet blank for Lady Mary's portion, he had ventured to confess:

> It is making court ill to one fine Woman [Lady Rich] to shew her the regard we have for another, and yet I must own there is not a period of this Epistle but squints toward another [Lady Mary's] over-against it. . . . Your penetrating eyes cannot but discover how all the letters that compose these words lean forward after Lady *M*'s letters, which seem to bend as much from mine, and fly from them as fast as they are able. Ungrateful letters that they are! which give themselves to another man [Lady Rich's husband, by whom Lady Mary's "letters" will be read] in the very presence of him who will yield to no mortal in knowing how to value them.

In the covering letter to Lady Mary that accompanied this, he acknowledged himself her servant "to some degree of Extravagance." It was the right word. Only extravagance, in its double sense of roving fantasy and conspicuous excess, can adequately describe the character of the correspondence he was to hold with Lady Mary from August 1716, when she departed with her husband for Adrianople and Constantinople, where he was to be British envoy to the Sultanate, and October 1718, when they returned.

A "cultivated infatuation"

In a classic instance of personal feeling breaking through a socio-literary convention, Prince Hamlet first inscribes some rather silly Petrarchan verses in a letter to Ophelia, then interrupts himself to exclaim: "O dear Ophelia, I am ill at these numbers. I have no art to reckon my groans. But that I love thee best, O most best, believe it!" Though the situation is of course very different, the effects of what appears to be at times a rather similar collision give a special interest to the letters Pope wrote to Lady Mary during her twenty-six months abroad.

The convention in Pope's case is that of epistolary gallantry, growing somewhat old-fashioned in his day but still serviceable. Epistolary gallantry, it is well to bear in mind, is a species of flirtatious game, governed, if not by rules, at least by norms. It demands most of all a witty imagination because its object is to flatter in unusual and pleasing ways. It often inspires delicate feats of exaggeration because exaggeration preserves the carnival tone and the comic distance without which the whole game might collapse into bouts of heavy

breathing. And, further, epistolary gallantry invites sexual undertones because the smoke of so much compliment palls quickly if there
is not thought to be somewhere a fire. Alike creative or destructive
according to its use, the undercover fire reminds both parties that the
game *can* be played seriously and for high stakes.

Pope handles the convention with the skill we expect from him.
Much that he chooses to say to Lady Mary takes the form of consciously droll scenarios, in which the ostensible fervor of the message
is exploded by the absurdity of the medium. In one fantasy, he and
Congreve pay a weekly rite to her memory, in which they "strow
Flowers of Rhetorick, and offer such Libations to your name as it were
a Prophan[en]ess to call Toasting." In another, he lies dreaming of her
on moonshiny nights like "Endymion gaping for Cynthia in a Picture." Never a day passes but she is present to his reveries and dreams,
all the conversations he has had with her returning to his memory,
"and every Scene, place, or occasion where I have enjoyd them . . . as
livelily painted, as an Imagination equally warm & tender can be capable to represent them."

Sometimes he entertains himself with the notion of meeting her
abroad, and when he does, he is put in mind of Leander, who drowned
while swimming the Hellespont to reach his beloved Hero. Unless, in
fact, she herself crosses the Hellespont, she will know the true Asia
only "in such a dim & remote prospect, as you have of Homer in my
Translation"—a copy of the current volume of which he is sending
her. Or alternatively, he is put in mind of the troubadour Geoffrey
Rudel, who went on a pilgrimage to Jerusalem to die in the arms of the
Countess of Tripoli, who thereupon built him a tomb of porphyry,
inscribed his epitaph on it in Arabic verse, had his poems copied out
and illuminated with gold, then "was taken with Melancholy, and
turnd Nun"—all which, except the last, he persuades himself Lady
Mary would do for *him*. In one letter, he supposes himself tracing her
steps across Europe in an eastward hegira that discovers at the same
time the stages of her conversion from Christianity to Islam:

> At this Town, they will say, She practised to sit on the Sofa; at that
> village, she learnt to fold the Turbant; here she was bathd and
> anointed; & there she parted with her black Full-bottome [wig]. At
> every Christian Virtue you lost, and at every Christian Habit you
> quitted, it will be decent for me to fetch a holy Sigh, but still I shall
> proceed to follow you.

In another letter, he is part of her retinue, filling his pockets with
antique Roman coins or lugging "an old Busto" behind her, his

friends in England imagining that the object of his journey is to tread on "Classic Ground," while he is whispering "other reasons" in her ear. An idyll that he develops with particular loving care is that of commissioning Lady Mary to bring him back a "fair Circassian Slave":

> But I beg you to look oftener than you use to do, in your Glass, in order to chuse me one I may like. If you have any regard to my happiness, let there be something as near as possible to that face, but if you please, the colours a little less vivid, the eyes a little less bright. . . . Take care of this, if you have any regard to my Quiet; for otherwise instead of being her Master, I must be only her Slave.

Serious issues treated seriously are rare. One occurs early on, following a first letter from across the Channel in which Lady Mary has evidently indicated some sense of loss:

> I am glad, Madam, your native Country uses you so well as to justify your regret for it: It is not for me to talk of it with tears in my eyes; I can never think that Place my Country, where I can't call a foot of paternal Earth my owne.

If the situation for Roman Catholics becomes intolerable enough, would he emigrate to Italy? On the whole, no:

> . . . I believe, I should be as uneasy in a Country where I saw Others persecuted, by the Rogues of my own Religion, as where I was so myself by those of yours. And it is not impossible but I might run into Turkey in search of Liberty; for who would not rather live a free man among a nation of Slaves, than a Slave among a nation of free men?

The gleam of humor does not disguise the gravity of the emotion.

On other occasions, a playful surface will disclose sober questionings. Thus he imagines a reunion with Lady Mary in Lombardy, scene of some celebrated amours between a "fair Princess" and "her Dwarf"; or declares himself capable like her "of following one I lov'd, not only to Constantinople, but to those parts of India, where they tell us the Women best like the Ugliest fellows, as the most admirable productions of nature, and look upon Deformities as the Signatures of divine Favour"; and then reminds her when he next writes that there is more to a poet than his body:

> . . . if my Fate be such, that this Body of mine (which is as ill-matchd to my Mind as any wife to her husband) be left behind in the journey, let the Epitaph of Tibullus be set over it.

Hic jacet immiti consumptus morte Tibullus,
Messalam, terra, dum sequiturque, mari.
Here stopt by hasty Death, Alexis lies,
Who crost half Europe, led by Wortley's eyes!

At one point in this same letter, he sails close to the wind indeed. "I shall hear at Belgrade," he writes, concluding his fantasy of Lady Mary's conversion to Islam,

how the good Basha receivd the fair Convert with tears of joy, how he was charm'd with her pretty manner of pronouncing the words Allah, and Muhammed, and how earnestly you joind with him in exhorting Mr Wortley to be circumcised. But he satisfies you by demonstrating, how in that condition, he could not properly represent his Brittannick Majesty. Lastly I shall hear how the very first Night you lay at Pera [i.e., in Constantinople], you had a vision of Mahomet's Paradise, and happily awaked without a Soul. From which blessed instant the beautiful Body was left at full liberty to perform all the agreeable functions it was made for.

Is there a form of erotic displacement here, a fantasized exchange of identities such as rejected lovers are prone to indulge, or is it all art and entertainment? It would be hard to say. Still harder for a passage like the following, where what he wishes her to receive from and feel for her husband seems to be partly a vehicle for his own ardent wishes:

May that Person for whom you have left all the world be so just as to prefer you to all the world. . . . May you continue to think him worthy of whatever you have done, . . . ever look upon him with the eyes of a first Lover, . . . surrounded with all the Enchantments and Idæas of Romance and Poetry. In a word, may you receive from him as many pleasures and gratifications as even I think you can give.

And yet harder to judge, I incline to think, is the sort of dramatic outburst to which he gives voice in late 1717, having just learned that the Wortley Montagus have been called home:

I can keep no measures in speaking of this subject. I see you already coming, I feel you as you draw nearer, My heart leaps at your arrival: Let us have You from the East, and the Sun is at her service.
I write as if I were drunk, the pleasure I take in thinking of your

return transports me beyond the bounds of common Sence and decency.

Assailed with so much rhetoric and feeling (whether genuine or not) over a period of two years, Lady Mary behaved as a sensible woman should. She gives him to understand from the start that she is prepared to dismiss all he says as raillery, though she may, now that a suitable distance divides them, be persuaded to suppose him serious since she detects an inclination in herself to believe in "miracles." But apart from such minute concessions to the "personal" dimension, she holds firm. To all his fanciful inventions, her response is a well-observed but low-key and quite impersonal travelogue, bristling with enough exotic details of costume and custom to make the heart of a less determined swain quail. Hence viewed in one light, their correspondence is the story of a comic impasse. He seeks a regard from her that it is folly in him to ask and that it would be folly in her to bestow, even were she so inclined. In another light, however, moments of wry pathos appear. He longs desperately—as he did in all his relationships with women, and as we know today that cripples and other afflicted persons regularly do—to know the degree and nature of his acceptance, especially now that it can be conveyed by letter without face-to-face embarrassment:

> If Momus his project had taken of having Windows in our breasts, I should be for carrying it further and making those windows Casements: that while a Man showd his Heart to all the world, he might do something more for his friends, e'en take it out, and trust it to their handling.

And again, somewhat later in their exchange:

> I foresee that the further you go from me, the more freely I shall write, & if (as I earnestly wish) you would do the same, I can't guess where it will end? Let us be like modest people, who when they are close together keep all decorums, but if they step a little aside, or get to the other end of a room, can untye garters or take off Shifts without scruple.

"Take all thou e're shalt have, a constant Muse"

Still, whatever degree of sincerity we assign to Pope's protestations, it is impossible to disagree with the wise critic who once called it punningly a cultivated infatuation. To understand how much so, we need only turn to the letters he was writing during this same period to the Blount sisters, where he is not so much upon parade, and where even the highest flights of fancy seem less modish—as with Mrs. Nelson's preparations for the Pretender and the Honorable Thomas Gage's Flanders mares. When he compliments the Blounts—partly because they are unmarried and their social status closer to his own, but partly too, perhaps, because there is a deep stratum of affection, at least on his side—he can be at once more forthright and more playful:

> I can't express the Desire I have of being Happy with you a few days (or nights, if you would give me leave). . . . For in very deed Ladies, I love you both, very sincerely and passionately. . . . In earnest, I know no Two Things I would change you for, this hot Weather, except Two good Melons.

Or, having piqued (he hopes) their imaginations by telling them that a friend in Oxford, whither he is now bound, has sent him word where harlots are to be found there:

> I defy them and all their works, for I love no meat but Ortolans, and no women but you. Tho indeed that's no proper comparison but for fatt Dutchesses; For to love you, is as if one should wish to Eat Angels, or drink Cherubim-Broath.

When the Blounts and he are on good terms, which is by no means always the case (the correspondence contains evidences of several misunderstandings to whose causes we have no clue), he can affectionately tease Teresa (in a letter to Martha) for her love of finery and frolicking—

> Let your faithless Sister triumph in her ill-gotten Treasures; let her put on New Gowns to be the Gaze of Fools, and Pageant of a Birth-night! While you with all your innocence enjoy a Shadey Grove without any leaves on, & dwell with a virtuous Aunt in a Country Paradise—

and in the same letter poke gentle fun at Martha for her addiction to romance reading—

> It is usual with unfortunate Young Women to betake themselves to Romances, and therby feed & indulge that melancholy which is occasioned by the Want of a Lover: . . . I presume it may be so far your present case, as to render the five Volumes of the Grand Cyrus no unseasonable Present to you—

while delivering himself simultaneously, as the quotations suggest, of a few big-brotherly home truths for each.

At such times, when he feels secure in their regard, scattered glimpses of the inner man show through. He tells them of a proposal of Lord Harcourt's, at whose seat in Oxfordshire he worked on the Homer in the summers of 1717 and 1718:

> Here, at my Lord Harcourt's, I see a Creature nearer an Angel than a Woman, (tho a Woman be very near as good as an Angel)[.] I think you have formerly heard me mention Mrs Jennings as a Credit to the Maker of Angels. She is a relation of his Lordships, and he gravely proposed her to me for a Wife, being tender of her interests & knowing (what is a Shame to Providence) that she is less indebted to Fortune than I. I told him his Lordship could never have thought of such a thing but for his misfortune of being blind, and that I never cou'd till I was so: But that, as matters now were, I did not care to force so fine a woman to give the finishing stroke to all my deformities, by the last mark of a Beast, horns.

Or he tells them of a study-visit to nearby Oxford, where certain painful ironies flood his mind as he contemplates the homage paid him in a seat of learning and contrasts it with the frugal allotment of that commodity he is able to command from women:

> I conform'd myself to the College hours, was rolld up in books & wrapt in meditation, lay in one of the most ancient, dusky parts of the University, and was as dead to the world as any Hermite of the desart. If any thing was awake or alive in me, it was a little Vanity. ... For I found my self receivd with a sort of respect, which this idle part of mankind, the Learned, pay to their own Species. ... Indeed I was so treated, that I could not but sometimes ask myself in my mind, what College I was founder of, or what Library I had built? Methinks I do very ill, to return to the world again, to leave the only place where I make a good figure, and from seeing myself seated with dignity on the most conspicuous Shelves of a Library, go to contemplate this wretched person in the abject condition of lying at a Lady's feet in Bolton street [where the Blount sisters with their mother were now living].

Or he tells them of a nostalgic day at Binfield, spent in seeing old friends, wandering old haunts, and composing a "Hymn" that ended "with a deep Sigh"—

All hail! once pleasing, once inspiring Shade,
Scene of my youthful Loves, and happier hours!
Where the kind Muses met me as I stray'd,
And gently pressd my hand, and said, Be Ours.

Take all thou e're shalt have, a constant Muse:
At Court thou may'st be lik'd, but nothing gain;
Stocks thou may'st buy & sell, but always lose;
And love the brightest eyes, but love in vain!—

following which, an inexplicable melancholy had kept him company as he completed his journey to Oxford by moonlight:

Nothing could have more of that Melancholy which once us'd to please me, than that days journey: For after having passd thro' my favorite Woods in the forest, with a thousand Reveries of past pleasures; I rid over hanging hills, whose tops were edgd with Groves, & whose feet water'd with winding rivers, listening to the falls of Cataracts below, & the murmuring of Winds above. The gloomy Verdure of Stonor [Oxfordshire seat of the Stonor family, friends of the Popes] succeeded to these, & then the Shades of the Evening overtook me, the Moon rose in the clearest Sky I ever saw, by whose solemn light I pac'd on slowly, without company, or any interruption to the range of my thoughts.

"That Melancholy which *once* us'd to please me"—from this phrase and the Binfield "Hymn" it is easy to divine one of the more compelling subjects that fell within the range of his reflections. For the thoughts of a young man at twenty-nine are usually long, and the nostalgias that arise at about that age for lost childhoods and missed opportunities (sometimes more imaginary than real) can only have been sharpened in Pope's case by the consciousness that in the relationships where he longed most for success the future looked as unpromising as the past. Was it this consciousness that impelled him, when balancing the melancholy brought on by loving the brightest eyes in vain against the palpable blessing of his friendship with the two sisters, to write: "after all, He must be a beast that is [unhappy], with two such fine women for his friends. Tis enough to make any man easy, even such an one as Your humble Servant"—and then, in a quick surge of feeling that seems to mix bitterness with self-pity, to substitute "creature" for "man"? Certainly there is a compound of these emotions at the opening of the letter, where he remarks:

> You can't be surprized to find him a dull Correspondent, whom
> you have known so long for a dull Companion. ... I am pretty
> sensible, that if I have any wit I may as well write to show it, as not;
> because any Lady that has once seen me will naturally ask, what I
> can show that is better?

And the compound recurs with some vehemence, a few weeks or
months later, when in a moment of obvious discomfort he tries to
settle himself to a reasonable resolution of matters that have never
been resolvable on rational terms:

> I Take this occasion to tell you once for all, that I design no longer
> to be a constant Companion when I have ceas'd to be an agreable
> one. ... You must not imagine this to proceed from any Coldness,
> or the least decrease of Friendship to you. If You had any Love for
> me, I should be always glad to gratify you with an Object that you
> thought agreable. But as your regard is Friendship & Esteem; those
> are things that are as well, perhaps better, preservd Absent than
> Present. A Man that you love is a joy to your eyes at all times; a
> Man that you Esteem is a solemn kind of thing, like a Priest, only
> wanted at a certain hour to do his Office: Tis like Oyl in a Sallet,
> necessary, but of no manner of Taste.

Then in a paragraph particularly intended for Teresa and reminiscent of the fantasies he had expressed to Lady Mary about the Princess
and her Dwarf, he comes to the point:

> Let me open my whole heart to you: I have some times found
> myself inclined to be in love with you: and as I have reason to know
> from your Temper & Conduct how miserably I should be used in
> that circumstance, it is worth my while to avoid it: It is enough to
> be Disagreable, without adding Fool to it, by constant Slavery. I
> have heard indeed of Women that have had a kindness for Men of
> my Make; but it has been after Enjoyment, never before; and I
> know to my Cost you have had no Taste of that Talent in me,
> which most Ladies would not only Like better, but Understand
> better, than any other I have.

What galled most, as the final two clauses show, was that the
women he valued did not, like the Countess of Tripoli, set store by a
man because he was blessed with the divine gift of poetry. All they
were interested in, or so he believed, was little Mr. Pope the enter-
tainer, the ingenious master of compliments, the provider of casual
amusements in the same vein as the antics of a lapdog or pet monkey.

How well he understood his position with Teresa, and by extension with women generally, may be gauged from some lines first printed in 1721, but perhaps written in a fit of pique as their relationship was worsening two or three years earlier. They bear the title *Verses Sent to Mrs. T.B. with his Works. By an Author* and perhaps accompanied a copy of his *Works* of 1717, bound, as almost all of Pope's presentation copies are, in red morocco with gold lettering—though the color in the next to last line possibly glances also at the uniforms of glamorous young army officers and that in the last line at Teresa's consuming interest (because she was extravagant) in South Sea Stock and other forms of gain:

> This Book, which, like its Author, You
> By the bare Outside only knew,
> (Whatever was in either Good,
> Not look'd in, or, not understood)
> Comes, as the Writer did too long,
> To be about you, right or wrong;
> Neglected on your Chair to lie,
> Nor raise a Thought, nor draw an Eye;
> In peevish Fits to have you say,
> *See there! you're always in my Way!*
> Or, if your Slave you think to bless,
> *I like this Colour, I profess!*
> *That Red is charming all will hold,*
> *I ever lov'd it—next to Gold.*

The very fluctuations of feeling in Pope's regard for the Blount sisters give it a proximity to real experience that his inflated tenders to Lady Mary lack.

CHAPTER 15

"THIS SUBTLE THIEF OF LIFE, THIS PALTRY TIME"

"Is it, in heav'n, a crime to love too well?"

From such hopes, fears, hurts, thoughts—modified as always in that age by the accommodation of individual experience to some communal or generic norm—two of Pope's most haunting poems took shape: his *Elegy to the Memory of an Unfortunate Lady* and his *Eloisa to Abelard*: haunting partly because we have so little explicit information as to how or why they were written; partly, too, because they represent an indulgence of sentiment uncommon in Pope's longer works; and partly because they have evoked from their readers over the past two and a half centuries irreconcilable contrarieties of interpretation and evaluation.

In the *Elegy*, a male speaker is suddenly confronted by the beckoning ghost of a young woman still carrying the sword with which she has killed herself. He recognizes her, asks her (since her wandering on earth suggests that suicide has excluded her from heaven) whether there is no sympathy in those regions for great hearts and minds:

> Is it, in heav'n, a crime to love too well?
> To bear too tender, or too firm a heart,
> To act a Lover's, or a *Roman*'s part?
> Is there no bright reversion in the sky,
> For those who greatly think, or bravely die?

> (ll. 6–10)

Here, though the poem offers no clue, we are evidently to imagine the apparition's vanishing for a while, or at the very least withdrawing upstage. For the speaker now turns his attention to the "Pow'rs" of

heaven, among whom the "glorious fault" of ambition first appeared and from whom it still flows to kings, heroes, and a few
other chosen mortals distinguished by it, like the lady, from the
common herd whose life is a species of living death:

> Most souls, 'tis true, but peep out once an age,
> Dull sullen pris'ners in the body's cage:
> Dim lights of life that burn a length of years,
> Useless, unseen, as lamps in sepulchres;
> Like Eastern Kings a lazy state they keep,
> And close confin'd to their own palace sleep.
>
> (ll. 17–20)

Perhaps it was for her visible superiority to all these (the poem goes
on to speculate), and for her possession of the unqualified greatness
of soul which heaven in this poem seems to favor, that "Fate
snatch'd her early to the pitying sky" (line 24)—a reminder,
possibly, of Jove's action on behalf of Hercules, Ganymede, and
Romulus, but surely an odd way of describing suicide:

> As into air the purer spirits flow,
> And sep'rate from their kindred dregs below;
> So flew the soul to its congenial place,
> Nor left one virtue to redeem her Race.
>
> (ll. 25–28)

This last verse (elegiac practice often calls for a scapegoat) gives
way to an indictment of the young woman's uncle and guardian:
"Thou, mean deserter of thy brother's blood" (line 30). In some
undefined way, but apparently by coming between his ward and her
beloved, the guardian has precipitated her suicide. Now he is
invited to consider the appalling consequence of his behavior
("Cold is that breast which warm'd the world before," line 33) and
the retribution, if there is justice in the world, that he has drawn on
himself and his whole posterity—not the least part of which will be
the absence of all mourners as "frequent he[a]rses" (line 38) besiege
his gates:

> There passengers [passers-by] shall stand, and pointing say,
> (While the long fun'rals blacken all the way)
> Lo these were they, whose souls the Furies steel'd,
> And curs'd with hearts unknowing how to yield.
> Thus unlamented pass the proud away,

> The gaze of fools, and pageant of a day!
> So perish all, whose breast ne'er learn'd to glow
> For others' good, or melt at others' woe.
>
> (ll. 39–46)

With the uncle and his successors thus disposed of, the speaker returns to the apparition, who is now again addressed directly and whom we should perhaps imagine moving downstage center as the speaker details the indignities inflicted on her by her guardian's hard heart. No kinfolk attended her death, her funeral, or her burial;

> By foreign hands thy dying eyes were clos'd,
> By foreign hands thy decent limbs compos'd,
> By foreign hands thy humble grave adorn'd,
> By strangers honour'd, and by strangers mourn'd!
>
> (ll. 51–54)

No matter. Even though she will have no monument and her grave is barred from hallowed ground, there are healing powers in nature (one of Pope's deepest convictions) to counteract the transgressions of men:

> What tho' no friends in sable weeds appear,
> Grieve for an hour, perhaps, then mourn a year,
> And bear about the mockery of woe
> To midnight dances and the publick show?
> What tho' no weeping Loves thy ashes grace
> Nor polish'd marble emulate thy face?
> What tho' no sacred earth allow thee room,
> Nor hallow'd dirge be mutter'd o'er thy tomb?
> Yet shall thy grave with rising flow'rs be drest,
> And the green turf lie lightly on thy breast:
> There shall the morn her earliest tears bestow,
> There the first roses of the year shall blow;
> While Angels with their silver wings o'ershade
> The ground, now sacred by thy reliques made.
>
> (ll. 55–68)

For reasons left unclear in the poem—unless they too derive from her alleged "purer spirits" and the great mind that could not tolerate subjection—the body of this dead girl has sanctified the ground she is buried in and her ashes are now "reliques." Burial in a foreign land notwithstanding, there are flowers for her grave in perpetuity, tears from a mourner who can never fail, and, for monument, a tableau of angels. All the more astonishing that in the next paragraph something very like a graveside committal shrinks all that she was to a handful of dust, a destiny in no way different from that awaiting her proud persecutors:

> So peaceful rests, without a stone, a name,
> What once had beauty, titles, wealth, and fame.
> How lov'd, how honour'd once, avails thee not,
> To whom related, or by whom begot;
> A heap of dust alone remains of thee;
> 'Tis all thou art, and all the proud shall be!
>
> (ll. 69–74)

The succeeding lines, bringing the elegy to a rather unusual close, reveal for the first time the identity of the speaker. He is a poet, whose own death is felt to be not far off:

> Poets themselves must fall, like those they sung;
> Deaf the prais'd ear, and mute the tuneful tongue.
> Ev'n he, whose soul now melts in mournful lays,
> Shall shortly want the gen'rous tear he pays. . . .
>
> (ll. 75–78)

And he is also apparently—we are left to infer this—the lover whose suit, welcome to the lady but forbidden by the uncle, has led to the catastrophe of her suicide. Though reduced to dust, she lives on in his heart so long as he and his Muse live, and even when death comes (so I take the last couplet to imply), this product of his heart and Muse, this elegy that immortalizes her, will remain:

> Then from his closing eyes thy form shall part,
> And the last pang shall tear thee from his heart,
> Life's idle business at one gasp be o'er,
> The Muse forgot, and thou belov'd no more!
>
> (ll. 79–82)

There are passages of great beauty in this poem, as the reader will have noticed. Still, it is hard to resist the judgment that it is a pastiche of motifs and attitudes not very well accommodated to the whole in which they find themselves. If the unfortunate lady, as one critic has suggested, is "cast as a Roman lover" and the accent of the poet in addressing her is "Roman-elegiac," the obstacles to her being buried in hallowed ground (which account for her appearing as a ghost in the first place) quickly dissipate—and along with them the justification of that enchanting passage of inversions by which a conventionally

37. Elegy on the Death of an Unfortunate Lady. Mid-century broadside showing lines 69–74 in a musical setting by Matthew Greene. Composed in 1729.

By kind permission of the late R. H. Griffith.

unholy figure makes all about her holy, even to attracting the perpetual guardianship of angels. There is a question, in any case, as to
what supports her claim to these supernal powers. If it was indeed
fate that snatched her early to the pitying sky because only there could
a soul like hers be at home, how exactly does suicide come into it at
all? And if it does, why describe it here in such terms as blur our sense
of her defiant courage in taking her life and even raise the disturbing
question, was it necessary? What exactly were the circumstances she
confronted? The poem does not tell us. What grounds have we for
supposing that the lady's intransigence was more pardonable than
that of the "hearts unknowing how to yield?" The poem offers none.
And even if we imagine, as for young lovers we like to do, that only
the guardian is at fault, can we really defend a curse of death on his
entire line—kits, cats, bags, and wives—*in saecula saeculorum*? This is
the world of nursery rhyme and folktale. Surely it is not the same
world as that in which men and women "bear about the mockery of
woe To midnight dances and the publick show," or poets pay a
"gen'rous tear," or "eternal justice" rules. And what must be our
feelings—what indeed might be *her* feelings—towards a lover so
vengeful that he would deny escape not only to every child or woman
among her collateral relations, but to every other human being
whose breast fails to "melt at others' woe." As Hamlet might have
said, "It out-herods Herod. Pray you avoid it."

Thus the varying emotions that swirl through the *Elegy* seem fully
as incoherent as the central effort to mix the "hard" psychology of a
great-souled Roman suicide with the "soft" psychology of a
Christian burial. What one suspects may have happened is that a
thoroughly stagey incident, possibly lodged in the poet's imagination through his close association with Rowe, who at the time was
making great theatrical capital from such notoriously unfortunate
ladies as Jane Shore and Lady Jane Grey, was gradually energized by
his reading and his past and current sympathies with Mrs. Cope and
Mrs. Weston into a sort of magnetic constellation attracting all sorts
of personal impulses that had only the loosest connections (if any)
with the original fictional incident. Both Mrs. Weston and Mrs.
Cope, we may recall, were victims of men whom Pope thought
tyrannical, and in Mrs. Weston's case there was also a guardian, Sir
William Goring, of whom Pope wrote to Caryll: "he who put so
valuable a present [Elizabeth Gage, who became Mrs. John Weston]
into so ill hands shall . . . never have my good opinion . . .! and guard
all my friends from such a Guardian!" Ann Caryll Cope, moreover,
lived much of her life abroad, always in dire need of the financial

support that her bigamous husband never sent. Thus with a little poetic license she could be associated with foreign burials even though she was not dead. So also could—here we come perhaps to warmer associations—Lady Mary Wortley Montagu, whose death, though not by suicide, Pope expected might be the price of her not-less-than-Roman fortitude (he compares her, for instance, to Curtius, Portia, and Lucretia) in undertaking the perilous long trek across Europe to Istanbul. In addition, like the lady, she had been forbidden her choice of husband by that adamant guardian her father, who, then a marquess and now a duke, was certainly qualified for registry among the poem's "proud"; and though she had not established her independence of her guardian by killing herself, she had done so by arranging and boldly carrying out a dangerous elopement with a man her inferior in rank.

Neither would it be sensible in Pope's case to neglect the literary analogues, living so sensitively as he did in the experience of other climes and times. Of Ovid's eighteen heroic women, for example, protagonists of his so-called *Heroides*, of which in his *Sapho to Phaon* Pope had already translated the fifteenth, all are in one way or other victims of frustrated loves. For eight of them death is near as the poem closes. Six of the eight intend suicide, and at least three of these speak explicitly of the sword. Moreover, Ariadne, complaining to Theseus in the tenth (ll. 119–22), voices a concern that must have lurked in Pope's mind along with other matters as he composed his verses on the unfortunate lady's death in a foreign land:

> Am I then to die, and, dying, not behold my mother's tears; and shall there be no one's finger to close my eyes? Is my unhappy soul to go forth into stranger-air, and no friendly hand compose my limbs and drop on them the unguent due?

All or any of these thoughts may have been floating in the recesses of Pope's consciousness as the *Elegy* took shape. And doubtless there were others of which we know nothing, including, it may be, some such anticipations of his own death (Pope was much ill during 1716 and early 1717) as are recorded in the poem's final paragraph; or even (like most Catholics he had thought of emigration during this difficult year) of his own or others' deaths in a foreign land. Yet obviously the poem is not in any explicit sense biographical, despite the universal assumption to that effect in Pope's own day and after; nor does it seem principally concerned with the flamboyant story it tells, which it leaves at all points vague and at some points inchoate. Its actual deep substratum I take to be a mood, the sort of archetypal psychological configuration that probably gave rise to the genre of elegy in the first place. To begin with, the shock of loss. In the poem, centered on the suicide of an unfortunate young woman, this is made dramatic, and indeed melodramatic, by the appearance of her bleeding ghost, but the taut feelings of injustice and deprivation that undergird it may come from deep and far: the wrenching loss of Binfield; the uprooting of the Blount sisters and their mother from their Mapledurham home upon their brother's marriage (an action that Pope felt to be harsh and that he greatly deplored); the absence of Lady Mary on her journey into savage lands; the recent deaths of Sir William Trumbull and Wycherley, two of his oldest friends and mentors, the latter of whom, it will be recalled, he visited as he lay dying; not to mention the current persecution, and sometimes execution, of Jacobites, which could be held to have its own aspect of injustice, and the compulsion felt by a number of Roman Catholics who were entirely innocent, his good friend Edward Blount among them, to remove their family hearths at least for a while to the Continent. The feelings engendered by such occurrences might easily lend body to a narrative of loss resulting from a rash but heroic action.

The complementary emotion to the sense of loss in the elegiac syndrome, apart of course from the assignment of blame, often accompanied by a surge of anger at a crass world's or individual's, obtuseness or indifference, is consolation. Whatever has happened will be in some way compensated: there is a power of regeneration rooted in the very constitution of things that cannot finally be defeated; and though one must commit whatever has died or been lost to the common fate ("A heap of dust alone remains of thee"), there remains the leap of the heart that remembers while it lives, as also the leap of the poet's heart to commemorate beauty or virtue in a work that men will not willingly let die. It is at this deeply buried level, I think, that Pope's *Elegy* achieves its modest success, and, just possibly, gives us a glimpse of a defiant corner of his mind during one of the more difficult moments of his life.

"Thy image steals between my God and me"

In *Eloisa to Abelard*, on the other hand, the displacement of personal urges and anxieties into one of the great love stories of the world becomes far easier to trace.

Peter   Abélard,   the   brilliant   and   stormy   twelfth-century

theologian, was asked, it will be remembered, by one of the canons of
Notre Dame in Paris, Fulbert by name, to take over the education of his
niece Héloïse, already known throughout France for her love of learning. She was then about sixteen or seventeen, Abélard in his late thirties. Living in Fulbert's house the better to get on with his task, the new
tutor soon found himself immersed in extracurricular activities—
"There was more kissing than teaching; my hands found themselves at
her breasts more often than on the book"—and his pupil found herself
pregnant. To spare them both embarrassment, Abélard removed
Héloïse to the care of his sister in Brittany, where her child was born.
Soon after, despite resounding declarations by Héloïse that she did not
ask for marriage and would rather be Abélard's mistress than wife even
to Caesar, they returned to Paris and were clandestinely wed. At this
point, if we are to believe Abélard (his testimony is questionable since
he had much to gain ecclesiastically from keeping the marriage secret,
and is, by the way, our only source for his mistress's supposed indifference to marriage), Héloïse made a loving but disastrous mistake. To
avoid, as she thought, the dampening effects that marriage might have
on Abélard's advancement if broadcast to the world, she denied to
Fulbert that she was in fact married. And to escape his resulting fury,
she took refuge by Abélard's arrangement in a Benedictine convent,
where for a time she was simply housed without becoming a religieuse
and where Abélard continued to visit her as her husband. Ignorant of
this last fact and supposing that Abélard, having seduced his niece, had
now immured her in a religious life to be rid of her, Fulbert took an Old
Testament revenge: he hired two ruffians to enter Abélard's lodgings
by night and cut off his genitals. Héloïse, at her husband's request, soon
after became a Benedictine nun, and he in turn a Benedictine monk.
Eventually, he was allowed by the order to build a retreat near Nogent-
sur-Seine, which with characteristic ebullience he named the Paraclete
for the third person of the Trinity (a usage at the time forbidden) and
filled with students who still flocked to hear his lectures. Appointed,
later on, abbot of St. Gildas on the Brittany coast, he left the Paraclete
to Héloïse, who moved there with the body of sisters over whom she
had become abbess during the intervening years, and there, in due
course, a sort of autobiography of Abélard's misfortunes, purporting
to be written as a letter of consolation to a friend, fell into her hands. It
is at this moment that Pope's poem begins, as Abélard's letter fires the
passion that she has never been able to conquer and sends coursing
through her memory the whole history of their relationship, at once
the event that brought her to God and the event that separates her from
Him.

The poem's content is essentially Eloisa's anguished recapitulation of her seduction by Abelard, their mutual great love, the disaster that separated them and retired them to the life of convent and monastery, and her own present inability, try as she will, to give up her memories and dreams of her terrestrial husband to become whole-heartedly the bride of Christ. She thinks with longing of "the blameless Vestal's lot"—

> The world forgetting, by the world forgot.
> Eternal sun-shine of the spotless mind!
> Each pray'r accepted, and each wish resign'd. . . .
> For her th' unfading rose of *Eden* blooms,
> And wings of Seraphs shed divine perfumes;
> For her the Spouse prepares the bridal ring,
> For her white virgins *Hymenæals* sing;
> To sounds of heav'nly harps, she dies away,
> And melts in visions of eternal day.
>
> (ll. 208–10, 217–22)

Eloisa's own "dying" is of quite another sort. Whether she walks the grove outside the Paraclete, kneels at its altars, or takes part in its offices, "Thy image"—she confides to Abelard in the passionate outpouring precipitated by his letter—"steals between my God and me":

> When from the Censer clouds of fragrance roll,
> And swelling organs lift the rising soul;
> One thought of thee puts all the pomp to flight,
> Priests, Tapers, Temples, swim before my sight:
> In seas of flame my plunging soul is drown'd,
> While Altars blaze, and Angels tremble round.
>
> (ll. 271–6)

Nor is her trouble simply the perilous power of imagination, well known to Renaissance moralists. Her rational will is involved too; only it is torn. When she contemplates the possibility of heaven's replacing Abelard in her heart, she recoils from it:

> While prostrate here in humble grief I lie,
> Kind, virtuous drops just gath'ring in my eye,
> While praying, trembling, in the dust I roll,
> And dawning grace is opening on my soul:
> Come, if thou dar'st, all charming as thou art!

> Oppose thy self to heav'n; dispute my heart. . . .
> Snatch me, just mounting, from the blest abode,
> Assist the Fiends and tear me from my God!
>
> (ll. 277–82, 287–8)

Yet equally she longs for it, trying to dismiss Abelard from her thoughts and to welcome the rewards of a life fully dedicated to God:

> No, fly me, fly me! far as Pole from Pole;
> Rise *Alps* between us! and whole oceans roll! . . .
> Fair eyes, and tempting looks (which yet I view!)
> Long lov'd, ador'd ideas! all adieu!
> O grace serene! oh virtue heav'nly fair!
> Divine oblivion of low-thoughted care!
> Fresh blooming hope, gay daughter of the sky!
> And faith, our early immortality!
> Enter each mild, each amicable guest;
> Receive, and wrap me in eternal rest!
>
> (ll. 289–290, 295–302)

But the struggle and the anguish refuse to go away. Even when Eloisa imagines her death, which she believes to be not far off, the experience remains mixed. Abelard as vested priest, holding cross and taper to ward off the fiends who (in medieval belief) snatch at all souls as they issue from the body with the last breath, becomes indistinguishable for her from Abelard the lover, whose kiss will "Suck my last breath, and catch my flying soul!" And her corresponding wish for his death that it may be painless and watched over by heavenly powers merges with memories of his "fair frame"—"That cause of all my guilt, and all my joy"—with visions of a "trance extatic" in which all his pangs will be "drown'd"—and with imaginations of saints embracing him "with a love like mine"; all features appropriate, possibly, to the death of an abbot, but appropriate assuredly to a *Liebestod*.

As often with Pope's poems, the conclusion holds a personal application. Adapting the traditional funerary formula *Siste, viator* ("Wayfarer, stop!"), which urges the passerby to pause and reflect on the meaning or the content of the scene before him, Pope first allows Eloisa to imagine a pair of wandering lovers brought by chance or curiosity to the Paraclete, discovering there the common grave in which she and Abelard now lie together, and "with mutual pity mov'd" murmuring sadly, "Oh may we never love as these have lov'd!" (line 352). Or again, if someone in the midst of Mass at the

Paraclete—"when loud *Hosanna*'s rise"—should spare a glance for that grave "where our cold reliques lie" (here again we may wonder if these are Love's saints, or God's):

> Devotion's self shall steal a thought from heav'n,
> One human tear shall drop, and be forgiv'n.
>
> (ll. 357–8)

Eloisa's final modulation of the *Siste, viator* motif is to imagine a poet suffering from frustrations and deprivations similar to hers, who will record them and by recording them give her ghost (and presumably his own spirit) peace.

> And sure if fate some future Bard shall join
> In sad similitude of griefs to mine,
> Condemn'd whole years in absence to deplore,
> And image charms he must behold no more,
> Such if there be, who loves so long, so well;
> Let him our sad, our tender story tell;
> The well-sung woes will sooth my pensive ghost;
> He best can paint 'em, who shall feel 'em most.
>
> (ll. 359–66)

Readers familiar with Pope's poems generally will need no reminder that *Eloisa to Abelard* consorts somewhat oddly with the rest of them, considerably more oddly than the *Elegy*, which in many respects is simply an expanded epitaph. True, the poem's literary and cultural antecedents are plain enough. The original Latin letters reputedly exchanged by the lovers had been lately translated into English from a French version heavily pruned, revised, and at some dramatic points expanded by romance-minded writers of the age of Louis XIV, a circumstance that made Pope's venture timely. Tears were also in high fashion—considering her circumstances, weeping is inevitably Eloisa's chief relief—especially female tears of love or repentance. Here may be remembered the many Counter-Reformation paintings of the distraught Magdalene, forgiven in the end because she "loved much," or of those female saints from whose "lambent" eyes (a contemporary adjective ideally suited to this style of painting and its transparent blend of pathos with eros) a single round drop brims, or courses with pearly emphasis down a wasting cheek. In fact, the image of a female in distress, her woes brought upon her by some self-immolating high principle, entanglement in hopeless love, or cruel turn of fate—"Beauty and anguish," as Tennyson was to put it later in his *Legend of Fair Women*, "walking hand in hand The downward slope to Death"—is one of the most striking features of the psychological progression that leads from Dryden's Indamora through Rowe's Jane Shore, Lillo's Maria, Hogarth's Sarah Young, Richardson's Clarissa and Fielding's Amelia to that delicious moment confessed to by the German poet Johann Furchtegott Gellert, who boasts that while reading about the parting of Clementina and Sir Charles Grandison in Richardson's novel of that name, tears ran down his cheeks till they soaked his book, his handkerchief, and his writing table.

Though this fashion for troubled females may have expressed in part a rising consciousness of the legal and social trammels in which women were bound—a consciousness very plain in some of Pope's other poems and conceivably at play here in the "Relentless walls" and oppressive rules that immure Eloisa—it tended to confirm as well a stereotype of woman's anarchic slavery to her passions. In *Eloisa* itself, though clearly the poem means us to pity a protagonist trapped like a Racinian Bérenice or Phèdre in a world where nothing desirable is possible and nothing possible desirable, we are no more asked to suspend whatever judgment we feel the situation calls for than we are (to compare small things with great) in the case of Shakespeare's Constance, Ophelia, Desdemona, or Cleopatra. On the other hand, Pope has effectively seen to it for most readers that their judgments shall not be harsh. It has been said of Ovid's heroines, on whose lamentations Pope occasionally draws for details, that for the most part they are self-centered, self-pitying, morally weak, hurt, and angry, and much afraid that they have been betrayed, whereas Eloisa is cut from a different cloth. She never grows cynical about Abelard's love, truth, or genuine concern for her best interests, and refuses to play tricks with her own emotions:

> It is characteristic of her personality, of the nature of her love, and of the tone of her appeals to Abelard that when she slips, just once, into an argument that is not quite candid:
>
> > Ah, think at least thy flock deserves thy care,
> > Plants of thy hand, and children of thy pray'r,
> >
> > (ll. 129–30)
>
> she quickly recognizes that this is unfair to him and unworthy of herself:
>
> > See how the force of others' pray'rs I try
> > (O pious fraud of am'rous charity!)

38 Alexander Pope, between figures of the Unfortunate Lady and Eloisa. By William Blake. Oil and tempera, *c.* 1800.

Blake has framed Pope's head in both "the Poet's Bays" (viewer's left) and "Critick's Ivy" (viewer's right). *Essay on Criticism*, 706. Wimsatt, 66.20.

By kind permission of the City Art Gallery, Manchester.

> But why should I on others' pray'rs depend?
> Come thou, my father, brother, husband, friend!
>
> (ll. 149–52)

As the last line strongly intimates with its mingle of religious and secular relationships, Eloisa's experience has fused love and religion indissolubly. Every movement toward God is a movement toward Abelard, the human as well as priestly center of that personal history which has brought her to be God's votaress as well as his. Love of the saving doctrine has become inextricable from love of the saving doctor, yet love of the saving doctor violates the vows taken for his sake, which remain a divine as well as human bond (she has also taken marriage vows) between them. To give up her love for Abelard would be the action of a saint:

> I come, I come! Prepare your roseate bow'rs,
> Celestial palms, and ever-blooming flow'rs.
>
> (ll. 317–18)

To give up her longing for God would be the action of a legendary figure of romance:

> May one kind grave unite each hapless name,
> And graft my love immortal on thy fame.
>
> (ll. 343–44)

Yet either step, though it would end her torment, would be a surrender of some part of her reality, a partial denial of the identity that defines her as Eloisa rather than as the blameless Vestal, and a diminution (at least in human and dramatic terms) of her tragic stature and poetic interest.

"He best can paint 'em, who shall feel 'em most"

Sending a copy of *Eloisa* to Lady Mary in Constantinople in June of 1717, Pope coyly warned her of one passage "that I can't tell whether to wish you should understand it, or not." Doubtless the lines he had in mind were those in which the "future Bard," suffering from Eloisa's pangs—

> Condemn'd whole years in absence to deplore,
> And image charms he must behold no more—

will paint 'em best because he feels 'em most. About a year earlier he had written to Martha Blount to much the same effect: "The Epistle of Eloise grows warm, and begins to have some Breathings of the Heart in it, which may make posterity think I was in love. I can scarce find it in my heart to leave out the conclusion I once intended for it." If the conclusion *named* Martha, as seems to be implied, it was probably left out because she insisted (as she always did) on not being publicly identified either as addressee of his poems or as object of his affections. No matter. Whatever Pope might say about it to Lady Mary or, in 1717–1718, believe he meant by its intimations of love, the poem clearly belongs more to Martha's and Teresa's world than to Lady Mary's. Its immersion in Catholic feeling, as many Catholic readers have recognized, is more than skin-deep. Its glances at the various structures of devotional meditation—exercises particularly recommended by the handbooks of the Counter-Reformation to

struggling souls like Eloisa (one is aptly named *The Spiritual Combat*)
—are numerous, if sometimes sidelong, and well-informed. Several
of Eloisa's mental acts and visions, as Pope conceives them, bear a
surprising likeness to the meditative exercitant's "composition of
place" (i.e., particularized mental imaging of a scene), though in her
case used not to reify a moment in the life of Jesus, but to project her
own sense of entrapment and rebellion:

> Relentless walls! whose darksom round contains
> Repentant sighs, and voluntary pains:
> Ye rugged rocks! which holy knees have worn;
> Ye grots and caverns shagg'd with horrid thorn!
> Shrines! where their vigils pale-ey'd virgins keep,
> And pitying saints, whose statues learn to weep!
> Tho' cold like you, unmov'd, and silent grown,
> I have not yet forgot my self to stone.
>
> (ll. 17–24)

"Application of the senses," a related exercise designed to stir up
the affections that in turn move the will, obviously characterizes her
effort to warm to the raptures of the blameless vestal; though this
exercise is not sufficiently under her spiritual control to prevent its
suffusing those same raptures with erotic overtones or indeed to
prevent her transformation of the entire setting of the Paraclete into a
rendezvous of natural objects wooing and making love:

> The darksom pines that o'er yon' rocks reclin'd
> Wave high, and murmur to the hollow wind,
> The wandring streams that shine between the hills,
> The grots that eccho to the tinkling rills,
> The dying gales that pant upon the trees,
> The lakes that quiver to the curling breeze.
>
> (ll. 155–60)

Even the well-known "colloquy" and the meditation on death
appear among Eloisa's devotional resources. The meditation on death
is of course widely recommended in the manuals as the best means to
self-knowledge, which is to say, to knowledge of the vanity of the
things of this world, or, as Eloisa has it at the close of her own
meditation on this subject, to a proper sense of "What dust we doat
on, when 'tis man we love" (line 336). Colloquies, on the other hand,
are the direct conversations with God that most authorities held to be
the end-product of the meditative discipline. In these moments,
urges one of the best known of the spiritual directives, anticipating

almost uncannily the character of Eloisa's colloquies with Abelard in her letter, we are to speak to God, sometimes "as a sonne speaketh unto his Father"; sometimes "as a sicke man speaketh to a Phisitian, declaring unto him his infirmities, and desiring remedie thereof"; sometimes "as one that is guiltye speaketh to a Judge"; sometimes as a pupil speaks to his teacher, "requyring of him light, and Instruction," or else "as one friend speaketh unto another, when he talketh with him of some waighty affaire," or sometimes, even, "as the bride speaketh to her spouse in several Colloquyes, wherewith the book of Canticles is replenished." Here again, it might be said, Abelard has become both God's intermediary and his rival.

It is difficult to account for the extreme Catholic cast of this poem, so much unlike anything else that Pope ever wrote. Did his uprooting from Binfield together with the turmoil of his co-religionists at this period produce in him a special feeling of solidarity with the old faith and its practices, impelling him to write something substantial that, unlike the *Essay on Criticism* and *Rape of the Lock*, which some of his fellow-Catholics had disapproved, would be a work for his own people? The idea is tempting, but one cannot claim that the monastic vocation is treated here with much more respect than in the *Essay on Criticism*, where it had exposed him to censure. On the contrary. The rigor of Eloisa's surroundings and her sense of melancholy incarceration, if we suppose them to have any significance beyond fulfilling the demands of the narrative or reflecting the familiar accidie of conventual life, might be felt to communicate his distaste for all confining practices and dogmas. Or did a projected possible emigration of the Blount family, or of his own, give rise to a surge of emotions centering on separation, longing, and loneliness for which the newly published letters of Héloïse to Abelard offered an ideal vehicle? This idea too is tempting but probably does not go far enough. Both the *Elegy* and *Eloisa*, we notice, concern a woman's great love for a man, something Pope could only dream of; though in both poems, it is decidedly worth noticing, our attention is brought around at the close to a "poet" or "Bard" who has somehow, to borrow a phrase from Shakespeare's Enobarbus in *Antony and Cleopatra*, earned a place in the story: in the first instance by actually being the object of the Lady's sacrificial love; in the second by so sharing in the yearnings of his heroine that he can and does create them anew—as much for his inner audience of Lady Mary and the Blounts as for the larger readership who will buy his book at Lintot's shop.

Furthermore, whether Pope himself was conscious of it or not, the

Abelard and Eloisa story offered latent possibilities of emotional identification with both lovers. In Abelard, he might, if he chose, sense one kind of actuation of his own situation, both as it was and as he might wish it to be. Though there is no evidence whatever that Pope was sexually crippled, he had been penalized from boyhood by a dwarfish stature and deformity that seemed capable of bringing about similar frustrations so far as normal relations with women were concerned and were just as certain to last his lifetime. (Here it may be helpful to recall that in European countries, England was known as the kissing nation. To kiss a woman on greeting her had been a normal form of salute among polite Englishmen for centuries. One may easily guess at the embarrassment of this usage, whether one followed or side-stepped it, for a man of Pope's size.) On the other hand (going back to Pope's source), Abelard was deeply loved despite all. Hence at least in Pope's fantasy, he could be an emblem of hope. Had not a letter from him precipitated Eloisa's outpouring of passion? What if a letter of his own—to Lady Mary, say—should prove a comparable invitation?

With Eloisa, the potential identifications might go still deeper. Until the outpouring of this letter, she had had to suppress her passion, or at least be mute about it, because to do otherwise would have been to breach the rules of her society. In Pope's case, not to have suppressed passion would have subjected him immediately to ridicule for the same reason: how sensitive (like most cripples) he was to hostile laughter appears everywhere in his correspondence and throughout his career. Eloisa, moreover, once the dam is broken, realizes the ironies of her fate, or better—since realizes is too intellectual a term for what actually takes place—explores them by reenacting them in her letter to Abelard. Having done so, she does not flinch from the bleak future that for all her longings she foresees will be hers. In a sense, she exorcises her pain by recapitulating its history, as in modern psychiatric therapy, knowing at the same time that she must bear it out even to the edge of doom. It is not hard to believe, though it can never be proved, that in Pope something similar was at work. In the person of Eloisa, he could pour out his longing to be loved: to be loved greatly, for it would take a great love, he knew, to overlook his limitations—not just his size and twisted back but his perpetual illnesses. In her person, too, he could express his angry sense of imprisonment in a fate he had never asked for and done nothing to deserve, together with those sensations of profound melancholy—

> Black Melancholy sits, and round her throws
> A death-like silence, and a dread repose—

(ll, 165–66)

that grew on him sometimes in contemplating his future, as they had grown on him that moonlit night riding to Oxford, after his nostalgic revisit to Binfield, and after the realization, set down in those verses for the Blount sisters, that only the Muses would ever press *his* hand and say, Be Ours! And likewise in her person, he could dream:

> O curst, dear horrors of all-conscious night!
> How glowing guilt exalts the keen delight!
> Provoking Dæmons all restraint remove,
> And stir within me ev'ry source of love.
> I hear thee, view thee, gaze o'er all thy charms,
> And round thy phantom glue my clasping arms.
> I wake—no more I hear, no more I view,
> The phantom flies me, as unkind as you.
> I call aloud; it hears not what I say:
> I stretch my empty arms; it glides away:
> To dream once more I close my willing eyes;
> Ye soft illusions, dear deceits, arise!
> Alas no more!—methinks we wandring go
> Thro' dreary wastes, and weep each other's woe;
> Where round some mould'ring tow'r pale ivy creeps. . . .

(ll. 229–42)

To put the affinities of life with poetry in these terms is to put them too baldly, I am well aware. Yet the poem does open, I think, at some obscure subterraneous level, a window on Pope's sense of his situation at this time, and marks, perhaps, a personal urge to come to terms, imaginatively, poetically, dramatically, by means of an objective correlative, with the austere future that lay ahead. It is interesting, at any rate, that he never again undertook a poem so amorous of content or so passionate of style. What is yet more interesting as a mark of his genius is that, having created in the two *Rapes* of 1712 and 1714 the consummate version of the glittering gay belle of the *beau monde* of his time, end-product of a society deeply concerned for propriety, etiquette, and fashion, and end-product too of a distinguished line of Restoration comic ingenues, he could perfect so soon thereafter an anticipatory model, complete even to a medieval ambience, of the loving, self-giving culture heroine of the future, whose essential type, in many variants and by no means always in medieval contexts, would dominate the novel from Rousseau's Julie (in his own *La Nouvelle Héloïse*) to Emily Bronte's Catherine Earnshaw, and poetry from Byron's Haidée, Keats's Isabella, and Tennyson's Oenone to (at last only a wistful memory) the *Waste Land*'s Hyacinth Girl.

A publication and a death

Eloisa to Abelard and the *Elegy to the Memory of an Unfortunate Lady* made their first appearance in Pope's *Works* of 1717, published on 3 June simultaneously with the third volume of his Homer. It was a handsome book, issued in the same sumptuous quarto, folio, and large folio formats as the *Iliad* translation, printed on several qualities of paper, and embellished with engraved headpieces, tailpieces, and pictorial initials. The nine headpieces were especially engraved by Samuel Gribelin, whether after Pope's designs we do not know. But the first pictorial initial is certainly a work either drawn by him or drawn to his specifications. The initial itself, a large capital "I," stands like an ancient pillar, dividing two scenes. In one, the huge winged horse Pegasus strikes his foot against Mount Helicon to create Hippocrene, the mythic headwater of all poetry. In the other, Jove's lightning bolt strikes the ground and produces fire. From the sky above both scenes, the rays of a sunburst (or of Olympus?) stream down, charging the whole setting with an energy that reminds one of Van Gogh. Throughout his career, Pope never missed an opportunity to apprise his readers that the poet's calling (like that of the truly creative mind in all fields) rests on powers of whose sources we still know surprisingly little and whose contributions to the total health of mankind have perhaps been as indispensable as water and fire. It is a poet of our own day, not Pope, who reminds us, "We shall never have great poetry"—in the sense of great works of imagination whether in verse or prose—"unless we believe that poetry serves great ends." Pope believed.

The frontispiece of the *Works*, as was the habit of those times, shows the author. It is a larger than full-page folding plate, engraved by George Vertue from an oil by Jervas. Painted in the autumn of 1714, when the *Rape of the Lock* was still the talk of the town, and on sale in its engraved form at Lintot's shop by late August 1715, immediately following the acclaim that had greeted his Homer in June, the portrait depicts the poet-as-gallant or young-man-about-town: an image agreeing very well with such of the volume's contents as the *Rape*, the

39 Alexander Pope, aged about twenty-six. By Charles Jervas, *c*. 1714.
Wimsatt, 2.1.

Courtesy of the Bodleian Library, Oxford.

Essay on Criticism, and the complimentary poems for Teresa Blount, but perhaps less appropriate to the poet of the *Pastorals,* the *Messiah, Windsor-Forest,* the *Temple of Fame,* and to the new "man of feeling" discovered in the *Eloisa* and the *Elegy.* Lustrous curls of a full-bottomed wig falling far down over the shoulders make a flattering frame for the thin sharp face with its broad brow, wide soft eyes, long nose, and firm chin. The head, held a touch too proudly, rises above the stand-up collar of a white shirt whose fine lawn sleeve shows again at the wrist of the left arm, in full view (perhaps) because Jervas wanted to paint the elegant hand in which it terminates) across the breast of the dark blue jacket (it is so colored in the oil) that covers the shirt and by its dark mass keeps the painting in balance. It is a likeness worth study because it tells us so much about how Pope saw himself during the early part of the period we have been discussing, or at least how he wanted others to see him. The angle of the pose allows no hint of the humped back to escape; no viewer could possibly guess, unless he was forewarned—so fully does the body fill the canvas allotted to it—that the sitter was not a man of normal size and weight; and the total effect is stunning.

To some extent, without doubt, this sumptuous book produced by this handsome young man—as if, says one critic, he were already a classic—was a monument to vanity. Vanity may have been abetted, however, by a pragmatic suspicion that his life would not necessarily be long. The sense of relative security that modern medicine has induced is best appreciated by reading a seventeenth- or eighteenth-century correspondence, where the minor or chronic discomfort of one letter may be succeeded in the next, as if magically, by what we now know must have been some version of coronary or pulmonary failure, an internal hemorrhage, a burst appendix, septicemia, acute uremia, or any of the thousand and one viral and bacterial killers for which today we always have names, frequently have lenitives, and sometimes have cures. In Pope's case, the uncertainties were multiplied, and his letters between 1716 and 1720 do not lack for hints that on occasion he had fears, like Keats, that he might cease to be. This edition of the *Works,* moreover, seems to have been largely Lintot's venture. It was not a subscription edition, and we have no record of Pope's profiting from it, apart from the 120 copies in royal quarto that he was to receive in return for copyright. This suggests that, however welcome the undertaking may have been to a young man's ego, it was essentially an effort by the publisher with the poet's help, and with some new important pieces, to compensate for the somewhat less than hoped return that his part in the Homer, the folio without plates, had brought in. Very likely the same double purpose will account for Pope's editing that same summer (Lintot published it on July 13) the small octavo *Poems on Several Occasions*. It was a miscellany that allowed him to preserve in print a handful of small poems and juvenilia that apparently he wished neither to own nor to suppress, while at the same time compiling an attractive item for Lintot's buyers by drawing in his distinguished friends, most notably John Sheffield, duke of Buckinghamshire, the admired author of *An Essay on Poetry* in the manner of Horace's *Ars Poetica*, and Anne Finch, countess of Winchelsea (some of whose "delightful pictures," along with a passage or two in *Windsor-Forest*, Wordsworth declared to be the only new images of external nature between *Paradise Lost* and Thomson's *Seasons!*). We do not know how well the miscellany volume sold, but we have no evidence that Pope himself received any rewards from it.

The *Works*, however, allowed him in its Preface to make his first public presentation of himself in prose. The essay, as we have it in print, is unassuming, formal, dignified, and in a quiet way witty: "In this office of collecting my pieces, I am altogether uncertain, whether to look upon myself as a man building a monument, or burying the dead." Johnson praises it for its "great spriteliness and elegance," Atterbury for its "Modesty, and good sense," and Joseph Warton, who in a moment of exaggeration called it "one of the best pieces of prose in our language," rightly admired its spare simplicity of style.

Essentially, in its first and more general portion, it is a conciliatory and commonsensical plea for greater tolerance by reader and critic in the reception of new authors. Even those who write poorly *mean* to please the public, and have no way of assuring themselves whether they can without publishing; and even if they sometimes continue to publish after the response has been negative, the public should reflect that the verdict often comes too late in life to permit a change of livelihood. (By 1728, when he wrote *The Art of Sinking in Poetry* and the first *Dunciad*, eleven years of further attacks on his work, person, and family had evidently expunged these charitable sentiments from his brain.) As for the writer who writes well, how shall he find this out if not by publishing? Yet when he does, he is all too often dismissed as a conceited puppy pursuing fantasies of immortality, when in fact he is trembling in his boots. If his work succeeds, he is immediately judged a genius and everyone feeds him full of flatteries which "put him in no small danger of becoming a Coxcomb" (a consummation not confined, alas, to the age of Pope), while at the same time other writers begin to be jealous of him and the ordinary man in the street suspicious: "A hundred honest Gentlemen [here speaks the author of the *Essay on Criticism*?] will dread him as a Wit, and a hundred innocent Women [and here the author of the *Rape*?] as a Satyrist."

As he moves from such general reflections to his personal apologia for bringing out this collection of 1717, one may marvel once again at the curiously peaceful co-presence in the same mind of an attitude toward literature inherited from court circles of the Renaissance and still vigorously alive in a society largely dominated by men of birth and privilege, and an attitude almost diametrically opposed that over the recent past had become midwife to a new view of literature as a professional activity to which, at least by serious practitioners, only the highest standards of performance should be brought. On the one hand, a doctrine according to which every gentleman should be something of a poet, but mainly as divertisement of his idle hours:

> I writ because it amused me; I corrected because it was as pleasant to me to correct as to write; and I publish'd because I was told I might please such as it was a credit to please.

On the other hand, the manifesto of a new age and of the program rigorously followed, as we have seen, by Pope himself:

> I fairly confess I have serv'd my self all I could by reading; that I made use of the judgment of authors dead and living; that I omitted no means in my power to be inform'd of my errors, both by my friends and enemies.

But then, without even swallowing hard, back to the traditional thesis!

> But the true reason these pieces are not more correct, is owing to the consideration how short a time they, and I, have to live: One may be ashamed to consume half one's days in bringing sense and rhyme together; and what Critic can be so unreasonable as not to leave a man time enough for any more serious employment, or more agreeable amusement?

Never during his lifetime will Pope be able to cease paying lip service to the old church even while observing all the requirements and indeed setting the standards of the new.

The collected *Works* was Pope's most important "public" event in 1717. The most important personal event was his father's death on 23 October. The death was sudden, evidently from a heart attack, as we saw in an earlier chapter, and the family's state of mind may be read in a note sent to Burlington asking for a few hartshorn drops (supposedly a relaxant and soporific) for his mother and the loan of a servant to be sent into the country to inform "a Relation of mine"—presumably his half-sister Magdalen at Hallgrove, near Bagshot. In his discomposure, he dates the note to Burlington "December 23." To the Blounts, in a briefer information of October 24, he writes: "My poor Father dyed last night. Believe, since I don't forget you this moment, I never shall."

"I am a Catholick, in the strictest sense of the word"

This sad occurrence altered Pope's life considerably. Apart from personal grief—there are suggestions in the correspondence that he did not care to see any but his closest friends for a while—there were new responsibilities. His mother was 74 and ailing. His old nurse, Mary Beach, was close to seventy. With only two very elderly women, plus a servant or two, now residing at 110 Chiswick Lane, his festive life along the Thames but more particularly his business life in London would have to be curtailed, long stays from home being under the new conditions inadvisable. Or so it may have seemed at the time. (Later he became famous for his summer "rambles.") Perhaps on this account, for a period during 1718 he considered building on a piece of ground belonging to Lord Burlington behind Burlington House in London: but then, dissuaded by the costs, and probably also by the ten-mile rule governing Roman Catholics, settled at Twickenham in the early months of 1719.

Shortly before this date, he had reaffirmed the commitment that required him to pay attention to such matters as Catholic penal laws. For it was hardly a fortnight after his father's death when Francis Atterbury, dean of Westminster and bishop of Rochester, with whom a warm friendship based on shared interests in literature and shared sentiments about the greatness of Milton had lately been growing up, wrote proposing that he convert now to the Established Church. In that time, as we saw earlier, the formal affiliation of a household was ordinarily set by the head of the family, which the poet now was. "When you have paid the Debt of Tenderness you owe to the Memory of a Father," Atterbury began,

> I doubt not, but you will turn your Thoughts towards improving that Accident to your Own ease and Happiness. You have it now in your Power to pursue that Method of Thinking and Living [i.e.,

whatever it is] which you like best. Give me leave, if I am not too early in my Applications of this hand [kind], to Congratulate you upon it, and to assure you, that there is no man living, who . . . would be more pleas'd to contribute any ways to your Satisfaction, or Service.

What clergyman would not wish to have the merit of bringing the period's leading poet into the national fold?

But he had reckoned without his man. Earlier on, in 1713, when Swift had made a similar proposal, Pope had replied with a style of fine raillery that must have entertained the then newly appointed dean of St. Patrick's (who believed himself to be, and was, a master in that mode) fully as much as his intended proselyte's refusal to take the proposal seriously can possibly have disappointed him. After a number of facetious suggestions, including the idea that he might make more money by selling off his faith by subscription than by any mere translation of Homer, Pope accedes to all the main Protestant tenets but cannot quite give up an old-fashioned belief in saving the souls of sinners by establishing masses in perpetuity. Though Old Dryden, for instance, was a Roman Catholic, he was also a poet, and no poet's soul is ever saved for less than £50; for a Socinian like Walsh, it will run at least to £100; and the sum required for Gay, a man cannot even guess at. Unfortunately, there is one more whose salvation he must insist on, but this will "prove of so much greater Charge than all the rest" that a subsidy from the Lord Treasurer is the only hope:

> The Person I mean is Dr Swift, a dignified Clergyman, but One who, by his own Confession, has composed more Libels than Sermons. If it be true, what I have heard often affirmed by innocent People, that too much Wit is dangerous to Salvation, this unfortunate Gentleman must certainly be damned to all Eternity. . . . Be it as it will, I should not think my own Soul deserved to be saved, if I did not endeavour to save his, for I have all the Obligations in Nature to him. He has brought me into better Company than I cared for, made me merrier, when I was sick, than I had a Mind to be, put me upon making Poems on Purpose that he might alter them, &c.

The letter goes on, witty to the end, permitting Swift to smile at his invitation to apostatize if it were seriously meant and to laugh at it if it were not: a delightful demonstration of affectionate tact. No such tone or content were of course appropriate to a bishop or to an invitation made in all seriousness, and Pope's reply in this difficult situation can only be called noble. Since it also supplies a good deal of insight into his convictions on a matter that most men and women in his day and some still in ours regard as the most important question of their lives, I shall quote from it freely:

> I am truly oblig'd by your kind condoleance on my Father's death, and the desire you express that I should improve this incident to my advantage. . . . It is true, I have lost a parent for whom no gains I could make would be any equivalent. But that was not my only tye: I thank God another still remains. . . . A rigid divine may call it a carnal tye, but sure it is a virtuous one: at least I am more certain that it is a duty of nature to preserve a good parent's life and happiness, than I am of any speculative point whatever. . . . For she, my Lord, would think this separation more grievous than any other, and I, for my part, know . . . little . . . of the success of such an adventure, (for an Adventure it is, and no small one, in spite of the most positive divinity.) Whether the change would be to my spiritual advantage, God only knows: this I know, that I mean as well in the religion I now profess, as I can possibly ever do in another. Can a man who thinks so, justify a change, even if he thought both equally good?

The poet then goes on to make the earlier-quoted statement that because he loved reading he had run through his father's whole library at around the age of fourteen: all of it Catholic-Protestant apologetics, and all of it leaving him convinced according to the book he had read last. He suspects that most "Seekers" are in the same case, and that when they finally decide "are not so properly converted as out-witted." He suspects, too, that Atterbury and he are already, in fact, of the same religion, "if we were throughly understood by one another; and that all honest and reasonable christians would be so, if they did but talk enough together every day; and had nothing to do together, but to serve God and live in peace with their neighbour."

> As to the *temporal* side of the question, I can have no dispute with you. It is certain, all the beneficial circumstances of life, and all the shining ones, lie on the part you would invite me to. But if I could bring myself to fancy, what I think you do but fancy, that I have any talents for active life, I want health for it; and besides it is a real truth, I have less Inclination (if possible) than Ability. Contemplative life is not only my scene, but it is my habit too.

Then follows the closest thing to a program of political and religious principles that Pope ever made:

In my politicks, I think no further than how to preserve the peace of my life, in any government under which I live; nor in my religion, than to preserve the peace of my conscience in any Church with which I communicate. I hope all churches and all governments are so far of God, as they are rightly understood, and rightly administred [Pope will return to this point in the *Essay on Man*]: and where they are, or may be wrong, I leave it to God alone to mend or reform them; which whenever he does, it must be by greater instruments than I am. I am not a Papist, for I renounce the temporal invasions of Papal power, and detest their arrogated authority over Princes, and States. I am a Catholick, in the strictest sense of the word. If I was born under an absolute Prince, I would be a quiet subject; but I thank God I was not. I have a due sense of the excellence of the British constitution. In a word, the things I have always wished to see are not a Roman Catholick, or a French Catholick, or a Spanish Catholick, but a true Catholick: and not a King of Whigs, or a King of Tories, but a King of England. Which God of his mercy grant his present Majesty may be.

Some timely adjustments

At the time, then, of his move to Twickenham, several of those choices that modern sociology likes to call life choices had been made by Pope, or made for him. On the side of his female acquaintance, much had already changed, or was fast changing. We inevitably know less of his feelings for Lady Mary once her return to England had interrupted any regular (and surely any "romantic") correspondence with one who had ceased to be an instance of Beauty-in-Peril in far places and was now simply a handsome bluestocking with court aspirations, and of a Whiggery so absolute that she could abide neither Swift nor his writings and was later on impelled to attack him outrageously with an obscene lampoon. For at least a while after their return, very friendly relations were kept up between Pope and the Wortley Montagus—he was instrumental, for example, during his first spring there in helping them find a residence in Twickenham—and it is quite possible that for a time Lady Mary continued to fascinate him; for the break was long in coming and doubtless had for background when it came, as most such breaks do, a history of petty resentments on both sides. As late as 1720, at any rate, he could still write in a letter to Gay, who had congratulated him on finishing the renovations to his Twickenham riverside villa:

> Ah, friend, 'tis true—this truth you lovers know—
> In vain my structures rise, my gardens grow,
> In vain fair Thames reflects the double scenes
> Of hanging mountains, and of sloping greens:
> Joy lives not here; to happier seats it flies,
> And only dwells where Wortley casts her eyes.

Very pretty, Mr Pope! But there was no future in that direction, as he well knew.

As for the Blount sisters, so many of Pope's letters to them are undated and undatable that to go about mapping the ups and downs of their relationship is like walking through a minefield. Suffice it to say that after his letter citing the kind of (imaginary?) women who have had a kindness "for Men of my Make" (probably late 1717 or early 1718), his letters to the two sisters, and particularly to Teresa, rarely recapture for long "their old verve and *joie*." A formal indenture that he drew up in early 1718, committing himself to pay Teresa an annual annuity of £40 for a period of six years or until she married, though it has understandably provoked a good deal of speculation, is perhaps most satisfactorily explained as a kind but misguided effort to enhance the income (from the Mapledurham estate by agreement with her brother) of which she was always in dire need, but which was sometimes unpaid, and was rarely paid on time. The agreement carries Pope's signature and that of two witnesses, but no corresponding endorsement or attachment from Teresa. Quite possibly she was furious at what could easily seem to her his presumption, and it is barely possible that a mystifying undated letter in the correspondence constitutes his written apology after an oral quarrel over the matter: he apologizing both for what she had taken to be his insufferable vanity in this action, and for his own effrontery in taxing *her* with vanity when she refused so practical a solution to the galloping consumption of her purse. But this is guesswork. What it is sufficient to say, once more, is that by the time of his removal to Twickenham, the relation with Teresa was deteriorating badly. Readers of the poem *Sent to Mrs. T.B. with his Works*, quoted earlier, will have little difficulty in guessing why. Only with Martha, more peaceable in temper, probably better endowed with pity, plainly less dependent than her sister on gowns, gallantries, gaming, and other traditional excitements of that beau monde where Whirl is King, did a durable friendship (which in Pope's case remained at least nine parts love) gradually evolve. To her, some fifteen years later, in his *Epistle to a Lady*, he would address the finest tribute that any eighteenth-century woman ever received.

Just now, however, the future must have looked considerably more shrunken through those clear unflinching eyes that Jervas in 1714 had so finely caught in his portrait of the artist as a young man. He had been taught by now, as we saw a moment ago, that the only passionate love affair in which he could hope to be the successful wooer would have to be conducted with his Muse. A second portrait of the poet by Jervas, undated, but painted (probably?) during one of his returns from Ireland between 1717 and 1720, teases one into wondering whether some such mood, or conclusion, is not being intentionally or unintentionally evoked. It shows Pope in the same sort of full-bottomed wig as before, with, again, fine lawn cuffs, this time emerging at the wrists of both sleeves, for we see the sitter at full length in a very large upholstered Queen Anne wing chair, one hand resting lightly on the chair's left arm, the other supporting his right cheek in a musing position that will be repeated in Kneller's portrait of 1722. He is dressed in white shirt and cravat, dark blue-gray jacket, waistcoat, breeches, and stockings, plus black shoes with yellow buckles. The crossed legs, the hand supporting the cheek, the other wrist limp on the chair arm, as well as the marked downward cast of the eyes, give the impression of a mind lost in reflection or even possibly "rapt" in the process of poetic composition. No attempt is made to disguise the thin legs or the fact that the chair's curved back looms large and high in contrast to the comparatively small figure rather perched upon its seat than occupying it.

Well above and to the right (our left) of the poet's head, resting on what appears to be an elaborate baroque mantel (it could be a plinth) is a sculptured head of Homer, which, as Pope's distinguished iconographer has pointed out, much resembles the head of Homer drawn by Jervas for the frontispiece of the first volume of the *Iliad* translation. The presence of the Homer seems explicable enough and may indeed be a clue to the reflections of the man in the large chair, who by 1718 had delivered four of the six promised volumes to his subscribers, but missed one in 1719, and was thereupon faced with supplying two for 1720. No, the teasing aspect of the painting is not Homer, but the young woman on our right (the poet's left). With darkish blonde hair and wearing a golden-brown dress, she stands tiptoe in her stocking feet on what seems to be a low stool, her shoulders, neck, head, and upward-reaching arms easily visible behind the curved chairback. Her left hand holds a book, which she may be reaching down from or replacing on a higher shelf while her right pushes up and away some sort of drapery or heavy curtain,

40. Alexander Pope, aged about twenty-nine. By Charles Jervas, *c.* 1717.
Wimsatt, 3.2.

Courtesy of the National Portrait Gallery, London.

almost as if she were engaged in an unveiling. Her face, seen in profile by us, is turned toward the figure in the chair, as are (less certainly) her eyes.

But who or what is she? If Teresa Blount, the likeness is poor, not at all the enchanting young woman (not, by the way, a blonde) whom Jervas captured in his portrait of the two sisters; nor does she at all resemble Martha. Are we, then, to see her as the female pole in a tussle of irreconcilables of which the other pole is poetry and Homer, as in Robert Burton's story of the young wife who could only distract her learned husband from his books by leaping onto his work table and lifting her skirts? If so, there is perhaps a little private Jervas joke in the lady's posture, which is modeled on that of at least two Italian compositions showing Herodias turning away from Herod with the head of John the Baptist on a salver? Or are we to suppose her the poet's Muse, his world now reduced, at least for this pictorial moment (and in real life for the long future), to a life of poetry alone, all his begetting doomed, as he had put it in the nostalgic letter from Binfield, to be merely of "Sons upon the Muses," and all his poetry, much as he valued it, serving finally but "to ease some Friend, not Wife," as he would put it later in the *Epistle to Dr Arbuthnot*, through the long discomforts of the invalidism that awaited him?

In any case, it would inevitably be a soberer existence from now on. Many of the friends with whom he had been merry in younger and more hopeful days were dead or gone now. Swift was in Dublin and wrote but occasionally. Jervas too was spending much time there, where he had many clients. Bolingbroke was in exile in France. Harley, after his stay in the Tower, had retired to his estate at Brampton Castle in Herefordshire. Henry Cromwell, if still in London, was probably avoiding Pope in view of his own loyal friendship with Dennis, and it is possible that the making of his will in 1717 and the donation of the letters Pope had written him to his former "Sappho," Elizabeth Thomas, at about the same time or shortly after, signifies a partial withdrawal to the country. Parnell, having visited his friends in England during the summer of 1718, died at Chester in October on his way home. Earlier, in April, John Caryll, Jr., with whom Pope had spent many happy hours in London before the latter's marriage, succumbed to the smallpox. That December Rowe also died, quite unexpectedly—he was only forty-four—and in January was followed by that lively spirit and "best good Christian" without knowing it, Dr. Garth. Pope would make new friends—*was* making new friends: Burlington, Bathurst,

Peterborow, and many another. Still, there is a glow about one's earliest companions during those short days when Time lets us play and be golden in the mercy of his means that is never quite recapturable. He was thirty, going on thirty-one. His youth had passed.

PART THREE

WORKS AND DAYS

1720–1733

CHAPTER 16

SUCCESS AND ITS REWARDS

"The noblest version . . . which the world has ever seen"

The decade following his removal to Twickenham was a period of profound readjustments in Pope's life—such readjustments as occur not infrequently during a man's thirties, bringing a gradual shift of interests and goals, even sometimes substantial alterations of personality, and usually accompanied by a vague unrest in which memories of roads not taken and doors now closed jostle uneasily with self-questionings about the future. In Pope we have reason to think that these sensations were acute. He was to engage during this decade in editing and additional translation, but only at the very end of it would he again write original poetry of major importance, a circumstance that possibly suggests some degree of imaginative exhaustion, depression, or distraction. During the same period, he was to be deprived of a number of friends by death (and of one by exile) while continuing to attend an aged and increasingly helpless mother: melancholy experiences that his intense immersion in the development of his miniature Twickenham estate and his program of summer rambles to the houses of sociable friends were presumably designed to mitigate. Most important of all among events requiring readjustment at this time, he had finished the *Iliad* translation. Its final two volumes were ready for subscribers on May 12, 1720.

Nine days before his thirty-second birthday, by a relentless application often interrupted by illness but never relaxed, Pope had completed the enormous labor that his own ambitions and the advice of old Sir William Trumbull had marked out for him while he was yet in his late teens. He had produced an English *Iliad* that for all its concessions to contemporary politeness and polish, traditional theories of epic elevation, and the complex rhetoric of the rhymed pentameter couplet was irrefutably a masterpiece in its kind. Addison and a few other Buttonians might grumble that Tickell's first book had more of Homer than his. Richard Bentley, greatest classical scholar of the age, may have called it "miserable stuff" or merely urged that though "it is a pretty poem, Mr. Pope, you must not call it Homer." Pamphleteers, including of course the irrepressible Dennis, would reiterate for years that the translator had no Greek. All such warnings went unheeded, once the generality of readers had found in the translation, as the demand for new editions throughout Pope's lifetime and for a century after indicates that they did, a poem which at the very least had to be acknowledged, in Coleridge's phrase, "an astonishing product of matchless talent and ingenuity," and could be acclaimed, as it was by Johnson, "the noblest version [i.e., translation] of poetry which the world has ever seen."

Pope's *Iliad* is not, of course, our *Iliad*. His notion of Homer's world is entirely untouched by the findings of nineteenth- and twentieth-century archaeology and anthropology. His conceptions of epic know nothing of oral performance and transmission, formulaic composition, multiple authorship, or epic cycles of the story of Troy antecedent to Homer's own works. Inevitably, he saw the poet he was translating through the tradition of commentary and imitation that had accumulated about him, first in his own Greece, then in the literature of Rome, and finally among writers of the European Renaissance. And, as always for Pope, the paramount "commentaries" were the poems of those who had performed greatly in the same mode, chiefly Vergil, Tasso, and Milton; but especially—as being both an ancient himself and an epic poet rated never less than second to Homer if not (by some) superior to him—Vergil. As he had urged others to do in his *Essay on Criticism*, he had done now himself:

> Still with *It self compar'd*, his *Text* peruse;
> And let your *Comment* be the *Mantuan Muse*.
>
> (ll. 128–29)

But of course other influences were at work. An important one was contemporary taste. Every historical period, as our own appreciates more keenly than any of its predecessors, reformulates the great poetry of the past partly by its own conceptions of that greatness and that past as well as by its own views of what constitutes poetry and the art of translation. When the work belongs, as Homer's works do, to a very distant past indeed, one of which we ourselves know little and earlier centuries knew less, the infusion from the translator's own time will inevitably be considerable. In the *Iliad*'s third book, for

example, the goddess Aphrodite, having saved Paris from an igno-
minious defeat on the battlefield at the hands of Helen's husband
Menelaus, spirits him away to the city and then in the guise of an old
serving woman summons Helen from her colloquy on the walls with
the old men of Troy to join her lover for a bout of love making. In a
literal rendering, the invitation reads something like this:

> Come! Alexander [Paris's alternative name in the poem] wants you
> home. He is in the bedroom and on the carved marriage bed, all
> aglow with beauty and bright apparel—you would never guess he
> had just come from fighting but more likely was on his way to a
> dance or just now resting after dancing.
>
> (3:390–94)

Homer's Elizabethan translator, George Chapman, interprets this
for his own audience by making his disguised Aphrodite an Elizabethan waiting woman. She addresses her mistress as "Madame,"
urges her to "kind haste," plays off the seemly measures of a courtly
dance against the dusty disorder of the battlefield—an effect not in
Homer—and builds up with other details, also not in Homer, a seductive picture of a waiting lover's mood:

> Madam,
> My lord cal[l]s for you. You must needs make all your kind haste
>   home.
> He's in your chamber, stayes and longs, sits by your bed.
>   Pray come.
> 'Tis richly made and sweet; but he, more sweet, and lookes so cleare,
> So fresh and movingly attir'd that (seeing) you would sweare
> He came not from the dustie fight but from a courtly dance,
> Or would to dancing.
>
> (ll. 408–14)

In a widely used translation of our own day, on the other hand, not only
is the medium prose—a dilapidating of the original that would have
shocked Chapman and Pope yet is thoroughly characteristic of our
own culture, which is not notably comfortable with the formalities of
verse—but the episode has been so transformed by other considerations relevant to a modern audience that it could be mistaken for an
invitation to Lady Chatterley to make haste from the big house for a
quick tumble with the gamekeeper:

> Come here! she said, thi man wants tha at home. He is in thi room,
> on the bed, all finery and shinery! Tha'st never think he's fresh from
> fighten a man! More like just come from a dance, or just goen maybe!

Beside this, Pope's version must seem tame. Yet that it is further from the original, although distanced in the opposite direction, it would be difficult to claim. In *his* rendering, the contempt for Paris's unmanly conduct that Helen will give voice to in her reply to the old woman seeps through in the invitation itself, possibly asking us to remember that "Nymph" can be a term of some ambiguity at this period and that any "gay Dancer in the publick Show" serves a form of entertainment that lovers of British literature affected to despise:

> Haste, happy Nymph! for thee thy *Paris* calls,
> Safe from the Fight, in yonder lofty Walls,
> Fair as a God with Odŏurs round him spread
> He lies, and waits thee on the well-known Bed:
> Not like a Warrior parted from the Foe,
> But some gay Dancer in the publick Show.
>
> (ll. 481–86)

Moreover, in comparing Paris to a god lapped in fragrance, Pope singles out for stress the seductive powers of Aphrodite (her own usual attribute in classical poetry being a shower of sweet odors), who has not only snatched her favorite from the sweat of battle but bestowed on him for the moment something of her own style of allure. The translator's purpose, one gathers from his note, is to support what he believes is Homer's intention of "preserving still in some degree our good Opinion of *Helena*, whom we look upon with Compassion as constrain'd by a superior Power."

The effort to achieve this same effect on a larger scale—to win so far as possible the favorable opinion of his audience, not for Helen merely, but for Homer's world and people generally and the epic poetry that gives them being; or, as Sir William Trumbull had written in his original charge to him, to make Homer "as useful and instructive" to the present times as he had been found to be by Horace when he read him at Praeneste and judged him a wiser teacher than all the philosophers combined—this effort governs Pope's translation from start to finish. His personal response to Homer was, we know, intense; moreover, the desire to absorb so great a writer would be nearly irresistible to a young man of poetic promise and ambition. And the urge to make him "available," make him, as Trumbull urged, contemporaneous and exemplary to the age, use him (consciously or unconsciously) as an Ajax's shield under whose vast authority war might be waged on forces that deprecated poetic imagination and poetic truth: this is likely to have been for Pope a decisive attraction. In the *Essay on Criticism*, under the guise of a treatise on criticism, he had powerfully asserted the creative power of "Wit," a term in which, for all its multiplicity of meanings, he had managed to keep uppermost the sense of imaginative insight and light, and so to relate it to the creative power of "Nature," whose effects were also definable as insight and light: "One *clear, unchang'd*, and *Universal* Light." The translation of Homer, though we need not suppose that this was part of a considered campaign, gave him an opportunity to strike a second blow for light and insight, now under the title of Invention. John Locke and others might divide the imaginative and comparing powers of the mind from the judicious and discriminating, and prefer the latter; but Homer—and indeed all the other great poets—were there to prove them wrong. Pope refrains from saying this in so many words, but he makes his Preface a paean to the supremacy of imagination and a testimony to its indivisibility from judgment, as he had earlier done with wit and judgment in the *Essay on Criticism*.

Imagination, says the Preface, lies at the heart of poetry and is the distinctive attribute of genius in all fields:

> Homer is universally allow'd to have had the greatest Invention of any Writer whatever. . . . Nor is it a Wonder if he has ever been acknowledg'd the greatest of Poets, who most excell'd in That which is the very Foundation of Poetry. It is the Invention that in different degrees distinguishes all great Genius's: The utmost Stretch of human Study, Learning, and Industry, which masters every thing besides, can never attain to this. It furnishes Art with all her Materials, and without it Judgment itself can at best but *steal wisely*: For Art is only like a prudent Steward that lives on managing the Riches of Nature. Whatever Praises may be given to Works of Judgment, there is not even a single Beauty in them to which the Invention must not contribute.

The Preface contains much more in this vein, all of it in homage to the poet generally regarded as the father of poetry and to the power of poetic imagination, which here, in a work already three thousand years old, could still hold children from play and old men from the chimney corner. Pope was fully aware of the inevitable "pastness" of Homer, though, as we have seen, his notion of the nature of that pastness differed enormously from ours. It was precisely the pastness of poetry as a serious vehicle of truth and the obsolescence of poetic insight that the new Cartesian, Hobbesian, and Lockean forms of discourse too much insisted on; and though Pope as a child of his times was neither exempt from nor in particular instances hostile to these forms, the case for poetry was what he never gave up. To all "modernist" depreciation of the ancients, to all tendencies to underrate or rule out poetic truth, Homer's two great epics constituted a massive refutation. Here was an ancient—in fact, of secular authors then known, the most ancient—whose poems were undeniably "histories":

> When we read *Homer*, we ought to reflect that we are reading the most ancient Author in the Heathen World; and those who consider him in this Light, will double their Pleasure in the Perusal of him. Let them think they are growing acquainted with Nations and People that are now no more; that they are stepping almost three thousand years backward into the remotest Antiquity, and entertaining themselves with a clear and surprising Vision of Things no where else to be found, and the only authentic Picture of that ancient World.

Yet, "through the Strength of this amazing Invention," his work contained so much that was "present," so obviously recognizable as truth for today as well as yesterday, "that no man of a true Poetical Spirit is Master of himself while he reads him."

Pope's aim in the translation was therefore to bring Homer to his readers in both capacities: as recorder of an historical world now gone, and as maker of a poetic world that endures. The procedures required or at least encouraged by this strenuous task tell us, as might be expected, a good deal more about Pope and his age than about Homer. He is frank to acknowledge in a general way the *Iliad*'s gross representations of the Olympian gods and the frequently "vicious" conduct of its heroes:

> Who can be so prejudiced ... as to magnify the Felicity of those Ages, when a Spirit of Revenge and Cruelty reign'd thro' the World, when no Mercy was shown but for the sake of Lucre, when great Princes were put to the Sword, and their Wives and Daughters made Slaves and Concubines?

But in the course of translating, partly no doubt without realizing it, partly because the critical tradition within which he worked recognized in Homer one of the great poet-teachers, he added his own touches to the long cumulative process of "civilizing" the Homeric text. What was barbarous, he softened, and what was gross or vulgar he mitigated, rather in the manner of Racine, in whose plays, it has been wittily observed, nobody ever sneezes.

Hence, Homer's unselfconsciousness in treating the responses of

41. Alexander Pope, aged about thirty. By Sir Godfrey Kneller, *c.* 1718. Pope holds a Greek text of the *Iliad*, open at Book Iota (9), with which the third volume of his translation begins. Wimsatt, 5.1.

Private collection. Photograph: Courtauld Institute of Art.

men and women to each other comes through in Pope highly colored
by an inherited socioliterary vocabulary that to us is downright
funny: "Delightful *Greece*, the Land of lovely Dames." To support
"the Majesty of Epic Poetry, where every thing ought to be great and
magnificent"—a majesty in large part introduced after the time of
Homer—he repeatedly magnifies effects that in the original are
already overblown. Mars's roar of pain, for example, when
wounded, is compared in Homer's Greek to the noise of "nine or ten
thousand" warriors clashing in battle; in Pope's English, it is the
noise of "shouting Millions." The translator is further impelled, this
time by the closed couplet's epigrammatic inclinations as well as by
the contemporary fondness for succinct verbal formulations which
makes that couplet the period's verse norm, to speak with a
generalizing sententiousness or pithiness considerably beyond what
is already present in the original. Homer's "No good comes of
chilling grief"—spoken by Achilles to Priam as the latter mourns
Hector in the poem's final episode—has been variously rendered in
our own century as

> —no profit cometh of chill lament (prose, 1925)
> —there is no profit in freezing lamentation (prose, 1938)
> —weeping is cold comfort and does little good (prose, 1950)
> —   There is not
>   any advantage to be won from grim lamentation (verse, 1951)
> —   Tears heal nothing,
>   drying so stiff and cold (verse, 1974).

The thought typically strikes from Pope a more aphoristic note,
relating the particular occasion to a tight-lipped endurance of the
miseries of the human condition at large—miseries that he knew
personally a good deal about: "To mourn, avails not: Man is born to
bear." To tease in this way a particular utterance toward something
more generic (and often, therefore, more easily recognizable by
eighteenth-century readers) is everywhere a distinguishing mark of
Pope's practice.

Characteristic, too, is omission or reformulation of "offensive"
material. Since the wisdom of the day held that an epic poem's purpose was to edify, excite wonder, and invite emulation, he faced his
most difficult decisions with those elements in Homer's text that
seemed to him—or would, he knew, seem to his readers—too
homely, vulgar, indecorous, or trivializing of the great actions of
heroes to meet the standards of the genre. What was an English
translator to do when Homer compared Ajax to an ass, having just

compared him to a lion? What he *might* do, Pope knew perfectly
well and states with some eloquence in his note:

> This whole Passage is inimitably just and beautiful; we see *Ajax*
> drawn in the most bold and strong Colours, and in a manner alive
> in the Description. We see him slowly and sullenly retreat
> between two Armies, and even with a Look repulsing the one,
> and protecting the other. . . . [Homer] compares him first to the
> Lion for his Undauntedness in Fighting, and then to the Ass for
> his stubborn Slowness in retreating; tho' in the latter Comparison
> there are many other Points of Likeness that enliven the Image:
> The Havock he makes in the Field is represented by the tearing
> and trampling down the Harvests; and we see the Bulk, Strength,
> and obstinacy of the Hero, when the Trojans in respect to him are
> compared but to Troops of Boys that impotently endeavour to
> drive him away.

Still, ass at the time was a "low" term, from its associations with
the barnyard—"the word *Asinus* in *Latin*, and *Ass* in *English* are the
vilest imaginable," Pope adds in his note—and since a translator
owes something to the age in which he lives, "this induced me to
omit the mention of the word *Ass* in the Translation." On similar
grounds, Homer's assertion (during a particularly intense moment
of the fighting around the body of Patroclus) that Athena filled the
breast of Menelaus with the daring of a fly seems to Pope anti-
climactical. His note again acknowledges that there is "no
Impropriety in the Comparison, this Animal being of all others the
most persevering in its Attacks"; but "the Littleness and Insig-
nificancy of this Creature" impel him to change it nevertheless to a
"vengeful Hornet (Soul all o'er)."

Most shattering of all to post-Homeric notions of epic dignity and
morality was the conduct of Homer's gods. This of course had been a
stumbling block for admirers since before Plato's time, and it is here
that Pope takes his boldest liberties in an effort to accommodate a
pantheon that is sometimes vicious, often spiteful, and almost always
irresponsible (*their* wounds heal!) to an acceptable heroic norm. In his
notes, he allows himself to resort, though sometimes impatiently, to
the elaborate allegorism that had gathered round Homer's two epics
since the sixth century B.C. and enabled his divinities' deeds and
motives to be resolved into effects of the several elements (air, earth,
water, fire) or of various human attributes (prudence, wrath,
patience, love), thus saving the appearances, so to speak, for Homer
as moral teacher and even "improving" the instruction:

The Allegory of this whole Book lies so open ... that it is a wonder how it could enter into the Imagination of any Critick, that these Actions of *Diomed* [who was warned by Athena not to fight with any god but nevertheless took on Mars and Venus, wounding them both] were only a daring and extravagant Fiction in *Homer*, as if he affected the *Marvellous* at any rate. The great Moral of it is, that a brave Man should not contend against Heaven, but resist only *Venus* and *Mars*, Incontinence and ungovern'd Fury.

In the translation itself, where this sort of fudging is quite unfeasible, Pope's recourse is to move Homer's deities as far in the direction of a Vergilian-Miltonic sobriety as the text in front of him when stretched to its outer limits will permit. One illustration will suffice. In the poem's first book, Zeus and Hera quarrel. Hera has seen the sea goddess Thetis, mother of Achilles, in the attitude of a suppliant at Zeus's knee and suspects he may have promised her some sort of honoring of her son that will benefit the Trojans, whom she hates. On this suspicion, she reproves her spouse, and an altercation follows that Zeus brings to an end with a threat of force. How to render such a speech from the supreme Olympian, "Father of Gods and Men"?

Dryden, a master of disdainful obloquy and gifted always with a keen antipathy to rebelliousness, had rendered it as if spoken by a harrassed Restoration husband dressing down his prying wife:

> To whom the Thund'rer made this stern Reply;
> My Houshold Curse, my lawful Plague, the Spy
> Of *Jove*'s Designs, his other squinting Eye;
> Why this vain prying, and for what avail?
> *Jove* will be Master still and *Juno* fail.
> Shou'd thy suspicious Thoughts divine aright,
> Thou but becom'st more odious in my Sight,
> For this Attempt: uneasy Life to me
> Still watch'd, and importun'd, but worse for thee.
> Curb that impetuous Tongue, before too late
> The Gods behold, and tremble at thy Fate.
> Pitying, but daring not in thy Defence
> To lift a Hand against Omnipotence.
>
> (ll. 751–63)

Not surprisingly, when the quarrel is reconciled some lines later, and Hephaestus, the gods' lame metalworker, passes about the loving cup, Dryden's Olympian scene begins to resemble a Covent Garden tavern (cf. *they lov'd*, which is assuredly not in Homer), complete with willing barmaids or women of the town:

The Feast continu'd till declining Light:
They drank, they laugh'd, they lov'd, and then 'twas Night. . . .
Drunken at last, and drowsy they depart,
Each to his House; . . .
                              The Thund'ring God
Ev'n he withdrew to rest, and had his Load.
His swimming Head to needful Sleep applied;
And *Juno* lay unheeded by his Side.

                                        (ll. 806–7, 810–11, 812–15)

Sexual politics with a vengeance! as Pope points out in an amusing note dissenting from Dryden's "Severity upon the Ladies." Also a very far cry from his own notion of this episode.* Here is *his* version of Zeus silencing Hera:

Then thus the God: Oh restless Fate of Pride,
That strives to learn what Heav'n resolves to hide;
Vain is the Search, presumptuous and abhorr'd,
Anxious to thee, and odious to thy Lord.
Let this suffice; th' immutable Decree
No Force can shake: What *is*, that *ought* to be.
Goddess submit, nor dare our Will withstand,

* Pope reproves Homer's commentators ancient and modern, including Dryden, for the zeal with which they have seized on the episode as an excuse to lecture women and indicates his preference for the solution of Homer's French translator, Anne Dacier, who had argued that in this passage "Homer design'd to represent the Folly and Danger of prying into the Secrets of Providence. 'Tis thrown into that Air in this translation, not only as it is more noble and instructive [the terms should be noticed] in general, but as it is more respectful to the Ladies in particular."
  Pope also takes Dryden to task for allowing the gods' laughter to arise from the awkward hobbling movements of the lame Hephaestus as he passes the loving cup. He reminds his readers that this notion is not in Homer and censures with some dignity a species of ridicule of which he himself has had painful experience: "Homer tells you the gods did laugh [Pope follows here the comment of Eustathius], yet he takes care not to mention a word of lameness. It would have been cruel in him, and Wit out of Season, to have enlarg'd with Derision upon an Imperfection which is out of one's Power to remedy" (1:771n). When his rival Tickell compounded the error by following Dryden both in the gods' laughter at lameness and in respresenting the effect of lameness to be a hopping motion, he jotted beside the passage in his copy, seemingly with the curt contempt of one who has reason to know better: "Lame men limp not hop" (*Collected in Himself*, p. 456).

> But dread the Pow'r of this avenging Hand;
> Th' united Strength of all the Gods above
> In vain resists th' Omnipotence of *Jove*.

(ll. 726–35)

We have moved appreciably from Covent Garden in the direction of Mount Sinai and of Pope's own *Essay on Man*.

Pope's *Iliad*, then, is not Homer's, as Bentley with justice (but somewhat naively) said. Unlike many versions before and since, however, it has claims to being a poem. To cite its favorite sorts of departure from the strict Homeric text, as here, is only to emphasize that Pope has done what any responsible translator of poetry must always do. He must decompose the work, long or short, to its constituent elements (in Homer their sheer abundance and heterogeneity constitute a special challenge), select from the resulting miscellany and clutter those materials that answer best to his own conception of the whole (including the smaller wholes that make it up), and then reconstitute these in a creation growing from the original, but new. The final test of the achievement will be the amount of imaginative energy that flows inside the new creation, shaping configurations which are held together by poetic force and which however different from those of the original yet resemble them in being true galaxies, spin-offs of a central sun.

It is this quality of Pope's *Iliad* that gives Johnson's praise its measure of truth; continues to convince seasoned twentieth-century classicists that, though every age must and should interpret the great classical works for itself, Pope is still Homer's "best" translator; and drew from Gerard Manley Hopkins, no mean judge (at a time when Pope's stock both as man and poet was at its nadir) the thoughtful verdict: "When one reads Pope's Homer with a critical eye, one sees, artificial as it is, in every couplet that he is a great man."

"An elegant retreat"

In the same month in which the final volumes of the *Iliad* appeared, Pope celebrated in a letter to his good friend Robert Digby, not without a certain poetical "Pomp of Style," as he put it, the coming of spring to his new Twickenham domain:

> No Ideas you could form in the Winter can make you imagine what *Twickenham* . . . is in this warmer Season. Our River glitters beneath an unclouded Sun, at the same time that its Banks retain the

Verdure of Showers. Our Gardens are offering their first Nose-
gays; our Trees, like new Acquaintance brought happily together,
are stretching their Arms to meet each other, and growing nearer
and nearer every Hour [it takes an anxious gardener to consider his
plantings in terms of hours!]: The Birds are paying their thanks-
giving Songs for the new Habitations I have made 'em: My
Building rises high enough to attract the eye and curiosity of the
Passenger from the River, where, upon beholding a Mixture of
Beauty and Ruin, he enquires what House is falling, or what
Church is rising?

He had been building and planting in the new setting for a year
now, and the letter clearly tingles with the exhilaration every house-
holder feels when at last results begin to show. From an original
building probably quite as nondescript as those seen flanking the
house in an engraving of 1735, he eventually shaped a dwelling that in
plan and ornamentation approximated the characteristic form of
most eighteenth-century English adaptations of the North Italian or
"Palladian" villa. His personal version, as the engraving shows,
comprised a central block with slightly recessed and lowered wings,
the north wing fitted with bow windows framed in Ionic pilasters,
and the center block rising from its grotto arch at basement level to
(by 1735) a balustraded platform at the level of the *piano nobile*, then
to a balustraded balcony supported on Tuscan pillars at the chamber
level, and thence past a narrow attic to a highly decorated cornice
topped by a hipped roof.

As a villa, historians of architecture remind us, the house belonged
to a category of dwellings whose characteristic one-three-one
window arrangement announced plainly to the world the modesty of
its interior accommodations together with its corresponding claim to
be "more in the nature of a retreat than an advertisement of its
owner's standing." "Elegance, compactness, and convenience" were
the amenities it proposed in lieu of the spaciousness and opulence of
the Great House, which was invariably a status symbol and in particular instances during the long ministry of Robert Walpole sometimes became tarnishingly associated with gross feeding at the public
trough. And if its interior had a particular emphasis, that emphasis
was on friends. Their portraits by Jervas, Kneller, Richardson, and
many more constituted the decoration of his rooms, some four dozen
in all. "*Mihi & Amicis*," he told Fortescue in 1736, "and indeed Plus
Amicis quam Meipsi" ["More for my friends than for myself"],
would be a proper motto over his gate, and five years later he informs

42. Pope's Villa: Twickenham. Detail from an engraving by Andreas(?) Rysbrack, 1735.

"There, my Retreat the best Companions grace."

Imit. Hor., Sat. II, i:125

Courtesy of the Lewis Walpole Library, Farmington.

another friend and frequent visitor that he is now indeed "putting over my door at Twitnam, *Libertati & Amicitiae*." In no small house of which we have records is there found such concentration on a single theme. Pope's villa, in other words, could increasingly seem to him, and to others, expressive of his deepest values as man and poet, and together with its gardens and grotto could facilitate (or so at least I have elsewhere argued) the role of satirist and social critic he was eventually to assume.

Before the house lay a well-cropped lawn sloping to the Thames, which gave easy access by water, and behind, quite out of sight in the 1735 engraving, the developing plantations of which the letter to Digby speaks. The scope of Pope's garden was about five acres (measuring approximately 250 yards by something over 100), which before many years had passed he had packed as full and patterned as intricately, with as many quiet little mirrorings, reversals, and surprises as compete for our attention in his best couplets. Besides a small vineyard and an orangery, it held hothouses for the experimental culture of pineapples, still an uncommon and highly prized fruit; a small orchard containing at least fig trees, both espaliered and standard, in addition to rare varieties of French pear; and a large kitchen garden, where he grew broccoli, fennel, and asparagus (scarce at this date), perhaps, like his father, artichokes, and very possibly the "Cabbidge," "Spinage," endive, lettuce, beans, beets, and herbs he mentions in his poems. He seems also to have grown "Jamaica strawberries"—at least in the fall of 1731 he planted some, "which are to be almost as good as Pineapples"—and to have kept bees.

This was the domestic aspect. The landscaping aspect encompassed straight avenues and winding interlaced paths, sunny openings and seemingly dense woods, and a succession of continually shifting contrasts through the use of trees and plants of varying forms, textures, and gradations of green, including the solemn dark hue of the cypresses that after his mother's death led up to the obelisk in her memory. There was also an amphitheater (this possibly only for a time), quincunxes, groves, a wilderness and a bowling green, a shell temple and three mounts, one of them tall, with a seat at the top under a spreading tree, upon which after a rough and circuitous climb one could take one's ease and contemplate much of the panorama beneath. "It was a singular effort of art and taste," wrote Horace Walpole many years after, "to have impressed so much variety and scenery on a spot of five acres." This was emphatically the view of an anonymous visitor who saw the garden within three years of Pope's death and described it rapturously in a letter to a friend:

> I would next give you some particular Idea of the Garden, but am
> afraid I shall fail . . .: for that free natural Taste, and unaffected
> Simplicity, which presides every where in the Plan, wanders so
> much from all common Forms and stated Fashions, that a Wood or
> a Forest doth not much more deviate from Rule: . . .

The visitor closes his account with a sentence that would have pleased
Pope, as much by its assumption of a certain affinity of values relating
the man to the place as by its actual praise. This is not, he notes, "a
Place that bears the high Air of State and Grandeur, that surprizes you
with the vastness of Expence and Magnificence; but an Elegant
Retreat of a Poet strongly inspired with the Love of Nature and
Retirement; and shews you, with respect to these Works, what was
the Taste of the finest Genius that this or any other Age has produced."

From the grass plot in front of the house to the shell temple in the
garden ran a subterranean way entered through the rusticated arch
that is so conspicuous a feature at ground-level center in the
engraving of 1735. This was Pope's grotto. Originally no more (one
suspects) than a convenient route through the villa's basement, but
excavated further so as to reach the shell temple after considerably
underpassing what was then the main London/Hampton Court road
running by the house on that side, it too, like the five acres opposite,
was gradually elaborated. Already by the summer of 1722, it seems to
have inspired from a visitor an account that Pope termed "poetical."
Three years later, he himself describes for a friend the condition he
has currently brought it to, which—with its orbicular central lamp
flanked by mirrors on which are captured the objects and events of the
outer world as in a "moving Picture"—seems now not so much
"poetical" as an actual metaphor and emblem of the poet's trade:

> From the River Thames you see thro' my arch [and through the
> grotto-tunnel] up a Walk of the Wilderness to a kind of open
> Temple, wholly compos'd of Shells in the Rustic Manner; and
> from that distance under the Temple you look down thro' a
> sloping Arcade of Trees [lining the walk to the grotto on the
> garden side and eventually roofing it with foliage], and see the Sails
> on the River passing suddenly and vanishing, as thro' a Perspective
> Glass. When you shut the Doors of the Grotto, it becomes on the
> instant, from a luminous Room, a *Camera obscura*; on the Walls of
> which the Objects of the River, Hills, Woods, and Boats, are
> forming a moving Picture in their visible Radiations: And when
> you have a mind to light it up, it affords you a very different Scene;

43. A fanciful view of Alexander Pope's garden. By William Kent, *c.* 1725–30. A boat on the Thames may be seen through the Grotto aperture, as one of Pope's Bounces approaches a pair of figures, the taller probably intended to represent Kent, the shorter Pope.

it is finish'd with Shells interspersed with Pieces of Looking-glass in angular forms; and in the Cieling is a Star of the same Material, at which when a Lamp (of an orbicular Figure of thin Alabaster) is hung in the Middle, a thousand pointed Rays glitter and are reflected over the Place.

By the end of Pope's life, following a new surge of "grottofying" (as he called it) from about 1740, the area had been further trans-

44. Alexander Pope in his Grotto. By William Kent, *c*. 1725–30? The grotesques overhead may or may not be Kent's jesting interpretation of a poet's "maggot Muse." Wimsatt, 15.

By kind permission of the Trustees of the Chatsworth Settlement. Photograph: Courtauld Institute of Art.

formed. The part of the tunnel beneath the house had been enlarged, the space diversified into rooms, a spring Pope had earlier uncovered there developed into a system of rills and pools enhanced by optical reflection in overhead mirrors, and the whole layout encrusted with ores carefully placed to give the illusion of a natural mine: ores from all parts of England and indeed the world. Our best account of this phase is again from the visitor of 1747:

> Cast your Eyes upward, and you half shudder to see Cataracts of Water precipitating over your head, from impending Stones and Rocks, while Salient Spouts rise in rapid Streams at your Feet: Around, you are equally surprized with flowing Rivulets and rolling Waters, that rush over airey Precipices, and break amongst Heaps of ideal [i.e., mirror-imaged] Flints and Spar. Thus, by a fine Taste and happy Management of Nature, you are presented with an undistinguishable Mixture of Realities and Imagery.

A diverting toy, no doubt, for the child in Pope, who, as in most of us, never quite grew up. But surely an impractical one, considering the English climate, as Samuel Johnson with his usual hard sense did not fail to point out. Such a spot, all the more to a man with Pope's ailments, can have been bearable only in summer and then only on warm days. Yet that the place had a profound appeal to his imagination, the money and care he lavished on it clearly show. Was it simply that it reminded him of the famous caves, often furnished with a nymph or nymphs, of which he had read in such favorite poets as Ovid and Homer? Can the murmur of its waters have helped induce in him, as the sound of water is often said to do, states of trance or meditation, like those we hear of in the testimony of other poets, when one is laid asleep in body to become a living soul, or sinks so deep in hearing music that you are the music while the music lasts? Did he pause to consider that a teasing symbolism might lurk in making the main walkway between the river and his garden a sort of dark underworld passage, where, as in the *Aeneid* he knew so well and the *Odyssey* he was soon to translate, the lost wanderer looking for his home must forgo the familiar world to consult a world of shadows and a blind seer named Teiresias or a prophet-father named Anchises? Could one only gain, or regain, the lost Garden, after passing through a darkness filled like life itself with "an undistinguishable Mixture of Realities and Imagery." Or was it merely that the glimmering twilight of the grotto made his own and his visitor's emergence into the resplendent scene that lay beyond it a more gratifying experience?

Which—if any—of these connections or intentions the poet actually entertained, we have no way of guessing. Perhaps none. Yet he can hardly have been ignorant of the associations between caverns and consciousness that he plays with in his own Cave of Spleen in the *Rape of the Lock*, and seems to draw on further in the *Dunciad*'s Cave of Poetry and Cave of Truth—associations possibly reaching back in his case to his boyhood in Plough Court. Moreover, the long tradition that made grots and caves the appropriate haunt of frugal virtue, true philosophy, and a wisdom tempered by detachment from the values of court and city cannot have escaped the attention of one who could later rally George II's Queen Caroline on the incongruity of placing a bust of the courtly Dr. Samuel Clarke in her "Hermitage" at Richmond. All of which inclines one to reflect that the Twickenham situation and what the poet set out to achieve there may have been in some unconscious or possibly even conscious sense expressive as well as emblematic. For us, at any rate, a fine propriety is clear. On the one side lay the traffic of the river, the great world seen in a passing show, accessible at will through a procession of refracted images. On the other lay the instruments and emblems of a life of contemplation: his shell temple; his "Mount" with its "Forest Seat or Chair," overlooking his small domain; his walks leading in and out of "Wildernesses"; and, from 1735, the obelisk to his mother—"a plain Stone Pillar resting upon a Pedestal," inscribed:

> Ah Editha!
> Matrum Optima.
> Mulierum Amantissima.
> Vale.★

Thus between the evermoving river with its transient scenes and figures and the garden with its quiet temple, the poet in his cave—whatever that cave may have represented to him—was intermediary and interpreter.

Plus Amicis quam Meipsi

Whatever his inward fancies about his Twickenham estate, Pope was understandably proud of it. It was the first home of which he himself had been head, the first he had been free to make over as he chose, the

---

★ ["Ah Edith! / Best of Mothers / Most Loving of Women. / Farewell."]

first circumstanced by size, setting, comfort, salubrious situation, and proximity to London to become a center for visitations by his acquaintances and friends. This was a service that appealed to him. He likes to think of himself, both in his poems and in his letters, as one engaged in the preservation of ancient but disappearing hospitalities. "My house," he writes his Yorkshire friend Hugh Bethel during the mid-1720s, "is like the house of a Patriarch of old, standing by the highway and receiving all travellers." What if the penal laws did interdict a Catholic from ownership:

> My lands are sold, my Father's house is gone;
> I'll hire another's, is not that my own,
> And yours my friends? thro' whose free-opening gate
> None comes too early, none departs too late.
> (Imit. Hor., Sat. II, ii, 155–58)

Come at any rate they did, in a procession broken between 1719 and 1744 only when Pope or his mother was severely ill (she died in 1733), or Pope was away on one of his summer jaunts. Many came to dine or sup, some to talk business, others to stroll the grounds or inspect the grotto. Sometimes they even came to romp. In a charming letter of October 1721, Pope describes a visit from his friend Edward Blount's youngest daughters: "I still see them walking on my Green ..., and gratefully remember (not only their green Gowns [i.e., stains from tumbles] but the Instructions they gave me how to slide down, and trip up the steepest Slopes of my Mount." Often the poet's closest friends made stays of several nights, weeks, or even, as when Swift visited England in 1726 and 1727 for the first time since 1714, months, though broken of course by rambles elsewhere. One of the earliest guests came to convalesce. This was Mary Lepell, the lively and beautiful young woman, maid of honor to Princess Caroline, to whom along with the Misses Bellenden and Griffith, he had addressed his *Court Ballad*. She is visiting, he tells a friend in March 1720, "in hopes of a recovery by our air from a dangerous illness" (the Twickenham/Richmond area was famous for its supposed good air), and he is "now constantly engaged at home in attending" on her. Her recovery was apparently satisfactory, for within a month, on April 21, she became the wife of John Hervey, later, as already mentioned in these pages, Pope's bitter enemy. One wonders if she ever recalled at that time this quite exceptional kindness on the part of one about whom her husband was then saying in a poem written in collaboration with Lady Mary Wortley Montagu:

> If Limbs unbroken, Skin without a Stain,
> Unwhipt, unblanketed, unkick'd, unslain,
> That wretched little Carcass you retain:
> The Reason is, not that the World wants Eyes;
> But thou'rt so mean, they see, and they despise.

Another of the villa's early visitors was Robert Digby. Even before Pope's letter to him of 1 May 1720 welcoming spring to Twickenham, he had come for a short stay and liked what he saw. Second son of William, fifth baron Digby (known in his own time as the "good" Lord Digby), young Digby shared with Pope a chronic semi-invalidism together with a warm capacity for friendship and an old-fashioned upbringing, complete in Digby's case with parental instructions for behavior (while pursuing his studies at Oxford) that are refreshingly less worldly than those tendered by Shakespeare's Polonius to Laertes. To choose almost at random: "Take this for a fixt & certain principle that nothing can be a price for your Integrity." "Consider well before you promise but never consider whether you shall perform." "Be civil to all the World. . . . Humility is so far from being below a Man of Quality that it becomes no other so well." Such reports of the fifth baron as have survived him suggest that he had earned the right to voice such counsels by the scrupulousness with which he followed them himself.

In the Pope household, young Digby evidently encountered observances and attitudes that he had come to know were rare:

> I had many . . . pleasures from your letter; that your mother remembers me is a very sincere joy to me; I cannot but reflect how alike you are; from the time you do anyone a favour, you think your selves obliged as those that have received one. This is indeed an old-fashioned respect, hardly to be found out of your house.

Following a second visit in 1723, he further expresses his admiration, with a reference to "honour" that inclines one to wonder whether there had not already entered into their conversations some such dreams of a social order based on *noblesse oblige* and responsible stewardship as were to undergird the poet's satires and epistles of the 1730s. "I have as you guess," Digby writes, "many philosophical reveries in the shades of Sir Walter Raleigh [the Digby seat at Sherborne was built by Raleigh], of which you are a great part. You generally enter there with me, and like a good Genius applaud and strengthen all my sentiments that have honour in them. This good office which you have often done me unknowingly, I must acknowledge now, that my own breast may not reproach me with ingratitude . . . when I would muse again in that solemn scene."

Pope's return visit to Sherborne the following summer equally produced food for thought. After describing with great excitement the "romantick" landscape of the place and the dramatic proximity of the Tudor house to the ruins of a Norman tower overrun and destroyed by the parliamentary armies during the Civil War, when its royalist garrison tried to hold it for the king, Pope continues, in a letter to Martha Blount:

> I cannot make the reflection I've often done upon contemplating the beautiful Villa's of Other Noblemen, raisd upon the Spoils of plunderd nations, or aggrandiz'd by the wealth of the Publick. I cannot ask myself the question, "What Else has this man to be lik'd? what else has he cultivated or improv'd? What good, or what desireable thing appears of him, without these walls? I dare say his Goodness and Benevolence extend as far as his territories.

Pope speaks here of a Tory lord with Stuart sympathies. But the point at issue, as his only reference in verse to the fifth baron (some fourteen years later) shows, is not the direction of a man's convictions but the quality of his loyalty to them: what the fifth baron had reminded his son was called "Integrity." The lines in question couple Digby's name with that of Dr. John Hough, Bishop of Worcester, among "the truly Brave"—"The one," Pope adds in his note, "an assertor of the Church of England in opposition to the false measures of King James II. The other as firmly attached to the cause of that King. Both equally men of principle, and equally men of honour and virtue."

Summer rambles and landscaping friends

Visits of this sort to country houses large and small were, from an early date, but most especially after he had established a reciprocal place of entertainment at Twickenham, a regular feature of Pope's life. He was a "gadder," to use the homely term the duchess of Buckingham expected his mother to use. Much of the time in pain, ever restless (we have noted before the "April weather" of his mind), he seems to have found release and freedom for his imagination in the movement from house to house, garden to garden, friend to friend, uncomfortable though travel usually made him. Probably, too, the presence of assured intimates in surroundings grown familiar and

45. Allen, 1st Earl Bathurst (1684–1775). By Sir Godfrey Kneller, 1719.

> To balance Fortune by a just expence,
> Join with Œconomy, Magnificence;
> With Splendour, Charity; with Plenty, Health;
> O teach us, BATHURST!

Epistle to Bathurst, 223–26.

Private Collection. Photograph: Courtauld Institute of Art.

beloved brought him a needed security, a sort of countering reassurance of affection that could not fail to be important for one who was so often under cruel attacks, even if sometimes he had himself provoked them. Other impulses were possibly operating as well. Men and women habitually in pain often gain a degree of physical together with psychological relief from change, if for no other reason than that it brings new distractions: and Pope was well aware, as in later life he confessed to his friends the Orrerys, that being away from home in the role of guest puts far greater pressure on an invalid to fight back the peevishness and exasperation that accompany physical distress than exists at home, where he feels freer to let go.

Thus the summer rambles afforded therapy in several kinds and in no kind more healing, we may guess, than in the part he took in the improvement efforts that in the eighteenth century were under way on almost every estate in England. Particularly absorbing pleasures of this kind he had with many friends, earliest, perhaps, with Bathurst. Allen Bathurst, first baron Bathurst, one of the Tory peers created to save the Peace of Utrecht, was to be in due course the dedicatee of one of Pope's major efforts in sociopolitical criticism:

> The Sense to value Riches, with the Art
> T' enjoy them, and the Virtue to impart, . . .
> O teach us, Bathurst! yet unspoil'd by wealth!
>
> (ll. 219–20, 226)

A generous man of large proportions, Bathurst indulged appetites that were equally outsized. He was considerably a womanizer, though the father of seventeen legal offspring by his wife Frances Apsley—nine still living in 1729. He was also a robust trencherman and tippler who rarely needed to let physicians near him and accordingly lived to be ninety-one.* (Even at ninety, concluding a long

---

* Like Sir William Trumbull, he preached the value of exercise, and, when Pope was staying with him in the years before his weakness prevented such activities, the two men engaged in regular walks and outridings on the estate, partly for this purpose. Later, these became less possible. Pope to Martha Blount, September 1728, and to Bathurst, 7 November 1728 (2: 512, 525). An unpublished letter of Bolingbroke's to Sir William Wyndham, 20 February 1731 (Bolingbroke papers, Petworth House), records his entertaining recollection that the portly Dr. George Cheyne, who had published a treatise on diet, "with a gallon of milk coffee, and five pounds of Biscuit before him at Breakfast, declaimed to Pope, and me, against the enormous immorality of using exercise to promote an appetite. But a much better Casuist, and a much better Physician too, . . . even the foresaid Lord of Cirencester, prescribed exercise to prevent indigestion . . . and to promote

dinner party from which his son—a less agreeable ministerial type who became Lord Chancellor and burnt his father's papers lest the king learn of Stuart sympathies—had just excused himself, he is reported to have looked about the table with a twinkle and to have said, "Come, now the Old Gentleman's gone, let's crack another bottle.") The Brobdingnagian schemes of afforestation and landscaping that he applied to his vast estates at Cirencester in Gloucestershire even included a playful plan, never executed, for uniting the Thames and Severn underground in a Spenserian marriage of rivers.★ Appropriately to these other characteristics, he was a courageous and great-hearted supporter of the underdog and persecuted. This no doubt accounts in part for his deep affection for Pope, whom he is continually inviting to come stay with him at one or other of his various establishments in Gloucestershire, Buckinghamshire, or London. "I wou'd quit the finest Walk on the finest day in the finest Garden to have your Company at any time," he writes on one such occasion; and on another, with a smiling threat:

> ... if you refuse coming I'll immediately send one of my wood-Carts & bring away your whole house & Gardens, & stick it in the midst of Oakly-wood [part of Bathurst's Cirencester estate] where it will never be heard of any more, unless some of the Children find it out in Nutting-season & take possession of it thinking I have made it for them.

Pope, in turn, seems to have looked up to Bathurst as to an older brother (he was, in fact, four years Pope's senior) and writes him with

---

the most sensible benefit of insensible perspiration." (For bringing this letter to my attention, I am indebted to Peter Martin's fine study, "*Pursuing Innocent Pleasures*": *The Gardening World of Alexander Pope* (New Haven: Archon Books, 1984.) See also Bathurst to his cousin Lord Strafford, July 17, 1736. (Wentworth Papers, p. 519.)
★ Pope to Digby, [May] 1722 (2: 116), describes his own and Bathurst's fantasies of the Cirencester estate in future, including "the Pavillions that are to glitter, the Colonnades that are to adorn them: Nay more, the meeting of the *Thames* and the *Severn*, which (when the noble Owner has finer Dreams than ordinary) are to be led into each other's Embraces thro' secret Caverns of not above twelve or fifteen Miles, till they rise and openly celebrate their Marriage in the midst of an immense Amphitheatre, which is to be the Admiration of Posterity a hundred Years hence." As Lees-Milne points out (p. 44), the fancy became a fact. In 1789, "the $2\frac{1}{4}$ mile Sapperton tunnel with its crenellated Gothic and its sober classical openings" was dug under Bathurst's estate, "and the Thames and Severn Canal formally opened by King George III in person."

an openness of feeling that early eighteenth-century epistolary manners ordinarily preclude:

> You cannot know, how much I love you, & how gratefully I recollect all the Good & Obligation I owe to you for so many years. I really depend on no man so much in all my little distresses, or wish to live & share with no man so much in any Joys or pleasures. I think myself a poor unsupported weak Individual, without you.

Charles Mordaunt, third earl of Peterborow, also crossed Pope's horizon at about this period and was likewise a receptive host to gardening improvements. At first, Pope visited him most often at his address in Bolton Street, where the Blount sisters with their mother now lived, or at his house in Parson's Green, Fulham, where the first tulip tree bloomed in England. (Peterborow was a collector of botanical rarities.) In later years, the poet would spend weeks on end with Peterborow and his unacknowledged countess, Anastasia Robinson, formerly an opera diva, at his spectacular hillside estate called Bevis Mount, overlooking the sea at Southampton—a place, in Pope's description of it, "beautiful beyond imagination," where he found it congenial to compose, and where his host, from about 1730, as usual with the poet's active participation, covered a gravelly hill with exquisite gardens and laced them with paths "so prettily diversify'd that it appears to be a very large garden, tho' in reality it is a very small spot"—as at Twickenham. One of them came to be called "Pope's Walk."

Of a lean wiry physique, aquiver with nervous energy and impetuous to the point of violence—"His Body active as his Mind," writes Swift, though "A Skeletor in outward Figure"—Peterborow, born in 1658, had left Cambridge at sixteen for the sea, serving against the Moors at Tangier in the time of Charles II. Later, as a zealous Whig passionately opposed to James II, he took part in William III's invasion, landing with him at Torbay, levying sympathizers in the West Country, and occupying Exeter. Subsequently, under Anne, owing to the intrepid ease with which he seemed to have taken Barcelona and Valencia during the Spanish campaigns of 1705–6, he won a glittering contemporary reputation for military genius, which later researches have shown to be in some part a self-generated myth. The truth, apparently, is that he was one of those people in whom imaginative inventions bubble up continuously like water from a spring and who, instinctively and almost (as it were) protectively, impose their own dashing colors on the drabness of fact. His affinity with Pope, he once remarked, came from their souls being composed

46. Charles Mordaunt, 3d Earl of Peterborow (1658–1735). By Sir Godfrey Kneller.

> And He, whose Lightning pierc'd th' Iberian Lines,
> Now forms my Quincunx, and now ranks my Vines.
> *Imit. Hor., Sat.* II, i: 29–30.

of "the same restless atoms, which makes . . . [us] perhaps desirous of more than we deserve but [desiring] to be sure of more than we obtaine." It was perhaps this roving quality of his mind together with the warmth, cheerfulness, and extreme generosity of his nature that drew so many writers to him: in addition to Pope and Gay, Berkeley the philosopher, Voltaire, Arbuthnot, Swift (who in a characteristic moment of gruff affection called him "the ramblingest lying rogue on earth"), and several more.

Through Peterborow, affecting at this period a gallant courtship of Mrs. Howard, Pope extended his acquaintance with the woman whose chaperonage he had asked in inviting Mary Lepell and the two other maids of honor to a rendezvous with himself and Gay in his *Court Ballad.* Since the accession of George I, Henrietta Hobart Howard, estranged wife of Charles Howard, younger son of the eighth earl of Suffolk, had been woman of the bedchamber to the Princess of Wales and her husband groom of the bedchamber to the King. Almost penniless from Howard's gambling and other dissipations, they had crossed to Hanover shortly before Queen Anne's death to cultivate the new regime and had been lucky; though at one point, unable to obtain credit because of her husband's notorious debts, Henrietta had been obliged to sell her lustrous head of hair to pay for an expedient dinner party. From about 1720, she drifted into a liaison with the Prince of Wales that flickered like a spent candle for more than a dozen years without (apparently) ever attaining on either side anything that could be called a flame. The Prince, as Hervey later put it, looked upon a mistress "rather as a necessary appurtenance to his grandeur as a Prince than an addition to his pleasures as a man," and Henrietta Howard, for her part, though the model of "good sense, good breeding, and good nature" that Hervey also describes, had little tinder in her makeup.

Later, she was severely blamed by Swift for failing to obtain something from the Court for her friends, most notably Gay (though he clearly cherished hopes of something for himself as well), especially when in 1727 her royal lover became George II. But Mrs. Howard was never an achiever in that sense. She emerged from the royal embrace in 1733 with extremely modest gains, partly because she was not grasping, but partly too because the King, whatever his extracurricular attachments, was guided by his wife, and she, though affecting superficially to be very fond of her bedchamber woman, hated her and humiliated her by subjecting her to the most menial tasks about her person. One may doubt, in other words, that Henrietta Howard ever had the influence necessary to elicit anything very desirable, even

47. Henrietta Howard, Countess of Suffolk (1681–1767). Engraving by John Harris after an unknown artist, *c*. 1715–25.

> Not warp'd by Passion, aw'd by Rumour,
> Not grave thro' Pride, or gay thro' Folly,
> An equal Mixture of good Humour,
> And sensible soft Melancholy.
>
> *On a Certain Lady at Court*, 5–8.

Courtesy of the National Portrait Gallery, London.

for the unoffending Gay in the period before *The Beggar's Opera*, from a monarch most of whose decisions of all kinds were reached in consultation with the Queen, and the Queen's, in turn, in consultation with Sir Robert Walpole, who had little use for poets.

Still, it is possible to wonder, with Swift, how hard she tried. Everything we know about her suggests a certain passivity beneath the obvious charm. With a settlement of £11,500 placed at her disposal by the Prince in 1723, some twenty-five acres of land were acquired for her at a spot along the Thames in Twickenham called Marble Hill; an impressive Palladian mansion (today beautifully renovated) took shape there over the next four or five years under the oversight of the eighth earl of Pembroke and the builder Roger Morris; and handsome landscaping, about which unfortunately we have little exact information, was carried out for her by Pope and the professional gardener Charles Bridgeman, with an assist from Bathurst. Yet there is little evidence to show that she herself was deeply or passionately engaged in these activities. Possibly the bitter disenchantment of her marriage to a debauched rake, who for years persecuted her and sought to exploit her for gain, had somewhat numbed her by the time she knew Pope and his circle. Perhaps, alternatively, she was by innate temperament one of those charming persons who delight in life and friendship but are incapable of investing very deeply in either. This implication has sometimes been drawn from Pope's jesting comment in 1734 to Martha Blount as he set out for Bath, whither Martha and Mrs. Howard (now Countess of Suffolk from the title's having fallen to her husband) had preceded him:

> Lady Suffolk has a strange power over me: She would not stir a days Journey either East or West for me, tho she had dying or languishing Friends on each Quarter who wanted & wishd to see her. But I am following her chariot wheels 3 days thro Rocks & Waters, & shall be at her feet on Sunday night. I suppose she'l be at Cards, & receive me as coldly as if I were Archdeacon of the place. I hope I shall be better with you.

But as the comment was obviously set down to be communicated by Martha to her companion for the amusement of both, it cannot be taken very seriously as criticism. Certainly Pope never tired of defending her against Swift's censures; lamented her loss as well as his own from the death of Gay; sent frequent bulletins about her health to mutual friends in letters during the 1730s; and as late as 1739, when she had given him a quilt, entrusted Martha Blount, who hated punning, with the equivocating message: "Pray tell my Lady Suffolk . . .

that I think of her every night constantly, as the greatest Comforter I
have, under her Edderdown Quilt." It is therefore extremely unlikely
that he intended the impervious "Cloe" in his *Epistle to a Lady* to be a
portrait of Lady Suffolk, as later eighteenth-century gossip supposed:

> Virtue she finds too painful an endeavour,
> Content to dwell in Decencies for ever.
> So very reasonable, so unmov'd,
> As never yet to love, or to be lov'd.

(ll. 163–66)

He may have drawn a trait from her (though even this is uncertain:
the world has never lacked for examples of outstanding social charm
in combination with extreme inward reserve amounting to indifference), as every author draws on people and incidents from life. But
he can hardly be supposed to have wished to injure a woman he so
much admired in a poem addressed to one who admired her equally
and was his own dearest friend. Nor can he be very credibly supposed
to be describing the same personality in the portrait above, which he
published in 1735, and the stanzas below, published only three years
earlier, their subject identified in both contemporary transcripts as
Mrs. Howard—who was in fact somewhat deaf:

> I know the thing that's most uncommon;
> (Envy, be silent and attend!)
> I know a Reasonable Woman,
> Handsome and witty, yet a Friend.
>
> Not warp'd by Passion, aw'd by Rumour,
> Not grave thro' Pride, or Gay thro' Folly,
> An equal Mixture of good Humour,
> And sensible soft Melancholy.
>
> "Has she no Faults then (Envy says) Sir?"
> Yes she has one, I must aver:
> When all the World conspires to praise her,
> The Woman's deaf, and does not hear.

What Pope, Bridgeman, or Bathurst accomplished in laying out
Mrs. Howard's landscape remains uncertain. The same is true of the
second earl of Oxford's Wimpole in Cambridgeshire, about which
we know certainly only that in the spring of 1726 he writes Pope that
he is "extreamly busie" there, but "will not tell you ... of my
designs till you come to the place and see it with your own eyes and
you shall have power to alter and I am sure you will be amending,

anything I shall think of." It is not clear, however, that Pope ever visited Wimpole apart from one ramble in the summer of 1727; and though he seems to have stayed now and then at Down Hall (the house Oxford had helped Matthew Prior purchase after his release from the imprisonment imposed by the Whigs for his role in negotiating the Peace of Utrecht), his relationship with Lord Oxford was obviously less horticultural than literary and bibliothecal. Oxford was one of the most generous of men (though not one of the best estate managers); and, as even the tough-minded George Vertue acknowledged, "every branch of Learning and [its] professors he kindly received & made himself acquainted with their merrit, and to his utmost promoted and protected them." Them—and their works as well; for to his father the first earl's already large library of books, manuscripts, and antiquities he added at a rate that by the time of his death in 1741 had brought him close to bankruptcy. Wimpole had to be sold in 1740, and soon after it the vast library of books. The manuscripts from all quarters of the globe—a very nearly priceless collection—passed at the desire of both Edward Harley and his lady, in an act that was far more benefaction than sale, to the newly founded British Museum for £10,000.

A remark made by Lady Oxford to Lady Mary Wortley Montagu a few weeks after Pope's death presumably indicates that she disliked him. With his many discomforts, he can never have been an easy guest. She was in no sense an intellectual or wit herself and may, quite reasonably, have found such conversation distasteful or a waste of time. Perhaps she had heard him say something she found offensive; or perhaps it was simply that he had written offensively of her close friend Lady Mary. Though greatly fond of Prior, who died early in her married life, and, in her younger days, on excellent terms with Swift, there is little evidence that during her maturity she was much drawn to any of the group who had once gathered about her father-in-law and whom her husband was proud to count among his friends. Since by the time she made the remark ("It is true Pope is Dead. I did not mention it, knowing the Contempt you have for worthless People"), she knew what the literary and bookish side of her husband's life had cost the family estates, it would not be at all surprising, nor would it be unpardonable, if her definition of worthless people and her animus against them had recently expanded. Earlier, in any event, she was not above accepting the poet's hospitality at Twickenham and kept her disapproval—which, if it stemmed from Lady Mary, must have included Swift—so well concealed that they knew nothing of it, Swift going so far as to call her "Sister Harriet" because he had been in the habit of referring to her husband, with whom in the time of Queen Anne he had been a fellow-member of the Brothers Club, as Brother Harley.

Her husband, at any rate, loved them all and was loved by them. Swift called him "the person of the world for whom I have the greatest love and esteem," and Pope, when he believed his mother to be dying in 1724, sat down to open his troubled heart to Oxford as one of the few who would have a true feeling of "This melancholy Circumstance." Such deep trust and reliance were, he knew, mutual. "I will allow nobody," Oxford had written only a few weeks before,

> to esteem, to value, or love you more than I do, and I do so from the conviction that you are the Best Poet, the truest Friend, and the Best natured man; these are characters that are extreamly amiable but very seldom fall to the share of one man to possess in such a degree as you do.

Yet of all his noble friends, it was Bathurst with whom Pope felt most completely at his ease, and with whom he seems to have collaborated most fully in landscaping projects of all kinds. He had known Bathurst since Scriblerus Club days, but it was from about 1718 that he increasingly sought refuge at one or other of Bathurst's houses: in St. James's Square, Westminster; Richings Park, Buckinghamshire (only seventeen miles from London); and Cirencester House in eastern Gloucestershire. Sometimes he may have been fleeing the seasonal social whirl of Twickenham. It is from Bathurst's, we notice, that in the last letter we have from him to Lady Mary Wortley Montagu (15 September 1721) he offers her his villa to use for a musicale, having been denied by his landlord the privilege of lending her the harpsichord that apparently the house contained when leased. Throughout 1721–22, when the newly arrived composer G. B. Bononcini was seeking a reputation in London operatic circles and for a time lived in Twickenham, Pope was considerably involved in musical affairs. He seeks tickets for the Blount sisters to a benefit for Anastasia Robinson, still at this date singing but soon to be married secretly to Peterborow ("Mrs. Robinson haunts Bononcini, you follow her, and I plague you," his friend Atterbury writes); he solicits his friends, obviously with some success, for subscriptions to Bononcini's *Cantate*, published in 1721; he hears at Buckingham House on 10 January 1723 a pair of odes he has written for insertion in his friend the Duke's adaptation of Shakespeare's *Julius Caesar* performed by Mrs. Robinson and others to Bononcini's settings; and the following year he may himself have

48. Edward Harley, 2d Earl of Oxford (1689–1741). Drawing by
George Vertue.

> Is there a Lord . . .
> Who copies . . . OXFORD'S better part,
> To ease th' oppress'd, and raise the sinking heart?
> *Epistle to Bathurst*, 239, 243–4.

contributed the words for a cantata, to be sung at her farewell benefit performance by the diva Margaritta Durastanti.

If demands of this sort upon his time became heavy, a visit to Richings or Cirencester could always rescue him. At Richings, Bathurst jokingly complained, he had even been forced to buy a tin standish, since his poetical guest was always in need of ink and pens. Probably he did at various times compose there, but the special attraction of Richings was the garden, which Bathurst, no doubt with his guest's eager collaboration, was "improving." By the time he sold the place in 1739, it had a canal some 1600 feet long, down which one could drift through variegated scenes to a greenhouse filled with orange trees and oleanders, many small woods with winding paths as at Twickenham, a rude cave—no grotto! but having its own spring—overhung with periwinkle, little arbors "interwoven" with lilac, woodbine, mock orange, and laurel, a broad Long Walk "under prodigiously high overarching beeches" (Bathurst was one of the century's greatest arborealists, but these must have been planted earlier), and an ancient bench covered—so attests the Countess of Hertford, whose husband purchased the property from Bathurst—with verses inscribed by Addison, Pope, Prior, Congreve, Gay, and others. The only inscription she quotes sounds much like Pope, anticipating (perhaps) the themes of careful father, reckless son developed in his *Epistle to Bathurst*:

> Who set the trees shall he remember
> That is in haste to fell the timber?
> What then shall of thy woods remain,
> Except the box [i.e., the dice box] that threw the main.★

Still, it was on Cirencester Park, judged by a twentieth-century authority in these matters to be still (in 1950) "perhaps the most spectacular park in England," that Bathurst and Pope, and most notably the former, spent their chief efforts, mapping, drawing, and contriving in a manner that illustrated long before Pope wrote his famous line what it means to "Consult the Genius of the Place in all." Between Cirencester and Sapperton, Bathurst had put together a holding of around 4,000 acres, 3,000 of them eventually forest (of which 1,000 were of his own planting), composed, like the vast forest Pope grew up in, of successive woods and glades, hills and plains, but threaded, unlike Windsor Forest, with unbroken broad vistas reaching between solid plantations of beech, oak, elm, or conifer and

★ The number called by the caster before he casts the dice.

punctuated with intersections and rond-points featuring architectural objects much as Pope had used statues and urns at Twickenham. Down the broadest avenue of all could be seen the handsome steeple of Cirencester church; down another, a house in the woods designed by Bathurst and Pope in 1721 but later extended and gothicized into a structure called Alfred's Hall; and down a third by 1741 (Pope had been urging it since 1736) "a Dorick pillar near 60 feet high, with ye statue of Q. Ann upon it as big as the life."★ At one rond-point, known as The Seven Rides, where many vistas converged, stood and still stands a small stone summer house known as "Pope's Seat." Some such similarly titled structure could once, and in several instances still can, be seen in a number of the great gardens of England's eighteenth century. Poetry today seldom fares so well.

It was in this environment that Pope spent many of his happiest hours. Sometimes in much company, for, as he says in one letter, his host "invites hither every Woman he sees, & ev'ry Man." Perhaps it was on some occasions of that kind, when the last books of the *Iliad* translation were still in progress, that at breakfast he would read aloud—"with great rapture," says Bathurst—the Greek verses he had been working on in bed, followed by his own draft rendering of them, and then fall to comparisons. Sometimes he and Gay would be there together, Gay as felicitously carried on the wings of imagination to the bower in Oakley Wood "as ever Don Quixote was to an Enchanted Castle." And sometimes, alone, he would paint for Lady Scudamour, his friend Digby's Twickenham cousin, an invitation to "a better Life in the Elysian Groves of *Cirencester*, whither I could almost say in the style of a Sermon, the *Lord bring us all. . . .* Thither may we tend, by various ways to one blissful Bower: Thither may Health, Peace, and Good Humour wait upon us as Associates:

★ The description is Milles's, f 127. He also says of the house in the woods: "There is likewise a little old house situated in the thickest part of ye wood, to which Lord Bathurst has given a very romantick appearance by building some walls in an irregular manner & in a Gothic taste, in order to have it look like the ruins of a castle. Lord Bathurst has a pheasantry here, & sometimes dines & drinks here." Edward Stephen's *A Poem on the Park and Woods of . . . Allen Lord Bathurst* (2d ed., Cirencester, 1748), referring to the house in a note as "a most curious Imitation of Antiquity, and surrounded with a great Variety of most agreeable Walks," tells an amusing story of the elderly female servant who was its caretaker: "*No Doubt,* says a Gentleman who came to see it, *this Building must be very ancient; it can't be less than Five or Six Hundred Years old.* O, *Sir,* replies the Woman, *my lord intends soon to build a House Six Hundred Years older.*"

Thither may whole Cargoes of Nectar (Liquor of Life and Long-aevity!) by mortals call'd *Spaw-water*, be convey'd, and there (as *Milton* has it) may we, like the Deities,

> On flow'rs repos'd, and with fresh garlands crown'd,
> Quaff Immortality and Joy."

And usually, of course, in addition, there was the sparkling benefi-cent presence of Bathurst himself, of whom even in his very ripe age the author of *Tristram Shandy* was to write to his "Eliza":

> This nobleman, I say, is a prodigy; for at eighty-five he has all the wit and promptness of a man of thirty. A disposition to be pleased, and a power to please others beyond whatever I knew: added to which, a man of learning, courtesy, and feeling.

"The amiable Simplicity of unadorn'd Nature"

How far Pope's work at Twickenham and elsewhere helped establish the freer and supposedly more "natural" style of landscaping that gradually replaced the geometrizing Dutch and French styles favored during his boyhood has lately become a matter of some debate and is likely to continue so, since precise evidence (as often in gardening matters) remains in short supply. Horace Walpole credits him with having advised William Kent, in some respects the foremost land-scapist of the day, in the design of certain famous gardens of the "liberated" kind, and we know that he was instrumental in recom-mending the professional gardener Charles Bridgeman, whose instincts were moderately libertarian, to important patrons and seemingly in some instances "collaborated" or "advised." Yet it would be difficult to say what, exactly, this means. Three points only seem beyond dispute. He stood always ready to put his own consider-able knowledge of horticulture, his keen enthusiasm for the new fluid relationships of house to garden and park and the countryside beyond, and also what Horace Walpole was moved to call on at least one occasion his "exquisite judgment" in the disposition of light and shade at the disposal of any friend. His own gardens became, during his lifetime as well as after it, a magnet for tourists, strangers and friends alike, and were regarded by many contemporaries, including the visitor from Newcastle earlier quoted, as an example of what could be achieved by using art to imitate and consummate nature's own forms. The poet Thomson even ventures to name Pope's garden along with Cirencester, Chiswick, Stowe, and the royal gardens at Richmond as exemplary to the age, and the eighteenth-century Irish garden historian, Cooper Walker, suggests that from Pope's practice at Twickenham Swift's good friend Dr. Patrick Delany may have learned "to soften into curve the obdurate and straight line of the Dutch, to melt the terrace into a swelling bank, and to open his walks to catch the vicinal country."

Also, of course, there were the poet's two "essays" on landscaping, one in prose, one in verse. Not that anything he proposed was altogether new. The ideas in his *Guardian* of 1713 attacking topiary and praising "the amiable Simplicity of unadorned Nature" are all traceable in earlier writers—Temple, Shaftesbury, Addison, not to mention a succession of brief references in writers of the previous century—though certainly never before expressed with such satiric gusto or illustrated so persuasively with examples from the admired ancients, especially Homer's description of the Gardens of Alcinous, which he includes in the argument in his own brilliant translation. Much the same may be said of the *Epistle to Burlington*, published almost two decades later. This, in his remarks to Spence before it had taken shape, he called his "gardening poem," and it does contain a considerable amount of sound landscaping counsel. But again, none of it is strictly new, not even the influential admonition to consult the genius of the place or the famous summary (in two lines) of intelligent gardening in the new style as Pope understood it: "He gains all points, who pleasingly confounds, Surprizes, varies, and conceals the bounds." Not so simple a recipe as it looks!

What must have given both pieces any horticultural influence they had was the telling way in which horticultural matters were related to larger values of good sense and constructive use. Along with this went the typically early eighteenth-century implication that there are traditions, rules, and cultural norms by which the sillier impulses of one's naked subjectivity may be regulated and educated, and the characteristically though not exclusively Popian principle that traditions, rules, and cultural norms, valuable as they may be, are never by themselves enough:

> Yet shall (my Lord) your just, your noble rules
> Fill half the land with Imitating Fools;
> Who random drawings from your sheets shall take,
> And of one beauty many blunders make;
> Load some vain Church with old Theatric state,
> Turn Arcs of triumph to a Garden-gate;

> Reverse your Ornaments, and hang them all
> On some patch'd dog-hole ek'd with ends of wall,
> Then clap four slices of pilaster on 't,
> That, lac'd with bits of rustic, makes a Front [i.e., facade]
> Or call the winds thro' long Arcades to roar,
> Proud to catch cold at a Venetian door;
> Conscious they act a true Palladian part,
> And if they starve, they starve by rules of art.
>
> *Epistle to Burlington* (ll. 25–38)

Anyone who looks closely at the towerscape of Manhattan island in the late twentieth century will understand what Pope is saying.

What has to be emphasized in any sensible conclusion to this matter is that the new gardening, and Pope's or any other gardener's part in it, must be seen in historical perspective. The eighteenth century saw the development of the armchair from the upright wooden spine-splints of earlier days; the manufacture of upholstered furniture; re-arrangements of space both within and without the country house to deemphasize its symbols of hierarchy and power and feature those of sociability and play, thus suiting it better to what we now call the nuclear as distinguished from the institutional or tribal family; a gradual, if glacially slow, uncramping of women's bodies; and a growing toleration of marriages for love. Even in textiles the change was dramatic. In the sixteenth century, the young bride-to-be of the Duke of Clèves had to be carried to the ceremony, such was the weight of her status-signifying costume. In the seventeenth, poets are beginning to be ravished by "Robes loosely flowing, haire as free," not to mention the occasional "erring Lace," "tempestuous Pet-ticoat," or "lawn about the shoulders thrown Into a fine distraction." Pope's "graceful negligence," one suspects, is simply one of the heirs to such sentiment, now applied to verse making. His "Grace beyond the reach of Art" in poetry seems perfectly compatible with what Horace Walpole felt about his garden, "twisted and twirled and rhymed and harmonized." And his continual pleas in letters, particu-larly to new correspondents, that the exchange should be kept free of conventional epistolary compliment, like his jocular protest against the obliquities of women's undergarmenting in his imitation of Horace's bawdiest satire—

> But if to Charms more latent you pretend,
> What Lines encompass, and what Works defend!
> Dangers on Dangers! obstacles by dozens!
> Spies, Guardians, Guests, old Women, Aunts, and Cozens!

Could you directly to her Person go,
Stays will obstruct above, and Hoops below,
And if the Dame says yes, the Dress says no—

(*Imit. Hor., Sat.* I, ii, 126–32)

have, surely, a real even if not precisely definable relationship both to
a general *Zeitgeist* or shifting sensibility (whatever we may mean by
those rather dubious terms) as well as to the results that his own
personal distaste for the patterns of French and Dutch landscaping,
natural to one reared in Windsor Forest, had brought about on five
acres in Twickenham.

CHAPTER 17

EMBARRASSMENTS AND GRIEFS

"She waits, or to the Scaffold, or the Cell"

Meanwhile, there had been surprisingly little interruption of Pope's literary labors following the publication of the *Iliad*. Scarcely three months after its last two volumes appeared in May of 1720, we hear of his borrowing from Atterbury a copy of "Chapman," presumably Chapman's Homer—which can only mean that he was already meditating his translation of the *Odyssey*. This, after many delays, he completed and published in five volumes in 1725–26—not, however, without extensive collaboration from his friend the rector of Sturston, William Broome, who had helped him with extracts from Eustathius for his *Iliad* notes and now contributed eight of the twenty-four books of the *Odyssey* besides its entire prose commentary. Another friend, Elijah Fenton, whom Pope had perhaps come to know when he was living as tutor with the Trumbull family in Easthamstead, contributed four books. Pope himself engaged for twelve, wrote the critical "Postscript" comparing the two Homeric epics and the distinctive styles required to render them, and oversaw with exemplary care and energy the undertaking as a whole.

To have taken up again so exacting a task after so short an interlude argues, one is bound to suspect, a financial pinch. The building and gardening he was busy with at Twickenham must have called for considerable outlays and had come, moreover, just at a time when he may have lost part of his earnings from the *Iliad* in the widespread bankruptcy following the collapse of the South Sea Bubble. Gay, at any rate, thought so and wrote to Swift in early 1723: "He has engag'd to translate the Odyssey in three years, I believe rather out of a prospect of Gain than inclination, for I am persuaded he bore his part in the loss of the Southsea." What may add weight to Gay's perhaps informed guess is that at about this time we also hear of a subscription edition of Shakespeare's plays for the benefit of the publisher, the younger Jacob

Tonson (nephew of the Jacob who had published the *Pastorals*), with Pope as editor at a fee of £100.

For whatever reasons, Pope kept himself busy. During 1720–21, he was engaged partly in preparing Parnell's poems for publication. On his visit to England to see his old friends in the summer of 1718, Parnell had asked this favor (Pope alludes to it in the acknowledgments at the close of the *Iliad*), very probably knowing that he had not long to live: he died, as we saw earlier, on the journey home. "I am erecting the best Monument I can," Pope tells Jervas in a letter of probably 1720. "What he gave me to publish, was but a small part of what he left behind him, but it was the best, and I shall not make it worse by enlarging it." Hearing of this prospect in Ireland, Swift added his own plea. If a posthumous collection was to appear, Pope *must* "bestow a few Verses on his friend Parnels memory."

When the collection was published in late 1721, it was prefaced with a poem addressed not to Parnell, however, but "To the Right Honourable, Robert [Harley], Earl of Oxford, and Earl Mortimer." Harley (as we saw earlier) after two years in the Tower under Whig charges of high treason was now living quietly on his estate at Brampton Castle in Herefordshire, the Whigs having found it impossible to make the indictment stick. There was method in this deviance on Pope's part. For the poem makes it obvious that as he brooded on the memorial to Parnell it expatiated, as so often happens in his work, into something more inclusive and generic. It would be a memorial to Parnell, but also to Harley, to Swift, and to a time that as he looked back on it now seemed golden. It would be a tribute to a poet but also to a statesman who had loved and valued poets; and, most especially, to those claims for the moral and civil functions of poetry that he would maintain throughout his career: functions that center in a particular way of seeing.

Hence the poem addresses itself directly to Harley, treating the death of "his" poet Parnell as an illustration of the Homeric theme that no gifts or blessings can save a mortal from his fate, though modified here to fit the figure of the poet with his traditional pipe or reed, "stopped" now by a bonier finger:

> Such were the Notes thy once-lov'd Poet sung,
> Till Death untimely stop'd his tuneful Tongue.
>
> (ll. 1–2)

To the happiness of such company, the poem goes on (at this point adding Swift), Harley used often to escape from the vexations of his central position in the temple of the Goddess of Getting-on:

49. Robert Harley, 1st Earl of Oxford (1661–1724). By Sir Godfrey Kneller, *c.* 1714.

"Fond to forget the Statesman in the Friend."
Epistle to ROBERT Earl of OXFORD, and Earl MORTIMER, 8.

Courtesy of the National Portrait Gallery.

> For him, thou oft hast bid the World attend,
> Fond to forget the Statesman in the Friend;
> For *Swift* and him, despis'd the Farce of State,
> The sober Follies of the Wise and Great;
> Dextrous, the craving, fawning Crowd to quit,
> And pleas'd to 'scape from Flattery to Wit.
>
> (ll. 7–12)

Not even the great minister of state—more poignant, not even the Muse herself—can postpone or dispel the moment of death: "Dear to the Muse, to Harley dear—in *vain*!" Yet the Muse, even if not the statesman, has access to life in another dimension—in fact, insists on it: "*In vain* to Desarts thy Retreat is made." Represented in the poem by Harley's Parnell, by Swift, and, very quietly, with careful avoidance of the word "I," by the author of the poem as well, the Muse, who brings a way of seeing unaffected by vicissitude, "forbids the Good to dye"—so Pope will put it again in the very last of his satires—and opens "the Temple of Eternity":

> In vain to Desarts thy Retreat is made;
> The Muse attends thee to the silent Shade:
> 'Tis hers, the brave Man's latest Steps to trace,
> Re-judge his Acts, and dignify Disgrace.
> When Int'rest calls off all her sneaking Train,
> When all th' Oblig'd desert, and all the Vain;
> She waits, or to the Scaffold, or the Cell,
> When the last ling'ring Friend has bid farewel.
> Ev'n now she shades thy Evening Walk with Bays,
> (No Hireling she, no Prostitute to Praise)
> Ev'n now, observant of the parting Ray,
> Eyes the calm Sun-set of thy Various Day,
> Thro' Fortune's Cloud One truly Great can see,
> Nor fears to tell, that MORTIMER is He.
>
> (ll. 27–40)

The poem is a tribute and ends as a tribute should in a dazzle of praise. But, as the critic who has read this poem with the greatest sensitivity reminds us, it is not dazzle alone. Pope was not blind to Harley's faults:

To "bid the World attend" is a finer compliment to Parnell's wit than to a statesman's sense of responsibility; there is some ground for political uneasiness in the word "Fond"; no statesman should despise "the Farce of State" lest he should come too near to despising the state itself; nor can we admire the statesman who likes his pleasures to the point of having acquired a "dexterity" in "escaping" to them, even if it is only from the "craving, fawning Crowd." Harley, Pope says outright, did suffer a "Fall"; during two years of unduly prolonged imprisonment (owing to alleged Jacobite sympathies) he faced "the Scaffold or the Cell." Nor does Pope blink what is least pleasant in Harley's rustication; he has made a "Retreat" after his "Fall," and that to the "Desarts" on the Welsh border [site of Brampton Castle], where instead of buzzing with curiosity the "Shade" is silent; he is under a "Cloud," and a "Disgrace" that stands in need of being given its dignity. The climax of Pope's poem is a blaze, but the recovering eye is aware that Harley is human after all.

And aware, too, we might add, that despite all these qualifications poetry is never history.

A "horrid conspiracy" and a "scandalous Libel"

To write of a suspected Jacobite leader in this exalted vein took as much courage (or folly) in the tense scare atmosphere of the early 1720s as it had when in his *Iliad* Preface of 1715 Pope had praised Bolingbroke only a few weeks after the latter had fled to France and the Pretender. As things turned out, there would soon be moments when he may have wished he had been more discreet. Between 1716 and 1719, two further plots for a Stuart restoration, one involving Spain, one Sweden, had been afoot; and though vigilance at home and an effective secret service abroad had combined with bad luck and a total lack of united leadership on the Stuart side to defeat these efforts, the government continued uneasy. And with reason. The Whig ministers, naturally with the warm support of the Hanoverian king, had ever since the rising of 1715 so ruthlessly proscribed Tories from sharing in the political reward system (on the trumped-up grounds that they were uniformly Jacobite at heart) that no matter how little sympathy most of the party had with ideological Jacobitism, they were steadily under pressure to rally to the Stuart cause as the only alternative to an exclusionary policy that the Whigs appeared intent upon maintaining indefinitely. The conclusion of at least one Jacobite observer as late as 1750 was that "if it were not for proscription, there would not be a Jacobite in England."

Then came the South Sea stock crash of 1720–21, so disastrous that it reduced some families to penury. When it became apparent that the ministry and its minions had been manipulating the market for some time to their own advantage and that inquiries into the full extent of the corruption were to be systematically blocked in the Commons, partly (so the rumors went) because the Court, having been kept abreast of developments, had made a killing before selling out, the emotional climate for a Stuart restoration was ripe. Arthur Onslow, then Whig M.P. from Guildford and a future Speaker of the House, acknowledged later that if the Pretender could at that time have landed at the Tower, "he might have rode to St. James's with very few hands held up against him."

In situations like this, as every politician knows, no domestic pacifier is so effective as the threat of armed invasion from abroad. And fortunately for the government, there was again in 1721–22 an intention of this sort, supported chiefly by some of the wilder-eyed Jacobite exiles on the Continent. Though it had almost no prospect of success (as the government was well aware through its agents, who were planted like moles in the movement's innermost networks), it could with a little ministerial cunning be nursed up to look like a clear and present danger to the Hanoverian dynasty. The man who sized up and seized this opportunity was Sir Robert Walpole. Without much doubt, Walpole was not in this matter a mere opportunist: he had a genuine paranoia about Jacobitism that could raise oaks out of acorns in his mind overnight. Yet there is no doubt, either, that he knew a sound political gambit when he saw it. To be credited with the uncovering of a plot against the throne, followed by, if possible, some sensational trials, sanguinary executions, and other familiar expedients for influencing opinion, would fix him forever in the affections of George I, who, though hardly brilliant, was bright enough to know that his hold on the affections of the English nation was just now something less than ironclad. Already, to quote from an authoritative recent history of these matters, Walpole "had earned the respect and gratitude of the Hanoverian ruling clique, from the monarch downwards, by his devoted and successful efforts to ensure that justice was thwarted" in the South Sea affair by screening as many offenders as possible from retribution, thus earning both future votes and the title (which he never lived down) of "Skreen-Master General." Now he would crown that accomplishment by *un*-screening some Jacobites, forcing through Parliament a suspension of the Habeas Corpus Act, imposing on Roman Catholics a fine of £100,000, and, in what has been described as "a classic example of the use of the armed forces not to defend but manipulate a society," would stir further panic by setting up an encampment of thousands of soldiers in Hyde Park.

In command (so far as any single individual was ever in command) of the opposite front in England at this juncture was Pope's friend Francis Atterbury. Not by inherited loyalties a Stuart supporter, profoundly hostile to Roman Catholicism, the Pretender's faith, never a Jacobite in any sense till 1716, when to him as to many Tories a Stuart restoration began to look like the sole means of breaking the Whig stranglehold on church and state, he had agreed in 1716 to assume the leadership of English Jacobitism, though not till five years later was he actually involved in the planning or execution of any of the Continental Jacobites' invasion attempts. Foolishly, in 1721, he agreed to a preposterous plan by which the Duke of Ormonde, who like Bolingbroke had fled to the Pretender after being impeached in 1715, would invade England during the General Election of April 1722. In a letter sent to the Continental Jacobites in March of that year, he warned them of the folly of their scheme but did not actually dissociate himself from it and continued his correspondence with the Pretender and his agents abroad and at home, none of it, however, in his own hand, and much of it in cipher.

Through its listening posts the government was fully apprised of the intention and also of its collapse: no invasion took place. But by August 1722, Walpole thought he had enough clues from messengers, informers, and fringe conspirators (such as Christopher Layer, who, having been given assurances by Walpole that Walpole shamefully did not keep, was executed as a traitor) to risk his grand move. On the ninth of that month, Atterbury as Dean of Westminster presided over the vast Abbey funeral of the Duke of Marlborough, when Pope stayed overnight with him at the Deanery to "moralize," as he put it, "on the vanity of human Glory."* It proved to be the Dean's last act in office. On Friday the twenty-fourth, he was summarily seized, the Deanery and his country retreat at Bromley were ransacked, and he himself was unceremoniously hurried off to the Tower. To borrow the words of Atterbury's best biographer, Walpole had now "staked his political career on a successful prosecution":

* To Atterbury, July 27, [1722] (2:127). For a brilliant account of the funeral, the pomp and circumstance of which were indeed staggering, see James Sutherland's *Background for Queen Anne* (1939), pp. 204–24. Like every event of the period, the funeral had a political aspect, serving from the Whig point of view as a grand public reproach to the Tories on behalf of the great leader they had disgraced ten years before.

50. Francis Atterbury (1662–1732). By Sir Godfrey Kneller, *c.* 1713.

"How pleasing ATTERBURY's softer hour!
How shin'd the Soul, unconquer'd in the Tow'r!
One Thousand Seven Hundred and Thirty-Eight, Dialogue 1: 82–83.

By kind permission of the governing body, Christ Church, Oxford.

For the next nine months he was to devote himself day and night to proving to the satisfaction of the King and Parliament that there had been a grave threat to national security and that Atterbury had been the principal director of this "detestable and horrid conspiracy." ... Indeed in later years Speaker Onslow had no hesitation in pointing to the trial of Bishop Atterbury as the real beginning of Walpole's premiership. It was, he wrote, the "most fortunate and greatest circumstance of Mr. Walpole's life. It fixed him with the King, and united for a time the whole body of Whigs to him, and gave him the universal credit of an able and vigilant Minister."

While Walpole settled down to find the evidence that would make his career (suspension of the Habeas Corpus Act allowed him time to carry on this search while the accused, though nowhere yet proved guilty, languished in prison), Pope was at work arranging and revising for publication the papers and poems of John Sheffield, Duke of Buckinghamshire. This, like the edition of Parnell, was an act of piety to a dead friend (the Duke had died on 24 February 1721), but in this case an act initiated while the friend was 'yet living and carried through posthumously at the behest of his tempestuous Duchess, natural daughter of James II. Though she gave Pope a great deal of trouble by her overbearing demands on his time, not merely for the niceties of the inscription honoring her husband in the book but for the design of the monument she was erecting to him in the Abbey, the Duke's works appeared at last in two handsome volumes published by Alderman John Barber on 24 January 1723. Two days later, an order from Lord Carteret, the Secretary of State, authorized a search of Barber's premises and seizure of the books, "because," said the *British Journal*, "in some Part of these Volumes great Reflections are cast upon the late happy Revolution"—so happy, apparently, that it could be a treasonable offense to "reflect" on any part of it. The government's interest lay actually, as the warrant shows, in two prose pieces in the first volume: "Some Account of the Revolution" and "A Feast of the Gods." Written years before about an event still further in the past, even their most daring sentences did not go beyond what many perfectly patriotic John Bulls had been saying for three decades. In "Some Account," for instance, that "the pretended Cause" of the Prince of Orange's coming "was for redress of *Grievances*: the real one needs not to be mentioned, and will be easily imagined." And in "A Feast of the Gods," on the Dutch: "Some mention was made of a certain People remarkable for industry, and for having no one good quality besides."

Little wonder that Pope was worried (as well as probably astounded) by the government's action. Only the preceding November he had cautioned Broome that public announcement of the *Odyssey* translation must wait upon certain "contingencies," one of which has surely been correctly identified as the potential damping effect on any subscription effort of his known close friendship with a man then awaiting trial for high treason, a friendship made all the more suspicious by his own often satirized "popery." Now a book of his editing had been seized as "a seditious and scandalous Libel." Furthermore, according to *The British Journal*, he himself was taken into custody, probably for questioning. What actually took place, we can only guess. By February 13, enemies (possibly some of the old crowd at Button's) were at him in the newspaper *Pasquin* and elsewhere with the charge that he had obtained Carteret's license to print the Duke of Buckingham's works by showing only a selection of the Duke's papers—a lie, since it was not he but Barber who had obtained the license. But it caused Pope enough anxiety about its possible public effects to draw from him a letter to Carteret, in which a reference to having recently waited upon his lordship quite possibly alludes to some hearing or interview following his arrest.

One (probably secondary) purpose of the letter was to assure the secretary that he had not looked through all the Sheffield papers at the time Barber obtained the license to print. The statement may or may not be true, but it could hardly, in any case, excuse his not showing the items to Carteret once he had unearthed them, if he thought they were likely to be regarded as subversive. Clearly, he did not. What one suspects happened is that when the secretary's officers went through the papers at the time of Barber's application to print in the spring of 1722, long before the seizure of Atterbury, they saw nothing that particularly disturbed them, at least nothing worth making an issue of, since the writings dealt with no event more recent than the transition from James II to William III and the Duke's Stuart sympathies in that matter were sufficiently well known. But then came the imprisonment of a major prelate and Walpole's program for keeping public opinion in a chronic state of alarm. The appearance of the papers of an eminent peer (whose duchess was a Stuart and known for Jacobite activity) through a publisher with Jacobite connections, under the editorship of a well-known papist, may have seemed too good an opportunity to miss, particularly if the hurly-burly about their seditious character was being pressed in the first place by government underlings inimical to Pope, as the poet seems originally to have thought.

The other and probably primary intent of Pope's letter to Carteret was to offer to abandon his *Odyssey* project as a bridge to stating that neither his friendship with Atterbury, which he does not propose to renounce, nor his determination to preserve his poetical independence should in fairness be used to brand him a rebel to the state. It is an impressive statement of a position from which Pope never wavered:

> Give me leave my Lord to pay you my thanks for your Intentions to promote my design on Homer; but allow me to add, that if I am, (however innocently) under the least displeasure of the Government: I desire not to be oblig'd by those that dislike or think me unworthy. Indeed my Lord I love my Country, better than any Personal friend I have; but I love my Personal Friend so well, as not to abandon, or rail at him, tho' my whole Country fell upon him. And I assure your Lordship, tho' the King has many Subjects much more valuable than my self, he has not one more Quiet; no Man is more Sensible of the Indulgence I enjoy from my Rulers, I mean that which is common to every Subject from the Protection of a free Government. But as to any particularly, I take my self to be the only Scribler of my Time, of any degree of distinction, who never receiv'd any Places from the Establishment, any Pension from a Court, or any Presents from a Ministry. I desire to preserve this Honour untainted to my Grave.

If the Secretary cared to attach a flicker of irony to a Roman Catholic's acknowledging the "Indulgence" of rulers who systematically oppressed men and women of his persuasion, were about to post a bill in Parliament to assess them £100,000 for the expenses of a "plot" that was not of Roman Catholic origin, and had held one of their own Anglican prelates for six months, under draconian conditions, almost inaccessible to visits even from his own children; or if the secretary chose to catch another flicker of the same in the "Honour" a certain poet found in dissociating himself from such an "Establishment," "Court," and "Ministry," that would be, of course, his privilege.

In the event, the offending material in the Sheffield *Works* was trashed out and the mutilated book allowed to be sold. The government's gain by the suppression would seem to have been minimal. That shameless entrepreneur and expert in underground publishing, Edmund Curll, soon had a pamphlet in circulation appealingly called *The Castrations* with both forbidden items intact, and these found separate publication again at the Hague in 1727, now entitled *Buckingham Restored*. Meanwhile, an edition of the *Works* with no castrations of any kind was issued without government interference in 1726, and others later on. All which might lend credence to the theory that the 1723 suppression was not without its links to the government's campaign to keep Jacobitism in the forefront of the public's mind till Atterbury could be tried.

The Atterbury Trial

The trial came in May. Well before, Walpole had reluctantly realized that he lacked the sort of evidence required for conviction in a court of law, and even, possibly, for a successful impeachment. He would have to proceed by a bill of pains and penalties, which required only that a majority of each House be prepared to vote into law a parliamentary bill inflicting specified criminal penalties on the accused. The trial, in other words, would be political rather than juridical, and since the Whigs had the votes, it would be at bottom a charade—as Atterbury warned Pope in April. On Monday, May 6, it began. The task on Walpole's side was to prove that the detailed narrative he had painstakingly put together out of bits and scraps of information from a multitude of sources over a period of months was basically true; that for the bishop's side, to show that the whole account was a fabrication, designed to destroy the Tory leadership by pinning to it a Jacobite label.

During the first days of examining and cross-examining witnesses, neither side appeared to have gained a decisive edge. On the Thursday, May 9, Atterbury's servants, under severe cross-examination, stuck immovably to their testimony that no such comings and goings as Walpole's narrative called for had ever to their knowledge taken place either at the Deanery or Bromley. On the next day, the tenth—among other witnesses, and in a fine state of nerves (to judge from his comments to Spence later on)—Pope was summoned to the stand. According to the Lord Chancellor's brief and cryptic notes, his testimony stated that he often saw Atterbury, frequently lodged with him, sat in the same room, never heard any company refused admittance while he was there, came in at all hours himself yet never knew the subject of discourse to be suddenly changed—in short, had seen or heard nothing whatever to suggest that the bishop was concerned in a plot. Both he and the servants are likely to have been telling the truth so far as they knew it. Atterbury was a circumspect man.

On the eleventh (Saturday), it was Atterbury's turn. He spoke for two hours in his own defense, with a brief interval for rest—he was sixty-one, and not well: less well since his harsh treatment in the

Tower—carefully skirting by ingenuities of language, as his biographer points out, the lie direct; since, though genuinely ignorant of much of the peripheral material that Walpole had turned up, he knew he was on the central point guilty. His chief and telling theme was the absence of credible evidence:

> After a twelve month's search for the contrivers and conductors of this scheme, no consultations appear to have been held, no money to have been raised, and (which is stranger) no arms, officers or soldiers, to have been provided. Not a man of the army is engaged in it. A poor Bishop has done all, and must suffer for it.

Many in the room were moved, Pope unquestionably. Obviously in a state of high emotion, he wrote Atterbury that night:

> To tell you that my heart is full of your Defense, is no more than I believe the worst enemy you have must own of his. . . . Their Passions and Consciences have done you right, though their Votes will not. . . . Let me take the only Occasion I have had in the whole Series of your misfortunes, to congratulate you; not you only, but Posterity, on this Noble Defense. I already see in what Lustre that Innocence is to appear to other Ages, which this has overborn[e] and oppressed. . . . Thanks be to God, that I a Private man, concerned in no Judicature, and employed in no Publick cause, have had the honour, in this great and shining incident . . . to enter, as it were, my Protest to your Innocence, and my Declaration of your Friendship.

Monday the thirteenth brought the two antagonists into dramatic confrontation. To refute the charge that the plot was a wholesale invention, Walpole took the stand personally. With the quick intelligence, mastery of detail, and unshatterable poise that were to make him one of the nation's most effective leaders, even if at some moments and in some actions a scoundrel, he met Atterbury's sharpest cross fire with a patience in refutation and a refusal to be sidetracked from his insistence on the bishop's Jacobite involvement that compelled admiration. Predictably, two days later, when the Lords' vote came, it was for the bill, 83 to 43, despite some eloquent pleadings by Atterbury's supporters and a statement by William, first earl Cowper, one of the staunchest and most honored of Whig statesmen, that to incriminate a man as they had done by political, not legal, procedures was a disgrace to British justice.

51. Sir Robert Walpole, 1st Earl of Orford (1676–1745). By Michael
Rysbrack, *c.* 1726–30.

> Seen him I have, but in his happier hour
> Of Social Pleasure, ill-exchang'd for Pow'r.
> *One Thousand Seven Hundred and Thirty-Eight, Dialogue* 1: 29–30.

The penalty written into the bill was banishment in perpetuity. No British subject was to communicate with the bishop except with privy-seal approval, and if he should ever in future set foot in the kingdom, that action would be an instant felony, unpardonable even by the king. (Walpole had seen to the bishop's punishments when the bill was drawn.) When Atterbury requested release from the Tower to facilitate the sale of his effects and preparation for a new life abroad, this privilege was denied him. Friends and relatives, however, were allowed to visit. Those among the lords who had spoken in his defense came to take their last farewells. Bathurst, who was one of them, also took up a collection among country Tories to piece out the bishop's modest income, while government newspapers ran false stories of his great wealth, and Benjamin Hoadly, Bishop of Hereford and sycophant extraordinary, attacked his fallen enemy in a series of savage articles signed Britannicus in the government's *London Journal*, for which he was promoted to the rich see of Salisbury the same year. Pope, who had somehow managed to procure a conversation with Atterbury (through a grating) while he awaited trial, now came again on the last evening, June 17, and was given the bishop's Bible as a memorial of their friendship. The next day, the prisoner was taken down the Thames to a waiting ship, which carried him to Calais. There, pretending to be ill in his inn so as not to have to meet with him, was Bolingbroke en route to England, having gained release from his own exile by convincing the government that he was through with Stuart claims forever. On learning of his presence, Atterbury is reported to have commented, with a grim smile, "Then I am exchanged!"

A felony close home

Pope himself soon had additional worries. On May 17, two days after Atterbury's conviction, Parliament passed Walpole's bill mulcting English Catholics for the supposed expenses of the "plot." On the twentieth, only ten days after he had appeared before the Lords on behalf of a now convicted traitor and scarcely more than three months after coming under suspicion for his connection with the "seditious" writings of the Duke of Buckinghamshire, his half-sister Magdalen's husband, Charles Rackett, was arrested by government officers, along with two servants and his son Michael, for deer stealing.

The Racketts lived at Hall Grove, Windlesham, on the petticoat edge of Windsor Forest. Charles, whose family connections seem to be mainly with Hammersmith, is set down in the parish register there in 1695 as "Charles Racket, gentleman," husband of Magdalen and father of Mary—Mary being probably his and Magdalen's firstborn. As we saw, the girl died in infancy, and we do not hear of her again; but eventually there were five sons who lived to grow up, Michael (the eldest), Bernard, Henry, John, and Robert. Also in that year, "Charles Rackett of Hammersmith, in the parish of Fulham, in the country of Middlesex" bought Whitehill House in Binfield of Gabriel Young (the man who later gave Pope a copy of Chaucer) and three years later sold it to his father-in-law. At about that same time an old yeoman family named Attfields sold Hall Grove to a Mr. Mountagu, who in turn sold it to a "Mr. Ragette"; while in 1715 "Elizabeth Rackett, widow" (Charles's mother?) "surrendered messuage called le Great House with buildings orchard and gardens, 2 a[cres] in Hammersmith" to "Charles Rackett of Windlesham, Surrey, gentleman," who promptly relinquished it, presumably by sale or lease, to two Londoners, a barrister and a goldsmith. One thus gets the impression of a certain affluence in the Rackett line, and this seems to be confirmed by one of the state documents bearing on the arrest, which describes Charles Rackett as "Mr. Ragget of Hall Grove near Bagshot, worth £20,000."

The grounds of the arrest are clear enough. According to one summary in the government's notes on the case, "Mr. Rackett, his Son and his Servants Horses & Dogs frequently were seen hunting and maliciously destroying the Deer in Windsor Forest." More precisely, a gamekeeper of Swinley Walk reported to the authorities in October that on three occasions the preceding summer (June 25 and 30 and July 1) he had seen three men hunting deer in the Forest and on the third occasion had followed them to Hall Grove, where he found Michael Rackett and two Rackett servants dressing their kill. He had asked to see the father and the father had offered him a guinea to forget it.

There was nothing at all new in this, and conceivably another year the keeper might have pocketed his hush money and departed with a warning not to repeat the offense. But this was 1722; there had been for some time an increasing lawlessness in parts of the royal forests—to some extent, it may be, in response to a shift from the easy-going, not rigorously policed forest administration of the past to the new tighter surveillance governing all regulations pertaining to property in the era of the Hanoverians. Bands of men wearing masks or with blacked faces were tangling with gamekeepers in the royal and even great private demesnes. Bullyings, extortions, pitched fights, even killings had occurred. Obviously, order—though perhaps it was rather the new order than the old—was threatened and had to be restored.

This was the year, moreover, of Walpole's witch hunt; Atterbury had been seized in August; and there seems to have been suspicion in government quarters, understandable even if for the most part unfounded, that the men involved in the masked gangs might be, or had been, recruited by Jacobite agents or for Jacobite activities. May of 1723, the month the Racketts and a number of others were arrested, was a particularly fruitful moment in the Walpole scenario. Not only was Atterbury sent to exile and Christopher Layer executed, but Parliament (almost, it appears, without discussion) passed the Black Act, a more comprehensive disgrace to British justice than any occasional trials of peers by bills of pains and penalties. Named for its special stress on poachers who disguised their faces with blacking, the act at one blow raised an uncommon number of existing criminal offenses to capital offenses and created new ones: "offenses against public order, against the administration of criminal justice, against property, against the person, malicious injuries to property of varying degrees—all came under the statute and were punishable by death." Poaching of game when armed or disguised was prominent among the named offenses, and if the poaching took place in any of the royal forests such as Windsor, it was a capital offense regardless.

In these circumstances, it is not hard to see why Michael Rackett, whose name appears on a government list of "Berkshire Blacks" in the document above-mentioned, along with those of his father and the two servants, is signalized as "absent." Evidently he fled, and for the rest of his life—at the very least for the next sixteen years—lived abroad, unable to return safely to England even when as late as 1739 (the last time we hear of him) his affairs as heir to the Hall Grove property demanded it. The father's case is more puzzling. On "A List of the Blacks Taken by Captain Brereton," a government paper accessory to the list just cited, the word "Jacobites" is set down beside the entry "Mr. Ragget of Hall Grove near Bagshot . . . and his son Michael, his 2 Servants and Horses and Dogs," and the same designation beside the name of one other. Against two other names is the notation: "suspicion of High Treason." Taken up on May 20, Charles Rackett was bound over under surety of £500 to appear at the Court of King's Bench on the twenty-fifth.

That is the last we hear of his case. What happened? The English historian who has studied with exemplary care the backgrounds and implementation of the Black Act proposes four possibilities. (1) Pope successfully intervened in his brother-in-law's behalf with some of his powerful friends. When on June 21 he thanks Lord Harcourt, one of the Lords Justices of the Regency Council during the King's absence in Hanover, for "many & great favours," this may have been one of them. (2) Rackett's case was transferred to the assizes, which were a common venue for forest offenses, and perhaps even held over till the next year—the records being not now discoverable. An undated fragment of a letter in which Pope speaks of having to go "to Oxfordshire for some time" could refer to such a turn of events, though it could equally well refer to the work being carried on at Oxford by his assistants on the Shakespeare edition. (3) Rackett may have been at Hall Grove in July 1723, but this is not certain, for the relevant letter is possibly of 1722. In any event, this is the last we hear of him before 1728, when he died—we do not know how or where. Does this signify something? Did he by any chance skip bail and leave the country? If so, this might account for Pope's mysterious statement, in a letter to Michael Rackett in 1739, that the Rackett fortunes had been impaired "by Mortgages, Law Suits, and by your Father's Neglect [i.e., absence?], as well as by the Sums of money and Bonds he took away with him before he Dyed." Conceivably, it was with these assets that he established a modest annuity for Magdalen through Lady Carrington, a fellow Roman Catholic living in Paris. At the time of his death, there is evidence that the estate was involved in a chancery suit—without much doubt, for unpaid debts or mortgages. It is even possible that within this comparatively short span of years, an estimated worth of £20,000 had shrunk to a small annuity and a property heavily charged with claims. (4) A final possibility accords easily with the first. The threat of prosecution was "kept hanging for a year or two, or indefinitely," over Rackett's head:

> Walpole was a hard man to bargain with. He was by no means likely to have allowed a Catholic gentleman and a reputed Jacobite, against whom, and against whose son, he had a good case of association with Blacking, to go free without obtaining something in return. The father might be left unprosecuted; but some large sum of money might have been exacted for that, as well as an undertaking that the son remain an outlaw. Meanwhile, the prosecutions might remain dormant. Michael, if in France, might well have burned his fingers further in the Jacobite cause. . . .
> Walpole would stand to gain one other asset. He had two hostages to hold against Alexander Pope. Pope had seemed, in the

early months of that deeply disaffected year, 1723, to be moving towards open criticism of the Walpole regime. He had given testimony on behalf of his friend, Francis Atterbury, the Jacobite Bishop of Rochester, when on trial in May before the House of Lords; and his correspondence with the Bishop, when imprisoned in the Tower, was well known. This can have pleased Walpole very little. But from June onwards—and until Charles Rackett's death in 1728—Pope had to tread warily. It is my impression that, for several years, he did.

Until further information comes to light, the consequences of the Rackett family's being identified, rightly or wrongly, with the Berkshire Blacks and involved in the newly capital crime of deer stealing from a royal forest, will remain in doubt; though I would hazard the guess that 1723 is too early for Walpole to have had any consuming interest in putting Pope in leading strings. The episode must, however, have added to the several complications delaying circulation of the poet's Proposals for his *Odyssey* subscription, which did not finally appear till January 1725, only three and a half months before the first three volumes were issued.

"*Years following Years, steal something ev'ry day*"

The year 1723—easily, as we have seen, one of Pope's most difficult and disheartening—was succeeded by several that in most ways brought little to cheer him. The loss of Atterbury by exile was compounded the next year by the death of Robert Harley, never of course an intimate and of an earlier generation, yet one of Pope's heroes, as the verses quoted earlier testify, and representative of a golden moment in his life as well as the father of a dear friend of his own age. "No man honourd the last Earl of Oxford more," he wrote immediately to the son; "no man loves the present better." The next year (1725) added a loss more tender. Mary Beach, his nurse as an infant and a much-loved servant who had been a member of the family for close to forty years, died at seventy-seven. Though we know little else about her, she is again and again referred to affectionately by Pope's friends and, at an earlier time, is jokingly said to have fallen so in love with Parnell that she might consider marrying Parnell's manservant just to be employed by his master. "My poor old Nurse," Pope writes Edward Harley two days after the event, "who has lived in constant attendance & care of me, ever since I was an Infant at her breast, dyed the other day":

I think it a fine verse, that of your Mr. Prior.

> . . . and by his side
> A Good man's greatest loss, a faithful Servant dy'd!

and I don't think one of my own an ill one, speaking of a Nurse,

> The tender Second to a Mother's cares.
>
> Hom. *Odyss.* 7 [:16]

Surely this Sort of Friend, is not the least, and this sort of Relation, when continued thro Life, Superior to most that we call so.

A few months later, quite unexpectedly, less than two years in fact after the poet's visit to Sherborne in 1724, Robert Digby died at the age of thirty-four—

> Just of thy Word, in ev'ry Thought sincere,
> Who knew no Wish, but what the World might hear.

So Pope wrote of him in an epitaph that not long after he was obliged to enlarge to include Digby's sister Mary, with whom he had also been on teasing affectionate terms. Within three months of Digby's death, his friend of long standing, Edward Blount, whose daughters had romped up and down his Great Mount, was also gone. A delightful man, sharing as a fellow Roman Catholic in some of Pope's deepest concerns, but also capable of returning the "chariot" he had borrowed from the poet with an entertaining parody of Horace followed by several equally entertaining sentences in prose:

> Let some the Booby Hatch [a small carriage],
> or Berlin Praise
> Let others sing of Coaches close, or open chaise
> Your Chariot will a better Theme afford,
> If Phoebus, and your nine but give the word;
> Like your Wheels my numbers then should Roll
> And with a Lofty Head I'de Knock the Pole;
> Nor Greece nor Rome like this e're Chariot drove
> Fit for the Goddess or the God of Love:
> For want of Talent, proper Art and Time
> For foolish Prose I quit the loosest Rhyme, etc.

I know not where I have got this small Itch of Rhyming but as when people are stung with the Tarantula, they are play'd to, and dance till they are cur'd, so I have stirr'd about in my Rhymes till I am very well cur'd, and as free from the least humour tending to

Edward Blount; Esq.
of · Blagden·in
Devon—

52. Edward Blount (?–1726). Artist unknown. Possibly French.

". . . of whose many virtues we had an experience of so many years." Pope to Caryll, 30 August 1726, following Blount's death.

Private Collection.

that distemper as ever I was in my life: I have tak'n the Bark [bark of the Cinchona tree, from which quinine for the treatment of fevers is made], which I hope will prevent its return.

Blount's death left Pope "very melancholy," as he wrote to their mutual friend Hugh Bethel:

> Whoever has any portion of good nature will suffer on these occasions. . . . I hope to trouble you as little as possible, if it be my fate to go before you. I am of old Ennius his mind, *Nemo me decoret lachrymis* ["Let no one honor me with tears"]—I am but a *Lodger* here: this is not an abiding City. I am only to stay out my lease, for what has Perpetuity and mortal man to do with each other?

Or, as he was to put it some ten years later (it is characteristic of him to anticipate in letters themes that will occupy him in verse only long after) in a passage touching particularly on Bathurst's vast schemes at Cirencester: "*Man?* and *for ever?* Wretch, what wou'dst thou have?"

> Join *Cotswold* Hills to *Saperton's* fair Dale,
> Let rising Granaries and Temples here,
> There mingled Farms and Pyramids appear,
> Link Town to Town with Avenues of Oak,
> Enclose whole Downs in Walls, 'tis all a Joke!
> Inexorable Death shall level all,
> And Trees, and Stones, and Farms, and Farmer fall.
> (*Imit. Hor. Ep.* II, ii, 252, 257–63)

One imagines that it was on some of these losses of the 1720s (to which in early 1729 Congreve was added, touching Pope, as he wrote to Gay, "nearly": "It is twenty years that I have known him. Every year carries away something dear with it") along with the later ones of Arbuthnot and Gay himself that Pope's mind was turning when he wrote in the same poem, with a delicacy of understanding of the erosions of time that has rarely been matched:

> Years foll'wing Years, steal something ev'ry day,
> At last they steal us from our selves away.
> (*Imit. Hor. Ep.* II, ii, 72–73)

One may hear in that little word *away* (if one listens) a still sad music that is like hearing in a seashell the muted roar of the sea.

These years brought also a worsening of Pope's tubercular malady and its side effects. His disorders became more frequent and lasted longer. Hardly a year, moreover, passed without at least one very serious illness for his mother, who was now in her eighties and on several occasions near death. In 1730, dozing (one supposes), as old people do, she fell into the fireplace she was sitting by, and though luckily rescued before any flame touched her body, "it consumed the clothes she had on, at least a yard about." Later, his imagination would situate these long periods of attending her in a striking metaphor of a child returning to its parent the care it has received:

> Me, let the tender Office long engage
> To rock the Cradle of reposing Age—
> (*Epistle to Dr. Arbuthnot*, ll. 408–9)

but at the time it was a strenuous and often melancholy task, "much like watching over a Taper that is expiring; & even when it burns a little brighter than ordinary is but the nearer going out."

"The Morals blacken'd, when the Writings 'scape"

His affection for the Blount sisters had now for some years centered in Martha. Yet Teresa continued to trouble him for other reasons. His reports to Caryll, even if considerably discounted, give evidence that the frustrations of vanishing youth, moderate means, and the consequent prospect of perpetual spinsterhood for one not at all temperamentally inclined to it were breeding in her some of the traits of a virago. We hear more than once of "outrage" to her mother ("striking, pinching, pulling about the house") and of much tyrannizing over her sister, who is too accommodating and timid, Pope feels, to stand up to her. Toward the close of the decade, there seems to have been some sort of not very happy affair between Teresa and a married man, which Pope fears will reflect disgrace on the whole family for having been insufficiently firm in dealing with it. "[Your god-daughter], indeed," he warns Caryll, "may share the shame of being thought conscious of her [sister's] proceedings, if not a party in them."

Slander and gossip, in the meantime, gathered about his own sexual conduct and his relationship with Martha. In a pamphlet published soon after the death of the Duke of Buckinghamshire, a certain Monovaria, who is obviously his duchess Katherine, is said to have taken a doctor for lover, whose "only Rival is as eminent for his Person as for his *Genius*." On this rival, "whose *Form* is the best *Index* of his Mind," if Monovaria now and then showers some of her favors, "it must be only to appease the *Manes* of her husband: he was his *Friend* when he was living, and therefore ought to be considered as his *Representative* now he is dead." What prompted the author of these sentences, a minor scribbler not known to have had any grounds for animus against Pope, to such fantastical scurrilities, it is impossible to say; but that his principal victim is Pope there is no doubt, for he also makes him the object of the Unfortunate Lady's passion and the cause of her suicide, his person being "as amiable as his *Muse*, and certainly not to be seen by *any of the Sex* without some fatal effect; especially if big with Child."

Three years later, in a vulgar *roman à clef* by Eliza Haywood, it is Marthalia (identified in the Key as Mrs. Bl[oun?]t who is vilified: "the most dissolute and shameless of her Sex." She is married, we are told, to the "old Servant" of a necromancer, the latter identified in the Key as the father of Pope's recently dead friend, the younger Craggs, who is himself represented as the lewd Melanthus. The servant suffers, from an incurable disease, and so, in fact, does Marthalia, though hers is of another species:

> Some . . . of late have severely repented trusting themselves in her embraces, and cursed the artificial Sweets and Perfumes, which hindered them from discovering those Scents, that would have been infallible Warnings of what they might expect in such polluted Sheets.

If Mrs. Haywood's ugly thrust is actually aimed at Martha Blount, as in view of the names it seems difficult to deny, it conceivably reflects gossip that had been going about in some circles since at least 1722. Though in July of that year idle chatter had it that Pope and Lady Mary Wortley Montagu "keeps so close yonder that they are a talk to the whole town," an innuendo that in their case could not possibly include marriage, by September Pope is having to assure Broome that reports of his intending to leave his "easy single state" are quite groundless: "as idle, as the news people invent, merely because they are idle." The rumor of a secret marriage to Martha was not, however, easily quashed. It reared up more than once during Pope's life, and when he died there were those who were surprised that his will, which reserved for her life use of his estate, did not name her his wife.

Yet more disturbing during the 1720s were reports of a different kind. "A very confident asseveration," he writes Caryll in 1725, has been spread over the town

> that your god-daughter, Miss Patty and I lived 2 or 3 years since in a manner that was reported to you as giving scandal to many: that upon your writing to me upon it I consulted with her, and sent you

an excusive alleviating answer; but did after that, privately and of myself write to you a full confession; ... and that she, being at the same time spoken to by a lady of your acquaintance [Caryll's wife], ... did absolutely deny to alter any part of her conduct, were it ever so disreputable or exceptional. Upon this villanous lying tale, it is further added by the same hand, that I brought her acquainted with a noble lord, and into an intimacy with some others, merely to get quit of her myself. ...

I wish those very people had never led her into anything more liable to objection, ... than I hope my conversation or kindness are. She has in reality had less of it these two years past than ever since I knew her; and truly when she has it, 'tis almost wholly a preachment, which I think necessary, against the ill consequence of another sort of company, which they by their good will would always keep, and she, in compliance and for quiet sake keeps more than you or I could wish.

To deal with you like a friend, openly: you know 'tis the whole misfortune of that family to be governed like a ship—that is, the head guided by the tail, and that by every wind that blows in it.

What Pope seems to be saying here, if language means anything, is that the slander originated with Teresa.

A shabby business all round

There can have been little time, however, for one engaged simultaneously with an edition of Shakespeare and a translation of the *Odyssey* to brood. Both undertakings proved unexpectedly vexatious. From the beginning, in order to ease the labor and speed completion, the *Odyssey* translation was planned to be a collaborative effort with his friends Fenton and Broome. But as with most literary collaborations, there were delays, jealousies, and misapprehensions. The reward for Pope lay in the subscriptions he could command privately, prior to the public announcement; the reward for his auxiliaries would lie in the subscriptions they too could command privately plus their share in whatever subscriptions resulted from the public proposals. This at any rate was the arrangement that Pope suggested to Broome in November 1724 and that Broome readily accepted, with the instruction to Pope to proceed "as if there were no person concerned" in the work but himself.

Fair enough—in fact, since the marketability of the work depended altogether on Pope's reputation, generous. But the fatal flaw in their arrangements from the outset was a consensus that their collaboration should be kept secret: in the first place, to avoid injury to the subscription, which might well appear less attractive were it known that parts of the translation were to be by other hands; and in the second—a notion that appears to have had special appeal for Broome, who was well-to-do—to garner prestige for the collaborators when it was found (as they hoped it would be) that their contributions could not be distinguished from Pope's. The deception does none of them credit, least of all Pope, who no doubt pressed the hardest for secrecy because he had the most to gain or lose. True, he did vaguely acknowledge in the public Proposals (10 January 1725) "that the future Benefit of *this Proposal* is not solely for my own use, but for that of *Two of my Friends*, who have *assisted me*"—driven thereto, one suspects, only by the already widespread public awareness of the partnership, for which Broome's inability not to boast seems to have been principally responsible. And there was truth also, of course, in what Broome declared in the final note to Book 24:

> It was our particular request, that our several parts might not be made known to the world till the end of the work; and if they had the good fortune not to be distinguished from [Pope's], we ought to be the less vain of it, since the resemblance proceeds much less from our diligence and study to copy his manner, than from his own daily revisal and correction. The most experienced Painters will not wonder at this, who very well know, that no Critic can pronounce even of the pieces of *Raphael* or *Titian*, which have, or which have not, been worked upon by those of their school? when the same Master's hand has directed the execution of the whole, reduced it to one character and colouring, gone over the several parts, and given to each their finishing.

In painting, unquestionably, there had been a long tradition of works, even very great works, bearing the contribution of one or more studio hands in addition to the master's, as in our own day ghostwriting and fiction factories have become a commonplace of the literary market. Possibly it helped salve the consciences of the three participants to think of their endeavor in this light, and certainly, Pope did not shirk his duties as the "Master's hand." We see him repeatedly in the correspondence urging on his colleagues, reworking their verses, admonishing them to stricter discrimination of differences in the Greek text, comparing Broome's notes with those of the current French Homerist, Anne Dacier, while assuming as well all the tasks of administration: negotiation with Lintot, supervision of the bookmaking, commissioning of the copper plates for the engravings from William Kent.

Still, it was a shabby business all round. Even when reasonable extenuations have been made (that politics delayed completion and publication, that delay gave time for the collaboration to become widely known, that knowledge of the full extent of the partnership might shrink the public subscription from which Broome and Fenton were to benefit), it cannot be judged other than a dishonest cover-up for the sake of gain, Broome—without doubt at Pope's behest—admitting publicly (in the note just cited) to a mere three books of the eight he had actually translated, and Fenton to only two of four. The necessary distinction was made bluntly by an article in the *London Journal* only a few months after the first three volumes were delivered to subscribers. Having taken notice of the "the late Translation of *Homer's Odyssey*, which was . . . proposed to be done by the Translator of the *Iliad*," but in which, it is reported, "other Persons have had the chief Hand . . . and . . . do not pretend to deny it," the writer came to the heart of the matter:

> I shall not say any thing concerning the Persons who are supposed to be our *Poetical Undertaker*'s Deputies in this Affair, because were they as able to translate *Homer* as even their *Taskmaster* himself, yet to have one or more Authors obtruded upon us, without our Knowledge or Consent, under the Name and Character of another to whom we have subscribed, is *Quackery* and *C—licism* in the greatest perfection.

Apart from the bigoted thrust at Catholicism, the verdict stands.

One would like to think that some misgivings and regrets about his conduct of this enterprise,★ even though its full consequences were

★ The inevitable consequence of the concealment was a justified resentment on the part of both colleagues (2:344, 385, 390, 398, 423, 470–71, 487–89, 499–500). This was especially true of Broome, whose longings for poetic fame made concealment of more than half his actual contribution understandably objectionable, even though in the beginning he had approved of secrecy. His retribution evidently took the form of saying that Pope was no master of Greek—asserted how often or to whom we do not know, but publicly enough, at any rate, to reach Pope's ear (2:500). It also took the form of claiming (in the Preface to his *Poems on Several Occasions* of 1727, p. 3) all the notes of the *Odyssey* translation without acknowledgment of any supervision or revisal by "the Master's hand," and of inserting (in the "Advertisement" affixed to the same Preface, p. [xvi]) a nicely equivocal sentence that could be read by Pope's accusers, by Pope himself, and by any knowing member of the Town as a severe indictment: "The Author has not Inserted yet to unfold, made their way into that complex of feelings that drew from him, in the late spring or summer of 1724, ten lines that strike a

into this Collection any part of *his Translation of the Odyssey, published by Mr. Pope*" [italics mine]. It was these thrusts, one guesses, that decided Pope to include the initials "W.B." among the writers identified in his *Art of Sinking in Poetry* (1728) as "Parrots" ("they that repeat *another's words* in such a *hoarse, odd Voice,* that makes them seem *their own*"—ch. 6), and to cite there also (ch. 7) a couplet from Broome's "Epistle to My Friend Mr. Elijah Fenton" for its inexact lumping together of the signs of the zodiac as "Monsters," despite the presence among them of Gemini, Virgo, Libra, Sagittarius, and Aquarius, along with perfectly ordinary animals. It is only fair to add that Pope cites in the same chapter, as well as elsewhere in the *Art of Sinking,* clumsy and pretentious couplets from his own early work; and that a critic to whom Fenton showed the "Epistle" when it first reached him in manuscript, and who insisted as the price of his counsel on not being identified to Broome, advised striking out the entire passage in which the zodiac couplet appeared. Not impossibly this was Pope himself, with whom Fenton, domiciled at Twickenham, was frequently in touch.

Inclusion in the *Art of Sinking* prompted Broome, in return, to compose part of "a new Session of Poets." Here, following the line of Pope's worst enemies, he represented him as "a monkey of man,/Through av'rice ill-clad, maliciously wan," and then, with reference to the alleged Ovidian qualities of his Homer, as "the ghost of Thersites repeating old Naso." Not pretty. To Broome's great credit, however, he seems never to have finished and certainly did not publish this exercise in spite, though he cannot have been pleased to find himself entered in the 1729 *Dunciad,* not precisely as a dunce, but as the somewhat trying collaborator that the correspondence shows him to have been:

> Hibernian politicks, O Swift, thy doom,
> And Pope's translating three whole years with Broome.

One may reasonably wonder if the couplet, with its accompanying note stressing the pecuniary rewards Broome had received for his work, did not come in response to Broome's contention, characteristically not kept to himself, that he had been meanly paid (see 2:344). On the latter point, he was quite in the wrong. (See Sherburn, *Early Career,* p. 259, and *TE,* 7: xlv–xlvi.)

The *Dunciad* editions of 1729 contained "A List of All our Author's Genuine Works," claiming (accurately) only "Twelve Books of the *Odyssey,* with some parts of other Books, and the *Dissertation* by way of *Postscript* at the end." After an interruption of friendship lasting till 1735, Pope quietly and once more acknowledged in his *Works* of that year that only half the *Odyssey* translation, and none of the notes, belonged to him. Broome showed an answering willingness to let bygones be bygones in refusing Curll's invitation to publish Pope's letters, acknowledging also that there had never been any contract stipulating a stated reward for his work (2: 479, 495–97). Pope then canceled the *Dunciad* reference, and the friendship was resumed—unavoidably, one thinks, rather scarred. The history of literary collaborations has rarely been happy, even for temperaments far less touchy and ambitious than those of Pope and Broome.

note not elsewhere found in the body of his work. On 7 May 1724, Harry Mordaunt, a nephew of Peterborow's and an officer in the guards, having paid his debts, written to his relatives, and composed a farewell couplet—"But the truest laudanum of all Is resolution and a ball"—shot himself. Pope's lines refer to this event and give us a very rare glimpse of a mind deeply troubled. Perhaps only by ill health, his own and his mother's, which had been exhausting him that spring. Perhaps by grief for friends lately dead. Perhaps by love, its fires not yet entirely banked. Perhaps by all these, with some infusion of discomfort or discouragement about himself:

On a Late Birth Day. 1724.

With added Days, if Life bring nothing new,
But, like a Sieve, let ev'ry Pleasure thro';
Some Joy still lost, as each vain Year runs o'er,
And all we gain, some pensive Notion more!
Is this a Birth-Day? ah! 'tis sadly clear
'Tis but the Fun'ral of the former Year.
If there's no Hope, with kind, tho' fainter ray
To gild the Evening of our future Day;
If ev'ry Page of Life's long Volume tell
The same dull Story—Mordaunt! thou did'st well.

As for the material results of the *Odyssey* undertaking, they were excellent. Pope made from it approximately what he had made from the *Iliad*, despite the fact that Lintot drove a far harder bargain on copy money and soon earned Pope's lasting resentment by announcing a subscription to the translation for his own benefit within a few days of Pope's announcement and at a saving over Pope's quartos of a guinea on the large folio and of £2–11 on the small. True, he had bound himself for ten years not to print his copies in the quarto format or on paper like that of the quartos or with the same engravings Pope used (though he was free to use others); but these differences seemed unlikely to be decisive for the general public, from whom Broome and Fenton, having been lazy about personal solicitations, expected their reward. They did not, in fact, do as badly as feared. According to the detailed study of these matters referred to earlier in connection with the *Iliad* proceeds, Broome received £400 as his share of the public subscription (i.e., one third for his eight of twenty-four books translated), plus £100 from subscriptions he had himself obtained, plus £100 for contributing the notes. Fenton had £200 for his share of the public subscription, and, questionably, another £100 for subscriptions personally obtained. Pope had £600, again prorated according to his share in the translation, which was twelve books of the twenty-four. Over and above this, however, he had the entire proceeds from the earlier solicitation, personal and through friends, that he assured Broome in his November letter was now complete. It was this group of subscriptions that made his fortune, numbering in the neighborhood of one thousand, with thirty-four well-placed subscribers taking between them two hundred and forty sets, or an average of seven sets apiece. All this can only have been gratifying, so far as the upkeep of his Twickenham household and the new Catholic taxes were concerned; but the deception had cast a shadow on his reputation that was real and had given enemies an opening for attacks that would not readily be closed.

CHAPTER 18

FROM SHAKESPEARE TO SWIFT

Editing Shakespeare

The other major claimant to Pope's attention at this period was the subscription edition of Shakespeare for the benefit of the younger Jacob Tonson, who had now taken over the firm from his more distinguished uncle. Pope served simply as editor for his fee of £100, with additional expense money set aside for assistance from Gay, Fenton, and one or two others working on the project in Oxford. The motive on Tonson's part was quite evidently to exploit Pope's reputation as a critic and man of taste, and to do so with a sumptuous edition in six quarto volumes offered at a profitable five guineas the set. He hoped further, as his equivocating first advertisement of the undertaking makes clear, to have it appear that the subscription was really for Pope, thinking in that way to enlarge it. But this Pope refused. Apart from the deception involved, which presumably seemed to him, as it would to the rest of us, less acceptable when another's gains were in question, there was a considerable risk that the subscription, if thought of as his, might draw off potential subscribers to the *Odyssey*; and there was a virtual certainty that he would be accused of avarice if he appeared to be asking support of two costly subscriptions at the same time. He was therefore careful, when he issued his *Odyssey* proposals in January 1725, to open them with the statement: "I take this occasion to declare that the *Subscription* for *Shakespear* [advertised disingenuously by Tonson the preceding November and December as "Mr. Pope's Shakespeare"] *belongs wholly* to Mr. *Tonson*."

The edition itself is a fascinating book—the combined and somewhat confusing result of two ways of looking at the past and at the functions of literature. As with Homer, Pope seeks to make Shakespeare intelligible and instructive to contemporary readers. (The plays onstage were another matter and had their own long tradition of managerial editing and adaptation, as they have still.) To this end, he uses the authority of his Preface to remind contemporaries that despite several characteristics which both he and they hold to be faults, Shakespeare is "justly and universally elevated above all other Dramatic Writers." His characters are, in fact, so persuasive as expressions of human reality—which is to say, in Pope's terms, of "Nature"—that "'tis a sort of injury to call them by so distant a name as Copies of her." His skills in tragedy (here Pope sees more clearly than Johnson, who thought tragedy less congenial to Shakespeare than comedy) are as masterly as his comic skills:

> The *Power* over our *Passions* was never possess'd in a more eminent degree, or display'd in so different instances. Yet all along, there is seen no labour, no pains to raise them; no preparation to guide our guess to the effect . . .: But the heart swells, and the tears burst out, just at the proper places: We are surpriz'd, the moment we weep; and yet upon reflection find the passion so just, that we shou'd be surpriz'd if we had not wept, and wept at that very moment.
>
> How astonishing it is again, that the Passions directly opposite to these, Laughter and Spleen, are no less at his command! that he is not more a master of the *Great*, than of the *Ridiculous* in human nature; of our noblest tendernesses, than of our vainest foibles; of our strongest emotions, than of our idlest sensations!

The same extraordinary insight is manifest in Shakespeare's command of appropriate reflections: "he seems to have known the world by Intuition, to have look'd thro' humane nature at one glance, and to be the only Author that gives ground for a very new opinion, That the Philosopher and even the Man of the World, may be *Born*, as well as the Poet." True it is that the plays are not conceived "on the model of the Ancients," where all is normally worked out within strict limits of time, place, and action; but this sort of structure was neither the expectation nor within the experience of the audiences for which he wrote, and to "judge therefore of Shakespear by *Aristotle*'s rules, is like trying a man by the Laws of one Country, who acted under those of another."

With the same aim (however misguided) of protecting Shakespeare's standing as an artist, Pope began a process of exclusion which was to continue for two centuries and occasionally persists today.

Passages that he judged it would demean Shakespeare to be thought to have written, he either degraded to the foot of the page (some fifteen hundred and sixty lines in all, including, predictably, many such "low" speeches as the Porter's soliloquy in *Macbeth*, which he doubtless excluded on the same principles as the "ass" simile in Homer and which even Coleridge assigned to some other hand than Shakespeare's, writing "for the mob") or simply left out. He left in, for example, Macbeth's vision of his bloody hands never washing clean but making the green ocean red (2.2.59–62), but he left out, degrading it to the foot of the page, the line which said that those hands would "The multitudinous seas incarnadine" (61).

With equally laudable ends in view, he made a point of drawing attention to passages that seemed to him notable for some special distinction of form or content by placing beside them in the margin a vertical line of commas—a practice he followed also in his own books when pleased. If an entire scene happened to be chosen, he distinguished it with a star, as he does, for example, 2.1 and 2.2 of *Macbeth*, the two scenes that include the murder of Duncan. For "performing the better half of Criticism, namely the pointing out an Author's excellencies," this was, he thought, a shorter and less ostentatious method "than to fill a whole paper with citations of fine passages, with *General Applauses*, or *Empty Exclamations* at the tail of them."

By 1725 the beginnings of a consensus in identifying Shakespeare's best moments had accumulated, and with this consensus Pope's selections frequently correspond. Far the larger number of them are those that linger in every reader's mind today: Portia on the quality of mercy, Falstaff impersonating Henry IV in the tavern, Jaques methodizing the seven ages of man, Iago insinuating into Othello's mind the possibility that Desdemona has betrayed him, Prospero brooding on "such stuff as dreams are made on," and so on through some one hundred and sixty instances in the thirty-six plays Pope prints as Shakespeare's. Yet Pope's judgments are never simply choric: only about half of the passages he directs attention to had been singled out before. He withholds his commas from Hamlet's "To be, or not to be," though it was one of the most admired speeches then as now; he singles out five passages from *Antony and Cleopatra*, at that time not a popular play (of particular interest is his marked approbation of the entire droll dialogue between Cleopatra and the countryman who delivers the asp in a basket of figs, an episode one might have thought he would overlook or even degrade to the foot of the page as "low"); he takes seven from *Titus Andronicus*, a play usually scorned—one of them the lovely lines on the qualities of Lavinia before her hands were cut off and her tongue torn out—and eleven from *Timon of Athens.*

One may notice in his selections from the last named, and indeed to some extent generally, a significant attraction to passages of moral criticism. Shakespeare's reflections on the corrupting power of gold; on the falsity or effeteness of courtiers or, for that matter, of men in gray flannel suits, who make a life of flattery and servility (Pope will not forget these when he comes to draw Sporus, his own great portrait of the courtier type); and on the perversions of justice by wealth or power—

> In the corrupted currents of this world,
> Offence's gilded hand may shove by justice,
> And oft 'tis seen, the wicked prize itself
> Buys out the law—
>
> (*Hamlet*, 3.3.60–63)

such reflections obviously have the same sort of appeal for him as the verses he had found in his copy of Chaucer on the corruptions of monks and friars, and had signalized with commas in the same way. Corollary to these preferences, one finds, as one might expect, much comma-ing of sentiments pastoral or meditative on the superiority of the quiet life of self-examination to the frantic treadmill of "painted pomp":

> 'Tis certain, Greatness once fall'n out with fortune,
> Must fall out with men too: what the declin'd is,
> He shall as soon read in the eyes of others
> As feel in his own fall: for men like butterflies
> Show not their mealy wings but to the summer,
> And not a man, for being simply man,
> Hath any honour, but honour for those honours
> That are without him: as place, riches, and favour,
> Prizes of accident as oft as merit.
>
> (*Troilus and Cressida*, 3.3.75–83)

Lines of this stamp, relevant to all time, must have struck Pope as particularly applicable to his own time and personal experience. His verses to Robert Harley had lately touched, in fact, on this same matter of worldly greatness in decline, finding in "rejudgment" of the world's and fortune's judgments the supreme challenge for the poet's Muse, who is not to look with "the eyes of others" or to fly with mealy wings, but rather—so he would reimagine it later on—in the manner of eagle or angel soaring into the very Eye of Day:

> Ye tinsel Insects! whom a Court maintains,
> That counts your Beauties only by your Stains,
> Spin all your Cobwebs o'er the Eye of Day!
> The Muse's wing shall brush you all away.
> (*One Thousand Seven Hundred and Thirty-Eight: Dial. 2:* 220–23)

It is impossible, I think, to read these verses thoughtfully, or many another passage in the satires and epistles of the 1730s—or, for that matter, the fourth epistle of the *Essay on Man*, which seeks to realize a frame of mind and a conception of reality in which men and women do have honor mainly as men and women—without recognizing that the thorough reading of Shakespeare which Pope undertook at this time was the best imaginable preparation, along with Homer, Horace, and Vergil, for his subsequent career. As an observant critic pointed out some years ago, "Pope shares with Shakespeare not only targets for satire but also the ethical standards by which the vices and follies are judged."

When it came to editing the plays themselves, Pope delivered a far more questionable performance. Their texts had come down to him through four successive folios (1623, 1632, 1663–1664, 1685), each adding to and sometimes compounding by miscorrection the printing-house errors of its predecessors. Thus "important letters" (in *The Comedy of Errors*, 5.1.138) became in later folios "impoteant letters" and was miscorrected in the last to "impotent letters": Pope was the first to retrieve the original reading. Eighteen of the plays that he was including, moreover (he omitted *Pericles*, partly no doubt because it had been omitted from the first two folios), had a collateral line of descent in separate quarto printings published before the first folio and in many instances reprinted again and again throughout the seventeenth century. Some of the early quarto texts were obviously garbled and abbreviated, yet here and there seemed to preserve a plausible addition or variant reading not found in the folio text. Other quartos plainly had excellent texts; yet these too, because they lacked subsequent revisions, differed from the folio text at many small points and sometimes in larger ones. To illustrate from *Hamlet*, there was a "bad" quarto of 1603, a very "good" quarto of 1604, and two reprints of the latter before the folio of 1623. The folios added some eighty-odd lines that did not appear in the quartos, but omitted well over two hundred lines that had been present in the 1604 quarto and continued to be present in the nine quarto reprints up to 1703. If you sat down to read *Hamlet* in the quarto text, you would find the hero meeting a Norwegian contingent off to do battle for a piece of ground not big enough to bury those who would give their lives for it, and moved thereby to his fifth soliloquy, "How all occasions do inform against me. . . . What is a man, If his chief good and market of his time Be but to sleep and feed?" Yet if you read the play in the folio text, you would encounter none of this; all but the first dozen lines of the scene had been cut. Meantime, to muddy the editorial waters still further, quartos of a few plays were floating about with texts extracted directly from the folios and merely printed up by enterprising publishers in the convenient quarto format. Something of the bibliographical darkness in which the early editors of Shakespeare had to work may be gauged from Tonson's advertising in 1722, with a view to Pope's edition, for the loan of prefolio quartos of several plays first published in the first folio.

Darkness covered other areas as well. The first English dictionary built on historical principles and showing systematically the evolution of word meanings through examples of usage lay thirty years in the future. Very little was known of Elizabethan grammar, syntax, vocabulary, or spelling, and that little only by a very few, of whom Pope was not one. English usage had changed and begun to standardize to the point at which common Shakespeareanisms like "the most unkindest cut of all," "Words to the heat of deeds too cold breath gives," "You have seen Cassio and she together," "torn to pieces with [i.e., by] a bear," seemed marks of illiteracy rather than bygone conventions. Then there was the slang of the age, often short-lived. Who would necessarily guess that "fishmonger" was slang for pimp and "nunnery" for whorehouse? or that a "prig" is a thief, a "bung" a pick-pocket, and to "crack" is to boast? or, to move away from slang, that "silly" women are merely helpless women and "silly sooth" the simple truth. Obsolete or nonce spellings were an equal hazard. No editorial glosses in the quartos and folios told one that "sedule" meant schedule, "philome" film, "berrord" bearward, "wrenching" rinsing, "spleet" split, and so on through hundreds of what by Pope's time were impenetrable oddities—as were many more ordinary words, some of them common enough now, that had dropped out of use during the seventeenth century to be revived (if revived at all) not till the late eighteenth or early nineteenth century: "incarnadine" being one, along with "rood," "henchman," "brooch," and so on. And then, of course, worst of all, were the actual mistakes from the careless printing of the early editions, which would give a reader, among thousands of other missignals, a "temple-haunting Barlet" for a "temple-haunting martlet," or "His highness comes post from Marcellus," which is to say, from Marseilles.

Such was the state of affairs when Pope's friend, the playwright Nicholas Rowe, went to work on the first "edited" collection of the plays, which he published in 1709. He too was employed by Tonson (in his case, Jacob senior), who was evidently eager to consolidate his claim in preparation for the new more protective regulations (the copyright act of Queen Anne) to be put into effect the next year.

Rowe's finest contribution was by all odds his life of Shakespeare (the first), based in part on information provided by Betterton and simply reprinted by later editors for more than a century. He also unearthed—somewhat surprisingly, since his acquaintance with the quartos was limited and haphazard—the *Hamlet* lines extant in the quartos but not in the folios, and of a total of around two hundred and thirty restored in his own text something over half. Like all early editors, though more conservative in this respect than most, when he found something that puzzled him, he proposed an emendation, including one amusing one that shows the same impulse to save appearances for Shakespeare that Pope was soon to show more effusively. Could the man who had written some of the world's greatest plays have possibly put into the mouth of Hector an allusion to Aristotle, who lived hundreds of years later than the supposed war at Troy? Obviously not: the text had to be corrupt; and accordingly in Hector's sharp reminder to his fiery brothers that their arguments for retaining Helen at such cost in lives are superficial—

> not much
> Unlike young men, whom Aristotle thought
> Unfit to hear moral philosophy—
> (*Troilus and Cressida*, 2.2.65–67)

"Aristotle" gave way to "graver sages"—as he would do also in Pope's edition.

In the main, however, Rowe's contribution lay in standardizing and tidying up—in other words, in making comprehension easier for the readers of his time and thus widening, as Pope's edition for all its faults also helped to do, Shakespeare's *reading* audience. Rowe provided the plays with lists of *dramatis personae*. He inserted the localities of scenes. He saw to it that a given character was consistently referred to in stage directions and speech headings by a single name, instead of—as in *The Comedy of Errors*, say—as "Aegeon," "Merchant of Syracuse," "Merchant," "Merchant Father," and

"Father." Though he seems not to have worried much about act and scene divisions till he reached his final volumes containing the tragedies, from that point on he introduced them wherever they were wanting, as they often were. For the rest, apart from correction of grammatical errors and false spellings, he left the text pretty much as he found it, using the fourth folio of 1685 for copy text and thus perpetuating all the misreadings accumulated in the folio line of descent, save for the few he personally amended.

It would have been well for Pope if he had been as conservative. Many of his editorial principles were sound enough. According to his own account in the Preface,

> I have discharg'd the dull duty of an Editor . . . with a religious abhorrence of all Innovation, and without any indulgence to my private sense or conjecture. . . . The various readings are fairly put in the margin, so that every one may compare 'em: and those I have prefer'd into the Text are constantly *ex fide Codicum*, upon authority. The Alterations or Additions which *Shakespear* himself made, are taken notice of as they occur.

Even his practice was partly sound. He rejected the six pseudo-Shakespearian plays that had crept into the third folio, though he threw out along with them *Pericles*, about Shakespeare's share in which editors still argue. He sought out the early editions through advertisements in the press, obtaining access to at least one quarto (not necessarily, however, always the best: he had *first* quartos of only six) of every play of which quartos are known save *Much Ado About Nothing*, and to both the first and second folios. He continued, too, much more systematically the modernizing and regularizing that Rowe had begun. And he concentrated immense effort on metrical regularization and on the relineation into verse of passages he thought mistakenly printed as prose, an area in which his impress is still felt.

Nevertheless, he botched the job badly—by our standards. It is usually said of Pope's work that once he had assembled the early editions, he was too lazy or negligent to collate them with care. There is more than a grain of truth in this, since no eighteenth-century editor collated anything with the scrupulous attention that goes into the making of the best texts of a standard author today, including Pope. But the real problem lay elsewhere. Pope wanted, in his way, to recover what Shakespeare wrote—to recognize that the past had an integrity of its own: hence his going to great trouble to bring together the early editions. Toward that same objective, he and his helpers compared texts (when they did compare them) with

astonishing vigilance, considering the habits of the age. This is easily
verified by noting the minute importations from the quarto texts that
Pope's edition introduces *within* lines and passages which otherwise
follow the folio text. Or, to illustrate that vigilance with an example
from a play that has no quarto text, here is part of Macbeth's meditation on the prospect of murdering Duncan as it appears in any modern
edition. Such acts of violence, Macbeth is telling himself, bring judgment here as well as at the last day; so that

> we but teach
> Bloody instructions, which, being taught, return
> To plague th' inventor: this even-handed Justice
> Commends th' ingredience of our poison'd chalice
> To our own lips.

Folios two through four, and therefore Rowe, whose text is based on
four, make nonsense of this by omitting most of line 10:

> we but teach
> Bloody instructions, which being taught return
> To plague the ingredience of our poison'd chalice
> To our own lips.

Pope restores line 10 from the first folio; inevitably accepts the
obvious correction of "prison'd" (F 1) to "poison'd (F 2–4 and Rowe);
replaces the obsolete "ingredience" with "ingredients," of which he
probably took "ingredience" to be a misspelling; and then, quite
wantonly, guided by nothing but his own sense of the image implicit
in the figure of Justice taking the poison offered to another and
bringing it back to "th' inventor," replaces "Commends" with
"Returns"—in which he is followed by every other eighteenth-
century editor down to (but not including) Johnson.

Some "Negligence of Revisal"

"Pope's Shakespeare," in other words, is far more the result of over-
confidence than of sloth. Like the other early editors, he imagined
that the route to a proper text lay in comparing the readings of the old
editions, culling out the best of these, and, despite his caveat in the
Preface against innovations, omitting or degrading to the bottom of
the page passages in which he thought Shakespeare had written beneath himself, while at the same time introducing changes (like
"Returns" in the example above) whenever he felt he knew how the

received text could be "clarified" or "improved" to the state in which a great artist would surely have left it. He was encouraged in these rash procedures by a mistaken belief that the reference in the first folio by Shakespeare's fellow actors Hemmings and Condell to "stolne and surreptitious copies, maimed, and deformed by the frauds and stealthes of injurious imposters" [i.e., the "bad" quartos] was their way of putting down all editions prior to theirs; and since he knew from experience that some of these editions were in fact good, the apparent falsification encouraged him to doubt the reliability of their claims as well. This (in his view) being the parlous condition of the only tools an editor had to work with, what alternative was there but to use his own judgment in retrieving what Shakespeare wrote, while supplying, as his foremost priority, a text of Shakespeare that contemporary readers could understand and admire?

There *was* an alternative, however, and in 1726, the year after his own edition had appeared, it was brought somewhat irreverently to his attention. The author was Lewis Theobald. The book was a nearly two-hundred-page quarto volume with the title (as modest as brief): "SHAKESPEARE restored: Or, A SPECIMEN of the Many ERRORS, As Well *Committed*, as *Unamended*, by Mr. POPE In his Late EDITION of this POET. DESIGNED Not only to correct the said EDITION, but to restore the True READING of SHAKE-SPEARE in all the *Editions* ever yet publish'd." And the alternative proposed to Pope's undisciplined eclecticism was an equally eclectic method, but one to some extent abated and directed by a substantial knowledge of Elizabethan and Shakespearean usage and vocabulary. This Theobald had gained from much reading in the literature of the period (he once said he had read eight hundred of its plays), which had brought him to the crucial realization that an author's usage in one place is usually best explained by his usage elsewhere, or, when this fails, by the usage of his contemporaries. Putting this principle and his wide reading into practice, he was able, as his biographer remarks, "to ride to success on the interest created by Pope's edition"—which is to say, to exhibit a sufficient number of oversights, errors, and omissions resulting from Pope's use of and sometimes failure to use the texts available to him to establish that he had not done his work well—certainly not as well (this is the most glaring of the intended implications of *Shakespeare Restored*, pointed to also in the "Specimen" of its title) as it *might* have been done by a certain Lewis Theobald had he been asked, and *would* be done if any publisher were to ask in future. (Tonson, as a matter of fact, soon did, and Theobald's own edition of the plays appeared in 1734.)

It should not be supposed, however, from its success in improving on Pope that *Shakespeare Restored* is a brilliant exercise in textual criticism. It is the first genuinely critical treatment of the text and it contains some brilliant particulars; but as a whole it makes tedious reading. Better than two thirds of its pages are given over to proposed improvements in Pope's text of *Hamlet*, and where these are readings recovered from the early editions (not found in Pope because he used for copy text the second edition of Rowe, and Rowe's copy text was the fourth folio), they are usually the readings of the best modern texts as well. But much space is given to a finical obsession with punctuation whether or not it affects the sense—"Commas and points they set exactly right," Pope will concede when he recalls this breed of critic in *Arbuthnot* (line 161)—and much also to conjectural emendations, thirty-three in all (several of them far sillier than anything to be found in Pope), of which only one is of importance and sometimes survives today. The remaining third of *Shakespeare Restored* is devoted to proposing "restorations" in other plays, and here Theobald does some of his best work. The best known of these is his justly admired emendation, in the description of Falstaff's death in *Henry V*, of the baffling line "for his nose was as sharp as a pen, and a Table of green fields." Of the final five words here Pope had ignorantly tried to make sense by supposing them a stage direction: "a Table was here directed to be brought in, it being a scene in a tavern where they drink at parting. . . . Greenfield was the name of the Property-man in that time who furnish'd [such] implements." Theobald offered instead the conjecture: "for his nose was as sharp as a pen, and a' babled of green fields." As he himself tells us, he had found among the marginalia made in one of his editions by a former owner the conjecture "and a' talk'd of green fields," and took the matter from there.

Many other admirable clarifications appear in this part of *Shakespeare Restored*. But—as everywhere in the book—they are accompanied and sometimes almost crowded out by so much nonsense, so many tiresome displays of irrelevant learning, self-gratulations, gloatings—

I cannot but wonder the Editor did not trace the Author's Thought in this Place, as it is evident he did not, both by the Text, and Gloss upon it; but it leaves me the Pleasure of explaining, beyond Exception, a Passage, which this ingenious Gentleman did not so much as guess at. Upon the first Reading, I immediately suspected it should be restor'd—

and, most annoying of all to Pope, no doubt, such insinuating reproaches of the *editor* when it is the *restorer* who is wrong, that one
readily understands his resentment, entirely apart from the humiliation of being, in other instances, shown up for ignorance. One
example of Theobald's maddening self-assurance whether wrong or
right will suffice. In the following sentences he lays the ground for his
emendation of "Perigenia" (named in *A Midsummer Night's Dream* as
one of Theseus's former mistresses) to "Perigune."

> The faulty Passages which I have hitherto alledged, I think, are
> mostly such, as called for the Assistance of *Judgment* to set them
> right [the implication with respect to Pope is clear]: There are other
> Places again, which are corrupted in our Author, that are to be
> cur'd by a strict Attention to the Author himself, and by taking
> *History* [again, an insinuation, soon made overt] along with us. . . .
> Diligence in this Respect is certainly the Duty of an Editor: And
> yet that a due Care, even in this Part, has been hitherto wanting,
> the Instances I am now going to subjoin will manifestly prove.

At this point, in his own opinion, Theobald moves in for the kill,
quite unaware, apparently, that he is now invoking the kind of
evidence he properly disapproved when used by Rowe (followed by
Pope) to reject "Aristotle" for "graver sages."

> None of the old Classicks tell us of such a Person as *Peregenia*, with
> whom that Hero had an Affair: Restore therefore the Place, from
> the Authority of the *Greek* Writers [here the familiar charge that
> Pope had no command of that language is probably intended and
> seems to be driven home by what follows]:

> > Did'st thou not lead him thro' the glimm'ring Night
> > From PERIGUNE, whom he ravished?

> Here we have the Name of a famous Lady, by whom *Theseus* had
> his Son *Melanippus*. She was the Daughter of *Sinnis* the cruel
> Robber . . .; and Plutarch and Athenaeus are Both express in the
> Circumstance of Theseus's ravishing her, which is so exactly
> copied by our Poet. The former of Them adds, (as *Diodorus Siculus*,
> *Apollodorus*, and *Pausanias*, likewise tell us), that he kill'd her
> Father into the Bargain.

It is hardly surprising that the phrase "learned lumber" recurred to
Pope's mind when describing Theobald's library in *Dunciad*, Book 1.
 Theobald was no stranger to Pope at this time. They may first have
met, in fact, as far back as 1713–14, when Pope was beginning work

on the *Iliad*. Theobald, though trained as an attorney, had like many others of that breed in every period turned to literature and during 1713–14 had contracted with Bernard Lintot to do translations of the tragedies of Aeschylus, four tragedies by Sophocles, all the satires and epistles of Horace, and the entire *Odyssey*. (Diffidence seems not to have been his forte.) Engaged by such similar enterprises, it is difficult to believe that the two translators, by whom Lintot evidently hoped to rival Tonson as a "classical" publisher, did not at some point cross paths, even if only at Lintot's shop. However that may be, by 1726 they had had at least distant contacts, of which the details are now obscure. In 1715, for instance, a pamphlet later attributed by Pope to Theobald and a player named Griffin (Theobald had early begun to write for the stage) contained a vicious attack on Pope and Gay, calling "me," Gay wrote to Caryll, "a blockhead, and Mr. Pope a knave," as well as a milder attack on Gay's farce *The What D'ye Call It*, to which contemporaries believed Pope had been a considerable contributor. Even in the milder part of the pamphlet, probably Theobald's part, Pope cannot have enjoyed the scornful reference to his "Wit and Manners": "Popery and Knitting [in one passage of the play] are so admirably well put together, as things of equal Importance, that any man, who has but read the Celebrated Rape of the Lock, cannot be at a loss for the Author of these Lines."

On the other hand, in early 1717, Theobald's short-lived journal *The Censor* had generous praise for Pope's *Iliad*, and in 1721 Pope subscribed for four copies in royal paper of Theobald's miscellany *The Grove*. Perhaps the speedy resurgence of hostility in Theobald's mind came about through the Sheffield affair. Curll the scavenger had long found it profitable to publish soon after any prominent writer's death a hastily assembled edition of his works, attended by a yet more hasty life, always inaccurate and frequently scandalous—which made him (said Dr. Arbuthnot) "one of the new terrors of death". In early 1722, he advertised an undertaking of this kind with respect to the Duke of Buckinghamshire, the life to be "by Mr. Theobald" and "compleated from a Plan drawn up by His Grace"! As the Duchess's own authorized edition with Pope as supervising editor was being prepared at this time, someone—as likely the Duchess as the editor, or possibly Alderman John Barber the publisher—invoked from the House of Lords the protection accorded peers and others in high place against this sort of potential libel or *scandalum magnatum*, and the life had to be dropped. Theobald would quite understandably attribute this reverse to Pope even if it were the Duchess's or Barber's doing, and this in turn might help account for the fact that in addition to being a work of serious and often successful Shakespearean scholarship *Shakespeare Restored* is a clear-cut act of war.

For what seems usually to be overlooked in assessing the grounds for Theobald's eventual enthronement as king of dunces is that both the pedantries and brilliancies of his book are threaded through with what could hardly be read by its victim as other than a fine malice. It is not a work designed simply to set the record straight on Shakespeare by showing a fumbling editor how it ought to have been done. It is partly that, because Theobald wants to show what he has to offer, as he has every reason and right to do. But it is also a book designed to gall, embarrass, and humiliate by every stratagem he can devise. Though he lays claim at the start of his Introduction to immense admiration for Pope—"so high an Opinion of his Genius and Excellencies, that I beg to be excused from the least Intention of derogating from his Merits . . . [and am] very loth even to do [Shakespeare] Justice at the Expence of *that other* Gentleman's Character"—it is only moments until (like Shakespeare's Antony in his funeral speech on Caesar: "For Brutus is an honorable man!") he has launched a prolonged effort to destroy that character. It begins mildly, with little innuendoes like: "The second Edition in Folio, . . . which is one of those that Mr. *Pope* professes to have collated [p. 3]." Or: "The Propagation of this Fault is manifestly owing to the Negligence of Revisal [p. 16]." Or: "The same Error has slipt the Editor's Diligence [with a slight hovering emphasis upon the word?] in another of our Author's Plays [p. 30]." Or: ". . . this Passage either seems to have been rectified by Chance, or some others, where the same Phrase occurs, have been revised with a strange Carelessness [pp. 47–48]."

From time to time, the game is spiced with slurs at Pope's Catholicism. The "religious Abhorrence of Innovation" that Pope had promised (but did not consistently observe)—could that be "downright *Superstition*"? Shakespeare's writings are not so venerable that we should be "excommunicated from good Sense" or show "the Indolence of that good honest *Priest*, who had for thirty Years together mistakingly, in his Breviary, read *Mumpsimus* for *Sumpsimus*; and being told of his Blunder, and sollicited to correct it, *The Alteration may be just,* said he; *but however, I'll not change my old* MUMPSIMUS *for your new* SUMPSIMUS." This is a Roman priest, of course, contentedly mired in papist error, and he is followed on later pages by the usual hits at Pope's papal "infallibility" as editor, and at the "invincible darkness" [read: "ignorance"] which in Catholic doctrine can free a sinner from his [in this case, editorial] "sins."

The climax Theobald builds to comes at p. 75:

> The next [of Pope's errors] . . . is a *Slip* of such a kind, that I don't
> know to whose Account, properly, to place it. There are many
> Passages of such intolerable Carelessness interspers'd thro' all the
> six Volumes, that were not a few of Mr. *Pope's Notes* scatter'd here
> and there too, I should be induced to believe that the Words in the
> Title Page of the *First* Volume,—COLLATED, *and* CORREC-
> TED *by the former* EDITIONS, *By Mr.* POPE,—were plac'd there
> by the *Bookseller* to enhaunce the *Credit* of his *Edition*; but that he
> had play'd false with his *Editor*, and never sent him the Sheets to
> revise. [This echoes, innocently (?), the charge made against Pope,
> when publication of Sheffield's works was stopped, that he had not
> sent all the sheets to Carteret.] And, surely, this must have been the
> Case sometimes: For no Body shall perswade me that Mr. *Pope*
> could be awake, and with his Eyes open, and revising a Book
> which was to be publish'd under his Name, yet let an Error, like
> the following, escape his Observation and Correction.

The error in question is half a line repeated, one of the commonest
of compositor's mistakes, and Theobald is quite right that Pope
should have been troubled by it. But is the suggestion that the bookseller failed to send the editor the sheets for revisal a kindly make-
believe generously offered? Hardly. It is the hangman adjusting the
noose:

> But because it may seem a little too hard, upon a single Instance of
> this kind, to suspect that the Sheets might not be *all* revised by the
> Editor, as I just now hinted; I'll subjoin another *flagrant* Testimony
> of the same sort of Negligence.

This time the error is a line entirely omitted, which again Pope
should have caught. After this, it only remains to kick away the trap
and leave the victim twisting in the wind:

> . . . the Fault appear[s] to have arisen from a Negligence of, or
> rather from the Want of *revising at all*. But that this Suspicion of
> mine may not appear a meer *gratis dictum*, I'll now give the Reason.
> . . . The Case is, a Material Line is left out in this Passage, by Mr.
> *Pope's* Impression; which very Line is left out of another Edition,
> . . . likewise publish'd by Mr. *Tonson* about ten years ago [Rowe's
> second edition, which Pope had used for copy text]; so that it seems
> most probable, that the Press was set to Work and corrected by this
> . . . Edition; without any Collation with the old Editions

mentioned in Mr. *POPE*'s Table of Editions at the End of his *Sixth Volume*.

Pope's failure was to catch a serious printing fault that had crept into his copy text, one he would have caught if his collations had been as thorough as his title page and preface claim. Theobald was quite right to censure him. But this is not Theobald's main point. His main point, here and everywhere, is to imply that Pope's list of editions used at the end of Volume 6 is a hoax and that no collations were actually made at all. This was false, and Theobald knew it. Though it is true (as one of our own century's greatest bibliographers stated long ago) that he was almost as unsystematic in his collations as Pope, using the early editions "much as Pope had done, consulting them whenever it struck him that there was anything suspicious in the text before him; but only occasionally, in plays which especially interested him, collating them throughout," the collations he did make could not fail to reveal to him some of Pope's genuinely valuable contributions to the clarification of Shakespeare's text: Of these, he has nothing whatever to say.

If, then, we imagine ourselves reading *Shakespeare Restored* in Pope's shoes, we may readily recognize the storm of conflicting emotions that assailed him. Embarrassment at being shown up for the textual amateur he was. Deeper embarrassment from the revelation that he had not made the profit from the early editions that with more effort combined with more learning and experience he could and should have. Outrage at the false implication that he had made no effort at all. Resentment that no acknowledgement was made of his undeniable improvements, however sporadic, of the currently available texts. Cold fury, we may suspect, at the sneers disguised in professions of admiration, proffered by an opponent who, while clearly beating him at his own game, just as clearly showed himself something of a conceited pedant, one whom Johnson would describe later on in the century (too harshly but not entirely without reason) as "a man of heavy diligence, with very slender powers."

Theobald voices in his Introduction the hope that his labors on Shakespeare may gain him "some little Share of Reputation." This hope was very soon to be fulfilled in a manner that he had not anticipated and one that in all probability would have been rather different if Swift had not chosen that same year for a visit to his old friends in England. For it was Swift—as during his visit the two friends sat looking through their papers for materials to make up a collection or two of "miscellanies"—who saved from the burning the first sketch of the *Dunciad* and "persuaded his friend to proceed in it."

"For England hath its own": Swift's first visit

Swift's first visit, lasting from about mid–March of 1726—as it happened, the same month in which *Shakespeare Restored* appeared—to mid–August, was half triumph, half carnival. Triumph, partly because he came victorious from his recent contest in the matter of "Wood's halfpence." This had been a proposed imposition of suspect copper coins on the Irish monetary system for the exclusive profit of an English entrepreneur named William Wood, to whom for a consideration the Walpole government had granted the necessary patent. Understandably, inflationary fears rose like wildfire; the Irish parliament protested vigorously but without effect; and at this point Swift intervened. Writing as an ordinary tradesman, a drapier, he created in a succession of five pamphlets (issued between February and December 1724) the common voice by which an impoverished and oppressed but fainthearted nation roused itself sufficiently to say no to a mother country that recognized no responsibility to any of its wards apart from the exploitation of their trade and the use of their positions in church and state for English placemen. All of the *Drapier's Letters* in their ultimate implications were subversive, since behind them lay a vision of an independent Ireland; and one, the fourth, was so overtly seditious—"to let you see that by the laws of GOD, of NATURE, of NATIONS, and of your own COUNTRY, you ARE and OUGHT to be as FREE a people as your brethren in England"—that the printer was taken into custody and a price of £300 set upon its author's anonymous head. The public mood was by now such, however, that the government at Whitehall was reluctant to act. Though everybody knew the Drapier's identity, and broadsides circulating on the streets quoted 1 Samuel 14:45—

> And the people said unto Saul, Shall Jonathan die, who hath wrought this great salvation in Israel? God forbid: as the Lord liveth, there shall not one hair of his head fall to the ground, for he hath wrought with God this day. So the people rescued Jonathan that he died not—

no one was punished. And from 25 August 1725, when it was learned in Dublin that Wood's patent had been surrendered, Swift became a national hero. It was a pyrrhic victory, as no one knew better than himself: the government had yielded the small point in order to evade the large: there were to be no more forums for talk of independence. Nothing would be altered in the long run.

Still, it had been an exhilarating contest of wits, and, for the time being, a triumph, with the result that Swift came back to England trailing glory. For writers like Pope and Gay, never heartily reconciled to the regime and soon to become outspokenly critical, it must have seemed an inspiriting example of the potential social and political influence of the written word. For Bolingbroke, now redomiciled in England and seriously seeking to compound an image of government that would lay party passion aside, draw the best talent from all quarters, and restore the ancient British constitution by correcting the inbalance which (in his view) the power of the moneymen and stockjobbers had introduced into it, Swift's success was also inspiriting, and he was promptly invited to contribute to the newly established opposition journal, *The Craftsman*. Evidently he declined. His interest, at first at least, lay in convincing the Whitehall ministry to heed the grievances of its colony across the Irish Sea. When in two interviews with Walpole soon after his arrival he undertook to do so, not only without success but with the discovery that there was no hope whatever of reaching an accommodation that would resettle him in England short of sacrificing all his principles, he became for the future, along with Pope, one of the administration's sharpest critics.

On first arrival in London, Swift took lodgings for a fortnight or two in Bury Street next door to the Royal Chair coffee house. There his host of old friends thronged to greet him, finding him, as Pope wrote excitedly to Edward Harley, "in perfect health and spirits, the joy of all here who know him." There Arbuthnot, in particular, came to lead the new arrival "a course thro' the town, with Lord Chesterfield [and] Mr. Pulteney": names that suggest an early effort to attach him to the Whig–Tory combination with which Bolingbroke was also affiliated, whose present aim was to unseat Walpole. Something of the exuberance of these first reunions comes through in lines by Pope, not written immediately at the moment but recalling a little later its happy sense of a lost traveler returned, a friend repossessed:

> Jonathan Swift
> Had the gift,
> By fatherige, motherige,
> And by brotherige,
> to come from Gutherige,
> But now is spoil'd clean,
> And an Irish Dean.
> In this church he has put
> A stone of two foot;

> With a cup and a can, Sir,
> In respect to his grandsire;
> So Ireland change thy tone,
> And cry, O hone! o hone!
> For England hath its own.

The explanation of these jaunty lines is that on his way down from Holyhead Swift had stopped by the church at Goodrich (or Gotheridge), near Ross-on-Wye, and indicated his intention to donate a chalice ("A cup and a can, Sir") and to set up a tablet ("A stone of two foot") in memory of his grandfather Thomas Swift, who had been its vicar for thirty-four years. Pope's "O hone!" a corruption of "Ohone," a Gaelic cry of lamentation, apparently alludes in this instance to a late seventeenth-century ballad in which, likewise, Tories were credited with getting back their own:

> What have the Whigs to Say?
> O hone! O hone!
> Tories have got the day.
> O hone! O hone!

From about April, for close to four months, Swift made Pope's house in Twickenham intermittently his home. There were interruptions, of course. Visits to Arbuthnot in London, where the talk was much on the "wild boy," a creature lately found going on all fours in one of the forests of Hanover and promptly imported for the king's entertainment (Swift must have wondered if he were not reliving his own Gulliver's experience as a freak on exhibition in Brobdingnag), after which he was committed to the care of Arbuthnot for "education." Someone—probably Arbuthnot himself, at least in part—blew up a pamphlet for the occasion, splendidly entitled: *It Cannot Rain but it Pours . . . .: Of the wonderful wild man that was nursed in the woods of Germany by a wild beast, hunted and taken in toils; how he behaveth himself like a dumb creature, and is a Christian like one of us, being called Peter; and how he was brought to Court all in green, to the great astonishment of the quality and gentry.* One paragraph in particular must be by Gay, Pope, Swift, or Arbuthnot, since along with Bolingbroke they are the only persons likely to have been familiar with *Gulliver*, still in manuscript at this time:

> He [the wild boy] takes vast pleasure in conversation with horses; and going to the mews to converse with two of his intimate acquaintances in the king's stables, as he passed by, he neighed to the horse at Charing Cross [an equestrian statue of Charles I], being

as it were surprised to see him so high: he seemed to take it ill that the horse did not answer him.

Other London visits, either at this time or possibly when Swift returned the following summer, may have included at least one to a Masonic lodge. Speculative Freemasonry—in the sense of a fraternity no longer having any but symbolic links with masonry as a trade—was still in its infancy at this period but growing fast. Six English lodges around the turn of the century had become thirty by 1723, the majority in London. A list cumulative to 1723 of the members of the lodge at the "Bedford-head in Covent Garden" (lodges were still designated in these early days by the tavern at which they met) shows plainly the name of "Dr. Arbuthnott." And a similar list cumulative to 1730 for the "Goat at the Foot of the Hay Market" shows with equal clarity the name of "Mr. Alexr. Pope." A little farther down that list the name "John Swift" appears. Since these lists are not the original lodge lists with personal signatures, but copies entered by a clerk in the minute book of the Grand Lodge, it is tempting to suppose that Swift joined when Pope joined, "John Swift" being in that case the clerk's conjectural expansion of an original "J. Swift." However this may be, it is clear that Pope was a member by 1730, only eight years before a papal bull prohibited (as it still does) Roman Catholics from accepting membership. The reason for the interdict is clear. One of the chief stipulations of the Masonic order was that in the interests of harmony political and religious affiliations must be left at the door. The important *Constitutions* drawn up by James Anderson in 1723 exclude both the "stupid Atheist" and the "irreligious Libertine," but otherwise oblige members only "to that Religion in which all Men agree, leaving their particular Opinions to themselves; that is, to be 'good men and true,' or Men of Honour and Honesty, by whatever Denominations or Persuasions they may be distinguish'd, whereby Masonry becomes the 'Center' of 'Union,' and the means of conciliatory true Friendship among Persons that have remain'd at a perpetual Distance."

Though such libertarian doctrine can hardly have appealed to the papacy, especially as Freemasonry in Catholic countries rapidly developed a strong anticlerical bias, it accords very comfortably with what we know of Pope's own impatience with fine points of dogma, and it seems genuinely to have had, within the English lodges at least, the desired ecumenical effect. One notices, for instance, among the members of the lodge to which Arbuthnot belonged a very broad spectrum of clergy, physicians, lawyers, merchants, and gentlemen.

53. From the 1723 membership list of the Lodge of Freemasons meeting at the Bedford Head Tavern, Covent Garden. Arbuthnot's name is the twentieth, reading down.

By kind permission of the United Grand Lodge of England.

Goat at the Foot of the Hay Market:

Mr. Isaac Dubois Mar.
Mr. Gam.l Massiot:} Wardens
Mr. William Bodle}
Mr. William Stephenson.
Mr. Elias Russell.
Mr. Peter Russell.
Mr. Edward Eldridge.
Mr. John Beauford.
Mr. Paul Dubois.
Mr. Andrew Halke.
Mr. Richard Stone.
Mr. Abraham Foiseau.
Mr. William Crawford.
Mr. Andrew Halke.
Mr. Alexr. Pope.
Mr. Thos. Buck.
Mr. Peter St. Pair.
Mr. Peter Jubart:
Mr. Michael Luige.
Mr. William Williams.
Mr. William Forrest.
Mr. John Swift.
Mr. Josias Amelo.
Mr. Clement Meem.
Mr. Thos. Briggs.
Mr. Robert Timpson.
Mr. Thos. Munn.
George Rooke Esqr.
Mr. Eligh. Mansur.
Mr. Henry Cowpland.
Mr. Hampson Bishop.
Mr. Jos: Ruswale.
Mr. William Smith.
Mr. John Savage.
Mr. John Barns.

54. From the 1730 membership list of the Lodge of Freemasons meeting at the Goat Tavern at the foot of the Haymarket. Pope's name is fifteenth, reading down, and Swift's, if it is Swift's, twenty-second.

By kind permission of the United Grand Lodge of England.

It was, in fact, the astronomer and natural philosopher, J. T. Desaguliers, who together with Anderson helped found the London Grand Lodge, and its first Grand Master was a peer, John, Duke of Montague, installed on 24 June 1721 at Stationers' Hall after a procession through London streets. The London Grand Lodge endured and is now the oldest Masonic Grand Lodge in existence, but the more loosely organized individual lodges often disappeared, or perhaps sometimes amalgamated with each other, after a few years. Of the Goat at the Foot of the Hay Market, nothing is known later than 1735.

For the two friends domiciled at Twickenham, there were also country rambles. One to Lord Bathurst at Cirencester and possibly another to his gardens at Richings. One—at least one—to Lord Burlington at Chiswick, where at the close of what appears to have been a merry occasion, Swift was presented with a copy of Fréart de Chambray's *Parallèle d'Architecture antique et de la moderne* (Paris, 1712), inscribed: "I give this book to Dr. Jonathan Swift, Dean of St. Patrick's, Dublin; in order to constitute him Director of Architecture in Ireland, especially upon my own Estate in that Kingdom. Cork and Burlington, June 27, 1726. Witness: A. Pope." Other destinations during that spring and summer included Lord Cobham's Stowe, Henrietta Howard's Marble Hill (of whose wine cellars, Swift wrote the following winter, "Mr. Gay and I are to have free access, when you are safe at Court; for, as to Mr. Pope, he is not worth mentioning on such occasions"), and Peterborow's house at Parson's Green. At the latter address, on August 3, a farewell dinner was held in Swift's honor, which Pope's having to miss (because of illness) elicited the next day a typically Swiftian gruff burst of affection:

> I had rather live in forty Islands than under the frequent disquiets of hearing you are out of order. I always apprehend it most after a great dinner; for the least Transgression of yours, if it be only two bits and one sup more than your stint, is a great debauch; for which you certainly pay more than those sots who are carry'd drunk to bed. My Lord Peterborow spoiled everybody's dinner, but especially mine, with telling us that you were detained by sickness. Pray let me have three lines under any hand or pothook that will give me a better account of your health; which concerns me more than others, because I love and esteem you for reasons that most others have little to do with, and would be the same although you had never touched a pen, further than with writing to me.

I am gathering up my luggage, and preparing for my journey: I will endeavour to think of you as little as I can, and when I write to you, I will strive not to think of you; this I intend in return to your kindness; and further, I know no body has dealt with me so cruelly as you, the consequences of which usage I fear will last as long as my life, for so long shall I be (in spite of my heart) entirely Yours.

Nevertheless, for all its excursions and celebratory wassails ("Yesterday My Lord Bolingbroke and Mr. Congreve made up five [with Swift, Gay or Arbuthnot, and Pope] at Dinner at Twickenham"), the visit was essentially a working and planning interlude. While Gay devised his *Fables* and Arbuthnot worked on his *Table of Ancient Coins, Weights, and Measures*, both to be published the next year, Pope and Swift at Twickenham culled through their collection of hints, sketches, and past publications to make up a miscellany or two—actually, in the end, the selections filled four volumes. Among the papers looked at, without doubt, was the anthology of "solemn nonsense"—"high flights of poetry"—that Pope and probably others of the Scriblerus group had begun collecting for one of the Club projects as early as 1714. These, very possibly because of the new inspiration provided by Swift and by the many reunions of the surviving Scriblerians, Pope collected during the next year or two into a humorous parallel to Longinus's famous treatise ΠΕΡΙ ΥΠΣΟΥΣ ("On 'Elevation' in Style"), but directed instead at poetic "descents" and entitled ΠΕΡΙ ΒΑΘΟΥΣ: *Or, Martinus Scriblerus His Treatise of the Art of Sinking in Poetry*. It may well have been Swift who made the creative suggestion that here was not only a potential Scriblerus piece, as had been all along intended, but a bright sequel, in its way, to his own *A Tale of a Tub*, with the "moderns," like a certain few critics of our own day, quite insensible of their inanities:

> It hath been long (my dear Countrymen) the Subject of my Concern and Surprize, that whereas numberless Poets, Cricks, and Orators have compiled and digested the Art of *Ancient Poesie*, there hath not arisen among us one Person so publick spirited, as to perform the like for the *Modern*. Altho' it is universally known, that our every-way-industrious Moderns, both in the Weight of their *Writings*, and in the Velocity of their *Judgments*, do so infinitely excel the said Ancients.
>
> (Ch. 1)

Also present among Pope's accumulations seems to have been a fragment of a satire on dullness that he may have initiated as early as

1719 or 1720, pillorying the kind of verse used to flatter Lord Mayors
at their annual pageants along with the breed of poets who stooped to
write it. According to Swift, it was he himself who "put Mr. Pope on
writing the poem, called the *Dunciad*," and Pope testifies to the same
effect when he says in a note to the poem that Swift was "in a sort" its
author:

> For when He, together with Mr. *Pope* . . . determin'd to own the
> most trifling pieces in which they had any hand, and to destroy all
> that remain'd in their power, the first sketch of this poem was
> snatch'd from the fire by Dr. Swift, who persuaded his friend to
> proceed in it.

What perhaps actually happened has been persuasively reconstructed:

> Swift was staying with Pope when Theobald's book came out, and
> if Pope was annoyed by Theobald's criticisms no one would know
> it better than Swift. The idea, therefore, of making Theobald the
> hero of the poem may have come from Swift, and it may have been
> just this happy suggestion that persuaded the dissatisfied author to
> try again. Now, at one stroke, Theobald was to supply the poet
> with a hero for his poem, and the editor of Shakespeare with the
> sort of revenge that he was best fitted to take. The poem, which
> had originally been a satire on dull poets, would now satirize dull
> critics as well: it would thus be a typical production of the
> Scriblerus Club.

For the greatest of the Scriblerian productions was also being
passed about that summer and probably given its final polish. This
was *Gulliver's Travels*, outgrowth of an early notion that Scriblerus
should see the world, but now totally transformed by a decade of
Swift's broodings on English politics, the sufferings of Ireland, the
follies of collectors and virtuosi, the miserable frustration and stag-
nation in an uncongenial setting of what he knew were his own
remarkable powers, and the ageless spectacle of human greed,
cruelty, hatred, lust, and pride. Peterborow's farewell party took
place on August 3. On August 8, probably in Gay's hand to avoid
identification, Lemuel Gulliver's supposed cousin "Richard Sympson" wrote Motte the publisher enclosing a sample of his seafaring
cousin's *Travels*—entrusted to him (he said) some years ago—which
he would now like to see published. Motte replied favorably on the
eleventh. "Sympson" shot off a note on the thirteenth to insist that
both volumes be issued together and not later than Christmas, and
two days later was off to Dublin. Soon after, in the mysterious way

that its author and (apparently) Pope had agreed on, Motte received the manuscript, "dropped at his house in the dark [probably by Pope or Gay, possibly by Swift's friend Erasmus Lewis] from a Hackney-coach," and on October 28 it was published.

Among the load of imitations, keys, tributes, and replies that tumbled from the presses during the next twelvemonth, none was more noteworthy than a pamphlet entitled *Several Copies of Verses on Occasion of Mr. Gulliver's Travels*—five poems in several styles, largely the work of Pope but possibly with assistance from Arbuthnot and Gay. One of the five, "A Lilliputian Ode," is addressed to Gulliver by the name assigned him in Lilliput, Quinbus Flestrin, and begins:

> In Amaze
> Lost, I gaze!
> Can our Eyes
> Reach thy Size?
> May my Lays
> Swell with Praise
> Worthy thee!
> Worthy me!
> Muse inspire
> All thy Fire!
> Bards of old
> Of him told,
> When they said
> *Atlas* head
> Propt the Skies:
> See! and believe your Eyes!

Another, an address to Gulliver by "*the Unhappy* HOUYHNHNMS, *now in Slavery and Bondage in England*," rejoices that someone has at last published the virtues of their native stock:

> You went, you saw, you heard: With Virtue fraught,
> Then spread those Morals which the *Houyhnhnms* taught.
> Our Labours here must touch thy gen'rous Heart,
> To see us strain before the Coach and Cart;
> Compell'd to run each knavish Jockey's Heat!
> Subservient to *New-market*'s annual cheat!
> With what Reluctance do we Lawyers bear,
> To fleece their Countrey Clients twice a Year?
> Or manag'd in your Schools, for Fops to ride,

> How foam, how fret beneath a Load of Pride!
> Yes, we are slaves—but yet, by Reason's Force,
> Have learnt to bear Misfortune, like a Horse.

In a third poem, bewildered by her husband's estrangement from her, Mary Gulliver recapitulates her tender feelings at all the dangers to which he has been exposed and wonders how she may win a happier reply than the one she now hears when she awakes at night, alone, to find her Gulliver gone:

> I wake, I rise, and shiv'ring with the Frost,
> Search all the House; my *Gulliver* is lost!
> Forth in the Street I rush with frantick Cries:
> The Windows open; all the Neighbours rise:
> *Where sleeps my* Gulliver? *O tell me where?*
> The Neighbours answer, *With the Sorrel Mare.*

A shorter poem, one whose content is easily imagined, comprises the "Words of the KING of BROBDINGNAG, *As he held Captain Gulliver between his Finger and Thumb for the Inspection of the Sages and learned Men of the Court.* The remaining poem, no. 2 in the published series, is sheer enchantment. It is the last appearance in Pope's work of the miniaturizing imagination that pervades the *Rape of the Lock*, and solid evidence of his recent readings in Shakespeare's *Midsummer Night's Dream.* The verses purport to be the lament of the gigantic little girl Glumdalclitch for the loss of her living toy Grildrig—Gulliver's Brobdingnagian name. Her first thought is that he has fallen into the vinegar cruet, where he used to fish, and drowned: "She dragg'd the Cruet, but no *Grildrig* found." Then other horrors spring to mind:

> Art thou in Spider's web, entangled hung?
> Or by some Flea with mortal venom stung?
> Dost thou bewilder'd wander all alone
> In the green Thicket of a Mossy stone?
> Or tumbl'd from the Toadstool's slippery round
> Perhaps all Maim'd lye grovelling on the ground?
> Or happier bosom'd in the Folded Rose,
> Or sunk within the peaches down repose?
> Or in a Bean-shell venture from the shore
> And brush the dangerous deep with strawy Oar?

As with any real mother, all the little exploits by which he has endeared himself flood her mind:

55. Jonathan Swift (1667–1745). By Francis Bindon, 1735. The scroll is inscribed: "Travels by Lemuel Gulliver. The Voyage to the Country of the Houyhnhnms." In the background are seen some natives of that country.

> Whether thou chuse Cervantes' serious air,
> Or laugh and shake in Rab'lais' easy chair,
> Or in the graver Gown instruct Mankind,
> Or silent let thy morals tell thy mind.
>   Pope in a letter to Swift, 22 October 1727.

Courtesy of the National Portrait Gallery, London.

> And shall I set thee on my hand no more,
> And see thee leap the lines and traverse o'er
> My spacious palm; in Stature scarce a Span
> Mimick the Actions of a Real Man?

(This was a role Pope knew all too well.)

> Shall I ne'er see thee turn my watches key
> As Seamen at a Capstain Anchors weigh?
> Or laugh to see thee walk with cautious tread,
> A dish of Tea like Milk-pail on thy head.
> Or mow from racy plumbs the sav'ry blew,
> And swill in Acorn cups the morning dew,
> Or gulp the yelks of Ants delicious eggs,
> Or at the Glow-worm warm thy frozen legs?
> Or chase the mite that bore thy cheese away.

In the end, she breaks down in such a Brobdingnagian flood of tears as would pickle all the herring caught off the Grand Banks of Newfoundland:

> The plenteous Pickle shall preserve the Fish,
> And *Europe* taste thy Sorrows in a Dish.

"I am very uneasy here": Swift's second visit

By the time these poems appeared, Swift was again in England and again staying with Pope. Old friends were as attentive as ever, and there was a new acquaintance of some note. Voltaire had fled to England the preceding spring, and by now, thanks to his charm, wit, and remarkable progress in the spoken language, had won admittance to all circles, including Walpole's, from whose government he received in May of 1727 a payment of £200, whether as a tribute to talent or an acknowledgment of information supplied or hoped for (he had known Bolingbroke in France and moved easily among the Opposition) has never been certainly established. He had shown his epic poem on France's Henri IV to Bolingbroke while still in France (first published there in 1723 as *La Ligue*, but in England in 1728 as *La Henriade*) and through this connection had had some correspondence about the poem with Pope. Though it is not clear just when the two met, by September 1726 Voltaire was sufficiently acquainted with Pope to write him an informal complimentary note of commiseration on his damaged hand. (Bringing Pope home from Dawley at night, early that month, Bolingbroke's coach had capsized in crossing the river Crane, "& the Glass being up," as Arbuthnot quickly wrote Swift, "which he could not break or get down, he was very near drowned." The footman, himself mired in the ooze, managed to pull free just in time to shatter the glass and haul the poet through the opening, but at the price of Pope's being cut deeply in two of his fingers on the right hand, the use of which for some time he lost.) Voltaire's impressions of his first meeting with Pope as recorded in Goldsmith's memoir of him have a special interest as the only appraisal we have of this kind from an acute foreign observer. Voltaire, says Goldsmith,

> has often told his friends, that he never observed in himself such a succession of opposite passions as he experienced upon his first interview with Mr. Pope. When he first entered the room, and perceived our poor melancholy English poet, naturally deformed, and wasted as he was with sickness and study, he could not help regarding him with the utmost compassion. But, when Mr. Pope began to speak, and to reason upon moral obligations, and dress the most delicate sentiments in the most charming diction, Voltaire's pity began to be changed into admiration and at last even into envy. It is not uncommon with him to assert, that no man ever pleased him so much in serious conversation, nor any whose sentiments mended so much upon recollection.

Through Pope, or possibly Bolingbroke, Voltaire was introduced to Swift early on in this second visit and by June was writing enthusiastic letters of introduction to facilitate the journeys in France with which Swift was then planning to occupy a part of the summer.

As with most sequels, however, Swift's second visit was somehow less sparkling and recuperative than its predecessor. The death of George I on June 11 made the French journey, or so Bolingbroke and others urged, impolitic. With the Prince, who had long been at odds with his father, now assuming the throne, there was hope in several quarters of Walpole's dismissal and the reinstatement of a more even-handed policy toward Whig and Tory alike. In Swift's words:

> The Talk is now for a moderating Scheme, wherein nobody shall be us'd the Worse or Better for being call'd Whig or Tory, and the King hath received both with great Equality; shewing Civilities to several who are openly known to be the latter. I prevailed with a Dozen that we should go in a Line to kiss the K—— and Q——'s Hands. We have now done with Repining, if we shall all be us'd

well, and not baited as formerly; we all agree in it, and if Things do not mend it is not our Faults: We have made our Offers: If otherwise, we are as we were.

In the upshot, Walpole was not dismissed, and those who had been optimistic remained "as we were." For Swift, already in his sixtieth year and condemned now to indefinite exile in Ireland, there to "die like a rat in a hole," the disappointment was profound. His only even slightly hopeful avenue of approach to Court favor in future would be through Henrietta Howard, to whom he addressed shortly after George I's death one of his most winning pieces. It is imagined in the poem that her Marble Hill, now supposed subject to abandonment owing to her removal nearer to St. James's, meets Richmond Lodge as one neighbor might meet another, for they were only separated by about two miles across the Thames. The Lodge is likewise emptied of its former occupants, the Prince and Princess of Wales, whose summer residence it had been but who will hereafter be too exalted for such modest quarters. The two houses commiserate. My Master, says Richmond Lodge, from being wealthy as a prince will now be poor as a king and always in debt. Nobody will come to visit *me* at all, Marble Hill mourns in return:

> No more the Dean, the grave Divine,
> Shall keep the Key of my (no) Wine;
> My Ice-house rob as heretofore,
> And steal my Artichokes no more;
> Poor *Patty Blount* no more be seen
> Bedraggled in my Walks★ so green:
> Plump *Johnny Gay* will now elope;
> And here no more will dangle *Pope*.

(ll. 43–50)

★ Swift expands on this in a letter to Lady Frances Worsley, who pretended to be jealous of his avuncular carryings-on (when last in England) with flirtatious girls, including "dirty Patty." Swift replies: "As to Patty Blount, you wrong her very much. She was a neighbour's child [to Pope], a good Catholic, an honest girl and a tolerable courtier at Richmond [i.e., in the Princess's circle]. I deny she was dirty, but a little careless, and sometimes wore a ragged gown, when she and I took long walks. She saved her money in summer only to be able to keep a Chair at London in winter. This is the worst you can say: and she might have a whole coat to her back if her good nature did not make her a fool to her mother and sanctified sister Teresa." (4 November 1732; Swift, *Correspondence*, 4: 79.)

Not only that, but I shall be snapped up by one of these new-style capitalists:

> Some *South Sea* Broker from the City,
> Will purchase me, the more's the Pity,
> Lay all my fine Plantations waste,
> To fit them to his Vulgar Taste;
> Chang'd for the worse in ev'ry Part,
> My Master *Pope* will break his Heart.
>
> (ll. 67–72)

My best hope, says Richmond Lodge, is to be given to the new very young Prince of Wales, for "he'll be Prince these fifty Years":

> I then will turn a Courtier too,
> And serve the Times as others do.
> Plain Loyalty not built on Hope,
> I leave to your Contriver, *Pope*:
> None loves his King and Country better,
> Yet none was ever less their Debtor.
>
> (ll. 79–84)

To which suggestion, Marble Hill replies: Then let him eschew all palaces and be solely mine—"let him come and take a Nap,"

> In *Summer*, on my verdant Lap:
> Prefer our Villaes where the Thames is,
> To Kensington, or hot St. James's;
> Nor shall I dull in Silence sit;
> For 'tis to me he owes his Wit;
> My Groves, my Echoes, and my Birds,
> Have taught him his poetick Words.
> We Gardens, and you Wildernesses,
> Assist all Poets in Distresses,
> Him twice a Week I here expect,
> To rattle Moody [the gardener] for Neglect;
> An idle Rogue, who spends his Quartridge [quarter's wages]
> In Tippling at the *Dog* and *Partridge*;
> And I can hardly get him down
> Three times a Week to brush my Gown [i.e., lawn]
>
> (ll. 85–100)

Whereupon the two grave ladies take a courteous leave:

Richmond-Lodge. I pity you, dear *Marble-Hill*;
But hope to see you flourish still.
All Happiness—and so adieu.
Marble-Hill. Kind *Richmond-Lodge*, the same to you.

(ll. 101–104)

A further disappointment, added to Swift's loss of his French excursion and the growing certainty that nothing in the government would alter in his favor, was that things at Twickenham were less happily circumstanced for his accommodation this summer than they had been in 1726. This summer, Pope's mother was extremely ill, her life being sometimes despaired of, and in consequence of his assiduous attendance on her, he and his guest were alike sometimes deprived of, or obliged to postpone, visits to friends' country-houses that would have been joyous and restorative. During the latter part of the summer, Pope too was ill, as was Swift himself, his old disorders of deafness and giddiness worsening unbearably. "Ten days ago," he writes to his Dublin intimate Thomas Sheridan in August,

> my old Deafness seized me, . . . but which is worse, about four Days ago my Giddiness seized me . . .; what will be the Event, I know not; one thing I know, that these deaf Fits use to continue five or six weeks, and I am resolved if it continues, or my Giddiness, some Days longer, I will leave this Place, and remove to Greenwich, or somewhere near *London*, and take my Cousin *Lancelot* to be my Nurse. . . . I am very uneasy here, because so many of our Acquaintance come to see us, and I cannot be seen; besides Mr. Pope is too sickly and complaisant.

What Swift meant by this last assertion becomes clear in a letter sent to Pope from Dublin soon after his return there, replying to his friend's remonstrance that he had been "sorry to find you could be easier in any house than in mine." "I find it more convenient to be sick here," Swift writes, "without the vexation of making my friends uneasy":

> I should be a very ill judge, to doubt your friendship and kindness. But it hath pleased God that you are not in a state of health, to be mortified with the care and sickness of a friend: Two sick friends never did well together; such an office is fitter for servants and humble companions, to whom it is wholly indifferent whether we give them trouble or no. The case would be quite otherwise if you were with me [there had been talk in Pope's letter of a possible visit to Ireland]; you could refuse to see any body: here is a large house

where we need not hear each other if we were both sick. I have a race of orderly elderly people of both sexes at command, who are of no consequence [Swift's view of inferiors is not always endearing, though sometimes it is largely disguise], and have gifts proper for attending us; who can bawl when I am deaf, and tread softly when I am only giddy and would sleep.

With the special mistrust of showing emotion that was so much a part of Swift's nature, he forebore to mention to any of his English friends (though some suspected) the cause that most of all prompted his restlessness and moodiness that summer, and, psychosomatically, perhaps increased even the severity of his familiar symptoms. This was the grave illness of Stella. Even during the preceding summer, he had lived constantly with the fear that any post might bring word of her death, confiding (again to Sheridan) in July:

> I have yours just now of the 19th, and the Account you give me [of Stella's rapid decline], is nothing but what I have some Time expected with the utmost Agonies. . . . I look upon this to be the greatest Event that can ever happen to me, but all my Preparations will not suffice to make me bear it like a Philosopher, nor altogether like a Christian. There hath been the most intimate Friendship between us from her Childhood, and the greatest Merit on her Side that ever was in one human Creature towards another —Nay if I were now near her, I would not see her; I could not behave myself tolerably, and should redouble her Sorrow.—Judge in what a Temper of Mind I write this.—The very time I am writing, I conclude the fairest Soul in the World hath left its Body. .

As these sentences so painfully show, one among the many motives impelling Swift's visits to England in these years was the dread of having to be a witness of Stella's suffering and, most especially, of her death. In his anguish of mind, he was prepared, indeed, to wait out the event in England, and once it had occurred, if his health permitted, flee to France "to forget myself." Only when Sheridan in high alarm took it upon himself to write Pope that "a particular Friend of the Dean's" was "upon the brink of another World" did he summon all his courage and pack for Dublin. He arrived there, considering the errand he came on, with time to spare. Stella died on Sunday, 28 January 1728. That evening, after some visitors were gone, he began to write his now famous narrative of the life and character of Mrs. Esther Johnson, his friend for some thirty-five years. It begins:

56. Esther Johnson (Swift's "Stella") 1681?–1728. By James Latham, undated.

> Say, *Stella*, was Prometheus blind,
> And forming you, mistook your kind?
> No: 'twas for you alone he stole
> The fire that forms a manly Soul.
> >   Swift, "To Stella, Visiting Me," 85–8.

Courtesy of the National Gallery of Ireland, Dublin.

This day, being Sunday, January 28, 1727–8, about eight o'clock at night, a servant brought me a note with an account of the death of the truest, most virtuous, and valuable friend, that I, or perhaps any other person, was ever blessed with. She expired about six in the evening of this day; and as soon as I am left alone, which is about eleven at night, I resolve for my own satisfaction, to say something of her life and character.

He was unable to finish the narrative that night. But on January 30, the night of her funeral, and of her burial, as she had wished, in the main aisle of the cathedral, he took it up again:

This is the night of the funeral, which my sickness [his giddiness, no doubt, but probably also the grief he could not bear to show in public] will not suffer me to attend. It is now nine at night; and I am removed into another apartment, that I may not see the light in the church.

The long tribute that follows, composed at intervals, opens with the sentence: "With all the softness that became a lady, she had the personal courage of a hero," and ends, in the last paragraph but one:

She loved Ireland much better than the generality of those who owe both their birth and riches to it; and having brought over all the fortune she had in money, left the reversion of the best part of it, one thousand pounds, to Dr. Steevens's Hospital. She detested the tyranny and injustice of England, in their treatment of this kingdom. She had indeed reason to love a country, where she had the esteem and friendship of all who knew her, and the universal good report of all who ever heard of her, without one exception.

Swift is reported by Sir Walter Scott to have preserved a lock of Stella's hair in an envelope on which he had written, "Only a woman's hair"—that "only" a quintessentially Swiftian way of holding pain at arm's length, like his "Vive la bagatelle!" So widely read in seventeenth-century literature as he was, one cannot but wonder whether, as for an earlier poetical dean, the thought had crossed his fancy of being carried to his long home—which in the end was in the cathedral close to Stella—wearing a bracelet of bright hair about the bone.

A remarkable harvest

At home in Dublin that fall, awaiting the event he could not bear to contemplate, Swift had news from his English friends that in another mood might have brought him consoling reflections. On October 22, in a joint letter of Pope and Gay, he learned that the mock-epic poem whose germ he had snatched from the burning, and to the evolution of which he had contributed we do not know how much, was now ready to be published, with some form of high tribute to him. A tribute, as he would learn more precisely when the variorum edition of the poem reached him in 1729, founded first of all on the epic convention that in invoking a muse or a god one tries out many names to find the one most likely to please—

> O thou! whatever Title please Thine ear,
> Dean, Drapier, Bickerstaff, or Gulliver!—
>
> (1: 17–18)

but, second, and more generally, on the implication that his presence in Dublin was sufficient of itself to displace Dulness's oncoming Golden Age from Irish soil to English:

> From thy Baeotia tho' Her Pow'r retires,
> Grieve not at ought our sister realm acquires:
> Here pleas'd behold her mighty wings out-spread,
> To hatch a new Saturnian age of Lead.
>
> (1: 23–26)

In the same letter, he heard from Gay that his *Beggar's Opera* was finished. As far back as 1716, he had suggested to Gay, knowing his talent for mock-pastoral, that he might find his profit in "a Newgate pastoral, among the whores and thieves there." And while we may or may not be disposed to believe that this hint (made in a letter to Pope) lingered in Gay's mind for a decade, it is at least a curious coincidence that Swift's visits were followed by the composition of a ballad opera that did, in fact, concern itself with whores, thieves, and Newgate, though modified, to be sure, as Scriblerus's travels had been modified, by its author's experiences in the meantime, and his observations, reflections, and intuitions about the world in which he found himself. One intuition he seems to have had was of a growing inclination—perhaps inevitable in a society in which, following the passage of the Black Act, more and more offenses against property were magnified into capital crimes—to make heroes of culprits sentenced to the gallows, as if gratifying some obscurely felt defiance of a political and social order in which, as Shakespeare's King Lear had once said, "See how yond justice rails upon yond simple thief. . . . Change places, and handy-dandy, which is the justice, which is the thief?" The last words of the Beggar in Gay's *Opera* summarize this kind of sentiment with a nonchalance that makes it only the more cutting:

> Through the whole piece you may observe such a similitude of manners in high and low life, that it is difficult to determine whether . . . the fine gentlemen imitate the gentlemen of the road, or the gentlemen of the road the fine gentlemen.—Had the play remain'd, as I at first intended, it would have carried a most excellent moral. 'Twould have shown that the lower sort of people have their vices in a degree as well as the rich: And that they are punish'd for them.

The *Opera* manages to catch too the profound latent xenophobia of the age. There is an antipathy to foreign importations to which any nation becomes subject when it senses that something deeply indigenous, something essential to its "economy" in the root senses of that word, is under threat from without. And it would not be unfair to guess, I think, that the vehement prejudice of many at that time (including Pope) against Italian opera—the opera of which Gay's own *Opera* makes continuous fun and in the face of which its songs flaunt native English sentiments expressed in honest kersey English words set to traditional English tunes—carried in suspension antipathies to other forms of foreign infiltration, such as an Italian-opera-loving German court, where German hangers-on were paid with English pounds and pence. The tunes Gay had chosen, ranging from ancient favorites like "Chevy Chase" and "Old Simon the King" through street ballads, drinking songs, and still-popular hits from the Restoration stage, were well suited to elicit in his audiences, though he may have been quite unconscious of this, a happy sense of a secure world, once familiar and widely shared, that was now receding, almost lost, in fact, in the commercializing attitudes incorporated in Peachum —and tainting, in the end, even the "gentlemen" of the road. Pervasive throughout, as well, is the evidence of Gay's own experience with the Court. There he had dangled among other suitors whose success or failure he soon saw to be as dependent on the designs of the Walpole ministry as were the fortunes of the *Opera*'s pickpockets and highwaymen on the designs of Peachum. "How exhilarating," it has been astutely suggested, "a cultural affirmation of this sort"—with its upsurge of English solidarity and nose-thumbing—"must have been in 1728 to . . . men and women voiceless and doubly depressed by the absence, the previous year, of any changes at the death of George the first."

On 29 January 1728, one day after Stella's death, Gay's *Opera* was produced at Lincoln's Inn Fields. Though the audience seemed at first hesitant to make up its mind, the evening ended (as Pope, who was present, later told Spence) in "a clamour of applause," and the play proceeded to an unprecedented run of sixty-two consecutive performances. Some five weeks later, on March 8, the third volume of Swift's and Pope's *Miscellanies* was issued. This contains *The Art of Sinking in Poetry*, a work that, as noted earlier, would very possibly never have been written at that time or in that form apart from the stimulus provided by the reunion of the Scriblerians—particularly, I would myself suspect, apart from the stimulus provided by the author of *A Tale of a Tub*, whose assault upon the "Moderns" it renews in a manual for their use on how to write badly and defend the results.

> It is therefore manifest that *Mediocrity* ought to be allow'd, yea indulg'd to the good Subjects of England. Nor can I conceive how the World has swallow'd the contrary as a Maxim, upon the single Authority of that *Horace*? Why should the *Golden Mean*, and Quintessence of all Virtues, be deem'd so offensive only in this Art? Or *Coolness* or *Mediocrity* be so amiable a Quality in a Man, and so detestable in a Poet?
>
> However, far be it from me to compare these Writers with those *Great Spirits*, who are born with a *Vivacité de pesanteur*, or (as an *English* Author [Shakespeare] calls it) an *Alacrity of sinking*; and who by *Strength of Nature* alone can excell. All I mean is to evince the *Necessity* of Rules to these lesser Genius's, as well as the *Usefulness* of them to the Greater.
>
> (Ch. 3)

When, some two months after *The Art of Sinking*, the *Dunciad* appeared (on May 18), Swift could have felt, had he wished, that the harvest of his English visits had been bounteous indeed. As he wrote to Gay on March 28, "The Beggers Opera hath knockt down Gulliver; I hope to see Pope's Dullness knock down the Beggers Opera; but not till it hath fully done its Jobb." There was in fact, of course, no likelihood of any of these works knocking down the other or finishing its "Jobb." Quite the contrary. Each in its own way continues to ask us questions about ourselves and the societies we have built or tolerated to which in the latter decades of the twentieth century we can make only embarrassed and sometimes shameful answers.

CHAPTER 19

TAKING WRITING
SERIOUSLY

"The Cloud-compelling Queen"

The *Dunciad* of 1728, though today much sought after by collectors and all but impossible to obtain, is an unprepossessing little pamphlet of fifty-two pages, bearing no author's name. Its full title is *The Dunciad. An Heroic Poem. In Three Books*; and its imprint— "Dublin, Printed, London Re-printed for A. Dodd"—lays a claim to Irish origins that its small size and rather seedy character as a specimen of bookmaking may have been intended to support. In marketing libelous or seditious political pieces, it was no new thing for printers and booksellers to pretend to publication in Ireland or on the Continent as a way of throwing pursuers off the scent. Very possibly Pope had this precedent in mind, for he can hardly have been unaware of the poem's explosive potentialities. As his friend Richard Savage (subsequently also Johnson's friend during the early years of sleeping on bulks in London) describes the occasion,

> On the Day the Book was first vended, a Crowd of Authors besieg'd the Shop; Entreaties, Advices, Threats of Law, and Battery, nay Cries of Treason were all employ'd to hinder the coming out of the *Dunciad*: On the other Side, the Booksellers and Hawkers made as great Efforts to procure it.

A twentieth-century publicist's dream!

What Pope had also in mind, no doubt, in giving the book its Dublin imprint, was to cast some responsibility on Swift. Had the poem appeared, as first planned, in the third volume of their *Miscellanies* (also 1728), effective legal identification of the author would have been rendered comfortably moot by the dual and even multiple authorship claimed for all of those collections by the preface to the first. A Dublin imprint regained this lost advantage by associating the work with one who had indeed played a part in its beginnings and, far more important, was secure on the thither side of the Irish Sea from physical retaliation. It also helped support the fiction, wittily developed in the poem's "The Publisher to the Reader," that the pamphlet in its present form was issued without authority, and so (as in fact, of course, happened) must be replaced as soon as possible by an authorized edition, the anticipated demand for which Pope had shrewdly enhanced by inserting in his version a very large number of initials, asterisks, and blanks calculated to pique curiosity about the names they concealed. Even the name of the hero dunce, Lewis Theobald, though printed out in full, was "translated" (like Bottom wearing the ass's head in *A Midsummer Night's Dream*) into a foolish tumble of syllables rhyming with "ribald."

In the poem as a whole, Pope assumed for background Vergil's story of the founding of Rome. Aeneas's destiny, it will be recalled, was to rescue from burning Troy (in addition to his son and father) the *lares* and *penates* of his house—which is to say, in substance, the austerity, gravity, dignity, piety, and strict observance of duty that Vergil's contemporaries liked to think of as "Roman." The national image they defined in this way was largely a reaction to the alleged luxuries and effeminacies of the East, to which, in the form of Cleopatra and her allies, their leadership had very nearly succumbed only twenty years before. (Englishmen from Shakespeare's time on would engage in a similar exercise with reference to a supposedly effete Italy or France, and "innocent" nineteenth-century Americans would behave likewise vis-à-vis the "corrupting" Old World of Europe.) These solid Roman virtues it was Aeneas's task to transplant to a new home in Italy and there found on them a civilization. Its eventual seat would be the city that later times would call the Eternal City, and its mission, divinely ordained as in all such inventions, would be to impose everlasting peace on a contentious world through a Roman *patrocinium* or protectorate. (How long, one wonders, will these juggling terms continue to delude?)

Tibbald's destiny parallels Aeneas's. He is to lead a similar westering movement of the *lares* and *penates* of Grub Street, Rag Fair, and other unsavory neighborhoods of the old City of London. The City had been long established in the mythology of the wits as home to a stolid, tasteless, dissenting, and money-grubbing bourgeoisie centered on the areas about the Royal Exchange. But it had also for some decades, in fact as well as myth, offered its immediately out-lying suburbs such as Holborn, Stepney, and Clerkenwell to be the haunt of London's poor, most of its criminal element, and, from about Dryden's time, subsisting in various states of respectability and squalor, its new class of hack writers supplying an enlarging literate public with its daily fix of news, scandal, ballads, letters from a gentleman in the country to a gentleman in the city, pornographic novels, animadversions, humble addresses, sermons, dedications, invectives, and lampoons.

But now—so the thesis of the *Dunciad* ran—this taste for "masscult" and "midcult" (I borrow the terms from an astringent observer of our own cultural scene) was seeping westward to contaminate the traditional national power centers and arbiters of taste in parliament, the peerage, and the court, all situated in Westminster. Thus "The Action of the *Dunciad*" (to draw on Pope's own account of it published the next year in the *Dunciad Variorum*), "is the removal of the Imperial seat of Dulness from the City to the polite world; as that of the Aeneid is the Removal of the empire of *Troy* to *Latium*." Though only an allegorical fiction, to be sure, the interests and habits of George I—"an honest blockhead," according to Lady Mary Wortley Montagu—combined with those of his son, who made no secret of his contempt for books and learning, to give it the coloration of truth. At this Pope seems to hint. His manuscript version of the *Dunciad*'s opening, very possibly written before the accession, describes the transmission of sovereignty he is about to celebrate as a wholly literary event:

> Say what the cause that still this taste remains,
> And when a Settle falls, a Tibbald reigns.

The printed version, published less than a twelvemonth after George II came to the throne, leaves the whole matter of succession significantly vague:

> Say from what cause, in vain decry'd and curst,
> Still *Dunce the second reigns like Dunce the first?*

Almost certainly an early excursion into the mode of political innuendo that Pope will handle with such brilliance in the satires to come.

Book 1 of the poem describes the consecration of the hero to his task (it turns out to be his coronation as well) by the one divinity that Grub Street natives recognize: the goddess Dulness, "Daughter of Chaos and Eternal Night" (l. 10). Her palace, situated in the purlieus of St. Giles Cripplegate, is a ramshackle ruin of a sort this area of London once supplied in abundance and is described in the poem (altogether appropriately to its tenant) as "yawning" even while it "nods." Open to the weather, it lay in odorous proximity to Rag Fair and other nearby marts of second-hand clothes, festering in a rancid maze of lanes and narrow streets largely populated by purveyors of that other species of used merchandise which Hogarth commemorates in his "Harlot's Progress." Tawdry, soiled, and—as for the clothes—usually stolen, the several attributes of Dulness's environment, including her ramshackle dwelling, figure forth vividly the qualities of the writings that she and her minions proliferate.

A dazzling passage early in this book gives us Dulness in her throne room, meditating, as a good divinity should, on ultimate mysteries of being and becoming:

> Here she beholds the Chaos dark and deep,
> Where nameless *somethings* in their causes sleep,
> Till genial *Jacob*, or a warm *third-day*★
> Calls forth each mass, a poem or a play.
> How hints, like spawn, scarce quick in embryo lie;
> How new-born nonsense first is taught to cry;
> Maggots† half-form'd, in rhyme exactly meet,
> And learn to crawl upon poetic feet.
> Here one poor *Word* a hundred clenches makes,
> And ductile dulness new meanders takes;
> There motley *Images* her fancy strike,
> *Figures* ill-pair'd, and *Similes* unlike.
> She sees a Mob of *Metaphors* advance,
> Pleas'd with the madness of the mazy dance:
> How *Tragedy* and *Comedy* embrace;
> How *Farce* and *Epic* get a jumbled race;
> How *Time* himself stands still at her command,
> Realms shift their place, and Ocean turns to land.
> Here gay *Description Aegypt* glads with showers;
> Or gives to *Zembla* fruits, to *Barca* flowers;‡
> Glitt'ring with ice here hoary hills are seen,
> Fast by, fair vallies of eternal green,
> On cold December fragrant chaplets blow,
> And heavy harvests nod beneath the snow.
>
> (1: 43–66)

★ Jacob is, of course, the publisher Tonson, *genial* in the sense of procreative as well as amiable. The proceeds of a third day's performance were in Pope's time the sole profit of a playwright.
† In the double sense of grubs and mental crotchets.
‡ Barca is a desert in Libya; Zembla a polar region.

Such passages, of which the *Dunciad* contains many, communicate a complex attitude and tone. We are not, of course, to overlook in them the satirist's reductive scorn, highlighting here and everywhere the enemy's anarchic sprawl by a masterful display of order. "All of Pope's accumulated skills," one of the poem's most perceptive commentators has observed, "help this effect: . . . the sharply defined couplets, the decisive rhymes, the unfailing clarity":

> Set against this we have a series of vacillations and muddles. . . . Everything *within* the picture is *dark, deep, in embryo, half-form'd, ductile, motley, ill-pair'd, mazy, jumbled.* The constituent parts are *nameless somethings* . . .; other nouns suggest the same quality— *mass, spawn, non-sense, mob, madness—*

to which may be added *meanders.* Yet we are not to overlook, on the other side, the exuberance with which the poet invents the grotesque psychic activities by which he imagines the workings of an imagination out of control. He does not contemplate these activities with a shudder or a blaze of fury, though unquestionably the ease with which he moves among them contributes at some level to the belittling effect, as if a renowned figure skater were suddenly to materialize among the struggling crowd on a village pond. Plainly, something in Pope responds to the secret resources of dulness, elaborates them with visible delight, even educes from them a strange beauty—for the ear as well as the eye:

> Glitt'ring with ice here hoary hills are seen,
> Fast by, fair vallies of eternal green,
> On cold December fragrant chaplets blow,
> And heavy harvests nod beneath the snow.
>
> (1: 63–66)

In the final line, notably, the heaviness, sleepiness, and inverted norms expressive of the dunce world have been sublimed into a suggestive image of opposites possibly reconciled, fruitfulness attained despite odds. In passages like this, it has been well said, the poet aims not "to ridicule and dismiss, but to amplify and explore":

> With a part of his sensibility, he is able to feel a kind of anarchic enchantment in dulness. That [his] poem . . . is capable of a full human response to the thing it chiefly opposes makes the final rejection more telling, and is a measure of the greatness of the work.

The "good old Cause"

Next introduced after its goddess, the poem's hero is discovered in his library. Like the Son in *Paradise Lost*, he bears his progenitor's image, "full exprest"; but like the fallen angel Satan of the same poem, newly arrived in hell, he reacts to the landscape lying all about him with "huge dismay." As well he might! For the shelves gleam with enormous leather folios housing the achievements of both the duncical brotherhood of poets and the voluminous commentators and explicators to whose lineage, it is implied, Theobald on Shakespeare belongs:

> But high above, more solid Learning shone,
> The *Classicks* of an Age that heard of none;
> There *Caxton* slept, with *Wynkin* at his side,
> One clasp'd in wood, and one in strong cow-hide:
> There sav'd by spice, like mummies, many a year,
> Old Bodies of philosophy appear.
> *De Lyra* there a dreadful front extends,
> And there the groaning Shelves *Philemon* bends.
>
> (l: 117–24)

Here too, however, as in the meditations of the goddess, the prevailing ridicule seems tempered by fascination. The passage springs from a friendlier subconscious attitude to ancient pedantries than we usually imagine, or, if this overstates the case, the lines carry at least an undertone of such excitements as an imaginative youth, eager to educate himself, might first have known in the spooky flicker of the firelight on a dark November Windsor Forest afternoon: the shine of leather bindings, the faint scent of aromatic beeswax ("spice") rubbed into them and now set free by the fire's warmth, and then the suddenly dawning fancy that the shelves he stared at were a kind of catacomb or charnel house or boneyard, where the mighty dead, asleep in their niches, could at any instant choose to "appear" (like the elder Hamlet's ghost), and with their dreadful fronts extended, the very boards "groaning" under their gigantic weight, send delicious terrors down a boyish spine.

From these imposing materials and his own unvendible creations, Tibbald builds an altar in the approved epic style and prayerfully recounts before it his services to Dulness's "good old Cause." For eighteenth-century readers, the phrase at once identified the goddess with the rise of the dissenting groups, heavily engaged in commerce, whose great grandfathers could be and often were branded by

Anglicans and Catholics with the charge of regicide; whose grand-fathers and fathers had made up much of the grumbling "crowd" of Dryden's *The Medal* and *Absalom and Achitophel* determined to ex-clude James II from the throne; and whose current members, many of them outstanding figures of the new capitalism, now furnish—so Pope's verses imply—patrons for the kind of writing that Tibbald and his fellow-dunces produce.

> *Dulness!* whose good old cause I yet defend,
> With whom my Muse began, with whom shall end! . . .
> Ah! still o'er *Britain* stretch that peaceful wand,
> Which lulls th' *Helvetian* and *Batavian* land. . . .
> There, thy good *Scholiasts* with unweary'd pains
> Make *Horace* flat, and humble *Maro*'s strains;
> Here studious I unlucky Moderns [e.g., Shakespeare] save,
> Nor sleeps one error in its father's grave,
> Old puns restore, lost blunders nicely seek,
> And crucify★ poor *Shakespear* once a week.
> For thee I dim these eyes, and stuff this head,
> With all such reading as was never read;
> For thee supplying, in the worst of days,
> Notes to dull books, and Prologues to dull plays;
> For thee explain a thing 'till all men doubt it,
> And write about it, Goddess, and about it.
>
> (ll. 135–36, 145–46, 149–60)

Bidding, at last, an anguished farewell to his brain-children, he ignites the sacrificial pile and with the same feelings as Aeneas in the midst of burning Troy watches it consume:

> The opening clouds [of smoke] disclose each work by turns,
> Now flames old *Memnon*, now *Rodrigo* burns,
> In one quick flash see *Proserpine* expire,
> And last, his own cold *Aeschylus* took fire.
> Then gush'd the tears, as from the Trojan's eyes
> When the last blaze sent Ilion to the skies.
>
> (ll. 197–202)

At this moment, however, Dulness appears and douses the pyre with a conveniently damp sheet from one of Ambrose Philips's unfinished poems. She bids her suppliant attend her to her "sacred Dome"—which is to say, to the ruin described earlier amongst the

---

★ Referring to "cruxes" of interpretation as well as torture.

other purveyors of used goods—and there, as if in Westminster
Abbey, crowns him her king of dunces. While the sacred ointment is
being administered—in this instance, opium—a queer sort of bird
descends and settles on the new monarch's head: "Something
between a H[eidegger] and Owl." As an owl, it is, of course,
Athena's bird, representative of the wisdom by which an epic hero
(an Aeneas, above all) is or should be guided. As an owl, it is also a
stupid bird, representative of folly masquerading as wisdom, and
hence well suited to adorn a mock hero. As a mysterious apparition,
evidently a mark of favor from on high, it is presumably a parody of
the dove seen by John the Baptist above the head of one whose shoe-
latchet he held himself unworthy to unloose, thus certifying Tibbald
as not merely king but king of kings, and reminding us who read that
the power of Pope's feelings about the collapse of culture comes from
their being, finally, religious feelings. It is not by accident or exclusively in fun that at the outset of the second book he will confer on
Camillo Querno, Leo X's papal buffoon, and, by extension, on Tibbald, the Hanoverian buffoon (whose theatrical gimcrackery was
popular with royalty and its courtiers), the title of "Antichrist of
Wit"; or that at the conclusion of the third book, even in this earliest
version, an apocalyptic darkness supervenes:

> *Let there be darkness!* (the dread pow'r shall say)
> All shall be darkness, as it ne'er were Day.
>
> (3: 281–82)

Finally, in its resemblance to the notoriously ugly manager of the
opera house in the Haymarket, John James Heidegger (whom Fielding
dubbed "Count Ugly"), the owlish bird signifies a decay of standards
explicitly among that group whom Pope believed *noblesse*, or at least
privilege, should especially *oblige*: the "great Patricians" invoked at
the poem's opening as responsible for the transit of the Smithfield
muses to the west. They were the chief supporters and frequenters of
Heidegger's opera-house masquerades, entertainments that became
so offensive for their disorderliness and their encouragement of
sometimes brothel-like behavior that a Middlesex grand jury presented him the year after Pope's lines were published as a "principal
promoter of vice and immorality." A yet more salient fact for Pope,
we may guess, is that these affairs enjoyed the patronage of George II,
who soon after his accession appointed Heidegger his master of the
revels. Thus the new King Tibbald's Heideggerian mark of grace is
shared by another new king, and Dunce the second reigns like Dunce
the first in more "Domes" than one.

The succeeding two books of the poem chronicle the promised westward expansion. Though Dulness crowns her new king in Rag Fair, hard by the Tower, the epic games she lays on to honor his accession take place at the spot where Drury Lane meets the Strand at the very edge of the jurisdiction of Westminster. In this general area, embracing Fleet Street to the east with its booksellers, including Edmund Curll, and Covent Garden just slightly west, formerly a fashionable residential quarter but now declining into the city's best-known bagnio, people of all backgrounds thronged, some, we are told, coming to visit Mother Douglas's or Tom and Moll King's tavern-*cum*-bawdy house (he was an Eton man!) straight from Court, "in full dress, with swords and bags [bagwigs], and in rich brocaded coats". The melting pot aspect of the area comes through amusingly enough in Pope's register of the "heroes" who rush to honor their monarch in the games:

> An endless band
> Pours forth, and leaves unpeopled half the land,
> A motley mixture! in long wigs, in bags,
> In silks, in crapes, in garters, and in rags;
> From drawing rooms, from colleges, from garrets,
> On horse, on foot, in hacks, and gilded chariots [pron. *charets*]
> All who true Dunces in her cause appear'd,
> And all who knew those Dunces to reward.

(2: 1–8)

A succession of coronation games ensues. First, the publishers strive in a footrace to seize a fleeing poet's likeness—this is Pope's comment on the inclination of the trade to whip up a market for hackwork by assigning it on the title page to an author of note. The chief contestants are Lintot and Curll, the former vastly outstripped by the latter until, like Ajax in Homer and Nisus in Vergil, Curll slips on some ordure deposited by one of his own authors—here again a metaphorical realization of his ventures into obscene and smear publishing. Even so, with the help of Cloacina the sewer goddess, who for obvious reasons favors him, he rises—"Renew'd by ordure's sympathetic force"—to win the race, only to find that the author he pursues is indeed illusory. Dulness comforts him with an appropriate reward—

> Be thine, my stationer! this magic gift;
> C[ook] shall be *Prior*, C[oncane]*n Swift*;
> So shall each hostile Name become our own,
> And we too boast our *Garth* and *Addison*.

(2: 117–20)

For good measure, she adds a tapestry registering the fates to be expected by Dulness's devotees: pillorying, scourging, blanket tossing (Curll had been tossed by the scholars of Westminster School for publishing, as usual without authority, a work of one of their number), and, Pope's own earlier gift to him, the vomit:

> There kick'd and cudgel'd R[idpath] might ye view,
> The very worsted still look'd black and blue:
> Himself [i.e., Curll] among the storied chiefs he spies,
> As from the blanket high in air he flies,
> And oh! (he cry'd) what street, what lane but knows
> Our purgings, pumpings, blanketings and blows?
> In ev'ry loom our labors shall be seen,
> And the fresh vomit run for ever green!
>
> (2: 129–36)

It has been remarked by critics that Pope often builds effects of striking epic richness in the *Dunciad* only to let them be broken down, disfigured, stained. As the word "vomit" here disfigures the lovely cadence and possibly pastoral implication of the verse in which it occurs, so the subject matter of the whole passage disfigures one of the most touching self-recognition scenes in ancient poetry. This is the scene in which Aeneas beholds the conquest of his native Troy represented on the walls of Dido's Carthage, and, weeping, cries out: *sunt lacrimae rerum, et mentem mortalia tangunt* ["Even here, in this far place, there are tears for our misfortunes; even here suffering touches the human heart".] A stain indeed!

Subsequently, Curll is also victor (the annotated *Dunciad Variorum* of the next year will remind readers that heroic exploits mean enough for heroes of this caliber are not easily found) in a urinating contest, whose symbolism speaks for itself. His rival in this event, William Chetwood, included doubtless because he published the roman à clef in which Martha Blount was called "the most dissolute and shameless of her sex," manages only a rainbowlike curve:

> So *Jove*'s bright bow displays its watry round,
> (Sure sign, that no spectator shall be drown'd).
>
> (2: 155–56)

"Not so from shameless C[url]*l*":

> Impetuous spread
> The stream, and smoking, flourish'd o'er his head.

Then follows, like Chetwood's rainbow, an epic simile comparing

Curll's performance to that of fabled Eridanus, the river represented anciently by poets as rising to the skies and flowing through
them:

> So, (fam'd like thee for turbulence and horns,)
> *Eridanus* his humble fountain scorns,
> Thro' half the heav'ns he pours th' exalted urn;
> His rapid waters in their passage burn.
>
> (2: 161–66)

The allusions are unquestionably insulting: Chetwood is definitely
a failure, quite outclassed in what later times will call the activities
of the yellow press, unable even to direct his own small affair; and
Curll, though something of a genius in the disposal of poisonous
wastes, is (allegedly), over and above his well-documented
"turbulence," both a cuckold and a sufferer from venereal pangs.
There is no mistaking the contempt. Yet the tone becomes almost
affable as the grotesque comparisons pile up, the high-style eu-
phemisms are set to skating gracefully on the thinnest ice, and
even an illusory sense of dispassionate conscientious appraisal is
made to emerge from such an apparent insistence on accuracy as
the fact that Curll, like Eridanus, waters only "half" the heavens.

It is this sense of high clowning, of an imagination freely
frolicking and at times itself entertained, even convulsed, by the
rich absurdities to be unveiled when modern dunces are viewed
against older traditions they no longer understand or follow, that
gives the *Dunciad* its unique status in Pope's career. He will write
other satires, far more withering satires, satires with a longer or
more immediate public reach; but he will write nothing ever again
(except later versions of the *Dunciad*) that will show so clearly (as
was said of Shakespeare's Antony, whose delights were dolphinlike
and showed his back above the element they lived in) a great comic
invention "at play."

"Let there be darkness"

Two of Pope's finest exhibitions of this kind are found in the
diving contest in this book and the Pisgah-like vision of imperial-
power-to-come granted Tibbald in the next. The diving game
takes place at roughly noon in the vicinity of Bridewell Bridge,
one of London's most noisome areas,

> where *Fleetditch* with disemboguing streams
> Rolls the large tribute of dead dogs to *Thames*,
> The King of Dykes! than whom, no sluice of mud
> With deeper sable blots the silver flood.
>
> (2: 249–52)

The discolorations of filth that Fleet Ditch—in Pope's time, essentially an open sewer running from Holborn to the Thames—offers to London's great waterway represent the discolorations that the products of the dunces, especially their party writers (of whom the annotated *Dunciad Variorum* will declare the following year that they "stick at nothing," "delight in flinging dirt,' and "slander in the dark by guess") are presumed to offer to the canons of literature. For the best performances in pollution, Dulness now offers her awards, and the contestants come forward, Dennis in the lead. He tries for extra momentum by diving from the height of a barge stranded in the Ditch at low tide, and apparently his effort is effectual—he is never heard from again:

> The senior's judgment all the crow'd admire,
> Who but to sink the deeper, rose the higher.
>
> (2: 267–68)

The same fate appears to overtake the next contestant, Laurence Eusden, a bibulous cleric totally without talent, who had been made poet laureate on Rowe's death in 1718 as if to confirm in advance the thesis of the *Dunciad* about the Hanoverian "patricians." The dives of several others intervene and Eusden is given up for lost till, "sudden," in a burst of thunder like Jove himself, he rises transformed:

> Greater he looks, and more than mortal stares;
> Then thus the wonders of the Deep declares.
> First he relates, how sinking to the chin,
> Smit with his mien, the *Mudnymphs* suck'd him in,
> How young *Lutetia* softer than the down,
> *Nigrina* black, and *Merdamante* brown,
> Vy'd for his love in jetty bow'rs below;
> As *Hylas* fair was ravish'd long ago.
> Then sung how, shown him by the nutbrown maids,
> A branch of *Styx* here rises from the *Shades*,
> That tinctur'd as it runs with *Lethe*'s streams,
> And wafting vapors from the *Land* of *Dreams*,
> (As under seas *Alphaeus*' secret sluice

Bears *Pisa*'s offerings to his *Arethuse*)
Pours into *Thames*: Each City-bowl is full
Of the mixt wave, and all who drink grow dull.
How to the banks where bards departed doze,
They led him soft; how all the bards arose;
Taylor, sweet bird of *Thames*, majestic bows,
And *Sh*[adwell] nods the poppy on his brows;
While M[ilbour]n there, deputed by the rest,
Gave him the cassock, surcingle, and vest;
And "Take (he said) these robes which once were mine,
"Dulness is sacred in a sound Divine."

(2: 292-314)

We do not need to catch—though it must have delighted contemporaries—the comparison of the laureate Eusden, whose habitual hard drinking was well known, to Silenus, usually presented in art as a fat naked drunkard riding on an ass. In classical poetry, he is a nature god like Proteus, who, if caught, can be made to reveal secrets. Taken prisoner by shepherds in Vergil's sixth eclogue, he wins his freedom by singing a succession of events read by some as a pessimistic prophecy of man's fate—beginning with the Creation and happy Golden Age but ending in various kinds of dehumanization brought on by the failure of men and women to control their egoistic drives: not far from the *Dunciad*'s own theme. One of the events Silenus sings in Vergil is the rape of Hylas by river nymphs. Another, equally recognizable in Pope's parody, is the experience of the poet Gallus, who is led by a muse to the sacred precincts of Apollo, "where all the choir of Phoebus rose to do him honour," and where the poet Linus, already received there, surrenders to him the reeds once played on by the poet-theologian Hesiod. In Pope's adaptation, it is the Reverend Luke Milbourne, vicious enemy of his idol Dryden, who passes on to Eusden the ecclesiastical instruments guaranteeing dulness in a sound divine.

All this we can miss without failing to enjoy the romp that Pope is having in other ways. In (for starters) his droll parody of the epic voyage to the underworld and the revelation vouchsafed there—in this instance, discovery of the secret sluice by which City dulness is fed. Or in the visitation of the epic hero to his great predecessors in the Elysian Fields—here a trio of seventeenth-century poets whose feats in verse had been a laughingstock for generations. Most winning of all, perhaps: in the smiling ease with which he aerates the viscous matter of Fleet Ditch with nymphs as mellifluous in name as any that haunt the Ilissus: Nigrina, Lutetia, Merdamante—delectable inspirations of the comic muse. (If one imagines how Swift might have handled this scene, one gets some sense of the healing and sublimating powers of which Pope's imagination was capable.) Taylor, Shadwell, and Milbourne, when Pope wrote, were universal figures of fun—Shadwell, despite Dryden's *MacFlecknoe*, somewhat less than the other two because his plays were still played—and Pope treats them as such. Yet his lines allow them at the same time an eccentric dignity. John Taylor the Water-Poet, a "swan" of Thames because he had been for a time a Thames waterman as well as a producer of vast quantities of bad verse, "bows" with a certain "majesty"; the playwright Shadwell, who had died of an overdose of opium and here wears on his brows a circlet not of bay but of poppy, "nods" as a sleepy monarch might nod, with authority as well as ennui; and Milbourne, though Pope disliked him intensely for his treatment of Dryden (he lived till 1720 and may have been known to Pope), is imagined showing Eusden a well-meant even if ironically undercut generosity. There is ridicule of the trio throughout the passage, but one looks in vain for spite.

The second book ends with a contest in which the object is to stay awake while the verse and prose of two exceptionally prolific dunces are read aloud. There are no winners. But the new king, himself now somnolent on Dulness's lap following the severe exertion of watching the day's celebrations, experiences a dream. In his dream the ghost of his predecessor on the throne, the City Poet Elkanah Settle, long in charge of Lord Mayors' pageants and other catchpenny entertainments (germs, as Pope sees it, of the skits and pantomines that Tibbald was currently composing for the theater manager John Rich in the West End) accosts him and leads him to a mountain top. From there, like Moses, Aeneas, and Adam in *Paradise Lost*, viewing the panorama of past, present, and future, he sees the everwidening, more and more westerly expanses over which Dulness has now established her own *matrocinium*. Throughout, it is Settle who speaks:

> "Old scenes of glory, times long cast behind,
> Shall first recall'd, rush forward to thy mind;
> Then stretch thy sight o'er all her rising reign,
> And let the past and future fire thy brain."

> (3: 55–58)

In the Orient, where learning had its origins, an emperor burns the imperial library that there may be no learning beyond what dates from his reign (ll. 65–70). In the South, the expansionist Muslim caliphate fires the library of the Ptolemies, whose inscription was *Medicina Animae*—"Healing for the Soul" (ll. 71–74). Meantime, the barbarians of the North sweep down upon the Roman empire, in lines that bring vividly home the fragility of all civilizations, though our own invaders may arrive somewhat more impersonally by fission or fusion:

> "How little, see! that portion of the ball,
> Where faint at best the beams of Science [learning] fall.
> Soon as they dawn, from *Hyperborean* skies,
> In dulness strong, th' avenging Vandals rise!
> Lo where *Maeotis* sleeps, and hardly flows
> The freezing *Tanais* thro' a waste of snows,
> The North by myriads pours her mighty sons,
> Great Nurse of *Goths*, of *Alans*, and of *Huns*.
> See *Alaric's* stern port, the martial frame
> Of *Genseric*! and *Attila's* dread name!
> See! the bold *Ostrogoths* on *Latium* fall;
> See! the fierce *Visigoths* on *Spain* and *Gaul*."

Even in Rome itself, as her emperors become converts to a new faith, the arts fall victim as relics of past heresy:

> Lo *Rome* herself, proud mistress now no more
> Of arts, but thund'ring against *Heathen* lore;
> Her gray-hair'd Synods damning books unread,
> And *Bacon* trembling for his brazen Head;★
> Lo statues, temples, theatres o'erturn'd,
> Oh glorious ruin! and [Apelles] burn'd.
>
> (3: 93–98)

The change, alas, does not make for fewer wars—in Britain, wars even about the correct dating of Easter:

> See'st thou an *Isle*, by Palmers, Pilgrims trod,
> Men bearded, bald, cowl'd, uncowl'd, shod, unshod,
> Peel'd, patch'd, and pieball'd, linsey-woolsey brothers,
> Grave mummers, sleeveless some, and shirtless others.
> That once was *Britain*—Happy! had she seen
> No fiercer sons, had *Easter* never been.
>
> (3: 99–104)

★ Referring possibly to Roger Bacon's brazen defiance of the prevailing attitudes in carrying on scientific experimentation as well as to the result attributed to it in later legend: a brazen head that talked.

But now all points to an unresisted fruition: for

> see [!] my son, the hour is on its way,
> That lifts our Goddess to imperial sway:
> This fav'rite Isle, long sever'd from her reign,
> Dove-like, she gathers to her wings again.

(3: 109–12)

There follows at this point a long muster of the Goddess's chief champions—all of it biting, much of it funny—after which Settle, like God the Father in Milton and Flecknoe in *MacFlecknoe*, announces the successor Son, foretold in ancient prophecies, who will reconstitute Dulness's Golden Age and maintain her rule *in saecula saeculorum*:

> This, this is He, foretold by ancient rhymes,
> Th' *Augustus* born to bring *Saturnian* times!
> Beneath his reign, shall E[usde]n wear the bays,
> C[ibbe]r preside, Lord Chancellor of Plays,
> B[enson] sole Judge of Architecture sit,
> And A[mbros]e P[hilip]s be preferr'd for Wit! . . .
>   Then, when these signs declare the mighty Year;★
> When the dull Stars roll round, and re-appear;
> *Let there be darkness*! (the dread pow'r shall say)
> All shall be darkness, as it ne'er were Day;
> To their first Chaos Wit's vain works shall fall,
> And universal Dulness cover all!

(3: 269–74, 279–84)

Though this conclusion will become far grander—sublime, some will call it—in later versions of the poem, one notices that its curious shudder of comic terror is already in place. The entropy that matters, as Pope and the Scriblerians knew in their very bones, is entropy of imagination.

"Beyond the range of horses' asses"

Publishing the *Dunciad* was in many ways the greatest folly of Pope's life. Though it was already a masterpiece of sorts and would metamorphose through successive stages over a period of fifteen

---

★ The *Annus Magnus* or period of time within which the constellations return to their first stations and all begins anew.

years into one of the most challenging and distinctive works in the history of English poetry (a kind of luxuriant late flowering of certain Renaissance traditions and values in the face of the crescent edge that was to prove to be Romanticism), it bore bitter fruit. It brought the poet in his own time the hostility of its victims and their sympathizers, who pursued him implacably from then on with a few damaging truths and a host of slanders and lies; while in later times, it brought the severe disapprobation of all who judge personal satire, caricature, and ridicule inappropriate vehicles of high art, whether on moral or esthetic grounds. During two and a half centuries of an equally brilliant but very different poetry, woven largely of explorations of the self and for the most part astonishingly impervious to social or political concerns, the number of disapprovers has proved to be great, and Pope's reputation has suffered, still in fact suffers. What can possibly have impelled him to do what he did?

Sheer arrogance in part, we may guess. An implication that he and his friends enjoyed something like a monopoly of literary genius begins to poke up disconcertingly at about this time in the letters of the group, especially those of Pope and Bolingbroke;

> I know nothing that moves strongly but Satire, and those who are asham'd of nothing else, are so of being ridiculous. I fancy if we three [Pope, Swift, and Bolingbroke] were together but for three years, some good might be done even upon this Age; or at least some punishment made effectual, toward the Example of posterity, between History, Philosophy [Swift was at work on *The Four Last Years of the Queen*, Bolingbroke busy in historical and theological study], and Poetry, or the Devil's in it. Nay, and I think 'tis all among ourselves; at least, I yet see none likely to dispute it with us.

The attitude has much to do, one suspects, with the disappointments befallen the group since they started out so propitiously together in Anne's time; with the need to keep up morale through fantasies of triumphant vindication by posterity; and with that "saving-remnant" syndrome which has so often throughout history stiffened the spines of men and women who either were or perceived themselves to be repositories of some variety of "true faith." In Pope, who happens to be the author of the above sentences, it may have stemmed also from the usual compulsion of men who are physically very small to take up a compensating posture of reckless courage. Whatever the explanation, it is not a particularly ingratiating frame of mind, even when expressed jocosely, as it was in Pope's manuscript epigraph for the poem, happily canceled. For this position he intended originally a

Fronti Fides

MARTINI SCRIBLERI VERA EFFIGIES

Ad origin: delin: G.D.   *Herman Van Kruys sculp.*

57. Martini Scribleri Vera Effigies. Delin[eavi]t G. D. Herman Van Kruys sculp[sit]. Frontispiece to *Pope Alexander's Supremacy and Infallibility Examin'd* (1729), a pamphlet attack evoked by the Dunciad *Variorum.*

"G. D." may be Pope's long-standing enemy, George Duckett, co-author of the proposed *The Hump Conference,* later retitled *Homerides,* in 1715. Above, p. 277. The design manifestly exploits the traditional association of simians with imitation (Pope as imitator of the ancients in his work and as a poor imitation of a man in his body), but may refer also to his signature in the form to which his enemies customarily abbreviated it: "A. P—E."

stanza of Spenser's *Faerie Queene* (1.1.23) in which the Red Cross Knight battling Error's viperous offspring is compared to a "gentle Shepheard in sweete even-tide" brushing away a cloud of stinging gnats. Pope as Red Cross Knight, or even as shepherd brushing away gnats with (as the stanza has it) "clownish" hands, would have offered his enemies an opening not so deep as a well, perhaps, nor so wide as a church door, but enough.

But if there was arrogance, there was also legitimate resentment. Whatever else the poem might be, it was a determined effort to settle scores with a mob of scribblers (many of them unknown to him personally and hostile from no discernible motive except envy) who had made bold to sneer at him in print for nearly twenty years. The attacks of a few he had himself provoked, as by his ill-advised lines on Dennis in the *Essay on Criticism* and the emetic administered to Curll. Once attacked, moreover—his *Narrative of Dr. Robert Norris* on Dennis's madness is a case in point—he had by no means invariably held his peace. Still, until 1728, he could rightly feel that he had been far more sinned against than sinning. His shape, his parents, his politics, his religion, and his character—one or other or all—had been year after year crudely and cruelly attacked. So, very often, had his friends, Swift, Gay, and Arbuthnot in particular, and Martha Blount. So had all writings of his that found their way to press. Though these last were fair game for critics, as he was himself the first to admit (and, besides, had been admiringly received by the great majority of readers), the continual nitpicking meanness of the published censurers of his work and their determined denial that merit of any sort could be found in it was bound to rub hard at any author's pride.

Only once during this entire period did any of Pope's writings receive what might be called an appraisal without prejudice. This was in *An Essay on Pope's Odyssey*, published in two parts in 1726 and 1727 by the young Oxonian Joseph Spence, in whom, to quote Johnson, "Pope had the first"—and, we may add, during his lifetime his last—"experience of a critick without malevolence, who thought it as much his duty to display beauties as expose faults; who censured with respect, and praised with alacrity." The criticism, as Spence described it himself many years later after Pope's death, when a possible life of Pope was under discussion, was by no means perfunctory:

I don't know whether it may be worth while to mention that Mr Pope's friendship for me, (wch was continu'd, without any the least interruption, for 18 years,) began on my writing a Criticism, against him. T'was not perhaps so very ill-natur'd as Criticisms had generally usd to be; but still was blunt, & rough enough, in many places.

Spence's memory did not deceive him. Though he had gone out of his way to acknowledge Pope's genius, the passages he arraigns in his first volume considerably outnumber those he praises; and despite the fact that the manuscript of the second was communicated to the poet for his perusal and correction, the proportion of praise to blame in that volume is not radically different. What the manuscript shows is that Spence sometimes softened or curtailed his censure of individual passages in response to Pope's citation of evidence in support of his (or his collaborators') rendering, or, more rarely, in response to a *mea culpa* and a plea for mercy—e.g., "these are great faults, pray don't point 'em out, but spare yr Servant" [Spence did]; or "This is bad indeed" [Spence didn't]. Yet in no substantial way did the critic relax his insistence that the translation as a whole was too often decorative, overopulent, pompous, on the one hand, or, on the other, in many places too low and too lame. The following passage, preceded and succeeded by specific quotations from several books of the transla-tion, is typical of the strictures that Pope accepted without a quibble, coming as they did from a qualified judge with no axe to grind:

> A little or pretty thought dress'd up in grand words, is like the Cupid, in one of Coypel's pieces, who is crept into Mars's armour, and looks as if he was endeavouring to strut about in it: whilst a great thought in little words, puts one in mind of that tall gentleman we saw one night at the masquerade, dress'd like an infant; and dangling its hands, as if it were perfectly helpless.

Not only did Pope take censures of this kind without a quibble: he sought out their young author and made him a lifelong confidant and friend. Though he was sometimes vengeful and could hate with the best, the stereotype that he was a monster of spleen, or decidedly unlike the rest of us, it is time we outgrew.

The mix of wounded vanity and frayed patience, infused with exuberant comic energy, that produced the 1728 *Dunciad* held other ingredients that come more clearly to the fore in the *Dunciad Variorum* of the following year. In this redaction, though he enlarged the poem itself by less than a hundred lines, Pope incorporated all the parapher-nalia required to make the book a parody of a typical eighteenth-century learned edition of a classical literary text. The new version, he wrote Swift, was to be presented "in all pomp," not only with the dedication to Swift made public, but with "Proeme, Prolegomena, Testimonia Scriptorum, Index Authorum, and Notes Variorum"—not to mention six appendices and a short bibliography of "All our Author's Genuine Works." When it appeared, still anonymous though everyone now knew the author, it was a work of substance in a small-quarto format with pages more than twice the size of those in 1728 and more than twice as many of them, all bristling with notes by that early Scriblerian invention, Martinus Scriblerus, who raises quite unawares on every imaginable occasion Montaigne's famous question, "Whereto serveth learning, if understanding be not joyned to it?"

In part, of course, this travesty drew inspiration from Pope's anger at being shown up for the untrained textualist he was; in part, too, from a pardonable distaste for the elaborate self-glorifying monument of learned lumber under which in *Shakespeare Restored* Theobald had all but buried the genuine lights he could shed on perplexing passages. But other yeasts were at work as well. It is as impossible to read through the drolly ironical notes of the *Dunciad Variorum* as it is to recall certain passages of the *Essay on Criticism* or of *The Art of Sinking in Poetry* without remarking the uneasy (not to say scornful) mistrust which has traditionally divided the artist of whatever persuasion—painter, poet, dancer, musician—from the professional scholar or critic in the same field, no matter how "professional" in his own outlook that same artist may be. A gifted poet of our own day, himself a professor of literature, attended not long since a session of papers on Swift delivered at an annual meeting of a professional scholarly association. After it, he wrote a poem. The commentaries it reacts to may have been good, bad, or indifferent—no matter. For the poet, there had been something terribly missing in that room, which his poem undertakes to restore (later, the poet sent the poem to a friend, also an English professor who had been at the meeting, inscribed in a book of Swift's poetry).

> I promised once if I got hold of
> This book I'd send it on to you.
> These are the songs that Roethke told of,
> The curious music loved by few.
> I think of lanes in Laracor
> Where Brinsley MacNamara wrote
> His lovely elegy, before
> The Yahoos got the Dean by rote.

Only, when Swift-men are all gone
Back to their chosen fields by train
And the drunk Chairman snores alone,
Swift is alive in secret, Wayne:
Singing for Stella's happiest day,
Charming a charming man, John Gay,
And greeting, now their bones are lost,
Pope's beautiful, electric ghost. .

Here are some songs he lived in, kept
Secret from almost everyone
And laid away, while Stella slept,
Before he slept, and died, alone.
Gently, listen, the great shade passes,
Magnificent, who still can bear,
Beyond the range of horses' asses,
Nobilities, light, light and air.

In its own backhanded ironic way, the *Dunciad Variorum* also reminds us of nobilities, and light, and light and air.

A further general concern, likewise not peculiar to Pope, which the *Dunciad Variorum* pricked out in bold letters for its readers was the alarming spread in that time of what we nowadays call literary consumerism. This phenomenon is so imbedded in our own culture it hardly occurs to us to be surprised that most books today, even very good ones, are headed for a shelf life "shorter than that of the hardier vegetables" (to quote from a current comment on the publishing scene), and in consequence, as some of our more thoughtful observers have been warning us, what we like to think of as the American character, or even our own individual characters, run a serious danger of becoming lost in an ever enlarging wilderness of miscellaneous subjectivity, overgrowing us from all sides as a jungle overgrows a pillar. In Pope's time, this situation was on its way. The Gutenberg age, though not yet in full flower, was well-budded; and the steady growth of London, together with some slight increase of literacy in the population and a marked decline (so it was perceived by many at the time, and to an extent it was true) in the standards of connoisseurship and patronage set by the court and the ministry of Walpole, was bringing about as fast as could be reasonably expected what Johnson would call an Age of Authors, meaning an age of hacks.

It is not now, as in former times, when men studied long, and passed through the severities of discipline, and the probation of publick trials, before they presumed to think themselves qualified for instructers of their countrymen; there is found a nearer way to fame and erudition, and the inclosures of literature are thrown open to every man whom idleness disposes to loiter, or whom pride inclines to set himself in view.

Just so, some twenty-seven years earlier, Pope had put it himself in the *Dunciad Variorum*, speaking of the author of that poem through the person of Scriblerus its editor. "He lived in those days, when (after Providence had permitted the Invention of Printing as a scourge for the Sins of the learned) Paper also became so cheap, and printers so numerous, that a deluge of authors cover'd the land: Whereby not only the peace of the honest unwriting subject was daily molested, but unmerciful demands were made of his applause, yea of his money, by such as would neither earn the one, or deserve the other." Writing had, in fact, become the last resort of "the shifty, needy, and incompetent"—the judgment is not Pope's, but that of a twentieth-century historian of the book trade in those times. And while Pope undoubtedly meant his association of duncery and poverty in the poem and its notes to insult and annoy those who had annoyed and insulted him, there was real truth in his insistence that in general the dunces had made love to failure by neglecting their proper talents in favor of activities for which they had no genuine gift.

"Fragments, not a Meal"

Many of Pope's deepest feelings, however, as expressed in the notes variorum and other learned parodies of the 1729 *Dunciad*, had much longer roots. They sprang from a controversy that had been going on since the Renaissance but had recently entered a new phase: the so-called Quarrel of the Ancients and Moderns. By the close of the seventeenth century, it was acknowledged in most quarters, despite some pockets of resistance in writers like Swift and his then employer, Sir William Temple, that, in the fields we now call scientific, contemporary learning had advanced far beyond anything to be found among the ancients. In the area of the arts and literature, on the other hand, except by some rhapsodists in France, where a puff for the contemporary was a way of flattering the age of Louis Le Grand, the highest achievements of the ancients were usually conceded to be unsurpassed, even by those who were in sympathy "moderns."

It was at about this time that a new antagonism arose from the embers of the old. The dispute now was not about the value of ancient texts, but to what use they should be put. Traditionalists, far the most numerous group, saw in the literary culture of the classics the fountainhead of a responsible cosmopolitan education: affording knowledge of the world, teaching the principles of good and bad governance, delineating the expectable powers, limits, and temptations of human nature, civilizing the passions and refining the manners, and (in the old sense in which historical and literary studies were held to be, essentially, philosophy teaching by example) supplying guidance for the conduct of life. The third Earl of Shaftesbury had summed up the position succinctly if smugly in declaring:

> A good Poet, and an honest Historian, may afford Learning enough for *a Gentleman* [not yet, it should be recalled, a term of reprobation]. And such a one, whilst he reads these Authors as his Diversion, will have a truer relish of their Sense, and understand 'em better, than a Pedant with all his Labours, and the assistance of his Volumes of Commentators.

On the other side of this question (actually, of course, there were not many on either side who took an extreme or unmixed position) stood the practitioners of a comparatively new form of philological learning and antiquarian research. In the long run, their approach to ancient culture would diversify into the technical studies we know today as palaeography, epigraphy, papyrology, numismatology, archaeology, and many more. Gradually, through the next two centuries, they would open up aspects of the ancient world, including many glimpses of its underside and backside, that contrasted disconcertingly with the view from the rather limited but much loved educational preserve that a long line of sixteenth- and seventeenth-century humanists and schoolmasters had carved out of the ancient authors, particularly the Romans. The main thrust of the new classicism during Pope's time, however, was aimed at rectifying corrupt and unintelligible passages in the ancient texts, a process that began early to be called "verbal criticism." Its tools, understandably, were learned commentaries on Roman or Greek manuscripts, monuments, inscriptions, coins; dictionaries, grammars, and indexes; interminable footnotes; and frequent collections of proposed emendations of difficult readings up and down the length and breadth of Greek and Latin literature unaccompanied by any whole texts. All of this, at the time, tended to identify these new labors with dismemberment rather than restoration, with bits and pieces instead of wholes. Or, as Pope would eventually say in his final *Dunciad* through the mouth of a leader of this new school and naming three of his collaborators:

> In ancient Sense if any needs will deal,
> Be sure I give them Fragments, not a Meal;
> What Gellius or Stobæus hash'd before,
> Or chew'd by blind old Scholiasts o'er and o'er.
> The critic Eye [of "verbal criticism"], that microscope of Wit,
> Sees hairs and pores, examines bit by bit:
> How parts relate to parts, or they to whole,
> The body's harmony, the beaming soul,
> Are things which Kuster, Burman, Wasse shall see,
> When Man's whole frame is obvious to a *Flea*.
>
> (4: 229–38)

The last line contains more than a casual insult. Since it was a favorite theological argument of the day that it was as absurd for human beings to imagine imperfections in a God-created cosmos from their obviously limited point of vantage as it would be for flies or fleas to pontificate about the human (or any other) frame from their equally limited purview, the line insinuates that "a love to parts," as Pope had called it in his *Essay on Criticism*, threatens one's capacity to grasp wholes in every department of experience.

Pope's speaker in the foregoing lines is Richard Bentley, not only the ablest English classicist of his time and one of the great classical scholars of all time, but in the skills of verbal criticism an undisputed master. The lines first appeared in print in the fourth book of the *Dunciad*, published by itself in 1742 before being incorporated into the revised poem in four books the following year; but manuscript evidence suggests that this or an equivalent passage was originally planned for the *Dunciad Variorum*. By 1729, for all the depth and range of his erudition and the razor-sharp analytical powers of his mind, Bentley had become in the public view something between a fool and a boor. Not—it is sad to have to add—without grounds.

In 1699, he had been appointed Master of Trinity College, Cambridge, and very soon established such an arbitrary despotism over his colleagues that for thirty years Master and Fellows were at odds and frequently in litigation. In 1717, by a slippery maneuver he helped vote himself into the Regius Professorship of Divinity, with a handsome stipend, while retaining the Mastership of Trinity in defiance of a statute expressly forbidding the Regius Professor to hold other office. This he capped the same year by extorting from newly created honorary Doctors of Divinity four guineas each for his own

58. Richard Bentley (1662–1742). Engraved after Sir James Thornhill, 1710.

"Roman and Greek Grammarians! know your Better."

Dunciad, 4: 215.

Courtesy of the National Portrait Gallery, London.

pocket, and when in consequence the Vice-Chancellor's Court deprived him of his degrees (D.D., M.A., B.A.) he brought an action against the university to recover, which, this time, he rightly won. Eventually, in 1734, after exhausting every imaginable ruse and delaying tactic, he was found guilty of misuse of college property and violation of college statutes. But the sentence, loss of the Mastership, was never carried out. The deprivation had to be executed by the college's Vice-Master, and the Vice-Master, Richard Walker, a Bentley satellite—had he not been he could not have survived in the Vice-Mastership—refused to undertake it. For eight more years, Bentley continued to "Master" Trinity College even after he had been legally deprived. A formidable man!

The temperamental details are worth stressing because they help explain some of the characteristics of verbal criticism as Bentley—and, in his shadow, Lewis Theobald—practiced it. Bentley's favorite subject, it seemed to many of his contemporaries and not merely those hostile to him, was himself, even in his most learned works. He was given to remarking on his cleverness in having reached a particular emendation or reconstruction. He liked to indulge in sarcasms on the ignorance of his predecessors and even of his day-to-day associates—being rather too apt, as his biographer remarks, to try to efface or expunge those who differed from him as if they were inferior readings in a bad manuscript. And he did not hesitate to present himself as endowed with powers of textual divination which in his own view entirely equalled (thus foreshadowing a habit of mind fashionable in some quarters in the 1980s), if indeed they did not surpass, whatever art or genius might have been possessed by the poet on whom he was then commenting. So intoxicating, indeed, were the sensations stirred among its devotees by this new form of criticism that as early as 1694 Bentley's mild-mannered friend, the Reverend William Wotton, a thoughtful man, addicted but not mindlessly to modernist positions on all fronts, could speak of it with a solemn wonder hardly to be credited:

There are Thousands of Corrections and Censures upon Authors to be found in the Annotations of Modern Critics which required more Fineness of Thought, and Happiness of Invention, than, perhaps, twenty such Volumes as those were, upon which these very Criticisms were made [and] . . . which often raise a judicious Critic as much above the Author upon whom he tries his Skill, as he that discerns another Man's Thoughts, is therein greater than he that thinks.

It was, of course, complacencies like these in the emendatory school that most infuriated. Lofty condenscensions of critic to creator. Boastful claims that no man could consider himself educated unless he recognized even in the best ancient texts swarms of errors clamoring to be rectified. Assertions of undying "glory" and "honour"—surely an instance of Coypel's Cupid creeping about in armor too big for him—to be won by restoring "Sense" to even a single ancient sentence, especially if done by altering only a letter or two (as in Theobald's unnecessary and quite wrong emendation of the purgatorial punishment of the ghost in *Hamlet* from "confin'd to fast in fires" to "confin'd to roast in fires"). Above all, a peremptory self-assurance expressed in brassy tones. Though savagely unfair, Swift's portrait of Bentley in his *Battle of the Books* captures vividly the characteristics of the man and his school as a hostile eye saw them. A captain of the Moderns, he wears armor "patch'd up of a thousand incoherent Pieces" and a helmet whose visor is "Brass." He attributes the successes of the Ancients in the battle so far to the stupidity of the generals on his own side, who—"with great Submission"—he allows are "all a Pack of *Rogues*, and *Fools*, and *Son's of Whores*, . . . and *confounded Loggerheads*, and *illiterate Whelps*, and *nonsensical Scoundrels*"—Swift's version of Bentley's style in controversy. He is then faced down by one of these same generals, who details the effects that *ought* to emanate from humane studies but from Bentley's have not: sure proof that his way of dealing with them is wrong:

> *Miscreant* Prater, said he, *Eloquent only in thine own Eyes,* . . . *Thy* Learning *makes thee more* Barbarous, *thy Study of* Humanity, *more* Inhuman; *Thy* Converse *amongst Poets more* groveling, miry, *and* dull. *All Arts of* civilizing *others,* render *thee* rude *and* untractable; Courts [Bentley was Royal Librarian and had rooms in St. James's] have *taught thee* ill Manners, *and* polite Conversation *has finished thee a* Pedant.

Hence contemporary resistance to the new school of criticism arose not simply, or even mainly, as has sometimes been proposed, from the pique of individuals shaken up by it, as Pope had been shaken up by Theobald's *Shakespeare Restored* or Temple by Bentley's *Dissertation on the Letters of Phalaris*, which showed what Temple had assumed were among the oldest surviving pieces of ancient prose to be a forgery of some six or seven hundred years later. The best part of a century would have to go by before the harvest of Bentley's labors could be set free of its chaff and his own personality, and the man be recognized for the genius he was. In the meantime, what most of his contemporaries saw was a patronizing self-congratulatory manner, carried even to the pedantry of claiming he had thought independently of improvements in which others had anticipated him: a manner and claim found equally in *Shakespeare Restored*, where most of Bentley's habits, including that of burying the point at issue in a catacomb of citations, are systematically aped. What they also saw in Bentley and his followers were disturbing violations of sound textual procedures in men who professed to be infallible. In his edition of Terence, for example, published in 1726, the same year with *Shakespeare Restored*, Bentley offered by his own proud count a thousand emendations for six surviving plays. Since Bentley never touched anything that he did not in some degree adorn, a certain number of these broke new ground by reason of his imperfect but yet pioneering grasp of Latin dramatic meters; the rest, however, were simply the result of preferring his own taste to Terence's. His edition of Horace, fifteen years earlier, had created yet more of a scandal. Here, in what was already one of the soundest classical texts the eighteenth century possessed, he interpolated (no tentative marginal proposals for him!) well over seven hundred conjectures, guided almost entirely by his critical "intuition," which supplied him, he said, with more, and more reliable, improvements than the manuscripts.

Small wonder that men of learning as well as educated readers were shocked. As Broome complained vigorously in the preface to his *Poems* of 1727, with reference, one presumes, to both the Horace and Theobald's recent conjectural rampage in *Shakespeare Restored*:

> The question is not what the Author might have said, but what he has actually said; . . . not whether a different Word will agree with the sense and turn of the Period, but whether it was used by the Author. If it was, it has a good Title still to maintain its post, and the authority of the Manuscript ought to be followed rather than the fancy of the Editor.

Small wonder, too, that verbal criticism was seized on by Pope in the *Dunciad Variorum* as the best possible background music to his induction of appropriate offenders into the chivalric order of duncehood. It is an obbligato that sometimes makes itself heard with an all but serious urgency:

> Two things there are, upon which the very Basis of all verbal Criticism is founded and supported: The first, that the Author could never fail to use the very best word, on every occasion: The second, that the Critick cannot chuse but know, which it is. This

being granted, whenever any doth not fully content us, we take upon us to conclude, first that the author could never have us'd it, And secondly, that he must have used That very one which we conjecture in its stead.

More often, it is sounded in burlesque:

Book 1. Verse 8. *E'er Pallas issu'd from the Thund'rers head. E'er* is the contraction of *ever*, but that is by no means the sense in this place: Correct it, without the least scruple, *E're*, the contraction of *or-ere*, an old *English* word for *before*. What Ignorance of our mother tongue!

But it is kept prominent throughout. Announced vigorously in the poem's first annotation, it recurs often in the notes variorum, takes over even the *Errata* at the end, and, with particular attention to Bentley, branches out into variations in Appendix 4—a collection of absurd emendations to Vergil complete with notes in Bentleian Latin, of which the last concludes: "Reader, farewell! While you are making these little corrections, I'll be getting on with something important" (*Vale! dum haec paucula corriges, majus opus moveo*).

When we look back on all these alarums and excursions from our own point in the late twentieth century, certain conclusions emerge. The rearguard action that Pope and his friends, and many more, fought against the new dispensation was, in their time, partly a defense of that critical civility whose virtues he had made the climax of his *Essay on Criticism* nearly twenty years before: "Still *pleas'd* to *teach*, and yet not *proud* to *know*"; "Not *dully prepossest*, nor *blindly right*"; "Modestly bold, and Humanly severe" (ll. 632, 634, 636). Partly, too, it was a defense of critical flexibility and common sense, opposing both those who (in every age) freeze their subject matter into formulas and fashions—Pope had not spent time in his youth with Henry Cromwell for nothing—and those (to quote Broome again) who "make it the supreme business of life to repair the ruins of a decay'd Word." Johnson was forgetful when he asserted that it was only after and because of *Shakespeare Restored* that Pope became "an enemy to editors, collaters, commentators, and verbal criticks." Quite the reverse. An acute consciousness of the abuses and misuses of learning—its love of display, its power to magnify trifles, its marked tendency to ossify (even to "petrify a Genius to a Dunce")—suffuses much of his major work, from that moment in 1712 when he first proposed in the pages of *The Spectator* his mock *Account of the Works of the Unlearned*, on through the *Essay on Criticism*, the *Art of Sinking in Poetry*, the *Dunciads* of 1729, 1742, and 1743, and the *Memoirs* of that editor, collator, commentator, and verbal critic *par excellence*: Martinus Scriblerus.

It becomes equally apparent on looking back that Pope and his friends were on the wrong side, at least in one sense. So far as the thing they were battling to preserve was a classical mystique—a notion that into the history of essentially only two great peoples and two great literatures had been somehow gathered, as into the imagined inscription on Keats' urn, all that we know on earth and all we need to know, they were engaged in a losing fight and for mistaken ends. The additions to understanding that the new advances in the philological and other disciplines were bringing and would continue to bring did unquestionably threaten the claim of the classics to be the universally indispensable five-foot shelf. "To know Homer or Pythagoras too well," as a historian of this controversy has remarked,

> was to open a gulf that divided them from modern life, rather than identifying them with it. It was in the end to make them useless in any immediate practical fashion. Of what value was the teaching of a poet who sang his songs aloud to a group of tribal warriors whose manners and customs seemed closer to the American Indian [as the French critics in particular liked to point out] than to the eighteenth-century gentleman?

We have seen already to what straits Pope was sometimes driven in trying to give that question a reassuring answer. Once the new learning was fully in place (though this was not to happen in Pope's lifetime), such defensiveness would no longer be required. Homer's world and all the other inventions of ancient literature could then be valued for what they were as imaginative and historical artifacts, not as models for emulation in a myth created by the European Renaissance centuries after their own creation and probably first enunciated to the world in Petrarch's exclamation: "What is all history but the praise of Rome!"

But there was another side to this coin. Bentley and his followers were right that knowledge, being cumulative, can never be stayed to fit the needs of a particular group or time. For this reason, their contributions, even most of Bentley's, have long been absorbed into the working stock of classical philology or whatever other discipline may be concerned, and their books accordingly, as Pope says of the Scotists and Thomists in the *Essay on Criticism*, "now," for most readers, "in Peace remain, Amidst their *kindred Cobwebs* in *Duck-Lane*" (ll. 444–45). Swift's *Battle*, on the other hand, and the *Dunciad Variorum*, which in so many ways takes its cue from Swift, remain as lively today as when they were written, being not only works of art, which are never cumulative, but also true comic inventions, like the *commedia dell'arte* itself, in which the assigned roles never alter, only the assignees. As Pope chose to put it himself, "the *Poem was not made for these Authors, but these Authors for the Poem*: And I should judge they were clapp'd in as they rose, fresh and fresh, and chang'd from day to day, in like manner as when old boughs wither, we thrust new ones into the chimney." Looking over our own late twentieth-century scene, few would have trouble collecting replacements.

"Athanasius contra Mundum"

Readers today are sometimes tempted to view the figures of the *Dunciad* as they might view one of those village scenes common in Dutch painting—a crowd of what look like miniature men and women skating or dancing or simply scurrying to what seem to be a hundred different destinations, with here and there perhaps a small static group so absorbed in some transaction or entertainment as apparently to be oblivious of the rest. Parts of the poem might in this way remind us of a Brueghel. Some of its more grotesque touches might suggest a Bosch. Always—and this much was intentional on Pope's part—it will remind us of Milton's devils or fallen angels as they explore their new abode in hell or indulge in sports to pass the time while their great leader makes his foray to new-created Earth:

> Part on the Plain, or in the Air sublime
> Upon the wing, or in swift Race contend,
> As at th' Olympian Games or *Pythian* fields? . . .
> Others with vast *Typhoean* rage more fell
> Rend up both Rocks and Hills, and ride the Air
> In whirlwind; Hell scarce holds the wild uproar.
>
> (2: 528–30, 539–41)

London is afflicted with a similar problem during the dunces' epic noise-contest. The producers become indistinguishable from their product and individuals are reduced to decibels—

> 'Twas chatt'ring, grinning, mouthing, jabb'ring all,
> And Noise and Norton, Brangling and Breval,
> Dennis and Dissonance—
>
> (2: 229–31)

until at last the din (representing, as Johnson said, the new literature that required no severities of discipline or probation of public trials) has penetrated with its echoes and reechoes the whole metropolis west of Chancery Lane.

To indulge in such comparisons is, of course, to acknowledge fictionality. As twentieth-century readers of historical plays and novels soon become acutely conscious, actual persons on entering a work of fiction forfeit something, perhaps much, of their historical reality and become subject to the needs and themes of the new world they have been placed in, like Joan of Arc, say, in Schiller's play about her, where (history be damned) she dies not at the stake but in battle. For modern readers of the *Dunciad*, too, owing to a similar effect of esthetic and temporal distance, there intervenes a recognizable even if sometimes tricky distinction between the figures who populate the poem and the live contemporaries or long-dead forefathers in Dulness's family tree upon whose names the poem bestows a gratuitous immortality. Obviously, Lewis Theobald is not Tibbald or, as the poet sometimes spells it (as if it couldn't really matter): Tibald, Tibalds, and Tibbalds. His library though esoteric, probably contained neither De Lyra (in "five vast Folio's," as Pope's note says) nor the complete works of the Duchess of Newcastle (in twelve!). And any hill from which one can view Dulness's expanding empire all the way from the Great Wall of China to Savoy House in the Strand is by definition as fictional as the view itself. Perhaps the nearest analogy, therefore, to Pope's manipulation of Theobald and the other dunces is the work of the political cartoonist. In *his* sketches of living figures, a salient trait or two is seized and magnified till it subsumes the entire personality, and the whole man or woman, like the Cheshire Cat in *Alice in Wonderland*, disappears into a cruel or stupid grin. We can see, when we examine the cartoon coolly, that its victim has been caught up in and made subsidiary to an idea, an indictment, a miniature drama. But we can see, too, that if we ourselves or any of our close friends or political heroes happen to be victimized, our detachment ebbs fast. A "true" self, as we like to imagine it, has been mutilated, shrunk; and if this happens to have taken place in a very funny cartoon called the *Dunciad*, one of the most effective shrinking machines ever invented, we are outraged.

Understandably, they were. Pope's half-sister Magdalen told Spence that after publishing the poem (and she might well have added, *The Art of Sinking in Poetry*) there was a period during which Pope never sallied forth (it was his habit to stroll upriver from time to time to visit the Fortescues at Richmond) except in the company of

Bounce, his Great Dane, and with pistols in his pocket. He may have been well advised. Already by 1 June 1728, in fact, hardly more than a fortnight after the first *Dunciad*'s appearance, the story circulated that two "Gentlemen" had met with him in Ham Walks (a then somewhat parklike area just across the Thames from Pope's house) and disciplined him severely. They had recognized him, of course, "partly by his back," whereupon one of the two had hoisted him on his own back, holding him there

> whilst the other drew out, from under his Coat, a long birchen Rod, (as we are inform'd made out of a Stable Broom) and . . . did . . . strike Master Pope so hard upon his naked Posteriors, that he voided large Quantities of Blood, which being yellow, one Dr. A[rbuthno]t his Physician, has since affirm'd, had a great Proportion of Gall mix'd with it, which occasion'd this said Colour.

Left "weltring," he was found by one "Mrs. B[lount] a good charitable Woman," who "took him in her Apron, and buttoning up his Breeches, carried him to the Waterside," where a boat was procured to take him home.

In view of Magdalen's testimony about Bounce and the pistols, the story is probably pure fiction, though it is worth noting that Pope took the trouble to repudiate it publicly on June 14 in *The Daily Post*. Perhaps he feared that, however fictional in this instance, the idea might catch on; more likely, he found its patronizing tone toward Martha as well as himself too humiliating to go unchallenged. In any event, the dunces kept up a paper war. At the end of two months, Lord Oxford was writing to Swift that "Pope stands by himself Athanasius Contra Mundum"—

> there is never a Newspaper comes out but he is favord with a letter, a poem and Epigram[,] even to a Distich[,] from the newmorous [probably Oxford's strained pun?] Herd of Dunces and Blockheads that are in and about London and the Suburbs thereof—

and Gay was lamenting from Amesbury, where he now spent most of his time with the Queensberrys, that any word he gets of Pope these days is from advertisements in the newspapers,

> by which one wou'd think the race of Curl[l]s was multiplied; and by the indignation such fellows show against you, that you have more merit than any body alive could have. Homer himself hath not been worse us'd by the French. I am to tell you that the Duchess . . . is always inclin'd to like any thing you do; that Mr. Congreve

admires, with me, your fortitude; and loves, not envys your performance, for we are not Dunces.

If there is a hint of wonderment in both these comments that Pope should have lavished so much poetic energy in chastising (mainly) nonentities—and nonentities at that who had access to publishers—the wonderment must have sometimes been shared by the poet himself. For now all the old canards came circling back to light upon his head and hang about his neck. He was a Jacobite, a traitor, a plagiary, a defrauder of the public, a would-be despot. Here the long-hackneyed plays upon his name could be revived, as in *Pope Alexander's Supremacy and Infallibility Examin'd* (1729), whose engraved frontispiece shows the poet crouched over a stack of his own works and wearing a papal tiara. He was also, to be sure, a lump, a toad, a venomous spider, and a monkey dropping filth. In this last connection, since he usually signed himself "A. Pope," his names could be tortured into A-P-E; and, in the engraving above mentioned, his tiara-crowned head rests on a monkey's shape. His verse, it goes without saying, is mere singsong and jingle-jangle, his *Rape of the Lock* obscene, his burlesque of Sternhold and Hopkins blasphemous, his *Iliad* a travesty of the original because he knows no Greek, his Shakespeare a costly hoax, everything good in the *Odyssey* the product of collaborators. And now he has turned his poisonous pen on the poor souls who write for a living, by his very ridicule making it more difficult for them to find work!

Actually, to the extent that the poorer dunces ever made any money from their writings, mortgaged as they were to the booksellers (as Pope too might have been had he not had both the talent and the gumption to break free), the paper war generated by the *Dunciad* worked in their favor. For a period of three or four years, any squib let loose by a dunce against Pope had a guaranteed audience at least among the other dunces and among coffee-house literati who made it a point to know the latest tittle-tattle. Indeed, as one pamphleteer acknowledged during a later campaign against Pope,

> The more we rail, the more bespatter,
> 'Twill make our *Pamphlets* sell the better.

Pope's own unpardonable offense against the living dunces (many of whom had attacked him first) lay precisely in this area: *his* works always sold. A cripple, a papist, a betrayer of that model of virtue the great Addison, of whom in the Pope-Swift *Miscellanies* he had now released the portrait quoted in an earlier chapter (few knew at the

59. The PHIZ and CHARACTER of an *Alexandrine* Hyper-crick & Com-[m]entator. Artist and engraver unknown, though possibly those named in the variant of this design used for frontispiece to *Pope Alexander's Supremacy and Infallibility Examin'd* (above, p. 474). An earlier state of this engraving announces it is "Sold by the Print-sellers of London and Westminster," *c.* 1729.

Below the title, selections from Dryden and Lee's *Oedipus*, l. 1: 135–58, beginning: "Nature her self shrank back when thou wast born, / And cry'd the Work's not mine —" Below Dryden and Lee, four lines from Pope's *Iliad* describing the crippled Thersites (2: 257–8, 267–8). The earlier state has instead Psalm 36: 1–4.

time that the treachery lay the other way, and those who did weren't telling), this runt of a poetaster had made enough profit from his work to entertain noble friends and live like a gentleman in a Thames villa. Incredible. How account for it? Servility, flattery, knavery, malice! No dunce seems ever to have noticed that when Pope ridiculed them he sounded like this, even in his most ordinary vein—here he describes the mustering of troops for the final assault on Westminster:

> Jacob, the Scourge of Grammar, mark with awe,
> Nor less revere him, Blunderbuss of Law.★
> Lo Bond and Foxton, ev'ry nameless name,
> All crowd, who foremost shall be damn'd to Fame?
> Some strain in rhyme; the Muses, on their racks,
> Scream, like the winding of ten thousand Jacks:†
> Some free from rhyme or reason, rule or check,
> Break Priscian's head,‡ and Pegasus's neck;
> Down, down they larum, with impetuous whirl,
> The Pindars, and the Miltons, of a Curl[l].
> "Silence, ye Wolves! while Ralph to Cynthia howls,
> And makes Night hideous§—Answer him ye Owls!
> "Sense, speech, and measure, living tongues and dead,
> Let all give way—and Durgen¶ may be read."
>
> (3: 149–162)

Whereas when they attacked him, whether in verse or prose, it was mainly unrelieved invective:

> The Mind that inhabits his little Glass-case is like Assa foetida in a Thumb-bottle, or flat Vinegar in a broken Crewet; ill within, and worse without Doors: . . . his life is a Corrosive, that eats first on itself, then on other people; . . . His Bow, as his Back informs you, is too weak, and his Arrows too short and blunt for Execution, therefore he tips them with the native *Arsenic* of his own Malice.

★ Giles Jacob (1686–1744), like Theobald, had been trained as an attorney and was author of a law dictionary.
† A machine for turning the spit when roasting meat. Most jacks were wound up like clocks.
‡ I.e., violate grammar (Priscian was an early sixth-century grammarian).
§ With reference to an execrable poem by James Ralph (1705–62) entitled *Night*.
¶ An attack on Pope in answer to the 1728 *Dunciad* by Ned Ward (1667–1731), to which Pope now answers in the 1729 *Dunciad*.

> What he calls writing is his poisoning Paper and Reader; he lives on Scandal, like a Maggot on Putrefaction, or a Fly on Excrement.

However inured to this sort of thing Pope may have become by years of experience, the *Dunciad* aftermath cannot have been a happy time for him, the less so since it was his own imprudent effort to brush the gnats away that had brought them back in force with renewed stings and lavish droppings.

CHAPTER 20

A WIDER VIEW

"Consult the Genius of the Place in all"

An ordeal much worse was yet to come. For many years, Pope told his friend Lord Burlington in a letter of 4 April 1731, he had cherished the notion of leaving "some Testimony of my Esteem for your Lordship among my Writings." To this end, he had now composed an epistle to the Earl, which he enclosed, possibly for use in a new volume of Palladio's drawings that Burlington seems to have been planning at the time, but touching, in any case, on a variety of topics suited to "the Apollo of the Arts": building, landscaping, collecting, and the concern for "sense," "taste," and appropriate "use" that ought to govern in them all. To an extent, in other words, it was a poem on prodigality, destined in the long run to balance an epistle to Bathurst that would concern itself with avarice:

> 'Tis strange, the Miser should his Cares employ,
> To gain those Riches he can ne'er enjoy:
> Is it less strange, the Prodigal should waste
> His wealth, to purchase what he ne'er can taste?
> Not for himself he sees, or hears, or eats;
> Artists must chuse his Pictures, Music, Meats:
> He buys for Topham,★ Drawings and Designs,
> For Pembroke Statues, dirty Gods, and Coins;
> Rare monkish Manuscripts for Hearne alone,
> And Books for Mead, and Butterflies for Sloane.
> Think we all these are for himself? no more
> Than his fine Wife, alas! or finer Whore.
>
> (ll. 1–12)

"Collecting" as a status symbol has never been more accurately described.

Showing off, the epistle continues, is what gets people into

★ The persons named were all well-known connoisseurs and collectors. The prodigal buys "for" them in the sense that they can appreciate his acquisitions, as he cannot.

trouble. Throwing money at the problem won't save them. Taste may—but only if it keeps in vitalizing touch with "Sense":

> Good Sense, which only is the gift of Heav'n,
> And tho' no science, fairly worth the sev'n:
> A Light, which in yourself you must perceive;
> Jones and Le Nôtre have it not to give.
>
> (ll. 43–46)

In building and gardening, sense shows itself most surely in a concern to understand what the situation calls for: "Consult the Genius of the Place in all." If you do this respectfully, if you treat the landscape with the consideration taught by the classical and chthonic notion that every natural scene is informed by an indwelling "presence," all else will follow:

> That tells the Waters or to rise, or fall,
> Or helps th' ambitious Hill the heav'n to scale,
> Or scoops in circling theatres the Vale,
> Calls in the Country, catches opening glades,
> Joins willing woods, and varies shades from shades,
> Now breaks or now directs [makes straight], th' intending Lines;
> Paints as you plant, and, as you work, designs.
>
> (ll. 58–64)

Failing that, you will do everything wrong; and after a number of brief instances of this kind of disappointment, the epistle settles down on its prime example: Timon's villa. There everything is wrong because it exists for show:

> To compass this, his building is a Town,
> His pond an Ocean, his parterre a Down:
> Who but must laugh, the Master when he sees,
> A puny insect, shiv'ring at a breeze!
>
> (ll. 105–8)

Before the house, a basin into which two Cupids "squirt." Behind it, and to the north, a large lake that makes the wind's bite sharper. In the garden, boring symmetries ('Grove nods at grove, each Alley has a brother"—117), much topiary (always in Pope's view an assault on nature), and no play of water to support landscaping arrangements apparently intended to suggest attributes of sea and river.

Ostentation rules everywhere at Timon's villa. His library is not his in the sense that he possesses it by enjoying it: much of it consists of antiquarian items he has been told are valuable, the rest of wood painted to look like book backs. In his chapel, again, high fashion reigns, not worship. In music, something inappropriately jiggish. In the murals, scenes unintentionally or intentionally erotic. For sermon, an unctuous Dean who knows how his bread is buttered.

> And now the Chapel's silver bell you hear,
> That summons you to all the Pride of Pray'r:
> Light quirks of Musick, broken and uneven,
> Make the soul dance upon a Jig to Heaven.
> On painted Cielings you devoutly stare,
> Where sprawl the Saints of Verrio or Laguerre,
> On gilded clouds in fair expansion lie,
> And bring all Paradise★ before your eye.
> To rest, the Cushion and soft Dean invite,
> Who never mentions Hell to ears polite.
>
> (ll. 141–50)

The meal that follows—Pope here draws on one of the oldest of satiric themes, "the bad dinner"—becomes a kind of comic nightmare. The dining room is marble, so that every foot-scrape of the fifty servers grates. The meal is like a temple ceremonial: "A solemn Sacrifice, perform'd in state," with courses succeeding each other so fast there is hardly time to partake, let alone savor.

> In plenty starving, tantaliz'd in state,
> And complaisantly help'd to all I hate,
> Treated, caress'd, and tir'd, I take my leave,
> Sick of his civil Pride from Morn to Eve;
> I curse such lavish cost, and little skill,
> And swear no Day was ever past so ill.
>
> (ll. 163–68)

The sole compensations are the realization that all this expenditure (as we say today) at least makes jobs, and the conviction, which ran very deep in Pope and probably goes back to his years in Windsor Forest, that the natural world contains some sort of retributive and resuscitative power that will at last heal over its wounds as grass heals over a raw grave:

> Yet hence the Poor are cloath'd, the Hungry fed;
> Health to himself, and to his Infants bread
> The Lab'rer bears: What his [Timon's] hard Heart denies,
> His charitable Vanity supplies.

★ The word could carry a sexual meaning in Pope's time, as here.

> Another age shall see the golden Ear
> Imbrown the Slope, and nod on the Parterre,
> Deep Harvests bury all his pride has plann'd,
> And laughing Ceres re-assume the land.

(ll. 169–76)

In the end, the lines tell us (with a confidence that in this ecologically threatened time we may well envy), the land will be reappropriated. Harvests yellowing in the sun will replace the gold that is now wasted here. The sterility of the place and its way of life will be buried as if by an inundation of the sea. And a new scene will take shape—what used to be called a smiling or a laughing scene—in which the oldest of mysteries, whose Greek name is Ceres, continues to be consummated.

Though the *Epistle to Burlington* continues to a triumphant close, part of which we looked at earlier, it is only with Timon's villa we need be now concerned. That the whole conception is a composite fiction will be evident to those who have traveled much among English country houses. Some of Pope's more remarkable details, like the urinating Cupids at the entrance, the "gaping Tritons" in the dining-hall that "spew to wash your face," the pian-terreno study from which the owner greets his guests after a climb of ten terraces, not to mention the "Lake" and the ocean-sized "pond" in a terrain that elsewhere seems to be afflicted by total drought: the germ of these may have been planted by things actually seen or heard of but in their present form they are unlikely to have existed outside of Pope's imagination and were certainly never found at one location.

No matter for that. The poem had hardly issued from the presses (on 13 December 1731) when a scandalous charge rose like a rank mist from what seemed all quarters at once. Timon's villa, it was said, was actually "Cannons," the opulent Berkshire estate of James Brydges, first duke of Chandos, to whom, it was further charged, Pope was indebted for a gift of money variously quoted as £500 or £1,000. Typical ingratitude, typical meanness, typical turning on a friend—so clamored the dunces as with one voice. But Pope had anxieties more troubling. Chandos was only slightly known to Pope, who had never visited his estate, but was on very friendly terms with many of the poet's friends, Arbuthnot, Bathurst, and Bolingbroke among them, and particularly intimate with Burlington, to whom the poem was addressed. To him, therefore, the alleged satire on Chandos was bound to be acutely embarrassing, and Pope, after taking counsel with Burlington—"Either the whole Town then, or I, have lost our Senses; for nothing is so evident, to any one who can read the Language, either of English or Poetry, as that [the] Character of Timon is collected from twenty different absurditys and improprieties: & was never the Picture of any one Human Creature . . . I beg to know what are your Lordships sentiments, that I should do in this unaccountable affair?"—took to the public prints to repudiate the falsehood with all possible vigor:

> But the Application of it to the D. of Ch. is monstrous; to a Person who in *every particular* differs from it. 'Is his Garden crowded with *Walls*? Are his Trees cut into *Figures of Men*? Do his Basons want *Water*? Are there *ten steep Slopes* of his Terrass? Is he piqued about *Editions* of *Books*? Does he exclude all *Moderns* from his *Library*? Is the *Musick* of his Chappel bad, or *whimsical*, or *jiggish*? On the contrary, was it not the best composed in the nation, and most suited to grave Subjects; witness *Nicol[as] Haym*'s, and Mr. *Hendel*'s [Handel's] noble *Oratories* [Oratorios]? Has it the Pictures of naked Women in it? And did ever Dean Ch[et]w[oo]d preach his Courtly Sermons there?' I am sick of such Fool Applications.'

"This way of Satire is dangerous"

But the damage had been done. Though there is no sign that Pope's friends believed it, and though Chandos assured Pope by letter that he did not believe it either, the slander, like most slanders, was impossible to discredit with finality, since like every Great House in England "Cannons" had features that with a little stretching could be alleged to have been in Pope's mind. The duncyes had now shown what they had it in their power to do with any poem he might in future issue. And not the hack-writing dunces merely. If we may believe *A Master Key to Popery* (an ironical pamphlet Pope threw off at about this time but never published, proving by the same reasoning his enemies used that the poem attacked not merely Chandos but all of his closest friends), several persons in high places were implicated in the uproar, including several well known in court and ministry. From the evidence available, it is difficult to resist the conclusion that Pope came to feel the outcry had been "orchestrated." Certainly, it had taken hold with speed, been bruited widely (not in Rag Fair only, but at court) and shown a unanimity in identifying Timon that was little short of astounding. It would be a while, he warned in an open letter prefixed to the third edition of the poem, before he used an assumed name again:

A. Pr. a Plaisterer white washing & Bespattering   D. Taste
B. any Body that comes in his way   E. a standing Proof
C. not a Dukes Coach as appears by ye Crescent at one Corner   F. a Labourer

Price 6ᵈ

60. A retort to Pope's *Epistle to Burlington*, showing him "whitewashing" the Palladian gate of Burlington House, spattering all and sundry below, including the coach of the Duke of Chandos. Burlington himself (on the ladder with new mortar) and Kent, his protégé (towering above Raphael and Michelangelo on the roof) are as much the objects of the satire as Pope.

Privately owned.

This way of Satire is dangerous, as long as Slander rais'd by Fools of the lowest Rank, can find any Countenance from those of a Higher. . . . I will leave my Betters in the quiet Possession of their *Idols*, their *Groves*, and their *High-Places*; and change my Subject from their *Pride* to their *Meanness*, from their Vanities to their *Miseries*: And as the only certain way to avoid Misconstruction, to lessen Offence, and not to multiply ill-natur'd Applications, I may probably in my next make use of *Real* Names and not of Fictitious Ones.

Under the circumstances, a little bravado was pardonable. But nothing, as it turned out, could alter what had happened. A falsehood of considerable damage to his character had been pinned to him and, thanks to the credulity of Samuel Johnson, would be passed down from biographer to biographer well into our own time.

In Pope's own career, the Chandos affair was also something of a watershed. Unlikely to have played the decisive role alone, it may well have been among the last factors determining a change of attitude on his part toward the ministry and court. During the middle through late 1720s, owing to Fortescue's influence, Pope was to all appearances on reasonably good terms with Walpole, sometimes attended the Sunday dinners at his house in Chelsea, and if by any chance he *had* made an agreement with the minister for the protection of Charles Rackett, he kept the bargain. Thanks to Walpole, in turn, a copy of the *Dunciad Variorum* was officially received by the king on 12 March 1729, a favor that obviously helped legitimize the poem and enhanced its "social" prestige. Though a little hard to believe in view of George II's known views on literature, Arbuthnot assured Swift a week later that the king had even "perused" the book and pronounced its author "a very honest Man."

No peaceable accommodation could, however, be expected to last forever between interests so irreconcilable. There were too many grounds for Pope and his friends to be discontent with Walpole and he with them. He had shown no receptiveness to Swift's concerns about English treatment of Ireland or to his longing for transfer back across the Irish Sea. He had seen to it that nothing was offered Gay, by a government that paid out thousands in emoluments to hireling propagandists like Henley, beyond the post of Gentleman Usher to the Princess Louisa, aged two, when Gay was forty-two. This "honor" the poet had declined, endeavoring (in a letter it is a pity we do not have) "in the best manner I could, to make my excuses to her Majesty," who was, after all, the Princess's mother and might take offense. In the autumn of 1729, Walpole had also banned from performance *Polly*, Gay's sequel to the *Beggar's Opera*, which like the original, though a very poor second to it in quality, thrust hard at ministerial corruption. When some of Gay's titled sympathizers began a subscription for a printed edition, one of them, Kitty Hyde, Duchess of Queensberry, was exiled from the court for venturing to solicit subscribers within the sacred precincts of St. James's. A year later, not without some justification since he had his finger in every pie, Walpole was blamed when the Duke of Grafton, the Lord Chamberlain, was allowed (or encouraged?) to choose as successor in the laureateship to the alcoholic Eusden an author with no claims to poetic power whatever, Colley Cibber. As an immediate epigram ran, possibly by Pope,

> Tell, if you can, which did the worse,
> Caligula or Gr[afto]n's Gr[a]ce?
> That made a Consul of a Horse,
> And this a Laureate of an Ass.

On the other side, there were equal provocations. Though himself no reader of poems, Walpole must soon have been alerted to the possibility that "Dunce the second," in the poem he had with his own hand presented to the King, might refer as easily to a royal dunce as to Lewis Theobald. Further, when one of his many literary outriders (several publishers including Pope's enemy Curll and his supposed good friend Samuel Buckley were either by appointment or self-appointment among his gleaners and informers at various times) came upon and undoubtedly showed his master Swift's praise of Pope's independence in his *A Libel on D[octor] D[elany]*—

> Hail! happy *Pope*, whose gen'rous Mind,
> Detesting all the Statesmen kind,
> Contemning *Courts*, at *Courts* unseen,
> Refus'd the Visits of a Queen;
> A Soul with ev'ry Virtue fraught
> By *Sages*, *Priests*, or *Poets* taught;
> Whose Filial Piety excels
> Whatever *Grecian* Story tells:
> A Genius for all Stations fit,
> Whose *meanest Talent* is his Wit:
> His Heart too Great, though Fortune little,
> To lick a *Rascal Statesman*'s Spittle—

(ll. 71–82)

Walpole's "straightforward nature," as his biographer describes it, could only have been confirmed in the conviction that such men were incapable of doing as they were told.

At the time (early 1730), there had been as yet no public parting of the ways. Consequently, Pope found Swift's praise (which made him the occasion of insults to both the Queen and the First Minister) considerably disconcerting and wrote at once to Fortescue to put some distance between himself and it. It was one thing for an Irish national hero to pen such lines in Dublin, quite another to be their beneficiary and scapegoat as a papist living ten miles outside of London for a reason:

> I've had another Vexation [besides a violent cold], from the sight of a paper of verses said to be Dr Swift's, which has done more by praising me than all the Libels [of the dunces] could by abusing me, [that] Seriously troubled me: As indeed one indiscreet Friend can at any time hurt a man more than a hundred silly Enemies. I can hardly bring myself to think it his, or that it is possible his Head should be so giddy.

Still, he was beginning in his own letters of the period to take sly shots privately at Walpole, as his editor points out. Thus in what seems a kind of apology for his failure to gain government support for Gay, despite the influence that he might be imagined to wield through Fortescue or other friends, he writes no later than the following August:

> Dear Gay,—If my friendship were as effectual as it is sincere, you would be one of those people who would be vastly advantag'd and enrich'd by it. I ever honour'd those Popes who were most famous for Nepotism, 'tis a sign that the old fellows *loved Somebody.* ... And now I honour Sir *Robert Walpole*, for his extensive Bounty and Goodness to his private Friends and Relations [Walpole's use of government places for members of his family was notorious] But it vexes me to the heart when I reflect, that my friendship is so much less effectual than theirs; nay so utterly useless that it cannot give you any thing, not even a Dinner, at this distance.

In the midst of this generally worsening climate on both sides, one must wonder whether the two occasions during the summer of 1730 when Pope sought to wait upon Sir Robert, only (as he wrote Fortescue) to find him "ingaged," were the result of some coolness on the minister's part or merely coincidence. A year earlier, he had written Fortescue of his appeal to Sir Robert to ignore whatever falsehoods

61. A view in the gardens of Chiswick House. Drawing by Jacques Rigaud, *c.* 1730.
By kind permission of the Trustees of the Chatsworth Settlement. (Below, p. 753.)

might be spoken of him by Lady Mary Wortley Montagu (for their
relation had now come to this), and it is not at all unlikely that these
later requests for an audience had a similar or related objective. In
any event, when the great Chandos slander was initiated, Pope was
obviously angered that so many of its circulators were court and
ministry associates. For him, as suggested earlier, this may have
been the final piece of evidence that he could never, even with
Fortescue's loyal help, count on Walpole as a reliable friend.

Meantime, Walpole had his own piece of evidence from which to
draw analogous conclusions about Pope: his admiring friendship
with Henry St. John, Lord Bolingbroke. Under the latter's leadership, a loose coalition of Tories, disappointed Whigs, and (from
Walpole's point of view) young interlopers who imagined they
were political idealists was just beginning to press uncomfortably
on his most vulnerable spot: the corruption by which he firmed his
power.

"Superior to anything I have seen in human nature"

Bolingbroke is surely one of the most sparkling, puzzling, and controversial figures of the eighteenth century. Ten years older than Pope, born of an illustrious Wiltshire family divided between Cavaliers and Roundheads (his grandmother was the daughter of Cromwell's Chief Justice), he was educated either at Eton or at a dissenting academy (no one knows for sure), and then by two years on the Grand Tour (1698–1700). During this time he kept in close touch by letter with Sir William Trumbull, his "pattern," as he calls him in one letter, "Dear Patron, Master, and Friend," in another. Returning to England in 1700, he married, assumed in 1701 the family parliamentary seat at Wootton Bassett, and began the extraordinary career that took him to the post of Secretary of War (1704), then to one of the two Secretaryships of State (1710), made him a Viscount (1712) as well as a chief architect of the Peace of Utrecht (1713), and, finally, through his procrastinations and shillyshallyings about the Hanoverian Succession, left him an ousted minister (1714), vulnerable to the usual charges of high crimes and misdemeanors certain to be brought by the victorious Whigs and an angry new king. When he was warned by several friends, apparently including Marlborough, who had been one of his early heroes and whose protégé he had formerly been, that he might be in serious danger of his life, and when surrender of all his papers was demanded by the new Whig ministry in mid-March 1715, he panicked—as his by that time hated rival Robert Harley did not—and fled on the twenty-seventh of that month, disguised as a French ambassadorial servant, to safety across the Channel. A motion of impeachment carried against him unanimously on June 10 no doubt helped incline him to seek service with the Pretender, whose Secretary of State he was from July 1715 to March 1716: months, unfortunately, that included the '15, for whose failure he was with doubtful justice made scapegoat by many Jacobites, including his master James.

Pope, it seems reasonable to surmise, may have met Bolingbroke early through Trumbull. If not through him, then certainly a few years later through Parnell, Swift, or Arbuthnot, the latter two of whom, along with Prior, formed the literary phalanx within the Brothers Club, founded by Bolingbroke in 1711 for "The improvement of friendship, and the encouragement of letters." By early 1713, at any rate, Pope was sufficiently intimate with both Bolingbroke and Oxford to be chosen by Addison (as we saw earlier) to show them his *Cato* and assure them it was not a "party-play." Only two months, in

62. Henry St. John, Viscount Bolingbroke (1678–1751). Attributed to Jonathan Richardson, *c.* 1730–35?

> There *St. John* mingles with my friendly Bowl
> The feast of Reason and the Flow of Soul.
>
> *Imit. Hor., Sat.* II, i: 127–28.

Courtesy of the National Portrait Gallery, London.

fact, before Bolingbroke's flight to France, Pope records a few days' visit with him on a journey from London to Binfield, evidently at the Bucklebury estate in Berkshire that he had acquired through his marriage. What was talked about we have no way of guessing, but one suspects that it may have been on this occasion that the poet submitted the manuscript of the first volume of the *Iliad* translation to his friend and received permission to acknowledge in the Preface "That such a Genius as my Lord *Bolingbroke*, not more distinguished in the great Scenes of Business than in all the useful and entertaining Parts of Learning, has not refus'd to be the Critick of these Sheets, and the Patron of their Writer." Even at that moment, which was January 1715, such a tribute to a Tory minister already expelled from those "great Scenes" and under heavy suspicion (much of it, we now know, justified) of malfeasance in office would not have been exceptionally prudent. When actually it *was* published, more than ten weeks after Bolingbroke's flight to France, it seemed a bold statement indeed, as Swift was quick to point out—all the bolder coming from a papist. And since the printing-house practices of those days would have permitted that or any other page of the book to be canceled, revised, and reprinted a hundred times over in a period of ten weeks, the fact that no revision was made tells us something about Pope as well as about a devotion that was to last all his life.

Pope had many heroes. It seems to have been a requisite of his nature, and not simply of his size, that he look up to people: Trumbull, Swift, Arbuthnot, Jervas, the Harleys, Bathurst, Burlington, Peterborow; in the first years in London, Wycherley; in the last years of his life, Warburton. In a loose way and up to a point, one may even relate the complexion of certain poems to the influence of certain individuals, in addition to those bearing friends' names in their titles. Trumbull to *Windsor-Forest*, for example. Walsh, Wycherley, and Henry Cromwell to the *Essay on Criticism*. The Blount sisters and the Addison and Steele of the *Spectator* and *Tatler* to the *Rape of the Lock*. Martha Blount and Lady Mary Wortley Montagu to *Eloisa*. Swift to the two *Dunciads* of 1728–1729. Bolingbroke to the *Essay on Man* and, in some degree to the Horatian poems. Warburton to the final *Dunciads* of 1742–1743. It was Bolingbroke alone, however, who inspired in Pope an intensity of admiration almost uncanny. That lord, he told Spence, "is something superior to anything I have seen in human nature"; and when on another occasion Spence himself remarked: "I really think there is something in that great man which looks as if he was placed here by mistake," Pope replied (though we need not suppose the reply was unaccompanied by a smile):

There is so; and when the comet appeared to us a month or two ago
I had sometimes an imagination that it might possibly be come to
our world to carry him home, as a coach comes to one's door for
other visitors.

"People of real genius," the poet William Shenstone remarked later,
"have strong passions; people of strong passions have great par-
tialities; such as Mr. Pope for Lord Bolingbroke." It is an explanation
that will perhaps do as well as any.

Bolingbroke resettled in England in 1725. He had received the
royal pardon in 1723 and made a hurried visit at that time, almost
encountering in Boulogne, it will be remembered, Atterbury, who
was going into exile as he was coming out. But it was not till two
years more had passed that Parliament spelled out the conditions of
his stay, restoring his rights of property but withholding (which was
wormwood) both his title and his seat in the Lords—in other words,
all hope of participating in English politics from within. Walpole
was taking no chances. Not even Walpole, however, had he wished,
could have won reentry into parliamentary affairs for a minister who
had twice turned his coat (after the débâcle with the Pretender he had
immediately started negotiations with George I). Now, moreover,
though partly from self-interest, partly also from the detachment
distance gives, Bolingbroke had grasped clearly that there was no
future for the Tories, ever, till all connexions with the Stuarts had
been cut—connexions that Walpole, as we have seen, found sometimes indispensable when he needed literally to "scare up" support
against them. He was also groping his way toward the maverick
conviction that England's best future lay in a bipartisan government
of moderates from both parties under a common tie of loyalty to the
Hanoverian Succession. With a history of disloyalty and views as
uncongenial as these to Tory and Whig alike, Bolingbroke was lucky
to win his way back to England at all, and if Walpole, who detested
him, had been as firmly cemented in the favor of George I at this time
as he later was with George II and Queen Caroline, it is improbable he
would have succeeded.

Bolingbroke's old literary friends, of course—Pope, Swift, Gay,
Arbuthnot—were cognizant of his escape to the Pretender and of his
political views and ambitions generally, but quite insensible, it seems
clear, of the many darker shadows in his career and personality, a
disability that equally afflicted Walpole's friends and is probably to be
duplicated wherever friends of men in power or of men struggling to
be in power are found. What his literary friends saw—except that

now he had gained a greater maturity and breadth from his studies in philosophy, divinity, and history while in exile—was the spell-binder whom in 1711 Swift had pronounced

> the greatest young man I ever knew; wit, capacity, beauty, quickness of apprehension, good learning, and an excellent taste; the best orator in the house of commons, admirable conversation and good manners;

and against whose "Wit and Eloquence," "Grace and Address," in both speaking and writing, there was "little Help," since, like the skilled debater he was, "he charmed all who had not a deep Discerning"—which in this context, for this is Steele writing in 1715, probably means no more than "all who had not the deep discerning to be Whigs."

As an appropriate setting for the image of retired leisure that Bolingbroke chose to project on his return to England (he hoped for a time, by lying low, to persuade the ministry to remove his political deprivations), he bought Dawley Manor, near Uxbridge in Middlesex. This was a property of more than four hundred acres of park plus some twenty-odd acres adjoining the house, all of it at the time, it appears, laid out in the formal manner of Le Nôtre, with long radial avenues down which one could gaze and congratulate oneself on one's central position of power, so plainly evinced, or, if one had the dissenting Calvinist background of some of the wealthier Whig magnates who were putting up country houses, one could bask in this unimpugnable evidence of one's membership in heaven's Elect. To set himself apart from such grandeurs, Bolingbroke immediately changed the name of his estate to Dawley Farm, and though he was teased for it by his friends, had murals of farm implements painted in grisaille on his dining room walls. "I now hold the pen for my Lord Bolingbroke," Pope writes Swift in 1728, apparently in the midst of a haying scene,

> who is reading your letter between two Haycocks, but his attention is sometimes diverted by casting his eyes on the clouds, not in admiration of what you say, but for fear of a shower. ... Now his Lordship is run after his Cart, I have a moment left to my self to tell you, that I overheard him yesterday agree with a Painter for £200 to paint his country-hall with Trophies of Rakes, spades, prongs [pitchforks], &c. and other ornaments merely to countenance his calling this place a Farm.

Nonetheless, the symbolism was evidently important to Bolingbroke. Not only could it recall the Roman ideal of the farmer statesman or general like Cincinnatus (an ideal that left its mark on eighteenth-century America too), ever ready, if called, to move to the conduct of greater affairs. It could also specifically flout the image of conspicuous waste associated in many minds with the Whig moneymen, while asserting in its stead those principles of good stewardship, and close interdependence of land and landlord, with which the squires who made up much of the Tory party liked to identify.

The Great House, Bolingbroke altered sufficiently to allow a flattering versifier in 1731 to describe it as a villa: "See! Emblem of himself his *Villa* stand!" (line 18) And the land, too, though he seems to have handled it essentially as a *ferme ornée*, he farmed or had farmed for him to the extent of realizing £700 a year. To that extent, the image expressed the facts.

From this symbolic center for about a decade, 1726–35, Bolingbroke conducted his forays into political journalism and intrigue. His first essays for *The Craftsman*, the new antiministerial newspaper supported also by his friend, the dissident Whig William Pulteney, appeared in January 1727, after he had abandoned all hope of an accommodation with Walpole to recover his political privileges. During the next nine or ten years, his contributions to this journal may have numbered as many as a hundred. And though their aim, of course, was to bring about a climate of opinion suitable for unseating Walpole, he framed this objective in extended overviews of British constitutional history expressing a genuine apprehension, not unreasonable at the time and shared by many, that by a collusion between the throne, its chief minister, and the new money-capitalism (as opposed to the old landed capitalism), that great foundation stone of English liberties, an independent parliament, was being chipped away. Bolingbroke's prescription for arresting this process—which with his patrician personality and his record of political instability he was totally incapable of carrying out—has been the butt of much patronizing criticism, most recently for offering "a politics of nostalgia," as in part it did. Yet there is nothing necessarily misguided in efforts, quixotic though they may turn out, to retain or restore values deeply rooted in the national past, even if the efforts are at the same time, as most such efforts are, self-serving. Nostalgia, indeed, if that is the right word for assessing the achievements of a disappointing present in the light of images from an idealized past, is an everpresent ingredient in the tussle of contending interests that make up a healthy society or a thoughtful individual and are as recognizable today as in Bolingbroke's time. For all that he was not a great thinker, he did give voice to proposals, caveats, visions, and powerful emotions to which many sound minds down at least to Disraeli's time responded, including the second president of these United States, who said of his *Dissertation upon Parties* (a series of essays first published in *The Craftsman*): "This is a jewel, there is nothing so profound, correct, and perfect on the subject of government, in the English or any other language."

Meantime, frequent visits between Twickenham and Dawley (the two "villas" were only four miles apart) whetted Pope's interest in philosophic "studies" of the sort his friend had undertaken in France and was now continuing at his English farm. In the age of Huygens (d. 1697), Hooke (d. 1703), Newton (d. 1727), and Halley (d. 1742), it was all but impossible to remain uninterested in questions of cosmology and cosmogony, and we may recall in this connexion the profound impression that Whiston's astronomical lectures made on Pope when he heard them at Button's in 1713. By 1726 (the *Odyssey* behind him), he had apparently, under the stimulus of Bolingbroke's conversation and much reading of his own, begun to entertain the thought of grappling seriously in verse with some such range of topics as eventually found their way into the *Essay on Man*. Such, at any rate, one may take to be the implication of Broome's verses affixed to the final *Odyssey* note urging him to devote himself now to "heavenly subjects" and "fair Virtue's cause." But the intention, if there was one, had to be postponed. Swift's two visits with their revival of Scriblerian themes, Theobald's lacerating attack on his Shakespeare, Curll's highly embarrassing publication at this same moment of his youthful unbuttoned letters to Henry Cromwell, and the accumulating irritation of many unprovoked attacks all helped dictate the excursion into satire from which the *Art of Sinking* and the *Dunciad* resulted.

Now, by the summer of 1729, he was ready for a new departure. Maybe some "epistles in Horace's manner," he told Fenton that June. Maybe even some sort of "system of Ethics in the Horatian way," he told Swift in November. Certainly, at the very least, a body of work that, on the one hand, could counter the impressions of his character circulated by the dunces, and, on the other, gratify the wishes of such friends as Atterbury, who had urged him, probably on receiving the *Dunciad Variorum* in Paris, to turn his talents to themes more appropriate:

Remember, Virgil dy'd at 52, and Horace at 58; and, as bad as both their Constitutions were, Yours is yet more delicate and tender. Employ not your precious Moments, and great Talents, on little Men, and little things: but choose a Subject every way worthy of you; and handle it, as you can, in a manner which nobody else can equal, or imitate.

Of the work that these considerations were to foster, later dubbed by Pope his *opus magnum*, we get our first extended glimpse in a letter from Bolingbroke to Swift on 2 August 1731:

Does Pope talk to you of the noble work which, att my instigation, he has begun . . . ? The first Epistle which considers man, and the Habitation, of man, relatively to the whole system of universal Being; the second which considers Him in his own Habitation, in Himself, & relatively to his particular system, & the third which shews how an universal cause "works to one end, but works by various laws," how Man, & Beast, & vegetable are linked in a mutual Dependancy, parts necessary to each other & necessary to the whole, how human societys were formed, from what spring true Religion and true Policy are derived, how God has made our greatest interest & our plainest Duty indivisibly the same, these three Epistles I say are finished. The fourth he is now intent upon. . . . The Epistles I have mentioned will compose a first Book. The Plan of the Second is settled.

Bolingbroke's "settled" was wildly optimistic. Around *An Essay on Man*, both at the time and for some years after, a staggering array of complementary pieces—enough to compose a second and even a third book—were conceived, though not written, their number and shape fluctuating like the pseudopods of a hungry amoeba. What Pope finally managed to bring to fruition (out of a welter of hints and possibilities that included at one time or other poems on avarice, prodigality, wit, reason, education, happiness, civil and ecclesiastical polity, the knowledge and characters of men and women, and several more) was a set of four additional "ethic" epistles, loosely, sometimes very loosely, linked to the *Essay on Man* and to each other, each addressed to a different and appropriate friend. The earliest of these, that to Burlington, though initially designed to introduce a collection of Palladio's drawings, as we saw earlier, was brought under the collective umbrella and placed fourth when the epistles were published together. The next earliest, placed third in the collective arrangement, was an epistle on the use of riches, addressed to

Bathurst. The first and second in position, though latest to be composed, were a poem on the characters of men addressed to Lord Cobham, Pope's host during his many visits to Stowe, and a poem on the characters of women addressed "To a Lady," which is to say, to Martha Blount.

"O teach us, BATHURST!"

Complementing the poem to Burlington, the *Epistle to Bathurst* dwells less on lords than on the newly rich merchant classes. Its objects of ridicule are not building and landscaping on country estates but sharp business practice in the City. And though abuse through prodigality can never be entirely excluded from any poem about riches, the emphasis in *To Bathurst* is far more on parsimony, accumulation, and avarice. Pope had had his say about the current ruling class, a class he plainly saw was abdicating its cultural responsibilities and losing ground as a political and social force. In this poem, he would press his views of a rising class that much too often acknowledged no responsibilities at all, or if it did, did so in such remarkably astringent and self-righteous ways as have furnished writers down to our own day (sociologists and political theorists as well as novelists and poets) with some of their major preoccupations:

> The grave Sir Gilbert holds it for a rule,
> That "every man in want is knave or fool":
> "God cannot love (says Blunt, with tearless eyes)
> "The wretch he starves"—and piously denies:
> But the good Bishop, with a meeker air,
> Admits, and leaves them, Providence's care.
>
> (ll. 103–8)

To Bathurst, in short, was to be a sermon. Not simply in the Horatian sense of *sermo* as an argument or discourse (including especially the notion of satirical discourse), but a sermon too in the more ordinary sense of an edifying address setting forth for a self-declared Christian or at least allegedly humane audience, with a wealth of parables and examples, what is to be sought, what shunned. Like a sermon, the poem fairly bristles with allusions to a text to which, presumably, such an audience, especially a dissenting audience with its stress on Scriptural texts, could not comfortably admit indifference, e.g.—

> Yet, to be just to these poor men of pelf,
> Each does but hate his Neighbour as himself;
>
> (ll. 109–10)

or:

> 'Tis GEORGE and LIBERTY that crowns the cup,
> And Zeal for that great House which eats him up.★
>
> (ll. 207–8)

At the same time, over the idea of what is to be shunned, Pope lets his comic imagination grandly play, building a grotesque cartoon out of current fiscal abuses seen as if altered by a time warp to transactions "in kind." These for the politician:

> Oh! that such bulky Bribes as all might see,
> Still, as of old, incumber'd Villainy! . . .
> A Statesman's slumbers how this speech would spoil!
> "Sir, Spain has sent a thousand jars of oil;
> "Huge bales of British cloth blockade the door;
> "A hundred oxen at your levee roar."
>
> (ll. 35–6, 43–6)

And these for the domestic scene—details that may very well reach back to Pope's childhood near Leadenhall market:

> His Grace will game: to White's a Bull be led,
> With spurning heels and with a butting head.
> To White's be carried, as to ancient games,
> Fair Coursers, Vases, and alluring Dames.
> Shall then Uxorio, if the stakes he sweep,
> Bear home six Whores, and make his Lady weep?
> Or soft Adonis, so perfum'd and fine,
> Drive to St. James's a whole herd of swine?
>
> (ll. 55–62)

Even gold, which is variously associated throughout the poem with Phaeton's doomed attempt to drive the horses of the sun (line 12) and other acts of *hubris*, had in the old days a certain inhibiting virtue, being heavy and likely to give the game away by jingling (line 67). But now all is paper, primitive, to be sure, beside the microchip, but more susceptible to abuse than metals by a quantum leap:

★ Psalms, 69: 9. "For the zeal of thine house [O God] hath eaten me up."

Blest paper-credit! last and best supply!
That lends Corruption lighter wings to fly! . . .
A single leaf shall waft an Army o'er,
Or ship off Senates to a distant Shore;
A leaf, like Sibyl's, scatter to and fro
Our fates and fortunes, as the winds shall blow:
Pregnant with thousands flits the Scrap unseen,
And silent sells a King, or buys a Queen.

(ll. 69–78)

The evocation in the last passage of the palm leaves on which the Cumaean sibyl was reputed to scratch her prophecies when possessed by the god—implying, it would seem, that prophecy and the divine overview on which it depends have given way under the new dispensation to "fortune-hunting" of another kind—strikes a note that vibrates throughout the poem. Are riches, or any other good, a gift from heaven, as in the parable of the talents, or our own "lucky hit" (ll. 377–78)? Does the accessibility of earth's beauty and bounty to our use call for ownership or stewardship? What blessing can wealth bring if hoarded—as by old Cotta, a City merchant who has bought himself a country estate only to invert the whole way of life that gave such estates their meaning?

Like some lone Chartreux stands the good old Hall,
Silence without, and Fasts within the wall;
No rafter'd roofs with dance and tabor sound,
No noontide-bell invites the country round;
Tenants with sighs the smoakless tow'rs survey,
And turn th' unwilling steeds another way:
Benighted wanderers, the forest o'er,
Curse the sav'd candle, and unop'ning door;
While the gaunt mastiff growling at the gate,
Affrights the beggar whom he longs to eat.

(ll. 189–98)

Contrariwise, what good can wealth do us if we merely run through it, like Charles II's Duke of Buckingham?

In the worst inn's worst room, with mat half-hung,
The floors of plaister, and the walls of dung,
On once a flock-bed, but repair'd with straw,
With tape-ty'd curtains, never meant to draw,
The George and Garter dangling from that bed
Where tawdry yellow strove with dirty red,

> Great Villiers lies—alas! how chang'd from him,
> That life of pleasure, and that soul of whim! . . .
> No Wit to flatter, left of all his store!
> No Fool to laugh at, which he valu'd more.
> There, Victor of his health, of fortune, friends,
> And fame; this lord of useless thousands ends.
>
> (ll. 299–306, 311–14)

But the two images to which Pope entrusts his deepest feelings in the poem are those of the Man of Ross and Balaam. The Man of Ross was an actual person. A native of Ross in Herefordshire who died in 1724, he rapidly became a legend for his good works. By correspondence with old Jacob Tonson, who had a place in that county, and from other sources as well, Pope took pains to assemble the most explicit information he could get about him, though admitting he might probably, with a poet's license, give it here and there an extra brush stroke. What he produced was his own eighteenth-century version of a conception that is even now not quite dead, though moribund, in some American and English small towns: a sketch of the ideal townsman or civic leader, who anticipates in attitudes if not in means or setting Fielding's Squire Allworthy and his many fictional successors.

The Man of Ross, according to both other contemporary evidence and Pope's verse, had set up a small waterworks and reservoir for the inhabitants of Ross, enclosing it in a stone wall of which the gates still stand. He had planted a nearby eminence with trees, making there for himself and his fellow townsmen a long shaded walk "commanding a beautiful prospect of the Wye," which is today a park. He repaired and raised the spire of the ancient parish church, and he took over, to the extent of his ability, the obligations today assumed, or expected to be assumed, by the state:

> Behold the Market-place with poor o'erspread!
> The MAN of Ross divides the weekly bread:
> Behold yon Alms-house, neat, but void of state,
> Where Age and Want sit smiling at the gate:
> Him portion'd maids, apprentic'd orphans blest,
> The young who labour, and the old who rest.
> Is any sick? the MAN of Ross relieves,
> Prescribes, attends, the med'cine makes, and gives.
> Is there a variance? enter but his door,
> Balk'd are the Courts, and contest is no more.
>
> (ll. 263–72)

There is a degree of pastoralism here—we are not to take this at quite
face value. The vigorously voiced approval of the Wye and Severn
smilingly warns us of that—

> Pleas'd Vaga echoes thro' her winding bounds,
> And rapid Severn hoarse applause resounds—
>
> (ll. 251–52)

as does the tacit comparison of the Man and his waterworks to the
miracle of Moses commanding water for his people: "From the dry
rock who bade the waters flow?" There is a degree of epic in the
portrait too: here is a succession of feats that only a muse can sing:

> But all our praises why should Lords engross?
> Rise, honest Muse! and sing the MAN of Ross.
>
> (ll. 249–50)

And if the scene points too heavily toward a Dickensian paternalism
to please most of us today, reared as we are among computerized
welfare systems in a psychological culture less inclined to applaud
personal benefactions of the kind attributed to the Man of Ross than
to identify them as a form of subconscious aggression, it nevertheless
manages to convey at its close a withering Dickensian scorn of the
Podsnappery in all of us that has got us into this frame of mind.
"Thrice happy man!" Bathurst exclaims when the story is done,

> enabled to pursue,
> What all so wish, but want the pow'r to do!
> Oh say, what sums that gen'rous hand supply?
> What mines, to swell that boundless charity?"

To which comes the quiet answer:

> Of Debts, and Taxes, Wife and Children clear,
> This man possest—five hundred pounds a year.
>
> (ll. 275–80)

   Pope's antithesis to the story of the Man of Ross—his real name,
though Pope knew it, is never used in the poem's text, evidently to
enhance his archetypal character like the Old Testament's man of Ur
and man of Uz—is the story of Balaam, some of whose details may
derive from the poet's cockney childhood. Balaam lives in the heart
of the merchandizing City, not far from Lombard Street perhaps, in
the shadow of the monument that he and his kind had erected after the
Great Fire to place responsibility for it on the Roman Catholic

minority: a lie, as Pope's verses make clear, thrust in the very face of heaven:

> Where London's column, pointing at the skies
> Like a tall bully, lifts the head, and lyes;
> There dwelt a Citizen of sober fame,
> A plain good man, and Balaam was his name.
>
> (ll. 339–42)

For most of Pope's contemporaries, the name was itself a clue. In the Book of Numbers, the prophet Balaam is offered rewards by the king of Moab if he will curse the Israelites, who are pressing in upon his land. Balaam refuses, being a God-fearing man, but when the promised rewards grow great enough, he capitulates (so later Biblical writers interpreted his story), managing still to withhold the curse that the Lord had forbidden him to utter, yet in some obscure way seducing the Israelite newcomers into worshipping Moabite idols, for which the Lord punishes them with a great plague. Hence Balaam came to stand in later writings as one guilty of "covetous practices," one "who loved the wages of unrighteousness," and his career as the career of a man who sold out.

Pope's treatment of Balaam is more ironical. He sells out, of course, like his namesake, when the stakes go high enough. His first windfall comes when "two rich ship-wrecks bless the lucky shore" of some lands he owns in Cornwall, an event which in that country was not always providentially arranged but sometimes effected by the natives with misleading lights, or even, if the vessel were simply stranded, by boring holes in its hull to ensure its not getting off and thus becoming subject to the law of "prize." Whatever the situation with Balaam's prizes (Pope is silent on this point), the new wealth gives him his first step up the social ladder:

> Sir Balaam now, he lives like other folks,
> He takes his chirping pint, and cracks his jokes:
> "Live like yourself," was soon my Lady's word;
> And lo! two puddings smoak'd upon the board.
>
> (ll. 357–60)

A second windfall arrives in the shape of a huge diamond, fleeced from its finder by a shipping agent and from the shipping agent by Balaam, who, with some adjustments of conscience manages to keep it for himself:

Some scruple rose, but thus he eas'd his thought,
"I'll now give sixpence where I gave a groat,
"Where once I went to church, I'll now go twice—
"And am so clear too of all other vice."

(ll. 365–68)

From this point on, good fortune follows good fortune till Balaam has become one of England's merchant princes:

Behold Sir Balaam, now a man of spirit,
Ascribes his gettings to his parts and merit,
What late he call'd a Blessing, now was Wit,
And God's good Providence, a lucky Hit.
Things change their titles, as our manners turn:
His Compting-house employ'd the Sunday-morn;
Seldom at Church ('twas such a busy life)
But duly sent his family and wife.
There (so the Dev'l ordain'd) one Christmas-tide
My good old Lady catch'd a cold, and dy'd.

(ll. 375–84)

The rest of the story is all downhill, though (like most of the rest of us when similarly bemused), Balaam imagines his direction is up. He now travels in the best circles, meets a woman of quality, marries her, and of course leaves the City for the West End. There he "joins . . . The well-bred cuckolds in St. James's air" and in due course becomes an M.P. To provide for his son, he buys him a commission in the army, where he "drinks, whores, fights, and in a duel dies." To aggrandize his daughter, he buys her a Viscount, who reciprocates by bestowing on her "a Coronet and P-x for life." Then the second Lady Balaam loses heavily at play. As her husband must take up her debts, he is driven to accept a bribe from France. (France's chief minister, Cardinal Fleury, was widely believed to have gained a sympathetic hearing for French interests in England's Parliament by methods normally institutionalized today under the heading of foreign aid):

The House impeach him; Coningsby harangues;
The Court forsake him, and Sir Balaam hangs.

(ll. 397–98) .

Pope's tone, it will be noticed, is like a shrug. He can afford this offhand manner because he has set his sordid story against the background of the Book of Job. There, it will be recalled, Satan wagers with the Lord that by taking Job's riches he can make Job curse Him:

And the Lord said unto Satan, Hast thou considered my servant Job, that there is none like him in the earth, a perfect and an upright man, one that feareth God, and escheweth evil? Then Satan answered the Lord, and said, Doth Job fear God for nought? Hast thou not made an hedge about his house, and about all that he hath on every side? thou hast blessed the work of his hands, and his substance is increased in the land. But put forth thy hand now, and touch all that he hath, and he will curse thee to thy face.

(1: 7–10)

It is Job's loyalty to God that is thus at issue, in a test that one suspects reminded Pope's Catholic friends of certain other "tests"—closer home—which also made religious loyalty difficult. Riches had been seized in these cases too, and were always liable to seizure or penalty, as after the '15, or whenever an excuse could be found. In any case, as Pope's story puts it, back in the days when Balaam was "a plain good man," or, as the extremer sects liked to say, one of the "Elect,"

> The Dev'l was piqu'd such saintship to behold,
> And long'd to tempt him like good Job of old:
> But Satan now is wiser than of yore,
> And tempts by making rich, not making poor.

(ll. 349–52)

Accordingly, it is "the Prince of Air" who brings on the lucky shipwrecks. It is "the Tempter," assuming the form that Jove assumed for the rape of Danae, who after the diamond episode adds to the traditional forms of gain the new ones:

> The Tempter saw his time; the work he ply'd:
> Stocks and Subscriptions pour on ev'ry side,
> Till all the Dæmon makes his full descent,
> In one abundant show'r of Cent. per Cent.,
> Sinks deep within him, and possesses whole,
> Then dubs Director, and secures his soul.

(ll. 369–74)

And this time Satan wins:

> Wife, son, and daughter, Satan, are thy own,
> His wealth, yet dearer, forfeit to the Crown:
> The Devil and the King divide the prize,
> And sad Sir Balaam curses God and dies.

(ll. 399–402)

It is, however, a Pyrrhic victory, for as Pope has warned us from his opening lines, Balaam's religion has never been more than a tissue of outward observances, a lie thrust in the face of heaven: even lines 341–42 look different when read again.

> Where London's column, pointing at the skies
> Like a tall bully, lifts the head, and lyes;
> There dwelt a Citizen of sober fame,
> A plain good man, and Balaam was his name;
> Religious, punctual, frugal, and so forth;
> His word would pass for more than he was worth.
> One solid dish his week-day meal affords,
> An added pudding solemniz'd the Lord's:
> Constant at Church, and Change [the Royal Exchange];
>   his gains were sure,
> His givings rare, save farthings to the poor.
>
> (ll. 339–48)

Clearly, a poem for all seasons. And if we recall that in the Opposition press, Robert Walpole was sometimes represented in the guise of Satan as Tempter, possibly a rather daring poem for its own season too.

CHAPTER 21

THE PROPER STUDY

"Hope humbly, then"

The *Epistle to Bathurst*, though complete or nearly so when that to Burlington appeared, Pope held back for more than a year. This may have been partly from his preference for letting his things "lie by" him for periods of varying length during which the advice of friends could be consulted and second thoughts entertained. In this instance, moreover, there was the disheartening clamor occasioned by the possibly deliberate mistaking of Timon's villa for Chandos's "Cannons" to be taken into account. Pope was not about to enhance the uproar by releasing a new poem that, as he had promised, carried some real names. The thought must also have occurred to him that postponing the poem (which he intended to publish with his name on it) till he was ready with the *Essay on Man* (planned for anonymous publication) would strengthen the impression that the *Essay*, so unlike any work for which he was yet known, must be by another hand and thus help it obtain a fair hearing. This, at any rate, is how he finally chose to handle things. He brought out the poem to Bathurst on 15 January 1733, another poem, also signed, on February 15, and then, anonymously, on February 20, March 19, and May 8, through a publisher he had never before used, the first three epistles of the *Essay on Man*.

The ruse succeeded admirably. An acquaintance of Pope's not in on the secret reported to a friend on March 13 that the Town was currently reading, along with the poem to Bathurst, "An Essay on Man by a New Author"—not the easiest subject "to succeed in," he added, but here "treated with a greatness of Thoughts and a force in the expression which shew a true Genius." At about the same time, according to letters from Pope to Caryll, some readers were attributing the new work to one or other well-known clergyman, "Dr. Croxall, Dr. Secker, and some others" solemnly denying it. What must have gratified Pope most of all was that several of the dunces went on record at this time with tributes they could not afterward decently retract. Leonard Welsted, for instance, who over the past three years had publicly dismissed all of Pope's poetry as plagiarized, pieced together from stolen "half Lines, till the tun'd verse went round, Complete, in smooth dull unity of Sound," and had branded Pope himself

A Soul corrupt, that hireling Praise suborns!
That hates for Genius, and for Virtue scorns!

was now sufficiently incautious to write the unknown author that he had found the *Essay* "what I had long despaired, a performance deserving the name of a poet. . . . It is, indeed, above all commendation, and ought to have been published in an age and country more worthy of it, If my testimony be of weight any where, you are sure to have it in the amplest manner." This little comedy was intensified in April, when a second dunce, Bezaleel Morrice, by whom Pope's effort to translate Homer had been declared "weak," "modish," "spruce," "effeminate," simply a proof of his avarice and conceit, hailed the new poem unreservedly in his own imitation of it called *An Essay on the Universe*:

Auspicious bard! while all admire thy strain,
All but the selfish, ignorant, and vain.

As Pope confided to Richardson on March 2, a glut of praise was succeeding to the glut of reproach raised by the alleged satire on Chandos in the *Epistle to Burlington*: "I am as much overpaid this way now as I was injur'd that way before."

There were reasons for the poem's outstanding success. For one thing, it dealt with matters of consuming interest to contemporary minds. Pope's lifetime, it will be recalled, was a period when the sea of faith, to borrow Arnold's haunting metaphor from *Dover Beach*—already in slow recession for at least two centuries—was beginning to make audible to almost any ear "its melancholy long withdrawing roar." Thirty years before Pope was born, Milton had been able to use the Eden story to locate the origins of human suffering in the ambitious self-centered unruly nature that we all recognize as postlapsarian humanity and so "assert Eternal Providence, And justify the ways of God to men." But even for Milton and at that time this had been a tour de force, accomplished only by conceptualizing the story at all important points. In *Paradise Lost*, the prohibition of the apple is no longer an adventitious command beset with mysteries as it is in Genesis, but a rationalized symbol of obedience or disobedience, its meaning thus internal. And the consequences of eating it are again rationalized and internalized in the rebellion of the passions, symbolized explicitly in Eve's and Adam's immediate act of lust.

With the writings of Hobbes, Locke, and Newton in every thoughtful mind, this story had lost its literal usefulness. It lived on as an imaginatively appealing episode in the total scheme of revealed salvation evolved by the Christian community in its early centuries, and therefore enjoyed strenuous protection (though rarely detailed attention) in eighteenth-century churches of all persuasions. Meantime, however, any number of cosmogonies totally at odds with it prowled about the doors and sometimes were even received inside, at least as far as the back pews. One effect of Hobbes's materialist philosophy (strengthened by native Leveller inclinations during the Civil Wars as well as *libertin* influences from across the Channel) had been to stir interest in the ancient Democritean-Epicurean-Lucretian thesis that the world is a fortuitous concourse of atoms, in which all that happens happens by merest chance; gods, if there are gods, sit serenely above it all, detached spectators like an audience at a play; beyond death lies pure oblivion. Except to atheists, who were perhaps already greater in number than we suspect, such doctrines had only negative appeal. But their powerful presentation in the brilliant hoarse music of Lucretius's *De Rerum Natura* was on all sides much admired. John Evelyn, the diarist, translated Book 1 even under the Commonwealth, awarding its author first place among "the whole Assembly of Epick Latine Poets." Dryden translated portions of five of the six books, praising Lucretius for his "sublime and daring genius" and "the perpetual torrent of his verse." Thomas Creech of Wadham College, Oxford, translated the entire poem in 1682 and edited it in Latin in 1695, making it yet more widely known.

By Pope's time, therefore, what was obviously required for continuing Milton's defense of providence in an acceptable contemporary idiom, as the first paragraph of the *Essay on Man* announces its intent to do, was a work of breadth and stature that could match the poetical attractions of *De Rerum Natura* while countering its thesis of atomic happenstance on its own broadly rational speculative terms. Blackmore, Pope's favorite whipping boy, had made a plunge in this direction in 1712 with a poem called *Creation*: a dreary exercise in bombast highly praised by Addison and Dennis because (or so one likes to think) they were blinded by its pious content. Now there was to be a new contestant. In letters while Pope was working on the *Essay*, in his confidences to Spence, in the astonishing number of direct allusions to Lucretius's text to be found in his, most of all, perhaps, in the peremptory tone singled out by Dryden as the Latin poet's most distinctive attribute and plainly appropriated throughout much of the *Essay*, there is abundant evidence that Pope wished his poem to be read, at least in some degree, as a modern *De Rerum Natura*.

A *De Rerum Natura* based, however, on tenets more congruent with what the astronomers and cosmographers as well as the philosophers and psychologists of his own time were saying. To make this clear, Epicurus and his visionary mode of knowing are set aside at the very outset of the work, immediately following the induction. We can only reason about either man or God, says Pope, taking up at once an empiricist's position, from the evidence available to us. In man's case, that is limited to this terrestrial scene, and in God's to His manifestations in our world. One could do better, doubtless, if one had superhuman powers:

> He, who thro' vast immensity can pierce,
> See worlds on worlds compose one universe,
> Observe how system into system runs,
> What other planets circle other suns,
> What vary'd being peoples ev'ry star,
> May tell why Heaven has made us as we are.
>
> (1:23–28)

These are the powers that Lucretius claims for Epicurus. Epicurus, he says, traversed in imagination the immense All, pierced even beyond its flaming limits, and brought back knowledge of its principles: knowledge whereby religion is at last defeated and trampled underfoot, and we by that victory raised to the sky. A likely story! Pope's lines imply. At any rate, of no use to the rest of us, who both lack "pervading" souls and have seen enough of the complexities of even our own system as revealed by Newton and his followers to be wary of expansive claims:

> But of this frame the bearings, and the ties,
> The strong connections, nice dependencies,
> Gradations just, has thy pervading soul
> Look'd thro'? or can a part contain the whole?
>
> (1:29–32)

A more widely influential complex of ideas about which Pope also registers some reservations at the beginning of his poem is that which swirled about the ancient conception of the cosmos as a Chain or Scale [i.e., Ladder] of Being. The implications of a tightly linked and

full creation derivable from the metaphor of the chain, and of hierarchy and due degree from the metaphor of the scale, had now been
empirically confirmed (so it seemed) by the apparently limitless
species revealed under the microscope, especially if they were extended to the stellar worlds that were also becoming visible in growing numbers as telescope lenses improved. It was thus beginning to be
possible in Pope's time, as in the Whiston lectures that so stirred him
as a young man, to entertain a conception of a hierarchical universe—whether conceived as a chain of beings:

> Vast chain of being, which from God began,
> Natures æthereal, human, angel, man,
> Beast, bird, fish, insect! what no eye can see,
> No glass can reach! from Infinite to thee,
> From thee to Nothing!
>
> (1: 237–41)

or as a scale of creaturely powers:

> Far as Creation's ample range extends,
> The scale of sensual, mental pow'rs ascends:
> Mark how it mounts, to Man's imperial race,
> From the green myriads in the peopled grass—
>
> (1: 207–10)

created by God for reasons not accessible to human reason (apart from
Scripture) and constantly preserved by his power flowing through it.
As Whiston, one of Newtonianism's chief publicizers, had remarked
in a sermon a few years earlier: "If the Almighty should supersede or
suspend his constant Providential Power for one single Hour, all the
World would be dissolved and dissipated, and all the noble Bodies
therein, Suns, Planets, Comets, Vegetables, and Animals would at
once be destroyed."

On the other hand, a similar though stricter system, deduced *a
priori* in ancient times from the supposed nature of Being itself, was
also much in vogue during the later seventeenth century and on
through Pope's day. On this reasoning, the one Perfect Being (who is
also the One as distinguished from the Many) entered on the act of
creating the Many because it is the nature of such perfect Being to
communicate its own perfections to the fullest extent possible in all
possible forms. Hence the cosmos became a continuum of beings
from the highest orders to the lowest, with no gaps: a *plenum
formarum*. And though this scheme required from Christian
theologians a good deal of intricate footwork to preserve the

Supreme Being's freedom of action in opposition to the necessitarian logic of Spinoza, it became for some considerable while their favorite metaphysics, even to the conclusion, however qualified, that this universe had to be the best of possible universes because that is the only sort of universe an all-wise or all-good Being could/would choose. In the words of the Cambridge Platonist and Anglican divine, Ralph Cudworth:

> Nor is the Deity therefore *Bound* or *Obliged* to do the *Best*, in any way of *Servility* (as men fondly imagine this to be contrary to his *Liberty*) much less by the Law and Command of any Superiour (which is a Contradiction) but only by the *Perfection* of its own *Nature*, which it cannot possibly deviate from, no more than Ungod it self.

Pope had little use for such *a priori* reasoners. In the final *Dunciad* of 1743, they are the takers of "the high Priori Road," who reason downward till they doubt of God. For "instead of reasoning" (says the *Dunciad*'s note at this point) "from a *visible World* to an *invisible God*," they took the other road,

> and from an *invisible God* (to whom they had given attributes agreeable to certain metaphysical principles formed out of their own imaginations) reasoned *downwards* to a *visible world* in theory, of Man's Creation; which not agreeing, as might be expected, to that of God's, they began from their inability to account for *evil* which they saw in his world, to doubt of that God.

The *Essay on Man* likewise disposes of this school of thought with some celerity. It encapsulates its line of argument—

> Of systems possible, if 'tis confest
> That Wisdom infinite must form the best,
> Where all must full or not coherent be,
> And all that rises, rise in due degree—
>
> (1: 43–46)

but only as a conditional premise ("if 'tis confest") leading to a conclusion—

> There must be somewhere such a rank as Man—
>
> (line 48)

that differs in no important way from the observation of the empiricist already stated—

Of Man what see we, but his station here?—

(line 19)

save in the limitation of God by human logic implied in the use of "must."

In short, says Epistle 1, we know little for certain about the totality of the cosmos except that we live and die in our own corner of it. We cannot guess whether in that larger totality we serve some purpose utterly beyond our understanding. Possibly our destiny includes a life after death, but we cannot be sure of that and certainly have no grounds on which to demand it. What we are given during this life is hope, which, if we will let it, can be our present comfort. For humble minds, as unfamiliar with demanding versions of immortality as with Christian greed, it plainly is a comfort:

> Lo! the poor Indian, whose untutor'd mind
> Sees God in clouds, or hears him in the wind;
> His soul proud Science never taught to stray
> Far as the solar walk, or milky way;
> Yet simple Nature to his hope has giv'n,
> Behind the cloud-topt hill, an humbler heav'n;
> Some safer world in depth of woods embrac'd,
> Some happier island in the wat'ry waste,
> Where slaves once more their native land behold,
> No fiends torment, no Christians thirst for gold!
> To Be, contents his natural desire,
> He asks no Angel's wing, no Seraph's fire;
> But thinks, admitted to that equal sky,
> His faithful dog shall bear him company.

(1: 99–112)

The remainder of the first epistle is given over to implicit contrasts between these trusting attitudes and those arising from contemporary theologies, whether based on the notion that the universe was created to pleasure man—

> Ask for what end the heav'nly bodies shine,
> Earth for whose use? Pride answers, "'Tis for mine: . . .
> Seas roll to waft me, suns to light me rise;
> My foot-stool earth, my canopy the skies"—

(1: 131–32, 139–40)

or on an excess of confidence that what God is and does must fall within bounds established by the human mind:

> If plagues or earthquakes break not Heav'n's design,
> Why then a Borgia, or a Catiline? . . .
> From pride, from pride, our very reas'ning springs;
> Account for moral as for nat'ral things:
> Why charge we Heav'n in those, in these acquit?
> In both, to reason right is to submit.
>
> (1: 155–56, 161–64)

The goal of these and other mockeries of presumption is the triumphant assertion of faith with which the first epistle ends. Allowing for its different idiom, this closely parallels Raphael's advice to Adam before the fall in *Paradise Lost*:

> Solicit not thy thoughts with matters hid,
> Leave them to God above, him serve and fear;
> Of other Creatures, as him pleases best,
> Wherever plac't, let him dispose: joy thou
> In what he gives to thee, this Paradise
> And thy fair *Eve*: Heav'n is for thee too high
> To know what passes there; be lowly wise:
> Think only what concerns thee and thy being;
> Dream not of other Worlds, what Creatures there
> Live, in what state, condition or degree,
> Contented that thus far hath been reveal'd
> Not of Earth only but of highest Heav'n.
>
> (8: 167–78)

"Be lowly wise" is a restriction that particularly appealed to Pope, as his own vindication of "Eternal Providence" clearly shows. God, though *in* all—though it is *His* power that

> Warms in the sun, refreshes in the breeze,
> Glows in the stars, and blossoms in the trees, . . .
> As full, as perfect, in vile Man that mourns,
> As the rapt seraph that adores and burns—
>
> (1: 271–72, 277–78)

also transcends and disposes all, and not necessarily in a manner we can understand:

> Know thy own point: This kind, this due degree
> Of blindness, weakness, Heav'n bestows on thee.
> Submit—In this, or any other sphere,
> Secure to be as blest as thou canst bear:
> Safe in the hand of one disposing Pow'r,

Or in the natal, or the mortal hour.
All Nature is but Art, unknown to thee;
All Chance, Direction, which thou canst not see;
All Discord, Harmony, not understood;
All partial Evil, universal Good:
And, spite of Pride, in erring Reason's spite,
One truth is clear, "Whatever is, is RIGHT."

(1: 283–94)

"But what composes Man, can Man destroy?"

But the repositioning of human expectations required by new
cosmogonies was only one of several issues stirring excited speculation in Pope's day. Under no less intense scrutiny was the nature of
human motivation. Are human beings, as Hobbes had contended,
driven exclusively by selfish individualism, so intransigent and
bellicose that they can live together in society only under an absolutist government designed to keep them from each other's throats? Or
do they possess, as a considerable school of anti-Hobbesian thought
insisted, both self-affections and benevolent affections under the control of an innate moral sense? On the Hobbesian view, how can there
be any such thing as "virtue"—what, in fact, *is* virtue? To be reckoned virtuous, must an action be caused by a benevolent affection, as
the third earl of Shaftesbury had claimed? Or is performing an action
that the world calls virtuous—say, risking one's life for a friend—
only a more complex form of self-gratification and thus essentially
egoistic: a more noble form of self-love, perhaps, but self-love still?
Come to think of it, do we more appropriately judge an act by its
motive or its result? If private self-interest, which can also be termed
greed, produces actions that conduce to general prosperity—here we
rub elbows with a concern closely tied to the rationalizing of the new
capitalist forces set free by the settlement of 1688—must it still be
registered morally as a vice? or as a public benefit and hence a virtue?

   And what do all these considerations say about human nature? Is
the high-powered egoism so visible in an expanding market society
to be thought one of the corruptions accruing from the Fall, since
which time, as Richard Baxter put it, "self is become all to corrupted
nature, as God was all to nature in its integrity"? Or is this impulse,
despite the teaching of the great classical Stoics (who differed from
the radical Puritans mainly in believing that passions *can* be quelled
by individual effort), actually salutary—the energy source of all

activity, virtuous or otherwise? May it not even be the case, in fact, that by virtue of this inheritance from the Fall man is now "a more excellent Creature" than before he fell?

It was among questions of this nature that the author of the second epistle of the *Essay*, published in late March some five weeks after the first, could be seen picking his way. He had closed the earlier epistle on the note of submission that any vindicator of God's ways must finally strike: the frame of mind ascribed to Job after the voice speaks to him from the whirlwind, or the frame of mind claimed by Montaigne toward the close of a life often punctuated by prolonged cruel sufferings from the kidney stone: *Tout bon il a faict tout bon* ("Himself all good, he has made all things good"). Now it was time to turn the attention of his readers from the cosmic scene to the psychological and ethical, from footless metaphysical speculation on the attributes of the divine nature to careful notation of the attributes of human nature. Pope makes this transition in what are probably the best-known lines of the poem, basing himself heavily on Pascal but expressing also his own deepest convictions:

> Know then thyself, presume not God to scan;
> The proper study of Mankind is Man.
> Plac'd on this isthmus of a middle state,
> A being darkly wise, and rudely great:
> With too much knowledge for the Sceptic side,
> With too much weakness for the Stoic's pride—
>
> (ll. 1–6)

here Pope repudiates both the Pyrrhonist's total mistrust of reason and the Stoic's excess of confidence in it—

> Chaos of Thought and Passion, all confus'd;
> Still by himself abus'd, or disabus'd;
> Created half to rise, and half to fall;
> Great lord of all things, yet a prey to all;
> Sole judge of Truth, in endless Error hurl'd;
> The glory, jest, and riddle of the world!
>
> (ll. 13–18)

Though the terms differ dramatically, Pope says much here that any post-Freudian culture will recognize as pertinent.

Plainly, the prime difficulty for human nature in Pope's view of it is that it is not single and integral, but dual, even plural. Like most writers outside of the Stoic school and the extremer Calvinists, he assigns positive value to the passions, accepting the traditional division of human nature into reason and appetitive instinct, and regarding the passions as useful rather than reprehensible expressions of this instinct. Though human beings have affinities with the Godlike-rational, they must recognize in themselves (as the Stoics failed to do: hence their "pride") equally strong affinities with the animal-sensitive, realizing that the task laid on them is to reconcile both characters in some form of constructive synthesis:

> Passions, like Elements, tho' born to fight,
> Yet, mix'd and soften'd, in his [God's] work unite:
> These 'tis enough to temper and employ;
> But what composes Man, can Man destroy?
> Suffice that Reason keep to Nature's road,
> Subject, compound them, follow her and God.
>
> (2: 111–16)

It is in this connection that the conception of a "ruling" passion becomes important for Pope's scheme. If we may assume, as some psychologies of our own day suggest, that human beings pass from chaotic to better organized states by ways we still know little about, the ruling passion may be called Pope's guess as to one of the ways. The idea had many antecedents, particularly in the French moralists beginning with Montaigne, but Pope develops it to a degree and ascribes to it a multiplicity of functions not duplicated elsewhere. In a sense, it is the psychic counterpart of his "Genius of the Place" in landscaping, a power which one must "consult" and with which one must collaborate. Lacking this passion, human nature would be a vessel tossed in contrary directions by the aimless succession of its desires; having it, that nature goes with some steadiness to its main objectives: the same directive effect as that assigned to habit by Aristotle and by modern behaviorist theories. This conception is central to the second epistle of the *Essay*, where it is obvious that Pope presents human character as a creative achievement, something built out of chaos as God built the world. The direction planted in the individual character is a *datum*, but what the individual makes of it, and whether it leads to good or evil, depends on skill and will:

> Thus Nature gives us (let it check our pride)
> The virtue nearest to our vice ally'd;
> Reason the byass turns to good from ill,
> And Nero reigns a Titus, if he will.
>
> (2: 195–98)

The other significance of this passion for Pope's theory relates to the divine plan. Sent by God, it serves within His providential scheme not only to steady our characters in their pursuit of the apposite objective, but to differentiate these objectives so that the world's work may be accomplished, and to distinguish the satisfactions resulting from them so that each person may have his or her own special form of contentment:

> Let pow'r or knowledge, gold or glory, please,
> Or (oft more strong than all) the love of ease;
> Thro' life 'tis follow'd, ev'n at life's expence;
> The merchant's toil, the sage's indolence,
> The monk's humility, the hero's pride,
> All, all alike, find Reason on their side.
>
> (2: 169–74)

God's direction and supervision of ruling passions (students of early capitalist theory will be reminded here of God's harmonizing of economic self-interests in the system put forward by Adam Smith) is thus a phase of Pope's vindication of providence as well as of his ethics. The object of both, at this point in the poem, is to show that the pluralism of the human psyche, however ticklish in the management it requires and though like any good it may be abused, is to be accepted with gratitude and resignation as the gift of a wise and benevolent Creator.

In writing of the ruling and other passions in this double context, Pope uses expressions which, though confusing, are thoroughly characteristic of his time and his subject matter. Psychological treatises of the sixteenth and seventeenth centuries are likely to deviate, on successive pages, from describing passions as tempests that shamefully debauch the soul to describing them as necessary solicitations to virtuous action; and, correspondingly, from a Shaftesburyan and rigorist definition of virtue (virtue is action not motivated by the affective or "lower" elements in human nature) to a Mandevillian quasi-utilitarian one (virtue is action having good effects, to which the passions are frequently the best incentives). Pope's own language about the passions must always be read in this light, and most particularly in this epistle. Thus he speaks of the formation of human character as though it were simultaneously an individual achievement and a free gift of God, like grace; of reason as a god within the mind and also a deluded queen; of the ruling passion as a disease and yet divine; of good and evil as absolutes known intuitively and yet in practice blurred beyond distinction:

> This light and darkness in our chaos join'd,
> What shall divide? The God within the mind. . . .
> Tho' each by turns the other's bound invade,
> As, in some well-wrought picture, light and shade,
> And oft so mix, the diff'rence is too nice
> Where ends the Virtue, or begins the Vice.
>
> (2: 203–4, 207–10)

In the same way, shifting between rigorist and utilitarian terminologies, he calls the results of affective actions good, their self-regarding motives bad. The consequence is that while he is celebrating on one hand the utility of the passions, he is on the other constantly referring them to a context of frailties, vanities, imperfections, and wants. The pursuits to which our passions spur us, it appears, genuinely beautify our days, but we must not fail to acknowledge them, in the long run, painted clouds:

> Mean-while Opinion gilds with varying rays
> Those painted clouds that beautify our days;
> Each want of happiness by Hope supply'd,
> And each vacuity of sense by Pride:
> These build as fast as knowledge can destroy;
> In Folly's cup still laughs the bubble, joy.
>
> (2: 283–88)

Likewise, nature's law is kindly—nature being here the inclusive rational-affective condition all human beings share—yet the life that nature in this sense leads to is a poor play, signifying not very much, and lighting mainly the incorrigible child in all of us to rest:

> Behold the child, by Nature's kindly law,
> Pleas'd with a rattle, tickled with a straw:
> Some livelier plaything gives his youth delight,
> A little louder, but as empty quite:
> Scarfs, garters, gold, amuse his riper stage;
> And beads and pray'r-books are the toys of age:
> Pleas'd with this bauble still, as that before;
> Till tir'd he sleeps, and Life's poor play is o'er!
>
> (2: 275–82)

Somewhere in the middle distance one catches the accents of Shakespeare's Jaques and beyond him, far away, just faintly audible, Macbeth.

One of Pope's habits in this poem, possibly a strategy to keep before his readers the complexities of human reality in contrast to the elaborate floor plans of philosophers, is to stress how differently the same phenomena appear when viewed within differing contexts. The hierarchy of beings, for example, is brought before us in the first epistle as a "dread ORDER," its forbidding size serving primarily to shrink and humble its rebellious human component. In the second epistle though this order appears but briefly, its angels are used to depreciate the greatest scientist of the age (one whom Pope genuinely admired), pointing out, no doubt with a superior smile, "a Newton as we shew an Ape." On the other hand, this same gradational structure wears a far benigner aspect when we meet with it next, in the third epistle, as a "chain of Love." In this epistle, the hierarchy of beings combines ancient notions of the creation of all things by Eros with contemporary Newtonian principles of attraction and with Newton's own explicit hypothesis that behind his mathematical formulas lay something far more deeply interfused: "a powerful ever-living Agent, who being in all Places, is more able by his Will to move the Bodies within his boundless uniform Sensorium, and thereby to form and reform the Parts of the Universe, than we are by our Will to move the Parts of our own Bodies." Through a chain of love thus informed, Pope can now assert, in opposition to Lucretius and Hobbes, the doctrine of interdependence that is to be the theme of this epistle and the means of rehabilitating human nature:

> Look round our World; behold the chain of Love
> Combining all below and all above.
> See plastic Nature working to this end,
> The single atoms each to other tend,
> Attract, attracted to, the next in place
> Form'd and impell'd its neighbour to embrace.
> See Matter next, with various life endu'd,
> Press to one centre still, the gen'ral Good.
> See dying vegetables life [animal life] sustain,
> See life dissolving vegetate again:
> All forms that perish other forms supply,
> (By turns we catch the vital breath, and die)
> Like bubbles on the sea of Matter born,
> They rise, they break, and to that sea return.

(3: 7–20)

Pride, of course, is still the great enemy, fueling the destructive impulses by which human beings undertake to set themselves apart from this fellowship of creatures. Like the subordination stressed in the first epistle and the duality of human nature expounded in the second, the fellowship of creatures in the third is a law of God that men and women in their separatist moods are always ready to imagine they have superseded. Hence their assumption that creatures below them exist merely for their exploitation—an attitude in our time beginning to meet with some resistance from biologists concerned for the total gene pool—which (according to the traditional but not necessarily misleading lore that Pope follows here) eventually fathers a like assumption with respect to their fellow human beings:

> The Fury-passions from that blood began,
> And turn'd on Man a fiercer savage, Man.
>
> (3: 167–68)

The true facts are, this epistle throughout insists, that human creatures and all other creatures of the visible creation have been made mutually dependent, the instinctive nature of the latter oriented so unerringly within its limits that reason has no cause to preen:

> Say, where full Instinct is th' unerring guide,
> What Pope or Council can they need beside?
> Reason, however able, cool at best,
> Cares not for service, or but serves when prest,
> Stays till we call, and then not often near;
> But honest Instinct comes a volunteer; . . .
> This too serves always, Reason never long;
> One must go right, the other may go wrong.
>
> (3: 83–88, 93–94)

Human societies originate like animal societies from sexual drives. The arts supporting human societies are usually elaborations of processes found among the other creatures. And even in its highest manifestations civilized life represents a conscious application, not a repudiation, of the mutuality divinely established in the terrestrial and cosmic whole:

> Where small and great, where weak and mighty, made
> To serve, not suffer, strengthen, not invade,
> More pow'rful each as needful to the rest,
> And, in proportion as it blesses blest,
> Draw to one point, and to one centre bring
> Beast, Man, or Angel, Servant, Lord or King.
>
> (3: 297–302)

"More pow'rful each as needful to the rest"

To this theme of an arrogant separatism blinding the human animal to its own best interests, the fourth epistle supplies an additional dimension. Man, who has been looked at successively with reference to his place in the cosmos, his own compound nature, then his need for and inclination to society, is now considered with reference to happiness—

> Oh Happiness! our being's end and aim!
> Good, Pleasure, Ease, Content! whate'er thy name:
> That something still which prompts th' eternal sigh—
>
> (4: 1–3)

and particularly with reference to those much sought-after goods that every individual has to learn for himself are largely illusory: riches, rank, aristocratic bloodlines, power military or political, even exceptional intellectual genius. Any of these, in addition to exacting a price whose extent and nature are unforeseeable, can quickly turn to ashes in the owner's hands. (In speaking of the disappointments that may attend intellectual genius, the poet addresses Bolingbroke directly: did he also think of the misshapen body that, so far as he knew, made part of the price in his own case?) In any event, he is careful to open his account of these goods with lines reiterating the thesis of the earlier three epistles that humanity's self-serving effort to set itself apart—in this instance to find happiness in pursuits unworthy of it—is blasphemous as well as vain:

> O sons of earth! attempt ye still to rise,
> By mountains pil'd on mountains, to the skies?
> Heav'n still with laughter the vain toil surveys,
> And buries madmen in the heaps they raise.
>
> (4: 73–76)

Traditional instances of pride warring on heaven (the Titans and the insurgent kings of the second Psalm) are invoked here to underscore the meaning of preoccupation with material goods. As if to certify, in fact, that such goods have no moral standing, Providence goes out of its way to distribute them unevenly, and, where they most abound, to stress their consequences. Decorations would you have? "Mark how they grace Lord Umbra, or Sir Billy." Gold? "Look but on Gripus, or on Gripus' wife." Talent? "Think how Bacon shin'd, The wisest, brightest, meanest of mankind." Reputation after death? "See Cromwell, damn'd to everlasting fame!" Or do you long for all of these goods together?

If all, united, thy ambition call,
From ancient story learn to scorn them all.
There, in the rich, the honour'd, fam'd and great,
See the false scale of Happiness complete!
In hearts of Kings, or arms of Queens who lay,
How happy! those to ruin, these betray:
Mark by what wretched steps their glory grows,
From dirt and sea-weed as proud Venice rose;
In each how guilt and greatness equal ran,
And all that rais'd the Hero, sunk the Man.
Now Europe's laurels on their brows behold,
But stain'd with blood, or ill exchang'd for gold,
Then see them broke with toils, or sunk in ease,
Or infamous for plunder'd provinces.
Oh wealth ill-fated! which no act of fame
E'er taught to shine, or sanctify'd from shame!
What greater bliss attends their close of life?
Some greedy minion, or imperious wife,
The trophy'd arches, story'd halls invade,
And haunt their slumbers in the pompous shade.
Alas! not dazzled with their noon-tide ray,
Compute the morn and ev'ning to the day;
The whole amount of that enormous fame,
A Tale, that blends their glory with their shame!

(4: 285–308)

Latent in Pope's mind here, as the manuscripts of the poem show, was the career of the Duke of Marlborough. But he was wise to leave the features shadowy in printing it. The covert references to the modern instance are expediently muted but at the same time tellingly reasserted by the generalized historic pattern of guilt and greatness in which they are subsumed. Or to put it another way, the "ancient story" has recurred, has become modern all over again, and thus "ancient" in a richer and more damning sense.

Yet for all its sharp indictments, the mood the poem encourages in its readers is not finally negative. Quite the reverse. Though pride and narcissism make our common nature a different kind of threat in each epistle, all four phases of the poem conclude with images of reconciliation, and there is an unmistakable progression in them. The whole in which we find ourselves in the lines earlier quoted on the One and Many is stupendous and minimizing: we are present, but mainly as the lower term of a disproportion of which the upper term is the highest order of created things. Unlike the seraph, we lack the beatific vision, we are vile, and we complain. Still, the force that lights the stars and through the green fuse drives the flower informs us too. At the close of the second epistle, it is plain that we have come a certain way. Though fools where God is wise, individualists pursuing selfish ends that are only to be reconciled with the larger scheme by a superior power, we are now squarely at stage center and at least capable of virtues. If our ways of fulfilling ourselves seem, when looked at from a higher view, partly delusive as well as genuine, they are after all an aspect of our reality with which the higher view must come to terms: "In Folly's cup still laughs the bubble, joy." Pity mingles with irony in the poet's sketch of man the eternal child.

For these passional, instinctive, self-concerning elements in human nature are forces helping us toward a wider range of sympathies. Through compassion as well as pride, interest, and luxury, we subserve the fellowship of lower creatures, sometimes against our will. Our self-considering instincts guide us into wedlock, family, commonwealth. Misapplied, they can carry us to superstition and despotism, but rectified, to true religion and government by law. In the image of conciliation with which the third epistle closes, man is no longer minimized or self-deluded, but the composer of "th' according music of a well-mix'd State," an agent able to reproduce in his society the harmony of opposing forces visible in God's creation, delineating thus His shadow if not His image, and though "supported," also supporting:

> Man, like the gen'rous vine, supported lives;
> The strength he gains is from th' embrace he gives.
> On their own Axis as the Planets run,
> Yet make at once their circle round the Sun:
> So two consistent motions act the Soul;
> And one regards Itself, and one the Whole.
>
> (3: 311–16)

In the corresponding passage of the fourth epistle, man no longer reflects the shadow but the image. When he has thrown an ever-widening circle of acceptance, good will, and love about the vast whole in which he finds himself—extending the embrace he gives to include neighbors, enemies, and the entire kingdoms represented by men and women, animals, and plants—self-love transcends itself in charity, eros in agape, and humanity reflects to heaven an experience of complex unity creatively achieved among dissimilars, which is akin to and the mirror image of the complex unity of existents sustained in the mind of God:

> God loves from Whole to Parts: but human soul
> Must rise from Individual to the Whole.
> Self-love but serves the virtuous mind to wake,
> As the small pebble stirs the peaceful lake;
> The centre mov'd, a circle strait succeeds,
> Another still, and still another spreads,
> Friend, parent, neighbour, first it will embrace,
> His country next, and next all human race,
> Wide and more wide, th' o'erflowings of the mind
> Take ev'ry creature in, of ev'ry kind;
> Earth smiles around, with boundless bounty blest,
> And Heav'n beholds its image in his breast.
>
> (4: 361–72)

Beginning with a reminder of a paradise we have lost—the "Garden, tempting with forbidden fruit"—the poem ends with a paradise to be regained.

As a whole, it will by now be clear, the *Essay on Man* represents the day side of Pope's visionary imagination, as the *Dunciad* represents the night side. In the *Dunciad*, things fall apart. We are made acutely conscious of a world whose creatures are intensely self-absorbed, solipsistic atoms rocketing about in an eternal now, oblivious of past or future. Even the expanded famous close, written for the Variorum *Dunciad* of 1729, presents a system of seemingly isolated particulars, each acting separately in its own interest and therefore in vain. Light dies, stars fade "one by one," "Art after Art goes out," "Truth" is buried under mountains of "heap'd casuistry":

> See Physic beg the Stagyrite's★ defence!
> See Metaphysic call for aid on Sence!
> See Mystery to Mathematicks fly!
> In vain! they gaze, turn giddy, rave, and die.

The verses last quoted from the *Essay*, however, and those immediately preceding them proffer a countervision of embrace, ingathering, and coherence:

> Self-love thus push'd to social, to divine,
> Gives thee to make thy neighbour's blessing thine.
> Is this too little for the boundless heart?

★ Aristotle's.

Extend it, let thy enemies have part:
Grasp the whole worlds of Reason, Life, and Sense,
In one close system of Benevolence.

To this order, redeemed from the chaos of separatism, human beings despite their frailties—indeed, in part because of them—may legitimately aspire.

"The destruction of the orchard"

Voltaire called the *Essay* "the most beautiful, the most useful, and the most sublime didactic poem ever written in any language." Samuel Johnson, though on different grounds, also gave it high praise. He did not care for what he took (sometimes wrongly, I believe) to be its doctrines, and, moreover, thought them derived from Bolingbroke, whose heterodoxy he despised. But he acknowledged that they were "never till now recommended by such a blaze of embellishment or such sweetness of melody":

> The vigorous contraction of some thoughts, the luxuriant amplification of others, the incidental illustrations, and sometimes the dignity, sometimes the softness of the verses, enchain philosophy, suspend criticism, and oppress judgment by overpowering pleasure.

Coming from a critic who did not use words idly, Johnson's "overpowering pleasure" gives food for thought. Even in 1974 an English poet and critic is found comparing Pope in his *Essay on Man* to a Blakean angel sitting in the sun and the poetry itself to the music of the spheres.

But such sentiments are admittedly today exceptional. Poems in the genre of the *Essay* are not, as the saying goes, our thing. Neither, for that matter, are greater poems like *Paradise Lost*. Neither is the long poem generally: witness Browning's psychological cliffhanger, *The Ring and the Book*, once read aloud in every literary family and in a century of Browning societies. To tell truth, poems whether long or short are not particularly our thing, though many volumes containing them annually appear and are reviewed, given prizes, and read—mainly by other poets. The idea that a poem of some thirteen hundred odd lines could run through dozens of editions in its author's lifetime and be translated into eighteen or twenty European languages (into some of them as many as twelve to twenty times in its first century of existence) strikes us nowadays as slightly indecent: proof, surely, that the work must be bad. As for the corollary idea that a poet might seriously endeavor to gather up, in a language suited to communication with a general audience, many of the central concerns of his society and time, this seems today almost equally unimaginable, and with reason. The imaginations of our own poets, notably in this second half of the twentieth century, have been engaged by other matters, not necessarily less exacting; and nothing that can be called a general audience, much less a shared vocabulary of literary and philosophical experience for addressing it, remains.

Pope was luckier. He could shape for the entire literate public of his time a world view which was both traditional and very "modern"; which gathered up the muddle and miscellany of things in a comprehensive intellectual order; which brought together in one imaginative time and space (to choose a single instance from many) the rapt seraph of Biblical theology and the retractable membrane protecting a mole's eye ("the mole's dim curtain"), only recently discovered by the new science of zoology; and which, best of all, as much in the disciplined concision of the individual couplet as in the shifting perspectives and polarities of the poetic whole, enacted, so far as language can enact, the faith it was proposing: that the muddle and miscellany were in fact subject to a plan and the centrifugal freedoms of the individual caught up in a larger motion that imposed on them a form:

> On their own Axis as the Planets run,
> Yet make at once their circle round the Sun. . . .

In couplet, poem, man, society, cosmos—just as in the ancient intuitions of Heraclitus and the new demonstrations of the Newtonians (past and present here again brought into a mutually supportive relationship)—it was the tension of opposing forces that made the structure one.

At the same time, though its author may or may not have been conscious of this, the poem voiced some of the major anxieties of its period, anxieties that in other forms have troubled later periods equally if not more. One, clearly, is the problem of authority and its sanctions. The *Essay*'s heavy stress on "Order" as the first law of heaven and its correspondingly dramatic images of anarchy ("All this dread ORDER break? for whom? for thee?"), though no doubt they owe something to the awe attending on Newton's revelation of the delicate balance of forces in the solar system, can hardly have been uninfluenced by a century of rapid and stunning change—political, social, religious, economic, and intellectual. It was a century that had seen civil war, the execution of a king, the expulsion of another, profound readjustments of values and powers as the business middle classes jostled the landed gentry and aristocracy, and even more profound readjustments of attitudes and loyalties as three different ruling dynasties, each in some degree foreign, took over and had to be "absorbed."

A period anxiety shows itself again perhaps in the poem's recurrent emphasis on the interdependence of things, including the interdependence of human beings in their families and societies. This is not, I think, simply Pope's response to Hobbes's picture of natural society as a war of all on all. It springs partly from his own deepest intuitions of the atomistic individualism working in the age (a phenomenon attested to by many), as it moved compulsively toward such definitions of success as are implicit in the career of Balaam, and, psychologically, toward such aspects of self-concern and self-exploration as in their youthful heyday produced the glories of Romantic poetry, but now, in their old age and decadence, as an astute observer during these latter decades has pointed out, serve chiefly to carry the pursuit of happiness "to the dead end of a narcissistic preoccupation with the self."

And then, finally, as cause for worry both conscious and subconscious, that arresting figure: the glory, jest, and riddle of the world. Pope does not use the term Faustian, but it is clearly the Faustian rebellious side of man's potential that disturbs him. In Marlowe, the Faustian figure chooses doom and goes to it. In Milton, one such figure chooses and goes to it, taking many with him; two others choose and are saved by mercy. In Pope, though man is granted power to see things straight, to recognize the intricate interdependence of things, and, if he will, to found upon it a contentment that will secure him, his separatist and exploitative pride threatens not his own species only but all, and, indeed, the entire system of relationships that includes him:

> On superior pow'rs
> Were we to press, inferior might on ours:
> Or in the full creation leave a void,
> Where, one step broken, the great scale's destroy'd.
>
> (1: 241–44)

Pope's conditional suggests that there is an option open. Faustian man *can* press. And though Pope had no other way of understanding this than as a philosophical possibility, we know now that it is more.

"Human beings," one of the most distinguished medical biologists of our time has written,

> are getting themselves, and the rest of the world, into deeper and deeper trouble, and I would not lay heavy odds on our survival unless we begin maturing soon. Up to now, we have been living through the equivalent of an early childhood for our species. We have not been here any length of time, in evolutionary terms, and no wonder we are still young, with nothing but frontal lobes, thumbs, language, and culture to rely on for our shelter and survival. We could fumble and do it wrong. Thermonuclear war is the worst case to contemplate, enough in itself to cause the crash of our species, but we have other threats to make against our lasting existence: overpopulation and crash, deforestation and crash, pollution and crash, a long list of possible bad dreams come true, the sounds, always outside the window offstage, of the destruction of the orchard.

That almost every reference in this quotation would have left Pope dazed is a measure of how much our world has changed from his. But the destruction of the orchard—*that* he would have understood, without needing to read Chekhov. That had happened before. In Genesis. And it could happen again:

> Could he, whose rules the rapid Comet bind,
> Describe or fix one movement of his Mind?
> Who saw its fires here rise, and there descend,
> Explain his own beginning, or his end?
> Alas what wonder! Man's superior part
> Uncheck'd may rise, and climb from art to art:
> But when his own great work is but begun,
> What Reason weaves, by Passion is undone.
>
> (2: 35–42)

Including the Passion of Superpowers.

"The finest Image of a Saint expir'd"

Pope published the third epistle of his *Essay* on May 8, 1733, intending, one suspects, that the fourth should follow some four or five weeks later, as had been the case with the earlier parts. But on June 7, after a period of several years during which her memory sometimes flickered and there were lapses into or at least toward second childish-

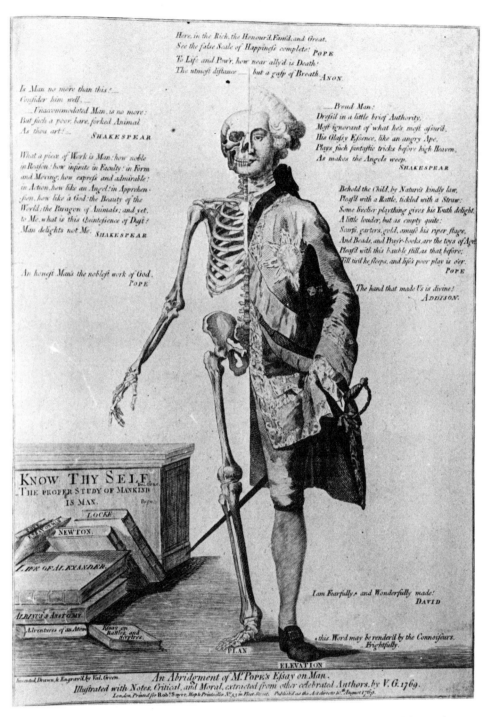

63. An Abridgment of Mr. Pope's *Essay on Man*. Drawn and engraved by Valentine Green, 1769.

Privately owned.

ness and mere oblivion, Edith Pope died. Without a groan or sigh, according to her son, and having, as he wrote Jonathan Richardson on the third day after the event,

> upon her countenance such an expression of Tranquillity, nay almost of pleasure, that far from horrid, it is even amiable to behold it. It wou'd afford the finest Image of a Saint expir'd, that ever Painting drew; and it wou'd be the greatest obligation which even That obliging Art could ever bestow on a friend if you cou'd come and sketch it for me. . . . I will defer her interment till tomorrow night.

Despite the controlled tone, there was still a certain agitation, as Pope's first giving the letter a January date suggests, and as his earlier announcement of her death to Fortescue makes clear:

> It is indeed a Grief to mee which I cannot express, and which I should hate my own Heart if it did not feel, & yet wish no Friend I have ever should feel.

And then, in two sentences as if applying to himself the account he had been giving of human nature in the *Essay*: "All our Passions are Inconsistencies, & our very Reason is no better. But we are what we were Made to be."

In the evening of June 11, evidently after Richardson had made the sketch requested of him, Mrs. Pope was buried in St. Mary's, Twickenham. Evening, it will be recalled, was the usual time for a Roman Catholic burial in Protestant ground, there being as yet no legal papist alternative. Those chosen to carry her coffin, after a custom much honored in those times as bringing with it an emolument of clothing and perhaps money, were six of the poorest and oldest men of the parish, and the bearers of her pall were six of the oldest and poorest women. In Mrs. Pope's case, probably more than custom was involved. The compliment to his mother that the poet inserted in the *Essay's* fourth epistle, now not to appear till the following January, claims her as "a parent to the poor" as well as to himself. However this may be, St. Mary's as an arm of the Establishment was obliged to exact the usual humbling ounce of flesh. The bearers, both men and women, all wore mourning—"except Gloves and Hatbands, which were not allowed to the Minister, nor any Body to follow the Corpse."

For Pope, the consciousness of loss was acute, more so probably than is the norm. Habit alone would have been disoriented by the sudden removal (however much expected) of a center of concern so

J. Richardson delin 1731.   *C. Carter fecit Aqua forti 1774.*

64. Edith Pope (1643–1733). Engraving by Charles Carter after a drawing (1731) by Jonathan Richardson.

> Or why so long (if long in life can be)
> Lent Heav'n a parent to the poor and me?
>
> *Essay on Man*, 4: 109–10.

Privately owned.

faithfully attended over so many years. But there was also deep affection. An affection likely to have been enhanced as she and her son grew older by the mutual nursing services required of each other by two partial invalids, and also by the warmth of an undoubtedly passionate man to whom nature had denied, or so he thought, attachments of another kind. Indeed, if we may believe his half-sister, Pope seems to have been as oversolicitous in the care of his mother as sometimes in the service of his friends. "Mrs. *Pope*," Magdalen Rackett told Richardson in 1742,

> complain'd that most children plagu'd their Parents with Neglect; that He did so as much the other way, perpetually teasing her with his Overfondness & Care, & pressing her to Eat this & that; & Drink another Glass of Wine; and so assiduous as never to let her be at Liberty, & chuse for her self. Gave her great Uneasiness this way.

Though assuredly it was trying, no one who has watched the very old wither away unawares through self-starvation and dehydration, or has felt the unexceptionable human urge to establish contact, by whatever means, with a consciousness that is more and more often seen to be partly or wholly oblivious of its surroundings, will be confident that Pope's zeal was altogether misplaced.

How closely in her earlier stronger days during the 1720s Edith Pope was able to follow her son's career and what sort of psychological support she brought him, we are not likely at this date to learn. Though inevitably conscious of his fame and of the many friends and admirers who passed through their house at Twickenham, was she also acquainted with that portion of his life alluded to in the Preface of his 1717 *Works* as "a warfare upon earth"? Did she see or hear of the steady stream of pamphlet and newspaper attacks, which after his reprisal in the *Dunciad* rose to a torrent? And did he, on his side, let his acute sensitivity to such slurs (which he always tried to pretend was indifference) show in her presence: his pardonable anger and embarrassment, for instance, when Timon's villa was slanderously identified as Chandos's "Cannons" and he was charged on all sides with ingratitude? Or was this dimension of his world largely *terra incognita* to her?

Whatever the right answer to these questions, it is probably safe to say that her twilit condition during the spring of 1733 spared her knowing one of the most crushing blows ever dealt her son. This was the blow delivered by two representatives of the highest centers of power in the land—Lady Mary Wortley Montagu, her son's former

65. The obelisk in Alexander Pope's garden in memory of his mother. Watercolor by John Chessell Buckler, signed and dated 1826.

By kind permission of the Houghton Library, Harvard University.

intimate but now enemy, whom she had known well, and Lord Hervey, vice-chamberlain to the king, but also husband of the beautiful Mary Lepell, who thirteen years before had come to convalesce in the good air of Twickenham under their mutual care.

PART FOUR

"MY COUNTRYS POET"

1733–1744

CHAPTER 22

PERSONALITIES AND POLITICS

"Its proper Pow'r to hurt each Creature feels"

At some point during the 1720s, relations between Pope and Lady Mary had seriously soured—we do not know why. One rather silly story has it that she inspired his aversion by returning, unwashed, some sheets she had borrowed while entertaining guests at her house in Twickenham. Another, hardly more convincing (though Lady Mary is apparently its source), attributes their estrangement to Pope's jealousy of the young duke of Wharton, whom she began to see much of for a few years following 1722. Lady Louisa Stuart, Lady Mary's granddaughter, reports as coming from her grandmother a yet different account. At some ill-chosen time, she says

> when she least expected what romances call a declaration, he [Pope] made such passionate love to her, as, in spite of her utmost endeavours to be angry and look grave, provoked an immoderate fit of laughter; from which moment he became her implacable enemy.

This explanation, though tempting, is suspicious on three counts. It has against it Pope's painfully acquired wariness about exposing his crippled self to humiliations (the same sort of wariness that prompted him to think immediately of being cuckolded by some handsome Lord Foppington when in 1717 his friend Harcourt suggested he marry a Harcourt relation). It is precisely the sort of explanation that a woman who wished to hold a male enemy up to scorn would be likeliest to invent. And it remains considerably astonishing that it appears nowhere in Lady Mary's written attacks on Pope, published or unpublished; surely it would have been the most effective weapon in her armory. It cannot, on the other hand, be altogether ruled out. In affairs of the heart, as we all know, one sudden impulse can shrivel

66. *The Rejected Poet* (Pope's proposal of love to Lady Mary Wortley Montagu). By W. P. Frith, *c.* 1854. The scene is, of course, imaginary, and the likeness of the painter's Lady Mary to the actual Lady Mary not impressive.

Courtesy of the Wolverhampton Art Gallery.

up all the wariness in the world like a moth in a candle flame. An episode of this kind would, moreover, help account for the lasting vehemence of Pope's animosity against her as well as for what appears to have been on her part an increasingly psychotic hatred of him, though her feeling, which extended to several of his friends, must have been in part political. Even as late as 1757, thirteen years after Pope's death, twelve years after Swift's, and six after Bolingbroke's, she showed an English friend who visited her in Venice (in 1739 she had left England to live abroad) how her close-stool was painted like the backs of books by these three. She had known them well, she said. "They were the greatest Rascals, but she had the satisfaction of shitting on them every day."

Pope's own explanations of the break, though they do not rule out Lady Mary's, hang together convincingly enough to warrant equal consideration. As early as 1724, in a letter to Bathurst, he associates her mysteriously with an unexplained "fiction" which he calls greater than is "necessary to Poetry" and one he cannot hope to unravel. If the allusion is to some sort of satire directed at either Bathurst or himself, which he understands Lady Mary to be handing about, this is the first in a series of complaints on that score. Rightly or wrongly, from about this time on, he seems to have convinced himself that either by her encouragement or by her pen she was covertly responsible for certain of the attacks made on him—for example, the *Popp upon Pope* of 1728, which represented him as having been whipped in Ham-walks and gathered up in Martha Blount's apron, or the later *One Epistle to Mr. Pope* (1730), evidently a composite work, which after raking up as many untruths as possible about the poet himself, made very free in its final lines with Swift's relations with Vanessa:

> So when Vanessa yielded up her charms,
> The blest Cadenus languish'd in her arms;
> High, on a peg, his unbrush'd beaver hung,
> His vest unbutton'd, and his God unsung;
> Raptur'd he lies; Deans, Authors, are forgot,
> Wood's Copper Pence, and Atterbury's Plot;
> For her he quits the tithes of Patrick's fields,
> And all the Levite to the Lover yields.

Not surprisingly, in view of the appetite in Lady Mary's fashionable circles for scandalous gossip, all the keener if reported in clever verse, Pope further convinced himself that she was palming off some of her productions in this vein as his.

The upshot of these convictions, whether founded or otherwise, was that concealed but pointed allusions to Lady Mary began to slide into his verses and hitch in his rhymes. A squib published in the Pope–Swift *Miscellanies* of 1728—about a hen that hatched more chicks than she could rear—had the insinuating subtitle, doubtless sufficient in itself to alert the cognoscenti: "To a Lady who father'd her Lampoons upon her Acquaintance," and concluded with the advice: "Such, Lady *Mary*, are your Tricks; But since you hatch, pray own your Chicks." The early *Dunciad* of 1728 found an occasion to refer to the practice of English madams in pretending to foreign visitors that their inventory included titled ladies, and referred to it in such a manner as at once to impugn the venereal soundness of a particular lady and allow the author an escape-hatch if needed:

> (Whence hapless Monsieur much complains at Paris
> Of wrongs from Duchesses and Lady Mary's).
>
> (2: 127–28)

Even the *Epistle to Bathurst*—"On the Use of Riches"—managed without breaking stride to take sly note of two ladies, one of them Robert Walpole's mistress Maria Skerrett, the other her good friend Lady Mary Wortley Montagu, totting up resources to support an addiction of the sort already alluded to in the *Dunciad* lines:

> Ask you why Phryne★ the whole Auction buys?
> Phryne foresees a general Excise.
> Why she and Lesbia† raise that monstrous sum?
> Alas! they fear a man will cost a plum.‡
>
> (ll. 121–24)

Meantime, if we may believe Pope, there were activities on Lady Mary's side that gave *him* concern. September 1729 finds him complaining to Fortescue, as if in answer to a query,

> I have seen Sir R[obert] W[alpole] but once since you left. I made him then my confidant in a complaint against a lady, of his, and once of my, acquaintance, who is libelling me, as she certainly one

---

★ The name of a celebrated Athenian courtesan, who grew very rich from the liberality of her lovers; hence applicable to Maria Skerrett, who, according to Lord Hervey (p. 86) received from Walpole, besides an annual allowance, £5,000 by way of "entrance money."
† Lesbia, evoking Sappho's Lesbos, suited equally a poetess like Lady Mary—in 1735 Pope altered Lesbia to Sappho.
‡ A plum was the sum of £100,000.

day will him, if she has not already. You'll easily guess I am speaking of Lady Mary. I should be sorry if she had any credit or influence with him, for she would infallibly use it to bely me; though my only fault towards her was, leaving off her conversation when I found it dangerous.

Some light is possibly cast on Pope's meaning by a statement of Lady Mary's to Spence, when he met her in Italy in 1741:

I got a third person to ask Mr. Pope why he had left off visiting me. He answered negligently that he went as often as he used to. I then got Dr. Arbuthnot to ask what Lady Mary had done to him? He said that Lady Mary and Lord Hervey had pressed him once together (and I don't remember that we were ever together with him in our lives) to write a satire on some certain persons, that he refused it, and that this had occasioned the breach between us.

"Lord Fanny" (Hervey) and "Lady De-la-Wit" (in all probability Lady Mary) are further credited in his unpublished "Master Key to Popery" of 1732 with leading roles in spreading slander about "Timon's Villa" and, in his likewise unpublished "Letter to a Noble Lord" of the following year, with misuse of his name:

Had I ever the honour to join with either of you in one *Ballad*, *Satire*, *Pamphlet*, or *Epigram*, on any person *living* or *dead*? Did I ever do you so great an injury as to put off *my own Verses* for yours, especially on *those Persons* whom they might *most offend*?

What seems clear, at any rate, is that by 1733 patience on both sides was wearing thin. In a manuscript reply to his *Dunciad*, which it would have been surprising if she did not circulate among her courtier friends, Lady Mary had transferred the "Palace" of Dulness to Pope's grotto, dismissed *The Beggar's Opera* as fit only for "Male and female Fools," referred to Swift as "Trampling on Order, Decency, and Laws," and written of Arbuthnot, even while she was using him to convey to Pope her denial of having taken part in *One Epistle*, that he was "Born in that Realm where Nastyness gives Joy, And scratching all the solitary hours employ." Whether Pope, who also had many friends at Court, heard rumors of this piece; or thought by 1733 that he knew of fresh attacks on himself or new libels being circulated in his name; or still smarted from the Timon/ Chandos slander or some other gossip in which he suspected she had played him false; or was simply moved to spleen by the bout of illness during which he wrote the poem—whatever the provocation,

imagined or real, he seems to have decided that now was the time for
a sharper flick of the lash. In his *First Satire of the Second Book of Horace,
Imitated* (published in mid-February with his name on it as part of his
scheme to dissuade the public from imagining the *Essay on Man* could
also be his), he began with a relatively mild allusion to Hervey as
"Lord Fanny." This was a name that both associated Hervey with the
Roman poetaster Fannius, whom Horace likewise had laughed at,
and emphasized the femininities of bearing and appearance, including
face-painting, that had made him the butt of London ridicule for
some time:

> There are (I scarce can think it, but am told)
> There are to whom my Satire seems too bold,
> Scarce to wise *Peter* complaisant enough,
> And something said of *Chartres* much too rough.
> The Lines are weak, another's pleas'd to say,
> Lord *Fanny* spins a thousand such a Day.
>
> (ll. 1–6)

Though scornful, there was nothing notably egregious about such
language, which had often enough been used of Hervey by others.
But having gone on from this, in the wake of Horace, to propose that
every creature is by nature granted its own appropriate form of
aggression, he concludes that satire must be his, just as Lady Mary
and certain other Establishment favorites also have theirs:

> Slander or Poyson, dread from *Delia*'s Rage,
> Hard Words or Hanging, if your Judge be [*Page*];
> From furious *Sappho* scarce a milder Fate,
> P—x'd by her Love, or libell'd by her Hate:
> Its proper Pow'r to hurt, each Creature feels,
> Bulls aim their horns, and Asses lift their heels,
> 'Tis a Bear's Talent not to kick but hug,
> And no man wonders he's not stung by Pug:*
> So drink with *Waters*, or with *Chartres* eat,
> They'll never poison you, they'll only cheat.
>
> (ll. 81–90)

Why Lady Mary took this particular insult, outrageous as it was,
more to heart than the one placing her in brothels is difficult to see.
Her reaction put her in the awkward position of seeming to acknowledge a disrepute that she might have let go glancing by. For as Lord
Peterborow reminded her with infuriating exactness (in a letter

* Common name for a pet monkey.

possibly phrased by Pope) when she called on him as intermediary to inquire into Pope's intentions, there were and had been many English "Sapphos":

> He said to me what I had taken the Liberty to say to you, that he wonderd how the Town could apply those Lines to any but some noted common woeman, that he should yet be more surprised if you should take them to your Self, He named to me fower remarkable poetesses & scribblers, Mrs. Centlivre Mrs Haywood Mrs Manly & Mrs Been [Aphra Behn], Ladies famous indeed in their generation, and some of them Esteemed to have given very unfortunate favours to their Friends, assuring me that Such only were the objects of his satire.

Possibly, Lady Mary thought the clue in "P—x'd" too pointed to be ignored. Not because she had syphilis, though Horace Walpole, by no means always a reliable witness, at a later time thought so. Nor even because she was a plainly marked victim of the smallpox. Her fame had long been deservedly established for defending the practice of inoculation, which she had observed in the East, and for abetting its spread in England despite vociferous opposition. "P—x'd by her love" had therefore an extra depth, almost enabling it to function as a compliment while at the same time identifying its victim and, possibly, if it came to legal prosecution, confusing the issue. In any event, one can hardly blame her for her anger at the insulting allegation dropped in so casually among other allegations believed by many to be truths. Page, for example, *was* in fact something of a judicial sadist, and there had been a scandal, carefully hushed up, involving a supposed attempt by "Delia" (Lady Mary Deloraine, governess to the younger princesses and soon to be their father's whore) to poison a rival. And it may be, further, that Lady Mary's resentment was spurred by Lord Hervey, himself now a sufferer as "Fanny" and perhaps eager for revenge. A degree of collaboration, at any rate, took place, and a poem appeared on March 9, essentially Lady Mary's but apparently with assistance from Hervey, entitled *Verses Address'd to the Imitator Of the First Satire of the Second Book of Horace. By a Lady*. In this, Pope received the fiercest verbal thrashing of his life. It rehearsed the usual themes—that Pope was baseborn, knew no Greek, wrote only crabbed verse, hated all mankind ("To thee 'tis Provocation to exist"), returned, for Chandos's generosity, ingratitude—but reserved its cruellest lines for his deformity:

> But how should'st thou by Beauty's Force be mov'd,
> No more for loving made, than to be lov'd?
> It was the Equity of righteous Heav'n,
> That such a Soul to such a Form was giv'n.
>
> (ll. 48–51)

Alas, if Lady Mary's tale of a "declaration" may be trusted, he had been by beauty's force far too deeply moved. Ensuing verses on his "wretched little Carcass" have been quoted on an earlier page. From these, as a recent historian of contemporary attacks on Pope phrases it, she rises "in the appalling final lines . . . to a full command of the rhetoric of hate," comfortably forgetting in the first two of them that however scurrilous and vindictive Pope had been, he had not struck from ambush—he had put his name to his work, as she had not:

> Then whilst with Coward Hand you stab a Name,
> And try at least t'assassinate our Fame;
> Like the first bold Assassin's be thy Lot,
> Ne'er be thy Guilt forgiven, or forgot;
> But as thou hat'st, be hated by Mankind,
> And with the Emblem of thy crooked Mind,
> Mark'd on thy back, like *Cain*, by God's own Hand;
> Wander like him accursed through the Land.
>
> (ll. 105–12)

To compare this passage or indeed any part of *Verses to the Imitator* with Pope's couplet on "Sappho" is to discover the esthetic virtues of brevity and irony. Still, the gauntlet had been thrown, however crudely, and Pope was not the man to hesitate to take it up. For the next five years, he rarely failed to dedicate a line or two of his Horatian poems to Lady Mary, touching mainly on her slatternliness and her own and her husband's tightfistedness, two points where there is much evidence he was on solid ground, but also, and repeatedly, on her sexual promiscuity, about which, not surprisingly, despite her unsavory reputation in some quarters in her own time, it is impossible to be positive. As with her story of his "declaration," it is the sort of insult a deeply wounded man might well make up.

On her side, Lady Mary was not idle. In 1734, evidently irritated by Pope's tributes to Bolingbroke in both the *Essay on Man* and the offending imitation of Horace, she composed a set of verses addressed as if by him to Bolingbroke. Their general character may be gauged from the following sample, where Pope is imagined to be saying to his guide, philosopher, and friend:

> You, learned Doctor of the publick Stage,
> Give gilded poison to corrupt the Age;
> Your poor Toad-eater I, around me scatter
> My scurril jests, and gaping Crouds bespatter.

(ll. 59–62)

This anemic effort she had sense enough not to publish, but there is no reason to suppose it did not circulate in manuscript, and if word of it reached Pope, who already knew, or believed he knew, that her *Verses to the Imitator* had been presented to the King and Queen, it can only have suggested that a cabal was forming against him at the highest levels. That same year, this time with a more temperate treatment of Pope, she attacked Swift, in print, but again anonymously, for writing *The Lady's Dressing Room*, first published in 1732. Characteristically Swiftian in its stress on unsavory and even nauseating realities underlying glittering outsides, *The Lady's Dressing Room* is explained in Lady Mary's poem as the dean's revenge after visiting a certain "Betty" of easy virtue and failing to achieve what he came for:

> The Rev'rend Lover with surprise
> Peeps in her Bubbies, and her Eyes,
> And kisses both, and tries—and tries.

(ll. 67–69)

Like her *Verses to the Imitator*, the poem is more abuse than wit and conveys a disheartening sense of what time, personal sufferings of much bitterness (her husband proved intolerable and her son worthless), and, probably most of all, that thickening carapace of cynicism with which, like the hermit crab, she had grown accustomed to shielding her softer feelings, could do to the enchanting gay young woman who had dazzled Pope so many years before. When the dean, unsuccessful, asks his money back, the best Lady Mary can do with his light o' love's reply is a kind of fatigued obscenity:

> What if your Verses have not sold,
> Must therefore I return your Gold?
> Perhaps you have no better Luck in
> The Knack of Rhyming than of——
> I won't give back one single Crown
> To wash your Band, or turn your Gown.
>   I'll be reveng'd you saucy Quean
> (Replys the disapointed Dean)
> I'll so describe your *Dressing-Room*

The very *Irish* shall not come.
She answer'd short, I'm glad you'll write,
You'll furnish paper when I sh——e.

(ll. 90–101)

As we saw earlier, with Bolingbroke and Pope he *did* finally furnish a receptacle.

"An answer from Horace"

The poem into which Pope dropped his explosive "Sappho" couplet is not only one of his most assured masterpieces, but in its calculated offhand way the nearest thing to a poet's manifesto that he had so far ventured. He wrote it, apparently in a day or two, at Lord Oxford's house in Dover Street, while lying ill in early 1733 of what was being called at the time an "Epidemical Distemper"—doubtless some variety of what we now know as flu, which had been spreading that winter over Europe as well as England. One fragment of the manuscript of the poem is, in fact, a medical instruction, on the back of which the poet has scribbled several lines.

The work was clearly intended to be a codicil, or, as it has been called, a "rearguard," to the two earlier epistles to Burlington and Bathurst. The *Epistle to Burlington*, though centered mainly on the grotesque results of misguided prodigality in collecting, building, and landscaping generally, *could* be read as censure of the philistinism of the new class of war-rich and pension-rich Whig magnates, with one of the richest of whom, perhaps significantly, Pope's enemies had instantly chosen to identify the master of "Timon's Villa." The *Epistle to Bathurst* had been far bolder. Pope obviously had not anticipated the misapplication of "Timon" that aroused such outcries, but he knew that in *To Bathurst* he was treading perilous ground, and for that reason kept the poem back two years, no doubt improving it in the interval, as was his custom. Most of the wrongdoers referred to in it—embezzlers, forgers, rapists, tricksters, tightfisted oppressors of the poor, bribe takers like Sir Balaam—were representative of the seamier groups that had found protection under the current chief minister, whose "shadowy figure" hovers in the poem's background, "just as it hovered over the politico-morality of the age." Little wonder that on March 29, referring at least partly to this poem, Bathurst wrote Swift that Pope had promised him a visit—and a good thing too! he implied. "He has made the town too hot to hold him."

What Pope's position at this point obviously called for, *vis-à-vis* his reading audience and the public generally, was clearer definition. He needed a precedent or procedure that would give these poems or any other commentaries that as a serious writer he might be moved to make about the times he lived in, an unmistakable provenance. Not in disappointed ambition or native spleen (the only two motives allowed by the ministry's beneficiaries and defenders), but in a responsible civic concern, and, for his own individual protection, in what poets, including satirists, had liked to think for generations was their traditional classical freedom to speak out. "If he is a good writer," Ernest Hemingway is reported to have said, speaking of the writer's trade, "he will never like the government he lives under." This expresses a romantic conviction, still largely dominant in Western countries today, that the artist is alienated necessarily from the body politic. No view could be further from Pope's own. For him, the poet was or should be part and parcel of the body politic, and his task remained what it had been, at least in theory, for both his classical and his Renaissance forerunners: to discourage evil-doing by dragging it to the light and burying it with obloquy, and to quicken excellence of all kinds by offering it eternal fame. As Shakespeare was fond of saying at the close of sonnet after sonnet with reference to his love:

> So long as men can breathe, or eyes can see,
> So long lives this, and this gives life to thee—

so Pope, once his satirist's mantle was on, found himself wedded to an analogous claim:

> Truth guards the Poet, sanctifies the line,
> And makes Immortal, Verse as mean as mine.
> (*One Thousand Seven Hundred and Thirty-Eight:*
> *Dial. 2:* 246–47)

It was just here that the notion of imitating Horace proved invaluable. Horace had censured his times and yet been protected by men in great place like Maecenas and Augustus. He had promised fame to virtue, infamy to vice, to folly lasting ridicule, and so far as the eighteenth century was concerned, had made good on his boast: to educated readers, his Tigellius and Crispinus were as well known as their own contemporary mountebanks and bores. Horace, therefore, made the ideal poetic precedent. Juvenal would never do, having been banished from Rome, probably by Domitian, for some satirical indiscretion. Neither would Persius, whose clotted style and comparative abstraction from the particulars of daily life in Rome did not easily accord with the shifting rainbow of incident and the quicksilvery crescendos and diminuendos of tone of which translating many thousands of lines of Homer had given Pope a mastery unparalleled. Yes: of the Roman satirists, Horace had to be the man; though once behind his mask a resourceful poet could (as Pope did) develop hints, tones, and stances from all three.

Choice of the *First Satire of the Second Book*, Pope tells us, was Bolingbroke's suggestion. Stopping by to visit the poet during his illness at Lord Oxford's and thumbing through a copy of Horace that lay on the bed table till he reached this satire, he had "observed how well that would hit my case." One suspects the little conversation may not have ended there. For when Pope completed his imitation, he had transformed Horace's poem (in which Horace persuades the eminent Roman jurist Gaius Trebatius Testa that the penalty reserved in Roman law for "libels"—*mala carmina*—is irrelevant to his own poems because they are *bona carmina* and because in any case Augustus is his patron) into a defense of satire and free expression yet more deliciously spirited than the original and, at the same time, a comically scathing challenge to the Walpole ministry and its world.

Horace's satire "hit his case" because it allowed Pope to make his present position and future intentions clear, apparently under the countenance of a highly respected world poet. By following his Roman predecessor in choosing for interlocutor a lawyer who was part of the governmental establishment to hear a defense of criticisms that were aimed directly at that establishment, he could intimate his awareness of potential danger. By rejecting, like Horace, the lawyer's advice that if he could not stop writing altogether (which would be far the best) he should write to glorify the regime, he could take public account of what must, on occasion, have been proposed to him by Fortescue or other administration friends, and what, even if never actually proposed, must sometimes have been desired or expected of him, as chief poet of the age. Further, with just a slight adjustment of Horace's demurrer—that to praise Augustus properly called for a higher style than he could command—Pope could convey the absurdity of writing poetry at all about a family so prosaic as the royal house of Brunswick. Either it would have to be epic bombast in the Sir Richard Blackmore style, which would fix the king forever in the grotesque museum of comedy, his passion for warlike postures and tendency to temper tantrums caught in the very noise and swagger of the verse—

What? like Sir *Richard*, rumbling, rough and fierce,
With ARMS, and GEORGE, and BRUNSWICK crowd the Verse?
Rend with tremendous Sound your ears asunder,
With Gun, Drum, Trumpet, Blunderbuss & Thunder?

(ll. 23–26)

or else it would have to be insipid panegyric for the distaff side, such
as would put even the Nine Muses to sleep and only a Colley Cibber
could bear to write:

Then all your Muse's softer Art display,
Let *Carolina* smooth the tuneful Lay,
Lull with *Amelia*'s liquid name the Nine,
And sweetly flow through all the Royal Line.

(ll. 29–32)

The last verse, with its hovering pun on "Line"★ and its delicate
intimations of the havoc to be expected if this poet's ink actually did
flow through the entire family, seems a particularly exquisite
invention.

With an even slighter adjustment, he could convert Horace's statement about using his satiric weapon only when attacked into a
comparison between himself and Walpole, whose hypersensitivity to
criticism he affects to share in the very moment that he chafes it
further with allusions to standing armies (always regarded as a threat
to parliamentary independence); to Cardinal Fleury's alleged dicta-
tion of England's peace policy toward Spain despite Spanish
depredations on English shipping that were much resented by City
merchants; and to what *looks* like a flamboyant warning:

Satire's my Weapon, but I'm too discreet
To run a Muck, and tilt at all I meet;
I only wear it in a land of Hectors,
Thieves, Supercargoes, Sharpers, and Directors. . . .
Peace is my dear Delight—not *Fleury*'s more:
But touch me, and no Minister so sore.
Who-e'er offends, at some unlucky Time,
Slides into Verse, and hitches in a Rhyme,
Sacred to Ridicule! his whole Life long.

(ll. 69–72, 75–79)

★ A pun presumably involving "loin" (as the seat of generative power:
OED, 2b, in Pope's day often phonetically indistinguishable from "line") as
well as "line" = verse and "line" = lineal descendants.

So much for satire as a means to self-defense should it come to that: Pope promises to give as good as he gets, and in the next three verses slips in three names of persons close to Walpole, as if in evidence of his prowess: "Delia," Sir Francis Page, and "Sappho."

"Such as Sir Robert would approve"

What yet remains unresolved, however, is the status of the satirist as licensed censor of vice and folly, which was the purpose of applying "to Council learned in the Law" in the first place. To this question, Pope now turns with particular eloquence. Horace had cited in self-defense his famous predecessor Lucilius:

> What! when Lucilius first dared to compose poems after this kind, and to strip off the skin with which each strutted all bedecked before the eyes of men, though foul within, was Laelius offended at his wit, or he [the younger Scipio Africanus] who took his well-earned name from conquered Carthage? Or were they hurt because Metellus was smitten, and Lupus buried under a shower of lampooning verses? Yet he laid hold on the leaders of the people, and upon the people in their tribes, kindly in fact only to Virtue and her friends. Nay, when virtuous Scipio and the wise and gentle Laelius withdrew into privacy from the throng and theatre of life, they would turn to folly, and flinging off restraint would indulge with him in sport while their dish of herbs was on the boil.
>
> (ll. 62–74)

This was the passage, as a writer in the *Craftsman* had urged in a debate with the government's spokesmen on freedom of the press, in which, "like an honest brave Man," the Roman poet tells Trebatius he will continue to write satire. It is also the passage that Pope had cited in a letter to Swift as "my own single motive" for writing the imitation. In reworking the lines, he replaces Lucilius with his own English and French precedents of Dryden and Boileau, without however losing the force of the Roman antecedents, whose names remain visible on the left-hand page. (Always in editions of Pope's lifetime, and for some while thereafter, the relevant portions of the Latin original, sometimes injected with additional meanings by typographical devices, faced his English and in their own way commented on it, and vice versa.) Against this background, he then puts the question to his lawyer that Horace puts to Trebatius. Is the privilege of satire that was conceded to Lucilius when he flayed moral offenders without forfeiting the favor of those in power—and to Horace, who won the protection and friendship of Augustus—and to Boileau, who even had a pension under the French establishment, and under an absolutist king at that—and to Dryden, who was never harried by either of the Stuart kings he wrote under and spasmodically had money from: is this privilege not still available today, the poet asks, especially to one who has no political obligations and counts, in fact, almost as many Whigs as Tories among his friends?

The expected answer is of course yes—provided the writer can muster the necessary courage, which, as the drift of the whole poem to this point has shown, is required to be somewhat greater under George Augustus and Walpole than under the Roman Augustus, the Sun King, or Charles and James, who were all supporters of poets:

> Could pension'd *Boileau* lash in honest Strain
> Flatt'rers and Bigots ev'n in *Louis*' Reign?
> Could Laureate *Dryden* Pimp and Fry'r engage,
> Yet neither *Charles* nor *James* be in a Rage?
> And I not strip the Gilding off a Knave,
> Un-plac'd, un-pension'd, no Man's Heir, or Slave?
> I will, or perish in the gen'rous Cause.
> Hear this, and tremble! you, who 'scape the Laws.
> Yes, while I live, no rich or noble knave
> Shall walk the World, in credit, to his grave.
>
> (ll. 111–20)

These are the traditional accents of the defiant satirist, standing his ground "whatever should be the Consequence," as the *Craftsman* writer had put it. Did they have for Pope a personal urgency as well, springing from the challenge he must have known this poem was flinging to a sensitive first minister? An answer may be found, I think, in the lines that introduce the ones just quoted:

> What? arm'd for *Virtue* when I point the Pen,
> Brand the bold Front of shameless, guilty Men,
> Dash the proud Gamester in his gilded Car,
> Bare the mean Heart that lurks beneath a Star;
> Can there be wanting to defend Her Cause,
> Lights of the Church, or Guardians of the Laws?
>
> (ll. 105–10)

Contemporaries attuned to the argot of the day cannot have missed these allusions, however glancing, to a "bold Front," a "proud Gamester" (in fact, "the" proud Gamester), and a Garter "Star": attributes appropriated to Walpole for many years. Yet there was nothing anyone could pin down, nothing he could even resent unless he first were willing to accept the charge that Walpole's singularity and eminence in vice were such that these terms could apply to no one else; whereas in fact the impudence of villains' faces was a stereotype, London was notorious for successful gamesters in luxurious circumstances (not least among them the Colonel Chartres who had figured so prominently in the *Epistle to Bathurst*), and "mean" Garter-wearers could be cited all the way back to the founding of the order by Edward III. An equal ambiguity lay in wait further along in the passage. What were "you, who 'scape the Laws" if not the usual great villains of satiric theory, so eminent that no power but that of publicity (as our own day has almost continuously had reason to discover) can reach them? Yet there was one particular "great villain" who, according to Opposition literature, had again and again escaped the laws, though it was hoped his luck would not hold forever. Were *all* great villains to "hear this, and tremble," or was it, primarily, one?

Whatever the right reply to these questions may be, once they cross the mind, Pope's maiden imitation of Horace appears in a somewhat changed light. Perhaps it is a "rearguard" to the earlier works, not only in pleading the cause of satire before the court of public opinion, but even in seeking to communicate some sense of the particular kind of publicizing power that this particular satirist commands, visibly acted out. Perhaps it is for this reason that the poem begins with three names of persons well known to be of Walpole's train and representative of his influence: Peter Walter (Pope sometimes calls him Waters), the grasping New Man of aristocratic household finance, who left many a nobleman whose estates he looked after in straitened circumstances—not, however, including the Duke of Newcastle, Walpole's Secretary of State; Francis Chartres, Walpole's runner and informer, known for good reason as "Rape-Master General" of Great Britain as his master was "Skreen-master General," a multiple scoundrel, but "protected"; and Lord Fanny, effete courtier and literary dabbler, Walpole's chief palace agent to the queen. Perhaps it is for this reason, too, that Pope goes out of his way to sneer at the royal family, and at Cibber, their and Walpole's laureate; at Denis Bond, lately incriminated in both the Derwentwater Estates and the Charitable Corporation scandals, where Walpole had notably screened villainy; at standing armies, Cardinal Fleury's influence, and England's alleged defeats in the European political card game called in contemporary slang "Quadrille": at (very close home now) bold Fronts, Gamesters, and Garter Stars; and, finally, in the very last lines of the poem, at the great name itself:

> P[oet]. *Libels* and *Satires*! Lawless Things indeed!
> But grave *Epistles*, bringing Vice to light,
> Such as a *King* might read, a *Bishop* write,
> Such as Sir *Robert* would approve—
>   F[riend]. Indeed?
> The case is alter'd—you may then proceed,
> In such a Cause the Plaintiff will be hiss'd,
> My Lords the Judges laugh, and you're dismiss'd.

There is, of course, a flick of irony in this conclusion at the entire power structure—king, church, and ministry. In Augustan England, a "King" did *not* read; the kind of "Bishop" Pope had in mind did *not* attack vice; and Sir Robert—that strong-minded ruler who opposed all inquiries into fraud on the ground, Hervey tells us, that these might become so habitual with Parliament as someday to "affect himself, his family, and posterity"—could hardly be supposed to approve of bringing any vice whatever to light. Does the passage also have in reserve, besides this, a delicate thrust for the minister alone? It may well be. The prompt capitulation of the legal interlocutor when the approval of Sir Robert is mentioned, followed by the capitulation of the "Judges," seems calculated to underscore the Opposition point that England was ruled by a man and not by laws. To quote from his supporter Lord Hervey again, despite "many . . . crying instances of flagrant injustice and oppression, which he could not defend," he "yet declined to correct [these] by any extraordinary method, though, in the ordinary courts of justice, he and all the world knew it was impossible to come at the offenders, put any stop to the offences, or give any redress to the injured."

In no other poem before 1738 does Pope engage the activities and personalities of the Walpole regime with such peculiarly personal intensity and (possibly reflecting the confidence of early 1733, when it seemed that Walpole's removal might be imminent) a tone that so clearly blends ridicule with something almost like threat, and both with a parade of strength. To Horace's register of weapons, Pope rather strikingly adds the disquieting proposition (though it would have drawn no more than a horselaugh from Walpole, who felt about fame as Falstaff feels about honor) that he will reserve his censure of vice in the highest places for posterity:

> Publish the present Age, but where my Text
> Is Vice too high, reserve it for the next:
> My Foes shall wish my Life a longer date. . . .
>
> (ll. 59–61)

To Horace's simple resolve to continue writing satire, Pope adds the oddly self-conscious claim that he will "perish" if need be, and follows this with what appears to be a combination of warning and defiance quite foreign to the Latin original: "Hear this, and tremble! you, who 'scape the Laws." Similarly, for Horace's rather vague *magnis*, great persons who will protect him as Scipio and Laelius protected Lucilius, Pope substitutes two clearly identified "champions": the one, Lord Peterborow, still an almost legendary conqueror in the Spanish wars of Marlborough's time and a gentleman of the old school whose contempt for the Hanoverian court seems never to have been disguised; the other Walpole's most implacable enemy and, in Pope's view presumably, best successor if the government should fall:

> To VIRTUE ONLY and HER FRIENDS, A FRIEND,
> The World beside may murmur, or commend.
> Know all the distant Din that World can keep
> Rolls o'er my *Grotto*, and but sooths my Sleep.
> There, my Retreat the best Companions grace
> Chiefs, out of War, and Statesmen, out of Place.
> There *St. John* mingles with my friendly Bowl,
> The Feast of Reason and the Flow of Soul:
> And He, whose Lightning pierc'd th'*Iberian* Lines,
> Now, forms my Quincunx, and now ranks my Vines,
> Or tames the Genius of the stubborn Plain,
> Almost as quickly, as he conquer'd *Spain*.

If Pope, in adapting this satire, did have in view not simply the usual apologia of the satirist but the more wide ranging intentions that Bolingbroke's participation at the genesis of the poem might suggest, his first Horatian performance was a prophetic one indeed. The questions it raised on the responsible uses of power—power of the king, power of the minister, power of the law, and, particularly, power of the poet-satirist—were to remain a staple theme of much of his finest poetry during the rest of his career.

The attitudes toward court and administration expressed in this first of Pope's surviving Horatian imitations had doubtless been gathering in his mind for some while. At the moment, he may have

67. Alexander Pope in his "Roman" image. Marble bust by L. F. Roubiliac, *c.* 1740. Incised at margin: *Uni aequus virtuti atque eius amicis* ["To Virtue only and her Friends a Friend"], Horace's tribute to Lucilius in *Sat.* II, i: 70, which Pope appropriates. Wimsatt, 59.1.

Private collection.

been responding also to the euphoria then current among Opposition leaders from the belief that Walpole's projected "Excise Scheme," rumored since the late summer of 1732, could be made to cause him and the court such irreparable loss of face in Parliament and before the country that a change of ministry would follow. During the period of the poem's composition and publication, and in the immediately following weeks till April 10, when Walpole withdrew his proposal, hostility to the minister and court had never been higher, and satirical lampoons, engravings, ballads, as well as sober petitions and presentments of extreme displeasure from the shires and boroughs multiplied to give vent to it.

The plan itself was in most ways sensible and desirable. Its aim was to replace the customs duties levied on wine and tobacco, ever subject to evasion through smuggling, falsified accounts, and other more ingenious deceits, with an excise tax collectible at any point between port and final sale, and therefore far more difficult to dodge. The moneys thus reclaimed for the royal treasury were to be used to make permanent the previous year's reduction in the land tax, and with a parliamentary election coming up the following year, Walpole was not oblivious of the support this would gain for candidates favorable to himself. As his aide Delafaye wrote to his envoy in Paris in early March, "Half the land tax taken off, and no more remaining than 1 s. in the pound, which was never known before since the revolution, . . . must be of service against the next election; for it will no doubt be known who voted pro and con."

Unfortunately for its success, the plan involved a considerable increase in the number of government functionaries, all of them empowered with rights of entry to warehouses and other depositories—even, it was claimed by the bill's enemies, to shops and homes. Hence in this respect it lent itself easily to interpretation as a ministerial plot to enhance the government's police power, intrude on privacy, and enlarge the opportunities for bribery, collusion, and the hatching of a new flock of placemen—these last anxieties not surprising in view of the record the administration had already compiled on such matters. By late March and early April, as a result, the "Opposition" was no longer the undisciplined miscellany of Whigs and Tories who called themselves by that name and for one reason or another, whether ambition, disgruntlement, policy disagreement, or even, sometimes, idealism, resented Walpole's ways of doing business. The opposition now embraced almost the entire nation (consumers, merchants, even the squires it was supposed to benefit) and was reacting vigorously not only to the fears already mentioned but to the Great Fear that this new excise on wine and tobacco was but a try-out for a "general Excise" on all goods: an eventuality about which Pope had already mischievously hinted in his *Epistle to Bathurst* that Maria Skerrett might have inside information:

> Ask you why Phryne the whole Auction buys?
> Phryne foresees a general Excise.
>
> (ll. 121–22)

In the upshot, however, as if he had suddenly regained the acumen he seemed to have lost when pushing the bill so stubbornly for so long, Walpole retracted the measure, there was a day or two of riotous rejoicing in the streets, and while it was clear he had lost some ground and opened rifts that might be troublesome to him later, he had not lost enough to imperil the 1734 elections, which he survived with his majority slightly more precarious but still intact.

By this date in Walpole's career, few literary men, if they took the slightest pride in their profession, could feel comfortable in the vacuum created by his indifference to literature as such. As a careful student of their situation has lately commented, "for perhaps the first time in England, the most talented writers of a generation faced a government which made no bones about its hostility to men of letters and its contempt for their role in society." True, the responsibility for this state of affairs should not be laid entirely at Walpole's door: he was symptom as well as cause. Affairs of government were now more demanding, as England inched further toward an upper-middle-class and mercantile society. The men of business "Sense," whom we met earlier in considering Pope's *Essay on Criticism*, were taking over from the men of "Wit," who were themselves by now becoming a different and more specialized professional breed. Most significant change of all perhaps: for reasons sound and unsound, social preconceptions were leaning away from the last lingering intimations of the "Renaissance man" or "complete gentleman" ideal and toward the maxim which Walpole's own practice so vividly expresses and which still dominates, though now possibly under some stress, industrial societies today: that men of imagination have no head for government or business, and that men of government and business should leave all matters of imagination to their wives.

Thus there was much in the age besides Walpole to pique the vanity of the writing class, who could not forbear looking back to a time when one of their predecessors (Addison) had been a secretary of state, another (Prior) an envoy plenipotentiary in Paris, and a writer

of at least moderate distinction (Rowe) in possession of the laureateship. But there was likewise much in the age to give the most ordinary conscience pause, whether fired by traditions of leadership or
not. In a society where the belief still survived that those in high
places should set a high example and so earn the respect they demanded, the very king himself was a figure of derision: a strutting
braggart, known to be led by the nose by his wife and Walpole,
fonder by far of Hanover than of England, capable of puerile fits of
anger during which he did not hesitate to kick whatever or whoever
was nearest him, and a scorner of all wit and learning. In the words of
his own vice-chamberlain, he

> used often to brag of the contempt he had for books and letters; to
> say how much he hated all that stuff from his infancy; and that he
> remembered when he was a child he did not hate reading and
> learning merely as other children do upon account of the confine-
> ment, but because he despised it and felt as if he was doing some-
> thing mean and below him.

In his speech, and often in his family relations, he was brutal. When
his daughter Anne, the Princess Royal—offered the option of rejecting a match proposed for her with the Prince of Orange, who was
seriously deformed—decided she would marry him even if he were a
baboon (seeing no other future for herself than a spinsterish depen-
dency), he replied, "Well, then there is baboon enough for you."
Later, when she suffered a false pregnancy and sympathy was
expressed by those around her for her disappointment, "the King,"

> who had taken every occasion, since the bustle the Princess Royal
> had made and the expense she had put him to, to show the little
> affection he felt for her, said he could not imagine why any of her
> friends should be sorry for anything but the foolish figure she made
> in not being able to tell whether she had a child in her belly or not,
> for as to her having none, he thought it much better so than other-
> wise; or why anybody should think it such a misfortune that one
> crooked beggar should not people the earth with more crooked
> beggars.

Music, on the other hand, the king genuinely enjoyed, and he
staunchly supported Handel. But since his taste ran heavily toward
Italian opera, it did his standing little good with those who had
flocked to Gay's *Beggar's Opera* precisely because they felt it to be true
British heart-of-oak. He was also a brave man, the last of England's
monarchs to lead troops into battle, and in his personal habits so

reliable, though not necessarily so scrupulous, as to make the court anguishingly dull for those who had to attend it. In fact, says Hervey, writing to Horatio Walpole, his brother Robert's envoy at the Hague at the time, "if you look in your Almanack for the Day of the Week, & at your watch for the hour of the Day, every thing in the Palace moves . . . in such a tick-tack Pendulam-regularity, that . . . you may be able in Holland to know every thing we do in England, full as well as the most exact & minute Journalist could be able to inform you."

Through his chief minister, this improbable monarch presided over a scheme of things (of which doubtless he was mostly unaware) in which the degradation of the London poor and their destruction by disease and poverty—

> The grave Sir Gilbert holds it for a rule,
> That "every man in want is knave or fool"—

reached a statistical high point that had not been matched since the Great Plague of 1665. The gin habit, imported from Holland along with William III, had become by the 1730s in all the poorer areas of London as settled a resource against the misery of consciousness as heroin today in the ghettos of the South Bronx—save that enough gin to put a man or woman in a stupor could be had for tuppence. By 1737, despite a government prohibition of 1736, laughably enforced, there were seven thousand gin shops in the suburbs of London alone, without counting the City, and as with most other criticisms of the status quo at this period, if any one expressed alarm, supporters of the government could be counted on to ask insinuatingly why it concerned *him*:

> And must no Egg in Japhet's Face be thrown,
> Because the Deed he forg'd was not my own?
> Must never Patriot then declaim at Gin,
> Unless, good man! he has been fairly in?
> (*One Thousand Seven Hundred and Thirty-Eight:*
> *Dial. 2:* 189–92)

Meantime, the rich grew richer. In 1721, the combined holdings of the Marlborough and Godolphin families in Bank of England stock amounted to £104,600; thirty years later, to £347,417. The "grave Sir Gilbert" Heathcote, one of the Bank's founders and later its governor, whose indifference to the poor Pope indicates in the lines earlier quoted, died in 1733 with an estimated fortune of £700,000. Sir John Clerk, visiting London and its environs from Penicuik in 1727, speaks with awe of the luxurious Greenwich mansion of Sir Gregory

68. Gin Lane. Engraving by William Hogarth (3d state, 1751).

"Must never Patriot then declaim at Gin,
Unless, good man! he has been fairly in?"
One Thousand Seven Hundred and Thirty-Eight: Dialogue 2: 191–2.

Page, a merchant's son, who is worth, he is told, £900,000. Some of these great fortunes were perhaps honestly made, at least according to the *mores* of the period. Swindles and embezzlements, however, were also the order of the day, as Pope did not hesitate to advertise in his *Epistle to Bathurst*. And not only the order of the day: if engaged in by men of sufficient rank or wealth, they were immune from serious punishment. Lord Chancellor Macclesfield, for instance, amassed over £100,000 by selling masterships in chancery, and when he was at last tried and convicted, the King offered to help him pay his £30,000 fine. Denis Bond, whose concern for the poor Pope memorializes along with Heathcote's, though expelled the House of Commons in 1731 for one fraud and the next year found guilty of another, each involving large sums of money and a breach of public trust, was spared even a fine. As a matter of fact, within three years he was elected a church warden of fashionable St. George's, Hanover Square, and died wealthy. As for Walpole himself, though no surviving evidence connects him unmistakably with the transfer of public funds to his own account, no one has been able to show how a man in his position could so speedily have come by such immense wealth honestly, and no one denies that he supported his mistress Molly out of public money, while siphoning attractive perquisites for most members of his family from the same well. His eldest son had £7,000 annually from one post, his second son £3,000 from another, and his youngest son, Horace, the collector and gifted letter writer, £3,400 from several. All this, of course, in addition to the immense sums expended secretly to control county elections, assure ministerial majorities in the two Houses, and suppress so far as possible hostile opinion, while, at the same time, through his own army of gazetteers, arguing the curious proposition that legitimate criticism of his devious courses somehow lost legitimacy if it came from politically ambitious rivals. A speaker's motives in asserting that two and two make four presumably have little effect upon the sum.

Opinion today is therefore beginning to back away from the adulation of the Walpole ministry carried on in most historical quarters during the past two centuries. That he was unquestionably one of England's greatest parliamentary leaders and on some occasions and in certain contexts a great statesman as well goes without saying. That he brought his country through one of its most difficult and strife-torn periods, kept it out of continental wars, and saw it grow rich and strong is also true. These were achievements of a high order. But the cost was also high. When he was finally defeated in January 1742, only two years before Pope's death and three before his own, he left behind him a moral malaise that cannot be laughed away and that even Johnson's lines in *London* (1738) only partly catch:

> Here let those reign, whom Pensions can incite
> To vote a Patriot black, a Courtier white;
> Explain their Country's dear-bought Rights away,
> And plead for Pirates in the face of day;
> With slavish tenets taint our poison'd Youth,
> And lend a lye the confidence of Truth.
>
> (ll. 51–56)

"Modern cynicism," one of England's most eminent historians has lately written, referring to the modes of governing established during Walpole's two decades of ascendancy:

> applauds the skilful techniques employed, and justifies the means by reference to the end, which was constitutional parliamentary government unruffled by popular revolutions. But this begs the question; had another choice been made, a better or at least a different kind of government could have emerged much earlier. Had the Septennial Act not been passed [giving each parliament a tenure of seven years and thus attenuating the influence of voters except at widely spaced intervals], had a firm line been taken with electoral corruption, had the abuse of patronage been curbed, had a proper system of government accounting been instituted and all placemen barred from the House of Commons [reforms repeatedly defeated by Walpole's "skilful techniques"], the face of eighteenth-century England could not have been worse, and might well have been better.

By the early 1730s, in other words, when the effects of Walpole's control of almost every aspect of political and institutional life (elections, newspapers, the post office—which was instructed to open private letters—even the stage) were becoming increasingly clear, it was possible to be repelled by it, whether or not one had a political axe of one's own to grind. And if one were a poet, believing, as many educated Englishmen in those days did, in the moral and civilizing role traditionally assigned to the arts, poetry and drama in particular, it was difficult *not* to be repelled by it. It is interesting, as noticed earlier, that Pope's period of personal intercourse with the minister through Fortescue's good offices came to an end about 1730, the year Colley Cibber was appointed to the laureateship after considerable speculation that the Court's current new toy, a so-called child of nature like its earlier wild boy, but this time a self-educated farm laborer named Stephen Duck, was to have the post. Though as a Catholic Pope could have no aspiration to this office for himself, the choice of a total incompetent like Cibber and the apparently serious consideration given to Duck (whose poetry he rightly diagnosed as weakly derivative, but for whom, personally, he went out of his way to be kind) must have struck him as arising from a flaunting indifference to the art he prized if not from a conscious contempt for it. All the more contemptuous if, as a sentence in one of Swift's letters to him seems to hint, he had interceded in vain with Viscount Townshend, Robert Walpole's brother-in-law, for a suitable candidate of his own.

More intimate vexations

More intimate vexations may also have been at work. His exiled friend, Francis Atterbury, the former Dean of Westminster with whom he had continued to correspond after it became a felony to do so, died in Paris on 4 March 1732. The English government's response was at no point magnanimous. There followed first, as Atterbury's most recent biographer describes it, "an unseemly struggle, virtually over the corpse," between agents of the British ambassador in Paris, agents of the Pretender, who was now settled in Rome, and agents of Louis XV's minister, Cardinal Fleury, for control of the papers: a struggle which Fleury won. Apparently unconvinced, when Atterbury's coffin arrived in British waters in the custody of his son-in-law, Pope's friend William Morrice, on April 30, agents acting for Walpole impounded the coffin and Morrice's baggage on the fabricated charge that they contained contraband French lace, then arrested Morrice himself, and hustled him off to be quizzed by the two secretaries of state, while an undersecretary combed through the purely domestic letters that Fleury had allowed Morrice to bring home. Nothing with anti-Jacobite value having been found, Morrice's effects were returned to him on May 6 along with his father-in-law's body; but the order was given that maimed rites only were to be allowed, without publicity and without the presence of the then dean, chapter, or choir. Accordingly, when on May 22 Atterbury's body was at last received into the Abbey for burial in the vault which he had long ago prepared and which already held his wife and his two daughters, the coffin was unceremoniously stowed overnight in a workmen's lumber room. It was thence removed the following day for a service performed by a single minor canon in a church empty save for Morrice and two of Atterbury's former chaplains. This whole pettish story Pope would soon have had from Morrice, and we may guess that it did not endear the Walpole administration to him.

Two years earlier there had been a rather more sumptuous Abbey interment. In this instance, the body lay in state in the Abbey's Jerusalem Chamber, a room whose accumulating associations with personages of distinction in church and state would eventually make it what it is today: something in the nature of a national shrine. Also, in this instance, the interment took place with "great Funeral Pomp and Solemnity," and the pallbearers were six gentlemen of high political and social consequence, among them Lords Delawar and Hervey. The body accorded these honors was that of Anne Oldfield. A gifted actress, she had been careful not to imitate the unfaithful servant of the parable by burying her very considerable talent in the greenroom, but had put it out to use in ways that seem not to have altered greatly between 1713, when Pope wrote the epigram about Damon being "at her," and 1725, when James Thomson, newly in London, wrote his friend Cranstoun after first seeing her perform: "Mrs. Oldfield has a smiling jolly face[,] acts very well in comedy but best of all, I suppose, in bed. She twines her body and leers with her eyes most bewitchingly."

As Pope subsequently composed, in the summer of 1734, his sardonic comment on the funeral fanfare for Anne Oldfield—

> The Tribe of Templars, Play'rs, Apothecaries,
> Pimps, Poets, Wits, Lord *Fanny*'s, Lady *Mary*'s,
> And all the Court in Tears, and half the Town,
> Lament dear charming *Oldfield*, dead and gone!
> Engaging *Oldfield*! who, with Grace and Ease,
> Could joyn the Arts, to ruin, and to please—
>
> (*Imit. Hor., Sat.,* I, ii: 1–6)

did he recall what he had been told of the empty church around Atterbury? It is tempting to think so. In the mishmash of trades, persons, and sexes, Smithfield and St. James's, in the opening three lines, he catches at any rate something of the mishmash of values and motives that he had already made the argument of his *Dunciad* and that the two contrasting Abbey scenes must have seemed to confirm.

Soon Pope was to visit the Abbey himself, on one of the most melancholy errands of his life. On 4 December 1732, exactly nine months after Atterbury, Gay died. He was forty-seven. He had come up to the Queensberrys' London house a little ahead of the rest of the family "on some business" that apparently had to do with putting his new play *Achilles* in rehearsal. And while there, as Pope wrote immediately to inform Swift, "An inflammatory feaver hurried him out of this life in three days." Arbuthnot, who with two other physicians attended him, speaks (as they often did in those days) of "a mortification of the bowels," and Pope of "acute torment" during his final hours from pains in his bowels and breast. Thus the disorder in its final phase can have included anything from a diseased gall bladder to a perforated ulcer to acute peritonitis brought on by a ruptured appendix to cancerous stoppage of the colon. In Arbuthnot's experience, at any rate, "it was the most precipitate case I ever knew."

Gay's lying in state took place at Exeter Exchange. This was an area now almost entirely given over to undertakers as formerly to prostitutes: a transformation in corporeal services that would have moved Gay to drolleries had he been alive. On Saturday, December 23, in the late evening, his coffin was conveyed to the Abbey, "drawn," we are told in a Curll "biography" that instantly appeared, "in a Hearse trimmed with Plumes of Black and White Feathers, attended with three mourning Coaches and six Horses." A newspaper report informs us that the six pallbearers were "the Right Hon. the Earl of Chesterfield, the Lord [Viscount] Cornbury, the Hon. George Berkeley [not Pope's friend the philosopher, but Lady Suffolk's friend and later her husband, who was no doubt in some sense 'representing' her among the pallbearers], the Hon. Levison Gower, Esq., General [James] Dormer, and Alexander Pope, Esq." and that the funeral was attended, in addition, "by several Persons of Distinction." "His Remains," the Curll biography adds, "were deposited in the South-cross-Isle"—what is today called the Poets' Corner—"over against Chaucer's Tomb," from which prominence, as we saw earlier, it has in our time been relegated to a humbler position and total invisibility.

The blow to Pope was stunning. "Good God!" he exclaims in the same letter to Swift (a letter that from some intuition of misfortune Swift left unopened for five days), "how often are we to die before we go quite off this stage? in every friend we lose a part of ourselves and the best part. God keep those we have left!" He and Gay had for some time, of course, been seeing each other less than in the old days, now that Gay was domiciled with the Queensberrys at Amesbury, which was far better for his worsening "colic" than the irresistible indulgences of London (he had been taken totally, in fact, off wine), though not always better for his spirits. "Your letter is a kind one," Pope writes on one occasion, "but I can't say so pleasing to me as

Life is a jeft; and all things fhow it.
I thought fo once; but now I know it.

69. John Gay (1685–1732). Gay's monument in Westminster Abbey. By Michael Rysbrack. Pope's epitaph for him is just below his own, but not visible here.

Left me to see neglected Genius bloom,
Neglected die! and tell it on his Tomb.
Epistle to Dr. Arbuthnot, 257–58.

By kind permission of the Warburg Institute.

many of yours have been, thro' the account you give of the dejection of your spirits":

> I wish the too constant use of water does not contribute to it. .... I also wish you were not so totally immers'd in the country; I hope your return to Town will be a prevalent remedy. ... I wish it partly for my own sake: We have liv'd little together of late, and we want to be physicians for one another. It is a remedy that agreed very well with us both, for many years, and I fancy our constitutions would mend upon the old medicine of *Studiorum similitudo*, etc. I believe both of us want whetting.

Whetting, yes! Gay throve on the crackle of wit. And writing at a slightly earlier date, apparently soon after Gay had been put onto a special diet, and obviously striving to make him smile, Pope teases:

> How comes it that Providence has been so unkind to me, (who am a greater object of compassion than any fat man alive) that I am forc'd to drink wine, while you riot in water, prepar'd with oranges by the hand of the Duchess of *Queensberry?* that I am condemn'd to live on a Highway side, like an old Patriarch, receiving all Guests, ... while you are wrapt into the *Idalian* Groves★, sprinkled with Rose-water, and live in Burrage†, Balm, and Burnet‡ up to the chin, with the Duchess of *Queensberry?*

But now the most lovable of companions—*socius peramabilis*, as he would put him down in his Elzevir Vergil—was gone, leaving such a gap in the attractions of England that he fears Swift will never again visit. Swift and he had teased each other for years, ever since the two earlier visits, with proposals to unite at last in England or Dublin or even in France to pass their declining days together, each knowing at the same time, one senses, that it would never happen and would never work. They were each too subject to illness, too vain—Swift, now very deaf, growing cranky and demanding in his old age and always pretending to be more so than he was; Pope, frail, doubtless often irritable from headache and other ailments, altogether unable to match the Dean in his strenuous regimen of walking and riding, and eternally wrapped up in poetical or other literary schemes, either on his own behalf or on behalf of the whole group who had once banded

★ From Mount Ida, haunt of the gods.
† Borage, whose leaves floated in wine or other beverage were supposed to produce a brew good for the heart.
‡ A salad green, at one time thought to be helpful to the liver.

70. Catherine ("Kitty") Hyde, Duchess of Queensberry (1700–1777). Pastel by Charles Jervas.

> If QUEENSBERRY to strip there's no compelling,
> 'Tis from a Handmaid we must take a Helen.
>
> *Epistle to a Lady*, 193–94.

Courtesy of the Courtauld Institute Galleries. Photograph: Courtauld Institute of Art.

together in Queen Anne's time and whose memorialist he more and more felt himself to be. Still, under all the proposals about ending their lives together, there did at least persist the expectation on both sides that Swift would make a further visit to England. Now, that hope too might be gone.

> I shall never see you now I believe; one of your principal Calls to England is at an end. Indeed he was the most amiable by far, his qualities were the gentlest, but I love you as well and as firmly. . . . Adieu. I can add nothing to what you will feel, and diminish nothing from it. Yet write to me, and soon. Believe no man now living loves you better, I believe no man ever did. . . . Once more adieu, and write to one who is truly disconsolate.

In a letter of the following day, probably to Martha Blount, the mood is yet darker. Gay's death reminds him of another to come:

> The subject is beyond writing upon, beyond cure or ease by reason or reflection, beyond all but one thought, that it is the will of God.
> So will the death of my Mother be! which now I tremble at, now resign to, now bring close to me, now set farther off: Every day alters, turns me about, and confuses my whole frame of mind. . . .
> I am unfeignedly tired of the world, and receive nothing to be call'd a Pleasure in it, equivalent to countervail either the death of one I have so long lived with [Gay], or of one I have so long lived for. . . . I sit in her room, and she is always present before me, but when I sleep. . . . I have shed many Tears, but now I weep at nothing. I would above all things see you.

It is against this background of disgust with the régime (Gay's death can only have reminded Pope of its preference for Cibber and Duck) and against these feelings of isolation, soon to be deepened by the death of Arbuthnot, that the note of defiance sounded in the first Horatian imitation and repeated sometimes more shrilly thereafter is perhaps best understood. After Arbuthnot's death in February 1735, only Swift and himself remained of the group of like-minded friends who in 1713–14 had nursed high hopes for themselves and each other, and for the future of letters in England in their time. But Swift was too far away now to be of comfort. Entombed in Dublin, like a defeated Titan, by a government understandably disinclined to promote to a benefice nearer home the man who had single-handedly bested it in the matter of Wood's halfpence, he was effectually out of

touch with the ebb and flow of English events. Under these circumstances, it is hardly surprising that Pope came more and more to see
himself as the last surviving representative of a certain body of attitudes and values, and to present himself, on some occasions and in
certain poems, as a sort of Leonidas defending these values as if at
Thermopylae against barbarian hordes. On the corruption of the age,
for instance:

> Yet may this Verse (if such a Verse remain)
> Show there was one who held it in disdain.
> > (*One Thousand Seven Hundred and Thirty-Eight:*
> > *Dial. 1:* 171–72)

Or on the power of the satirist:

> Yes, I am proud; I must be proud to see
> Men not afraid of God, afraid of me:
> Safe from the Bar, the Pulpit, and the Throne,
> Yet touch'd and sham'd by *Ridicule* alone.
> > (*One Thousand Seven Hundred and Thirty-Eight:*
> > *Dial. 2:* 208–11)

Equally unsurprising, I would venture, is his increasing inclination—witness both the poems and the letter-publishing schemes
that soon begin to occupy him as well as the final refurbishing and
publication of the *Memoirs of Scriblerus*—to assume the role of historian and elegist to a school of geniuses or near geniuses of which he
knew himself to be one.

CHAPTER 23

A MAN OF
MANY MOODS

"Belisarius, *Old and Blind*"

Meanwhile, as always after a great loss, there was life to be got on
with, and Pope threw himself into the frenzy of writing and publishing already partly described—the *Epistle to Bathurst* appearing in
mid-January, the first Horatian imitation in mid-February, the first
epistle of the *Essay on Man* on February 20, the second and third
epistles in March and April. During the same period, in January, he
had been back and forth to Kensington to visit Peterborow; recovering at Lord Oxford's from his own version of the "Epidemical
Distemper"; writing the epitaph for Gay's monument quoted earlier
in this book; and advising with the Duke of Queensberry about the
disposition of Gay's as yet unpublished works. The comic opera
Achilles that Gay had not lived to see onstage was performed at the
Covent Garden Theatre on February 10 before "a crouded and splendid Audience" (so runs a news account)—Pope and the Queensberrys, we may guess, among them.

Perhaps he also used the occasion to prepossess the theater's manager John Rich in favor of his young friend Robert Dodsley's *Toy
Shop*, which he had looked over in manuscript a few days earlier and
whose author he soon helped with £100 to set himself up in the book
trade. Late in the month, he was off to the Windsor Forest area on
some unidentified errand, presumably to advise his sister either about
a claim in chancery against her late husband's estate that had now
devolved on her, or about an action for debt that may have been
lodged at about this time against her seafaring son John. Early March
finds him busying himself with a Palladian portico for his house with
the architectural aid of Burlington; seething also—this we have to
guess at, but it appears a plausible guess—under the abuse heaped on
him by Lady Mary and Lord Hervey in the *Verses to the Imitator*

published on March 8; and assuring Fortescue on the same day that the desire communicated to him from Sir Robert Walpole that the couplet on Lady Mary be expunged or altered cannot now be honored, since the lady has taken her own "Satisfaction" in a libel. None of this interfered, however, on the eighteenth, with his urging his Scots friend David Mallet, author of an as yet unpublished poem called *Of Verbal Criticism* protesting the excesses of Bentley, Theobald, and others of that school, to postpone publication "till after he [Theobald] has had a Benefit-Night for a Play of his call'd *Secret Love* or some such name; It may perhaps, else, be some pre-judice to him." To which is added in a final paragraph:

> I have not forgot J[ohn] Dennis; if you find occasion, pray Extend my Debt to you by giving him a little more.

Pope had, it seems clear, been contributing financial aid to Dennis surreptitiously through Mallet—how long we do not know. It was a generosity he extended later that year by soliciting a contribution from Aaron Hill, and, still later, by using all his influence with his noble friends to make the performance of Cibber's *The Provok'd Hus-band*, acted at the Haymarket for Dennis's benefit on December 18, a success. The result was evidently all that had been hoped. The theater was "crowded," we are told, and HRH the Prince of Wales "was pleased to send twenty Guineas as a present" directly to the benefi-ciary. An epigram published in one of the London newspapers three days before the event caught perhaps the truest sense of what was going on:

> *Epigram. Occasion'd by the Interest that has been made,*
> *for a splendid Appearance of Ladies, at the Haymarket*
> *Theatre, on Tuesday next, for the Benefit of Mr. Dennis.*
>
> Where gen'rous *Morals* curb vindictive Wit,
> Till [i.e., to the point at which] P[o]pe forgives
>   what angry D[enni]s writ;
> And, hem'd with *Beauties*, in the *Critick*'s Cause
> Half the gay Town, to grace his Circle, draws:
> Pleas'd, we revolve the Scene, with just Surprize;
> And *hail* the *Golden Age*, that seems to rise:
> When *Lambs* wou'd Thorns, from wounded *Lyons*, draw,
> And smile—*assistant* to the *pressive* Paw!

In a *Prologue, For the Benefit of Mr. Dennis, 1733*, evidently written at the time for the performance but first published anonymously in 1741, the lamb went further. Comparing Dennis to Justinian's great general Belisarius (reputed to have been blinded and allowed to die in beggary by that emperor despite outstanding service in driving the Goths and Vandals from Italy and north Africa) he managed a tribute to the old critic that could also be read as a reproof to Justinian's current British counterparts:

> As when that Hero, who in each Campaign
> Had brav'd the *Goth*, and many a *Vandal* slain,
> Lay Fortune-struck, a Spectacle of Woe!
> Wept by each Friend, forgiv'n by ev'ry Foe:
> Was there a gen'rous, a reflecting Mind,
> But pitied *Belisarius*, Old and Blind?
> Was there a Chief, but melted at the Sight?
> A common Soldier, but who clubb'd his *Mite*?
> Such, such Emotions should in *Britons* rise,
> When prest by Want and Weakness, *Dennis* lies.
>
> (ll. 1–10)

There is, of course, laughter as well as compliment in the prologue's remaining lines—indeed, there would have had to be to keep the poet honest to his convictions and to underwrite the sincerity of the praise. Yet the amused glance at Dennis's eccentricities is not allowed to deflect the poem from its main, and generous, point: however ridiculous and fierce the old critic may have shown himself to be at times, he is now in want and that should be sufficient warrant to open purses:

> *Dennis*, who long had warr'd with modern *Huns*,
> Their Quibbles routed, and defy'd their Puns;
> A desp'rate Bulwark, sturdy, firm, and fierce,
> Against the *Gothick* Sons of frozen Verse;
> How chang'd from him, who made the Boxes groan,
> And shook the Stage with Thunders all his own!★
> Stood up to dash each vain Pretender's Hope,
> Maul the *French* Tyrant, or pull down the Pope!
> If there's a *Briton*, then, true bred and born,
> Who holds Dragoons and Wooden–Shoes in scorn;

★ Dennis had invented a new method of producing stage thunder for his tragedy *Appius and Virginia*, which failed. In "all his own," Pope may allude to the story that Dennis, when his new method of making stage-thunder continued to be used in other plays, went into a paroxysm of fury and exclaimed: 'Sdeath! that's *my* thunder." Perhaps Pope's other implication (available by 1733 to very few besides himself) is that the *audience's applause* was not thunderous.

If there's a Critick of distinguish'd Rage;
If there's a Senior, who contemns this Age;
Let him to–Night his just Assistance lend,
And be the Critick's, *Briton*'s, Old–man's Friend.

                                                    (ll. 11–24)

"Content with little"

Earlier, during that same spate of publishing in February and March,
Pope wrote drafts of at least two additional poems. If, as one suspects,
these are further evidence of an effort to bury his feelings of loss in hard
work, it may be significant that each is addressed and pays homage to a
long-loved friend, almost as if he had turned subconsciously for comfort to known points of refuge and support. One of the two poems is
his *Epistle to a Lady*, addressed to Martha Blount, though owing to her
modesty (or discretion?) she was never to be named in it, and apparently completed in an early version by mid-February. The other, finished by March 20 and addressed to his Yorkshire friend Hugh Bethel,
one of Burlington's large circle in that county, is his adaptation of the
satire in Horace next following the one he had already imitated: the
second satire of the second book. The poem for Martha, first published
in 1735 and never offered to the public complete till Pope was on his
deathbed in 1744, will detain us more fittingly at a later point. The
poem for Bethel, on the other hand, belongs very much to the poet's
political and personal situation at the time it was composed.

The Latin original is a typical Horatian discourse on the desirability
of keeping to the mean in all things, most especially in eating, because
to do so is to liberate oneself from distresses and enslavements. The
extreme emphasis on food in its first two thirds—oysters, trout,
thrush, grouse, peacock, gull, pike, turbot, shellfish, pig—and on the
tumults in the gut that come from promiscuously stuffing it is almost
enough to make one wonder if Pope was put in mind of this poem, in
some dim subliminal way, by thoughts of Gay's habitual self-
indulgences in this department and their consequence. Or his own, for
that matter. The evidence about Pope's eating habits is contradictory,
but the general impression one receives is that while plain living was
and had to be his practice owing to the weakness of his constitution,
this was punctuated from time to time by excesses, especially when
dining with congenial friends—whose company, as Trumbull had
reminded him years before, spurred efforts to hold his own that were
lethal to his health. Thus though he himself cites the lavish eating and

drinking in Swift's hospitable Dublin circle as a serious impediment to a visit, and though Swift often comments on how little Pope manages to consume, William Kent in 1738 calls him "the greatest Glutton I know," and Bathurst writes to Lady Suffolk, in 1734:

> You do well to reprove him about his intemperance; for he makes himself sick every meal at your most moderate and plain table in England [Bathurst's view of his own]. Yesterday I had a little piece of salmon just caught out of the Severn, and a fresh pike that was brought me from the other side of your house [Marble Hill] out of the Thames. He ate as much as he could of both, and insisted upon his moderation, because he had made his dinner on one dish.

A closer look, however, yields grounds for Pope's interest in *Satire* II, ii that are probably more pertinent to his actual motives than his or Gay's digestion. Much of the Latin "sermon" on moderation is put into the mouth of Ofellus, a friend of Horace's youth who had been uprooted from his ancestral holdings in order that Octavian's veterans might be rewarded and resettled (an early version of the "Veterans' Bonus") after the decisive victories of 42–39 B.C. Yet Ofellus had always lived so frugally by choice that he could digest with equanimity the difference between being owner and being tenant. A similar sacrifice had been exacted from Vergil, and for the same reasons, though later his lands were restored to him by Octavian. Likewise from Horace, who had fought for Brutus and Antony against Octavian. And likewise, too—or so it could easily be felt by the victim, merely for the fault of being as Roman Catholics on the "wrong" side—from Pope and his family when forced to give up Binfield. For Pope, in short, the Latin poem held both personal and political resonances. Political, furthermore, in that it could be adapted to hint at several of the ways in which English values were felt to be changing for the worse in the new "me-first" economy associated by the Opposition with Walpole's management:

> "Right, cries his Lordship, for a Rogue in need
> "To have a Taste, is Insolence indeed:
> "In me 'tis noble, suits my birth and state,
> "My wealth unwieldy, and my heap too great."
>
> (ll. 111–14)

To which Bethel, who is Pope's Ofellus, replies with a countryman's metaphor of great beauty and simplicity not found in the Latin—

> Then, like the Sun, let Bounty spread her ray,
> And shine that Superfluity away—
>
> (ll. 115–16)

followed by an indictment of the lack of public spirit and civic responsibility in the new dynasty and the new breed of titled men:

> Oh Impudence of wealth! with all thy store,
> How dar'st thou let one worthy man be poor?
> Shall half the new-built Churches round thee fall?
> Make Keys,★ build Bridges, or repair White-hall:
> Or to thy Country let that heap be lent,
> As M[arlbr]o's was, but not at five per Cent.
>
> (ll. 117–22)

In the final portion of the Latin poem, Ofellus describes the simplicity of his earlier life to explain the little change that loss of patrimony has made in it. For the English poem, the poet transfers this description to himself and effects something of a small miracle in doing so. Though he appears simply to be illustrating his effort to live up to the precepts of Bethel/Ofellus—

> Thus Bethel spoke, who always speaks his thought,
> And always thinks the very thing he ought:
> His equal mind I copy what I can,
> And as I love, would imitate the Man—
>
> (ll. 129–32)

he actually transforms them from an economic prudentialism that stresses self-denial and provident action against the always uncertain future to an idealized liberality resulting from wise and free acceptance of the limits that nature sets. Sets for the human condition generally—an awareness never far from Pope's consciousness, as may be noticed in poems as different as *The Rape of the Lock* and *An Essay on Man*. But sets likewise for each individual, as Pope with his crippled body and alien status as a Roman Catholic had more reason than most to see:

> His equal mind I copy what I can,
> And as I love, would imitate the Man.
> In *South-sea* days not happier, when surmis'd

★ I.e., Quays. Many London churches were at this time in drastic need of repair, and the ruins of Whitehall palace, destroyed by fire under William III (save for the Banqueting Hall) still lay about in heaps.

> The Lord of thousands, than if now *Excis'd*;
> In Forest planted by a Father's hand,
> Than in five acres now of rented land.
> Content with little, I can piddle here
> On Broccoli and mutton, round the year;
> But ancient friends, (tho' poor, or out of play)
> That touch my Bell, I cannot turn away.
>
> (ll. 131–40)

The reference in "out of play" to the two exceptional talents seen sharing the poet's Twickenham retirement in the earlier imitation, Bolingbroke and Peterborow, seems unmistakable. But there is no posture of defiance this time, no hint that being out of play is a waste of powers attributable to Walpole, no air of boasting: "To VIRTUE ONLY and HER FRIENDS, A FRIEND"—"Envy must own I live among the Great" (II, i: 121, 133). Instead, we are given one of the most charming pictures in English poetry (visionary, to be sure: a man's reach should exceed his grasp, or what's a heaven for?) of a way of life in which limit has become freedom, the dancer indistinguishable from the dance, and the apparent bondage of the rhymed pentameter couplet an opening to the gracious rhythms of skilled conversational speech:

> 'Tis true, no Turbots dignify my boards,
> But gudgeons, flounders, what my Thames affords.
> To Hounslow-heath I point, and Bansted-down,
> Thence comes your mutton, and these chicks my own:
> From yon old wallnut-tree a show'r shall fall;
> And grapes, long-lingring on my only wall,
> And figs, from standard and Espalier join:
> The dev'l is in you if you cannot dine.
> Then chearful healths (your Mistress shall have place)
> And, what's more rare, a Poet shall say *Grace*.
>
> (ll. 141–50)

Political discontents continue to sputter to the surface, but they are not allowed to break the mood of serene urbanity by means of which, for this moment, and within the fiction of this poem, Pope sublimates what must have been, in fact, a very keen sense of the uncertainties and perils attendant on a satirist who had now made the town too hot to hold him:

> Fortune not much of humbling me can boast;
> Tho' double-tax'd, how little have I lost?
> My Life's amusements have been just the same,

> Before, and after Standing Armies came.
> My lands are sold, my Father's house is gone:
> I'll hire another's, is not that my own,
> And yours my friends? thro' whose free-opening gate
> None comes too early, none departs too late;
> (For I, who hold sage Homer's rule the best,
> Welcome the coming, speed the going guest.)
>
> (ll. 151–60)

As doubtless he would have done in real life, Swift breaks in at this point to offer a necessary caution. It is a provident caution, slightly exaggerated here, but at bottom not much unlike many he actually gave to Gay in his letters. Swift was given to worrying about incomes and perquisites, for his friends as well as himself:

> "Pray heav'n it last! (cries Swift) as you go on;
> "I wish to God this house had been your own:
> "Pity! to build, without a son or wife:
> "Why, you'll enjoy it only all your life."
>
> (ll. 161–64)

Pope was thinking here, we may guess, of his new portico, which was costing him a great deal. And the warning that Swift voices, we may also guess, is intended to function in the poem as a reflection of sobering thoughts that in one compartment of his mind Pope, too, has entertained. Within the poem, however, he will rise above them. He will welcome the limitations laid on by the nature of things in order to be free of them, give way to the turning wheel in order to remain steadfast at the center:

> Well, if the Use be mine, can it concern one
> Whether the Name belongs to Pope or Vernon?*
> What's *Property*? dear Swift! you see it alter
> From you to me, from me to Peter Walter,†
> Or, in a mortgage, prove a Lawyer's share,
> Or, in a jointure, vanish from the Heir,
> Or, in pure Equity (the Case not clear)
> The Chanc'ry takes your rents for twenty year:
> At best, it falls to some ungracious Son

---

* Thomas Vernon, owner of Pope's leased "five acres" at Twickenham.
† The fleecing "scrivener" of the earlier imitation (l. 89), who at the moment was snatching up bankrupt estates in Dorset.

Who cries, my father's damn'd, and all's my own.
Shades, that to Bacon could retreat afford,
Become the portion of a booby Lord;
And Hemsley* once proud Buckingham's delight
Slides to a Scriv'ner or a City Knight.
Let Lands and Houses have what Lords they will,
Let Us be fix'd, and our own Masters still.

(ll. 165–80)

Self-possession is the only possession that is ours to keep.

"This image of a natural scene quietly transfigured by human art," a perceptive critic has lately written, referring to the entire passage, "is an emblem not merely of an acceptance of natural process, a surrender to time and loss, but also of their modest human redemption."

> And time and loss may be compensated in other ways as well. "I am pleased," Pope wrote to Ralph Allen in 1736, "to think my Trees will afford Shade and Fruit to Others, when I shall want them no more. And it is no sort of grief to me, that those will not be things of my own poor Body, but it is enough they are Creatures of the same Species, and made by the same hand that made me."

One senses in such passages (as so often with our own exemplary sentiments) that Pope is expressing not quite what he actually feels, but what he knows he ought to feel and wishes for his own ease of mind to learn to feel. For the true "blessed state," as he knew from his reading in the Roman poets as well as from that great sentence in Epicurus which permeates most of them, springs from "an attitude of mind which imposes the limits ordained by nature."

"Our depths who fathoms, or our shallows finds?"

His mother's death that June—"allways . . . a shock," as his Twickenham neighbor William Pulteney wrote their mutual friend John Caryll, "to a good-Natur'd Mind," however much expected—made Pope more restless than ever. Though his comings and goings resist precise sorting out, it is clear that he had made up his mind to spend as much of the summer as possible with old friends and as little of it as

* Helmsley, in Yorkshire, sold after Buckingham's death (described in the *Epistle to Bathurst*) to a City banker.

possible at home, which "is become so melancholy to me." Till late
June, he lingered in Twickenham, no doubt visiting and being visited
on consolatory errands by nearby intimates like Martha Blount, the
Fortescues, the two Richardsons, father and son, the Burlingtons,
and Bolingbroke, but also responding, in the way bereft persons
often do, by settling all his own affairs ("paying all I owe, and
disposing all my papers, &c.") as well as his mother's.

His first real journey was to Stowe, and possibly there were
reasons. He had long been on easy terms with its owner, Sir Richard
Temple, whom he had been visiting on his rambles since 1725.
Temple, some nineteen years his elder, had in youth, it seems, read
law, making the acquaintance of William Congreve, who was then
similarly employed and in whose company, "six nights in seven," we
are told, he looked upon the wine when it was red, a propitious
nativity for Congreve's crippling lifelong gout. Later, during the
French wars under Anne and again in the campaign against Spanish
ports in 1719, Temple so distinguished himself in battle that he was
quickly raised to the rank of lieutenant general (after Walpole's fall he
would be made a field marshal), created Viscount Cobham, and
given the colonelcy of the "king's own" horse. A staunch Whig, he
had supported the Walpole administration loyally until the spring of
1733. On the excise bill he balked; and when in May Walpole quashed
in the Commons an inquiry into the practices of the South Sea Company's directors—this time not only into what they had done long
ago with the very large sums supposed to have been restored to the
company following the conviction of some of the worst of their
number for embezzlement in 1721–22, but also into subsequent de-
ceptions which (according to Lord Hervey, Walpole's supporter in
this matter as in all others) "permitted a set of annual rascals [the
directors] to cheat the Company without being punished, in order to
let England cheat Spain without being discovered"—several in the
Lords objected, Cobham among them. Though defeated in the
voting, they lodged a protest in writing that in polite language called
a spade a spade. They noted the "arts" that had been used to divert
parliament from its duty in pursuing this inquiry, stressed the
encouragement that impunity for present offenders would bring to
future ones, especially if "under the protection of some corrupt and
all-screening minister," and announced their own imperviousness to
"the influence of any man whatsoever, whose safety may depend on
the protection of fraud and corruption."

Retribution was swift. By Walpole, as Hervey puts it, "the signing
this protest was looked upon as the sin against the Holy Ghost which

was not to be forgiven." Those signers who had any sort of government employments were immediately turned out of them, and
Cobham, despite his high standing for long and meritorious service
in the field, was dismissed from his regiment: an action so arbitrary
and vindictive that it was perceived as scandalous on all sides. Salt
was added to the wound when the command was immediately given
to Walpole's son-in-law, the third earl of Cholmondeley, aged
thirty, the sort of fellow of whom Iago complains in Shakespeare's
Othello that he has "never set a squadron in the field Nor the division
of a battle knows, More than a spinster." The dismissal took place at
the close of Parliament on June 13. Pope arrived at Stowe early in
July. Since he liked to think of the poet's role in society as enjoying
the heroic character accorded it in Homer and in his own earlier lines
on Harley—

> In vain to Desarts thy Retreat is made;
> The Muse attends thee to the silent Shade:
> 'Tis hers, the brave Man's latest Steps to trace,
> Re-judge his Acts, and dignify Disgrace—
>
> (ll. 27–30)

it is conceivable that these two events are related. In fact, it may have
occurred to Pope at once that here was a double opportunity. By
addressing a major poem to Cobham, he could, on the one hand,
perform an act of personal loyalty and friendship; on the other, honor
publicly a man disgraced by Walpole for the very virtue most admirable in a public servant: independence of mind. His working papers
for the never-to-be-completed "Opus Magnum" almost certainly
contained by this time a sketch, or at least a set of brouillons, toward
the epistle designated as "Characters of Men and Manners" in the
manuscript exordium of his *Essay on Man*. Why not, it might readily
occur to him, develop this topic? It was certain to have appeal to the
shrewd and amused observer of human antics deducible today from
Van Loo's portrait of Cobham. Develop it in such a way as would set
off against the flux and mercury of our natures that element of
stability (whether called a ruling passion, as by Pope, or an acquired
habit of inner direction, as by some of today's sociologists, or simply
a genetic disposition) which allows us on occasion to be "our own
Masters still" and to take such stands against prevailing currents as
that for which Cobham was now paying the price?

All this is the purest speculation, of course. What we know is that
Pope made his earliest ramble that summer to Stowe, was able to
show a version of his *Epistle to Cobham* to Caryll when his travels led

71. Sir Richard Temple, 1st Viscount Cobham (1675–1749). By J. B. Van Loo.

And you! brave Cobham....

Epistle to Cobham, 263.

Courtesy of the National Portrait Gallery, London.

him to Ladyholt in September, and by November had received his addressee's approval of the compliment made him at the end. The epistle draws heavily on the poet's reading in Montaigne's *Essays*, which he had called "the very best Book for Information of Manners, that has been writ," especially on the essay entitled "Of the Inconstancy of Our Actions," whose general drift is epitomized in the following three sentences:

> If I speak variously of my self, it is because I consider my self variously. All contrarieties are there to be found, in one corner or another, or after one manner or another. Bashful, Insolent, Chast, Lustful, Prating, Silent, Laborious, Delicate, Ingenious, Heavy, Melancholick, Pleasant, Lying, True, Knowing, Ignorant, Liberal, Covetous, and Prodigal: I find all this in my self, more or less, according as I turn my self about; and whoever will sift himself, to the bottom, will find in himself, this volubility and discordance.

Taking such many-sidedness as his premise, Pope devotes much of the body of the epistle to a lively exposition of the difficulty if not near-impossibility of reading human character correctly. Books are no help. Observation is easily misled. The specimen we examine changes as we examine it. We read our own tastes and prejudices into our judgments. Nor do any person's actions necessarily mean what we conclude they mean. Their origin may lie in an impulse that, in Pope's description of it with analogies from dream life, looks arrestingly like today's notions of something underlying consciousness, a "sub"-conscious:

> Oft in the Passions' wild rotation tost,
> Our spring of action to ourselves is lost:
> Tir'd, not determin'd, to the last we yield,
> And what comes then is master of the field.
> As the last image of that troubled heap,
> When Sense subsides, and Fancy sports in sleep,
> (Tho' past the recollection of the thought)
> Becomes the stuff of which our dream is wrought:
> Something as dim to our internal view,
> Is thus, perhaps, the cause of most we do.
>
> (ll. 41–50)

The one fixative in Pope's scheme, as we saw in connection with his *Essay on Man*, is the "Ruling Passion." Assigned by Providence at conception, "cast and mingled" with our very frame, it persists for life and appears most dramatically (as, according to traditional wisdom, truth generally may be expected to do) at the moment of death. It was on this thought that Pope elected to hang his tribute. A succession of illustrative examples—among them, the ancient lecher who when death comes is tottering to his wench on knocking knees; the courtier of forty years whose last words are: "If—where I'm going—I could serve you, Sir?"; and the pretty actress whose final thought is of how her corpse will look—

> "Odious! in woollen! 'twould a Saint provoke,
> (Were the last words that poor Narcissa spoke)
> "No, let a charming Chintz, and Brussels lace
> "Wrap my cold limbs, and shade my lifeless face:
> "One would not, sure, be frightful when one's dead—
> "And—Betty—give this Cheek a little Red"—
> (ll. 242–47)

a succession of such examples, all illustrative of ruling follies, is made to close climactically with a single instance of a ruling virtue:

> And you! brave COBHAM, to the latest breath
> Shall feel your ruling passion strong in death:
> Such in those moments as in all the past,
> "Oh, save my Country, Heav'n!" shall be your last.
> (ll. 262–65)

Traveling to forget

Bolingbroke's Dawley also saw Pope that summer. As he had probably written much of the *Essay on Man* there on earlier occasions, it was natural to seek his friend's counsel in finishing the poem. Doubly natural, since, as the manuscripts show, he had intended from the beginning to make its peroration largely a eulogy of Bolingbroke. On August 9, he writes from Dawley to his friend Bethel that he expects to print this last epistle in about a fortnight. Yet during his September visit to Caryll, from roughly the ninth to the twenty-fourth, the work is still in hand; and having apparently been pressed by his host to give it a more unmistakably Christian stamp, he replies in a letter of late October that while it would be incongruous in so "philosophical" an argument to name "our Saviour" directly, he believes he can satisfy Caryll's scruple by magnifying Christian doctrine as the perfection of moral doctrine generally: "nay, and even . . .

quote the very words of the gospel-precept, that includes all the law and the prophets, *Thou shalt love God above all things, &c.*"

Publication of the epistle continued to be delayed, however, during another three months, and again, possibly, for a discernible cause. On October 27, just four days after the reply to Caryll, Bolingbroke began to publish in *The Craftsman* the series of papers that would eventually make up his *Dissertation on Parties*, the work so much admired by John Adams. Though undoubtedly composed with an eye on the forthcoming septennial election of 1734, they constitute an impressive history of the constitutional and religious differences dividing the Whig and Tory parties, of the steady superannuation of these differences by the course of events since 1688, and of the damage they now inflict on the common interests of the nation, being kept alive mostly in shibboleth and slogan:

> It is time therefore that all who desire to be esteemed good men, and to procure the peace, the strength, and glory of their country, by the only means, by which they can be procured effectually, should join their efforts to heal our national divisions, and to change the spirit of party into a diffusive spirit of public benevolence.

As the series was drawing toward its close (it was suspended for a time with the issue of February 2), Pope published on January 16 his epistle to Cobham, the newly outcast Whig whose ruling passion was his patriotism, and on the twenty-fourth the fourth epistle of the *Essay on Man*, winding down into twenty-six lines of handsome commendation of the best-known of outcast Tories:

> Come then, my Friend, my Genius, come along,
> Oh master of the poet, and the song! . . .
> Teach me, like thee, in various nature wise,
> To fall with dignity, with temper rise. . . .
> Oh! while along the stream of Time thy name
> Expanded flies, and gathers all its fame,
> Say, shall my little bark attendant sail,
> Pursue the triumph, and partake the gale? . . .
> Shall then this verse to future age pretend
> Thou wert my guide, philosopher, and friend?
> (ll. 373–74, 377–78, 383–86, 389–90)

The temptation to believe that this conjunction of events was in some degree premeditated tends to increase when one reflects how well Bolingbroke's appeal for changing party faction into a diffusive spirit of public benevolence accords with Pope's admonition to mankind to quell its appetite for separatism and "Grasp the whole worlds of Reason, Life, and Sense, In one close system of Benevolence." Despite their well-attested vanity, ambition, evasiveness, and love of intrigue, both men shared deeply a belief in the efficacy of reason and good will in the conduct of human affairs which, though possibly naive (in Bolingbroke's *Idea of a Patriot King*, if considered as political doctrine rather than propaganda, it is obtrusively naive), compares favorably with that announced by Walpole to the king when he said, with reference to the lords who had signed the protest, that "he knew ... the price of every one of them."

From Dawley, Pope went probably to Bathurst at Cirencester. A letter obviously written from there to Martha Blount sustains the note of restless gloom that he had confessed to her earlier and suggests that the visit was but brief:

> You cannot think how melancholy this place makes me: every part of this wood puts into my mind poor Mr. Gay with whom I past once a great deal of pleasant time in it, and another friend who is near dead, and quite lost to us, Dr. Swift. I really can find no enjoyment in the place; the same sort of uneasiness as I find at Twitnam, whenever I pass near my Mother's room.

The future too looks bleak:

> Life, after the first warm heats are over, is all downhill; and one almost wishes the journey's end, provided we were sure but to lye down easy, whenever the Night shall overtake us.

Ay, there's the rub. He has even dreamed all last night of his mother, he tells Martha—which is not, he knows, indicative of a desirable state of affairs within, lest one drop into a depression so noticeable the world will judge it lunacy.

The letter ends with a paragraph vaguely reminiscent of a will. The intention to free Martha of dependence on her family that will eventually result in his leaving her life use of his estate has already formed or is forming:

> It is a real truth, that to the last of my moments, the thought of you, and the best of my wishes for you, will attend you, told or untold. I could wish you had once the constancy and resolution to act for yourself [by living independently of her sister and mother], whether before or after I leave you (the only way I ever shall leave you) you must determine: but reflect, that the first wou'd make

me, as well as your self, happier; the latter could make you only so. Adieu.

Pope's last extended stop of this summer, following his September fortnight at Ladyholt with Caryll, was at Bevis Mount with Peterborow. This, along with Stowe, was becoming more and more his favorite spot on earth and increasingly congenial to his writing. While there this time, probably at some early date in October, his host took him to see Winchester College. "The Earl," we are told on the authority of William Whitehead, who was at the time a pupil (later a playwright as well as poet laureate), "gave ten guineas to be disposed of in prizes amongst the boys, and Mr. Pope set them a subject to write upon, viz. PETERBOROW." Submissions undoubtedly had to be in Latin verse. Six of the contestants captured prizes of a guinea each, and the remaining four guineas were laid out "for other boys" in subscriptions to a very beautiful edition of Horace then about to be published, with superb engravings by John Pine. Whitehead was one of the six who won a guinea.

"Hast thou, O sun! beheld an emptier sort?"

At Bevis Mount, Pope must have been polishing a poem that he published anonymously on November 5, about three weeks after his return. This was *The Impertinent, Or a Visit to the Court. A Satyr. By an Eminent Hand*. It is an adaptation of a satire by Donne, itself an adaptation of a famous Horatian satire. The Latin poem tells the story of Horace's encounter with a pretentious chatterbox and bore from whom, despite several efforts, he cannot break loose till luckily they meet up with the fellow's adversary in a lawsuit, by whom he is dragged away. Donne converts Horace's street encounter into a meeting at court with a courtier or court parasite, whose conceited, all-knowing, name-dropping palaver creates comedy, as in Horace, but also a certain unease, as if the courtier or someone within earshot might be a court spy, quick to impose treasonable implications on any chance remark. As critics have pointed out, though Donne had earlier converted from Roman Catholicism, his lingering sense of what it was like to belong to a suspect papist minority under the harsh laws of Elizabeth I (his own papist brother had been imprisoned in 1593 and the priest found with him hanged, drawn, and quartered) enables him to maintain here a complex mixture of exasperation, mock terror with an undercurrent of actual apprehension, and intense moral disgust as the law of the jungle is revealed in his interlocutor's conversation to be the governing principle of court life:

> He knows, he knows
> When the Queen frown'd, or smil'd, and he knows what
> A subtle States-man may gather of that;
> He knows who loves whom; and who by poyson
> Hast[e]s to an Offices reversion.

(Satire 4, 98–102)

How readily all this could play into the hands of an alert court critic some hundred and thirty years later may be seen in Pope's seemingly effortless adaptation of these and later lines, eliciting from a self-proclaimed court figure the same picture of its vices as that painted by the Opposition, and stressing, perhaps more strenuously than even Donne, the myriad ways in which power corrupts:

> When the *Queen* frown'd, or smil'd, he knows; and what
> A subtle Minister may make of that?
> Who sins with whom? who got his Pensioh *Rug,*★
> Or quicken'd a Reversion by a *Drug?* . . .
> Who, having lost his Credit, pawn'd his Rent,
> Is therefore fit to have a *Government?*†
> Who in the *Secret,*‡ deals in Stocks secure,
> And cheats th' unknowing Widow, and the Poor?
> Who makes a *Trust,* or *Charity,* a Job,§
> And gets an Act of Parliament to rob? . . .
> He tells what Strumpet Places sells for Life,
> What 'Squire his Lands, what Citizen his Wife?
> And last (which proves him wiser still than all)
> What Lady's Face is not a whited Wall?¶

(ll. 132–35, 138–43, 148–51)

★ Thieves' slang at the time for "safe"—"all squared away."
† A position, authority, or sinecure assigned by the government.
‡ Having political information affecting the market.
§ "A public service or trust turned to private gain"—*OED*. Pope alludes to funds established in the Charitable Corporation to provide cheap loans to the poor, but diverted by the directors to rich borrowers at higher interest and in some instances embezzled.
¶ Whiting was used to conceal skin blemishes, most especially those caused by venereal disease, but with reference here also to the whited sepulchres of Matthew, 23:27, "which indeed appear beautiful outwards, but are within full of dead men's bones, and of all uncleanness."

Back home at last, freed of his tormentor by the arrival of other court personages better worth toadying to, Donne falls into a dream (or nightmare) of the court resembling Dante's account of Hell.

The most picturesque of the several spectacles the dream presents is that of the court ladies meeting the court men—their voluminous bright apparel inviting a favorite nautical joke, as when Mercutio hails Juliet's nurse in Shakespeare's play as if he had sighted a warship: "A sail! A sail!"

> Now
> The Ladies come. As Pirats, which do know
> That there came weak ships fraught with Cutchanel,★
> The men board them; and praise (as they think) well,
> Their beauties; they the mens wits; both are bought.
>
> (ll. 182–90)

Pope's architectural couplet cannot achieve such condensation without doing itself injustice. What it can do is to extend the drama of the ladies' entrance, act out in syntax the confrontation of male and female forces (as if for an actual engagement at sea), catch character by the use of direct address, and give an extra shimmer to the whole through the multiplicity of erotic colorations liberated in this context by such traditionally equivocal terms as "Frigates," "Vessel," "Prize," "Top-gallant," "boarding," "bought," and the rest:

> Painted for sight, and essenc'd for the smell,
> Like Frigates fraught with Spice and Cochine'l,
> Sail in the *Ladies*: How each Pyrate eyes
> So weak a Vessel, and so rich a Prize!
> Top-gallant he, and she in all her Trim,
> He boarding her, she striking sail to him.
> "*Dear Countess!* you have Charms all Hearts to hit!"
> And "*sweet Sir Fopling!* you have so much wit!"
> Such Wits and Beauties are not prais'd for nought,
> For both the Beauty and the Wit are *bought*.
>
> (ll. 226–35)

But the pith and center of the dream for Donne is his realization that the people he has seen at court are indeed damned:

> Then,
> Shall I, none's slave, of high born or rais'd men
> Fear frowns; and my mistress Truth, betray thee

★ A red dye used as rouge.

For th' huffing, braggart, puft Nobility?
No, no, Thou which since yesterday hast been
Almost about the whole world, hast thou seen,
O Sun, in all thy journey, Vanity
Such as swells the bladder of our Court? I
Think he which made your Waxen garden⋆, and
Transported it, from Italy, to stand
With us at London, flouts [i.e., mocks] our Courtiers; for
Just such gay painted things, which no sap, nor
Tast have in them, ours are. . . .

(ll. 161–73)

Surely, at any rate—with their clear anticipation of his own
earlier

And I not strip the Gilding off a Knave,
Un-plac'd, un-pension'd, no Man's Heir, or Slave?—

(*Sat. II*, i, 115–16)

these must be the lines that attracted Pope at this particular moment
in his career, when he was still groping to establish his credibility as
a serious moral satirist by invoking the example of honored predecessors and endeavoring to hammer out a conversational couplet as
shapely as art could make it, yet as apparently impromptu as prose:

Not *Dante* dreaming all th' Infernal State,
Beheld such Scenes of *Envy*, *Sin*, and *Hate*.
Base Fear becomes the Guilty, not the Free;
Suits Tyrants, Plunderers, but suits not me.

(ll, 192–95)

Then with a jauntier tone ("Imagine it! Four and a half feet high,
and they pretend to be scared of me"), as if in the immediately
preceding line he might have to come too close for comfort to
current events:

Shall I, the Terror of this sinful Town,
Care, if a livery'd Lord or smile or frown?
Who cannot flatter, and detest who can,
Tremble before a *noble Serving-Man*?

(ll. 196–99)

⋆ Pope's own note refers to "A show of the Italian Gardens in Waxwork,
in the time of King James the First."

Too close again, which sends him scurrying for protection back to Donne and the court of Elizabeth:

> O my fair Mistress, *Truth*! Shall I quit thee,
> For huffing, braggart, puft *Nobility*?
> Thou, who since Yesterday, hast roll'd o'er all
> The busy, idle Blockheads of the Ball,
> Hast thou, O *Sun*! beheld an emptier sort,
> Than such as swell this Bladder of a Court?
>
> (ll. 200–205)

But Donne's wax garden will mean nothing to his readers in 1733. Why not a wax court? As a matter of fact, only two years earlier in March, there had been on show for a while in London "the COURT of FRANCE in Waxwork." Signalized in a note to those lines, this circumstance will serve as a lightning rod against prosecution without deflecting most readers' minds from the far more familiar "court of Great Brittain" exhibited by Mrs. Salmon in her wax museum in Fleet Street—the king, at least in Pope's description of the group, wearing the well-known Brunswick stare, and the "painted Puppets . . . only Dress and Face" doubtless including Hervey:

> Now pox on those who shew a *Court in Wax*!
> It ought to bring all Courtiers on their backs.
> Such painted Puppets, such a varnish'd Race
> Of hollow Gewgaws, only Dress and Face,
> Such waxen Noses, stately staring things,
> No wonder some Folks bow, and think them *Kings*.

Suitors bow to them at court, that is to say, and impressible young farmers from the country at Mrs. Salmon's. Or, as Shakespeare had put it succinctly in *King Lear*: "A dog's obey'd in office."

"And my answer to Arbuthnot," Lord Hervey wrote to his friend Henry Fox on 31 January 1734 (the month in which the *Epistle to Cobham* and the last epistle of the *Essay on Man* had both appeared), "when he asked me why I had been so very severe on Pope,"

> was, "because he was a rascal, had begun with me, and deserved it; and that my only reason for being sorry the verses were printed, which I did not design they should be, was because I thought it below me to enter into a paper war with one that had made himself by his late works as contemptible as he was odious."

The verses referred to were not those addressed *To the Imitator* and shared with Lady Mary, but a further foray of Hervey's own. In a foolish poem—as he says, not intended for publication, but foolishly sent to an indiscreet clerical acquaintance at Chichester—he had painted with his usual smart-set cynicism a portrait of his own and the court's habits and attitudes that is only somewhat less damning than Donne's:

> For Courts are only larger Familys,
> The Growth of each, few Truths, & many Lyes;
> Like you [the clergy] we lounge, & feast, & play, & chatter;
> In private Satirize, in Publick flatter.
> Few to each other, all to one point true,
> Which one I shan't, nor need explain. Adieu.
>
> (ll. 169–74)

At the end of the poem, allowed by its flattered recipient to be published on November 10 as *An Epistle from a Nobleman to a Doctor of Divinity.* . . . *Written from H[ampto]n C[our]t*, Hervey devoted some lines to attacking Pope. Most of them simply aired once more the mouldy falsehood that Pope was no poet but a "Jingler," who might have been tolerated had he not attempted satire but concluded his career instead with his three major works of plagiarism, the *Essay on Criticism*, the *Rape of the Lock*, and the Homer:

> Had he ne'er aim'd at any Work beside,
> In Glory then he might have liv'd and dy'd;
> And ever been, tho' not with Genius fir'd,
> By School-boys quoted, and by Girls admir'd.
> So much for P[o]pe.
>
> (ll. 159–63)

Coming from one of Walpole's staunchest henchmen, Queen Caroline's favorite confidant, and the Court's vice-chamberlain, even such toothless mumblings of the game as these had to be taken seriously: hence Arbuthnot's mission of inquiry. And they caused Pope sufficient anger to draw from him a full-dress answer in prose, "A Letter to a Noble Lord," dated only twenty days after the publication of Hervey's *Epistle*. Veined with sometimes telling irony, the "Letter" shows Pope seeking (without always finding) the right tone for an ordinary Englishman to take in responding to an assault from a peer of the realm. This was not an easy task in a time when Lady Mary Wortley Montagu could write with bland sarcasm to her daughter, ascribing the success of Pope and Swift entirely to the condescension of their aristocratic friends and readers: "It is pleasant to consider that had it not been for the good nature of those very mortals they contemn, these two superior Beings were entitled by their Birth and hereditary Fortune to be only a couple of Link Boys."

Though Pope's "Letter" is rather too long for maximum effect and his control of tone sometimes fails him, it remains a withering document, and in its best moments seizes and keeps the high ground, with a dignified reminder of the responsibilities that belong to birth and rank in a hierarchical society:

> I beseech your Lordship to consider the injury a Man of your *high Rank* and *Credit* may do to a *private Person*, under *Penal Laws* and many other disadvantages, not for want of *honesty* or *conscience*, but merely perhaps for having too *weak a head* or too *tender a heart*. It is by *these alone* I have hitherto liv'd excluded from all *posts* of *Profit* or *Trust*. As I can interfere with the *Views* of no man, do not deny me, my Lord, *all that is left*, a little *Praise*, or the common Encouragement due, if not to my *Genius*, at least to my *Industry*.
>
> Above all, your Lordship will be careful not to wrong my *Moral Character*, with THOSE under whose *Protection* I live, and thro' whose *Lenity* alone I can live with Comfort. Your Lordship, I am confident, upon consideration will think, you inadvertently went a little *too far* when you recommended to THEIR perusal, and strengthened by the weight of your Approbation, a *Libel*, mean in its reflections upon my poor *figure*, and scandalous in those on my *Honour* and *Integrity*: wherein I was represented as "*an Enemy* to Human Race, a *Murderer* of Reputations, and a *Monster* mark'd by God like *Cain*, deserving to wander accursed thro' the World."

As it turned out, this reply was never published in Pope's lifetime, only by Warburton in 1751. One explanation attributes its suppression to a request from Walpole; another, tentatively, to a possible desire of the Queen, "apprehensive that it might make her counsellor insignificant in the public esteem"; a third, to prudential considerations on the poet's part. Pope being the man he was, we ought probably to add to this list considerations of artistic effect. The "Letter" may very well have seemed to him, on reflection, entirely apart from these other possible restraints, too personal, topical, ephemeral, lacking esthetic distance and therefore long-term esthetic interest beyond the immediate occasion. Though doubtless he would not have put the matter in just these words, he must have sensed that for one writing in the tradition of the serious satirist, or, for that matter, in the larger encompassing tradition of the serious poet—seer, prophet, *vates*, fine cutting edge of the conscience and consciousness of his age—what mattered about Hervey was not what might have been offensive about his treatment of a certain A. Pope at this or that time or place (however much that particular poet might hate him on that account!), but what would be found representatively offensive about such a figure, always, everywhere, and by all. Hervey, in other words, need not be deprived of his moment in the spotlight of fame; it was simply that another medium than prose might better catch that representative aspect.

Pope was in his usual state of uncertain health that winter of 1734. Probably, however, not so afflicted that he could not rejoice when his friend George Berkeley the philosopher, currently dean of Derry, was appointed in January bishop of Cloyne. (In late April he would visit him at Burlington's in Chiswick to say farewell before his departure to Ireland, a farewell that proved to be their last since Berkeley did not return again to England for eighteen years.) January also brought the death and funeral of John Dennis, now in his eightieth year. One wishes it were possible to know whether Pope's kinder feelings for the impoverished old man extended to his keeping company with "the Friends and Acquaintances in mourning Coaches" (Mallet and Thomson, we may guess, among them) who on January 10 attended the body to St. Martin's in the Fields, where, according to the *Daily Post Boy*, it was "handsomely interred." No illness, surely, could have kept Pope from smiling at the news, in early February, of a public altercation between Bolingbroke's footman and Walpole's, in which the former gave the latter the drubbing of his life. Since the episode brings home with particular clarity the almost total politicization of the atmosphere in which English life was lived (and English poetry written) during these years, the high-spirited account of it sent to his twin brother in Berwickshire by Hugh Hume, later earl of Marchmont and one of Pope's executors and closest friends, is worth quoting:

> You must know that the Footmen have got a Clubb on the same day that their Masters have theirs[,] I mean the Lords. Among others that dropt in there . . . came the Footman of the Great Man, R[ober]t W[alpole] who upon some discourse said that his master could send all the Scotch L[or]ds home on their foot.* L[or]d B's

* I.e., that Walpole's influence over the upcoming elections will send packing the sixteen Scots peers currently representing Scotland in the Lords. His efforts to control the political complexion of this group by corruption were notorious.

footman being present desired to know who this bragadocio was that had sent his Sancho Pancha to bully them & . . . he told them that he was S. R. W. [,] upon which the other resolved to have a trial at Club Law & taking up his stick thressht the Gentleman till he could beat no longer and told him that was for his Master. The footman however after this threatned to sue him and going out mutter'd as if his master were in the Minority, upon which our modern St. Andrew Protector of the Scots follow'd & giving him another sound drubbing for his Master [,] in order to do an entire civil thing kick'd him over the Stair and told him that was for himself. When our Caledonian went home he told his Master that the yellow sleeved Squire threatened to sue him, but LB told him not to fear [,] that he would stand by him.

I hope you'll come [from Scotland] in time to manage this national quarrel.

Entertaining possibly, but in no way an accurate reflection of what was going on in the real world of parliamentary maneuver. There, as usual, the skill, sense, and patronage that united Walpole's supporters repeatedly turned the flank of an Opposition loosely knit by a common antagonism to the minister, but rarely of one mind on measures. An Opposition move, for example, to give life status to army officers in reprisal for the king's arbitrary dismissal of Cobham lost votes even from the most stalwart of Walpole's foes, the extreme right-wing Tories, because the measure would curtail the prerogatives of the crown. Similar moves—to restore triennial parliaments, pare the number of placemen, reduce the size of the standing army, make corruption in elections more difficult—were likewise handily defeated. Once the election results were in, moreover—this was by late May 1734—it was clear that the government had kept its majority, even if one slightly reduced, and so far as the sixteen Scots were concerned, had swept the board, as Walpole's footman had promised.

For the time being, obviously, things would go on at St. Stephen's as before. Bolingbroke's effort to unite the country behind a program of ecumenicism as to parties and of needed reforms as to procedures of government had failed, and Walpole, shrewd as always in his intuition of electoral results, had already been conducting since January, through his army of gazetteers, a campaign for "The Reasonableness and Necessity of Driving Bolingbroke out of the Kingdom." By coincidence or otherwise, Pope's fourth epistle of the *Essays on Man* with its high praise of Bolingbroke was published two days after the first essay in this campaign, and it is not unlikely that the attack as a whole influenced his decision to restore to that praise (in his collected edition of the four epistles published on April 20) two lines he had at first omitted:

> When Statesmen, heroes, kings, in dust repose,
> Whose sons shall blush their fathers were thy foes.
>
> (ll. 387–88)

If there were to be war, no one need doubt which side he had been on.

Stowe and its "Worthies"

That June, almost as soon as the new Parliament met, Pope's rambles took him again to Stowe. There he could count on an informality and freedom that he never failed to find rehabilitating. "Every one," he tells Martha Blount (the date is five years later, but it is doubtful that the way of life had much altered) "takes a different way, & wanders about till we meet at Noone. All the Mornings we breakfast & dispute; after dinner & at night, Musick & Harmony; in the Garden, Fishing; no Politicks and no Cards, nor much Reading. This agrees exactly with me, for the Want of Cards sends me early to bed. I have no complaints, but that I wish for you & can't have you." The company at Stowe could also be counted on. It would include an amiable and generous host ("one perfect in the Pleasing Art," Congreve had written), who knew how to give just enough structure to the entertainment of his guests but not too much, and who was evidently, like Pope himself when in spirits, quite a tease. "Stowe is in great beauty," writes one of Pope's fellow guests during this particular visit,

> the master of it in good health and excellent spirits, by which the major-general [James Dormer, longtime friend of Pope's, owner of nearby Rousham, at present with Pope a visitor at Stowe] gets a new tormentor; not that his old one (*Pope*) was not sufficient, who has really laughed himself fat at poor Jemmy's expense, who in proportion hath fretted himself lean.

Other sprightly guests often to be found at Cobham's were his two nephews, Gilbert West and George Lyttelton. The latter was soon to become secretary to the Prince of Wales and therefore deeply involved in the reformist "Young Patriot" movement, whose members, largely young Whigs opposed to Walpole, looked upon Pope as their moral inspiration. West, elder of the two, had just made his first bid for fame as a poet with a paper of verses addressed to Pope (it was sent to him for consideration in 1731 and published anonymously in 1732), describing in some detail, almost like a guide book, his uncle's gardens.

For Pope, these were, of course, the ultimate attraction. "If any thing under Paradise," he wrote to his friend John Knight in 1731, "could set me beyond all Earthly Cogitations, Stowe might do it, It is much more beautiful this year than when I saw it before, & much enlarged, & with variety." That was the great thing about Stowe: like Shakespeare's Cleopatra it was ever unpredictable, new areas being landscaped, new garden buildings rising, in the planning of both of which it is probably safe to say that Pope sometimes lent a discreet hand. As far back as 1725, when he seems to have first visited the place, the gardens were already "very noble" and richly ornamented with "Temples, . . . Statues, Obelisks, Pillars, and Porticoes." So many temples that one may well ask with the authors of a modern guide to Stowe whether Cobham did not find amusement "in visibly illustrating his family motto, *Templa Quam Dilecta*—'How delightful are thy temples!'"—not to mention his family name.

Stowe had in abundance what Cirencester lacked: water. On the parterre immediate to the house, a large stone-framed pond with its fountain. Lower, at the foot of a terraced slope lined with a double row of white poplars, an octagonal pond of some two and a half acres, with a sixty-foot obelisk, or guglia, in the midst, from the top of which rivulets could be made to jet out and drift like a constellation of diamonds onto the mirroring surface below. By a cascade on one side, overflow from the "Octagon" fed an eleven-acre lake, along whose border one could pause to rest, or to reflect on change and the perpetual metamorphosis of things, intended (perhaps) to be implied by the syrinx figure carved over the door of a small stone shelter called the hermitage. A prospect of the lake and its surrounding plantations probably still more stunning because framed by trees and fronted by greensward could be had from the nearby "Persian Pavillion," recently erected by William Kent: two square pavilions of rusticated stone joined by porticoes to a central templelike structure, inscribed on one of its walls within: Veneri Hortensi ["To the Venus of Gardens"]—the entire layout curved in the shape of a new moon. The next year, the cove ceiling of this central room would be painted with the story of Hellinore and Malbecco from the *Faerie Queene*.

From here, an inner winding route, filled with surprises, took one past a pyramid sixty feet high built by and now dedicated to the memory of Sir John Vanbrugh, designer, along with Bridgeman, of

72. A view in Stowe Gardens. Detail of an undated engraving after a drawing by Jean Rigaud, *c.* 1735. In the far middle distance is the Rotondo.

> Nature shall join you, Time shall make it grow
> A Work to wonder at—perhaps a STOW.
>
> *Epistle to Burlington,* 69–70.

Courtesy of Stowe School and kindness of George Clarke.

the Stowe landscape in its first phases. His, for example, was the long vista reaching down through the rows of poplars to the Octagon and, beyond it, to two small Doric temples, also of his making, whose walls, at least by 1735, had been painted *al fresco* with scenes from Guarini's pastoral tragicomedy *Il Pastor Fido*. Inside the pyramid, possibly suggested by Pope, who was fond of the sentiment and would soon give it a memorable rendering in his adaptation of the Horatian original from which it derives, were inscribed the lines:

> Lusisti satis, edisti satis, atque bibisti:
> tempus abire tibi est: ne potum largius aeque
> rideat, & pulset lasciva decentius aetas.
> ["You've play'd, and lov'd, and eat, and drank your fill:
> Walk sober off; before a sprightlier Age
> Comes titt'ring on, and shoves you from the stage:
> Leave such to trifle with more grace and ease,
> Whom Folly pleases, and whose Follies please."]

Imit. Hor., Ep. II, ii: 323–27)

If pursued further, the same winding course allowed one a succession of points of interest, each with its own changed perspective. A temple of Bacchus, for instance, also painted *al fresco* with Bacchic scenes. An obelisk named for the chaplain of Cobham's regiment of dragoons. A Circle of Saxon Deities ("Sunna, Mona, Tiw, Woden, Thuner, Friga, Saetern": names fossilized in our days of the week) rudely carved by Rysbrack. A secluded grotto familiarly dubbed the "Randibus" in honor of a local satyr named Conway Rand who happened also to be the local vicar. (Enchanted by watching a young domestic nymph swinging freely above his head in her unocclusive draperies, he became so enchanted that he pursued her to the spot later named for him, with what result history does not say.) And a brilliantly situated "Rotondo." This last had been modeled by Vanbrugh on the circular Temple of Vesta above the gorge at Tivoli that so haunted the imaginations of European and English painters from Claude Lorrain to Richard Wilson and beyond. From it, at Stowe, one could look west over the full extent of the Home Park with its grazing animals to Vanbrugh's pyramid; north, through a long avenue of trees to a Vanbrugh-designed pavilion, painted within with stories taken from reliefs in the Roman Capitolium and with imperial inscriptions from the same source; and east, along the length of a five-hundred-foot reflecting basin, to a statue of Queen Caroline, flanked on each side by statues of shepherds and shepherdesses, "dancing." Not far away in a fringe of trees, but still visible from the Rotondo, a Corinthian pillar with a plinth inscribed "Georgio Augusto" thrust thirty feet into the air a likeness of George II, making it all but impossible not to wonder if annual contemplation of this statue and its inscription had anything to do with the inception in Pope's mind of his own ironical address to "George Augustus" in his adaptation, published in 1737, of Horace's address to Caesar Augustus. In the same spirit, on the opposite side of the Great House from the gardens, where it greeted all arriving guests, stood an equestrian statue of George Augustus's father, George I—to whom Cobham owed his viscountcy—life-size in lead. In lead. Appropriate, Pope must occasionally have thought, for a dynasty that in the mythology of his *Dunciad* had hatched a new Saturnian age from that formidable metal (1: 26).

Most notable, however, among Cobham's garden Whiggeries had been till recently a squarish heavily buttressed building in a favored position overlooking the Home Park and lake, girded about with eight busts eventually to be called "the British Worthies." In their number, as a modern historian of Cobham's gardens has interpreted the display,

> were two sovereigns, and you might suppose that one of them would have been Queen Anne, for whom Lord Cobham had fought so stoutly and who had promoted him from colonel to lieutenant general. But no, with all her virtues Queen Anne was a Stuart. She was left out. The sovereigns were the great patriot Elizabeth, last before the Stuarts, with her poet Shakespeare; and William III, supplanter of the Stuarts, with his philosopher John Locke. Between was John Hampden, the local patriot from Aylesbury, who had drawn his sword against the Stuarts and died for the Parliament. There were also Bacon and Newton, who had clearly shown that Truth, though not of course its Divine Origin, was to be found by intellectual process and not by listening to what the priests had to say. There was no priest of any kind among the Worthies. [The priesthood's local representative, as we have seen, left something to be desired.] Finally there was Milton. He was there because he had written sublime poetry, but it was open to anyone to point out that he had also written letters for Oliver Cromwell. In short, the theme was "1688," Dutch William receiving by acclaim the title of British Worthy. The theme was anti-Stuart and anti-clerical.

Such, till very lately, had been the gardens' political complexion. But now changes were afoot. The building by the lake would be called hereafter the "Belvedere," and the residence of the "Worthies" had been shifted to a new area of the gardens under development by William Kent, appropriately named (for Worthies) "The Elysian Fields," and to a new building just now being referred to as "The Mausoleum," though before long it would be renamed "The Temple of British Worthies." Whatever its name, the new structure was semicircular and formed of two wings of small, attached, individually pedimented mausoleums, much like those seen in many burial grounds today. Where the wings joined, a somewhat larger central mausoleum rose above the rest, having as they did not, a steep pyramidlike roof from which a head of Mercury in an oval niche looked out upon a passing stream mirroring the entire structure. Eight individual mausoleums formed each wing, and in each mausoleum an inset niche held a Worthy's bust, with name and suitable inscription carved on a plaque above.

Of the sixteen niches thus provided, only nine by July 1735 were yet filled: eight with the busts aforementioned, brought from their earlier home, and one with the bust of Inigo Jones, who as grandfather of English Palladianism was an almost inevitable addition now that William Kent was in charge. During the next few years, before Pope's death, and probably very soon, five of the remaining seven niches would be assigned, and assigned in every case to figures important either in the sympathies or in the political actions of the resistance to Walpole. Edward the Black Prince was there—by his derring-do in France an implicit criticism of Walpole's French policy; but also a compliment to the present Prince of Wales, a lump of not very promising clay that for a while the Opposition hoped to fire into the likeness of a great future king. King Alfred also was there. He was an Opposition favorite because of their contention that English liberties began with the Saxons, not, as the government writers liked to argue, only in 1688. Further, he was credited in his inscription with having done everything that George II and Walpole ought to have done but hadn't: "The mildest, justest, most beneficent of Kings; who ... secur'd the Seas [a characteristic Opposition allusion to Walpole's peace policy, which allowed Spanish men-of-war to prey on English merchant shipping with impunity], protected Learning, ... crush'd Corruption, guarded Liberty, and was the Founder of the English Constitution."

Similar awakening feelings as to the importance of British naval power doubtless account for the presence in these niches of Sir Francis Drake and Sir Walter Raleigh. Drake, who had "carried into unknown Seas and Nations the Knowledge and the Glory of the British Name." And Ralegh, "Who endeavouring" [like the Opposition itself throughout the 1730s] to rouse the Spirit of his Master, for the Honour of his Country, against the Ambition of Spain, fell a Sacrifice to the Influence of that Court." (Possibly it is not altogether an accident that one of the services Pope would soon claim for the good poet in purifying the language of the tribe was that he could

> Command old words that long have slept to wake,
> Words, that wise Bacon, or brave Raleigh spake).

Of the three other busts, one was predictably that of Sir Thomas Gresham, founder of the Royal Exchange, symbol of the merchant group, whose support Walpole had largely forfeited by his refusal to challenge the Spanish depredations. Another was that of Sir John Barnard, who would also be celebrated in Pope's later poetry and for much the same reasons. M.P. for the City, in 1737 its Lord Mayor, he had become the leader of its attacks on Walpole's policies in the Commons. As a "Worthy" still alive, his bust had no inscription. One other bust likewise had no inscription because its original was living. This was Pope's. The inscription, not placed till 1764, can have been known only to his "beautiful electric ghost," but it would have pleased him:

> Alexander Pope,
> Who uniting the Correctness of Judgment to the Fire of Genius,
> by the Melody and Power of his Numbers,
> gave Sweetness to Sense, and Grace to Philosophy.
> He employ'd the pointed Brilliancy of Wit to chastise the Vices
> and the Eloquence of Poetry to exalt the Virtues of Human Nature;
> and being without a Rival in his own Age,
> imitated and translated, with a Spirit equal to the Originals,
> the best Poets of Antiquity.

One might almost guess from this account so far (and if one did, one would be quite right) that during these same 1730s a "Temple of Ancient Virtue" was erected, again in Kent's "Elysian Fields," paying tribute to four great ancients who by exemplary conduct, or principles, or both, had fought corruption on all fronts. Epaminondas, from whom "the Republick of Thebes receiv'd both Liberty and Empire." Lycurgus, who "instituted for his Countrymen the firmest Liberty and the soundest Morality." Socrates, "innocent in a most corrupt State, an Encourager of the Good, who ... reduced Philosophy from ... vain Disputations, to the Duties of Life, and the Advantages of Society." And, of course, also, as in Pope's own

Temple of Fame, Homer, "Bestower of Immortality", who "incites all . . . honourably to dare, and resolutely to suffer." Conceivably, one might even guess (again correctly) that hard by there stood a "Temple of Modern Virtue," significantly in ruins, and within its precincts a headless statue obviously intended to represent the absence of such qualities as those described above, but possibly also, for those who chose to see it that way, Sir Robert Walpole.

Thus from 1733 on, when Cobham was cashiered, Stowe gardens gradually responded. They had always been various, beautiful, meditative, and memorializing—soon to be added, in fact, was a memorial to Congreve. But now in the new eastern areas being opened up, they began to assume not only a more picturesque and painterly aspect, as Kent's work always did, but a political overlay incorporating the very themes sounded most often in Opposition writings of the period, including several of Pope's Horatian imitations: corruption, loss of liberty, and the decay of that "Virtue"—an Opposition term denoting courage, patriotism, and independence—which had once made Britain great, but was now fading (so it was alleged, not without a certain justice) under a rule that valued one's merit less than one's vote. By the late 1730s a perambulation about Stowe must have had for Pope some of the flavor of a tour of his own mind. "Pope's spirit," it was shrewdly remarked not long ago, still "hovers over Stowe."

> A walk round the gardens should make us return home and take down his poems; it will make us regret that no modern successor is available to lash the absurdities of our own age and the place-seekers, sycophants, and double-talkers who too often parade as cultural leaders.

CHAPTER 24

THE LADY AND THE DOCTOR

"Imitated. *Why imitated?*"

Pope's 1734 stay at Stowe lasted but a few days. From there he went on to Cirencester, rambling in his usual summer way, as Bolingbroke writes Swift on July 6, "from one friends house to another":

> He is now att Cirencester, he came thither from my Lord Cobhams; he came to my Lord Cobhams from Mr. Dormers [i.e., Rousham, where Pope and his traveling companions, the Honorable George Berkeley and General James Dormer stopped on the way to and from Stowe]; to Mr. Dormers from London, to London from Chiswick; to Chiswick from my Farm, to my Farm from his own Garden, and he goes soon from Lord Bathursts to Lord Peterborows, after which he returns to my farm again.

En route to Peterborow's, as a matter of fact, Pope stopped also at Tottenham, seat of Burlington's brother-in-law Lord Bruce, and called (in vain, for they were away) at Amesbury to see the Queensberrys. Nor did his peregrinations end in mid–September with Bevis Mount and Dawley. Having stopped in Hampstead for a day with Arbuthnot, who was now undergoing what he knew to be his last illness, and, at Twickenham, "having kiss'd Bounce (my only Friend now there)," he was off again with Bolingbroke about September 18 to Bath. Not, he insists in a letter to Bethel, because he expects any improvement of his health, but to join Martha Blount—who, as he reminds her in a letter announcing his and Bolingbroke's arrival, has been instructed by Dr. Arbuthnot that the mineral baths may be of service to her in heating her blood. "For," he adds, with a teasing pun that he knew would make her blush (and that later members of the Blount family carefully blotted out), "there is no Scandal in being in Heat."

Meanwhile, his six long weeks at Bevis Mount, including all of August and the first fortnight of September, had been exceptionally productive. Bevis Mount had sea air, a commodity by which eighteenth- and nineteenth-century medical opinion set much store. It had also, as Pope exuberantly wrote to Oxford during this visit, "the best Sea fish & River fish in the world, much tranquillity, some Reading, no Politiques, admirable Melons, an excellent Bowling-green & Ninepin alley." At Bevis Mount, moreover, there was not simply, as at many great estates, a seat or viewpoint all his own, but an actual small dwelling, with a noble prospect. "I write this," he tells Arbuthnot in an early August letter asking about his health, "from the most beautiful Top of a Hill I ever saw, a little house that overlooks the Sea, Southampton, & the Isle of Wight; where I study, write, and have what Leisure I please." And then, coming to the main point,

> Pray if it be not too uneasy to you, write to me now & then, or let some of your family acquaint me how you are? Is your Brother with you? If he is, let me be kindly rememberd to him, & to your Son & Daughters: I wish them sincerely well, & (what is the Best Wish I can form for them) I wish them the longer Life of so Good a Father.

Added delights of a stay at Bevis Mount were the expeditions on which Peterborow, as restless a man as Pope himself, liked to take his guests. The previous summer they had gone to see Winchester College. This time there was a visit to Beaulieu in a spectacular situation "on the sea" (actually on the Solent), home of Lady Mary Churchill, one of Marlborough's daughters, now duchess of Montagu, whose portrait Pope had painted (or rather, copied) in his youth when studying with Jervas. But the great excursion of the summer, as it turned out, was one that began by sea. Curious, as he put it, "to try if a Sea-Sickness would be supportable to me, in case I should ever run [flee] my Country," Pope took off with Peterborow as helmsman and three mariners down Southampton Water, their boat well victualled with "Cold Pye, Pig[e]ons, & Turkies" and supplied with wine purchased from some incoming French sailors, doubtless smugglers. Going ashore about five miles down the Water in search of a place to dine, they stumbled upon the ruins of Netley Abbey, a place, as they discovered later, not recorded by Camden in his *Britannia*, and quite unknown to Peterborow despite his long period of residence nearby. There they ate, using for seats the fallen capitals of two pillars, and for their table, the length of another fallen pillar.

After dinner, we strolld out again, & (going to visit the rest of the Ruins which we saw were very Extensive) found the Shell (all but the Covering) of a Church, not much less than the Body of that at Westminster, a whole side of windows entire, to the number of eight great arches; the End window over the Altar vastly high, & the whole wrought finely with old Gothic ornaments: one Part of the Roof, which seemd to have been under the Steeple, was yet standing, but lookd terribly [i.e., terrifying]; it was above 60 foot high, & hung like Net work, so thin & so fine over our heads: No part of Westminster abby is more ornamented.

There is a great deal more in the letter, which was written, as this kind of detailed description of romantic scenes almost invariably was, to Martha Blount. He plans to return to the abbey another day, he says, to add to the sheaf of drawings he has already made to show her when they meet. And he will, by the way, if all goes as planned, return home by way of "your old Monastery, Mapledurham":

thence look on Whiteknights (without troubling either of the Masters, for Sr Henry [Englefield] I hear is yet at Scarborow) & so lye in Windsor forest at Mr Dancastle's: This may be the last time I shall see those Scenes of my past Life, where I have been so happy, & I look upon one of them in particular in this Light, since it was there I first knew you.

Pope was working during this stay at Peterborow's on (probably) three poems. One was his third Horatian imitation, the bawdy second satire of Horace's first book, which conducts an argument for preferring innocent fornication with a strumpet to the more dangerous amenities of adultery:

> Give me a willing Nymph! 'tis all I care,
> Extremely clean, and tolerably fair,
> Her Shape her own, whatever Shape she have,
> And just that White and Red which Nature gave.
> Her I transported touch, transported view—

—here Pope (or is it the womanizing Bathurst? The poem seems deliberately ambiguous as to the speaker of these lines) manages a compliment to the duchess whose hospitality at Beaulieu he has just enjoyed and whose youthful beauty he remembers from his studio days—

And call her *Angel*! *Goddess*! *Montague*!
No furious Husband thunders at the Door;
No barking Dog, no Household in a Roar;
From gleaming Swords no shrieking Women run;
No wretched Wife cries out, *Undone*! *Undone*!
Seiz'd in the Fact, and in her Cuckold's Pow'r,
She kneels, she weeps, and worse! resigns her Dow'r.
Me, naked me, to Posts, to Pumps they draw,
To Shame eternal, or eternal Law.

(ll. 161–74)

A portion (or possibly a version) of this imitation, Pope had read aloud to the doubtless all-male company at Rousham, when stopping there on his way from Stowe to Lord Bruce's Tottenham. And if it occurred to any of those present to wonder why just now, at the age of forty-six, he had chosen to imitate this particular satire out of the entire Horatian canon of eighteen, they might have found their answer late the following December, when at last it appeared—anonymously—in print. For in print it had notes. Some of these were signed "Bent." for Richard Bentley. And those so signed were plainly intended to embarrass. Not merely by mimicking that editor's overbearing style—

> *Imitated.* Why Imitated? Why not translated? *Odi Imitatores!* ["I hate imitators"]. A Metaphrast had not [i.e., a literal translator would not have] turned *Tigellius*, and *Fufidius*, *Malchinus* and *Gargonius* (for I say *Malchinus*, not *Malthinus*, and *Gargonius*, not *Gorgonius*)★ into so many LADIES. *Benignus, hic, hunc,* &c all of the Masculine Gender: Every School-boy knows more than our Imitator [*TE*, 4: 74]—

but by applying it comically to sexual terms and situations in the Latin that in his own edition of Horace, for all its vast commentary, Bentley had in the main genteelly passed by:

> *Magno prognatum deposco consule Cunnum. A Thing descended from the Conqueror. A Thing descended—why* Thing? *the Poet has it* Cunnum; *which, therefore, boldly place here* [*TE*, 4: 82].

Similar NOTÆ BENTLEIANÆ (as the poem calls them) appear here and there throughout.

★ Pope's parody selects these particular emendations from Bentley's Horace because they are among the most pedantical and perverse, and require some of the longest and showiest defenses in the entire edition.

The occasion of this vulgar parody, we may guess—it can be no more than a guess— is that Bentley had recently made himself something of a public scandal by bringing out a new edition of *Paradise Lost*. In this he had argued that some eight hundred passages or parts of passages were spurious (signalized in his text by italic letter), but of course capable of appropriate restorations (provided by himself in the marginalia). To support these extraordinary procedures, he proposed a thesis that even the slightest consultation of the 1694 biography of Milton by his nephew would have rendered immediately untenable: that Milton had been ill served by an ignorant amanuensis whose copy his blindness did not allow him to set right, and even worse served by a rascally editor, who so abused the poet's trust "that *Paradise* under his ignorance and audaciousness may be said to be *twice lost*."

The public outcry was understandably loud. Not that Bentley's critics had nothing to learn from him. As Pope's friend Jonathan Richardson, who had been working for some years with his son on an "appreciation" of the poem from a painterly point of view, confessed candidly to a friend soon after the edition appeared,

> Bently has cut me out a deal of work, not to answer his Blunders, Conundrums, & Impertinences, but to read Milton with more Care & Attention than I have yet done [;] tho I have been almost an Adorer of him for above Forty Years, I discover Faults, or Incorrectnesses I had rather call 'em, wch I had not observd till Now, but withall New Beautys, & Those (I need not tell you) are a New Acquisition of Delight.

Bentley, in other words, compelled those who would refute him to read with the same rigor he had shown.

Still, the main objection stood. Bentley had taken the greatest long poem in English, its only finished epic, a work of intricately complex organization, awesome in its delicate and manifold gradations of imagery and mood, haunting in its verbal harmonies, and reduced it to a tract. Reduced it so thoroughly, in fact, that as a student of this controversy has lately remarked, his edition was not merely an "attack" on Milton, despite his honorable intentions, but an attack on poetry itself, obliterating those very freedoms to snatch a grace beyond the reach of art or prose without which it ceases to exist. This evidenced a degree of critical complacency not easy for a poet to overlook. And though he resisted the opportunity that Tonson promptly offered him to blow Bentley's textual theories sky high by

73. Jonathan Richardson (1665–1745). Self portrait, *c.* 1729.

". . . for that [sunrise] is an hour to find You & the Lark, awake & singing. That you may long preserve that Spring, in your Autumn of life! is the true Wish of Dear Sir Your A. Pope." Pope to Richardson [?August 17, 1738].

Courtesy of the National Portrait Gallery, London.

using (in a new edition to be edited by himself) Milton's manuscript of *Paradise Lost*, Book 1, which Tonson owned, Pope could rarely thereafter dismiss Bentley and what he stood for from his mind. The rowdy Horatian imitation with its Bentleyan notes he published in a folio edition on 21 December 1734, and, in a second folio edition, in mid-January 1735, just in time (though the conjunction of dates may be accidental) to serve as harbinger for the Richardsons' full-dress reply to Bentley in their *Explanatory Notes and Remarks on Paradise Lost*, issued on January 28.

"Yet mark the fate of a whole Sex of Queens!"

Also, while at Bevis Mount, Pope must have been putting the last hand, as he liked to call it, to the *Epistle to a Lady*, for Martha Blount. All his life, he had been a sensitive observer of women, had been required to be by his physical circumstances and his dread of ridicule. They fascinated him. Moved him to fear, wonder, and amusement—tender amusement as well as critical. And elicited a sympathy with the lot society had assigned them as pawns in the chess game of family aggrandizement that did not blind him to the alacrity with which they sometimes embraced their own destruction. In the early poem addressed probably to Teresa Blount with a copy of Voiture's letters, what he most dreads is the kind of future he summons up before her in "Paméla," perhaps the earliest of his admonitory portraits:

> The Gods, to curse *Pamela* with her Pray'rs,
> Gave the gilt Coach and dappled *Flanders* Mares,
> The shining Robes, rich Jewels, Beds of State,
> And to compleat her Bliss, a Fool for Mate.
> She glares in *Balls, Front-boxes*, and the *Ring*,
> A vain, unquiet, glitt'ring wretched Thing!
> Pride, Pomp, and State but reach her outward Part,
> She sighs, and is no *Dutchess* at her Heart.

(ll. 49–56)

Though she represents much else, *The Rape of the Lock*'s Belinda may herself be seen as potentially a victim of this cycle, captured in its earliest and most enchanting rosebud phase, yet touched already by the disquieting narcissism of those, female or male (consider the late twentieth-century rock star or professional athlete), whom society first makes its idols, then its slaves.

The *Epistle to a Lady* casts its net wider and at a later point. In a sense, it tells the story of what happens to the Belindas of the world once the rose is blowing or has blown. The tradition ultimately behind it is the genre of the satire against women, reaching back from some minor Restoration figures through Chaucer's Prologue to the Wife of Bath's Tale and certain excoriating Church Fathers to Juvenal's famous sixth satire—or diatribe, as it might more accurately be called. Pope alters the genre almost past recognition, replacing its characteristic hostility with an attitude that moves from detached amusement (the stereotypical male response) to awe, wonder, and commiseration, accompanied by a sense of deepening personal understanding and involvement. The structural metaphor that supports this progress is that of a guided tour of a gallery of female portraits, made in company with Martha Blount—though we soon discover that the guide is also to be the painter and to sketch the portraits as he goes:

> Come then, the colours and the ground prepare!
> Dip in the Rainbow, trick her off in Air,
> Chuse a firm Cloud, before it fall, and in it
> Catch, ere she change, the Cynthia of this minute.
>
> (ll. 17–20)

There were enough actual "galleries" of aristocratic women's pictures to give the idea topicality for the poet's readers and perhaps to have suggested it to himself. Peter Lely had painted a series called "The Windsor Beauties," and Pope's friend Sir Godfrey Kneller had painted another called "The Beauties of Hampton Court." The latter Pope probably knew both in its palace setting and in Kneller's resplendent house at nearby Whitton, where the painter had hung smaller copies of the Hampton Court beauties for his own gratification. In both series, portraits of individual women (adjusted, however, to so uniform a norm that one sometimes wonders if each painter did not work from a single archetypal sketch) have been given generalizing and emblematic touches that remind one of Pope's. Lely's countess of Rochester, for instance, plucks a blown rose against a background of cypresses and a burial urn: apparently a Lelyan version of the "Vanitas" or "Et in Arcadia Ego" theme. Kneller's Lady Essex points toward a ship at sea, believed here to be symbolic of hope, and his duchess of Grafton is shown surrounded by Platonic emblems of flux and permanence, earthly love aspiring to divine. Pope does not allegorize his figures in precisely this way, but one can readily discern the affinity of such generalizing modes with his own practice in producing a gallery of figures named Silia, Papillia, Narcissa, etc.

The poem takes for text a remark attributed by the poet to his companion, which he glosses in his note to signify that the "Characters of Women" are "not so strongly mark'd as those of Men, seldom so fix'd," and even more susceptible to inner contradictions:

> Nothing so true as what you once let fall,
> "Most Women have no Characters at all."
>
> (ll. 1–2)

From this it is an easy step to the mobility of the female temperament, as men, at least, have traditionally interpreted it ("Age cannot wither nor custom stale Her infinite variety"), here fittingly expressed within the gallery metaphor by the variety of roles in which individual women have allowed or required painters to depict them:

> How many pictures of one Nymph we view,
> All how unlike each other, all how true!
> Arcadia's Countess, here, in ermin'd pride,
> Is there, Pastora by a fountain side:
> Here Fannia, leering on her own good man,
> Is there, a naked Leda with a Swan.
> Let then the fair one beautifully cry,
> In Magdalen's loose hair and lifted eye,
> Or drest in smiles of sweet Cecilia shine,
> With simp'ring Angels, Palms, and Harps divine;
> Whether the Charmer sinner it, or saint it,
> If Folly grows romantic, I must paint it.
>
> (ll. 5–16)

Though some of the details here possibly derive from pictures Pope had seen, his primary reference is to a vogue at least as old as Botticelli, which, having reached its peak in England during the Restoration (when even Mrs. Samuel Pepys had herself painted as St. Catherine), was now beginning by the 1730s to be slightly funny. Still, the fashion died hard. Though Steele in 1705 was already making gentle game of it in the romantic longings of his Biddy Tipkin to be painted as the Amazon Thalestris, spear in hand and helmet on table, with a dwarf holding her milk-white palfrey in the background, Goldsmith as late as 1762 was still able to exploit its risible possibilities in the conversation piece painted of the vicar of Wakefield's family: his wife as Venus, one daughter as an Amazon, the other as a shepherdess, the two smaller children as Cupids, and the Vicar as himself, presenting to Venus his book on the Whiston controversy. Pope's use of the fashion, though enchanting, can only have helped deflate it.

A second subject matter, far less playful, swims into view as the poem turns to the manifold variegations of female personality and to inner "contrarieties" and contradictions that we would probably attribute today to the collision of internal individualizing energy with the period's sharply defined social code. Portraits characterized by extreme emotional and psychological instabilities now enter the poet's gallery and become occasion for attitudes of awe, wonder, terror, scorn, and pity. "Ladies," this part of the poem announces, "like variegated Tulips, show, 'Tis to their Changes half their charms we owe" (ll. 41–42). But the changes actually depicted betray the telltale frenzy, the cultivated eccentricity, the passion for bizarre and far-out behavior, which suggest that all is not well within. There is the peeress Philomedé, for one, who talks romance but settles for casual orgasm:

> What has not fir'd her bosom or her brain?
> Caesar and Tall-boy, Charles★ and Charlema'ne.
> As Helluo, late Dictator of the Feast,
> The Nose of Hautgout, and the Tip of Taste,
> Critick'd your wine, and analyz'd your meat,
> Yet on plain Pudding deign'd at home to eat;
> So Philomedé, lect'ring all mankind
> On the soft Passion, and the Taste refin'd,
> Th' Address, the Delicacy—stoops at once,
> And makes her hearty meal upon a Dunce.
>
> (ll. 77–86)

Or there is the Wit, Flavia. Always discontent with what the humdrum of reality has to offer, she burns her life away in flash and sputter, like damp gunpowder:

> Flavia's a Wit, has too much sense to Pray,
> To Toast our wants and wishes is her way;
> Nor asks of God, but of her Stars to give
> The mighty blessing, "while we live, to live."
> Then all for Death, that Opiate of the Soul! . . .
> Wise Wretch! with Pleasures too refin'd to please,

★ Tall-boy is an amorous young fool in Richard Brome's *The Jovial Crew*; Charles was the generic name in Pope's time for a footman.

With too much Spirit to be e'er at ease,
With too much Quickness ever to be taught,
With too much Thinking to have common thought:
Who purchase Pain with all that Joy can give,
And die of nothing but a Rage to live.

(ll. 87–91, 95–100)

Or there is Atossa—a figure larger than life, both pitiful and revolting. Mercurial, quarrelsome, violent, self-centered, frustrating and frustrated—who would not laugh if such a one there be? who would not weep if . . . ?

Full sixty years the World has been her Trade,
The wisest Fool much Time has ever made.
From loveless youth to unrespected age,
No Passion gratify'd except her Rage. . . .
Her ev'ry turn with Violence pursu'd,
Not more a storm her Hate than Gratitude.
To that each Passion turns, or soon or late;
Love, if it makes her yield, must make her hate:
Superiors? death! and Equals? what a curse!
But an Inferior not dependant? worse. . . .
Strange! by the Means defeated of the Ends,
By Spirit robb'd of Pow'r, by Warmth of Friends,
By Wealth of Follow'rs! without one distress
Sick of herself thro' very selfishness!

(ll. 123–26, 131–36, 143–46)

And finally there is Cloe, Atossa's opposite, appalling instance of the total dissolution of the individual into the formulary of the social code:

"With ev'ry pleasing, ev'ry prudent part,
"Say, what can Cloe want?" She wants a Heart. . . .
Virtue she finds too painful an endeavour,
Content to dwell in Decencies for ever.
So very reasonable, so unmov'd,
As never yet to love, or to be lov'd.
She, while her Lover pants upon her breast,
Can mark the figures on an Indian chest;
And when she sees her Friend in deep despair,
Observes how much a Chintz exceeds Mohair. . . .
Would Cloe know if you're alive or dead?
She bids her Footman put it in her head.

(ll. 159–60, 163–70, 177–78)

In the memorable conclusion of this review of worldliness, Pope seems almost to be recalling and enlarging his early summary of the fate of Pamela: "A vain, unquiet, glitt'ring, wretched Thing." Accommodating received traditions of female sexuality and desire of dominion to his theory of master passions, he assigns women two: "The Love of Pleasure, and the Love of Sway":

> That, Nature gives; and where the lesson taught
> Is still to please, can Pleasure seem a fault?
> Experience, this; by Man's oppression curst,
> They seek the second not to lose the first.
>
> (ll. 211–14)

On the other hand, since the only form of the second that the eighteenth century was normally disposed to honor in women was *sexual* sway, to secure the one gratification by means of the other frequently meant, especially in the enclaves of a court society, that queens like Pamela or Belinda lapsed quickly into queans like Philomedé: women as Thing into woman's Thing—

> Yet mark the fate of a whole Sex of Queens!
> Pow'r all their end, but Beauty all the means.
> In Youth they conquer, with so wild a rage,
> As leaves them scarce a Subject in their Age:
> For foreign glory, foreign joy, they roam;
> No thought of Peace or Happiness at home.
>
> (ll. 219–24)

And then, in lines possibly inspired by the tragic bravado of Chaucer's Wife of Bath's lament in the face of waning charms and slackening powers—

> But age, allas! that al wol envenyme,
> Hath me biraft my beautee and my pith.
> Lat go, farewel! the devel go therwith!
> The flour is goon, ther is namoore to telle;
> The bren,* as I best kan,† now moste‡ I selle;
> But yet to be right myrie wol I fonde§—
> (*The Wife of Bath's Prologue*, 474–79)

Pope draws back the curtain on a scene particularly relevant to his own society but duplicable in certain strata of most:

---

* The husks or chaff.   † Know.
‡ Must.   § Strive.

At last, to follies Youth could scarce defend,
'Tis half their Age's prudence to pretend;
Asham'd to own they gave delight before,
Reduc'd to feign it, when they give no more:
As Hags hold Sabbaths, less for joy than spight,
So these their merry, miserable Night;★
Still round and round the Ghosts of Beauty glide,
And haunt the places where their Honour dy'd.

(ll. 235–42)

They have given themselves to the world, and the world rewards them in kind:

See how the World its Veterans rewards!
A Youth of frolicks, an old Age of Cards,
Fair to no purpose, artful to no end,
Young without Lovers, old without a Friend,
A Fop their Passion, but their Prize a Sot,
Alive, ridiculous, and dead, forgot!

(ll. 243–48)

The two words that immediately succeed these lines come like an awakening from nightmare: "Ah Friend!" The affection in the sigh and the tribute in the address—friend being the one word in the language that denotes relationships of equality and permanence—exorcise between them the ghosts who, young, had no true lover, and, old, lacked a friend. The mobility of woman's nature, regarded as a mark of vanity or frivolity or propensity to evil, is left behind among other cast-off stereotypes of male "superiority." The fleeting moon is still the female planet, but relates now to the serenity of moonrise, not to the Cynthia of this minute:

Ah Friend! to dazzle let the Vain design,
To raise the Thought and touch the Heart be thine!
That Charm shall grow, while what fatigues the Ring
Flaunts and goes down, an unregarded thing.
So when the Sun's broad beam has tir'd the sight,
All mild ascends the Moon's more sober light.

★ The particular night on which eighteenth-century ladies of quality were at home to visits; but with overtones from (1) the night appointed by witches for their revels, (2) night as the time for amours, and (3) the night into which all "suns" of beauty set.

74. Martha Blount (1690–1763). Attributed to Sir Godfrey Kneller, undated.

To you gave Sense, Good-humour, and a Poet.
Epistle to a Lady, 292.

By kind permission of J. J. Eyston, Mapledurham House. Photograph: Courtauld Institute of Art.

Serene in Virgin Modesty she shines,
And unobserv'd the glaring Orb declines.

(ll. 249–56)

"That Charm shall grow." The words remind us that Pope's view of successful self-building calls for the same attention to the Genius of the Place, the same respectful use of the situation and materials supplied by nature, as enlightened gardening, where, if you do not violate or try to exclude them,

Nature shall join you, Time shall make it grow
A Work to wonder at—perhaps a STOW.

(*Epistle to Burlington*, 69–70)

Always in the background of his mind, whether he thinks of his boyhood "scene" at Binfield—

Where Order in Variety we see,
And where, tho' all things differ, all agree;

(*Windsor-Forest*, 15–16)

or the formation of human character—

These [the passions] mix'd with art, and to due bounds confin'd,
Make and maintain the balance of the mind:
The lights and shades, whose well accorded strife
Gives all the strength and colour of our life;

(*Essay on Man*, 2: 119–22)

or of the composition of a poem—"Bold" but also "Regular" (*Essay on Criticism*, ll. 243–52, esp. 252); or simply of the perfections he ascribes to Martha Blount, the notion of a harmony achieved from things and forces disparate or conflicting, a *concordia discors*, as it had been called traditionally by philosophers, asserts itself:

And yet, believe me, good as well as ill,
Woman's at best a Contradiction still.
Heav'n, when it strives to polish all it can
Its last best work, but forms a softer Man;
Picks from each sex, to make its Fav'rite blest,
Your love of Pleasure, our desire of Rest,
Blends, in exception to all gen'ral rules,
Your Taste of Follies, with our Scorn of Fools,
Reserve with Frankness, Art with Truth ally'd,
Courage with Softness, Modesty with Pride,
Fix'd Principles, with Fancy ever new;
Shakes all together, and produces—You.

(ll. 269–80)

With "you" the poet turns from his gallery of portraits to the living woman at his side. *Her* "character" is not of his making, but "Heav'n's." Nor is it, indeed, a woman's character as woman in the poem has been hitherto understood; for she is androgyne. And further, the celestial powers by which she has been shaped include both moon and sun. For though her sober radiance is like moonrise, as serene in Virgin Modesty as Diana, she has been from birth the ward of Phoebus, who has showered her with all his gifts but one:

> Be this a Woman's Fame: with this unblest,
> Toasts live a scorn, and Queens may die a jest.
> This Phoebus promis'd (I forget the year)
> When those blue eyes first open'd on the sphere;
> Ascendant Phoebus watch'd that hour with care,
> Averted half your Parents' simple Pray'r,
> And gave you Beauty, but deny'd the Pelf
> Which buys your sex a Tyrant o'er itself.
> The gen'rous God, who Wit and Gold refines,
> And ripens Spirits as he ripens Mines,
> Kept Dross for Duchesses, the world shall know it,
> To you gave Sense, Good-humour, and a Poet.
>
> (ll. 281–92)

"A sort of Bill of Complaint"

Through Martha Blount, while he was on his ramble that summer, Pope learned that the illness from which he had seen Arbuthnot suffering when he last visited him was believed by the doctor himself to be irreversible. "Tho I know you are as fit to Dye as any Man," he hastened to write, "I think no Man fitter to live for that very reason, or more Wanted by those who are in this world, both as a Comfort, and as an Example, to them." To which Arbuthnot had responded firmly:

A Recovery in my Case, and at my Age [he was now sixty-seven, having been born the same year as Swift], is impossible; the kindest Wish of my Friends is *Euthanasia* [i.e., an easy death (not, as now, one induced)]. Living or dying, I shall always be Your most faithful Friend.

Earlier in the letter, as this was in a sense a solemn occasion, the length of time remaining to him being quite uncertain, he had taken the opportunity to sum up their long relationship:

As for you, my good Friend, I think since our first acquaintance there has not been any of those little Suspicions or Jealousies that often affect the sincerest Friendships; I am sure not on my side. I must be so sincere as to own, that tho' I could not help valuing you for those Talents which the World prizes, yet they were not the Foundation of my Friendship: They were quite of another sort; nor shall I at present offend you by enumerating them.

As a "Last Request" (he goes on to say), he urges Pope to continue in his writings his *"Disdain & Abhorrence* of Vice," but not without some regard for his own personal safety. The qualification of the last phrase was, of course, a tacit warning of the dangers to be run in satirizing individuals by name. It is a warning that need not much surprise us, coming from Arbuthnot, who is said to have caned James Moore-Smythe for the abuse heaped on him (and on Pope) in *One Epistle to Mr. Pope*, as far back as 1730. The only problem with heeding it—if one believed, as the Scriblerians all did, that satire had a legitimate shaming and ridiculing function in the common-weal—was the one to which Swift had pointed in his *Battle of the Books*: in general satire "beholders do generally discover everybody's face but their own." Or as Pope put it in replying to Arbuthnot:

> General Satire in Times of General Vice has no force, & is no Punishment: . . . 'tis only by hunting One or two from the Herd that any Examples can be made. If a man writ all his Life against the Collective Body of the Banditti, . . . would it do the least Good, or lessen the Body?

One may discern dimly in this exchange some of the larger contours of the epistle that about three weeks later Pope told Arbuthnot he was composing in his honor and, a week afterwards, had finished—at least in first draft. The doctor's testimony that the foundation of their friendship lay not in Pope's poetic talent but in his qualities as a man touched a concern that was always primary for the poet and that any reader may trace at large in the epistle. The "charge," too, from a dying friend that he should stand his ground as a critic of the times while being careful not to get hurt could easily have helped shape the imaginary dialogue of the poem, as we have it, between a firm unyielding satirist and a somewhat more cautious counselor. Nor is it entirely inconceivable that Arbuthnot's stress on his friend's "Disdain & abhorrence of Vice" contributed something to those shadowy forces which impelled Pope's imagination to intuit, in his character of "Sporus," what was unquestionably vicious in Lord Hervey and the system of court sycophancy from which he profited; and to convert his own personal resentment, anger, fury, or whatever other passion we may think Hervey awoke in him into the most accomplished exhibition of moral disdain in the language.

Pope was able to compose the epistle with such speed because he had in hand several distinct pieces, published and unpublished, which he now evidently saw a way to knit together. One piece, in fact, was the substantial first draft (260 lines) of an unpublished poem addressed to his Scots friend William Cleland, whom we met earlier as a fancier of broccoli seed. Cleland, following a career of some distinction in the military, had been rewarded with a post as tax commissioner, though this seems not to have prevented him (if we may trust Swift) from "walking perpetually in the Mall, and fastning upon everybody he meets." Both in 1729, during the furor about the *Dunciad Variorum*, and again in late 1731, in face of the brouhaha raised by the poet's alleged attack on Chandos's "Cannons," Cleland had stepped forward uncompromisingly to Pope's defense—in the latter instance, possibly with some risk to his livelihood.

This never-published poem, whose opening lines compliment Cleland as a "Man, whose Heart has ner forgot a Friend," may well have been started in 1730, when attacks on everything to do with the author of the *Dunciad* were at their fiercest. Even in this primitive form, it answers reasonably well to the description Pope gives to Arbuthnot on August 25, 1734 of the poem about to be inscribed to him: "written by piece-meal many years . . .; wherein the Question is stated, what were, & are, my Motives of writing, the Objections to them, & my answers." Verses cropping out in the margins with unmistakable reference to his slanderers in the Chandos affair, together with other marginal accretions subsequently skimmed off for use in the imitation of the first satire of the second book of Horace, indicate that the theme of an *apologia* for his life and art continued to gestate in Pope's mind without as yet assuming anything like a final shape. Some of these additions belong no doubt to early 1732, when Pope also wrote his prose *Master Key to Popery* to ridicule the charges about Timon's villa. Others were obviously added during 1733, when, either in the spring after Lady Mary and Lord Hervey published *Verses to the Imitator*, or, in the autumn, after Hervey's further attack in his *Epistle to a Doctor of Divinity* evoked the poet's suppressed "Letter to a Noble Lord," the first lineaments of "Sporus" began to emerge in his mind.

Assembled at last and given by several breathtaking rearrangements within the manuscript a winning shape, the new epistle to Arbuthnot became a work of many layers, themes, and voices. First of all, as many readers will doubtless remember, it is an orchestration of opposing moods. Its opening paragraphs, harried and breathless, give us the tired literary lion fuming with the sorts of exasperation every eminent writer of almost any modern period is likely to have shared at some time or other, thanks to crackpots and scribblers who are out to reap the profit of his name:

> Shut, shut the door, good *John!** fatigu'd I said,
> Tye up the knocker, say I'm sick, I'm dead,
> The Dog-star rages! nay 'tis past a doubt,
> All *Bedlam*, or *Parnassus*, is let out.

(ll. 1–4)

No place is free of these intruders: they show up in his garden and grotto, stop him when he drives out in his chariot, arrive in his boat with his waterman, and beset him with special reinforcements on Sundays, when people who haven't paid their debts are exempt from arrest:

> Is there a Parson, much be-mus'd in Beer,
> A maudlin Poetess, a ryming Peer,
> A Clerk, foredoom'd his Father's soul to cross,
> Who pens a Stanza when he should *engross*?†
> Is there, who lock'd from Ink and Paper, scrawls
> With des'prate Charcoal round his darken'd walls?
> All fly to *Twit'nam*, and in humble strain
> Apply to me, to keep them mad or vain.

(ll. 15–22)

None of these hopefuls cares much for the hard work required to master a literary trade. All angle instead for a quick fix from the great man:

> "The Piece you think is incorrect: why take it,
> "I'm all submission, what you'd have it, make it."
>   Three things another's modest wishes bound,

---

* Pope's servant, John Searle.

† I.e., compose legal documents; but with overtones from its meaning "to swindle by cornering the market in land or a commodity."

My Friendship, and a Prologue, and ten Pound.
    Pitholeon sends to me: "You know his Grace,
"I want a Patron; ask him for a Place."
                  . . . "your Int'rest, Sir, with Lintot."
Lintot, dull rogue! will think your price too much.
"Not Sir, if you revise it, and retouch."

                                        (ll. 45–50, 62–4)

As the instances multiply, it becomes apparent that the poet has more in mind than simply the nuisance value of these intruders. What they unknowingly bring with them is the mind set of Johnson's "Age of Authors," when "the inclosures of literature [an arresting parallel in Johnson's sentence to the invaded grotto and garden of the poem] are thrown open to every man whom idleness disposes to loiter, or pride inclines to set himself in view." Individually, these solicitors seek an unearned success. Collectively, their importunities amount to a demand that literary standards be collapsed to their level or their level lifted by powers not their own. Not for them the days and nights of self-discipline implicit in the Horatian counsel, "Keep your Piece nine years," which Pope conveys to them. Not for them, either, the detachment of the artist, the necessary loneliness of the long-distance runner, signified by the Thames-side retreat into which they so confidently irrupt.

The poem thus places in immediate confrontation two definitions of literature and two views of writing as a profession that first came deeply into conflict in Pope's and Johnson's century and are with us still, most notably today in the by no means always successful struggle of the serious writer to keep from drowning in a Sargasso Sea of soft porn or other eyewash prepared to formula for the tired typist home at teatime. In the 1980s, those who reflect adversely on the current publishing scene are likely to trace its character to economic forces or the decline of critical leadership or the disappearance of the man of letters as winnower and guide. In the 1730s, many, including Pope, thought the answer lay closer home. In verses directly succeeding those cited, Pope invokes the fable of King Midas—not the episode of the golden touch, but the later one of his receiving ass's ears for stupidity in choosing Pan's music over Apollo's. Ostensibly, Pope uses the tale to explain how difficult it is to refrain from telling these conceited coxcombs the truth about their talents:

> 'Tis sung, when *Midas'* Ears began to spring,
> (*Midas*, a sacred Person and a King)
> His very Minister who spy'd them first,
> (Some say his Queen) was forc'd to speak, or burst.
> And is not mine, my Friend, a sorer case,
> When ev'ry Coxcomb perks them in my face?
>
> (ll. 69–74)

Covertly, however, Midas is George II, as managed by his Queen and First Minister, who have preferred Colley Cibber to the laureateship over a dozen better talents and even assigned a pension, not to a genuine writer, but to a collector's curiosity, Stephen Duck. To make the royal and ministerial reference unmistakable, Pope assigns to Arbuthnot at this point his first cautionary interruption:

> "Good friend forbear! you deal in dang'rous things,
> "I'd never name Queens, Ministers, or Kings;
> "Keep close to Ears, and those let Asses prick,
> "Tis nothing"—Nothing? if they bite and kick?
> Out with it, *Dunciad*! let the secret pass,
> That Secret to each Fool, that he's an Ass:
> The truth once told, (and wherefore shou'd we lie?)
> The Queen of *Midas* slept, and so may I.
>
> (ll. 75–82)

It is from this succession of opening chords—harsh, studiedly impatient—that the poem makes its way to its famous close, in calm of mind, all passion spent. Here the poet recaptures with pride (mixed with a certain envy, we might be justified in guessing) the solid virtues and simple pieties of his father's world in Binfield—

> No Courts he saw, no Suits would ever try,
> Nor dar'd an Oath, nor hazarded a Lye:
> Un-learn'd, he knew no Schoolman's subtle Art,
> No Language, but the Language of the Heart—
>
> (ll. 396–99)

recaptures them in memory and implores their attendance on his own future life at Twickenham: "Oh grant me thus to live, and thus to die!" Here also—so at least it is made to seem within the fiction of the poem—his chronic "disease," comprehending both the restless whirl and hurry of the literary celebrity and the physical aches and pains of deteriorating bone marrow can be alleviated, if only for this moment, by the lenitive influence of one to whom sickness of any sort had been unknown. And here, finally, a life that Arbuthnot has often been diligent in the past to save is now found diligent in its concern for the lives of others. In a sense, the patient momentarily becomes physician, possesses lenient, i.e., healing arts (Pope's adroit domestication of the traditional association of satirist with physician as curer of the diseases of the commonwealth); and a conversation that began with a vexed exclusionary command—"Shut, shut the door, good John!"—can end now with resignation and a double prayer:

> O Friend! may each Domestick Bliss be thine!
> Be no unpleasing Melancholy mine:
> Me, let the tender Office long engage
> To rock the Cradle of reposing Age,
> With lenient Arts extend a Mother's breath,
> Make Languor smile, and smooth the Bed of Death,
> Explore the Thought, explain the asking Eye,
> And keep a while one Parent from the Sky!
> On Cares like these if Length of Days attend,
> May Heav'n, to bless those days, preserve my Friend,
> Preserve him social, chearful, and serene,
> And just as rich as when he serv'd a QUEEN!
> Whether that Blessing be deny'd, or giv'n,
> Thus far was right, the rest belongs to Heav'n.
>
> (ll. 406–19)

Swung between these two contrasting scenes and poles of feeling comes the vindication of his career that Pope promised Arbuthnot in his August letter. Why did I write? Because, answers the author of one of the most artful poetries in English (doubtless with a grin), it was all so effortless: "I lisp'd in Numbers, for the Numbers came." Further, I hadn't many choices, either as a part invalid or—and here the lines insist that one read between them— as a Roman Catholic, to whom not much in the way of a "Calling" (ll. 128–129) is open. But why then publish? Desire of a poet's fame, of course, but fueled by praise or at least approval from the acknowledged arbiters of those days:

> *Granville* the polite,
> And knowing *Walsh*, would tell me I could write;
> Well-natur'd *Garth* inflam'd with early praise,
> And *Congreve* lov'd, and *Swift* endur'd my Lays.
>
> (ll. 135–38)

But don't imagine such reception insured my peace. Even in the days of the *Essay on Criticism, Windsor-Forest*, and the *Rape of the Lock*, I was assaulted by Dennis, Gildon, and the rest. Then the scholars got into the act. "A pretty poem, Mr. Pope, but you mustn't call it Homer." That was Bentley. *SHAKESPEARE RESTORED: or, A Specimen of the MANY ERRORS, As well Committed, as Unamended, by MR. POPE in his late EDITION of this POET. Designed not only to correct the said Edition, but to restore the TRUE READING of SHAKE-SPEARE in all the Editions ever yet publish'd.* That was Theobald.

> Pains, reading, study are their just pretence,
> And all they want is spirit, taste, and sense.
> Comma's and points they set exactly right,
> And 'twere a sin to rob them of their Mite. . . .
> Ev'n such small Critics some regard may claim,
> Preserv'd in *Milton*'s or in *Shakespear*'s name.
> Pretty! in Amber to observe the forms
> Of hairs, or straws, or dirt, or grubs, or worms;
> The things, we know, are neither rich nor rare,
> But wonder how the Devil they got there?
>
> (ll. 159–62, 167–72)

In brief, there is no secure way of staying on good terms with anyone afflicted with writer's itch:

> A man's true merit 'tis not hard to find,
> But each man's secret standard in his mind,
> That Casting-weight Pride adds to Emptiness,
> This, who can gratify? for who can *guess*?
>
> (ll. 175–78)

Even for men of true genius like Addison, there is always the potentially enervating effect of the "little Senate" (line 209): the cult, the claque, the bookstore "reception," the TV interview, each new work presented as profounder than the last. I never went in for that sort of thing, Pope continues. I left all that to the *littérateurs* with money, Bufo or Bubo and their like:

> Proud as *Apollo* on his forked hill,
> Sate full-blown *Bufo*, puff'd by ev'ry quill;
> Fed with soft Dedication all day long,
> *Horace* and he went hand in hand in song.
> His Library, (where Busts of poets dead
> And a true *Pindar* stood without a head)

Receiv'd of Wits an undistinguish'd race,
Who first his Judgment ask'd, and then a Place:
Much they extoll'd his Pictures, much his Seat,
And flatter'd ev'ry day, and some days eat:
Till grown more frugal in his riper days,
He pay'd some Bards with Port, and some with Praise,
To some a dry Rehearsal was assign'd,
And others (harder still) he pay'd in kind.

(ll. 231–44)

If only there were more such! They could take over all these people
who now come rushing into my garden. "Blest be the *Great*!" has to
be my way of saying thank you, both

for those they take away
And those they left me—For they left me GAY,
Left me to see neglected Genius bloom,
Neglected die! and tell it on his Tomb;
Of all thy blameless Life the sole Return
My Verse, and QUEENSB'RY weeping o'er thy Urn!

(ll. 255–60)

As for myself, I don't ask much—simply "a Poet's Dignity and
Ease," including the privilege of *not* writing at all, and especially the
privilege of not having libels attributed to me on the ground of
"Style":

Curst be the Verse, how well soe'er it flow,
That tends to make one worthy Man my foe. . . .
But he, who hurts a harmless neighbour's peace,
Insults fal'n Worth, or Beauty in distress,
Who loves a Lye, lame slander helps about,
Who writes a Libel, or who copies out: . . .
Who tells whate'er you think, whate'er you say,
And, if he lye not, must at least betray:
Who to the *Dean* and *silver Bell* can swear,
And sees at *Cannons* what was never there: . . .
A Lash like mine no honest man shall dread,
But all such babling blockheads in his stead.

(ll. 283–84, 287–90, 297–300, 303–4)

Varieties of prostitution

Let one sample suffice: the species of man who, by his own confession, makes a trade of flattery, lies, and gossip—the professional courtier and sucker-up, the Rosencrantz-and-Guildenstern figure, always on the make and so fully the creature of Power that the only name symbolically fit for him is "Sporus," the name also of Nero's catamite and castrated "wife." Let *that* man tremble!

At this point, even the prudent Arbuthnot kindles:

> "What? that Thing of silk,
> "*Sporus*, that mere white Curd of Ass's milk?
> "Satire or Sense alas! can *Sporus* feel?
> "Who breaks a Butterfly upon a Wheel?"
>
> (ll. 305–8)

Point conceded. Still, let's not forget that *this* specimen is more than butterfly. He is the ultimate toad and toady, characteristic offspring of a system where the creature has no choice but to run from the cur, the dog *is* obeyed if in office, and the human self becomes, as in the career of Balaam, the "possession" of some external agent, demonic or otherwise:

> Whether in florid Impotence he speaks,
> And, as the Prompter breathes, the Puppet squeaks;
> Or at the Ear of *Eve*, familiar Toad,
> Half Froth, half Venom, spits himself abroad,
> In Puns, or Politicks, or Tales, or Lyes,
> Or Spite, or Smut, or Rymes, or Blasphemies.
>
> (ll. 318–22)

If there is something deeply ambiguous about Sporus, it is only partly because he looks like a girl. Mainly, he expresses the doubleness and duplicity that all power systems spawn: on the one hand, flattery of the dog in office to make one's way, on the other, a corrosive cynicism creating disgust in others and perhaps eventually self-disgust:

> Amphibious Thing! that acting either Part,
> The trifling Head, or the corrupted Heart!
> Fop at the Toilet, Flatt'rer at the Board,
> Now trips a Lady, and now struts a Lord.
> Eve's Tempter thus the Rabbins have exprest,

75. John, Baron Hervey of Ickworth (1696–1743). Attributed to John Fayram, *c.* 1735–40.

> "Like you, we [courtiers] lounge, & feast, & play, & chatter,
>   In private Satirize, in Publick flatter."
> [John Hervey], *An Epistle from a Nobleman to a Doctor of Divinity* (1733).

By kind permission of the National Trust, Ickworth.

A Cherub's Face, A Reptile all the rest;
Beauty that shocks you, Parts that none will trust,
Wit that can creep, and Pride that licks the dust.

(ll. 326–33)

That the portrait springs from an intense personal hatred of Lord Hervey requires no emphasis. From the poet's point of view, he is an aristocratic dapperwit who can dismiss a sober writer's entire life work as plagiarism—one is reminded of Lady Mary's complacent comparison of Pope and Swift to linkboys. He is also, from the poet's point of view, a possible political threat to safety, being a confidant of Walpole's and, literally and almost daily, at the ear of the Queen, perhaps feeding both the same kind of abuse he had published or helped publish in cold type in *Verses to the Imitator* and *An Epistle to a Doctor of Divinity*. Nor is there any question but that the portrait, like all satirical portraits, is "unfair", though it says nothing about Hervey that others had not said before. Representations of actual persons in art, as we have had occasion to notice in connection with Theobald as Tibbald and should bear in mind when examining any of Pope's portraits, are inevitably "unfair," whether the intent is hostile or friendly, because inevitably interpretive. This is a limitation of sorts, to be sure, but not one that need prevent a great writer or painter from coming up with an arrangement that we find to be in some sense truer than the glaring chaos and wild heap of irrelevant detail of which any actual historical person, or moment, normally consists. If the interpretation is then embodied in some larger plan—a novel, say—the modifications of historical reality will be still more pronounced, since what was already an arrangement must be additionally tailored to fit the role assigned it in the larger whole: Amy Robsart and Queen Elizabeth, for example, in Scott's *Kenilworth*, or J. P. Morgan in E. L. Doctorow's *Ragtime*, or, to return to Pope, Hervey in the *Epistle to Arbuthnot*.

For inside the poem, we are asked to understand, Sporus is simply the climactic instance of a form of prostitution bedeviling the entire society that the poem depicts. What those invaders of the poet's grotto and garden come seeking is flattery, not appraisal of their work. What they propose in return is also flattery, doubly embarrassing in being proffered for the wrong reasons—

All my demurrs but double his attacks,
At last he whispers, "Do [i.e., revise it], and we go snacks"—

(ll. 66–67)

or directed to the wrong attributes:

> There are, who to my Person pay their court,
> I cough like *Horace*, and tho' lean, am short,
> *Ammon*'s great Son one shoulder had too high,
> Such *Ovid*'s nose, and "Sir, you have an *Eye*—"
> Go on, obliging Creatures, make me see
> All that disgrac'd my Betters, met in me.
>
> (ll. 115–20)

This is the sort of thing, the poem goes on to emphasize in its three famous portraits, that destroys morality as well as literature. Look at Atticus, who developed such an addiction to his little Senate and its applause that he became incapable of welcoming new talent. Or look at Bufo, gormandizing on fulsome dedications while neglecting Dryden, the one true poet of his generation, much as other patrons since, on the same grounds, have neglected Gay. In any such sequence of moral failures, the commanding position unquestionably belongs to Sporus because he combines with the jealousy of Atticus and the vanity of Bufo a triviality and even nihilism that only comparison to Eve's toad in Milton's Eden can precisely catch. Each of these portraits, it has been wisely said, is a conscious evocation of a route that the idealized speaker of the poem might have taken, but chose not to—

> Not proud, nor servile, be one Poet's praise
> That, if he pleas'd, he pleas'd by manly ways—

and the poem as a whole, with its "concern for merit, scorn of patronage, and humility in private life is a lecture to the times on the principles by which a literary man should live." What has also been wisely said is that though Atticus, Sporus, and a certain number of Pope's other portraits take their beginnings from personal antagonism, they are transfigured by his imagination into warnings of universal application, as recognizable today as in the 1700s:

> When Pope satirizes an individual, it is as if he set fire to an effigy: the effigy crackles, blazes, and is burned up; but in the process it ignites a wider conflagration, and in the flames we see, brightly illuminated, the hateful figure of Folly or Vice itself.

This is certainly what happens with Lord Hervey as Sporus, as any reader of his *Memoirs* will attest:

> Somehow Pope intuited from Hervey's drawing-room manner substantially everything which we can dredge up from the *Memoirs* and couch in psychological terms. He expressed what he perceived

in the language available to him and hence portrayed Sporus/ Hervey as Evil incarnate— a judgment which we are apt to think unjust. But Hervey's character was a chaos of obsessive impulses; he represented a rampantly selfish individualism which was anathema to Pope's reverence for the moral tradition and the possibilities of private and civic order.

Or to put the matter in the only slightly different terms of the distinguished parliamentary historian who is Hervey's editor:

A further influence which went to the moulding of Hervey's outlook was that of his political set. He was one of Walpole's young men and it is well known that Walpole made a point of debauching the political morals of his boys, preaching a rationalised scoundrelism, systematically deriding political decencies, and using his prestige and influence, with considerable success, to lower the tone of public life.

To the degree and nature of that success, Sporus is perhaps the most sensitive index we have and the one that will last longest.

CHAPTER 25

A SENSE OF AUTUMN

Gallant gestures

The Epistle to Dr. Arbuthnot was published on 2 January 1735, just twenty-five days (the text of the first edition shows unmistakable signs of haste) before the doctor's death at his house in Cork Street. There Pope and Chesterfield visited him the previous evening to make their farewells. Like Gay, he died in extreme pain from a so-called "inflammation of his bowels," but remained clear-headed to the last, and took his leave, of us, says Chesterfield, "with tenderness, without weakness." Tenderness, to be sure; but to make a good end, as it was usually called in those days, required an abundance of fortitude as well.

Similar fortitude, if not greater, Pope was obliged to witness later that year in his friend Peterborow. Now seventy-seven, that intrepid old soldier had been subject for some years to illnesses of increasing seriousness, largely attacks of the stone with the resultant stoppages. He had come close to death—in fact, been reported for dead—during the "Epidemical Distemper" of early 1733, a circumstance that may have influenced Pope to couple him with Bolingbroke for affectionate praise in his first Horatian imitation. By 1735, he was once more in great difficulties, so much so that, having vainly sought relief during the late spring at Bath and at Bristol, he had consented to be cut for the stone and was now in midsummer seeking to recuperate at Bevis Mount from the agonies attendant on that operation in those surgically primitive times. A letter sent at this period of extreme suffering to Lady Suffolk, about whom, when she was still Mrs. Howard and he in his early sixties, he had composed a charming love song, conveys much about the man, both the theatricality of his imagination and his invincible high spirits. He has been reading the life of the emperor Julian, he tells her. Not prepossessing in the whole, but "With what majesty does the emperor meet his fate! showing how a soldier, how a philosopher, how a friend of Lady Suffolk's ought . . . to die."

> I want to make an appointment with you, Mr. Pope, and a few friends more, to meet you upon the summit of my Bevis hill, and thence, after a speech and a tender farewell, I shall take my leap toward the clouds (as Julian expresses it), to mix amongst the stars; but I make my bargain for a very fine day, that you may see my last amusements to advantage.

It is not recorded that even the "conqueror of Spain" could have arranged so dramatic a lift off. But Pope did receive from him in mid-August a plea that he hurry to Southampton to say good-bye before Peterborow sailed for warmer climes—bringing Bathurst with him if possible. "To see the Last of an old Hero, the last Sparks of such a Noble Flame, it will be a thing to dwell on [in?] our memory & to talk of in our old age"—such was Pope's message to Cirencester. But as so often, it was Pope who set everything aside and went, uncomfortable though long journeys now made him. Peterborow, he soon found, was to be spared nothing in the way of physical torment:

> I lay in the next room to him, where . . . he was awake, & calld for help most hours of the night, sometimes crying out for pain: In the morning he got up at nine, & was carryd into his Garden in a Chair: he fainted away twice there. He fell about 12 into a violent pang which made his limbs all shake & his teeth chatter, & for some time he lay cold as death.

Still, he played the game manfully by the rules it was then customary to observe. After his wound was dressed, "he grew gay, & Sate at dinner with ten people." Day after day he lay on his couch and received all comers, including any resident of Southampton who wished to call on him—only "when his Pains come, he desires them to walk out, but invites them to stay & dine or sup." With Pope, during a visit of some six or seven days, he talked animatedly of working on memoirs that would justify Queen Anne against the imputation of having wished to bring in the Pretender; and of finishing—no doubt with Pope's help, for the poet returned twice the next summer to oversee such operations—some horticultural improvements that his countess could enjoy after him.

For she was now, at long last, his acknowledged Countess. Never one to do any thing by halves, he had gathered together in the spring of this year, with a grand theatrical gesture in a private room at St.

James's palace, all his kinfolk, to whom, after discoursing for some while on the manifold virtues of an unnamed female friend, he had at length introduced Anastasia, secretly his wife since 1722—whereupon, according to report, she fainted dead away. (She had refused to accept his addresses on any other terms, being as devout a Roman Catholic as he was an unbeliever.) Later, to make her future doubly sure—the priest who had married them was dead—he remarried her before witnesses at Bristol. All this, too, he confided to Pope soon after his arrival, very probably extracting from him a promise not only to carry out the landscaping works they had planned together, but to perpetuate their own affection in a continuing friendship with Lady Peterborow, as there is every evidence that Pope did. For a parting gift *in memoriam*, Peterborow gave the poet his watch—"That I might have something to put me every day in mind of him." It was a gift he had himself received in his military and ambassadorial days from Victor Amadeus II, the much admired king of Sardinia, whose abrupt abdication at the height of his power in 1730 had set tongues clacking all over Europe and been cited by Pope, in his *Epistle to Cobham*, as an instance of the impenetrability of human motives. After having it suitably inscribed, Pope wore it the rest of his life and passed it on to Dr. Arbuthnot's son George. It has now disappeared.

Soon after, with his lady, Peterborow took ship to Lisbon, died there in October (according to one report, from the "rash act" of eating grapes and immediately drinking water, which brought on "a flux"), was brought to Portsmouth on November 10 and buried at Turvey in Bedfordshire on the twentieth. "There is another string lost," Pope lamented to Swift that month, "that wou'd have help'd to draw you hither!" And to Bathurst, a month earlier:

> Your Lordship is almost my only [remaining] Prop. Two of those with whom my soul rested, & lean'd upon, are gone out of the Kingdom this Summer. [Bolingbroke, discouraged by the disunity of the Opposition, had in June taken up residence in France, whence he was not to return till 1738.] Every one that makes Life enjoyable to me is absent now.

He has begun, he adds, to feel old, and he was helped to that conclusion, it is tempting to think, by an adventure that had happened to him outside Oxford on his way from Peterborow's bedside to the refreshment of Stowe. He had come away—this is Spence telling his mother of the incident—"in a Chariot of his Lordships, that holds only one person, for quick travelling."

When he was got about 3 miles of Oxford, coming down a Hill in Bagly Wood, he saw 2 Gentlemen & a Lady setting as in distress by the way side. By them lay a chaise, overturn'd, & half broke to pieces; in the Fall of which the poor Lady had her Arm broke. Mr. Pope had the goodness to stop; & to offer her his Chariot to carry her to Oxford, for help; & so walk'd the three mile, in the very midst of a close sultry day, to us; & came in, the most fatigu'd you can imagine—

his thin face "lengthen'd at least two Inches beyond its usual appearance." Pope could never resist gallant gestures, ill-equipped though he was for them. A year later almost to the day, as he was handing a beautiful young woman down his landing stairs at Twickenham to her boat, she lost her footing, fell into the Thames, pulled him after her, and both nearly drowned.

"To put the image straight"

Pope was probably also confessing in his October letter to Bathurst an uneasiness that had less to do with growing old than with some of his recent publishing activities. "You animated my Youth, my Lord, Comfort my age!" he pleads:

> Let not th'insulting foe my fame pursue,
> But shade those Laurels that were rais'd by You.

Do not think this a florid Flamm*. . . . I feel the want of you in all my little distresses; if any other hurts me, I am like a Child that comes to complain to its best friend who has humourd it always; and if I play the fool, I want to complain to you against my self.

Though the letter gives no clue to the nature of his current distresses or of just how he has played the fool, we may reasonably suspect that he has in mind a certain publication of the preceding May. In April he had brought out with considerable pomp and circumstance Volume II of his collected *Works*, printed in the quarto and folio sizes necessary to accompany his Volume I of 1717 and the eleven volumes of the Homer, and assembling between two covers the *Dunciad Variorum*, the *Essay on Man*, and the epistles and satires addressed to several persons that we have already examined. No particular harm was to come from this apart from making his position on the Walpole

---

* Flattery.

administration abundantly clear, and the response to the volume, even of a good Whig like Thomas Herring, then dean of Rochester but later archbishop of Canterbury, may be taken as typical. He pronounced himself much put off by the compliments to Bolingbroke—but these had not prevented his buying the volume and finding that the brightness of the wit, the raised sentiments, the elegant turns, and the musical cadences charmed him "immensely."

In May, however, a fortnight or so after the *Works*, there had appeared a pair of volumes containing letters between Pope and a number of his early friends: Wycherley, Walsh, Cromwell, Congreve, certain unidentified ladies, Trumbull, Steele, Addison, Jervas, Digby, Gay, Edward Blount, and one or two more. These volumes were to cause more damage to Pope's reputation in the long run than any other project he would ever set hand to. What few at the time knew—possibly at first only Pope, his printer Wright, and his then publisher Gilliver—was that the poet himself had had these letters printed up over a period stretching back to 1729 and by a series of intrigues and intermediaries, including at one point a London actor dressed to look like a clergyman, had duped Curll into buying the unbound sheets and thus becoming their apparent publisher and unmistakably their first distributor. Curll had laid himself open to this trick by advertising in 1733 that he had one of his notorious "Lives" in press, this time of Alexander Pope, to embellish which he desired all gentlemen "willing to do Mr. Popes character justice"—a clear invitation to everyone distinguished by satiric notice in the *Dunciad*, the epistles to Burlington and Bathurst, and the *First Satire of the Second Book of Horace*—to convey their offerings with speed. This, Pope seems to have realized, was the chance of a lifetime. By initiating messages to Curll as if from several pseudonymous persons identified only by initials—messages hostile to Pope and hinting at access to his private letters and other possibly juicy tidbits—he could at the very least delay the proposed biography. And to do so could only be advantageous, since a typical Curll "Life," with its predictable slanders and misrepresentations, not to mention juster charges, might prove an item of some danger and certainly of embarrassment at a time when he was already locked in combat with Lady Mary and beginning to be out of favor with the court circle generally.

Further: if Curll, who had built his entire business on sensational publicity, could be coaxed into advertising that there were letters appertaining to peers in these promised materials, as he had been carefully led to believe, Pope's friends in the Lords could have both the books and their purveyor seized for examination on grounds of possible *scandalum magnatum*, and the latter perhaps enjoined from the harrassments for which he had become notorious. By the spring of 1735, when a bill for renewing the copyright act was before that body—a "Booksellers Bill," Pope called it, because he thought it overly protective of publishers and insufficiently protective of either authors or the public—this objective had become centrally important. Let Curll, who had already stood in the pillory for publishing pornography, be haled before the Lords on a matter as sensitive as the unauthorized publication of peers' letters, and a dramatic example would have been set of a type of mischief to which the act before the House offered no remedy, and which was just as obnoxious to any private man or woman as to a peer. Pope describes it feelingly two years later in his preface to the authorized edition of his correspondence which these ostensibly unauthorized (even if secretly self-generated) volumes had been used by him to justify:

> A Bookseller advertises his intention to publish your Letters: He openly promises encouragement, or even pecuniary rewards to those who help him to any; and ingages to insert whatever they shall send: Any scandal is sure of a reception, and any enemy who sends it skreen'd from a discovery. Any domestick or servant, who can snatch a letter from your pocket or cabinet, is encouraged to that vile practise. If the quantity falls short of a volume, any thing else shall be join'd with it ... which the collector can think for his interest, all recommended under your Name: You have not only Theft to fear, but Forgery.

Thus as an author you were deprived of the right of deciding for yourself "what pieces it may be most useful, entertaining, or reputable to publish, at the time and in the manner you think best." As an individual, you lost your right "even over your own Sentiments ... to divulge or conceal them." And as a member of society you were injured most grievously of all: "your private conduct, your domestick concerns, your family secrets, your passions, your tendernesses, your weaknesses, are expos'd to the Misconstruction or Resentment of some [and] to the Censure or Impertinence of the whole world." Though things did not happen before the Lords exactly as Pope had planned, he notes in capital letters in his later *Narrative* of this conspiratorial transaction: "By THIS INCIDENT THE BOOKSELLERS BILL WAS THROWN OUT" and closes with the hearty wish that at the next session of the Lords, "when the BOOKSELLERS BILL shall be again brought in," their Honours will be pleased "not to *extend the Privileges*, without at the same Time *restraining the Licence, of Booksellers.*"

Pope had other ends in mind as well. For one, the relief of knowing that *this* collection of his letters had been edited to suit his own sense of privacy and personal dignity—quite unlike those unbuttoned effusions he had tossed off in youth to Henry Cromwell, which Curll, after getting his hands on them through Cromwell's mistress, had published in two volumes in 1726. Volumes pieced out, as we have just heard Pope complain, with every sort of flotsam from "An Essay on Gibing" to "The Praise of Owls." Pope was determined that nothing of this sort should happen to him again. He had long ago discovered that most of his correspondents preserved his letters. He had, in fact, called in some from Caryll to mine for ideas for his *Guardian* papers as early as 1712. After the embarrassing Cromwell episode, he began to do so oftener. Unquestionably, he felt apprehension. Copies of his impassioned letters of support to Atterbury during his trial could be stolen from countless Tory country houses, as he may have guessed, and the letters exchanged during his friend's exile, technically a "criminal" correspondence, might quite possibly also, in view of ministerial vigilance, soon or late reach some printer's desk. Like every writer dependent on a public, Pope had to give as much consideration to what he was perceived to be as to what he was. His position as Roman Catholic, with whatever ardor or lack of ardor held, made him only more vulnerable. Owing to that position, it was still expedient for him, when Court was kept at Hampton Court, to decamp from his villa and go elsewhere, a consideration that may have sometimes extended his summer rambles. And it was evidently judged altogether inexpedient for him to remove to London for medical attention when he lay dying in the spring of '44, rumors of a massive French invasion to restore the Stuarts being already in the air. To this lifetime vulnerability as a recusant, he had of course added by his folly in becoming the scourge of Dunces, and, more recently, an outspoken supporter of the anti-Walpole dissidents.

There were, then, genuine grounds for Pope's concern about his letters, particularly about the way they might be presented to the public, either now or after his death, by some unsympathetic or unscrupulous publisher—some Curll of the future. Meantime, not to be ignored, there was considerable anticipatory satisfaction in turning the tables on the present Curll, conning him into buying and distributing correspondences already printed and therefore largely invulnerable to the impudent footnotes and leering digressions that normally accompanied his ventures into epistolary or biographical publication. If, in addition, as Pope doubtless hoped, the Lords saw fit to take some action against Curll following the seizure, vengeance would be sweet. For it can hardly be overstressed that there was much to avenge. During more than twenty years now, Curll had hovered over Pope's career and reputation like a particularly nauseous harpy with both sphincters set on "Go." He had organized his stable of hacks ("three in a bed at the *Pewter-Platter* Inn in *Holborn*") to rain down pamphlets on each new work as it appeared, filled the newspapers with unsavory publicity, worked up "Keys," often false, to identify Pope's pseudonyms, invented new scurrilities, perpetuated old lies, and offered, as in his advertisement of Pope's biography, access to print to every unfriendly or jealous pen: e.g., "For *both* those wretched Performances [the Odyssey translation and the Shakespeare edition], a large subscription has been carried on, purely through the sycophantick Meanness of the *Undertaker*, who crawls under the *Toilet* of every *Court-Lady*." As early as 1716, Defoe had called Curll "a contemptible Wretch," odious in his person, beastly in his language (he was, in fact, notably foul-mouthed), scandalous in his fame; and had wondered how his offenses could continue unpunished. For that early date, an answer would be hard to give. Later, however, despite his one stint in the pillory, it is probable he had a degree of protection from the government, with which from about 1718 on he seems to have been often in touch as an informer. In 1730, for example, we find him offering Walpole "some papers ... concerning Ld Bolingbroke, & the rest of Brindsden's★ Durham-Yard Assembly, who intend to overthrow you"; and in 1731 proposing himself as inspector of newspapers and advertisements to police infractions of the paper tax. If Pope was at all aware of Curll's relations with the ministry, it can only have added to his apprehension and dislike.

Alas for the plans of mice and men. For reasons unclear—though perhaps no more complicated than the failure of one of Pope's printers to get the final sheets printed and delivered before the books were seized—the Lords could turn up no correspondence about or from peers, Curll was set free, and Pope, who was present at the hearing, must inevitably have suffered a degree of public discomfiture, as must those peers who brought forward his complaint. True, the "Booksellers Bill" was thrown out for this session. But Curll, who had been in no way enjoined from pursuing his usual courses, and who toward

★ John Brinsden was Bolingbroke's secretary and agent.

the close of negotiations with Pope's emissaries had glimpsed the truth, began now to publish it along with his own new printings of the sheets he had bought, annotating the letters with all the irritating mockeries Pope had expected to avoid and inflating his successive volumes (he managed to blow Pope's two up to four) with ephemera from twenty-odd other authors living and dead—always remembering, in addition, to feature one or more of Pope's early gay-doggish compositions that he would have preferred to forget. As if to mark his triumph, Curll in early summer made "Pope's Head" his shop sign in Rose Street, Covent Garden. Retrospection on all or any of this would have sufficed to prompt Pope's remark to Bathurst that he had played the fool.

Yet if Curll had won the skirmish, Pope, in a sense, had won the war. He had managed to bring a selection of his letters before the public without the outcry upon his vanity that would have been forthcoming had he openly published them himself. (Curll, of course, claimed he had, but Curll's reputation being what it was, few could be expected to believe him.) For though many eighteenth-century writers composed their letters, as Horace Walpole once remarked of his own, with posterity standing behind their chairs and peeping, and though the *fictional* letter, whether used as vehicle for politics, philosophy, satire, confession, or, eventually, the novel, was as conventional a part of the daily scene as the lace on a gentleman's shirt, to offer one's actual correspondence to the public as one might offer it one's essays, poems, histories, novels, sermons, travelogues, was by early eighteenth-century standards unthinkable. Even at the century's end, though a nobleman, and plainly resolved to leave behind him an epistolary record of the men and manners of his times (in the great edition of our own day it comes to nearly fifty volumes), Horace Walpole did not venture such effrontery. Hence Pope's elaborate chicanery with Curll, carried on in part, no doubt, because he loved intrigue, but essentially because there was no respectable way of accomplishing his end.

And he *would* publish. Not exclusively, we may guess, because he was vain about what he had written, and wanted—as we realize today with some gratitude—to make his correspondence a part of his total literary output. This was undoubtedly a motive. But other interests must have been equally compelling. One, surely, was the need of any writer who turns seriously to political and moral satire to project an "ethos" or public sense of himself as an essentially decent human being: one whose censures spring not from spleen or misanthropy, but from a responsible concern for the common good and an appropriate sense of outrage when it is seen abused. For Pope, unquestionably, an intimately related interest would have been that of countering at least some of the distortions and defamations of his character which, unsurprisingly, it had pleased the dunces to multiply after 1728, and which, as had begun by 1733 to appear, it was the intention of certain persons at St. James's to keep alive and to augment. Whatever might have been his own role in provoking such assaults initially, he knew that the picture they painted of him as toad, spider, wasp, monkey, and general enemy of mankind was a gross lie and that the best way to explode it would be through the history of his friendships as preserved in letters.

One must recognize, too, in all of Pope's activities after, roughly, the publication of his epistle to Arbuthnot a growing sense of autumn. Increasingly, one sees him gathering up and in, as reapers do. He collects his recent pieces, beginning with the *Dunciad*, in a *Works, Volume II* (1735). He arranges his entire output from 1709 forward in the order in which he wishes posterity to see it and issues it in small-octavo volumes (1735–43), adding to their number as new poems appear. He sets the younger Jonathan Richardson to work collating the manuscripts of his poems with their texts as published and enters a selection of the manuscript variants in the new octavos: notes often equally contributory to the history of the poem and the history of the poet's mind. As the years speed by, he begins to consider returning to the large cluster of planned pieces (the *Opus Magnum*) of which the *Essay on Man* and the epistles to Burlington, Bathurst, Cobham, and Martha Blount made part; and to some extent out of this ambition gradually emerges a poem called *The New Dunciad* (1742), soon incorporated as a fourth book into the *Dunciad Variorum*, itself now (1743) totally revised. At some point during these years, too, he gets out the sheaf of papers, by various hands but perhaps substantially Arbuthnot's, which constitute the *Memoirs* of that distinguished pedant and virtuoso Martinus Scriblerus, and readies them for publication along with other Scriblerian items. A settling of personal affairs and a commemoration of himself among his band of friends and of a moment in his country's cultural history seem to be much on his mind.

Meantime, the elder Richardson had not been idle. Whether at Pope's instigation or for his own pleasure as admirer and draughtsman, he was turning out at this period (1734–38) likeness after likeness with pencil, pen, brush, and burin. One of his drawings depicts the poet looking like the Occleve portrait of Chaucer, another like the Faithorne portrait of Milton, and the undoubted masterpiece among his oils shows Pope in profile crowned with laurel. This is

76. Alexander Pope, laureated. By Jonathan Richardson, *c.* 1738. Wimsatt, 54. Courtesy of the National Portrait Gallery, London.

expressive evidence, one is inclined to think, not simply of Pope's admiration for two poets he had much drawn on, but of a kind of positioning by himself or Richardson in the line of poetic fame. Other evidence of this nature abounds. What Voltaire had remarked in the early 1730s as a reproach to France for indifference to men of letters like himself (that whereas in England a likeness of the chief minister might be seen over his own mantel, a likeness of Mr. Pope would be found in twenty noblemen's houses) became spectacularly true, at least as far as the second half of the statement is concerned, from 1735 on. To this period, apart from Richardson's multiple contributions, belong portraits by William Kent, Arthur Pond, William Hoare of Bath, the French medalist J. A. Dassier, and the Flemish painter J. B. Van Loo—several of their productions continuing to be available in copies by the master or by other copyists as well as in engravings and mezzotints. In 1738, perhaps on Pope's initiative, certainly at any rate with his hearty collaboration, the French sculptor L. F. Roubiliac made the most sensitive reading of the poet's face that has come down to us. This was a terra-cotta bust, immediately used by him as model for 'four superb marbles (1738–41) as well as several casts: all together constituting a Roubiliac type imitated through the remainder of the century in bronze, lead, basalt, porcelain, plaster, and almost any other material capable of being cut, impressed, or moulded.

For Pope, in short, as the dean of English historians of British portraiture has recently pointed out,

> vanity was intensified by the need to rectify the tragic twisted reality of his crippled body with an image worthy of the lucid beautifully articulated construction and spirit of his poetry—the need very literally to put the image straight. When the sum of his portraits is surveyed [more than sixty distinct types, matched during Pope's lifetime only by royalty], it reads like a willed highly controlled projection by Pope of his person into posterity—

and not of his person simply, but of "the poetic vocation itself, its classic dignity and its independence."

It is in this context that Pope's resolve to make his correspondence public is best understood. It was part of his effort to set the record straight, garner up the fruits of his career, project an edifying image to the after time, communicate his deep belief in the social worth of the poetic function, and erect a monument to himself and the gifted group of writers he had known. Like the portraits, which tactfully

77. Alexander Pope. Terra cotta bust by L. F. Roubiliac, *c.* 1738, Wimsatt, 57.1.

By kind permission of the Trustees of the Barber Institute of Fine Arts, The University, Birmingham.

refrained from revealing his warped and diminutive frame, concentrating instead on the face and its expressive eyes, this too would be a controlled image, calculated to minimize whatever was unflattering either to the personal ego or to the idea of the good poet as the good man—an equation once held dear by poets (notably dear by satirists!), though the moral term of the equation seems to have proved as elusive for most of them as for the rest of us. Selected, edited, arranged, and (possibly) where necessary supplied, his letters could be counted on to show—what was indeed the truth—that he had won the respect of honorable and talented men from the beginning. They would show him, in sober moments, stating with an elegant precision his views on matters as diverse as couplet versification and the errors of the Roman Church; romping and teasing, in lighter moments, with his more intimate associates; and, in the whole picture, radiating a healthy combination of sense, fun, affection, and good will that was the very reverse of the stereotype with which Grub Street and now the Court circle seemed determined to identify him.

Above all, his letters could be *used* to show what had actually happened between Addison and him. For the charge of ingratitude to Addison (whose spotless integrity was fast becoming as firm a datum in Whig literary mythology as the Satanism of Bolingbroke in the corresponding political mythology) had served the poet's enemies for many years, especially when seconded by later allegations with respect to Chandos, as irrefutable proof of his black villainy. The truth about this episode, Pope was therefore particularly eager to establish, even if establishing it meant inventing a partly fictional scenario.

And what a scenario it was! In the printed sheets conveyed to Curll, Pope had pieced out some of his early correspondences with one or more letters made up from parts of letters originally sent to his Sussex friend John Caryll. He had an abundance of these, because their epistolary exchange had begun in his teens and Caryll had always been obliging enough to return them. Of his letters to other early friends, he undoubtedly had fewer. In most instances, obviously, because he had written fewer; though in some—Congreve is probably a case in point—the sheer distinction and seniority of the correspondent may have made it too great a presumption to suppose either that his letters had been saved, or if saved, could be asked back. Thus we happen to know that Pope and Congreve corresponded from surviving letters of his to Pope. We may guess at the respect and affection felt on Pope's part from his having dedicated to Congreve his monumental translation of the *Iliad*. And we may easily imagine the poet's urge, as he began to assemble his letters for publication in the early 1730s, to record some testimony to this friendship in the collection. Having apparently no access to his actual letters to the playwright (who had died in 1729), he solved the problem by printing as from himself to Congreve at least two letters derived from his correspondence with Caryll and one whose origins remain unclear.

Similar treatment was accorded Addison. Here there had been a special reason not to seek the return of letters. Yet something in the published correspondence would have to represent a relationship that all knowledgeable readers knew had existed and gone bad. What to do? Once more, Pope turned to his Caryll correspondence. Four of the five letters printed in 1735 as from himself to Addison, he again made up from this source, with no discernible aim more sinister than to show that a literary friendship had existed. The fifth letter—dated only six months before his first volume of the *Iliad* was to appear and about four after he gives the first sign of knowing about Addison's alliance with Tickell—tacitly challenges his mentor to a confession by inviting him to look over and correct his own Books 1 and 2. Did Pope write and send this letter to Addison at the time, and because it was a masterly put-down keep a copy to show his friends? Nothing in the letter rules this possibility out. Or is it a refined and meditated version (emotion recollected in tranquility) of a letter that was actually sent in a different form? Or is it altogether an afterthought, a pure fiction like Hamlet's play within the play, which, without being literally true, is calculated to convey truth?

Puzzling questions of this kind also attend the two letters Pope printed as from Addison. There had been, as his statement in the *Iliad* preface testifies and no member of the Little Senate ever ventured to deny, one or more flattering letters from Addison to Pope about his Homer project, and these may be the ones that appear in Pope's 1735 collection. Again, nothing in the letters themselves precludes this. The reason we cannot be absolutely sure is that Pope could be devious on occasion and this may be one of the occasions. Yet even if we suppose the worst—that he fabricated all three letters from scratch, as the Victorian editors who first uncovered his reassignment of portions of his Caryll letters understandably thought—we have to recognize that he did not invent the story they tell. Addison did deceive him, as we saw earlier, did encourage and revise the rival translation after earlier offering Pope full support for his, and did not gather any subscriptions. The fabricated letters, if they are fabricated, simply make the duplicity crystal clear.

"I will preserve . . . all the memorials I can"

Trumpeted by a fanfare of claims and counterclaims in the newspapers as to their authenticity or lack of it, Mr. Pope's letters proceeded to enjoy a smashing success. They ran through some thirty
reprints, piracies, and so-called new editions during the next four
years and without much question their popularity established a precedent to which we owe something of the eighteenth century's interest in the preservation of personal correspondence generally. They
also exerted, at least in some quarters, the hoped-for rectifying effect
on the poet's image. Ralph Allen of Bath, for example, who would
eventually be the model for Squire Allworthy in *Tom Jones* but in the
1730s was still very busy accumulating a sizable fortune from his
upright and inventive management of a large sector of the British
postal service, found in the letters a man to be cherished. Though he
had been a reader of Pope for some while "and admired him for the
excellence of his genius" (this is Owen Ruffhead speaking in 1769, the
poet's first "official" biographer, who had his information from
within the Allen family), "the asperity of his satirical pieces was so
repugnant to the softness and suavity of that worthy man's disposition, that it in some degree estranged him from his intimacy. But no
sooner had he read over our author's letters, than he loved him for the
goodness and virtues of his heart." The new perspective led soon to
personal acquaintance, then to friendship.

Broome, too, Pope's coadjutor in the *Odyssey* translation, renewing their correspondence in the summer of 1735 after nearly
seven years' estrangement, testifies to the letters' influence. "The
humane companion," he writes to Pope, "the dutiful and affectionate
son, the compassionate and obliging friend, appear so strongly
almost in every page, that I can assure you I had rather be the owner of
the writer's heart, than of the head that has honour'd England with
Homer, his Essays, Moral Epistles, &c." It is perhaps worth stressing
that this is precisely what Pope (and Congreve, too, it will be recalled, when confronted by Voltaire) believed to be his own view of a
right ordering of priorities; and that despite his numerous fallings-
short, as, for example, in the hypocritical pretense that these volumes
had been published without his knowledge or approval, the man
discovered by Broome and Allen in the collection he edited and manipulated differs little from the man revealed in the far larger correspondence we possess today in autograph, just as it flowed from his
pen.

In the eighteenth century, however, the excuse of a corrupt or pirated edition was always good warrant for an "authoritative" one, and this, enthusiastically backed by Allen, Pope proceeded to effect in 1737, with a quarto and a folio designed for those who already owned his earlier publications in these larger formats. Meanwhile, stimulated doubtless by the triumph of the letters of 1735, he sought to forward what had become by now the most cherished of his memorializing schemes. He was extremely proud of his long intercourse with Swift and Bolingbroke, whose esteem, he tells Swift in an amusing letter of 1736, "is a greater honour to me by far, and will be thought so by posterity, than if all the House of Lords writ Commendatory Verses upon me, the Commons order'd me to print my Works, the Universities gave me publick thanks, and the King, Queen, and Prince crown'd me with Laurel."

> You are a very ignorant man; you don't know the figure his name and yours will make hereafter: I do, and will preserve all the memorials I can, that I was of your intimacy.

Though this is the rhetoric of compliment—the tone, however, kept comfortably astringent by the comic imagery of the House of Lords hotly scribbling execrable verses in honor of Mr. Pope, and of the King, Queen, and Prince agreeing, by 1736, on anything at all, much less on the disposition of laurels to poets—Pope clearly means what he says. "My sincere Love for this most valuable, indeed Incomparable Man," he writes to Lord Orrery a few months later, in 1737, speaking of their mutual friend the dean,

> will accompany him thro Life, & pursue his memory were I to live a hundred lives, as many as his Works will live, which are absolutely Original, unequald, unexampled. His Humanity, his Charity, his Condescention, his Candour, are equal to his Wit, & require as good and true a Taste to be equally valued. When all this must dye (this last I mean) I would gladly have been the Recorder of so great a part of it, as shines in his Letters to me, & of which my own are but so many acknowledgments.

Here one of Pope's aims is to urge upon Orrery, then in Dublin, the reasons why Swift should be persuaded to return his letters. The compliments to Swift are presumably intended as much for the dean's ear as for Orrery's; and we have every reason to doubt that Pope really regarded his own letters as "but so many acknowledgments." Still, discount the language as we may, there can be no question that in consulting his own glory with posterity he believed himself to be contributing to that of his friend at the same time. Few words survive from his pen more touching than those in which, four years later, knowing that they would never meet again, and made aware by Orrery's as well as Swift's reports of the rapidly worsening amnesia, deafness, and giddiness which within some seventeen months were to bring the dean before a commission *de lunatico inquirendo*, Pope looks back over their long friendship with such a valedictory tenderness as might make one think he foresaw his friend's fate:

> My Dear Friend, When the Heart is full of Tenderness, it must be full of Concern at the absolute Impotency of all Words to come up to it. You are the only Man now in the world, who cost me a Sigh every day of my Life [because of their enforced separation], and the Man it troubles me most, altho' I most wish, to write to. Death has not used me worse in separating from me for ever, poor Gay, Arbuthnot, &c, than Disease & Distance in separating You so many years. But nothing shall make me forget you, and I am persuaded you will as little forget me; & most things in this world one may afford to forget, if we remember, & are remembered by, our Friends. . . . Think it not possible that my Affection can cease but with my last breath.

In the interval between these two expressions of concern, what appears to be a real-life comedy of intrigue, mystification, and deceit was played out (possibly by both men) that could scarcely have been bettered onstage by Plautus or Ben Jonson. To Pope's disingenuous complaints of Curll's rascality in purloining and publishing the collection of 1735, Swift replied disconcertingly that no such apprehension need be entertained about the letters sent to *him*: they were all carefully guarded from prying eyes and would be, by strict orders given his executors, immediately destroyed upon his death—"which my bad state of health makes me expect every month." After all, he adds, what did their correspondence have to offer? No "Turns of Wit, or Fancy, or Politics, or Satire"—nothing but "mere innocent friendship." The suspicion that Swift is here pulling Pope's leg can hardly be avoided. He had long before this (1730) twitted the poet with harboring schemes of epistolary fame, "almost from your infancy." To which Pope had answered that he had indeed kept some letters of friends, including Swift's, which he might some day wish to bring together in a volume as evidence (here Pope's concern with the dunces' vilification of his character becomes apparent) of a life passed in "Innocent amusements & Studies," with the good will of "worthy and ingenious Men." So, he adds, with some but surely less than the whole truth, "do not therefore say, I aim at Epistolary Fame:

78. Jonathan Swift (1667–1745). Attributed to R. Barker.

The Rights a Court attack'd, a Poet sav'd.

Imit. Hor., *Ep* II, i: 224.

Present location unknown.

... The Fame I most covet indeed, is that, which must be deriv'd to me from my Friendships." Swift, in other words, knew from early on that Pope planned to make public a record of their acquaintance. Hence the threat to burn his letters has all the earmarks of a piece of solemn fooling.

Similarly tongue-in-cheek (one is tempted to conclude) is his appraisal of their content. Both men, most particularly Swift from the comparative security of his Irish deanery, had indulged a good many sentiments about politics, not to mention satire, witty turns, fancies (among others, that of permanent cohabitation in either Dublin or Twickenham), along with elaborately solemn posturings from time to time (not of course entirely posturings) about the slings and arrows of outrageous fortune, the slippage of their literary talents, their weariness of the world, and other topics on which it was appropriate for eighteenth-century sages to give the high rhetorical horse free rein. To suppose therefore that the greatest ironist in the language is not teasing Pope with an at least partly calculated coyness during the negotiations that ensued requires a considerable act of will and one that is only further strained by what appear to be the stages of a planned or at least semiconscious delaying action. First, the determination to burn the letters, expressed on 3 September 1735. Then the concession that, yes, they should be returned to Pope but only on Swift's death, made on 22 April 1736. And then, finally, the agreement, reached on 31 May 1737, that they should be given to Orrery at once for conveyance to Pope—only now, however, where the dean had once been confident he had saved "*Every Scrap*" of Pope's writing, it appeared there was actually "a chasm ... of six years," 1717–1722—an announcement that in view of Orrery's reports of the dean's advancing forgetfulness and ill health, of "Designing People, who swarm about him" ("the Dean is guarded, not defended, by Dragons and all the monstrous Animals of the Creation"), and of Orrery's own apprehension, when the chasm became known, that those letters "are on your Side o' the Water and in very improper Hands," gave Pope some bad moments.

Clouding the picture further for us today are three additional possibilities. One is that Swift genuinely wished not to return Pope's letters because he knew that his own, sure to be published with them, were ecclesiastically and politically indiscreet. This is possible but, in view of the modest changes he made on the printed text eventually submitted to him by Pope, unlikely. Another—which has some support from a statement made later by George Faulkner, Swift's Dublin publisher—is that Swift was himself at about this time toying with the idea of publishing his correspondence. And a third, as likely as any because of Swift's repeatedly expressed wish that Pope dedicate a poem to him (in addition to the *Dunciad*), is that he feared an epistolary memorial to their friendship might attenuate his chances of a poetical one.

Whatever may be the truth about Swift's "shyness," as Lord Orrery called it, in giving up the letters, Pope received them back in the summer of 1737 through Orrery's mediation (except for those belonging to the sizable chasm, which still exists), and the second act of the comedy began. Now, as with the earlier collection, the object was to publish without seeming to have done so. To this end, a packet addressed to Swift in Dublin appeared mysteriously on a day in late May 1740 at the Bath lodgings of one Samuel Gerrard, who was about to return to his native Ireland. A few months earlier, while still in Bath at the Allens' (he stayed that year till about mid-February), Pope had become acquainted with Gerrard and evidently asked to be alerted before he returned home in order that a letter to Swift might be conveyed in his care. When Gerrard obliged, probably toward mid-May, Pope replied from Twickenham that, another opportunity for transmitting a letter to Swift having arisen and been seized, he had nothing now for Gerrard to deliver except his usual love and esteem. Pope's intention, of course, was to distance himself as far as possible from the mysterious packet about to be delivered to Gerrard's door.

Arrived in Swift's hands and opened, the packet turned out to be (not surprisingly) printed sheets of a selection of letters from Pope to Swift and Swift to Pope, appropriately edited (on the one hand) to emphasize their mutual affection, dignity, and general indifference to the censures of a crass world and (on the other) to expunge all references that showed Pope seeking to recover his correspondence. Swift, who was himself something of a master in the art of surreptitious publishing and who had already said of Pope's letters in returning them that they contained nothing requiring "to be left out," saw at once what was going on, inserted some small revisions in the text, and turned the sheets over to Faulkner, his publisher, for a Dublin reprint—the normal Irish procedure with works originating in London. But Pope could not endure to leave it at that. Since Orrery, along with those who attended on the dean, particularly his cousin Mrs. Whiteway, had been accessory to Pope's recovery of his side of the correspondence, and since the dean himself had every reason to assume that the packet of printed sheets came from that source, Pope's hypersensitive vanity about not appearing to be vain drove him to leave no stone unturned, no lie untold, that would situate the origin of the printed sheets in Ireland. The letter accompanying them, for example (copied out, of course, by some scribe or amanuensis), implied in every sentence that the senders were Irish, that the letters would be lost to posterity if this, the sole extant copy, were destroyed, and that it thus lay in the dean's power alone to decide the fate of an exchange which gave at one and the same time "so amiable a Picture of your own excellent Mind" and "so strong a Testimony of the Love and Respect of those who nearest know, and best can judge of it."

To protect his flank, Pope was further obliged to ask to see this clandestine production—as if he did not already know it as well as his own thumbprint—together with the two sheets of it that by the end of July Faulkner had printed. Faulkner, as an honorable man, acquiesced, and there ensued one critical moment when it seemed that Pope's protests might forestall altogether the Irish reprint by which his own authorized London edition was to be justified. But the moment fortunately passed. Pope managed to transmit through Orrery a vague consent to Faulkner's completing the impression; made sure, again through Orrery, that the clandestine text should be returned to him when Faulkner finished with it; and at length, on 16 April 1741, published his London quarto and folio edition of the letters, suitably enough companioned, since Swift had been the moving spirit of the Scriblerus Club of 1713–14, by the *Memoirs of Scriblerus* and other miscellaneous Scriblerian prose. Roughly two months later, Faulkner's Dublin edition, by which Pope falsely claimed that his own edition had been provoked, made its appearance, and, probably at about the same time, a now extremely rare edition showed up in the bookshops, in which Pope was using up the sheets of the clandestine impression of which he had sent a copy to Dublin in the care of Samuel Gerrard. At all this, if he was at the time in command of his memory, Swift must either have groaned or grinned: he was well enough schooled in the intricacies of printing to have understood from the start that a set of printed sheets would undoubtedly be but one set among many; and he was too shrewd a reader of small signals not to have noticed that when the letter accompanying the packet advised printing on the grounds that "In doing so You shall oblige all Mankind in general, and *benefit any deserving Friend* in particular," the last six words, four of them apparently underscored in the original, invited interpretation as a very explicit signal indeed.

Certainly, Pope's conduct in this episode was discreditable by any standard. That Swift recognized what was going on and took part in it by revising the clandestine sheets for Faulkner to reprint in no way excuses his friend, who, once into the intrigue, lied and lied again to maintain his cover, besides, on more than one occasion, imputing dishonest motives to Mrs. Whiteway. True, Orrery unquestionably frightened him with unfounded slurs on the character and intentions of those around the dean during negotiations for the letters. True, also, that deceitful as his machinations were, they had no object more sinister than that of getting his best letters before the public and by this means presenting a suitably retouched and edifying image of himself to posterity in the company of an admired friend (or rather, two admired friends, since several of the letters were joint compositions of himself and Bolingbroke and several of Swift's replies were directed to both)—an objective held quite blameless by our own society and sought for in any given season by autobiographies without number. To this it may be further added that if we owe the preservation of this correspondence to Pope, as conceivably we may (since it is impossible to guess what Swift's executors might have done with it if by any chance he was serious when he said he had ordered it to be burned), some gratitude must be mixed with our distaste. Even so, when all extenuating considerations have been balanced in, Pope's willingness throughout the affair to lay his own scheming on the backs of others is painful to behold. Had the Recording Angel who, in Sterne's *Tristram Shandy*, erases Uncle Toby's mild offense from heaven's register with a tear, been in a similarly charitable frame of mind between 1735 and 1741, he would have required for Pope the services of Hecuba.

CHAPTER 26

COUNTRY AND COURT

"Ah spare me, Venus!"

For nearly two years after the release of his early letters through Curll, Pope published little. Not that he was idle—for him an unthinkable condition except when deathly ill. He was scrupulously revising texts for the new small-octavo editions of his works (clear evidence of the degree to which the face of publishing was changing and of Pope's awareness of the extent and character of his growing audience), four of which appeared during 1736; busy, too, pruning his letters of inelegancies and indecorums for the stately authorized edition of 1737; and somewhere in the intervals between these demanding tasks (probably during his two visits to Lady Peterborow at Bevis Mount in June and October 1736) finding time to adapt two of Horace's finest epistles for publication in April and May of the following year. Being the good businessman he was, he chose usually to publish new works between January and June, when Parliament was normally in session, the town full, and anything new—scandal, politics, opera, theater, and, most especially, a new piece from the pen of Mr. Pope—in considerable demand.

Not surprisingly, then, only two relatively small poems saw print at this time. Both, however, are memorable for the glimpses they allow of interior moods, in the one piece exuberantly expressed, in the other with a wistfulness only partly playful and self-mocking. The later of the two, published officially on 9 March 1737, but unofficially a few days earlier in a newspaper, is an adaptation of Horace's "Ode to Venus." Here the Roman poet, representing himself to be getting on in years and no longer the man he was when Cinara (an early mistress) ruled him, pleads with the goddess to stop assaulting him with amorous desires. These, he says, belong more properly to young men like his good friend the lawyer, Paulus Maximus: let Venus make *him* her means to conquest over the distaff half of humankind, and let *his* house become for a new generation the center of merriment, dance, and song. And yet, even now—the poet adds—thoughts of Ligurinus (another and more recent flame: like so many Romans, Horace was a lover of boys as well as women) stirs the fading embers; and in his dreams he seems for a moment to catch and hold him, only to find that his cruel shade glides from his arms to dissipate itself in the surrounding landscape.

Pope's adaptation alters the poem slightly, but significantly, and in such a way as to accommodate both the recent discomfiture of a friend and his own never quite repressible feelings for Martha Blount. Horace's years under the spell of Cinara become for the English poet the golden time between, say, 1712 and 1714, before the dynasty changed and the little band of literary friends was forced to break up. In those days, it had been exciting to be in love with love. In those days, his *Rape of the Lock* had taken the drawing rooms and boudoirs as well as the coffee houses by storm. And—happiest circumstance of all in those days—the Little Climacteric of age forty-nine to which his next birthday would be bringing him (with the formidable fifties lurking in ambush just around the bend) had been hardly so much as a flyspeck on an horizon that seemed to stretch forever in a great rosy dawn.

> Again? new Tumults in my Breast?
> Ah spare me, Venus! let me, let me rest!
> I am not now, alas! the man
> As in the gentle Reign of My Queen *Anne*.
> Ah sound no more thy soft alarms;
> Nor circle sober fifty with thy Charms.
> Mother too fierce of dear Desires!
>
> (ll. 1–7)

Similarly, Horace's Paulus Maximus becomes for Pope his Scots friend William Murray. A thriving young barrister, who in later life was to become first earl of Mansfield and one of the great lord chancellors, Murray had at just this moment in his career (so, at any rate, his biographer John Campbell, himself a chief justice, tells us) lost out in a love match from being thought by the young lady's father insufficiently in funds—a loss that Pope's poem undertakes humorously to assuage. "To Number five direct your Doves," the English poem admonishes Venus (calling up a wonderfully droll picture of the chariot of the great Cyprian settling to a three-point landing in King's Bench Walk, where at no. 5 Murray had chambers); "Make but his riches equal to his Wit," and he will outshine all rivals, win the Chloe of his choice, and command the gay social scene of a Thames villa, where "every Grace and Muse shall throng."

As for himself, the poet acknowledges, those joys are gone:

> Adieu! fond hope of mutual fire,
> The still-believing, still-renew'd desire;
> Adieu! the heart-expanding bowl,
> And all the kind Deceivers of the Soul!
>
> (ll. 33–36)

So, at least, it pleases him to say, and perhaps in part believe. Yet for the English poet as for the Roman, the banked coals still shimmer:

> —But why? ah tell me, ah too dear!
> Steals down my cheek th' involuntary Tear?
> Why words so flowing, thoughts so free,
> Stop, or turn nonsense at one glance of Thee?
>
> (ll. 37–40)

For though he long since has put away hope of kindling in his female counterpart of Ligurinus a "mutual fire," and though, when he clasps her in dreams, she always breaks from him, he cannot prevent himself from looking longingly after as her swift quicksilvery shade recedes and mixes with the elements:

> Now shown by Cynthia's silver Ray,
> And now, on rolling Waters snatch'd away.
>
> (ll. 47–48)

Cinara's sovereignty over Horace's early life has been replaced by the very different sovereignty of "My Queen *Anne*" over Pope's; but thoughts of the latter's Ligurinus are another matter. In the official printed version of March 9, line 37 reads as above, addressed to an unnamed woman. In the one surviving autograph manuscript of the poem, it reads: "But why? ah Celia still too dear," using the stock name made famous by Ben Jonson and by lesser poets in droves. But in the newspaper text, quite obviously unauthorized and a considerable embarrassment no doubt to both addresser and addressee, the name reads unashamedly "Patty" (Martha Blount's nickname), as it must have done in some exceptionally private copy released by a friend to the press; and the whole quatrain, beautifully catching the crosscurrents of sheepish tenderness and confusion that every man who has ever loved a woman knows, assumes an endearing intimacy.

79. Alexander Pope with his dog Bounce. By Jonathan Richardson, *c*. 1718. Wimsatt, 9.1.

Hagley Hall. Reproduction by kind permission of the Viscount Cobham. Photograph: Courtauld Institute of Art.

"We Country Dogs love nobler Sport"

The other poem, written in a different key altogether, was published about a year earlier. All his life long, so far as can now be ascertained, Pope had kept dogs. In Binfield, there had been the dog that followed him about as he had followed Wycherley when first being introduced to literary London. Though this dog's name is unknown, if by any chance it was the same animal that Gay calls "a f[riend of his] and of yours" in a letter of 1716 to Parnell, it was a male named Bounce. The dog standing by Pope's knee and looking fondly up at him in a painting by Richardson of about 1718, is very possibly the same, a large tan-colored hound with "A. Pope" inscribed on his collar. By 1729, when the *Dunciad* had made Pope the object of physical threats, he took with him for his walks upriver to visit the Fortescues, along with his pistols, "a great faithful Danish dog" (as his sister describes it), again named Bounce and presumably of the same general configuration as our present-day Great Dane; and this is clearly the configuration of the very large animal accompanying the small stooped human figure in the riverfront view of Pope's villa that Curll, to annoy him, had engraved in 1735 and put on sale at his shop.

This Bounce, presumably, is the one to which George Lyttleton (Cobham's nephew, it will be recalled, and one of the group of young anti-Walpolians who now often gathered at Stowe and who looked to Pope for a certain kind of poetical-patriotic inspiration) refers in a letter of the following year:

> I am now so much recoverd that I grow very impatient to get away from Bath. You need not be told that the Desire of seeing you is one great cause of that impatience, but to show you how much I am Master of my passions, I will be quiet here for a week or ten days longer, and then come to you in most outrageous Spirits, and Overset you like Bounce when you let her loose after a regimen of Physick, and Confinement.

Rather a fetching scene. Tiny poet, great dog, and a relationship in which, as many besides Pope have discovered, a damaged body makes no difference.

It is this Bounce that Pope makes his heroine in the other poem of this period. It was issued in early May 1736, under the title *Bounce to Fop. An Heroick Epistle from a Dog at Twickenham to a Dog at Court. By Dr. S[wif]t*, and reissued soon thereafter in Dublin by Swift's printer, Faulkner, minus the attribution "By *Dr. S[wif]t*". That Swift did, however, have a hand in it seems clear from contemporary evidence, and in its earlier now unrecoverable Ur-form perhaps the sole hand. In that event, the original *may* have been some verses of disdainful disenchantment with the ways of courtiers, tossed off during or soon after his second English visit, when he came to see that his hopes of advancement or, better yet, retranslation to an English living through the influence of the royal mistress, Mrs. Howard, were headed for disappointment.

But this is guesswork. The poem as we now have it, whatever it was at first, is a jocular conceit on the contrast of Country Dogs and Court Dogs. There is the usual disdain of courtiers, with particular glances at Lord Hervey, of whom Fop appears to be in some degree the intended *alter ego*, as Bounce is in some degree of Pope, even to the point of making what appears to be an oblique allusion either to his "Letter to a Noble Lord" or to "Sporus":

> To thee, sweet *Fop*, these Lines I send,
> Who, tho' no Spaniel,⋆ am a Friend.
> Tho, once my Tail in wanton play,
> Now frisking this, and then that way,
> Chanc'd, with a Touch of just the Tip,
> To hurt your Lady-lap-dog-ship;
> Yet thence to think I'd bite your Head off!
> Sure *Bounce* is one you never read of.
>
> (ll. 1–8)

Predictably, Fop is conceded all the menial talents that induce kings to bestow the ribbons of the various Orders (Garter, Bath, and Thistle) as well as the white staffs of office:

> Fop! you can dance, and make a Leg,
> Can fetch and carry, cringe and beg,
> And (what's the Top of all your Tricks),
> Can stoop to pick up *Strings* and *Sticks*.
> We Country Dogs love nobler Sport.
>
> (ll. 9–13)

Likewise, hers is the knack traditionally (but also most recently by Hervey himself) attributed to courtiers of soiling and even nipping behind their backs those who must be fawned on to their faces. Fop's master, it goes without saying, is a "pilf'ring Lord," presumably Robert Walpole, supported by a system that encourages such extractions from the public till:

⋆ Hervey is compared to a spaniel in one of the verses on Sporus not quoted above.

> Before my Children set your Beef,
> Not one true *Bounce* will be a Thief;
> Not one without Permission feed,
> (Tho' some of J[ohnston]'s★ hungry Breed)
> But whatsoe'er the Father's Race,
> From me they suck a little Grace.
> While your fine Whelps learn all to steal,
> Bred up by Hand on Chick and Veal.

(ll. 49–56)

Meanwhile, back on the Thames shore at Twickenham, Bounce romps happily with *her* whelps:

> See *Bounce*, like *Berecynthia*, crown'd
> With thund'ring Offspring all around,
> Beneath, beside me, and a top,
> A hundred Sons! and not one *Fop*.

(ll. 45–48)

She reviews with a mother's pride (in what is also a review of prominent Whig and Tory peers out of favor with the court) the promising careers of her family to date:

> My Eldest-born resides not far,
> Where shines great *Strafford*'s† glittering Star:
> My second (Child of Fortune!) waits
> At *Burlington*'s Palladian Gates:
> A third majestically stalks
> (Happiest of Dogs!) in *Cobham*'s Walks:
> One ushers Friends to *Bathurst*'s Door;
> Or fawns, at *Oxford*'s, on the Poor.

(ll. 57–64)

And she names one particular aspiration that she feels it is probably too much to hope can ever be realized, yet, if it could be, might secure for the next English monarch a different order of counselors from those that surround George II:

★ James Johnston (1655–1737), a staunch Hanoverian, former Scottish Secretary of State and Pope's Twickenham neighbor at what was then called "Governor Pitt's" house, now Orleans House. His dog was evidently a canine Lothario.
† Thomas Wentworth (1672–1739), third earl of Strafford, knight of the Garter since 1712, Pope's friend and neighbor in Twickenham.

> And O! wou'd Fate the Bliss decree
> To mine (a Bliss too great for me)
> That two, my tallest Sons, might grace,
> Attending each with stately Pace,
> Iülus'* Side, as erst Evander's,*
> To keep off Flatt'rers, Spies, and Panders,
> To let no noble Slave come near,
> And scare Lord Fannys from his Ear:
> Then might a Royal Youth, and true,
> Enjoy at least a Friend—or two:
> A Treasure, which, of Royal kind,
> Few but Himself deserve to find.

(ll. 69–80)

At such a consummation, her joy would admit no bounds, material or temporal:

> Then Bounce ('tis all that Bounce can crave)
> Shall wag her Tail within the Grave.†

(ll. 81–82)

In a codicil that clearly dates this part of the poem to late 1733 or early 1734, when the last epistle of the *Essay on Man* was about to be published, Bounce announces in her own inimitable doggerel much the same intention on her master's part as that which he himself had disclosed at the end of his first Horatian imitation: a shift to satiric comment on the political regime:

> And tho' no Doctors, Whig or Tory ones,
> Except the Sect of *Pythagoreans*,
> Have Immortality assign'd

---

* Alternate name for Ascanius, Aeneas's son, to whom here the Prince of Wales is paralleled: hope of the Opposition, as Ascanius was of the venture to found Rome. Evander, friendly king of the Italian lands where Rome will one day rise, goes attended by two guardian dogs (*Aeneid*, 8: 461–67).
† Actually Bounce did not have to wait so long. The Prince, who had made Pope a complimentary visit in the autumn of 1735, accepted one of her pups some months after this poem appeared, its collar inscribed with probably the most widely quoted couplet Pope ever wrote:

> I am his Highness' Dog at Kew;
> Pray tell me Sir, whose Dog are you?—

keeping just visible, however, beneath the witticism, a note of distaste for the parasitic scheme of things that gives the verses their double sense.

To any Beast, but *Dryden's* Hind:★
Yet Master *Pope*, whom Truth and Sense
Shall call their Friend some Ages hence,
Tho' now on loftier Themes he sings
Than to bestow a Word on *Kings*,
Has sworn by *Sticks*† (the Poet's Oath,
And Dread of Dogs and Poets both)
Man and his Works he'll soon renounce,
And roar in Numbers worthy *Bounce*.

(ll. 83–94)

"Walk sober off"

Bounce proved to be a knowledgeable prophet. Over the next two years, poem after poem streamed from Pope's pen. In 1737 (besides the *Ode to Venus*), *The Second Epistle of the Second Book of Horace, Imitated by Mr. Pope* (April 28), and three weeks later, *The First Epistle of the Second Book of Horace, Imitated* (May 19). The earlier poem, though it names no addressee, is probably addressed to Pope's Rousham friend, James Dormer, whose advancement in 1735 to the rank of lieutenant general (he had held the colonelcy of the Sixth Foot since 1720 and was promoted to that of the First Troop of Horse Grenadier Guards in February 1738) it quite possibly celebrates—as well, perhaps, as his membership in Cobham's growing circle of antiministerial dissidents, to which its first verse may well allude: "Dear Col'nel! Cobham's and your Country's Friend!" Dormer, it will be remembered, was the well-upholstered "Jemmy," whose bulk, according to the Hon. George Berkeley, quoted earlier, Pope's teasing had reduced to sylphlike inanition by the time their party reached Stowe from Rousham in the summer of 1734.

Superficially a humorous survey of all the reasons for not writing poems now that he has reached maturity (while in fact actually writing one), the epistle to Dormer allows Pope to expand his presentation, begun in the earlier satires, of a way of life and system of values alternative to those of court and town. In a succession of

---

★ Dryden's *The Hind and the Panther*, in which the hind, "immortal and unchang'd," represents the Roman Church, to which Dryden had become a convert.

† Also, of course, "by Styx" (the underworld river): strongest of all oaths. Above, p. 162.

brilliant glimpses, it catches up those aspects of a madding world that make secession from it unavoidable for any person who aspires to grow wise, most particularly a poet. These range, jestingly, and sometimes not so jestingly, from the initial alienation imposed on Pope by the Penal Laws—

> Bred up at home, full early I begun
> To read in Greek, the Wrath of Peleus' Son.
> Besides, my Father taught me from a Lad,
> The better Art to know the good from bad. . . .
> For Right Hereditary tax'd and fin'd,
> He stuck to Poverty with Peace of Mind;
> And me, the Muses help'd to undergo it;
> Convict a Papist He, and I a Poet—

through the frantic hurly-burly of the contemporary London scene:

> How shall I rhime in this eternal Roar?—
>
> (line 114)

the sleaziness of current literary standards:

> Call *Tibbald Shakespear*, and he'll swear the Nine
> Dear *Cibber!* never match'd one Ode of thine—
>
> (ll. 137–38)

and the pathetic scramble for forms of permanence not granted to mortals:

> *Man*? and *for ever*? Wretch! what wou'dst thou have?—
>
> (line 252)

to a renunciatory close (highly typical of both classical Stoic "wisdom" and Pope's personal experience at age forty-nine of a new world a-dawning) such as was already inscribed at Stowe.

> You've play'd, and lov'd, and eat, and drank your fill:
> Walk sober off; before a sprightlier Age
> Comes titt'ring on, and shoves you from the stage:
> Leave such to trifle with more grace and ease,
> Whom Folly pleases, and whose Follies please.
>
> (ll. 323–27)

Less than a century later, Keats will reconstitute this sentiment in the idiom of his own personality and period:

> Thou wast not born for death, immortal bird!
> No hungry generations★ tread thee down—

and roughly a century after that, Yeats, in the idiom of *his* personality and period:

> What shall I do with this absurdity—
> O heart, O troubled heart—this caricature,
> Decrepit age, that has been tied to me
> As to a dog's tail?

All three, of course, as attitudes temporally formed, change with the whirligig of time. What does not seem to change is the pain that produces them.

"Great Friend of LIBERTY!"

The second poem, significantly anonymous, but not likely to elude attribution by any reader with an ear, was a version of Horace's epistle to Augustus, addressed with an irony almost as winning as it is withering to George Augustus of Hanover, now England's George II. Him it lauds in the grandiose style of the court panegyrists of the period, including that of the royal birthday odes of the laureate Colley Cibber, overturning every compliment (since, as the poem is careful to point out toward its close, "Praise undeserv'd is Scandal in disguise"), into a calculated insult:

> While You, great Patron of Mankind, sustain
> The balanc'd World, and open all the Main;
> Your Country, chief, in Arms abroad defend,
> At home, with Morals, Arts, and Laws amend;
> How shall the Muse, from such a Monarch, steal
> An hour, and not defraud the Publick Weal?

(ll. 1–6)

This of a monarch who had no taste for any art but music, and even that taste, because it favored masquerades and Italian opera, despised by many of his subjects. A monarch whose administration had indeed opened all the "Main," but rather to Spanish freebooters than to his country's merchant ships (Pope's intent one suspects, in using that

---

★ Keats perhaps has in mind Malthusian theories, but is also responding to the fugitive nature of human things, like Pope and Horace and many another before him.

telltale term); and several of whose "Laws," at least in the literal form of measures passed and recorded in paper "bills," had been blown up and burnt by some of those on whom they bore most heavily with an explosion of gunpowder in Westminster Hall on July 14, 1736. A monarch, furthermore, who far from inculcating either "Morals" or *mores* had gross personal habits, indulged a barbarous temper (often by kicking anyone within range), loathed his son, whored his younger daughters' governess, and now, even now (even as Pope was drafting these lines in the summer or fall of 1736) was making the beast with two backs in the "Arms abroad" of his new Hanoverian mistress, Amelie Sophie Marianne von Walmoden, subsequently to be imported into England for his entertainment like the Westphalian ham he also favored. For such ironies, as one of the best of Pope's critics remarked long ago, there is no redress.

To salute in lines of this nature the reigning monarch himself, who by long-standing convention could do no wrong, but could only be misled by evil counselors, was a conspicuously daring not to say reckless move on Pope's part. But the country was in such a state of disaffection—serious riots broke out in many parts of the kingdom during 1736, and when one of them (at Spitalfields in July between English and Irish weavers) was broken up by constables, both sides merged into a single angry crowd cursing the Germans and huzzaing for James III—that the government felt the need to act cautiously. We know from a note of Alderman Barber's that the Privy Council toyed with the idea of taking Pope into custody for his blunt tribute to Swift in this poem as Ireland's savior from Wood's halfpence. It was that line the authorities pounced on. But there was subtler criticism in the verses surrounding it, which praise the dean both for willing his estate to found an asylum for the insane, and for being (like all true poets in Pope's view) the transmitter to posterity of infamy and fame:

> Let Ireland tell, how Wit upheld her cause,
> Her Trade supported, and supply'd her Laws;
> And leave on SWIFT this grateful verse ingrav'd,
> The Rights a Court attack'd. a Poet sav'd.
> Behold the hand that wrought a Nation's cure,
> Stretch'd to relieve the Idiot and the Poor,
> Proud Vice to brand, or injur'd Worth adorn,
> And stretch the Ray to Ages yet unborn.

(ll. 221–28)

The passage as a whole compliments Wit and Poetry as exemplified in Swift for shouldering responsibilities that any proper shepherd of his people (such is the clear implication of every line) would have regarded as the first duties of the throne. The entire poem, in fact, despite its amusing Horatian deprecations of the poetic itch—

> Yet Sir, reflect, the mischief is not great;
> These Madmen [poets] never hurt the Church or State:
> Sometimes the Folly benefits mankind;
> And rarely Av'rice taints the tuneful mind.
> Allow him but his Play-thing of a Pen,
> He ne'er rebels, or plots, like other men.
>
> (ll. 189–94)

> My Liege! why Writers little claim your thought,
> I guess; and, with their leave, will tell the fault:
> We Poets are (upon a Poet's word)
> Of all mankind, the creatures most absurd:
> The season, when to come, and when to go,
> To sing, or cease to sing, we never know;
> And if we will recite nine hours in ten,
> You lose your patience, just like other men—
>
> (ll. 356–63)

records vividly the abdication of the king and court from their ancient function as center and guide of the nation's culture and moral life and their replacement in that role, as most governments continue to be replaced today, by the conscience of the serious writer and social critic—in this particular instance, the satirist.

The Privy Council, we are told, decided not to proceed against Pope on the ground that Swift's Drapier activities took place "in the late king's time." But this can only have been a face-saving maneuver. They could see as readily as any why, in the lines immediately preceding the tribute to Swift, Pope chose to stress poetry's utility as a refiner of speech, and they knew perfectly well whose graceless English (George Augustus never seriously undertook to master the language of the people who had made him king) was being laughed at:

> What will a Child learn sooner than a song?
> What better teach a Foreigner the tongue?
> What's long or short, each accent where to place,
> And speak in publick with some sort of grace.
>
> (ll. 205–8)

Nor could they easily have missed in the same passage his contempt for precisely that species of institutionalized flattery which ministerial writers existed to turn out, which any poet who took his public function seriously would have to repudiate to retain his self-respect, and which the author of this poem could be seen to be in the act of repudiating by converting compliment to ridicule before their very eyes:

> I scarce can think him [the poet] such a worthless thing,
> Unless he praise some monster of a King,
> Or Virtue, or Religion turn to sport,
> To please a lewd, or un-believing Court.
>
> (ll. 209–12)

Perilous stuff! Yet how could a government deal with it without calling public attention to what it had to hope few would notice and fewer still have the effrontery to apply to George II? especially as Pope had created a diversion by shifting focus suddenly in the next line to Charles II, in whom it was the obligation of dutiful Hanoverians to see, if not a monster, at least "New woes again."

The three words just quoted come from one of the interpolations which were made in Dryden's play *King Arthur* when it was revived in late 1735 and which have the signal virtue (all too plainly they have no other) of bringing before us the tone of Court propaganda, to which Pope's epistle is in some sense a formal rebuttal. The second of these interpolations, purporting to be Merlin's prophecy to King Arthur of Britain's great glories to come, offers a thumbnail sketch of British history that gives short shrift to most of it. Brushing quickly by the far past, depositing on each subsequent era an unenlightening cliché, and omitting Queen Anne altogether (the only Stuart whom in 1735 it still might be dangerous to depreciate?), the prophecy rises in a language as unspeakable as its content to climax in a horse, emblem of the House of Hanover:

> And Lo [says Merlin], it opens to my wondrous View . . .
> A Reign of many Tyrants [the Commonwealth]—Restoration,
> New Woes again [Charles II]—an Abdicated King [James II],
> A glorious Stranger—born for Reformation
> And Britain's peace [William III]—and Lo a little forward
> Where from the German Shore a Stately Horse
> Advances, joining to our British Lyon.
> England[,] date thence the whitest Hour of State[—]
> Thence in a Gay Successive Order Shine

> Peace and her Golden Train—nor can the Eye
> Of long Futurity foresee a Change,
> But happiness must last till Time decay.

Inanities of this caliber, which abound throughout the 1730s, help one understand the motivating force behind Pope's ironies and the grounds of his increasing effort to engage satirically the debasements—moral, cultural, political, and linguistic—that he believed he saw about him on all sides.

"Persuasion tips his tongue"

The first eight months of 1738 brought a veritable downpour of new poems. On January 23, the *Sixth Epistle of the First Book of Horace Imitated*; on March 1, *An Imitation of the Sixth Satire of the Second Book of Horace*; on March 7, the *First Epistle of the First Book of Horace Imitated*; on May 16, *One Thousand Seven Hundred and Thirty-Eight. A Dialogue Something like Horace*; on June 22, *The Universal Prayer. By the Author of the Essay on Man*; and on July 18, *One Thousand Seven Hundred and Thirty-Eight. Dialogue II*. With this last piece, Pope's Horatian phase comes to an end. In fact, apart from a few very minor things, his publishing career also comes to an end—for a period of nearly four years. There were reasons, as we shall see.

The Sixth Epistle of the First Book was again addressed to young Murray, who at about this time must have been at work on the eloquent appeal he was to deliver in March before the Commons in support of the merchants' protest against Spanish encroachments on their shipping: an appeal that was essentially an attack on Walpole's foreign policy. In days to come, Murray was to be a speaker of immense forensic reputation, particularly excelling, in the judgment of Edmund Burke, in drawing up the statement of a case. "This of itself," Burke commented, "was worth the argument of any other man." At this early stage, however, he was still perfecting his oratorical gift under the elocutionary tutelage of Pope, the latter, as one of Murray's biographers suggests, having "caught in the beauty of Murray's voice echoes of those tones which had earned for himself the title of 'the little nightingale.'" The epistle itself, in any case, though it descants amiably enough on some of Horace's and also Pope's favorite theses about the art of living, is not among the poet's best and even manages to commit, at one point, the kind of crashing bathos at which he had poked such ridicule in *The Art of Sinking in Poetry*. "Grac'd as thou art with all the Power of Words," he remarks

80. William Murray, 1st Earl of Mansfield (1705–1793). By J. B. Van Loo.

Grac'd as thou art, with all the Pow'r of Words.

Imit. Hor., Ep. I, vi: 48.

Courtesy of the National Portrait Gallery, London.

promisingly in his tribute to his young friend; but then: "So known, so honour'd at the House of Lords" (ll. 48–49). A resounding anticlimax that later, it is said, Colley Cibber immortalized:

> Persuasion tips his tongue whene'er he talks,
> And he has chambers in the King's Bench Walks.

Still, the poem's not being among its author's best is unlikely to have improved the court and ministry's opinion of it. They cannot have been much pleased to see "the gifts of Kings" (i.e., orders of merit, peerages, lucrative appointments) dismissed with the same scorn as "the Mob's applauses"; or the future career of their young opponent William Murray compared to that of Cicero (who had exposed Catiline, often in Opposition writing a cant name for Walpole) or to that of Clarendon (Charles II's lord chancellor, who when his royal master sought to encroach on parliamentary independence resisted him with such determination—so, at any rate, ran the Opposition's propaganda—as led to his dismissal, trial for treason, and exile). All this, of course, in implied contrast to the behavior of the present minister. That the poem alluded only eight lines further along to similar integrity on the part of Clarendon's great grandson, Henry Hyde, Viscount Cornbury, one of the so-called Young Patriot group who were also giving Walpole trouble, only sharpened the affront. For it was well known that on his return from the Grand Tour, having been offered a very handsome government pension by his brother-in-law Lord Essex, Cornbury had refused it with the reply: "How could you tell, my Lord, that I was to be sold? or at least, how could you know my price so exactly?" Hence the poem's advice to all restless pursuers of illusory goods—

> Would ye be blest? despise low Joys, low Gains;
> Disdain whatever CORNBURY disdains—

carried a political as well as philosophical message, as did also its later reference to the king's refusal to raise the Prince of Wales' allowance following his marriage (ll. 83–84)—a characteristic stinginess deplored by many of his own supporters.

"A Story of two Mice"

On March 1, the epistle to Murray was followed by an adaptation of Horace's *Sixth Satire of the Second Book*. This time Pope rose brilliantly to the challenge—in fact, a double challenge. On the one hand, Horace, among whose many celebrations of the reflective retired life as against the hurly-burly of the urban rumor mill and gold rush, this

81. Henry Hyde, Viscount Cornbury (1710–1753). By George Knapton.
The cup is inscribed "Res Publica".

> Would ye be blest? despise low Joys, low Gains;
> Disdain whatever CORNBURY disdains.
>
> *Imit. Hor., Ep.* I, vi: 60–61.

By kind permission of The Society of Dilettanti. Photograph: Courtauld
Institute of Art.

is surely the most delectable; on the other hand, Swift. Swift had adapted roughly the first half of this poem as long ago as 1714, using it with great charm to commemorate his intimacy with Harley, while protesting (not without a certain pride) that the minister's demand for his presence in London interfered with his enjoyment of the "Country Seat" now provided him in Ireland—which, however, as he does not fail to remind his mentor, he would willingly relinquish for a similarly funded post in Britain, somewhere "this side Trent."

As one might guess from this beginning, the part of Horace's poem that most captures Swift's imagination, or at least elicits his liveliest response, is the part delineating the precious bane of being known to be (in Horace's case) Maecenas's, (in Swift's) Harley's confidant and friend:

> "Tomorrow my Appeal comes on,
> "Without your help the Cause is gone—
> The Duke expects my Lord and you
> About some great Affair, at Two—
> "Put my Lord Bolingbroke in mind,
> "To get my Warrant quickly sign'd. . . .
> "I doubt not, if his Lordship knew—
> "And, Mr. Dean, one word from you." . . .
>
> (ll. 71–6, 81–2)

Several passages in this vein so brilliantly evoke power even while the poet is busy disclaiming it and insisting that his weekly tours with Harley down to Windsor (the very name a further claim to influence) are merely companionable sorties,

> Where all that passes, *inter nos*,
> Might be proclaim'd at Charing–Cross,
>
> (ll. 99–100)

that the return to country joys which follows seems, for Swift, remarkably formulaic and almost, indeed, to invite an ironic reading:

> Oh, could I see my Country Seat!
> There, leaning near a gentle Brook,
> Sleep, or peruse some ancient Book,
> And there in sweet oblivion drown
> Those Cares that haunt the Court and Town.
>
> (ll. 128–32)

Coming from Swift, such lines tease one into hearing beneath them a subliminal small voice retracting every syllable.

At this point, Pope takes over. He is plainly on his mettle to make of the remainder of the poem, in which Horace develops the attractions of retirement, as felicitous an adaptation as Swift had made of the section on urban wheeling and dealing, and to make it in Swift's favorite meter and so far as possible in his idiom. Sleep, oblivion, and ancient books are therefore speedily left behind (as they are also in the Latin) for a scene of idealized domesticity in which even Bounce and her puppies appear to be included and where chitchat, laughter, and unassuming sociability—

> My Friends above, my Folks below,
> Chatting and laughing all-a-row,
> The Beans and Bacon set before 'em,
> The Grace-cup serv'd with all decorum.
> Each willing to be pleas'd, and please,
> And even the very Dogs at ease—
>
> (ll. 135–40)

do not necessarily preclude considerations of a graver sort:

> Here no man prates of idle things,
> How this or that Italian sings,
> A Neighbour's Madness, or his Spouse's,
> Or what's in either of the *Houses*,
> But something much more our concern. . . .
> What good, or better, we may call,
> And what, the very best of all.
>
> (ll. 141–5, 151–2)

From this frame of mind, it is a short step indeed to the fable of the country mouse and city mouse with which Horace concludes his poem and which Pope retells with a grace and verve not likely to be soon matched in English. The country mouse, like Bounce in the earlier poem, embodies the kind of hardihood and self-reliance that every urbanizing nation seems at some point in history to have associated with country living, and at some later point in history to have feared (not always in the long run wrongly) it might be losing. The city mouse—in Pope's version typically, like Fop, a courtier—illustrates the ease with which a people can become dependent if it allows itself to do so, or, especially, as the Opposition liked to think, if actively encouraged by Walpolian hand-outs.

To prepare the entertainment of his city cousin the country mouse goes all out, but always within the modest limits of his means:

> A frugal Mouse upon the whole,
> Yet lov'd his Friend, and had a Soul;

Knew what was handsome, and wou'd do 't,
On just occasion, *coute qui coute*.
He brought him Bacon (nothing lean)
Pudding, that might have pleas'd a Dean;
Cheese such as men in Suffolk make,
But wish'd it Stilton for his sake;
Yet to his Guest tho' no way sparing,
He eat himself the Rind and paring.

(ll. 161–70)

Alas, to no avail. Though the city mouse is gentleman enough not to show his revulsion at the food ("He did his best to seem to eat"), he cannot conceal his conviction that this is no way for any self-respecting mouse to live. Off they go, accordingly, to town; to the kind of quarters in the West End that "Our Courtier" mouse has grown used to, living on the luxurious leavings of the rich and powerful:

('Twas on the night of a Debate,
When all their Lordships had sate late.) . . .
Palladian walls, Venetian doors,
Grotesco roofs, and Stucco floors: . . .*
The Guests withdrawn had left the Treat,
And down the Mice sate, *Tête à tête*.

(ll. 187–88, 193–94, 198–99)

The "moral" is soon evident: ancient, hackneyed, but not without a certain continuing pertinence even for nations with trillion-dollar national debts. While the city mouse enjoys the role of docent—

Our Courtier walks from dish to dish,
Tastes for his Friend of Fowl and Fish;
Tells all their names, lays down the law,
Que ça est bon! Ah goutez ça!
That Jelly's rich, this Malmsey healing,
Pray dip your Whiskers and your Tail in,"

(ll. 200–5)

and the country mouse the role of willing scholar—

"I'm quite asham'd—'tis mighty rude
"To eat so much—but all's so good.

---

* The City Mouse's habitation—"a tall house near Lincoln's-Inn" (l. 186)—is rather plainly the dwelling of the Duke of Newcastle, a further stroke of satire since Newcastle, though incorrupt himself, was Walpole's chief paymaster and manager of corrupt elections.

"I have a thousand thanks to give—
"My Lord alone knows how to live"—

(ll. 208–11)

a sudden hubbub is heard from the servants' hall, and in rush all those who equally depend on rich men's leavings (and livings): chaplain, butler, dogs, and cat:

O for the Heart of Homer's Mice,
Or Gods to save them in a trice!
(It was by Providence, they think,
For your damn'd Stucco has no chink)
"An't please your Honour, quoth the Peasant,
"This same Dessert is not so pleasant:
"Give me again my hollow Tree!
"A Crust of Bread, and Liberty."

(ll. 216–23)

Although some years after publishing this piece Pope confided to Spence that the dean "did not think it at all a right imitation of his style," it is probably safe to say that no one so far has come closer.

"Is this my Guide, Philosopher, and Friend?"

Up to this point, the government's gazetteers and other minions had left Pope pretty much alone in print, except, possibly, for covert operations. Curll, we know, was in touch with Walpole as an informer, at least sporadically, from about 1718, and while this arrangement must have had to do chiefly with keeping tabs on printers and booksellers who handled Opposition material, it probably did not diminish his taste for embarrassing Pope when opportunity offered. That eccentric cleric, John Henley, better known as "Orator Henley," was also in Walpole's pay and kept up from about 1730 a stream of gutter abuse of the poet, both from his pulpit in the so-called Oratory Chapel in Lincoln's Inn Fields and in his newspaper *The Hyp-Doctor*, issued from 15 December 1730 to 20 January 1741. The paper's title may be freely translated as "Physician-for-what ails us," the "Hyp" or "Hyps" being a slang term at the time for low spirits or hypochondria; and "what-ails-us" (it needs no emphasis) signified in that day as in ours whatever the government in power happened not to like, especially criticism, or any revelation in the media of its backstairs intrigues. Although Henley had been awarded in the *Dunciad* the niche he so richly deserved, it is difficult to believe that his sixteen-year animus against Pope owed nothing of its stamina to his annual retainer of £100 (some said £200) from a first minister he was content to address as "The Delegate of Caesar and of God."

We shall doubtless never learn at this late date the precise truth about the relationship of Walpole and Pope after their apparent break around 1730. The minister, however, seems not to have been altogether divorced from the general anti-Pope campaign of that decade if we may trust the testimony of the respected antiquary William Oldys. Oldys records in his *Journal* that, going to call on the widow of Thomas Odell (miscellaneous writer, theater manager, and builder of the playhouse at Goodman's Fields) shortly after his death in 1740, he was shown some of Odell's papers:

> ... mostly poems in favor of the ministry, and *against Mr. Pope.* One of them printed by the late Sir Robert Walpole's encouragement, who gave him ten guineas for writing, and as much for the expence of printing it; but through his advice it was never published, because it might hurt his interest with Lord Chesterfield, and some other noblemen, who favored Mr. Pope for his fine genius.

Since Chesterfield supported Walpole in the debate on the size of the standing army in early March 1733, but threw his weight soon after against the Excise Bill and was almost immediately punished by dismissal from his court appointment as lord steward (following which, the two men were permanently estranged), the period of the minister's concern for his "interest" with Chesterfield probably falls somewhere in the first two months of 1733. Odell's poem, in other words, seems likely to have been readied for use soon after the *Epistle to Bathurst* and the first Horatian imitation made it clear that Pope was abandoning his previously cherished position of neutrality for guerrilla war.

Though, according to Oldys, only one of Odell's attacks on Pope was subvented by Walpole, the presence of several others among his papers is a valuable reminder that at least some, and perhaps many, of the anonymous assaults on Pope at this period may have been made by persons with no special personal incentive (there is no evidence, for instance, that Odell was acquainted with Pope, and he does not appear in the *Dunciad*) beyond a desire to establish their credentials with the ministry and perhaps be singled out to join its battalion of knights of the quill. Conversely, it is only fair to recognize that the unanimous antipathy to Walpole among serious writers probably

sprang as much from his indifference to the writer's métier (except as
it might be turned to immediate advantage in support of the regime)
as from moral or political considerations. An Opposition that
counted among its leaders men like Pulteney, Bolingbroke, and,
later, Chesterfield—writers all—and among its supporters at this
period Fielding, Pope, Swift, Thomson, and, until they died,
Arbuthnot and Gay, as well as many lesser authors well known in
their day, was inevitably attractive to other aspirants to literary fame.
It might reasonably be argued, moreover, that here as sometimes
elsewhere Walpole was simply in advance of his time. If his indifference to matters literary reflects in part his own personal biases and
those of his royal master, as unquestionably it does, it may equally
reflect, in a shrewd man of business, some dim or perhaps not so dim
apprehension of the class-and-cultural shiftings, long under way by
the 1730s, whose result (referred to on an earlier page) was to push
apart the pursuits of governance and learning, strip poetry, along
with humanistic studies generally, of the high public function to
which poets like Spenser, Milton, Pope, and Shelley successively
(and vainly) laid claim, and reassign all such activities for the most
part to the quite literally private sector of the poet's and reader's
interior world.

But all this, of course, is outrageous speculation. All that can be
securely said is that with the publication of Pope's next Horatian
adaptation, *The First Epistle of the First Book*, dedicated by Horace to
Maecenas and by Pope to Bolingbroke, it became quite suddenly
respectable to attack the poet by name in the government's news
organs. Previously, this had been all but unheard of. Official policy
seems to have been to ignore his and other respected writers' references to corruption or slurs on the royal family, perhaps on the
ground that to pursue any other course only increased their circulation; perhaps too, however, because there was still a certain lingering
disrepute in being perceived by the general public to be a government
against which all writers of any talent were as one man arrayed. The
government's vulnerability on this score became only the more acute
when in 1737 Walpole forced through the Licensing Act for the stage,
the evidence supporting his move being an inexcusably obscene and
insulting farce ridiculing the king, which some thought the minister
had himself commissioned to gain his end.

With the appearance of this new poem, ministerial strategy dramatically changed. It was a tense moment politically on both sides.
Queen Caroline's death the previous November had cost Walpole his
staunchest ally in the royal family and his best leverage on the king. In

addition, the almost hysterical dislike, not to say loathing, with which both king and queen had long regarded their son—"I always hated the rascal," said the king, "false, lying, cowardly, nauseous, puppy;" "My dear first-born," said the queen, "is the greatest ass, and the greatest liar, and the greatest canaille [scum], and the greatest beast, in the whole world, and . . . I most heartily wish he was out of it"—had by this time borne its predictable fruit in the formation of a rival court gathered about him and his princess and their first child, to which most of those whom the government had alienated now happily flocked. This too was an event to give Walpole concern.

On the other hand, the Opposition was partly paralyzed as usual by the contradictory objectives of the Whigs, Tories, Jacobites, and other groups composing it. Bolingbroke—for all his faults an invaluable idea man—had been in a sense drummed out of the kingdom, his reputation so battered by the government press and by Walpole himself in a powerful speech before the Commons (a man "void of all faith or honour, and betraying every master he has ever served") that he was now a clear embarrassment to the cause, no longer trusted by the Opposition Whigs, especially his former close colleague William Pulteney. For that matter, many in the Opposition groups no longer trusted Pulteney, reckoning—rightly, as it turned out—that he would drop his principles like hot poultices on the first offer of a peerage. When, therefore, on February 3, their forces in parliament were again defeated on a motion to reduce the size of the standing army, discouragement prevailed. Sizing up their inability to act together, Hugh Hume, future third earl of Marchmont, confided to a Scots associate: "I know not what posterity may think of us, but I am of opinion they can scarcely think worse of us generally, than what we deserve."

March 3, however, brought a second chance. This time the effort was to call in question the earnestness of the ministry's efforts to solve the problem of the Spanish raids on British shipping by commandeering all papers bearing on its negotiations with Madrid. Walpole, managing to soften the motion but not to defeat it, wisely stalled for time in which to search out the documents (paper shredding was not yet among a government's options), and further debate was postponed till March 15. It was in this interval of suspense, on March 7, that Pope's epistle appeared. Politically, it says little that in one way or other he had not managed to say before. A glance at the king's domination formerly by his wife and now by his new mistress (ll. 62–63); a glance at Walpole's unblemished record in screening malefactors in high places (ll. 95–96); a glance at the court as destroyer

82. Hugh Hume, 3rd Earl of Marchmont (1708–1774). By Pierre Falconet, 1769.

"I shall never see any Good or any Evil happen in this Country, but I shall immediately ask myself the question, How will it please or displease Lord Marchmont? and I shall set my own Mind by that." Pope to Marchmont, 22 June 1740.

Courtesy of the National Galleries of Scotland, Edinburgh.

of virtues (ll. 118–19): none of these charges was new and all were less cutting than many he had made before. (Nothing, after all, could ever quite top the implications he had directed at the rule of the king and his first minister in calling Lord Hervey their Sporus.) Morally, the same is true: as one might expect of an imitation of Horace, the poem hews to a line handed down by poets, philosophers, and prophets ever since Amos came out of the hills of Tekoa crying, "Hate the evil and love the good. . . . Let judgment run down as waters and right- eousness as a mighty stream":

> 'Tis the first Virtue, Vices to abhor;
> And the first Wisdom, to be Fool no more.
> But to the World, no bugbear is so great,
> As want of figure, and a small Estate. . . .
> Alike in nothing but one Lust of Gold,
> Just half the land would buy, and half be sold:
> Their Country's wealth our mightier Misers drain,
> Or cross, to plunder Provinces, the Main:
> The rest, some farm the Poor-box, some the Pews;
> Some keep Assemblies, and wou'd keep the Stews. . . .
> While with the silent growth of ten per Cent,
> In Dirt and darkness hundreds stink content.
>
> (*Imit. Hor., Ep.* I, i: 65–8, 124–29, 132–33)

Most of the poem, for that matter, like its Horatian original, had less to do with either politics or public morals than with some not altogether light-hearted self-questionings, as real for Pope as for his Roman model. How far into age, for instance, can one expect one's poetic gift to last?

> A Voice there is, that whispers in my ear,
> ('Tis Reason's voice, which sometimes one can hear)
> "Friend Pope! be prudent, let your Muse take breath,
> "And never gallop Pegasus to death;
> "Lest stiff, and stately, void of fire, or force,
> "You limp, like Blackmore, on a Lord Mayor's horse."
>
> (ll. 11–16)

And even if that be not a problem (as it certainly was not yet for one who could make verse so tellingly enact both Pegasus' gallop and the ponderous limp of the Lord Mayor's elderly steed), does there not come a time in every life when energies must be reoriented toward that self-possession, self-sufficiency, and self-discipline which the ancients called the *summum bonum* and the proper study of mankind?

> That task, which as we follow, or despise,
> The eldest is a fool, the youngest wise;
> Which done, the poorest can no wants endure,
> And which not done, the richest must be poor.
>
> (ll. 43–46)

Yet how achieve a consummation that seems to run against the very grain of human nature: its mutabilities, incongruities, predilection for ephemera:

> You laugh, half Beau half Sloven if I stand,
> My Wig all powder, and all snuff my Band;
> You laugh, if Coat and Breeches strangely vary,
> White Gloves, and Linnen worthy Lady Mary!
> But when no Prelate's Lawn with Hair-shirt lin'd,
> Is half so incoherent as my Mind,
> When (each Opinion with the next at strife,
> One ebb and flow of follies all my Life)
> I plant, root up, I build, and then confound,
> Turn round to square, and square again to round;
> You never change one muscle of your face,
> You think this Madness but a common case, . . .
> Careless how ill I with myself agree,
> Kind to my dress, my figure, not to Me.
> Is this my Guide, Philosopher, and Friend?
>
> (ll. 161–72, 175–77)

There was certainly not much in all this to raise a ministry's mislike. The poem's offensiveness, obviously, lay in the compliments it paid to Bolingbroke (that "Greatest of all Criminals," as the gazetteers had for some time decided), and, probably more important, paid at a moment when Walpole was coming under heavy fire from the literary Opposition generally. One of the world's dullest "epics" had sold like hot cakes the preceding spring because it was seen to be a manifesto for patriotic resistance to ministerial corruption, while at the same time, despite the Great Criminal's absence abroad, a new generation of gifted young men was rallying to the program of political idealism that he had been unfolding in his writings since 1730, many of these as yet circulating only in manuscript. Whatever political theorists may conclude about the practicality of Bolingbroke's proposals, or psychologists about the nature of his motives (doubtless not very different from the usual politician's mix of consuming ambition and genuine conviction), his teachings were

shrewder than Walpole's in at least one respect: they called for qualities of altruism, public spirit, and personal rectitude such as the
young, almost always more generous than their elders, have
throughout history often fervently responded to, and in the group
variously known as "Cobham's Cubs," the "Cousinhood," and the
"Young Patriots" they were doing so now.

Young Patriots

There was young Cornbury—"polish'd Cornbury," Thomson calls
him in his *Seasons*—at present twenty-eight. His sentiment in rejecting the proffered pension was altogether in tune with Bolingbroke's program for a politics of "patriotism" and with Jacobite
sympathies of his own. Later he would write his cousin, striking a
note not often heard in the Walpole years: "Every thought of mine is
now confined to serve this country while I live, and manure it when I
die." There was also young Murray, whom we have met before, aged
thirty-three. Besides taking on Walpole as spokesman for the merchants' grievance against Spain, he had become counsel for the city of
Edinburgh in its resistance to the bill of disenfranchisement and other
penalties promoted by the Walpole ministry against it. In 1736, a
certain John Porteous, British captain of the city garrison, between
whom and the citizens of Edinburgh there had long been bad blood,
ordered his men to open fire on a crowd assembled to protest the
execution of a smuggling merchant, Andrew Wilson. Though the
evidence in such situations is always cloudy, the crowd does not
appear to have been getting out of hand and Porteous does appear to
have commanded his men to shoot at the protesters rather than over
their heads. In any event, some eight persons were killed, twice as
many wounded. Porteous, tried by Scots judges and sentenced to be
hanged, was immediately pardoned by Queen Caroline, acting as
regent that summer while her husband was "in Arms abroad." This
infuriated the people of Edinburgh (raising the vexed question of
judicial hegemony and all those other Scots–English tensions that
persist even today) to the point at which some of them, several re-
portedly in high place and disguised as women, broke into the prison,
seized Porteous, and ceremoniously carried out the sentence of their
court. In the end, thanks partly to Murray's efforts, working with the
duke of Argyll, not a Scot was punished, other penalties were shrunk
to a token, and the ministry and court in London digested a rankling
defeat. Though strictly speaking not a member of the Young Patriots,

Murray was friendly with them all and an equal admirer of Bolingbroke's.

Included centrally in the group were the Grenville brothers: Richard, twenty-seven in 1738, and George, twenty-six, both nephews of Cobham, both subsequently important figures in the ministries of the midcentury, though often on opposite sides; Richard's brother-in-law William Pitt, just turned thirty—"the Great Commoner," as English history would know him later——eventually prime minister and first earl of Chatham, one of Parliament's most gifted speakers and Murray's lifelong rival, though at this time united with him in opposing Walpole; and George Lyttelton, whose age was twenty-nine. Made secretary to the Prince of Wales in 1737, Lyttelton was in some sense, despite his unfitness for the task, whip and spokesman for the group. In the background stood Cobham, uncle to the Grenvilles and to Lyttelton, at whose Stowe a communion of purpose seems to have been first consolidated during the summer of 1735; Chesterfield, of an intermediate generation, now (after the *Craftsman*'s demise) helping to establish *Common Sense*, a new Opposition journal; and Pope. A little to one side, like Murray, but along with Pope probably Bolingbroke's greatest admirer in England, stood Murray's fellow Scot, Hugh Hume, now Lord Polwarth, but soon, on the death of his father, to be third earl of Marchmont. He, like Pitt, was thirty.

An extraordinary group! all, of course, ambitious; some very ambitious indeed; and no Sir Galahads among them. Yet all, during their youth, and some throughout their careers brought a standard of integrity to political life that had been rare before. Cornbury's views we have sampled. Pitt astonished his colleagues repeatedly by refusing to reap the illicit profits by long custom attached to his various posts. Lyttelton, too gawky, clumsy, and naive for enduring political success, was nevertheless for several years a power to be reckoned with through his influence with the Prince and was not for sale. No more was Marchmont. Walpole in public might reflect with scorn on young unseasoned politicians; but his true estimate is better indicated by his willingness to offer Thomas Pitt, who controlled several seats in the House, "any terms" to keep his younger brother William and his brother-in-law Lyttelton out of it, and by his care to prevent Marchmont, whose speaking abilities he did not underestimate, from serving in the House of Lords as a representative Scots peer. With the same shrewdness (for which there are other names), he had seen to it that Bolingbroke, when pardoned in 1724, was not restored to the House of Lords. And in early 1736, when young Pitt

83. George Lyttelton, 1st Baron Lyttelton (1709–1773). Engraving by
G. H. Every after Reynolds.

> Free as young Lyttelton, her cause pursue,
> Still true to Virtue, and as warm as true.

Imit. Hor., Ep., I, i: 29–30.

alluded ironically during his maiden speech to the despatch and generosity of the king in arranging a marriage for the prince that everyone knew he had done all in his power to delay or prevent, though Walpole could not expel him the House, he took the next best revenge by depriving him of his post in the army as cornet of horse.

Thus if Walpole's opponents exaggerated their country's danger, as political Oppositions tend to, one can nevertheless see why "Virtue" ("To Virtue only, and her Friends, a Friend")—meaning essentially to put the good of the commonwealth above one's own—became in the thinking of many at this time the indispensable condition of "Liberty" ("Give me again my hollow Tree! A Crust of Bread, and Liberty")—meaning essentially escape from Walpole's control by jettisoning those desires for eminence and riches that so easily rendered one his "Slave." For the degree and nature of that control was no longer a laughing matter. In the words of his most recent biographer, summing up his position by the middle 1730s:

> For ten years he had dominated the political life of the country, defeating intrigue, grinding down opposition. . . . He became so used to his own greatness that he no longer bothered to adjust himself to circumstances. His sensibilities hardened. His language, always coarse, became brutal; his attitude to friends and foes franker, more unguarded. . . . He grew impatient of criticism, regarded with hostility men of strong will who would not accept his yoke, bullied weaker characters with a coarseness and brutality that shocked. . . . And, of course, he found it difficult to brook rivals; his career is littered with the broken careers of gifted men who crossed his path—Pulteney, Carteret, Townshend, Chesterfield, Cobham —and apart from Hardwicke, a man of massive moral integrity and great intelligence, and one or two others, he surrounded himself with faint replicas of himself or fools and flatterers. . . . Not only was his power resented; . . . his whole manner of life bred detestation. . . . He paraded his wealth . . . ; his huge ungainly figure sparkled with diamonds and flashed with satin. And he gloried in his power, . . . and let the whole world know that he was master.

Possibly because of the attitudes just described, more probably because he sensed a possible threat in the rise of the Young Patriot group, all at the moment hostile to him and friendly with the prince, all deriving something of their ideology from Bolingbroke and something of their personal inspiration from Pope, with whom they met at Twickenham, Stowe, and elsewhere, Walpole gave his gazetteers free rein when the epistle to Bolingbroke appeared. Month after month for

more than a year, the government news-organs, as well as poems and
pamphlets not impossibly government inspired, handled severely
and sometimes savagely both the reprobate poet who could praise
such a criminal as Bolingbroke (the compliments paid him earlier in
the *First Satire of the Second Book* and the *Essay on Man*, at that time
mostly ignored, now came in for attention) and the scandalous
satirist who could perversely use the work of Horace and Donne to
embarrass a virtuous administration: a trick all the guiltier since he
himself was by no means (as Lord Hervey put it somewhat later in
what was essentially a summary of the ministry's position) the virtuous figure he affected to be, but "a *bad Companion*, a *dangerous
Acquaintance*, an *inveterate, implacable Enemy*, *no body's Friend*, a *noxious
Member of Society*, and a *thorough bad Man*." One can only admire the
fervor with which persons in high place have always been drawn to
the New Testament's position on the casting of stones.

CHAPTER 27

OPEN CHALLENGES

"But Horace, *Sir, was delicate, was nice"*

Among Pope's earliest assailants in the government press that spring was one who challenged him on his own poetical ground. Speaking of Bolingbroke, this gazetteer wrote:

> Far, far from Courts, hence, wisely trust for Fame
> To *Twick'nam*'s Bowers, and the Banks of *Thame*,
> By gentle Bard be sung in gentle Strain,
> And the calm *Hero* of a *Couplet* reign;
> So may thy Virtues tinkle in our Ear,
> Thy *Honour spotless*, and thy *Soul sincere*;
> Safe from thy Arts, so may thy harmless Praise
> In harmless Song our *Doubt* and *Pleasure* raise;
> Our *Doubt*, so true a *Briton* e'er cou'd be;
> Our *Mirth*, to find that *B—ling—ke* is *He*.

For Pope, from any point of view, these had to be fighting words. Not merely because they belittled Bolingbroke, for whom his devotion cannot easily be exaggerated, or because they mocked his famous line on Addison. In their sneering "tinkle," "gentle Bard," and "gentle Strain," not to mention "harmless Song" and "calm Hero of a Couplet," they belittled poetry as well. They treated it with the same disdain that the administration had shown in appointing a Cibber poet laureate. In particular, they expressed that segregation of wit from "sense," of imagination from the serious business of society, which Pope had fought against throughout his career, and which every serious artist is obliged to fight against if he is not to see his willingness to scorn delights and live laborious days dismissed as trifling. Such patronizing attitudes, voiced again and again by the administration's gazetteers, but especially during that month of high political excitement (April 1738), when Opposition hopes were reviving for a victorious showdown on the Spanish question (Walpole had won in March, but indecisively) could not go unchallenged.

Nor did they. In two of the most eloquent poems of his career,

Pope demonstrated to his own satisfaction and the admiration of posterity that a great poet's poetry does not "tinkle," need not be "harmless," and is, in fact, first cousin to that other art "whose end, both at the first and now, was and is, to hold, as 'twere, the mirror up to nature, to show virtue her own feature, scorn [i.e., what is to be scorned] her own image, and the very age and body of the time his form and pressure."

The earlier of the two, *One Thousand Seven Hundred and Thirty Eight. A Dialogue Something like Horace,* chiefly holds up its glass to what is to be scorned. One of its two voices is that of the poet—any poet, but here of course with particular reference to Pope himself—defending his turf, his weapon, his right to use it. The other voice is that of a "Friend": a typical ministerial timeserver whose advice may be taken to represent both the establishment and the cautionary or Sancho Panza side of the poet's own heroic quixoticism, still opting naively for virtue in a world gone mad. Using many of the same arguments as the government's gazetteers, this spokesman launches an attack ostensibly on the abuses of satire, but actually on satire generally and, if considered in its ultimate implications, on poetry as anything other than an entertaining toy. Nobody, says he, could object to a poet's writing poems if they could be counted on to serve the interests of the regime; or to his writing satires, even, if they did not name names; or to his naming names if he excluded persons currently in power or if what he said about them were presented in Newspeak. For "*Horace,* Sir," urges the friend, pointing unconsciously to the reason why Pope had called this poem "*Something like*" (but not entirely like) the Roman poet:

> was delicate, was nice;
> *Bubo* observes, he lash'd no sort of Vice:
> *Horace* would say, *Sir* Billy *serv'd the Crown,*
> Blunt *could do Bus'ness,* H[u]ggins *knew the Town,*
> In *Sappho* touch the *Failing of the Sex,*
> In rev'rend Bishops note some *small Neglects,*
> And own, the *Spaniard* did a *waggish thing,*
> Who cropt our Ears, and sent them to the King.
> His sly, polite, insinuating stile
> Could please at Court, and make AUGUSTUS smile:
> An artful Manager, that crept between
> His Friend and Shame, and was a kind of *Screen.*

(ll. 11–22)

As in our own day, euphemism and corruption work hand in hand.

For heaven knows, the "Friend" continues, there are "safe" subjects enough to keep you out of mischief. For instance, all those things and people that aren't really "with it" any more:

> Why, yes: with Scripture still you may be free;
> A Horse-laugh, if you please, at *Honesty*;
> A Joke on JEKYL, or some odd *Old Whig*,
> Who never chang'd his Principle, or Wig:
> A Patriot is a Fool in ev'ry age,
> Whom all Lord Chamberlains allow the Stage:
> These nothing hurts; they keep their Fashion still,
> And wear their strange old Virtue as they will.
>
> (ll. 37–44)

Even the rich and powerful need not be immune if you show a little tact: "If Satire know its Time and Place, You still may lash the Greatest—in Disgrace." Satire causes trouble only when it turns on people who deserve it. A good satirist has better sense:

> To Vice and Folly to confine the jest,
> Sets half the World, God knows, against the rest;
> Did not the Sneer of more impartial men
> At Sense and Virtue, balance all agen.
> Judicious Wits spread wide the Ridicule,
> And charitably comfort Knave and Fool.
>
> (ll. 57–62)

Perhaps so, replies the "Poet," but haven't you noticed how the common people get out of hand when no one reproaches vice in their betters?

> *Virtue*, I grant you, is an empty boast;
> But shall the Dignity of *Vice* be lost?
> Ye Gods! shall *Cibber*'s Son, without rebuke
> Swear like a Lord? or *Rich* out-whore a Duke?
> A Fav'rite's *Porter* with his Master vie,
> Be brib'd as often, and as often lie?
> Shall *Ward* draw Contracts with a Statesman's skill?
> Or *Japhet* pocket, like his Grace, a Will?
> Is it for *Bond* or *Peter* (paltry Things!)
> To pay their Debts or keep their Faith like Kings?
>
> (ll. 113–22)

You will agree that such vice in low places is shocking? We must activate those great social therapists, the Church and the Law, which have never hesitated to prescribe to the powerless:

> This, this, my friend, I cannot, must not bear;
> Vice thus abus'd, demands a Nation's care;
> This calls the Church to deprecate our Sin,
> And hurls the Thunder of the Laws on *Gin*.
>
> (ll. 127–30)

To tell truth, there is an essential distinction in these matters of vice and virtue that you ministerial types sometimes overlook. Virtuous behavior is the same wherever found, whether in an itinerant Quaker woman raising funds for medical treatment of the indigent in Edinburgh (l. 133), or in "humble Allen" of Bath, always a generous and usually an anonymous contributor to those in need (ll. 135–36). (Allen was soon to join with Pope in guaranteeing the support of the feckless poet Richard Savage, and during the terrible winter of 1740, when it was so cold that horse races were held on the Thames and sheep were roasted over open fires on the ice, employed hundreds of additional men in his Bath stone quarries to keep their families alive.)

> *Virtue* may chuse the high or low Degree,
> 'Tis just alike to Virtue, and to me;
> Dwell in a Monk, or light upon a King,
> She's still the same, belov'd, contented thing.
>
> (ll. 137–40)

Not so with Vice, old chap. A little countenancing from people like you and it is amazing how she changes:

> Vice is undone, if she forgets her Birth,
> And stoops from Angels to the Dregs of Earth:
> But 'tis the *Fall* degrades her to a Whore;
> Let *Greatness* own her, and she's mean no more:
> Her Birth, her Beauty, Crowds and Courts confess,
> Chaste Matrons praise her, and grave Bishops bless.
>
> (ll. 141–46)

And though I know you didn't intend to take matters this far when we began our little dialogue, let me show you now, as in a Roman triumph, or in one of those allegorical *Trionfi* that the Renaissance painters were so fond of, just how far we have come under the cynical principle of your master (and of *his* master) that everything is for sale:

> In golden Chains the willing World she draws,
> And hers the Gospel is, and hers the Laws:
> Mounts the Tribunal, lifts her scarlet head,
> And sees pale Virtue carted in her stead!
> Lo! at the wheels of her Triumphal Car,
> Old *England*'s Genius, rough with many a Scar,
> Dragg'd in the Dust! his Arms hang idly round,
> His Flag inverted trails along the ground!
>
> (ll. 147–54)

Most appalling of all, however, is the prostitution implicit in the entire system, hopeful Sporuses rushing to be castrated, as far as the eye can see:

> See thronging Millions to the Pagod run,
> And offer Country, Parent, Wife, or Son!
> Hear her black Trumpet thro' the Land proclaim,
> That "Not to be corrupted is the Shame." . . .
> All, all look up, with reverential Awe,
> On Crimes that scape, or triumph o'er the Law:
> While Truth, Worth, Wisdom, daily they decry—
> "Nothing is Sacred now but Villany."
>
> (ll. 157–60, 167–70)

Except of course to that solitary defender before the walls of Troy, for whom "this Verse (if such a Verse remain)" will "Show there was one who held it in disdain." (ll. 171–72.)

"The Affront is mine, my Friend, and should be yours"

The poem we have been looking at was published on 16 May 1738, four days after Pope's friend, the future earl of Marchmont, had told a correspondent in Scotland that in his view the Opposition was "at an end," and one day after a bill put forward in the House to force Walpole's hand on war with Spain had been handily defeated despite the Opposition's best showing in some time. Two months later, on July 18, Pope published a sequel: *One Thousand Seven Hundred and Thirty-Eight. Dialogue II*, which clearly communicates in its final lines his disillusionment with the movement he has been supporting.

Disillusionment is not, of course, all that the poem conveys. It begins with an ironic tour de force as the egregious everpresent "Friend" and voice of expediency reminds the "Poet" that Nicholas

Paxton, Walpole's official censor of dissident opinion, will say it's "all" a libel—meaning by "all," one gathers, both this and the earlier companion piece with its "Triumph" of Vice, but possibly also such additional subversive items as the *Epistle to Augustus.* Replying, the Poet chooses to take "libel" in the sense of statements which misrepresent because they understate rather than exceed the truth. If his poetry is really found libelous, it can only be because he has failed to keep abreast of the Age of George II:

> Fr. 'Tis all a Libel—*Paxton* (Sir) will say.
> P. Not yet, my Friend! to-morrow 'faith it may;
> And for that very cause I print to day. . . .
> Vice with such Giant-strides comes on amain,
> Invention strives to be before in vain;
> Feign what I will, and paint it e'er so strong,
> Some rising Genius sins up to my Song.
>
> (ll. 1–3, 6–9)

This introduces an accomplished piece of stichomythic exchange as the Poet shoots down the Friend's charge of injury in naming names:

> *Fr.* Spare then the Person, and expose the Vice.
> *P.* How Sir! not damn the Sharper, but the Dice?
> Come on then Satire! gen'ral, unconfin'd,
> Spread thy broad wing, and sowze on all the Kind.
> Ye Statesmen, Priests, of one Religion all!
> Ye Tradesmen vile, in Army, Court, or Hall!
> Ye Rev'rend Atheists!—*Fr.* Scandal! name them, Who?
> *P.* Why that's the thing you bid me not to do. . . .
> The pois'ning Dame—*Fr.* You mean—*P.* I don't.—*Fr.* You do.
> *P.* See now I keep the Secret, and not you.
> The bribing Statesman—*Fr.* Hold! too high you go.
> *P.* The brib'd Elector—*Fr.* There you stoop too low.
> *P.* I fain wou'd please you, if I knew with what.
> Tell me, which Knave is lawful Game, which not?
>
> (ll. 12–19, 22–27)

For instance, could I name a dean, provided I spare a bishop? (Pope has in mind here, for his dean, as some contemporary readers would know, Thomas Sawbridge, Dean of Ferns and Leighlin, indicted for rape in 1730, and, for his bishop, Lancelot Blackburne, Archbishop of York, whose current mistress sat at the head of his table when he entertained and his illegitimate son by an earlier mistress as chaplain at the foot.)

> *Fr.* A Dean, Sir? no: his Fortune is not made,
> You hurt a man that's rising in the Trade.
>
> (ll. 34–35)

But surely, says the Poet, this means that only wretches may be stigmatized:

> Have you less Pity for the needy Cheat,
> The poor and friendless Villain, than the Great? . . .
> Then better sure it Charity becomes
> To tax Directors, who (thank God) have Plums;
> Still better, Ministers; or if the thing
> May pinch ev'n there—why lay it on a King.
>
> (ll. 44–45, 48–51)

There you go again, says the Friend. Why must your poetry always be censure? Why can't you ever say something nice about people? Oh but I have done, and do, the Poet replies, seizing the opening he has made for himself: "God knows, I praise a Courtier where I can" (line 63). Sometimes I praise bishops too:

> *Secker* is decent, *Rundle* has a Heart,
> Manners with Candour are to *Benson* giv'n,
> To *Berkley*, ev'ry Virtue under Heav'n.
>
> (ll. 71–73)

Still, I won't deny it: the people I like best to praise are people out of power, with whom the ugly question of self-serving flattery cannot arise. People like those I knew in my youth, mostly good Whigs, turned out of office when the Tories took over in 1710: Somers, Halifax, Shrewsbury, Carleton, Stanhope (ll. 74–81). Or a Tory, say, like Atterbury, exiled in 1723, when the political currents changed (ll. 82–83). Or those in bad odor with the government right now: Pulteney, Chesterfield, Argyle, Wyndham (ll. 84–89):

> Names, which I long have lov'd, nor lov'd in vain,
> Rank'd with their Friends, not number'd with their Train.
>
> (ll. 90–91)

You are not to think, though, that I praise only friends. I never dined with the Man of Ross or Sir John Barnard, but that hasn't prevented my celebrating their virtues. True, I do not compliment at random: approval is meaningless if everyone is approved:

> Enough for half the Greatest of these days
> To 'scape my Censure, not expect my Praise:
> Are they not rich? what more can they pretend?
> Dare they to hope a Poet for their Friend?
>
> (ll. 112–15)

In the line just quoted, as often elsewhere in this dialogue, "Poet" associates the actual individual poet who is speaking with the large exemplary figure of "the Poet" in his historic bardic role: seer, prophet, conscience, memorialist, and even purifier of the language of his tribe—a role that sets him somewhat apart from the easy come and go of everyday acquaintanceships. And it is emphatically as an individual poet's enactment of this larger generic function that the remainder of the dialogue is written. The cautionary Friend raises the question that every member of a community must continually answer, and no one with more urgency than the writer, be he drama- tist, novelist, journalist, or poet, because of his privileged access to public opinion: "If you're not hurt personally by the wrong-doing in your world, what's it to you?" For the poet speaking in his character as "Poet," there can be but one answer:

> Ask you what Provocation I have had?
> The strong Antipathy of Good to Bad.
> When Truth or Virtue an Affront endures,
> Th' Affront is mine, my Friend, and should be yours.
> Mine, as a Foe profess'd to false Pretence,
> Who think a Coxcomb's Honour like his Sense;
> Mine, as a Friend to ev'ry worthy Mind;
> And mine as Man, who feel for all mankind.
>
> (ll. 197–204)

In matters of public morality, in other words, no man is an island; we are all parts of a single continent; therefore never send to ask for whom the bell tolls—it tolls for *thee*.

On the same principle, as spokesman for an ideal, Pope presumes to close his poem with an affirmation of the integrity of the Poet and the value of his task that perhaps no poetry without benefit of irony can quite sustain. Yet the effort is impressive. In their apparent self- confidence, the lines look forward to the Romantics and to such famous self-coronations as Carlyle's treatment of the man of letters:

> Men of letters are a perpetual Priesthood, from age to age. . . . In the true Literary Man there is thus ever, acknowledged or not by the world, a sacredness: he is the light of the world; the world's

Priest;—guiding it, like a Sacred Pillar of Fire, in its dark pilgrimage through the waste of Time.

> Yes, I am proud; I must be proud to see
> Men not afraid of God, afraid of me:
> Safe from the Bar, the Pulpit, and the Throne,
> Yet touch'd and sham'd by *Ridicule* alone.
>   O sacred Weapon! left for Truth's defence,
> Sole Dread of Folly, Vice, and Insolence!
> To all but Heav'n-directed hands deny'd,
> The Muse may give thee, but the Gods must guide. . . .
> Truth guards the Poet, sanctifies the line,
> And makes Immortal, Verse as mean as mine.
>   (ll. 208–15, 246–47)

But in the solemnity of their intention and in their awareness of a sometimes not easily healable breach between the Poet and the social order, the lines remind too of Milton, resolved to say what society needs to hear despite his having fallen on evil days and evil tongues—"In darkness and with dangers compass'd round, And solitude." Though strongly believing in "Order," as we have seen throughout his work and notably in the *Essay on Man*, Pope knew that no order is to be accepted, as one of his most distinguished critics has reminded us, "passively":

It requires its martyrs and witnesses to demonstrate against any betrayal of standards, wherever this is found, in the Establishment or out of it; and for Pope the basis of this witness must always be the individual sensibility of the poet, which gives him access to truths which are concealed from others by the disorders of real life.

> Ye tinsel Insects! whom a Court maintains,
> That counts your Beauties only by your Stains,
> Spin all your Cobwebs o'er the Eye of Day!
> The Muse's wing shall brush you all away:
> All his Grace preaches, all his Lordship sings,
> All that makes Saints of Queens, and Gods of Kings,
> All, all but Truth, drops dead-born from the Press,
> Like the last Gazette, or the last Address.
>   (ll. 220–27)

"In golden Chains the willing World she draws"

Yet the "Order" of any given time is likely to exact a price for conscientious objection (if it acknowledges such individualism at all), and in the final paragraph mentioned earlier, in which he discloses his disenchantment with the Opposition as a political movement, Pope defiantly anticipates it.

> Yes, the last Pen for Freedom let me draw,
> When Truth stands trembling on the edge of Law:
> Here, Last of *Britons*! let your Names be read;
> Are none, none living? let me praise the Dead,
> And for that Cause which made your Fathers shine,
> Fall, by the Votes of their degen'rate Line!
>
> (ll. 248–53)

Are the allusions in these lines to some portending or threatened retributive action by the government entirely a dramatic fantasy? Possibly not. On 8 July 1738, ten days before the poem was issued, Bolingbroke—always in need of money since he had no income from the St. John estates prior to his father's death in 1742—returned to England to sell Dawley, and, until that transaction could be effected (a period of some nine months, as it turned out), settled as Pope's guest in Twickenham. The reappearance of the "Greatest of all Criminals" cannot have been comforting to the government, possibly still less this close domestic affiliation with one who was both the country's leading poet and its administration's most trenchant critic. We know, too, that at some point, probably almost at once on Bolingbroke's arrival, though possibly during an earlier visit, Pope's windows were broken as Bolingbroke and, it is said, also Bathurst were dining with him. The incident is mentioned in the poem with no holds barred as to its language:

> What? shall each spur-gall'd Hackney★ of the Day,
> When *Paxton*† gives him double Pots and Pay,
> Or each new-pension'd Sycophant, pretend
> To break my Windows, if I treat a Friend;
> Then wisely plead, to me they meant no hurt,
> But 'twas my Guest at whom they threw the dirt?
>
> (ll. 140–45)

★ Hack writer: but Pope's adjective insists also on the term's other meanings: (a) horse worn out; (b) horse for hire—both slipping easily into (c) prostitute.
† Nicholas Paxton, Walpole's watchdog over the press.

Immediately preceding this passage, moreover, is a backhanded compliment to Walpole on his easy-going charm that Pope told Fortescue the minister must take "for no small one, since in it I couple him with Lord Bol[ingbroke]": the last company, as Pope well knew, in which Walpole would care to be complimented, even if the compliment to him (ll. 133–37) had been studded with fewer burrs and that to Bolingbroke—"Oh All-accomplish'd St. JOHN" (line 139)—less lavish.

From that same letter (July 31, 1738) we learn that Pope has recently met with Walpole at the latter's request—how recently he does not say. But we may guess with some plausibility that the summons occurred not too long after the appearance of the first dialogue in May with its scathing final scene of "thronging Millions" rushing to lay their possessions before the Golden—in this instance not Calf but—"Pagod." Portuguese for "idol," but perhaps carrying an English pun as well, the term "Pagod" had been memorably applied to George II in a "vision" published in the Opposition paper *Common Sense* only the year before. There, in what is obviously the state chamber at St. James's, a satyr figure, his large rump of solid gold directed toward his worshippers (in allusion to the king's coarse habit of turning his ample backside on any who displeased him), addresses the assembled company in words that Pope's portrait of the triumph of vice may have been intended to recall:

> Hearken unto my Voice, all ye People, and offer up unto me yourselves, your Sons, and your Sons Sons; your Wives and your Daughters, your Man-servants and your Maid-servants! Hearken unto my Voice, all ye People, and offer up unto me Vessels of Silver, and Vessels of Gold. I say unto you Vessels of pure Gold, your own and your Neighbours Vessels! so shall ye find Favour in my sight, and the Man who changeth his Rod into a Serpent, shall fill you with good Things.

Sure enough, when the gifts have been placed, the man with the rod (also known for his great belly as Gaster Argos = Walpole) casts it on the pavement; and though there is no indication that his action produces any "good Things" for the offerers, the rod, changing to a huge serpent, despatches the offerings with relish:

> For no sooner had he beheld the Vessels of Gold, but seizing them one after another, he gulp'd them down with all their Contents and Appurtenances, in less time than a Dunghill Cock would have pick'd up a dozen Barley-corns from a Threshing Floor; and yet

84. Satiric engraving of 1737 to accompany the fable of the Golden Rump in the Opposition journal *Common Sense*.

"See thronging millions to the Pagod run."
One Thousand Seven Hundred and Thirty-Eight, Dial. 1: 157.

Privately owned.

he did not seem to be half filled or satisfied with his Meal, but looked about for more Food of the same Kind. I once thought he would have snapt at those Parts of the Pagod which were formed of Gold, when the CHIEF MAGICIAN [i.e., Gaster Argos] taking him by the Tail, he became a small Rod or Wand, as before.

One must sympathize with Walpole if he decided that in recalling this scurrilous piece in his apotheosis of Vice (to say nothing of the apotheosis itself), Pope was going too far. And if he had any inkling, as he probably did not, that the salaaming to "Vice" in the opening lines of Pope's portrait—

> But 'tis the Fall degrades her to a Whore;
> Let Greatness own her, and she's mean no more:
> Her Birth, her Beauty, Crowds and Courts confess:
> Chaste Matrons praise her, and grave Bishops bless:
> In golden Chains the willing World she draws—

referred not simply to courtly bootlicking in general but to a particular reception that had taken place at St. James's early that spring—

> Last Friday Sir Robert Walpole declared his marriage to Mrs. Skerrit by whom he had two daughters during his late lady's lifetime. She was the same day introduced to Court and received with great marks of distinction by his Majesty and [Queen Caroline being dead] the Princess Amelia. The Duchesses of Newcastle and Richmond contended earnestly which of them should have the dishonourable honour of presenting her to the King, but at length Mrs. Walpole, Horace Walpole's wife [Sir Robert's sister-in-law], did the office, as the nearest relation, and to shew that Sir Robert marrying his whore was by consent of his family—

one must commend him for his patience in merely warning Pope—if indeed he did so much. What must not, of course, be overlooked is that from the point of view of many contemporaries besides Pope, Walpole's action in flouting custom, innocuous or even admirable as it may appear today, seemed simply one more instance of his arrogant use of power and one more depressing demonstration of the truth (then, now, and presumably for ever) of

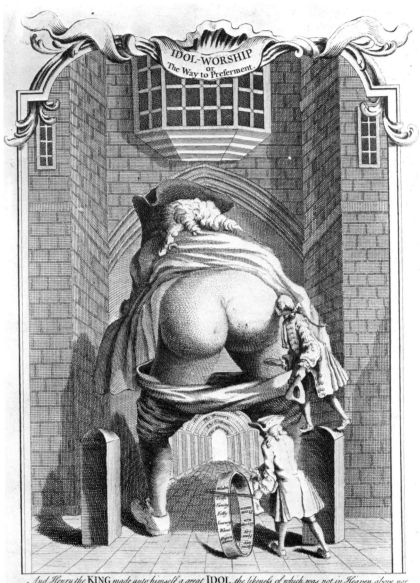

IDOL-WORSHIP
or
The Way to Preferment.

And Henry the KING made unto himself a great IDOL, the likeness of which was not in Heaven above, nor in the Earth beneath; and he reared up his Head unto ȳ Clouds, & extended his Arm over all ȳ Land; His Legs also were as ȳ Posts of a Gate, or as an Arch stretched forth over ȳ Doors of all ȳ Publick Offices in ȳ Land, & whosoever went out, or whosoever came in, passed beneath, & with Idolatrous Reverence lift up their Eyes, & kissed ȳ Cheeks of ȳ Postern.

Chronicle of the Kings, page 51

85. Satiric engraving of *c.* 1740 in criticism of the supposed sycophancy encouraged by Walpole's system of control.

Privately owned.

that hoary proverb: "Learn to lick betimes: you know not whose tail you may go by."

"The man reborn in the poems"

Glancing back over the roughly ten-year span that divides Pope's early *Dunciads* from the second dialogue of *One Thousand Seven Hundred and Thirty-Eight*, one is struck by certain preoccupations and recurrent themes. One, we have seen, is political, enlarging gradually to become a principal interest by the end of the period. Another, also mentioned earlier, is the urge to memorialize his friendships, himself, and an ethically oriented way of life at Twickenham, expressive, as he puts it in his verses to Arbuthnot, of "a Poet's Dignity and Ease." And a third, often intertwined with these, is a paramount concern with image, which must be paused over for a moment if we are not to misinterpret it. Through the portraits of his artist friends, the carefully edited letters, and the poems themselves (considered as a continuum of self-presentations), Pope makes an understandable and, one would guess, largely self-conscious effort to counter the charges of misanthropy, spite, and cruelty leveled at him, also understandably, by the wincing dunces. Particularly from 1733, when he assumes explicitly the mantle of Horace, the succession of satires and epistles projects, with varying degrees of emphasis and at varying length, a personality combining great affability and charm with that "manliness" which he cites as his aspiration in his verses to Arbuthnot and which Marchmont singles out in describing him to Boswell as the distinctive quality of his conversation.

About these "public" selves of writers, sometimes called *personae*—the selves who speak to us from their works—the dramatic and almost inevitably idealized selves in whom they hope to live for their own and future generations—much doubt has been sometimes voiced. Yeats put the necessary point a half century ago with his usual vividness when he said that the man who sits down to breakfast is not the man reborn in his poems. Essentially, the distinction reaffirms the fictionality of fictions. It declares, among other things, that up to a point the degree and character of an author's presence in a work of art are aspects of its artifice, determined like its other elements by selection, coherence, and the requirements of "composition." Thus an old Leech Gatherer, for example, appears in Wordsworth's poem *Resolution and Independence* as the very type of noble self-reliance, sticking without complaint to a wearisome and

dwindling livelihood on the moors, and hence bringing to the
despondent Wordsworth who encounters him new resolve and
hope—as if "from some far region sent, To give me strength by apt
admonishment." We happen to know, however, that the poet met
this figure not on the moors but on a highway, that the "Old-man"
had given up gathering leeches and now lived by begging, and that
the whole moving scenario, in which he appears first as a huge stone,
then as a sea beast sprawled in the sun, and finally as an exemplum of
human fortitude and patience, searching for leeches with his staff in
the muddy waters of a moor pond, is an invention of the poet's fancy.
Apt admonishment indeed! Is our appropriate response to this knowledge to tax Wordsworth with a fraudulent presentation of the incident and himself? Hardly, though this is the judgment to which
nineteenth-century theories of artistic sincerity inexorably point.
The appropriate response is to recognize that all literary events are
"made" events and to return to the poem with renewed gratitude for
the powers of mind, feeling, and imagination that can turn such
unpromising materials, the depressing substance of things seen,
almost inside out to compose the substance of things not seen into
one of the great moments of Romantic natural supernaturalism.

Mutatis mutandis, the development of Pope's public self in the
poems of the 1730s is similarly, in part, a literary event. It has roots,
to be sure, in that vanity which impels us all to present to the world a
more or less flattering image of ourselves, much intensified for Pope,
one would guess, by his mean stature and deformity, and possibly
encouraged further from boyhood onward by the lingering mistrust
of Roman Catholics in the dominant culture. It may have other and
deeper roots as well. Sociologists will see in it a species of ressocializ-
ation. Nature had set him apart with a crippling and disfiguring
disease. Upbringing had set him apart through membership in a
disfranchised and always somewhat suspect minority. The *Dunciad*
and other assaults, sometimes unprovoked, both on those he believed
to be public nuisances and on his own enemies, had set him yet
further apart, in the minds of those who did not know him or who
sought revenge, as a figure of pure malevolence. The resulting urge to
redefine, almost re-create himself, within the poems and elsewhere,
is readily understandable in this context, as is his resolution, conscious or unconscious, to build a poetic world in which he is seen
surrounded not by jealous dunces or supercilious courtiers, but by
admired and admiring friends.

"Out of his friends," it has been wisely said, "Pope made something more than the largely fortuitous assemblage of acquaintances

which is all that most people can make of their friends; he made them into his own image of the ideal community he would wish to write for and to live in." And more often than not, we notice, it is a community whose members, like himself, circumstances have in some respect circumscribed and set apart: Swift, cast away in Dublin; Gay, unpensioned despite "a hundred [courtly] friends"; Arbuthnot, *formerly* servant to "a QUEEN"; Martha Blount, "deny'd the Pelf" which buys a husband—though possibly this is a blessing in disguise. Besides which, of course, in Pope's view, there were all those exclusions of great talent from influence on public affairs, all those "Chiefs, out of War, and Statesmen, out of Place"—men whom, as his biographer says, Walpole had broken or who were alienated by his methods.

But though answering in part, it may be, to some such psychological needs, the personality who speaks to us in the poems of the 1730s was shaped with at least equal force, and far more explicitly, by the traditional requirements of formal verse satire. To convince, as we saw earlier, the satirist must persuade us that he speaks from his own observation and with the compulsion that comes from the natural antipathy of a plain decent man to vicious goings-on about him and the scorn of a man of sense for fashionable foolishness. Hence the unavoidable centrality and egoism of the seeing eye, expressed as "I," even if the satirist should happen to be (unlike Pope) a paragon of modesty. Not that the speaker in formal satire need be wholly free of failings. Unspecified "Spots" he may, like the rest of us, pardonably admit to; we only become irritable when they are named. A certain testiness, perhaps, when injured—"But touch me, and no Minister so sore"—is not unbecoming. And since a susceptibility to fits of self-congratulation is present in all of us—

> Thus we dispose of all poetic Merit,
> Yours *Milton*'s Genius, and mine *Homer*'s Spirit—
> (*Imit. Hor., Ep.* II. ii: 135–36)

it is reassuring to see that our speaker recognizes and can parody it. Were he to acknowledge, in addition, a lamented even if as yet unmastered inconstancy of mind—"One ebb and flow of follies all my Life"—that too is forgivable, even (Montaigne says) normal, and may rather enhance than impair our necessary faith in what the satirist has to tell us. For as Defoe had been quick to point out to those who believed that the kettle was not black if the pot was black that called it so (and who always in that belief set to work to blacken the pot):

If none but faultless Men must reprove others, Lord ha' Mercy upon all our Magistrates; and all our Clergy are undignified [i.e., stripped of their special status] and suspended at a blow.

Lord ha' mercy also, we might add today, on all the other trades and professions, not to mention any parent striving to rear a child.

Still, whatever the venial faults to which a satirist lays claim as proof of his being no prig, his personality in his work as a whole must show us that his values are values we can approve and that his anxiety for the common welfare is real. To borrow a memorable phrase from a pioneering figure in the twentieth-century study of satire, he must be a member of that "invisible church of good men, few though they may be, for whom things matter":

> So impudent, I own myself no Knave:
> So odd, my Country's Ruin makes me grave.
> (*One Thousand Seven Hundred and Thirty-Eight, Dial. 2*: 206–7)

Inevitably, then, Pope assumes in these poems such virtues and attitudes as the culture of his period prized or at least affected to prize, whether or not the man who sat down to breakfast actually possessed them or possessed them in the degree stated. Courage, patriotism, friendliness, lasting loyalties, charitable benefactions, extreme generosity in helping others find employment or advancement, assiduous attention (despite the impatience expressed in the epistle to Arbuthnot) to promising younger writers, high standards of performance in his own work—these and other flattering attributes, with only slight qualifications here and there, Pope could genuinely claim; though it is worth noting that about many of them—his considerable acts of charitable support, for instance—the public personality within the poems is silent. What that personality usually wishes to display instead is the gentlemanly or even lordly air of serene superiority (whether to blows of fortune or censures of hostile critics or sneers at his unprepossessing person) which an aristocratic culture still living off the accumulated capital of classical philosophies of self-sufficiency, self-cultivation, and self-containment tended to encourage:

1.   To VIRTUE ONLY and HER FRIENDS A FRIEND,
        The World beside may murmur, or commend.
        Know, all the distant Din that World can keep
        Rolls o'er my Grotto, and but sooths my Sleep.
                            (*Imit. Hor., Sat.* II, i: 121–4)

2.   Fortune not much of humbling me can boast;
Tho' double-tax'd, how little have I lost? . . .
My lands are sold, my Father's house is gone;
I'll hire another's, is not that my own? . . .
Let Lands and Houses have what Lords they will,
Let Us be fix'd, and our own Masters still.

(Imit. Hor., Sat. II, ii:
151–52, 155–56, 179–80)

3.   Did some more sober Critic come abroad?
If wrong, I smil'd; if right, I kiss'd the rod. . . .
   Were others angry, I excus'd them too.

(Epistle to Dr. Arbuthnot, 157–58, 173)

4.   Gold, Silver, Iv'ry, Vases sculptur'd high,
Paint, Marble, Gems, and Robes of *Persian* Dye,
There are who have not—and thank Heav'n there are
Who, if they have not, think not worth their care.

(Imit. Hor., Ep. II, ii:
264–67)

5.   What is 't to me (a Passenger God wot)
Whether my Vessel be first-rate or not?
The Ship it self may make a better figure,
But I that sail, am neither less nor bigger.

(Ibid., 296–99)

6.   I left no Calling for this idle trade. . . .

(Epistle to Dr. Arbuthnot, 129)

Shall I, in *London,* act this idle part?
Composing Songs, for Fools to get by Heart?

(Imit. Hor., Ep. II, ii:
125–26)

Farewell then Verse, and Love, and ev'ry Toy.

(Imit. Hor., Ep. I, i: 17)

O sacred Weapon! left for Truth's defence. . . .
Truth guards the Poet, sanctifies the line,
And makes Immortal, Verse as mean as mine.

(One Thousand Seven Hundred and Thirty-Eight,
Dial. 2: 212, 246–47)

Some of these expressions accord with Pope's personality as we know it from other sources and express convictions that, in general, he lived by. Others doubtless voice convictions that he wished to live by, or liked to delude himself into thinking he lived by, but rarely, in fact, put into practice. This would be particularly true of the serenity he pretends to with respect to criticism, though even here it is fair to recall that in the face of Spence's censures of his *Odyssey* translation he did kiss the rod, and even from such mean and picky denunciations as Dennis's of the *Essay on Criticism* was able to draw improvements for the next edition. Sometimes, as with the passages gathered under no. 6, the attitudes expressed even by his public self are at odds, as we know they were in his private life; and as they were, also, with respect to the restless mobility of mood that he clearly recognized in himself ("One ebb and flow of follies all my Life"), ever undoing the masterful self-command that he shared the sensibility of his age in approving, at least with lip-service ("Let Us be fix'd and our own Masters still"). The man reborn in the poems says nothing, of course, of the satisfactions to be had by the man at breakfast from a well-placed vengeful barb (a satisfaction he took often with certain individuals like Lady Mary after their falling-out); or of the public lies told to protect the *Odyssey* collaboration from exposure, largely at Broome's expense; or of the private lies and intrigues required to obtain his letters from Swift—for even if we allow that the end was pardonable, even desirable, the means were shabby.

Partly, then, the public Pope is an invention. He answers to the needs and develops a great many of the predictable themes of the genre he is writing in, as established by his Roman predecessors: the values of the examined life, plain fare, scorn of riches, withdrawal from the madding crowd, country pleasures, moral independence, openness of heart and house—all of them perhaps intended to be subsumed in Pope's comment on his deathbed that "nothing . . . is meritorious but virtue and Friendship, and indeed friendship itself is only a part of virtue." The public figure is also partly molded, like Wordsworth in *Resolution and Independence*, by the demands of the individual poem. He may be "young" if the situation calls for it, as when he wrote, "Dear Sir, forgive the Prejudice of Youth," though he was actually fifty when the line was written. He may go out of his way to be exceptionally agreeable:

> Thus Bethel spoke, who always speaks his thought,
> And always thinks the very thing he ought:

His equal mind I copy what I can,
And as I love, would imitate the Man—
(Imit. Hor., Sat. II, ii: 129–32)

or disagreeable:

> *Fr.* This filthy Simile, this beastly Line,
> Quite turns my Stomach—*P.* So does Flatt'ry mine;
> And all your Courtly Civet-Cats can vent,
> Perfume to you, to me is Excrement—
(One Thousand Seven Hundred and Thirty-Eight,
Dial. 2: 181–84)

mischievously naive:

> There are (I scarce can think it, but am told)
> There are to whom my Satire seems too bold—
(Imit. Hor., Sat. II, i: 1–2)

coldly contemptuous:

> Yet let me flap this Bug with gilded wings,
> This painted Child of Dirt that stinks and stings—
(Epistle to Dr. Arbuthnot, 309–10)

touchingly personal:

> This subtle Thief of Life, this paltry Time,
> What will it leave me, if it snatch my Rhime?
(Imit. Hor., Ep. II, ii: 76–77)

and so on through whatever modulations of feeling the pattern of the particular satire or epistle is constructed to convey.

And yet, however much the Pope "composed" within this succession of poems may differ at various points and in certain discernible ways from the historical A. Pope of Twickenham, it would be short-sighted to dismiss him as an impostor. For he is in some sense the poet's ideal rendering of the best in himself, like Roubiliac's rendering of a face to which more than one contemporary attributed a genuine classical nobility. The end product, we might call him, of Pope's last and greatest Ovidian metamorphosis, realized in the poetry even if never on the flesh and bone. And the poems in which he appears, moving gracefully from grave to gay and lively to severe, register under various guises an archetypal drama that was as personal and self-involving for their author as it is exemplary and timeless for us. The poems were personal for Pope because their characteristic argument (often stated, sometimes more implied than stated) between a compromising "Friend," interested only in expediencies, and an uncompromising "Poet," interested in principles, raised questions about how to survive in a corrupt world that were entirely real for a little hunchback who must from time to time have wondered what his great literary prestige, if laid at the feet of king and minister, would bring. Both speakers, in other words, Friend as well as Poet, represent "strains," in both senses, within the experience of Pope himself; for whom it would no doubt have been extremely convenient on some occasions to have followed the advice of his time-serving interlocutors, and who perhaps, when warned by Fortescue, sometimes did so; just as it was exhilarating and appealing on other occasions to see himself and conduct himself as if he actually were *ultimus Romanorum.* The very structure of these poems, in other words, may have possessed for Pope a psychic as well as poetic utility, affording him a theater for his own ambivalent feelings about the society that had bred him and excluded him, caressed him and hurt him.

"An Englishman in his Grotto"

But there was also, of course, the public side, for Pope was not given to wearing his heart upon his sleeve. Whatever psychic wellsprings may have contributed to their genetic history, the satires and epistles of the 1730s, as we know them, have obviously been shaped by a conscious artist into an expression of himself that is public and available to all. In the figure of his poet-hero and in the figure of the remonstrating supporter of Things-As-They-Are, Pope dramatizes afresh, with an engaging charm, the tension to which each of *us* must respond in our relations with our community: the will to master its complexities, occupy its high places, bask in the glow of its affection and applause ("Envy must own I live among the Great"), set over against the will to be free of the world's subtle slaveries, pay Caesar no more than Caesar's due, and preserve something integral and serene from the powerful undertow of compromise, expediency, corruption, and sheer busy-ness that no community on earth has ever been without: "Yet may this Verse (if such a Verse remain) Show there was one who held it in disdain."

In the upshot, thanks to the intrepid spokesman he had invented for these poems, A. Pope of Twickenham became a symbolic figure as centrally inspiring to Opposition pamphleteers as he was allegedly in his own person to the young patriots surrounding the Prince of Wales. As early as 1733, an anonymous poem written as if by Pope to Lord Hervey evokes the image of the plain good poet living in retirement by standards that are in themselves an implicit indictment of courtly servitudes:

> As for my Part, I chuse to live remote,
> Nor will I be induc'd to turn my Coat;
> I hear, but yield not to the *Syren*'s Note.
> Let others in Brocaded Silks and Sattins
> Appear abroad, while I attend my *Mattins*.
> My Home-spun Lindsy Wolsy pleases me,
> Nature's Intent it answers, and I see
> With Unconcern, each dapper, spruce *Toupee*.
> Your pretty Face and Shape I envy not,
> But rest content with what has been by Lot:
> My rural Mansion is to me a Court,
> Tired with the Town I thither do resort;
> Divide my Hours between my Friends and Study,
> And sometimes sit and chat with honest Cuddy.★

In 1740, having been celebrated frequently in this vein for his preeminence in "Virtue's Cause," he is made the hero of a fancied confrontation with Walpole in two pamphlets entitled respectively *Are These Things So? . . . From an Englishman in his Grotto to a Great Man at Court* and *The Great Man's Answer to Are These Things So?* In substance, the first is an address to the Great Man, couched in inferior verse but in Pope's general manner, made by a virtuous retirement figure whose accents are often drawn from or based on Pope's previous poems.

> My sole *Ambition* o'er myself to reign,
> My *Avarice* to make each Hour a Gain;
> My *Scorn*—the Threats or Favours of a Crown,
> A Prince's Whisper, or a Tyrant's Frown;
> My *Pride*—forgetting and to be forgot,
> My *Luxury*—lolling in my peaceful Grott.
> All Rancour, Party, Pique, expung'd my Mind,
> Free or to *laugh* at, or *lament* Mankind;
> Here my calm Hours I with the wise employ,
> And the great *Greek*, or *Roman* Sage enjoy;

★ Gay—one of whose characters in *The Shepherd's Week* has this name.

Or, gayly bent, the Mirth-fraught Page peruse,
Or, pensive, keep a *Fast-day* with the Muse.
Close shut my Cottage-Gate, where none pretends
To lift the Latch but Virtue and her Friends;
Tho' pardon me—a Word, Sir in your Ear,
Once, *long ago*, I think I saw YOU here. ★

(pp. 1–2)

Despite his isolation, however—"all Hermit as I live"—this speaker loves his country deeply and has been troubled by reports reaching him of her degeneracy, of her famed dominion of the seas lost to "Gaul and Spain," her parliaments grown servile, her great men who dare speak out "Stripp'd of all Honour, Dignity, and Rule," her moral health "Polluted," her "Commerce" fled. "Are These Things So?" the "Englishman in his Grotto" asks the "Great Man at Court," or are they simply slanders of the out-party—"Of those who *want*, or who have *lost* a *Place*?" If the latter, why not defend yourself in detail—for example, with sentiments like the following:

"In my dear Country's Service now *grown gray*,
Spotless I've walk'd before you to this Day,
My Thoughts laid out, my precious Time all spent
In the hard *Slavery* of *Government*; . . .
You have my SONS too with you, who bow down
Beneath the weighty Service of the Crown;
My COUSINS and their COUSINS too—hard Fate!
Are *loaded* with the Offices of State;
And not *one Soul* of all my Kindred's free,
From *sharing* in the Publick Drudgery."

(p. 8)

But if the charges, on the other hand, are true—if, just for instance,

all your Kindred, BROTHER, SONS, and COUSINS,
Have *Titles* and *Employments* by the *Dozens*;
And for as many *Sidesmen* as are wanted,
New Places are contriv'd, *new Pensions* granted—

(p. 10)

then you should reflect on what awaits you once your hour is out. It will not be the recognition that attends those who were "as Good as Great";

★ Walpole had visited Pope at Twickenham in 1725.

No! with the *Curs'd* your Tomb shall foremost stand,
The GAVESTON's and the WOLSEY's of the Land.
      Your EPITAPH.
In this foul Grave lies HE,
Who dug the Grave of British *Liberty.*

(p. 11)

Therefore: "Quit the Reins before we're quite undone."

The second pamphlet shifts from address to direct dialogue, as its subtitle indicates: *A Dialogue Between His Honour and the Englishman in His Grotto.* Whether by typographical accident or design, the grotto poet has now become "*the* Englishman," representative of the whole nation, but he remains, for all that, the retired Twickenham spokesman deeply disquieted by his country's peril:

HAIL blest *Elizium*! sweet, secure Retreat;
Quiet and Contemplation's sacred Seat!
Here may my Life's last Lamp in Freedom burn:
Nor live to light my Country to her Urn.

(p. 1)

Hearing an enormous fracas at his grotto door, the speaker sends "John" (Pope's John Searle, who is asked to shut his door in *Arbuthnot*) to investigate:

      . . . what Tempest shakes my Cell?
Whence these big Drops that Ooze from ev'ry Shell?
From this obdurate Rock whence flow those Tears?
Sure some *Ill Power's* at hand.

(p. 1)

The "*Ill Power*" proves of course to be Walpole, the Great Man, come for a personal call on the English Man:

G.M. Well, solemn Sir, I'm come, if you think fit.
To solve your Question. E.M. Bless me! pray, Sir, sit.
G.M. The Door! E.M. No Matter, Sir, my Door won't shut:
Stay here, *John*; we've no *Secrets.* G.M. Surly Put!*
How restiff still! but I have *what* will win him
Before we part, or else the Devil's in him.

(p. 2)

---

* Country bumpkin.

The interesting feature of the debate that follows—on the usual subjects: the throttled fleet, standing armies, misue of Secret Service funds, briberies, taxes, and so on,—is that Walpole is given some of the arguments that went farthest, in a period when nothing like modern party discipline was known, to excuse his system of place-men and pensioners:

> Free P[arliamen]ts! mere stuff—What would be done?
> Let loose, five hundred diff'rent Ways they'd run;
> They'd Cavil, Jarr, Dispute, O'return, Project,
> And the great Bus'ness of *Supply* Neglect;
> On *Grievances*, not *Ways* and *Means* would go.
>
> (p. 5)

He is also given the arguments that in his time served those who did not suffer from any refined sense of *meum* and *tuum* (here it is impor-tant to remember that some did: Walpole's brother-in-law Townshend left office poorer than he entered it) to justify their spoils of office:

> Besides, who'd drudge the *Mill-Horse* of the State;
> Curst by the Vulgar, envy'd by the Great;
> In one fastidious Round of Hurry live,
> And join, in Toil, the *Matin* with the Eve. . . .
> Who'd cringe at *Levees*, or in *Closets*—Oh!
> Stoop to the *rough* Remonstrance of the *Toe?*★
> Did not some Genius whisper, "That's the Road
> To Opulence, and Honour's bless'd Abode;
> Thus you may aggrandize yourself, and Race."
>
> (p.11)

Moreover, he is finally allowed to set against the "Epitaph" of the preceding pamphlet a résumé of his achievements as he sees them, with an epitaph of his own:

> I want no *Grave-Stone* to promulge my *Fame*,
> Nor trust to *breathless Marble* for a *Name*,
> BRITANNIA's self a *Monument* shall stand
> Of the *bless'd Dowry* I bequeath my Land:
> Her Sons shall hourly my *dear Conduct* boast;
> They *best* can speak it, who will *feel* it most.
> But if some grateful Verse *must* grace my Urn,

★ Referring to the King's habit of kicking when displeased.

> Attend ye *Gazeteers*—Be this the Turn—
> *Weep*, Britons, *weep*—*Beneath this Stone lies* He,
> *Who set your Isle from dire Divisions free*
> *And made your various Factions all agree.*

(p. 12)

It is very nearly the epitaph pronounced on Walpole by yesterday's historians.

All this is irony, however, not prescience, as the ending of the poem makes clear. Finding he has nothing to say that will mollify the grotto-speaker's "starch'd unbending temper," the Great Man gets up to go, proposing to leave behind "his last *best* answer . . . in *Writing*." The "Writing" proves to be a thousand-pound banknote, which the English Man scornfully tears up. A pension, a place, a title, and a decoration are similarly scorned. Whereupon:

> [G.M.] Farewell then Fool—If you'll accept of *Neither,*
> You and your *Country* may be *damn'd* together.

(p. 13)

Though the compliment paid him as the conscience of the Opposition may have pleased Pope, he must have been appalled by the quality of the verse.

CHAPTER 28

LAST HEROES

A turning point

The year 1738 merits a certain prominence on the map of eighteenth-century English literature as well as in the story of Pope's career. It is then that we encounter the first major work by the man who was to dominate the literary scene for the next four decades, as Pope had done for the previous three. It was published almost on the same day as the first of Pope's two *Dialogues*: Samuel Johnson's adaptation of Juvenal's third satire, entitled *London*. Unfortunately the two men never met. But Pope recognized, as he had a habit of doing, the marks of genius in the anonymous author—he will soon be "déterré" ["unearthed"], he assured his friend Jonathan Richardson on learning that the poem was by an obscure man named Johnson—and tried during the next several months to find him a position. At first, it appears, as tutor to a friendly nobleman's son; subsequently, as master of a school in Leicestershire, which, unfortunately for Johnson's hopes but fortunately for the glory of English letters, insisted on the baccalaureate degree that poverty had blocked Johnson from acquiring. (He had been obliged to break off his studies at Pembroke College, Oxford, after little more than a year.) Much later in the century, Joshua Reynolds, who knew of Pope's efforts to help Johnson, observed to him that he seemed to be much flattered by them. "Who," Johnson replied, "would not be flattered with the solicitous inquiry of such a man as Pope?"

For Pope himself, 1738 was distinctly a turning point. His health, as usual, was precarious, and he had turned fifty in May—an event perhaps not unconnected with two epitaphs composed at about this time. Playful rather than solemn, both are obviously designed to convey that spirited mood of careless independence which he apparently found requisite to his personal self-esteem, especially when under attack. One of the two, possibly elicited by the now steady drumbeat of insult from ministerial gazetteers, has something of the quality of a self-conscious shrug:

EPITAPH

On Himself

Under this Marble, or under this Sill,
Or under this Turf, or e'en what they will;
Whatever an Heir, or a Friend in his stead,
Or any good Creature shall lay o'er my head;
Lies He who ne'er cared, and still cares not a Pin,
What they said, or may say of the Mortal within.
But who living and dying, serene still free,
Trusts in God, that as well as he was, he shall be.

The other epitaph, more obviously a response to his present
unpopularity with government and court, registers his views in its
title as well as in its content:

EPITAPH

For One who would not be buried in Westminster Abbey.

HEROES and KINGS! your distance keep.
In peace let one poor Poet sleep,
Who never flattered Folks like you:
Let Horace blush, and Virgil too.

Though somewhere behind both poems there probably lie thoughts
inspired by the recent completion in the Abbey of Rysbrack's monument to Gay with Pope's epitaph inscribed on it and by his own
current efforts (with the help of Burlington and Dr. Mead) to raise
funds for an Abbey monument to Shakespeare, one need not read
very deeply in them to sense, as well, the intimations of mortality
that age fifty usually brings, even if highly colored in this instance by
their author's care to appear not to care.

The year 1738 also stands out in Pope's life on other counts. It
brings to a close his career in formal verse satire, in the "Horatian"
style generally, and—almost—in poetry itself. It marks the beginning of an uproar about the alleged heterodoxy of the *Essay on Man*,
Warburton's belligerently ingenious *Vindication* of which brought
Pope the last of his great friendships—if indeed that is the right word
for a relationship which (it has been wittily said) made Pope a
Christian and Warburton a bishop. And it was the year in which,
during Bolingbroke's long stay with him, Pope was entrusted with a
copy of his friend's essay on *The Idea of a Patriot King*, with a commission to print up a few copies for private circulation among close

86. The monument by Peter Scheemakers erected to Shakespeare in the Abbey in 1738 through the efforts of many, but particularly those of the Earl of Burlington, Dr. Richard Mead, and Pope. The reproachful inscription above Shakespeare's head—"Erected by Public Love [i.e., Subscription] 124 years after his death"—could well be Pope's.

Courtesy of the Dean and Chapter of Westminster.

Opposition friends: a commission that his adulation of Bolingbroke led him to exceed (with disastrous consequences after his death) by printing fifteen hundred copies for future circulation and making a small number of discreet softenings in the text. These are episodes to be looked at in turn.

For nearly four years following his two *Dialogues*, Pope published no major poems and very few of any sort. Doubtless he was tired. The tide of inventive energy which had sustained his failing body for over a decade—through the two *Dunciads* of 1728 and 1729, through the *Essay on Man* and its satellite epistles to several friends, and then through some fifteen poems in the general manner of Horace and Donne—may quite possibly have been ebbing by 1738; while at the same time the sheer labor of composition (a theme on which he had been eloquent in several of the Horatian pieces) mounted correspondingly and likewise its capacity to distract from pursuits of a more personal kind: "Have I no Friend to serve, no Soul to save!"

Fatigue, however, if fatigue there was, seems to have been seconded by other pressures. A note to the second of his Dialogues, allegedly Pope's, but not published till after his death in Warburton's 1751 edition of his *Works*, characterizes the poem as "a sort of PROTEST against that insuperable corruption and depravity of manners, which he had been so unhappy as to live to see" and which now made "Ridicule . . . as unsafe as it was ineffectual." We know, further, from the same letter to Fortescue (July 31, 1738) in which he mentions having lately seen Walpole, that he was then contemplating a third Dialogue. According to Warburton, this was yet "more severe and sublime than the first and second," and, "being no secret, matters were compromised. His enemies agreed to drop the prosecution, and he promised to leave the third Dialogue unfinished and suppressed."

Though we have no clue to the actual events these statements glance at (warnings? threats? negotiations? gentlemen's agreements?), the conclusion appears inescapable that, in some sense, Pope was silenced. The intensifying assaults on ministerial corruption, and, doubtless more important, the undeviating declared allegiance of the most respected literary figure of the age to the chief minister's bitterest opponent, whatever else they may have accomplished, gave aid and comfort to dissidents of every stripe and helped foster a climate of opinion hostile to the regime. And they were deeply resented. This much is clear from the virulence of the already mentioned government attacks on Pope's person and character during 1738 and early 1739, one particularly unfriendly writer going so far as to name him among "the Six Incendiary Chiefs" (the others being Bolingbroke, Pulteney, Wyndham, Chesterfield, and Carteret—the latter also now in opposition) seeking to trouble the repose of a contented people. The office of Poet has seldom been paid a higher compliment; and though it may be, as a distinguished poet of our own century has said, that poetry makes nothing happen, it is extraordinary how often in the historical record those in authority have elected to muzzle it. Pope published nothing major again till about five weeks after Walpole fell.

Warburton to the rescue

Unfortunately for his peace of mind, the assault on his satires coincided with a great clamor raised against the *Essay on Man*. Until 1738, its reception in England had been overwhelmingly favorable. Its author had here or there been censured for addressing the poem to a bad man, namely Bolingbroke, but not for his doctrine. On the Continent, too, from its first publication onward, but especially from 1736 when a translation into French prose by Etienne de Silhouette appeared and ran through four editions in a year, the *Essay* enjoyed an extraordinary popularity. One of the best-known French men of letters of the time, the Jesuit Tournemine, after reading the poem in the new prose translation, reported that any reader not already corrupted by infidelity would draw from it sound nourishment, enlarged views, and useful maxims. "I am charmed by Pope," Tournemine had said; "he is a penetrating thinker and a poet truly sublime."

This assessment of the *Essay*, though confirmed in the same year by an official organ of the Jesuits, the *Mémoires de Trévoux*, was suddenly retracted in 1737 and the poem condemned in the name of both morality and religion. For this reversal, a translation of the poem into French verse, published in the interim, seems to have been primarily responsible. The translator, J. F. du B. Du Resnel, undertook to confer on the *Essay* more of the system and method which were favored by the Latin mind and just then much in fashion throughout Europe as thinkers of various persuasions undertook to schematize the new secular theorizing about man's nature and his universe. To this end, a multitude of passages in the poem were deleted, others added, still others transposed, expanded, or contracted, and the whole was so altered, despite extensive omissions, as to stretch thirteen hundred lines to two thousand and render the result substantially unrecognizable as Pope's. Even the title was revised to imply something especially ambitious: having decided on a reissue of his earlier translation of the

Essay on Criticism, Du Resnel brought out the two together as *Les Principes* [!] *de la Morale et du Goût*.

Meantime, the French translations had reached Lausanne, where Jean-Pierre de Crousaz, a Swiss professor, seized the opportunity he thought he saw in them for attacking, by way of Pope, all the newer secular speculations that seemed to him to impugn traditional orthodoxies about God's and man's free will. In 1737, he published an *Examen* of the poem, based on Silhouette's prose, and, the following year, a *Commentary*, based on Du Resnel's verse. A more unhappy confrontation of minds and methods can hardly be imagined. On the one hand, a critic whom a French historian of this episode has described as a "mathématicien, philosophe et pédagogue, ... terriblement affairé ["busy-body"] et pédant," understanding no English, less interested in literature than in infidelity, and explicating the poem as if its subject matter were a branch of algebra. On the other hand, the elusive couplets of the work itself, some perhaps consciously ambiguous, many containing terms and concepts which are equivocal in the very nature of language, many others requiring for interpretation a context of intellectual and literary history that Crousaz did not choose to supply, and the whole problem further complicated for a foreign writer by translations each differing from the other and from the original. The result was that Crousaz devoted much of his attention to criticizing expressions nowhere to be found in Pope's English and assailing propositions that his victim would have found as unacceptable as he. What remains when all irrelevancies are stripped away is a tedious, if successful, demonstration that the poem shows logical contradictions of the sort that philosophical systems have always been found to contain even when erected by skilled philosophers and that poets have habitually utilized to preserve aspects of experience which logicians overlook. In fairness to Crousaz, it must be added that certain concepts and expressions used by Pope have (and have had since their first use by Plato and his followers) fatalistic implications if carried farther than Pope carries them.

Despite its egregious faults, the attack was damaging. Crousaz's prestige as a theologian and logician, and particularly his disingenuous method, which carefully associated the doctrines of the *Essay* with various allegedly infidel philosophies while professing to separate it from them and repeatedly criticized the poem for assertions that he had every reason to know (through Silhouette's more literal translation) the original did not contain, were ideally suited to alarm the orthodox and give a handle to the poet's enemies. In late November 1738, just when the campaign of the gazetteers was in full cry, Curll, whose minions had previously left the poem unassailed, advertised a translation of Crousaz's *Commentaire* with the observation that it was "a critical Satire upon the Essay on Man," and promised to "pursue M. Crousaz in his Attacks upon Mr. Pope regularly." (Actually, the translation dealt with only part of the *Commentaire* and was considerably condensed as well.) Almost simultaneously, on the twenty-third, a complete translation of Crousaz's *Examen* appeared, containing, the advertisement said, "a Succinct View of the System of the Fatalists, and a Confutation of their Opinions; . . . and an Enquiry what View Mr. Pope might have in touching on the Leibnitzian [according to Crousaz, a fatalist] Philosophy." The translator was Elizabeth Carter, later a famous Bluestocking, who had visited Pope's gardens and found them rapturously agreeable the preceding July, and who was now engaged to various scriptural chores, including the Crousaz project, by the publisher of the recently founded *Gentleman's Magazine*, Edward Cave. Available at the same shop, the advertisement noted, was a complete translation of the *Commentaire*, with notes. This, we now know, was by Elizabeth Carter's friend, Samuel Johnson—one of the many booksellers' commissions by which he was in those days scratching out a livelihood. Here again, for a moment, his life and Pope's very nearly come together.

Advertisements of such tendency, continuing through the fall and winter, were followed on 13 March 1739 by the announcement of William Ayre's *Truth. A counterpart to Mr. Pope's Essay on Man. Epistle the first*; and on June 13, by the announcement of *Truth . . . Epistle the Second*, "opposing his [Pope's] Opinions of Man as an Individual." Little wonder that Pope took alarm and gratefully accepted the refutation of Crousaz that the Reverend William Warburton of Brant Broughton, Lincolnshire, had been publishing for several months, quite unsolicited, in the *History of the Works of the Learned*. Here was a *deus ex machina* indeed! For though Warburton's *Vindication* (as it was eventually called) strained passages in the poem toward literally pietistic senses they were not equipped to bear, and claimed for it, further, a ratiocinative rigor impossible and probably undesirable in poetry, his work had two considerable merits. It gave an analysis of the argument far more consonant than Crousaz's with any meaning we may suppose the poet to have had, and it recognized in the proposition that this *has* to be the best of *possible* worlds because made by an all-good, all-wise, and all-powerful Being, a respectable premise and conclusion of long standing. Susceptible they might be to fatalistic deductions, but they had nevertheless enjoyed a long untainted history among Christian theologians, including "the most celebrated and orthodox *Fathers* and *Divines* of the ancient and modern Church."

Sheltered by Warburton, the *Essay* met but one more public attack before Pope's death. This too came from across the Channel, where, in a pious poem of 1742, Louis Racine, the playwright's son, addressed Pope as an "abstract Reasoner, who ... in his stolid Anglican way will reply, *All is for the best*," and called the *Essay* a nursery of heretical opinions. These, he said, had become common in France since the appearance there of Pope's poem and had led some to find in it a system that was perhaps, in fact, not that of its author. The kindly suggestion of the last clause opened the way to an exchange of letters between the two, in which Pope declared flatly (and correctly) that his work was misrepresented by the translation of Du Resnel, in which Racine had read it, and added that his religious views, far from being "those of Spinoza, or even of Leibnitz," were, on the contrary, "conformable to those of Mons. Pascal & Mons. Fénélon: the latter of whom I would most readily imitate, in submitting all my Opinions to the Decision of the Church." The choice of two eminent anti-rationalists—in fact, fideists (the second a distinguished apostle of quietism whose mystical views had been condemned by the papacy in 1699)—can hardly have been accidental.

Where this leaves us with reference to Pope's own deepest convictions, it is not easy to say. The evidence is as conflicting as one suspects the views were themselves. All that we know of Pope before or after writing the *Essay* suggests that he was a man of religious temper even if not particularly devout, far more warmly interested by the ethics of Christianity than by the dogmas whose divisive consequences he could see in the society around him as well as in his own incapacitated political lot. We know too that he had written for the poem an address to the Savior modeled on Lucretius's address to Epicurus, which was omitted on the advice of his friend, Bishop George Berkeley. This address must have said, one supposes, something like but also unlike what Lucretius says of the philosopher, that he alone had looked into the heart of things and brought back truths to set men free of the fear of death. How far, if at all, it committed Pope to doctrines like the Incarnation or the divinity of Jesus cannot now be guessed, yet it can hardly have been obtrusively Unitarian or Pope would not have shown it to Berkeley. Nor would Pope, astute judge of audiences that he was, have vented an opinion certain to bring the English public about his ears. To this evidence may be added the fact that he set down at the end of Epistle 1 in the earliest surviving manuscript of his poem, "Thy will be done, in Earth as it is in Heaven." The superscription says nothing precise, of course, about his religious views, but it is not likely to have been the sentiment of a man taking part in a conspiracy, as one of his Victorian editors presumed, to write down the Christian or any other religion.

On the other hand, during the period when the *Essay* was being written, Pope undoubtedly had leanings toward the "deism" of his day, if for no other reason than that it skirted the perpetual wranglings of individual creeds and sought to isolate a minimal common ground acceptable to all. Bolingbroke's influence—surely considerable, though in the absence of any very precise documentation difficult to assess and tempting to exaggerate—would have pressed him in this direction, and some of the poet's friends have left statements suggesting that at this time he was, in fact, like Bolingbroke, a professing deist. The only piece of evidence that bears directly on his intentions *in the poem*, however, is the comment of the younger Jonathan Richardson, the painter's son, that the poet never dreamed of interpreting his poem as Warburton was to do until "the general alarm of its fatalism, and deistical tendency" broke out, "of which ... we talked with him (my father and I) frequently at *Twickenham*, without his appearing to understand it otherwise, or ever thinking to alter those passages, which we suggested as what might seem the most exceptionable." Richardson's statement can be taken in several ways. If it means, as some have believed, that Pope intended and approved a generally fatalistic, deistic, and even anti-Christian meaning in the *Essay*, it is nonsense, since it conflicts with everything we know about the author, the poem, and the author's sense of audience. If it means, as others have supposed, that Pope, though not interested in a general attack, wished certain passages to be unmistakably heterodox, it conflicts with the strong desire evinced by the poet in letters to his friend Caryll to keep the poem at least within the general pale of Christian acceptability. It *need* mean no more than that like other poets Pope proved enigmatic when queried about his meanings, solemnly refusing to combat interpretations of the parts that he did not see how any careful reader of the whole could make.

All things considered, the most eligible conclusion appears to be that at the time of writing Pope wished to have it both ways. He liked to house, at least in fancy (as his poems tell us), with both Whig and Tory, Locke and Montaigne, Aristippus and St. Paul. He unquestionably had sympathies with the liberal theology which was stirring the great religious controversies of his time; but also, as his commerce with Catholic friends and his life at Twickenham with his mother show, sympathies with an older view. Quite possibly he conceived his poem to be an exercise in conciliation like his *Essay on Criticism*, an effort to map a middle ground between extremes in even more ways than its preface declares. It does not unequivocally embrace traditional Christian views, but it does not unequivocally oppose them; and it keeps some of them present by implication just beneath the text. In this respect, it resembles those collections of eighteenth-century sermons in which a first series in defense of religion on "natural" grounds is combined with a second series in defense of revelation. Pope has telescoped the two and submerged the second, but the duality of the poem in this respect answers to a profound duality in the age and, very probably, in his own mind. How many of us today, if we reflect on such matters at all, have clear and settled convictions or convictions that are not a tapestry of many strands?

Warburton and Pope

By late 1738, in any event, unquestionably alarmed by attacks on his politics which came very close to branding him a traitor, and perhaps even more alarmed (in what was always a dangerous situation for a Roman Catholic) by attacks on his religious views as expressed in the *Essay on Man*, Pope settled with relief for Warburton's *Vindication*, the first portion of which appeared that December. Soon after, in January 1739, he sent its author an effusive letter of thanks, the first of several, and in April 1740, these led to a meeting of the two in London, followed by a week or ten days during which Warburton was Pope's guest at Twickenham.

In imagination, the encounter tickles the funnybone, like the long-ago association with Wycherley. A large, rawboned, burly man, "of a frame that seemed to require a good supply of provisions to support it," Warburton was ready and willing to impress his host with his principled and "philosophical" frugality; while the comparatively tiny poet, whether to impress in turn or from a wish to offer only the best, tossed the country-mouse philosophy of his poems and of his ordinary diet out the window, producing at their first dinner a conversation of which he later gave Spence this entertaining record:

"Shall I help you to some lobster?"

"No, I thank you."

"What, do you never eat any?"

"I never did."

"You hate it then!"

87. William Warburton (1689–1779). Engraving by Thomas Burford after Charles Philips. The inscription on the manuscript under Warburton's hand is "The Divine Legation of Moses," title of his best-known work.

"... the greatest general critic I ever knew."

Pope to Spence, no. 509.

Courtesy of the National Portrait Gallery, London.

"I can't tell."

"You had as good try, how you like it."

"No, as I have never tasted it, I don't know why I should get a taste to it now."

Pressed to partake also of some Cyprus wine, Warburton responded with similar garrulity: "We have desires enough. Why should we add to them?"

One readily sees why some who did not know Warburton well took what one of them called his "impenetrable taciturnity" to be the mark of a fool. But they were quite wrong. Though overbearing, belligerent, and disputatious in his writings (effectively disputatious, since he had practiced for some years as an attorney before taking orders), Warburton was a man of exceptional learning, with analytical powers of a high intensity, and a most agreeable companion. Pope thought him "the greatest general critic I ever knew" for "seeing through all the possibilities of things," and evidence abounds to suggest that his occasional taciturnity may have been more political than temperamental: a way of getting his bearings in a new situation (for he was determined to shine) before venturing to participate. Once at ease with an individual or a group, he was (a contemporary tells us) "surprisingly communicative."

> His memory is prodigious, and his fancy enchanting. His diligence is equal to the vivacity of his parts, and the fluency and correctness of his conversation is beyond most men. I regard him, however, as a genius of so high rank, that, unable to contain himself within the narrow limits of ordinary capacities, he *spurns the dull earth, and soars above the skies*; or, to use an expression of his own concerning Mr. Bayle [author of the great biographical dictionary of that name], "strikes frequently into the province of paradox."

It was presumably this fondness for spurning the ordinary and seeking out tasks more eccentric and attention-getting that drew Warburton to grapple with Pope's poem in the first place and to try to break it to the saddle, even if, like the Homeric critics, as a friend soon reminded him, it meant reading into Homer things that Homer "never dreamt of." His own view, at least for public consumption, was that "The Infidels and Libertines prided themselves in thinking Mr. Pope of their party. I thought it of use to Religion to show so noble a Genius was not."

Actually, in springing to Pope's defense at this time, Warburton was behaving even more paradoxically than anyone but himself and his friend Lewis Theobald, hero of the 1728–29 *Dunciads*, knew. Only nine years before, three anonymous letters contributed by Warburton to the *Daily Journal* had defended Theobald by attacking Pope with an abusiveness and, indeed, an obscenity hardly to be matched elsewhere in hostile Popeana. (It is considerably to Theobald's credit that he allowed no word of this to escape him, at least none that reached Pope.) Yet more remarkable: When in 1733–34 the *Essay on Man* first appeared, Warburton is reliably reported to have read weekly essays refuting it to a club of Pope's enemies to which he then belonged, and to have written, though he did not publish, a treatise proving it to be "atheism, spinozaism, deism, hobbism, fatalism, and what not." To have moved by 1738 from an opinion so damning to the laudatory sentiments of the *Vindication* was an exercise in paradox such as must have choked even Momus, the Greek God of blame, though whether with tears or laughter it would be hard to decide.

The relationship that in 1740 sprang up between the poet and his defender was therefore not without self-interest: each had something to gain from the association, and knew it—Pope, a protector; Warburton, an opener of doors. Even during their first week together, Pope began the process of introducing his new acquaintance to his circle of powerful friends, through one of whom in the near future Warburton's fortune would be made; while Warburton, having the preceding autumn published the separate essays of his *Vindication* as a book, to Pope's great satisfaction and relief, now responded with such warmth to proposals for extending the *Essay* (proposals which eventually gave rise to the final *Dunciads* instead) that from 1740 till Pope's death he became his chief confidant in the project and, indeed, to the extent of providing enthusiastic support and some of its Scriblerian mock-notes, a collaborator.

In the long run, the material advantages of the relationship fell largely to Warburton. Not only was he introduced by Pope to Ralph Allen (1741), whose niece he married (1746), whose heir he ultimately became (1766), and whose influence raised him first to be dean of Bristol (1757), then bishop of Gloucester (1760); from Pope also, as an outright legacy, he received the property of all the poet's works in print—a legacy that over the editions of his lifetime cannot have been worth less to him than four or five thousand pounds—eighty to a hundred thousand pounds in today's money. Pope's own gains were more problematical. True, he now had a gifted controversialist standing like a sturdy breakwater between himself and any who might choose to attack him through the *Essay on Man*—Curll, for example. He had also an editor who was eager to cooperate with him in preparing a definitive edition of his works, with learned commentary in the grand manner. As it turned out, perhaps fortunately, only the *Essay on Criticism*, the *Essay on Man* with its four attendant epistles to friends which Warburton later named the *Moral Essays*, and the final *Dunciad* in four books were equipped by the time Pope died with a full panoply of Warburton's heavy-handed notes. The Warburton edition of the complete works, a more perfunctory affair in a smaller format and with briefer comment did not appear till 1751, when the poet had been seven years dead. And a memorial biography, which Spence might have written (considerably to the benefit of Pope's reputation) if it had not been annually looked for from Warburton's pen, was in the end farmed out to a hack and first saw the light of day in 1769, a full quarter century after its subject's decease. Even the editorial responsibility he held in the works, Warburton occasionally abused, inserting notes in later *Dunciad* editions to pay off personal scores.

Still, during the four years remaining to Pope after Warburton and he met, something like a friendship, or at the very least a mutual admiration society, took shape on both sides. Pope, ever inclined to hero worship, placed Warburton on a pedestal almost equal to that of Bolingbroke: "the Only Great Man in Europe who knows as much as He." And when in 1741 Oxford offered him an honorary Doctorate of Laws and, at about the same time, Warburton an honorary Doctorate of Divinity, but then owing to the pettishness of certain dons withdrew the offer to Warburton, Pope declined his own honor firmly. "I will dye before I receive one," he wrote Warburton, "in an Art I am ignorant of, at a place where there remains any Scruple of bestowing one on you, in a Science of which you are so great a Master. In short I will be Doctor'd with you, or not at all."

Warburton, for his part, besides providing Pope with inspiriting assistance of several sorts while he yet lived, considered himself the guardian of his memory when he died. As he gave out books from Pope's library in later life (these too he had inherited), he inscribed them in Latin as a "Gift from Alexander Pope, easily first of Poets, best and friendliest of men," and even in his last years, though by then well gone in senility, he is reported to have come suddenly alert, during a conversation when Pope was being censured, with the exclamation, "Who talks against Pope? He was the best of friends and the best of men." Not—to tell truth—that as a guardian of Pope's memory, he did it much good. To be defended by Warburton was rather like being defended by a giant saurian, whose thrashing tail could inflict as much damage on the object defended as its savage muzzle on assailants.

"St. John! whose Love indulg'd my labors past"

After Pope's death, as it oddly happened, the chief assailant was
Bolingbroke. Declared by Pope's will custodian of his manuscripts
(as Warburton of his printed works), Bolingbroke soon made two
troubling discoveries. The first was that the *Epistle to a Lady*, in the
expanded form in which it was left by the poet, already set in type
but not published, contained among other added "characters" the
one called "Atossa," quoted earlier in these pages. This was also
extant, it appears, as Pope's character sketches usually were, in
separate form among his papers. Though "Atossa" has its longest
roots in the stereotype of the female Fury (virago, shrew,
termagant: the same stereotype that Shakespeare turns to comic use
in his famous Kate of *The Taming of the Shrew*), Pope's contemporary inspiration came from two imperious and quarrelsome
women, both by the 1730s notorious among the *beau monde* for
their pride, self-will, and sometimes altogether infantile behavior.
One of them was Sarah Jennings Churchill, "Marlbro's Termagant
Dutchess," as a contemporary calls her, who also remarks with
astonishment that in her London house near St. James's she had had
the face and hands in a portrait of her granddaughter Lady Anne
Spencer actually "blacken'd"—to match, so it is explained to him,
"the colour of her heart." "What was right," another contemporary
remarked after her death, this time a woman, "she seemed to do by
Caprice, & what was Cruel by Intention. Her Revenge never dyed &
for her gratitude it could hardly be said to have existed. . . . But I
think I have said more than enough of one of whom no good can be
spoken." The last statement is extreme, for there were good sides as
well as bad to Sarah Churchill, but it serves to convey some notion
of her contemporary reputation.

The other figure in Pope's mind—no doubt companioned there,
like Marlborough's duchess, by his observations of a social type
common among all "Whom an unbounded prosperity lets loose to
their own wills"—was Katharine Darnley Sheffield, Duchess of
Buckinghamshire, whose London house (considerably altered over
the years) is now the British royal family's Buckingham Palace. As a
natural daughter of James II, she was accustomed to claiming for
herself all the privileges of excess and from others all the deferences
that she fancied her royal blood warranted. Though she too was not
without her virtues, her dark side comes through most vividly in
Horace Walpole's verdict that she was "more mad with Pride than
any mercer's wife in bedlam" and in her own reported statement

on church sermons that "it was monstrous to be told you have a heart as sinful as the common wretches that crawl the earth."

Though we are now entering the realm of inference and speculation, it is probably fair to say that in some early manuscript form largely lost to us, the character now named "Atossa" had a different name, at least a certain number of different lines, and, insofar as it was meant to suggest any actual person, was meant to suggest Sarah Churchill. In that state, it would have made an arresting companion piece to the character of her husband that Pope sketched out tentatively for his vanity-of-human-wishes survey in Epistle 4 of the *Essay on Man*, but then wisely developed for publication into the more general and marmoreal verses beginning:

> There, in the rich, the honour'd, fam'd and great,
> See the false scale of Happiness complete!
>
> (4: 287–88)

All this, as chief inspirer of the *Essay*, Bolingbroke must have known, at least during the years 1731–34, when Pope was working on the poem and he himself was still at Dawley. What he probably did not know was that in the decade since, doubtless owing in part to a growing friendship between Sarah Churchill and Pope after she joined the Opposition (stereotypes have a way of dissolving when we come to know the individual they obscure), doubtless too for reasons we cannot now recover, the portrait had been revised. Revised so far, in fact, that as a detailed history of this episode has shown, every line of the version printed in the enlarged *Epistle to a Lady* left behind at Pope's death may, and some lines must, be taken as referring to the Duchess of Buckinghamshire. The current name "Atossa," moreover, had no relevance at all to Sarah Churchill, but fitted Katharine Darnley almost like a glove, the Persian princess Atossa having been a daughter of Cyrus the Great and a sister of his son Cambyses as Katharine Darnley was daughter of James II and half-sister of the Old Pretender.

Curiously, in going over Pope's papers, Bolingbroke failed to recognize the reorientation of the portrait. It may simply have been that we tend to see what we expect to see, and *some* of the verses, especially those on pride of rank and outrageous caprice, could legitimately be taken to apply to either duchess. It may have been that a manuscript version existing among Pope's papers had not yet been wholly freed of lines that seemed to glance at the duchess of Marlborough and this affected his reading of the final form as well. Or it may simply have been, with Marlborough's duchess actively importuning him for any of Pope's papers that might reflect on the Marlborough name, he was hasty and mistook what he had for what she wanted. At any rate, with Marchmont apparently as witness, he destroyed what he took to be a manuscript satire on Sarah Churchill and forced Warburton to suppress for several years the printed *Epistle to a Lady* along with the three other epistles (to Bathurst, Burlington, Cobham) making up the collection with which it had been intended to be published.

So far, no harm done, though one may reasonably wonder at the precipitancy with which Bolingbroke concluded that in planning to publish "Atossa" Pope was somehow breaking faith with the Duchess of Marlborough, despite a "favor" that according to Bolingbroke he had lately accepted from her, and which he said Marchmont knew about too. No second or third thoughts—"friendly" thoughts, such as might have prompted him to read what Pope proposed to print with more attention—seem to have troubled him then or afterward. Accordingly, when a few weeks later news of the secret printing of his *The Idea of a Patriot King* was brought to his attention, he was even less amenable to extenuating reflections. Not that his anger was unjustified. Quite the reverse. Pope had plainly exceeded whatever mandate he had received for printing a few copies for private distribution among friends. Worse, he had very possibly tidied up and revised the text here and there (as he was always tidying up and revising his own texts) in order that it might shine out more gloriously when the day of publication at last arrived. That would of course be after Bolingbroke's death—in case Bolingbroke had failed in the meantime to publish the piece himself—and would be undertaken by that far too officious yet affectionately well-intentioned guardian of his friends' reputations, Alexander Pope. Bolingbroke, sixty in 1738, had not for some time been in such health as made it an untenable guess that he might predecease his admirer. Six years later, in the spring of 1744, when Pope knew that it was *he* who would go first—knew it for many weeks—he took no steps to have the printing destroyed, despite the fact that at some point during his final months he consigned a number of his own papers to the fire. Clearly, he did not anticipate his friend's extreme reaction, and, equally clearly, his friend was as little disposed in this instance as in the other to consider qualifying his judgment of "treachery."

Even so, no public harm had yet been done to Pope. In 1745, however, word came to Bolingbroke's ear that the life of the poet which Warburton was said to be writing would be critical of the alleged maleficent influence of a certain lord and might animadvert with some asperity on the said lord's reactions to the surreptitious printing of his *Patriot King*. (Much as Pope wished them to, and believed, naively, that only good could come of it if they did, it is by no means irrefutably certain that Warburton and Bolingbroke ever met. What is more nearly certain is that, either in writing or conversation or both, Warburton evinced contempt for some of Bolingbroke's "philosophy," which Bolingbroke as cordially returned.) Urged by Pope's friend Lyttelton not to stir a hornet's nest, Warburton held off: he was still on the make, and besides, on the main question, however innocent or even admirable the motives, Pope's action was demonstrably wrong.

Bolingbroke was not on the make. He was a tired sick man in his sixty-seventh year, cheated (from his point of view) of the fulfilment of most of his life's ambitions. He was pardonably resentful of the trespass on his property. He may, as his biographer contends, have wished to show Warburton what strong cards he held against Pope if it came to a public showdown. And, unquestionably, he was piqued. Only a rankling and rather pettish jealousy of the ascendancy gained by Warburton over Pope in the four years after their meeting, when Bolingbroke was much in France, can explain his willingness to defame in public one of his oldest and warmest friends after he was dead and unable to defend himself. This he did by publishing in 1746 a six-page pamphlet containing *Verses Upon the Late D—ss of M—. By Mr. P—*. After this title came "Atossa," to which he appended as explanation:

> These Verses are Part of a Poem, entitled *Characters of Women*. It is generally said, the D—ess gave Mr. Pope £1,000 to suppress them. He took the Money, yet the World sees the Verses; but this is not the first Instance where Mr. P's practical Virtue has fallen very short of those pompous Professions that he makes in his Writings.

The fairest assumption is that Bolingbroke genuinely believed this story, though each of its details rests on questionable evidence and its two main points as to the identity of "Atossa" and the treachery of Pope in publishing a character of the duchess of Marlborough after accepting a fee to suppress it are misapprehensions. Even so, such treatment of a dead friend seems contemptible. Perhaps it is explained as kindly as it can be if we call it the retaliation of "injured merit" against one who has presumed to accord a rival the deference once reserved to himself. (Warburton's position *vis-à-vis* the last of Pope's poems—the *New Dunciad*, and the final *Dunciad* in four books—somewhat resembles Bolingbroke's during the composition of the *Essay on Man*, and Bolingbroke may have been resentful of this, though of course his absence in France was of his own making.) Or perhaps such actions are ultimately inexplicable, one more proof, as Pope might have put it, of the gross thieveries of time; or one more characteristic expression of what he had called in his *Essay* that "Chaos of Thought and Passion, all confus'd": the human psyche.

But this was not the end. Bolingbroke had not signed the "Atossa" pamphlet of 1746, though many guessed its source—some indeed had obtained transcripts of the portrait, presumably with the Duchess of Marlborough's name attached—and if, as he had said in his note, "the World now sees the Verses," their release could hardly be laid at any door save that of the man who had control of the poet's manuscripts. Nevertheless, Bolingbroke's first "owned" attack on his friend did not come till 1749. In that year, moved to a response by the serial publication of extracts from his *Idea of a Patriot King* in the January, March, and April issues of *The London Magazine*, he decided to use the occasion to publish an "authorised" text of the work, combining it with his *Letter on the Spirit of Patriotism* (addressed to Cornbury in 1736 but never published) and an essay *On the State of Parties at the Accession of King George the First*. Lyttelton, asked to accept the honor of being its dedicatee, declined: the political situation had changed enormously in the ten years since the *Patriot King* was written, and so had Lyttelton's place in it. Further, he could see no virtue in publishing at this moment a collection certain to stir controversy, since there was a very great difference between fragments "stole into print in a magazine" and a *bona* fide complete edition under Bolingbroke's name. He must have been yet more put off when he learned from his correspondent's reply that while Bolingbroke would omit, as requested, "any marks of my esteem or affection for *you*," he was "forced to reveal the turpitude of a man with whom I lived long in the intimacy of friendship." In an "Advertisement" affixed to the three works, published in May, he did so with some fanfare.

For this second act of revenge, as for the first, it would be hard to say just whence the irresistible "force" came. Bolingbroke could easily have justified his edition on the simple unglossed grounds that the magazine text derived from a source that had been tampered with. There was no requirement that he attribute the tampering to Pope. Nor have we, in fact, any certainty as to how much or how little tampering Pope did, since, as Bolingbroke's most recent biographer remarks, Pope's significant alterations (if any) may have been accepted by Bolingbroke and incorporated in the new 1749 edition; in which case they can still less be justly adduced as grounds for an indictment. What we are left with once again is an inexplicable impulse to strip from his old friend's memory the last ounce of honor:

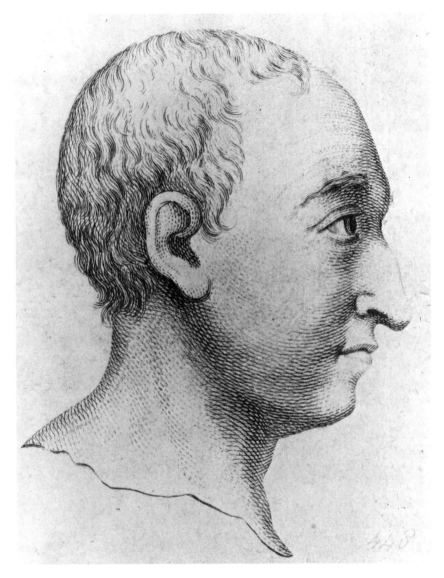

88. Henry St. John, Viscount Bolingbroke (1678–1751). Engraver unknown; undated. Perhaps 1751–52?

St John, whose love indulg'd my labours past
Matures my present, and shall bound my last!

Imit. Hor., Ep. I, i: 1–2.

Courtesy of the National Portrait Gallery, London.

an impulse that renders it impossible to read the closing verses of
the *Essay on Man* (to say nothing of countless passages in the correspondence) without something like a sigh for the tears of things:

> Oh! while along the stream of Time thy name
> Expanded flies, and gathers all its fame,
> Say, shall my little bark attendant sail,
> Pursue the triumph, and partake the gale?
> When statesmen, heroes, kings, in dust repose,
> Whose sons shall blush their fathers were thy foes,
> Shall then this verse to future age pretend
> Thou wert my guide, philosopher, and friend?

Sophocles says we should count no man happy till he is dead.
Clearly an optimistic view.

Good years

Happily for everyone concerned, during the remaining years of
Pope's life, 1738–44, all such dismaying eventualities lay hidden in
the seedbed of time. These were good years for him, on the whole,
despite the further encroachments of his disabilities and a deepening
disenchantment as he looked about him at what evidently seemed, if
we may judge by his forceful depictions of it in the final *Dunciads*, a
general trivialization of the national life and, notably, of the institutions expected in those days to foster it: court, nobility, church,
school, and university. True, we hear oftener in these years of colds,
headaches, failing eyesight, rheumatisms, asthmas, and bouts of
indigestion—the last hardly surprising since he never quite learned
to curb his impulse to overeat when warmed by the company of
friends, and sometimes to overdrink, even with the knowledge that
much wine was lethal to him.

Particularly mischievous for his dietary regimen were his
occasional feastings and libations with Lord Burlington's protégé
William Kent, designer, landscapist, and from 1740 Jervas's
successor as the king's principal face painter. He had gourmandizing
tastes far more sophisticated than Pope's, and, as the latter confided
in a metaphorical report to Kent's patron, might hope to paint like a
Raphael and look like an Angelo if he would but "cleanse his Pencil,

& purify his Pallat★ of all that greasy mixture and fatt Oyl they have contracted." Otherwise, he must expect by his "Carnality"† and by his "Carnivoracity" not to imitate Raphael "in any thing but his untimely End."

There was much teasing of this sort between poet and painter (as the droll Maggot-Muses circling the poet's head in Kent's sketch of him in his grotto presumably testify), and between each of them and their mutual good friends, the Burlingtons. Lady Burlington, considerably a romp, seems to have amused herself that fall (1738) by sending Pope the gazetteers' worst attacks on him with epigrammatic retorts by herself masquerading as his, and one suspects that it was largely to humor her, in a comparable banter on Kent at about this time, that Pope wrote one of his funniest and most endearing letters, petitioning Burlington not to let a tree be cut down at Chiswick to make way for one of Kent's landscape "improvements." Except for the signatures of the Burlington entourage and neighbors, the letter is entirely Pope's:

The Petition of

Dorothy Countess of Burlington, Dorothy & Charlot Boyle
Spinsters, Charles Duke of Grafton, Geo. Lord Euston, Sir
Clemt Cottrel Knt. Alexr. Pope Gent. & Chs. Brunevall Gent.
and others—
To the Right Hon. the Earl of Burlington,
Humbly Shewing

That whereas a Certain Tree lying, being, & standing in or on the Grounds of your Lordship, at or before or on one side or the other of a Certain Edifice of your Honour's called the Casino, hath possessed occupied and held, for the space of twenty or twenty one years or thereabouts, over or under, the said Ground Place and Bank, and suffered & endured all the Changes & Vicissitudes of Wind Water & Weather in the Worst of Times. And whereas a certain Upstart Terras, hath arisen & stood opposite (tho at great distance) to your Honour's said Tree, above & before mentioned & described, which said Terras hath and can suffer no molestation, Let, or hindrance from any Shadow, Root or Branch of your said Tree, which both continued faithfully fixed to the Premises, nor ever stirred, or attempted to stir, from his said place, notwithstanding which the said Terras hath, by the Instigation of Sathan,

---

★ Palate as well as palette.
† Used here for Burlington's benefit with a pun on "Carnation," a painter's management of flesh tints.

89. Dorothy Savile, Countess of Burlington (1699–1758). By Charles Jervas, *c.* 1721–25?

> But sure you'll find it hard to spoil
> The Sense and Taste of one that bears
> The Name of *Savile* and of *Boyle*.
> *On the Countess of B[urlington] cutting Paper*, 14–16.

By kind permission of the Trustees of the Chatsworth Settlement. Photograph: Courtauld Institute of Art.

& of William Kent, his agent and Attorney, conspiring thereunto,
devised and plotted, and do at this time devise plot & conspire the
Destruction, Abolition, Overthrow & Total Subversion of This
Your Honour's Tree[,] the said Tree to cut down, or saw down, or
root up & grub up, & ruin for ever: We, Your Honour's humble
Petitioners who have many years known, accustomed & frequented
the said Tree, sitten, reposed or disported under the Shade thereof[,]
yea and seen the said William Kent, the Agent & Attorney of the said
Sathan, solace himself with Syllabubs, Damsels, and other Benefits
of Nature, under the said Tree, Do, for ourselves & our Posterity,
most earnestly, & jointly as well as Seperately [*sic*], petition & pray,
that the said Tree may remain, subsist, continue & flourish in his
place, during his or her natural Life (not being absolutely certain of
the Sex of the said Tree) to enjoy the Small Spot of Ground on which
God & your Lordship's Ancestors of ever blessed memory have
placed it. And Your Honours most humble Petitioners, as in Duty
bound, shall ever pray &c. &c.

	D. Burlington	A. Pope	B. Fairfax Euston
	D. Boyle	Charles Bruneval	F. Fairfax
Grafton	C. Boyle	Clement Cottrell	

This was also the period, it will be recalled, when Bolingbroke was
Pope's guest at Twickenham for some months: seeking an acceptable
price for Dawley, composing the essay on the patriot king that was to
cause such havoc to Pope's reputation after his death, and lending
what influence he could to the Young Patriot effort to rally a now
fatally splintered Opposition around the Prince of Wales. There were
unquestionably many meetings of a political nature at the villa, to
some of which Pope alludes in his *Verses* on his grotto, which must
have been germinating at about this time, though first published in
1741:

> Here nobly-pensive St. John sate & thought.
> Here patriot Sighs from Wyndham's bosom stole.
>
> (ll. 10–11)

Between the Prince of Wales and Pope, Lyttelton worked hard to
promote an intimacy: "Be therefore as much with him as you can,
Animate him to Virtue, to the Virtue least known to Princes, though
most necessary for them, Love of the Publick; and think that the
Morals, the Liberty, the whole Happiness of this Country depends on
your Success"—not exactly a light assignment for one small poet.
And the Prince made what was possibly an overture (though perhaps

90. Frederick, Prince of Wales (1707–1751). Drawing by Jonathan Richardson, *c.* 1736.

> Let him—no trifler from [his father's?] school,
> Nor like his [father's father?] still a fool—
> Be but a man!
>> *One Thousand Seven Hundred and Forty*, 87–88.

he was merely acknowledging the poet's earlier gift of a Bounce puppy) by bestowing several urns for use in Pope's "laurel circus" as well as marble busts of Spenser, Shakespeare, Milton, and Dryden to adorn his library. Nevertheless, where royalty was concerned, Pope was always skittish, as we have had reason to see. Though at least once he dined with the Prince at Kew, apparently during 1738, he had very nearly to be forced into it by Lyttelton, and there is an anecdote of this period, which though it may not be authentic, gives a reliable account of Pope's sentiments:

> The Prince said: "how shall we reconcile your love to a Prince with your professed indisposition to Kings, since Princes will be Kings in time?" "Sir," replied Pope, "I consider royalty under that noble and authorized type of the Lion; while he is young, and before his nails are grown, he may be approached and caressed with safety and pleasure."

These affairs, together with Pope's pride in showing off Boling-broke to their many mutual friends, undoubtedly taxed his slender stores of energy, and by late autumn of 1738 he is confiding to his Yorkshire friend Hugh Bethel, who also had serious health problems:

> I hope the Season is now coming that drives Friends together, as it does Birds, into warm Coverts & close Corners: [Bethel usually spent part of the winter months in London] That we may meet over a Fire, & tell the Stories of the Year. Indeed the Town Hours of the Day suit as ill with my Stomach [at this period dinner was usually taken around three in the afternoon], as the Wintery & dark Nights do with my Carcase. . . . Take care of your Health; follow not the Feasts (as I have done) of Lords, nor the Frolicks of Ladies.

Still, despite the dissipations, which seem to have been rather frequent at least into 1739, Pope was able to maintain through several of the years remaining to him what will seem to most of us a demand-ing schedule: rambles in the summer, long winter visits with the Allens in Bath, a continuous flow of letters to friends, frequent enter-taining of guests at Twickenham, regular forays into London to dine or consult with his printers, continuous superintendence of the addi-tions and changes taking place in his gardens and grotto (as all gar-deners know, never to be altogether "finished"), and, what is perhaps most remarkable of all, a substantial amount of literary activity—if not for himself, at least for others. During the latter months of 1738, for instance, he was seeing through the press for Gay's heirs the second volume of *Fables* (the sort of literary executorship he had earlier assumed for Parnell). He was also considering and probably taking the lead in the complicated revisings of Swift's ironic poem on his own death (*Verses on the Death of Dr. Swift*), intended by the dean's English friends to represent him more winningly to both current readers and posterity than the version he had actually sent for publication. The same well-intentioned itch to "improve," so habitual with his own compositions, so obviously annoying when let loose without permission on the work of others, would not long after be applied to the text of the *Patriot King* and so establish at least one of the conditions leading to Bolingbroke's vendetta. Swift, who was also displeased, promptly published his own original text of the *Verses* in Dublin. In defense of Swift's English friends it is only fair to add that the poem they made from the verse he sent, partly through omissions, partly through excerpting lines from an earlier poem by him on the same subject, is still felt by some readers today to be the more effective poem of the two; and, further, that they were without much doubt encouraged in the liberties they took by Swift's own, and his friend Orrery's, alarming reports from Dublin about the condition of his mind and memory: a condition they may have thought the poem reflected.

Meanwhile, Pope seems to have been playing a considerable consulting role in the cluster of historical-allegorical Opposition plays put forward for the stage during 1738–39, possibly to test the mettle of the new Licensing Act. Two of the authors most involved, his friends Thomson and Mallet, moved in the orbit of the prince, and their offerings (no worse than the norm of the period, but not much better) were spiced for contemporaries with topical innuendo. David Mallet's *Mustapha*, for instance, first performed on 13 February 1739, told the story of Solyman the Magnificent, misled by a wicked adviser into imagining his son Mustapha disloyal to him and hence into having him disposed of. The application to the king, to Walpole, and to the enforced exile of the prince from St. James's was obvious, and doubtless mainly for this reason—it has little else to recommend it—the play enjoyed an exceptional run of fourteen nights. Pope, to whom Mallet had read the script almost act by act while composing it, attended the opening performance and was so delighted by James Quin, London's leading tragedian at the time, as Mustapha that he went backstage at the close to congratulate him—which in turn so delighted Quin that he insisted on holding the poet's scarlet cloak for him as he took his leave.

Having let through his fingers a play so offensive, the Lord Chamberlain came belatedly to life and suppressed two others that were already in rehearsal. One, Henry Brooke's *Gustavus Vasa*, based on an incident of Swedish history involving usurpation of power by figures vaguely reminiscent of George II and Walpole, has won a niche in theater history as the first play banned by the Act and a place in the biography of Samuel Johnson as the occasion of one of his few excursions into Swiftian irony: his *Compleat Vindication of the Licensers of the Stage*, issued in May after the suppression in March. The second play banned was James Thomson's *Edward and Eleonora*, which likewise has few other claims to immortality. Mainly a harmless tearjerker—its Prince Edward (later England's Edward I) is stabbed by a poisoned dagger while on a crusade to the Holy Land and saved by his loving princess, who sucks the poison from his wound—it carried in one speech by Edward's faithful adviser "Gloster" an admonition that might remind audiences of Walpole's exclusion of the prince and his associates from governmental posts, and it celebrated a loving couple who could, if one insisted, be identified with the Prince and Princess of Wales.

Thomson had a year earlier, however, slipped by the censor a much more insinuating piece, his adaptation of Aeschylus' *Agamemnon*. Though not intended primarily as propaganda, the play made available some broad analogies between Agamemnon's return to Argos with a Trojan concubine in tow after his ten years at Troy and George II's return to Britain after a seven-month stay in Hanover, not exactly in company with his new German concubine, Madame Walmoden, but ready and willing to have her imported. A fainter though more dangerous analogy—rendered almost inoperative by the queen's unexpected death in late 1737—permitted comparisons between the privileges of rule accorded to Aegisthus by Clytemnestra during Agamemnon's absence and those accorded by Caroline to Walpole during the absence of the king.

Pope's connection with the play is problematical. It probably went no deeper than judicious reading and appraisal, perhaps enhanced by suggestions and the prestige of his name with certain theater managers, which it had become habitual for many writers of the day, especially his friends, to ask of him. He was, we know, present at the play's opening on 6 April 1738. Possibly because his public appearances in these years were rare, possibly too because his recent poems had been making his political dissent very clear and this was presumably a somewhat anti-Establishment, pro–Prince of Wales audience, his entrance is said to have been greeted with a burst of applause. One later account, from a source usually reliable, goes further. Disappointed, it tells us, that the play's first-night reception was not all that had been hoped, "a club of wits, with Mr. Pope at the head of them, met at the theater next morning, and cut, and slash'd like dexterous surgeons," excising a young-love subplot altogether and moving the last scene of the fourth act into the fifth. Whether this is true or not, the play went on to a successful run of nine nights. The pathetic part of Cassandra was played by Susannah Cibber, wife to Colley Cibber's rascally son Theophilus. (She was a sister of the composer Thomas Arne, whose "Rule, Britannia"—written in 1740 at the height of the war with Spain to conclude his setting of the Mallet-Thomson masque *Alfred* and first performed on August 1–2 at Cliveden House, then a country seat of the Prince—gave Britain the best, musically speaking, of all patriotic songs). Trained, and well trained, by her husband, her father-in-law, and Aaron Hill, Susannah Cibber was to become one of the period's leading tragediennes and frequently played opposite Garrick.

Garrick's name is a useful reminder that not all of Pope's interest in the stage during these years sprang from a wish to help friends or embarrass the ministry. According to the actor's own report, he "had the honour to act thrice in the presence of Pope" between that Monday, 19 October 1741, when he burst like a thunderclap on the London theater scene in the title role of Shakespeare's *Richard III*, and, say, late 1743, after which time Pope was doubtfully in sufficient health to attend. It was not his initial appearance in the role of Richard, but apparently his fifth, performed a fortnight later on November 2, that Pope witnessed and that Garrick later described *con amore* to his friend Percival Stockdale:

> When I was told that POPE was in the house, I instantaneously felt a palpitation at my heart; a tumultuous, not a disagreeable emotion in my mind. I was then in the prime of youth; and in the zenith of my theatrical ambition. It gave me particular pleasure that RICHARD was my character, when POPE was to see, and hear me. As I opened the part, I saw our little poetical hero, dressed in black, seated in a side-box near the stage; and viewing me with a serious, and earnest attention. His look shot, and thrilled, like lightning through my frame; and I had some hesitation in proceeding, from anxiety, and from joy. As RICHARD gradually blazed forth, the house was in a roar of applause, and the conspiring hand of POPE shadowed me with laurels.

To Lord Orrery, who was sitting with him, Pope is said to have commented, "That young man never had his *equal* as an actor, and he will never have a rival."

Garrick's acute consciousness of Pope's presence gives some measure of the esteem in which during these later years (apart, no doubt, from court circles) the poet was held. When he attended the auction of his friend Edward Harley's pictures in March 1742 (Harley had died the preceding year, enormously in debt and close to alcoholism), the young Joshua Reynolds, aged nineteen, just then starting his career in the portrait studio of Thomas Hudson, was also in attendance and in later life described the occasion to Boswell, who characteristically set it down as a little scene:

> The room was much crowded. Pope came in. Immediately it was mentioned he was there, a lane was made for him to walk through. Everyone in the front rows by a kind of enthusiastic impulse shook hands with him. Reynolds did like the rest and was very happy in having the opportunity. . . . Sir Joshua said he had an extraordinary face, not an everyday countenance—a pallid studious look; not merely a sharp keen countenance but something grand, like Cicero's.

The comparison to Cicero may have had as much to do with the poet's standing at the time as an outspoken champion of public virtue as with his actual appearance.

His own enthusiastic response to Garrick's acting is also in its way revealing. Unlike many of us, he seems to have retained to the end of his life a capacity to react warmly and intelligently to excellence in areas quite foreign to his own skills and experience. When Richardson's *Pamela* appeared in 1740, he charged his Bath acquaintance, Dr. George Cheyne, who knew Richardson, to make his warm compliments to the author, having read the book "with great Approbation and Pleasure," even to the extent of staying up much of the night to finish it. Of the merits of Mark Akenside's *Pleasures of Imagination* (1744)—whose unlikeness to his own usual habits of thought and expression appears plainly in the following sample:

> O ye Northumbrian shades. . . .
> How gladly I recall your well-known seats
> Belov'd of old, and that delightful time
> When all alone for many a summer's day,
> I wandered through your calm recesses, led
> In silence by some powerful hand unseen—

he was similarly appreciative. This is no every-day writer, he told Dodsley when approached for a judgment (Dodsley thinking the asking price a little high): don't be niggardly!

"The Most Noble Man in England"

Following the sale of Dawley and Bolingbroke's return to France (he would be back but only for short visits in the years before Pope's death), Pope settled into the pattern of life earlier mentioned, combining his old habit of summer rambling with long winter stays near Bath in vain pursuit of some alleviation of his maladies. In 1739, for instance, after Bolingbroke's departure in April, he was off by late June to Stowe. Thence, in a rather touching letter of July 4, he writes Martha Blount that the "New" part of the gardens, laid out by Kent from about 1735 as "The Elysian Fields," is "beyond all description." "Adieu," he says abruptly at one point—can there have been floating somewhere in his mind Shakespeare's Antony's dream of Cleopatra in fields similarly named ("Where souls do couch on flowers, we'll hand in hand, And with our sprightly port make the ghosts gaze")?—"I'm going into the Elyzian Fields, where I shall meet your Idæa [image]." And again, in a later passage of the same letter designated "9 at night": "Adieu once more. I'm going to dream of you."

From such thoughts, however, he was soon off to Adderbury to visit the Duke of Argyll, who had lately broken with Walpole. Then to Hagley, seat of Sir Thomas Lyttelton, his young friend's father—here, according to his own report, he made sketches for three new garden buildings. Then to Rousham to see General Dormer. After that to Cornbury, where he was again to advise on some garden alterations. And after that to Oxford to spend a day or two with Lady Grizel Murray, high-spirited cousin of his friend Marchmont.

That same autumn, he began his series of protracted hibernations with the Allens. During the first of these, which lasted from roughly mid-November till early February, he pushed on first to try the waters of Bristol's Hot Well, describing excitedly to Martha Blount how, as one approached the city, a long arm of the sea reaching into it between quays built up with houses on either side gave the illusion of "hundreds of Ships, their Masts as thick as they can stand," jostling in the middle of a city street:

> This street is fuller of them, than the Thames from London Bridge to Deptford, & at certain times only, the Water rises to carry them out; so that at other times, a Long Street full of ships in the Middle & Houses on both sides looks like a Dream.

The rocky terrain of the Bristol neighborhood also riveted his attention. Partly, as all his "travel" letters to Martha show, because he knew her appetite for detailed scenic description; but also, we may guess, because his current project for enlarging his Grotto into a sort of mineralogical "Musæum" was sensitizing him to the hues and textures of stone. "On that rocky way," he tells her, describing his progress from Bristol to the location of the Hot Well outside, "rise several white Houses, and over them red rocks, and as you go further, more Rocks above rocks, mixd with green bushes, and of different colourd stone. . . ."

> When you have seen the Hills seem to shut upon you & to stop any further way, you go into the House [sheltering the Well] & looking out of the Back door, a vast Rock of 100 foot high, of red, white, green, blue & yellowish Marbles, all blotch'd & variegated strikes you quite in the face, & turning on the left, there opens the River at a vast depth below, winding in & out, & accompanied on both sides with a Continued Range of Rocks up to the Clouds, of a hundred Colours, one behind another.

It is not hard to see whence at least one of the inspirations for the Grotto's final geological character was derived.

Little of lasting value to Pope's health came from these annual hibernations, but there were other satisfactions. Allen's circle of Bath friends became his own, and he in turn introduced to Allen many whom it could do a rising man of business and government concessionaire no harm to know: Burlington, Cornbury, Fortescue, Lyttelton, Murray, possibly Pitt, to mention only a few. Through one of Allen's circle, Dr. William Oliver, news of the new Grotto undertakings reached the Reverend William Borlase, a gifted antiquary, mineralogist, and classical scholar, who contributed giant shipments of rare minerals and fossils from the Cornish mines, together with precise information as to how the lodes in which they were found in nature could be approximated in arrangements at Twickenham. These, artfully set in among the great quantities of Bath stone given by Allen for the Grotto's new rough-hewn arches and rude chambers, were to help create, as Borlase put it, "a natural cave in which the passenger may even entertain himselfe with all the delicacies of subterraneous nature, and more justifiably delay his entrance for a while into the Elyzium it leads him to."

It is also from Oliver that we receive a striking picture of what was apparently an immediately companionable relation between guest and host. Pope—Oliver wrote to Borlase soon after making his

91. Pope's Grotto in its later "geological" phase, still with a fine view through to the Thames. Watercolor by John Chessell Buckler, signed and dated 1826.

By kind permission of the Houghton Library, Harvard University.

acquaintance—is "the freest; humblest, most entertaining Creature you ever met with":

> He has sojourned these two months with our great Countryman [like Oliver and Borlase, Allen was a Cornishman]. . . . They are extremely happy in each other; the one feeling great Joy in the good Heart, and Strong Sense of his truly generous Host, while the other, with the most pleasing Attention, drinks in Rivers of Knowledge continually flowing from the Lipps of his delightful Stranger.

Whatever Allen's feelings may have been about being bathed in rivers of knowledge, Pope's delight in his host's good heart was unalloyed. Here was a Man of Ross who could afford to go well beyond five hundred pound a year. He "suffers no misery near him," Pope wrote to Fortescue that January. "Whoever is lame, or any way disabled, he gives weekly allowances to the wife or children: Besides large supplies of other kinds to other Poor."

> God made this Man rich, to shame the Great; and wise, to humble the learned. I envy none of you in Town the Honours you may have received at Court . . . : I have past this Christmas with the Most Noble Man of England.

Three years afterward, unhappily, this exemplary friendship came under a severe strain and was never quite perfectly restored. It all happened in the summer of 1743, when Pope and Warburton were already in residence with the Allens, collaborating on the supposed definitive edition of Pope's works with Warburtonian notes. Martha Blount, having several times been urged to accept the Allens' hospitality, decided on this occasion to do so, as prelude to a longer stay in Bristol with her own close friend Lady Gerard. George Arbuthnot, the doctor's son, now a London solicitor, had also accepted an invitation to be the Allens' guest on the understanding that he and Pope were to have a housekeeping arrangement of their own in a nearby manor house, formerly Mrs. Allen's family home, which her husband had lately purchased. For reasons not clear, but perhaps owing to some objection of his wife's to this use of the house, Allen, who had at first seemed to agree to the plan (no doubt to please Pope) now decided against it and insisted that all his guests should live together in the great house, Prior Park, erected some two years before on a hillside with a ravishing distant view of Bath. The new arrangement, which involved a direct imposition on the Prior Park household that he had not intended, did not appeal to Arbuthnot, as Pope had sought vainly to persuade Allen it would not, and, accordingly, soon after his arrival,

92. Ralph Allen (1694–1764). By Thomas Hudson, *c.* 1740.

> Let humble ALLEN, with an aukward Shame,
> Do good by stealth, and blush to find it Fame.
> *One Thousand Seven Hundred and Thirty-Eight, Dial.* 1: 135–6

By kind permission of the Bishop of Worcester.

Pope and he set off to pay a scheduled brief visit to Bathurst at Cirencester, then pushed on to Bristol to partake of the Hot Well. Martha
Blount, who had arrived at Prior Park only shortly before Arbuthnot,
was to continue for a few days with the Allens, then go to join Lady
Gerard.

What precisely happened at this point, or slightly earlier, is anyone's
guess. Clearly, there developed upon Martha's arrival or very soon
after it a "mutual dissatisfaction," as Allen put it later, between
Martha and his wife. Indeed, if Martha's story is to be taken at face
value along with certain remarks of Pope's, there was already an ed-
giness in Mrs. Allen's behavior toward Pope by the time Martha
arrived. It is quite possible, for instance, that she had never been particularly pleased by her husband's extreme generosity to his poetical
friend; or that the inevitable inconvenience and added responsibility of
having an invalid in the house for long periods these several years past
had tried her patience; or that she judged the poet had come to feel
altogether too much at his ease in their private Zion; or that the new
plea to borrow the manor house for a month was simply one irritation
too many.

In any event, after Pope's and Arbuthnot's departure, there was
what Martha Blount took to be a distinct chilliness in the air toward
her. As she complained in a deeply depressed note to Pope,

> I packed up all my things yesterday, the servants knew it, Mr. &
> Mrs. Allen never . . . so much as asked me how I went or where, or
> when. . . . Mr. Warburton takes no notice of me. . . . they have not
> one of 'em named your name, nor drank your health since you went.
> They talk to one another without putting me at all in the
> conversation.

One rumor had it at the time that Martha had asked the use of Allen's
coach to go to the mass-house in Bath, but was refused; or, alternatively, was allowed to go, but instructed to take the back ways and
dismount at a distance, since this was the year of Allen's mayoralty in
Bath. Understandable caution, if true, but not notably generous to a
lone female Roman Catholic in view of the kindnesses showered
openly on her male Roman Catholic friend.

Another report, this one given many years later by Gertrude Tucker,
Allen's niece, who within two years at the age of eighteen was to
espouse William Warburton aged forty-six, stated that "every Morning" during their stay at Prior Park Martha Blount went to Pope's
room between six and seven o'clock and that they could be heard
talking together "earnestly" there for a long time; after which, when

they came down to breakfast, "Mrs. B: usd alys to ask him how he had rested that night." Since Pope does speak angrily of "Listeners at doors" and of the possibility that Mrs. Allen "must have had some very unjust & bad thing suggested to her against you" [Martha Blount] in his letters dealing with this affair, there may be truth in Gertrude Tucker's testimony. On the other hand, in view of Pope's state of health at the time and his long years of rather obvious yearning for a species of intimacy denied him, the inference she and her aunt may have chosen to draw from it seems less than plausible. If, as Martha claims, she sensed early on that her presence was not welcome and that, from her point of view, Pope was being treated "rudely," Pope's bedroom before the household was up would have offered the best, perhaps the only, available privacy, and her efforts to persuade him that all was not well, especially if he inclined to set them down to oversensitivity, would easily have made the tone of their conversation "earnest."

So, as Allen's biographer has well stated it, what had been meant on all sides to be a joyous house party turned into a fiasco, "and of the quartet of Popean visitors only Warburton stayed on, triumphantly in possession of the rich Mr. Allen's friendship." Pope did not stay at Prior Park on his way home from Bristol, but with Dr. Oliver; yet one notices that by early September he has taken the initiative in trying to mend matters, after which he and Allen resume a regular, friendly, but perhaps somewhat tentative and cautious correspondence during the remaining nine months of Pope's life. A clause in Pope's Will bequeathing Allen £150—"being to the best of my Calculation, the Account of what I have received from him; partly for my own, and partly for Charitable Uses"—may show that Pope's sense of the discourtesies suffered by Martha Blount had not quite been assuaged, but it is easily made too much of. As he had borrowed exactly that amount from Allen in early 1740 to help his outlawed nephew Michael Rackett buy an army position (as the custom then was) in France or in Spain, this may have been primarily a way of repaying that debt while continuing to indicate (the will was drawn five months earlier than the Good Friday conversation in 1744, when the two men finally closed over the wound) some sense of having been wronged. Men are often more zealous to defend those they love—Allen his wife, Pope Martha Blount—than themselves. And if on being told of the bequest Ralph Allen did say, "Poor Mr. Pope was always a bad accomptant," he was certainly correct in that judgment. As Marchmont informed Boswell, "Pope could not keep his own accounts. [His entries] were all on one page and did not distinguish 'received' from 'paid.'"

CHAPTER 29

LAST POEMS

Back to the drawing board

Through the winters from 1739–40 to 1742–43, nevertheless, the long periods at Prior Park supplied Pope with an ideal setting. For relaxation with company he respected. For doctoring—his circle of medical friends in Bath soon included, besides Oliver, Jeremiah Pierce the surgeon, George Cheyne, apostle of plain diets, and David Hartley, whose associationist psychology was to exercise a profound influence on Wordsworth as well as initiate the British associationist school linked with the name of James Mill. And for work. Work that for a time seemed to be pointing in an altogether new direction. We know from Dr. Cheyne, for example, that Pope was persuaded, at least in a genial moment, to contemplate undertaking an English verse rendering of the Psalms, the individual poems to be marketed at a shilling each and the proceeds consigned to "some universal Charity." Two of the Psalms, Cheyne tells his friend, the author of *Pamela*, "he has done at my Desire to Admiration." Brilliant or mediocre (more likely the latter), the two poems actually finished would have lent insights into Pope's thought and feeling that it is a pity we have been denied. As manuscripts, they were perhaps in the bundle left to Bolingbroke, which in consequence of his pique about the printing of *The Idea of a Patriot King* seems to have been mislaid or destroyed.

Plans have survived for other work that lies equally off Pope's usual path and invites curiosity. There were to have been some odes ("in the sublime style," according to one report), which I am inclined to identify with the "two odes, or moral poems, on the *Mischiefs of Arbitrary Power*, and *the Folly of Ambition*," whose plans (the poems themselves were apparently and perhaps fortunately never written) have been preserved. The first, on arbitrary power, was to show a peaceful landscape on the slopes of Aetna or Vesuvius—flowering pastures, fields of grain, lush vineyards and olive orchards, shepherds and farmers indulging themselves blissfully in dance and song and sunburnt mirth—till suddenly the mountain erupts, torrents of lava

93. *Landscape with Classical Ruins* by Pope's and Gay's friend John Wootton. This painting hung in Pope's villa and is expressive of themes important to him.

By kind permission of J. J. Eyston, Mapledurham House. Photograph: Courtauld Institute of Art.

pour down its sides, and the whole laughing scene is swept away. The other "ode" was to utilize a variation on a theme once very familiar in poetry: "Stop, traveler, and reflect on what you see"—whether it be, as in *Eloisa*, the "pale marble" of a mutual grave, or, as for many who had crossed the Alps only in imagination as well as those who had crossed them in reality, the vast eloquent ruins of Rome: "the Niobe of nations"—"the grave, the city, and the wilderness." In this instance, the traveler's curiosity is aroused by a majestic heap of stone lying in an entirely desert country, and he inquires about it from the only living soul to be found there: a shepherd, who (as so often in eighteenth-century Rome) had built his shelter against a moldering wall. From the rubble of history and legend that he supplies, the traveler eventually makes out that these are the remains of Blenheim, all that is apparently now left of the Marlborough name and of the once spirited and cultivated people who built that palace for "the Deliverer of Europe".

The connections here with the disquisition on "Fame" in the *Essay on Man* (4: 237–58) and with the passage in the same epistle (287–308) beginning

> There, in the rich, the honour'd, fam'd and great,
> See the false scale of Happiness complete!

are obvious enough, as is the glance backward at a theme which had first engaged Pope seriously in *The Temple of Fame*. What is perhaps more significant at this stage in his life is the keen sense communicated by these poem-plans, taken together, of the suddenness with which disaster strikes, the blindness of human beings generally to any obvious peril that they assume will never threaten *them*, and the utter desolation of what remains as around the shattered face of Ozymandias, king of kings, the low and level sands stretch far away.

For another and far larger work on which Pope must have been meditating during some of these winter visits, we have a very full sketch, and, in addition, the opening lines. This was to have been a blank verse epic, paralleling in some respects the *Aeneid*, in which the mythical Trojan Brutus, Aeneas's grandson, sets out from his homeland with a few compatriots to found the ideal commonwealth. Pope had long cherished an intention to expound his views on church and state, much of this material designed at one time for a niche in the *Opus Magnum*. But as he told Spence on a later occasion, to have said all he wanted to say would have brought both establishments about his ears. An epic fiction, he seems to have decided, offered the right solution, and could possibly have the further advantage of giving

imaginative life to certain aspirations of the Young Patriots, who
looked to him for that form of leadership. "Some sparks of Publick
Virtue are yet Alive," Lyttelton was writing him in November 1741,
the same month in which we have evidence that his plan for an epic
was becoming known,

> which such a Spirit as Your's might blow into a flame, among the
> Young men especially; and even granting an impossibility of Re-
> forming the Publick, your Writings may be of Use to private
> Society; The Moral Song may steal into our Hearts, and teach us to
> be as good Sons, as good Friends, as Beneficent, as Charitable as
> Mr Pope, and sure *That* will be Serving your Country, though you
> cant Raise her up such Ministers, or such Senators as you desire. In
> short; my dear Friend, though I am far from supposing that if you
> don't write, you *Live in Vain*; . . . yet as your Writings will have a
> still more extensive and permanent Influence, . . . and may do
> Good to Mankind in better Ages and Countries, if not in This, I
> wou'd have you Write till . . . at least Weakness of Health shall
> Oblige . . . you to lay down your Pen.

In the plan of the poem itself, it is early decided that no site in the
familiar known world will do for the proposed community, since
there is none in which corruption has not prevailed, including Troy
itself, which the Almighty has punished for its sins by allowing it to
be overthrown. Brutus must therefore push beyond the Pillars of
Hercules into the vast unknown of the Atlantic. Many delays,
councils, altercations in the ranks, hostile receptions by native
peoples, and splintering off of colonies unable or unwilling to go on
take place; and one sees that the poet has left himself ample room and
verge enough for both delectable lotus-eating scenes of self-
indulgence and resonant admonitions by Brutus (and the Celestials
who support his venture) to renounce temptation and keep the great
end in view—all sufficiently applicable, one might guess, to the
Patriots' efforts to resolve the ditherings of the Opposition. Tenerife
in the Canaries is visited, where one group elects to stay on in that
"land of laziness," as it is called, despite the suggestive propinquity
of its snow-topped volcanic peaks. Eventually, after adventures and
misadventures too numerous to be mentioned here, but including a
costly battle on the coast of Norway, where a great storm has driven
them, a mind-boggling aurora borealis (such as England had experienced during Pope's youth), a hurricane, a shipwreck, and a volcanic
eruption, Brutus arrives at southwest Britain and lands at Torbay.
Predictably, not all parts of Britain welcome the new commonwealth

with open arms. Among its enemies are certain priests, conjurers, and magicians, along with such fabled giants as Corinæus and Gogmagog. But Brutus's ruling principle is benevolence (first cousin of the expatiating understanding and compassion celebrated in the fourth epistle of the *Essay on Man*), as Aeneas's was *pietas*. Compelling only where he has to, persuading by example where he can, allowing no one in his company to prey either upon the land or its people, he eventually brings about the good (it is impossible from our vantage point in the late twentieth century not to smile a little) that an epic hero should. The virtues of good government and true religion (a religion, one suspects, though nothing in the plan itself defines it, that eliminates all notions of eternal torment, avoids sectarian exclusiveness and pride, places its central emphasis on love of God and neighbor—this time as in the *Essay*'s third epistle) prevail, and the poem ends.

There is much more in the plan as we have it—a celestial "machinery" with good and evil angels, individual episodes of temptation, violence, courage, love, a *dramatis personae* already supplied with names and capsule characterizations. But surely its most compelling feature is the eight-line blank-verse invocation, with which the poem was to open:

> The Patient Chief, who lab'ring long arriv'd
> On Britain's shores and brought with fav'ring Gods
> Arts Arms & Honour to her Ancient sons:
> Daughter of Memory! from elder Time
> Recall; and me with Britains Glory fird,
> Me far from meaner Care or meaner Song,
> Snatch to the Holy Hill of spotless Bay,
> My Countrys Poet, to record her Fame.

Nostalgic, of course—as in a sense an epic must be, seeking always (like Shakespeare's Henry V at Agincourt) to foster present virtues by rooting them in the past. Touching, too, it seems to me. For one feels in Pope's dream of an epic poem at his late stage of literary history, to say nothing of this late stage in his career, that quality of his genius which Johnson stresses so eloquently as its eminent characteristic:

> a mind active, ambitious, and adventurous, always investigating, always aspiring; in its widest searches still longing to go forward, in its highest flights still wishing to be higher; always imagining something greater than it knows, always endeavouring more than it can do.

And yet one feels equally, in his failure to carry the project further, that other distinctive and balancing aspect of his genius noticed earlier: a fine dry sense of what he could not do and what he could.

Most of all, to be sure, it is the Miltonism of these introductory eight lines that strikes, though they have a gravity and timbre of their own. A Miltonism more allusive than strictly imitative, I believe a careful reader may conclude. For here with some emphasis and deliberation Pope declares himself of Milton's party. Not as a poet of equal rank—though Pope was vain, he knew there were countries beyond his reach, and though he censured Milton freely for his fallings-off, he never forgot from what heights he fell. Rather, he claims company with Milton as the bearer, like his great predecessor, of a dream for England: the dream of a regenerated land, such as Blake, in his own way, will dream again at the century's end:

> I will not cease from Mental Fight,
> Nor shall my Sword sleep in my hand,
> Till we have built Jerusalem
> In England's green and pleasant land.

It is a safe bet that Pope's *Brutus*, if executed, would not have ranked among the world's great epics, or perhaps even its readable long poems. What is thought-provoking about it, however, is that Pope should have had such a poem seriously in mind. As the *Dunciad* of 1729 and the *Essay on Man* confront each other as the night side and day side of his imagination, so in a way *The New Dunciad* of 1742 faces *Brutus*. Follow the world and the world's ways, says *The New Dunciad*, and sooner or later your own particular Troy will join the other Troys it buries. But it *can* be different, says *Brutus*: the world is all before you, where to choose.

Most poignant of all, perhaps, coming as it does from a member of a mistrusted minority and illuminating with a fine defining light the spirit that glows behind the political and social criticism of the satires and epistles, is the invocation's close: "My Countrys Poet, to record her Fame."

"Cibber and I are, luckily, no friends"

Yet while the epic languished, unattempted, one work of substance did emerge from the protected leisure made possible by the Allens' hospitality, first at their Widcombe house and then at Prior Park. This was the *New Dunciad*—"my Widcomb Poem," as Pope himself refers to it—first published on 20 March 1742. Though in several respects a greater achievement than the earlier *Dunciads*, it created nothing like the same stir, partly because it was in some passages riddling and even obscure (Pope may have thought this necessary to avoid prosecution even though Walpole was no longer in office) and partly, as he explained to Bethel, because the satire was oftener general than individual: "Men not being singled out from the Herd, bear Chastisement better, (like Gally slaves for being all linkd in a String, & on the same Rank)."

One galley slave, however, decided to take it amiss: the laureate, Colley Cibber. Though referred to in the poem only once (and then mildly, and not by name), Cibber had been for years a favorite butt of Pope's in earlier work. The antipathy of the two reached as far back, in fact, as 1717 or earlier. In that year a collaborative farce by Gay, Arbuthnot, and Pope was staged with considerable success. In it, taking the part of a fatuous playwright named Plotwell, Cibber was required by the script to speak lines that were a satire on himself—a circumstance which suggests that ill feeling had already begun. Pardonably enough, Cibber soon had his revenge by interpolating into his revival of Buckingham's *The Rehearsal* some slighting allusions to the earlier farce. According to contemporary reports (of the truth of any of which it is impossible to be sure), Pope then accosted Cibber, called him a rascal, said that he would cane him if he could, and that if he persisted in this mischief, his friend Gay would give him a come-uppance. The following night, when Cibber repeated the inter-polated lines, Gay appeared in the green room afterward as promised, fisticuffs ensued, and, depending on which of the several reports one believes, Gay or Cibber had the worst of it.

More significant, without much doubt, in shaping Pope's estimate of Cibber for the rest of his life was the actor-playwright's presenta-tion at the end of that same year of his propaganda comedy, *The Non-Juror*, based on Molière's *Tartuffe*. This was a piece of cheap political opportunism. It mocked in many of its speeches and situa-tions recognizable persons and events brought to notoriety by the government's often brutal efforts during the previous year to wipe out religious nonconformity along with Jacobitism: efforts which included the execution at Tyburn of two nonjuring clergymen, not for *acts* of treason but for their rejection of what in their eyes was the "Schismatical Church" and their adherence to the "Non-juring Church, which has kept itself free from Rebellion and Schism." Un-questionably, many nonjurors were activists and plotters. But many more were Jacobites-of-conscience, passive even though honestly

94. Colley Cibber (1671–1757). By George Beare.

> Alas! few Verses touch their nicer Ear;
> They scarce can bear their *Laureate* twice a Year.
>
> *Imit. Hor., Sat.* II, i: 33–4.

Present location unknown.

convinced that nothing had yet taken place to free them from their sworn duties to the house of Stuart. And some were simply upright Dissenters like Isaac Watts, the Protestant hymn writer, or equally upright Roman Catholics like Pope's friend Henry Englefield, or upright Anglicans like William Digby, who could not swallow down in conscience the studied Erastian language (language that also repudiated central doctrines of the Roman church) in which the oaths were couched.

Catering to stock responses, branding all nonjurors either hypocrites or dupes, the play has been justly termed "a blatant exercise in demagoguery, produced after the cause it purported to defend was already won." Though it met with immense immediate success, it offended many, not merely those who were its victims (such as Pope, whose works were three times mentioned as if to remind audiences of the best-known literary nonjuror of the day), but those on the Hanoverian side who could see the cynicism of squeezing huzzas and snickers from genuine recent sufferings and complex questions of conscience for which some of their fellow Englishmen had been willing to lose their lives. Cibber himself subsequently dated the beginnings of his unpopularity from this play, and appears to have believed, too, that it was the major consideration in his being awarded the laureateship in 1730. Quite possibly he was right on both counts, since he dedicated the printed play to the king and received £200 for it. To any impartial eye, let alone such a partial eye as Pope's pardonably was after the event, this episode was enough to establish Cibber once and for all as Literary Toad Eater Extraordinary to the Hanoverian regime. And his twice-a-year performances from 1730 on as Poet Laureate could only enhance his claim to that title:

> Behold in ev'ry Face, imperial Graces shine,
> All native to the Race of George and Caroline.
>
> (1730)

In the *Dunciad* of 1729, Pope had "handled" Cibber, and occasionally in later poems after his appointment as laureate, but in the main casually, and with, as it were, only partly obtruded claws. (In 1737, in fact, in *To Augustus*, he had sincerely praised his play the *Careless Husband*.) But after Cibber published his autobiography (entitled *An Apology for the Life of Colley Cibber*) in 1740, he had reasons to move him to a more central position in his consciousness. Much in the manner of Theobald in *Shakespeare Restored*, while professing to conciliate, the *Apology* actually recapitulated all the traditional charges as to Pope's vanity, avarice, and malice, pieced out by the further claim that he was jealous of Cibber's success (including his sexual success with women despite advancing years) and that when he included him in his satires it was only to make money by the use of an illustrious name. These were "personalities" not likely to be kindly received by Pope from any source and least of all from this one, who, despite his well-deserved reputation as actor and playwright, had in his later years been chiefly known for execrable flatteries of the royal family, and, after the appearance of his *Apology* in 1740, invaluable though the book is for theater history, as a kind of incorrigible exhibitionist and public buffoon. In Samuel Johnson's words, probably set down in 1741:

> Augustus still survives in Maro's strain,
> And Spenser's verse prolongs Eliza's reign;
> Great George's acts let tuneful Cibber sing:
> For Nature formed the Poet for the King.

There had been, in short, sporadic feuding between the two men for years, and Pope, even as he composed the *New Dunciad* in 1741, may have been looking forward to the day when it could be entailed on the earlier *Dunciad* as its climactic book, and the entire poem then renovated for the reception of Cibber:

> Lift up your Gates, ye Princes, see him come!
> Sound, sound, ye Viols, be the Catcall dumb!
> Bring, bring the madding Bay, the drunken Vine;
> The creeping, dirty, courtly Ivy join.

(1: 301–4)

Such change of heroes would have much to recommend it. Theobald was ancient history by now, and his actual edition of Shakespeare, when at last published in 1734, had won acclaim. Cibber, on the other hand, was considerably an ass and perpetually in the public eye. As laureate, he thrust in the face of heaven the taste of the minister and king who had appointed him. As court sycophant, he demeaned what Pope believed was the proper dignity of a subject and the proper role of a poet. And as an actor-manager, a manipulator skilled in "staging," a personality with "cheek," he had begun of recent years to serve the Opposition press as Robert Walpole's *alter ego*. Writing of the ministerial manipulator so famous for his own cheek that he was called Sir Robert Brass, they could pretend to be talking only of Colley Cibber.

All these thoughts may have been roosting in Pope's brain while he worked on the *New Dunciad*, or they may not. They must at any rate have gathered there like homing pigeons when, five months or so after the *New Dunciad* appeared, with its lone reference to the laureate sleeping on the goddess Dulness's lap, Cibber published a pamphlet of some sixty-odd pages entitled *A Letter From Mr. Cibber to Mr. Pope, Inquiring into the Motives that might induce him in his Satyrical Works, to be so frequently fond of Mr. Cibber's name.* It too reiterated the usual charges, with expansions, but when it reached the lines in the *Epistle to Dr. Arbuthnot* that seem really to have rankled—

> Whom have I hurt? has Poet yet, or Peer
> Lost the arch'd Eye-brow, or Parnassian Sneer?
> And has not Colley still his Lord, and Whore—

Cibber chose to be "reminded" of a story (alluded to earlier in these pages) about a youthful escapade when a merry Lord, himself, and Pope visited "a certain House of Carnal Recreation":

> where his Lordship's Frolick propos'd was to slip [one notices the hunting term] his little Homer, as he call'd him, at a Girl of the Game, that he might see what sort of Figure a Man of his Size, Sobriety, and Vigour (in Verse) would make, when the frail fit of Love had got into him; in which he so far succeeded, that the smirking Damsel, who serv'd us with Tea, happen'd to have Charms sufficient to tempt the little-tiny Manhood of Mr. Pope into the next Room with her: . . . But I . . . observing he had staid as long as without hazard of his Health he might, . . . without Ceremony, threw open the Door upon him, where I found this little hasty Hero, like a terrible *Tom Tit*, pertly perching upon the Mount of Love! But such was my Surprize, that I fairly laid hold of his Heels, and actually drew him down safe and sound from his Danger. My Lord, who staid tittering without, . . . upon my giving an Account of the Action within, began to curse, and call me a hundred silly Puppies, for . . . spoiling the Sport; to which . . . I reply'd: pray, my Lord, consider what I have done was in regard of the Honour of our Nation! For would you have had so glorious a Work as that of making *Homer* speak elegant *English*, cut short by laying up our little Gentleman of a Malady, which his thin Body might never have been cured of?

It was a shrewd gambit, brilliantly executed. For Pope it was dynamite: the most shattering ridicule of his wretched carcass that had ever been delivered, far exceeding Lady Mary's. Almost overnight, engravers seized on the incident, and with their several variations on the "Tom Tit" situation befringed the rails of Bedlam and Soho.

95. An engraver's rendering of Cibber's anecdote, 1742.

Privately owned.

Pope's fury can easily be imagined—in fact, this is probably the occasion the Richardsons describe, when Pope tried to keep up a front by saying, "These things are my diversion," while his face writhed with chagrin and pain. But fury cools. And when Pope's had cooled, he must have known he had his enemy—his greatest enemy in the sense that Cibber had come to represent everything he believed a poet should not be, an enemy both to esthetic standards and to independence of court servilities—in the hollow of his hand. If he had earlier considered making Cibber his king dunce, he had now the perfect justification from the public's point of view. If he had not—and there are factors that incline one to wonder—his work was cut out for him (the four-book *Dunciad* seems to have been completed within three months of the publication of Cibber's *Letter*), but the change could only benefit the poem. With Cibber as king of dunces, it could point its finger from the very outset at the true begetters of Dulness's new empire: George II and his stage manager: Cibber-Walpole.

Cibber made a point of boasting in his pamphlets against Pope at this time that he would pursue him to the end and would have the last word. But as Pope replied in an epigram that rapidly became famous:

> Quoth *Cibber* to *Pope*, Tho' in Verse you foreclose,
> I'll have the last Word; for by G–d, I'll write prose.
> Poor *Colley* thy Reas'ning is none of the strongest.
> For know, the last Word is the Word that last longest.

One feels for Cibber. He was indeed a coxcomb, but he had many virtues not honored in the *Dunciad*. Which should remind us once more, of course, that poetry is never history.

A ruining City?

The poem that Pope published in late 1743 is the last and in some ways least perfect, but in scope and power the grandest of his poems. The revised *Dunciad* in four books "is not," to appropriate some wise words from a recent comment on it, "a 'well-made' work." "It is a big harsh poem with a lot of violent work to do, which it does with some waste and awkwardness that are incidents of its energy, defects of its virtues." Somewhat like the *Iliad*, one might say (comparing great things with small), where also a civilization is at stake. Or like the *Aeneid*, where a civilization falls because it deserves to fall from its own pride, folly, gullibility, and decadence. Or like *Paradise Lost*, on which Pope allusively draws in establishing the dunces' London as a

species of Hell and in enclosing all his poem's acts and persons, however commonplace, in a great religious metaphor. Even the *Divine
Comedy* has been cited as an analogue of sorts. There, as in Pope's
poem, historical persons in large numbers, enmeshed in the narrative
of a "progress" largely symbolic, assume symbolic implications of
their own; and there, too, as with the dunces, what men or women are
seen doing or undergoing becomes an index to what they are or have
been. Nor can it be entirely amiss in this connection to recall two
poems, large in suggestiveness if not in substance, closer to our
own times. Like "death's other kingdom" in *The Hollow Men*, the
Dunciad's London has no room for lost violent souls, only for stuffed
men, leaning together—in fact, at times "conglobed" (4:79) together—headpiece filled with straw. And if in the *Dunciad* we see a
whole society sick because there is sickness at the power centers, so in
the myth behind *The Waste Land* the land lies waste because the king is
sterile. The resemblances by no means, however, end there:

> Both *The Waste Land* and *The Dunciad* can make us feel what it
> would be [like] to redeem the time by redeeming the heritage [the
> Bible, the achievements of Greece and Rome, the works of the
> great European poets, dramatists, historians, philosophers: all that
> with which our own century is beginning to lose contact]. ... In
> both poems the redeeming creative act occurs, or seeks to occur,
> within the zone of what variously excites it, resists it, or is funda-
> mentally hostile to it. ... In Pope, a witty allusiveness and comic
> verve holds the mirror up at close range to arts of servile imitation
> and mere sensational opportunism. In Eliot, a difficult but true
> coherence is won from, but still within, distracted and demoral-
> ized states of awareness. [In the one poem], custard, lavatory
> paper, dab-chicks, pies, Lord Mayors' processions, John Locke,
> Vergil, Welsted, and Aphrodite; [in the other], cardboard boxes,
> the Cannon Street Hotel, Lil's husband, Mrs. Porter, Spenser, the
> gashouse, Dante, and a pocket full of currants.

One sometimes wonders whether Wordsworth, in specifying as the
distinctive attribute of Romantic poetry "the real language of men,"
can ever have looked at the Horatian poems or the *Dunciad* at all.

By virtue of its compositional history, Pope's poem is also, of
course, a cumulative work, which accounts in part for its
awkwardness and waste. It incorporates the three books of the
Dunciad Variorum of 1729; it adds as a fourth book *The New Dunciad* of
1742; and it brings about such alterations in the earlier books as make
them *almost* a proper habitat for the new king dunce, Colley Cibber,

as well as an inviting prelude to the activities of Queen Dulness on her accession to the British throne. In one way of looking at it, the poem thus encompasses a nearly complete record (a few of its lines date back in their first versions as far as 1708 or earlier) of Pope's experience as a writer, crippled, quick-tempered, highly sensitive to slights, at times vengeful, carving out a career by sheer genius and relentless application in the face of envy, religious bigotry, and almost continuous slander.

The lines grow warm with personalities and quarrels, but they glow also with genuine concern for standards and with vivid satiric realizations of the forces—intellectual, social, economic, political, and psychological—that in the poet's time and from his personal vantage point were sapping the nation's cultural vitality. "When the *free* Spirit of a Nation," the third earl of Shaftesbury had written in 1712 (moved by the comfortable glow of a Whiggish war nearly won to predict that after it Britain would be the principal seat of the arts), "turns it-self this way, [i.e., to these occupations] Judgments are form'd; Criticks arise; the publick Eye and Ear improve; a right Taste prevails." To such mindless jingoism, though it is unlikely that Pope had Shaftesbury in mind, the *Dunciad* is one poet's answer, and, to this extent, reflects the views of a particular individual in a particular time and place, even though some of us might be constrained to admit that the forces singled out as debilitating have lost little of their capacity to debauch us with the passage of the years.

Yet the poem may be seen to harbor, also, a more universal theme with distinct tragic undertones. It is the same theme that in their varying ways the works named above carry in suspension and often at their very core: most particularly Milton's poem, which structures his experience of the Puritan revolution (with its high hopes shattered) in the frame of the second and third chapters of Genesis, because he recognizes in both events the same sad story of human self-betrayal, humility and idealism giving way to arrogance, love sent packing by a demonic will to power. In the *Dunciad*'s own day, therefore, its evocation of world's end at the close, though famed for its eloquence and grandeur (Pope's voice, we are told, trembled as he read it aloud to Spence, and Johnson in later years, hearing this, pronounced that "well it might, for they are noble lines") constituted only the most recent contribution to the long succession of visions of apocalypse by poet, prophet, sage, and seer—all, like Cassandra, condemned not to be believed. (Carlyle, too, it is reported, said wistfully during his last days, "They call me a great man now, but not one believes what I have told them.")

Today we are not so sure. Are these repeated intuitions of a Ruining City and an oncoming Great Darkness by any chance true apprehensions of a scheme of things in which consequence follows deed, as Shakespeare thought in writing *King Lear*, along with others before him?

> For the stars of heaven and the constellations thereof shall not give light: the sun shall be darkened in his going forth, and the moon shall not cause her light to shine.
> Then will I cause to cease from the cities of Judah and from the streets of Jerusalem, the voice of mirth, and the voice of gladness, the voice of the bridegroom, and the voice of the bride: for the land shall be desolate.

Or are they simply, as in the Cave of Poverty and Poetry, the half-formed maggots of overheated poetic brains? Doubtless the latter. Surely the latter. And yet. . . .

> What is the city over the mountains
> Cracks and reforms and bursts in the violet air
> Falling towers
> Jerusalem Athens Alexandria
> Vienna London
> Unreal.

Which can also be said in prose, though it is the prose of a great poet:

> We had long heard tell of whole worlds that had vanished, of empires sunk without a trace, gone down . . . into the unexplorable depths of the centuries, with their gods and their laws, their academies and their sciences, pure and applied, their grammars and their dictionaries, their classics, their romantics and their symbolists, their critics and the critics of their critics. . . . We were aware that the visible earth is made of ashes and that ashes signify something. Through the obscure depths of history we could make out phantoms of great ships laden with riches and intellect; we could not count them. But the disasters that had sent them down there were, after all, none of our affair. . . . [Today] we see that the abyss of history is deep enough to hold us all. We are aware that a civilization has the same fragility as a life. The circumstances that could send the works of Keats and Baudelaire to join the works of Menander are no longer inconceivable; they are in the newspapers.

It is in this line of succession that the *Dunciad* holds its niche.

"The uncreating Word"

The 1729 version, it will be remembered, slants toward its famous ending with a mountain-top vision of Dulness's past and future conquests. The barbarians fall upon Rome, the Moslems on Spain, the medieval papacy on pagan art, the monks on Britain. And these advances are soon to be crowned (so in 1729 the old king-dunce, Settle, prophesies to his heir, Tibbald, and in 1743 to his newer heir, Cibber) through a collective descent on St. James's by all the lunacies, infatuations, and, most especially, the perverse applications of intelligence that Dulness, in Pope's sense of the term, represents.

In general, in these early books, the movement is systolic. Persons and things tend to move outward from centers of idiocy to touch, taint, deafen, overwhelm, possess. The typical image is that of the reverberating bray of the long-eared crowd tethered at the gate of a rich City merchant who has been put on a diet of ass's milk (very possibly a vivid reminiscence from Pope's childhood days in Plough Court), which discharges its echoes all the way from Threadneedle Street to Westminster Hall:

> As when the long-ear'd milky mothers wait
> At some sick miser's triple-bolted gate,
> For their defrauded, absent foals they make
> A moan so loud, that all the Guild awake,
> Sore sighs Sir G[ilbert], starting at a bray
> From dreams of millions, and three groats to pay!
> So swells each Windpipe; Ass intones to Ass. . . .
> Long Chanc'ry-lane retentive rolls the sound,
> And courts to courts return it round and round:
> Thames wafts it thence to Rufus' roaring hall,
> And Hungerford re-ecchoes, bawl for bawl.
>   (2: 237–43, 251–54) [1729]

Exceptions to this centrifugal tendency occur, as when the tribes press in from outside upon the Roman empire or when the Smithfield Muses and their admirers, some of them in costumes as seedy as their values—

96. Alexander Pope. Bust in stone. Sculptor unknown, probably late eighteenth
century after a painting by William Hoare. This is the only known bust of Pope
showing him in a cap. Not in Wimsatt.

Courtesy of Mr. and Mrs. Donald Gadge, of Hanworth near Twickenham.

> A motley mixture! in long wigs, in bags,
> In silks, in crapes, in garters, and in rags;
> From drawing-rooms, from colleges, from garrets—
>
> (2: 17–19) [1729]

migrate, not only from all quarters of the old City and its purlieus but seemingly from all England, to the West End. For the most part, however, the accent in the earlier books is on dissemination.

The fourth book's emphasis is on centering, and the groups it features are considerably more uppercrust:

> None need a guide, by sure Attraction led,
> And strong impulsive gravity of Head:
> None want a place, for all their Centre found,
> Hung to the Goddess, and coher'd around. . . .
>   Nor absent they, no members of her state,
> Who pay her homage in her sons, the Great; . . .
> Patrons, who sneak from living worth to dead,
> With-hold the pension, and set up the head;
> Or vest dull Flatt'ry in the sacred Gown;
> Or give from fool to fool the Laurel crown.
>
> (4: 75–78, 91–92, 95–98)

As the book opens, we see that the victory prophesied by Settle has already taken place. Bloodlessly, of course. Partly because it has, in fact, involved no change, but only the unveiling of what under the Hanoverians have been the true facts all along. And partly, too, we may suspect, because a decadent society, as one of the greatest poets of our own century has reminded us, yearns for surrender as the mosquito yearns for its swamp:

> Some just back from the frontiers
> tell us there are no more barbarians.
> —What will become of us with no barbarians?
> They were our one way out.

It is appropriate, therefore, that the first of Dulness's subjects to address her after she has mounted her new throne should be the effete allegorical figure of Italian Opera:

> a Harlot form soft sliding by,
> With mincing step, small voice, and languid eye;
> Foreign her air, her robe's discordant pride
> In patch-work flutt'ring, and her head aside;
> By singing Peers up-held on either hand.
>
> (4: 45–49)

And that Cibber, the new king, is found asleep on his goddess-mother's lap, in which condition he continues for the duration of the poem. "Nor ought this, well considered, to seem strange in our days," interposes that indefatigable annotator Scriblerus (with a quick glance back at Queen Caroline's control of George II during the Walpole era), "when so many *King-consorts* have done the like."

Dulness, now approached by a throng of favor-seekers—

> There march'd the bard and blockhead, side by side,
> Who rhym'd for hire, and patroniz'd for pride—
>
> (4: 101–2)

and delighted, moreover, by some pioneering eighteenth-century versions of today's cost-effective, tax-deductible, corporate gratuities to the arts, (4: 105–14), is just indulging a burst of joyous anticipation—

> "So by each Bard an Alderman shall sit,
> A heavy Lord shall hang at ev'ry Wit,
> And while on Fame's triumphal Car they ride,
> Some Slave of mine be pinion'd to their side"—
>
> (4: 131–34)

when "lo! a Spectre rose."

The specter proves to be the ghost of the famous Dr. Busby, headmaster of Westminster School, whose skill with the birch was legendary, and who, while showing Charles II about the buildings, kept his hat on, "lest the boys should think that there was anyone greater than himself." He curries favour with the new queen by reminding her that he and his kind contribute powerfully to quenching whatever tendencies toward independent thinking might endanger the status quo:

> "Whate'er the talents, or howe'er design'd,
> We hang one jingling padlock on the mind."
>
> (4: 161–62)

For this service, having witnessed its effectiveness since the time of James I, the queen is duly grateful:

> "For sure, if Dulness sees a grateful Day,
> 'Tis in the shade of Arbitrary Sway. . . .
> May you, may Cam, and Isis preach it long!
> 'The RIGHT DIVINE of Kings to govern wrong.'"
>
> (4: 181–82, 187–88)

Cam and Isis [Cambridge and Oxford], as if corporealized by the mere mention of their names, immediately appear in full academic regalia. Many of them, still loyal to Aristotle's physics despite the findings of Newton and the new physics generally, are appropriately and punningly described as a *"block*ade" and numbered in terms ordinarily reserved for collectivities of fish, or sheep and cattle:

> Prompt at the call, around the Goddess roll
> Broad hats, and hoods, and caps, a sable shoal:
> Thick and more thick the black blockade extends,
> A hundred head of Aristotle's friends.

Their spokesman is Richard Bentley, master of Trinity College, Cambridge, whom we have met before. Like Busby, he would keep his hat on in the royal presence, save that his servile vice-master reverently removes it. He nods to the monarch rather than bow like the rest. He addresses her with a quite unacceptable demotic epithet. And he admits, modestly, that he can do more for her single-handed than all his colleagues combined:

> "Mistress! dismiss that rabble from your throne:
> Avaunt—is Aristarchus yet unknown?
> Thy mighty Scholiast, whose unweary'd pains
> Made Horace dull, and humbled Milton's strains.
> Turn what they will to Verse, their toil is vain,
> Critics like me shall make it prose again."

In general, the grand achievements of duncery in Book 4 are to fragment, dilapidate, trivialize, and misconstrue. Its critics revive the great texts, but "murder first, and mince them all to bits" (4: 120). The schoolmasters divorce what is said from how, and, excluding the former, confine their charges "in the pale of Words" till death (4: 160). The university men, like Bentley, are careful to give their students "Fragments, not a Meal" (4: 230); to nitpick among hairs and pores; and to congratulate themselves (in a manner that seems curiously familiar in the 1980s) on minute eccentric explications:

> For thee explain a thing till all men doubt it,
> And write about it, Goddess, and about it.
>
> (4: 251–52)

Only by such men and methods does it become possible to "petrify a Genius to a Dunce," "bring to one dead level ev'ry mind," and guarantee political subservience; or, as Bentley assures George II himself in an early but suppressed version of this episode (circa 1729–30): "I make them loyal, learn'd I suffer none."

Then follows what is perhaps the *Dunciad*'s most brilliant invention. An important strategy throughout the poem is to evoke images, scenes, and actions of great pith and moment, only to degrade them in a kind of perpetual reenactment of the dunces' devastation of their cultural heritage, among whose monuments and voices they scurry deaf and blind. Thus, as we saw earlier, a single word poisons the lovely line in which Curll (like Aeneas in Dido's Carthage viewing scenes of the Trojan War—already legendary) wistfully remembers the effects of Pope's emetic: "And the fresh vomit run for ever green" (2: 148 [1729]). In much the same way, the diving and other games in Book 2 disfigure the epic ideal of noble emulation and suggest the befoulment of heroic values through befoulment of the words and activities in which these values are recorded. And again in this manner, the crowd-pleasing shenanigans of the contemporary London stage in Book 3 cheapen the associations that for most Western peoples have gathered about such conceptions as the Day of Judgment, the Day of the Lord, the Four Last Things, the End of the World—

> All sudden, Gorgons hiss, and Dragons glare,
> And ten-horn'd fiends and Giants rush to war.
> Hell rises, Heav'n descends, and dance on Earth,
> Gods, imps, and monsters, music, rage, and mirth,
> A fire, a jigg, a battle, and a ball,
> 'Till one wide conflagration swallows all.
>
> (3: 231–36 [1729])

Not to mention the yet more solemn feelings that in classical antiquity used to attend the notion of a new Annus Magnus, or, in Christian times, the creation of "a new heaven and a new earth; for the first heaven and the first earth were passed away"—

> Thence a new world, to Nature's laws unknown,
> Breaks out refulgent, with a heav'n its own;
> Another Cynthia her new journey runs,
> And other planets circle other suns:
> The forests dance, the rivers upward rise,
> Whales sport in woods, and dolphins in the skies;
> And last, to give the whole creation grace,
> Lo! one vast Egg produces human race.
>
> (3: 237–44 [1729])

"God's business," as the Stoic Epictetus used to call it—creation, cosmology, cosmogony, eschatology—has shrunk to show business: a shrinkage that television evangelists continue to exploit.

"This is that good AENEAS"

In the fourth book, the supreme trivialization is that of the classical and Renaissance ideal of wisdom ripened by commerce with men and cities: the Grand Tour. Pope's lines plainly remember Horace's advice to young Lollius: Be like Ulysses. Learn about manners and men. But don't succumb to Sirens' songs or Circe's cup; for if Ulysses had done so, he would have become the shameful and silly slave of a harlot mistress. Closer home, they remember Ben Jonson's adaptation of this counsel for his young friend William Roe, who is admonished to observe, select, and transform (as the bee does in making honey). Go, Jonson urges,

> Countries, and climes, manners, and men to know,
> T' extract, and choose the best of all these [i.e., men] knowne,
> And those [i.e., manners] to turne to bloud, and make thine owne.

Yet remain such that on your return we may rejoice that

> This is that good AENEAS past through fire,
> Through seas, stormes, tempests: and imbarqu'd for hell,
> Came backe untouch'd. This man hath travail'd well.

In short, go but stay; let the wheel turn around a still center; gather food like the bee from far sources, but let it nourish what you already are; grow but don't change your nature—either to a grub or to a butterfly.

Pope's parody of all this—hardly so much a parody as an exposition of what in many instances actually took place—is a wonderfully droll travelogue detailing the kinds of experience that the rich young scions of the great families of the day, dunces of the ruling class, were extracting and turning "to bloud"—frequently with additions that ensured a miserable, not to say paretic, old age. After a youth totally undisciplined, denied nothing, rotten even before ripe, the typical specimen of this group first makes a spectacle of himself in London, then repeats his act on a bigger stage abroad:

> "Thro' School and College, thy kind cloud o'ercast,
> Safe and unseen the young Aeneas past:
> Thence bursting glorious, all at once let down,
> Stunn'd with his giddy Larum half the town.
> Intrepid then, o'er seas and lands he flew:
> Europe he saw, and Europe saw him too."
>
> (4: 289–94)

France he visits, of course: a France where the nobility's sole function is to adorn the court, bed the ladies, and flatter the king—much too like, Pope's lines seem to imply, what has been happening in England. Italy likewise is on all Grand Tour itineraries: a country no longer tuned to Roman Republican virtues, but plunged in political and religious torpor, victim of castrations in more senses than one, playground and brothel to the united idlers of the world:

> "There [in Europe] all thy gifts and graces we display,
> Thou, only thou, directing all our way!
> To where the Seine, obsequious as she runs,
> Pours at great Bourbon's feet her silken sons;
> Or Tyber, now no longer Roman, rolls,
> Vain of Italian Arts, Italian Souls:
> To happy Convents, bosom'd deep in vines,
> Where slumber Abbots, purple as their wines:
> To Isles of fragrance, lilly-silver'd vales,
> Diffusing languor in the panting gales:
> To lands of singing or of dancing slaves,
> Love-whisp'ring woods, and lute-resounding waves."
>
> (4: 295–306)

There is a bite, of course, in the lines; yet also a warm, vivid, and as-it-were Venetian coloration as the poet imagines a decadence that both repels and draws:

> "But chief her shrine where naked Venus keeps,
> And Cupids ride the Lyon of the Deeps"

—one remembers those paintings in which Mars's arms are donned by Venus's *amorini*—

> "Where, eas'd of Fleets, the Adriatic main
> Wafts the smooth Eunuch and enamour'd swain."
>
> (4: 309–10)

All this is from the speech made to the new queen by the young man's tutor or governor in introducing him. The "governor" (taking his cue, no doubt, from Locke's dictum that "The great work of a *Governour* is to fashion the Carriage and form the Mind") has prepared his charge for meritorious service to the court by helping him acquire the amenities and civilities appropriate to that calling—

> "Led by my hand, he saunter'd Europe round,
> And gather'd ev'ry Vice on Christian ground;
> Saw ev'ry Court, heard ev'ry King declare
> His royal Sense, of Op'ra's or the Fair;
> The Stews and Palace equally explor'd."
>
> (4: 311–15)

Furthermore, by bringing back in their train the young man's favorite Circe, he has enabled him to carry out his primary obligation to his class. "See," he says to the queen,

> "to my country happy I restore
> This glorious Youth, and add one Venus more.
> Her too receive (for her my soul adores)
> So may the sons of sons of sons of whores,
> Prop thine, O Empress! like each neighbour Throne,
> And make a long Posterity thy own."
>
> (4: 329–34)

There are moments when one wonders whether Pope was not secretly sympathetic to the idea of a republic.

"If the comedy still bites"

Much else in this "big harsh poem" warrants quotation, because much of it is very funny and at the same time oddly noble. But space forbids. Suffice it to say that the Grand Tour is succeeded by episodes in which Pope has a great deal of sport with collectors and virtuosi, as he would have today with an art-auction market in which fifteenth-rate "Old Masters" go for hundreds of thousands and Victorian cottage tearjerkers for thousands—not to be looked at in either case, but salted away in bank vaults. As one of the commentators on the *Dunciad* quoted earlier is careful to point out, "Looking at Pope from our own days, one thinks how nice it would be to have him back: our times could use him."

Then follows the passage, quoted earlier in connection with the

Essay on Man, about taking "the high Priori Road" in religious philosophy and reasoning downward till God evanesces (Pope's intuitions become uncannily predictive at this point) into "Nature" (Romantic pantheism) or "matter" (scientific materialism), or "some Mechanic Cause" (today renamed "The Big Bang") or, most commonly of all, into Faustian man's own invention: "Make God Man's Image, Man the final Cause" (4: 478). From this point it is only a step to the final apotheosis of darkness. Molded by the influences cited throughout the fourth book, the collective gilded youth of England are now formally dedicated in a body to the service of their new monarch. Time was, to be sure, when such a group would have been "Mark'd out for Honours," even "honour'd for their Birth"; but things are different now:

> Now to thy [Dulness's] gentle shadow all are shrunk,
> All melted down in Pension, or in Punk!
>
> (4: 507, 509–10)

Eagerly the young heirs drink from the Circean cup that an old "Magus" [Walpole, but also any other conjuror of great estates] holds out to them. Some will sell themselves for star and garter; some for "Int'rest" ("Int'rest, that waves on Party-colour'd wings"); some, deprived of any serious function by the minister's monopoly of power, will make a life of frivolities: hunting, drinking, foreign opera and foreign divas, *haute cuisine*, collecting (4: 517–64). All equally, however, will honor their monarch's charge: "My Sons! be proud, be selfish, and be dull."

> More had she spoke, but yawn'd—All Nature nods:
> What Mortal can resist the Yawn of Gods?
>
> (4: 582, 605–6)

What mortal indeed? As the Great Sleep takes over the realm, one remembers uncomfortably that some of the best minds of the last two decades have placed boredom, apathy, the shrinking threshold of individual attention (and "the great goose-cackle of mob-acquiescence," as D. H. Lawrence once called it in an inspired moment) just below nuclear war and overpopulation among the afflictions most likely to destroy the West. One is hardly surprised, therefore, that when the poet calls on the Muse to name the names of those most responsible for capitulating to the ultimate barbarian within, the time turns out to be not three minutes to midnight, but midnight:

> She comes! she comes! the sable Throne behold
> Of *Night* Primæval, and of *Chaos* old!
>
> (4: 627–30)

Her first assault, like that of all despots, is on the creative imagination:

> Before her, *Fancy's* gilded clouds decay,
> And all its varying Rain-bows die away.
> Wit shoots in vain its momentary fires.
>
> (4: 631–33)

Her second is on the arts and sciences, imagination's languages. Then all at once her mysterious power is everywhere. There is panic in the streets, hysteria, madness, death:

> See skulking *Truth* to her old Cavern fled,
> Mountains of Casuistry heap'd o'er her head!
> *Philosophy*, that lean'd on Heav'n before,
> Shrinks to her second cause, and is no more.

And then the dark:

> See *Mystery* to *Mathematics* fly!
> In vain! they gaze, turn giddy, rave, and die.
> *Religion* blushing veils her sacred fires,
> And unawares *Morality* expires.
> Nor *public* Flame, nor *private*, dares to shine.
>
> (4: 641–44, 647–51)

(If Pope was indeed silenced for a period after 1738, he may have been thinking of that here.)

> Nor *human* Spark is left, nor Glimpse *divine*!
> Lo! thy dread Empire, CHAOS! is restor'd;
> Light dies before thy uncreating word:
> Thy hand, great Anarch! lets the curtain fall;
> And Universal Darkness buries all.
>
> (4: 652–56)

A very pretty poem Mr. Pope, but you must not call it prophecy. So Dr. Bentley, one imagines, would have said, with as usual a certain justice. And yet, as one of the poem's best commentators has lately observed,

The world of *The Dunciad* is still familiar enough: great cities continue to create garbage, hack writers to satisfy our huge appetite for trifles, pedants to traffic in banalities masked as profundities, and scholiasts to "explain a thing till all men doubt it.["] . . . In the dialect of our own protesting dunces, we cart our loads of crap to market, and it is still possible for an advertised English "poet" to piss in a public pot at a city festival under the patronage of the Arts Council [and we might add here, for an American artist to attract funds for enveloping whole islands in colored Saran Wrap]. . . .

If the comedy still bites, however, the revelation still illuminates. . . . At precisely the point where Pope dramatizes the pathos of his own expendable art, . . . that art is at its most assured. If "Universal Darkness" has not yet buried all it is because the dead wits at least are still alive, reaching us from outside our own vortex. Creativity is a condition of life; without it, at the end of an exhausting cosmic day in Grub Street, we are composed (indeed composted) to everlasting rest.

"Affectionately yours—Amica"

One reader of Pope's final *Dunciad* had not been at all pleased with Cibber's *Letter*. This was "Amica." She called it a vomit.

Amica is a younger contemporary of Pope's, whose actual identity is not known. She left behind her a small body of letters and poems, which indicate acquaintance with some of Pope's circle and, eventually, with him. She passionately admired Pope's poetry—in a shy way, seems to have loved him *for* his poetry. Once, at least, perhaps oftener, she walked in Pope's gardens alone in his absence—it is through her, in fact, that we know such trivia as that Pope kept bantam chickens. In due course, she held what must have been a very limited correspondence with him, of which we have only her side and perhaps only selected parts of that. Having sent him, early on, some of the poems she had been writing in his praise, she seems to have been reminded from several quarters that "ladies" do not make advances. But in the end, one gathers, she met the man she so much idolized and enjoyed for the short time before his death a kind of friendship with him, warmer doubtless on her side, where it seems to have been almost a love affair, than on his.

Though her letters as we have them are very short, and the poems very bad, Amica's little packet of her writings, culled and copied out for the perusal of a friend, have virtues. They allow us a close-up look at the kind of rapture Pope's poetry inspired in at least one eighteenth-century mind. (Johnson's "overpowering pleasure," coming from a far more sophisticated source, should not be forgotten here.) They give us also a reassuring sense of the patience of which the poet was capable even when ill and old; for her overtures (so much like a teen-ager's crush, though she was apparently a mature young woman and married) must have embarrassed him. And they open a hazy but entertaining glimpse of what was undoubtedly the last "new" friendship in a life that had engendered many. The record Amica has left us, though considerably absurd, is somehow touching, for as Benedick reminds us seasonably at the close of Shakespeare's *Much Ado*, "man is a giddy thing, and that is my conclusion."

Amica's first record of her enthusiasm for Pope is dated 1737. He is already to her "a god-like Poet"; and when she reads his various works, though her soul is at first consumed in "Thought," her mind soon wanders into speculation about what the poet she has never seen is like. She knows what "vulgar Scandals" say about his physical characteristics, but since, after all, his soul lives there,

> its Mansion I 'd approve,
> And tell him, *I am his Platonic Love.*

From another poem of the same year, we learn that it is no longer through his "charming Mind" alone that she knows him. For she now carries a miniature of him with her:

> Oft on the Lilliputian God I look,
> That is confin'd within my Pocket-Book;

and the general effect of such communings is to send "Reason" packing:

> For whil'st I scan each sacred Feature o'er
> I am transform'd to an Idolater.

A year later, she finds herself transported by the two dialogues of *One Thousand Seven Hundred and Thirty-Eight.* She is now aware, however, of the attacks on his character by the gazetteers, who censure him for "Pride," "Caprice of Temper," and all sorts of other evils, some even asserting that

> his extensive Mind
> To superstitious Tenets is confin'd.

She herself, she says, prefers to think him "Of no Persuasion save divinely good," witness his own testimony in the second dialogue:

> "Nor think that Friendship only prompts my Lays,
> "I follow Virtue. . . . Where she shines, I praise."

By 1739, Amica has sent Pope, seemingly through the mediation of his surgical friend, Cheselden, one of her poems, probably the earliest one, in which she said that, whatever his physical frame, she would approve it because it contained his great soul. Now, in a poem directly addressed to Cheselden, she reprimands him for suggesting that the poet could possibly have misconceived her meaning:

> He has perhaps my Rhymes jocosely read,
> And you misconstru'd [pron. miscónstered] ev'ry Word he said;
> Tis true, on Paper I did him adore,
> I took that Liberty . . . *but took no more.*

She is sure Pope will forgive her this little trespass, if that is what it is, and reprieve her "injurd Honour"—all the more because he will understand it is not easy for women, with their "Frame too curious," their "slight Texture," and their "Want of Education," to know what is "wise." Subsequently, as appears from another poem of this year, Cheselden offered the opportunity to meet Pope at his Chelsea surgery. This invitation she rejects because she might indeed fall in love with him:

> Obscure on Earth, I rather chuse to be
> His bright Attendant in the Milky Way—

that after-home of great souls, it will be recalled, where Peterborow too intended to expatiate.

An actual letter to Pope (the first in the collection), dated 1740, continues to refer to Cheselden's invitation. Nothing but the generosity of the poet's temper, she tells him, and the delicacy of his thought, gives her courage to say how surprised she was by the alarm he expressed (evidently to Cheselden) "at the Thoughts of seeing a Woman, who has so candidly expressed her Sentiments in your Regard." Lest she be thought more at fault than she really is, she will now enclose everything she has ever written about him. (Can she, one wonders, have enclosed the verses about the Lilliputian god within her pocketbook?) Let him not imagine for a moment that she is put out by his alarm. No such thing. Such a "Sentiment of Honour" disposes her to "Adoration," and allows her to hope he will forgive and permit her to subscribe herself "Your Friend." A further explanatory poem on this subject, dated 1741, puts the question: "Can we grow fond of those We seldom see?"—with emphasis apparently on *see*, since according to the later letter of this year in which she describes her stroll in his garden, she had not at that time "so much as spoke" to him. And if we do grow fond of those we seldom see, the poem continues, surely it must be set down to esteem and friendship rather than love of another sort? Whatever he thinks of her, Pope must not suppose her "Bad as poor *May* [the young woman married to old January in the Chaucerian story Pope had modernized in his youth], when lifted in the Tree."

This was a rather remarkable allusion for one brought up as a lady to be making to an elderly gentleman in those days and one not calculated to allay any unease he might have about the nature of her feelings for him. But worse was to come. "Some," she continues,

> affirm, I'm intimate with you,
> And I have wish'd their false Assertions true.
> For when A Woman has her Self forgot,
> 'Tis then she wishes for she knows not what.

But then quite suddenly, as if unsaying everything just said and bidding him wait to censure her till her conduct *is* improper in the ways described (or, alternatively—for the lines are perhaps revealingly ambiguous—desiring a resolution of her problem through some immediate overt rejection by him), she urges:

> But blame my Conduct, when I'm so remiss,
> Reprove, nay call me Maudling [maudlin] Poetess;
> Condemn these Lines, and all I've wrote before,
> Say any Thing, that I may write no more.

At about this point, Pope or Martha Blount, or both, must have decided things were getting out of hand. The letter in which Amica describes her walk in the poet's garden is written to a female friend, who is thanked for her "tender Cautions." It is attended by a poem announcing in its title that it was sent to Pope on seeing him with Martha Blount, which reads in part as follows:

> Just Heav'n forbid, that I a Thought should know
> Which may contribute to Another's Woe; . . .
> May you each offer'd Friendship disapprove
> Whil'st charming B[loun]t do's visit, and can love!

Cheselden, evidently, also took some judgmental action, even going so far as to intimate she must be out of her head—to which he got the starchy and rather pretty (even if poetically atrocious) retort he deserved:

> Your Caution I with pleasure did receive,
> For which my Compliments of Thanks I give;
> I know there's room enough in Bethlehem [Bedlam]
> Both for my Self, and Mr. Ch[eseld]en.

By 1742, Amica's notes to Pope are beginning to be signed "Affectionately Yours." She is still in great awe of him. But she has learned everything about him that she can. One of her poems, titled "Mr. Pope's Supper," even stresses the Horatian simplicity of his diet, which on the occasion she has apparently heard about consisted of spinach, eggs, butter, bread, some cold fish, and Indian-Root, the last item glossed as "A Sort of Endive that grows in his Garden." An accidental glimpse of him landing from the Thames onto his grass plot moves her to verse. So does an accidental meeting with him (can it have been on another stroll in his garden?), when he gallantly gives up his seat to her. And her own dwelling by this time, thanks, as she says, to an indulgent husband, has become a veritable Pope museum. "I have indeed," she admits to a friend, "plac'd Mr. Pope in every Room in my Apartments." On the mantel in her bedroom, apparently a bust of Pope with prints of Homer and Horace on either side. In her "middle Room," another bust, located "in a fine Cabinet, fill'd with the best Edition of his Works." And in "the further Room," whether as bust or painted portrait is not clear, he is seen between Swift and Gay with Congreve below. The letter ends, not surprisingly, "I long to see you, tho' I expect to be chid."

At one point during 1742, when Martha Blount apparently felt called on to intervene directly with a note, Amica sends it on to Pope, with an appeal to him as arbiter:

> I shall make no Scruple, Sir, as Mrs. B[loun]t directs, of asking your Pardon for having so often intruded upon your time, and Patience, as I have; And I think my Self criminal enough, to deserve the Reflection of the Ladies; but I can't be alarm'd at the Thoughts of laying my Self open to Your Censure; . . . because, I am positive the most severe Sentence you can pass, will be mixt with so much Judgement and Justice, as becomes the Greatness of Your Soul. I shall not venture to trouble you with more, but beg

leave this Once to express, that I am, *Mr. Pope*, With an infinite Deal of Respect, Your ever obliged & affectionate Friend, Amica.

In the upshot, he was forbearing with her. She continued to send him poems, despite her promise. She felt free to express regret that her friend Dr. James Douglas, obstetrician and collector of Horace, now lately dead, had been named in the 1743 *Dunciad*, even if not unfavorably. For he—and here obviously she is confessing something as well as defining something—had been her mentor and good angel. He admired Pope's work, as she did, but he warned her against the power it had upon her fancy: if

> I too much should honour ev'ry Line,
> He'd say, *"that I was partial to a Crime;"*
> If I for Eloisa shed a Tear,
> His just Reproof would ever be severe;
> He'd tell me, Tho' I was Another's Wife,
> *"You fill'd up every Hour of my Life";* ...
> I complaisantly gave him all his Way,
> Yet smil'd to think, how far from Truth he'd stray;
> But tho' he never rightly understood
> The Case, he meant these Lessons for my good.

Our last glimpse of Amica before Pope's death is a letter of the spring of 1744:

I am greatly alarm'd at your being worse; Let me conjure you to send the Poems back, if you have not corrected the whole; for if I should be so unhappy as to survive so dear a Friend as your self, I can never be persuaded to have them printed. [Persuaders might have been difficult to find.]

I will be at Twickenham to morrow if I hear you are better by the Bearer; and will Sir bring each one of Yours, that I have been favour'd with, that you may be assur'd, in Case of your Removal, I will not boast of that Friendship, which you so prudently, in regard to my Character, have conceal'd. I can say no more but that I am with just Esteem, Most valuable Man, Affectionately Yours.

She kept her word. Her encounters with Pope and what she felt for him are here made public for the first time.

CHAPTER 30

DEATH

By now Pope's deteriorating health had become visible to all, even at moments to himself. As long ago as 1740, speaking of his "asthmatic Complaint" (actually the effect of his shrinking lung cavity as spine and rib-cage gave way), he had told Allen that his case was incurable, must therefore "become painful first, & then fatal."

The painful phrase arrived early in 1743, bringing him a constant ache in the chest and, at his worst times, a pulmonary dysfunction so extreme that "I can scarce walk, or go up a pair of Stairs, or move much in my bed, without quite losing breath." At about the same period, despite a painful probing he had undergone three years earlier to alleviate the stricture in his urethra, his urinary difficulties returned—either, one suspects, from a developing prostatitis or some degree of kidney failure, with its threat of dropsy. His eyes too were dimming. No longer able to read much after nightfall, he managed by employing readers. "I pick up a poor Scholar or two," he tells Orrery in January 1743, ". . . to sit & read to me, and I drink in return with them, especially if they are of the University [Oxford academics had gained a certain fame for tippling], sometimes rather too much (for me I mean)." And probably rather too much for his kidneys as well.

Old habits, nevertheless, died hard. He took spring, summer, and early autumn rambles that year. In late March, to Kent, to visit Cobham's nephew Gilbert West and his family, and bring them all back for a fortnight's stay at his villa. In late July and early August, to Bath and Bristol, at which time the peevish dignity of either Martha Blount or Mrs. Allen, or both, caused the temporary estrangement from the Allens noticed earlier. And in September, a tour of friends at Cornbury, Rousham, Amesbury, and Oxford, from the last of which places he again escaped (as he laughingly wrote Orrery, who had made a vain attempt to budge the group opposing the offer of a degree to Warburton) "un-doctored." Nor was there any noticeable let-up during the following several months in his attention to minutiae in the new edition of his works with notes by Warburton, which was to be, he thought, his best monument; or in his preparations to purchase

97. Alexander Pope. Drawing by an unknown artist, *c.* 1740?

An unusual pose, the poet being obviously offguard, as in Lady Burlington's sketch of him at cards and William Hoare's drawing of him at full length.

By kind permission of the Henry E. Huntington Library and Art Galleries.

a house in London, which would after his death be Martha's; or in his determination to retain, so far as illness permitted, his former way of life unchanged.

In the late fall and early winter he was much at Battersea with Bolingbroke and Marchmont (on his father's death at age ninety in 1742, Bolingbroke had at last inherited the family estate there) in lively conversations which one could wish to have heard. Pope was not, Marchmont told Boswell in 1778, "un homme à bons mots":

> His conversation was something better—more manly. A flow of vivacity. But it was necessary he should lead the conversation. If other people talked together, he fell asleep.

"I am older than anybody imagines," he observed to Marchmont, apparently by way of explanation. "One day is as much to me as three to others." Yet even so, by fits and starts, his energy was astounding. When not off to Battersea, he was likely to be in London seeing to his publishing affairs, dining with a friend, or consulting doctors, in whose profession he seems always to have taken an intellectual as well as personal and valetudinary interest. In late November, he pictures himself and Jonathan Richardson, who now also suffered grievously from an "asthma," sitting together over a cup of sack some night that winter, chattering "like two Parrots"; but whether this appealing fancy was ever realized we do not know.

For some time now—we can only guess how long—his body had required the support of "an iron case." So Marchmont testifies (who saw his warped and shriveled figure lifted out of it after he was dead), adding: "like a man whom you hang in chains." The grotesque comedy of the comparison, so characteristic of Pope's own imagination, inclines one to wonder whether it may not originally have been his; and, further, whether his iron case, so like a cage, so chill perhaps to the touch in winter, may not have suggested the rather haunting image of himself as a small bird that he resorts to twice during the dreary early months of 1744—as, for instance, in this reply to one of Bolingbroke and Marchmont's invitations to Battersea:

> My dear Lords,—Yes, I would see you as long as I can see you, & then shut my eyes upon the world, as a thing worth seeing no longer. If your charity would take up a small Bird that is half dead of the frost, and set it a chirping for half an hour, I'll jump into my Cage, & put myself into your hands to morrow, at any hour you send.

It is around this time, in early 1744, that his awareness of having entered the last and fatal stage of his disease becomes unmistakable. In December of 1743, he made his will, asking that his body be buried in Twickenham church; be carried to the grave, as his mother's had been, "by six of the poorest men of the parish," each of whom would receive a suit of mourning clothes for his pains; and have no other monument than the austere tablet he had set on the church wall for his parents, with simply the addition to its inscription: *et sibi: Qui obiit anno 17—, aetatis—*. To Spence, who on that December day was among the witnesses to his signature, he gave the further instruction: "The ceremony and every thing else [to be] as plain as the epitaph." About a month later, in January, he noted with some sense of urgency: "I *must* make a perfect edition of my works, and then I shall have nothing to do but die." Mid-February brought the first of several crises. For a few moments—he was again visiting at Battersea—he all but lost breath entirely. Cheselden, fetched posthaste from Chelsea, where he was now surgeon to the Royal Hospital, responded in the manner of those days by bleeding him. The patient, happily, survived both the attack and its treatment.

During the remaining three and a half months of Pope's life, the decay of his faculties was progressive though intermittent. During March and April, he is still able to be whisked about in a two-horse chariot for short journeys on warm days. He can still keep an intelligent eye on Warburton's annotations for the great edition. He visits nearby friends and is visited by many, among them the Allens, with whom (at least externally) amicable relations have been restored. (His last surviving letter is to Allen, dated May 7.) And he commands enough of his old charm to send Orrery, on April 10, one of his most winning letters, responding to news of the death of their Bounce. *This* Bounce, presumably one of the many sons of the Bounce celebrated in *Bounce to Fop*, had been given to the Orrerys for their country seat in Somerset in the summer of 1742; but just now, in March, only twenty-one months later, he has been bitten by a mad dog and has had to be put down. Pope has evidently been spared the details:

> I dread to enquire into the particulars of the Fate of Bounce. Perhaps you conceald them, as Heav'n often does Unhappy Events, in pity to the Survivors, or not to hasten on my End by Sorrow. I doubt not how much Bounce was lamented: They might say as the Athenians did to Arcite, in Chaucer:
>
> > Ah Arcite! gentle Knight! why would'st thou die,
> > When thou had'st Gold enough, and Emilye?

> Ah Bounce! ah gentle Beast! why wouldst thou dye
> When thou hadst Meat enough, and Orrery?

For what in nature could Bounce want, at Marston? What should
any one, Man or Beast, want there, but to live always under the
benigne Influence of Lady Orrery? I could dye more resign'd any
where else: I should not be so patient to suffer there, as among
those people here, who are less hurt by anothers Suffering, &
before whom therfore I make no conscience to complain, nay to
roar, or be as peevish as the devil.

Yet despite these and other favorable signs, his condition is clearly
worsening. We hear in this same letter of new symptoms: swellings
of the legs and "convulsive Catchings all over my body." From other
letters, we learn that Cheselden is about to try an unidentified
"Experiment . . . upon me," not impossibly a further effort to relieve
retention of urine. And by the end of the month, a new doctor has
been called in. This was Thomas Thompson, recommended to Pope
by his friend Bethel, a physician (according to Johnson) of considerable self-assurance, who, promptly and not without some justification from those swollen legs, "chang'd the nature of my disease from
an Asthma to a Dropsy; & certain it is, he has drawn from me a great
quantity of pure water by stool." Thompson continued to purge
Pope so steadily for several days running that he was credited by some
with hastening his death—not least, it appears, by Pope's usual
doctor, Simon Burton, physician to St. George's Hospital and royal
physician in ordinary, who mistrusted the violence of Thompson's
methods, but evidently had no serious alternative to propose. Pope's
friend Mallet, after a two-day visit with him on May 18 and 19,
summarizes the situation for Lord Orrery with a grim irony:

> After having been treated several months for an asthma by some
> eminent physicians [these would have been Burton; probably
> Richard Mead as well, one of the most respected doctors of the
> day, Pope's friend for many years; and, if Mallet uses "physician"
> loosely, Cheselden the surgeon, another friend of long standing]
> without the least abatement of that supposed distemper, there
> comes at last Dr. Thompson, who asserts that his illness is a dropsy
> of the breast, and that the asthmatic complaint is only a conse-
> quence of it. He says too that he can cure him, weak and attenuated
> as he is. For this end he ordered Mr. Pope several doses of physic,
> with what judgment I will not say, but they have evacuated him
> into absolute inanition.

After Pope's death, a story widely circulated spoke of an actual physicians' quarrel in Pope's sick room, Burton protesting Thompson's purgatorial scheme, Thompson defending it, and Pope silencing both men with the instruction that a postscript be added to the next edition of his *Dunciad*:

> Dunces, rejoice! forgive all censures past,
> The greatest dunce has kill'd your foe at last.

Other versions of the sick room quarrel give the epigram to Burton himself; while one version, highly jocular, pictures Burton, Thompson, and Cheselden all present together, Cheselden finally saving the poet's life by surreptitiously halving Thompson's dose and Pope consigning the other half to his horse:

> As Burton and Thompson were set upon Pope,
> The former despairing, the latter cry'd, "Hope:
> "For, faith Sir, I dread not this aqueous matter,
> "The Nerves be your care, let mine be the water;
> "D' you rouse up the Senses with Castor and Borax,
> "Whilst Jalap for me shall empty the Thorax.
> "The case is a Dropsy, Mead & Burton are Fools,
> Mr. Pope must have just Twenty two Stools."
> Poor Burton assented, and each took his Station,
> Whilst Cheselden watch'd the grand Operation;
> And happy for Pope that the Surgeon was there,
> For the half that he gave him did double its Share.
> What remain'd you will think was repeated, of course?
> No, No, Popes no Dunce—He gave it his Horse;
> Because Mr. Cheselden thought it less Hurt
> And not so unseemly shou'd he die in his Dirt.
> Poor Pope thus escap'd tho' something the Worse—
> I'll tell you tomorrow how it fared with his Horse.

In his account of Pope's condition to Orrery on May 19, Mallet goes on to say:

His strength, as well as his senses, is, I think, irrecoverably impaired. I staid with him all Friday evening and Saturday without being able to understand a word of what he would have said to me, till towards noon that I had him carried into the garden. There he recovered into some coherence of thought, talked intelligibly and rationally for above an hour, but grew weary, would return into the house, where I left him, without the satisfaction of taking a last farewell of him [i.e., Pope was no longer rational]. I beg pardon, my Lord, for this melancholy detail, but it is the overflowing of a heart that long loved and esteemed him as a good man, no less than an excellent writer.

At what point in his progress toward darkness Pope began to be afflicted with these twilit lapses, it is difficult to say with assurance. Marchmont, usually a reliable witness, told Boswell in 1778 that Pope was "quite gone in his judgment" for three months; but this, recalled at a distance of thirty-four years, seems irreconcilable both with Pope's own letters of the period and with Spence's rather full record of his conversations with him during his last months and weeks. There the earliest intimation of the onset of senile dementia occurs on May 10, when Pope tells his visitor that the previous Sunday (May 6) he had suffered the humbling experience of losing his mind "for a whole day." Instances multiply thereafter. A day or two later, he had the not uncommon experience of the very ill in finding the room grow dark, or, as he himself put it, "of seeing everything . . . as through a curtain." On the fourteenth he had color problems ("seeing false colours on objects"), an equally familiar phenomenon in extreme illness, and on the fifteenth his behavior was such as to draw from Cheselden, well-read in Shakespeare, an echo of Ophelia's despairing cry about Hamlet: "His mind is like a fine ring of bells, jangled out of tune."

From about this time on, visions and hallucinations began to occur, some of them bizarre. On one occasion, "pointing up in the air with a very steady regard," he exclaimed "What's that?" and then, turning his gaze back to Spence, "with a smile of pleasure and with the greatest sweetness," answered his own question: "'Twas a vision." At another time, when Mallet was keeping vigil with him (very probably during his visit of May 18–19), he said he had just had a vision of "an odd kind": His own head had opened, Apollo had risen out of it, Mallet's head had also opened, Apollo had gone into it, then both heads had closed. In this instance, one may perhaps fairly sense some vivid boyhood experience, such as most of us have when we first read of Athena springing full-armed from the head of Zeus, short-circuiting with his sense of himself as leading poet of the age, or perhaps merely with the description Fortescue had given of him in that *Spectator*-style "vision" of their long-ago youth.

Other reported incidents defy explanation. Once when Robert Dodsley, the publisher he had years before set up in business, was sitting with him, he asked suddenly: "What great arm is that I see coming out of the wall?" Does this relate in some addled way to the arm of God as conceived by a small boy's wandering mind at Mass? to childhood memories of nocturnal terror? to some illogical conflation of imagery from Homer's world of derring-do? to a shadow cast by sunlight streaming through a barred pane? Similarly inpenetrable as to source and significance is the exclamation recorded by Horace Walpole in a letter dated May 29, the day before Pope died:

> Pope is given over with a dropsy, which is mounted into his head; in an evening, he is not in his senses; t' other day at Chiswick he said to my Lady Burlington, "Look at Jesus there! How ill they have crucified him!"

One's first impulse is to suppose Pope spoke of a painting he and Lady Burlington had before them, the more so as his last recorded visit to Chiswick was made on March 30. But no trace of such a painting survives among the records of Burlington's collections; nor is the remark quite what one is likely to say, in one's right mind, about a *painting* of the crucifixion; nor would Chiswick have been an impossible journey in mid to late May (a time that accords a good deal better than March 30 with Walpole's "t' other day") for one who could and did take the two-mile drive from his villa to Bushy Park the day before his death. The remark must continue to stand, I am inclined to think, with its mysteries unresolved—these being, after all, no greater than those of the mind itself; or of what becomes of it, or it becomes, on its way to the undiscovered country from whose bourn no traveler returns.

All these aberrations were, of course, accompanied by intervals of lucidity—so, at least, we "normals" have agreed to call it. On the same day on which Cheselden compared his mind to a fine ring of bells out of tune, and just after Thompson had been telling him in how many ways he was getting better, Pope was able to greet his friend Lyttleton as he came into the room, with a flash of that wit which had endeared him to so many: "Here am I, dying of a hundred good symptoms!" Even twelve days later, in one of his good moments, he was able to quote accurately his own lines on his life having been divided between extravagance and prudence:

> I, who at some times spend, at others spare,
> Divided between Carelessness and Care.

The quotation came to him as he was speaking apologetically of having so little to leave to his friends; for friends and friendship were now much on his mind, as they had been throughout his life. Over the years, we may recall, his house had become something like a monument to that theme, every room in it hung with portraits of those he had loved and admired. As much may be said of his work. If no other poetry in English contains so many sharp and unforgettable censures, it is equally true that no other poetry so swarms with glowing and affectionate tributes to friends: tributes that the essayist Charles Lamb would read aloud in the next age with tears and, throwing down the book, exclaim, "Do you think I would not wish to have been friends with such a man as this?" Now, in his final days, after the fashion of an age in which dying was still a public act, he desired to have as many of his friends as possible about him. "Like Socrates," it had occurred to him on one occasion in early May, when he was sending about advance copies of what is today called the deathbed edition of his four epistles to Burlington, Bathurst, Cobham, and Martha Blount: "Here am I, like Socrates, distributing my morality among my friends, just as I am dying." To which Spence had replied: "I really had that thought several times when I was last with you, and was apt now and then to look upon myself like Phaedo."

And so, knowing these were final days, they came. For if it was his duty to make a good end in their presence, it was theirs to attend him toward that one event in his life and theirs (and ours) which, if it be not now, yet will come. Some made a single visit and stayed to dine. As few as five days before he died, says Spence, he was at table "when others would have been on a death bed," his wizened withered figure provoking from Anne Arbuthnot, the doctor's daughter, who was present at one such entertainment, the shocked aside, "Lord have mercy upon us! This is quite an Egyptian feast!" Others came for a day or two, or more than once, like David Mallet. And some—Bolingbroke, Marchmont, Nathaniel Hooke (a friend of Pope's later years, at that time serving on his recommendation as secretary and historian to the old Duchess of Marlborough, who was writing her memoirs), and the ever-loyal Spence—seem to have been towards the end in almost continuous attendance. On the twenty-first, when it was thought for a while that the last moments had come, Bolingbroke cried—"for [a] quarter of an hour like a child," Spence informs us, breaking out into exclamations on the order of "Oh great God! What is man?" but this did not prevent him (says another account) from flying into "a great fit of passion and indignation" when he discovered after his arrival on the twenty-ninth that Pope had received the sacraments that morning, at the suggestion of Hooke, a fellow Roman Catholic, who had probably been one of his schoolmates at Twyford. This was not at all to Bolingbroke's deistic taste, and possibly it was to quiet him that Cheselden (who usually made no disguise of his own atheism) remarked, "There is no hopes for him here; our only hopes for him must be ——" To which Bolingbroke, as uncomfortable with the idea of immortality as Pope was convinced of it, replied, "Pshaw! We can only reason from what is: we can reason on actualities, but not on possibilities." Life, in other words, with its little sureties and exigences, never fails to go on. As a poet of our own day has handsomely reminded us, the ploughman sticks to his ploughing, the sun to its shining, and the ship to its sailing, no matter that Icarus is falling out of the sky.

It was said later that Martha Blount neglected Pope in his last illness. That this judgment is at least partially incorrect we may gather from Spence's note that "Mrs. Blount's coming in gave a new turn of spirits or a temporary strength to him." Johnson is more damning. He states that one day during his illness when Pope was resting outdoors on the Thames side of his house Martha arrived by water. Pope asked Bolingbroke to go down and hand her up the lawn, but Bolingbroke, disinclined, crossed his legs and sat still, and Marchmont performed the courtesy instead. When he reached her side, Martha is reported to have said to him, "What, is he not dead yet?" It is impossible to be sure whence Johnson had this story, so obviously intended to discredit Martha. It does not sound much like Marchmont, who so far as we know relayed no such information in his conversation with Boswell in 1778; and who, as a warm admirer of Bolingbroke's, is unlikely to have stressed the detail about his rudeness. It would come quite plausibly, on the other hand, from any source close to Warburton, who hated Bolingbroke, did not care for Martha Blount, warmly espoused the Allen side in the Allen–Blount dispute, and eventually married Allen's niece and heiress. To be sure, Martha may have made the remark in question and perhaps in these very words. One would still, before judging her, need to know how close in tone she came to "What, is he not yet out of his pain?"—which is to say, "Am I not out of mine?"

For Pope, though the remark if intended cruelly would have hurt him, no change of attitude was thinkable: love is not love which alters when it alteration finds. Whether she wanted them or not, he had told her in his verse epistle, Phoebus had given her sense, good humor, "and a Poet." Or as he wrote in his last surviving letter to her earlier that spring, urging that she soon decide where she wished to live in town:

Would to God you would Quicken your haste to settle, by reflecting what a pleasure it would be to me, just to see it, and to see you at ease; & then I could contentedly leave you to the Providence of God, in this Life, & resign my Self to it in the other! I have little to say to you when we meet; but I love you upon unalterable Principles, which makes me feel my heart the same to you as if I saw you every hour. adieu.

À dieu it was. Not much more than two months after writing this, he was dead. On June 1, Mallet reported to Orrery:

On Monday last [28 May] I took my everlasting Farewell of him. He was enough himself to know me, to enquire after Mrs. Mallet's Health, and anxiously to hasten his Servant in getting ready my Dinner, because I came late. The same social Kindness, the same friendly Concern for those he loved, even in the minutest Instances, that had distinguished his heart through Life, were uppermost in his Thoughts to the last.

He dyed on Wednesday [30 May] about the Middle of the Night, without a Pang, or a Convulsion, unperceived of those that watched him, who imagined he was only in a sounder Sleep than ordinary.—But I cannot go on.

At about the same time, Spence, who had been among those watchers, set down in his notes: "Mr. Pope died the thirtieth of May, in the evening, but they [i.e., we] did not know the exact time, for his departure was so easy that it was imperceptible even to the standers-by. May our end be like his!"

The long disease was over, "my countrys poet" gone.

APPENDIX

Tax Records for the Broad Street Ward and the Langbourne Ward (hereafter abbreviated as BSW and LW), now preserved at the CLRO, afford a few useful clues to Pope's father's career. ("Box" refers to "Assessment Box.")

We first meet up with him in 1671, when he is twenty-five. He is then apparently living in the parish of St. Benet Fink with another lodger named Sampson in the house of one Abra Debuxbilles—from the name, probably a Huguenot. His tax is twelve shillings on goods appraised at two hundred pounds. (BSW: Box 57. 7. Subsidy 22 and 23 Charles II, c. 3. [Date is ca. June, 1671.] F 12, verso.) Two years later, he is definitely living in the parish of St. Benet Fink, with two other lodgers named Beaver and Terry, in the house of Susana Kemp. This time his tax (not a subsidy tax) is given as two shillings for the first quarter of 1673. (BSW: Box 19, MS. 7. 18 Month Tax. P. 19.) The same figure is given for (each of?) the second and third quarters. (BSW: Box, 22. 18. [Collection warrant dated "July, 1673."] P. 19.) His obligation for the fifth quarter of the eighteen-month tax is again two shillings, but his landlords are now Jasper Cloet and Nicholas Wood. (BSW: Box 14, MS. 2 [Warrant dated 6 April 1674.] P. 19.)

When the extant records again carry his name, he is himself a "Landlord" like his neighbors Cloet and Wood. For this he pays one pound eleven, and since he pays also two shillings under the heading "Inhab[itants]," he has presumably married Magdalen. (BSW: Box 61, MS. 21. "As Assessment made . . . for the Building of 30 Shippes of War . . . by . . . Warrant b[e]aring date Sept. the 4th 1677." P. 20.) By 23 April 1678, his household is described as "Alexand[e]r Pope wife and a boy," plus "Mary"—apparently Mary Beach—who receives board and lodging and wages of "£2" a year. For himself and family his tax is thirteen shillings; for Mary, three. The "boy," of course, was the earlier Alexander, whose care was soon entrusted to his aunt, Mary Stavely, and whose burial at Pangbourne on 1 September 1682 (above, pp. 3, 21) was recorded by her husband, the Rev. Ambrose Stavely. (BSW: Box 11, MS. 9. Poll Tax 1678. [Warrant dated 23 April 1678.] P. 40.) That same year Mr. Pope is taxed two shillings sixpence for his family and one shilling sixpence for his "Inhabitants," doubtless Mary again, by another assessment for building thirty warships, warrant dated 18 April 1678. (BSW: Box 62, MS. 22. P. 20.)

In 1679, as we know from other sources, Magdalen died. Accordingly, the records of 1680 show that Pope is again a lodger, this time in the house of his neighbor Nicholas Wood. No tax figure is set down, though doubtless one was assessed on the new basis. Mary the servant has perhaps gone to Pangbourne with the children. (BSW: Box 25, MS. 13. [Warrant dated 24 July 1680.] 6 Months Tax "for Disbanding the Army." P. 17.)

The next appearance of Pope's father in the extant records has to do with still another assessment for building "thirty shipps of warr," of which the collection warrant is dated 11 July 1688. This is James II's response, evidently, to the news that his son-in-law, Dutch William, has an invasion army in preparation. Pope is now a "Landlord" again and in the Lombard Street Precinct. As landlord, he is assessed two pounds, which probably includes himself and his wife Edith Turner Pope (though young Pope was born in May), and for "Inhabitants"—plausibly Mary, back from Pangbourne, where she must have lately lost a child of her own?—one shilling and six. (LW: Box 29, MS. 23. P. 8. Lombard Street Precinct.)

A year after this, in July 1689, a "List of the names of Papists with their addresses and trades" gives "Alexander pope of the p[ar]ish of St. Edmond Lumbardstreet[,] Merchant" and "Edith pope wife of the said Alexander Pope." (LW: Sessions Records—Sessions Minutes 60, July 1689.) By warrant dated 31 July of that year—for a levy granted by Act of Parliament to William and Mary: ". . . No more than two penc[e] in the pound to be Rated upon houses pr. month"—Pope as landlord is taxed five shillings and six, and five shillings also for inhabitants, which suggests that his household is increasing. The little girl Magdalen is certainly by now back from Pangbourne. (LW: Box 26, MS. 16. P. 9. Lombard Street.) For a similar levy in 1690, its warrant dated 16 May, the assessment list describes the Pope household as follows:

papist.   Alexander pope unfree Mer[c]h[an]t house & poll
           his Wife and two Children
           three Serv[an]ts.

Three sets of figures appear: 21 [shillings] 02 [pence]; 6 [shillings]; and a total: 21 [shillings] 08 [pence]. Since the figure "21" overwrites a figure "10" (the tax set down for Pope's next door neighbor), this may represent the double taxing of Roman Catholics, which was to last throughout Pope's lifetime. One earlier name in this tax list carries the note "doubly charged"; another has the note "reputed papist," but the "reputed" seems to have saved him from double taxing, at least as recorded here. (LW: Box 12, MS. 1. P. 13.)

Our first intimation that the Pope family may be considering departure from the city, perhaps in consideration of the act of 1689 prohibiting papists from habitation closer to London than ten miles, appears in the Vestry Minutes Book of St. Edmund the King, Lombard Street (Guildhall Library, MS 4266/1). There it is recorded under 18 December 1691 (p. 91) that:

Whereas Mr. Alexander Pope hath desired to Fine for Constable[,] Questman[,] and Scavenger [Quest-Men were chosen yearly by each ward to look into abuses and misdemeanors, especially those having to do with weights and measures]—It is therefore This Day Ordered that the said Mr. Pope bee excused from the said Office[,] hee having paid Fourteen pounds into the Church Wardens hands as his Fine for the same. And it is also Ordered That if hee shall leave the Ward at Midsomer next the halfe of the said Fine viz: Seaven Pounds shall bee repaid to the said Mr. Pope by the Church Warden.

The decision of Mr. Pope to "fine" signifies nothing, as the job was a thankless one and many chose to pay rather than serve (he himself had twice "fined" earlier: Vestry Minutes Book, pp. 74, 98); but the provision for reimbursement if he shall leave the ward after the first half of 1692 hints that removal may be under consideration. Conformably, Pope is taxed as follows in what is presumably a first-quarter assessment of the 1692 Poll Tax [Act of 3 William and Mary, c. 6]:

Alexander Pope Merch[an]t & wife		1	2	–
John Taverner } serv[an]ts			2	–
Mary Baron				
		1	4	

(LW: Box 32. MS. 5. P. 11. Lombard Street Prec[inc]t); whereas in the assessment record for the second quarter of the same tax, we find "George Ouldner" [probably, "Oldner": see below], a lighterman, and his wife "In Popes hous." Their tax is eleven shillings instead of Pope's one pound two, with two shillings added for two children, two more for two servants, and one for "Mr. Poopes Servante." (LW:

Box 20. 17. [Warrant dated ca. July.] 1692 Poll Tax. 2d Quarter. P. 11. Lombard Street Precinct.) Though this looks as if Pope were again double-taxed as a papist, the difference may lie simply in the annual one-pound surtax that this levy laid on "gentlemen, clergy . . . , merchants and brokers." (D. V. Glass, "Socio-Economic Status and Occupations in the City of London at the End of the Seventeenth Century," in A. E. J. Hollaender and William Kellaway, *Studies in London History* [London: Hodder & Stoughton, 1969], pp. 373–89.) In the fourth quarter, "Oldner" is assessed twelve shillings for himself and his wife, a shilling each for two children and two servants, and a shilling each for "Mr. Popes serv[an]t & John Taverner." (LW: Box 36, MS. 12. [Warrant dated 12 December 1692.] P. 9. Lombard Street Precinct.)

It seems reasonably clear that in each of the last three entries above we are talking about Mary Beach, earlier the infant poet's wet nurse, and John Taverner, alias Banister, the family's priest. Why "Mr. Poopes Servante" continued on in the house after Oldner took over, we cannot guess, but it was perhaps a favor done the Pope family, whilst it was seeking out new quarters, by a man whose trade as lighterman might make him well acquainted with an importer of "Hollands." Some further accommodation of the sort may account for the presence of the Popes' servant and priest in the fourth quarter. Conceivably, Oldner may have been buying out Mr. Pope's business and stock, for in a 1693 list of "Names of householders and stock-holders" ("4s in the £ tax"), Oldner is assessed under "Rents" one pound ten and under "Estates" three shillings; and in a corresponding list of 1694 he is assessed under "Rent" for the same amount and under "Stock" for six shillings. (LW: Box 13, MS. 28. P. 10; and Box 17, MS. 4. P. 11.) By June 1696, Oldner too had gone from these premises. (LW: Box 11. MS. 18.) About the Popes, the likeliest guess (above, pp. 37–8, 44) is that they went from Plough Court to Hammersmith.

ABBREVIATIONS

Apology	*An Apology for the Life of Colley Cibber, with An Historical View of the Stage during His Time*, ed., B. R. S. Fone (University of Michigan Press, 1968).
Ault	Norman Ault, *New Light on Pope* (London: Methuen, 1949).
BL	British Library (MSS.).
Boyce	Benjamin Boyce, *The Benevolent Man: A Life of Ralph Allen of Bath* (Harvard University Press, 1967).
Brownell	Morris Brownell, *Alexander Pope and the Arts of Georgian England* (Oxford: Clarendon, 1978).
Carruthers	Robert Carruthers, *Life of Alexander Pope* (1857).
CLRO	Corporation of London Record Office (MSS.).
Collected in Himself	Maynard Mack, *"Collected in Himself": Essays Critical, Biographical, and Bibliographical on Pope and Some of His Contemporaries* (Delaware University Press, 1982).
Correspondence	*The Correspondence of Alexander Pope*, ed., George Sherburn, 5 vols. (Oxford: Clarendon, 1956). The word *Correspondence* is omitted, and volume and page appear within parentheses when the reference to Pope or his correspondent is already clear.
Dennis	*The Critical Works of John Dennis*, ed., E. N. Hooker, 2 vols. (Johns Hopkins University Press, 1943).
Dickinson	H. T. Dickinson, *Bolingbroke* (London: Constable, 1970).
Dilke	C. W. Dilke, *Papers of a Critic*, 2 vols. (1875).
Dryden *Poems*	*The Poems of John Dryden* ed., James Kinsley, 4 vols. (Oxford: Clarendon, 1958).
E-C	*The Works of Alexander Pope*, eds., Whitwell Elwin and J. W. Courthope, 10 vols. (1871–89).
E-CS	*Eighteenth-Century Studies*
Early Career	George Sherburn, *The Early Career of Alexander Pope* (Oxford: Clarendon, 1934)
Egmont	HMC: *Diary of Viscount Percival afterwards First Earl of Egmont*, 3 vols.
Ehrenpreis	Irvin Ehrenpreis, *Swift: His Life, His Works, His Times*, 3 vols. (London: Methuen, 1962–83).

The Garden and the City	Maynard Mack, *The Garden and the City: Retirement and Politics in the Later Poetry of Pope* (University of Toronto Press, 1969).
Guerinot	J. V. Guerinot, *Pamphlet Attacks on Alexander Pope, 1711–1744* (London: Methuen, 1969).
HL	Huntington Library (MSS.).
HMC	Historical Manuscripts Commission.
Halsband, *Life*	Robert Halsband, *The Life of Lady Mary Wortley Montagu* (Oxford: Clarendon, 1956).
Hervey	John Lord Hervey, *Some Materials towards Memoirs of the Reign of King George II*, ed., Romney Sedgwick. 3 vols. (London: Cresset, 1931).
Horace Walpole	*The Complete Correspondence of Horace Walpole*, ed., W. S. Lewis *et al*. 45 vols. (Yale University Press, 1937–83).
Johnson	Samuel Johnson, "Pope", *Lives of the Poets*, ed., G. B. Hill, 3 vols. (Oxford: Clarendon, 1905), volume 3.
Journal to Stella	Swift's *Journal to Stella*, ed. Harold Williams, 2 vols. (Oxford: Clarendon, 1948).
Lady MWM, *Letters*	*The Letters of Lady Mary Wortley Montagu*, ed., Robert Halsband, 3 vols. (Oxford: Clarendon, 1965).
Lady MWM, *Poems*	Lady Mary Wortley Montagu, *Essays and Poems and Simplicity—a Comedy*, eds., Robert Halsband and Isobel Grundy (Oxford: Clarendon, 1977).
The Last and Greatest Art	Maynard Mack, *"The Last and Greatest Art,"*: *Some Unpublished Poetical Manuscripts of Alexander Pope* (Delaware University Press, 1984).
Lees-Milne	James Lees-Milne, *Earls of Creation: Five Great Patrons of Eighteenth-Century Art* (London: Hamish Hamilton, 1962).
NLS	National Library of Scotland (MSS.).
"New Anecdotes"	George Sherburn, "New Anecdotes of Alexander Pope", *Notes and Queries*, n. s. 5 (1958): 343–49.
POAS	*Poems on Affairs of State: Augustan Satirical Verse, 1660–1714*, ed., G. DeF. Lord *et al*., 7 vols. (Yale University Press, 1963–74).
PQ	*Philological Quarterly*.
PRO	Public Record Office, London (MSS.).
"Pope's Books"	"A Finding List of Books Surviving from Pope's Library," in Maynard Mack, *"Collected in Himself"* [see above], Appendix A: nos. 1–176.

Pope, *Prose*	*Prose Works of Alexander Pope*, ed., Norman Ault (Oxford: Blackwell, 1936).
RES	*Review of English Studies*.
Rogers, *Major Satires*	R. W. Rogers, *The Major Satires of Alexander Pope* (University of Illinois Press, 1955).
Ruffhead	Owen Ruffhead, *The Life of Alexander Pope* (1769).
SEL	*Studies in English Literature*.
SRO	Scottish Record Office (Edinburgh).
SP	*Studies in Philology*.
Sedgwick	Romney Sedgwick, *The House of Commons, 1715–1754*, 2 vols. (London: HMSO, 1970).
Sherburn, "Letters"	George Sherburn, "Letters of Alexander Pope," *Review of English Studies*, n. s. 9 (1958): 388–406.
Spence	Joseph Spence, *Observations, Anecdotes, and Characters of Books and Men*, ed., J. M. Osborn, 2 vols. (Oxford: Clarendon, 1966).
Stone	Lawrence Stone, *The Family, Sex, and Marriage in England, 1500–1800* (London: Weidenfeld and Nicolson, 1977).
Swift, *Correspondence*	*The Correspondence of Jonathan Swift*, ed., Harold Williams, 5 vols. (Oxford: Clarendon, 1963).
Swift, *Poems*	*The Poems of Jonathan Swift*, ed., Harold Williams, 3 vols. (Oxford: Clarendon, 1937).
Swift, *Prose*	*Swift: Prose Works*, ed., Herbert Davis *et al.*, 14 vols. (Oxford: Blackwell, 1939–68).
TE	*The Twickenham Edition of the Poems of Alexander Pope*, ed., John Butt *et al.*, 11 vols. (London: Methuen, 1938–68).
VCH	Victoria County Histories.
Wentworth Papers	*Selections from the Private and Family Correspondence of Thomas Wentworth, 3d Earl of Strafford*, ed., J. J. Cartwright (1883).
Wimsatt	W. K. Wimsatt, *The Portraits of Alexander Pope* (Yale University Press, 1965).
Works (1751)	Pope, *Works*, ed., William Warburton, 9 vols. (1751).

NOTES

Chapter 1, A London Childhood

3 *"Hollands":*
As Edith Pope put it to Spence, her husband "dealt in Hollands wholesale" (Spence, no. 11). A merchant's trade was often in kind, however, and might include other goods as well: see above, p. 21.

3 *Special tribute, rarely offered:*
"St. Benet Fink, Churchwardens' Accounts, 1610–1700," Guildhall Library, MS. 1303/1: "Rec^d: of M:^{r} Alexander Pope for Buriall of his wife Ground and great Bell 18.4." The fee paid for use of the "great Bell" was 5 shillings (such at least the records indicate it was in 1681). This was an outlay of some moment when Mr. Pope's total annual rate charge came to 8 shillings 8 pence, and it seems in most cases to have served as a dissuasive. Of the fifteen burials of 1679 among which Magdalen Pope's is listed, only one other had the great bell.

For the date of Magdalen's burial, see the "Burial Register" of St. Benet Fink (also in the Guildhall Library: MS. 4098) for 1679, p. 18: "12th Augst: Buried Magdilin the wife of Allixander Pope." This entry seems to have been the source for Joseph Hunter in *Pope: His Descent and Family Connections* (1859), p. 14, though he records it slightly differently. The year is clearly 1679, not 1678 as George Sherburn has it (*Early Career*, p. 32).

Burial of Roman Catholics in Anglican graveyards, once frowned on by the Establishment, had become commonplace after the Restoration, though the actual burial services were usually said by the priest before the corpse left the house and the interment more often than not (until 1700) took place at night. See John Bossy, *The English Catholic Community, 1570–1850* (New York: Oxford University Press, 1976), p. 142.

3 *Burial notice of the infant son*
Pangbourne Parish Register, D/P 91/1/3, f 3v, now in the Berkshire Record Office, to whose archivist, Amanda Arrowsmith, as well as to the Pangbourne Parochial Church Council I am indebted for assistance. The entry carries the usual formula—"for whom Affidavit was brought"—required from 1678 by legislation prohibiting the use of material other than wool for shrouds. Still on the books in Pope's time, the prohibition is referred to amusingly by "Narcissa" in his *Epistle to Cobham*, 242ff, quoted above at p. 600.

3 *Looked for a wife to mother them:*
Then yet more than now, a mother's death left a father with young children "helpless." "As quickly as possible he [a widowed father] farmed out his children to a grandmother, a sister, or a sister-in-law, or went through the tiring process of remarrying." Randolph Trumbach, *The Rise of the Egalitarian Family: Aristocratic Kinship and Domestic Relations in Eighteenth-Century England* (New York: Academic Press, 1978), p. 240. When (for example) Mary Wortley Montagu's mother died her father immediately packed the children off to *his* mother.

3 *Marriage with Edith Turner:*
Hunter, *Descent*, p. 14, supposes that Edith's marriage to Alexander took place as late as 1686 or even 1687, on the ground that young Alexander arrived in the spring of 1688. The one certainty we have is that Edith was remembered with a small legacy as "Mistress Edith Turner" in a will dated 17 June 1684. Thus at that point she was still single. Mary Edmond, "Limners and Picture-Makers: New Light on the Lives of Miniaturists and Large-Scale Portrait Painters Working in London in the Sixteenth and Seventeenth Centuries," *Walpole Society Publications*, 47 (1978–80): 112. I owe this reference to Valerie Rumbold's outstanding research into the Turner family: "Alexander Pope and the Religious Tradition of the Turners," in *Recusant History*, 17 (1984): 17–37.

4 *Dangerous distempers:*
John Evelyn, *Diary*, 15 and 29 April 1688. See also Dryden's *Britannia Rediviva*, 169–74.

4 *Forty-fifth birthday:*
   Hunter, *Descent*, p. 34, gives the date of Edith's baptism as 18 June 1642, an error in which he is followed by Sherburn (*Early Career*, p. 32). Actually, the year was 1643, Hunter having failed to notice in the Worsborough (Yorks) register the indication of a new calendar year beginning on Ladyday in March 1643. I am grateful for this correction to Valerie Rumbold, whose work on the Turner family is cited above.

4 *Five wise virgins and five foolish ones:*
   Hunter (pp. 25–45, especially p. 39) and also Robert Davies, *Pope: Additional Facts Concerning His Maternal Ancestry* (London, 1858), pp. 41–52.

4 *An Anglican clergyman:*
   See above, p. 21.

4 For Pope's father's apprenticeship see *Early Career*, pp. 30–1.

5 For John Evelyn's remark see his *Diary*, 6 December 1680. Evelyn speaks specifically here of Titus Oates, but the other informers, though less brazen, were equally unscrupulous.

5 On the plot generally, see J. P. Kenyon's excellent *The Popish Plot* (London: Heinemann, 1972). Kenyon is sometimes more critical of the occasional "tactlessness," "self-confidence," or provocative behavior of certain papists than outraged by the brutal violations of their lives and rights. For a first-rate impartial account of the plot's backgrounds and after-effects, see John Miller, *Popery and Politics in England, 1660–1688* (Cambridge: Cambridge University Press, 1973). The Catholic historian J. C. H. Aveling, in *The Handle and the Axe: The Catholic Recusants in England from Reformation to Emancipation* (London: Blond and Briggs, 1976, pp. 207ff), offers persuasive evidence of the extent to which papists contributed to the scare: in some instances by the provocative behavior to which Kenyon calls attention; in others, perhaps more damagingly, through petty jealousies and group antagonisms, sometimes leading to such wild denunciations of Roman Catholics by Roman Catholics that it is not surprising Protestants were alarmed. Aveling's evidence is important in explaining the speed and thoroughness with which the panic ballooned and assumed, in his words, "a life of its own." Equally influential, at some subliminal level, must have been a suspicion among the more judicious Protestants (as among whites in the American Old South) that they had sown the wind for generations and could expect to reap a whirlwind.

5 *Ransack the coffins for contraband arms:*
   Popish Plot, p. 84.

5 *Pope burnings:*
   On Pope burnings, see Sheila Williams, "The Pope-Burning Processions of 1679, 1680, and 1681," *Journal of the Warburg Institute*, 21 (1958): 104–18: O. W. Furley, "The Pope-Burnings of the Late Seventeenth Century," *History*, 44 (1959): 16–23; David Allen, "The Role of the London Trained-Bands in the Exclusion Crisis," *English Historical Review*, 87 (1972): 300–1; and John Miller, *Popery and Politics* (1973), pp. 73–4, 131, 183–7, 189, 259, 261.

8 *"Yᵉ Pope and Yᵉ Divel in a dialogue":*
   Charles Hatton to Christopher Hatton, 22 November 1677. *The Hatton Correspondence*, ed., E. M. Thompson (1878), 1: 157.

8 *The screams of those burning cats:*
   Some British historians, from Macaulay down, have chosen to underplay the ugly side of these saturnalia, e.g., "*All* men made merry at a bonfire, regardless of who had lit it and why"—David Allen ("London Trained-Bands"), p. 300 (italics mine). Other instances abound.

8 *Another Pope burning, in 1677:*
   Miller, *Popery and Politics*, pp. 183–4.

8 *Where we know the Popes were situated:*
   A Collection of the Names of the Merchants living in and about the City of London (1677), leaf G2r. Broad Street lay in the parish of St. Benet Fink.

8 *An assault that never came:*
   Popery and Politics, p. 185.

8 *The best defense a good offense:*
   See Richard Baxter, *A Key for Catholics, To Open the Jugling of the Jesuits* (1659), ch. 45, especially pp. 315–23; William Denton, *The Burnt Child dreads the Fire* (1675), pp. 4, 31

("*Levellers, Agitators, Independents,* Fifth Monarchy Men, Quakers, &c. . . . are but Badgers, Working Holes for the Foxes, the Jesuits"), 56–64; and Peter du Moulin, *A Vindication of the sincerity of the Protestant Religion In the Point of Obedience to Sovereignes. Opposed To the Doctrine of Rebellion, authorized and practiced by the Pope and the Jesuits* (1664), especially pp. 53–61 ("When the business of the late bad times is once ripe for an history, . . . it will be found, that the late rebellion was raised and fostered by the arts of the Court of Rome," p. 58)—most of the content of these pages was reissued in 1673 as *The Great Loyalty of the Papists to K. Charles I.* See in addition William Prynne, *A True and Perfect Narrative* (1659), pp. 19–20, 43, 57–63, especially 62–3. (Prynne was undoubtedly the most influential expounder of the doctrine of Jesuit and papal responsibility for the rebellion and the regicide: see his preface to *The First and Second Part of a Seasonable Legal and Historical Vindication,* 1655.)

9 *"Of a corpse whose fragments":*
This notice comes, I believe, from a contemporary newspaper, whose precise date and title I have not been able to recover from an accidentally mutilated note. Fuller accounts of the episode appear in *Publick Occurrences Truely Stated,* 21 and 28 February 1688, and in *The London Gazette,* 27 February–1 March and 1–5 March 1688.

9 *Lord Russell's declaration:*
Anchitel Grey, *Debates of the House of Commons from the Year 1667 to the Year 1694,* 10 vols. (1763), 7:146. Quoted in Kenyon, *Popish Plot,* p. 1.

9 *Andrew Marvell:*
An Account of the Growth of Popery, and Arbitrary Government in England (1677), p. 4.

9 *Whether the Pope was or was not Antichrist:*
A Sermon Preach'd November 5, 1678 at St. Margaret's Westminster, Before the Honourable House of Commons (1678), pp. 29, 28.

9 *"That holy thing that shall be born of her":*
Ephemeris Vitae Abrahami Pryme [Abraham de la Pryme], *or, A Diary of My Own Life,* ed., Charles Jackson (1870), p. 11.

9 *"God's English-men":*
Areopagitica, in *Complete Prose Works,* vol. 2, ed., Ernest Sirluck (New Haven: Yale University Press, 1959), p. 553.

10 *Letter* and *Anatomy:*
Pamphlets published in 1687 and 1688 by George Savile, first marquis of Halifax. They confirmed many in the belief that James II's inclination to free all worshippers from special laws and test acts in order to free also his fellow Catholics was an insidious plan to establish popery and extirpate Protestantism.

10 *Lost the child by miscarriage:*
Narcissus Lutrell, *A Brief Historical Relation of State Affairs from September 1678 to April 1717,* 6 vols. (Oxford, 1857), 1:422 (27 November 1687), 439 (11 May 1688). See also *Public Occurrences,* no. 13, and *Upon the King's Voyage to Chatham . . . and The Queens Miscarriage Thereupon,* both cited in POAS, 4: 238, 242–3.

11 *"Still the Superiors move . . . raising Micro-Cosmal Wars":*
John Gadsbury, *Ephemera: or a Diary Astronomical, Astrological, Meteorological. For the Year of our Lord, 1688.* The last line of the March prognosis may refer to the negative response James had received from the gentry in 1687, when he asked their assistance in electing a parliament that would repeal the Penal Laws.

11 *James II had lately fled:*
He was careful to drop the Great Seal in the Thames as he went. See HMC: *Stuart Papers* (1902), 1: 77, and Turner (*James II*), p. 444.

12 Pope records the day and time of his birth in his Elzevir Vergil: "Natus Maji 21, 1688, Hora Post Merid. 6 3/4." (E–C, 1: p. ix. The location of the book itself is no longer known.) See also Spence, no. 1.

12 *"Pope's birthplace":*
Spence (no. 2), from information communicated by Pope himself and his close friend Nathaniel Hooke in 1738, says that the poet was born "in the city of London in Lombard Street (at the house which is now one Mr. Morgan's, an apothecary"). The name Morgan is troublesome since no apothecary by that name is known in the area at this time, as Dilke pointed out emphatically in reviewing Carruthers's biography of Pope (1: 214 ff). An apothecary named Sylvanus Bevan did, however, carry on a business at No. 2 Plough

Court and was still doing so in 1738 when Pope and/or Hooke spoke. Dilke theorized—I think rightly—that Spence's Morgan is Pope's, Hooke's, or Spence's mnemonic error for Bevan. There is nothing surprising in Pope's not specifically naming Plough Court. Residences in courts were normally described by the name of the street they abutted, and it is perfectly possible too that by 1738 Pope had forgotten the Court's name. See E. C. Cripps, *Plough Court: The Story of a Notable Pharmacy, 1715–1927* (London: Allen and Hanbury, 1927), pp. 4ff.

13 *Before the onset of adult cares:*
Elements of this mood are already present in Gray's *Ode on a Distant Prospect of Eton College* (1747).

13 *"A person without a voice":*
Collected Writings, ed., David Masson, 14 vols. (Edinburgh, 1889), 1:9. On this and other matters mentioned in this paragraph, see a fascinating essay by Patricia Meyer Spacks, "Notes on Autobiography and the Life Cycle," *Boston University Journal*, 25 (1977): 7–17. Instructive also are J. H. Hagstrum's "'Such, Such Were the Joys': The Boyhood of the Man of Feeling," Clark Library Papers (University of California Press, 1972), and Philippe Ariès's classic study, *L'Enfant et la vie familiale sous l'ancien régime* (Paris: Plon, 1960).

13 *Launched on his career as a poet:*
"Transcript of what Mr. Pope, dictated to Mr. Jonathan Richardson Senr. at Twickenham 5th August 1739." Bodley MS. Eng. lett. d. 59, f. 80–1. (Printed in "New Anecdotes," pp. 346–48—but there wrongly dated 1730). The early eighteenth-century attitude toward childhood is expressed typically by Steele in *The Spectator*, no. 263 (1 January 1712): ". . . Growth towards Manhood [is] so desirable to all."

14 *Even to be hung up on a hook:*
Swaddling obviously expresses in extreme form the theory of education that obtained in most Western nations till well into the eighteenth century. The child is to be shaped and molded; his freedom must be restricted in order that his limbs may grow straight; his personality, far from trailing clouds of glory or unfolding from within like a flower, needs all the props and disciplines society can supply, including, at a later age, the birch at school. Whatever we may think of these procedures now, the men and women who were formed by them, or at least survived them, seem not appreciably inferior to those who are formed by, or survive, our own.

14 *Psychological results remain unknown:*
Lawrence Stone, *The Family, Sex and Marriage in England in 1500–1800* (New York: Harper and Row, 1977), pp. 161–2. Swaddling is passionately ruled out by Cornelius Scriblerus for his son Martinus (*Memoirs of the Extraordinary Life, Works, and Discoveries of Martinus Scriblerus*, ed., Charles Kerby-Miller, New Haven: Yale University Press, 1950, pp. 100–101). Since he is continually an object of satire, this may mean that Dr. Arbuthnot and/or Pope viewed swaddling favorably. Locke had doubts about it (*Some Thoughts Concerning Education* (1693) in *Educational Writings*, ed., J. L. Axtell, Cambridge University Press, 1968, p. 123), and Rousseau later opposed it strongly (*Emile*, Book I, ed. and tr., Allan Bloom, New York: Basic Books, 1979, pp. 42–44). The first physician to attack the practice in print seems to have been Dr. William Cadogan in his *Essay upon Nursing and the Management of Children* (1748).

14 *"Scarce able to hold himself erect":*
Johnson, pp. 83, 197. Johnson draws here on "Particulars respecting the Person of Mr. Pope," *Gentleman's Magazine*, 45 (1775): 435.

14 *Foster nurses:*
On wet nursing, see Trumbach (*Rise of the Egalitarian Family*), pp. 198ff; also, Stone (*Family, Sex, and Marriage*), pp. 99–101, 426ff. The nursing period varied greatly, though the norm was about a year. There was much pressure on the foster nurse from the child's parents to forgo sexual activity during this period, and she was often domiciled in the household to ensure compliance.

15 *"Nutrix mea fidelissima":*
E-C., 1: ix. Pope also commemorated her on a stone that is now set in the outside wall at the chancel end of St. Mary's Twickenham, and reads: "TO THE MEMORY OF / MARY BEACH / WHO DIED NOV. 5 1725 AGED 78 / ALEX. POPE, WHOM SHE NURSED IN / HIS INFANCY AND CONSTANTLY AT- / TENDED FOR THIRTY-EIGHT

YEARS / IN / GRATITUDE TO A FAITHFUL OLD SERVANT, / ERECTED THIS STONE." The difference from the age recorded in the diary may be a correction but more probably shows a lapse of memory.

15 *"My aunt of most blessed memory"*:
Spence, no. 14. As Elizabeth Turner is not mentioned in the notation of 1692 (below, p. 829—*48: Pope's tutor*), it is possible she did not join the Popes till after the death of her sister Christiana Cooper (above, p. 19).

15 *Had freed him of the bellyache*:
The Diary and Will of Elias Ashmole, ed., R. T. Gunther (Oxford: no publisher, 1927), p. 45 (14 August 1651).

15 *"Issue-pease"*:
24 January 1681. *The Works of Sir Thomas Browne*, ed., Geoffrey Keynes, 6 vols., (London: Faber & Faber, 1931), 6: 207–8.

15 *Boyle's prescriptions*:
Works, 6 vols. (1772), 5: 363, 319, 320, 326. Times were, however, changing. In an anonymous satirical pamphlet of 1715, Pope's friend Dr. Garth is shown paying a professional visit to the sickbed of Gilbert Burnet, bishop of Salisbury, and saying of this collection: "Sir, I am sorry to see you so ill; but *Egad* I think you deserve it, if this Piece of *Quackery* has been your *Regimen*: An idle, trifling Collection of old Womens, Corn-Cutters, and Farriers *Recipes*: Is this a Directory for a Man of your Parts and Sense?" (*Notes and Memorandums of the Six Days Preceding the Death of a late Right Reverend Prelate*, p. 16). Even so, the collection was widely used by the unsophisticated.

16 *Escaped acquaintance with its cures*:
In describing this book in "A Finding List of Books Surviving from Pope's Library" (*English Literature in the Age of Disguise*, ed., M. E. Novak (University of California Press, 1977), p. 240, I attributed the signature to Pope. Though it is rarely possible to be entirely sure about signatures, I now believe, after comparing it with Pope's father's signature, that it belongs to him and not to his son. See "Pope's Books," no. 27.

16 *"Mr. Pope's life was in danger"*:
Spence, nos. 3–4.

17 *"A Step towards Manhood"*:
Axtell (*Educational Writings*), p. 172.

17 *"Prettier than in his coats"*:
Anne, Lady North, to her son Sir Francis North, 10 October 1679. Roger North, *The Lives of the Right Hon. Francis North, Baron Guilford; the Hon. Sir Dudley North; and the Hon. and Rev. Dr. John North*, ed., Augustus Jessopp (1890), 3: 215. See also Roger North, *Autobiography*, ed., Jessopp (1887), pp. 215–16.

17 *The high quality of the painting*:
The portrait is reproduced in color as frontispiece to Wimsatt, and described on pp. 3–6. On the fame of Cooper both as miniaturist and lutenist see Daphne Foskett, *Samuel Cooper, 1609–72* (London: Faber and Faber, 1974), pp. 47ff.

19 *"All wit and courtesy"*:
Foskett, p. 53.

19 *A charming miniature of Christiana*:
Foskett, Plate 58. The Cooper miniature of Christiana was purchased in 1722 by Pope's good friend Edward Harley, collector extraordinary. R. W. Goulding, "The Welbeck Abbey Miniatures," *Publications of the Walpole Society* (1916), 4: 91.

19 *A miniature of their mother*:
This was Thomasine Newton Turner (d. 1681), who gave her husband William (1597–1665) thirteen daughters and three sons. Two of the sons died supporting the king in the battles of the Civil Wars—"in Honour's Cause," to adopt Pope's words in his *Epistle to Dr. Arbuthnot* (388). The third son became a general in the armies of Spain. Three of the daughters died in infancy or early childhood, and the other ten divided down the middle into Catholics and Protestants, as we saw earlier. Edith Turner Pope, one of the youngest of the daughters, apparently derived her Christian name from her paternal grandmother Edith Gylming. See Hunter, *Descent*, Sherburn, *Early Career*, Edmond, "Limners and Picture-Makers," Rumbold, "Pope and the Turners," and Davies, *Pope*—above, p. 820—*3: Marriage*.

19 *"Books, Pictures and Medals":*
 For Christiana Cooper's will, see Foskett, pp. 97–9. She died on 24 August 1693. Dilke points out (1: 189ff.) that Mrs. Cooper's choice of Pope at so young an age to be residuary legatee of the Cooper family's books tends to bear out the many reports of his precocity.

19 *His cups "of precious agate":*
 G. C. Williamson in *The Miniature Collector* (London: Jenkins, 1921), p. 65. Though the story itself is not inherently implausible, the evidence that Dr. Williamson adduces for it—in the form of "a document" once preserved and "a tradition" *still* preserved in the Pope family—is obviously unacceptable. Pope had no heirs of body and the family name died with him in 1744, only Magdalen and her issue surviving. One suspects there may be some sort of confusion here with the family of Alexander Pope, the painter and miniaturist (1763–1835), whose third wife was the widow of Francis Wheatley, R. A. (as Christiana was of Samuel Cooper) and a painter herself.

19 *Erected at the poet's father's expense:*
 Foskett (*Samuel Cooper*), p. 58, records the opinion of Richard Goulding (*The Welbeck Abbey Miniatures* [Oxford, Clarendon, 1916], p. 92) that the letters C.A.P.D. at the end of Cooper's epitaph stand for *curavit Alexander Pope dedicari* ("Erected by Alexander Pope"). In the L.C.C. *Survey of London*, 19 (1938): 79, they are interpreted to mean *Caritas Amicorum Ponendum Decrevit* ("Affectionately erected by his friends"). A more persuasive solution than either of these has been suggested to me by the Council of the Catholic Record Society: *Cuius Animae Propitietur Deus* ("May God be gracious to his soul"), often found on the gravestones of Roman Catholics. Cooper's burial in St. Pancras Old Church, where at this period many prominent London papists found their long home (H. B. Wheatley, *London Past and Present* [3 vols., 1891], 3: 17–18), and the presence of C.A.P.D. in his inscription are very strong indications that he was a Roman Catholic like his wife. I am grateful to Rosemary Rendal, Secretary of the Catholic Record Society, for pursuing this matter for me.

19 *Of Edith, the three images now known:*
 Wimsatt, p. 150, n. 17; p. 151, n. 20, pp. 173–6. The drawing discussed here is not reproduced.

20 *"The Prater"; "a parent to the poor and me":*
 For the first phrase, see the duchess of Buckinghamshire to Pope [1725?] (*Correspondence*, 2: 303 and n.). As Sherburn remarks, Mrs. Pope may have had personal contact with Compton when he was M.P. for East Grinstead, not far from West Grinstead, where the Caryll family lived. The second phrase is from the *Essay on Man*, 4: 110.
 Whatever other virtues Edith Pope possessed she clearly had the tact necessary to get along with the astonishing variety of Pope's friends and to hold her own on familiar terms with several of "the great." Though the remark was mainly intended to put down Pope, Lady Mary Wortley Montagu said of her in 1735. "[I] will add one praise to his mother's Character that (tho' I only knew her very old) she allways appear'd to me to have much better sense than himselfe." (*Correspondence*, 3: 449.)

20 *The beauty of the face in ripe age:*
 Ecclesiasticus, 26: 17.

20 *This winter-flower:*
 10 June 1733 (*Correspondence*, 3: 374).

20 *"Her mother also died in 1681":*
 On the Yorkshire Turners, see Hunter (*Descent*), and Davies (*Pope*). Hunter says, p. 44 (but without giving his evidence), that the sister who lived with Edith and taught the poet to read was deformed. If this is correct, Christiana and Edith, and later Edith and her husband, may have felt a special responsibility for her.

20 *Three households of Turner kin:*
 The available London households were those of Thomasine Turner, one of the unmarried sisters about whom very little is known; Alice Turner Mawhood's son Samuel (1655–1736), "woollen-draper of Snowhill, near Smithfield" (E. E. Reynolds, "The Mawhoods of Smithfield and Finchley," *Recusant History*, 1 [1955]: 59–60); and Christiana Turner Cooper. Since Christiana was left a widow in 1672 in very good circumstances, with a royal pension continued to her (spasmodically) after her husband's death, one may guess that Edith and Elizabeth were domiciled with her, as, possibly, the very personal nature of Christiana's

legacies to them also suggests. The legacy to "Mistress Edith Turner" also came from a member of Christiana's circle and hence strengthens the likelihood.

21 *The poet's father:*
On the Pope side, see F. J. Pope, "The Paternal Ancestors of Alexander Pope," *Notes and Queries*, 11th series, 7 (1913), 281–3; Hunter (*Descent*), pp. 13–25; and Sherburn (*Early Career*), pp. 27ff.

21 *"William was in chancery":*
Sherburn (*Early Career*), pp. 29–30; F. J. Pope ("Paternal Ancestors"), p. 283. details are given in Chancery Proceedings, Reynardson 86/84 (the complaint being dated 27 May 1684 and the reply 6 June 1686), but it is impossible to determine from these documents who was in the right.

21 *"Some sort of rift":*
"A Letter to a Noble Lord," E-C., 8: 253. This comment is also noticed in *Early Career*, p. 30. For Pope's quarrel with Hervey, see above, Chapter 22.

21 *The certain prospects of war:*
One of William's main concerns in accepting the invitation to England was to throw the weight of English arms and money into the European coalition against Louis XIV of France.

24 *He was worth some £10,000:*
This is Spence's figure (no. 12) from Martha Blount, who apparently had it from Pope. It is also Sherburn's estimate (*Early Career*, p. 34). From the few clues we have, Warburton's guess of £15,000 to £20,000 seems excessive, as Sherburn also notes.

24 *"Twenty-nine years in privacy":*
Weekly Journal, quoted by Carruthers, p. 160n. I have not been able to confirm Carruthers's information. The sole notice of Pope's father's death known to me is in the *Weekly-Journal, or Saturday's Post*, 26 October 1717, and says nothing of his years of "privacy," but does call him, at this early date, "Father to Mr. Pope the famous Poet."

24 *Likeness of Pope's father:*
See Wimsatt, p. 151, n. 21.

24 *"You'll do nothing but get enemies":*
Spence, no. 82.

25 *"These are not good rhymes":*
No. 11. Fortunately for Pope's future, his father did not agree with Locke, who held it "the strangest thing in the World that a Father should desire or suffer [a son's poetic gift] to be cherished or improved." Axtell (*Educational Writings*), p. 284. Though it is no doubt frivolous, one cannot help wondering whether Pope's characteristic later association of poetic rewards with custards and puddings—"Weighs . . . solid pudding against empty praise," "Yet eat in dreams the custard of the day," "cloy'd with custard and with praise" (*Dunciad*, 1; 52, 90, 247); "Fed with soft Dedication all day long" (*Epistle to Dr. Arbuthnot*, 233)—had its origins in an extra or more tempting slice of egg-pie (for such custard then was) rendered to a small boy for "good rhymes."

26 *The "Simplicity of a Prophet":*
6 December 1707 (*Correspondence*, 1: 35).

26 *Lyly's* Euphues:
Works, ed., R. W. Bond (Oxford: Clarendon, 1902), 1: 195.

26 *"The best of men":*
Spence, no. 12.

Chapter 2, Lessons

29 *A paradise of dainty devices:*
Cripps. I draw here on Appendix II (pp. 214ff), which reproduces the "schedule" of the house as recorded in the Bevan lease.

31 *"The Cave of Pope":*
See *The Garden and the City*, ch. 2.

31 *"All that had been written on both sides":*
Pope to Atterbury, 20 November 1717 (*Correspondence*, 1: 453).

31 *A street sign featuring a plough:*
  Bryant Lillywhite, *London Signs. A Reference Book of London Signs from Earliest Times to about the Mid-Nineteenth Century* (London: Allen and Unwin, 1972), pp. 412ff.

32 *The grasshopper still to be seen:*
  See J. B. Martin, *"The Grasshopper" in Lombard Street* (London, 1892).

32 *History has so far betrayed legend:*
  The ballad is printed in Percy's *Reliques of Ancient English Poetry*, 3 vols. (1765), vol. 2, poem no. 35. Sir Thomas More, who knew her, testifies to Mistress Shore's attractions. *Life of Richard III*, ed., R. S. Sylvester, in *Complete Works*, 2 [1963]: 54–7. That her husband was a mercer seems to have been first pointed out by C. L. Scofield, *Life and Reign of Edward IV*, 2 vols. (London: Longmans, 1923) 2: 163. That she was born Elizabeth Lambert is shown by Nicholas Barker, "The Real Jane Shore," *Etoniana*, no. 125 (4 June 1972), pp. 383–97; no. 126 (2 December 1972), pp. 399–407.

32 *Samuel Pepys . . . ill-starred summer of 1665:*
  Diary, 10–11 June; 6, 9–10 August 1665.

32 *Area swarmed with shops and coffee-houses:*
  Bryant Lillywhite, *London Coffee Houses. A Reference Book of the Coffee Houses of the Seventeenth, Eighteenth, and Nineteenth Centuries* (London: Allen and Unwin, 1963), pp. 330ff. Other merchants' coffee houses of note were Garroway's at no. 4 and Jonathan's at no. 20 in Exchange Alley, which sliced through at the east end of Lombard Street to Cornhill and the Exchange.

32 *A head crowned with the papal tiara:*
  Lillywhite (*London Signs*), p. 416.

32 *St. Paul's still building:*
  The final stone was placed in 1710.

33 *From folio to 13mo:*
  Diary, 9 September 1666.

34 *One of the City's "High Streets":*
  T. F. Reddaway, *The Rebuilding of London after the Great Fire* (London: Jonathan Cape, 1940), p. 294. For popular attitudes see *London in Flames, London in Glory: Poems on the Fire and Rebuilding of London, 1666–1709*, ed., R. A. Aubin (New Brunswick: Rutgers University Press, 1943).

34 *"Well builded and inhabited":*
  John Strype, *A Survey of the Cities of London and Westminster*, 2 vols. (1720), 1: 162–3.

34 *"The most healthy City in the World":*
  John Woodward, *An Account of Some Roman Urns, . . . With Brief Reflections upon the Ancient and Present State of London. In a Letter to Sir Christopher Wren* (1713), pp. 4–5. The letter is dated 23 June 1707.

34 *The bells pealed sometimes all day:*
  See, for example, the *Post-Boy*, 14–16 September 1697.

34 *William III's cavalcade:*
  Luttrell (*Brief Historical Relation*), 4: 306–7 (16 November 1698.)

35 *The Lord Mayor and retinue:*
  Thomas de Laune, *The Present State of London: or, Memorials Comprehending a Full and Succinct Account of the Ancient and Modern State Thereof* (1681), p. 255. On the "SS collar" worn by the Lord Mayor, see OED—"*Collar of SS*": "an ornamental chain consisting of a series of S's either joined together side by side or fastened in a row." The emblem was originally worn as a badge by adherents of the House of Lancaster, but was later absorbed into the official insignia of various magistracies.

36 *Journey on Lord Mayor's Day:*
  The splendors of each Lord Mayor's Day (October 29) are regularly described in contemporary newspapers.

37 *"Gigantic Forms in Cars triumphal ride":*
  See the manuscript variants preserved by Pope's friend Jonathan Richardson, Jr., recorded in *The Last and Greatest Art*, p. 131.

37 *"Sometimes infantile and sometimes maniac":*
  Emrys Jones, "Pope and Dulness," *Proceedings of the British Academy*, 54 (1968): 231–63.

37 *A new accommodation was being found:*
   See Appendix, p. 816.
37 *A Roman Catholic refuge:*
   A Roman Catholic convent had been established there, used by Charles II's Queen as a religious retreat.
39 *The elaborate penal system:*
   On the penal laws, see Miller, *Popery and Politics*, chs. 3–5; M. D. R. Leys, *Catholics in England, 1559–1829* (London: Longmans, Green, 1961), pp. 93ff; Philip Hughes, *The Catholic Question, 1688–1829* (London: Sheed and Ward, 1929); John Warner, *The History of English Persecution of Catholics*, ed. T. A. Birrell, 2 vols. (London: The Catholic Record Society, 1953: vols. 47–8); R. R. Madden, *The History of the Penal Laws Enacted Against Roman Catholics* (1847), ch. 16; and J. M. Aden, *Pope's Once and Future Kings: Satire and Politics in the Early Career* (University of Tennessee Press, 1978), chs. 1–2.
41 *"That dreadful Fire":*
   Edward Hatton, *A New View of London* 2 vols. (1708), 1: 56–7. Hubert was a misguided and partly demented creature who claimed to have inside knowledge of what he said were papist and French intentions, and was hanged for it.
41 *"The stoppage of passengers to read it":*
   Wheatley (*London Past and Present*), 3: 127.
41 *"The Pillar":*
   Hatton (*New View*), 1: 56–7.
41 *"To look big & lye":*
   Pope's *Epistle to Bathurst . . . with an edition of the manuscripts*, ed., E. R. Wasserman (Baltimore: the Johns Hopkins Press, 1960), p. 139.
44 *"A man that hath a soul":*
   "The Character of a Trimmer": *Complete Works*, ed. J. P. Kenyon (Penguin Books, 1969), p. 84. Halifax here assumes what was for his time an advanced liberal position, advocating a degree of mitigation in the treatment of the Catholic minority in order that it might gradually find its true "interest" in conversion from "old error" to "new truth." Though well intended, the wholly materialistic assumptions that the argument rests on and its coolly patronizing tone must have been infuriating to genuine believers of all persuasions.
44 *A rhyme on the last word spoken:*
   W. J. Bate, *John Keats* (Cambridge: Harvard University Press, 1963), p. 8. The anecdote is first recorded by Benjamin Haydon, the painter.
44 *"Lisp'd in numbers":*
   The phrase had the further virtue of asserting a playful connection between himself and Ovid, of whose comment on his own childhood in *Tristia* (4.10: 25–6) Pope's line is very nearly a translation. (Below, p. 913—*641: For the numbers came.*)
44 *Homer—"when I read him in my childhood":*
   Pope to William Broome, 16 June 1715 (1: 297).
44 *"In that great edition with pictures":*
   Spence, nos. 29–30.
45 *"A sort of rapture only in reflecting on it":*
   Spence, no. 30.
45 *"A wild Paradise":*
   TE, 7: 3.
45 *"Wonderfully diversify'd":*
   Ibid., p. 7.
45 *Certain great scenes in the poem:*
   Iliad, 6: 594ff (in Pope); pp. 156–7 in John Ogilby, *Homer his Iliads Translated* (1660); 24: 585ff (in Pope); in Ogilby, pp. 513–15.
46 *Images not easily forgotten:*
   Plates 11, 41, and 48 (see also 37 and 40).
46 *There, on a single page:*
   Page 3.
47 *Homer's "Rapture and Fire":*
   Pope to Ralph Bridges, 5 April [1708] (1: 44).

47 *"By copying printed books"*:
Spence, no. 14.

48 *Under the regular tutelage:*
Ibid. The priest may, however, have been living with the family for some time: see the following note.

48 *Pope's tutor:*
On Taverner, see Godfrey Anstruther, *The Seminary Priests: a dictionary of the secular clergy of England and Wales 1558–1850*, (3 vols., Ware: St. Edmund's College), 3: 1660–1715 (1977), 219ff. Anstruther overlooks, however, the information provided by R. W. Rogers ("Notes on Alexander Pope's Early Education," in *South Atlantic Quarterly*, 68 (1969), p. 238) from a poll-tax list of 1692 (CLRO: Assessment Box 32, MS. 5), which registers "Alexander Pope, merchant and wife" and two servants "Mary Baron" and "John Taverner" as living in the parish of St. Edmund the King in Lombard Street. Rogers suggests, I suspect rightly, that "Mary Baron" is Mary Beach. "John Taverner" could easily be a conflation of Taverner with the first name of one of his aliases, "John Davies." See also Appendix, pp. 815–16.
Though it has been repeatedly stated in accounts of Pope's early education that Taverner took over Twyford School in 1696, Anstruther points out that no contemporary evidence connects Taverner with either Silkstead or Twyford; nor have I been able to discover any.

48 *Pope had acquired the rudiments:*
Spence, nos. 17, 18. If the "year" with the priest began when Pope was "about eight," he would have been nine when sent to school. The statement in no. 15 that Pope learned his "accidence" at Twyford I take to mean that he continued at school what the priest had begun.

48 *Roman Catholic Schools:*
A manuscript in Lambeth Palace Library, entitled "Account of ye Popish Schole at Silkstead, near Winchester" and dated 1695/6 (A. C. F. Beales, *Education under Penalty: English Catholic Education from the Reformation to the Fall of James II, 1547–1689* [London: Athlone Press, 1963]), pp. 220ff, establishes beyond doubt that there were three active Roman Catholic schools in the Winchester neighborhood—Silkstead, Twyford, and a "Third School"—and names the adults associated with them. The author of the "Account" describes Twyford as "a Nursery to Silkstead"; but a letter dated 8 March 1696, published in Anstruther's account of Taverner, makes it clear that trouble has developed between the two schools, seemingly because Twyford intends "to vie with Silkstead" despite what appears to have been an agreement to the contrary "under hand and seal."

48 *"Only one year":*
Spence, no. 18.

48 *"Taken from thence on that account":*
Spence, nos. 15, 19–20.

48 *A letter not wholly to be trusted:*
This letter is reprinted in Spence, vol. 2, p. 609: "Appendix to No. 18."

49 *For the common gratification of all:*
What has been said of the young Sam Johnson at school may also be said of the young Pope: "Denied physical attractions [in Pope's case at this age not so much attractions as size] and skill at games, with no inherited wealth or social position, he knew he could be looked up to only because of the superiority of his mind and pen." J. L. Clifford, *Young Sam Johnson* (New York: McGraw-Hill, 1981), p. 51.

49 *A struggling school at Marylebone:*
The school was certainly operative by 1696. See "Copy of a Letter of Mr. Dean a Popish schoolmaster at St. Mary le bon at which Schole were found about 16 Schollars, & it was broken up by the Justices of the Peace by order of the Lord Lieutenant of [sic] ye duke of Bedford about Midsomer 1696," *Publications of the Catholic Record Society*, 56 (1964): 138. Deane's letter, dated 27 March 1696, inquires of the father of one of his students why the boy is so long detained at home and states (prematurely) that the school has "mett with no disturbance for these Times" and none is anticipated. Since Pope seems to have been with Deane at both Marylebone and Hyde Park Corner (Spence, no. 15), Deane must have reopened for a time at Marylebone after this forced closing.

49 *On the conversion of Deane:*
Anthony à Wood says in *Athenae Oxonienses*, ed., Philip Bliss (5 vols. in 4, 1813–20),

4: 450, that Deane converted "much about the same time that his master [at University College] Mr. Oba [diah] Walker did, in March, an. 1685, whose creature and convert he was." Wood also gives the name under which Deane stood in the pillory.

49 *"Printed by one who lodg'd in the same House":*
    Whitehall Evening Post, 18 March 1735. (Quoted in *Correspondence,* 2: 428n.)

49 *"Where Down-street was afterwards built":*
    The Life of Alexander Pope; with Remarks on his Works (London: Weaver Bickerton, 1744), pp. 12–13.

49 *Pope used to stroll to the playhouse:*
    Johnson, 3: 84. Johnson probably had this from Pope's friend Warburton, who notes in his edition of Pope's *Works* (1751), 4: 17, that Pope at Hyde Park Corner was "suffered to go to the Comedy with the greater boys."

49 *In prison for a "seditious" pamphlet:*
    Pope to John Caryll, 28 March [1727] (2: 428–9). Sherburn infers that the school friends in question were John Caryll, Jr., Charles Dormer, a "Mr. Webb," and possibly William Lewis, the bookseller (*Early Career,* p. 39n), who in 1711 published the *Essay on Criticism.* On Webb, see *Correspondence,* 3: 274.

49 *"A number of speeches from the Iliad":*
    Spence, no. 33.

49 *The gardener as Ajax:*
    For the gardener's playing Ajax, see Johnson, 3: 84, whose source appears again to be Warburton, *loc. cit.* The two passages in the *Iliad* where it would be most advantageous to have the part of Ajax played by a full-grown adult appear at 7: 206–313 and 17: 120 to the end of the book. (In Pope, 7: 249ff; 17: 143ff.)

50 *"Dressed after the pictures in Ogilby":*
    Pope, *Works,* ed., Warburton (1751), 4: 17n.

50 *"All his life a dupe":*
    2: 428–9. Deane's death notice in the *General Evening Post,* 5 November 1735, notes that he "lately lived wholly upon charitable contributions."

50 *The religious regimen at Standon:*
    Rogers ("Notes"), pp. 239–40.

50 *"And contempt of the world":*
    Henry Turberville, *An Abridgement of Christian Doctrine . . . Catechistically Explained, by way of Question and Answer* (1680; 1st ed., 1649), p. 23.

51 *Looking back on his schooldays:*
    Spence, nos. 14, 17–18.

51 *"Used to amuse himself with Drawing":*
    Bickerton (*Life*), p. 14. H. G. McCurdy, *The Personal World* (New York: Harcourt, Brace and World, 1961), p. 149, points out that children who have had much contact with adults tend to gravitate to social relationships of a maturer kind than those offered by their peers, which seem to them disappointingly childish.

52 *Rote-minded instruction:*
    For a typical specimen of seventeenth-century pedagogy, see *Notes on the Method and Education of Youth in Merchant Taylors' School in the year 1671,* quoted in *Merchant Taylors' School: Its Origin and Present Surroundings* (Oxford: Blackwell, 1929), pp. 50–51.

52 *Ben Jonson's picturesque phrase:*
    Conversations with William Drummond, in *Works,* eds., Herford and Simpson, 11 vols. (Oxford: Clarendon, 1925–52), 1: 138. As the famous Elizabethan schoolmaster, Richard Mulcaster, had put it in a revealing sentence, "the Rod may no more be spared in Schooles, than the Sword may in the Prince's hand." *Positions* (1581), p. 81.

52 *"I cou'd never leave it off since":*
    Complete Works, ed., Montague Summers, 5 vols. (London: The Fortune Press, 1927), 3: 139.

52 *"Without any manner of improvement":*
    The Life, Unpublished Letters, and Philosophical Regimen of Anthony, Earl of Shaftesbury, ed., Benjamin Rand (London: Swann Sonnenschein, 1900), p. 281. About a century earlier, Robert Cecil had made the same complaint about his son as he came down from Cambridge! Algernon Cecil, *A Life of Robert Cecil, First Earl of Salisbury* (London: Murray, 1915), p. 369. For Pope's marginalia in his copy of Montaigne see "Pope's Books," no. 121.

Chapter 3, Traditions

53 *Some 350 souls:*
    For the population of Binfield, see William Money, "A Religious Census of the County of Berkshire in 1676," in *Berks, Bucks, and Oxon Archaeological Journal*, 5 (Reading, 1899), pp. 22–6. This recapitulates Seth Ward's "An Account of the number and proportions of Popish Recusants, Obstinate Separatists, and Conformist inhabitants of Berkshire under the Jurisdiction immediate of the Bishop of Sarum" and gives for Binfield a population of 345, of whom 24 are Roman Catholics and 3 are Separatists. This is the largest number of Roman Catholics ascribed to any Berkshire parish except Ufton, seat of the Catholic Fermors, whose daughter Arabella was to become the heroine of the *Rape of the Lock*. E. P. Thompson, *Whigs and Hunters* (Penguin Books, 1975), p. 33, notes that this figure applies only to adults, and even for that group remains disputable. The figure for Binfield in the more reliable census of 1801 has grown to 1045.

53 *"Very small":*
    Lucius Fitzgerald, "Pope at Binfield," in *Home Counties Magazine*, 2 (1900): 54. I am much indebted to this article for information about the Popes' house and the holdings that went with it. Several Binfield deeds seem to have been available to Fitzgerald that I have not been able to examine. An engraving of the house as it looked in the late nineteenth century is included with Fitzgerald's article, and a mid-nineteenth-century engraving appears in Thomas Dugdale's *England and Wales Delineated* of 1854. On the latter, the mad Victorian painter Richard Dadd based a small oil variously called "Pope's House" and "The Gardener," now in a private collection. See Patricia Alldridge, "'The Late Richard Dadd,' 1817–1886," *Catalogue of an Exhibition at the Tate Gallery* (1974), no. 189.

53 *Better than "Places of greater Entertainment":*
    25 June 1711 (1: 124).

53 *Known in those days as "Whitehill House":*
    According to Fitzgerald, the house was successively called throughout the eighteenth and nineteenth centuries "Whitehill House," "Binfield Lodge," "Pope Lodge," "The Firs," and "Arthurstone." A differing nomenclature, found in *VCH: Berkshire*, eds., William Page and P. H. Ditchfield, 3 vols. (London: St. Catherine's Press, 1923): 120 and nn, appears to be less well documented than Fitzgerald's and takes no account of his research. Through much of the present century, the house has been known as "Pope's Manor" and under that title was advertised for sale in 1977 (with now 34 acres of land, staff cottages, swimming pool, and tennis court) at £500,000 (London *Times*, 17 June 1977). Pope would have been amused. For an illustrated description of the interior of the house as altered by the 1950s, and of the furnishings of the then current owner, see *The Antique Collector* (1951), pp. 81–9.

53 *Wokingham:*
    In Pope's day, usually spelled "Oakingham" or "Okingham."

54 *"And begot such sons upon the Muses":*
    13 September 1717 (1: 428). Alternatively, Pope may refer to the wood he calls "Priest-Wood"—"whose Trees I yet have some concern about." To Thomas Dancastle, 7 August 1716 (1: 352). This lay along the southeast edge of Binfield Parish and the north edge of Easthamstead Parish.

54 *"Here Pope sung":*
    See Fitzgerald ("Pope at Binfield"), p. 58. Also *Gentleman's Magazine*, vol. 86, pt. 1 (1816): 589–90, and *The Mirror of Literature, Amusement, and Instruction*, 16 June 1827. The original tree was blown down about 1825, but the inscription appears to have been renewed from time to time on others, once as late as 1893. *VCH: Berkshire*, 2: 120. The initiator of the inscription is variously said to have been Pope's friend George Lyttelton, later first baron Lyttelton, or Lady Gower of nearby Bill Hill, whose husband John, Lord Gower, Pope sometimes solicited for aid in good works—notably on one occasion for the benefit of young Samuel Johnson (*Correspondence*, 4: 194).

54 *A late commentator with a professional competence:*
    Norman Ault, pp. 88–9. Before becoming an editor and literary historian, Ault was a professional commercial artist. To his account of Pope's painterly training (which, however, was taken under Charles Jervas in 1713 and therefore most probably postdates such

passages as this one from *Windsor-Forest*) must be added the influence of a very considerable tradition of seventeenth-century landscape description in which many of the principles of poetical landscape representation (e.g., keeping a foreground and background, achieving variety without clutter, effective managing of contrasts) had already been worked out. Thus contrasts of light and shadow play a large part in the *Windsor-Forest* passage along with contrasts of high and low, near and far, tame and wild, fertile and waste, all being organized (as some of the adjacent unquoted lines make clear) toward a paradigm of *concordia discors*—the paradigm that Pope uses to exemplify both the "good" landscape and the "good" society in which "a Stuart reigns." With respect to his "blueish Hills," one may note Henry Peacham's instruction that "If you lay your Lantskip in colours, the farther you goe, the more you must lighten it with a Thinne and ayerie blew, to make it seem farre off." *Graphice: or the Most Auncient and Excellent Art of Drawing and Limning* (1612), p. 41. The archetypal passage here may be Leonardo's "You know that in an atmosphere of equal density the remotest objects seen through it, as mountains, in consequence of the great quantity of atmosphere between your eye and them, appear blue. . . . Hence you must make the nearest building above the wall of its real color, but make the more distant ones less defined and bluer . . .; . . . if one is to be five times as distant, make it five times bluer." *Notebooks of Leonardo da Vinci*, ed., Edward MacCurdy (New York: Reynal & Hitchcock, 1939), p. 880.

56 *Unmistakably scenes about Binfield:*
   E. P. Thompson, pp. 289–9, traces a connection between Pope's cheerful picture of life in the Forest and the newly mild administration of the forest laws under Anne. In quite a different vein, John Barrell places Pope's glorification of the Windsor area as a harmony of many functions and terrains ("Where Order in Variety we see, And where, tho' all things differ, all agree") within a collective effort, partly unconscious, partly (it seems) conspiratorial, to uphold aristocratic delusions about the condition of the rural poor. *The Dark Side of the Landscape* (Cambridge University Press, 1980), p. 50.

56 *"Did nothing but write and read":*
   Spence, no. 27.

56 *The size of his "Hartichokes":*
   Sir William Trumbull to Pope, 15 June 1706 (*Correspondence*, 1: 17).

57 *"Beautiful hills and vales intermixed":*
   Joseph Poté, *Les Délices de Windsore: Or, a Description of Windsor Castle and the County Adjacent* (1751), p. 84.

57 *"My Queen Anne":*
   The First Ode of the Fourth Book of Horace (1737), l. 4.

57 *No damned humbug about merit:*
   Lord Melbourne, who refused the honor for himself. His quip is variously quoted. See Charles Dickens, *Dictionary of the Thames* (1880), p. 261; *Oxford Dictionary of Quotations* (Oxford University Press, 1966), *sub.* Melbourne; and David Cecil, *Melbourne* (New York: Bobbs, Merrill, 1954), p. 177.

58 *"Heartless Henry . . . headless Charles":*
   "Windsor Poetics: Lines Composed on the Occasion of His Royal Highness the Prince Regent Being Seen Standing between the Coffins of Henry VIII and Charles I in the Royal Vault at Windsor." See also the improved later version entitled "On a Royal Visit to the Vaults. Or Caesar's Discovery of C. I. and H. 8 in Yᵉ Same Vault."

58 *The sin from which followed trials and disorders:*
   The nation's guilt for shedding Charles's "innocent blood" formed the chief theme of the Church of England's annual service commemorating his execution.

59 *"Non est imitabilis Anna":*
   The statue was placed in 1707.

59 *No other attention given Elizabeth I:*
   It would, of course, have been unbecoming in a Roman Catholic to mention her elder sister Mary. By Pope's time, moreover, English Catholics generally deplored Mary's persecutions and her marriage with Philip II of Spain. For a different view of the poet's attitude to Elizabeth I, see Vincent Carretta, "Anne and Elizabeth: The Poet as Historian," *Studies in English Literature*, 21 (1981): 425–38.

60 *Depredations by Henry:*
> G. M. Hughes, *A History of Windsor Forest, Sunninghill, and the Great Park* (1980), esp. pp. 45–6. Pope may also have remembered Dryden (*The Hind and the Panther*, 1: 350ff).

60 *"Prosecutor, judge, and jury":*
> J. A. Froude, *History of England from the Fall of Wolsey to the Defeat of the Armada* (1870), 3: 246. Froude's glorification of the attack on the religious houses has to be read to be believed.

60 *The abbey pillaged:*
> On the fate of Faringdon and the pillaging of the abbey, see J. C. Cox, "The Religious Houses of Berkshire", *VCH: Berkshire*, 2 (London: Constable, 1907), pp. 68–72. Defoe's statement (in his *Tour Thro' the whole Island of Great Britain*, ed., G. D. H. Cole [London: Peter Davies, 1927], 1: 293) that Reading Abbey is so far demolished "that scarce any Remains of it are found, or the place of it known" is quite wrong. Much stands today, and yet more stood in 1779 when Henry Englefield made a plan of the ruins. (*VCH: Berkshire*, 3: 339).

62 *Small company of Catholic faithful:*
> Lucius Fitzgerald states that when Bishop Richard Challoner visited Binfield in 1741, he found a congregation of fifty Catholics under the care of the Reverend Thomas Adams. "Alexander Pope's Catholic Neighbours," *The Month*, 145 (1925): 329. The figure evidently derives from E. H. Burton's *The Life and Times of Bishop Challoner*, 2 vols. (London: Longmans, Green, 1909), 1: 176, where it is said to be the figure set down in Challoner's notebook of his visitations.

62 *"Some private Devotion":*
> [John Gother], *Instructions for Confession, Communion, and Confirmation* (1744), p. 142; *Instructions and Devotions for Hearing Mass* (1740), pp. 7–8. These manuals went through many editions before and after 1700, but as they were contraband, their imprints are usually uninformative and their survival has been haphazard.

62 *Substantial demands on the individual member:*
> See especially John Bossy, *The English Catholic Community, 1570–1850* (London: Dartman, Longman, and Todd, 1975), ch. 6.

63 *"The fasting and praying was too much for him":*
> Frances Dillon, Lady Jerningham, to Charlotte Jerningham, Lady Bedingfield, "Good Friday night" [1799], in *The Jerningham Letters, 1780–1843*, ed., Egerton Castle (2 vols., 1896), 1: 150. Quoted in Bossy, *English Catholic Community*, pp. 115–16.

63 *"Drunk or Scandalous"—"Grave & Godly":*
> 10 April 1710 [Easter Monday] (1: 81).

63 *Complying with a friend's inclinations:*
> 19 October 1709 (*Ibid.*, 1: 74).

63 *A basic truth about himself:*
> "Collected in Himself", pp. 365ff. For a fuller treatment, see J. A. Winn, *A Window in the Bosom: The Letters of Alexander Pope* (New Haven: Archon Books, 1977), esp. ch. 3.

63 *Oysters and wit:*
> 25 January 1711 (1: 114–15).

64 *Escaping the family prayer-bell:*
> 1 March 1713. First published in *The Scriblerian*, 9 (1976), 1–7. See also "*Collected in Himself*," p. 463.

64 *"(For that's the way to heav'n)":*
> *Epistle to Miss Blount, on her leaving the Town, after the Coronation*, ll. 11–22 (*TE*, 6: 125).

Chapter 4, Preparations

66 *"The happiest part of my life":*
> Spence, no. 24. Cf. Boswell, *Life of Johnson*, 1: 428 (11 July 1763): "A man ought to read just as inclination leads him; for what he reads as a task will do him little good."

66 *All these experiences appear in Pope's poetry:*
> *Iliad*, 14: 397; *January and May*, l. 624; *Spring*, l. 42; *Odyssey*, 11: 729; *Epistle to Burlington*, l. 174.

66 *One of the first poems he ever wrote:*
  See "The River," ll. 13–20, in Howard Erskine-Hill, "Alexander Pope at Fifteen: A New Manuscript," *RES*, n.s. 17 (1966): 278.

67 *"Childhood's green enclosure bound":*
  Phineas Fletcher, *Piscatorie Eclogs* (1633), Eclog 1, sta. 5.

68 *"I chose myth":*
  Kathleen Raine, *Defending Ancient Springs* (Oxford University Press, 1967), p. 123.

69 *A translation of Ovid's story of Arethusa:*
  The grounds for attributing this translation to Pope, never publicly acknowledged but included in a miscellany that he edited cheek by jowl with an acknowledged translation, are given together with the text in Ault, pp. 38–48.

71 *"Those visions of my childhood":*
  See "Pope's 1717 Preface, with a Transcription of the Manuscript Text," in *Augustan Worlds*, ed., J. C. Hilson, M. M. B. Jones, and J. R. Watson (Leicester: Leicester University Press, 1978), p. 104 (nn. 10, 15).

71 *No further or higher ambitions:*
  Rhetorical modesty has of course been practiced by poets since earliest times. E. R. Curtius (*European Literature and the Latin Middle Ages* [New York: Pantheon, 1953] pp. 83–85) calls it a topos and traces it to Cicero. But surely it is already present in the epic poet's invocation of the Muse.

72 *"A mighty hunter, like Nimrod":*
  Journal to Stella, 31 July 1711.

73 *"Cruelty to put a living Creature to Death":*
  Guardian, no. 61 (21 May 1713).

73 *His spaniel at his heels:*
  19 October 1709 (1: 73). Later on, at Twickenham, Pope had a succession of dogs resembling Great Danes, all named Bounce. If he had kept a large dog while at Binfield, forest regulations would have required that it be "lawed"—i.e., have its three foreclaws cut off to lame it against chasing deer.

73 *"May your gun never fail":*
  18 February [1717] (1: 393). That Pope himself did not participate is perhaps the implication of his remark to Caryll (19 April 1714: 1: 219): "I fully purpose . . . to see Ladyholt in two or three months, and save the lives of some innocent birds by keeping you a few hours in the day from taking the field." In 1787, a correspondent of the *European Magazine* (12: 365) reported an inscription "written in a sporting book," as follows: "This Art of Gunnery / is presented to that keen sportsman, / And my very good friend, John Somers, Esq. / By Alexander Pope, / who himself detested *that art*,—and every art of killing." I am indebted for this reference to Professor Arthur Sherbo. The phrasing of the inscription, quite unlike any other Pope is known to have written and (in my opinion) quite unlike *him*, seems suspect. The only book of that title (if it is indeed the title) with which I am familiar is Nathaniel Nye's *The Art of Gunnery* (1684). John Somers, addressed so familiarly, can hardly be Baron Somers, who for a time was lord chancellor and died in 1716, but must be a lesser man of that name. As for the donor, neither of the possible alternatives—Alexander Pope the Scottish divine (d. 1782) or Alexander Pope the actor and miniaturist (1763–85)—seems particularly probable.

74 *His having carried pistols for a time:*
  Spence, no. 265.

74 *"The pitiful destruction it depicts":*
  Ault, p. 90.

76 *The true aim of learning:*
  Of the Advancement of Learning, Book 1, *Works*, ed. Spedding-Ellis-Heath (1857), 3: 294.

76 *Pope in the Spectator:*
  No. 406 (16 June 1712).

76 *"Without any design but that of pleasing myself":*
  Spence, no. 24.

76 *Taught to read only for words:*
  Ibid., no. 29.

77 *His favorites among the classical poets:*
     Ibid., no. 30. The very bad hand belonged to Thomas Stephens, who in 1648 published a translation of the first five books of the *Thebaid*.
77 *His favorites among the English poets:*
     Ibid., no. 43.
77 *To render passages and to imitate the styles:*
     Ibid., no. 45.
77 *Correct the lopsided and haphazard education:*
     Pope, *Works* (1751), 4: 211n. See also Spence, no. 50.
77 *"He stuck to it, went thither":*
     Spence, no. 26.
77 *Skin-deep Italian:*
     Scipio Maffei, *Merope* (Verona, 1745), p. 180. See also G. E. Dorris, *Paolo Rolli and the Italian Circle in London, 1715–1744* (The Hague: Mouton, 1967), p. 234.
78 *"To read our authors in the original":*
     Émile Audra, *L'Influence française dans l'oeuvre de Pope* (Paris: Champion, 1931), p. 138.
78 *An anthology of their work:*
     Selecta Poemata Italorum Qui Latine scripserunt. . . . Accurante A. Pope, 2 vols. (1740).
78 *Tolerably well read in French:*
     For French authors in Pope's library (in French), see "Pope's Books," nos. 24, 25, 26, 38, 40a, 62, 64, 88, 120.
78 *"May keep me always humble":*
     To John Caryll, 25 June 1711 (1: 120).
78 *"Mistook the excess of his genius for madness":*
     Spence, no. 28.
79 *"A madman or . . . a very great poet":*
     Ibid.
79 *"I had only dream'd of them":*
     To John Caryll, Jr., 5 December 1712 (1: 163).
80 *"I live among the great":*
     The First Satire of the Second Book of Horace Imitated, l. 133.
80 *"They are not so properly converted, as outwitted":*
     To Atterbury, 20 November 1717 (1: 453).
81 *"Queen Mary, and Elizabeth":*
     "Pope's Books", no. 164.
81 *"Done by fools in the presence of fools":*
     The Praise of Folly ed. and tr., H. H. Hudson (Princeton University Press, 1941), p. 33.
81 *Erasmus became a lifelong hero for Pope:*
     He owned Erasmus's *Works* eventually in the imposing 11-volume Leyden edition by Jean Le Clerc (1703–6), which he passed on in his will to Bolingbroke.
82 *"The unrevenging spirit of primitive Christianity":*
     To Caryll, 18 June 1711 (1: 118).
82 *"Not more Wise than Montaigne, but less honest":*
     Collected in Himself, p. 431.
83 *"Just like me!":*
     Ibid., p. 427. Montaigne, book 1, ch. 26; Cotton, 1: 301.
83 *"But make them to espouse it":*
     Cotton, 1: 304.
83 *"Who supply flatteries for a price":*
     TE, 5, frontispiece.
83 *"And to the Guelph a Gibelin":*
     Montaigne, book 3, ch. 12; Cotton, 3: 431.
84 *"Whereas it skreens, nourishes and incites them":*
     Montaigne, book 2, ch. 17; Cotton, 2: 184–5.
84 *The . . . thinking from which that poem grew:*
     It is very much worth noting that Montaigne's essays had been on the papal *Index* of books forbidden to good Roman Catholics since 1676, twelve years before Pope was born.

85 *"Is a catching and an incurable Disease":*
On Pope's books generally, see *Collected in Himself,* pp. 307–21, and for his *Don Quixote,* "Pope's Books," no. 35. The quoted passage is at 1: 52 in the edition Pope owned.

86 *"And that you have the Book":*
Sir William Trumbull to his nephew Ralph Bridges, 5 August 1707 ("New Anecdotes," p. 343).

86 *Renovation of his Twickenham waterfront:*
See *The Garden and the City,* pp. 37–40.

86 *Of certain contemporary ways of life:*
Epistle to Burlington, ll. 159–60.

86 *That neither of his predecessors had quite achieved:*
Ep. II, ii: 72–79; *Collected in Himself,* p. 157.

Chapter 5, First Heroes

88 *Held by the Dancastles since late in the sixteenth century:*
Fitzgerald ("Pope's Catholic Neighbours"), pp. 329–30.

88 *A neighbor as amanuensis:*
References to Dancastle's transcriptions of Pope's *Iliad* appear in *Correspondence,* 1: 351, 393, 443, 445, 519; 2: 8, 9, 19.

88 *The happy days when he had used to see them:*
Correspondence, 1: 352, 445, 524, 579.

88 *"Learned & Politique Gentleman":*
Pope to Englefield, 8 August 1707, in *R.E.S.,* n.s. 9 (1957): 393–4. Cf. Wycherley to Pope, 22 March 1706 (1: 15), in which Wycherley sends his services to "that factious [facetious] young Gentleman Mr. E and tell him, if I come into Berkshire, I will make him hollow as lowd, in the Tavern at Reading as he did at the Coffee House in London till he dances with his own Dayry Maids." In a letter of 22 November 1707 (1: 32), he is "that Wagg, Mr. *Englefyld.*"

89 *Who heartily admired Pope:*
Spence, no. 101.

89 *"Vir facetissimus":*
Pope, *Works* (E–C, 1: ix).

89 *He had once seen Dryden:*
Spence, no. 57. See also Pope to Wycherley, 26 December 1704 (1: 2): "I was not so happy as to know him: *Virgilium tantum vidi";* and Spence, vol. 2: p. 611. In a later letter to Wycherley (29 November 1707: 1: 34) Pope cites a simile that Dryden used "in conversation." This is probably from report, though it could conceivably mean that when Pope saw Dryden (at Will's, the unverifiable story goes), he also heard him holding forth.

89 *Reputed the greatest actor of his time:*
Pepys called Betterton the best actor in the world (*Diary,* 4 November 1661). Barton Booth, who often played with him, said "Divinity hung round that man!" Thomas Davies, *Dramatic Miscellanies,* 3 vols. (1783–4), 3: 32. Pope describes him in his Memorial List as the Roscius of his time who made his exit to the applause of all good men.

92 *"An artful* Climax":
Anthony Aston, *A Brief Supplement to Colley Cibber, Esq.; His Lives of the Late Famous Actors and Actresses* [1747], reprinted in Colley Cibber's *Apology,* ed., R. W. Lowe, 2 vols. (1889), 2: 300.

92 *"They in some Measure partook of the Astonishment":*
The Laureat: or The Right Side of Colley Cibber (1740), p. 31. The account is attributed to "a Gentleman who has frequently seen Mr. *Betterton* perform this part."

92 *"Both without Competitors":*
Apology, pp. 59–60.

92 *Pope's man of men:*
See his identification of Dryden with Vergil in the letter to Wycherley (above, n. 89);

his entry in the Memorial List, where Dryden is "semper venerandus, poetarum princeps"; and Spence, nos. 55–7. It is only fair to add that almost all of Pope's early acquaintances had been Dryden's friends and probably fanned the young aspirer's admiration.

92 *Who had given him his coronation suit:*
    John Downes, *Roscius Anglicanus* (1708), p. 21. When playing Owen Glendower in Orrery's *Henry V*, Betterton wore the Coronation Suit again. (*Ibid.*, p. 28.)

92 *Pope received much of the lore:*
    Betterton also seems a plausible source for some of the lore in Pope's *Shakespeare* (1725), e.g., the assertion that *The Two Noble Kinsmen* is wholly by Shakespeare.

92 *Pope's interest in 17th-century drama:*
    For the individual plays in Pope's library, see Spence, no. 428; for the collections, "Pope's Books," nos. 16, 60, 99. Pope seems to have been familiar also with some of the tragedies of Thomas Goffe (or Gough), Kyd, Marston, Massinger, and Webster: Spence, no. 427.

93 *"In the hand of Betterton":*
    Johnson, *Lives*, 3: 108. See also Caryll to Pope, 23 May 1712 (1: 142) and Walter Harte's testimony in Pope's *Works*, ed. Warton (1797), 2: 166. Betterton's adaptations appeared in Lintot's *Miscellaneous Poems and Translations* (1712), partly edited by Pope, under the title: *Chaucer's Characters, or the Introduction to the Canterbury Tales* (pp. 245ff) and *The Miller of Trompington, Or, the Reve's Tale from Chaucer* (pp. 301ff). Lintot paid £5.7.6 for them on 28 April 1710, presumably to Mrs. Betterton.

93 *"One of Mr. Betterton":*
    Pope to Caryll, 31 August 1713 (1: 189).

93 *"The legend of Saint Genevieve":*
    Spence, nos. 34, 35. It is possible (from the analogy of the *Legenda Aurea*) that Pope would refer to the "legend" of St. Genevieve when he meant the life of the patron saint of Paris (ca. 422–512), who is credited as a young girl with having saved the city from sack by Attila. More probably, he was taken at this tender age with the story of St. Genevieve of Brabant (legend from start to finish) which offers a touching recognition scene toward the close when her husband Siegfried follows a deer to the forest shelter where his wife (supposedly executed at his order many years before on a false charge of infidelity) has been living on roots and berries and bringing up their son with the help of a friendly deer. The couple are reunited but Genevieve dies soon after.

93 *"Think on the dignity of Tragedy":*
    1: 18, 67, 136.

93 *"I had taken such strong resolutions":*
    Spence, no. 34. Betterton apparently suggested that he should rewrite his epic on Alcander (above, p. 94n) as a tragedy.

94 *A firm sense of his own limits:*
    See the comment of Pope's young friend Walter Harte (*The Amaranth, or Religious Poems*, 1767, p. 140): "Amongst Mr. Pope's great intellectual abilities, good sense was his most distinguishing character: for he knew precisely, and as it were by a sort of intuition, what he had power to do, and what he could not do." Joseph Warton in his *Essay on the Genius and Writings of Pope*, 2 vols. (1782), 1: 307n, claims that Pope attempted a tragedy on Timoleon, the Greek liberator and enemy of tyrants; but "not satisfying himself laid it aside." There is no other authority for this story. If it is true, it indicates once more Pope's sense of his limits. Together with his interest in Gracchus, if that too was real, it suggests the political direction in which his conception of the tragic hero ran.

94 *A blank verse epic on Brutus:*
    Above, pp. 771–4.

94 *Wycherley's mistress as well:*
    Pope's version of this story, which may have come from Wycherley himself, is given in Spence, no. 79: "Wycherley was a very handsome man. His acquaintance with the famous Duchess of Cleveland [the title Charles II had conferred on her] commenced oddly enough. One day as he passed that Duchess's coach in the Ring [a circular road for coach-driving in Hyde Park at that time], she leaned out of the window and cried out loud enough to be heard distinctly by him, 'Sir, you're a rascal! You're a villain!' Wycherley

from that instant entertained hopes. He did not fail waiting on her the next morning, and with a very melancholy tone begged to know how it was possible for him to have so much disobliged her Grace. They were very good friends from that time."

94 *"He charges in iron":*
George Granville, first baron Lansdowne, "A character of Mr. Wycherley and his Writings," in [Charles Gildon], *Memoirs of the Life of William Wycherley* (1718), pp. 25–6.

96 *By the time he and Pope came to be acquainted:*
Pope's first letter to Wycherley is dated 26 December 1704. Known only through Pope's own editions, the letter has been questioned and may indeed have been misdated, since it is not clear that Pope already knew Congreve and Trumbull, as the letter implies. What seems certain, at any rate, is that the acquaintance began early. In an undated letter in which Pope is spoken of as "not above Seventeen or Eighteen", George Granville, first baron Lansdowne, proposes to introduce both him and Wycherley to an unidentified "Harry" (Lansdowne, *Works*, 1732, 1: 436–7), and before he was eighteen the publisher Jacob Tonson had seen some of the *Pastorals* in the hands of Congreve and Walsh (*Correspondence*, 1: 17). The Harry of Granville's letter is probably Henry Sheers, military engineer and translator of Polybius, who was one of those through whose hands the manuscript of the *Pastorals* passed. Pope had turned seventeen on 21 May 1705.

96 *A collection of verse:*
Miscellany Poems: Satyrs, Epistles, Love-Verses, Songs, Sonnets, Etc. (1704).

97 *Masculine friendships:*
From Wycherley, who had studied under him at Westminster School, Pope may also have heard those stories of Busby's floggings that make him so vivid an apparition in the *Dunciad* (4: 139ff). Above, p. 788.

97 *Addressing an admiring letter to him:*
The date of the letter, following at once on Christmas day, suggests that the meeting occurred during a holiday visit by Wycherley to the household of a country friend: Englefield, Betterton, Caryll, possibly Trumbull. There is also a letter of 17 May 1704 from Wycherley to Caryll (Add. MS. 28,618, f. 85) which makes it clear that the playwright has been invited to the latter's country seat that spring. If Wycherley took up the invitation on his return from Bath, this could have been the occasion of his meeting Pope, or of a second encounter.

97 *"The little Nightingale":*
John Boyle, fifth earl of Orrery, *Remarks on the Life and Writings of Dr. Jonathan Swift* (1752), p. 225. After her quarrel with Pope, Lady Mary Wortley Montagu devised her own version of this: "Some called Pope little nightingale—all sound and no sense." Johnson, 3: 83n.

97 *"Excessively gay and lively":*
Spence, no. 10. Both Wycherley and Sir William Trumbull speak admiringly of Pope's conversation (15 June 1706, 11 November 1707—1: 17, 29–30). Also above, p. 804.

98 *Superior to anything Vergil had done:*
Walsh to Wycherley, 20 April 1705 (1: 7).

98 *"As I was us'd to do Mr. W in the Towne":*
Pope to Cromwell, 19 October 1709 (1: 73).

99 *"Compliment . . . the Smoak of Friendship':*
25 March 1705 (1: 5).

99 *"Every Man Partakes of the Praise he gives":*
7 April 1705 (1: 6). DeQuincey compares the correspondents to "village cocks from neighboring farms, endeavouring to overcrow each other." *Collected Writings* (Edinburgh, 1889), 4: 255–56.

99 *Five years among the précieuses:*
At Angoulême, where Julie d'Angennes (wife of the Marquis de Montausier and daughter of Madame de Rambouillet, leader of the Précieuses) kept a provincial salon, Wycherley was educated for several years during his teens (?1655–1660) and was, he told John Dennis, "often admitted to the conversation of that Lady, who used to call him the Little Huguenot." (Dennis, 2: 409). Pope's testimony (Spence, no. 76) is that he became acquainted there with Mme de Rambouillet herself, but a sheet of Spence's biographical notes on Wycherley taken down from Pope's conversation (Osborn Collection, Spence

Papers, Box 7) shows that the poet was confusing Julie with her mother. Pope shows the same confusion in the lines quoted at p. 248. One of the best-known frequenters of Mme de Montausier's salon was Voiture, past master of the style of compliment, irony, and delicate raillery that Wycherley here applies to Pope.

99 *He visited the old man almost twice a day:*
     Spence, no. 82.

100 *Two years of time-consuming labor:*
     Ibid., no. 83. The degree of Wycherley's eventual impatience with a process of revision that he had himself solicited and continued to encourage may be seen in his reply of 22 November 1707 (1: 34). Pope has indicated in his own letter some of the ways in which he is undertaking to bring "method" to Wycherley's poem on Dulness. Wycherley's reply, for a "Plain Dealer", is uncomfortably feline: "And now for the pains you have taken to recommend my *Dulness*, by making it more methodical, I give you a thousand thanks; since true and natural *Dulness* is shown more by its pretence to form and method, as the sprightliness of Wit by its despising both." Pope's response seems exemplary. He pulls no punches, but raises the level from innuendo to frank discourse and says nothing mean:

> I must take some Notice of what you say, of "My pains to make your Dulness methodical;" and of your hint, that "The sprightliness of Wit despises method." This is true enough, if by *Wit* you mean no more than *Fancy* or *Conceit*; but in the better Notion of *Wit*, consider'd as propriety, surely Method is not only necessary for Perspicuity and Harmony of parts, but gives beauty even to the minute and particular thoughts, which receive an additional advantage from those which precede or follow in their due place. . . . I will not disguise any of my Sentiments from you: To *methodize* in your Case, is full as necessary as to *strike out*; otherwise you had better destroy the whole Frame, and reduce them into *single Thoughts* in Prose, like *Rochfoucault*, as I have more than once hinted to you."

Part of the difficulty between the two poets plainly arises from their different understanding of the nature of "Wit" (above, pp. 169–70), the rest from Wycherley's impatience with the toil of versification. In his copy of Montaigne, beside the sentence—"If there be Invention, and that the Wit and Judgement have well perform'd their offices, I will say here is a good poet but an ill Rhymer"—Pope notes marginally. "Mr. W____y." ("Pope's Books," no. 121).

100 *"Expressed in a different turn":*
     Spence, no. 87. See also Wycherley to Pope, 11 and 27 April 1710; Pope to Wycherley, 15 April and 2 May 1710 (1: 82–7). To Cromwell Pope remarks ruefully on 28 October (1: 100): "I value Sincerity the more, as I find by sad Experience the practise of it is more dangerous; Writers rarely pardoning the Executioners of their Verses, ev'n tho themselves pronounce sentence upon them."

100 *"I went to see him on his death-bed":*
     Spence., nos. 77n, 95, 96, 97.

100 *"Decessit Gul. Wycherley":*
     Works (E-C 1: ix). Wycherley actually died 31 December 1715. Pope's error is doubtless owing to the fact that he made this entry only at some date after entering the death of Parnell, which came in late 1718—in other words, after an interval of nearly three years. For conflicting accounts of the circumstances surrounding the playwright's death, see Pope to Edward Blount, 21 January 1716 (1: 328–9); Spence, nos. 92–5; and H. P. Vincent, "The Death of William Wycherley," *Harvard Studies and Notes*, 15 (1933) 219–42. As there was no reason for Pope to manufacture the account he gave Blount, and as Wycherley had, as Pope says, expressed the intention to disappoint his nephew by marrying just before death so as to burden with a widow's jointure the estate the nephew would receive— Wycherley to Pope, 11 August 1709 (1: 70)—the depositions in the chancery case brought by the nephew (first published by Professor Vincent) must be placed in perspective. It is clear from Spence, no. 92, that Pope eventually knew there had been a cheat.

102 *"The best Critick of our Nation":*
     In the *Postscript* to his translation of Vergil (1693). *Poems*, p. 1462.

102 *A free dispensary for the poor:*
     On the backgrounds and progress of the quarrel between the apothecaries and the

College of Physicians, see Sir George Clark, *A History of the Royal College of Physicians of London* (2 vols., Oxford: Clarendon, 1966), 2: 427–79, esp. 465ff. The best modern edition of the poem is in POAS, 6 (ed. Frank H. Ellis): 58–128.

102 *Inscribed "Donum Autoris"*:

See "Pope's Books," no. 67. This is a copy of the fifth edition. Since in 1706 a sixth edition appeared (of which Pope also had a copy but not inscribed—*ibid.*, no. 68), we may plausibly guess that Garth gave him his copy of the fifth between 1703 and 1705. Pope told Spence that he was "early acquainted" with Garth (no. 74).

102 *Like a eunuch's founding a seraglio*:

Pope to Martha Blount, [*post* 24 November 1714] (1: 268); Swift, *Journal to Stella*, 10 April 1711. Radcliffe was a skilled physician but often rude, high-handed, and capricious. The detail of Garth's red cloak is from Lady Mary Wortley Montagu's town eclogue: "Saturday," where Garth appears as "Machaon" (l. 78).

102 *"And Charitable Temper"*:

Abel Boyer, *Annals of King George* [I]. *Year the Fifth* (1720), p. 441. See also Albert Rosenberg, "Last Days of Sir Samuel Garth," in *Notes and Queries*, 204 (1959), 272–4.

103 *"Great Approbation and Applause"*:

Sir George Clark (*Royal College of Physicians*), 2: 472; Charles E. Ward, *The Life of John Dryden* (Chapel Hill: University of North Carolina Press, 1961), pp. 317–18; and esp. Edmund Malone, *Prose Works of John Dryden*, 4 vols. (1800), 1: 372–81. The quoted words are from Ned Ward's eyewitness account of the funeral in *The London Spy* (London: Casanova Society, 1924), p. 425.

103 *Glowing tribute*:

The tribute lay in the fact that Garth coupled *Windsor-Forest* with one of the most admired poems of the age, John Denham's *Cooper's Hill* (1650), as "those two excellent Poems."

103 *Good nature*:

"One of the best-natured men in the world" (Spence, no. 105); "the best natur'd of men" (Pope to Jervas, [1720?] (2: 25); "Well-natur'd *Garth*" (*Epistle to Dr. Arbuthnot*, 1735, l. 137).

103 *"As plain . . . as old Montagne"*:

See also, especially, Pope to Lady Mary Wortley Montagu, 18 August [1716] (1: 353), and *Collected in Himself*, p. 304.

104 *A habit of "performance"*:

It is possible that Pope's somewhat enigmatic comment to Spence (no. 565)—"I was acquainted with old men when I was young, which has brought some habits upon me that are troublesome"—bears on this.

104 *More studied in their own responses*:

Pope's younger friend John Boyle, fifth earl of Orrery, probably recalls something of this nature when he says of Pope (*Remarks on the Life and Writings of Dr. Swift*, 1752, pp. 224–5): "He has given his imagination full scope, and yet has preserved a perpetual guard upon his conduct. The constitution of his body and mind might early incline him to habits of caution and reserve. The treatment which he met afterwards from an innumerable tribe of adversaries confirmed these habits." See also *Collected in Himself*, pp. 372–75.

104 *"Homo candidus"*:

E–C, 1: ix.

104 *A considerable career*:

On Trumbull's career, see his own "Sir William Trumbull's Life *annaliter*," *Gentleman's Magazine*, vol. 60, pt. 1 (1790): 4–5. It is reprinted in Ruth Clark, *Sir William Trumbull in Paris, 1685–1686* (Cambridge: Cambridge University Press, 1938), pp. 2–3.

105 *Competing at translations*:

B. S. Donaghey, "Alexander Pope and Sir William Trumbull's Translations of Boethius," *Leeds Studies in English*, 1 (1967): 71–9.

105 *"At last almost every day"*:

Spence, no. 71.

105 *Easthamstead Walk*:

A detailed account of forest law is given in John Manwood's *A Treatise of the Laws of the Forest*, issued in a number of editions and revisions from 1598 to 1741.

105 *The family of Pope's sister*:

Above pp. 402ff.

105 *"A model patron":*
Wycherley to Pope, 13 November 1708 and 23 May 1709 (1: 54, 62). The French writer was Pierre Sylvestre. His friend, Pierre Bayle, whose critical and biographical *Dictionary* Pope was later fond of reading, seems to have had thoughts at one time of dedicating the book to Trumbull, to whom he sent a copy. Bayle to Trumbull, 17 April 1696, in Clark (*Trumbull in Paris*), pp. 177–80.

105 *Trumbull and Dryden's Aeneid:*
Poems ed., James Kinsley 4 vols. (Oxford: Clarendon, 1958), p. 1425.

107 *"Poor little Pope":*
Sherburn, "New Anecdotes," pp. 343–44.

107 *"Get out of all Tavern-company":*
6 March 1741 (1: 212).

107 *To replace the formal university training:*
George Sherburn, *Early Career*, p. 42.

107 *Books that Pope has recommended:*
Sherburn, "New Anecdotes," pp. 343–4.

107 *Collection of Milton's minor poems:*
Trumbull to Pope, 19 October 1705 (1: 10).

107 *Fidelity to the Greek:*
Sherburn, "New Anecdotes," p. 344.

107 *A self-proclaimed atheist:*
From the pamphlet cited earlier on his visit to the sickbed of Gilbert Burnet (above, p. 824 —15: *Boyle's prescriptions*), it is plain that Garth's free-thinking ways were well publicized. An anonymous poem of 1710 (*The Apparition*) gives him the epithet "Blaspheming."

108 *Different sorts of moral conduct:*
Pope twice refers to the disparity between Garth's supposed convictions and his behavior. In his high-spirited *Farewell to London* of 1715, he takes his leave of Garth among others—"the best good Christian he, Altho' he knows it not," ll. 15–16. Four years later on Garth's death, he comments: ". . . if ever there was a good Christian, without knowing himself to be so, it was Dr. *Garth*." (To Jervas [1720?] (2: 25).

108 *"Nothing is desperate in the condition of good men":*
Works, 3 vols., (Aberdeen, 1751), 2: 20. The relative unimportance of doctrine seems to be the clear implication of the *Essay on Criticism*, ll. 396–7, and of Pope's defense of these lines to Caryll (1: 118, 126). See also *Essay on Criticism*, 440–7, though the language is guarded. The later statement in the *Essay on Man* is quite uncompromising (3: 305–6).

108 *What religious persecution meant for its victims:*
See especially the letters sent to him while in France by his fellow countryman, James Bruce, then resident at Nantes, whose house, property, and wife had been seized by Louis's dragoons. Clark (*Trumbull in Paris*), pp. 33–5, 46, 55–6.

108 *"The last Infirmity of noble Minds":*
Possibly the earliest appearance of a tenacious misquotation of what Milton called "That last infirmity of Noble mind." One wonders whether Pope habitually misread the line or (in publishing his letters in 1735) misread what he had written to Trumbull.

109 *"The only solid blessings":*
12 March 1714 (1: 213). Much in this passage anticipates the theme of expanding benevolence in the *Essay on Man*, Epistle 4. One may reasonably suspect, from Pope's reference to "awakenings" of friendship, that this letter belongs some years earlier than 1714, the date assigned it in *Correspondence*—the more decidedly so in that his letter to Trumbull of 17 March shows that his last letter to him was of 26 February.

110 *If we may believe the hints:*
Included in Walsh's *Letters and Poems, Amorous and Gallant* (1692), especially letter 3 (p. 7) and letter 6 (p. 15). Some portions of the MSS. of these, with other poems not published, and two unpublished letters (all seemingly from his gay youth) are now in the British Library. Phyllis Freeman, "Two Fragments of Walsh Manuscripts," RES, n.s. 8 (1957): 390–401.

110 *"Left Cupid in the lurch":*
"Some Account of William Walsh, Esq.," *Works* (1736), p. 124.

110 *His statements about his work:*
    Works (1717), Preface; *Epistle to Dr. Arbuthnot*, 11. 128–9. On the sixteenth-century formation of this attitude, see the lively account by J. W. Saunders in *Essays in Criticism*, 9 (1959): 139–64.

110 *Congreve and Voltaire:*
    Letters concerning the English Nation (1733), p. 140.

111 *"The impertinent Frenchman was properly answer'd":*
    Letters of Charles and Mary Lamb, ed., E. W. Marrs, Jr. (Ithaca: Cornell University Press, 1976), 2: 274.

111 *"Impossible, you should be forgotten":*
    Aaron Hill to Pope, 28 January 1731 (3: 168).

111 *"My Morality . . . must make me Beloved, or Happy":*
    Ibid., 3: 172.

111 *"He encouraged me much":*
    Spence, no. 173.

112 *Technicalities like the hiatus . . .:*
    Several of these matters are discussed by Pope in a letter ostensibly addressed to Walsh, dated 22 October 1706. (Some have thought the letter suspect because of its resemblance to a letter sent to Cromwell dated 25 November 1710. This skepticism may be well founded. It is possible, however, to explain the resemblance by supposing that in each case the discussion was based on observations collected in a commonplace book or notebook—the sort of collection one can easily imagine Pope making as preparation for his *Essay on Criticism*).

112 *Or perhaps both:*
    Perhaps Walsh meant no more than Perrault meant when he allowed that contemporary poets might have less genius than the revered ancients but were more correct. *Parallèle des anciens et des modernes*, 3 vols., ed., H. R. Jauss (Munich: Eidos, 1964), 3: 153–5.

112 *"My opinion of the particulars":*
    20 April 1705 (*Correspondence*, 1: 7).

112 *Carried the corrections of Walsh:*
    Spence, no. 31.

112 *Some leaves surviving with the manuscript:*
    These are printed in *TE*, 1: 477–82. For photographs, see *The Last and Greatest Art*, pp. 62–9.

116 *A degree of familiarity with Italian writers:*
    24 June 1706 (1: 18).

116 *"A dreadful long Journey":*
    Sherburn, "New Anecdotes," p. 343. Pope may have had the use of Walsh's horses, or his coach, from Worcester to Abberley (1: 29).

116 *"Famous for Fertility and bad Roads":*
    See Arthur Whaley's diary of a journey to Worcester in 1735. British Library Add. Ms. 5842, f. 244.

116 *Ever lay eyes on him again:*
    Sherburn, "New Anecdotes," p. 343.

117 *Far along toward a final text of the Pastorals:*
    The third *Pastoral*, last to be written, Walsh did not see till he came to town for the opening of Parliament in November 1707. Walsh to Pope, 9 September 1706 (1: 21–2).

Chapter 6, First Publications

121 *"I have been most mercifully repriev'd":*
    To Cromwell, 1 November 1708 (1: 51–52). Tonson was first in correspondence with Pope about publishing a pastoral work of his on 20 April 1706 (1: 17). A letter from the poet to Sir William Trumbull's clerical nephew Ralph Bridges, 11 March 1708, indicates that publication was expected that spring (Sherburn, *Letters*, p. 395). Possibly it was put off because of excitement over the Pretender's abortive attempt to land in Scotland in March. It was evidently postponed again in the fall of 1708, perhaps this time because of public mourning for Queen Anne's consort George of Denmark, who died October 28.

121 *"All the best Judges like your Part of the Book":*
17 May 1709 (1: 59).
122 *"What Authors lose, their Booksellers have won":*
20 May 1709 (1: 60–1). Pope's couplet probably responds to Wycherley's reference to Tonson, 13 May 1708 (1: 50), as "Pimp, or Gentleman-Usher to the Muses".
122 *"Chief Merchant to the Muses":*
Edward ("Ned") Ward, *The Secret History of Clubs* (1709), p. 360.
122 *That Dryden had overseen:*
The six volume series (begun in 1684), of which *Poetical Miscellanies: The Sixth Part* is the last, was widely known as "Dryden's Miscellany," since he had contributed heavily to the four volumes published in his lifetime and was assumed to have had a lion's share in their arrangement.
122 *Tonson buys copyrights:*
On Tonson's publishing career, see K. M. Lynch, *Jacob Tonson, Kit-Cat Publisher* (Knoxville: University of Tennessee Press, 1971) especially chapters 4–6, and H. M. Geduld, *Prince of Publishers, A Study of the Work and Career of Jacob Tonson* (Indiana University Press, 1969). Cf. Egmont's comment a quarter of a century later (*Diary*, 3: 161—17 March 1735): "I was made acquainted this day with a subscription of ten guineas a man by divers noblemen and gentlemen in favour of ingenious authors to rescue them from the tyranny of printers and booksellers, who buy their works at a small rate, and while they almost starve them make fortunes by printing their labours. Thus Tonson the bookseller got very many thousand pounds by publishing Dryden's works, who hired himself to write for a starving pay."
123 *"Always a sharp Eye towards his own Interest":*
Ward (*History of clubs*), p. 361.
123 *Kit-Kat hints for his printing ventures:*
Explanations of the origin of the Kit-Kat Club vary. Ward's version seems to me to suit what we know of Tonson's personality and business sense. See also John Macky, *A Journey Through England* (1714), 1: 188, and John Oldmixon, *History of England*, 3 (1735): 479. For explicit evidence of Tonson's role as underground purveyor of Whig propaganda, see Frances Harris, "Jacob Tonson and the 'Advice to the Electors of Great Britain'" (*Factotum*, no. 16, February 1983, pp. 13–15).
123 *"To make new Knights of Wit":*
The Kit-Kats. A Poem (1708), p. 6. ("Chapters" are meetings of the entire body of a knightly order.)
123 *"I am the Touchstone of all Modern Wit":*
William Shippen, *Faction Display'd* (1704), ll. 374–85. In *POAS*, 6: 667. A story recorded by Malone, *Prose Works of John Dryden*, 4 vols. (1800), 1: 525, relates that Dryden, having sent to Tonson for an advance and been refused, despatched a messenger to him with the three lines and the instruction: "Tell the dog, that he who wrote these lines, can write more." A different account is given in a letter of Richard Powys to Matthew Prior in 1698. Dryden is here said to have composed the lines to accompany a sketch of Tonson by Godfrey Kneller. (See *HMC*; Bath MSS, 1908, 3: 238–9, where the lines are given with a slight difference and the second and third reversed.)
124 *"A Phaenomenon worth seeing":*
To Edward Harley, 11 February 1731 (3: 176). Tonson's version of the dictionary, enlarged with further articles on English authors, appeared in four huge folios in 1710.
124 *"Art of driving shrewd bargains":*
Lynch (*Jacob Tonson*), p. 68.
124 *All of five pence a line:*
Lintot paid £7 for the 2-canto *Rape* on 21 March 1712 and £15 for the 5-canto version on 20 February 1714. John Nichols, *Literary Anecdotes of the Eighteenth Century*, 9 vols. (1812–15), 8: 299–300.
124 *The prospects of the writing class:*
Hogarth was to perform a very similar feat for the artist. See R. A. Paulson, *Hogarth: His Life and Times* (Yale University Press, 1971), 1: 352.
125 *Given by a Binfield neighbor:*
The neighbor was Gabriel Young, owner of Whitehill House before Pope's father purchased it. See "Pope's Books," no. 36, and above, p. 403.

125 *"I read Chaucer still":*
    Spence, no. 411. Pope must have been sensitive also to Chaucer's personal version of the authorial figure who both is and is not to be mistaken for the author, a version that has several points of similarity with the one that he himself evolved.
126 *"Here is God's Plenty":*
    Dryden, *Fables Ancient and Modern* (1700), Preface. *Poems*, p. 1455.
127 *"So varied in discourse":*
    Walter Savage Landor, *To Robert Browning*, ll. 8–10.
127 *On the merest whim:*
    What seems to be a vivid reminiscence of *January and May* appears in one of the discarded couplets of the *Dunciad* MSS.: "On Sumer's neck his Arms here Autumn flings/And naked Winters marry blooming Springs." *The Last and Greatest Art*, p. 102.
128 *"And so bifel":*
    I use the numeration and text of F. N. Robinson, *The Poetical Works of Chaucer* (Boston: Houghton Mifflin, 1933).
130 *"The heroic view of tragic life":*
    J. T. Sheppard, *The Pattern of the Iliad* (Methuen, 1920), p. 119.
130 *"Give glory to another, or another to us":*
    Iliad, 12: 322–8. I use the Loeb Library translation of A. T. Murray.
130 *"The trumpets of heroism rang out":*
    E. T. Owen, *The Story of the Iliad* (New York: Oxford University Press, 1947), p. 125.
133 *"A common Sacrifice to Honour fall":*
    Sarpedon's speech to Glaucus in the 12th of Homer, ll. 18–29. *Poetical Works*, ed., T. H. Banks (New Haven: Yale University Press, 1928), pp. 179–80.
133 *"Have try'd their Strength":*
    Charles Gildon, *The Complete Art of Poetry* (1718), p. 157.
134 *"Successful attempts to do something small":*
    The Sacred Wood (London: Faber & Faber, 1920), p. 152.
134 *"In mores tempora priscos":*
    Consolation of Philosophy, book 2, metrum 5, 11.
134 *"Discontent of the civilized with civilization":*
    Arthur Lovejoy and George Boas, *A Documentary History of Primitivism and Related Ideas in Classical Antiquity* (The Johns Hopkins University Press, 1935), p. 7.
134 *"Fly hence, our contact fear!":*
    The Scholar Gypsy, ll. 201–6. One of the most perceptive discussions of the pastoral impulse generally is William Empson's *Some Versions of Pastoral* (London: Chatto and Windus, 1935).
135 *"Follow'd the employment" of sheep-herding:*
    "A Discourse on Pastoral Poetry" (*TE*, 1: 25). Though published first in Pope's *Works* of 1717, this introduction is present in the manuscript that passed among Pope's early friends.
136 *"Rococo vignettes":*
    Georgio Melchiori, "Pope in Arcady: The Theme of *Et in Arcadia Ego* in His Pastorals." In *Essential Articles for the Study of Alexander Pope* (New Haven: Archon Books, 1968), p. 151.
136 *"As gorgeous as those court masques":*
    A. J. Sambrook, "An Essay on Eighteenth-Century Pastoral, Pope to Wordsworth (1)," *Trivium*, 5 (1970): 25.
136 *"Landscapes of Poussin and Zuccarelli":*
    R. A. Brower, *Alexander Pope: The Poetry of Allusion* (Oxford: Clarendon, 1959), p. 24.
137 *Romanticism . . . lay . . . well ahead:*
    All such categorizations must, of course, be understood as highly ambiguous conveniences, since many elements of Romanticism are already present in the literature and the thinking about literature of Pope's time (e.g., Addison's *Spectator* series on the pleasures of the imagination, appearing only three years after Pope's *Pastorals*); just as many elements associated with Neoclassicism persist well into the next century and are not totally invisible today. B. H. Bronson, in "When Was Neoclassicism?" (*Studies in Criticism and Aesthetics, 1660–1800*, eds., Howard Anderson and J. S. Shea, University of Minnesota Press, 1967, pp. 13–35) is particularly fine on this point.

137 *The Poussin paintings . . . "Et in Arcadia ego":*
    Anthony Blunt, *Poussin* (New York: Pantheon–Random House, 1967), pp. 114, 304; plates 56, 225.
138 *"Constant braving of death":*
    Melchiori ("Pope in Arcady"), p. 157.
138 *The traditional melancholy of the genre:*
    This mood has been variously explained as the consequence of taking real sorrow into the fictive Agreeable Place (Irwin Panofsky, "Et in Arcadia Ego," *Philosophy and History*, eds., Raymond K. Pibansky and H. J. Paton [New York: Harper and Row, 1963], pp. 227–31); or of recognizing that the Agreeable Place is only a fiction or at least not suited to continuous habitation (Theodore Rosenmayer, *The Green Cabinet* [University of California Press, 1969], pp. 224–31).
139 *"To dwell on Mantuan Plains":*
    "The Sixth Pastoral, or Silenus", ll. 1–2.
140 *No other land "may vie with Italy's glories":*
    Georgics, 2: 136–9. I give H. R. Fairclough's Loeb Library translation.
140 *A "double groping":*
    See T. M. Greene, "Petrarch and the Humanist Hermeneutic," *Italian Literature: Roots and Branches. Essays in Honor of Thomas Goddard Bergin*, eds. G. Rimanelli and K. J. Atchity (New Haven: Yale University Press, 1976), pp. 201–24.
141 *"The Gods of Poetry":*
    TE, 7: 7.
141 *"Time Conquers All":*
    Notably modifying Vergil's "Love conquers all" (*Amor vincit omnia: Eclogues*, 10: 69), the phrase obviously sums up the seasonal cycle of Pope's *Pastorals* and just possibly hints at new poetical undertakings in the more strictly time-bound modes of georgic (*Windsor-Forest*) and epic (Statius, Homer).
142 *Linkèd sweetness, long drawn out:*
    For a different view of Pope's accomplishment in the *Pastorals*, see M. C. Battestin, *The Providence of Wit: Aspects of Form in Augustan Literature and the Arts* (Oxford: Clarendon, 1974) ch. 2. On structure and versification, see Pat Rogers, "Rhythm and Recoil in Pope's *Pastorals*," *E-CS*, 14 (1980–81), 1ff.

Chapter 7, Deluding Fancies, Real Discomforts

143 *A letter to a friend:*
    To Cromwell, 11 July 1709 (1: 68–9).
144 *Ben Jonson's Horatian adaptation:*
    "The Praises of a Country Life," ll. 1–8 (Horace, *Epodes*, 2).
145 *"The garret, and the jail":*
    The Vanity of Human Wishes, l. 160. "Patron" later replaced "garret."
145 *A first cousin once removed:*
    He was baptized on 15 January 1659 at Clifton, Bedfordshire, the second son of Thomas Cromwell (1609–60), who was first cousin to Oliver. His will was proved on 5 July 1728, and he was buried in St. Clement Danes.
145 *Pope may have met him through Granville:*
    This is George Sherburn's suggestion in *Early Career*, p. 60.
145 *Squadron of the Spanish armada:*
    This was not the great Armada of 1588 but a smaller Spanish fleet that Grenville met off the Azores.
145 *As early as 1705:*
    Pope to Wycherley, 26 October 1705 (1: 11).
145 *"Speculative Angle":*
    To Cromwell, 29 August 1709 (1: 70).
145 *A translation from Ovid's repertory:*
    Cromwell had been a contributor in 1692 to Charles Gildon's *Miscellaneous Poems on*

Several Occasions. In the 1712 Lintot Miscellany in which the 2-canto *Rape of the Locke* appears, he is represented by two translations from the *Amores*: "To His Mistress" (2: 16) and "The Dream" (3: 5). Attributed to him in the West papers (BL: Add. MS. 34, 744: f. 54) are translations of *Amores*, 1: 5 and 3: 3.

145 *In a tye-wig:*
    Johnson, p. 92.

145 *"With red Breeches":*
    "Mr. Pope's Welcome from Greece[:] a copy of Verses wrote by Mr. Gay upon Mr. Popes having finisht his Translation of Homers Ilias," l. 136.

145 *Somewhat deaf:*
    See also 1: 51.

146 *One of Pope's verse-letters:*
    12 or 13 July [1707] (1: 25).

146 *"Pockets stuffed out with Poetry":*
    From a description of him by Elizabeth Thomas (Cromwell's "Sappho") in her account of herself called *The Life of Corinna* (1731), p. 53.

147 *A nosegay from the flower-booths:*
    I take this to be the meaning of Pope's allusion in his letter to Cromwell of 7 May 1709 (1: 57). See, however, the sketch of him in disarray at 1: 47.

147 *"Leading up a Spanish-Pavan":*
    Elizabeth Thomas (*Corinna*), pp. 192–3.

147 *"A satyr's face":*
    To Pope, 14 June 1709 (1: 65).

147 *"You are a polite person":*
    19 February 1709 (1: 56).

147 *Don Quixote . . . three satiric personalities:*
    See Elizabeth Thomas (*Corinna*), pp. 96, 98, 144, 283, 286.

147 *"A Jest to the rest of the World":*
    Ibid., p. 96.

147 *Stiff pedant and arch-critic:*
    In Addison's *Tatler*, no. 165 (29 April 1710), Sir Timothy Tittle challenges a young woman who has laughed heartily while watching a particular stage comedy to "show me a single rule that you could laugh by."

148 *"The best-natur'd of Mortalls":*
    10 May [1711] (1: 116). On Cromwell's "softness," see also Wycherley to Pope, 6 December 1707 (1: 36): "Soft Cromwell salutes you." The terms "gentle" and "gentleness" are also used of him by Pope at 1: 46 and 116; by Wycherley at 1: 56 and 80, and by Elizabeth Thomas (*Corinna*) at p. 283.

148 *"Country putt":*
    To John Caryll [February 1720] (2: 31).

148 *"Writ tolerably smooth Verses":*
    Charles Gildon, *Memoirs of William Wycherley* (1718) p. 16. As Sherburn notes (*Early Career*, p. 46n), "Rustick Parent" contains an "envenomed reference to the recent death of Pope's father." There is other evidence of Pope's early "rusticity." Charles Wogan (later Chevalier Charles Wogan in the service of the Pretender), apparently one of the few men of about his own age whom Pope knew in his Binfield days, speaks in a letter to Swift (27 February 1722–3: *Swift, Correspondence*, 4: 113 and n.) of his friend Pope, with whom he had lived for two or three summers in Binfield "in perfect union and familiarity" and whom he had had "the honour to bring up to London, *to dress a la mode,* and introduce at Will's coffee-house." (Italics mine.)

148 *The manuscript, which survives:*
    In the Pierpont Morgan Library. It is photographically reproduced with a transcript in *The Last and Greatest Art*, pp. 74–90.

149 *Promising more "Obedience":*
    7 May 1709 (1: 57).

149 *A month later, a further letter:*
    10 June 1709 (1: 63).

149 *"Habitual outrageousness"*:
    The phrase belongs to T. R. Steiner, "The Heroic Ape," *Eighteenth-Century Life*, 5 (1979): 47. His study of Pope's relations with "Corinna" is forthcoming.

149 *"Where I feel Affection"*:
    18 March 1708 (1: 42). See also Pope to Cromwell, 24 June and 30 December 1710 (1: 90 and 112).

149 *"Malicious untruths"*:
    19 October 1709 (1: 73).

150 *"At once nasty & diverting"*:
    29 August 1709 (1: 70–1).

150 *"Sad-dog" pose*:
    W. J. Thomas, "Dryden, Pope, and Curll's 'Corinna'," *Notes and Queries*, 12 (1855): 277–9.

150 *"Even as Sapho & Mr. Cromwell"*:
    11 July 1709 (1: 67–8). It seems possible though not likely that Pope had read Boccaccio's story about putting the Devil in Hell (Day 3, Story 10). If the anecdote is fiction, the hint of it may have been put into Pope's mind by Wycherley's letter of 12 March 1706 (1: 14), where he speaks of being in a coach with a siek woman, who, if well, "deserv'd better Jumbling, than that of the Coach nay she might have deserv'd Jumbling in a Coach in Covent Garden, when it moves whilst the Wheels stand still."

151 *"Of little Size"*:
    24 June 1710 (1: 89). Pope's verses are adapted in part from Rondeaux 32 and 34. *Oeuvres de Voiture: Lettres et Poésies*, ed. M. A. Ubicini, 2 vols. (Genève: Slatkin reprints, 1967), 2: 319–21. The "Sappho" to whom Pope desires Cromwell to show these lines is not (as suggested in J. A. Hagstrum's *Sex and Sensibility: Ideal and Erotic Love from Milton to Mozart*, University of Chicago Press, 1980, p. 138) Lady Mary Wortley Montagu, but Cromwell's "Sappho," the Elizabeth Thomas (*Corinna*), who greatly embarrassed Pope by selling these incautious letters, given her by Cromwell when he left her, to Edmund Curll.

152 *"What have I to do with Jane Gray"*:
    Pope evidently knew that a play on this theme was being written, or planned, by his friend Rowe, though it was not acted till 1715. He was witness to Rowe's agreement with Lintot for the publication of *Jane Shore* some ten months before it was performed. See A. W. Hesse, "Pope's Role in Tonson's Loss of Rowe," *Notes and Queries*, 24 (1977): 234–5.

152 *"I'll e'en compose my own Tragedy"*:
    21 December 1711 (1: 137–8).

152 *"That little Alexander the women laugh at"*:
    25 January 1711 (1: 114).

153 *The disease that crippled him*:
    That Pope's affliction came from Pott's Disease is the conclusion of Marjorie Nicolson and George Rousseau in their careful study, with medical assistance, of the progress of the disease and its symptoms: "*This Long Disease My Life*": *Alexander Pope and the Sciences* (Princeton: Princeton University Press, 1968), pp. 7–82—on which I gratefully draw. Pope himself seems to have thought his disability congenital, according to some unpublished lines in the manuscript of the *Epistle to Dr. Arbuthnot*. These are reproduced in *The Last and Greatest Art*, pp. 434–5.

153 *An acute observer of its effects*:
    See *The Chirurgical Works of Percival Pott*, 5 vols. (1783), 5: 394–481.

155 *"The mouths of crooked persons"*:
    Presumably Reynolds alludes to the thickening of the upper lip noted by Pott among the other symptoms of the disease.

155 *Reynolds on Pope's appearance*:
    James Prior, *Life of Edmund Malone* (1860), p. 429.

155 *Telling Spence in 1728*:
    No. 69.

155 *"Phlebotomy and blisters"*:
    Pope to Caryll, 15 April 1731 (3: 190).

156 *Frequent violent pain:*
Pope speaks of a lame arm and lame thigh in April 1726 (2: 373), of a lame arm in September of that year (2: 402), and of a lame shoulder in February 1731 (3: 176).
156 *"I can walk 8 or 10 Miles":*
15 January 1731 (3: 161).
156 *"Like an insect" . . . "God mend me!":*
Pope to Hugh Bethel, 20 February 1744 (*Correspondence*, 4: 499), and *The World*, no. 53 (13 December 1753). (This number of *The World* is by R. O. Cambridge, a resident of Twickenham from 1751.)
156 *Like an eighteenth-century thermometer:*
21 December 1712 (1: 165). In his striking image, Pope is possibly remembering Arbuthnot's John Bull, whose "Spirits rose and fell with the Weather-glass." (Above, p. 192.)
156 *"Like the picture of January":*
To John Caryll, Jr., 5 December 1712 (1: 163).
156 *"Built round in his very bed":*
30 October [1719?] (2: 17).
156 *"Like a small Bird":*
[January 1744] (4: 490–1).
156 *"I do not think I ever shall enjoy any health":*
7 November [1728] (2: 525).
158 *"The condition of an old fellow of Threescore":*
[Late 1728] (2: 530).
158 *"They had been employed with Mr. Pope":*
Gentleman's Magazine, 45 (1775): 435, and Johnson, pp. 197, 199.
158 *An image applied by Wycherley:*
19 February 1709 (1: 54).

Chapter 8, New Wine in Old Bottles and the Discovery of Envy

159 *The chamber next to Wycherley:*
Wycherley to Pope, 13 November 1708 (1: 53–4).
159 *London in late June:*
11 July 1709 (1: 68–9).
160 *Statius's Thebaid:*
A preliminary draft of the translation seems to have been complete by 31 October 1709, when Trumbull writes his nephew that Pope is copying it out "fairly." Sherburn, "New Anecdotes," p. 343.
160 *It attracted Pope's attention in his boyhood:*
Spence, no. 30.
160 *Above all Latin epics save the Aeneid:*
Somewhat to Spence's surprise: see nos. 44, 551–2. The *Thebaid* was not included in the usual English school curriculum; in Roman Catholic countries it was, and Pope very probably encountered it through one of his tutor-priests or at one of his Roman Catholic schools.
160 *"The cruel daylight of the mind":*
From Statius's description of Oedipus, brooding upon his crime and pain, at the beginning of the poem, l. 52. The Roman poet's talent for imaginative personalizing of abstractions must also have appealed to Pope, who had a similar gift. A particularly famous example ("Clementia") appears at *Thebaid*, 12: 481 ff.
160 *Political undercurrent of his own:*
For a full discussion, see J. M. Aden, "'The Change of Scepters, and impending Woe': Political Allusion in Pope's Statius," *PQ*, 52 (1973): 728–38. A somewhat more exploratory and conservative view is taken in Howard Erskine-Hill's "Literature and the Jacobite Cause," in Eveline Cruickshanks, ed., *Ideology and Conspiracy: Aspects of Jacobitism, 1689–1759* (Edinburgh, John Donald, 1982), pp. 49–69. That Pope published an anti-William epigram as early as 1705 is argued by David Nokes, "Lisping in Political Numbers," *Notes and Queries*, 24 (1977): 228–9.

167 *"The maturest age and longest experience":*
Johnson, p. 94. Taine, who echoes this opinion, adds: "In this subject, of which the treatment demands the experience of a whole literary life, he was at the first onset as ripe as Boileau." *A History of English Literature*, tr., Henry Van Laun (1883; repr. New York: Unger, 1965), p. 335.

167 *Quintilian, Rapin, and Bossu:*
Spence, nos. 94, 95.

168 *"Whether he has read it or not":*
Tatler, no. 165, 29 April 1710. For an even severer view of critics as collectors of faults, always attracted to the noblest writers "as a Rat to the best Cheese," see Swift's "Digression concerning Critics" in *Tale of a Tub*, section 3.

169 *"Contemporary coffee house and drawing room":*
Swift's *Polite Conversation*, not published till 1738 but begun as early as 1704, gives a fine sense of such banalities, even while raising them to a higher satiric power. So also, by implication, does Virginia Woolf's *Orlando*, ch. 4.

169 *"A propriety of thoughts and words":*
The *Author's Apology for Heroic Poetry and Poetic License* (1677); *Of Dramatic Poesy and other Critical Essays*, ed., George Watson, 2 vols. (London: J. M. Dent, 1962), 1. 207: "From that which has been said, it may be collected that the definition of wit (which has been so often attempted, and ever unsuccessfully by many poets) is only this: that it is a propriety of thoughts and words, or, in other terms, thoughts and words elegantly adapted to the subject." Pope was sensible of this change and in his efforts at revising Wycherley's poems comes down hard on the side of propriety in Dryden's sense. (Above, p. 839—100: *Two years . . . labor.*) In the *Essay*, he seems intent on establishing the hegemony of wit (as mother of invention) over judgment (as guardian of decorum).

169 *"A quibble was the fatal Cleopatra":*
In the preface to his edition of Shakespeare (1765). *Dr. Johnson on Shakespeare*, ed., W. K. Wimsatt (Penguin Books, 1969), p. 68.

169 *To seduce British virtue to its ruin:*
Blackmore's *Satyr* begins: "Who can forbear, and tamely silent sit, And see his Native Land undone by Wit." See on the episode as a whole R. M. Krapp, "Class Analysis of a Literary Controversy: Wit and Sense in Seventeenth-Century English Literature," *Science and Society*, 10 (1946): 80–92, and R. C. Boys, *Sir Richard Blackmore and the Wits* (Ann Arbor: University of Michigan Press, 1949). The change in attitudes is sharply visible in Defoe's view of the literary establishment in *Reformation of Manners* (1702), ll. 1044–6:

> Now view the Beau's at *Will*'s; the Men of Wit,
> Of Nature nice, and for discerning fit:
> The finish'd Fops, the Men of Wig and Snuff. . . .

169 *"Perfect cheats":*
II xi and III x.

169 *"False wit":*
See Addison, for example, in two influential *Spectators*, nos. 61 and 62, 10 and 11 May 1711.

170 *"Fancy without Judgement not":*
Leviathan (1651), p. 43. The conflict ascribed to wit and judgment in Hobbes's time and later has some obvious affinities with that between *l'esprit de finesse* and *l'esprit de géométrie* in Pascal, and both apparently relate to that ancient rift between poetic and ratiocinative modes illustrated in Plato's resort to fable as well as dialectic, and exemplified in Buddhist thought in the distinction between *prajna* and *vijnana*. On this last, see especially Victor Turner, *Dramas, Fields, Metaphors* (Cornell University Press, 1974), pp. 46 ff.

170 *Signify little more than a "joke" or a "joker":*
The foregoing two paragraphs are indebted to chapter 12 of W. K. Wimsatt, Jr., and Cleanth Brooks, *Literary Criticism: A Short History* (New York: Knopf, 1957).

174 *The great practitioners of criticism are reviewed:*
Much has been written on the structure of Horace's *Ars Poetica* but the most persuasive account is still W. K. Wimsatt's "*Jam Nunc Debentia Dici*," *Arion*, 9 (1970): 132 ff. A beautifully balanced study of Horace's poem as a whole is C. O. Brink's *Horace on Poetry*,

volume 2: *The "Ars Poetica"* (Cambridge University Press, 1971). Pope's tripartite division of his own subject, though not identical with Horace's, clearly relates to it.

175 *Pope extends his literary-critical ideal to its widest implications:*
The imagery of the poem has been discussed with particular sensitivity by Patricia Meyer Spacks in "Imagery and Method in the Essay on Criticism." For the uses and meanings of "Wit" in the *Essay*, see especially E. N. Hooker, "Pope on Wit: The *Essay on Criticism*," and William Empson, "Wit in the *Essay on Criticism*." These essays are reprinted in *Pope: Recent Essays*, eds., Maynard Mack and J. A. Winn, pp. 106–30, and in *Essential Articles*, ed., Maynard Mack, pp. 185–207 and 208–26.

176 *"Perhaps the best that English poetry can shew":*
Johnson, p. 229. It is revealing, one is bound to think, that Pope's objective correlative for the labors of a literary (or any other) education should be a longed-for journey across the Alps to Italy and Rome. So much in Johnson's work concerns the need to revise and enlarge innocent or narrow views that it is not surprising the lines moved him.

177 *His aunt Elizabeth Turner:*
Elizabeth Turner died, according to the entry in Pope's Elzevir Virgil (above, p. 15), on 24 January 1710; Betterton on 28 April.

178 *"The best Cure in the world for Ambition":*
12 October 1710 (1: 98).

178 *"In the light of traditional knowledge":*
D. B. Morris, "Civilized Reading: The Act of Judgement in *An Essay on Criticism*," *The Art of Alexander Pope*, eds., Howard Erskine-Hill and Anne Smith (London: Vision Press, 1979), pp. 36–7.

179 *"A System of rules, as evry art has":*
Dennis, 2: 283.

179 *"Irritable, suspicious, and envious":*
Ibid., 2: xi.

179 *"Was deaf to every Merit but his own":*
Francis Manning, *Poems Written at Different Times* (1752), p. 254.

179 *"The furious petulance, the jealous start":*
Aaron Hill, "Verses, on the Death of Mr. Dennis," ll. 5–7.

179 *"'Sdeath!":*
Benjamin Victor, *An Epistle to Sir Richard Steele, On his Play, call'd The Conscious Lovers* (1722), p. 28.

180 *Practices hardly distinguishable from embezzlement:*
On Dennis's chancery suit against his mother and the suit of others against him for misappropriation of funds, see F. S. Tupper, "Notes on the Life of John Dennis," *ELH: A Journal of English Literary History*, 5 (1938): 211–17.

180 *Thought by contemporaries to be capable:*
Life of Dennis (1734), p. 23; Swift, *Prose*, 4 (1957): 250; Theophilus Cibber, *Lives of the Poets*, 5 vols. (1753), 4: 221–2.

180 *A humorous couplet by Dennis written in his youth:*
Spectator, nos. 40, 47. Later, however, Addison seems to indicate his evaluation of Dennis's Milton criticism by making no mention of it in his eighteen *Spectators* on *Paradise Lost* published during 1712.

180 *Victim of a conspiracy or cabal:*
He had been further satirized under the title "Diphthong, a Critic" in Charles Johnson's *The Generous Husband* (act 2, scene 1), produced at Drury Lane the preceding January 20. There Secundum says of him, "He thinks he is the Chancellor of Parnassus and believes his Decrees are irreversible." While Diphthong is on stage, he shows Dennis's usual contempt, this time for the play he is in.

182 *"About thrice":*
Dennis, 1: 396; 2: 370.

182 *Territories he had long claimed to rule:*
Eighteen years later, Dennis was still claiming in his "Remarks" on the *Dunciad* that the *Essay on Criticism* was the effect of Pope's "impotent Envy and Malice, by which he endeavour'd to destroy the Reputation of a Man who had publish'd Pieces of Criticism, and to set up his own." *Ibid.*, 2: 370.

183 *"Too often Obscurity and Confusion"*:
   Ibid., 1: 413–14.
184 *"The Life of half a Day"*:
   Ibid., 1: 416–17.
184 *No more cruel review:*
   Early Career, p. 91.

Chapter 9, "A Few Lasting Dependable Friendships" and a Dream for England

185 *"A Master-piece in its kind"*:
   No. 253, 20 December 1711. Gay came to Pope's defense in a mock dedication to Dennis of his farce *The Mohocks* (never acted, but published 15 April 1712), where he says: "As we look upon you to have the Monopoly of *English* Criticism in your Head, we hope you will very shortly chastise the Insolence of the *Spectator*, who has lately had the *Audaciousness* to show that there are more Beauties than Faults in a Modern Writer."
185 *"One of the greatest genius's that this nation has bred"*:
   21 April 1713. Sherburn, "New Anecdotes," p. 345.
186 *"Seemed ye Genius of ye Place"*:
   The manuscript of this piece, plainly in Fortescue's hand, is now in the Pierpont Morgan Library. It was identified erroneously as Pope's by A. L. McLeod in *Notes and Queries*, 198 (1953): 334–7, and correctly as Fortescue's by John Butt in *idem*, 200 (1955): 23–5. Earlier in the Morgan Library catalogue, it had been attributed to Gay. In the sentence I quote, Fortescue first wrote "wonderful," which I have retained in my transcription rather than his revision, "great."
186 *Even its failures:*
   Teresa Blount should perhaps be added to this list, although we have no clear evidence that Pope behaved badly to her, only that he came increasingly to disapprove what he took to be her frivolity and was, much later, severe in his letters to Caryll on her conduct toward her sister and mother as well as on what appears to have been her liaison with an unidentified lover.
187 *"As much more friendship as death has depriv'd us of in him"*:
   The quotations are from letters dated 3 September 1726, 2 October 1727, October, 1730, and 6 December 1732 (2: 395, 447–8; 3: 138, 336).
187 *"None like you, living or dead"*:
   [February–March 1728/9] (3: 20).
187 *Pope met Gay:*
   Apparently through Cromwell, through whom he offers his "Service" in a letter of 15 July 1711 (1: 125).
187 *Pope's description of him:*
   In the collations of the *Dunciad* manuscripts made by Jonathan Richardson, Jr. before the MSS. were destroyed. See *The Last and Greatest Art*, p. 104.
187 *Congreve is reputed to have said of him:*
   Spence, no. 242.
187 *"Never design'd him to be above two and twenty"*:
   To Pope, 16 July 1728 (2: 505).
187 *More provident friends, Swift and Pope in particular:*
   Swift's letters to Pope and Arbuthnot are filled with concern for Gay's financial well-being and with hints for his Muse. Pope's assistance was closer at hand, and with him at Binfield and later at Twickenham, Gay sometimes made his home for considerable periods. Reminiscing to Richard Savage in 1736, four years after Gay's death, when Savage seems to have been completing a life of Gay, Aaron Hill stresses Pope's role in reviving Gay's poetic aspirations, which had withered upon the death of Queen Anne (cf. also Arbuthnot to Swift, 19 October 1714, *Swift Correspondence*, 2: 137), and in supporting him with "more *solid* improvements" as well—"for I remember a letter, wherein he invited him to partake of his fortune, (at that time but a small one) assuring him, with a very *un-poetical* warmth, that, as long as himself had a *shilling*, Mr. *Gay* should be welcome to *Six-pence* of it; nay to *Eight-pence*, if *he* could contrive but to live on a *groat*." (Hill to

Savage, 23 June 1736. *Works of Aaron Hill*, 4 vols. [1753], 1: 339–40.) Hill had been intimate with Gay, whom he had employed during part of Gay's early years in London (ca. 1708–11) as a secretary while editing *The British Apollo*. On the other hand, the letter he seems here to be recalling is of 16 October 1727 (2: 454). Parnell also gave money from his writings to Gay. Pope to Parnell [1717] (1: 395 and n); Goldsmith, Life of *Dr. Parnell*, in *Works*, ed., Arthur Friedman (Oxford: Clarendon Press, 1966), 3: 412.

187 *To die "worth upward of £3,000":*
     Spence, no. 247.

187 *"The dignity of genius":*
     "Gay." *Lives*, 2: 282.

189 *"Here lies Gay":*
     Gay's letter asking Pope to place the two-line epitaph on his gravestone is dated in February–March 1729, by Sherburn (3: 19–20), and, more correctly, I think, in October 1727, by C. F. Burgess, *Letters of John Gay* (Oxford: Clarendon, 1966), pp. 65–6. Gay cautions in his letter that the couplet is not to be taken as a communication made after death but as his "present Sentiment in Life." In the Poet's Corner, the monument with its inscription is today missing, having been removed in 1938 to the triforium to reveal two thirteenth-century wall paintings. *Notes and Queries*, 176 (1939): 52–3.

189 *An offer to serve as Pope's executor:*
     Pope offers him release from that service in a letter of 23 January 1740 (4: 222) on the ground that it "might . . ., now, be less convenient to you than formerly." He may refer to the fact that Fortescue had been transferred to the Court of Common Pleas in 1738 and, in Pope's mind at least, was already a candidate for the Mastership of the Rolls (4: 126); or it may refer to the political embarrassment an important government functionary might undergo from being publicly associated with one who had written so much against the Court and the Walpole ministry, including the suppressed "1740." As Sherburn points out (4: 222n), Fortescue did not serve as executor and is not mentioned in Pope's surviving will.

190 *"Pleased that you do it in the latter":*
     18 February 1733 (3: 351). The title of the poem in the surviving manuscript also assigns it to Fortescue. See *The Last and Greatest Art*, p. 172.

190 *"Ridens Fortescuvius":*
     Jervas to Pope [1716?] (1: 340: the actual phrase is *ridente Fortescuvio*).

191 *"Common Law is nothing but reason":*
     To Spence (no. 137), Pope confirms his authorship of this parody and Fortescue's participation in it.

191 *In a rhyme of 1714:*
     "Scriblerus" (apparently Parnell) to Robert Harley, Earl of Oxford, 12 June 1714 (1: 230).

191 *"Most ingenious political satire in our language":*
     History of England, ch. 24. *Works*, 8 vols. (1866), 4: 427.

191 *The recent "Plague of Frogs":*
     Sir John Knight, for example, had complained publicly in Commons of the "Great Noise and Croaking of the *Frog-Landers*." *Speech in the House of Commons against the Naturalizing of Foreigners* (1694), p. 7.

194 *"Quite the reverse of John in many Particulars":*
     The History of John Bull, eds., A. W. Bower and R. A. Erickson (Oxford: Clarendon Press, 1976), p. 9.

194 *"Shuffle" of his gait:*
     Swift to Arbuthnot, 25 July 1714; Swift to Pope, 29 September 1725 (Swift *Correspondence*, 2: 82; 3: 104). See also Pope to Robert Digby, 1 September [1724] (2: 253). For Arbuthnot's reputation as something of a glutton, see Chesterfield's "character" of him in his *Letters*, ed., Lord Mahon (1845).

194 *"Drives Sorrow from the Heart":*
     Line 123.

194 *Scattered manuscripts on the floor:*
     On Arbuthnot's musical skills, see Sir John Hawkins, *General History of the Science and Practice of Music* (1776) 5: 270n, and, especially, Judith Milhous and R. D. Hume, "New

Light on Handel and the Royal Academy of Music in 1720," *Theatre Journal*, 35 (1983): 151, where Arbuthnot's name is listed as one of the Academy's first directors and as its emissary to negotiate with Anastasia Robinson, a leading singer (later Lady Peterborow). The minutes of the next meeting record a vote "That Mr. Pope be desir'd to propose a Seal with a suitable Motto to it, for the Royal Academy of Musick" (p. 153). On Arbuthnot's laughter, see Orrery's *Remarks on the Life and Writings of Jonathan Swift* (1752), p. 256; on his inattention, Swift to Gay and the duchess of Queensberry, 10 July 1732 (3: 298), and on the scene with his children, Chesterfield's *Letters*, ed., Lord Mahon (1845), 2: 447. (Chesterfield's character sketch of Arbuthnot is first printed in this edition.)

195 *"In a manner improves my Theory"*:
To Swift, 12 August 1714 (*Swift Correspondence*, 2: 122). See also to Swift, 19 October 1717 (*Ibid.*, 2: 136).

195 *"For he shall never be disappointed"*:
Pope to Fortescue, 23 September 1725; Pope to Gay, 16 October 1727 (2: 323, 453).

195 *"Quite azure as the heavens"*:
Spence, no. 125.

195 *Most versatile writer of the age:*
In inscribing a copy of his *Travels in Italy*, presented before politics divided them, Addison recognizes Swift as "the greatest Genius of the Age." Thomas Birch to Philip Yorke, earl of Hardwicke, 10 August 1765. BL: Add. MS. 35,400, f. 272b.

196 *Promised much but offered nothing:*
Swift's disappointment is evident from a manuscript notation in his copy of Everte Jollyvet's *Poésies Chrétiennes* (1708): "Given me by my Lord Halifax May 3 1709. I begg'd it of him, & desir'd him to remember it was the only favour I ever received from him or his Party." Thomas Birch to Philip Yorke, earl of Hardwicke, 10 August 1765. BL: Add. MS. 35,400, ff. 272b–273a.

196 *Published long after his death:*
The work was published in 1758.

196 *Military and naval supply:*
Marlborough, for example, received £63,000 from Sir Solomon Medina and Antonio Alvarez Machado for the contract to supply bread to the army.

198 *"An unintelligible jargon"*:
Examiner, no. 13 (2 November 1710). Swift, *Prose*, 3: 7.

198 *Sophistical masterpieces:*
For a searching discussion of Swift's political writings of this period see Ehrenpreis, 2: 406 ff., 481 ff., 696 ff.

199 *"Destroying the Landed-Interest"*:
The quotations are from *The Conduct of the Allies:* Swift, *Prose*, 6: 55–6, 58, 58–9. As W. A. Speck points out, one must not lose sight of the fact that under the propaganda, however extreme, lies a genuine anxiety. "Conflict in Society," *Britain after the Glorious Revolution*, ed., Geoffrey Holmes (London: Macmillan, 1969), p. 137.

199 *"Read it"*:
Journal to Stella, 9 March 1713.

199 *Celebration of the Tory peace:*
The possibility of Swift's influence is noted by Ehrenpreis, 2: 593n.

199 *Personal coda with which the present poem ends:*
From Pope's note in his octavo editions, 1736–43. *TE*, 1: 175.

200 *An important Whig concern:*
It has been capably argued that Pope's attack on the Norman Williams (William I and William II), which occurs in this part of the poem, extends by innuendo to William III—like the other Williams a foreigner, an invader, a keen hunter whose death was precipitated by a fall while hunting, and (in the political arguments of those who wished to show that the Revolution came about not by James's abdication or by true succession) a conqueror. See J. R. Moore, *"Windsor-Forest* and William III," *Modern Language Notes*, 66 (1951): 451–4; and E. R. Wasserman, *The Subtler Language* (Johns Hopkins University Press, 1959), ch. 4. The claim is now widely accepted and may be sound. It must be confessed, however, that none of Pope's lines can be connected more than superficially with William III, and that the poet has left his intentions (if they go beyond the Normans)

uncharacteristically obscure. In the *Essay on Criticism*, for example (ll. 543–53), he leaves no doubt that it is to William his indictment applies. One must reckon it surprising, too, that no contemporary enemy of Pope's, not even the Argus-eyed John Dennis, noticed the opportunity thus offered for a charge of treason; and that the evils attributed to the Norman Williams have very litttle to do with the charges normally leveled by anti-Williamites against William III.

202 *"Justice planted her latest steps":*
  Georgics, 2: 136 ff, 171 ff, 458 ff.

203 *"That their kings may be brought":*
  Isaiah, 2: 3–4; 60: 3, 5, 11; 65: 21–2. I give the King James version. The Douai differs only slightly, mainly in the more accurate "abound" for "flow together."

206 *"A model for the future":*
  E. W. Leach, *Vergil's Eclogues: Landscapes of Experience* (Ithaca, N.Y.: Cornell University Press, 1974), p. 217.

207 *The city upon a hill:*
  For a thoughtful and considerably more political view of the poem, see Pat Rogers, "'The Enamelled Ground': The Language of Heraldry and Natural Description in *Windsor-Forest*," *Studia Neophilologica*, 45 (1973): 356–71; and for a view isolating some cracks or fissures occasioned by revision of the original poem into a poem on the Peace, see A. J. Varney, "The Composition of Pope's *Windsor-Forest*," *Durham University Journal* (1974): 57–67.

Chapter 10, Solemnities and Frivolities

208 *Pope also met Steele:*
  Probably through Caryll, who had come to know Steele during negotiations with Lord Cutts (whose secretary Steele was at the time) for return of Caryll's outlawed uncle's confiscated estates. In a letter to Caryll of 4 September 1711 (1: 134), Pope thanks him for an unidentified "application" to Steele on his behalf. One suspects Caryll may have asked Steele to put in a good word for the *Essay on Criticism*, so viciously mauled by Dennis, in the pages of the *Spectator*. Addison's favorable notice of the poem came that December.

208 *"That he spoke Truth":*
  The Present State of Wit, in a *Letter to a Friend in the Country* (1711), p. 13.

208 *"I will make you acquainted":*
  20 January 1712 (1: 141).

208 *The clerical household of Lancelot Addison:*
  Early on, Addison himself entertained thoughts of entering the church, and something of clerical demeanor seems to have hung about him. Old Jacob Tonson, who did not like either priests or Addison, held he was "a priest in his heart" (Spence, no. 191), and Mandeville is said to have called him a "parson in a tye-wig" (*Addisoniana*, 2 vols., 1: 7).

210 *"In any other man":*
  Spence, no. 148.

210 *"With as much ease as any one could write it down":*
  The quotations are from Spence, no. 822, and from Steele's preface to Addison's *The Drummer* (1722), p. x. When later on, however, Addison's position as a secretary of state required him to speak in Parliament, he gave a poor account of himself.

210 *Where women were concerned:*
  Bonamy Dobrée has some interesting remarks on this point in his *Essays in Biography, 1680–1726* (London: Oxford University Press, 1925), pp. 257–8, 277ff. His view is shared by F. W. Bateson, "The *Errata* in the *Tatler*," *Review of English Studies*, 5 (1929): 164–6. See also Peter Smithers, *The Life of Joseph Addison* (Oxford: Clarendon Press, 1968), pp. 364–6. Pope told Spence (no. 188) that Addison and Steele were a couple of H[erma-phrodite]s, i.e., homosexuals. But I know of no other evidence for this description.

211 *A copy of Thomas à Kempis:*
  "Pope's Books," no. 159.

211 *"My greatest Good!":*
  TE, 6: 5–7.

212 *A climax at the close:*
   Later set to music and present in many hymn-books today.
213 *Cruelty to animals; "Receipt"; taste for topiary:*
   Guardian, nos. 61 (21 May), 78 (10 June), 173 (29 September 1713).
214 *"For the sake of little* Tydeus":
   Nos. 91–2 (25 and 26 June 1713). Norman Ault, who argues plausibly that Pope must
   have written more *Guardians* than can now be identified, submits his own choices in Pope,
   Prose. A note in what appears to be Teresa Blount's hand on a copy of the original issue of
   Guardian, no. 149 (1 September 1713) assigns this paper to "Mr. Pope & Mr. Gay."
   (Mapledurham Papers).
214 *Two inches taller than Swift:*
   Spence, no. 844.
214 *"No better Eclogs in our Language":*
   28 October (1: 101).
215 *A second puff:*
   Tatler, no. 12 (7 May 1709); *Spectator*, no. 400 (9 June 1712).
215 *Tribute to Philips for avoiding it:*
   Nos. 223 and 523.
215 *"His eldest-born Philips":*
   Nos. 22, 23, 28, 30, 32 (6, 7, 13, 15, and 17 April 1713). The quotation is from no. 32.
215 *Expressing a "pretty Rusticity":*
   Nos. 22, 28, 30.
216 *Without catching its satirical tone:*
   Bonamy Dobrée (*Essays in Biography*) argues that Steele was not taken in (pp. 268–70).
   This seems to me improbable since it requires us to suppose him knowingly involved in
   depreciating two staunch Whigs (Philips and Tickell), whose works he and Addison had
   publicly praised. Some cancelled lines of the *Dunciad*—from the description of the heroic
   game of staying awake with which Book 2 concludes—may refer to this episode:

> To Him who nodding steals a transient Nap,
> We give Tate's Ovid, & thy Virgil, Trap[p].
> Unable Heads that Sleep and Wake by fits,
> Win Steel[e], well-sifted from all Alien Wits.

   Steele might be thought a companionable reward for those only awake by fits, on account
   either of his missing the irony of *Guardian*, no. 40, or of his ignoring Pope's work entirely
   in the five *Guardians* praising Philips, of which he was then thought to be the author. (See
   for the canceled lines *The Last and Greatest Art*, pp. 98, 146.)
216 *In the coffee houses:*
   By October the prank had become well-known. Pope to Caryll, 17 October 1713 (1:
   193).
217 *"Who live the Day to see":*
   From Philips's *Eclogue IV*, ll. 47–8. Sidney had earlier censured Spenser for "framing his
   stile," in pastoral "to an old rustick language." *Apology for Poetry*, in *Elizabethan Critical
   Essays*, ed., Gregory Smith (Oxford: Clarendon, 1904), 1: 196.
217 *"But something Better":*
   In a satirical epigram only lately published (*Review of English Studies*, n.s. 33, 1982),
   Parnell interprets the Pope-Philips-Tickell (or Steele) episode in the light of *Metamor-
   phoses*, 11: 146–79, where Pan and Apollo hold a singing contest and all give the victory to
   Apollo save Midas, on whom Apollo promptly bestows ass's ears:

> The Rustick [Philips] to his Fauns withdrew;
> Whilst on ye silver wing
> Sweet Phoebus for Parnassus flew
> To hear his Homer sing [i.e., Pope began translating the *Iliad*]
> Yet ere he went to Midas said,
> Ile fitt you for your Jears
> So took two leaves from off his head,
> And stuck them in his ears [i.e., Pope wrote *Guardian*, no. 40 making an ass of Philips].

219 *"The doctrine of Liberty very seasonable":*
    Addison, *Works*, 4 vols. (1721), Preface, p. xiv.
220 *"The Ruin of the WHIG Party":*
    Political State, 5 (1713): 380. In February that year there had been a Pope burning, with "the Pretender on his Left, in a French Dress, with a wooden Shoe hanging on his left Arm, and in his right Hand a Candle, which he held to the Pope and the Devil, as proper Emblems of the Blessings we are to receive from one, bred up in the Idolatry of Rome, and the Tyranny of France." (*Flying-Post*, 7–10 February 1713.) Queen Elizabeth's accession day, November 17, brought a second burning, the processioners carrying lighted torches "as far as the Royal Exchange & back again to Charing Cross, where in a Bon-fire of eight load of Fagots," Pretender, Devil, and Pope were again consumed. Henry Moore to Teresa Blount, 19 November 1713. Mapledurham Papers.
220 *"Either in boxes, pit, or gallery":*
    Hervey Letter Books, ed., S. H. A. Hervey, 3 vols., (Wells, 1894), 1: 370.
220 *"Never designed it as a party-play":*
    Spence, no. 153. See also *Journal to Stella*, p. 652. Many Whigs, however, chose to see in Cato a representation of Marlborough, and in his young admirer, Prince Juba, Marlborough's great admirer, the Elector of Hanover, who would one day be England's king. For a more inflammatory Whig interpretation, see the notice in *The Flying Post*, 30 April–2 May, where the villainy of Sempronius (the play's traitor) is said to be matched by that of all who "outwardly pretend mighty Zeal for Liberty but inwardly are willing for a Popish Pretender." On the opposite side, see a pamphlet purporting to show that Marlborough, "in endeavouring to be *a General for Life*," resembles the play's Caesar: *Mr. Addison turn'd Tory: Or, The Scene Inverted: Wherein It is made to appear that the Whigs have misunderstood that Celebrated Author* (1713).
220 *"Against a perpetuall dictator":*
    To Caryll, 30 April 1713 (1: 175). See also Spence, no. 156, and Cibber's *Apology*, pp. 250–1. The "home stroak," however, comes from a letter of Peter Wentworth to his brother, Lord Strafford, 28 April 1713. (*Wentworth Papers*, p. 330.)
220 *"Mr. Addison's play was acted":*
    Berkeley to Sir John Percival, 16 April 1713. Benjamin Rand, *Berkeley and Percival* (Cambridge: Cambridge University Press, 1914), pp. 113–14. Pope's report to Caryll (1: 175) places Addison behind the scenes at least part of the time, sweating with concern for fear the applause "proceeded more from the hand than the head. This was the case too of the prologue-writer, who was clapped into a staunch Whig sore against his will, at almost every two lines." Gay remarks in a letter to Maurice Johnson of April 23 (*Letters*, p. 3), apropos of the audience's clapping "Particular parts" of both play and prologue, that "the couplet—

> These tears shall flow from a more gen'rous Cause,
> Such tears as Patriots shed for dying Laws—

never faild of raising a loud Clap." The opening night audience had been carefully "packed" by Steele to guarantee the play's success (see his preface to *The Drummer*, 1722, p. x), a circumstance that perhaps accounts for Addison's concern about the sincerity of the applause and Pope's embarrassment by it. An excellent discussion of the play in its contemporary context is Malcolm Kelsall's "The Meaning of Addison's *Cato*," in *Review of English Studies*, n.s. 17 (1966): 149–62.
222 *(As Pope told Caryll):*
    In the letter cited above.
222 *"Miscarriage of twenty good ones":*
    Dennis, 2: 43.
222 *"Resolv'd to remain in the wrong":*
    Ibid., pp. 41, 43.
223 *Seventeen days after the* Remarks upon Cato:
    Dennis published on July 11, Pope on the 28.
223 *"I shall die in the Bastile":*
    Pope, *Prose*, p. 156.

223 *"Cover'd with a* Longinus":
    Ibid., pp. 157–9.
224 *"Excess of his Frenzy"*:
    Ibid., pp. 166–7. Pope may also have replied to Dennis soon after his attack on the *Essay on Criticism* by publishing the anonymous squib entitled *The Critical Specimen.* See Pope, *Prose,* pp. xi–xviii and 3–18. It shows the author, whether Pope or another, making good use of Cervantes.
224 *Its success had aroused Pope's envy:*
    See Dennis, 2: 324–5, 371.
225 *"Was sorry to hear of it"*:
    Pope, *Correspondence,* 1: 184.
225 *"Teach the rest to sneer"*:
    Early Career, p. 113.

Chapter 11, In the Studio and on the Town

226 *An interest in drawing:*
    His letter to the *Spectator* of 4 November 1712 (no. 527), a few months before his settling down at Jervas's, records a fan he had lately painted with the story of Cephalus and Procris and presented to a "Lady" (*TE,* 6: 46–7). The fan later came into the possession of Sir Joshua Reynolds, who used to show it to his students as the product of an amateurishness to be avoided, "the work of one who paints only for amusement." Allan Cunningham, *The Lives of the Most Eminent British Painters and Sculptors* (1831) 1: 234. Quoted in Wimsatt, *Portraits* (p. 11), to which I am indebted at several points in my account of Jervas.
226 *Studied subsequently in Paris and Rome :*
    Jervas writes to Sir John Ellis from Paris in 1698 (May 26 and June 24), where he is studying the Louvre's collection of antique statues in plaster casts, and from Rome in 1700 (March 20). BL: Add. MS. 28,882, f. 292, and 28,885, f. 121. He is still in Rome on 24 February 1703, when he writes to Bishop John Hough. Wimsatt, p. 8.
226 *In glowing terms:*
    No. 4 (19 April 1709).
227 *"Knight of the Garter"*:
    Most or all of these portraits would presumably be copies of Jervas's work. The Garter Knight is probably the Duke of Kent, for whose installation in August 1713 Jervas was supposed to paint him in his Garter robes. Jervas to Sir William Trumbull [Summer 1713], Sherburn, "Letters," pp. 397–8.
228 *"A Figure like anything in Heaven or in Earth"*:
    The first quotation is from Lord Killanin, *Sir Godfrey Kneller and His Times* (London: Batsford, 1948), p. 48. The second is preserved in a notebook of Zachary Pearce's at Westminster: MS. 64896, p. 18. See also the letter of Richard Hill to Sir William Trumbull, who has been inquiring about Jervas's qualifications to do a portrait of his wife Judith: "He . . . will certainly make a good picture of my Lady; the only danger is it may chance not to be so like as we could wish." HMC Downshire, vol. 1, pt. 1 (1924), p. 900.
229 *"The waters under the earth"*:
    23 August 1713. *Correspondence,* 1: 188. In a letter to Swift of 8 December 1713 (1: 200), Pope reverses the joke to compliment Jervas on having "grievously offended" by making such likenesses.
229 *No Leonardo:*
    The portrait is now at Scone, having been in the possession of the earls of Mansfield since the time of the first earl, who was Pope's friend, young William Murray, later Lord Chief Justice. Sir John Hawkins reports (in his edition of Johnson, *Works,* 1787, 4: 90) Murray's telling him that the Betterton portrait was the only picture that Pope actually "finished" in the painters' sense, since the weakness of his eyes prevented. As for the poet's efforts with Swift, see Parnell's epigram, first published by C. J. Rawson and F. P. Lock in *RES,* n.s., 33 (1982): 150—

> On Mr. Pope drawing D: Swifts Picture.
>
> One author has anothers head begun
> Lett no man say it might be better don
> For since they both are Witts Ime very glad
> To find he has not drawn him twice as bad.

Happily for eighteenth-century studies, a complete edition of Parnell's poems with much new material, edited by C. J. Rawson and F. P. Lock, is now in press.

229 *In the Studio:*
Pope to Caryll, 12 June 1713 (1: 177).

229 *"Here first their entry made":*
For the poems from which these stanzas are taken, see *TE*, 6: 48–50. (Kathleen Mahaffey, "Pope's 'Artemisia' and 'Phryne' as Personal Satire," *RES*, n.s. 21 (1970): 466–71, believes the two sketches to be a dyptich of George I's two mistresses, Madame Kielmannsegge and Ehrengard Melusina Schulenberg). Another perhaps slightly later sketch (c. 1715) of about this period is relegated in *TE*, 6: 419–20, to "Attributed Poems" and not there reprinted. It is found, however, in Voltaire's "Small Leningrad Notebook" (T. Bestermann, ed., *Voltaire's Notebooks*, 2 vols. [Geneva, 1952], 1: 33) with the title "Of Mr. Popp upon M-stress Poltney," and since it has what I take to be genuine Popean touches, I reproduce it here (as a possible addition to the canon) in Voltaire's text. Its subject is the metamorphosis of Maria Gumley, daughter of John Gumley, a glass manufacturer, and reputedly at an earlier time mistress to Bolingbroke, on becoming the wife of William Pulteney:

> With scornful mien, and various toss of hair
> Fantastick, vain, and insolently fair[,]
> Gra[n]deur intoxicates her guiddy brain.
> She speaks ambitions, and she moves disdain[.]
> Far other carriage graced her virgin life[,]
> But Gombley's daughter's lost in Poltneis wife.
> O cou'd they [thy] Sire renowned in glas produce
> One faithful mir[r]or for his daughter's use[,]
> Wherein she might her haughty errors trace[,]
> And by reflexion learn to mind her face[,]
> Her wonted sweetness to her form restore[,]
> Be what she was, and charm mankind once more.

The poem is also given to Pope (with added couplet) in BL: Add. MS. 4456, ff 100, 102.

230 *"Something to commend":*
The last couplet in this passage seems to owe something to, or be owed something by, another epigram of Parnell's, *RES*, n.s., 33 (1982): 156.

> Once Pope under Jervais resolv'd to adventure
> & from a Good Poet Pope turnd an ill painter
> So from a Good Painter Charles Jervais we hope
> May turn an ill Poet by living with Pope
> Then Each may perform the true part of a friend
> While each will have something to blame or commend.

230 *To walk on "classic Ground":*
It is almost impossible to exaggerate the hold that Rome had on an educated eighteenth-century imagination. Gibbon's experience is typical: "But at the distance of twenty-five years I can neither forget nor express the strong emotions which agitated my mind as I first approached and entered the *eternal city*. After a sleepless night, I trod, with lofty step, the ruins of the Forum; each memorable spot where Romulus stood, or Tully spoke, or Caesar fell was at once present to my eye; and several days of intoxication were lost or enjoyed before I could descend to a cool and minute investigation." *Autobiography*, ed., M. M. Reese (London: Routledge and Kegan Paul, 1970), p. 84.

231 *Sought out "conversation":*
Pope to Caryll, 1: 177.

231 *Politically like-minded coterie:*
Bonamy Dobrée, *Essays in Biography, 1680–1726* (London: Oxford University Press, 1925), p. 264. Button himself was not particularly prepossessing, if we may believe the

anonymous *Apollo's Strategem: or, Button Unmasqu'd. A Tale* (1719), which otherwise is complimentary to the group.

231 *"Do nothing else but laugh":*
   Spence, no. 249. See also *Correspondence*, 1: 190, where after Rowe's spending a week at Binfield with him, Pope comments on his "vivacity and gayety of disposition."

231 *The medium that passed with poets of the mid-century for blank verse:*
   From 1725 to 1728, Young published a sequence of witty satires on fame entitled *The Universal Passion*. Though marred by gross flatteries and flat stretches, they are among the more sparkling productions of their kind before Pope's work of the 1730s, which they influenced. Young's blank verse *The Complaint, or Night Thoughts on Life, Death, and Immortality*—a kind of *In Memoriam* on stilts, lacking only Tennyson's genius—was published in parts between 1742 and 1745.

232 *"Writes to honest T[ickell]":*
   In *Horace, umbrae* are the uninvited guests who tag along with the distinguished guest (*Sat. II*, vii, 22; *Ep. I*, v, 28). Pope's Umbra has been variously identified as Walter Carey and as Addison's cousin Eustace Budgell. The latter seems to me more likely. See *TE*, 6: 140–1, but also J. M. Osborn, "Addison's Tavern Companion and Pope's 'Umbra,'" *PQ*, 42 (1963): 217–25.

232 *A series of subscription lectures:*
   Whigs, generally, were inclined to be sympathetic with the newer intellectual movements in theology and science.

233 *"Unphilosophize us into mere mortals":*
   14 August 1713. (1: 185–6). For comment on Whiston's influence, see George Sherburn, "Pope and 'The Great Shew of Nature,'" *The Seventeenth Century: Studies in the History of English Thought and Literature from Bacon to Pope*, ed., R. F. Jones (Stanford University Press, 1951), pp. 306–15; also Marjorie Nicolson and George Rousseau, *"This Long Disease My Life": Alexander Pope and the Sciences* (Princeton: Princeton University Press, 1968), part 3.

234 *"Has ever conduced so immediately to morals as this":*
   To Caryll [February 1713?] (1: 173). Pope is reporting his response to reading the play in manuscript—which "drew tears from me in several parts of the fourth and fifth acts." According to Spence, nos. 174 and 175, Pope suggested several small revisions, which were accepted.

234 *"Leads directly to the Heart":*
   TE, 6: 99–100. The epigram was occasioned by an earlier one on a lady who had wept while watching *Cato* and is obviously intended to poke fun at some of the extremer forms of affective (or, as it is oftener called today, reader-response) criticism. Poetry, as Pope stresses in his *Essay on Criticism* and *Epistle to Augustus*, must move the feelings; but this is quite another thing from asking it to open the sphincters or (A. E. Housman's test!) make the bristles rise while shaving.

235 *"When Cato's clapped, Damon will be so too":*
   To Caryll, 30 April 1713 (1: 176). In *TE*, 6, this poem appears (quite wrongly, it seems to me) among poems of doubtful authorship. Pope's sidelong introduction of it as an "epigram, which was dispersed about the coffee houses in Holy Week, and is much approved of by our wits," the style and content of the verse, and the circumstance that the appearance of unidentified lines *not* by Pope himself in his letters to Caryll would be all but unprecedented (the only exception occurs in his letter of 12 June 1713 and is self-explanatory) incline me to belive it genuine.

235 *Its original "founding" purpose:*
   The fullest account of the Club and its productions is found in *The Memoirs of Scriblerus*, ed., Charles Kerby-Miller (Yale University Press, 1950).

237 *"But injudiciously in each":*
   Pope to Spence, no. 135.

237 *"His Mistress anima rationalis":*
   June. Swift *Correspondence*, 2: 42.

238 *"Haec olim meminisse juvabit":*
   Pope, *Correspondence*, 1: 216–17.

238 *"Fertile in stratagems and jeux d'esprit":*
   Kerby-Miller, p. 28.

238 *The Latin he had just composed:*
    Goldsmith, *Life of Thomas Parnell, D.D.* (1770), pp. 45–6.

238 *The marks of his oversight:*
    Many fragments of this work and others were burnt by Pope shortly before his death. Spence, no. 139; BL: Add. MS. 35, 396, f. 250.

Chapter 12, "Humour, Wit, a Native Ease and Grace"

239 *A friend's word that she is unfaithful:*
    Above, p. 837—93: *The legend.*

239 *John Weston was coming to dinner:*
    Correspondence, 1: 119 and n., 123, 132, 142–3, 428. See also Dilke, 1: 128ff.

239 *"Pity and comfort, the distressed":*
    28 May 1712 (1: 143).

239 *One of John Caryll's cousins, Anne Cope:*
    Caryll's first cousin, she married a Captain Cope whose first name is unknown. On rejoining his regiment in Minorca, Cope married bigamously another woman and remained deaf to all appeals for support. Efforts to put pressure on him through army channels seem to have been unavailing. Dilke (*Papers of a Critic*), 1: 142ff., and Howard Erskine-Hill, *The Social Mileu of Alexander Pope* (New Haven and London: Yale University Press, 1975), pp. 74–6.

240 *"Handsomer than all others":*
    19 July [1713] (1: 181). At 1: 205 he speaks of Mrs. Marriot as an old acquaintance, but this may be in jest.

241 *"Fishponds, Arbours, Mrs. Betty M[arriot]!":*
    [1714?] (1: 205–6).

241 *Which he published at twenty-four:*
    TE, 6: 62–5.

242 *Giving his poems for maidenheads:*
    Above, p. 151.

242 *Teresa some three months longer than Martha:*
    September [1714] (1: 258).

242 *Prospects for making suitable marriages:*
    Lyster Blount's will, dated 15 May 1710, provided £1,500 for each daughter, plus the proceeds of his personal estate divided between them, plus £1,000 to each on her marriage and £2,000 more (to be divided?) "payable to my said Daughters in and by certain Indentures bearing the same date with this my will." Later documents revised these handsome bequests to modest annual payments from the estate. Mapledurham Papers.

243 *"Sic positae quoniam suaves":*
    Wimsatt, *Portraits,* p. 10.

243 *Another of Pope's poems to Teresa:*
    "To a Young Lady, on her leaving the Town after the Coronation," ll. 45–6:

        Just when his fancy points your [Teresa's] sprightly eyes,
        Or sees the blush of Parthenissa [Martha] rise.

In a later reading, "soft Parthenia" replaces "Parthenissa." Pope's half-sister Magdalen, on the other hand, thought Martha something of a romp (i.e., mischief-lover) and Pope quite mistaken about her character. In the light of the entire record of their friendship, this seems suspect, though Magdalen may have been right in thinking her brother too easily deceived by people generally. Bodley Ms. Eng. lett. d. 59, f. 81; "New Anecdotes," p. 349.

243 *"The best of any Lady in England":*
    25 May 1712 (1: 143).

243 *Teresa . . . read nothing:*
    Pope to Martha and Teresa Blount [? September 1714] (1: 252).

243 *Frame fashionably japanned:*
    The value of the furnishings in "Mad: Martha's Roome" is estimated at £11.17.9; in "Mad. Teresa's Roome" at £25.12.6. Mapledurham Papers.

247 *Chose finally not to embrace:*
  The Mapledurham archives contain letters not only from Henry Moore of Fawley Court (located just north of Henley about twenty miles from Mapledurham) in which Teresa figures as "Zephalinda," Martha as "Parthenissa," and he as "Alexis" (J. T. Hillhouse, "Teresa Blount and 'Alexis,'" *Modern Language Notes*, 40 (1925): 88–91), but from other admirers as well. All make it clear that from girlhood she was praised for her great beauty, vivacity, "uninterrupted flow of spirits," and "good youmer," i.e., humor. (Mapledurham Papers: an unidentified correspondent to Teresa, undated; and Helen Eyre to Teresa, 4 May 1704.)
248 *"Laugh them together":*
  Spence, no. 104.
251 *Contemporary Rosicrucian lore:*
  Not to be forgotten, however, is Milton's *Comus*, ll. 298–301, and *Rape*, 2: 65–8; also *Comus*, ll. 453–61, and *Rape*, 1: 35–42. Pope "commas" in his copies ("Pope's Books," nos. 115, 118) both *Comus* passages. For a fine treatment of Pope's use of Milton, see David Fairer's *Pope's Imagination* (Manchester University Press, 1984).
251 *Fortunes of epic heroes:*
  See on all this the discussion and notes in *TE*, 2: 81–212. For a selection of criticism old and new, see *Pope: The Critical Heritage*, ed., John Barnard (London: Routledge Kegan Paul, 1973), pp. 93–113; *Pope: The Rape of the Lock. A Casebook*, ed., J. D. Hunt (London: Macmillan, 1968); *Pope: The Rape of the Lock*, ed., G. S. Rousseau (Englewood Cliffs: Prentice-Hall, 1979). Not to be overlooked are J. S. Cunningham's *The Rape of the Lock* (London: Edward Arnold, 1961), and Charles Martindale, "Sense and Sensibility: The Child and the Man in the *Rape of the Lock*," *Modern Language Review*, 78 (1983): 273–84.
253 *"An overturned bell without a clapper":*
  Guardian, no. 114.
255 *"The most consummate Work of it":*
  No. 116 (5 January 1710).
257 *Beautifully displayed dark curl:*
  In the correspondences of her youth, Teresa is usually addressed as "Zephalinda," a pseudonym nicely expressive of her zephyrlike wayward personality. One surviving fragment, however—this from a male correspondent—indicates that she was also addressed as "Bellinda." Mapledurham Papers.

Chapter 13, Insurrections Large and Small

258 *Had life in it:*
  One should not forget that the minute Jacobite army won two engagements against the regulars before succumbing at Culloden.
  On the Jacobite movement generally, including the '15, see G. H. Jones, *The Main Stream of Jacobitism* (Harvard University Press, 1954); Sir Charles Petrie, *The Jacobite Movement* (London; Eyre and Spottiswoode, 1959); C. Sinclair–Stevenson, *Inglorious Rebellion: The Jacobite Risings of 1708, 1715, 1719* (London: Hamish Hamilton, 1971); R. C. Jarvis, *Collected Papers on the Jacobite Risings*, 2 vols. (Manchester University Press, 1971–2); P. S. Fritz, *The English Ministers and Jacobitism between the Rebellions of 1715 and 1745* (Toronto University Press, 1975); Bruce Lenman, *The Jacobite Risings in Britain, 1689–1746* (London: Eyre Methuen, 1980); and F. J. McLynn, "Issues and Motives in the Jacobite Rising of 1745," *The Eighteenth Century*, 23 (1982): 97–133. See also an early paper by P. Purcell, "The Jacobite Rising of 1715 and Roman Catholics," *English Historical Review*, 44 (1929): 418–32.
258 *Other claims made themselves felt:*
  For an especially fine account of controversies and confusions in the grounds on which William III's takeover was argued to be justifiable or unjustifiable, see J. P. Kenyon, *Revolution Principles: The Politics of Party, 1689–1720* (Cambridge University Press, 1977). See also Geoffrey Holmes, *British Politics in the Age of Anne* (London: Macmillan, 1967); and Eveline Cruickshanks, *Political Untouchables: The Tories and the '45* (New York: Holmes and Meier, 1979), esp. ch. 1, together with her essay in the Jarvis collection cited

above. Also of particular help is Mark Goldie, "The Revolution of 1689 and the Structure of Political Argument; An Essay and an Annotated Bibliography of Pamphlets in the Allegiance Controversy," *Bulletin of Research in the Humanities*, 83 (1980): 473–564. On Pope in particular, see two valuable essays by Howard Erskine-Hill, "Alexander Pope: The Political Poet in His Time," *E-CS*, 15 (1981–2): 123–48, and "Literature and the Jacobite Cause: was there a Rhetoric of Jacobitism?" *Ideology and Conspiracy*, ed. Eveline Cruickshanks (1982).

259 *Corresponding with the enemy:*
Marlborough, for instance, sent the Pretender £2,000 in August of 1715, no doubt as a form of insurance. Roxburgh club: *Stuart Papers*, 2 vols. (1889), 1: 401, 407.

259 *"Quite another thing":*
John Byrom, "An Admonition against Swearing. Address'd to an Officer in the Army," *Chetham Society Publications*, n.s. 30 (1894), 572. Byrom was a poet of sorts and a Fellow of Trinity College, Cambridge.

260 *"Destitute of regular troops":*
William Cobbett, *The Parliamentary History of England*, 36 vols. (1806–20), 10: 402–3.

260 *Earn five pence a day:*
Daniel Defoe, *A Tour through the Whole Island of Great Britain*, ed., G. D. H. Cole, 2 vols. (London: Peter Davies, 1927), 2: 162.

260 *Harvests of the Tyburn tree:*
See *Albion's Fatal Tree: Crime and Society in Eighteenth-Century England*, eds., Douglas Hay, Peter Linebaugh, J. G. Rule, E. P. Thompson, and Cal Winslow (New York: Random House, 1975), pp. 17–117.

261 *"The kiss of death":*
Lenman (*Jacobite Risings*), p. 124.

261 *Immediately following the queen's death:*
From the Queen's death onward, the country was full of rumors. On August 6, Lady Mary Wortley Montagu writes agitatedly from Yorkshire to her husband in London of a fleet allegedly seen off the coast of Scotland. Lady MWM, *Letters*, 1: 215.

263 *"Expectation of the Successor":*
23 September 1714 (1: 254). Since this letter is known only from Pope's editions, it may have been edited before publication. That he did not excise the ambiguous allusion to "the Successor" is perhaps evidence that it was not.

263 *"Chosen City-Poet":*
23 July 1715 (1: 307–9).

264 *"So wicked a spirit as that of persecution":*
16 August 1714 (1: 241). The first eight words of the quotation are taken from the letter as Pope published it. They seem to have been inadvertently omitted from the copy of Pope's manuscript letter made by Caryll's scribe, from which Sherburn prints.

264 *"At least to wish generously":*
16 December 1715 (1: 324).

265 *[Lives] "taken off in cold [blood]":*
11 November 1715 (1: 320–1). See also Blount to Pope [September, 1714?] (1: 248): "It is much at one to you and me who sit at the helm, provided they will permit us to sail quietly in the great ship."

265 *Noncommittal or quite uncomplimentary:*
His references to James II and Charles I are noncommittal; those to James I and Charles II not complimentary.

266 *"Looked upon with affection":*
20 March 1716 (1: 335–6). Pope's views could, however, be shared by Jacobites of many complexions, convinced that their best hope was for a peaceful Restoration, as in 1660.

266 *"With Notes to each Book":*
Though no copy of the "Proposals" for the translation is known to survive, an advertisement in the third edition of the *Rape of the Lock* probably preserves the gist of them (*TE*, 7: xxxvi n).

267 *"Changed the face of printed English":*
The comment is by Nicholas Barker, himself an expert in these matters, reviewing (*Times Literary Supplement*, 3 September 1976) David Foxon's superb Lyell Lectures, *Pope*

and the Eighteenth-Century Book Trade, to be published (one hopes) shortly. In this and the succeeding paragraphs, I draw on Foxon's work, esp. ch. 2.

267 *Contract with Lintot on March 23, 1714:*

Egerton Charter 129. In some respects, this document foretells the end of the patronage system less dramatically but more effectively than Johnson's famous letter to Lord Chesterfield. Pope's limitation of the quarto and its special features to his subscribers was his insurance against additional copies being printed off and sold at the same or a lower price to casual purchasers. In that event, those who had helped underwrite a new and perhaps risky undertaking by committing money to it in advance (in Pope's case, the down payment of two guineas) enjoyed no advantage or could even be placed at a disadvantage vis-à-vis the ordinary book buyer who dropped in off the street. The virtue of the limitation may be seen in a remark of Edmund Gibson's, future bishop of London and author of the monumental *Codex Juris Ecclesiae Anglicanae* (1713), who explained to a friend when that book appeared following a successful subscription that the whole body of booksellers sought to obtain and sell copies at the subscribers' or even at a discount price in order to discredit subscription publishing, since it had the advantage of allowing an author both to initiate a publication and receive a due reward from it. If they were to succeed, Gibson notes, they will "have Authors entirely at their mercy, which is the great point they aim at." BL: Add. MS. 45,511: ff. 101–2: to Robert Nelson, 26 December 1713.

267 *Three thousand copies in four days:*

Pope to Caryll, 13 March 1714 (1: 214).

268 *Duodecimo editions did handsomely:*

Six such editions were issued in Pope's lifetime, and from the two of 1720 alone David Foxon (Lyell Lectures) calculates Lintot's profit to have been approximately £2,250. In the long run, Lintot and his son must have fared nearly as well as Pope.

268 *"Did not fall out of heaven":*

Pat Rogers, "Pope and His Subscribers," *Publishing History*, 3 (1978): 7–36. This splendidly executed piece of work covers Pope's Shakespeare and the *Odyssey* as well as the *Iliad* translation. For an illuminating complementary essay stressing class and political connections among the *Iliad* subscribers (with a glance toward those of the *Odyssey*), see Matthew Hodgart's "The Subscription List for Pope's *Iliad*, 1715," *The Dress of Words: Essays on Restoration and Eighteenth-Century Literature in Honor of Richmond P. Bond*, ed., R. B. White, Jr. (University of Kansas Press, 1978), pp. 25–34.

268 *For the new translator:*

"Extract from the MS. Diary of White Kennet." Quoted in Swift, *Correspondence*, 5: 228–9.

268 *"Tagged with two guineas":*

The dates of the three confidences to Caryll are January 9, March 19, and April 19 (1: 207, 215, 218–19).

268 *Did not actually appear till May:*

No copy is known. It would be instructive to be able to compare his list of subscribers at that date with the list published in volume I.

269 *Homer's effects or hints:*

Pope pays considerable attention to these in his notes to the translation.

269 *Frightened lest it never end:*

Spence, no. 197.

270 *"His blindness":*

The quotations are from Pope to Parnell, 25 May or 1 June 1714 (1: 225–6), Spence, no. 197; and Pope to Caryll, 25 July 1714 (1: 238). For Homer's curing him of poetry, see his letter to Caryll, [13] July [1714] and to Broome, 16 June [1715] (1: 236, 297).

270 *"Even to buy books":*

Spence, no. 192.

270 *Return was substantially reduced:*

Pope to Caryll, 13 July [1714] and 16 August 1714 (1: 236–7, 242 and n.).

270 *Unspecified but guessable:*

Though in these early years offers of a pension were occasionally made to Pope despite his religion (his friend Craggs would have concealed it in the Secret Service list), he seems always to have begged off, fearing, no doubt, for his independence. See Spence, nos. 228–30; *Correspondence*, 1: 271, 457; and *Imit. Hor., Ep. I*, vii 65–7.

272 *Misunderstandings could almost be counted on:*

That Addison detested Roman Catholicism, which he held up to contempt in his *Letter from Italy* (1704) and which, in the *Spectator* (no. 201, 20 October 1711), he called "one huge overgrown Body of childish and idle Superstitions," cannot have made the friendship easier to maintain; nor can his pronounced dislike of Bolingbroke.

272 *"Fine Flamms":*

To Caryll, 31 July 1710 (1: 94). Pope attributes the phrase to Robert Sydney, fourth earl of Leicester, a friend of Wycherley's. He uses the term again in the manuscript of his 1717 Preface. ("Pope's 1717 Preface, with a Transcription of the Manuscript Text," *Augustan Worlds*, eds., J. C. Hilson, M. M. B. Jones, and J. R. Watson (Leicester, 1978), p. 99, l. 128), and at *Correspondence*, 3: 500.

272 *He had got a clap:*

Pope to Fortescue, 18 March [1725] (2: 290).

272 *"Never so serious an Occasion":*

Jervas to Pope [1716?] (1: 341). Machiavelli makes a similar confession to Guicciardini: *The Chief Works*, tr., A. H. Gilbert (Duke University Press, 1965), 2: 993.

272 *When drunk more charming than when sober:*

Edward Blount refers to the kind of welcome the poet liked best, "which is, to be free to . . . do what you have most a mind to." To Pope, 30 August 1719 (2: 11). On the poet's great charm when he chose to exert himself, see Grace Cole to Frances Seymour, countess of Hertford, 14 October 1729. H. S. Hughes, "A Romantic Correspondence of the Year 1729," *Modern Philology*, 37 (1939): 198. Hervey gives his opinion in a letter to Stephen Fox, 4 September 1731. *Lord Hervey and His Friends*, ed., the Earl of Ilchester (London: Murray, 1950), pp. 83–4. Chesterfield's comment, which is similar, occurs in his "character" of Pope, *Characters by Lord Chesterfield Contrasted with Characters of the Same Great Personages by other respectable Writers* (1778), pp. 14–16. Pope's "drunken" letter to Elizabeth, duchess of Hamilton [1717], appears in *Correspondence*, 1: 436–8. Sherburn suggests that the supposed intoxication of the author may be a jocose fiction corresponding to a recent letter he had received from the duchess [June 1717?], written by G. Maddison (probably her secretary)— "My Lady Dutchess being drunk *at this present* & not able to write," etc. (1: 404). One notes, however, that a letter to Martha Blount of [December 1716] ends: "I am Melancholy—and Drunk" (1: 379) and that William Kent writes to Burlington, 28 November 1738 (4: 150) of Pope's being "very drunk last sunday night." In the opinion of Dr. William King, principal of St. Mary's Hall, Oxford (*Political and Literary Anecdotes*, 1819, pp. 20–21), Pope in his later years hastened his death by dram drinking—as favorite an anodyne then as now. (King was, however, a teetotaler, which may have influenced his opinion.) Johnson (p. 199), who may have had his information by way of King's Oxford circle, adds that Pope affected to be angry when offered a dram, but nevertheless drank it.

273 *"Slept all the time you have been with me":*

9 September 1732 (3: 313). For other instances of Pope falling asleep in company, see Pope to Caryll, 15 December 1713 (1: 204), Pope to Sarah, duchess of Marlborough [1740?] (4: 259); Johnson, p. 198; and of course the well-known lines (13–14) in the *Epistle to Fortescue* (*Imit. Hor., Sat. II*, i, 13–14).

> I nod in Company, I wake at Night,
> Fools rush into my Head, and so I write.

273 *"Delicate, easy, and engaging":*

John Boyle, fifth earl of Cork and Orrery, *Remarks on the Life and Writings of Jonathan Swift* (1752), p. 145.

273 *"The first man of the age":*

Thomas Tickell's preface to his edition (1721) of Addison's *Works*. Addison's need to instruct, edify, and be in some way exemplary is seen at its worst in the well-known anecdote about his summoning his dissolute stepson Lord Warwick to his deathbed to "see in what peace a Christian can die." Edward Young, *Conjectures on Original Composition* (1759), pp. 101–2. It must not be overlooked, however, that to the same impulse we owe much of what is most valuable in the *Spectator*.

273 *"Equally full information"*:
Works, ed., Lady Trevelyan, 8 vols. (1866), 7: 54. Macaulay's eyebrow-raiser about the novel is on pp. 97–8. Something of the same balance has been cited as the salient characteristic of Addison's thought by Edward and Lillian Bloom, "Addison and Eighteenth-Century 'Liberalism,'" (*Journal of the History of Ideas*, 12 [1951]: 560–83.) It is a characteristic that can, however, eventuate in blandness—Arnold called Addison's writing "perfect in lucidity, measure, and propriety," but in ideas "perfectly trite and barren"—and that has suggested to some observers a certain timidity of outlook or inability to commit (Bonamy Dobrée, "The First Victorian," *Essays in Biography, 1680–1726* [1925], p. 257).

274 *Transmute dross to gold:*
Spence, nos. 157–8.

274 *"Well said, Dick":*
Reprint of the 1743 first edition by the Golden Cockerel Press (1930), p. 48. For the same "unmistakable note of the literary oracle patronizing a lesser man" (in this instance Ambrose Philips), see Peter Smithers' *The Life of Joseph Addison* (Oxford: Clarendon, 1968), p. 93.

274 *By one of Addison's friends:*
Thomas Burnet: see *TE*, 6: 100. Being the man he was, Addison undoubtedly found Pope's ribald streak offensive in itself, even in such mild expressions of it as the little epigram entitled *Two or Three; or a Receipt to Make a Cuckold*. This seems to have been circulating in the coffee houses ("Alexis" to Teresa Blount, 30 September 1713: Mapledurham Papers) as early as 20 September 1713, just about the time Button's was turning against Pope; appeared again, anonymously, in Lintot's *Miscellany Poems* (2nd ed., published 3 December 1713); and was then republished with ascription to Pope by Edmund Curll and John Oldmixon in 1714 (*Poems and translations. By Several Hands*, p. 211). I give the *TE* text, which follows that of *Miscellany Poems*.

Two or *Three* Visits, and *Two* or *Three* Bows,
Two or *Three* civil Things, *Two* or *Three* Vows,
Two or *Three* Kisses, with *Two* or *Three* Sighs,
Two or *Three* Jesus's—and let me dyes—
Two or *Three* Squeezes, and *Two* or *Three* Towses,
With *Two* or *Three* thousand Pound lost at their Houses,
Can never fail Cuckolding *Two* or *Three* Spouses.

275 *"Alike reserv'd to blame, or to commend":*

"I had been up very late the night before you did me the honour to call on me, but as I have very seldome an occasion for such an excuse I hope it will not hinder you from comeing this way to let me know where I may wait upon you, and in the meantime return you my humble thanks for the noble entertainment you have sent me and which I have hitherto found in everything that comes from your pen." (fMS Eng 1336 (1). Houghton Library, Harvard University, for whose kindness in allowing me to publish, I am deeply grateful).

275 *"Cannot repeat without Vanity":*
TE, 7: 23. See also Spence, no. 161.

275 *To forward the subscription:*
1: 196. On the genuineness of this letter, whose substance both Sherburn and Walter Graham accept, see *Correspondence*, 1: 196n, and *The Letters of Joseph Addison* (Oxford: Clarendon, 1941), p. 280.

275 *No deeds, only words:*
To Caryll, 1 May 1714 (1: 220).

276 *"With very high commendations":*
Spence, no. 162.

276 *The entire Iliad:*
Details of the agreement are given in R. E. Tickell, *Thomas Tickell and the Eighteenth-Century Poets* (London: Constable, 1931), pp. 38–9. Tickell was to receive 500 guineas for the twenty-four books (the difference in copy-money suggests an obvious reason for Pope's preference of Lintot over Tonson), but if Books 1–4 failed to sell satisfactorily, the contract lapsed.

276 *An Oxford origin which he came to doubt:*

According to Pope's story to Spence (no. 163), corroborated by Spence's further inquiries, Tickell's closest friend at Oxford, the poet Young, denied that he could have made any such translation while there—and, Pope adds, "Tickell himself, who is a fair and worthy man, has since in a manner as good as owned it to me." Thomas Hearne, who was Bodley's second in command during Tickell's tenure as Fellow of Queen's, took a less charitable view of the man: "This Tickle is a vain conceited Coxcomb, & not able to write any thing solid, nor indeed intelligibly." *Collections*, 3: 318.

276 *"Interlined by Addison":*

Mist's Weekly Journal of 11 June 1715 attributes the authorship to "Mr. Tickel and a Person who made his Fortune by one Campaign [Addison's very successful poem of 1704 about the Duke of Marlborough's victories]." An anonymous spoof entitled *Homer in a Nut-Shell*, published the same month, found the *Iliad* "incomparably done by Mr. Pope" and looked forward to the *Odyssey*, "design'd to be infinitely better Translated by Mr. Tickell, alias Addison." Steele, in the dedication of his 1722 edition of Addison's failed play, *The Drummer*, a piece Tickell had omitted from the collected *Works*, refers to Tickell as "the reputed Translator" and challenges him to bring out a second book of Homer now that Addison is dead. Later in the century, Joseph Warton reported (*Essay on the Genius and Writings of Pope*, 2 [1782]: 246) that he had been told by several of Addison's and Pope's contemporaries—Edward Young, the poet Walter Harte, Lord Bathurst, and Lord Lyttelton—that the translation was "certainly" Addison's. Watts's evidence, however (*Addisoniana* [1803], 1: 167), seems conclusive. See also R. E. Tickell (*Tickell and the Eighteenth-Century Poets*), ch. 3. It may well have been Addison's habit of advertising his skill in improving the work of others—"O Sir, 'twas quite another thing when first it was brought to me" (Spence, no. 157)—that caused the translation to be ascribed to him rather than to Tickell.

276–77 *Pamphlets to ridicule his venture:*

Evoked by the supposition that he was to publish (as advertised the previous December) in early March.

277 *"Performance of your Articles":*

The quotations are from *The High-German Doctor*, 10 December 1714, *Aesop At the Bear-Garden*, published 10 March 1715, and *Homerides*, published 7 March 1715. Cited by Guerinot, pp. 19, 25, 23, 22.

277 *Remained in place:*

The two men were George Duckett and Thomas Burnet, the latter a son of Gilbert Burnet, bishop of Salisbury. Burnet in London writes Duckett in Dorset, on 2 February 1715, that their *The Hump Conference* is to appear "just a fourtnight before his [Pope's] first Volume"—still expected in March. On February 19 he tells Duckett he has shown the poem to Addison, who advised changing what was to have been a dialogue piece into a narrative and "to strike out all Reflections upon the poor fellow's person." He has also softened the title to *Homerides*, he adds, but "that Pope may see I coud be sharp upon his Person if I woud, I have placed the Greek Sentence [about Thersites] at the head, but have not translated it." After publication, Burnet writes Duckett on March 26, apparently answering a protest against the shift in policy, that it would have been a mistake to have printed *The Hump Conference* as it originally stood because Pope's person draws sympathy: readers are even resentful of the Thersites motto. Then he adds, in a sentence that (rightly or wrongly) accuses Addison of self-serving, "I believe you guess right, that Addison did this out of no manner of good will to me." *Letters of Thomas Burnet to George Duckett, 1712–1722*, ed., D. N. Smith (Roxburghe Club, 1914), pp. 80, 81, 85. These passages are quoted also in Guerinot, p. 21. The Greek motto is from the *Iliad*, 2: 216–19 (translation mine).

278 *Pope published on June 6:*

A specimen copy of Book I of the *Iliad* seems to have been circulated among potential subscribers as early as January 1715. This may have been a printed copy, as Sherburn conjectures (*Early Career*, p. 139n), in which case there were doubtless other copies and one is left wondering why no such specimen has ever been seen. Perhaps, in fact, the specimen copy was in Pope's beautiful printing hand. We know from Gay (*Letters*, ed., C. F. Burgess [Oxford: Clarendon, 1966], p. 8) that after some weeks of study and translation in the country with Parnell, Pope had come to town by 8 June 1714, "with him the first Book of Homer," presumably for the purpose of passing it about and attracting subscribers.

278 *"The latter has more of Homer":*
1: 294, 305.

278 *"Overheateth the Oven":*
George Savile, first marquess of Halifax, "Moral Thoughts and Reflections," *Complete Works*, ed., Walter Raleigh (Oxford: Clarendon, 1912), p. 237.

278 *It came from Addison's future stepson:*
Edward Henry Rich, earl of Warwick, whose mother Charlotte, the countess dowager of Warwick, Addison married in August 1716. As he was a profligate eighteen-year-old at the time, who did not approve of his mother's marrying Addison, his testimony is open to question. It seems more credible that he interpreted what may have been a simple act of generosity on Addison's part—ten guineas, say, bestowed on an ever-needy Gildon—as a reward for having attacked Pope as "Sawney Dapper" in his *A New Rehearsal* of 1714 (reissued 1715).

279 *"The Art of Criticism":*
Spectator, no. 523 (20 December 1711). Ault argues persuasively (p. 109) that Pope replies to this charge of Addison's in the closing lines of his *Temple of Fame* (published in 1715 but in progress earlier), which explicitly repudiate the idea of rising on "the fall'n Ruins of Another's Fame" (l. 520).

279 *Most famous poem,* The Campaign *(1705):*
H. B. Wheatley and Peter Cunningham, *London Past and Present*, 3 vols. (1891), 2: 198.

279 *Highest honor along with Swift:*
Epistle to Augustus, 213–20 (*Imit. Hor., Ep. II*, i).

279 *The Roman poet whom the eighteenth century loved best:*
As Addison had once intended to publish his *Dialogues* in 1713, Pope's tribute may have been written before the quarrel. Still, it was in 1721 that he allowed it to be published in Addison's *Works*.

280 *Epistle to Dr. Arbuthnot:*
I give the passage as it finally appeared in the *Epistle*. For earlier versions, see *TE*, 6: 142ff, 283ff. Some of the thoughts that went into it are already present in a letter of 15 July 1715 (1: 306–7).

282 *Suspension of hostilities that followed:*
Spence, no. 166. Jervas, early on, made apparently unavailing efforts to reconcile his two friends (1: 244–5, 262). In a letter to Philip Yorke, first earl of Hardwicke, 10 August 1765, Thomas Birch reports having just seen some of Swift's papers (sent him by a bookseller), among them a copy of the *Epistle to Dr. Arbuthnot* with a note—beside the Atticus passage?—saying that Addison and Pope "were at last reconciled by my advice." (BL: Add. MS. 35,400, f. 272b). The remark is somewhat mystifying since Swift was in Dublin from 1714 till 1726, and Addison was dead when Swift visited England in 1726 and 1727. William Ayre, in his hastily put together *Memoirs of the Life and Writings of Alexander Pope* (2 vols., 1745), 1: 100–2, tells of an attempt by Steele and Gay to reconcile the two men that eventuated in an even greater hostility and thereby precipitated the Atticus lines. According to Ayre, Steele persuaded them to meet, Gay being present. Whereupon instead of the apology or conciliatory spirit that apparently Pope, Steele, and Gay expected, Addison gave Pope the dressing down of his life, saying his vanity was "too great for his Merit," his Homer "an ill-executed thing and not equal to *Tickell*'s," and his verse in general always much improved after he [Addison] and Steele had corrected it. (Here he evidently had in mind *The Messiah*, which was first published in the *Spectator* and for one verse of which Steele suggested a revision that Pope adopted—as Addison, for all we know, may equally have done.) Then, according to Ayre, Pope gave Addison as good as he got, and the two having parted in some heat and "without any Ceremony," Pope soon after (Ayre says "immediately") composed the portrait.

It is certainly not psychologically implausible that the anger underlying Pope's lines should have been exacerbated or brought to a head by some such particular meeting, and the fact that this is the only piece of information in Ayre's *Memoirs* whose source is not readily traceable to printed matter available to him gives it a more interesting status than anything else in his book. But this, of course, says nothing about its actual reliability. One detail is certainly unreliable: no poet ever wrote lines of such exquisite precision and perception "immediately" after an angry encounter.

282 *"Has an entertaining wit":*

The gist of Addison's compliment (which may pardonably have seemed to Pope to lose some of its gloss by appearing in a newspaper mostly given over to sneers at Jacobites, Roman Catholics, High Church Tories, and all others who could not share in its editor's easy adulation of the Hanoverian regime) is that "the illiterate among our Countreymen [i.e., those who lack the classical languages]" may learn to judge the most perfect of epics, the *Aeneid*, from Dryden's translation; and that the parts of Homer that Pope has so far published "give us reason to think that the *Iliad* will appear in English with as little Disadvantage to that immortal Poem." A suspicious reader—which let us hope in this instance Pope was not—might wonder just how far the final eight words of that sentence were intended to double back on themselves, especially if he recalled *Spectator*, no. 279 (19 January 1712), where Addison had taken Dryden to task for allowing thoughts "affected and unnatural," or "mean and vulgar," or both, to misrepresent Vergil's "just and natural" sentiments. Burnet's tribute was more generous, allowing that Pope had "nothing in his whole Poem that is not Homer's, but the Language. And I think one may say of his Translation, as one wou'd of a copy by Titian of one of his own Pictures, that nothing can be better but the Original" (p. 89). See also Burnet to Duckett, 1 June 1716. *Letters of Thomas Burnet*, p. 99. For fuller accounts of the Addison-Pope relationship and quarrel, see *Early Career*, ch. 5, and Ault, ch. 6.

282 *Apologize for an unspecified injury done him:*

Spence, no. 187. Addison did not explain to Gay what the injury was, but acknowledged that he had injured him "greatly" and that if he lived "he would make it up to him"—presumably by his influence with the government.

Chapter 14, High Life

283 *Already one of Pope's friends:*

Pope's friendship with Bolingbroke, most often associated with the period after 1724 on his return from exile, probably began much earlier. Pope told Spence that Bolingbroke was one of his oldest acquaintances (no. 150), and this could well be, since they had a warm mutual friend in Sir William Trumbull, whom Bolingbroke like Pope admired and with whom he corresponded off and on for a dozen years (1698–1710). It seems hardly likely that two such close friends of Sir William's, despite their difference in age (Bolingbroke was ten years Pope's senior), should never have encountered each other at Easthamstead. In any event, they would speedily have met through Swift, Gay, or another during the period of the Tory ministry. We know that in January 1715, for instance, two months before Bolingbroke's flight to France, Pope stopped off to visit him at Bucklebury, his Berkshire estate, for "a few days" in the course of a journey of his own to Binfield. (Pope to Congreve, 16 January 1715, 1: 275). Though there is question about the dating of this letter, nothing impugns the information it contains.

283 *What was happening in the Ministry:*

For an admirably detailed account, see Ehrenpreis, 2: 730ff.

284 *"Ignorant of the Three last weekes":*

11 July [1714] (1: 234–5).

284 *"Be as Heaven pleases":*

1: 336–7.

285 *"Providence his Guide":*

[? March] 1716. First published by Claude Rawson in "Some Unpublished Letters of Pope and Gay, and Some Manuscript Sources of Goldsmith's Life of Thomas Parnell," *RES*, n.s., 10 (1959): 377.

285 *How far the bill . . . might be carried:*

As Sherburn notes (*Early Career*, p. 159: see also p. 36 and *Correspondence*, 1: 344n), there was much selling and conveyancing of real estate by English Roman Catholics at this time, owing especially to uncertainties about the extent of the tax to be imposed. Thus

Henry Eyre writes to John Caryll, 23 April 1716 (BL: Add. MS. 28, 227, f. 304): "The substance [of the pending bill] in short is that all papists shall at the quarter sessions c[ourt] give in their names and an account of their Real Estates that they may be made liable to be taxed *to make good the charges of this unnatural Rebellion*" (italics mine). There may have been also for the Popes some question as to the validity of their title to the Binfield property, once it fell under the close scrutiny of a hostile administration. Since Roman Catholics were legally barred from acquiring real estate, Pope's father had conveyed it soon after purchase to two of his wife's Protestant nephews, in trust for his son. Such conveyances, though usually winked at, had little standing if the penal laws were strictly enforced.

285 *Renewed pressure to take the oaths:*
      The deadline set was 23 January 1716.

285 *"Whatever I suffer":*
      Berkshire Record Office, Q/RRp 4, 49. This is also quoted in Erskine-Hill, "Alexander Pope: The Political poet in His Time," *Eighteenth-Century Studies*, 15 (1981–82), 143.

286 *"Those who pay double Taxes":*
      Collected in Himself, p. 429.

286 *Were liable in periods of stress:*
      Pope to Sir William Trumbull, 29 November 1715. *Collected in Himself,* p. 467.

286 *"Asylum for their old age":*
      20 April [1716] (1: 339).

286 *"Large Gardens behind":*
      John Bowack, *The Second Part of the Antiquities of Middlesex* (1706), pp. 43 [actually 47], 48. Another seventeenth-century resident of Chiswick was Sir John Denham, whose best-known lines, describing verse in a river metaphor—

> Though deep, yet clear, though gentle, yet not dull,
> Strong without rage, without ore-flowing full—

answer superbly even now to the actual character of the Thames, despite some pollution, in the Chiswick area.

286 *Apparently a tyro performer:*
      James Lees-Milne, p. 112.

288 *"His music is ravishing":*
      [March 1716?] (1: 388). On his return from the Grand Tour Burlington had put Handel in charge of his music, given him chambers in Burlington House, and made Castrucci his concert master. In view of the ancient canard that Pope was insensible to music, his adjective should be noticed. See also the duchess of Hamilton's invitation that he join her for water music on the Thames (1: 404–5); and Brownell, pp. 368–71. On Pope's relations with Handel as well as his responsiveness to music, see also Brownell's pioneering "Ears of an Untoward Make: Pope and Handel," in *Musical Quarterly*, 62 (1976): 555–70.

288 *His paintings arrive:*
      Pope to Jervas, 9 July 1716 (1: 347).

288 *"Blushing Peach":*
      An Epistle to the Right Honourable Earl of Burlington: A Journey to Exeter (not published till 1720 but written in 1716), ll. 3–4.

288 *Burlington's estates in Yorkshire:*
      1: 350–1.

289 *"The Pudding excellent":*
      [November, 1716] (1: 374).

289 *"Th'Idea's of your mind":*
      Besides being an enthusiastic amateur of music, Burlington was an architect and draftsman of some skill. George Vertue, whose standards were high, allowed him "great Judgement in Architectonical Knowledge & true manner & Tastes." *Note Books*: The Walpole Society, 22 (1933–34), 3: 139. Horace Walpole, who called him "Apollo of the Arts," also gave him "every quality of a genius and artist, except envy." *Anecdotes of Painting*, eds., James Dallaway and R. L. Wornum, 5 vols. (1826), 4: 216–17. For his role in the development of English neoclassicism and especially of a Palladian style that in England successfully countered the extremes of rococo dominant at the period in Continental building, see Geoffrey Webb, "The Letters and Drawings of Nicholas

Hawksmoor Relating to ... Castle Howard": (The Walpole Society, 19 [1930–31], 114–15), and Rudolf Wittkower, *Palladio and English Palladianism* (London: Thames and Hudson, 1974), esp. chs. 8–10. For a lively and informative account of the man and his achievements, see Lees-Milne, pp. 103–69, and for his and Lady Burlington's relations with Pope, see J. M. Osborn, "Pope, the 'Apollo of the Arts,' and His Countess," *England in the Restoration and Early Eighteenth-Century: Essays on Culture and Society*, ed., H. T. Swedenberg (University of California Press, 1972), ch. 5.

290 *"With a fa, la, la"*:

Pope calls his poem *The Court Ballad* and specifies that it is to be sung to the tune of "To all you Ladies now at Land," a favorite ballad air to which the light-hearted stanzas usually sung had been written by Charles Sackville, sixth earl of Dorset, while serving at sea in November 1664. Pope himself had contributed to the ballad's popularity by printing it in his and Lintot's *Miscellaneous Poems and Translations by Several Hands* (1712). Lady Rich (l. 45) was wife of Sir Robert Rich and sister of Anne Griffith, mentioned above. Mistress Howard (l. 46) was Henrietta (Hobart) Howard, later mistress to George II both as Prince of Wales and for a time as king. (Above, pp. 375–8.) The king (l. 51) is wished safe landing because he had been on a visit to Hanover and was in the course of return, landing on 18 January 1717. The allusion to standing armies is topical as well as equivocal: whether or not the country should keep soldiers under arms in peacetime was an ancient sore point of parliamentary controversy that in the current session had been notably acrimonious. "Limitations" (l. 55), though I find no OED or other dictionary support for this, is possibly a contemporary slang term for some sort of feminine undergarment. A more esoteric but perhaps more correct interpretation of this word, together with a persuasive account of the political shadings of the poem is given by Pat Rogers in "Pope's *Court Ballad*: A Reconsideration [forthcoming]."

291 *"With what appetite they may"*:

An amusing adaptation of Shakespeare's Henry VIII's remark to Wolsey after deposing with him the evidence of his perfidy: "Read o'er this, And after this, and then to breakfast with What appetite you may."

291 *"The grace to stay away"*:

Pope to Teresa and Martha Blount, 13 September 1717 (1: 426). See also Pope to the same [June 1717] and to Charles Rackett [7 September 1717] (1: 409, 424). Horace Walpole recalls being frightened of Madame Kielmannsegge as a boy because of her "enormous figure," "fierce black eyes," "two acres of cheeks spread with crimson," and "an ocean of neck that over-flowed & was not distinguished from the lower part of her body." *Reminiscences*, ed., Paget Toynbee (Oxford: Clarendon, 1924), pp. 29–30. In her time she was regarded as one of the king's mistresses. More recently it has been argued that she was (whether or not his mistress) his half-sister as well.

291 *"Within 2 hours sail of Chiswick"*:

[6 August 1717] (1: 417–18). See also Pope to Caryll, 7 June 1717 (1: 411).

292 *"By keeping foolish company"*:

18 January 1718 (1: 461–2).

292 *"The Fault is yours"*:

TE, 6: 232.

293 *Ensure the completion of the Homer*:

Above pp. 779–81. Though doubtless coincidence, it is curious that one of Pope's two "Choruses" written for John Sheffield's play *Brutus*, either shortly before or during 1716, should contain the lines (*TE*, 6: 153):

> What is loose love? a transient gust,
> Spent in a sudden storm of lust,
> A vapour fed from wild desire,
> A wandring, self-consuming fire.

293 *"So circumstanced as he pretends"*:

Spence, no. 251.

293 *Underwent painful surgery for it*:

Pope to Fortescue, 17 September 1740, and to Bethel, 26 September [1740] (4: 267, 268).

293 *"Fear of a c[lap] . . . without grounds":*
   Spence, no. 252. Cheselden's comment was made in August, three months after Pope's death.

293 *With as much prosperity as the swan:*
   Though Pope's enemies accused him of every imaginable frailty and humiliated him by every means they could invent, they rarely charged him with impotence. With the exception of one or two cursory allusions (as in *Sawney and Colley* (1742), p. 7: "As impotent in Spite as Love"), quite the reverse. In a pamphlet of 1721 ([Richard Morley], *The Life of the late Celebrated Mrs. Elizabeth Wisebourn, vulgarly call'd Mother Wybourn,* p. 33) he is accused of having an affair with, of all people, John Sheffield's widow, the duchess of Buckinghamshire. Lady Mary Wortley Montagu, in a bitter lampoon written after their quarrel, indicted Pope for (allegedly) pretending to amorous conquests he never made—Judith Cowper supposedly one of them; but her point is not that Pope is incapable but much too deformed to attract a woman. Actually, she says, though they boast of such successes with gentlewomen, Pope and Lord Bolingbroke "seek for Mistrisses in dirty Lanes," where Pope is the luckier in only getting "clapp'd" while Bolingbroke gets "pox'd." "P[ope] to Bolingbroke," Lady MWM, *Poems,* pp. 279–84. (The lampoon, never published, is said by the editors to date between July 1734 and June 1735.) One may note also that it does not occur to Cibber in describing the alleged brothel encounter, though his purpose is to hold Pope up to ridicule, to ascribe to him the sort of failure that would have made him most ridiculous of all. Equally germane to the question of the poet's sexual adequacy is the circumstance, mentioned earlier, that Gay could be misled by Arbuthnot into believing Pope had got himself clapped.
   Whatever doubts contemporaries may have entertained about Pope's sexuality, the whirligig of time brought in its revenges. In the anonymous *Aristophanes, Being a Classic Collection of True Attic Wit* (1778), pp. 34–5, it is said of him:

> The manners of Pope were by no means so immaculate as those of a Christian theist should be. Mrs. Martha Blount he kept as a mistress till the day of his death. Pope quarreled only with Lady Mary Wortley Montagu, because she gave him some pungent reasons to remember her favours. Not knowing the kindness she had rendered him, he obliged poor Martha Blount in the same way. It was the doleful condition, occasioned by the intimate friendship of Lady Mary, which gave rise to the lines on Sappho, that are so lamentably descriptive of the poet's disorder. I could illustrate the natural powers of Mr. Pope by many curious anecdotes: but it is well known that the proportion of parts allotted to his share were considerable. The first women of taste in the kingdom admired his abilities.

293 *Pope met Lady Mary Wortley Montagu:*
   Lady Mary was roughly a year Pope's junior (born 26 May 1689), daughter of the marquis of Dorchester, through whose hands Pope's manuscript *Pastorals* had passed and who had lately been elevated by the new regime to be duke of Kingston. Edward Wortley, eleven years older than she, was grandson of Edward Montagu, first earl of Sandwich, but his father, a second son, had taken the name Wortley on marrying an heiress of that name, with the result that Edward was usually called Wortley Montagu. He and Lady Mary were married in August 1712, and at first all was well. An unpublished letter of August 1713, although she had already by then met with some of Wortley's neglects, closes with the words, "This night last year I gave my selfe to you. Was that to do again, I would repeat the Gift, tho from all mankind I could chuse a Master." (Quoted here by kind permission of the owner.) But disenchantment gradually overcame devotion. Pope was acquainted with her at least by 23 July 1715, when he wrote from London to the Blount sisters (in the news-mongering letter already quoted) that he expects "further Advices" from her that afternoon.

295 *Fashionable court-nymphs and court-swains:*
   Halsband, *Life,* p. 52. James Brydges, first duke of Chandos, who reports the ladies' pun on "pity" and "pitted" (26 January 1716) also reports when sending the eclogues to a friend (20 February 1716) that they were written by one whose wit he admires much more than her person (*Early Career,* p. 204).

296 *"Lady of Quality":*
    One of the three may have been a collaborative work of Lady Mary and Gay. On this, see Lady MWM, *Poems*, p. 182, and Robert Halsband, "Pope, Lady Mary, and the *Court Poems* (1716)," *Publications of the Modern Language Association*, 68 (1953), 237–50.

296 *"By giving him a vomit":*
    20 April [1716] (1: 339).

296 *The revenge was brutal:*
    Pope subsequently published, perhaps as late as November 1716, *A Further Account of the most Deplorable condition of Mr. Edmund Curll, Bookseller, Since his being Poison'd on the 28th of March*. Perhaps because of the detachment that time had brought, this is a very funny pamphlet indeed, with Curll suffering an hallucination in which all the bad books he has ever published (flying at him like attacking ghosts) extort from him imprecations which show Pope's mastery of a vernacular quite as remarkable as his polite style:

> Now *G-d damn* all *Folio's, Quarto's, Octavo's* and *Duodecimo's!* Ungrateful Varlets that you are, who have so long taken up my House without paying for your Lodging?— Are you not the beggarly Brood of fumbling *Journey-men*; born in *Garrets*, among *Lice* and *Cobwebs*, nurs'd upon *Grey Peas, Bullocks Liver*, and *Porter's Ale?*—Was not the first Light you saw, the *Farthing* Candle I paid for?—Did you not come before your Time into *dirty Sheets* of brown Paper?—And have not I cloath'd you in double *Royal*, lodg'd you handsomely on *decent Shelves*, lac'd your *Backs* with *Gold*, equipt you with splendid *Titles*, and sent you into the World with the Names of *Persons of Quality!* [etc.]

297 *"Venomous and impious misanthropy":*
    Early Career, p. 165.

299 *"More of Jordan than of Helicon":*
    A Satyr against Hypocrites (1655), p. 5; and *The Church-History of Britain* (1655), p. 406.

299 *"As do's this POPISH Squire":*
    The Flying Post, 12–14 July 1716. See Ault, ch. 8; *Early Career*, p. 181. Whatever Pope's intentions, the verses were quite understandably thought to mock the psalm as well as its stilted English rendering and so were open to the charge of blasphemy. Pope, as a Roman Catholic nonjuror, was sufficiently alarmed to publish an equivocating denial of authorship in two London newspapers, where in asserting an ignorance of the identity of those who had brought about its publication that was probably real, he made himself seem to disclaim all connection with the piece.

300 *"Dennisissime":*
    Early Career, p. 178.

300 *"Nor of our Species":*
    Dennis, 2: 103ff.

301 *Could be injurious indeed:*
    For an opposing view, see Halsband ("Pope, Lady Mary, and the *Court Poems*), p. 249.

301 *Martha Blount had suffered from the disease:*
    Martha Blount noted in her copy of *The Offices of the B.V. Mary in English* (1687) (Mapledurham Papers) that she contracted smallpox on 16 April 1714. Accordingly, the letter in *Correspondence* now dated "[Late October 1714]" (1: 264–5) should be placed in April of that year.

302 *"Knowing how to value them":*
    [July 1716] (1: 346). The covering letter is at 1: 345. Lady Rich was wife of Sir Robert Rich and sister of Anne Griffith.

302 *British envoy to the Sultanate:*
    In early 1716, Pope had arranged a meeting for Wortley with Sir William Trumbull, who had held the post formerly, "to advise about the value and profits of [the] Embassy." Sherburn, *Letters* (16 February 1716), p. 406.

304 *"I must be only her Slave":*
    1: 357, 439, 405, 406–7, 441, 369, 440, 441 (see also 364). He threatens, perhaps sometimes a trifle more than playfully, to meet her in Italy—which, according to a letter of George Berkeley's, he had entertained "some half-form'd design" to visit as early as 1714

(1: 221). Very likely it was the advice of Dr. Arbuthnot and, much later on, a brief actual experience of what seasickness could do to the congestion of his chest cavity that dissuaded him from ever undertaking during his lifetime a long journey by ship.

304 *The gravity of the emotion:*
    1: 384, 385.

305 *"All the agreeable functions it was made for":*
    1: 365, 364, 369.

306 *"Beyond the bounds of common Sence and decency":*
    1: 355, 440 (see also 1: 389).

306 *To believe in "miracles":*
    1: 361.

306 *"Take off Shifts without scruple":*
    1: 353, 384.

306 *A cultivated infatuation:*
    Wimsatt, p. 33. See also Patricia Meyer Spacks, "Imaginations Warm and Tender: Pope and Lady Mary", *South Atlantic Quarterly*, 83 (1984): 207–15.

308 *A few big-brotherly home-truths for each:*
    1: 409, 428, 375.

309 *"Interruption to the range of my thoughts":*
    1: 430–31, 430, 429, 429–30.

310 *"What I can show that is better?":*
    1: 426. The revision from "man" to "creature" is very clear in the autograph letter (Mapledurham Papers). For a parallel sentiment to that of the opening of the letter, see 2: 290.

310 *"A kindness for Men of my Make":*
    Pope seems still to be remembering Astolfo's wife and the dwarf (*Correspondence*, 1: 365) from *Orlando Furioso*, Canto 28. The hope certainly does not die with Pope. In Lermontov's *A Hero of Our Time*, after noting that Werner is short, thin, weak, has one leg shorter than the other, a head disproportionately large, and bumps on his skull, Pechorin observes: "There have been cases of women falling madly in love with such people, preferring their ugliness to the beauty of the freshest, rosiest-cheeked Endymions."

310 *"Than any other I have":*
    1: 455–6.

310 *The divine gift of poetry:*
    Not exactly a new complaint. Ovid laments that his poetry does not bring him the favor of women in Pope's two favorite *Amores*, 3.8 and 3.11a (1: 92); and Sappho, in the fifteenth of the *Heroides* (ll. 33ff.), urges Phaon that though nature may have denied her physical beauty and made her *brevis* (short in stature), he should consider the beauty that nature has bestowed on her in her gift of song: lines that Pope had translated in his *Sappho to Phaon*, ll. 37–42, with, one suspects, a certain fellow-feeling. See on this *Collected in Himself*, p. 382.

311 *"I ever lov'd it—next to Gold":*
    The Mapledurham House library contains a pirated octavo reprint of Pope's *Works* of 1717 (Griffith, no. 103), which it is tempting to think may be the book Pope sent. It is bound in red gold-tooled morocco (the binding Pope used for gift copies) and the lower half of its half-title has been cut away. The one difficulty with the theory is that Pope would have had to write his poem rather small and probably in double columns to get it into the limited space. Possibly he did so, and then an angry Teresa (or a later member of the family) excised the offending half page. Just as possibly, the mutilation has some other explanation. Pope may have based his poem partly on a reminiscence of Montaigne's pretended (?) vexation that his *Essays* "only serve the Ladies for a common moveable, a Book to lie in the Parlour Window." *Essays*, tr., Charles Cotton, 3 vols. (1685–93), 3: 98. In his own copy, Pope writes beside this sentence: "For ye/Ladies." *Collected in Himself*, p. 429.

Chapter 15, "This Subtle Thief of Life, This Paltry Time"

315 *"Roman-elegiac":*
    R. A. Brower, *Alexander Pope: The Poetry of Allusion* (Oxford University Press, 1959), p. 64.

317 *Jane Shore and Lady Jane Grey:*
With the Lady's much-stressed greatness of soul, compare Calista in Rowe's *Fair Penitent*, who, complaining that woman's lot is to go from rigid father to tyrannical husband, cries: "Wherefore are we born with high Souls, but to assert our selves, Shake off this vile Obedience they exact, And claim an equal Empire o'er the World?"

317 *Victims of men whom Pope thought tyrannical:*
Above, pp. 239–40.

317 *"Guard all my friends from such a Guardian":*
1: 232.

318 *The poem not biographical:*
For a delightful review of early biographical theories about the Lady, see Ian Jack, "The Elegy as Exorcism: Pope's 'Verses to the Memory of an Unfortunate Lady,'" *Augustan Worlds*, eds., J. C. Hilson, M. M. B. Jones, and J. R. Watson (Leicester, 1978), pp. 69–83.

320 *An Old Testament revenge:*
Not simply in the sense of equitable retaliation, but in the sense of Deuteronomy, 23: 1: "He that is wounded in the stones, or hath his privy member cut off, shall not enter into the Congregation of the Lord."

320 *A letter . . . fell into her hands:*
On the Abélard-Héloïse story and its retelling, see especially Etienne Gilson, *Héloïse and Abélard*, tr., L. K. Shook (University of Michigan Press, 1960); D. W. Robertson, Jr., *Abélard and Héloïse* (New York: Dial Press, 1972); and *The Letters of Abélard and Héloïse*, tr., Betty Radice (Penguin Books, 1974).

321 *"Steals between my God and me":*
The poem's (and the story's) version of the eternal triangle, in which, however, the heavenly lover also fills the role of stern father standing between daughter and mortal lover. For a remarkable analogy to Eloisa's situation, torn between earthly and celestial loves, see Charlotte Bronte's *Jane Eyre*, where the heroine remarks (at the close of ch. 9 of vol. 2): "My future husband was becoming to me my whole world; and, more than the world; almost my hope of heaven. He stood between me and every thought of religion, as an eclipse intervenes between man and the broad sun. I could not, in those days, see God for his creature: of whom I had made an idol."

324 *His handkerchief, and his writing table:*
Autograph letter, 3 April 1755, to Count Hans Moritz von Bruhl. Speck Collection, Yale University. It is slightly differently translated in René Wellek and Austin Warren, *Theory of Literature* (New York: Harcourt, Brace, 1949), p. 114.

324 *"Unworthy of herself":*
Hoyt Trowbridge, "Pope's 'Eloisa' and the 'Heroides' of Ovid", *Racism in the Eighteenth Century*, ed. H. E. Pagliaro (Case Western Reserve University Press, 1973), p. 20.

326 *"The conclusion I once intended for it":*
1: 407, 338.

327 *"The lakes that quiver to the curling breeze":*
For some of the further associations of this passage, see J. D. Hunt, *The Figure in the Landscape: Poetry, Painting, and Gardening during the Eighteenth Century* (The Johns Hopkins University Press, 1976), pp. 71–3.

328 *"Wherewith the book of Canticles is replenished":*
Louis de la Puente, *Meditations upon the Mysteries of our Holie Faith*, 2 vols. (St. Omer, 1619). Quoted in L. L. Martz, *The Poetry of Meditation* (Yale University Press, 1954), p. 37. One may note too that the poem begins (ll. 8, 9, 13–14) with something very like the exercitant's salute to the Name above all other Names.

329 *A normal form of salute among polite Englishmen:*
See Stone, pp. 520–1.

331 *"Unless we believe that poetry serves great ends":*
Wallace Stevens, *Opus Posthumous* (New York: Knopf, 1957), p. 245.

331 *Engraved from an oil by Jervas:*
Wimsatt, p. 16.

333 *Already a classic:*
John Butt, "Pope's Poetical Manuscripts" (Warton Lecture on English Poetry), *Proceedings of the British Academy*, 40 (1954), 23.

333 *And sometimes have cures:*
A characteristic instance is the swift death of Pope's friend, young Simon Harcourt, aged 36, in Paris on 12 July 1720, as reported to his father by Bolingbroke, with whom he was staying at the time (BL: Add. MS. 15,916, ff. 33–4): "the night before last he had a strong fitt [i.e., ague] both cold, & hott, it went off gradually & with very strong sweating, this instead of disheartning encouraged ye Physitians. They expected ye intermission to give him the proper remedys, but on a sudden his sweat stopp'd entirely, his extremitys became cold, & all the methods that were used to bring heat into him, & to restore his sweats proved ineffectual, in short my Lord he dy'd at three this morning."

333 *Receive in return for copyright:*
Pope's emolument from the edition was 120 copies on royal quarto, which presumably he was free to give to friends or sell or both. David Foxon's Lyell lectures, *Pope and the Eighteenth-Century Book Trade*, ch. 2.

334 *Poems on Several Occasions:*
This is the book reissued by Norman Ault as *Pope's Own Miscellany* (1935).

334 *"Or burying the dead":*
TE, 1: 9.

334 *Admired its spare simplicity of style:*
Johnson, p. 135; Atterbury to Pope [December, 1716] (1: 378); and Joseph Warton, *Works of Alexander Pope*, 10 vols. (1797), 1: 1n.

334 *"In no small danger of becoming a Coxcomb":*
See also his remark to Caryll, 31 July 1710 (1: 94). Much of the content of the 1717 Preface is anticipated in Pope's early correspondence with his friends, especially with Caryll.

335 *"Or more agreeable amusement":*
TE, 1: 6, 7–8, 8. In an unpublished letter of ca. 1716 (summer), Francis Chute tells his correspondent John Audley that he has lately visited Rousham, Oxfordshire estate of the Dormers, where he has found Pope translating Homer: "He speaks with much indifference of the affair but works on, & the other day read to me a good part of the 9th book, so far He is advancd and I doubt not must, & will goe through; for his indolence I take to proceed from art; but that is entre Nous." Osborn Collection, Beinecke Library, Yale University. Even thorough-going hacks like John Oldmixon found it gratifying to say: "Poetry has not been the Business of my Life; I should reckon it among my Misfortunes if it had." *Poems on Several Occasions* (1695), Preface. The manuscript of the 1717 Preface shows a Pope far less on parade—rather charmingly confidential and self-deprecating, in fact, as he reminisces about his childhood when, with a juvenile epic and "panegyrics on all the Princes of Europe" in hand, he thought himself "the greatest Genius th[a]t ever was"; or writes nostalgically of his visions of those days, "wch like the fine Colours I then saw wh[e]n my Eyes shut, are vanished for ever." See "Pope's 1717 Preface," *Augustan Worlds*, pp. 96–106.

336 *"Since I don't forget you this moment, I never shall":*
1: 447. Contrary to supposition, Pope's father was buried in Chiswick (on 26 October), as the Burial Registers of the parish church plainly show. He is named, to be sure, in the family epitaph Pope placed in St. Mary's, Twickenham, but the inclusion in such epitaphs of family members buried elsewhere was not uncommon.

336 *In the early months of 1719:*
For details of this removal, see *The Garden and the City* (Toronto University Press, 1969), pp. 9ff.

337 *"To contribute any ways to your Satisfaction or Service":*
8 November 1717 (1: 451).

337 *A delightful demonstration of affectionate tact:*
8 December 1713 (1: 198–201).

339 *"God grant his present Majesty may be":*
20 November 1717 (1: 453–5).

339 *As he well knew:*
Sending the verses to her sister in April 1722, Lady Mary says she has "stiffle'd" them here and begs they may die the same death in Paris. *Letters*, 2: 15.

340 *"Their old verve and* joie*":*
     J. H. Hagstrum, *Sex and Sensibility: Ideal and Erotic Love from Milton to Mozart,* (University of Chicago Press, 1980), p. 140.
340 *Pope's annuity to Teresa:*
     The document reads as follows:

> This Indenture made the tenth day of March in the fourth year of our Sovereign Lord George by the Grace of God of Great Britain France and Ireland King and in the Year of our Lord one thousand seven hundred and seventeen between Alexander Pope on the one part and Teresa Blount spinster on the other witnesseth that the said Alexander Pope for and in consideration of divers causes him the said Alexander Pope thereunto moving hath given granted and confirmed and by these presents doth give and grant to the said Teresa Blount an Annuity of forty pounds for and during the term of Six years if both the said Alexander Pope and she the said Teresa Blount shall so long live to be paid yearly on the twenty fifth day of March being the feast of the Annunciation of the Virgin Mary [in England, spring quarter day and originally first day of the calendar year] free and clear of all Taxes whatsoever provided nevertheless that in case the said Teresa Blount shall marry that then from and immediately after such marriage the said Annuity of forty pounds shall cease and determine and the said Grant thereof be utterly void and of none effect and it is hereby further declared to be the true intent of these presents and of the Parties to the Same and the said Teresa Blount doth for herself her heirs executors and Administrators and Assigns covenant grant and agree to and with the said Alexander Pope his Heirs Executors Administrators and Assigns that in case the said Teresa Blount shall happen to dye living him the said Alexander Pope [i.e., while Pope is living] that then and not otherwise the Heirs Executors and Administrators of the said Teresa Blount within six months immediately after her decease shall and will pay back unto the said Alexander Pope or his Assigns all and every such sum or sums of mony as hath or have been paid unto the said Teresa Blount or her Assigns for and on account of the said Annuity of forty Pounds from the commencement of the Same home to the time of the Death of the said Teresa Blount or to the expiration of the said term of years which [ever] shall first happen in witness whereof the said parties to these presents their hands and seal interchangeably have sett the day and year first above written.
> Signed sealed & deliver'd
> in the presence of us,
> Margret Littleboyce
> Greg[or]y Sturzatker   Alex: Pope

     Above the first line of the Indenture, a different hand has written in pencil: "George 1st," and a still different hand, in ink; "anno / 1717." New Style, this is 1718. Mapledurham Papers.
340 *A mystifying undated letter:*
     2: 25–6. Sherburn dates the letter [1720?], but acknowledges it could as well fall in 1718, where I am inclined to place it.
341 *A second portrait by Jervas:*
     Wimsatt, 3: 2.
343 *Suppose her the poet's Muse?:*
     For an attractive discussion of the portrait from this point of view, see D. B. Morris, *Alexander Pope: The Genius of Sense* (Harvard University Press, 1984), pp. 305–16.

Chapter 16, Success and Its Rewards

347 *Exhaustion, depression, or distraction:*
     See *Collected in Himself,* pp. 385–7.
347 *Deprived of friends by death:*
     Young Simon Harcourt died unexpectedly in Paris on 12 July 1720; the younger Craggs, whom Pope memorializes in the last ten lines of his "To Mr. Addison," succumbed to smallpox on 16 February 1721; John Sheffield, duke of Buckinghamshire, died on the twenty-fourth of that same month; and in September of that year, Matthew Prior.

347 *Ready for subscribers on 12 May 1720:*
   In a terminal note dated "March 25, 1720" (*TE*, 8: 578–9), Pope dedicated the translation to Congreve (who had himself translated selections from Book 24) as "a Memorial of my Friendship, with one of the most valuable Men as well as finest Writers, of my Age and Countrey." Gay celebrated its completion in "Mr. Pope's Welcome from Greece," where the undertaking is seen as a dangerous sea voyage now happily ending in a progress up the Lower Thames to the huzzas of shoals of friends.

348 *"You must not call it Homer":*
   For the first version of this anecdote, see Thomas Bentley, *A Letter to Mr. Pope, Occasioned by Sober Advice from Horace* (1735), p. 14; for the second, see Johnson, 3: 213n. According to a third version (*Gentleman's Magazine*, 43 [1773]: 499–500), Bentley said, "the verses are good verses, but the work is not Homer, it is Spondanus"—i.e. dependent on Jean de Sponde's Latin rendering. This sounds rather more like some third party's explication of what Bentley might have meant than like his own native woodnotes wild, which were normally in the style of his comment about Joshua Barnes, a not deeply learned professor of Greek at Cambridge from 1695, that he knew about as much Greek as a Greek blacksmith. R. C. Jebb, *Bentley* (London: Macmillan, 1902), p. 35.

348 *The translator had no Greek:*
   See Dennis's *Remarks upon Mr. Pope's Translation of Homer* (1717), 2: 115, where Pope, as usual, is an author "absolutely without Merit."

348 *"Noblest version . . . the world has ever seen":*
   Coleridge, *Biographia Literaria*, ed., Shawcross, 2 vols. (Oxford: Clarendon, 1907), 1: 11; Johnson, p. 119.

348 *Among writers of the European Renaissance:*
   For a succinct informative account of Homer criticism and interpretation down through the centuries, see Howard Clarke, *Homer's Readers: a Historical Introduction to the Iliad and Odyssey* (University of Delaware Press, 1981).

349 *"Or just goen may be":*
   W. H. D. Rouse, *The Iliad* (New York: New American Library, 1938) p. 46.

350 *"Gay dancer in the publick Show":*
   The implied slur gains force from Hector's rebuke to Paris earlier in this book, where the emphasis on "show" is entirely Pope's invention ("When *Greece* beheld thy painted Canvas flow, And Crowds stood wond'ring at the passing Show," 3: 67–8), and also from Paris's reference (again Pope's invention) to his duel with Menelaus taking place as if on a "Stage" (3: 99–100). Pope's departures from the original are more often than not, as here, designed to heighten the moral significance of a situation. See also P. J. Connelly, "Pope's *Iliad: Ut Pictura Translatio*," *SEL*, 21 (1981): 444.

350 *"Constrained by a superior Power":*
   3: 479n.

350 *"Wiser . . . than all the philosophers combined":*
   9 April 1708 (1: 46).

351 *"To which the Invention must not contribute":*
   TE, 7: 2. Pope's firm intention to defend poetic imagination seems confirmed by his omission in the published Preface of qualifying assertions about its luxuriance in Homer that he had set down in the manuscript (*TE*, 10: 424–26); also Connelly ("Pope's *Iliad*"), p. 445.

352 *"That ancient World" . . . "While he reads him":*
   TE, 7: 14, 4.

352 *"Made slaves and concubines":*
   Ibid., p. 14.

354 *"Land of Lovely Dames":*
   Pope, 9: 577.

354 *"Shouting Millions":*
   Homer, 5: 860; Pope, 5: 1055.

354 *"Man is born to bear":*
   Homer, 24: 524; Pope, 24: 660. The five preceding translations are, in order, those of A. T. Murray (Loeb), W. H. D. Rouse, E. V. Rieu, Richmond Lattimore, and Robert Fizgerald.

355   *"The word* Ass *in the translation"*:

Homer, 11: 558ff; Pope, 11: 682ff and 668n. Two further considerations may have influenced Pope. "Ass" had been so long applied by transference to mean a fool or dolt that a connotation of this nature could hardly be excluded from any context involving Ajax, whose post-Homeric reputation for stupidity may be studied in Shakespeare's *Troilus and Cressida*. Further, since by 1650 (H. F. Wyld, *History of Modern Colloquial English* (Oxford: Blackwell, 1921), p. 299) *r* following a vowel and preceding a consonant had largely ceased to be sounded, a contamination of "ass" by "arse" may already have been sufficiently under way to make the word unsuitable (in the eighteenth-century view) for epic. Eric Partridge in *Shakespeare's Bawdy* (1948) gives some to my mind not entirely convincing evidence of Shakespeare's use of ass as arse. Pope's use is plainer: *TE*, 6: 660.

355   *"Soul all o'er"*:

17: 570; Pope, 17: 642. For an informative and learned study of Pope's notes and their sources, see H.-J. Zimmermann, *Alexander Popes Noten zu Homer: Eine Manuskript- und Quellenstudie* (Heidelberg:; Carl Winter, 1966).

355   *Since before Plato's time:*

Opposition began early. Easily the best-known fragment of Xenophanes (6th century B.C.) is his complaint that Homer and Hesiod ascribe actions to the gods that are unpardonably shameful even in mortals.

356   *"Incontinence and ungovern'd Fury"*:

Pope, 5: terminal note.

358   *As Bentley with justice said:*

As Paul Valéry remarks (*Oeuvres*, Pléiade edition, 2: 638–9), "Les traductions des grands poètes étrangers ce sont des plans d'architecture qui peuvent être admirables; mais elles font évanouir les édifices mêmes, palais et temples . . ." ["Translations of the great foreign poets are architectural blueprints, which may well be admirable; only they make the edifices themselves, palaces, temples disappear"].

358   *Pope is still Homer's "best" translator:*

Outstanding studies of the *Iliad* translation are D. M. Knight's *Pope and the Heroic Tradition* (Yale University Press, 1951), Steven Shankman's *Pope's Iliad: Homer in the Age of Passion* (Princeton University Press, 1983), and H. A. Mason, *To Homer through Pope: An Introduction to Homer's Iliad and Pope's Translation* (New York, 1972). See also R. A. Brower, *Mirror on Mirror* (Harvard University Press, 1974), chs. 4–5, and Clarke, *Homer's Readers*. Especially notable is the comment of George Steiner, writing in the *Times Literary Supplement* (16 November 1982), p. 1259: "Informed literacy is far from allowing the fact—yet, surely, it is obvious—that Pope's *Iliad* is a masterpiece in its own right and an epic which, so far as English goes, comes second only to Milton."

358   *"That he is a great man"*:

Further Letters of Gerard Manley Hopkins, ed., C. C. Abbott (Oxford University Press, 1956), p. 222. For some of the qualities accruing from Pope's effort to shape configurations with genuine poetic force (however different from Homer's own), see *TE*, 7: Introduction, and, more recently, P. J. Connelly, "Pope's Iliad," pp. 439–56.

359   *"What Church is rising?"*:

1 May 1720 (2: 44).

359   *Opulence of the Great House:*

John Summerson, "The Classical Country House in Eighteenth-Century England," *Journal of the Royal Society of the Arts*, 107 (1958–59): 551–2, 571.

361   *The role he was eventually to assume:*

See *The Garden and the City*, ch. 2, and *Alexander Pope's Villa* (London: GLC, 1980), an annotated and illustrated catalogue of an exhibition arranged at Marble Hill House by Morris Brownell.

361   *About five acres:*

See Pope's testimony to Bethel, *Imit. Hor.*, *Sat. II*, ii, 136; Horace Walpole to Horace Mann, 20 June 1760 (21: 417); *The Garden and the City*, p. 9n; and especially A. J. Sambrook, "The Shape and Size of Pope's Garden," *E-CS*, 5 (1972): 453–4.

361   *And to have kept bees:*

On the comparative rarity of broccoli at this period, see the letter of Pope's friend William Cleland, 1 November 1726 (SRO: RH 9/18/15): "As for your broccoli, sure you are mistaken in saying broccoli is a kind of asparagus. . . . I am more mistaken than either of you if they are anything but Italian sprouts or coleworts. . . . I know they are the rarest thing of that kind to be had here, for I remember Mr. Pope was talking to a friend of his and myne of a promise of some of that seed as the greatest favour My Lord Peterborough had done him. . . . I hope Mr. Pope will help me to some." Pope seems to have experimented with pineapple-growing from about 1734. G. S. Rousseau, "Pineapples, Pregnancy, Pica, and Peregrine Pickle," in *Tobias Smollett*, eds., G. S. Rousseau and P.-G. Boucé (Oxford University Press, 1971), pp. 102–3. For the strawberries, see *Correspondence*, 3: 233–4, and for the bees, 3: 114. Another visitor to Pope's garden mentions not only the hum of his bees, but encounters with bantam chickens as she strolled, confirming his sketch in his imitation of Horace (*Sat.* II, ii) of the simple fare offered to his guests: "and these chicks my own." From a manuscript entitled *Epistolary Conversation In Verse and Prose. Between a Lady, under the Name of Amica, And her Friends*. Above, pp. 796–801.

361 *"A singular effort of art and taste"*:
   The History of the Modern Taste in Gardening, ed., I. W. U. Chase (Princeton University Press, 1943), p. 28.

362 *"The Taste of the finest Genius"*:
   "An Epistolary Description of the late Mr. Pope's House and Garden at Twickenham," *Newcastle General Magazine*, 1 (1748): 25–8. (Reprinted entire in *The Garden and the City*, pp. 237–43.) On the "naturalness" of Pope's gardening, as it seemed to eighteenth-century taste, see also G. Hampshire, "Johnson, Elizabeth Carter, and Pope's Garden," *Notes and Queries*, n.s. 19 (1972): 221–2. Bluestocking, friend of Johnson, and eventually a contributor to his *Rambler*, Elizabeth Carter visited Pope's garden in 1738, describing later in a letter to a friend the "agreeable wildness" of its disposition of laurels and trees, "a Retreat equal to the Muses' own Parnassus" atop its Great Mount with a vista to the Thames ("'tis no wonder they pay such frequent visits to Mr. Pope"), and the whole layout "the nearest Thing I ever saw to those beautiful descriptions which I was before afraid existed only in the Imagination of Poets." Discussions of Pope's garden that should not be missed are found in J. D. Hunt, "Pope's Twickenham Revisited," in *British and American Gardens in the Eighteenth Century*, ed., R. P. Maccubbin and Peter Martin (Williamsburg: The Colonial Williamsburg Foundation, 1984); Ronald Paulson, "The Poetic Garden," in his *Emblem and Expression* (Harvard University Press, 1975); Peter Martin's just-now-published "*Pursuing Innocent Pleasures*"; *The Gardening World of Alexander Pope* (New Haven: Archon Books), and Brownell.

362 *An account Pope termed "poetical"*:
   Pope to Broome, 9 July [1922] (2: 125).

363 *"Rays . . . are reflected over the Place"*:
   To Edward Blount, 2 June 1725 (2: 296–7).

365 *England and indeed the world*:
   The progression seems to have been from *Musæum* in the sense of a haunt for the Muse or Muses to *Musæum* in the modern sense. But as Pope's *Verses on a Grotto* (1741) clearly show, the first significance was never lost.

365 *"Mixture of Realities and Imagery"*:
   "An Epistolary Description" in *The Garden and the City*, p. 239.

365 *A more gratifying experience?*:
   For additional speculations on the grotto, see *The Garden and the City*, ch. 2. For particularized information about its probable structure and content in its later phases, see the letters from William Borlase in "*Collected in Himself*," pp. 501–14. For some superb remarks on possible expressive aspects of both garden and grotto, see A. D. Nuttall, "Fishes in the Trees," *Essays in Criticism*, 24 (1974): 29–30.

366 *In her "Hermitage" at Richmond*:
   Epistle to Burlington, 78. During the early years at Twickenham Pope was editing Shakespeare and he marks for approbation in his edition (1725) the famous speech of Belarius (*Cymbeline*, 3.3. 1–26), who lives in a cave and extols a life of virtuous hardship as "nobler than attending for a check [rebuke], Richer than doing nothing for a robe, Prouder than rustling in unpaid silk," etc. See also Pope to Edward Blount, 3 October 1721 (2: 86).

367 *"Receiving all travellers"*:
   9 August (2: 386).

367 *"The Steepest Slopes of my Mount"*:
   3 October 1721 (2: 86).
367 *"At home in attending" on her*:
   To Broome, 24 March 1720 (2: 41).
368 *"And they despise"*:
   Verses Address'd to the Imitator of the First Satire of the Second Book of Horace (1733),
   ll. 68–72. See Isobel Grundy, "Verses Address'd to the Imitator of Horace: A Skirmish
   between Pope and some Persons of Rank and Fortune," *Studies in Bibliography*, 30 (1977):
   96–119, and Lady MWM, *Poems*, pp. 265ff. On resentments and provocations leading to
   the quarrel, see Halsband, *Life*, chs. 8–9; his *Lord Hervey, Eighteenth-Century Courtier*
   (1973), chs. 8–10; and above, pp. 553ff, 607ff, 644ff.
368 *"It becomes no other so well"*:
   "Some few Maxims & Rules for your Conduct," ca. 1714. Digby Family Papers:
   Birmingham Reference Library, Deposit 73132, List 13, no. 159.
368 *"Hardly to be found out of your house"*:
   21 May 1720 (2: 47).
369 *"Muse again in that solemn scene"*:
   14 August 1723 (2: 192).
369 *"As far as his territories"*:
   22 June [1724] (2: 239). Pope's attraction to the Digby family as representing an aristocratic integrity "now almost lost in this Nation" (2: 252) is admirably explored in Howard
   Erskine-Hill's *The Social Milieu of Alexander Pope* (Yale University Press, 1975). ch. 5.
369 *"Equally Men of honour and virtue"*:
   Epilogue to the Satires: Dialogue 2: 236, 240–1 and n.
369 *Expected his mother to use*:
   Katherine Sheffield, duchess of Buckinghamshire, to Pope [1725?] (2: 303). On Pope's
   summer travels among friends' houses, see the sensitive account in Pat Rogers' "Pope's
   Rambles" in *Augustan Worlds*, eds., J. C. Hilson, M. M. B. Jones, and J. R. Watson
   (Leicester, 1978), pp. 107–19.
371 *Where he feels freer to let go*:
   10 April 1744 (4: 517–18).
371 *On almost every estate in England*:
   As a writer in *Common Sense*, 15 December 1739, amusingly notes: "Every Man now, be
   his fortune what it will, is . . . *in Mortar* and *moving of Earth.*
371 *Nine still living in 1729*:
   Daily Post, 8 September 1729. For a fascinating sketch of Bathurst's life and personality,
   see Lees-Milne, ch. 1. To his amorous sensibilities Lady Mary Wortley Montagu's lines
   bear witness: Lady MWM, *Poems*, p. 243.
372 *"Let's crack another bottle"*:
   Lees-Milne, p. 28.
372 *"Thinking I have made it for them"*:
   [June, 1725?] (2: 299); 19 September 1730 (3: 134). See also 20 July [1732] (3: 299–300).
373 *"A poor unsupported, weak Individual, without you"*:
   6 August 1735 (3: 480–1). Also, 7 November 1728 (2: 525).
373 *Where the first tulip tree bloomed in England*:
   Charles Hatton to Christopher Hatton, 4 July 1688. *Correspondence of the Family of
   Hatton*, ed., E. M. Thompson, 2 vols. (1878), 2: 87.
373 *Where he found it congenial to compose*:
   To Anne Craggs Knight, 5 August 1734 (3: 426). On its inspiration to composition, see
   Pope to Fortescue, 21 September [1736] (4: 33).
373 *"Tho' in reality it is a very small spot"*:
   Jeremiah Milles, "An Account of a Tour in Hampshire and Sussex, 15–20th September
   1743." BL: Add. MS. 15, 776, f. 258. Milles's "Tours" are being edited for the press.
373 *"A Skeleton in outward Figure"*:
   "To the Earl of Peterborow," ll. 52, 51. Pope calls Peterborow and Bathurst "the two
   most impetuous men" he knew (3: 405–6).
375 *"Of more than we obtaine"*:
   BL: Add. MS. 22, 625, ff. 112–13.

375 *"The ramblingest lying rogue on earth":*
   Journal to Stella, 23 November 1710. In the spring of 1728, and perhaps on other occasions, 1726–28, he was host to Voltaire for extended periods. See C. B. Chase, *The Young Voltaire* (1926), p. 159, and Peterborow's letters to Dr. Richard Towne in *Collected in Himself*, App. B. For an evenhanded account of his strengths and weaknesses as a military man, see Colin Ballard's *The Great Earl of Peterborough* (1929). William Stebbing, in his *Peterborough* of 1890, finds so many questions about him unanswered and unanswerable that he believes he will always "continue, as statesman, soldier, courtier, lover, to occupy his old place on the borderland of fable" (p. 227). There he is securely placed also in Delarivière Manley's *New Atlantis*, where he appears under the name Horatio as "a Prince in his Aspect," all his lineaments "noble," his eyes bright with "a Brightness participating of the Sun." *Novels of Mary Delarivière Manley*, ed., Patricia Köster, 2 vols. (Gainesville, Fla.: Scholars' Facsimiles, & Reprints, (1971), pp. 4ff. John Macky, *Memoirs of the Secret Services of John Macky*, ed., Spring Macky (2d ed., 1733), pp. 64–6, describes him as brave and generous, "always in Debt," mistrusted by all political parties owing to his "natural Giddiness," and "an open Enemy to *Revealed Religion*." The last point probably requires some qualification in view of his tolerant acceptance of the religious convictions of his wife, who was a devout Roman Catholic and kept a personal priest.

375 *To pay for an expedient dinner party:*
   The anecdote is from Horace Walpole's *Reminiscences*, ed., Paget Toynbee (Oxford: Clarendon, 1924), pp. 58–9. John Griffin also records it, with credit to Walpole, in his manuscript Commonplace Book, ca. 1797. Beinecke Library, Osborn Shelves, C 16.

375 *Had little tinder in her makeup:*
   Hervey, 1: 42.

377 *With an assist from Bathurst:*
   Pope urges Martha Blount in his letter from the Digbys' Sherborne, (above, p. 369) to assure Mrs. Howard that he has spent many hours while there in studying plans for her (2: 240). The following summer, Martha informs Mrs. Howard that Pope has just returned from Lord Cobham's Stowe, "full of plans for buildings and gardens" to be placed at her service. BL: Add. MS. 22, 626, ff. 9–10. Swift, too, calls Pope "Contriver of the Gardens" in a whimsical note to his poem, "A Pastoral Dialogue between Richmond Lodge and Marble Hill": above, pp. 448–50. For Bridgeman, see Peter Willis's opulent and brilliant *Charles Bridgeman and the English Landscape Garden* (London: Zwemmer, 1977).

377 *Marriage to a debauched rake:*
   She was finally granted conjugal freedom by papers of agreement in early 1728 (2: 478).

378 *"Under her Edderdown Quilt":*
   [17 December 1734] (3: 434); 27 December 1739 (4: 212).

378 *"The Woman's deaf, and does not hear":*
   On a Certain Lady at Court. (TE, 6: 250–1).

379 *"Amending anything I shall think of":*
   22 April (2: 376–7).

379 *One ramble in the summer of 1727:*
   This was in July 1727 (2: 441, 444, 450). Projected but canceled visits are referred to at 2: 257, 260, 268, 317, 327. Rambles that *may* have included Wimpole are mentioned at 2: 310, 381, and 3: 46. Even if one or more of these last actually included Wimpole, I find no ground for assuming with Johnson (3: 202) and Lees-Milne, p. 190, that Pope visited there often; still less for A. S. Turberville's notion (*A History of Welbeck Abbey*, 2 vols. [London: Faber and Faber, 1938–9], 1: 346) that he "was given the run of the household and indeed lived part of the year in it." Unless these statements rest on evidence that is nowhere cited (Turberville even speaks mysteriously of "facile amours"!), it appears that Wimpole is being confused with Oxford's London house in Dover Street, where the poet did on some occasions make himself at home (notably when ill and in need of city physicians), composing there, perhaps among other pieces on other occasions, his imitation of Horace's *First Satire of the Second Book.*

379 *Negotiating the Peace of Utrecht:*
   Pope to Oxford, 3 March 1726: 10 August 1731 (2: 369; 3: 216). Down Hall had reverted to Lord Oxford on Prior's death in 1721.

379 *"Promoted and protected them":*
   Note Books (Walpole Society), p. 64. Vertue, though himself of Harley's circle, was no

one's creature. See also Zachary Grey's "Memoirs of the Harley family" (in William Cole's transcription), BL: Add. MS. 5834, ff. 145–68.

379 *Written offensively of her close friend Lady Mary:*

Johnson's anecdote (p. 202) of Pope and Lady Mary quarreling at the Oxfords' dinner table with such vehemence that one or other would quit the house has little inherent credibility and rests on no verifiable evidence. It was roundly denied by Lady Mary's granddaughter when the *Lives of the Poets* first appeared, and further controverted by Lord and Lady Oxford's daughter, the duchess of Portland, who pointed out that neither her father nor her mother would have been so gauche as to invite Lady Mary and Pope at the same time after their quarrel. Lady Louisa Stuart, *Biographical Anecdotes of Lady M. W. Montagu,* reprinted in Lady MWM, *Poems,* p. 38. Further, nothing we know of Pope or Lady Mary assures us that either would have been rude at the table of a friend. Johnson's picture of Pope's capricious behavior toward Oxford when his guest, apparently from the same unidentified hostile source, seems similarly questionable in view of the deep affection evident in their letters.

379 *"Knowing the Contempt you have for worthless People":*

Lady Oxford to Lady Mary, 18 August 1744. BL: Harley MS (on deposit by the Duke of Portland), quoted in Lady MWM, *Letters,* 2: 339n. It is to Lady Mary's credit that she spoke up warmly against rash judgments when her daughter called Lady Oxford stupid (Stuart, *Biographical Anecdotes,* p. 39), thus reversing her own 1712 pronouncement that she was "peevish," "ill-temper'd," "stupid," and "the most insipid thing breathing" (Lady MWM, *Letters,* 1: 115).

379 *Her animus against them had recently expanded:*

According to the earl of Orrery, writing to Swift in 1741 (Swift, *Correspondence,* 5: 205), "The deceased earl has left behind him many books, many manuscripts, and no money: his lady brought him five hundred thousand pounds, four of which have been sacrificed to indolence, good-nature, and want of worldly wisdom." This was also John Barber's view. (*Ibid.,* 5: 115. 27 July 1738).

379 *Not above accepting hospitality at Twickenham:*

Pope wrote of her in 1726 (2: 364), referrring to her love of country quiet rather than the giddy gossip of the town: "she is of so particular a make, & so errant [arrant] a Wife, & so meer a Good Woman, that little is to be hopd of her as a fine Lady." In 1728 (2: 493, 516), he is expecting a visit from the Oxfords at Twickenham.

380 *Was loved by them:*

Jeremiah Milles (*Journal:* July 1735. BL: Add. MS. 15, 776, ff. 44–5) notes portraits at Wimpole of "Spencer, Shakespeare, Cowley, Butler, Denham, Dorset, Prior, Pope, & Swift." Sir John Evelyn, who visited Wimpole on 3 January 1734 (*Journal:* 8 January 1731–12 January 1734, preserved at Christ Church, Oxford) gives the same list but omits Butler and Denham, and adds Ben Jonson.

380 *"This melancholy Circumstance":*

Swift, *Correspondence,* 2: 289; Pope, 2: 270.

380 *"In such degree as you do":*

25 September 1724 (2: 261). In 1727, Oxford presented Pope with a gold cup and salver, for which he is wittily (but a little ponderously) thanked on 26 December (2: 465–6).

380 *The harpsichord the house contained:*

From Pope's letter of apology to Lady Mary (2: 82–3), it appears that he leased his Twickenham property under rather severe restrictions from his landlord Thomas Vernon, though it is not at all clear why these should cover furnishings; or why, in the letter, he should be obliged to wonder whether these restrictions might also apply to his loan of the house.

380 *His friend Atterbury writes:*

To Teresa Blount [c. 2 February 1720] (2: 31); Atterbury to Pope (2: 123).

382 *The diva Margaritta Durastanti:*

2: 99n; 2: 135n and *TE,* 6: 151–55, 440.

382 *In need of ink and pens:*

To Pope, 19 September 1730 (3: 133).

382 *"Except the box that threw the main":*

Frances, Countess of Hertford, to Henrietta Louise, Countess of Pomfret, 17 April and 21 May 1740, *Correspondence,* (2d ed., 3 vols., 1806), 1: 246–8, 272–3.

382 *"Consult the Genius of the Place in all":*
Christopher Hussey, "Cirencester House—II. The Park," *Country Life,* 23 June 1950. For earlier accounts of the park, see *ibid.*, 8 August 1908; Mary Pendarves (later Mrs. Delany) to Swift, 24 October 1733 (Swift, *Correspondence,* 4: 198–9); Jeremiah Milles (*Journal*), ff. 127–8 (a visit ca. 1736); "A Tour in Wales, 1769," *HMC* Report on the MSS. of the earl of Verulam (1906), pp. 247–8 (anonymous); Samuel Rudder, *A New History of Gloucestershire* (1779) p. 355; [Simeon Moreau], *A tour to Cheltenham Spa: or, Gloucestershire display'd* (1783), pp. 146–8; the *Torrington Diaries,* ed., C. B. Andrews, 4 vols. (London: Eyre and Spottiswoode, 1934–38), 1: 258–9 (a visit in 1787). For a fully informed recent account, see Peter Martin, *"Pursuing Innocent Pleasures"* (just issued), and Brownell, pp. 188–95.

383 *Then fall to comparisons:*
To Lady Mary Wortley Montagu, 15 September 1721 (2: 82); Boswell, *Life of Johnson,* ed., G. B. Hill and L. F. Powell, 6 vols. (1934–50), 3: 403. Bathurst's hospitality sometimes overtaxed his accommodation, so much so that on one occasion (as Swift grumbles) he, Gay, and Pope had to lodge in one of his farmhouses and walk two miles to dinner: a farmhouse that (according to Mary Pendarves) "the day you left it, it fell to the ground; conscious of the honour it had received . . . it burst with pride." Swift, *Correspondence,* 4: 199.

383 *"As ever Don Quixote was to an Enchanted Castle":*
To Bathurst, 5 July 1718 (1: 477).

384 *"Quaff Immortality and Joy":*
To Robert Digby, 20 July 1720 (2: 50).

384 *"Man of learning, courtesy, and feeling":*
Letters, ed., L. P. Curtis (Oxford: Clarendon, 1935), p. 304.

384 *Difficult to say what, exactly, this means:*
For two masterful efforts to sort out these perplexities and give Pope his due (some may think more than his due), see Brownell, esp. chs. 5–6, and Peter Martin's more recent study cited above.

384 *"Exquisite judgment":*
Walpole (*Modern Taste in Gardening*), p. 29. Later in the century, following the further "liberation" sponsored by Lancelot Brown and the young Humphrey Repton, the artifice of Pope's garden (as of his couplet) came under censure. Joseph Heely, *Letters on the Beauties of Hagley, Envil, and the Leasowes,* 2 vols. (1777), 1: 43.

385 *"To catch the vicinal country":*
J. C. Walker, *An Essay on the Rise and Progress of Gardening in Ireland* (Dublin, 1791), p. 18. Pope is (questionably?) given credit for influencing Swift's as well as Delany's taste by Edward Malins and the Knight of Glin, *Lost Demesnes: Irish Landscape Gardening 1660–1845* (London: Barrie and Jenkins, 1976).

385 *"And conceals the bounds":*
Spence, no. 310; *Epistle to Burlington,* ll. 55–6.

386 *Changes in the country house:*
Mark Girouard's study of these matters in *Life in the English Country House* (Yale University Press, 1978) is already a classic. On the larger changes, see Stone.

Chapter 17, Embarrassments and Griefs

388 *His translation of the Odyssey:*
Atterbury to Pope, August 1720 (2: 52).

388 *"His part in the loss of the Southsea":*
3 February. Gay, *Letters,* p. 42.

389 *Editor at a fee of £100:*
The contract is dated 22 May 1721. Houghton Library, Harvard University: MS Eng. 233.13.

389 *Acknowledgments at the close of the* Iliad:
TE, 8: 578.

389 *"Verses on his friend Parnels memory"*:
2: 24; Swift to Ford, 6 January 1719: *Letters of Swift to Ford*, ed., David Nichol Smith (Oxford: Clarendon, 1935), p. 74.

389 *"And Earl Mortimer"*:
TE, 6: 238–40.

391 *"The Temple of Eternity"*:
One Thousand Seven Hundred and Thirty-Eight: Dialogue 2: 234–5.

392 *"Harley is human after all"*:
Geoffrey Tillotson, "Pope's 'Epistle to Harley': an Introduction and Analysis," in his *Augustan Studies* (1961), pp. 162–83. A splendid essay by a splendid man to whom eighteenth-century studies have long been in debt. See also Peter Martin, "Some Background to the Rhetoric of Blame in Pope's 'Epistle to Harley,'" *South Atlantic Bulletin*, 37 (1972): 3–9.

392 *"Not be a Jacobite in England"*:
This was Thomas Lister, Tory M.P. for Clitheroe (Sedgwick, *Commons*, 2: 219).

393 *"Very few hands held up against him"*:
HMC: Onslow Papers, 14: 9, p. 504. Quoted in Bruce Lenman, *The Jacobite Risings in Britain, 1689–1746* (London: Eyre Methuen, 1980), p. 258.

393 *"Efforts to ensure that justice was thwarted"*:
Lenman, p. 197.

393 *"Skreen–Master General"*:
The Garden and the City, pp. 131, 132n, 183.

393 *"But manipulate a society"*:
Lenman, p. 201.

394 *Pope's friend Francis Atterbury*:
On Atterbury's career and eventual attraction to the Stuart side, see especially G. V. Bennett, *The Tory Crisis in Church and State, 1688–1730* (Oxford: Clarendon, 1975)—essentially a life of Atterbury.

396 *"An able and vigilant Minister"*:
Bennett, p. 258.

396 *While the friend was yet living*:
Sheffield had given Pope permission to edit and alter his poems for Pope's miscellany of 1717, "not only as my friend but the best judg I know" (1: 386), and the superintendence seems to have continued. For the edition of 1723 he made about sixty small revisions in Sheffield's best known poem, *An Essay upon Poetry*. Spence, no. 85 and n.

396 *"The late happy Revolution"*:
2 February 1723.

396 *"Having no one good quality besides"*:
Pp. 71–2, 170.

397 *His own often satirized "popery"*:
2: 145 and n.

397 *"A seditious and scandalous libel"*:
A copy of Carteret's order, dated 26 January (executed the next day) may be found in *Copies Taken from the Records of the Court of King's Bench . . . for seizing persons suspected . . . of being the authors, printers, and publishers of libels* (1763), p. 26.

397 *Probably for questioning* :
Pat Rogers was the first, I believe, to call attention to the statement about custody ("Pope and the Social Scene," *Writers and Their Background: Alexander Pope*, ed., Peter Dixon [1972], p. 129), though Sherburn, *Early Career*, p. 224, quotes from the same notice. Professor Rogers rejects the story as rumor; yet Pope's being taken to Carteret for questioning (and in that sense into custody) seems to me probable in view of the political tensions at the time. Moreover, the MS. *Journal* of Mary Caesar, a warm Jacobite and wife of one (as well as a good friend of Pope's), states flatly that Pope was questioned about the volumes—the charge then "Dropt but the Books . . . no longer to be sold in Full Beauty", i.e., unexpurgated. See Howard Erskine-Hill, "Under Which Caesar? Pope in the Journal of Mrs. Charles Caesar, 1724–41," *RES*, n.s. 33 (1982) 436–44.

397 *Barber who had obtained the license*:
Pope to Carteret, 16 February 1723 (2: 159–60): *Pasquin*, 20 February 1723; and Sherburn, *Early Career*, 224–8.

397 *Clearly he did not:*
Though he can hardly have been ignorant of the insinuatingly Jacobite slant of "Some Account of the Revolution," his obvious sensitivity in his correspondence to the suspicion his intimacy with Atterbury might arouse, makes it difficult to believe he would have published at this time anything he judged actionable.

397 *Public opinion in a chronic state of alarm:*
Paul S. Fritz, *The English Ministers and Jacobitism between the Rebellions of 1715 and 1745* (University of Toronto Press, 1975), p. 105, quotes from PRO, SP 35/32, f. 225: "The public was bombarded almost ceaselessly with news 'of plots, conspiracies, and gaols [and] scarcely an hour passes but what some one or other is taken up and running reports [are circulated] of more that are to be seized.'" In such an atmosphere, it is not surprising that Bathurst (again, according to Mary Caesar's *Journal*) feared that the Sheffield edition would be ordered by the Lords to be burnt by the common hangman.

397 *Government underlings inimical to Pope:*
Tickell was Under Secretary of State at this time, his brother Richard also had a post in that office, and George Duckett, possible author of the offending *Pasquin*, was employed along with other Buttonians in the Treasury. Pope's letter to Edward Harley, communicating his friend Lord Harcourt's advice that this was not a propitious time to push the *Odyssey* subscription, *may* hint that he thought Buttonians involved in the hue and cry raised by the Sheffield papers: "If our Governors are displeas'd at me, Im not fond of being the Slave of the Publick against its will, for three years more. Let the Odyssey remain untranslated, or let them employ Mr. Tickell upon it" (2: 159). See also Pope to Harcourt, 20 February (2: 161). The anonymous author of *An Impartial History of . . . Mr. John Barber* (1741) alleges that Barber was sent to Italy in 1722 by the duchess of Buckinghamshire carrying £50,000 for the Pretender (her half-nephew). That Barber did go to Italy, ostensibly for his health, is true. Whether he carried funds for the Pretender and, if so, from what source, remains debatable.

398 *"To preserve this Honour untainted to my Grave":*
2: 160. One inevitably wonders whether the £200 paid Pope by the ministry in 1725, ostensibly in honor of his *Odyssey* translation and registered by him (it seems) in the form of subscription copies for the royal family, represented a belated gesture in palliation of an indignity done the nation's leading poet.

399 *Other editions later on:*
A few copies survive as issued, others with the excised pieces reprinted and reinserted, others, with the censored material copied out by hand and bound in. Many such copies were probably circulating *sub rosa* even in 1723. On 29 February 1724 (according to the *Evening Post* of that date) the *Works* were "Republished." Uncensored editions followed in 1726, 1740, and 1753.

399 *As Atterbury warned Pope in April:*
10 April 1723 (2: 165).

399 *From his comments to Spence later on:*
Spence, no. 234 and n. See also Pope to Lord Harcourt [6 May 1723] (2: 171–2), asking how to handle the questioning if it focused on his being a papist.

399 *That the bishop was concerned in a plot:*
BL: Add. MS. 34, 713, f. 30. Pope's appearance for the defense is noted in the Lords *Journals* (22: 194). The substance of his testimony as set down in the Lord Chancellor's jottings is repeated also in William Wynne's *Defense of Francis, late Lord Bishop of Rochester* (1723), p. 41. On the thirteenth, Reeve, counsel for the bill against Atterbury, acknowledged Pope's testimony but pointed out that Atterbury had doubtless conversed with many persons "to whom he would communicate nothing of an Affair of this Nature." *Complete Collection of State Trials*, 6 (1730): 452–3. This was also the dismissive view of "Britannicus" in the *London Journal* of September 14, who, however, went out of his way to flatter Pope as "the *Best modern Poet* of our *Nation*." *Pasquin*, as usual, chose the low road (20 May 1723): "As a farther Proof of my Innocence, I have produced the worthy Mr. P—pe, a professed *Roman Catholick*, who has deposed that he used frequently to visit me, and that I never mentioned this *Scheme* to him; but constantly entertained him with agreeable Panegyricks upon the *Protestant Religion* and the *Church of England* as by Law established."

400 *"And must suffer for it":*
The speech is found in Atterbury's *Miscellaneous Works*, ed., John Nichols, 5 vols. (1788–89), 5: 387.

400 *"My Declaration for your Friendship":*
　　This letter and Pope's earlier passionate outpouring of April 20, promising that he will find a way to show his respect and love for Atterbury that "no Bills can preclude, nor any Kings prevent"—presumably, that is, in poetry—became widely known and are found in many contemporary transcripts, one pair of which was actually published in Boulogne in 1731 with attribution to the Jacobite Duke of Wharton. See "Letters of Pope to Atterbury in the Tower," *Collected in Himself,* pp. 125–33.

400 *A disgrace to British justice:*
　　See the summary in the *Historical Register* (1724), pp. 90–2. A protest against procedure by bill was also lodged by Bathurst (*ibid.*), who then, turning to the Bench of Bishops, observed that "he could hardly account for the inveterate Hatred and Malice some Persons bore the learned and ingenious Bishop of *Rochester,* unless it was that they were intoxicated with the Infatuation of some of the wild *Indians,* who fondly believe they inherit not only the *Spoils,* but even the *Abilities* of any great Enemy they kill."

402 *"Then I am exchanged":*
　　Bennett, p. 276. See also Thomas Birch's article on Atterbury in the revision of Bayle's *General Dictionary Historical and Practical,* 5 vols. (1735), 2: 413.

403 *Sold it to his father-in-law:*
　　Lucius Fitzgerald, "Pope at Binfield," *Home Counties Magazine,* 2 (1890): 53–61, and Sherburn, *Early Career,* p. 36.

403 *Rackett properties in real estate:*
　　Owen Manning and William Bray, *History and Antiquities of the County of Surrey,* 3 vols. (1814), 3: Appendix, clxii; Hammersmith Court Roll transcripts, May and 18 July 1715 (these last kindly communicated to me by L. F. Hasker, Borough Librarian).

403 *"Worth £20,000":*
　　For this and what follows on the Rackett case I am indebted to the brilliant research of E. P. Thompson, published in *Whigs and Hunters: The Origin of the Black Act* (London: Penguin, 1975), especially his Appendix 2 ("Alexander Pope and the Blacks"), earlier published in the *Times Literary Supplement* (7 September 1973) in elaboration of and reply to Pat Rogers's "A Pope family scandal," *ibid.,* 31 August 1973. See also Rogers's important article on the Waltham Blacks, *Historical Journal,* 17 (1974): 465–86, and the further evidence assembled on possible Jacobite links by Eveline Cruickshanks and Howard Erskine-Hill, "The Black Act and Jacobitism," to be published soon. A "principal target" (Rogers, p. 470) of the Berkshire Blacks was the estate of the earl of Cadogan, an unattractive bullying figure and one of the government's most fervent supporters in its harsh treatment of dissidents.

404 *"Punishable by death":*
　　Leon Radzinowicz, *A History of English Criminal Law* (London: Stevens, 1948), 1: 77. Quoted in Thompson, p. 22.

406 *"For several years, he did":*
　　Thompson, p. 287.

406 *"No man loves the present better":*
　　22 May 1724 (2: 232).

406 *Just to be employed by his master:*
　　Pope to Parnell [25 May or 1 June 1714] (1: 225).

407 *"A faithful servant, dy'd":*
　　"An Ode, Humbly Inscrib'd to the Queen," 159–60. (Slightly misquoted.)

407 *"Superior to most that we call so":*
　　7 November 1725 (2: 336–7).

407 *Teasing, affectionate terms:*
　　TE, 6: 313–16. Robert Digby died 21 April 1726; his sister Mary, 31 March 1729.

409 *"I hope will prevent its return":*
　　30 August 1719 (2: 10–11). Edward Blount died 17 July 1726. On his cherished hope of effecting an accommodation between those of his faith and the Hanoverian government, see Eamon Duffy, "'Englishmen in Vaine': Roman Catholic Allegiance to George I," *Studies in Church History,* 18 (1982): 345–65.

409 *"To do with each other":*
　　9 August 1726 (2: 397).

409 *"Something dear with it"*:
[Early 1729] (3: 3). Congreve died 19 January 1729. To him Pope had dedicated his translation of the *Iliad*.

410 *"At least a yard about"*:
To Caryll, 22 October 1730 (3: 142).

410 *"Is but the nearer going out"*:
To Harcourt, 20 February 1723 (2: 161). See also 3: 51.

410 *"If not a party in them"*:
20 July 1729 (3: 41). See also 3: 36; Swift to Martha Blount, 29 February 1728 (2: 476): ". . . if Teresa beats you for your good, I will buy her a fine whip for the purpose."

411 *"Especially if big with Child"*:
[Richard Morley], *The Life of the late Celebrated Mrs. Elizabeth Wisebourn*, published in May 1721, pp. 33, 44. See Guerinot, pp. 80–2; and Sherburn, *Early Career*, p. 294.

411 *"In such polluted Sheets"*:
Memoirs of a Certain Island, published in September 1724. See Guerinot, pp. 90–1.

411 *"A talk to the whole town"*:
Quoted in Lady MWM, *Letters*, 2: 15n.

411 *"Merely because they are idle"*:
18 September 1722 (2: 134).

411 *His will did not name her his wife*:
Swift's marriage to Stella has been affirmed with as little solid evidence.

412 *"By every wind that blows in it"*:
25 December 1725 (2: 353–4).

412 *"No person concerned" in the work but himself*:
[November 1724] and 4 December 1724 (2: 271, 273).

413 "Friends *who have* assisted me":
No copy of the proposals is known to survive, but this sentence is quoted from them in the quarto *Dunciad* of 1729, pp. 10–11. See also Foxon, ch. II, iii.

413 *"Given to each their finishing"*:
TE, 8: 378.

414 *Engravings from William Kent, etc.*:
TE, 7: xlii–xlvi.

414 *"C—licism in the greatest perfection"*
London Journal, 17 July 1725 (letter signed "Homerides").

416 *Shot himself*:
The details are from Voltaire's account of the episode in his "Small Leningrad Notebook." *Voltaire's Notebooks*, ed., Theodor Bestermann, 2 vols. (Geneva: Institute et Musée Voltaire, 1952) 1: 39. See also *The Daily Post*, 9 May 1724.

416 *"Mordaunt! thou did'st well"*:
TE, 6: 247. As the *TE* editor remarks, the first six verses here eventually reappeared in the final version (1738) of "To Mrs. M. B. on her Birthday," first sent to Martha on her thirty-third birthday, 15 June 1723.

417 *An average of seven sets apiece*:
On the publishing and remunerative aspects of the *Odyssey* translation, see Foxon, ch. II, iii. Information on the character of the subscription list will be found in the analysis by Pat Rogers, "Pope and His Subscribers," *Publishing History*, 3(1978): 7–36.

Chapter 18, From Shakespeare to Swift

418 *His fee of £100*:
For evidence that this *was* his fee, and not the sum of £297.12 named by Johnson (Pope, 3: 138), see Foxon, ch. II, iii.

418 *"Belongs wholly to Mr. Tonson"*:
Quoted in the quarto *Dunciad* of 1729, pp. 10–11.

419 *"Who acted under those of another"*:
Quotations in the foregoing paragraphs are from Pope's Preface, pp. ii, iii, iv, vi.

420 *Passages degraded to foot of page:*
Far fewer, it should be remarked, than were excluded by certain later editors.

420 *Pope's selections frequently correspond:*
For a compact, lucid, and searching account of Pope's applauses and censures throughout the edition, see especially Peter Dixon, "Pope's Shakespeare," *Journal of English and Germanic Philology*, 69 (1964): 191–203, on which I draw in this and the following paragraph. See also John Butt, *Pope's Taste in Shakespeare* (Oxford University Press, 1936); James Sutherland, "The Dull Duty of an Editor," *RES*, 21 (1945): 202–15; and J. A. Hart's MS. Yale dissertation, "Alexander Pope's Edition of Shakespeare: A Critical Study" (1943).

422 *"By which the vices and follies are judged":*
Dixon, "Pope's Shakespeare," p. 201.

423 *First published in the first folio:*
Evening Post, 5 May 1722. A first-rate brief discussion of the history of Shakespeare's text will be found in Paul Bertram, *White Spaces in Shakespeare* (Case Western Reserve University Press, 1981); a detailed account in W. W. Greg, *The Editorial Problem in Shakespeare* (2d ed., Oxford, 1951.)

425 *"Taken notice of as they occur":*
P. xxii.

425 *His impress is still felt:*
Not necessarily for the better, if we wish to recover precisely what Shakespeare wrote and how he and his fellow actors spoke it. See Bertram, pp. 55–7.

425 *To bring together the early editions:*
One ground of his resentment against Theobald (below, pp. 426–33) was that he did not come forward with assistance when the Shakespeare was announced and advertisements were placed soliciting early editions. Though Pope had no right to expect Theobald to surrender his life's accumulation of notes, it would have been friendlier on Theobald's part to have let his hopes of publishing be known and to have lent what early editions he had. Lot 460 in the catalogue of his library when sold on 23 October 1744 consisted of "195 old English plays in Quarto, *some of them so scarce as not to be had at any price.*" It seems improbable that all these were acquired after Pope's edition was published in 1725.

426 *Importations from quarto into folio texts:*
There is an illuminating and persuasive study of Pope's practice in this matter in J. A. Hart's "Pope as Scholar-Editor," *Studies in Bibliography*, 23 (1970): 45–59.

427 *"The interest created by Pope's edition":*
R. F. Jones, *Lewis Theobald: His Contribution to English Scholarship* (New York; Columbia University Press, 1919), p. 30.

427 *Theobald's edition of the plays:*
The faults of *Shakespeare Restored* reappear throughout the edition. As Nichol Smith remarks (*Eighteenth Century Essays on Shakespeare* (Oxford: Clarendon, 1963), p. xlvi), "Theobald had not taste enough to keep him right when he stepped beyond collation."

428 *One emendation sometimes survives today:*
This is "sanctified and pious *bawds*" for the quarto and folio *bonds* in Polonius's warning to Ophelia that a prince's vows of love are likely to be hollow (*Hamlet*, 1. 3. 135). But since "bonds" in the sense of "pledges" also suits the context, many editors have gone back to the early reading.

428 *Took the matter from there:*
Pope's edition, 3: 422; *Shakespeare Restored*, p. 138; The original reading has, however, been defended. For a survey of interpretations, see E. G. Fogel in *Shakespeare Quarterly*, 9 (1958): 485–92.

429 *"Kill'd her Father into the Bargain":*
Shakespeare Restored, pp. 159–60.

430 *"The Author of these Lines":*
For Gay's comment, see *Correspondence* [April 1715] (1: 289). The remark about Popery and knitting is on p. 22 of the attack and refers to p. 5 of the farce.

430 *Generous praise for Pope's Iliad:*
The Censor, 5 January 1717.

430 *"One of the new terrors of death":*
   To Swift, 13 January 1733, when Curll was seeking materials for a life of Gay (Swift, *Correspondence*, 4: 101).

431 *"That other Gentleman's Character":*
   P. iii.

431 *His [in this case, editorial] "sins":*
   Pp. iv, 77, vi. One may note, too, how far Theobald goes out of his way to praise Dennis ("no Man in *England* better understands *Shakespeare*," p. 181), whom in the issue of *The Censor* cited above he had satirized as the ill-natured and ignorant "Furius." He pettishly claims priority for himself when a guess of Pope's has to be acknowledged plausible ("The *Editor* [i.e., Pope] is not the first who has had the same Suspicion: And I may say, because I can prove it by witnesses, it was a *Guess* of mine, before he had enter'd upon publishing *Shakespeare*," p. 82). And, with particular egregiousness, he ventures to "correct" (quite mistakenly) Pope's translation of a Greek word in the *Iliad* (pp. 146–7).

433 *" Only occasionally collating them throughout"*
   R. B. McKerrow, "The Treatment of Shakespeare's Text by His Earlier Editors, 1709–68. Annual Shakespeare Lecture, *Proceedings of the British Academy*, 19 (1933): 89–122.

433 *"Persuaded his friend to proceed in it":*
   Pope's note in the 1729 Dunciad. *TE*, 5: 201n. See also Pope to Swift, 12 October 1728 (2: 522).

434 *"Wood's halfpence".*
   For a full account, see *The Drapier's Letters to the People of Ireland*, ed., Herbert Davis (Oxford: Clarendon, 1935), and Ehrenpreis, 3: 187ff.

435 *One of the administration's sharpest critics:*
   Swift to Peterborow, 28 April 1726 (Swift, *Correspondence*, 3: 131–5) summarizes the second interview with Walpole and Ireland's grievances against England. Undoubtedly, Swift had cherished hopes of some accommodation for himself; but it was put about, of course, that he had been for sale. Two years later, 13 May 1728, the Rev. William Stratford writes to Lord Oxford (HMC: Portland papers, 7: 463): "It will be said now that he writes out of pique and revenge. It is given out that he was much disappointed when he was last here; that he was in hopes, by the interest he had with a certain lady [Henrietta Howard], to have exchanged his preferment in Ireland for as good in England. Nay, that at last he would have quitted all he had in Ireland for £400 *per annum* here, but could not get it."

435 *To unseat Walpole:*
   To Harley, 22 March, and to Fortescue, 2 April (2: 372, 373).

436 *"O hone! O hone!":*
   TE, 6: 251–2; *Roxburghe Ballads*, 5 vols. (1885), 5: 534.

436 *A freak on exhibition in Brobdingnag:*
   The boy was passed about as Gulliver had been. Swift writes to Tickell (now in Ireland) on 16 April: "the King and Court were so entertained with him, that the Princess could not get him till now." Swift, *Correspondence*, 3: 128.

437 *"Did not answer him":*
   P. 7.

437 *"Conciliatory true Friendship":*
   James Anderson, *The Constitutions of the Freemasons* (1723), p. 50. Arbuthnot's, Pope's, and Swift's (?) appearance on the lists of the Grand Lodge was first noticed by Rae Blanchard in "Was Sir Richard Steele a Freemason?" (*Publications of the Modern Language Association*, 63 (1948): 903–17. She lists among those who became members during the 1720s and 1730s (besides the three just mentioned) the poets James Thomson and Richard Savage; the painters Joseph Highmore, William Hogarth, and Sir James Thornhill; the actors John Mills, James Quin, and Theophilus Cibber; the peers Philip Duke of Wharton, John Duke of Montagu (he was Grand Master in 1721–22), and Philip Stanhope, Earl of Chesterfield; the Prince of Wales; and many more of lesser note. That Pope did not particularly warm to the secrecy of the order may be guessed from his *Dunciad* verses (4: 571–2), with the note: "Taciturnity is the *only* essential Qualification."

440 *Also country rambles:*
In a letter purportedly written by one "J. S." to Edmund Curll, dated 10 July 1736, an anecdote is told of a stay by "Lord *B*—. Dean *Swift*, and Mr. *Pope*" at an inn in Nettlebed, a mile or two northwest of Henley-on-Thames on the route to Oxford (and thence to Cirencester?) during which "Two very pretty *Impromptus* were written by Pope."
I. Under the picture of a Gentleman standing behind a Lady, combing her Hair.

> That *Man* will never Grace and Favour find,
> Who takes a *Maiden* by the Hair behind.

II. Under a Picture of Some Ladies at Prayers by a Bed-side.

> When Ladies say their Prayers at Night,
> 'Tis plain that All Things *don't go right*;
> But when All Things *do rightly stand*,
> *Ladies* have *something else in Hand.*

That the verses are genuine examples of even Pope's ephemera seems highly improbable. They accord too well with certain pruriences in the *Rape of the Lock* and in Pope's parody of the first Psalm that Curll had made a point of keeping in the public eye for years, especially as Pope's reputation for respectability grew. Nor is either their tone or the coloring of their "wit" (such as it is) in tune with Pope's work of 1726–27 (the years of Swift's visits) when this trip, if genuine at all, must have been taken and the verses written. The letter containing them occupies a separately paged half-sheet (in the Harvard copy) at the end of Curll's life of Gay, which he had first published in 1733, but, as was usual with him, kept reissuing till the edition was exhausted. I include the verses here as apocrypha not, I believe, elsewhere recorded.
440 *"Witness: A. Pope":*
Dorothea M. R. Benson, Baroness Charnwood, *An Autograph Collection* (London: Benn, 1930), pp. 25–6. On 23 January 1738, Swift passed the book on to his friend the painter Francis Bindon, delegating *him* "Director of Architecture through all Europe."
440 *"Not worth mentioning on such occasions":*
To Henrietta Howard, 1 February 1727 (Swift, *Correspondence*, 3: 196).
441 *"Entirely Yours":*
(2: 384). Swift left some silver cups for Pope at the end of this visit (2: 388, 470)—"with so kind an inscription" (388).
441 *"At Dinner at Twickenham":*
To Tickell, 7 July 1726. (Swift, *Correspondence*, 3: 137).
442 *"Persuaded his friend to proceed in it":*
TE, 5: 201n. Swift also assumes credit for the poem, humorously, in his "Dr. *Sw*—to Mr. *P*—*e*, while he was writing the *Dunciad*." Probably dashed off toward the end of his second visit in 1727, when his hearing difficulties returned, the poem claims that it was the two friends' new inability to communicate that allowed the *Dunciad* to proceed:

> *Pope* has the Talent well to speak,
> But not to reach the Ear:
> His loudest Voice is low and weak,
> The *Dean* too deaf to hear.
>
> A while they on each other look,
> Then diff'rent Studies chuse,
> The *Dean* sits plodding on a Book,
> *Pope* walks, and courts the Muse. . . .
>
> Yet to the *Dean* his Share allot;
> He claims it by a Canon:
> *That, without which a Thing is not*
> Is, *causa sine qua non.*
>
> Thus, *Pope*, in vain you boast your Wit;
> For, had our deaf Divine
> Been for your Conversation fit,
> You had not writ a Line.

442 *"Typical production of the Scriblerus Club"*:
   TE, 5: xiv.
442 *Was off to Dublin*:
   Swift, *Correspondence*, 3: 152–5.
443 *"From a Hackney-coach"*:
   Pope to Swift, 16 November 1726 (2: 412). It is possible that this is Pope's way of telling Swift that he has carried out the commission assigned him.
443 *Possibly with assistance from Arbuthnot and Gay*:
   TE, 6: 266–81. The text used here is from Harley's variant transcript (*TE*, 6: 271–72).
446 *Voltaire's role never certainly established*:
   The charge that Voltaire was a spy for Walpole seems to originate with Ruffhead's *Life of Pope* in 1769 (p. 214 and n), and therefore probably with Warburton, who as a bishop was naturally hostile to Voltaire's freethinking. For the documentary evidence on this matter, see Calhoun Winton, "Voltaire and Sir Robert Walpole: a New Document," *PQ*, 46 (1967): 421–4; and Pat Rogers, "Voltaire and Walpole: A Further Note," *ibid.*, 48 (1969): 279. Voltaire was graciously received by George I in January, 1727.
446 *Commiseration on his damaged hand*:
   2: 399.
447 *The use of which for some time he lost*:
   2: 401; also, 2: 399, 403. The fingers were lame and still paining him a year later (2: 516).
447 *"Sentiments mended so much upon recollection"*:
   Memoirs of M. de Voltaire, Works, ed., Arthur Friedman, 5 vols. (Oxford: Clarendon, 1966); 3: 253. Friedman suggests that Goldsmith's information came from Edward Young, who saw much of Voltaire during his stay in England. Voltaire is said to have remarked that Peterborow had taught him the art of despising riches, Walpole the art of acquiring them, but Harley alone "the secret of being contented" (3: 252).
447 *Journeys in France*:
   Voltaire to Swift, 16 [June 1727] (Swift, *Correspondence*, 3: 214).
448 *"We are as we were"*:
   To Sheridan, 24 June 1727 (Swift, *Correspondence*, 3: 219).
448 *One of his most winning pieces*:
   "A Pastoral Dialogue between Richmond-Lodge and Marble-Hill." Swift, *Poems*, 2: 407–11.
450 *"Too sickly and complaisant"*:
   12 August (Swift, *Correspondence*, 3: 229).
451 *"Only giddy and would sleep"*:
   Pope to Swift, 2 October 1727, and Swift to Pope, 12 October (2: 447, 452).
451 *"Hath left its body"*:
   27 July 1726 (Swift, *Correspondence*, 3: 147).
451 *"To forget myself"*:
   To John Worrall, 12 September 1727 (*ibid.*, 3: 238).
451 *"Upon the brink of another World"*:
   Pope to Sheridan, 6 September [1727] (2: 445).
451 *His friend for some thirty-five years*:
   Swift, *Prose*, 5: 227ff.
454 *High tribute to him*:
   2: 454–6.
454 *"Among the whores and thieves there"*:
   To Pope, 30 August 1716 (1: 360).
455 *"The death of George the first"*:
   Yvonne Noble, "The Beggar's Opera Restored to the Comic Mode by the Power of Song," [MS., pp. 4–5].
456 *"A clamour of applause"*:
   Spence, no. 245.
456 *"It hath fully done its Jobb"*:
   2: 484.

Chapter 19, Taking Writing Seriously

457 *"Great Efforts to procure it":*
A Collection of Pieces in Verse and Prose, which have been publish'd on Occasion of the Dunciad. By Mr. Savage (London, 1732), p. vi. (It is possible that the description was actually written by Pope.)

458 *Roman self-discipline vs. Eastern indulgence:*
Horace's "Cleopatra ode" (1: 37) is notably revealing on this point, as is the *Aeneid*, 8: 675–713.

458 *A* Roman *patrocinium or protectorate:*
Cicero's euphemism in *De Officiis*, 2.7.

459 *Dedications, invectives, and lampoons:*
On the reality, myth, and functions of Grub Street, see the informative and thoughtful chapters in Pat Rogers' *Grub Street: Studies in a Subculture* (London; Methuen, 1972). Also, Ian Watt, *The Rise of the Novel* (Berkeley: University of California Press, 1957), ch. 1.

459 *An astringent observer of our own cultural scene:*
Dwight Macdonald, *Against the American Grain* (New York: Random House, 1962), pp. 3–75.

459 *"Removal of the empire of Troy to Latium":*
TE, 5: 51.

459 *According to Lady Mary Wortley Montagu:*
"[Account of the Court of George I]," in *Poems*, p. 86.

459 *"A Tibbald reigns":*
From the compilation of *Dunciad* manuscript variants made by Jonathan Richardson, Jr. in the mid-1730s. See *The Last and Greatest Art*, p. 101.

461 *"Non-sense, mob, madness":*
Pat Rogers, *An Introduction to Pope* (London: Methuen, 1975), p. 128.

461 *"The greatness of the work":*
Howard Erskine-Hill, *Pope: The Dunciad* (London: Edward Arnold, 1972), p. 31. See also the delightful comments of A. D. Nuttall in "Fishes in the Trees," *Essays in Criticism*, 24 (1974): 27–8.

464 *Owl to adorn a mock hero:*
Some early editions of the *Dunciad* have a frontispiece showing an owl perched on an altar of very large and heavy tomes written by sundry dunces; in others the frontispiece shows an ass laboring under a load of similar tomes, again with an owl perched on top. For an illuminating discussion of the function served by these and other *Dunciad* engravings, see E. F. Mengel, "The Dunciad Illustrations," in *Pope: Recent Essays*, pp. 749–73; and, for additional information, William Kuppersmith, "Asses, Adages, and the Illustrations to Pope's *Dunciad*," *Eighteenth-Century Studies*, 8 (1974–5): 206–11.

464 *Whom Fielding dubbed "Count Ugly":*
Count Ugly, "Sur-intendant des plaisirs d'Angleterre," makes one of the *dramatis personae* in Fielding's revised *Pleasures of the Town* (1734), the puppet show attached to his *The Author's Farce* (1730). (His exceptional ugliness is further witnessed to by the painter John Wootton: HMC: Portland Papers, 6 (1901): 26.) Pope was not the only one to feel that the masquerades were unbecoming. Egmont noted, 23 January 1729: "These masquerades are the corruption of our youth and a scandal to the nation, and it were well to be wished the king would not encourage them. The bishops have addressed in a body against them, ... but all to no purpose." On the grand jury action, see *The Monthly Chronicle for the Year 1729*, vol. 2: appendix, p. 43, where the entire presentment is printed. See also Hogarth's emblematic "Masquerade Ticket," inscribed "A Sacrifice to Priapus" and showing the lion and unicorn of the royal arms in unseemly positions. For a fascinating account of masquerades throughout the century. See "Eros and Liberty at the English Masquerade," by Terry Castle, in *Eighteenth-Century Studies*, 17 (1983–4): 156–76.

465 *"In rich brocaded coats":*
E. B. Chancellor, *Annals of Covent Garden* (London: Hutchinson, 1930), pp. 63–5, and Hugh Phillips, *Mid-Georgian London* (London: Collins, 1964), pp. 142–3.

468 *"Slander in the dark by guess"*:
 TE, 5: 133.

473 *"To dispute it with us"*:
 Bolingbroke and Pope to Swift [March 1732], 3: 276.

475 *A cloud of stinging gnats:*
 In much the same vein, Pope assures Swift a few weeks before publishing the *Dunciad* that "This Poem will rid me of those insects" (2: 481), though he admits in the same letter that "if it silence these fellows, it must be something greater than any Iliad in Christendome."

475 *"And praised with alacrity"*:
 P. 143.

476 *"Rough enough, in many places"*:
 BL: MS. Egerton 1960. ff.8–8v. Quoted by Austin Wright, *Joseph Spence: A Critical Biography* (Chicago: University of Chicago Press, 1950), p. 10. Wright gives a reliable account of Spence's approvals and demurrers.

476 *Proportion of praise to blame not radically different:*
 Pope's marginalia on Spence's manuscript are reprinted in *TE*, 10: 594–605.

476 *"As if it were perfectly helpless"*:
 An Essay on Pope's Odyssey, 2 (1727): 135–6.

477 *"And Notes Variorum"*:
 28 June 1728 (2: 503).

477 *"If understanding be not joyned to it?"*:
 "Of Pedantisme" (Book 1, Essay 24, tr. Florio).

478 *"Nobilities, light, light and air"*:
 James Wright, "Written in a Copy of Swift's Poems for Wayne Burns." *Collected Poems* (Middletown, Connecticut: Wesleyan University Press, 1969), pp. 194–5.

478 *A current comment on the publishing scene:*
 The New Yorker, 13 December 1982, p. 37.

479 *"To set himself in view"*:
 "A Project for the Employment of Authors," *Universal Visiter*, April 1756, in *Works*, 11 vols. (Oxford, 1825) 5: 357.

479 *"Or deserve the other"*:
 TE, 5: 49.

479 *Historian of the book trade in those times:*
 A. S. Collins, *Authorship in the Days of Johnson* (London: Routledge, 1927), p. 14.

479 *Activities for which they had no genuine gift:*
 Pope raises this question in his "Letter to the Publisher" in the *Dunciad Variorum* (*TE*, 5: 15):

> . . . must poverty make nonsense sacred? If so, the fame of bad authors would be much better taken care of, than that of all the good ones in the world. . . . It is not charity to encourage them on the way they follow, but to get 'em out of it: For men are not bunglers because they are poor, but they are poor because they are bunglers.

 For similar sentiments, see *Spectator*, no. 404 (13 June 1712).

480 *"His Volumes of Commentators"*:
 Characteristics (1711), 1: 122.

480 *Unaccompanied by any whole texts:*
 Jeremiah Markland's *Epistola Critica* (1723) consists of emendations of several dozen authors, without texts. Bentley's emendations of Philemon and Menander also appeared in this form (1709) and so, of course, did Theobald's *Shakespeare Restored* (1726). R. F. Jones has an excellent chapter on "The Rage for Emending" in his *Lewis Theobald* (New York: Columbia University Press, 1919).

481 *"Is obvious to a Flea"*:
 In no. 49 of Gay's *Fables* (1727), a man after surveying sky, earth, and sea and supposing them all made for him exclaims: "I cannot raise my worth too high; Of what vast consequence am I!" To which comes the answer: "Not of th' importance you suppose, Replies a Flea upon his nose: . . . 'Tis Vanity that swells thy mind. What, heav'n the earth for thee design'd! For thee! made only for our need; That more important Fleas might feed."

483 *After he had been legally deprived:*
R. C. Jebb, *Bentley* (London: Macmillan, 1902), pp. 192–3.
483 *Inferior readings in a bad manuscript:*
Ibid.
483 *Endowed with powers of textual divination:*
J. H. Monk, *Life of Richard Bentley* (1830), p. 243.
483 *"Greater than he that thinks":*
Reflections on Ancient and Modern Learning (2d ed., 1697), pp. 382–3.
484 *Errors clamoring to be rectified:*
Markland's *Epistola Critica*, p. 2. See also Styvan Thirlby's dedication to his *Justini Philosophi et Martyris Apologiae duae* (1722). Though an opponent of Bentley's, he takes the same complacent view of the value of verbal criticism and later contributed emendations to Theobald's edition of Shakespeare.
484 *Undying "glory" and "honour":*
Bentley, *A Dissertation upon the Epistles of Phalaris* (2d ed., 1699), pp. 92, 276. Theobald, *Shakespeare Restored*, p. 193 (citing Bentley's emendations of Philemon and Menander as his model and inspiration).
484 *"Has finished thee a Pedant":*
A Tale of a Tub. To which is added The Battle of the Books, ed., A. C. Guthkelch and D. N. Smith (Oxford: Clarendon, 1920), pp. 252–3.
486 *Majus opus moveo:*
TE, 5: 96, 195, 221.
486 *"Commentators, and verbal criticks":*
Pp. 138–9.
486 *"Account of the Works of the Unlearned":*
No. 457 (14 August 1717).
487 *Martinus Scriblerus:*
Though worked over spasmodically by various Scriblerians from 1713, the *Memoirs of Scriblerus* were at last pulled together and published by Pope in his prose *Works* of 1741.
487 *The universally indispensable five-foot shelf:*
This is not to deny that Rome's long history has supplied a treasury of exemplary events for analysis and reflection in the light of our own situation. Cf. Geoffrey Barraclough in the *New York Review of Books*, 14 (29 January 1970): 52. "For anyone who believes in the 'relevance' or actuality of history, there is less to be gained, in the present world, from scrutinizing anxiously the Origins of the Second World War than from studying Caesar and the Roman revolution, which may be paralleled sooner than we think in our own society."
487 *"To the eighteenth-century gentleman?":*
J. M. Levine, "Ancients and Moderns Reconsidered," *Eighteenth-Century Studies*, 15 (1981): 83. A thoughtful reexamination to which I am in debt.
487 *"The praise of Rome!":*
Quoted as from Petrarch by David Thompson, ed., *The Idea of Rome from Antiquity to the Renaissance* (University of New Mexico, 1971), p. xi. (I have not yet, however, been able to locate it in Petrarch's own texts.)
488 *"New ones into a chimney":*
TE, 5: 205–6.
489 *We are outraged:*
In a lively essay dealing partly with that famous anthology of bad verse, *The Stuffed Owl*, put together in 1930 by Wyndham Lewis and Charles Lee, Hugh Kenner asks wittily: "What is the *Dunciad* itself ... but a huge synthetic eighteenth-century *Stuffed Owl*, confected with loving taxidermy, out of the skins of a thousand sparrows?" "The Man of Sense as Buster Keaton," *The Counterfeiters; an historical comedy* (Indiana University Press, 1968), p. 60.
490 *Pistols in his pocket:*
No. 265.
490 *A boat to take him home:*
A Popp upon Pope: Or a True and Faithful Account of a late Horrid and Barbarous Whipping, Committed on the Body of A. Pope, a Poet (1728), pp. 3–4. The title deliberately echoes that of Pope's pamphlet on the emetic administered to Curll.

491 *"We are not Dunces"*:
   27 July and 2 August 1728 (2: 507, 508).
491 *"Our* Pamphlets *sell the better"*:
   Sawney [i.e., Alexander Pope] *and Colley* [Cibber], *A Poetical Dialogue* (1742), p. 5.
493 *Execrable poem by James Ralph entitled* Night:
   Edward Young to Thomas Tickell, 5 February 1728. *The Correspondence of Edward Young
   1683–1765*, ed., Henry Pettit (Oxford: Clarendon, 1971), p. 61: "There's lately published
   a Piece calld Night, but there is not in it one single star yt I can find."
494 *"A Fly on Excrement"*:
   John Henley, *The Hyp-Doctor*, 11 May 1731.

Chapter 20, A Wider View

495 *"My Esteem for your Lordship among my Writings"*:
   3: 187–8.
496 *"Have it not to give"*:
   Doubtless it was sentiments of this kind that impelled Nicholas Hawksmoor, who was
   working at the time on the Mausoleum at Castle Howard, to write his employer humor-
   ously: "I . . . hope the poet Mr. Pope will not set his satir upon us for 't." Geoffrey Webb,
   "Letters and drawings of Nicholas Hawksmoor," *Walpole Society*, 19 (1931): 129.
498 *"Ceres re-assume the land"*:
   Pope may be recalling one of the most moving lines in Latin poetry: *iam seges est ubi
   Troia fuit* ("Now there is a cornfield where Troy was"). Ovid, *Heroides* 1: 53 ("Penelope to
   Ulysses"). Cf. also Henry Wotton, celebrating a country life in *Reliquiae* (1651), p. 533:
   "And gold ne're here appears, Save what the yellow Ceres beares." "Laughing" Ceres may
   come from Vergil's *laetans segetes*, as *TE* suggests, 3.2.154; but see also Psalms, 65: 13:
   "The valleys also are covered over with corn; they shout for joy, they also sing" and
   Edward Buckler's verses based on it (*A Buckler*, 1640, leaf B3): "And yonder fruitful
   valleys overnight Did laugh and sing, they stood so thick with corn."
498 *£500 or £1,000:*
   As the *TE* editor notes (3.2.173), this part of the charge may have been fabricated from
   Chandos's subscribing for twelve sets of the *Iliad* and ten sets of the *Odyssey*; though both
   subscriptions would amount to only £128/2.
499 *"Do in this unaccountable affair"*:
   3: 259. It was Lady Betty Germain's opinion that neither Pope's wit nor his sense armed
   him sufficiently "against being hurt by Malice" and that he was "too sensible of what fools
   say." To Swift, 11 January 1732; *Swift, Correspondence*, 4: 1.
499 *"I am sick of such Fool Applications"*:
   William Cleland to John Gay [16 December 1731] 3: 254–7. The letter appeared in the
   Daily Post-Boy. Though signed by Cleland, it was probably written entirely or in large
   part by Pope.
499 *Including several well known in court and ministry:*
   The *Master Key* is reprinted in *TE*, 3.2.176–88. See especially pp. 178–9.
501 *"Real Names and not . . . Fictitious Ones"*:
   TE, 3.2.132.
501 *"A very honest Man"*:
   TE, 5: 60.
501 *"To make my excuses to her Majesty"*:
   Gay and Pope to Swift, 22 October 1727 (2: 455).
502 *"A Laureate of an Ass"*:
   The Grub Street Journal, 24 December 1730. The epigram is reprinted in *TE*, 6: 450
   among doubtful pieces.
503 *As his biographer describes it:*
   J. H. Plumb, *Sir Robert Walpole: The King's Minister* (London: Cresset Press, 1960),
   p. 175.
503 *"His Head should be so Giddy"*:
   20 February 1730 (3: 91).

503 *"Not even a Dinner, at this distance":*
        18 August 1730 (3: 125). Possibly Pope had heard of Eusden's illness at this time and wished he had influence to obtain the laureateship for Gay.

504 *By Lady Mary Wortley Montagu:*
        [October 1730] and 13 September [1729?] (3: 139 and 53).

505 *No one knows for sure:*
        Walter Sichel, *Bolingbroke and His Times*, 2 vols. (London: Nisbet, 1901), 1: 146, assumes the school was Eton; but H. T. Dickinson, *Bolingbroke* (London: Constable, 1970), pp. 3–4, gives grounds for believing it was one of the dissenting academies.

505 *"Dear Patron, Master, and Friend," in another:*
        Quoted by Dickinson, p. 7, from the Trumbull MSS.

505 *Whose protégé he had formerly been:*
        Bolingbroke composed the tribute incised in 1728 on the column erected to Marlborough at Blenheim (David Green, *Sarah, Duchess of Marlborough* [London: Collins, 1967], p. 249) and also paid him homage in *The Craftsman* (1 May 1731): "a great Man; . . . as great as human Nature is capable of producing."

505 *Fled to safety across the Channel:*
        Other explanations are possible. Bolingbroke may have believed he could strengthen the Pretender's cause to the point at which it might speedily triumph, the prospects for a Restoration having never looked more promising than in 1715.

505 *"The encouragement of letters":*
        Bolingbroke to Orrery, 12 June 1711, *The Letters and Correspondence of Henry St. John*, ed., Gilbert Parke, 4 vols. (1798), 1: 246–7.

507 *Pope's visit to Bucklebury:*
        Pope to Congreve, 16 January 1715 (1: 275). Though this may be a conflated letter, or may have been written, as with some others of Pope's letters, to a different correspondent, I see no reason to doubt its contents.

507 *"The Patron of their Writer":*
        TE, 7: 24.

507 *As Swift was quick to point out:*
        28 June 1715 (1: 301–2).

508 *"As a coach comes to one's door for other visitors":*
        Spence, nos. 274, 275. The strength of Pope's attachment to Bolingbroke, with whom he had kept in touch while the latter was in France, comes through vividly in his letter of gratitude to Lord Harcourt, who had helped bring about the reconciliation with the English court (21 June 1723: 2: 175) and also in his announcement to Swift [August 1723] (2: 184) that "Lord Bolingbroke is now return'd (as I hope) to take me, with all his other Hereditary Rights."

508 *"Such as Mr. Pope for Lord Bolingbroke":*
        "On Men and Manners," in *Works*, 3 vols., (1765), 2: 245.

509 *Maturity from his studies in exile:*
        Referring apparently to these, Pope writes Swift, 15 October 1725 (2: 332): "Lord B. is the most *Improv'd Mind* since you saw him that ever was without shifting into a new body." It is likely he is also referring to Bolingbroke's leaving off the sexual and alcoholic excesses that had made his younger days notorious.

509 *"Admirable conversation . . . and good manners":*
        Journal to Stella, 3 November 1711 (2: 401). Twenty years later he is still "reckoned the most Universal Genius in Europe" in Swift's *Verses on the Death of Dr. Swift* (written 1731, published 1739), l. 196n.

509 *"Who had not a deep Discerning":*
        The Englishman, 8 August [1715], ed., Rae Blanchard (Oxford: Clarendon, 1955), p. 288.

509 *One's membership in heaven's Elect:*
        Pope ridicules this ultimately Calvinist assumption in his *Epistle to Bathurst*, where both men agree that wealth is "No grace of Heav'n or token of th' Elect" (l. 18).

509 *Farm implements on his dining room walls:*
        That they were painted in grisaille I infer from the anonymous *Dawley Farm* (1731), which compliments Bolingbroke for having no gaudy colors in his Rural "Hall" and from

which I quote l. 18 at p. 510. The poem is printed in *TE*, 6: 452–5. Though possibly revised by Pope, it is not, I am convinced, of his making. If in revising another's work he contributed the line "The Feast of Reason, and the Flow of Soul," this would account for his feeling free to borrow it back as l. 128 of his first Horatian imitation.

509 *"To countenance his calling this place a Farm":*
28 June 1728 (2: 503). See also Pope to Bathurst, 7 November [1728] (2: 525).

510 *Realizing £700 a year:*
Letters . . . by the late . . . Lady Luxborough to William Shenstone (1775), p. 170.

510 *Essays for The Craftsman:*
See Simon Varey's valuable collection, *Lord Bolingbroke: Contributions to the Craftsman* (Oxford: Clarendon, 1982).

511 *"In English or any other language":*
Adams' marginal comment in his copy. Placed by a particular passage, the comment appears to apply to the work as a whole. See Zoltan Haraszti, *John Adams and the Prophets of Progress* (Harvard University Press, 1952), pp. 51, 54.

511 *"Fair Virtue's cause":*
TE, 10: 380.

511 *Unbuttoned letters to Henry Cromwell:*
Cromwell gave the letters to Elizabeth Thomas (his "Sapho" and "Sappho" in the correspondence), who then sold them to Curll (2: 437–41). Above, p. 151.

512 *"The Plan of the Second is settled":*
Fenton to Broome, 24 June [1729] (3: 37); Pope to Swift, 28 November 1729 (3: 81); Atterbury to Pope, 20 November 1729 (3: 77); Bolingbroke to Swift (3: 213–14).

512 *To the* Essay on Man *and to each other:*
For a detailed account of the project as planned and as completed see Miriam Leranbaum, *Alexander Pope's "Opus Magnum," 1729–44* (Oxford: Clarendon, 1977).

513 *Acknowledged no responsibilities at all:*
Marx argues that capitalism tends to elicit different personality types depending on its stage of development—in its early stages, the aescetic and perhaps grasping personality required for capital accumulation. It may be significant that one of the most popular plays of the first half of the eighteenth century was *Volpone*, produced one hundred and three times, and never more popular than during the period when Pope was writing this epistle. See R. G. Noyes, *Ben Jonson on the English Stage*, 1660–1776 (Harvard University Press, 1935), and Graham Nicholls, "Two Notes on Pope's 'Epistle to Bathurst,'" *Notes and Queries*, 219 (1974): 251.

515 *"Or buys a Queen":*
It is amusing to see Pope's satirical account of the characteristics of a money economy put forward *au serieux* about two centuries later by the distinguished sociologist Georg Simmel (*The Sociology of Georg Simmel*, ed. and tr., K. H. Wolff [New York, The Free Press, 1950], p. 355): "Three characteristics of the monetary form of value are relevant here: its compressibility, which permits one to make somebody rich by slipping a check into his hand without anybody's noticing it; its abstractness and qualitylessness, through which transactions, acquisitions, and changes in ownership can be rendered hidden and unrecognizable in a way impossible when values are owned only in the form of extensive, unambigously tangible objects; and finally, in its effect at-a-distance, which allows . . . its complete withdrawal from the eyes of the immediate environment."

516 *The Man of Ross was an actual person:*
Both on the man himself (whose name was John Kyrle) and on Pope's use of him in the epistle, see the sensitive chapter in Howard Erskine-Hill's *Social Milieu of Alexander Pope* (Yale University Press, 1975).

Chapter 21, The Proper Study

522 *"Which shew a true Genius":*
Thomas Edwards to Sir John Clerk, 13 March 1733 (*Notes and Queries*, 198 (1953): 338).

522 *"And some others" solemnly denying it:*
8 and 20 March (3: 353–4, 358).

523 *"And for Virtue scorns":*
    One Epistle to Mr. A. Pope (1730), p. 10; *Of Dulness and Scandal* (1732), p. 6.
523 *"To have it in the amplest manner":*
    Printed by Pope in his "Testimonies of Authors" (*TE*, 5: 43), a common feature of learned editions such as the *Dunciad Variorum* burlesques, but intended also to record the insults and slanders over a period of many years that the poem was written to avenge.
523 *A proof of his avarice and conceit:*
    An Epistle to Mr. Welsted; And a Satyre on the English Translators of Homer (1721), pp. 17, 20.
523 *"The selfish, ignorant, and vain":*
    TE, 5: 43.
523 *"As I was injured that way before":*
    3: 352.
524 *Making it yet more widely known:*
    An essay on the First Book of T. Lucretius Carus De Rerum Natura . . . by J. Evelyn (1696), leaf A7v. Dryden's selections from books 1–5 appeared in his *Sylvae* (1685).
525 *Read as a modern* De Rerum Natura:
    On the Lucretian aspects of the *Essay*, see especially Miriam Leranbaum, *Alexander Pope's "Opus Magnum", 1729–44* (Oxford: Clarendon, 1977), ch. 2, and Bernhard Fabian, "Pope and Lucretius: Observations on *An Essay on Man*," *Modern Language Review*, 74 (1979): 524–37. Fabian concludes: "The Essay on Man can be read as an attempt to restore, for an age of mechanistic philosophy, the unity of the macrocosm and the microcosm, which had been destroyed with the disruption of the old emblematic concepts in the . . . seventeenth century. It can [also] be read as an anti-Lucretian poem in the sense that Pope tried to devise a counterpart to the only ancient poem that presented a consistent exposition, on philosophical principles, of man and his place in the universe. . . . It is [likewise] a grand allusion to Lucretius that made him a part of the neo-classical canon of English literature in much the same way . . . that Pope's translation of the Greek epics made Homer a part of this canon." To this aspect, my edition of the poem in *TE* paid insufficient heed. See too the fine pages on Manilius in G. F. C. Plowden's *Pope on Classic Ground* (1983).
526 *"Would at once be destroyed":*
    Sermons and Essays (1709), p. 209.
527 *"Ungod it self":*
    The True Intellectual System of the Universe (1678), p. 874.
527 *"To doubt of that God":*
    TE, 5: 387.
528 *Limitation implied in the use of "must":*
    See F. E. L. Priestley, "Pope and the Great Chain of Being," *Essays in English Literature from the Renaissance to the Victorian Age*, eds., Millar MacLure and F. W. Watt (Toronto: University of Toronto Press, 1964), pp. 213–28. Professor Priestley seems to me fundamentally right in his contention that Pope's empirical stand at the opening of Epistle 1 rules out acceptance of the deductive version of the chain of being in favor of a conception of it shaped by the thought of the physico- and astro-theologists along lines dictated by the observed order and multitudinousness of things as presented by the telescope and microscope. The frequent blurring of the two ways of conceiving the chain in eighteenth-century writing is reflected in Pope, I believe; but in the Twickenham edition I took too little account of its empirical emphasis.
530 *"Whatever is, is RIGHT":*
    The last four words, taken out of context, spelled trouble for Pope later on, as we shall see. Though the ambiguities of language make it impossible to be altogether certain, it seems unlikely that in this context he meant more than believers have always maintained. See the notes at *TE*, 3.1: 51.
530 *And hence a virtue:*
    The most influential reply to Hobbes was that of Shaftesbury and his followers, anticipated and prepared by the so-called latitudinarian preachers of the late seventeenth century, who groped their way toward a more optimistic theory of human nature than that of Hobbes or his later ironical disciple Bernard Mandeville—one which, whether intentionally or not, gave sanction to the strenuous economic individualism that underlay

the revolution of 1688 and the "money" economy of Pope's time. See on these develop-
ments R. S. Crane, "Suggestions toward a Genealogy of the 'Man of Feeling,'" *English
Literary History*, 1 (1934): 220–70, and, more recently, M. C. Jacob, *The Newtonians and the
English Revolution* (Hassocks, Sussex: Harvester Press, 1976). On Mandeville, see F. B.
Kaye's superb commentary in his edition of *The Fable of the Bees*, 2 vols. (Oxford: Claren-
don, 1924).

530 *"Nature in its integrity"*:
   A Treatise of Self-Denyall (1660): Preface.

531 *"A more excellent Creature than before he fell"*:
   Timothy Nourse, *A Discourse upon the Nature and Faculties of Man* (1686), p. 109.

531 *"He has made all things good"*:
   D. M. Frame, *Montaigne's Essais: A Study* (Englewood Cliffs, N.J.: Prentice-Hall,
   1969), p. 52.

532 *Rather than reprehensible expressions of this instinct*:
   On the backgrounds of Pope's thinking about the passions and their relation to reason
   and to the general well-being of both individual and society, see D. H. White's admirably
   informed discussion in *Pope and the Context of Controversy: The Manipulation of Ideas in "An
   Essay on Man"* (Chicago: University of Chicago Press, 1970), chs. 4–7; B. A. Goldgar,
   "Pope's Theory of the Passions: The Background of Epistle II of the *Essay on Man*,"
   Philological Quarterly, 41 (1962): 730–43; and the introduction and notes to the poem in *TE*,
   3: 1.

535 *"To move the Parts of our own Bodies"*:
   Opticks (English translation, 1718), p. 379.

541 *"Ever written in any language"*:
   Lettres philosophiques [Letter 22], 1756 ed. and after. In his poem on the Lisbon earth-
   quake, however, Voltaire chose to take *Tout est bien* literally and argued that the sufferings
   caused by that disaster exploded such views. See *TE*, 3.1. xlv–xlvi.

541 *"Oppress judgement by overpowering pleasure"*:
   P. 224.

541 *To the music of the spheres*:
   Peter Levi, *Pope* (Harmondsworth: Penguin, 1974), p. 23. For a brilliant but, in my
   view, sometimes rather off-the-cuff consideration of the *Essay*, see A. D. Nuttall, *Pope's
   "Essay on Man"* (London: Allen and Unwin, 1984).

542 *Forces that made the structure one*:
   TE, 3.1. xxxiv.

543 *"A narcissistic preoccupation with the self"*:
   Christopher Lasch, *The Culture of Narcissism: American Life in an Age of Diminishing
   Expectations* (New York: W. W. Norton, 1978), p. xv.

544 *"The destruction of the orchard"*:
   Lewis Thomas, *The Youngest Science: Notes of a Medicine-Watcher* (New York: Viking,
   1983), pp. 247–8.

546 *"Wish no friend I have ever should feel"*:
   10 and 7 June 1733 (3: 374). When she died, Edith Pope was about a week short of 90.

546 *"Nor any Body to follow the Corpse"*:
   The Universal Spectator, 16 June 1733.

548 *"Gave her great uneasiness this way"*:
   Bodley MS. Engl. lett., d. 59, f. 89. "New Anecdotes," pp. 348–9.

Chapter 22, Personalities and Politics

553 *"He became her implacable enemy"*:
   Although Lady Mary tells her sister Lady Mar in April 1722, that she sees Pope "very
   seldom" these days (*Letters*, 2: 15), two brief notes of probably August or October, 1723,
   survive among the Homer MSS. (*Corr.* 2: 194, 204) to indicate that they were not yet
   estranged. By late 1726 a break had evidently occurred. Writing to Lady Mar not long after
   Gulliver's Travels appeared, she tells her that it is the work of Swift, Arbuthnot, and Pope,
   and adds, with a characteristically witty but extremely offensive insinuation, "to say truth

they talk of a stable with so much warmth and Affection I can't help suspecting some very powerfull Motive at the bottom of it."

The soiled bedding story comes from Pope's friend, the painter James Worsdale (James Prior, *Life of Edward Malone* [1860], p. 150); that concerning Wharton, from Spence (no. 751). Lady Louisa's account of a "declaration" appears in her "Biographical Anecdotes of Lady M. W. Montagu," reprinted in Lady MWM, *Poems*, p. 37. The Victorian painter W. A. Frith was so taken with the drama of the supposed "declaration" scene that he painted it twice (in 1851 and 1854), Lady Mary standing tall and amused, Pope crouched forward in a chair looking straight ahead with mixed anger and dismay. Above, p. 554.

553 *Marry a Harcourt relation:*
		Above, p. 308.
555 *"Shitting on them every day":*
		Robert Halsband, "New Anecdotes of Lady M. W. Montagu," in *Evidence in Literary Scholarship*, eds., René Wellek and Alvaro Ribeiro (Oxford: Clarendon, 1979), p. 245.
555 *Complaints on that score:*
		17 September (2: 258).
555 *"Levite to the lover yields":*
		Though *One Epistle* is now believed to be the work of Leonard Welsted and James Moore-Smythe, Lady Mary's name was early associated with it. Arbuthnot, who seems to have seen an advance copy of the poem (which abused Swift, Gay, Jervas, Atterbury, and himself as well as Pope) as early as October, 1729, wrote at once to Lady Mary, asking (apparently) whether it was being correctly ascribed to her pen (3: 59–60). In her reply she expressed such shock at the very idea, professed herself so eager to join him in punishing "so horrid a villany," and labored so derisively to make the attribution to her seem "a contrivance of Pope's" that her correspondent, who had a keen sense of the ridiculous, might have been forgiven if the affair had reminded him of Queen Gertrude's comment on the Player Queen in *Hamlet*: "The lady doth protest too much, methinks." He would, perhaps, have been yet more inclined to that view had he known of the sentiments she had expressed about him, Swift, and Pope after the publication of *Gulliver* and continued to express in verses in her private papers and in one instance in print—some of the nastiest verses in her manuscripts being reserved for the man whose "Candor, Generosity, & good sense" (she now assures him) "has obligd me to be with a very uncommon Warmth your real Friend." In fairness to Lady Mary it must be stressed, however, that there is no hard evidence of her participation in *One Epistle*, despite the claim to that effect made in the *Grub Street Journal* of 21 May 1730, after the poem was finally published on 28 April. That claim may have been inspired by Pope. To be equally fair to Pope, one would have to add that he too might be forgiven for mistaking certain couplets in the poem for Lady Mary's, including the final four on Vanessa.
556 *"Pray own your chicks":*
		The poem appeared in the *Miscellanies. The Last Volume* (1727) with the title "The Capon's Tale: To a Lady who father'd her Lampoons upon her Acquaintance."
556–7 *"As she certainly one day will him":*
		Pope's prediction proved to be correct. In Lady Mary's manuscript imitation of Horace's ninth ode of the third book (*Poems*, pp. 284–6), adapted as a dialogue between Walpole and William Pulteney, his one time Whig associate but now Opposition arch-enemy, Walpole recalls the days when

in all my Schemes you most heartily joyn'd
And help'd the worst Jobs [i.e. cheats] that I ever design'd.

557 *"When I found it dangerous":*
		3: 53.
557 *"Occasioned the breach between us":*
		Spence, no. 751.
557 *In all probability Lady Mary:*
		The name has been thought to refer to Lady Deloraine, governess to the younger princesses; but if we may believe Hervey, wit was a rare achievement with her. Hervey, p. xxiii. See also p. xxxix, where she is called a "pretty idiot," and p. 745, where she is "one of the simplest women who ever lived." Pope may have meant to include both

"Ladies" in the term, since he certainly thought of Lady Delorain as a hostile court-gossip. See *TE*, 3.2: 171; 4, 124 and 340.

557 *"Whom they might most offend"*:

Works (1751), 8: 260. (A meticulous edition of Pope's later prose, prepared by Rosemary Cowler, whose headnote to the "Letter" I have drawn on, is currently in press.) Further to be noted in connection with Pope's explanation is the fact that in some MS. lines composed for the *Epistle to Arbuthnot* (1735), he makes the identical point. These lines, which do not appear in the surviving MSS. of the *Epistle* but only in a collation made by Jonathan Richardson, Jr. from a scrap of the MS. apparently now lost (see *The Last and Greatest Art*, p. 454) expand somewhat on a single couplet (ll. 368–9) devoted to this matter in the published poem:

> Once, & but once, my heedless youth was bit,
> And lik'd that dang'rous Thing, a Female Wit;
> Safe, as I thought, tho all ye Prudent chid;
> I writ no Libels, but my Lady did.
> Great odds! in Am'rous or Poetic Game,
> When Woman's was the *Sin*, but Man's the *Shame*.

"Declaration" or not, in other words, professional ethics may also have played a part in his resentment. It was one thing to disown works (most writers in the period did), quite another, if Pope's charge is just, to assign them to someone they might injure.

557 *"All the solitary hours employ"*:

"Her Palace placed beneath a muddy road," in *Poems*, p. 247, ll. 89, 69, 97–8.

559 *"Such only were the objects of his satire"*:

3: 352.

559 *Horace Walpole thought so:*

Meeting her in Florence while on his travels, Walpole writes to his friend Henry Conway on 25 September 1740: "Did I tell you Lady Mary Wortley is here? She . . . is laughed at by the whole town. Her dress, her avarice, and her impudence must amaze anyone that never heard her name. She wears a foul mob, that does not cover her greasy black locks, that hang loose, never combed or curled; an old mazarine wrapper, that gapes open and discovers a canvas petticoat. Her face swelled violently on one side with the remains of a pox, partly covered with a plaister, and partly with white paint, which for cheapness she has bought so coarse, that you would not use it to wash a chimney." In a second letter written a week later to Richard West, he refers to her as "Moll Worthless", who, in rivalry for a young man she fancies, "to get him from the mouth of her antagonist," took him to a ball, "where there was no measure kept in laughter at her old foul tawdrey painted, plastered personage."Her biographer, Robert Halsband, believes that Walpole's description of her to her daughter many years later—"She was not handsome, had a wild staring eye, was much marked with the smallpox, which she endeavoured to conceal by filling up the depressions with white paint"—is fairer to her. *Life*, p. 204. Her notoriety while abroad seems to have been considerable. In reply to a letter in which Bethel, in Italy for his asthma, had evidently spoken of its extent, Pope writes (1 January [1742]; 4: 377): "I wish you had just told me, if the Character be more *Avaricious*, or *Amatory*? and which Passion has got the better at last."

559 *To poison a rival:*

On the poisoning scandal, see *TE*, 4: 367, and William King's *Scamnum, Ecloga* (1740), where the rival, Mary M'Kenzie, is named Pholoe and the poisoner, Delia. As the rival was the niece of John Caryll, Jr.'s wife, Pope would readily hear about it. Sir Francis Page's judicial reputation is discussed in *TE*, 4: 376; see also Clarence Tracy, *The Artificial Bastard: A Biography of Richard Savage* (Harvard University Press, 1953), pp. 83–7.

560 *"The rhetoric of hate"*:

Guerinot, p. 226. She continued to deny authorship of the *Verses* while protesting to Arbuthnot against the mild references to her in the *Epistle to Arbuthnot* (ll. 101, 369), assuring the doctor that the *Verses* were written without her knowledge "by a Gentleman" and thus demonstrating the readiness to transfer responsibility to others that Pope claimed to have met with in his own case.

560 *"Like* Cain*":*

It seems improbable, though not perhaps impossible, that Lady Mary (or Lord Hervey) intends to remind readers of an ancient political association conceivably not yet forgotten: "I take *Cain* to be the first Tory, and they were call'd Cainites till of late years; for a Tory and a Murderer are synonimous in the original. . . . Tory is an Irish Word, and signifies the same in *Irish* as *Cain* does in *Hebrew*, or *Murderer* in *English*." *The True Picture of an Ancient Tory* (1702), p. 4.

560 *Her unsavory reputation in her own time:*

Horace Walpole, again, had no doubts. See his "Anecdotes of Lady M. W. Montagu and Lady Pomfret" (*Correspondence*, 14: 242–7), where he is quite specific about the identity of her lovers before and after marriage (see also Spence, no. 1560), and includes some verses from Horace (*Odes*, 1. 3), which he retitles "To the Postchaise that carries Lady Mary Wortley Montagu (Wrote at Toulon 1741)," and then adapts as follows:

> The Queen of Lust from dangers ward thee,
> And hotter Helen's brothers guard thee!
> And may The King of Winds restrain
> Each storm that blows across the plain,
> Chaining up all, except one gale
> To scatter whiffs and cool her tail!
> O chaise, who art condemn'd to carry
> The rotten hide of Lady Mary,
> To Italy's last corner drive;
> And prithee set her down alive;
> Nor tumble off with jolts and blows,
> The half she yet retains of nose.

561 *Presented to the King and Queen:*

Works (1751), 8: 279.

561 *Lady Mary's poem:*

The Dean's Provocation for Writing the Lady's Dressing-room, published 8 February 1734. For her MS. draft, see her *Poems*, pp. 273–6, and, for an account of the poem, Robert Halsband's "'The Lady's Dressing Room' Explicated by a Contemporary," in *The Augustan Milieu*, eds., H. K. Miller, E. Rothstein, G. S. Rousseau (Oxford: Clarendon, 1970), pp. 225–31.

562 *Over Europe as well as England:*

Pope's bout with the disease seems to have come in the first days of February, since in late January he was well and going almost every day to Kensington to comfort Peterborow, who was extremely ill there and from whom it is possible that Pope contracted it. See Pope to Fortescue (3: 343); to Swift, 16 February 1733 (3: 349–50); and to Richardson [18 February 1733], *ibid.* If early February is the right guess for the date of the illness, Bolingbroke's report that the poem was printed about six days after it was written (Spence, no. 321) may be exact. On the prevalence of a serious "Distemper" at this period, see Charles Delafaye, Undersecretary of State, to the earl of Essex at Turin, 15 February 1733 (BL: Add. MS. 27, 732, f. 114b). Possibly it was from some lingering after-effect of this that Mrs. Pope died the following June, since it had often proved fatal, we are told, to the elderly. Henry Pelham to the earl of Essex at Turin, 29 June 1733 (*ibid.*, ff. 99a and b).

562 *Earlier epistles to Burlington and Bathurst:*

TE, 4: xiv.

562 *As was his custom:*

Additional political grounds for the timing are suggested in Vincent Carretta's "Pope's *Epistle to Bathurst* and the South Sea Bubble," *Journal of English and Germanic Philology*, 77 (1978): 212–31.

562 *"The politico-morality of the age":*

E. R. Wasserman, *Pope's Epistle to Bathurst: A Critical Reading with an Edition of the Manuscripts* (The Johns Hopkins University Press, 1960), p. 54.

562 *"Too hot to hold him":*

[21 March 1733] (Swift, *Correspondence*, 4: 131–2).

563 *"Will never like the government he lives under":*
Carlos Baker, *Ernest Hemingway: A Life* (New York: Scribner, 1967), p. 227.

564 *Stances from all three:*
On Pope's use of Perseus and Juvenal, see the incisive discussions by Howard Weinbrot in *Alexander Pope and the Traditions of Formal Verse Satire* (Princeton University Press, 1982), and by Howard Erskine-Hill, in *The Augustan Idea in English Literature* (London: Edward Arnold, 1983). Needless to say, imitation of any of the Roman satirists offered a certain protective value if one were in danger of prosecution; but Horace, as the satirist whom Augustus himself had protected, could be the most effective shield. See R. W. Rogers, *Major Satires*, pp. 78ff. Boileau also is often in Pope's mind. See especially his Satires 8 and 9.

564 *"How well that would hit my case":*
Spence, nos. 321–321a.

564 *His awareness of potential danger:*
Pat Rogers "Pope and the Social Scene," in *Writers and Their Background*, ed., Peter Dixon (London: G. Bell & Sons, 1972), pp. 131–6, persuasively calls attention to the coloration of this poem and others of Pope's satires, 1733–8, by procedures and terms of law. These he believes represent for Pope the new Whiggery of the bureaucratic state confronting and seeking to put down a dissident individualism.

565 *"Blunderbuss & Thunder":*
As often, Pope reserved the most dangerous lines (25–6) for the second edition.

566 *He will continue to write satire:*
2 November 1728. The debate and its relation to Pope's imitation are summarized in *The Garden and the City*, pp. 174–87.

566 *"Motive" for writing the imitation:*
16 February 1733 (3: 348).

566 *And vice versa:*
Neill Rudd has some valuable comments on this in his essay on Pope's Horatian imitation (*Ep. II*, ii) in *The Yearbook of Literary Studies* (1984). See also the essay by Frank Stack in *The Art of Alexander Pope*, eds., Howard Erskine-Hill and Anne Smith (London: Vision Press, 1979).

568 *Left many a nobleman in straitened circumstances:*
On Walter, both as individual cheat and symbol of hucksterism, see the fine chapter in Howard Erskine-Hill, *The Social Milieu of Alexander Pope* (Yale University Press, 1975).

568 *Chief palace agent to the Queen:*
For all his ladylike carriage and patrician complacencies, Hervey was a shrewd observer of court and national politics, an able defender of the Walpole regime, and, within limits, a sensitive psychologist. One must add the qualifying phrase, because though capable of warm affections (as for Stephen Fox, to whom he seems to have had a passionate homosexual attachment, and for the Queen, who made him a kind of foster-son in lieu of the Prince of Wales, whom both she and the King disliked intensely), Hervey appears to have been constitutionally incapable of imagining any motives for human actions except the basest. His *Memoirs*, therefore, though invaluable historically, rarely allow one to forget that they have been in some degree, consciously or unconsciously, shaped to justify his own cynicism by projecting a world to which such cynicism is the only sound response. Thomas Birch expresses a contemporary's view in noting (upon Hervey's death) that he has left memoirs "in which, it is highly probable, he will fully gratify both his peculiar resentments and the general Malignity of his Nature." To Philip Yorke, 27 August 1743. BL: Add MS. 35, 346: f. 137b.

569 *"Give any redress to the injured":*
Hervey, pp. 186, 365.

570 *The first of Pope's surviving Horatian imitations:*
We hear of other earlier imitations of Horace, but these have not survived. See "*Collected in Himself*," pp. 323–25.

572 *"Will be known who voted pro and con":*
To Lord Waldegrave, 3 March 1732. Quoted in Paul Langford, *The Excise Crisis: Society and Politics in the Age of Walpole* (Oxford: Clarendon, 1975), p. 40.

573 *"Contempt for their role in society":*
> B. A. Goldgar, *Walpole and the Wits: The Relation of Politics to Literature, 1722–42* (University of Nebraska Press, 1976), p. 6. Celebrating in his *Enquiry into the Present State of Polite Learning* (1759) the link he thought he discerned between patron and poet during the reign of Anne, Goldsmith adds: "But this link seems now entirely broken. Since the days of a certain prime minister of inglorious memory, the learned have kept pretty much at a distance."

574 *"Something mean and below him":*
> Hervey, p. 261.

574 *"Baboon enough for you":*
> *DNB,* sub George II. See also Hervey, p. 231, where the Princess's term is "monkey," and p. 271, where the Queen's term is "ce monstre."

574 *"With more crooked beggars":*
> Hervey, p. 423.

575 *"Be able to inform you":*
> 26 September 1735. CH (Houghton), MS. #2482.

575 *Not since the Great Plague of 1665:*
> M. Dorothy George, *London Life in the Eighteenth Century* (London: Paul, French, and Trubner, 1925), p. 25.

575 *Seven thousand gin shops:*
> As late as 1751, Henry Fielding, in his *Inquiry into the Causes of the Late Increase of Robbery,* p. 18, speaks of gin as "The principal sustenance of more than a hundred thousand people in the Metropolis."

575 *"He has been fairly in":*
> See also *One Thousand Seven Hundred and Thirty-Eight, Dial.* 1: 129–30, where Pope ridicules the government's concern with the morals of the poor rather than with villainy in high places.

577 *Worth £900,000:*
> "Travel Diary of Sir John Clerk" *SRO:* GD 18/2107, f. 7b (5 April). I suspect C. W. Dilke's belief that Page lies somewhere in the background of Pope's Sir Job (*Imit. Hor., Ep. I,* i: 138–47) is correct.

577 *£30,000 fine:*
> H. T. Dickinson, "Walpole and his critics," in *History Today,* 22 (1972): 412.

577 *Achievements of a high order:*
> Keeping Britain free of debilitating wars deserves a high place on the credit side of Walpole's balance sheet; but it must not be overlooked that a war, with its consequence in having to ask Parliament for costly votes of supply and new taxes, would have imperiled his personal control.

578 *"And lend a lye the confidence of Truth":*
> Four decades later Johnson (p. 289) had succumbed to the Whig interpretation of history, disposing of Thomson's long poem *Liberty,* 1734–36 (which shared some of the sentiments expressed in his own *London*) with the laughable explanation that "a long course of opposition to Sir Robert Walpole had filled the nation with clamours for liberty, of which no man felt the want, and with care for liberty, which was not in danger."

578 *"Modern cynicism":*
> Exemplified, for instance, in Sir Lewis Namier's contention that bribery was "not a shower-bath from above constructed by Walpole, the Pelhams, or George III, but a water-spout springing from the rock of freedom to meet the demands of the people"—we are to see in Walpole, it appears, a Moses providing for the Chosen. *The Structure of Politics at the Accession of George III* (London: Macmillan, 1929), 1: 128. Robert Walpole's son Horace put the point with less humbug in 1792: "Esteem is no principle of union. When men are paid, they must vote for what they are bidden to vote. They will have a thousand vagaries when at liberty to vote for what they fancy right or not." To Horace Mann, 5 May, *Correspondence,* 25: 275.

578 *"Might well have been better":*
> J. P. Kenyon, *Revolution Principles: The Politics of Party, 1689–1720* (Cambridge: Cambridge University Press, 1977), pp. 203–4.

578 *Even the stage:*
  Walpole did not resort to a Licensing Act till 1737, but he had already denied performance
to Gay's *Polly* (1730) and Fielding's *Grub-Street Opera* (1731).
579 *Duck was to have the post:*
  On Duck, see Spence's excited letter to Pope, 11 September 1730 (3: 132–3) and his *A full
and authentick account of Stephen Duck, the Wiltshire poet* (1731). (For a brief modern survey of
Duck's career, see Michael Pafford, "Stephen Duck, the Thresher Poet," in *History Today*,
27 (1977): 467–72.) Having caught Queen Caroline's fancy, Duck was invited to read some
of his poems "in the drawing-room at Windsor Castle." *The Universal Spectator* of 26 September noted that she had settled £30 a year on Duck and given him a little house at
Richmond "on account of his several ingenious Poetical compositions." Later he became
librarian of her Hermitage at Richmond, and still later, through the continued support of
Spence, rector of Byfleet, Surrey. The five words of Pope's that Spence jotted down in 1734
say all that is necessary about Duck's poetry: "Duck no imagination, all imitation" (no. 505
and n.).
579 *A suitable candidate of his own:*
  15 January 1731 (3: 162). If Pope did try to influence the selection, he may have regarded it .
as too late for Gay after the *Beggar's Opera* and *Polly* and have proposed another, possibly
James Thomson. Thomson and he had become acquainted in the mid-1720s soon after
Thomson's settling in London, probably through William Aikman the painter or David
Mallett, both fellow Scots whom Pope knew. Thomson pays tribute to Pope in *Winter*,
ll. 545–55 (1726), the first of his *Seasons*, and indicates that they were already acquainted. A
letter from Lord Tyrconnel to Mrs. Clayton, Queen Caroline's mistress of the robes, may
signify, however, that Pope's nominee was Richard Savage. Still at this time Savage's
patron, Tyrconnel asks Mrs. Clayton to remind the Queen that she had earlier declared her
approval of his poetry, and adds that Mr. Pope seconds that approval. *Memoirs of Viscountess
Sundon* (1837), 2: 241–42 (8 November, 1730).
579 *"Virtually over the corpse":*
  G. V. Bennett, *The Tory Crisis in Church and State, 1688–1730: the Career of Francis Atterbury* (Oxford: Clarendon 1975), p. 305. See also H. C. Beeching, *Francis Atterbury* (London:
Pitman, 1909).
579 *With his father-in-law's body:*
  More than two months later, however, the first culling from the papers is still in
Walpole's hands, and Delafaye, having made a second culling, is asking if he may return the
rest to Morrice (Delafaye to Walpole, 18 July 1732: CH (Houghton), MS. #2014).
579 *In a workmen's lumber room:*
  Bodleian Library. MS. Rawl, J. 4°. 4 [p. 167].
580 *Lords Delawar and Hervey:*
  The Universal Spectator, 31 October 1730. See also Halsband, *Hervey*, p. 103.
580 *"Leers with her eyes most bewitchingly":*
  James Thomson, *Letters and Documents*, ed., A. D. McKillop (University of Kansas Press,
1958), pp. 7ff. Thomson's first impressions, though quite unfair to Mrs. Oldfield's distinction as an actress, give something of her reputation for amours. For a more informed comment on her acting, see Thomson's own tribute to her in the Preface to his *Sophonisba* (1730).
581 *"Hurried him out of this life in three days":*
  Lord Gower in London to the Earl of Essex in Turin, 9 December 1732. BL. Add. MS. 27,
732, f. 72; Pope, 5 December 1732 (3: 334). The death notice as it appeared in the *Universal
Spectator*, 9 December 1732, almost certainly written by Pope, gives his view of his friend's
worth and, very quietly, his admonishment of the regime (and "the Great") for neglecting
to honor him:

> Monday last died of a violent Inflammatory Fever, at the Duke of Queensberry's
> House in Burlington-Gardens, Mr. John Gay: He was descended of a Gentleman's
> Family in Devonshire, and had been Secretary to the Embassy to Hanover in the last Year
> of Queen *Anne*, where he had the Honour of being *personally known by the Royal Family, to
> which he express'd his Loyalty and Affection in some excellent Poems*. He was one of the most
> eminent poets, and in some Parts of writing the most eminent of his Age. His personal
> Character was perfectly amiable, the most natural, inoffensive, and disinterested of

Men. His Conversation was sought by all who knew him, and his *Life chiefly pass'd in the Friendship and Society of Persons of the first Rank*. He left a moderate Fortune, *no Part owing to any Preferment*, but wholly to his own Labour and Prudence, [divided] between two Sisters. *No Place is vacant by his Death*.

He is to be interr'd in Westminster-Abbey, at the Expence of the said Duke, who will erect a Monument to the Memory of so facetious and excellent a Companion. [Emphasis mine.]

581 *"By several Persons of Distinction":*
      The Life of Mr. Gay (published on 1 February 1733), p. 72; *The Weekly Miscellany*, 30 December 1732.
583 *"With the Duchess of Queensberry":*
      23 October and 18 August 1730 (3: 142, **125**).
585 *"I would above all things see you":*
      5 and 6 December 1732 (3: 335, 336).

Chapter 23, A Man of Many Moods

587 *So runs a news account:*
      The Bee; or Universal Weekly Pamphlet, 17 February 1733.
587 *Set himself up in the book trade:*
      Pope to Dodsley, 5 February 1733 (3: 346); Johnson, p. 213. John Nichols (*Literary Anecdotes of the Eighteenth Century* [1812], 1: 300) tells us that Pope also set up Henry Woodfall as master of his own printing shop and lived to give Woodfall's grandson a half crown for reading to him fluently a page of Homeric Greek. It is believed that he may likewise have set up the printer John Wright and the publisher Lawton Gilliver. For the latter, at any rate, he solicited the writings of his friends and entrusted to his care the publication of several major works: The *Dunciad Variorum*, the epistles to Burlington, Bathurst, Cobham, and Martha Blount, the four epistles of the *Essay on Man* (using the name of John Wilford, an associate of Gilliver's, on their titles as a blind), the imitations of Horace, *Sat. II*, i, and *II*, ii, and the *Epistle to Arbuthnot*. There was some altruism at work in this, but also much hard business sense. If he became for his own time, "the pioneer of literature as an honourable and remunerative profession" (Arthur Collins, *Authorship in the Days of Johnson* [London: R. Holden, 1927], p. 123), he did so partly by insisting that the author's share in the proceeds from his work be appreciably enlarged over what it had been. This meant exercising some control of both costs and pricing, which meant, in turn, that it could be expedient to deal with newcomers whom he had helped to their start and with whom he could therefore insist on breaking the usual percentages. For a fascinating account of Gilliver's and Wright's careers, see J. W. McLaverty's "Lawton Gilliver: Pope's Bookseller," in *Studies in Bibliography*, 32 (1979): 101–24 (with its supplement, issued by the University of Keele) and his *Pope's Printer, John Wright: a preliminary study* (Oxford: Oxford Bibliographical Society, 1976: Occasional Publications, no. 11). Majestically in the background of all recent studies of Pope as publisher lurk David Foxon's as yet unpublished Lyell Lectures of 1979: *Pope and the Early Eighteenth-Century Book Trade*.
587 *Her seafaring son John:*
      3: 339, 353.
587 *The architectural aid of Burlington:*
      To Caryll, 8 March (3: 353); To Burlington (3: 356).
588 *Her own "Satisfaction" in a libel:*
      3: 354.
588 *"By giving him a little more":*
      3: 357–8. The actual title of Theobald's play was *The Fatal Secret*.
588 *"Assistant to the pressive Paw!":*
      3: 394, and *General Evening Post*, 20 December 1733. See also Ault, *New Light*, ch. 19. A subscription was afoot for Dennis in 1730, to which Atterbury from Paris contributed £100. Pope, who was in frequent touch with Atterbury through Morrice, may have assisted the London newspapers in carrying the news to him. Atterbury, *Epistolary Correspondence* (1783), 1: 262.

590 *"And be the Critick's,* Briton's, *Old-man's Friend":*
  TE, 6: 355–7.
590 *Burlington's large circle in that country:*
  On this group, see Pat Rogers, "The Burlington Circle in the Provinces: Alexander Pope's Yorkshire Friends," *Durham University Journal,* 67 (1974): 219–26.
591 *"Made his dinner on one dish":*
  3: 383; 2: 384; 4: 150; and *Suffolk Correspondence,* 2: 81.
594 *Gave to Gay in his letters:*
  Swift writes to Lord Oxford, 30 August 1734 (3: 429), with reference to the prudential role Pope assigns him here, that "I could willingly have excused his placing me not in that Light which I would appear," but realizes it was done with no ill intention. Actually, in lines added for the 1738 edition of his own imitation of Horace (*Sat. II,* vi: 9–12), Swift assigns to himself a sentiment very similar:

> But here a grievance seems to lie,
> All this is mine but till I die:
> I can't but think 'twill sound more clever,
> To me and to my Heirs for ever.

  Ehrenpreis believes these verses were inserted by Pope.
595 *"Made by the same hand that made me":*
  F. V. Bogel, *Acts of Knowledge: Pope's Later Poems* (Lewisburg: Bucknell University Press, 1981), p. 184 (quoting *Correspondence* 4: 40–1).
595 *"The limits ordained by nature":*
  Epicurus: The Extant Remains, ed., Cyril Bailey (Oxford: Clarendon, 1925), p. 139: frag. 85.
596 *His affairs as well as his mother's:*
  Pulteney to Caryll, 14 July; Pope to Caryll, 25 June (3: 375 and n).
596 *"Six nights in seven":*
  [Denys Sutton], "The faire majestic Paradise of Stowe," in *Apollo,* 97 (1973): 542.
597 *"Was not to be forgiven":*
  Hervey, pp. 186, 198, 200.
597 *Third earl of Cholmondeley:*
  Egmont, 11 June 1733 (1: 387).
597 *The manuscript exordium of his* Essay on Man:
  TE, 3.1, pp. 11–12; Miriam Leranbaum, *Alexander Pope's "Opus Magnum," 1729–44* (Oxford: Clarendon, 1977), p. 21.
597 *Van Loo's portrait of Cobham:*
  One of Van Loo's best, the portrait now hangs at Hagley Hall, in Cobham's time the seat of the Lytteltons.
599 *"This volubility and discordance":*
  Essays, tr. Cotton, book 2, ch. 1, 3 vols. (1685–93), 2: 9. Pope signalizes the passage quoted with his characteristic marginal inverted commas in his copy. ("Pope's Books", no. 121.)
600 *Had written much of the* Essay on Man *there:*
  Nicholson and Rousseau, pp. 39ff, make a strong case for this.
600 *Largely a eulogy of Bolingbroke:*
  The two manuscripts are reproduced photographically in Alexander Pope, *"An Essay on Man". Reproductions of the Manuscripts in the Pierpont Morgan Library and the Houghton Library* (London: Oxford University Press for the Roxburghe Club, 1962); both photographically and in transcript, in *The Last and Greatest Art,* pp. 190–418.
600 *To print in about a fortnight:*
  3: 380–1. While at Gosfield in Essex in July (this was the home of Anne Craggs, now Mrs. John Knight, sister of the admired friend of his youth whose monument in the Abbey he had supervised and whose epitaph he had composed), Pope was already working on the *Essays's* fourth epistle: see his letter to Fortescue 15 July [1732], *"Collected in Himself,"* p. 482.
601 *"Thou shalt love God above all things, &c":*
  3: 390.

601–2 *"A diffusive spirit of public benevolence"*:
   A Dissertation upon Parties (1735), p. 6.
602 *"The price of every one of them"*:
   Hervey, p. 193.
603 *"Adieu"*:
   3: 385–6.
603 *One of the six who won a guinea*:
   The story of the visit is told by William Mason in his memoir prefacing Whitehead's *Poems* (2 vols., 1788), 1: 6–7. Though the College archives retain no record of the visit, I see little reason to suspect Mason's story, which seems to have come directly from Whitehead himself by way of Thomas Balguy, who was a prebend of Winchester, 1758–95, and its archdeacon, 1759–71. Whitehead was in school at Winchester College from 1729 to 1735.
603 *Treasonable implications on any chance remark*:
   The best account of Donne's reworking of Horace, *Sat. I.* ix, into his own "Satire 4" is given by Howard Erskine-Hill, "Courtiers out of Horace," in *John Donne, Essays in Celebration*, ed., A. J. Smith (London: Methuen, 1972), pp. 273–307. (Now chapter 4 in his *The Augustan Idea in English Literature*, [London: Arnold], 1983.)
604 *Effortless adaptation of these lines*:
   For the text of Satire 4, I use that printed by Pope facing his English, save that I silently omit from the first of Pope's passages his ll. 103–4, which in the text of Donne we use today come later as ll. 127–8. Pope also "modernized" Donne's second satire in an early version made in Queen Anne's time and in a later one shaped to the topicalities of the 1730's. Both are printed in *TE*, 4: 129–45. If there was also an early version of Donne's fourth, as Pope's foreword (*TE* 4: 3) seems to claim, it has not survived.
607 *Her wax museum in Fleet Street*:
   TE, 4: 42, and Lady Mary Wortley Montagu to Lady Rich, 1 December [1716] (*Letters*, 1: 288); Rosamond Bayne-Powell, *Eighteenth-Century London Life* (London: Murray, 1937), pp. 166–7.
607 *"As contemptible as he was odious"*:
   Ilchester, p. 189. Hervey had noted to Stephen Fox on 6 December 1733 that "Pope is in a most violent fury; and j'en suis ravi" (*Ibid.*, p. 183).
608 *An assault from a peer of the realm*:
   Pope does not exaggerate when he describes in his "Letter" the impression conveyed by Hervey's poem of the court and aristocracy. Each of his "if" clauses has a direct source in Hervey's lines. "I should be obliged indeed to lessen this Respect [the respect due Hervey's rank], if all the Nobility . . . are but so many hereditary Fools, if the privilege of Lords be to want brains, if all their business is but to dress and vote, and all their employment in court, to tell lies, flatter in public, slander in private, be false to each other, and follow nothing but self interest. Bless me, my Lord, what an account is this you give of them? and what would have been said of me, had I immolated, in this manner, the whole nobility, at the stall of a well-fed Prebendary?"
609 *"Only a couple of Link Boys"*:
   23 June 1754. (*Letters*, 3: 57.)
609 *By Warburton in 1751*:
   Works (1751), 8. The portion here quoted is from pp. 278–9.
609 *Prudential considerations on the poet's part*:
   See *Corr.* 3: 6n; Spence, no. 7 and p. 615: Halsband, *Hervey*, p. 164; and E-C, 5: 263. A contemporary view of Pope's letter and probably the most reliable explanation of his withholding it from publication is given in a letter of late 1748 by the sister of Charles Yorke (son of the then Lord Chancellor), to whom Warburton, a close friend, had briefly entrusted it: "This day being a holyday, papa drove to Twickenham Park, accompanyed by myself & bro. Charles, who entertained us . . . with reading an excellent letter of Mr. Pope's to Lord Hervey, in answer to his [Hervey's] most abusive epistle to Dr. Sherwin. . . . It is a piece of great humour, expressing the highest contempt for the person addressed, & yet wrote with a greater air of temper than is usual to the satire of the writer. It was wrote a few days after the epistle it answers was published, & was sent printed instead of written, wch gave great apprehensions that it was intended for the perusal of the public, which Mr. Warburton . . . says was the case, but that Mr. Pope was dissuaded . . .

by some friends of the noble lord's, & particularly by *Horace* [Horatio] *Walpole*." (As the letter was in print, it fell to Warburton by Pope's will rather than to Bolingbroke, who presumably would have burnt it along with the other manuscripts entrusted to him.) George Harris, *The Life of Lord Chancellor Hardwicke*, 3 vols., (1847), 2: 353.

610 *Might better catch that representative aspect:*
Pope's own account of the matter (to Swift, 6 January 1734, 3: 401–2) is not revealing, though its last sentence deserves notice. There he claims the right to retaliate against all (such as Hervey) who belie him, yet "even this is a liberty I shall never take . . . unless they are enemies to all men as well as to me."

610 *Not return again to England for eighteen years:*
3: 403 and n. Berkeley presumably departed in the latter days of April since Egmont (2: 87) presented him to Walpole on the eighteenth "upon his going to Ireland."

611 *"To manage this national quarrel":*
12 February 1734. SRO: Douglass G D 206/ii/594.

611 *After the first essay in this campaign:*
In the *Daily Courant*, 22 January.

612 *"I wish for you & can't have you":*
4 July [1739] (4: 185–6).

612 *Congreve had written:*
"Of Pleasing; An Epistle to Sir Richard Temple," l. 66; in *Works*, ed., Montague Summers (London: Nonesuch, 1923), 4: 149.

612 *"Hath fretted himself lean":*
The Hon. George Berkeley to Lady Suffolk, [June] 1734 (*Suffolk Correspondence*, 2: 76). Berkeley (not the bishop), Dormer, and Pope had traveled to Stowe together.

613 *Describing his uncle's gardens:*
Apart from West's poem—*Stowe: The Gardens of the . . . Viscount Cobham*—which takes its readers on a complete tour of the gardens as they stood in the early 1730s, and B. Seeley, *A Description of the Gardens . . . at Stowe* (Northampton, 1744), which is an early tour guide, there are contemporary MS. accounts of their state and progress at various dates during Pope's lifetime: (1) in a travel diary of 1724 kept by an unidentified author (Yorkshire Archeological Society, MS. 328); (2) in Sir John Evelyn's journal (Christ Church, Oxford), 17 May 1725; and (3) in the "Travel Diary" of Jeremiah Milles (BL: Add. Ms. 15776, ff. 2–10), who visited Stowe in July, 1735. On Milles's account, which seems to have been overlooked by historians and which affords the fullest description we have of Stowe gardens in the mid-1730s, I have drawn heavily in the following paragraphs. Important modern accounts of eighteenth-century Stowe and its creator by Colin Anson, George Clarke, Desmond Fitzgerald, Michael Gibbon, and Denys Sutton are found in *Apollo*, 97 (1973); 542–98; and by Clarke and Gibbon in *The Stoic*, 24 (1970): 57–63 and 113–21.

613 *"& with variety":*
23 August (3: 217).

613 *Pope sometimes lent a discreet hand:*
An interesting but to my mind somewhat quixotic argument, allotting to Pope a decisive influence on the overall conception, is made by Susanne Lang in "Stowe and Empire: The Influence of Alexander Pope," *Architectural Review*, (1983): 53–6. For further discussion of this point, see Brownell, p. 195.

613 *"Pillars, and Porticoes":*
Sir John Evelyn, *op. cit.*

613 *" 'How delightful are thy temples!' ":*
Laurence Whistler, Michael Gibbon, George Clarke, *Stowe: A Guide to the Gardens* (1968), p. 6.

615–6 *Shepherds and shepherdesses, "dancing":*
Milles, f. 9.

616 *George I:*
It was inscribed *In medio mihi Caesar erit*, with reference to Vergil's fantasy (*Georgics*, 3: 12ff) of setting up in Mantua a temple where *in medio mihi Caesar erit templumque tenebit* ("At the center I will place Caesar and he will be master of the shrine").

616 *"The theme was anti-Stuart and anti-clerical":*
    M. J. Gibbon, "The History of Stowe—IX," in *The Stoic,* 24 (1970): 62.
617 *"The Founder of the English Constitution":*
    For the inscriptions, I use throughout the translations by Seeley (*Description of the Gardens*), who also gives the original Latin. His guide went through several editions, of which that of 1780 gives the inscription for Pope's bust, incised in 1764. All or most of the Latin originals are believed to be the work of Cobham's nephew and Pope's friend George (later first baron) Lyttelton.
619 *"Who too often parade as cultural leaders":*
    [Denys Sutton], " 'The faire majestic paradise of Stowe," *Apollo,* 97 (1970): 547–8.

Chapter 24, The Lady and the Doctor

620 *"He returns to my farm again":*
    3: 413.
620 *"There is no Scandal in being in Heat":*
    3: 415, 435. Sherburn (3: 435n) misplaces the excised words (they occur at the end of the letter) and does not decipher them.
621 *When studying with Jervas:*
    3: 430, 424, 426.
622 *"Is more ornamented":*
    Horace Walpole, visiting Netley in 1755, called it "the ruins ... of Paradise," and exclaimed (borrowing a phrase from Pope's description of imagined Italian abbots in the *Dunciad,* 4: 301–2): "Oh, the purple abbots! what a spot had they chosen to slumber in!" To Bentley, 18 September 1755. *Correspondence,* 35: 251.
622 *"It was there I first knew you":*
    11 August 1734. First printed by G. S. Rousseau, "A New Pope Letter," in *Philol. Quart.,* 45 (1966): 409–18. The drawings Pope made of Netley are not now known. Life at Bevis Mount was further punctuated during Pope's visit by a country witch hunt, the barbarities of which at that date, sanctioned by the local parson, make rather surprising reading. See *"Collected in Himself,"* pp. 487–90.
623 *The doubtless all-male company at Rousham:*
    The reading is mentioned by the Hon. George Berkeley in a letter in which he jots down the only two lines (ll. 112–13) he can remember. *Suffolk Correspondence,* 2: 78–9. By 6 July, Bolingbroke had been sent a draft of the poem, probably because, as he wrote Swift on that date (3: 414), with mock irritation, "The rogue has fixed a ridicule upon me [under the pseudonym Sallust, ll. 63–70], which some events of my life could seem perhaps to justify him in doing."
624 *"Paradise may be said to be* twice lost*":*
    Paradise Lost. A New Edition (1732). Preface, leaf *a verso.*
624 *"A New Acquisition of Delight":*
    To Ralph Palmer, 13 March 1732. NLS: MS. 3421, ff. 163–4. Richardson was not the only reader to derive insights from Bentley's literalism. We are told by Thomas Newton in his 1750 variorum edition of Milton's poem that the margins of Pope's copy of Bentley (to which Newton had access, though it is now unknown) contained exclamations of "*rectè, benè, pulchrè,* &c." For modern comment on this effect of Bentley's edition, see William Empson, *Some Versions of Pastoral* (London: Chatto & Windus, 1935), pp. 149–91.
624 *Without which poetry ceases to exist:*
    P. M. Briggs, "The Jonathan Richardsons as Milton Critics," *Studies in Eighteenth-Century Culture,* 9 (1979): 115–30.
626 *Pope could rarely dismiss Bentley from his mind:*
    On Tonson's overture and Pope's reply, see 3: 369, 291. The poet did, however, permit himself the "Notae Bentleianae" already cited and an epigram avowing that Bentley's "murder" of Milton's text could be looked on as retribution for Milton's having defended the "murder" of Charles I. *TE,* 6: 328, 332. This epigram, in Pope's hand, is at Mapledurham House.

626 *Issued on January 28:*

I have assumed that the chief motive in publishing the imitation was to ridicule Bentley along with the type of textual "restoration" that Pope's friend Mallet had also recently attacked in *Of Verbal Criticism*—with possibly as a subsidiary motive (for the timing) a willingness to help create a receptive atmosphere for the Richardsons' more "earnest" refutation. Other explanations are possible. Pope, it will be recalled, fairly often chooses to relax from an extended endeavor (such as the *Essay on Man* and the other epistles of the *Opus Magnum* had been) with a light-hearted or bawdy jeu d'esprit and may simply have been amusing himself and his friends. See Leonard Moskovit, "Alexander Pope's Purpose in *Sober Advice*," *Philol. Quart.* 44 (1965): 199. Alternatively (see R. W. Rogers, *Major Satires*, p. 71), he may have published the poem as an obvious obscene parody of his own manner, thus helping to justify his "Bill of Complaint" in the *Epistle to Arbuthnot*. If so, he hardly needed such additional evidence; he had been genuinely libeled quite often enough.

627 *Deepening personal understanding and involvement:*

For a particularly fine treatment of this aspect of the poem, see Meg Gertmenian, "Strangeness and Temper: Pope in the Act of Judgment," in *Studies in English Literature*, 22 (1982): 491–504. A definitive description of the poem's several textual states is found in Frank Brady, "Pope's *Epistle to a Lady*," *SEL*, 9 (1969): 447–63.

627 *Earthly love aspiring to divine:*

J. D. Stewart, "Pin-ups or Virtues? The Concept of the 'Beauties' in Late Stuart Portraiture," *William Andrews Clark Memorial Library Papers*, 14 (1973). George Vertue in *Note Books* (Walpole Society, Oxford, 1932), 2: 68, comments on seeing Kneller's Hampton Court series in a smaller size at Kneller's house.

628 *Named Silia, Papillia, Narcissa, etc.:*

In the background of Pope's performance lies, of course, the popular theory expressed as *ut pictura poesis* and such antecedents as Giambattista Marino's *Galeria* (verse descriptions of both real and imagined paintings and sculptures) and the popular seventeenth-century genre "Instructions to a Painter." See also Marvell's poem "The Gallery," where different portraits of his beloved, not all flattering, are said to be represented in his soul. An especially valuable account of the poem's tradition and its precursors is found in Jean Hagstrum's *The Sister Arts: The Tradition of Literary Pictorialism in English Poetry from Dryden to Gray* (University of Chicago Press, 1958).

628 *"Seldom so fix'd":*

TE, 3, 2: 46n.

629 *His book on the Whiston controversy:*

The Tender Husband, 4.2; *The Vicar of Wakefield*, ch. 16. Mario Praz has some entertaining pages on this vogue, which captured all Europe, in his *Mnemosyne: the Parallel between Literature and the Visual Arts* (Princeton University Press, 1970), pp. 7ff. A surge toward greater realism in portraiture seems to begin roughly in the 1730s, but the old habit lasted out the century.

630 *"Sick of herself thro' very selfishness!":*

The extraordinary virtuosity with which Pope distinguishes his portraits from one another in this poem and in others—not simply through qualities and actions ascribed to the character, but through diction, syntax, parts of speech, repetition and variation of a single word or sound (together with its meaning) should not go unnoticed. To choose only two very crude examples: in the portrait of Atossa, "she," "her," and "herself" appear 21 times in 44 lines; in that of Flavia, "to" and "too" make 16 appearances in 14 lines. Much subtler structural and verbal distinctions will be remarked by those wishing to look for them.

630 *"She bids her Footman put it in her head":*

As noticed earlier, an inclination among critics to suppose Cloe a portrait of Henrietta Howard seems insupportable in view of Pope's own frequent defense of her from Swift's cavils and the happy relationship between her and Martha Blount. Though the portrait is presumably a composite, one contemporary on whom Pope may much more probably have drawn is Lady Hervey—for satirizing whom he would have had a credible motive. An admittedly hostile contemporary word-sketch (by Charles Hanbury-Williams, now in the Holland House MSS., but quoted by Romney Sedgwick in his edition of Hervey's *Memoirs*, 1: xiv), presents her as follows: "Nature took great care of her person, but quite forgot her mind, which had this effect, that she was of the same mind with every person she talked to. . . . She was what was reckoned well bred, civil to flatness. . . . She affected to be lively, which was expressed by a smile and opening her eyes a little wider than ordinary, which ended generally in an exclamation of some things being charming. . . . She smiled without joy and cried without sorrow. Incapable of love and ignorant of friendship, affected in every word, motion, and (I believe) thought, she was a fine lady. . . . Her total real indifference to mankind has hindered her ever having a lover [but not perhaps a few pantings upon her bosom?]" According to Mary Wortley Montagu, she was not above *claiming* an intrigue with George I (*Letters*, 2: 58–9), who, according to Horace Walpole (*Correspondence*, 34: 259), did pursue her but without success. If, indeed, she had a lover or lovers (whether or not she could love in return) it might explain the curious clause in Hervey's will denying her any inheritance save what he was "obliged to . . . by their marriage contract" (Halsband, *Hervey* p. 304), or, as Lady Mary more picturesquely said (*Letters*, 2: 311), whatever he left her was "because I can not help it" (*Ibid.*, 2: 311). What seems clear, in any case, is that if there is a single flesh-and-blood original lurking in the shadows behind "Cloe," which I tend to doubt, that original is likelier to have been Lady Hervey than Lady Suffolk.

634 *A concordia discors asserts itself:*
For a particularly fine account of this aspect of Pope, see David Morris, *Alexander Pope: The Genius of Sense* (Harvard University Press, 1984).

635 *"To you gave Sense, Good-humour, and a Poet":*
The final verses gave Caryll hope that Pope and his goddaughter might conclude their long friendship in marriage, but he was quickly set right: " 'Tis a new sort of father [i.e., Phoebus] for marriage: he gave me long ago to Belinda, . . . and tis a mercy he has not given me to more ladies, but that I am almost as little inclined to celebrate that way [i.e., by dedicating poems to their charms], as the other" [i.e., marrying] (3: 451).

635 *"Your most faithful Friend":*
15 July 1734 (3: 416).

636 *"Offend you by enumerating them":*
Pope's Victorian editors, understandably suspicious following their discovery that in certain respects he manipulated his letters in preparing them for publication, tended to see deep meanings in the alteration of "scarcely any" (which Arbuthnot's original apparently had: see 3: 416, 423) to "not any"—as if Pope were concealing a breach in their relationship. Actually, to say "scarcely any" in writing to a friend about possible misunderstandings need be no more than a courteous way of acknowledging that while one can speak absolutely for oneself, one cannot speak absolutely for another, therefore must allow for the possibility that is expressed in "scarcely." What Pope was probably trying to prevent by his alteration was the very misreading that his Victorian editors fell into: there is not a shred of evidence that he and Arbuthnot were ever on any but the warmest terms.

636 *"Or lessen the Body?":*
3: 106n, 423.

637 *Saw a way to knit together:*
On the pieces and the process of integrating them, see *The Last and Greatest Art*, pp. 416–54.

637 *"And fastning upon everybody he meets":*
15 January 1731 (3: 162).

637 *With some risk to his livelihood:*
TE, 5: 11ff; *Corr.* 3: 254–7. Cleland's position in the government may well have determined the decision not to make him the addressee of the lines later absorbed into *Arbuthnot.*

637 *"& my answers":*
3: 428.

639 *Into which they so confidently irrupt:*
Some of Pope's poetical harassers were at least inventive. One of them, name unknown, whose petition is preserved in the Portland Papers at Nottingham University (PwV 114: 5) first tells the story of a certain Dinocrates (not, one imagines, the architect), who in his effort to win an audience at court gets himself up in a garb combining Hercules's lion skin with a hair-do "whimsically pretty/Ophelia-like, or Cousin Betty," and thus by sheer

outlandishness of appearance wins both an interview and the favor he asked. The writer's application of all this is that he stands similarly willing "to hazard all. And boldly mount, tho' but to fall":

> Fondly desirous of yr Praise
> Untunable my Voice I raise,
> Rudely into yr Presence press
> In this uncouth Fantastick Dress [of bad verse],
> Regardless what the World may say
> So but to You I make my way.

Another suppliant—this one John Banckes, who tells the story on himself in his *Works* of 1739 (2: 42–3)—sent some verses ending with the petition:

> The most I seriously would hope,
> Is, just to read the words A. Pope,
> Writ without sneer, or show of banter
> Beneath your friendly Imprimantur—

to which Pope replied with a subscription for two copies of his *Works*, and with the couplet:

> May these put money in your purse,
> For I assure you, I've read worse.
>   A. P.

641 *"For the numbers came":*
  Johnson (*Rambler*, 143) was the first to see the reminiscence here of Ovid's autobiographical lines in *Tristia*, 4. 10. 25f ("Of its own accord my poetry fell into meters, and whatever I sought to say turned out to be verse"). In view of Ovid's situation at this time, estranged from Augustus and in exile in Pontus, one wonders if Pope saw other resemblances as well between his career and the Roman poet's.

644 *As in the career of Balaam:*
  It is worth noticing in the *Epistle to Bathurst* that the Man of Ross "possest" what he had (l. 280), whereas Balaam is "possessed" *by* it (l. 373).

647 *"Principles by which a literary man should live":*
  Rogers, *Major Satires*, p. 87.

647 *"The hateful figure of Folly or Vice itself":*
  Ian Jack, *Alexander Pope* (British Council Pamphlets), 1954, pp. 21–2.

648 *"Of private and civic order":*
  C. A. Paglia, "Lord Hervey and Pope," in *E-CS*, 6 (1973): 370.

648 *"To lower the tone of public life":*
  Hervey, p. lix.

Chapter 25, A Sense of Autumn

649 *"With tenderness, without weakness":*
  From Chesterfield's "Character" of Arbuthnot, first printed in his *Letters*, ed., Lord Mahon (1845), 2: 447.

650 *"See my last amusements to advantage":*
  [July 1735.] *Suffolk Correspondence*, 2: 129–30. Peterborow's "love-song" is the once famous one beginning "I said to my heart between sleeping and waking."

650 *Pope's message to Cirencester:*
  19 August [1735] (3: 484).

650 *Improvements his Countess could enjoy after him:*
  To Martha Blount, 25 August 1735 (3: 487–8).

651 *Remarried her before witnesses at Bristol:*
  Colin Ballard, *The Great Earl of Peterborough* (London: Sheffington, 1929), pp. 283–4; F. S. Russell, *The Earl of Peterborough and Monmouth*, 2 vols., (1887), 2: 328–9.

651 *Continuing friendship with Lady Peterborow:*
    Pope probably visited Bevis Mount for the last time in 1740 (4: 252), when accompanying his ailing young friend Lord Cornbury as far as Southampton, whence Cornbury was to cross the channel to Spa. In 1741 (4: 358) he and Lady Peterborow were to meet in London.

651 *"To put me every day in mind of him":*
    To Swift [November 1735], 3: 509.

651 *To Dr. Arbuthnot's son George:*
    See Pope's will, printed in *The Garden and the City*, p. 264.

651 *Buried in Bedfordshire on the twentieth:*
    On Peterborow's travels, death, and burial, see *London Evening Post*, September 2; *General Evening Post*, September 9; *Fog's Weekly Journal*, October 4; *Daily Gazetteer*, October 8; *Daily Post-Boy*, October 27; *Old Whig*, October 30; *Read's Weekly Journal*, November 15; *Old Whig*, November 15; *General Evening Post*, November 15; *Read's Weekly Journal*, November 22.

651 *"Is absent now":*
    3: 509, 500.

652 *"Two Inches beyond its usual appearance":*
    4 September 1735 (3: 493). The event took place three days earlier on the first.

652 *Both nearly drowned:*
    Mary Pendarves to Swift, 2 September 1736. Swift, *Correspondence*, 4: 523. The young lady was apparently Catherine Talbot, later a writer of modest note, contributor to Johnson's *Rambler* and close friend of his Bluestocking friend Elizabeth Carter.

652 *"Complain to you against my self":*
    3: 500.

653 *Musical cadences charmed him "immensely":*
    To William Duncombe, 12 May 1735, *Letters to Several Eminent People* 2 vols. (1773), 2: 81–2.

653 *Than any other project he would ever set hand to:*
    On this episode, see especially J. A. Winn, *A Window in the Bosom: The Letters of Alexander Pope* (New Haven: Archon Books, 1977), pp. 203–21; Sherburn's edition of the *Correspondence*, 1: xii–xv; Pope's own *A Narrative of the Method* (1735); and Edmund Curll's version in *Mr. Pope's Literary Correspondence*, vol. 2 (1735).

653 *"Do Mr. Popes character justice":*
    Daily Journal, 31 March 1733.

654 *Insufficiently protective of either authors or the public:*
    On the bill and its possible relation to Pope's activities at this time, see James McLaverty, "The First Printing and Publication of Pope's Letters," *The Library*, 6th series, 2 (1980): 264–80. In the middle thirties a considerable effort was under way for a time to improve the remuneration of authors, in which Pope played a part. Another version of the bill came before the Lords in 1737 (Pope holding back publication of his authorized edition to benefit from it), but it was again thrown out (4: 65, 66, 69). See also Thomson to Hill, 11 May 1736 (Hill's *Letters*, 1751, pp. 75–8); Conyers Middleton to Warburton, 31 March 1737 (BL: Add. MS. 32, 457, 118); and Lady Peterborow to an unidentified friend [? Spring 1737] (National Register of Archives, Edinburgh).

655 *"Not to extend the Privileges . . . of Booksellers":*
    A Narrative of the Method (1735).

655 *"The Praise of Owls":*
    They were aptly titled *Miscellanea*. (Griffith, nos. 177–8.)

656 *"At the Pewter-Platter Inn in Holborn":*
    Thomas Amory, *The Life of John Buncle, Esq.* (1756), p. 383. See also Fielding, *The Author's Farce*, Act 2: sc. 3–7.

656 *"Crawls under the Toilet of every Court-Lady":*
    The Adventures of Pomponius [etc.] (1726), p. 28. Quoted in Guerinot, p. 94.

656 *His offenses could continue unpunished:*
    Quoted in Ralph Straus, *The Unspeakable Curll* (London: Chapman and Hall, 1927), p. 79.

656 *To police infractions of the paper tax:*
  To Walpole, 31 March 1730: Houghton MSS. 1839. For other instances, see Curll to
  Viscount Townshend, 25 April 1722 (SP 35/31, f. 85); Curll to Delafaye, 20 October 1725
  (SP 35/58, f. 170); to Delafaye, 21 February 1726 (SP 35/61, f. 75); to Mr. Hutchins (a
  King's Messenger), 6 September 1728 (SP 36/8, f. 113); to Walpole, 22 September 1733:
  Houghton MSS. 2046. Also, 4 June 1718, Defoe to Delafaye [?]: SP 35/12, f. 97v. Curll's
  plan for stricter imposition of stamp duties, with (evidently) himself as inspector, appears
  in Treasury Papers: T 29/27, p. 4; TI/276, ff. 45, 47. See further Ralph Straus, *The
  Unspeakable Curll* (London: Champman and Hall, 1927), pp. 93–94, and *Gentleman's Maga-
  zine*, 68 (1978): 190. See also the evidence on Curll as informer in Graham Midgeley's
  Orator Henley (Oxford: Clarendon, 1973), pp. 53–54.
656 *Delivered before the books were seized:*
  McLaverty ("Pope's Letters"), pp. 265–6.
657 *Standing behind their chairs and peeping:*
  To Lady Ossory, 27 September 1778. *Correspondence*, 33: 54.
660 *Found in twenty noblemen's houses:*
  Letters on the English Nation (1733), p. 191.
660 *Cut, impressed, or molded:*
  On the multiplication of likenesses of Pope at this period, see *Wimsatt*,
  pp. 97–347. On Richardson's work, see ch. 8, and especially no. 19(12). no. 37(1), and
  no. 54.
660 *"Its classic dignity and its independence":*
  David Piper, *The Image of the Poet: British Poets and Their Portraits* (Oxford: Clarendon,
  1982), pp. 58, 74.
664 *Interest in the preservation of personal correspondence generally:*
  Pat Rogers, *An Introduction to Pope* (London: Methuen, 1975), pp. 140–1.
664 *"The goodness and virtues of his heart":*
  Ruffhead, p. 406n.
664 *"His Essays, Moral Epistles, &c":*
  1 December 1735 (3: 512).
665 *"That I was of your intimacy":*
  17 August (4: 28).
665 *"Are but so many acknowledgments":*
  4 March (4: 59–60).
666 *"But with my last breath":*
  22 March 1741 (4: 337). Not that the strong bond was never tested by grievances. Pope
  was genuinely irritated when Swift in 1730 made him a compliment which was simultaneously a sneer at Walpole, with whom Pope was then still on amicable terms. Swift must
  have been equally annoyed by some of Pope's maneuverings to obtain the letters and by his
  failure to supplement the verses dedicating the *Dunciad* to him with an epistle addressed to
  him formally, such as that to Arbuthnot. The shrewdest account of the Swift-Pope
  friendship as seen in their letters is A. C. Elias's "Jonathan Swift and Letter-Writing," a
  Yale Ph.D. dissertation of 1973, regrettably not yet published. As Elias rightly remarks,
  "A touch of friction is natural between two brilliant and strong-willed friends." A somewhat severer view of Pope's publication of the letters is taken by Irvin Ehrenpreis in his
  definitive biography of Swift.
666 *"Meer innocent friendship":*
  3 September and 21 October 1735 (3: 492, 505, 5: 16).
666 *"Almost from your infancy":*
  26 February 1730 (3: 92).
668 *"Deriv'd to me from my Friendships":*
  [9 April 1730] (3: 101).
668 *Letters given to Orrery for conveyance to Pope:*
  3: 492, 4: 11, 72.
668 *"In very improper Hands":*
  4: 42, 52, 54, 72, 73, 75.
669 *Idea of publishing his correspondence:*
  4: 54n.

669 *His chances of a poetical one:*
On the attention that each man was giving to developing his image before posterity during the 1730s, see A. H. Scouten's valuable "Jonathan Swift's Progress from Prose to Poetry," in *The Poetry of Jonathan Swift*, ed., M. E. Novak (William Andrews Clark Library Publications, 1981), pp. 27–52.

669 *His usual love and esteem:*
17 May 1740 (4: 241–2).

670 *"And best can judge of it":*
[? May 1740] (4: 242–3, and 242n).

670 *Sent to Dublin in the care of Samuel Gerrard:*
On this so-called "clandestine" volume, see V. A. Dearing, "New Light on the First Printing of the Letters of Pope and Swift," *The Library*, 24 (1943): 74–80; A. C. Elias, Jr., "The Pope-Swift *Letters* (1740–4): Notes on the First State of the First Impression," *Publications of the Bibliographical Society of America*, 69 (1975); and *Collected in Himself*, pp. 93–105.

Chapter 26, Country and Court

674 *Assumes an endearing intimacy:*
On the several texts of the poem, see *TE*, 4: 148, and *Collected in Himself*, pp. 122–4.

676 *Pope had kept dogs:*
One of his earliest excursions in the translation of Homer was the passage on Odysseus's ancient dog Argus (*TE*, 6: 51–2) who crawls to greet him on his return and then dies at his feet. This he sent to his friend Cromwell in a letter of 19 October 1709, remarking that an age of twenty-plus (Odysseus had spent ten years at Troy and ten years getting home) was not impossible, "since I remember the Dam of my Dog . . . was 22 years old when she dy'd" (1: 74). On Pope's succession of dogs named Bounce, see Spence, pp. 629–30.

676 *A letter of 1716 to Parnell:*
Claude Rawson, "Some unpublished Letters of Pope and Gay," *RES*, 10 (1959): 320.

676 *"After a regimen of Physick, and Confinement":*
22 December [1736] (4: 48).

677 *Perhaps the sole hand:*
See on this Pat Rogers, "The Authorship of *Bounce to Fop*: A Re-examination," *Bulletin of Research in the Humanities* (1983): 241–68. Also, S. L. Macey, "*Bounce to Fop*: Alexander Pope and Henry Carey," *Bulletin of the New York Public Library*, 79 (1976): 203–8. That Pope was the final shaper of the poem in its present form seems to me unmistakable.

680 *"And roar in Numbers worthy Bounce":*
This paragraph, with its clear echo of the compliment earlier paid Pope (in *A Libel on Dr. Delany*) for his independence of courts and kings, seems a likely survivor from the Ur-poem by Swift.

680 *Whose advancement it quite possibly celebrates:*
Daily Gazetter, 3 February 1738. If by any chance Dormer knew early on of his coming promotion to the new colonelcy, Pope's "Dear Col'nel!" would have been additionally pertinent.

682 *"And not defraud the Publick Weal?":*
The king left for Hanover and the "Arms" of Madame Walmoden on 22 May 1736. Pope began the poem at Bevis Mount that June and finished it there that autumn. To Fortescue, 21 September [1736] (4: 33 and n).

683 *Explosion in Westminster Hall on 14 July 1736:*
William Coxe, *Memoirs of the Life and Administration of Sir Robert Walpole*, 3 vols. (1798), 3: 346ff.

683 *There is no redress:*
TE, 4: xxxviii. See H. D. Weinbrot's *Augustus Caesar*, Princeton University Press, 1978 .

683 *Huzzaing for James III:*
Coxe (*Memoirs of Walpole*), 3: 348ff.

683 *Ireland's savior from Wood's halfpence:*
To Swift, 23 June 1737. Swift, *Correspondence*, 5: 50.

685 *Emblem of the House of Hanover:*
Johnson plays satirically with the white horse of Brunswick in *Marmor Norfolciense* (1739).

686 *"Till Time decay":*
See Judith Colton, "Merlin's Cave and Queen Caroline: Garden Art as Political Propaganda," *E-CS*, 10 (1976): 1–20, esp. p. 14.

686 *"Worth the argument of any other man":*
Charles Butler, *Reminiscences* (1822), p. 132.

686 *"The little nightingale":*
C. H. S. Fifoot, *Lord Mansfield* (Oxford: Clarendon, 1936), p. 30.

688 *"In the King's Bench Walks":*
Quoted by Fifoot, p. 34.

688 *"Know my price so exactly":*
Spence, no. 324.

693 *"Not a right imitation of his style":*
Spence, no. 143. Pope essays a further imitation of Swift's style in his imitation of Horace, *Ep. I*, vii (published about 4 May 1739 in the octavo edition of his *Works*, 2.2, dated 1738). In this instance, Swift had converted ll. 46–98 of Horace's epistle (addressed to Maecenas) into an expostulation with Harley about his gift of the Deanery in Dublin. This, Swift finds, has so many expenses attached to it that he hastens (in the poem) to return it. Pope's imitation covers the initial forty-five lines of the Latin in Swiftian tetrameters, then breaks off, reminding his readers to find the rest in Swift.

694 *"The Delegate of Caesar and of God":*
See Graham Midgeley, *The Life of Orator Henley* (Oxford: Clarendon, 1973) pp. 50–5, 216–34; for the quotation, p. 221. The figure of £100 is Pope's (a biased but rarely inaccurate witness on such details), at *Dunciad* (1743), 3: 199n.

694 *"Who favored Mr. Pope for his fine genius":*
31 July [1749]. Quoted first in Disraeli's *Curiosities of Literature* (6 vols., 1834): 6: 385. Also, *Notes and Queries*, 2d s., 4 (1857): 447. It was presumably for this and similar services that Odell was rewarded with the post of assistant licenser of plays in 1738, the year after the Licensing Act was passed.

695 *Were as one man arrayed:*
B. A. Goldgar, *Walpole and the Wits: The Relation of Politics to Literature 1722–42* (University of Nebraska Press, 1976), ch. 1. An important book.

695 *Commissioned to gain his end:*
The farce, allegedly brought to Walpole by Henry Giffard, manager of the theater at Goodman's Fields (see the anonymous *An Apology for the Life of Mr. T[heophilus] C[ibber]*, pp. 93–4), was based on an equally insulting "Vision" published in the Opposition paper *Common Sense*, 19 March 1737, entitled "The Golden Rump." The "Vision" is given entire in *The Garden and the City*, pp. 143–7.

696 *"Wish he was out of it":*
Hervey, *Memoirs*, pp. 885, 844. See also pp. 98, 234–5, 306, 636, 671, 681, 744–75, 812–13, 816, 822, 888.

696 *"Betraying every master he has ever served":*
Quoted in Dickinson, *Bolingbroke*, p. 243. Walpole might have spoken yet more savagely had he known of Bolingbroke's foolish negotiations with Chauvelin, the French foreign minister, which ended in his taking a stipend from France (until his father's death he was always short of funds). That he did this to help support the Opposition press rather than for Jacobite intrigues would surely have struck both king and minister as a distinction without a difference. *Ibid.*, pp. 240–2.

696 *"Than what we deserve":*
Marchmont Papers, 2: 98.

699 *One of the world's dullest epics:*
Richard Glover's *Leonidas*.

700 *"Manure it when I die":*
To George Grenville, 3 August 1742. SRO: DA 501/T 3/A44/1970. See also *Grenville Papers*, ed., W. J. Smith, 4 vols. (1852), 1: 5.

701 *A new Opposition journal:*
The Pretender seems to have had a hand in inaugurating the paper through his agents and other Jacobites, one of whom reports that Pope will participate if his participation is kept secret. G. H. Jones, "The Jacobites, Charles Molloy, and *Common Sense*," *RES*, n.s. 3(1952): 144–7. Whether Pope actually took part remains undeterminable. As both Lyttleton, the Prince's secretary, and Chesterfield, now of the Prince's entourage, occasionally contributed, the Jacobite background of the journal was presumably not known to them. No more in all probability was it known to Pope, who in 1739 wisely refused to allow verses from the *Essay on Man* to be politicized by appearing there. To John Brinsden, 15 December 1739 (4: 209).

701 *"Any terms":*
Lord Rosebery, *Chatham* (London: Harper, 1910), p. 147, using evidence from the Camelford MSS. that I have not been able to consult.

703 *As cornet of horse:*
Hervey, p. 553.

703 *Rendered one his "Slave":*
Sir John Clerk of Penicuik, though a Walpole supporter, laments that English luxury "has made bribery & preferments absolutely necessary," for private patrimonies do not suffice. "A Tour into England in the Year 1733," SRO: GD18/2110, f. 88.

703 *"Let the whole world know that he was master":*
J. H. Plumb, *Sir Robert Walpole: The King's Minister* (London: Cresset, 1960), pp. 245, 249, 330, 331.

704 *"And a thorough bad Man":*
[John Lord Hervey], *A Letter to Mr. C[ib]b[er], on his Letter to Mr. P[ope]* (1742), p. 25. Detailed discussions of the newspaper and pamphlet warfare on Pope are found in H. D. Weinbrot's valuable *Alexander Pope and the Traditions of Formal Verse Satire* (Princeton University Press, 1982) and in B. A. Goldgar's *Walpole and the Wits*, pp. 166ff. Individual pamphlet attacks are listed and described in Guerinot. Slurs of one sort or other, often extensive, appeared in the government newspapers on 27 March; 3, 6, 11, 12, 16, 23 April; 11, 20, 26, 30 May; 15 June; 4, 5, 24, 26 August; 5, 15 September; 14, 19 October; 9, 21, 27 November; 19, 27, 30 December. Many of these focus sharply on Pope's praise of Bolingbroke.

Chapter 27, Open Challenges

705 *"To find that B—ling—ke is He":*
Daily Gazetteer, 6 April 1738.

708 *"Humble Allen":*
On Allen's numberless charities and benevolences, see Boyce, especially ch. 5; Pope, *Correspondence*, 4: 36, 92, 217, 221–2, 234, 371. On his contribution to the support of Savage, *ibid.*, 4: 180. Activities on the frozen Thames are colorfully described in a letter of Michael Blount II to Anne Mannock, 30 March 1740 (Mapledurham Papers).

709 *The Opposition was "at an end":*
Hugh Hume, later third earl of Marchmont, to Lord Montrose (*Marchmont Papers*, 2: 101).

713 *"Through the waste of Time":*
"The Hero as Man of Letters," *Works*, 30 vols. (1869), 12: 186.

713 *"The disorders of real life":*
G. K. Hunter, "The 'Romanticism' of Pope's Horace," *Essays in Criticism*, 10 (1960): 390–414.

714 *"At whom they threw the dirt":*
TE, 4: 321n. The most plausible place for this incident is during Bolingbroke's 1738 visit, when the government writers' campaign against him, and against Pope as his ad-mirer, was at its hottest. But the timing is difficult: Bolingbroke reached England on 8 July; writing to a friend on the fifteenth (4: 110), Pope seems not to expect Bolingbroke at Twickenham till after another "few days"; and the poem was published on the eighteenth. It is possible, however, to accommodate the incident if we suppose that Bolingbroke (as is

not in itself unlikely) made a journey to Twickenham soon after his arrival (to see Pope, deposit his belongings, and settle arrangements for his stay), then returned to London for a brief period of business before taking up residence as Pope's guest. On this hypothesis, the window-breaking episode can have occurred early enough to allow Pope to send six lines on the subject to his publisher Robert Dodsley in time for insertion. (That there was much frantic rewriting of these particular poems we know from Dodsley's later testimony in Johnson, p. 221). One notices, further, that if one omits ll. 138–45 from the poem as it now stands ll. 146ff follow very readily on ll. 136–7. Less plausibly, one may assign the incident to the earlier years of the decade, before Bolingbroke in 1735 transplanted himself to France.

717 *"Marrying his whore . . . by consent of his family"*:
Egmont, 3: 389. A similar point is made by the anonymous author of an imaginary underworld dialogue between Walpole's first and second wives (his first died in 1737, his second about three weeks after Pope's poem was published): *The Rival Wives; or, the Greeting of Clarissa and Skirra in the Elysian Shades* (1738). The intended connection between Pope's lines and the recent scene at court is vouched for by Spence and Warburton but was first fully laid open by J. M. Osborn in "Pope, the Byzantine Empress and Walpole's Whore." *RES*, n.s. 6 (1955): 372–82.

717 *His arrogant use of power*:
This point is wittily made in a contemporary epigram on the marriage recorded in BL: Add. MS. 5832, f. 146v, whose text I quote.
I can't conceive why, in Decline of Life, *Sir Blew-String* should betroth another Wife. Is it because he feels an amorous Rage, Thus swell'd with Fat, & thus excis'd with Age? He surely don't. In this, believe me, Friends, He but proves his ever constant Ends. He, long enur'd to plunder & defraud, Unmov'd by Virtue, & by Shame unaw'd, Directs to private Use a *public Whore*. And thus he robs the *Public* one Way more: The only way he had not robb'd before.
See also Egmont, 2: 471 (19 March 1732).

719 *Preoccupations and recurrent themes*:
For a brilliant reconstruction of recurrent motifs in Pope's thought and work, see R. A. Paulson's "Satire, and Poetry, and Pope," in *English Satire*, ed., William Frost [*William Andrews Clark Memorial Library Publications*, 1972), pp. 59–113.

719 *Much doubt has sometimes been voiced*:
On this vexed matter, see R. C. Elliott's admirable monograph, *The Literary Persona* (University of Chicago Press, 1982). For an opposing view, see Irvin Ehrenpreis, *Literary Meaning and Augustan Values* (University of Virginia Press, 1974).

721 *"To write for and live in"*:
Patrick Cruttwell, "Alexander Pope in the Augustan World," *Centennial Review*, 10 (1966): 17. One of the best essays ever written about Pope, which I am sorry not to have known sooner.

722 *"Suspended at a blow"*:
Reformation of Manners (1702), leaf A2.

722 *"For whom things matter"*:
L. I. Bredvold, in a Modern Language Association address.

724 *"Only a part of virtue"*:
Spence, no. 656.

727 *"The Great Man's Answer to Are These Things So?"*:
The pamphlets have been attributed to James Miller. They were printed by Pope's printer James Wright, possibly with Pope's knowledge. James McLaverty, *Pope's Printer, John Wright*. Oxford Bibliographical Society: Occasional Publication, no. 11 (1976).

Chapter 28, Last Heroes

732 *The two men never met*:
There was possibly a near miss. It has been suggested that when Elizabeth Carter, in Pope's absence, visited his garden in July of 1738, Johnson *may* have been with her. He did, at any rate, compose a very pretty Latin epigram about Miss Carter's plucking some laurels while there. For an episode several years earlier that might have but did not bring

the two men together, see W. J. Bate's eloquent *Life of Johnson* (New York: Harcourt Brace Jovanovich, 1977), pp. 91–3. According to Johnson's note on the fragmentary MS. of *London*, his poem was published on May 12; according to the newspapers, it was published on May 13, as was Pope's. Possibly Johnson's date is the date on which he first received finished copies, in which case the newspapers may still be right with respect to the first day of public sale.

732 *"Of such a man as Pope?"*:
    F. W. Hilles, *Portraits by Sir Joshua Reynolds* (New York: McGraw-Hill, 1952), p. 79n.

733 *"Well as he was, he shall be"*:
    Elizabeth (Robinson) Montagu mentions this epitaph in a letter to her father of (probably) 1738. HL: MO 4752.

733 *"And Virgil too"*:
    For the epitaphs, see *TE*, 6: 386 and 376. Also, David Morris's *Alexander Pope: The Genius of Sense* (Harvard University Press, 1984), esp. pp. 27–32.

733 *An Abbey monument to Shakespeare*:
    According to the *London Evening Post*, 30 April 1737, Gay's monument was opened to public view "yesterday evening." A news item of 21 December observes that proposals for the inscription on Shakespeare's monument should be sent to Pope and that the sum of £300 raised for the undertaking by benefits at Drury Lane and Covent Garden has been deposited in trust to Burlington, Dr. Mead, and Pope.

735 *"As unsafe as it was ineffectual"*:
    TE, 4: 327n.

735 *"The third Dialogue unfinished and suppressed"*:
    Works (1751), 4: xl. The poem referred to is evidently the unfinished and unpublished "1740" (*TE*, 4: 330–7), in which Pope's despair at the condition of the country (as he sees it) and his disenchantment with the irresolutions and bickerings of the Opposition stand out stark and clear—balanced, but only mildly, by his hope that the principles appropriate to a patriot king will take shape in the bosom of the Prince of Wales.

735 *"Six incendiary Chiefs"*:
    See *A Hue and Cry After Part of a Pack of Hounds, which broke out of their kennel in Westminster* (1739), p. 21.

736 *"A poet truly sublime"*:
    Essai sur l'Homme [tr. Etienne de Silhouette] (Paris, 1736), pp. xxxi–xxxiii. On the vicissitudes of the *Essay*'s reputation in France and the attacks by Crousaz, see especially Émile Audra, *L'Influence française dans l'oeuvre de Pope* (Paris: Champion 1931), pp. 92–4, and *TE*, 3.1: pp. xviii–xxi.

737 *Which logicians overlook*:
    On the distinctive aphoristic language of Pope's poem, see esp. David Morris, *Alexander Pope: The Genius of Sense* (Harvard University Press, 1984).

738 *History of the Works of the Learned*:
    Collected and published as *A Vindication of Mr. Pope's Essay on Man*, 15 November 1739.

739 *"Of the ancient and modern Church"*:
    Vindication (2nd ed., 1740), p. 18.

739 *"To the Decision of the Church"*:
    On the Racine episode, see *TE*, 3.1: p. xxii.

739 *His friend, Bishop George Berkeley*:
    Spence, no. 305.

739–40 *"As it is in Heaven"*:
    The Last and Greatest Art, p. 226. Relevant also to any estimate of Pope's considered views are his letter to Atterbury, quoted above, and his "hymn" or "prayer," published in 1738 as *The Universal Prayer*, but extant in four earlier and somewhat variant forms, the earliest probably composed in 1716 or thereabouts as a hymn. On these and the final version, see R. W. Rogers, "Alexander Pope's Universal Prayer," in *Journal of English and Germanic Philology*, 54 (1955): 613–24. As Professor Rogers notes, the general movement of the successive versions is toward "a more definitely Christian coloring," but all versions contain "discreet references" to the Fall and to Grace, all stress religious tolerance and charity, and all base virtue on conscience rather than heavenly rewards. The most notable changes in the later versions (after 1716) are that Pope makes his position on free will

unmistakable ("And binding Nature fast in Fate, Left'st Conscience free, and Will"—1736) and alters the "Omnipotent and Stern judge" of the 1716 version to "a god of goodness and mercy, who must provide the . . . aid necessary [i.e., Grace] for the individual man to live up to his ideals."

The Universal Prayer was superbly set to music in 1969 by the Polish composer Andrzj Panufnik. Its world premiere took place (four solo voices, full chorus, harps, and organ) on 24 May 1970 at the Cathedral of St. John the Divine in New York—Leopold Stokowski conducting. It was later performed under the same conductor in several other American cathedrals, London's Westminster Cathedral, and St. Mary's, Twickenham (20 June 1971). The New York Times reviewer described its setting as "the grandest most awesome kind of music," and Stokowski himself expressed the hope "that all faiths will realise the greatness of the poem and of the music, and that it will become often performed like the Ninth Symphony of Beethoven." The Westminster Cathedral performance was recorded.

740 Pressed him in this direction:
For a study of Bolingbroke's possible influence on Pope in religious as well as political matters, see B. S. Hammond, Pope and Bolingbroke (University of Missouri Press, 1984). The book's argument would be more persuasive if it took into account the fact that influence between two close friends is a two-way street.

740 "Might seem the most exceptionable":
One such passage it seems fair to guess, would be the curt dismissal of particularized creeds found at 3: 305ff. ("For Modes of Faith, let graceless zealots fight; His can't be wrong whose life is in the right.") Pope's convictions on this matter were formed early (Essay On Criticism, 396ff, 440ff: Correspondence, 1: 126–8, 331, 453–5) and never wavered: similar assertions appear in all versions of his Universal Prayer, 1716–40. It is extremely doubtful, however, that he intended these views—any more than the Cambridge Platonists and "Latitude Men" like Archbishop Tillotson, from whom he probably derived them—to rule out revelation. In fact, his insistence in the Essay that genuine faith begins and ends in love of God and Man echoes the most familiar of all New Testament summations: "On these two Commandments hang all the law and the prophets."

741 Just beneath the text:
For a lively "corrective" view of what lies beneath the text, see J. D. Canfield's "The Fate of the Fall in Pope's Essay on Man," The Eighteenth Century, 23 (1982): 134–50.

741 "A good supply of provisions to support it":
Bishop Thomas Newton, Works, (1872), 1: 116. Spence, no. 95n.

743 "Why should we add to them?":
Spence, no. 508.

743 "Seeing through all the possibilities of things":
Spence, no. 509. Though eventually hated by many for his boorish manners in disputation, Warburton's standing with his contemporaries was generally high. A. W. Evans, Warburton and the Warburtonians (Oxford University Press, 1932) especially ch. 16: a book to which I am much in debt in these paragraphs.

743 "The province of paradox":
Charles Yorke to his brother Philip, [May or June] 1746. George Harris, Life of Lord Chancellor Hardwicke, 3 vols. (1847), 1: 475. Quoted by Evans (Warburton), pp. 84–5.

743 "So noble a Genius was not":
Warburton to William Stukeley, in John Nichol's Illustrations, 2: 53. Quoted by Evans, p. 80.

744 "Fatalism, and what not":
Evans, p. 72, quoting The Family Memoirs of William Stukeley, 3 vols. (1882), 1: 127. See also Thomas Birch to Philip Yorke, 6 July 1751, quoting an early letter of Warburton's to Pope's enemy Concanen, in which he designates the motives of English poets in borrowing from their predecessors as pride in Milton, modesty in Addison, want of leisure in Dryden, and "Want of Genius" in Pope. BL: Add. MS. 35, 398, f. 4.

744 A hundred thousand pounds in today's money:
Johnson's estimate (Life of Pope, p. 170) is £4,000, but in view of the number of editions issued this seems to me conservative.

745 A memorial biography. To pay off personal scores:
This was the biography by William Ruffhead, valuable for certain items of information

derived from Warburton, but largely a string of quotations from the poems with shallow comments. On Warburton's insertions in the *Dunciad* notes, see his letter to Hurd, 10 February 1750, *Letters from a Late Eminent Prelate*, (1804), p. 41.

745 *"Who knows as much as He":*
To Allen, 6 March [1744] (4: 504).

745 *"Doctor'd with you, or not at all":*
12 August [1741] (4: 357).

745 *"Best and friendliest of men":*
"Pope's Books," e.g., no. 95.

745 *"The best of men":*
John Keble, *Occasional Papers and Reviews* (1877), p. 113. Quoted in Evans, p. 83.

745 *Its savage muzzle on assailants:*
Pope's friend Murray, for example, by that date Lord Mansfield, takes Warburton to task in a letter conveyed to him anonymously in 1756 for demeaning Pope's understanding in order to attack Bolingbroke. "In a work where Lord Bolingbroke is represented as a Monster, ... why is Pope ... brought in only as his Friend and Admirer? Why as approving of, & Privy to, all that was address'd to him? Why should he, who had many great Talents, & Amiable Qualities be described only by the slighting Epithets of *Tuneful & Poetical*? ... Had you ... shewn that Pope differed from Lord Bolingbroke, where he was in the wrong, ... that where he was right Pope improved, but never Servilely ... copied his Ideas, you would have done honor to your Friend, & yourself." BL: Egerton, 1959, ff. 32v, 33r.

746 *"The colour of her heart":*
Sir John Clerk of Penicuik, "A Tour into England in the Year 1733," SRO: GD18/2110, f. 42.

746 *"Of whom no good can be spoken":*
Elizabeth Montagu to Viscountess Wallingford, 24 December 1745 (*Collected in Himself*, p. 548). It is worth noticing in Bolingbroke's defense that Elizabeth Montagu, having got hold of a transcript of Atossa, also takes it to be a portrait of Sarah Churchill.

746 *"Lets loose to their own wills":*
Ibid.

747 *"Common wretches that crawl the earth":*
To Horace Mann, 24 December 1741 (*Correspondence*, 17: 253–4); M. Dorothy George, *Hogarth to Cruickshank* (London: Allen Lane, 1967), p. 15.

747 *Meant to suggest Sarah Churchill:*
TE, 3: 2: Appendix A.

747 *Must be taken as referring to the duchess of Buckinghamshire:*
V. A. Dearing, "The Prince of Wales' Set of Pope's Works," *Harvard Library Bulletin*, 4 (1950): 332.

748 *A manuscript satire on Sarah Churchill:*
Marchmont Papers, 2: 332–5. Bolingbroke did come close enough to the truth to realize that the portrait contained "several strokes" that could enable the Duchess of Marlborough to say "it was not intended to be her character." On the vexed matter of the "Atossa" portrait, see *TE*, 3.2: Appendix A, and, especially, Frank Brady, "Pope's *Epistle to a Lady*," *SEL*, 9 (1969).

748 *Despite a "favor":*
The "favor," one assumes, is the £1,000 specified by Bolingbroke in giving "Atossa" a separate publication to emphasize Pope's treachery. Possibly such a gift was made, though firm evidence on the point is lacking, as also on the intention of the giver. Bolingbroke jumped (much too happily, one thinks) to the conclusion that the Duchess's aim was to buy Pope off from publishing, or leaving to be published, any satire on herself or her husband, and that Pope by receiving the "favor" had entered into a contract with her not to publish. Supposing such an understanding actually existed, it was not Pope who violated it but Bolingbroke by publicly attaching her name to a character directed at the Duchess of Buckingham. More plausible, I believe, is the guess that the Duchess's gift, if indeed she made one at all in monetary form, was intended to help Pope buy a house in London that he had given up as too expensive. Pope to Sarah Churchill, [? June 1743] (4: 457–8). This would have been for Martha Blount's use.

748 *Even less amenable to extenuating reflections:*
On Pope's editing and printing of this piece, see the accounts in Johnson, *Life of Pope*, p. 193; F. E. Ratchford, "Pope and the Patriot King," *Texas Studies in English*, 6 (1926): 157–77; Giles Barber, "Bolingbroke, Pope, and the *Patriot King, The Library*, 19 (1964): 67–89; and Dickinson, pp. 277–94.

749 *Which Bolingbroke as cordially returned:*
Ruffhead, p. 219; G. H. Nadel, "New Light on Bolingbroke's *Letters on History,*" *Journal of the History of Ideas*, 23 (1962): 551–3; and Dickinson, pp. 278–82.

749 *Warburton held off:*
Bolingbroke to Mallet, 25 July 1745 (BL: Add. MS. 4948A, f. 419) and Lyttelton to Warburton (*A Selection from the unpublished papers of . . . William Warburton*, ed., Francis Kilvert, 1841, pp. 207–8). Both letters are quoted by Dickinson, p. 281.

749 *Verses Upon the late D—ss of M——. By Mr. P——:*
Griffith, no. 613.

750 *He did so with some fanfare:*
Lyttelton to Bolingbroke, April 14; Bolingbroke to Lyttelton, 15 April 1749 (BL: Add. MS. 4948A, ff. 442–442v, 420–1). The second letter is quoted by Dickinson, p. 291.

750 *Incorporated in the new 1749 edition:*
Dickinson, p. 292. Pope's revisions, it should be noted, were made in collaboration with Bathurst, one of Bolingbroke's warmest friends, and so far as they were not merely clarifications seem to have been intended to tone down severities, e.g., on the King (Spence, no. 285). According to Warburton, Pope expected to be declared Bolingbroke's literary executor if his friend should die first. [Warburton], *Letter to the Editor of the Spirit of Patriotism* (1749), pp. 13–14.

753 *"But his untimely end":*
Pope to Burlington, 19 January [1740] (4: 221).

753 *Masquerading as his:*
David Nokes, "Pope's Epigrams on William Kent: A New Manuscript," *Yearbook of English Studies* 5 (1975). See also Kent to Burlington, 12 September 1738, first published by H. A. Tipping in *Architectural Review*, 63 (1928): 180–3.

755 *"Shall ever pray &c. &c.":*
Correspondence, 4: 323–4. Nokes ("Pope's Epigrams") seems to me correct in placing this letter among the other japes of 1738.

755 *First published in 1741:*
I use the text Pope sent to Bolingbroke, 3 September 1740 (4: 262). See also *TE*, 6: 382–5.

757 *"Caressed with safety and pleasure":*
Lyttleton to Pope, 25 October 1738 (4: 138). See for the Prince's gift, 4: 170, 178; Pope's dining with him, 4: 139; Pope's comment to him about kings, Spence, no. 591, Ruffhead, p. 535n, Boswell, *Life of Johnson*, 4: 50.

757 *"Nor the Frolicks of Ladies":*
19 November 1738 (4: 147).

757 *Consult with his printers:*
He was engaged during this period in editing and printing his Swift correspondence (1740), preparing for his *Prose Works*, volume 2 (1741), composing the *New Dunciad* (1742), and making plans for his epic *Brutus* (unpublished).

758 *They may have thought the poem reflected:*
On the whole matter, see Ehrenpreis, 3: 708–13, and for a fuller discussion A. H. Scouten and R. D. Hume, "Pope and Swift: Text and Interpretation of Swift's Verses on His Death," *PQ*, 52 (1973): 205–31. Swift seems to have entrusted the *Verses* for London publication to Dr. William King, Principal of St. Mary Hall, Oxford. King consulted Pope and Orrery, and probably, since he was living with Pope, Bolingbroke as well.

758 *The mettle of the new Licensing Act:*
See Malcolm Goldstein, *Pope and the Augustan Stage* (Stanford University Press, 1958), ch. 3.

758 *Quin holding Pope's cloak:*
Thomas Davies, *Memoirs of the Life of David Garrick*, 2 vols. (1780), 2: 34.

759 *Greeted with a burst of applause:*
Johnson, p. 291.

760 *Moving the last scene of the fourth act into the fifth:*
    Benjamin Victor, *Original Letters, Dramatic Pieces, and Poems,* 2 vols. (1776), 2: 11.

760 *"He will never have a rival":*
    Memoirs of Percival Stockdale, 2 vols. (1809), 2: 153–4. *Thraliana,* ed., K. C. Balderston, 2 vols. (Oxford: Clarendon, 1942, 1: 132) names *King Lear* as the play in which Pope saw Garrick perform. Quite possibly Pope saw him in both plays. Garrick writes his brother Peter on 19 April 1742 that he has supped twice with Lyttelton, twice with Murray, "& Shall with Mr. Pope by his [Murray's] Introduction." As this is just the period when (after several less distinguished attempts) Garrick mastered the part of King Lear to immense applause, it seems not improbable that Pope went to see his new triumph before meeting him.

761 *"Something grand, like Cicero's":*
    F. W. Hilles, (*Portraits by Reynolds*), p. 79n.

761 *Staying up much of the night to finish it:*
    Cheyne to Richardson, 12 March 1741, in *Letters of Dr. Cheyne,* ed., C. F. Mullet (University of Missouri Studies, 18, 1943), p. 65. See also Pope, *Correspondence,* 4: 335n.

761 *Don't be niggardly!:*
    Johnson, "Akenside" (*Lives of the Poets,* 3: 412).

762 *"I'm going to dream of you":*
    4: 185–6.

762 *Visit with Lady Grizel Murray:*
    4: 188–90, and Lady Grizel Murray to her uncle, second earl of Marchmont, 30 July 1739. SRO: GD158/1449/69.

763 *"Colours, one behind another":*
    [?19 November 1739] (4: 201).

763 *"The Elyzium it leads him to":*
    Collected in Himself, pp. 501–31. The quotation is from p. 506.

765 *"The Lipps of his delightful Stranger":*
    Oliver to Borlase, 14 January [1740]. Quoted in Boyce, p. 86.

765 *"The Most Noble Man of England":*
    4: 221–2.

765 *Did not appeal to Arbuthnot:*
    There is some likelihood that Warburton and George Arbuthnot did not get on (4: 461). See also Boyce, pp. 146n, 207n.

767 *"Without putting me . . . in the conversation":*
    Correspondence, 4: 462; Spence, no. 361.

767 *One rumour had it:*
    BL: Add. MS. 35, 396, ff. 275v–6. Thomas Birch to Charles Yorke, 27 October 1744. Quoted by Rogers, *Major Satires,* p. 101n, and Boyce, p. 149n.

768 *"How he had rested that night":*
    Tovey, *Gray and His Friends* (1890), p. 281.

768 *His letters dealing with this affair:*
    4: 464, 510.

768 *"The rich Mr. Allen's friendship":*
    Boyce, p. 147.

768 *"Partly for Charitable Uses":*
    The Garden and the City, p. 264. The episode is difficult to assess. One must suppose that in signalizing the bequest, Pope meant to show a certain resentment of the Allen family's treatment of Martha Blount. On the other hand, the wording is hardly what a skilled ironist might have made it had he wished to express serious displeasure. Johnson's description of the wording as "petulant and contemptuous" seems excessive, and his attribution of Pope's action to the influence of Martha Blount ("he polluted his will with female resentment") rests on no authority save that of Warburton (Ruffhead, p. 576), who hated her. She herself told Spence (no. 360), when questioned about this clause in the will, that she had advised Pope to omit it, and there is as much reason to believe her as to believe Warburton.

768 *To help Michael buy an army position:*
    4: 161, 215, 217.

768 *"Always a bad accomptant"*:
   Ruffhead, p. 547n. Orrery suggests a stronger resentment on Allen's part: to Mallet, 14 July 1745; quoted by *E-C*, 8: 523. Allen is said to have also remarked that Pope would have come closer to the amount of his indebtedness if he had added "a cypher more" to the figure (Johnson, p. 196). It seems improbable, however, that Pope accepted contributions of money amounting to that large sum, since he had refused Allen's offer to pay for the authorized edition of his *Letters* in 1737 and was always on guard against the imputation that his favor could be bought. Quite possibly, Allen was thinking of the shipments of Bath stone he had provided for Pope's Grotto and the occasional workman he had supplied for his garden. These Pope might not unreasonably have thought acts of friendship rather than debts.
768 *"Did not distinguish 'received' from 'paid'"*:
   Boswell in Extremes, eds., C. McC. Weiss and F. A. Pottle (New York: McGraw Hill, 1970), p. 334 (12 May 1778).

Chapter 29, Last Poems

769 *"At my Desire to Admiration"*:
   Cheyne to Samuel Richardson, 12 March 1741, in *Letters of Dr. Cheyne*, ed., C. F. Mullet (University of Missouri Studies, 18, 1943), p. 65. Martin Battestin makes a persuasive case for believing that Pope also met Fielding at Allen's in the winter of 1741–42.
769 *Mislaid or destroyed*:
   Johnson, *Idler*, no. 65: "The performances of Pope were burnt by those whom he had perhaps selected from all mankind as the most likely to publish them;" *Life of Pope*, p. 192, where it is recorded that Dodsley, on "going to solicit preference as the publisher [of Pope's "Remains"], was told that the parcel had not yet been inspected."
769 *According to one report*:
   Charles Yorke to Philip Yorke 29 May 1744, in George Harris, *Life of Lord Chancellor Hardwicke*, 3 vols. (1847), 2: 89.
771 *"The Deliverer of Europe"*:
   Ruffhead, pp. 423–4.
771 *Both establishments about his ears*:
   Spence, nos. 302, 343.
772 *"To lay down your pen"*:
   7 November 1741 (4: 369). By 26 September 1741 Benjamin Martyn (who in 1737–38 had worked with Pope and Mead to raise funds for the Shakespeare Monument in Westminster Abbey and whose *Timoleon*, performed with great success on 26 January 1730 and thirteen nights following, is thought to have received contributions by Pope) had heard from Thomas Birch an account of plans for *Brutus* and is assuring him that "From the Greatness of the Subject & Pope's Genius," he expects "a performance equal to the Iliad or Aeneid." BL: Add. MS. 4313, ff. 128v–129r.
773 *Much more in the plan as we have it*:
   I follow here the sketch that Ruffhead gives, fuller than any other. See also Pope, *Correspondence*, 1: 425, Spence, no. 343; also E. D. Snyder, "Pope's Blank Verse Epic," *JEPG* 18 (1919): 580–3; Frederick Brie, "Pope's *Brutus*," *Anglia*, 63 (1939): 144–85; D. T. Torchiana, "Brutus: Pope's Last Hero," *JEGP*, 61 (1962): 853–67; and H.-J. Zimmermann, "Bemerkungen zum Manuskript und Text von Popes *Brutus*," *Archiv für das Studium der neueren Sprachen*, CIC (1962): 100–6.
773 *"Endeavouring more than it can do"*:
   P. 217.
774 *"My Widcomb Poem"*:
   4: 387.
775 *"On the same Rank"*:
   21–3 May 1742 (4: 396).
775 *Gay or Cibber had the worst of it*:
   George Sherburn's "The Fortunes and Misfortunes of *Three Hours after Marriage*," *MP*, 24 (1926); *Early Career*, pp. 193–9; J. H. Smith, ed., *Three Hours after Marriage*, Augustan

Reprint Society, nos. 91–2 (1961); Helene Koon, ed., *A Letter from Mr. Cibber to Mr. Pope*, Augustan Reprint Society, no. 158 (1973).

775 *"Free from Rebellion and Schism":*
D. H. Miles, "The Political Satire of *The Non-Juror*," *MP*, 12 (1915): 281–305, quoting from the statements left behind them by the two clergymen. See also W. M. Peterson, "Pope and Cibber's *The Non-Juror*," *MLN*, 70 (1955): 332–5.

777 *"Was already won":*
John Loftis, *The Politics of Drama in Augustan England* (Oxford: Clarendon, 1963), p. 72.

777 *The laureateship in 1730:*
Apology, pp. 282–4.

777 *"The Race of George and Caroline":*
From Cibber's first ode as laureate. His subsequent performance on 28 October 1732 "outdid his usual Outdoing" (to borrow one of his own famous locutions, *Apology*, p. 34):

> The Word that formed the World
> In vain did make Mankind;
> Unless, his Passions to restrain,
> Almighty Wisdom had design'd
> Sometimes a William or a George should reign.

778 *The use of an illustrious name:*
See T. B. Gilmore, Jr., "Colley Cibber's Good Nature and His Reaction to Pope's Satire," *Papers on Language and Literature*, 2 (1966): 361–71. Cibber is most dangerous when he hints (repeatedly) that Pope is disloyal to the Government in having disaffected friends (presumably Atterbury, Bolingbroke, and the Young Patriots generally); and most ridiculous when he works himself into a fine hypocritical lather at Pope's attacks on corrupt clergymen.

778 *"Formed the Poet for the King":*
Johnson's Poems, eds., D. N. Smith and E. L. McAdam, Jr. (Oxford: Clarendon, 1941), p. 114.

778 *Talking only of Colley Cibber:*
The author of *The Tryall of Colley Cibber*, 1740 (sometimes attributed in whole or part to Fielding), pp. 6–7, notes that though some think Cibber's *Apology* is only about the theater, it "may as properly be stiled an Apology for the Life of One [i.e., Walpole] Who hath played a very comical Part . . . on a much larger Stage than *Drury-Lane*." For other instances of the association of Cibber with Walpole and vice versa, see *The Garden and the City*, pp. 157–62.

779 *"Might never have been cured of?":*
A Letter from Mr. Cibber to Mr. Pope (1742), pp. 47–8. A convenient listing of items relevant to the Pope–Cibber quarrel from 1717 to 1744 is found in C. D. Peavy's "The Pope–Cibber Controversy: A Bibliography," in *Restoration and Eighteenth-Century Theatre Research*, 3 (1964): 51–5. See also the index in Guerinot.

781 *With chagrin and pain:*
Johnson, pp. 187–8. Sir John Hawkins, *Life of Johnson* (1787), p. 347.

781 *"The Word that lasts longest":*
TE, 6: 397.

781 *"Defects of its virtues":*
B. L. Reid, "Ordering Chaos: *The Dunciad*," in *Quick Springs of Sense*, ed., L. S. Champion (University of Georgia Press, 1974), pp. 95–6.

782 *An analogue of sorts:*
William Kinsley, "Varieties of Infernal Experience: Pope's *Dunciad* and Dante's *Inferno*," in *City and Society in the Eighteenth Century*, eds., Paul Fritz and David Williams (Toronto: Hakkurt, 1973), pp. 281–301.

782 *"A pocketful of currants":*
J. S. Cunningham, "Pope, Eliot, and The Mind of Europe," in *"The Waste Land" in Different Voices*, ed., A. D. Moody (London: Arnold, 1974), pp. 84–5.

782 *King dunce, Colley Cibber:*
Those parts of the first three books which are directed at abuses of learning apply to Cibber far less aptly than to Theobald.

783 *"A right Taste prevails"*:
   Letter concerning . . . Design (1712), in *Characteristics* (1732 ed.) 3: 398, 403.
783 *"For they are noble lines"*:
   From the Journal of Boswell's son (James, Jr., 1778–1822), 21 May 1796: "Spence told [Bennet] Langton that Pope having repeated the conclusion of his Dunciad to him his voice trembled." Langton told Johnson, "& well it might," said he, "for they are noble lines." Yale Boswell Papers (unpublished), cat. no. C 361. (Quoted here with permission.)
783 *"What I have told them"*:
   J. A. Froude, *Carlyle, 1795–1835*, 2 vols. (1882), 2: 495.
784 *"They are in the newspapers"*:
   Paul Valéry, "The Crisis of the Mind," *Collected Works*, ed., Jackson Matthews, 15 vols. (London: Routledge & Kegan Paul, 1957–75), 10: 23. See also Mario Praz, *Mnemosyne* (Princeton University Press, 1970), pp. 156–7.
787 *"They were our one way out"*:
   Constantin Cavafy, "Waiting for the Barbarians." [Translation mine].
788 *"So many King-consorts have done the like"*:
   TE, 5: 341.
790 *"Learn'd I suffer none"*:
   See *Collected in Himself*, pp. 339–43, and *The Last and Greatest Art*, p. 128. Collations from the manuscripts preserved by Jonathan Richardson, Jr., show that in 1729 or thereabouts Pope planned to unfold much of the action of Book 4 with "Tibbald" still as king.
791 *Silly slave of a harlot mistress*:
   Ep. I, ii: 18–25.
791 *"This man hath travail'd well"*:
   "To William Roe," *Epigrams*, no. 128,. ll. 2–4, 12–14. For valuable comments on this poem, see R. S. Peterson, *Imitation and Praise in the Poems of Ben Jonson* (Yale University Press, 1981), pp. 33–43.
793 *"And form the mind"*:
   John Locke, *Educational Writings*, ed., J. L. Axtell (Cambridge University Press, 1968), p. 198.
793 *"Our times could use him"*:
   Reid ("Ordering Chaos"), p. 96.
794 *Likely to destroy the West*:
   Denis Gabor, *Inventing the Future* (New York: Knopf, 1964); Robert Nisbet, *History of the Idea of Progress* (New York: Basic Books, 1980); Harlow Shapley, *Beyond the Observatory* (New York: Scribners, 1967). In their time, both de Tocqueville and Schopenhauer shared this conviction.
796 *"Composed (indeed composted) to everlasting rest"*:
   Philip Brockbank, "The Book of Genesis and the Genesis of Books," in *The Art of Alexander Pope*, eds., Howard Erskine-Hill and Anne Smith (London: Vision Press, 1979), pp. 209–10.
796 *This was "Amica"*:
   What follows is derived from a group of poems and letters transcribed by their author and collected by her into a sheaf entitled "Epistolary Conversation. In Verse and Prose. Between a Lady, under the Name of Amica, And her Friends." Below this title on her manuscript title page, she has inscribed two lines from Pope's *First Satire of the Second Book*:

   To Virtue only, and her Friends, a friend,
   The World beside may murmur, or commend.

Amica's identity remains at present unknown, though efforts to identify her continue. Her sheaf of transcripts is the property of a private collector.

Chapter 30, Death

802 *"Become painful first, & then fatal"*:
   17 July [1740] (4: 252).

802   *"Without quite losing breath":*
        20 March 1743 (4: 445).
802   *"Rather too much (for me I mean)":*
        13 January 1743 (4: 437).
802   *"Un-doctored":*
        4: 451, 461–4, 470, 472.
804   *"As three to others":*
        Boswell in Extremes, eds., C. McC. Weiss and F. A. Pottle (New York: McGraw Hill, 1970), p. 332.
804   *"Like two Parrots":*
        21 November [1743] (4: 484).
804   *"At any hour you send":*
        Boswell in Extremes, p. 332, and Pope, *Correspondence*, 4: 490. One is, of course, tempted to wonder if Pope ever recalled his own earlier verses (*Elegy to the Memory of an Unfortunate Lady*, 17–18):

> Most souls, 'tis true, but peep out once an age,
> Dull sullen pris'ners in the body's cage.

805   *"Nothing to do but die":*
        Spence, nos. 624, 622.
805   *Bleeding him:*
        To Bethel, 20 February [1744] (4: 499).
806   *"As peevish as the devil"*
        4: 517–18.
806   *To relieve retention of urine:*
        4: 516.
806   *"Pure water by stool":*
        Pope to Orrery [c. 5 May 1744] (4: 521).
807   *"How it fared with his horse":*
        BL: Stowe MS. 180, f. 210.
808   *"A good man, no less than an excellent writer":*
        4: 523.
808   *"Quite gone in his judgment" for three months:*
        Boswell in Extremes, p. 333.
808   *"Jangled out of tune":*
        Spence, nos. 633, 634, 636, 639.
808   *"'Twas a vision":*
        Ibid., no. 644.
808   *Then both heads had closed:*
        Ruffhead, pp. 532–3.
808   *"Coming out of the wall":*
        Warton, *Works*, 1: lxiv.
809   *"How ill they have crucified him!":*
        To Mann (*Correspondence*, 18: 449).
809   *"Divided between Carelessness and Care":*
        Spence, nos. 637, 648.
810   *"To look upon myself like Phaedo":*
        Spence, no. 631. See also M. R. Brownell, "'Like Socrates': Pope's Art of Dying," *SEL* 20 (1980): 407–30.
811   *"But not on possibilities":*
        Spence, nos. 649, 646, 647, 651.
811   *"A temporary strength to him":*
        Spence, no. 641. Earlier, when he was laid up with his urethral operation, she visited him often.
811   *"What, is he not dead yet?":*
        Pp. 189–90. Johnson's handling of the remark is discussed by Robert Folkenflik, "Johnson's Art of Anecdote," *Studies in Eighteenth-Century Culture*, 3 (1973), 171ff.

812 *"If I saw you every hour. adieu"*:
       25 March (4: 511).
812 *"But I cannot go on"*:
       4: 524.
812 *"May our end be like his!"*:
       No. 658.

INDEX

This index was prepared by Sydney W. Cohen with the assistance of Sondra Armer and others. Page numbers in italics refer to illustrations and their captions.

DATE DUE